LET'S

Alaska

& The Pacific Northwest
Including Western Canada

■ Let's Go writers travel on your budget.

"Guides that penetrate the veneer of the holiday brochures and mine the grit of real life." —*The Economist*

"The writers seem to have experienced every rooster-packed bus and lunar-surfaced mattress about which they write." —*The New York Times*

"All the dirt, dirt cheap." —*People*

■ Great for independent travelers.

"The guides are aimed not only at young budget travelers but at the independent traveler, a sort of streetwise cookbook for traveling alone." —*The New York Times*

"Flush with candor and irreverence, chock full of budget travel advice." —*The Des Moines Register*

"An indispensable resource. *Let's Go*'s practical information can be used by every traveler." —*The Chattanooga Free Press*

■ Let's Go is completely revised each year.

"Only *Let's Go* has the zeal to annually update every title on its list." —*The Boston Globe*

"Unbeatable: good sight-seeing advice; up-to-date info on restaurants, hotels, and inns; a commitment to money-saving travel; and a wry style that brightens nearly every page." —*The Washington Post*

■ All the important information you need.

"*Let's Go* authors provide a comedic element while still providing concise information and thorough coverage of the country. Anything you need to know about budget traveling is detailed in this book." —*The Chicago Sun-Times*

"Value-packed, unbeatable, accurate, and comprehensive." —*Los Angeles Times*

Let's Go Publications

Let's Go: Alaska & the Pacific Northwest 1999
Let's Go: Australia 1999
Let's Go: Austria & Switzerland 1999
Let's Go: Britain & Ireland 1999
Let's Go: California 1999
Let's Go: Central America 1999
Let's Go: Eastern Europe 1999
Let's Go: Ecuador & the Galápagos Islands 1999
Let's Go: Europe 1999
Let's Go: France 1999
Let's Go: Germany 1999
Let's Go: Greece 1999 **New title!**
Let's Go: India & Nepal 1999
Let's Go: Ireland 1999
Let's Go: Israel & Egypt 1999
Let's Go: Italy 1999
Let's Go: London 1999
Let's Go: Mexico 1999
Let's Go: New York City 1999
Let's Go: New Zealand 1999
Let's Go: Paris 1999
Let's Go: Rome 1999
Let's Go: South Africa 1999 **New title!**
Let's Go: Southeast Asia 1999
Let's Go: Spain & Portugal 1999
Let's Go: Turkey 1999 **New title!**
Let's Go: USA 1999
Let's Go: Washington, D.C. 1999

Let's Go Map Guides

Amsterdam	Madrid
Berlin	New Orleans
Boston	New York City
Chicago	Paris
Florence	Rome
London	San Francisco
Los Angeles	Washington, D.C.

Coming Soon: Prague, Seattle

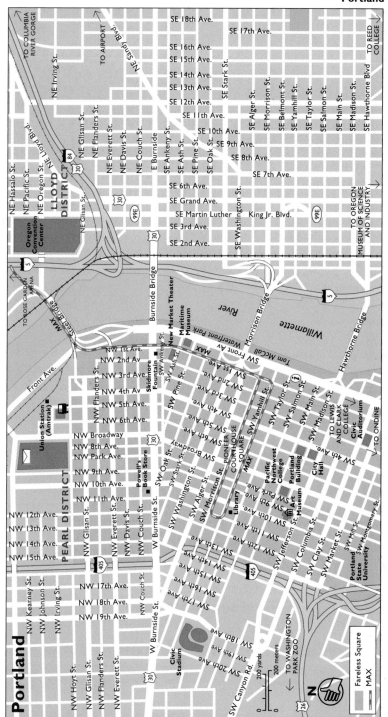

Portland

Seattle

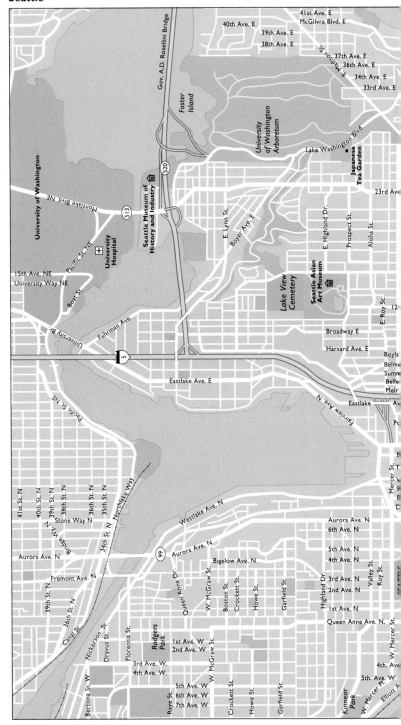

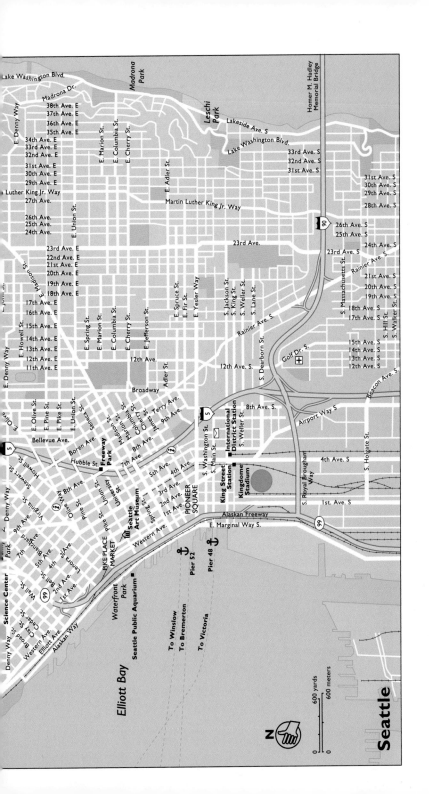

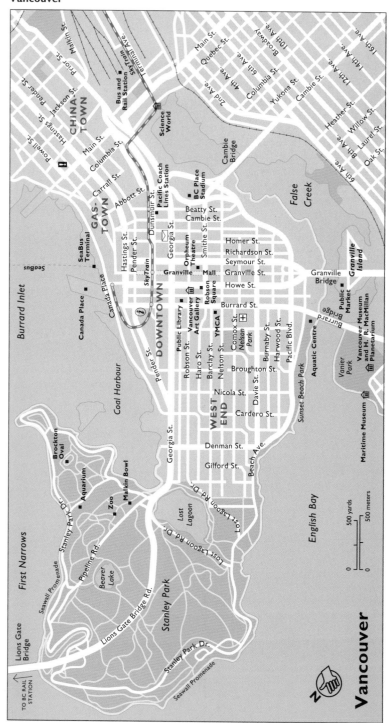

Vancouver

Vancouver

**Let's Go
Publications**

Let's Go
Alaska
& the Pacific Northwest
INCLUDING **Western Canada**

1999

Douglas Rand
Editor

Ben Florman
Associate Editor

Researcher-Writers:
**Kristy Garcia
Anne M. Johnson
Jennifer Laine
Thomas Lue
Rebecca Reider
Paul Todgham**

St. Martin's Press ❧ New York

HELPING LET'S GO

If you want to share your discoveries, suggestions, or corrections, please drop us a line. We read every piece of correspondence, whether a postcard, a 10-page email, or a coconut. Please note that mail received after May 1999 may be too late for the 2000 book, but will be kept for future editions. **Address mail to:**

> **Let's Go: Alaska & the Pacific Northwest**
> **67 Mount Auburn Street**
> **Cambridge, MA 02138**
> **USA**

Visit Let's Go at **http://www.letsgo.com**, or send email to:

> **feedback@letsgo.com**
> **Subject: "Let's Go: Alaska & the Pacific Northwest"**

In addition to the invaluable travel advice our readers share with us, many are kind enough to offer their services as researchers or editors. Unfortunately, our charter enables us to employ only currently enrolled Harvard-Radcliffe students.

How to Use This Book

Welcome to *Let's Go: Alaska & the Pacific Northwest Including Western Canada 1999*, a long title for a far vaster region. We road-tripping researchers and sedentary editors have cussed and kissed this book into being for the new year, and hope that you'll find it to be a more navigable, outdoor-intensive, Internet-relevant, sensitive, and sensical guide than ever before.

Just a few pages from here is the **Essentials** chapter, lovingly stuffed with general resources for budget travel, work and study, health concerns, transportation, and outdoor endeavors. The book's grand progression is north to south by political entity: **Oregon, Washington, British Columbia, Alberta,** the **Yukon,** and **Alaska.** (That's ORWABCABYTAK in postal lingo.) Each chapter begins with the biggest city or national park, and then unfolds in a hopefully intuitive progression.

Within the coverage of each city or park, **Orientation and Practical Information** come first, serving up a bevy of technical facts: **Transportation, Visitor and Financial Services, Local Services,** and **Emergency and Communications.** Next comes coverage of **Accommodations, Campgrounds,** and **Food,** listed with the highest quality first. Last come **Sights, Outdoors, Entertainment, Nightlife,** and **Events.** For small towns without such breakdowns, look for sights and outdoors first, with the usual arrangement afterward.

And now, a cavalcade of informative boxes:

This is a **warning box.** It's for fundamental, practical, important things, usually dealing with money or danger.

This Is a Graybox

It's for peripheral, arcane, entertaining things, usually dealing with outlandish conspiracy theories, wild get-rich-quick schemes, trenchant cultural or environmental essays, and revolting beverages.

THIS IS A HIGHLIGHT BOX

- Kicking off each major region, these brand-new flagships of box technology compress every unmissable attraction into attractive, easily digestible sentences.

This is a **listing pick.** Our researchers thought that this particular restaurant, bar, or accommodation was super-exceptional. Nefarious technical limitations prevent us from bestowing thumbs on perfectly deserving establishments in smaller towns, where glowing text will have to suffice.

Happy trails!

A NOTE TO OUR READERS

The information for this book was gathered by *Let's Go*'s researchers from May through August. Each listing is derived from the assigned researcher's opinion based upon his or her visit at a particular time. The opinions are expressed in a candid and forthright manner. Other travelers might disagree. Those traveling at a different time may have different experiences since prices, dates, hours, and conditions are always subject to change. You are urged to check beforehand to avoid inconvenience and surprises. Travel always involves a certain degree of risk, especially in low-cost areas. When traveling, especially on a budget, always take particular care to ensure your safety.

Table of Contents

Maps

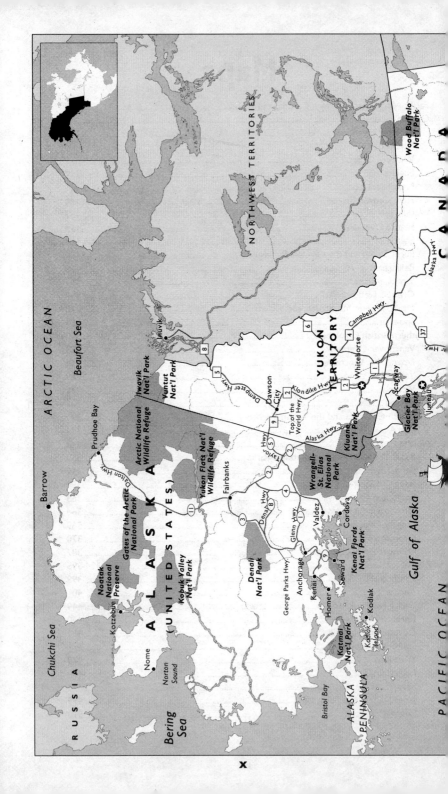

x

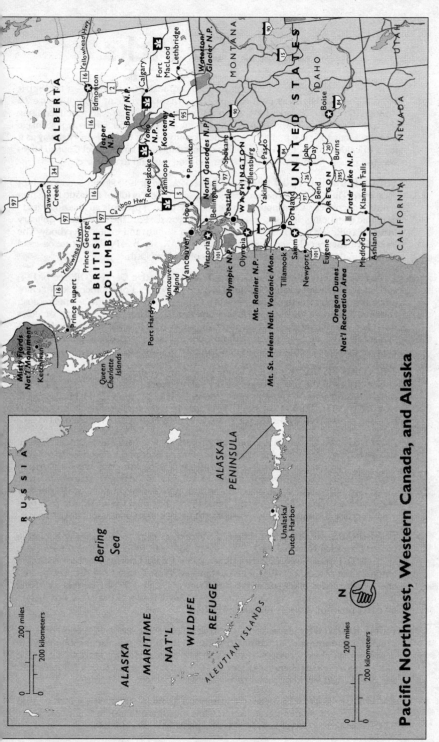

Pacific Northwest, Western Canada, and Alaska

Let's Go Picks

MIND-BLOWING DRIVES Cruising past post-apocalyptic renewal on the **Spirit Lake Memorial Highway** (WA; see p. 219)…that last verdant loop of **Route 20** through the North Cascades (WA; see p. 232)…massive hunks of stone and ice along the **Icefields Parkway** (AB; see p. 356)…making the **Dempster Highway** pilgrimage into the Arctic (YT; see p. 390)…breathless beauty in the **Richardson Highway** as it leads to Valdez (AK; see p. 438)…rolling over tundra on Nome's gravel **Council Highway** (AK; see p. 523) past fish camps, the sea, and the train to nowhere…

DROOL-INDUCING FOOD **Knead and Feed** (WA; see p. 178) simply serves the best soup ever. The entire **Okanagan Valley** (BC; see p. 296) is full of fantastic fresh fruit stands. Vancouver's **Commercial Drive** (BC; see p. 257) presents an amazing variety of ethnic restaurants amid exciting weeknight crowds. Portland's **Western Culinary Institute** (OR; see p. 63) throws a party in your mouth, and invites everybody. The **Wild Strawberry** (AK; see p. 507) and **Odie's** (AK; see p. 419) constitute oases of tastiness in the howling gastronomic desert of the Far North.

TRULY COOL MUSEUMS The **Oregon Trail Interpretive Center** (OR; see p. 144) and Sitka's **Sheldon-Jackson Museum** (AK; see p. 495) do a phenomenal job of enlivening history, the **Portland Art Museum** (OR; see p. 67) rules the aesthetic roost, and the **Anchorage Museum of History and Art** (AK; see p. 405) elegantly straddles the fence. The **Royal Tyrrell Museum** (AB; see p. 374) and **Head-Smashed-In Buffalo Jump** (AB; see p. 375) are without question the best possible places to view expertly-presented animal remains in the middle of nowhere.

THRILLING VISTAS This region is one great feast for the eyes; here are just a few choice dishes in the optical orgy: **Goat Peak Lookout** (WA; see p. 235), **Johnston Ridge Observatory** (WA; see p. 220), **Wreck Beach** (BC; see p. 261), **Maligne Lake** (AB; see p. 361), **Salmon Glacier** (BC/AK; see p. 337), the ferry dock in **Gustavus** (AK; see p. 504), **Mt. Eyak** (AK; see p. 442), and **Mt. Marathon** (AK; see p. 415).

AMPLE ANIMALS Avian fauna and bird voyeurs flock to **Malheur National Wildlife Refuge** (OR; see p. 139), while whales perform just astern off **Vancouver Island** (BC; see p. 268) and in the Inside Passage (AK; see p. 476). For a full week's worth of whale-watching, take the **ferry** from Bellingham, WA, all the way to Skagway, AK (see p. 34). Sea birds and marine mammals appear in profusion throughout **Glacier Bay National Park** (AK; see p. 503) and **Kenai Fjords National Park** (AK; see p. 416); a wildlife cruise through these waters is worth every budget-draining penny.

HIGH-GRADE HIKING A wide range of difficulty levels and sensory rewards await in **North Cascades National Park** (WA; see p. 234), **Mt. Rainier National Park** (WA; see p. 223), **Jasper National Park** (AB; see p. 357), **Lake Louise** (AB; see p. 355), and around **Sitka** (AK; see p. 493). The rainforested **West Coast Trail** (BC; see p. 288) and the **Alexander MacKenzie Heritage Trail** (BC; see p. 313) are perfect for insane hiking maniacs, but the trackless expanses of **Denali National Park** (AK; see p. 448) take first prize for vastness and sheer freedom.

PRIME NIGHTLIFE Seattle's strange **Sit and Spin** (WA; see p. 172) and Portland's pounding **Panorama** (OR; see p. 72) house all the urban undulations a body could desire, while Calgary's **Republik** (AB; see p. 372) is more ideal for punk wildness. The hidden **Howling Dog Saloon** (AK; see p. 466) and the **Chicken Creek Saloon's** (AK; see p. 473) wild weekend miner parties are way out there.

EXCEPTIONAL EVENTS Ashland's mammoth **Shakespeare Festival** (see p. 109) means seven straight months of theater, while the **Iditarod** finish in Nome (AK; see p. 523) guarantees no fewer than two weeks' partying in the darkness.

ESSENTIALS

PLANNING YOUR TRIP

■ When to Go

Traveling is like comedy—timing is everything. In Alaska, Western Canada, and the Pacific Northwest, the tourist season and the weather are the major timing concerns. In general, expect to share the warm weather between June and August with crowds of fellow tourists. In the off-season, crowds are smaller and rates are lower, but some of the sights and attractions may be closed, and winter travel can be treacherous and unpleasant. Snow, icy roads, and prohibitively cold weather (especially in northern Canada and Alaska) might limit both your movement and your desire to be outdoors.

Major holidays may also affect travel plans. On the biggest holidays, such as Independence Day (July 4) in the U.S. and Canada Day (July 1) in Canada, nearly every town has a celebration of some sort. Businesses and services may be closed, and both transportation and accommodations should be arranged some time in advance (see **Appendix**, p. 528).

CLIMATE

In Alaska and the Yukon, the weather varies from the coast inland. Summer and early fall are the warmest and sunniest times of year; even during the summer, however, wet, windy, and cold days should be no real surprise. In Alaska's Interior, the temperature ranges from around 70°F in summer to -30°F and lower in winter. Progressing farther north, summer days and winter nights become longer. North of the Arctic Circle, the sun does not set at all on the nights around the summer solstice in July, nor does it rise on the days around the winter solstice on December.

Average Temp. High/Low	January °C	January °F	April °C	April °F	July °C	July °F	October °C	October °F
Anchorage, AK	-6/-13	22/8	6/-2	43/28	18/11	65/51	5/-2	41/28
Banff, AB	-16/-7	3/19	-4/8	25/46	7/22	45/72	-1/10	30/50
Barrow, AK	-21/-28	-7/-19	-14/-22	6/-7	7/1	45/34	-7/-12	19/10
Calgary, AB	-2/-13	28/9	-11/-1	51/30	22/11	72/51	12/1	54/31
Eugene, OR	2/10	35/49	6/17	49/63	12/30	53/87	5/17	41/65
Fairbanks, AK	-28/-19	-19/-2	-6/5	20/41	11/22	53/72	-8/0	18/32
Port Angeles, WA	-1/6	31/43	4/12	40/54	9/19	49/66	6/13	43/56
Portland, OR	7/1	45/34	16/6	61/42	27/14	80/57	18/8	64/46
Seattle, WA	7/2	45/35	14/5	57/41	24/12	75/54	16/7	60/45
Spokane, WA	0/-7	32/20	14/2	57/35	28/13	83/55	14/2	58/36
Vancouver, BC	6/1	42/33	13/6	55/42	21/13	70/56	13/7	56/45
Victoria, BC	7/1	44/34	13/4	56/40	21/11	70/52	14/6	57/43
Whitehorse, YT	-47/2	-53/36	-15/17	5/45	5/26	41/79	-21/9	20/48

In British Columbia, Washington, and Oregon, the key weather-making factor are the mountains. To the east of the mountains it is relatively dry. West of the mountains it rains. A lot. In general, temperatures west of the mountains are more moderate than those east. Winters in coastal Washington and Oregon are soggy but not extremely cold. East of the Rockies, Alberta's temperatures are more extreme, with fine summers but harsh winters. See the **Inside Back Cover** for a temperature conversion chart.

■ Useful Information

TIME ZONES

Oregon, Washington, British Columbia, and the Yukon Territory are in the **Pacific Time Zone,** three hours earlier than Eastern Standard Time. Most of Alaska is in **Alaska Time,** one hour earlier than Pacific, four hours earlier than Eastern. Alberta is on **Mountain Time,** one hour later than Pacific, two hours earlier than Eastern.

GOVERNMENT INFORMATION OFFICES

Each state and province has its own travel bureau (listed below), which can recommend other useful organizations, send brochures and maps, and answer questions about the region. Contact the tourist bureau (often called the Visitor Information Center) in any city you plan to visit for more than a few days. Specific local tourist offices throughout Alaska, Western Canada, and the Pacific Northwest appear in the **Practical Information** section for each town or region, under **Visitor Information.**

Alaska Division of Tourism, P.O. Box 110801, Juneau, AK 99811-0801 (907-465-2010; fax 465-2287; email gonorth@commerce.state.ak.us; http://www.commerce.state.ak.us/tourism).

Travel Alberta, Commerce Place, 10155 102 St. 3rd floor, Edmonton, AB T5J 4G8 (800-661-8888 or 780-427-4321; fax 427-0867; http://www.albertahotles.ab.ca or http://www.discoveralberta.com/atp).

Tourism British Columbia, 1117 Wharf St., Victoria, BC V8W 2Z2 (800-663-6000 in BC, 250-387-1642 elsewhere; http://www.tbc.gov.bc.ca/tourism/tourism-home.html).

Oregon Tourism Commission, 775 Summer St. NE, Salem, OR 97310 (800-547-7842; fax 503-986-0001; http://www.traveloregon.com).

Washington State Tourism, Dept. of Community, Trade and Economic Development, P.O. Box 42500, Olympia, WA 98504-2500 (800-544-1800; http://www.tourism.wa.gov).

Tourism Yukon, P.O. Box 2703, Whitehorse, YT Y1A 2C6 (867-667-5340; fax 667-3546; email info@touryukon.com; http://www.touryukon.com).

TRAVEL ORGANIZATIONS

Council on International Educational Exchange (Council), 205 East 42nd St., New York, NY 10017-5706 (888-COUNCIL/268-6245; fax 212-822-2699; http://www.ciee.org). A private, not-for-profit organization. Administers work, volunteer, academic, internship, and professional programs world-wide. Also offers identity cards, including the ISIC and the GO25, plus a range of publications, like the useful (and free) magazine *Student Travels.*

Federation of International Youth Travel Organizations (FIYTO), Bredgade 25H, DK-1260 Copenhagen K, Denmark (45 33 33 96 00; fax 33 93 96 76; email mailbox@fiyto.org; http://www.fiyto.org). An international organization promoting educational, cultural, and social travel for young people. Member organizations include language schools, educational travel companies, national tourist boards, accommodation centers and other suppliers of travel services to youth and students. FIYTO sponsors the **GO25 Card** (http://www.go25.org).

International Student Travel Confederation, Herengracht 479, 1017 BS Amsterdam, The Netherlands (31 20 421 2800; fax 20 421 2810; email istcinfo@istc.org; http://www.istc.org) Nonprofit confederation of student travel organizations whose focus is to develop, promote, and facilitate travel among students.

HITTING THE BOOKS

On the road, knowledge is power. The mail-order travel shops listed below offer books with the scoop on specific travel issues. Some sell travel supplies as well.

Adventurous Traveler Bookstore, P.O. Box 1468, Williston, VT 05495 (800-282-3963; fax 677-1821; email books@atbook.com; http://www.AdventurousTraveler.com). Outdoor adventure travel books and maps for the U.S. and abroad. Their web site offers extensive browsing opportunities. Free 40-page catalogue.

Michelin Travel Publications, Michelin North America, P.O. Box 19008, Greenville, SC 29602-9008 (800-223-0987; fax 378-7471; http://www.michelin-travel.com). Offers 4 major lines of travel-related material: *Green Guides,* for sightseeing, maps, and driving itineraries; *Red Guides,* which rate hotels and restaurants; *In-Your-Pocket Guides;* and detailed, reliable road maps and atlases. All 4 are available at bookstores and distributors throughout the world.

Rand McNally, 150 S. Wacker Dr., Chicago, IL 60606 (800-333-0136; http://www.randmcnally.com). Publishes one of the most comprehensive road atlases of the U.S., Canada, and Mexico, available for $10 in their stores throughout the country, and in most other bookstores. Phone orders also available.

Specialty Travel Index, 305 San Anselmo Ave. #313, San Anselmo, CA 94960 (415-459-4900; fax 459-4974; email spectrav@ix.netcom.com; http://www.spectrav.com). Extensive listing of off the beaten track and specialty travel opportunities. $6, one-year subscription (2 copies) $10.

Superintendent of Documents, P.O. Box 371954, Pittsburg, PA 15250-7954 (202-512-1800; fax 512-2250; email gpoaccess@gpo.gov; http://www.access.gpo.gov/su-docs). Publishes *Health Information for International Travel* ($14), and Background Notes on countries ($1). Prices include postage. Open M-F 7:30am-4:30pm.

Travel Books & Language Center, Inc., 4931 Cordell Ave., Bethesda, MD 20814 (800-220-2665; fax 301-951-8546; email travelbks@aol.com). Sells over 75,000 items, including books, cassettes, atlases, dictionaries, and a wide range of specialty travel maps. Free comprehensive catalogue upon request.

Wide World Books and Maps, 1911 N. 45th St., Seattle, WA 98103 (206-634-3453; fax 634-0558; email travel@speakeasy.org; http://www.travelbooksandmaps.com/travelbk). Stocks travel guides, travel accessories, and hard-to-find maps.

INTERNET RESOURCES

Airline, hotel, hostel, or car rental reservations can all be made over the Internet, and the Internet can also be a means to connect personally with others abroad. **Net Travel: How Travelers Use the Internet,** by Michael Shapiro, is a thorough guide to all aspects of internet travel planning (US$25). The forms of the Internet most useful to budget travelers are the World Wide Web and Usenet newsgroups.

The World Wide Web

Search engines—services that search for web pages under specific subjects—can significantly aid the research process. **Alta Vista** (http://www.altavista.digital.com), and **Excite** (http://www.excite.com) are among the most popular. **Yahoo!** is a slightly more organized search engine; browse its travel links at http://www.yahoo.com/recreation/travel. Check out the Let's Go web site (http://www.letsgo.com) and find our newsletter, information about our books, an ever-expanding list of links, and more. For starters:

Alaska Home Page: http://www.state.ak.us
Alberta Home Page: http://www.gov.ab.ca/index1.html
British Columbia Home Page: http://www.gov.bc.ca
Oregon Home Page: http://www.state.or.us
Washington Home Page: http://www.state.wa.us
The Yukon Home Page: http:www.touryukon.com
Big World Magazine (http://www.bigworld.com) is a budget travel zine with a web page and a great collection of links to travel pages.

The CIA World Factbook (http://www.odci.gov/cia/publications/factbook/index.html) has tons of vital statistics on any nation. Check it out for an overview of a country's economy, or an explanation of their system of government.

Internet Guide to Hostelling (http://www.hostels.com) is just what it sounds like.

Microsoft Expedia (http://expedia.msn.com) offers a variety of web travel services: flight fare comparisons, maps, and reservations. FareTracker, a free service within Expedia, sends monthly mailings about the cheapest fares to any destination.

Rent-A-Wreck's Travel Links (http://www.rent-a-wreck.com/raw/travlist.htm) offers a surprisingly complete page of links.

Shoestring Travel (http://www.stratpub.com), is an alternative to Microsoft's monolithic site, this budget travel e-zine features listings of home exchanges, links, and accommodations information.

In addition to the above, relevant web sites are listed throughout the various sections of this Essentials chapter. Sites come and go like fickle lovers; a good web site one week might disappear the next, and then hit you with a palimony suit. For information on Internet access during your travels, see **Keeping in Touch: Email,** p. 51.

NEWSGROUPS Newsgroups are a forum for discussion of specific topics. One user posts a written question or thought, to which other users respond. The quality of discussion can be poor, and you often have to wade through piles of nonsense to come to useful information, but there are still a number of helpful newsgroups for travelers.

Usenet, a family of newsgroups, can be accessed from most Internet browsers. There are a number of different hierarchies of newsgroups. For issues related to society and culture, try the "soc" hierarchy (for example, **soc.culture.canada**). The "rec" (recreation) hierarchy is also good for travelers, with newsgroups such as **rec.fishing.fly.** The "alt" (alternative) hierarchy houses a number of different types of discussion, such as **alt.politics.socialism.trotsky** or **alt.culture.alaksa.** "Clari-net" posts AP news wires for many topics, such as **clari.sports.local.canada.brit_columbia.** Discussion quality changes rapidly, and new groups are always appearing, so it's worthwhile for a user to peruse the hierarchies to find appropriate topics.

■ Documents and Formalities

All applications for passports, visas, and other travel related documents should be filed several weeks or months in advance of your planned departure date; remember that you are relying on government agencies to complete these transactions. Demand for passports is highest between January and August, so try to apply as early as possible. A backlog in processing can spoil the most careful of plans.

When traveling, always carry two or more forms of identification, including at least one photo ID. A passport combined with a driver's license or birth certificate usually serves as adequate proof of identity and citizenship. Many establishments, especially banks, require several IDs before they will cash traveler's checks. Never carry all your forms of ID together; you risk being left entirely without ID or funds in case of theft or loss. Carry several extra passport-size photos that you can attach to the sundry IDs you will eventually acquire. If you plan an extended stay, register your passport with the nearest embassy or consulate.

PASSPORTS

Before you leave, photocopy the page of your passport that contains your photograph, passport number, and other identifying information. Carry one photocopy in a safe place apart from your passport, and leave another copy at home. These measures will help prove your citizenship and facilitate the issuing of a new passport if you lose the original document. Consulates also recommend that you carry an expired passport or an official copy of your birth certificate in a part of your baggage separate from other documents. Check your passport's expiration date: returning home with an expired passport is illegal, and may result in a fine.

If you do lose your passport, immediately notify the local police and the nearest embassy or consulate of your home government. To expedite its replacement, you will need to know all information previously recorded and show identification and proof of citizenship. A replacement may take weeks to process, and it may be valid only for a limited time. Some consulates can issue new passports within 24 hours if you give them proof of citizenship. Any visas stamped in your old passport will be irretrievably lost. In an emergency, ask for immediate temporary traveling papers that will permit you to reenter your home country.

Canada and U.S.: Citizens may cross the U.S./Canada border with only proof of citizenship (e.g. a birth certificate or a voter's registration card along with a photo ID; a driver's license alone will not be enough). U.S. citizens under 18 need the written consent of a parent or guardian; Canadian citizens under 16 need notarized permission from both parents.

Australia: Citizens must apply for a passport in person at a post office, passport office, or Australian diplomatic mission. An appointment may be necessary. A parent may file an application for a child who is under 18 and unmarried. Adult passports cost AUS$120 (for a 32-page passport) or AUS$180 (64-page), and a child's is AUS$60 (32-page) or AUS$90 (64-page). For more info, call toll-free (in Australia) 13 12 32, or visit http://www.austemb.org.

United Kingdom: British citizens, British Dependent Territories citizens, British Nationals (overseas), British Overseas citizens, and British subjects may apply for a full passport, valid for 10 years (5 years for ages under 16). Application forms are available at passport offices, main post offices, many travel agents, and branches of Lloyds Bank and Artac World Choice. Apply by mail (for an additional UK£10) to one of the passport offices, located in London, Liverpool, Newport, Peterborough, Glasgow, or Belfast. The fee is UK£31, or UK£11 for ages under 16. The London office offers same-day, walk-in rush service; arrive early. The formerly available British Visitor's Passport has been abolished; every traveler over 16 now needs a 10-year standard passport. The **U.K. Passport Agency** can be reached by phone at 0990 21 04 10.

Ireland: Citizens can apply for a passport by mail to either the **Department of Foreign Affairs,** Passport Office, Setanta Centre, Molesworth St., Dublin 2 (01 671 1633; fax 01 671 1092), or the Passport Office, Irish Life Building, 1A South Mall, Cork (021 272 525; fax 021 275 770). Obtain an application at a local Garda station or request one from a passport office. The new Passport Express Service, available through post offices, allows citizens to get a passport in 2 weeks for an extra IR£3. Passports cost IR£45 and are valid for 5 years. Citizens under 18 or over 65 can request a 3-year passport that costs IR£10.

New Zealand: Citizens can obtain passport application forms in New Zealand from travel agents or a **Department of Internal Affairs Link Centres.** Overseas, forms and passport services are provided by New Zealand embassies, high commissions, and consulates. Applications may be forwarded to the Passport Office, P.O. Box 10526, Wellington, New Zealand. Standard processing time in New Zealand is 10 working days for correct applications. The fees are adult NZ$80, and ages under 16 NZ$40. An urgent passport service is also available for an extra NZ$80. Different fees apply overseas; 9 posts including London, Sydney, and Los Angeles offer both standard and urgent services (adult NZ$115, under 16 NZ$58, plus NZ$115 if urgent). The fee at other posts is adult NZ$235, under 16 NZ$173, and a passport will be issued within 3 working days. Children's names can no longer be endorsed on a parent's passport—they must apply for their own, which are valid for up to 5 years. An adult's passport is valid for up to 10 years. More information is available at http://www.emb.com/nzemb or http://www.undp.org/missions/newzealand.

South Africa Citizens can apply for a passport at any **Home Affairs Office** or **South African Mission.** Tourist passports, valid for 10 years, cost SAR80. Those under 16 must be issued their own passports, valid for 5 years, which cost SAR60. If a passport is needed in a hurry, an emergency passport may be issued for SAR50. An application for a permanent passport must accompany the emergency passport application. The completion of an application usually takes 3 months or more from the time of submission. Current passports less than 10 years old (counting from the date of issuance) may be renewed until December 31, 1999; every citizen whose passport's validity does not extend far beyond this date is urged to renew it as soon as possible, to avoid the expected glut of applications as the millennium comes nigh. Renewal is free, and turnaround time is usually 2 weeks. For further information, contact the nearest Department of Home Affairs Office.

VISAS

A **visa** is an endorsement that a foreign government stamps into a passport which allows the bearer to stay in that country for a specified purpose and period of time. Most visas cost US$10-70 and allow you to spend about one month in a country, within six months to one year from the date of issue.

For more information, send for **Foreign Entry Requirements** (US$0.50) from the **Consumer Information Center,** Department 365E, Pueblo, CO 81009 (719-948-3334; http://www.pueblo.gsa.gov), or contact the **Center for International Business and Travel (CIBT),** 25 West 43rd St. #1420, New York, NY 10036 (800-925-2428 or 212-575-2811 from NYC), which secures visas for travel to and from all countries for a variable service charge.

U.S. AND CANADIAN ENTRANCE REQUIREMENTS

Foreign visitors to the United States and Canada are required to have a **passport** (see p. 4) and **visa/proof of intent to leave.** To visit either country, you must be healthy and law-abiding, and carry proof of your financial independence, such as a visa to the next country on your itinerary, an airplane ticket to depart, enough money to cover the cost of your living expenses, etc. A visa, stamped into a traveler's passport by the government of a host country, allows the bearer to stay in that country for a specified purpose and period of time. To obtain a U.S. or Canadian visa, contact the nearest embassy or consulate (see below).

UNITED STATES Travelers from certain nations may enter the U.S. without a visa through the **Visa Waiver Pilot Program.** Visitors qualify if they are traveling for business or pleasure, are staying for 90 days or less, have proof of intent to leave (e.g. a returning plane ticket), have a completed I-94W, and enter aboard particular air or sea carriers. Participating countries include Australia, France, Germany, Ireland, Italy, Japan, New Zealand, and the UK. Contact a U.S. consulate for more info; countries are added frequently.

Most visitors obtain a **B-2** or "pleasure tourist" visa. A B-2 costs $20 and is valid for six months. For general visa inquiries, consult the Bureau of Consular Affairs web page (http://travel.state.gov/visa_services.html). If you lose your **I-94 form** (the arrival/departure certificate attached to your visa upon arrival), you can replace it at the nearest **U.S. Immigration and Naturalization Service (INS)** office, though it's very unlikely that the form will be replaced within the time of your stay. **Extensions** for visas are sometimes obtainable with a completed I-539 form; call the forms request line at 800-870-3676. For more info, contact the INS at (800-755-0777 or 202-307-1501; http://www.ins.usdoj.gov).

CANADA Citizens of Australia, France, Germany, Ireland, Mexico, New Zealand, the U.K., and the U.S. may enter Canada without visas as long as they plan to stay for 90 days or fewer and carry proof of intent to leave. South Africans do need a visa to enter Canada. Citizens of all other countries should contact their Canadian consulate for more information. Contact **Citizenship and Immigration Canada** for the booklet *Applying for a Visitor Visa* at Information Centre, Public Affairs Branch, Journal Tower South, 365 Laurier Ave. W., Ottawa, Ontario K1A 1L1 (888-242-2100 or 613-954-9019; fax 954-2221; http://cicnet.ci.gc.ca.) **Extensions** are sometimes granted; phone the nearest Canada Immigration Centre.

EMBASSIES AND CONSULATES

Contact your nearest U.S. or Canadian embassy or consulate to obtain information regarding visas and passports to the United States and Canada. For **embassies and consulates** of other countries in Canada and the U.S., see p. 35.

U.S. Embassies: In **Australia,** Moonah Place, Canberra, ACT 2600 (02 6270 5000; fax 6270 5970); in **Canada,** 100 Wellington St., Ottawa, ON K1P 5T1 (613-238-5335 or 238-4470; fax 238 5720); in **Ireland,** 42 Elgin Rd., Ballsbridge, Dublin 4 (016 687 122); in **New Zealand,** 29 Fitzherbert Terr., Thorndon, Wellington (04 472 2068; fax 472 35 37); in **South Africa,** 877 Pretorius St., Arcadio 0083; P.O. Box 9536, Pretoria 0001 (012 342 1048; fax 342 22 44); in the **U.K.,** 24/31 Grosvenor Sq., London W1A 1AE (0171 499 90 00; fax 409 16 37).

U.S. Consulates: In **Australia,** MLC Centre, 19-29 Martin Place, 59th fl., Sydney, NSW 2000 (02 9373 9200; fax 9373 9125); 553 St. Kilda Rd., P.O. Box 6722, Melbourne, VIC 3004 (03 9526 5900; fax 9510 4646); 16 St. George Terr., 13th fl., Perth, WA 6000 (08 9231 9400; fax 9231 9444); in **Canada,** P.O. Box 65, Postal Station Desjardins, Montréal, QC H5B 1G1 (514-398-9695; fax 398-0973); 360 University Ave., Toronto, ON M5G 1S4 (416-595-1700; fax 595-0051); 1095 W. Pender St., Vancouver, BC V6E 2M6 (604-685-4311); in **New Zealand,** Yorkshire General Bldg., 4th fl., corner of Shortland and O'Connell St., Auckland (09 303 27 24; fax 366 08 70); in **South Africa,** Broadway Industries Centre, Heerengracht, Foreshore, Cape Town (021 214 280; fax 254 151); in the **U.K.,** Queen's House, 14 Queen St., Belfast, N. Ireland, BT1 6EQ (0123 232 82 39); 3 Regent Terr., Edinburgh, Scotland EH7 5BW (0131 556 83 15; fax 557 60 23).

Canadian Embassies and High Commissions: In **Australia,** Commonwealth Ave., Canberra ACT 2600 (02 6273 3844); in **Ireland,** Canada House, 65 St. Stephen's Green, Dublin 2 (014 78 19 88; fax 478 12 85); in **New Zealand,** 61 Molesworth St., Thorndon, Wellington (04 473 95 77; fax 471 20 82); in **South Africa,** 1103 Arcadia St., Hatfield, Pretoria 0028 (012 422 30 00; fax 422 30 52); in the **U.K.,** MacDonald House, 1 Grosvenor Square, London, W1X 0AA (0171 258 66 00; fax 258 63 33); in the **U.S.,** 501 Pennsylvania Ave., Washington, D.C. 20001 (202-682-1740; fax 682-7726).

Canadian Consulates: In **Australia,** Level 5, Quay West Bldg., 111 Harrington St., Sydney NSW 2000 (02 9364 3000; fax 9364 3098); in **New Zealand,** Level 9, Jetset Centre, 48 Emily Place, **Auckland** (09 309 36 90); in **South Africa,** Reserve Bank Building, 19th Fl., 360 St. George's Mall St., **Cape Town** 8001 (021 235 240; fax 234 893); in the **United Kingdom,** 3 George St., **Edinburgh,** Scotland, EH2 2XZ (0131 220 43 33; fax 245 60 10); in the **U.S.,** 22nd fl., 1251 Ave. of the Americas, **New York,** NY 10020 (212-596-1683; fax 596-1780); 550 Hope St., 18th fl., **Los Angeles,** CA 90071 (213-346-2700; fax 620-8827); 2 Prudential Plaza, 180 N. Stetson Ave. #2400, **Chicago,** IL 60601 (312-616-1860; fax 616-1877).

CUSTOMS: ENTERING

Unless you plan to import a BMW or a barnyard beast, you will probably pass right through customs with minimal ado. The U.S. and particularly Canada restrict the importation of firearms, fireworks, obscene literature and nudie flix. It is also illegal to import many perishable foods, including most fruits, vegetables, and meat products, because they may carry horrific pests. Officials may also seize articles made from certain protected species, so be ready to part with any illegal powdered rhino horn or koupreyskin boots. (See **Health,** p. 13, for info on carrying prescription drugs.)

UNITED STATES The following can be brought into the U.S.: $100 in gifts, $200 in personal merchandise, 200 cigarettes (1 carton), 50 cigars, and personal belongings like clothes and jewelry. Travelers age 21 and over may also bring up to 1 liter of alcohol, although state laws may further restrict this amount. Money (cash or traveler's checks) can be transported, but amounts over $10,000 must be reported. Customs officers may ask how much money you are carrying and your planned departure date to ensure that you'll be able to support yourself while in the U.S.

ESSENTIALS

The **U.S. Customs Service,** 1300 Pennsylvania Ave., Washington, D.C. 20229 (202-927-5580; http://www.customs.ustreas.gov), publishes a brochure with the snappy title *Customs Guidelines for Visitors to the United States,* detailing everything the international traveler might need to know about American customs.

CANADA Besides personal items, the following things may be brought in without duty: up to 1.14L of alcohol or a 24-pack of beer (as long you are of age in the province you are visiting), 50 cigars, 200 cigarettes (1 carton), 400g of manufactured tobacco, and gifts valued less than CDN$60. Exceeding the limited amounts results in a fine. For detailed info on Canadian customs and booklets on other Canadian travel information, write **Canada Customs,** 2265 St. Laurent Blvd., Ottawa, ON K1G 4K3 (800-461-9999 or 613-993-0534 outside Canada; fax 991-9062; http://www.rc.gc.ca).

CUSTOMS: RETURNING HOME

Upon returning home, you must declare all articles you acquired abroad and pay a **duty** on the value of those articles that exceed the allowance established by your country's customs service. Goods and gifts purchased at **duty-free** shops abroad are not exempt from duty or sales tax at your point of return; you must declare these items as well. "Duty-free" merely means that you need not pay a tax in the country of purchase. Restrictions generally apply to items such as alcohol, perfume, and tobacco and tobacco products. Contact the authorities listed below for specifics.

> **Australia: Australian Customs Service,** GPO Box 8, Sydney NSW 2001 (02 9213 2000; fax 9213 4000; http://www.customs.gov.au).
>
> **Canada: Canadian Customs,** 2265 St. Laurent Blvd., Ottawa, Ontario K1G 4K3 (613-993-0534). Phone the 24hr. **Automated Customs Information Service** at 800- 461-9999, or visit **Revenue Canada** at http://www.rc.gc.ca.
>
> **Ireland: The Revenue Commissioners,** Dublin Castle (01 679 27 77; fax 671 20 21; email taxes@iol.ie; http://www.revenue.ie), or **The Collector of Customs and Excise,** The Custom House, Dublin 1.
>
> **New Zealand: New Zealand Customs,** 50 Anzac Ave., Box 29, Auckland (09 377 35 20; fax 309 29 78).
>
> **South Africa: Commissioner for Customs and Excise,** Private Bag X47, Pretoria 0001 (12 314 9911; fax 328 6478), or consult the free pamphlet *South African Customs Information,* available in airports or from the Commissioner for Customs and Excise.
>
> **United Kingdom: Her Majesty's Customs and Excise,** Custom House, Nettleton Road, Heathrow Airport, Hounslow, Middlesex TW6 2LA (0181 910 3602 or 910 3566; fax 910 3765; http://www.open.gov.uk).
>
> **United States: U.S. Customs Service,** Box 7407, Washington D.C. 20044 (202-927-6724; http://www.customs.ustreas.gov). Ask for the brochure *Know Before You Go.*

YOUTH, STUDENT, & TEACHER IDENTIFICATION

Many U.S. establishments will honor an ordinary university student ID for student discounts. Still, the following two main forms of student and youth identification are extremely useful, especially for the accompanying **insurance** packages (see p. 15).

The **International Student Identity Card (ISIC)** is the most widely accepted form of student identification, procuring discounts for sights, theaters, museums, accommodations, meals, transportation, as well as other services. Present the card wherever you go, and ask about discounts even when none are advertised. In addition, cardholders have access to a toll-free **24hr. ISIC helpline** (800-626-2427 in the U.S. and Canada; 181 666 9025 in the U.K.; elsewhere call collect 44 181 666 9025) whose multilingual staff can provide assistance in medical, legal, and financial emergencies overseas. Most **budget travel agencies** (see p. 23) around the world issue ISICs. When you apply for the card, request a copy of the *International Student Identity Card Handbook,* which lists by country some of the available discounts. You can also write to **Council** for a copy (see p. 2). The card is valid from September to December of the following year and costs US$20, CDN$15 or AUS$15. Applicants must be at least 12 years old and degree-seeking students of a secondary or post-secondary school. Because of the proliferation of phony ISICs, many airlines and some other services require proof of student identity, such as a school ID card or a signed letter from the registrar attesting to your student status and stamped with the school seal. The **International Teacher Identity Card (ITIC)** (email isicinfo@istc.org; http://www.istc.org) offers the same insurance coverage, and similar but more limited discounts as the ISIC. The fee is US$20, UK£5, or AUS$13.

The **Federation of International Youth Travel Organizations (FIYTO)** issues a discount card to travelers who are under 26 but not students. Known as the **GO25 Card,** this one-year card offers many of the same benefits as the ISIC, and most organizations that sell the ISIC also sell the GO25. A brochure that lists discounts is free upon purchasing the card. Applying requires a passport-sized photo with your name printed on the back, plus a passport, valid driver's license, or copy of a birth certificate. The fee is US$20. Information is available on the web at http://www.ciee.org, or by contacting Travel CUTS in Canada, STA Travel in the U.K., Council Travel in the U.S., or FIYTO headquarters in Denmark (see **Budget Travel Agencies,** p. 23).

▓ Money Matters

By staying in the cheapest accommodations possible and self-preparing food from time to time, budget travelers from Alaska to Oregon can expect to spend anywhere from $10 to $60 per person per day. Transportation costs will increase these figures. Sacrificing health and safety isn't worth a cheaper tab—trips full of sickness, hunger, and muggings aren't fun.

CURRENCY AND EXCHANGE

It is cheaper to buy domestic currency than to buy foreign, so you should convert money to U.S. or Canadian dollars once there. Before leaving, however, it's a good idea to convert enough money to last a couple of days; this prevents problems if you arrive after banking hours or on a holiday. It's also wise to convert to the local currency before visiting seldom-touristed areas where banks may not recognize or exchange foreign currencies. Wholesale rates offered at banks are lower than those offered by other exchange agencies. If the bank has a surcharge for every exchange, converting in large sums will accrue fewer fees. Most international airports in Canada and the U.S. have currency exchange booths.

The Greenback (The U.S. Dollar)

CDN$1 = US$0.65	**US$1= CDN$1.53**
AUS$1 = US$0.60	**US$1 = AUS$1.68**
IR£1 = US$1.40	**US$1 = IR£0.72**
NZ$1 = US$0.50	**US$1 = NZ$1.99**
SAR1 = US$0.16	**US$1 = SAR6.26**
UK£1 = US$1.62	**US$1 = UK£0.62**

The main unit of currency in the U.S. is the dollar; the dollar is divided into 100 cents. Paper money is green in the U.S; bills come in denominations of $1, $5, $10, $20, $50, and $100. The U.S. has 1¢ (penny), 5¢ (nickel), 10¢ (dime), and 25¢ (quarter) coins, plus the elusive Susan B. Anthony silver dollar.

The Loonie (The Canadian Dollar)

US$1 = CDN$1.53	**CDN$1 = US$0.65**
AUS$1 = CDN$0.91	**CDN$1 = AUS$1.10**
IR£1 = CDN$2.14	**CDN$1 = IR£0.47**
NZ$1 = CDN$0.77	**CDN$1 = NZ$1.30**
SAR1 = CDN$0.24	**CDN$1 = SAR4.09**
UK£1 = CDN$2.47	**CDN$1 = UK£0.41**

ESSENTIALS

The main unit of currency in Canada is the dollar, not to be confused with the U.S. variety. Most Canadian businesses happily accept U.S. currency, their cheer fueled by the substantial hike they'll get with the exchange rate. Paper money comes in denominations of $5, $10, $20, $50, and $100, which are color-coded. Coins come in denominations of 1¢, 5¢, 10¢, 25¢, $1, and $2. The $1 coin is known as the **loonie** for the common loon *(Gavia immer)* on one face. Its recently introduced $2 counterpart has been dubbed the **toonie,** despite an obvious absence of toons.

> Except in the Western Canada section of this guide, and unless otherwise specified, all prices in this guide are in U.S. dollars.

SALES TAX AND TIPPING

State or provincial **sales taxes** are added to virtually all purchases in Canada and the U.S. Groceries are sometimes the sole exception. Oil-rich Alaska and Alberta have no state or provincial sales taxes. Alberta, like all of Canada, has a 7% federal **goods and services tax (GST).** Visitors can claim a rebate of the GST they pay on short-term accommodations (less than one month) and on most goods they buy to take home. This amount is significant, so be sure to save receipts and pick up a GST rebate form while in Canada. The total claim must be at least CDN$7 of GST (equal to $200 in purchases; each individual receipt must exceed CDN$50) and must be made within one year of the date of purchase. Further goods must be exported from Canada within 60 days of purchase. Contact **Revenue Canada, Visitor's Rebate Program,** 275 Pope Rd., Summerside, PEI C1N 6C6 (800-668-4748 in Canada; 902-432-5608 outside Canada).

In both Canada and the U.S., it is customary to **tip** waitstaff 15% for sit-down meals and cab drivers 15% of the fare, with variations depending on customer satisfaction. At the airport, porters expect a customary $1 tip per bag. **Bargaining** is generally fruitless and frowned upon. **Bartering** would be wackier still.

TRAVELER'S CHECKS

Traveler's checks provide a safe and easy ways to carry large sums of money, as they can be refunded if lost or stolen. Several agencies and banks sell them, usually for face value plus a small percentage commission. Keep some cash on hand in less-touristed regions, since small establishments may not accept traveler's checks.

Expect a fair amount of red tape and delay in the event of theft or loss of traveler's checks. Ask for a list of refund centers when buying checks (American Express and Bank of America have over 40,000 centers worldwide). To expedite the refund process, keep check receipts separate from checks and store them in a safe place or with a traveling companion. Record check numbers when cashing them and leave a list of check numbers with someone at home. Keep a separate supply of cash or traveler's checks for emergencies. Never countersign checks until you are prepared to cash them. Always bring your passport with you when you plan to use the checks. The following companies sell traveler's checks in U.S. and Canadian dollars:

American Express: 800-221-7282 in the U.S. and Canada; 800 25 19 02 in Australia; 0800 44 10 68 in New Zealand; 0800 52 13 13 in the U.K. Elsewhere, call U.S. collect 801-964-6665 or visit http://www.aexp.com. American Express traveler's cheques are the most widely recognized worldwide and the easiest to replace if lost or stolen. Cheques can be purchased for a small fee (1-4%) at American Express Travel Service Offices, banks, and American Automobile Association offices (AAA members can buy checks commission-free). Cardmembers can also purchase cheques at American Express Dispensers at airport Travel Service Offices and by ordering (800-ORDER-TC/673-3782). **checks for Two** can be signed by either of two people traveling together.

Thomas Cook MasterCard: 800-223-9920 in the U.S., Canada, or the Caribbean; call 0800 622 101 free or 1733 318 950 collect in the U.K.; from elsewhere call collect 44 1733 318 950. Commission 2% for purchases. Thomas Cook offices will cash checks commission-free; banks will make a commission charge.

VISA: 800-227-6811 in the U.S.; 0800 895 078 in the U.K.; elsewhere call collect 44 1733 318 949. Any of the above numbers can furnish the location of the nearest office. All Visa traveler's checks can be reported lost at these numbers.

CREDIT CARDS

Credit cards can be invaluable in the U.S. and Canada, and are sometimes expected or required. (For example, many car rental agencies require that you have a credit card.) Credit cards are also useful when an emergency leaves you temporarily without other resources. In addition, some cards carry services ranging from personal or car rental insurance to emergency assistance. Major credit cards can be used to extract cash advances from associated banks and ATMs; this can be a good bargain for foreign travelers because credit card companies get the wholesale exchange rate, which is generally 5% better than banks' retail rate. You will be charged ruinous interest if you don't pay off the bill quickly, though, so be careful when using this service. **American Express** cards also work in some ATMs, as well as at AmEx offices and major airports.

American Express (800-THE-CARD/843-2273) cards carry a hefty annual fee ($55; except the free student Optima card), but offer extensive travel-related services. **MasterCard** (outside North America, "EuroCard" or "Access") and **Visa** ("Carte Bleue" or "Barclaycard") are the most widely accepted credit cards. Both sell cards through banks. For lost or stolen cards call Visa at (800-336-8472) or Mastercard (800-037-7309). The following web sites locate Visa and MasterCard ATMs around the world:
http://www.visa.com/cgi-bin/vee/pd/atm/main.html?
http://www.mastercard.com/atm

ATM CARDS

There are tens of thousands of ATMs (automatic teller machines) all over in the U.S. and Canada, offering 24-hour service in banks, airports, grocery stores, gas stations, and beyond. ATMs allow you to withdraw local currency from your bank account wherever you are. There is often a limit on the amount of money you can withdraw per day (usually about US$500, depending on the card and account), and computer network failures are not unknown. The two major ATM networks in North America are **Cirrus** (800-4-CIRRUS/424-7787) and **PLUS** (800-843-7587; http://www.visa.com). Inquire at your bank about fees charged for ATM transactions.

EMERGENCY CASH

If you run out of money on the road, you can have more mailed to you in the form of a certified check, traveler's checks bought in your name, or through postal money orders, available at post offices (85¢ fee; $600 limit per order; cash only). Keep receipts, since money orders are refundable if lost. **Personal checks** from a distant home might not be accepted no matter how many shiny ID cards you have.

One of the easiest ways to get money from home is to bring an **American Express (AmEx)** card. AmEx allows Green Card holders to draw cash from their checking accounts at any of its major offices and many of its representatives' offices, up to $1000 every 21 days (no service charge, no interest). AmEx also offers **Express Cash** (800-CASH-NOW/227-4669; outside the U.S. call collect 336-668-5041), with ATMs located in airports, hotels, banks, office complexes, and shopping areas around the world. Express Cash withdrawals are automatically debited from a cardmember's checking account or credit line. Green Card holders may withdraw up to $1000 in a seven day period. There is a 2% transaction fee for each cash withdrawal, with a $2.50 minimum/$20 maximum. Unless using the AmEx service, cashing checks in foreign currencies usually takes weeks and a $30 fee to clear.

Money can also be wired abroad by **Western Union** (800-325-6000). In the U.S., call Western Union any time at 800-CALL-CASH/225-5227 to cable money with a Visa, Discover, or MasterCard within the domestic United States and the U.K. The rates for sending cash are generally $10-11 cheaper than with a credit card, and the money is usually available within an hour.

■ Safety and Security

For emergencies in the U.S. and Canada, dial **911**. This number works in most places. If it does not, dial 0 for the operator and request to be connected with the appropriate emergency service (i.e., police, fire, ambulance, etc.). In National Parks, it is usually best to call the **warden number** in case of emergency.

STREET SMARTS

Trust your instincts—they can be your most valuable asset. A gawking camera-toter is a more obvious target than a low-profile local look-alike. Try to appear that you know what you are doing and where you are going, even if you don't. Walking into a cafe or shop to check a map beats checking it on a street corner. Do not keep money or anything precious in your back pocket or in a fanny pack; use a neck pouch or money belt instead. Sleeping in a car or van parked in the city can be *extremely* dangerous—even the most dedicated budget traveler should not consider it an option. Be aware of your surroundings: a single block can separate safe and unsafe areas. If you feel uncomfortable, leave as quickly and directly as you can.

A good self-defense course can provide concrete ways to deal with different types of aggression. Community colleges frequently offer such courses inexpensively. **Impact, Prepare, and Model Mugging** (800-345-5425) can refer you to local self-defense courses in the United States. Course prices vary from $50-400. Women's and men's courses are offered.

TRAVEL ADVISORIES

Australian Department of Foreign Affairs and Trade (02 6261 9111) offers travel information and advisories at http://www.dfat.gov.au.

Canadian Department of Foreign Affairs and International Trade (DFAIT) provides advisories and travel warnings at http://www.dfait-maeci.gc.ca. Call them at 613-944-6788 from Ottawa or 800-267-8376 elsewhere in Canada; to receive extra travel tips, call 613-944-4000 for their free publication, *Bon Voyage*.

United Kingdom Foreign and Commonwealth Office provides official warnings at http://www.fco.gov.uk; you can also call the office at 0171 238 45 03. For official **United States Department of State** offers travel advisories available on its 24-hour hotline at 202-647-5225. Its website (http://www.state.gov), has travel information and publications.

DRUGS AND ALCOHOL

If you carry **prescription drugs** while traveling, it is vital to have a copy of the prescriptions readily accessible at U.S. and Canadian borders. The importation of **illegal substances** into Canada or the U.S. is, needless to say, illegal, and a punishable offense. Away from borders, police attitudes vary widely across the region, but the old standards—marijuana, LSD, heroin, cocaine—are illegal in every province and state. Those arrested for drug possession in the U.S. or Canada can be subject to a wide range of charges.

In Oregon, Washington, and Alaska, the **drinking age** is 21. British Columbia and the Yukon Territory prohibit drinking below the age of 19, while in Alberta the drinking age is 18. In both the U.S. and Canada, this law is strictly enforced. Particularly in the U.S., be prepared to show a photo ID (preferably some government document like a driver's license or passport) if you appear to be under 30. Sixty-five years after Prohibition, some areas of the U.S. are still "dry," meaning they do not permit the sale of alcohol at all, while other places prohibit the sale of alcohol on Sundays. Officials on both sides of the border take **drunk driving** very seriously—don't do it.

■ Health

Common sense is the simplest prescription for good health while traveling: eat well, drink and sleep enough, and don't overexert yourself. Travelers complain most often about their feet and their gut, so take precautions. Drinking lots of fluids can prevent dehydration and constipation, and wearing sturdy shoes, clean socks, and using talcum powder should help keep feet dry and happy. To minimize the effects of jet lag, reset your body's clock by immediately adopting the time of your destination upon arrival. Acclimatization to a new time zone usually takes two or three days.

BEFORE YOU GO

A good rule of thumb: if you can't live without something, bring a spare or make a backup plan. If you wear **glasses** or **contact lenses,** carry an extra prescription and arrange to have your doctor or a family member send a replacement pair in an emergency. In your passport or other document, write the names of any people you wish to be contacted in case of a medical emergency, and list any allergies or medical conditions of which doctors should be aware. **Allergy** sufferers should find out if their conditions are likely to be aggravated in the regions they plan to visit, and obtain a full supply of any necessary medication before the trip. Bring any **medication** you take regularly and may need while traveling, as well as a copy of the **prescription** and a statement of any preexisting medical conditions you may have—especially if you will be bringing insulin, syringes, or any narcotics into the U.S. or Canada.

Those with medical conditions (e.g. diabetes, allergies to antibiotics, epilepsy, heart conditions) may want to obtain a **Medic Alert** identification tag ($35 the first year, $15 annually thereafter), which identifies the condition and gives a 24-hour collect-call information number. Contact Medic Alert at 800-825-3785, or write to Medic Alert Foundation, 2323 Colorado Ave., Turlock, CA 95382. Diabetics can contact the **American Diabetes Association,** 1660 Duke St., Alexandria, VA 22314 (800-232-3472) to receive copies of the article "Travel and Diabetes," and a diabetic ID card, which carries messages in 18 languages explaining the carrier's diabetic status.

The **American Red Cross** publishes a *First-Aid and Safety Handbook* ($5) available for purchase by calling or writing to the ARC at 285 Columbus Ave., Boston, MA 02116-5114 (800-564-1234). Finally, an excellent source of general information on health for travelers is the **United States Center for Disease Control and Prevention,** Travelers' Health, 1600 Clifton Rd. NE, Atlanta, GA 30333 (404-332-4559; for traveler's hotline; 404-639-3311 for public inquiries; 800-227-8922 for STD hotline; 800-342-2437 for AIDS/HIV hotline; 800-243-7889 for TTY; fax 332-4565; http://www.cdc.gov).

COMMON WOES

For minor health problems, bring a compact **first-aid kit,** including bandages, aspirin or other pain killer, antiseptic soap or antibiotic cream, a thermometer, a Swiss Army knife with tweezers, moleskin, a decongestant for colds or allergies, motion sickness remedy, medicine for diarrhea or stomach problems, sunscreen, and insect repellent with DEET. If you suffer from any of the following ailments in a severe or prolonged form, seek medical help as soon as possible. For more detailed information, find *Backcountry First Aid and Extended Care* by Buck Tilton, published by ICS books.

Altitude sickness: Travelers to high altitudes must allow their bodies a couple of days to adjust to the lower levels of oxygen in the air before engaging in strenuous activities. Expect some drowsiness, and an amplification of the effects of alcohol.

Bee Stings: Potentially fatal for those who are allergic; if you are, always be prepared with an Ana-Kit or other treatment for anaphylactic shock. If suffering from restricted breathing after a sting, seek medical attention immediately.

Blisters: Second degree burns caused by friction, blisters are the bane of hikers everywhere. Proto-blisters (called hotspots) are more easily treated than full-blown blisters, so prevention is key. Warm wet feet are most prone to blisters. If a hotspot develops, replace wet socks with dry ones, clear the skin and cover the area with moleskin. If a blister occurs despite all preventative measures, keep the skin as cool and dry as possible, and surround the area with a doughnut of moleskin.

Diarrhea: Many people take over-the-counter medicine (such as Pepto-Bismol or Immodium) to counteract it, but be aware that such remedies can complicate serious infections. The most dangerous side effect of diarrhea is dehydration; a simple and effective anti-dehydration formula is 8 oz. of (clean) water with a ½ tsp. of sugar or honey, plus a pinch of salt. Decaffeinated soft drinks and salted crackers can also help. If you develop a fever or your symptoms don't go away after four or five days, consult a doctor. Also consult a doctor if children develop traveler's diarrhea, since treatment is different. This too shall pass.

Frostbite: Frostbite can be separated into two categories: superficial and deep. Superficially frostbitten skin is pale and numb, but moves when pressed. Victims should drink warm beverages, stay dry, and *gently and slowly* warm the frostbitten area with dry fabric or, even better, with steady body contact. *Never* rub or pour hot water on superficial frostbite; skin is easily damaged when frozen. Deep frostbite turns skin pale and numb, but it is hard to the touch. Find a doctor immediately. If means are available, rapidly rewarm in circulating water between 104-108°F—any hotter and heat damage occurs. Soft cotton should be placed between rewarmed digits, but any other contract should be avoided. Pain can be intense.

Giardia: Found in all too many rivers and lakes, *Giardia lamblia* is a bacterium that causes gas, painful cramps, loss of appetite, and violent diarrhea. To protect yourself, bring your water to a rolling boil for several minutes or purify it with iodine tablets before drinking or cooking with it.

Heat Stroke: Heat stroke is preceded by the dizziness and nausea of **heat exhaustion,** which is less serious and can be treated with rest, water, and salty foods (but not salt tablets, which are too concentrated). When sweating stops and body temperature rises, more dangerous heat stroke has begun. Cool the victim immediately with liquids, wet towels, and shade, concentrating on head and neck, and get medical attention even if the victim appears to have recovered. Relapses are common.

Hypothermia: A real danger in Alaska, Western Canada, and the Pacific Northwest. Symptoms include shivering, slurred speech, loss of coordination, exhaustion, hallucinations, or amnesia. The best way to treat hypothermia victims is to change their environment to keep their body heat from being lost: get the victim out of all wet clothes and into dry ones, and out of wind into shelter. *Do not let victims of advanced hypothermia fall asleep*—their body temperatures will drop further, and if they lose consciousness, they may die. To avoid hypothermia, stay dry and out of the wind. Dress in layers; wool, pile fleece jackets, and Gore-Tex rain gear insulate even when wet. Never rely on cotton, including denim jeans, for warmth; this "death fabric" sucks away heat when wet.

Lyme Disease: Tick-borne diseases, like Lyme disease, can be very serious. Lyme disease is not known to exist in Alaska, but may be a problem for travelers in the Pacific Northwest. Lyme is characterized by a circular rash of two inches or more that looks like a bull's eye. Other symptoms are flu-like: fever, headache, fatigue, or aches and pains. Left untreated, Lyme can cause dangerous problems in joints, the heart, and the nervous system. There is no vaccine, but Lyme can be treated with antibiotics if caught early. Removing a tick within 24 hours greatly reduces the risk of infection. Wear bug repellent when hiking, and check for ticks at least once a day; they are brownish and about the size of a pinhead. To be super-cautious, pull your socks up over your pant legs.

Mosquitoes: Perhaps the greatest threat to your *mental* health are the swarms of mosquitoes that descend very summer. Buy a bednet for camping, tuck long pants into socks, and wear long pants and long sleeves (fabric need not be thick or warm; tropic-weight cottons can keep you comfortable in the heat). Use insect repellents; **DEET** can be bought in spray or liquid form, but use it sparingly, especially on children. Another option is **Avon Skin-So-Soft,** which by some happy and mysterious accident frightens mosquitoes away while making skin silky smooth. Natural repellents can also be useful: taking **vitamin B-12** pills regularly can eventually make you smelly to insects, as can garlic pills. Still, be sure to supplement your vitamins with repellent. Calamine lotion or topical cortisones (like Cortaid©) may stop insect bites from itching, as can a bath with a half-cup of baking soda or oatmeal.

Poison Ivy, Poison Oak, Poison Sumac: These plants secrete oils that can cause unbearable itchiness, hives, and inflammation of the affected areas. Some people have allergic reactions with asthma-like symptoms; find medical help if this occurs. If you think you have come into contact with one of these plants, wash your skin with soap and cold water; heat dilates the pores, driving the poison deeper. An excellent soap is **Fels Naptha,** available at any good drug store. If rashes occur, calamine lotion, topical cortisones (like Cortaid), or antihistamines may stop the itching. Fight the near-irresistible urge to scratch; it will only spread the oil.

The Plague and **Relapsing Fever:** These diseases, which are transmitted through fleas and ticks, still occur in Western North America, though rarely. Treatment is available for both, and a vaccine can prevent the plague.

Rabies: If you are bitten by any animal, wild or otherwise, clean your wound thoroughly and seek medical help. Rabies can be fatal if it goes undetected.

Sunburn: Apply sunscreen liberally and often. You may not go to the Far North in search of a tan, but in summer the sun will be up for 20 or more hours a day. Sunscreens of Sun Protection Factor (SPF) 20 are strong enough for the fairest skin; higher ratings won't help and are more expensive. In case of severe sunburn and the formation of blisters, consult a doctor.

AIDS, HIV, STDS

Acquired Immune Deficiency Syndrome (AIDS) is a growing problem around the world. The World Health Organization estimates that there are around 30 million people infected with the HIV virus. The easiest mode of HIV transmission is through direct blood to blood contact with an HIV+ person; *never* share intravenous drug, tattooing, or other needles. The most common mode of transmission is sexual intercourse. Women now represent 40% of all new HIV infections. To lessen chances of contracting any sexually transmitted disease (STD), always use a latex condom. Condoms are widely available in Canada and the U.S.

For more information on AIDS, call the **U.S. Center for Disease Control's** 24-hour Hotline (800-342-2437). Contact the **World Health Organization,** attention Global Program on AIDS, Avenue Appia 20, 1211 Geneva 27, Switzerland (41 22 791 2111; fax. 41 22 791-0746) or the **Bureau of Consular Affairs,** #6831, Department of State, Washington, D.C. 20520 for statistics on AIDS internationally. Council's brochure, *Travel Safe: AIDS and International Travel,* is available at all Council Travel offices.

Sexually transmitted diseases (STDs) such as gonorrhea, chlamydia, genital warts, syphilis, and herpes are a lot easier to catch than HIV. It's a wise idea to actually look at a partner's genitals before having sex. Warning signs for STDs include: swelling, sores, bumps, or blisters on sex organs, rectum, or mouth; burning and pain during urination and bowel movements; itching around sex organs; swelling or redness in the throat, and flu-like symptoms with fever, chills, and aches. If these symptoms develop, see a doctor immediately. Condoms may protect you from certain STDs, but oral or even tactile contact can lead to transmission.

■ Insurance

Beware of offers for unnecessary coverage—your regular insurance policies might extend to many travel-related medical problems and property loss. **Homeowners' insurance** often covers theft during travel and loss of travel documents (passport, plane ticket, etc.), while many types of **medical insurance** (especially university policies) often cover medical costs incurred abroad. Travel insurance may still be worth considering, especially if the cost of trip cancellation, interruption, or emergency medical evacuation is greater than you can absorb.

ISIC and **ITIC** (see p. 8) provide $3000 of accident and illness insurance and $100 per day for up to 60 days of hospitalization. Cardholders have access to a toll-free 24-hour helpline (800-626-2427) whose multilingual staff provides assistance in medical, legal, and financial emergencies overseas. **Council** (see p. 2) offers a range of plans that supplement basic insurance coverage, with options covering medical treatment, hospitalization, accidents, baggage loss, and even charter flights missed due to illness. Most **American Express** cardholders (customer service 800-528-4800) receive automatic car rental insurance (collision and theft, but not liability) and travel accident coverage ($100,000 in life insurance) on flight purchases made with the card.

Insurance companies usually require a copy of the police report for thefts, or evidence of having paid medical expenses (doctor's statements, receipts) before honoring a claim. They may have time limits on filing for reimbursement. Always carry policy numbers and proof of insurance. Check with each insurance carrier for restrictions and policies. Most of the carriers listed below have 24-hour hotlines.

Access America, 6600 West Broad St., P.O. Box 11188, Richmond, VA 23230 (800-284-8300; fax 804-673-1491). Covers trip cancellation/interruption, on-the-spot hospital admittance, emergency medical evacuation, sickness, and baggage loss.

The Berkeley Group/Carefree Travel Insurance, 100 Garden City Plaza, P.O. Box 9366, Garden City, NY 11530-9366 (516-294-0220 or 800-323-3149; fax 516-294-1095). Offers two comprehensive packages with coverage for trip cancellation/ interruption/delay, accident and sickness, medical coverage, baggage loss/ delay, accidental death or dismemberment, and travel supplier insolvency. Trip cancellation/interruption may be purchased separately at $5.50 per $100 of coverage.

Globalcare Travel Insurance, 220 Broadway, Lynnfield, MA 01940 (800-821-2488; fax 617-592-7720; email global@nebc.mv.com; http://www.nebc.mv.com/global-care). Complete medical, legal, emergency, and travel-related services. On-the-spot payments and special student programs, including benefits for trip cancellation/ interruption. GTI waives pre-existing medical conditions, and provides coverage for the bankruptcy or default of cruise lines, airlines, and tour operators. Includes Worldwide Collision Damage Provision at no charge.

Travel Assistance International, by Worldwide Assistance Services, Inc., 1133 15th St. NW, Suite 400, Washington, D.C. 20005-2710 (800-821-2828 or 202-828-5894; fax 202-828-5896; email wassist@aol.com; http://www.worldwide-assistance.com). TAI provides its members with a 24hr. free hotline for travel emergencies and referrals in over 200 countries. Their Per-Trip (starting at $21) and Frequent Traveler (starting at $88) plans include medical (evacuation and repatriation), travel, and communication services.

■ Alternatives to Tourism

WORKING FOR A LIVING

There are few better way to immerse yourself in a culture than to become part of its economy. Finding work is often a matter of timing and luck. Jobs may come from local residents, hostels, employment offices, or chambers of commerce. Officially, you can hold a job in most countries only with a **work permit.** Temporary agencies often hire for non-secretarial placement as well as for standard typing assignments. Marketable skills, like touch-typing, dictation, computer knowledge, and experience with children can prove very helpful in the search for a temporary job. Volunteer (unpaid) jobs are readily available almost everywhere in Canada and the U.S; some provide room and board in exchange for labor. Consult newspapers and bulletin boards on college campuses for job listings.

Foreigners **must** apply for a **work visa** to work in the U.S. Working or studying in the U.S. with only a B-2 (tourist) visa is grounds for deportation. The first step toward acquiring a work visa begins at the U.S. consulate or embassy nearest you. **Council Travel** (see p. 23) runs a summer travel/work program which lets students spend their summers working in the U.S.; check your local Council agency for details. If you intend to work in **Canada,** you will need an **Employment Authorization,** obtained before you enter the country. Residents of the U.S., Greenland, and St. Pierre/Miquelon may apply for Employment Authorization at a port of entry. Your potential employer must contact the nearest **Canadian Employment Centre (CEC)** for approval of the employment offer. For more information, contact the consulate or embassy in your home country.

Canneries

Seafood harvesting and processing jobs are no pleasure cruise. While it is possible to earn a lot of cash in a brief time, you must be willing to put in long, hard hours at menial and unrewarding tasks. As the **Alaska Employment Service** eloquently states, "Most seafood processing jobs are smelly, bloody, slimy, cold, wet, and tiring because of manual work and standing for many hours. The aroma of fish lingers with workers throughout the season. Most get used to it. Those who can't generally leave." If you're still interested, the Alaska Employment Service (part of the Department of Labor) is a good source of information: call (Alaska area code 907) **Kodiak** 486-3105, **Anchorage** 269-4800, **Petersburg** 772-3791, **Sitka** 747-6921, **Ketchikan** 225-3181, **Homer** 235-7791, **Kenai** 283-2927, **Seward** 224-5276, or **Valdez** 835-4910.

Treeplanting

Planting trees is the Canadian equivalent of work in the canneries—the smell is better, but hours are long and hard, and the bugs can be indescribable. Canada requires its lumber companies to reforest the areas they log. Whether the planting can recreate Canada's old growth forests is a question of some debate; what the policy has created, though, is intense and potentially lucrative job opportunity in the forests of northern British Columbia and Alberta. Planters are usually paid between ten and thirty cents per tree; an experienced planter can plunk enough trees in the ground to earn CDN$200 a day. Most treeplanters are university students who work from late spring to mid-summer. The companies that hire them range from well-run, professional organizations to ragtag hippie collectives to exploitative rip-off operations. For more information, contact **Forestry Canada** (250-363-0600).

Organic Farming

Willing Workers on Organic Farms (WWOOF), operates in Canada and the U.S. (New England), among other countries. Membership in WWOOF allows you to receive room and board at a variety of organic farms, in exchange for agricultural toil. Those interested in WWOOF-ing can join WWOOF International ($10; apply to Dept.: Members Beau Champ, 24610 Montpeyroux, France) or become a member of WWOOF in the U.S. (New England Small Farms Institute, P.O. Box 937, Blechertown, MA 01007; $25; must be U.S. resident) or Canada (John Vanden Heuvel, RR2 Carlston Road, Blewett, Nelson, BC VIL 5P5; CDN $25).

STUDY OPPORTUNITIES

If you are interested in studying in the Pacific Northwest, Western Canada, or Alaska, contact the universities listed below for information about enrolling. As a first step, contact the **Institute of International Education (IIE)** (212-984-5413; fax 984-5358) 809 United Nations Plaza, New York, NY 10017-3580. A nonprofit, international and cultural exchange agency. Publishes *Academic Year Abroad* (US$43, plus $5 shipping), and *Vacation Study Abroad,* with information on short-term programs including summer and language schools ($37, plus $4 shipping).

Lewis & Clark College, 615 SW Palatine Hill Rd., Portland, OR 97219-7899 (503-768-7040 or 800-444-4111; fax 503-768-7055; email admissions@lclark.edu; http://www.lclark.edu).

Oregon State University, 104 Kerr Administration Bldg., Corvallis, OR 97333-2106 (541-737-4411; fax 541-737-2482; email osuadmit@ccmail.orst.edu; http://www.orst.edu).

Simon Fraser University, Office of the Registrar, Burnaby, BC V5A 1S6 (604-291-3224; fax 291-4969; http://www.sfu.ca); downtown branch at Harbor Center, 515 West Hastings, Vancouver, BC V6B 5K3 (604-291-5040).

University of Alaska Anchorage, 3211 Providence Dr., Anchorage, AK 99508 (907-786-1480; fax 786-4888; http://www.uaa.alaska.edu).

University of Alaska Fairbanks, Office of Admissions, P.O. Box 757480, Fairbanks, AK 99775-7480 (800-478-1UAF in Alaska; 907-474-7500 elsewhere; fax 474-5379; email fyapply@aurora.alaska.edu; http://zorba.uafadm.alaska.edu).

University of Alberta, 120 Administration Bldg., Edmonton, AB T6G 2M7 (780-492-3113; fax 492-7172; email registrar@ualberta.ca; http://www.registrar.ualberta.ca).

University of British Columbia, Office of the Registrar, 2016-1874 East Mall, Vancouver, BC V6T 1Z1 (604-822-3159; fax 604-822-5945; http://www.ubc.ca).

University of Calgary, 2500 University Dr. NW, Calgary, AB T2N 1N4 (403-220-6645; fax 289-1253; http://www.ucalgary.ca).

University of Oregon, Office of Admissions, 240 Oregon Hall, 1217 University of Oregon, Eugene, OR, 97403-1217 (541-346-3201; fax 346-5815; TTY 346-1323; email uoadmit@oregon.uoregon.edu; http://www.uoregon.edu).

University of Victoria, Admission Services, P.O. Box 3025, Victoria, BC V8W 3P2 (250-721-8119; fax 721-6225; http://www.uvic.ca).

University of Washington, Office of Admission, Schmitz Hall Room 320, Box 355840, Seattle, WA 98195-5840 (206-543-9686; fax 685-3655; http://www.washington.edu).

Washington State University, 370 Lighty Student Services Bldg., Pullman, WA 99163-1067 (509-335-5586; fax 335-4902; email admiss@wsu.edu; http://www.wsu.edu).

U.S. STUDENT VISAS Foreigners who wish to study in the United States must apply for either an **M-1 visa** (for vocational studies) or an **F-1 visa** (for full-time students enrolled in an academic or language program). An F-1 allows you to work part-time in an on-campus position. For information on how to obtain and submit the proper forms, and how to acquire an on-campus job, contact the international student office at the institution of interest.

CANADIAN STUDENT VISAS Foreigners who wish to study in Canada will need a **Student Authorization.** To obtain one, contact the nearest Canadian consulate or embassy. Be sure to apply at least four months ahead of time; it can take a long time to go through, and there is a processing fee. You will also need to prove to the Canadian government that you are able to support yourself financially. A student authorization is good for one year. If you plan to stay longer, it is extremely important that you do not let it expire before you apply for renewal. Canadian immigration laws permit full-time students to seek on-campus employment. For specifics, contact a Canadian Immigration Center (CIC) or consulate. Residents of the U.S., Greenland, and St. Pierre/Miquelon may apply for Student Authorization at a port of entry.

■ Packing

Pack lightly—this means you. Even if you have a car. The more you bring, the more you have to worry about. A good rule is to lay out only what you absolutely need, then take half the clothes and twice the money.

THE BACKPACK

If you plan to cover most of your itinerary on foot, a sturdy **frame backpack** is vital. **Internal-frame packs** mold better to your back, keep a lower center of gravity, and are excellent on difficult trails that require a lot of maneuvering. **External-frame packs** contain more compartments, keep the weight higher and distribute it more evenly, and can be more comfortable for long hikes over even terrain. Before buying a pack, weigh it and try it on. Make sure it has a padded hip belt that transfers weight from shoulders to hips. Any serious backpacking requires a pack of at least 4000 cubic inches. Allow an additional 500 cubic inches for your sleeping bag in internal-frame packs. Good packs cost anywhere from $150 to $500. Be wary of excessively low-end prices. Don't sacrifice quality. See **Camping and Hiking Equipment,** p. 45.

DRESS FOR SUCCESS

The clothing you bring will, of course, depend on when and where you're planning to travel. In general, **dressing in layers** is best when traveling and hiking.

Light Layers: Stick to natural fibers and lightweight materials. Start with a few t-shirts; they take up virtually no space and you can wear a sweatshirt or sweater over one on a chilly night. Pack a couple of pairs of shorts and jeans, as well as underwear, socks, a towel, and swimwear.

Heavy Layers: Even in summer, though, the Pacific Coast and Alaska can get quite cold. Bring heavier layers that insulate while wet, such as polypropylene, polar fleece, or wool. Never rely on cotton for warmth.

Rain: A waterproof jacket and a backpack cover will take care of you and your stuff. Gore-Tex is a fabric that's both waterproof and breathable; it's highly desirable if you plan on hiking. Avoid cotton as outer-wear, especially if you will be outdoors a lot.

Footwear: Well-cushioned athletic shoes or lace-up leather shoes are good for general walking, but for serious hiking a pair of water-proofed hiking boots is essential: they're lightweight, rugged, and dry quickly. *Break in your shoes before you leave home.* A double pair of socks—light absorbent cotton inside and thick wool outside—will cushion feet, keep them dry, and help prevent blisters. Talcum powder in your shoes and on your feet can prevent sores, and moleskin is great for blisters (see p. 13). Bring a pair of **flip-flops** for the fungal floors of communal showers.

ELECTRICAL CURRENT

Electricity is 110V AC in the U.S. and Canada, only half as much as that of most European countries. Visit a hardware store for an adapter (which changes the shape of the plug) and a converter (which changes the voltage). Do not make the mistake of using only an adapter, or you'll fry your appliances. Travelers who heat-disinfect their contact lenses should consider switching to a chemical disinfection system.

RANDOM USEFUL STUFF

Sleepsack: If planning to stay in **youth hostels,** make the requisite sleepsack instead of paying the hostel's linen charge. Fold a full size sheet in half the long way, then sew it closed along the open long side and one of the short sides.

Toiletries: Soap, shampoo, toothpaste, deodorant, razors, comb, brush, toilet paper, tampons, condoms, birth control, vitamins, sunscreen, lip balm, and insect repellent. Pack spillables in plastic bags to prevent chemical slicks within your luggage. Bring whatever you need to keep your contact lenses happy.

More useful than random: Alarm clock, batteries, waterproof matches, sun hat, needle and thread, safety pins, sunglasses, pocketknife, plastic water bottle, compass, towel, padlock, whistle, flashlight, earplugs, duct tape (for patching tears in anything), clothespins, maps, tweezers, garbage bags (for rain proofing anything).

More random but still useful: Notebook with pens, harmonica, bandanas, cheap novels, string, rubber bands, Walkman with headphones, lead-lined pouch (for protecting high-speed film from airport x-rays or storing Kryptonite).

■ Specific Concerns

WOMEN TRAVELERS

Women exploring on their own face additional safety concerns, but you can be adventurous without taking undue risks. Trust your instincts when choosing a place to stay; if you'd feel better somewhere else, move on. You might consider staying in hostels which offer single rooms that lock from the inside or in places that offer rooms for women only. Check communal showers before settling in. Stick to centrally-located accommodations and avoid solitary late-night walks or bus rides. **Hitching** is never safe for lone women, or even for two women traveling together. Look as if you know where you're going (even when you don't), and consider approaching women or couples for directions if you're lost or feel uncomfortable.

Dress conservatively, especially in rural areas. Wearing a conspicuous wedding band may help prevent unwanted overtures. The best answer to verbal harassment is usually no answer at all (a reaction is what the harasser wants). Don't hesitate to seek out a police officer or a passerby if you are being harassed. *Let's Go* lists emergency numbers (including rape crisis lines) in the **Practical Information** listings of most towns and cities. In emergencies, a toll-free call to **911** should result in immediate assistance. A **Model Mugging** course prepares you for a potential mugging, and can also raise your awareness of your surroundings and bolster your confidence (see **Safety and Security**, p. 12).

For info, contact the **National Organization for Women (NOW),** (email now@now.org; http://now.org) which has offices across the country that refer women travelers to rape crisis centers and counseling services. Main offices include 105 E. 22nd St., Suite 307, New York, NY 10010 (212 260 4422); 1000 16th St. NW, Suite 700, Washington, D.C. 20036 (202-331-0066); and 3543 18th St., Box 27, San Francisco, CA 94110 (415-861-8960; fax 861-8969).

Directory of Women's Media is available from the National Council for Research on Women, 11 Hanover Sq., 20th fl., New York, NY 10005 (212-785-7335; fax 785-7350). The publication lists women's publishers, bookstores, theaters, and news organizations (mail orders, $30).
A Journey of One's Own: Uncommon Advice for the Independent Woman Traveler, by Thalia Zepatos. Interesting and full of good advice, with a bibliography of books and resources. **Adventures in Good Company: The Complete Guide to Women's Tours and Outdoor Trips,** on group travel by the same author, costs US$17. Both books are available in bookstores across North America or can be ordered directly from the publisher. ($17; $2 shipping for the first book, 50¢ for each additional order). **Go Girl! The Black Woman's Book of Travel and Adventure,** Elaine Lee, editor. Includes 52 travelers' tales, advice on how to travel inexpensively and safely, and a discussion of issues of specific concern to black women. Available from The Eighth Mountain Press, 624 Southeast 29th Ave., Portland, OR 97214 (503-233-3936; fax 233-0774; email soapston@teleport.com).
More Women Travel: Adventures, Advice & Experience, by Miranda Davies and Natania Jansz (Penguin, $16.95). Essays by women travelers in several foreign countries, plus a decent bibliography and resource index. Contact Rough Guides, 345 Hudson St. 14th fl., New York, NY 10014 (212-366-2348; fax 414-3395; email rough@panix.com; www.roughguides.com/women).
Active Women Vacation Guide, by Evelyn Kay ($17.95; shipping is free for *Let's Go* readers). Includes listings of 1000 trips worldwide offered by travel companies for active women, and true stories of women's traveling adventures. Blue Panda Publications, 3031 Fifth St., Boulder, CO 80304 (303-449-8474; fax 449-7525)

OLDER TRAVELERS

Senior citizens are eligible for a wide range of discounts on transportation, museums, movies, theaters, concerts, restaurants, and accommodations, like the Golden Age Passport (see p. 43). If you don't see a senior citizen price listed, ask and you may be delightfully surprised. Agencies for senior group travel are growing in enrollment and popularity. Try **ElderTreks,** 597 Markham St., Toronto, ON, M6G 2L7, (800-741-7956 or 416-588-5000; fax 588-9839; email passages@inforamp.net; http://www.eldertreks.com) or **Walking the World,** P.O. Box 1186, Fort Collins, CO 80522, (970-498-0500; fax 498-9100; email walktworld@aol.com).

American Association of Retired Persons (AARP), 601 E. St. NW, Washington, D.C. 20049 (202-434-2277). Members over 50 receive benefits including the AARP Motoring Plan from AMOCO (800-334-3300), plus discounts on lodging, car rental, cruises, and sight-seeing. Annual fee $8 per couple; $20 for three years.
Elderhostel, 75 Federal St., 3rd fl., Boston, MA 02110-1941 (617-426-7788; email Cadyg@elderhostel.org; http://www.elderhostel.org). For age 55 or over (spouse of any age). Programs at colleges, universities, and other learning centers in over 70 countries on varied subjects lasting 1-4 weeks.
The Mature Traveler, P.O. Box 50400, Reno, NV 89513 (702-786-7419). Soft-adventure tours for seniors. Subscription $30.
National Council of Senior Citizens, 8403 Colesville Rd., Silver Spring, MD 20910-31200 (301-578-8800; fax 578-8999). Individuals or couples can receive hotel and

auto rental discounts, a senior citizen newspaper, and use of a discount travel agency. Memberships cost $13 per year, $33 for 3 years, or $175 for a lifetime.

No Problem! Worldwise Tips for Mature Adventurers, by Janice Kenyon ($16). Advice and info on insurance, finances, security, health, and packing, with useful appendices. Orca Book Publishers, P.O. Box 468, Custer, WA 98240-0468.

A Senior's Guide to Healthy Travel, by Donald L. Sullivan ($15). Can be found at http://www.amazon.com.

BISEXUAL, GAY, AND LESBIAN TRAVELERS

Prejudice against bisexuals, gays, and lesbians still exists in Canada and the U.S., but acceptance is growing. In larger cities and in major tourist and college towns, there is generally no need to compromise one's freedom. Outside these areas, regrettably, gay and lesbian travelers often must exercise caution to avoid harassment or aggression. Most major cities in both Canada and the U.S. have large, active gay and lesbian communities. Wherever possible, *Let's Go* lists local gay and lesbian information lines and community centers, as well as local hot spots.

Damron Travel Guides, P.O. Box 422458, San Francisco, CA 94142-2458 (415-255-0404 or 800-462-6654; fax 415-703-9049 or 703-8308; email damronco@damron.com; http://www.damron.com). The **Damron Address Book** ($15), lists bars, restaurants, guest houses, and services in the U.S., Canada, Mexico, and Europe which cater to gay men. The **Damron Road Atlas** ($16) contains color maps of 70 major North American and European cities, including gay and lesbian resorts and listings of accommodations and bars. The **Women's Traveller** ($13) lists over 7500 bars, restaurants, accommodations, bookstores, and services catering to lesbians. **Damron's Accommodations** lists gay and lesbian hotels around the world ($19). Mail order is available for an extra $5 shipping.

Ferrari Guides, P.O. Box 37887, Phoenix, AZ 85069 (602-863-2408; fax 439-3952; email ferrari@q-net.com; http://www.q-net.com). Gay and lesbian travel guides: **Gay Travel A to Z** ($16), **Men's Travel in Your Pocket** ($16), **Women's Travel in Your Pocket** ($14), **Inn Places** ($16). Available in bookstores or by mail order. Postage and handling $5 for the first item, $1 for each additional item mailed within the U.S. In Canada, first item $10. Overseas, call or write for shipping cost.

Gayellow Pages, P.O. Box 533, Village Station, New York, NY 10014 (212-674-0120; fax 420-1126; email gayellow@banet.net; http://gayellowpages.com). An annually updated listing of accommodations, resorts, hotlines, gay community centers, local hotlines and switchboards, among other things. U.S./Canada edition US$16.

International Gay and Lesbian Travel Association, 4331 N. Federal Hwy., Suite 304, Fort Lauderdale, FL 33308 (954-776-2626 or 800-448-8550; fax 954-776-3303; email IGLTA@aol.com; http://www.iglta.org). An organization of over 1350 companies serving gay and lesbian travelers worldwide. Call for lists of travel agents, accommodations, and events.

The Gay Vacation Guide: The Best Trips and How to Plan Them, by Mark Chesnut. Has a thorough listing of travel companies, and advice on how to use gay-friendly businesses and how to avoid problems while traveling ($14.95, shipping and handling $4 for the first order, $1 for each additional title). Carol Publishing, 120 Enterprise Ave., Secaucus, NJ 07094 (800-447 2665; fax 201-866 8159).

TRAVELERS WITH DISABILITIES

Hotels and motels in Alaska, Western Canada, and the Pacific Northwest have become increasingly accessible to disabled persons, and many national parks are trying to make exploring the outdoors more feasible. The free **Golden Access Passport,** honored at all U.S. National Parks entitles disabled travelers and their families to enter parks for free and provides a 50% reduction on all campsite and parking fees.

Arrange transportation well in advance to ensure a smooth trip. A number of major **car rental agencies** including **Hertz, Avis,** and **National** have hand-controlled vehicles at some locations (see **By Car: Renting,** p. 31). **Amtrak, VIA Rail,** and virtually all major **airlines** will accommodate disabled passengers if notified at least 72 hours in advance. **Greyhound** buses will provide free travel for a companion; if you are without a fellow traveler, call Greyhound (800-752-4841) at least 48 hours before you plan to leave and they will arrange to assist you. For transportation information in specific U.S. and Canadian cities, contact the local chapter of the Easter Seals Society.

Resources for Disabled Travelers

Facts on File, 11 Penn Plaza, 15th fl., New York, NY 10001 (212-967-8800). Publishers of *Resource Directory for the Disabled,* a reference guide for travelers with disabilities ($45 plus shipping). Available at bookstores or by mail order.

Moss Rehab Hospital Travel Information Service (215-456-9600, TDD 215-456-9602). A telephone information resource center on international travel accessibility and other travel-related concerns for those with disabilities.

Society for the Advancement of Travel for the Handicapped, 347 5th Ave. #610, New York, NY 10016 (212-447-1928; fax 725-8253; email sathtravel@aol.com; http://www.sath.org). Publishes a quarterly travel magazine, *Open World* (free for members; nonmembers US$13 subscription). Information on travel facilitation and accessible destinations. Annual membership $45, students and seniors $30.

Twin Peaks Press, P.O. Box 129, Vancouver, WA 98666-0129 (360-694-2462; fax 360-696-3210; email 73743.2634@compuserve.com; http://netm.com/mall/info-prod/twinpeak/helen.htm). Publishers of **Travel for the Disabled,** which provides travel tips, lists of accessible tourist attractions, and advice on other resources for disabled travelers ($20). Also publishes **Directory of Travel Agencies for the Disabled** ($20), **Wheelchair Vagabond** ($15), and **Directory of Accessible Van Rentals** (US$10). Postage $4 for first book, $2 for each additional book.

The Diabetic Traveler, P.O. Box 8223 RW, Stamford, CT (203-327-5832). A short quarterly offering advice to diabetics on flying, eating abroad and visiting extreme climates. A subscription ($19) includes a list of organizations worldwide.

Tours and Trips for Disabled Travelers

Directions Unlimited, 720 N. Bedford Rd., Bedford Hills, NY 10507 (800-533-5343; 914-241-1700 in NY; fax 914-241-0243). Arranges individual and group vacations, tours, and cruises for the physically disabled. Group tours for blind travelers.

Flying Wheels Travel Service, 143 W. Bridge St., Owatonne, MN 55060 (800-535-6790; fax 451-1685). Arranges trips for groups and individuals in wheelchairs or with other sorts of limited mobility.

TRAVELERS WITH CHILDREN

Family vacations demand careful pacing and planning ahead. When deciding where to stay, remember the special needs of young children, or invite disaster. If you pick a B&B, call ahead to make sure it's child-friendly. If you rent a car, make sure the rental company provides a car seat for younger children. Consider using a papoose-style device to carry a baby on walking trips. Be sure that your children carry some sort of ID in case of an emergency, and arrange a reunion spot in case of separation when sight-seeing. Finding private spaces for breast-feeding is sometimes a problem while traveling; pack accordingly or search for mother-friendly spots wherever you are. Restaurants often have children's menus and discounts. Most museums and tourist attractions have a children's rate, as do many airlines, trains, and bus companies.

Backpacking with Babies and Small Children ($9.95). Published by Wilderness Press, 2440 Bancroft Way, Berkeley, CA 94704 (510-843-8080 or 800-443-7227; fax 548-1355; email wpress@ix.netcom.com; http://wildernesspress.com). Third edition scheduled for release in August 1998.

How to Take Great Trips with Your Kids, by Sanford and Jane Portnoy ($9.95, shipping and handling $3). Advice on packing, how to plan trips geared toward the age of your children, and finding child-friendly accommodations. The Harvard Common Press, 535 Albany St., Boston, MA. 02118 (888-657-3755, fax 695-9794).

Have Kid, Will Travel: 101 Survival Strategies for Vacationing With Babies and Young Children, by Claire and Lucille Tristram ($9). Andrews & McMeel.

DIETARY CONCERNS

Travelers keeping **kosher** should contact synagogues for information on kosher restaurants; your own synagogue or Hillel may have access to lists of Jewish institutions across North America. The *Jewish Travel Guide* lists synagogues, kosher restaurants, and Jewish institutions in over 80 countries. Available in the U.S. from Sepher-Hermon Press, 1265 46th St., Brooklyn, NY 11219 (718-972-9010; $15 plus $3 shipping); in the U.K. from Vallentine Mitchell Publishers, Newbury House 890-900, Eastern Ave., Newbury Park, Ilford, Essex, U.K. IG2 7HH (0181 599 88 66; fax 599 09 84).

Vegetarian food is spreading its leafy tendrils to even the staunchest ranching communities of Alaska, Western Canada, and the Pacific Northwest. *Let's Go* often notes restaurants with good vegetarian selections in city listings. The **North American Vegetarian Society**, P.O. Box 72, Dolgeville, NY 13329 (518-568-7970), sells several travel-related titles in the U.S. and Canada.

GETTING THERE AND GETTING AROUND

■ Budget Travel Agencies

Campus Travel, 52 Grosvenor Gardens, London SW1W 0AG (http://www.campus-travel.co.uk). Forty-six branches in the U.K. Student and youth fares on planes, trains, boats, and buses. Offers **Skytrekker** (flexible student and youth airline tickets). Discount and ID cards for students and youths, travel insurance for students and ages under 35, maps, guides, and travel suggestion booklets. Telephone booking service: 0171 730 34 02 in Europe; 0171 730 21 01 in North America; 0171 730 81 11 worldwide.

Council Travel (888-COUNCIL/268-6245; http://www.ciee.org), the travel division of Council, is a full-service travel agency specializing in youth and budget travel. They offer discount airfares, railpasses, hosteling cards, guidebooks, budget tours, travel gear, and international student (ISIC), youth (GO25), and teacher (ITIC) identity cards. U.S. offices include: Emory Village, 1561 N. Decatur Rd., **Atlanta,** GA 30307 (404-377-9997); 273 Newbury St., **Boston,** MA 02116 (617-266-1926); 1153 N. Dearborn, **Chicago,** IL 60610 (312-951-0585); 10904 Lindbrook Dr., **Los Angeles,** CA 90024 (310-208-3551); 205 E. 42nd St., **New York,** NY 10017 (212-822-2700); 953 Garnett Ave., **San Diego,** CA 92109 (619-270-6401); 530 Bush St., **San Francisco,** CA 94108 (415-421-3473); 1314 N.E. 43rd St., **Seattle,** WA 98105 (206-632-2448); 3300 M St. NW, **Washington, D.C.** 20007 (202-337-6464).

STA Travel, 6560 Scottsdale Rd. #F100, Scottsdale, AZ 85253 (800-777-0112; fax 602-922-0793; http://sta-travel.com). A student and youth travel organization with over 150 offices worldwide, offering discount airfares, railpasses, accommodations, tours, insurance, and ISICs. Sixteen offices in the U.S. including: 297 Newbury Street, **Boston,** MA 02115 (617-266-6014); 429 S. Dearborn St., **Chicago,** IL 60605 (312-786-9050); 7202 Melrose Ave., **Los Angeles,** CA 90046 (213-934-8722); 10 Downing St., Suite G, **New York,** NY 10003 (212-627-3111); 4341 University Way NE, **Seattle,** WA 98105 (206-633-5000); 2401 Pennsylvania Ave., **Washington, D.C.** 20037 (202-887-0912); 51 Grant Ave., **San Francisco,** CA 94108 (415-391-8407). In the U.K., 6 Wrights Lane, **London** W8 6TA (0171 938 47 11). In New Zealand, 10 High St., **Auckland** (09 309 97 23). In Australia, 222 Faraday St., **Melbourne,** VIC 3050 (03 9349 6911).

Let's Go Travel, Harvard Student Agencies, 17 Holyoke St., Cambridge, MA 02138 (617-495-9649; fax 496-7956; email travel@hsa.net; http://hsa.net/travel). Railpasses, HI-AYH memberships, ISICs, ITICs, FIYTO cards, guidebooks (with every *Let's Go* title at a substantial discount), maps, bargain flights, and a complete line of budget travel gear. All items available by mail; call or write for a catalogue.

Travel CUTS (Canadian Universities Travel Services Limited), 187 College St., Toronto, Ont. M5T 1P7 (416-979-2406; fax 979-8167; email mail@travelcuts). Canada's national student travel bureau and equivalent of Council, with 40 offices across Canada. Also in the U.K., 295-A Regent St., **London** W1R 7YA (0171 637 31

61). Discounted domestic and international airfares open to all; special student fares to all destinations with valid ISIC. Issues ISIC, FIYTO, GO25, and HI hostel cards, as well as railpasses. Offers free *Student Traveler* magazine, as well as information on the Student Work Abroad Program (SWAP).

Traveler's Emergency Network (TEN), 4201 University Drive, Suite 102, NC 27707 (919-490-6055; 800-ASK-4-TEN/275-4836 for customer service; fax 493-8262; email ten@intrex.net; http://tenweb.com). Offers superlative affordable, flexible, and comprehensive annual travel assistance plans. Starts from $30 per year for individuals and $50 per year for families.

Usit Youth and Student Travel, 19-21 Aston Quay, O'Connell Bridge, **Dublin** 2 (01 677-8117; fax 679-8833). In the U.S.: New York Student Center, 895 Amsterdam Ave., New York, NY, 10025 (212-663-5435; email usitny@aol.com). Specializes in youth and student travel. Low-cost tickets and flexible travel arrangements all over the world. Supplies ISIC and FIYTO GO 25 cards in Ireland only.

■ By Air

The **airline industry** attempts to squeeze every dollar from its customers. To obtain the best fare, buy a round-trip ticket, stay over at least one Saturday, and travel during off-peak days (M-Th morning) and hours (overnight **red-eye** flights can be cheaper and faster than primetime). Call every toll-free number and don't be afraid to ask about discounts; if you don't ask, it's unlikely that they'll be volunteered. **Students** and others under 26 need never to pay full price for a ticket. **Seniors** can also get great deals; many airlines offer senior traveler clubs or airline passes with few restrictions, and discounts for their companions as well. Outsmart airline reps with Michael McColl's *The Worldwide Guide to Cheap Airfare* ($15), an incredibly useful guide.

Most airfares peak from mid-June to early September and around holidays; reserve a seat several months in advance for these dates. Call the airline a day before your departure to confirm your flight reservation, and get to the airport early to ensure you have a seat; airlines often overbook. (Of course, if your travel plans are flexible being "bumped" from a flight doesn't spell doom—you will probably leave on the next flight and receive a free ticket or cash bonus. If you would like to be bumped to win a free ticket, check in early and let the airline officials know.)

The commercial airlines' lowest regular offer is the **Advance Purchase Excursion Fare (APEX);** specials advertised in newspapers may be cheaper, but have more restrictions and fewer available seats. APEX fares provide you with confirmed reservations and allow "open-jaw" tickets (landing in and returning from different cities). Call as early as possible; these fares often require a one- to three-week advance purchase. Be sure to inquire about any restrictions on length of stay.

MAJOR AIRLINES

Within North America

North Americans use airplanes and cars more than buses and trains when taking long trips. Buses and trains take much longer and do not always offer savings equal to the added trouble (a cross-country train trip will take three to five days, compared with seven hours by plane).

Many U.S. and Canadian airlines offer special passes and fares to international travelers. You must purchase these passes outside of North America, paying one price for a certain number of flight vouchers. A voucher is good for one flight on an airline's domestic system; typically, travel must be completed within 30 to 60 days. The point of departure and destination for each coupon must be specified at the time of purchase, but travel dates may be changed during your trip, often at no extra charge. **US Airways, United, Continental, Delta,** and **TWA** all sell vouchers. Call the airlines for specifics. TWA's **Youth Travel Pak** offers a similar deal to students ages 14-24, including North Americans. **Greyhound Air of Canada** (800-661-8747; http://www.greyhound.ca) sells an international pass with unlimited use of Greyhound flights over a certain time period (7-day pass $209, 15-day $275, 30-day $375, 60-day $475).

AirTran, Consumer Relations, Dept. INT, 9955 AirTran Blvd., Orlando, FL 32827 (8000-247-8726; http://www.airtran.com). Special "X-fares" for 18-22 year-olds.

Air Canada, Consumer Relations, P.O. Box 14000, Station Airport, Dorval Quebec H4Y 1H4 (800-776-3000; http://www.aircanada.ca). Discounts for youths 12-24 on stand-by tickets for flights within Canada; advance-purchase may still be cheaper.

Alaska Airlines, P.O. Box 68900, Seattle, WA 98168 (800-426-0333; http://www.alaska-air.com).

America West Air, 4000 E. Sky Harbor Blvd., Phoenix, AZ 85034 (800-235-9292; http://www.americawest.com).

American Airlines, P.O. Box 619612, Dallas-Ft. Worth International Airport, TX 75261-9612 (800-433-7300; http://www.americanair.com).

Canadian Airlines, Customer Relations, Calgary Administration Building, 615 18th St. SE. Calgary AB T2E 6J5 (in Canada 800-665-1177, in U.S. 800-426-7000 or 250-624-9181; email comments@CdnAir.ca; http://www.scdnair.ca).

Continental Airlines, 2929 Allen Parkway, Houston, TX 77210 (800-525-0280; http://www.flycontinental.com).

Delta Airlines, Hartsfield International Airport, Atlanta, GA 30320 (800-241-4141; http://www.delta-air.com).

Northwest Airlines, 5101 Northwest Dr., St. Paul, MN 55111-3034 (800-225-2525; http://www.nwa.com).

TWA, 1 City Center, 515 N. 6th St., St. Louis, MO 63101 (800-221-2000; http://www.twa.com).

United Airlines, P.O. Box 66100, Chicago, IL 60666 (800-241-6522; http://www.ual.com).

US Airways, Office of Consumer Affairs, P.O. Box 1501, Winston-Salem, NC 27102-1501 (800-428-4322; http://www.usair.com).

From Europe

European travelers will experience the least competition for inexpensive seats during the off-season, but "off-season" need not mean the dead of winter. Peak-season rates generally take effect from mid-May until mid-September; don't count on getting a seat right away during these months. The worst crunch leaving Europe is from mid-June to early July; August is uniformly tight for returning flights. If you can, take advantage of cheap off-season flights within Europe to reach an advantageous point of departure for North America. (London is a major connecting point for budget flights to the U.S.; New York City is often the destination.) Once in the States, you can catch a coast-to-coast flight to make your way out West; see **Within North America,** above.

If you decide to fly with a commercial airline rather than through a charter agency or ticket consolidator (see below), you'll be purchasing greater reliability, security, and flexibility. Many major airlines offer reduced-fare options, such as three-day advance purchase fares: these tickets can only be purchased within 72 hours of the time of the departure, and are restricted to youths under a certain age (often 24). Check with a travel agent for availability. Seat availability is known only a few days before the flight, although airlines will sometimes issue predictions.

Airlines with international flights are: **British Airways** (800-247-9297), **Continental** (800-525-0280), **Northwest** (800-225-2525), **TWA** (800-221-200), **United** (800-538-2929), **Virgin Atlantic** (800-862-8621), and **IcelandAir** (800-223-5500). Smaller airlines often undercut major carriers by offering bargain fares on regularly scheduled flights. Competition for seats on these smaller carriers can be fierce—book early.

From Asia, Africa, and Australia

While European travelers may choose from a variety of regular reduced fares, Asian, Australian, and African travelers must rely on APEX (see p. 25). A good place to start searching for tickets is the local branch of an international budget travel agency (see **Budget Travel Agencies,** p. 23). **STA Travel,** with offices in Sydney, Melbourne, and Auckland, is probably the largest international agency around.

Qantas (800-227-4500), **United** (800-241-6522), and **Northwest** (800-225-2525) fly between Australia or New Zealand and the U.S. Advance purchase fares from Australia have extremely tough restrictions. If you are uncertain about your plans, pay extra for an advance purchase ticket that has only a 50% penalty for cancellation. Many travelers from Australia and New Zealand take **Singapore Air** (800-742-3333) or other East Asian carriers for the initial leg of their trip. **Delta Airlines** (800-241-4141), **Japan Airlines** (800-525-3663), **Northwest** (800-225-2525), and **United Airlines** (800-538-2929) offer service from Japan. A round-trip ticket from Tokyo to L.A. usually ranges between $1250-2500. **South African Airways** (800-722-9675), **American** (800-433-7300), and **Northwest** connect South Africa with North America.

CHARTER FLIGHTS AND TICKET CONSOLIDATORS

Charters are flights a tour operator contracts with an airline to fly extra loads of passengers to peak-season destinations. They are often cheaper than flights on scheduled airlines, although fare wars, consolidator tickets, and small airlines can beat charter prices. Delays are not uncommon, and companies reserve the right to change the dates of your flight or even cancel the flight a mere 48 hours in advance. To be safe, get your ticket as early as possible, and arrive at the airport several hours before departure time. Think carefully when booking your departure and return dates; you will lose all or most of your money if you cancel your ticket. Restrictions on the length of your trip and the time frame for reservations may also apply. Prices and destinations will change drastically from season to season, so be sure to contact as many organizations as possible in order to get the best deal. Try **Interworld** (305-443-4929), **Travac** (800-872-8800), **Rebel** (800-227-3235), or book through a travel agent.

Ticket consolidators resell unsold tickets on commercial and charter flights for very low prices, but deals include some risks. Tickets are sold on a space-available basis which does not guarantee you a seat; you get priority over those flying stand-by but below regularly booked passengers. The earlier you arrive at the airport the better, since passengers are seated in the order they checked in. There are rarely age constraints or length-of-stay limitations, but unlike tickets bought through an airline, you won't be able to use your tickets on another flight if you miss yours. This may be a good route to take if you are traveling on short notice (you bypass advance purchase requirements, since you aren't tangled in airline bureaucracy), on a high-priced trip, to an offbeat destination, or in the peak season (when published fares are jacked way up). Not all consolidators deal with the general public; many only sell tickets through travel agents. **Bucket shops** are retail agencies that specialize in getting cheap tickets. Look for their tiny ads in the travel section of weekend papers—the *Sunday New York Times* is a good source. Among the many reputable and trustworthy companies are, unfortunately, some shady wheeler-dealers. Before committing, contact the local Better Business Bureau to find out your company's track record. Get the company's policy in writing, insist on a **receipt** that gives full details about the tickets, refunds, and restrictions, and record of who you talked to and when.

Cheap Tickets, 6151 West Century Blvd. #100, Los Angeles, CA 90045 (800-377-1000 or 310-645-5054). Additional offices in San Francisco (415-5883700), Honolulu (808-947-3717), New York City (212-570-1179), Fullerton, CA (714-229-0131), and Seattle (206-467-7979).

Mr. Cheap's Travel, 9123 SE St. Helen's St. #280, Clackamas, OR 97015 (800-672-4327 or 503-557-9101; fax 800-896-8868; http://www.mrcheaps.com). Additional office in San Diego, CA (800-636-3273 or 619-291-1292).

NOW Voyager (http://www.nowvoyagertravel.com). Primarily a courier company, (see below), but performs consolidation with reliability rivaling that of most charter companies (97% of customers get on flights the first time) while maintaining considerably lower prices. NOW sells tickets over the internet at its web page.

For more consolidators and other useful information, consult Kelly Monaghan's *Consolidators: Air Travel's Bargain Basement* (US$8 plus $3.50 shipping) from The Intrepid Traveler, P.O. Box 438, New York, NY 10034 (email intreptrav@aol.com).

ESSENTIALS

COURIERS

Those who travel light should consider flying as a **courier**, where ridiculously low fares often come at the price of heavy restrictions. The company hiring you will use your checked luggage space for freight; you're usually only allowed to bring carry-ons. You are responsible for the safe delivery of the baggage claim slips (given to you by a courier company representative) to the representative waiting for you when you arrive—don't screw up or you will be blacklisted as a courier. You will probably never see the cargo you are transporting—the company handles it all—and airport officials know that couriers are not responsible for the baggage checked for them. **Restrictions** to watch for: you must be over 21 (18 in some cases), have a valid passport, and procure your own visa (if necessary); most flights are round-trip only with short fixed-length stays (usually 1 week); only single tickets are issued (but a companion may be able to get a next-day flight); and most flights are from New York. For a practical guide to the air courier scene, check out Kelly Monaghan's *Air Courier Bargains* ($15 plus $3 shipping), available from Upper Access Publishing (UAP), P.O. Box 457, Hinesburg, VT 05461 (800-356-9315; fax 242-0036; email upperaccess@aol.com), or consult the *Courier Air Travel Handbook* ($10 plus $3.50 shipping), published by Bookmasters, Inc., P.O. Box 2039, Mansfield, OH 44905 (800-507-2665; fax 419-281-6883).

STANDBY

Flying **standby** adds a certain ambiguous thrill to when you will leave and where exactly you will end up. Standby brokers do not sell tickets, but rather the promise that you will get to a destination near where you want to go from a location in a region you've specified, within a window of time (usually 5 days). Call in before your date range to hear all of your flight options for the next seven days and your probability of boarding; decide which flights you want to try to make, and then present a voucher at the airport, which grants you the right to board a flight on a space-available basis. This ritual must be followed again for the return trip. Flexibility of schedule and destination is often necessary, but all companies guarantee you a credit or refund if the available flights that fit your date and destination range are full. **Airhitch** (800-326-2009 or 212-864-2000 on the East Coast; 310-726-5000 on the West Coast; tel. 1 47 00 16 30 in Europe) and **Air-Tech Ltd.** (212-219-7000; fax 219-0066; email fly@airtech.com) are two prominent standby brokers.

Be sure to read all the fine print in your agreements with any such company—a call to the Better Business Bureau may be worthwhile. Be warned that it is difficult to receive refunds and that clients' vouchers will not be honored when an airline fails to receive payments in time.

■ By Train

Amtrak (800-USA-RAIL/872-7245; http://www.amtrak.com) is the only provider of inter-city passenger train service in the U.S. Most cities have Amtrak offices that sell tickets directly, but in some small towns they must be bought through an agent. The informative web page lists up-to-date schedules, fares, arrival and departure info, and allows reservations. **Discounts on full rail fares** include: 15% off for senior citizens, 15% off with a Student Advantage Card (call 800-96-AMTRAK/962-6872 to purchase a card for $20); 15% off for travelers with disabilities; 25% off for current members of the U.S. armed forces, active-duty veterans, and their dependents; 50% off for children under 15 accompanied by a parent; children under age two ride free on the lap of an adult. Circle trips and holiday packages can also save money. Call for up-to-date info and reservations. Amtrak also offers some **special packages:**

All-Aboard America: This fare divides the Continental U.S. into three regions—Eastern, Central, and Western.

Air-Rail Travel Plan: Amtrak and United Airlines allow you to travel in one direction by train and return by plane, or vice versa. The train portion of the journey can last up to 30 days and include up to 3 stopovers. A multitude of variations are available; contact **Amtrak Vacations** (see below) for details.

North America Rail Pass: Allows unlimited travel and unlimited stops over a period of either 15 or 30 days. A 30-day nationwide pass sells for $645 during peak season (June 1-Oct. 15) and $450 off-season; a 15-day nationwide pass costs $400 ($300 off-season). Call Amtrak for regional variants. The 30-day discount option available only to non-citizens of North America; the 15-day pass is available to all.

City Escapades: Tours of major American cities operated by Grayline. Tickets available from Amtrak stations; contact **Amtrak Vacations** (see below) for details.

Amtrak Vacations: 2211 Butterfield Rd., Downers Grove, IL 60515 (800-321-8684). An Amtrak-affiliated travel agency which offers packages in conjunction with airlines and hotel chains and, occasionally, provides discounts not to be found anywhere else. Programs vary throughout the year; call for details.

VIA Rail, P.O. Box 8116, Station A, Montreal, Québec H3C 3N3 (800-842-7733; http://www.viarail.ca), is Amtrak's Canadian analogue. **Discounts on full fares:** 40% off for students with ISIC, and youths under 24; 10% off ages 60 and over; 50% off for children ages two to 15, accompanied by an adult; children under two ride free on the lap of an adult. Reservations are required for first-class seats and sleeping car accommodations. **Supersaver fares** offer discounts of up to 50%. The **Canrail Pass** allows unlimited travel on 12 to 15 days within a 30-day period. Between early June and mid-October, a 12-day pass costs CDN$569; senior citizens, students and youths under 24 pay CDN$499. Off-season passes cost CDN$369, seniors and youths pay CDN$339. Add CDN$44 for each additional day of travel desired. Call for information on seasonal promotions, such as discounts on Grayline Sightseeing Tours.

For Alaskans in isolated regions, often the only link to civilization is the **Alaska Railroad Corporation (ARRC),** P.O. Box 107500, Anchorage, AK 99510-7500 (800-544-0552; fax 907-265-2323; email reservations@akrr.com; http://www.alaska.net/~akrr). North America's northernmost railroad covers 470 miles of track—connecting Seward and Whittier in the south with Anchorage, Fairbanks, and Denali N.P. farther north. See specific locations in this guide for fares, details, and additional rail options.

■ By Bus

Buses generally offer the most frequent and complete service between the cities and towns of Western Canada, the Pacific Northwest, and Alaska. Often a bus is the only way to reach smaller locales without a car. **Russell's Official National Motor Coach Guide** ($15 including postage) contains schedules of every bus route (including Greyhound) between any two towns in the United States and Canada. Russell's also publishes two semiannual *Supplements,* one which includes a **Directory of Bus Lines and Bus Stations** ($6), and one which offers a series of **Route Maps** ($6.45). To order any of the above, write Russell's Guides, Inc., P.O. Box 278, Cedar Rapids, IA 52406 (319-364-6138; fax 364-4853).

Greyhound (800-231-2222; http://www.greyhound.com), runs the largest number of routes in the U.S., though local bus companies may provide more extensive services within a specific regions. Schedule information is available at any Greyhound terminal or by calling the 800 number. Reserve with a credit card over the phone at least 10 days in advance, and the ticket can be mailed anywhere in the U.S. Otherwise, reservations are available only up to 24 hours in advance. You can buy your ticket at the terminal, but arrive early. Advance purchase is cheaper, so make reservations early. **Discounts on full fares:** 10% off for senior citizens; 50% off children ages two to 11; travelers with disabilities or special needs and their companions ride together for the price of one. 10% off with valid ID for active and retired U.S. military personnel and National Guard Reserves, and their spouses and dependents may take a round-trip between any two points in the U.S. for $169. With a ticket purchased 3 or more days in advance, two people can travel for the price of 1½.

Ameripass (888-454-7277). Allows adults unlimited travel for 7 days ($199), 15 days ($299), 30 days ($409), or 60 days ($599). Prices for senior citizens and students with a valid college ID are slightly less: 7 days ($179), 15 days ($269), 30 days ($369), or 60 days ($539). Children's passes are half the adult price. Before purchasing an Ameripass, total up the separate bus fares between towns to make sure that the pass is more economical, or at least worth the unlimited flexibility it provides. Most bus companies in the U.S. honor Ameripasses, but check for specifics.

International Ameripass: For travelers from outside North America. Primarily sold in foreign countries, they can also be purchased in either of Greyhound's International Offices, located in New York City and Los Angeles (800-246-8572). A 7-day pass is $179, 15-day pass $269, 30-day pass $369, 60-day pass $539. Call 888-454-7277 for schedule info. Orders can also be made over email (send request to Dialcorp!jetpo01!Greyhound@jetsave.mail.att.net).

Greyhound Canada (800-661-TRIP/8747 in Canada or 403-265-9111 in the U.S.; http://www.greyhound.ca) is Canada's main intercity bus company. The **British Columbia Student Pass** (CDN$119) allows four one-way trips anywhere in the province; a similar pass exists for **Alberta** (CDN$99). **Discounts:** seniors (10% off); students (10% off in Ontario, 25% off in West with purchase of CDN$15 discount card); a companion of a person with a disability rides free; ages 3-7 50%; under 3 free. If reservations are made 7 days or more in advance, a friend travels half off, and a passenger under 15 rides free with an adult.

Canada Pass offers unlimited travel for North American residents on all routes, including limited links to northern U.S. cities (7-day CDN$199; 15-day CDN$259; 30-day CDN$349; 60-day CDN$449).

International Canada Pass offers a similar deal for foreigner with slightly lower prices (7-day CDN$189; 15-day CDN$259; 30-day CDN$339; 60-day CDN$439). This pass can only be purchased overseas at select travel agencies, including those listed above for Greyhound Lines.

■ By Car

AUTO CLUBS

American Automobile Association (AAA), 1050 Hingham St., Rocklin, MA 02370 (800-AAA-HELP/222-4357; to sign up call 800-JOIN-AAA/564-6222; http://www.aaa.com). The best-known of the auto clubs. Offers free trip-planning services, road maps and guidebooks, emergency road service anywhere in the U.S., free towing, and commission-free traveler's checks from American Express with over 1000 offices across the country. Discounts on Hertz car rental, Amtrak tickets, and various motel chains and theme parks. AAA has reciprocal agreements with the auto associations of many other countries, which often provide you with full benefits while in the U.S. Basic membership fees are $55 for the first year with $39 annual renewal, and $30 yearly for additional family members.

Canadian Automobile Association (CAA), 1145 Hunt Club Rd. #200, Ottawa, Ontario K1V 0Y3 (800-CAA-HELP/222-4357; to sign up call 800-564-6222; http://www.caa.ca). Affiliated with AAA (see above), the CAA provides nearly identical membership benefits, including 24hr. emergency roadside assistance, free maps and tour books, route planning, and various discounts. Basic membership is CDN$53 and CDN$34 for family members.

Montgomery Ward Auto Club, 200 N. Martingale Rd., Schaumburg, IL 60173-2096 (800-621-5151). Provides 24hr. emergency roadside assistance for any car, unlimited trip routing, and up to $1500 for travel emergencies. Monthly membership ($79), with associate memberships available for ages 16-23 ($24 annually).

TIPS FOR THE ROAD WARRIOR

If you're driving in North America, road maps can be your best friend (but preferably not in any deep sense). **Rand McNally's Road Atlas,** has maps covering all of the U.S. and Canada, and is available at bookstores and gas stations for $10.

Before you leave, tune up the car, pack an easy-to-read manual and a compass, and learn a bit about minor automobile maintenance and repair—it may help you keep your car alive long enough to reach a reputable garage. Always carry: a **spare tire** and **jack, jumper cables, extra oil, flares,** a **flashlight,** and **blankets** (in case you break down at night or in winter). In summer, carry extra **water** for you and your radiator. In extremely hot weather, use the air conditioner with restraint; turning the heater on full blast will help cool the engine. If radiator fluid is steaming, turn off the car for half an hour—never pour water over the engine to cool it, and never lift a searing hot hood. Do not, even should the fancy arise, mix your gas with nitroglycerine.

Carry emergency **food and water** if there's a chance you may be stranded in a remote area. Always have plenty of **gas** and check road conditions ahead of time when possible, particularly during winter. Gas is generally cheaper in towns than at interstate service stops. The enormous travel distances of North America will require more gas than you might at first expect. To burn less fuel, make sure your tires have enough air, check the oil, and use the air-conditioner with restraint.

Sleeping in a car or van parked in the city is extremely dangerous—even the most dedicated budget traveler should not consider it an option. Be sure to **buckle up**—seat belts are required by law in almost every region of the U.S. and Canada. The **speed limit in the U.S.,** thanks to recent legislation devolving power to the states, varies considerably from region to region and road to road. Most urban highways retain a limit of 55 miles per hour (88km/hr.), while rural routes range from 65-80 mph (104-128km/hr.). The **speed limit in Canada** is generally 100km/hr. (63 mph).

In the 1950s, U.S. President Dwight "Ike" Eisenhower began the **interstate system,** a federally funded highway network. There is a simple system for numbering interstates. Even-numbered interstates run east-west, and odd ones run north-south, decreasing in number toward the south and west. If the interstate has a three-digit number, it is a branch of another interstate (i.e., I-285 is a branch of I-85) and is often a bypass skirting around a large city. An even digit in the hundreds place means the branch will eventually return to the main interstate; an odd digit means it won't.

RENTING

While the cost of renting a car for long distances is often prohibitive, renting for local trips may be more reasonable. National chains usually allow cars to be picked up in one city and dropped off in another but for a hefty charge. By calling a toll-free number you can reserve a reliable car anywhere in the U.S. and Canada. Drawbacks include steep prices and high minimum ages for rentals (usually 25). Many branches rent to ages 21-24, especially those with a major credit card to their name; there is an additional fee, however, and policies and prices vary from agency to agency. The website http://www.bnm.com/uage.htm specializes in locating car rental agencies willing to rent to people under the age of 25.

Alamo (800-327-9633; http://www.goalamo.com), most **Dollar** (800-800-4000) branches, and some **Thrifty** (800-367-2277; http://www.thrifty.com) locations allow ages 21-24 to rent for an additional daily fee of about $20. Some branches of **Avis** (800-230-4898; http://www.avis.com) and **Budget** (800-527-0700) rent to drivers under 25. **Hertz** (800-654-3131; http://www.hertz.com) policy varies by city. **Rent-A-Wreck** (800-421-7253; http://www.rent-a-wreck.com) specializes in supplying vehicles that are past their prime for lower-than-average prices; a bare-bones compact less than eight years old rents for around $20. There are also local agencies which serve a specific city or region, and these sometimes offer better deal; check **Practical Information: Car Rental** for specific towns in this guide.

Most rental packages offer unlimited mileage, although some allow only a certain number of miles free before a charge of 25-40¢ per mile takes effect. Most quoted rates do not include gas or tax, so ask for the total cost before handing over the credit card; many large firms have added airport surcharges not covered by the designated fare. Return the car with a full tank unless you sign up for a fuel option plan that stipulates otherwise. When dealing with any car rental company, be sure to ask whether the price includes insurance against theft and collision. There may be an additional charge, the collision and damage waiver (CDW), which usually comes to about $12-15 per day. If you use **American Express** to rent a car, they will automatically cover the CDW; call AmEx's car division (800-338-1670) for more information.

AUTO TRANSPORT COMPANIES

These services match drivers with car owners who need vehicles moved from one city to another. Would-be travelers give the company their desired destination, and the company finds a car that needs to go there. The only expenses are gas, tolls, and your own living expenses. Some companies insure their cars; with others, your security deposit covers any breakdowns or damage. You must be at least 21, have a valid license, and agree to drive about 400 mi. per day on a fairly direct route. Companies regularly inspect current and past job references, take fingerprints, and require a cash bond. Cars are available between most points, but it's easiest to find cars traveling coast to coast; New York and Los Angeles are popular transfer points. If offered a car, look it over first. Think before accepting a gas guzzler, since you'll be paying for fuel. With the company's approval, you may be able to share the cost with companions. Try: **Auto Driveaway,** 310 S. Michigan Ave. Suite 1401, Chicago, IL 60604-4298 (800-346-2277; fax 312-341-9100; email autodrv@aol.com; http://www.autodrive-away.com), or **Across America Driveaway,** 3626 Calumet Ave., Hammond, IN 46320 (800-619-7707 or 219-852-0134; fax 800-334-6931; http://www.schultz-international.com), also with offices in L.A. (800-964-7874) and Dallas (214-745-8892).

NORTHCOUNTRY DRIVING

Many major roads in Alaska and Northwestern Canada are still in **desperately bad shape.** Dust and flying rocks are major hazards in summer, as is road construction, which can slow highways with 10-30 mi. patches of gravel. Many roads in Alaska have been treated with calcium chloride to minimize the dust flying up from the road. It can be hard on your car's paint, though, and you should take every opportunity to wash your car. Melting and freezing permafrost causes "frost heaves," creating dips and twists in the road. Drive slowly on crummy roads; it will make the trip much easier on your car. Radiators and headlights can be protected from flying rocks and swarming bugs with a **wire screen** and/or plastic **headlight covers;** good **shocks** and a functional **spare tire** are essential. Winter snow cover can actually smooth the ride a bit; the packed surface and thinned traffic is easier driving, although the dangers of avalanches and driving on ice create a different set of concerns. Check **road conditions** before traveling. A number of information hotlines exist for just this purpose: for the **Alaska Highway,** call 250-774-7447 in BC; 867-667-8215 in the Yukon.

Vernon Publications, Inc., 3000 Northup Way #200, Bellevue, WA, 98004 (800-726-4707 or 425-827-9900; fax 425-822-9372; http://www.alaskainfo.com) offers two guides which include maps and detailed routes. **The MILEPOST** ($23) is a guide to the highways of Alaska and Northwestern Canada. **The Alaska Wilderness Guide** ($17) covers bush communities and remote areas of Alaska.

■ On Two Wheels

BY BICYCLE

Before you rush onto the byways of the Pacific Northwest, pedaling furiously away on your banana-seat Huffy Desperado, remember that safe and secure cycling requires a quality helmet and lock. A good helmet costs about $40—far cheaper than critical head surgery. U-shaped **Kryptonite** or **Citadel** locks run about $30 and carry insurance against theft for one or two years if your bike is registered with the police.

Scads of publications can help you get the most out of your bicycle. **Bicycle Gearing: A Practical Guide** ($8.95), available from The Mountaineers Books, 300 3rd Ave. W., Seattle, WA 98134 (800-553-4453; fax 206-223-6306; email mbooks@mountaineers.org; http://www.mountaineers.org/mbooks/mbooks.htm), discusses in lay terms how bicycle gears work, covering how to shift properly and get maximum propulsion with minimum exertion. **Anybody's Bike Book** ($12 plus $4.50 shipping) available from Ten Speed Press, Box 7123, Berkeley, CA 94707 (800-841-2665; fax 510-559-1629; email order@tenspeed.com; http://www.tenspeed.com), provides vital information on repair and maintenance during long-term bike sojourns. **The Packing Book** ($8.95) serves up various checklists and suggested wardrobes, addresses safety concerns, and imparts packing techniques. Rodale Press, 33 E. Minor St., Emmaus, PA 18098-0099 (800-848-4735 or 610-967-5171), publishes a number of books for the intrepid would-be cyclist, including **Cycling for Women** ($8.95 plus shipping) and **Bicycle Repair** ($5 plus shipping).

Adventure Cycling Association, P.O. Box 8308-P, Missoula, MT 59807 (406-721-1776; fax 721-8754; email acabike@aol.com; http://www.adv-cycling.org). A national, non-profit organization that maps long-distance routes and organizes bike tours for members. Membership $28 in the U.S., $35 in Canada and Mexico.

The Canadian Cycling Association, 1600 James Naismith Dr., #212A, Gloucester, ONT K1B 5N4 (613-748-5629; fax 748-5692; email general@canadian-cycling.com; http://www.canadian-cycling.com). Distributes maps and books like *The Canadian Cycling Association's Complete Guide to Bicycle Touring in Canada* (CDN$24), plus guides to specific regions of Canada, Alaska and the Pacific Coast. Also sells maps and books.

Backroads, 801 Cedar St., Berkeley, CA 94710-1800 (800-462-2848; fax 510-527-1444; email goactive@backroads.com; http://www.backroads.com). Offers tours in 23 states, including Alaska and parts of British Columbia. Trips range from a weekend excursion ($299) to a 9-day extravaganza ($1098).

BY MOTORCYCLE

Motorcycling is cheaper and more romantic than driving a car, but it still demands planning. Those considering a journey should contact the **American Motorcyclist Association,** 33 Collegeview Rd., Westerville, OH 43801 (800-262-5646 or 614-891-2425; fax 891-5012; email ama@ama-cycle.org; http://ama-cycle.org) or the **Canadian Motorcyclist Association,** Box 448, Hamilton, ON L8L AC4 (905-522-5705; fax 522-5716; http://www.niagara.com/~moto/cma). A membership ($29 per year) includes discounts on insurance, rentals, hotels, a subscription to *American Motorcyclist,* and a kick-ass patch. For another $25, members benefit from emergency roadside assistance, including pick-up and delivery to a service shop.

Motorcycles are incredibly vulnerable to crosswinds, drunk drivers, and the blind spots of cars and trucks. *Always ride defensively.* Dangers skyrocket at night. Helmets are required by law in many states. Americans should ask their State's Department of Motor Vehicles for a motorcycle operator's manual. The AMA web page (see above) lists relevant laws and regulations for all 50 states.

▓ By Ferry

Along the Pacific Coast, ferries are an exhilarating and often unavoidable way to travel. Practically none of Southeast Alaska is accessible by road; most of this area can be reached only by the **Alaska Marine Highway** (see below). Beyond providing basic transportation, the ferries give travelers the chance to enjoy the beauty of the coast. Ferry travel can become quite expensive, however, when you bring a car along.

ALASKA MARINE HIGHWAY

The **Alaska Marine Highway,** P.O. Box 25535, Juneau, AK 99802-5535 (800-642-0066; TDD 800-764-3779; http://www.dot.state.ak.us/external/amhs/home.html) consists of two unconnected ferry systems administered by one bureaucracy. The **southeast** system runs from Bellingham, WA and Prince Rupert, BC up the coast to Skagway, stopping in Juneau, Ketchikan, Haines, and other towns. The **southcentral/ southwest** network serves such destinations as Kodiak Island, Seward, Homer, Prince William Sound, and, occasionally, the Aleutian Islands. For both systems, the ferry schedule is a function of tides and other navigational exigencies. There is a slight additional charge for stopovers, and should be reserved at the same time as the rest of your itinerary. Plan ahead for all schedules, rates, and information.

Those who intend to hit the water running, and keep running, might check out the **AlaskaPass,** P.O. Box 351, Vashon, WA 98070-0351 (800-248-7598 or 206-463-6550; fax 800-488-0303 or 206-463-6777; http://www.alaskapass.com). It offers unlimited access to Alaska's railroad, ferry, and bus systems; a 15-day pass sells for $689, and a 30-day pass for $939. A pass allowing travel on 21 non-consecutive days over a 45-day period costs $979. The fare may seem expensive, but with a network that extends from Bellingham, WA to Dutch Harbor on the Aleutian Islands, the pass is a good deal for those who want to see a lot of Alaska in a short amount of time.

The full trip from Bellingham to Skagway takes three days—an adventure in itself, peppered with whales, bald eagles, and the majesty of the Inside Passage. All southeast ferries have free showers, cafes, and a heated top-deck "solarium" where cabinless passengers can sleep comfortably in a sleeping bag; some boats offer lectures on history and ecology. Free showers are also a bonus on all but the smallest boats.

OTHER PERFECTLY SEXY FERRIES

Information about fares, reservations, vehicles, and schedules varies greatly throughout the year. Be sure to consult each ferry company when constructing your itinerary in order to clear up any additional questions before finalizing your plans.

The **Alaska Northwest Travel Service, Inc.,** 3303 148th St. SW, Suite 2, Lynnwood, WA 98037 (425-787-9499 or 800-533-7381; fax 206-745-4946), is an agent for Alaska and British Columbia ferries, as well as a full service travel agency specializing in Alaska; they can book ferries, cruise ships, and airline reservations, and will plan individualized itineraries.

BC Ferries, 1112 Fort St., Victoria, BC V8V 4V2 (250-381-1401; fax 250-388-7754; http://bcferries.bc.ca/ferries). Passenger and vehicle ferry service throughout coastal British Columbia, with special facilities for disabled passengers. Service is frequent, and reservations are only required on the longer routes: Tsawwassen/ Gulf Islands, Inside Passage, Discovery Coast Passage, and Queen Charlotte Islands.

Black Ball Transport, Inc., 430 Belleville St., Victoria, BC V8V 1W9 (604-386-2202; fax 604-386-2207), Foot of Laurel, Port Angeles, WA 98362 (360-457-4491; fax 360-457-4493). Ferries daily between Port Angeles and Victoria, with a crossing time of 95min. $6.75 each way, car and driver $27.25, motorcycle and driver $16.50. Bicycles $3.25 extra. Advance reservations not accepted.

Washington State Ferries, 801 Alaskan Way, Seattle, WA 98104-1487 (800-84-FERRY/843-3779 or 206-464-6400 for schedule info; http://www.wsdot.wa.gov/ferries). Ferries to Sidney, BC, and throughout Puget Sound. No reservations, except for travel to the San Juan Islands or British Columbia. Service is frequent, but traffic is heavy—especially in summer, when waits of over an hour to board a ferry are not uncommon. Fares fluctuate, but stay reasonable.

■ By Thumb

Let's Go urges you to consider the risks and disadvantages of hitchhiking before thumbing it. Hitching means entrusting your life to a stranger who happens to stop beside you on the road. While this may be comparatively safe in some areas of Europe and Australia, it is **NOT** so in North America. We do **NOT** recommend it. Don't put yourself in a situation where hitching is the only option.

That said, if you feel that you have no other alternative and decide to hitchhike anyway, there are many precautions that must be taken.

Women traveling alone should never hitch in the United States. Don't hesitate to refuse a ride if you would feel in any way uncomfortable alone with the driver. If at all threatened or intimidated, experienced hitchers ask to be let out no matter how uncompromising the road looks, and they know *in advance* where to go if stranded and what to do in emergencies. In rural areas, hitching is reportedly less risky than in urban areas. Hitching is much more common in Alaska (see below) and the Yukon than farther south. All states prohibit hitchhiking while standing on the roadway itself or behind a freeway entrance sign; hitchers more commonly find rides near intersections where many cars converge.

HITCHING IN ALASKA

Many people hitchhike in Alaska, but it is not unusual to get stranded on a sparsely traveled route. A wait of a day or two between rides is not uncommon on certain stretches of the Alaska Highway. Alaska state law prohibits moving vehicles from not picking up stranded motorists, as the extreme weather conditions can be life-threatening. However, hitchhikers may only legally thumb for rides on the on-and-off ramps of highways—not on the highways themselves. Many hitchers carry a large sign clearly marked with a destination to improve the chances of getting a ride. Including "SHARE GAS" can make an added difference. Hitchers who catch a ride from Canada into Alaska on the Alaska Highway cross the **Alaska-Yukon border,** which involves a series of queries about citizenship, insurance, contraband, and finances, followed by an auto inspection. Hitchers can walk across the border to avoid these hassles.

ONCE THERE

■ Embassies and Consulates

For a more extensive list of embassies and consulates in the U.S., consult the web site (http://www.embassy.org). A similar compilation for Canada can be found at http://www.impactconsulting.com/embassyott. (For U.S. and Canadian **embassies and consulates overseas,** see p. 7.)

(For U.S. and Canadian **embassies and consulates overseas,** see p. 7.)

Embassies in the U.S.: Australia, 1601 Massachusetts Ave. NW, Washington, D.C. 20036 (202-797-3000); **Canada,** 501 Pennsylvania Ave. NW, Washington, D.C. 20001 (202-682-1740); **Ireland,** 2234 Massachusetts Ave. NW, Washington, D.C. 20008 (202-462-3939); **New Zealand,** 37 Observatory Circle NW, Washington, D.C. 20008 (202-328-4800); **South Africa,** 3051 Massachusetts Ave. NW, Washington, D.C. 20008 (202-232-4800); **United Kingdom,** 3100 Massachusetts Ave. NW, Washington, D.C. 20008 (202-462-1340).

Consulates in the U.S.: Australia, 630 5th Ave., New York, NY 10111 (212-408-8400), and Century Plaza Towers, 19th fl., 2049 Century Park East, Los Angeles, CA 90067 (310-229-4800); **Canada,** 1251 Ave. of the Americas, Exxon Building, 16th Fl., New York, NY 10020-1175 (212-596-1683), and Hope St., 9th fl., Los Angeles, CA 90071 (213-346-2700); **Ireland,** 345 Park Ave., 17th fl., New York, NY 10154 (212-319-2552), and 44 Montgomery St., Suite 3830, San Francisco, CA 94101 (415-

392-4214); **New Zealand,** 12400 Wilshire Blvd. Suite 1150, Los Angeles, CA 90025 (310-207-1605); **South Africa,** 333 E. 38th St., 9th fl., New York, NY 10016 (212-213-4880); **United Kingdom,** 845 3rd Ave., New York, NY 10022 (212-752-8400); 11766 Wilshire Blvd. #400, Los Angeles, CA 90025 (213-385-7381).

Embassies in Canada: Australia, 50 O'Connor St. #710, Ottawa, ON K1P 6L2 (613-236-0841); **Ireland,** 130 Albert St. #1105, Ottawa, ON K1P 5G4 (613-233-6281); **New Zealand,** 99 Bank St. #727, Ottawa, ON K1P 6G3 (613-238-5991); **South Africa,** 15 Sussex Dr., Ottawa, ON K1M 1M8 (613-744-0330); **United Kingdom,** 80 Elgin St., Ottawa, ON K1P 5K7 (613-237-1530); **United States,** 100 Wellington St., Ottawa, ON K1P 5T1 (613-238-4470).

Consulates in Canada: Australia, 175 Bloor St. E., suite 314, Toronto, ON M4W 3R8 (416-323-1155); **New Zealand,** 888 Dunsmuir St. #1200, Vancouver, BC V6C 3K4 (604-684-7388); **South Africa,** 1 Place Ville Marie #2615, Montreal, QC H3B 4S3 (514-878-9217), and 595 Burrard St. #3023, 3 Bentall Ctr., P.O. Box 49069, Vancouver, BC V7X 1G4 (604-688-1301). **United Kingdom,** 1000 de la Gauchetière W., Suite 4200, Montreal, QC H3B 4W5 (514-866-5863), and 1111 Melville St. #800, Vancouver, BC V6E 3V6 (604-683-4421); **United States,** 2 Place Terrasse Dufferin, CP 939, Québec City, QC G1R 4T9 (418-692-2095), and 1095 West Pender St., Vancouver, BC V6E 2M6 (604-685-4311).

■ Accommodations

Always make reservations, especially if you plan to travel during peak tourist seasons. The local crisis center hotline may have a list of persons or groups, as well as local shelters, who will house you in an emergency.

HOSTELS

Youth hostels offer unbeatable deals on indoor lodging ($5-25 per night), and they are great places to meet traveling companions from all over the world. Many hostels even have **ride boards** to help you hook up with other hostelers going your way. Hostels are dorm-style accommodations where the sexes sleep apart, often in large rooms with bunk beds. (Some hostels allow private rooms for families and couples, often for an additional charge.) You must bring or rent your own sleep sack or linen (see **Packing,** p. 18). Sleeping bags are often not allowed. Hostels frequently have kitchens and utensils available, and many have storage areas and laundry facilities. Some also require you to perform a daily communal chore.

Over 500 hostels are listed in **The Hostel Handbook for the U.S.A. & Canada** (Jim Williams, Ed.; available for $4 ($6 outside the U.S.) from Dept. IGH, 722 Saint Nicholas Ave., New York, NY 10031; email InfoHostel@aol.com; http://www.hostels.com/ handbook). Check out the **Internet Guide to Hostelling** at http://hostels.com. Reservations for over 300 Hostelling International (HI) hostels (see below) may be made via the **International Booking Network (IBN)** (202-783-6161), a computerized system that allows you make hostel reservations months in advance for a nominal fee. If you plan to stay in hostels, consider joining one of these associations:

Hostelling International-American Youth Hostels (HI-AYH), 733 15th St. NW, Suite 840, Washington, D.C. 20005 (202-783-6161, ext. 136; fax 783-6171; email hiayhserv@hiayh.org; http://www.hiayh.org). Maintains 35 offices and over 150 hostels in the U.S. Membership can be purchased at many travel agencies (see p. 23) or the HI-AYH national office in Washington, D.C. 1-year membership $25, under 18 $10, over 54 $15, family cards $35; includes *Hostelling North America: The Official Guide to Hostels in Canada and the United States*. Reserve by letter, phone, fax, or through the International Booking Network (see above).

Hostelling International-Canada (HI-C), 400-205 Catherine St., Ottawa, ON K2P 1C3, (613-237-7884; fax 237-7868; email info@hostellingintl.ca; http://www.hostellingintl.ca). Maintains 73 hostels throughout Canada. IBN booking centers (see above) in Edmonton, Montreal, Ottawa, and Vancouver; expect CDN$9-22.50 per

night. Membership packages: 1-year CDN$25, under 19 CDN$12; 2-year CDN$35; lifetime CDN$175.

HOTELS AND MOTELS

Many visitor centers, especially those off major thoroughfares entering a state, have hotel coupons. Even if you don't see any such coupons, ask. Budget motels are often clustered off the highway several miles outside of town, but the carless may do better to try the hostels, YMCAs, YWCAs, and dorms downtown. The annually updated **National Directory of Budget Motels** ($11) covers over 2200 low-cost chain motels in the U.S. **The Hotel/Motel Special Program and Discount Guide** ($8) lists hotels and motels offering special discounts. Also look for the comprehensive **State by State Guide to Budget Motels** ($13), from Marlor Press, Inc., 4304 Brigadoon Dr., St. Paul, MN 55126 (800-669-4908 or 651-484-4600; fax 651-490-1182; email marlor@ix.netcom.com).

It is fortunate that the Canadian hostel system is somewhat more extensive than that of the U.S., because the country has a dearth of cheap motels. U.S. budget motel chains cost significantly less than the chains catering to the next-pricier market, such as Holiday Inn. Chains usually adhere more consistently to a level of cleanliness and comfort than locally operated budget competitors; some even feature heated pools and cable TV. Contact these chains for free directories, and always inquire about discounts for seniors, families, frequent travelers, groups, or government personnel: **Motel 6** (800-466-8356); **Super 8 Motels** (800-800-8000; http://www.super8motels.com/super8.html); **Choice Hotels International** (800-453-4511); **Best Western International** (800-528-1234).

BED AND BREAKFASTS

As alternatives to impersonal hotel rooms, bed and breakfasts (private homes with spare rooms available to travelers, abbreviated **B&Bs**) range from the acceptable to the sublime. B&Bs offer an excellent way to explore an area with the help of a knowledgeable host, and some hosts go out of their way to be accommodating, accepting travelers with pets or giving personalized tours. Often the best part of your stay will be a home-cooked breakfast. However, many B&Bs do not provide phones or TVs, and bathrooms must sometimes be shared.

Several travel guides and reservation services specialize in B&Bs. Among the more extensive are **The Complete Guide to Bed and Breakfasts, Inns and Guesthouses in the U.S., Canada, and Worldwide** (US$17), which lists over 11,000 B&Bs and inns (available through Lanier Publications, P.O. Box D, Petaluma, CA 94953; 707-763-0271; fax 763-5762; email lanier@travelguides.com; http://www.travelguides.com). **Nerd World's Bed and Breakfasts by Region** (http://www.nerdworld.com/users/dstein/nw854.html) offers an excellent listing of international B&Bs. **Bed and Breakfast: The National Network of Reservation Services,** Box 764703, Dallas, TX 75376 (888-866-4262; fax 972-298-7118; email bdtxstyle1@aol.com; http://www.tnn4bnb.com), lists over 7000 B&Bs in the U.S., Canada, and the U.K. A travel kit will be mailed upon request. The **Northern Network of Bed and Breakfasts,** Box 954, Dawson City, YK Y0B 1G0 (867-993-5644; fax 993-5648; www.nnbandb.com), serves the same function for Alaska and northern Canada.

YMCAS AND YWCAS

Those **Young Men's Christian Association (YMCA)** that offer lodging are often located in urban downtowns, which can be convenient but a little gritty. YMCA rates are usually lower than a hotel's but higher than a hostel's, and may include use of libraries, pools, and other facilities. Many YMCAs accept women and families (group rates often available), but some will not lodge people under 18 without parental permission. All reservations must be made and paid in advance, with a traveler's check, money order, certified check, Visa, or MasterCard. Call the specific YMCA in question

for fees. For information or reservations (reservation fee $3, overseas $6), call **YMCA of the USA,** 101 North Whackers Dr., Chicago, IL 60606 (800-872-9622; fax 312-977-9063; http://www.ymca.net), which provides a listing of all the individual YMCAs in over 120 countries and in all 50 United States. The friendly staff provides information on prices, available services, and telephone numbers and addresses for the YMCA nearest to your travel destination. **For Ys in Canada,** contact the **Montréal YMCA** at 1450 Stanley St., Montréal, QC H3A 2W6 (514-849-8393; fax 849-8017) or the **YMCA Canada Customer Service Department** (416-928-3362).

Most **Young Women's Christian Associations (YWCAs)** accommodate only women, or occasionally, couples. Nonmembers are often required to join when lodging. For more information or a worldwide directory ($10), write **YWCA of the USA,** 726 Broadway, New York, NY 10003 (212-614-2700).

DORMS

Many **colleges and universities** in the U.S. and Canada open their residence halls to travelers when school is not in session—some do so even during term-time. No one policy covers all of these institutions, but rates tend to be low, and college campuses can be some of the best sources for information on things to do, places to stay, and possible rides out of town. *Let's Go* lists colleges renting dorm rooms in accommodations listings. College dorms are popular with many travelers, especially those looking for long-term lodging, so reserve ahead. Some schools require that you at least feign an interest in attending their institution. To contact colleges and universities in Alaska, Western Canada, and the Pacific Northwest, see **Study Opportunities,** p. 17.

HOME EXCHANGE AND RENTALS

Home exchange offers the traveler with a home the opportunity to live like a native, and to dramatically cut down on accommodation fees; usually only an administration fee is paid to the matching service. Once the introductions are made, the choice is left to the two hopeful partners. Most companies have pictures of members' homes and information about the owners (some will even ask for your photo). A listing of many exchange companies can be found at http://www.aitec.edu.au/~bwechner/documents/travel/lists/homeexchangeclubs.html. **Renting a home** may also be a good deal, depending on the length of stay and the desired services.

Intervac U.S., International & USA Home Exchange, P.O. Box 590504, San Francisco, CA 94159 (415-435-3497; fax 435-7440; email IntervacUS@aol.com; http://www.intervac.com). Part of a worldwide home-exchange network. Catalogues list over 10,000 homes in 30 countries worldwide. Members contact each other directly. You must pay for each catalogue you receive and list your home in a catalogue. Prices vary with each country; check the webpage for information.

The Invented City: International Home Exchange, 41 Sutter St., Suite 1090, San Francisco, CA 94104 (800-788-2489 in the U.S. or 415-252-114 elsewhere; fax 252-1171; email invented@aol.com). Listing of 1700 homes worldwide. For $50, you get your offer listed in one catalogue and receive three others. For $75, you can get unlimited access to the club's website database (http://www.invented-city.com), which contains all active homes for exchange.

■ Camping and the Outdoors

USEFUL PUBLICATIONS

A variety of publishing companies offer hiking guidebooks to meet the educational needs of novices and experts. For information about camping, hiking, and biking, write or call the publishers listed below to receive a free catalogue.

Family Campers and RVers/National Campers and Hikers Association, Inc., 4804 Transit Rd., Bldg. #2, Depew, NY 14043 (716-668-6242). Membership fee ($25) includes their publication *Camping Today.*

Sierra Club Bookstore, 85 Second St. 2nd fl., San Francisco, CA 94109 (800-935-1056 or 415-977-5600; fax 977-5793; http://www.sierraclub.org/books). Books on national parks, series on regions of the U.S., as well as *Learning to Rock Climb* ($14), *The Sierra Club Family Outdoors Guide* ($12), and *Wildwater* ($12).

The Mountaineers Books, 1001 SW Klickitat Way #201, Seattle, WA 98134 (800-553-4453 or 206-223-6303; fax 223-6306; email mbooks@mountaineers.org; http://www.mountaineers.org). Many titles on hiking (the *100 Hikes* series), biking, mountaineering, natural history, and conservation.

Wilderness Press, 2440 Bancroft Way, Berkeley, CA 94704-1676 (800-443-7227 or 510-843-8080; fax 548-1355; email wpress@ix.netcom.com; http://www.wilder-nesspress.com). Has over 100 hiking guides and maps of the western U.S. including *Backpacking Basics* and *Backpacking with Babies and Small Children* (each $11).

Woodall Publications Corporation, 13975 W. Polo Trail Dr., Lake Forest, IL 60045-5000 (800-323-9076 or 847-362-6700; fax 362-8776; email emd@woodallpub.com; http://www.woodalls.com). Covering the U.S., Mexico, and Canada, Woodall publishes the annually updated *Woodall's Campground Directory* ($20) and *Woodall's Plan-it, Pack-it, Go!: Great Places to Tent, Fun Things To Do* ($13).

For **topographical maps** of the U.S., write the **U.S. Geological Survey,** Branch of Information Services, P.O. Box 25286, DFC, Denver, CO 80225 (800-435-7627; fax 303-202-4693). Maps cost $4 payed in advance by Visa, MasterCard, check, or money order. The Canadian Map Office has recently been privatized, and all maps are sold by individual companies. For a list of companies, contact the **Canada Map Office,** 130 Bentley Ave., Ottawa ON, K1A 0E9 (613-952-7000; fax 613-957-8861).

NATIONAL PARKS

National parks like Alaska's Denali, Oregon's Crater Lake, and Alberta's Banff and Jasper protect some of America and Canada's most precious wildlife and spectacular scenery. The parks also offer recreational activities like hiking, skiing, and snowshoe expeditions; most have backcountry camping and developed tent campgrounds, others welcome RVs, and a few offer opulent living in grand lodges.

Entry fees vary from park to park. Pedestrian and cyclist entry fees tend to range from $2-7, while vehicles cost $4-10. Most national parks in the U.S. offer discounts such as the one-year **Golden Eagle Passport** ($50), which allows the bearer and family free entry into all U.S. parks. Visitors of age 62 and over qualify for the **Golden Age Passport** ($10), entitling them to free entry and a 50% discount on basic fees like camping. Ask for details at the entrance station of parks. The free **Golden Access Passport** offers free access to travelers with disabilities. Reservations are essential at the more popular parks in the Pacific Northwest; make them through **DESTINET** (800-365-2267 in U.S.). Visitor centers at parks offer excellent free pamphlets and information, and the **U.S. Government Printing Office** publishes *National Parks: Lesser-Known Areas* ($1.75).

Often less trammeled than their American counterparts, Canada's national parks are every bit as spectacular. Reservations are being offered for a limited number of campgrounds on a trial basis with a CDN$6.18 fee. For information or reservations, call Parks Canada at 800-213-7275 (http://parkscanada.pch.gc.ca). A patchwork of regional passes are available at specific parks.

National Park Service, 849 C St. NW, Washington, D.C. 20240 (202-208-6843; www.nps.gov).

U.S. Forest Service, Outdoor Recreation Information Center, 222 Yale Ave. N, Seattle, WA 98174 (206-470-4060; http://www.fs.fed.us).

Parks Canada, 220 4th Ave. SE, #552, Calgary, AB T2G 4X3 (800-748-7275 or 403-292-4401; email natlparks-ab@pch.gc.ca).

Alaska Public Lands Information Center, 605 W. 4th Ave. Suite 105, Anchorage, AK 99501 (907-271-2737; fax 907-271-2744).

STATE AND PROVINCIAL PARKS

In contrast to national parks, the primary function of **state and provincial parks** is usually recreation. Prices for camping at public sites are usually better than those at private campgrounds. Don't let swarming visitors dissuade you from seeing the larger parks—these places can be huge, and even at their most crowded they offer opportunities for quiet and solitude. Most campgrounds are first come, first camped, so arrive early; many campgrounds, public and private, fill up by late morning. Some limit your stay and/or the number of people in a group. For more information, visit:

Alaska Department of Natural Resources Public Information, 3601 C St., Suite 200, Anchorage, AK 99503 (907-269-8400; fax 269-8901; email pic@dnr.state.ak.us; http://www.dnr.state.ak.us/parks/index.htm).

Alberta Environmental Protection, 9820 106 St., 2nd Fl., Edmonton, AB T5K 2J6 (780-427-7009; fax 427-5980; email infocent@env.gov.ab.ca; http://www.gov.ab.ca/env/parks.html).

British Columbia Ministry of Environment, Lands, and Parks, P.O. Box 9398, Stn. Prov. Govt., Victoria, BC V8W 9M9 (250-387-4609; fax 387-5757; parkinfo@prkvctoria.elp.gov.bc.ca; http://www.elp.gov.bc.ca/bcparks).

Oregon State Parks and Recreation Department, P.O. Box 500, Portland, OR 97207-0500 (800-551-6949; fax 503-378-6308; email res.nw@state.or.us; http://www.prd.state.or.us).

Washington State Parks and Recreation Commission, P.O. Box 42650, Olympia, WA 98504-2650 (360-902-8500, info 800-233-0321; http://www.parks.wa.gov).

Yukon Parks and Outdoor Recreation, Box 2703, Whitehorse, YT Y1A 2C6 (867-667-5648; fax 393-6223; email joanne.butterworth@gov.yk.ca).

U.S. NATIONAL FORESTS

If national park campgrounds are too developed for your tastes, **national forests** provide a purist's alternative. While some have recreation facilities, most are equipped only for primitive camping; pit toilets and no running water are the norm. Entrance fees, when charged, are $10-20, but camping is generally free, or $3-4. **Reservations,** with a one-time $16.50 service fee, are available for most forests up to one year in advance, but they are usually unnecessary, except during high season at the more popular sites. For reservations, contact the **National Recreation Reservation Center,** P.O. Box 900, Cumberland, MD 21501-0900 (800-280-2267; fax 301-722-9802). For general information, including maps and the free *Guide to Your National Forests,* contact the **U.S. Forest Service** (see above).

Backpackers can enjoy specially designated **wilderness areas,** which are even less accessible due to regulations barring vehicles. **Wilderness permits** are required for backcountry hiking. They are generally free, though there is often a reservation fee. Permits can usually be obtained at the Forest Service office in the area; check ahead.

In Alaska, the Forest Service oversees more than 200 scenic and well-maintained **wilderness log cabins** for public use, scattered throughout the southern and central regions of the state. User permits are required, along with a fee of $15-50 per party per night. Call the Forest Service for reservations information. Most cabins have seven-day use limits (hike-in cabins have a three-day limit May-Aug.), and are usually accessible only by air, boat, or hiking trail. For general information, contact the Forest Service's regional offices. Any remaining questions that you have can probably be answered by the **Alaska Public Lands Information Center** (907-271-2737), which also mails out maps, brochures, and other information.

The U.S. Department of the Interior's **Bureau of Land Management (BLM),** Office of Public Affairs, 1849 C St. Room 406-LS, Washington DC 20240 (202-452-5125; fax 452-5125; http://www.blm.gov), offers a variety of outdoor recreation opportunities on the 270 million acres it oversees in ten western states and Alaska, including camping, hiking, mountain biking, rock climbing, river rafting, and wildlife viewing. These lands also contain hundreds of archaeological artifacts and historic sites. The BLM's many **campgrounds** include 20 sprinkled throughout Alaska, most of them free.

CAMPING AND HIKING EQUIPMENT

If you purchase **equipment** before you leave, you'll know exactly what you have and how much it weighs. Whether buying or renting, take the time to find sturdy, light, and inexpensive equipment.

Sleeping bags: Most good sleeping bags are rated by "season," or the lowest outdoor temperature at which they will keep you warm. Summer means 30-40°F, 3-season means 0°F, and 4-season or winter means below -50°F. Sleeping bags are made either of down (warmer and lighter, but more expensive, and miserable when wet) or of synthetic material (heavier, more durable, and warmer when wet). Prices vary, but might range from $65-100 for a summer synthetic to $250-550 for a good down winter bag.

Under your bag: If you're doing any serious camping, you'll need a **foam pad** ($15 and up) or **air mattress** ($25-50) to cushion your back and insulate you from the ground. Another good alternative is the **Therm-A-Rest,** part foam and part air-mattress, which inflates to full padding when you unroll it.

Over your head: The best tents are free-standing, with their own frames and suspension systems; they set up quickly and require no staking (except in high winds). Low-profile dome tents are best. When pitched, their internal space is almost all usable, which means little unnecessary bulk. Tent sizes can be somewhat misleading: 2 people *can* fit in a 2-person tent, but will find a 4-person more pleasant. If traveling by car, go for the bigger tent; if you're hiking, stick with a tent that weighs no more than 3-4 lb. Good 2-person tents start at $150, and 4-person tents at $400, but you can sometimes find last year's model for half the price. Be sure to seal the seams of your tent with waterproofer, and make sure it has a rain fly.

On your back: If you intend to do a lot of hiking, you should have a **frame backpack.** Sturdy backpacks cost anywhere from $125-500. This is one area where it doesn't pay to economize—cheaper packs may be less comfortable, and the straps are more likely to fray or rip. For more information, see **The Backpack,** p. 18.

Boots: Be sure to wear hiking boots with good **ankle support** that are appropriate for the terrain you are hiking. Your boots should fit snugly and comfortably over one or two wool socks and a thin liner sock. Be sure that the boots are broken in— a bad blister will ruin your hiking for days.

Other necessities: Rain gear should come in 2 pieces, a top and pants, rather than a poncho. Ponchos turn into rain-catching sails in high winds. **Synthetics,** like polypropylene tops, socks, and long underwear, along with a pile jacket, will keep you warm even when wet. When camping in autumn, winter, spring, or the great beyond, bring along a **space blanket,** which helps to retain body heat and doubles as a groundcloth ($5-15). Plastic **canteens** or **water bottles** are better than metal ones, and are virtually shatter- and leak-proof. Large, collapsible **water sacks** weigh practically nothing when empty and can significantly improve your lot in primitive campgrounds, though they can get bulky. Bring **water-purification tablets** for when you can't boil water. You'll need a **camp stove.** The classic Coleman starts at about $30. A **first aid kit, Swiss army knife, insect repellent, calamine lotion,** and **waterproof matches** or a **lighter** are essential camping items. Other items include: a **battery-operated lantern,** a **plastic groundcloth,** a **nylon tarp,** a **waterproof backpack cover** (although you can also store your belongings in plastic bags inside your backpack), and a **stuff sack** or plastic bag to keep your sleeping bag dry.

The mail-order firms listed below offer lower prices than those found in stores, but shop around locally to see what items actually look like and weigh. Remember that camping equipment is often more expensive in Australia and the U.K. than in North America. Local venues are listed under **Practical Information: Equipment Rental.**

Campmor, P.O. Box 700, Saddle River, NJ 07458-0700 (800-CAMPMOR/526-4784; 201-825-8300 outside the U.S.; email customer-service@campmor.com; http:// www.campmor.com). A wide selection of name brand equipment at low prices. 1-year guarantee for unused or defective merchandise.

Discount Camping, 880 Main North Rd., Pooraka, South Australia 5095, Australia (08 8262 3399; fax 8260 6240). Specializes in tents, but has other equipment as well.

Eastern Mountain Sports (EMS), 1 Vose Farm Rd., Peterborough, NH 03458 (603-924-7231). Stores throughout the U.S. Though slightly higher-priced, they provide excellent service and guaranteed customer satisfaction on most items. EMS doesn't have a catalogue, and they generally don't take mail or phone orders; call the above number for the branch nearest you.

Recreational Equipment, Inc. (REI) (800-426-4840; http://www.rei.com), stocks a comprehensive selection of REI-brand and other leading brand equipment, clothing, and footwear for travel, camping, cycling, paddling, climbing, and winter sports. In addition to mail order and an Internet site, REI has 49 retail stores, including a flagship store in Seattle, WA (222 Yale Ave. Seattle, WA 98109-5429).

L.L. Bean, Freeport, ME 04033-0001 (800-441-5713 in Canada or the U.S.; 0800 962 954 in U.K.; 207-552-6878 elsewhere; fax 207-552-3080; http://www.llbean.com). This monolithic equipment and outdoor clothing supplier offers high quality gear. Call or write for their free catalogue. Guaranteed 100% satisfaction on all purchases. Open 24hr., 365 days a year.

Mountain Designs, P.O. Box 1472, Fortitude Valley, Queensland 4006, Australia (07 3252 8894; fax 3252 4569). A leading Australian manufacturer and mail order retailer of camping and climbing gear.

Sierra Designs, 1255 Powell St., Emeryville, CA 94608 (800-635-0461 or 510-450-9555; fax 654-0705; http://www.mountaindesign.com.au). Especially carries small and lightweight tent models.

YHA Adventure Shop, 14 Southampton St., London, WC2E 7HA, U.K. (01718 36 85 41). One of Britain's largest outdoor equipment suppliers.

WILDERNESS CONCERNS

Stay warm, stay dry, and stay hydrated. The vast majority of life-threatening wilderness problems stem from a failure to follow this advice. On any hike, however brief, you should pack enough equipment to keep you alive should disaster befall. This includes water, high energy food, rain gear, and appropriate clothing and equipment (see above). Never rely on **cotton** for warmth. The "death fabric" is absolutely useless when wet (see **Packing,** p. 18).

Make sure to check all equipment for any defects before embarking on your adventure. Discovering that a tent pole is missing as the sun is going down miles from any signs of civilization is a good way to ruin a trip. Take the time before you leave to ensure everything is intact and in good working order.

Check **weather forecasts** and pay attention to the skies when hiking. A bright blue sky can turn to rain or even snow before you can say "hypothermia." If on a day hike and the weather turns nasty, turn back. If on an overnight, start looking immediately for shelter. Whenever possible, let someone know when and where you arc going hiking—either a friend, your hostel, a park ranger, or a local hiking organization. Do not attempt a hike beyond your ability, you may be endangering your life. A good guide to outdoor survival is *How to Stay Alive in the Woods,* by Bradford Angier (Macmillan, $8). See **Health,** p. 13, for information about outdoor ailments, basic medical concerns, and first-aid.

While protecting yourself from the elements, also consider protecting the wilderness from you. For the sake of those who follow you, practice **minimum impact** camping techniques. Leave no trace of your presence when you leave a site. Don't cut vegetation or clear new campsites. A campstove is the safer (and more efficient) way to cook, but if you must, make small fires using only dead branches or brush. Make sure your campsite is at least 150 ft. from water supplies or bodies of water. If there are no toilet facilities, bury human waste (but not paper) at least four inches deep and above the high-water line, 150 ft. or more from any water supplies and campsites. Always pack your trash in a plastic bag and carry it with you until you reach the next trash can.

IF YOU'RE BEING MAULED, YOU'RE TOO CLOSE

Alaska, Western Canada, and the Pacific Northwest are blessed with all three species of North American **bear:** polar bears live in the far north, while grizzly and black bears dwell everywhere else. If you're lucky, you may see one of these majestic furry sovereigns from the safety of a vehicle, a long distance, or both. If you're unlucky, or patently negligent, you may get between a majestic furry mom and her cubs, leading to **extreme danger.** While bears are not born people-eaters, they are also not cuddly stuffed animals, and must be taken very seriously.

The first and best defense against bear encounters is good old **mutual avoidance.** When hiking in a known bear area, make your presence obvious by **singing loudly or making other obvious noises**—tranquility is a small price to pay for security. While alerting bears with sound, do not attract them with food. As opportunistic omnivores, bears will seek out any grub that they can smell, and they can smell well. Keep camping sites clear of food scraps, and never cook in a sleeping area. Overnight, pack anything odoriferous in plastic bags: food, garbage, cooking utensils, soap, toothpaste, and used tampons. **Bear-bagging** is trickier than it sounds, unless it sounds to you like bagging a bear; make sure that you ask a ranger or other outdoor authority how to suspend all smelly possessions from a tree, away from curious paws. These precautions are as important to a bear's well-being as to a hiker's—bears that develop a taste for human food might develop a taste for humans *as* food, and are inevitably killed by wildlife authorities.

What to do in the event of a **bear encounter?** Ideas differ, but the main theme is to establish yourself as a non-threatening, non-prey entity. Wave your arms slowly above your head, speak firmly but not frantically ("Hey bear…stay away bear…"), and back away slowly. Most bears will lose interest and leave. If the bear charges, drop to the ground and curl up, with your backpack shielding your back and your arms shielding your neck. If you find this unsuccessful, defend yourself as best you can. In all situations, remain calm; loud noise and sudden movement can trigger an attack.

These procedures are founded on the fact that *you cannot outrun a bear*—they can cruise faster than the fastest human sprinter, uphill and through underbrush. If you get too close to a **moose,** on the other hand, run like hell. Again, you can't outrun it, but at least it won't mistake you for food.

OUTDOOR SPORTS

Canoeing, Kayaking, and Whitewater Rafting

The fast-flowing rivers in the Pacific Northwest, Western Canada, and Alaska is ideal for canoeing, kayaking, and whitewater rafting. Opportunities are noted throughout the book; travel agents and tourism bureaus can recommend others.

The **River Travel Center,** P.O. Box 6, Pt. Arena, CA 95468 (800-882-RAFT/7238; fax 707-882-2638), can plunk you in a whitewater raft, kayak, or sea kayak with one of over 100 outfitters. Trips range in length from one to 18 days and range in price from $80 (one day) to $2000 (extended). **Sierra Club Books** publishes a kayaking and whitewater rafting guide entitled *Wildwater* ($12). The club offers kayaking trips to the Pacific Northwest and Alaska every year. *Washington Whitewater* ($19) and *Canoe Routes: Northwest Oregon* ($13), published by The Mountaineers Books (see, p. 33) might also be of interest. The best bet is to contact the tourist office of the specific region in which you are interested (see **Government Information Offices,** p. 2).

Winter Sports

Tourism bureaus can help locate the best sports outfitters and areas for winter hiking, camping, skiing, snowshoeing, and dogsledding. *Let's Go* suggests options throughout the book. For Oregon and Washington skiing info (both downhill and cross-country), write the **Pacific Northwest Ski Areas Association,** P.O. Box 2325 Seattle, WA 98111-2325 (206-623-3777; fax 447-5897). The Sierra Club publishes *The Best Ski Touring in America* ($11), which also includes British Columbia and Quebec.

Pay attention to cold weather safety concerns. Know the symptoms of hypothermia and frostbite, and bring along warm clothes and quick energy snacks like candy bars and trail mix (see **Common Woes,** p. 14). Drinking alcohol in the cold can be dangerous: even though you *feel* warm, alcohol can slow your body's ability to adjust to the temperature, making you more vulnerable to hypothermia.

Fishing

From arctic char to king salmon, Alaska, Western Canada, and the Pacific Northwest enjoy incredible fishing. To take advantage of the region's well-stocked lakes and streams, contact the appropriate Department of Fisheries for brochures that summarize regulations and make sport fishing predictions. Some fishing seasons are short, so be sure to ask when the expected prime dates occur.

Alaska Department of Fish and Game Licensing Section, P.O. Box 25525, Juneau, AK 99802-5525 (907-465-2376; fax 465-2440; open M-F 8:30am-5pm). Nonresident 1-day fishing license $10, 1-day "salmon sticker" additional $10; 3-day $15, 3-day "salmon sticker" additional $15; $30 for 14 days; $50 for a year.

Alberta Environmental Protection Natural Resources Service, N. Tower Main Fl., Petroleum Pl., 9945 108 St., Edmonton, AB T5K 2G6 (780-427-6729; fax 422-9558).

British Columbia Environment and Lands, 10470 152 St., Surrey, BC V3R 0Y3 (604-582-5200; fax 930-7119).

Oregon Department of Fish and Wildlife, 2501 SW 1st Ave., P.O. Box 59, Portland, OR 97207 (503-872-5275). Nonresident 1-year fishing license $45, plus tags for salmon ($10.50), sturgeon ($6), and halibut ($6). One-day license covers all tags ($8.25; also 2, 3, 7 day licenses).

Washington Department of Fish and Wildlife, 600 Capitol Way, Olympia, WA 98501-1091 (360-902-2200). Nonresident game fishing license, good for 1 year, under 14 $20, over 14 $48. Nonresident personal use food fish license $30. Nonresident shellfish/seaweed license $20.

Yukon Government, Department of Renewable Resources, Fish and Wildlife Branch, 10 Burns Rd., P.O. Box 2703, Whitehorse, YT Y1A 2C6 (867-667-5221). Non-Canadian license CDN$5 for 1 day, CDN$20 for 6 days, CDN$35 for 1 year.

Licenses in the U.S. are available from many tackle shops, or can be purchased directly from the state department of fisheries. The sale of fishing licenses in Alberta and British Columbia has recently been privatized. Prices are consistent, but government agencies no longer sell licenses. To find Canadian fishing license vendors, call 1-888-944-5494. Nonresident fishing licenses cost CDN$18 for Canadians, CDN$36 for non-Canadians. Limited five-day fishing license for non-Canadians cost CDN$24.

Hunting

Regulations on hunting in Western North America are extensive. Certain animals may not be hunted, and others require special trapping licenses and permits. Rules are often specific to an area, so it's wise to start with a region's Fish and Wildlife department (listed above).

ORGANIZED ADVENTURE

Organized adventure tours offer hiking, biking, skiing, canoeing, kayaking, rafting, climbing, and archaeological digs. If you've got dough to shell, begin by consulting tourism bureaus, which can suggest parks, trails, and outfitters. The **Specialty Travel Index,** 305 San Anselmo Ave., Suite 13, San Anselmo, CA 94960 (415-459-4900; fax 459-4974; email spectrav@ix.netcom.com; http://www.specialtytravel.com), lists hundreds of tour operators worldwide. The **Sierra Club,** 85 Second St., 2nd fl., San Francisco, CA 94105-3441 (415-977-5630; fax 977-5795; email national.outings@sierraclub.org; http://www.sierraclub.org/outings), plans many adventure outings, both through its San Francisco headquarters and its local branches throughout Canada and the U.S. **TrekAmerica,** P.O. Box 189, Rockaway, NJ 07886 (800-221-0596; fax 201-983-8551; email info@trekamerica.com; http://www.trekamerica.com), organizes small group adventure camping tours throughout North and Central America. Trips run from seven days to nine weeks. **Footloose** (http://www.footloose.com) is their open-age adult program. **Alaska Wilderness Journeys,** P.O. Box 220204, Anchorage, AK 99522 (800-349-0064; fax 907-344-6877; email akwildj@alaska.net), organizes up to 10-day combination hiking, floating, and kayaking tours through Alaska as well as in Africa, Australia, and the Russian Far East.

■ Keeping in Touch

MAIL

U.S. MAIL Offices of the **U.S. Postal Service** are usually open Monday to Friday from 9am to 5pm and sometimes on Saturday until about noon; branches in larger cities open earlier and close later. All are closed on Sundays and national holidays (see p. 1).

Postcards mailed within the U.S. cost 20¢; letters cost 32¢ for the first oz. and 23¢ for each additional oz. To send mail to Canada from the U.S., it costs 40¢ to mail a post-card, 52¢ to mail a letter for the first oz., 72¢ for 2 oz., 95¢ for 3 oz., and 19¢ for each additional oz. The U.S. Postal Service requires that **overseas** letters be mailed directly from the post office and accompanied by a customs form. **Overseas rates** are post-cards 50¢, ½ oz. 60¢, 1 oz. $1, 40¢ per additional oz. **Aerogrammes,** sheets that fold into envelopes and travel via air mail, are available at post offices for 50¢. (All prices in US$.) Domestic mail generally takes three to five days; overseas mail, seven to four-teen days. Write **AIR MAIL** on the front of the envelope for speediest delivery.

The U.S. is divided into postal zones, each with a five-digit **ZIP code** particular to a region, city, or part of a city. Some addresses have nine-digit ZIP codes, used primarily to speed up delivery for business mailings. Writing the ZIP code on letters is essential for delivery. The normal form of address is as follows:

Marshall Lewy
Croatian Rappers, Inc. (title and/or name of organization, optional)
123 Apathy Avenue, Apt.#456 (address, apartment # if applicable)
Olympia, WA 98501 (city, state, zip code)
USA (country, if mailing internationally)

CANADIAN MAIL

In **Canada,** mailing a letter (or a postcard, which carries the same rate as a letter) to the U.S. costs 52¢ for the first 30g and 77¢ for 31-50g. To every other foreign country, a 20g letter costs 90¢, a 50g letter $1.37, and a 51-100g letter $2.25. The domestic rate is 45¢ for a 30g letter, and 71¢ for a letter between 31g and 50g. Aerogrammes cost 90¢. Letters take from seven to ten days to reach the U.S. and about two weeks to get to an overseas address by air. Canada Post's most reliable and pricey service is **Priority Courier,** which offers speedy delivery (usually next-day) to major American cities ($23.50 for a document). Delivery to overseas locations usually takes two days; for a document to Europe $35.50; to the Pacific $40; international $69. Guaranteed next-day domestic delivery between any two Canadian cities starts at $8.70 plus tax; cost varies depending on location. (All prices in CDN$.)

In Canada, **postal codes** are the equivalent of U.S. ZIP codes and contain letters as well as numbers (for example, L9H 3M6). The normal form of address is nearly iden-tical to that in the U.S.; the only difference is that the apartment or suite number can *precede* the street address along with a dash. For example, 3-203 Colborne St. refers to Room or Apartment #3 at 203 Colborne St.

GENERAL DELIVERY AND OTHER SERVICES

Depending on how neurotic/lov-ing your family and friends are, consider making arrangements for them to get in touch with you. Mail can be sent **general delivery** to a city's main branch of the post office. Once a letter arrives, it will be held for at least 10 days; it can be held for longer if such a request is clearly indicated by you or on the front of the envelope. Custom-ers should bring a passport or other ID to pick up General Delivery mail. Family and friends can send letters labeled like so:

Norman <u>FELL</u> (underline and capitalize last name for accurate filing)
c/o General Delivery
Main Post Office
Vancouver, BC V1L 2M6
CANADA (if mailing internationally)

American Express offices throughout the U.S. and Canada will act as a mail service for cardholders if you contact them in advance. Under this free **"Client Letter Ser-vice,"** they will hold mail for 30 days, forward upon request, and accept telegrams. The last name of the person to whom the mail is addressed should be capitalized and underlined. Some offices will offer these services to non-cardholders (especially those who have purchased AmEx traveler's checks), but you must call ahead to make sure. A complete list is available free from AmEx (800-528-4800) in the booklet *Traveler's Companion* or online at http://www.americanexpress.com.

If regular airmail is too slow, there are a few faster, more expensive, options. **Federal Express** (800-463-3339) is a reliable private courier service that guarantees overnight delivery anywhere in the continental U.S., at a significant price. The cheaper but more sluggish U.S. Postal Service **Express Mail** takes two days to deliver a parcel. Canada Post offers **Priority Courier** (next day delivery), **XPress Post**, and **SkyPak** for destinations in the U.S. and other countries. Rates vary by destination and weight.

TELEPHONES

Most of the information about telephone usage—including area codes for Canada and the U.S., foreign country codes, and rates—is in the front of any local **white pages** telephone directory. See this guide's **inside back cover** for relevant area codes.

The **yellow pages,** published at the end of the white pages or in a separate book, lists the numbers of businesses and other services alphabetically by the service or merchandise they provide. Federal, state, and local government listings are provided in the **blue pages.** To obtain local phone numbers or area codes of other cities, call **directory assistance** at 411. Dialing "0" will get you the **operator,** who can assist you in reaching a phone number and provide general information. You can reach local directory assistance and the operator free from any pay phone. For long-distance directory, dial 1-(area code)-555-1212. All area codes are listed at the end of a section's **Practical Information** listing.

You can place **international calls** from most telephones. To call direct, dial the international access code (from Canada and the U.S., the code is 011), followed by the country code, the area code, and the local number. Country codes and city codes may be listed with a zero in front (e.g., 033), but after dialing the international access code, drop successive zeros (with an access code of 011, dial 011 33). See the chart below for a list of country codes. Calls between Canada and the U.S. are not considered international calls. Dial them as you would a domestic long distance call: 1-(area code)-number. Be aware, however, that many toll free numbers in the U.S. (those that begin with 800 or 888) do not work from Canada, and vice versa.

Australia	Austria	Canada	Ireland	New Zealand	South Africa	United Kingdom	United States
61	43	1	353	64	13	44	1

You may want to consider getting a **calling card** if you plan to make a lot of international calls. The calls (plus a small surcharge) are billed either collect or to a calling card. Some companies will be able to connect you to numbers only in your home country; others will be able to provide many worldwide connections. For more information, call **AT&T** about its **USADirect** and **World Connect** services (888-288-4685; from abroad, call 810-262-6644 collect); **Sprint** (800-877-4646; from abroad, call 913-624-5335 collect); or **MCI WorldPhone** and **World Reach** (800-444-4141; from abroad dial the country's MCI access number). In Canada, contact **Bell Canada Canada Direct** (800-565-4708); in the U.K., **British Telecom BT Direct** (tel. (800) 34 51 44); in Ireland, **Telecom Éireann Ireland Direct** (800 250 250); in Australia, **Telstra Australia Direct** (13 22 00); in New Zealand, **Telecom New Zealand** (123); and in South Africa, **Telkom South Africa** (09 03).

Phone rates tend to be highest during the day, lower in the evening, and lowest on Sunday and late at night. Also, remember **time differences** when you call. See **Time Zones,** p. 2, for pertinent time zones.

EMAIL

With a minimum of computer knowledge and a little planning, users can beam messages anywhere for no per-message charges through **electronic mail** (known as **email**). One option is to befriend college students and ask if you can use their email accounts. If you're not the finagling type, **Traveltales** (http://traveltales.com) provides free, web-based email for travelers, and maintains a list of cybercafes, travel links, and a travelers' chat room. Other free, web-based email providers include **Hotmail** (http://www.hotmail.com), **RocketMail** (http://www.rocketmail.com), and **USANET** (http://www.usa.net). Many free email providers are funded by advertising, and some may require subscribers to fill out a questionnaire. Search through http://www.cyberiacafe.net/cyberia/guide/ccafe.htm to find a list of **cybercafes** around the world from which you can drink a cup of joe and email him, too.

If you're already hooked up to the infobahn at home, you should be able to find internet access numbers anywhere in the Pacific Northwest. If you're not connected, one comparatively cheap, easy-to-use access provider is **America Online,** 8615 Westwood Center Dr., Vienna, VA 22070 (800-827-6364).

THE PACIFIC NORTHWEST

In the 1840s, **Senator Stephen Douglas** ran his cane down a map of the Oregon Territory, tracing the spine of the **Cascade Range.** He argued, sensibly, that the mountains would make the perfect natural border between two new states. Sense has little to do with politics, of course, and the **Columbia River,** running perpendicular to the Cascades, became the border between Washington and Oregon. Yet even today, the range and not the river is the region's most important geographic and cultural divide: west of the rain-trapping Cascades lie the microchip, mocha, and music meccas of Portland and Seattle, while to the east sprawl tracts of farmland and an arid plateau.

Washington and Oregon are home to some of the most staggering landscapes in the U.S.: **seaside cliffs,** the moon-like **Mount St. Helens,** towering **Mt. Rainier,** and the plunging depths of **Hells Canyon.** In the 90s, the world has discovered the bounty of the Pacific Northwest; Portland and Seattle are currently two of the most popular and fastest growing cities in the U.S. Some residents fear that the region's laid-back way of life and tremendous natural beauty will be casualties of their own success. Emmet Watson's **"Lesser Seattle"** movement has gone so far as to publish negative statistics about the city in an attempt to stem the tide of migrating outsiders (especially Californians). Watson's crusade notwithstanding, residents of the Pacific Northwest are quick to welcome visitors to their beautiful home. Travelers need only keep in mind a few **regional quirks:** the typical driver does not like to honk, and pedestrians do not jaywalk in major cities. In Seattle and Portland, an umbrella is the mark of an outsider, though raincoats are allowed and Gore-Tex predominates. Finally, residents of the Beaver State wince to hear their home called or-i-GAHN, but will welcome you with open arms to OR-i-gun.

Early and Native History

Native Americans of the Pacific Northwest understood the Cascades' significance long before Senator Douglas dragged his cane along the map. Plateau tribes such as the **Palouse** and **Spokane** were on the move nine months of every year, hunting buffalo herds across the flat, dry region east of the Cascades. The arrival of horses from Mexico around 1730 profoundly boosted the inland tribes' hunting abilities, encouraging even greater nomadism. Coast dwellers such as the **Chinook,** in contrast, formed stable and stationary communities ruled by a hereditary chief and sustained by abundant resources. Salmon and other fish were plentiful, old growth forest provided a virtually endless supply of timber for building, and ample rainfall nourished an array of edible plants. Coastal society involved a complex fabric of intricate relationships between chiefs and community. In the custom of **potlatch,** chiefs gave away their possessions in a display of wealth and generosity that affirmed their privileged status within the group. Both cultures, inland and coastal, thrived until the onslaught of white trappers and settlers changed everything.

The Expedition of Lewis and Clark

U.S. President **Thomas Jefferson,** eager to attain "geographical knowledge of our own continent" and to strengthen American claims to the lands recently purchased from Napoleon, commissioned **Meriwether Lewis** and **William Clark** to explore the Pacific Northwest in 1803. These two proto-travel-researchers and their men were accompanied by the indomitable **Sacajawea,** a Shoshone translator, who proved invaluable to the party as both a bargainer for supplies and a peacemaker. This was lucky, since Lewis' attempts to impress the Shoshone with his limited command of their language involved rushing an armed warrior, waving madly, and yelling "I am your enemy!"

The expedition traveled about 4000 miles each way from St. Louis to the mouth of the Columbia River and back, accumulating and documenting flora and fauna while building stronger claims to a region that the U.S. and Britain still ostensibly shared. London, for its part, sent **Alexander Mackenzie** to cross the Rockies, and Captains **James Cook** and **George Vancouver** to map the Pacific Coast and its waterways. Vancouver charted the island that now bears his name, but inexplicably failed to notice the Columbia River, an oversight soon remedied by American **Robert Gray.** In 1818, Britain and the U.S. hammered out an agreement that divided their claims as far west as the Rockies at the **49th parallel,** but left the Oregon question unresolved.

Disaster and Dispossession

The arrival of Europeans in the Pacific Northwest was devastating to native communities. By the late 1800s, as much as 90% of the indigenous population had been wiped out by the machinations of white settlers, and by the unfamiliar diseases such as measles, small pox, and influenza that the settlers inadvertently carried. Missionary fervor, however genuine, often did little more than to help control and dispossess Native Americans. The tensions and misunderstandings generated by missionary activity destroyed lives on both sides, as when crusaders such as the Americans **Marcus and Narcissa Whitman** rushed west to Walla Walla to save the natives. When an epidemic of measles broke out among the Cayuse in 1847, the tribe blamed the missionaries. Marcus met his end at the tomahawk of **Chief Tilokaikt,** and Narcissa and ten others were killed shortly thereafter.

White settlers continued flocking to the region, and though Native Americans negotiated many land treaties with these newcomers, none were ever ratified by Congress. As the pressure over available land intensified, a number of small wars between the government and individual tribes broke out. These wars always ended in defeat for the tribes, who were then displaced to reservations on some of the worst land in the region. The **Nez Percé** tribe, led by the renowned **Chief Joseph,** fought the last and most famous war for its land in 1877. But the Nez Percé also were also defeated and herded onto reservations.

54-40 or Fight! (or Not)

Britain voiced strong opposition to American control of the Pacific Northwest, facilitating **James K. Polk's** election to the presidency in 1846 with an expansionist, militarist platform and a catchy slogan: "54-40 or Fight," a claim to all the land south of the 54°40´ parallel. Polk found the fight he wanted in Mexico rather than the Pacific Northwest, though, and proved content to settle for the 49th parallel as the dividing line between British and American territory. The southern half of America's Oregon Territory became the state of Oregon in 1859, and the more thinly populated territory to the north joined it 30 years later, reluctantly giving up the name "Columbia" (reserved for that pesky congressional district back east) and taking "Washington" (inexplicably left unreserved by that same bungling capital to confuse generations of geography students).

Birds, Bees, and Bill Gates

With those pesky Brits gone, present-day Oregon and Washington have found other problems to grapple with. Oregonians have struggled with the birds and the bees in arenas as disparate as **gay rights legislation** and sexual harassment (witness the 1995 scandal surrounding Senator Bob Packwood). Birds alone have also proven problematic, as the logging industry and environmentalists continue to butt heads over the endangered **northern spotted owl.** When Congress passed legislation to protect the owl, a federal court injunction banned logging in the public forests of the Pacific Northwest. Idle mills, unemployed loggers, and crippled local economies pushed the issue back into Congress in June 1994, and limited logging resumed under a complex new forest-use-and-protection plan. With the two states' once lucrative timber and fishing industries on the downturn, many Oregonians and Washingtonians are looking to cities like Seattle for fresh economic opportunities. Computer software companies based in the area are booming, and then booming some more, prompting Pacific Rim nations to strengthen their ties to the region. Yet some wonder if this slicker Pacific Northwest has lost touch with its history in acquiring a taste for coffee.

The Arts

The arts thrive in the soggy climate of the Pacific Coast. Long before European arrival, the relative leisure of the coastal way of life allowed indigenous peoples to devote time and energy to elaborate and sophisticated art forms such as masks, lodges, totems, dances, and songs.

Portland and Seattle funnel a 1% tax on capital improvements into the acquisition and creation of public art, and the Pacific Northwest offers numerous world-class venues. The **Oregon Shakespeare Festival** (see p. 109) in Ashland draws an annual audience of nearly half a million, while orchestral music aficionados flock to the **Bach Festival** in Eugene, OR, where Helmuth Rilling waves his baton. Seattle has a **repertory theater** community second in size only to those of Chicago and New York, and its **opera** is internationally renowned for its Wagner productions.

In popular culture, the region has made its mark with some of the smartest, sharpest talents of recent years. Filmmakers **Gus Van Sant** *(My Own Private Idaho, Drugstore Cowboy)* and **Cameron Crowe** *(Singles, Say Anything, Jerry Maguire)* are natives of the Pacific Northwest. **David Lynch** grew up in Spokane and produced the obtuse Oregon-based television series *Twin Peaks* in Snoqualmie (see p. 175). Oregon and Washington have each produced at least one cartoonist of twisted and undeniable genius: Portland's **Matt Groening,** creator of *The Simpsons* and *Life in Hell,* and Washington State alumnus **Gary Larson,** mastermind of *The Far Side.*

The Pacific Northwest is widely renowned for its Seattle rock scene, which exploded in the early 90s with the success of **grunge** rockers like Soundgarden, Pearl Jam, and Nirvana. While the record executives that once prowled the city signing contracts with everything in plaid have moved on, rock in the region is by no means defunct. An active, youthful population supports a range of excellent music and a vibrant nightlife not only in Portland and Seattle, but also in Eugene (second home of the Grateful Dead), Olympia, and even in smaller cities like Spokane and Bend. Seattle's **Bumbershoot** (see p. 174), a blow-out festival every summer of folk, street, classical, and rock, offers a great chance to sample the music of the Pacific Northwest.

Further Reading

The *Journals of Lewis and Clark,* by Meriwether Lewis and William Clark, tell the tale of the Pacific Northwest's most famous budget travelers. *Undaunted Courage,* by Stephen Ambrose, and *Sacajawea,* by Flora Warren Seymour, revisit that history and myth.

Jack Kerouac's *Dharma Bums* and Robert Pirsig's *Zen and the Art of Motorcycle Maintenance* continue the road-tripping tradition, but in fiction and with fur pants supplanted by denim. David Duncan's engaging and funny coming of age story, *The River Why,* wrestles with many of the environmental issues facing the region while demonstrating just how powerfully addictive fly-fishing can be. Raymond Carver's *Where I'm Calling From* describes the people of the Pacific Northwest in blunt and brutal prose. Sherman Alexie, in language no less harsh, depicts the condition of the Spokane tribe in his 1995 *Reservation Blues.* Other noteworthy books from and about the Pacific Northwest include *Snow Falling on Cedars,* a mystery novel by David Guterson set amid Japanese-American tensions in post-WWII Puget Sound; *The Lathe of Heaven* by science fiction author Ursula K. LeGuin; *Another Roadside Attraction* and *Even Cowgirls Get the Blues* by Tom Robbins; *The Lost Sun* by poet and former University of Washington instructor Theodore Roethke; and *Paul Bunyan* by James Stevens. The fearless Pacific Northwesterner, Ramona, from the series of the same name by Beverly Cleary, has inspired many a middle child.

Oregon

Over one hundred years ago, entire families liquidated their possessions and sank their life savings into covered wagons, corn meal, and oxen, high-tailing it to Oregon in search of prosperity and a new way of life. Today, Oregon remains as popular a destination as ever for backpackers, cyclists, anglers, beachcrawlers, and families alike. The caves and cliffs of Oregon's coastline are a siren call to tourists, and some coastal towns are enticing oases. Inland attractions include majestic Mt. Hood in the Cascade Range, the deep blue waters of Crater Lake National Park, Ashland's Shakespeare Festival, and North America's deepest gorge. Portland is casual and idiosyncratic—its name was determined by a coin toss—while the college town of Eugene embraces hippies and Deadheads. Bend, a tiny interior city with a young, athletic population, competes for the title of liveliest town. From excellent microbrews to snow-capped peaks, a visit to Oregon is still worth crossing the Continental Divide.

PRACTICAL INFORMATION

Capital: Salem.
Population: 3,082,000. **Area:** 97,060 sq. mi. **Motto:** "She flies with her own wings."
  Nickname: Beaver State. **Song:** "Oregon, My Oregon." **Flower:** Oregon grape. **Animal:** Beaver. **Fish:** Chinook salmon. **Rock:** Thunderegg. **Dance:** Square Dance.
Road Conditions: (800-977-6368 in OR; 503-588-2841outside OR; http://www.odot.state.or.us.
State Police: Northwest (503-378-2575), South (541-776-6111), East (541-617-0617).
Time Zone: Mostly Pacific (1hr. before Mountain, 3hr. before Eastern), with a small southeastern section in Mountain (1hr. after Pacific, 2hr. before Eastern).
Postal Abbreviation: OR.
Sales Tax: None. **Drinking Age:** 21. **Traffic Laws:** Seatbelts required.
Area Codes: Portland and the state's northwest corner 503; everywhere else 541.

■ Portland

Increasingly popular and populated, the City of Roses is still the quietest, mellowest, and rainiest big city on the West Coast. Although home to a thriving urban culture, Portland blends seamlessly with its majestic natural surroundings. With over 200 parks, the pristine Willamette River, and snow-capped Mt. Hood in the background, Portland is an oasis of natural beauty. The city government keeps it that way, regulating building height to preserve views and requiring all new buildings to have street-level retail space. With an award-winning transit system and pedestrian-friendly streets, Portland often feels more like a pleasantly overgrown town than a metropolis.

Driven indoors for the better part of the year by stubborn rain, Portlanders have nursed a love of art, music, and books. Culture is constantly cultivated in the endless theaters, galleries, and bookshops around town. Powell's City of Books engulfs an entire city block, making it the largest bookstore in the country. With the funds from a 1% tax on new construction, Portland fosters a growing body of outdoor sculpture and a series of open-air concerts. Local artists fill galleries and cafes with paint and plaster, and adorn the outdoors murals and street art. Improvisational theaters are in constant production, and open mic nights can be found almost anywhere in town. The city's venerable symphony orchestra, the oldest in the Western United States, adds tradition and class to Portland's pulsating cultural scene.

As the microbrewery capital of America, Portland is a flowing font of the nation's finest beer. During the rainy season, Portlanders flood neighborhood pubs and coffeehouses for shelter and conversation, but on rare sunny days, a battalion of hikers, bikers, and runners take advantage of their sylvan surroundings. The Willamette River and its wide park reach all the way downtown, and dense forests at the city's edge cloak miles of well-manicured hiking trails. Not too far out of town, Portlanders enjoy Mt. Hood to the east and the Pacific shore to the west. Portland has mastered this synthesis of urban and outdoor life, making it the best-kept secret on the coast.

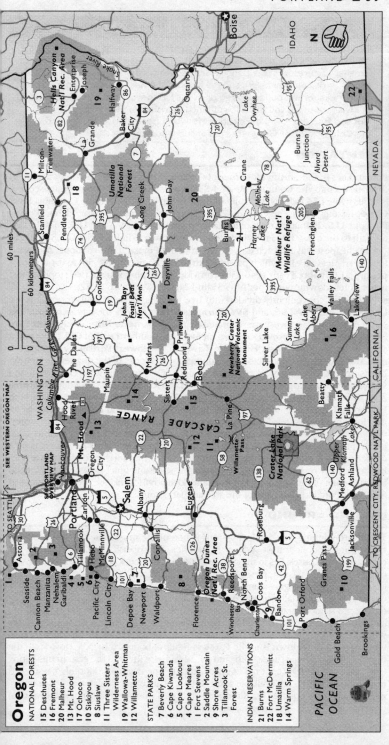

Oregon

NATIONAL FORESTS
15 Deschutes
16 Fremont
20 Malheur
13 Mt. Hood
17 Ochoco
10 Siskiyou
8 Siuslaw
11 Three Sisters
   Wilderness Area
19 Wallowa-Whitman
12 Willamette

STATE PARKS
7 Beverly Beach
6 Cape Kiwanda
5 Cape Lookout
4 Cape Meares
1 Fort Stevens
2 Saddle Mountain
9 Shore Acres
3 Tillamook St.
   Forest

INDIAN RESERVATIONS
21 Burns
22 Fort McDermitt
18 Umatilla
14 Warm Springs

OREGON

ⓘ HIGHLIGHTS OF PORTLAND

- Cerebral delights await at the **Portland Art Museum** (see p. 67) and the tome-stuffed **Powell's City of Books** (see p. 68).
- Greener pastures lie in the tranquil **Grotto** (see p. 68), the well-designed **Washington Park Zoo** (see p. 69), and the bloom-filled **Rose Garden** (see p. 69).
- Plenty of important ponderings go on at the kitsch-worshiping **24-Hour Church of Elvis** (see p. 67) and the cafe-crammed **Hawthorne St.** (see p. 64).
- Not too far from town, the exciting **Mt. Hood** (see p. 74) soars skyward, while the **Columbia River Gorge** (see p. 75) cuts a stunning rut.

ORIENTATION

Portland lies in the northwest corner of Oregon, where the Willamette (wih-LAM-it) River flows into the Columbia River. **I-5** connects Portland with San Francisco and Seattle, while **I-84** follows the route of the Oregon Trail through the Columbia River Gorge, heading along the Oregon-Washington border toward Boise, Idaho. West of Portland, **U.S. 30** follows the Columbia downstream to Astoria, but **U.S. 26** is the fastest path to the coast. **I-405** runs just west of downtown to link I-5 with U.S. 30 and 26.

The cheapest way to reach downtown from the **Portland International Airport** is to take Tri-Met bus #12, which passes south through town on SW 5th Ave. (45min., 4 per hr., $1.05). **Raz Tranz** (246-3301) provides an **airport shuttle** that stops at most major hotels downtown (2 per hr. 5:35am-12:05am; $9, ages 6-12 $2).

Portland is conveniently divided into five districts, by which all street signs are labeled: **N, NE, NW, SE,** and **SW. Burnside Street** divides the city into north and south, while east and west are separated by the **Willamette River. Southwest** Portland is known as **downtown,** but also includes the southern end of Old Town and a slice of the wealthier **West Hills. Old Town,** in **Northwest** Portland, encompasses most of the city's historic sector. The southernmost blocks of the quarter, around W. Burnside, are best not walked alone at night. Overlapping with Old Town and stretching north is the up-and-coming **Pearl District,** a rapidly rebuilding industrial zone. Farther north and west, NW 21st and NW 23rd St., collectively known as **Nob Hill,** are hot spots for boutique shopping. **Southeast** Portland contains parks, factories, local businesses, residential areas of all brackets, and a rich array of cafes, stores, theaters, and restaurants lining **Hawthorne Boulevard. Reed College,** with its wide green quads and brick halls, lies deep within the district. **Williams Avenue** cuts off a corner of the northeast sector, called simply the North. **North** and **Northeast** Portland are chiefly residential, punctuated by a few small and quiet parks; North Portland is also the site of the **University of Portland.** Drug traffickers base their operations in Northeast Portland, and parts of the area are dangerous.

GETTING AROUND

The award-winning **Tri-Met bus system** is one of the most logically organized and rider-friendly public transit systems in America. The **transit mall,** closed to all but pedestrians and buses, lies in the middle of downtown, between SW 5th and 6th Ave. Over 30 covered passenger shelters serve as stops and info centers. Southbound buses pick up passengers along SW 5th Ave.; northbound passengers board on SW 6th Ave. Bus routes fall into seven **service areas,** each with its own individual lucky charm: red salmon, orange deer, yellow rose, green leaf, blue snow, purple raindrop, and brown beaver. Shelters and buses are color-coded for their region. A few buses with black numbers on white backgrounds cut through town north-south or east-west. Most of downtown is in the **Fareless Square,** bounded by NW Hoyt St. to the north, I-405 to the west and south, and the Willamette River to the east. In this happy land, buses and **MAX** (light rail) are free, and no one ever dies. Monthly passes, bus maps, and schedules are available at the **Tri-Met Customer Assistance Office** in Pioneer Courthouse Square (for directions and fares outside this zone, see **Practical Information: Public Transportation,** below).

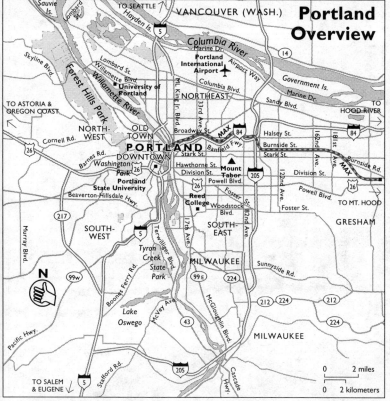

Portland Overview

Almost all downtown streets are **one-way,** with few legal left turns. **Street parking** is elusive and expensive: **meters** cost $1 per hour, usually limited from one to three hours. The city's **Smart Park** decks are common and well-marked (95¢ per hr.; $3 per hr. after three hours; $1.50 after 6pm; weekends $3 per day). **Tri-Met** is the best choice when spending the day downtown. **Jaywalking** is risky; cars will stop for you, but so will police, tickets in hand. It's a bit like using an umbrella—everyone will know you're not from Portland.

PRACTICAL INFORMATION

Transportation

Airplanes: Portland International Airport, 7000 NE Airport Way (460-4234). For transportation to and from the airport, see above.

Trains: Amtrak, 800 NW 6th Ave. (recording 273-4866; human 273-4865; reservations 800-USA-RAIL/872-7245), at Hoyt St. in Union Station. To: Seattle, WA (3 per day, $24); Eugene (2 per day, $12). Open daily 7:45am-9:15pm.

Buses: Greyhound, 550 NW 6th Ave. (243-2357 or 800-231-2222), at Glisan. To: Seattle, WA (11 per day, $20); Eugene (8 per day, $12); Spokane, WA (3 per day, $37); Boise, ID (4 per day, $35). Lockers $2 per 6hr. Ticket window open daily 5am-11:45pm; Station 5am-1am. **Green Tortoise** (800-867-8647) picks up at Union Station in the Amtrak building (see above). Confirm 2 days in advance. To: Seattle, WA (Tu and Sa 4pm, $15); San Francisco, CA (Su and Th 12:30pm, $49).

Public Transportation: Tri-Met 701 SW 6th Ave. (238-7433; http://www.tri-met.org), in Pioneer Courthouse Sq. Open M-F 8am-5pm. Several **information lines**

OREGON

Portland

ACCOMMODATIONS

A Ben Stark Hostel
B 4th Avenue Motel
C Portland HI-AYH

500 yards
500 meters

TO AIRPORT
TO COLUMBIA RIVER GORGE
TO OREGON MUSEUM OF SCIENCE AND INDUSTRY
TO LEWIS AND CLARK COLLEGE
TO REED COLLEGE
TO ONDINE
TO B
TO WASHINGTON PARK ZOO

Rose Garden Arena

Willamette River

Union Station (Amtrak)

Powell's Book Store

Civic Stadium

Portland State University

Library

City Hall

Portland Building

Civic Auditorium

Skidmore Fountain

Burnside Bridge
Morrison Bridge
Hawthorne Bridge

Fareless Square

Transit Mall

PIONEER COURTHOUSE SQUARE

MAX

84
30
99E
5
405
26
30
99E

NE Hassalo
NE Everett St.
NE Burnside St.
Sandy Blvd.
Lloyd Blvd.
Steel Bridge
Front

Stark St. SE
12th Ave. SE
SE 7th Ave.
SE Grand Ave.
SE Martin Luther King Jr. Blvd.
SE 3rd Ave.
SE 2nd Ave.

20th Ave.
16th Ave.

SE Morrison St.
SE Belmont St.
SE Yamhill St.
SE Taylor St.
SE Salmon St.
SE Main St.
SE Madison St.
SE Hawthorne Blvd.

NW Kearney St.
NW Johnson St.
NW Irving St.
NW Hoyt St.
NW Glisan St.
NW Flanders St.
NW Everett St.
NW Davis St.
NW Couch St.
NW Burnside St.

NW 23rd Ave.
NW 21st Ave.
NW 19th Ave.
NW 17th Ave.
NW 14th Ave.
NW 10th Ave.

NW 1st Ave.
NW 2nd Ave.
NW 3rd Ave.
NW 4th Ave.
NW 5th Ave.
NW 6th Ave.
NW Broadway Ave.
NW Park Ave.

SW Front Ave.
SW 1st Ave.
SW 2nd Ave.
SW 3rd Ave.
SW 4th Ave.
SW 5th Ave.
SW 6th Ave.
SW Broadway
SW Park Ave.
SW 9th Ave.

SW Ankeny St.
SW Ash St.
SW Stark St.
SW Washington St.
SW Alder St.
SW Morrison St.
SW Yamhill St.
SW Taylor St.
SW Salmon St.
SW Main St.
SW Madison St.
SW Jefferson St.
SW Columbia St.
SW Clay St.
SW Market St.

Willamette River

available: **Call-A-Bus** info system (231-3199); fare info (231-3198); updates, changes, and weather-related problems (231-3197); TDD information (238-5811); senior and disabled services (238-4952) lost and found (238-4855). Buses generally run 5am-midnight, reduced on weekends. Fare $1.05-1.35, ages 7-18 80¢, over 65 or disabled 50¢; free in the downtown **Fareless Square** (see **Getting Around,** above). All-day pass $3.25. All buses have bike racks ($5 lifetime permit available at area bike stores). **MAX** (228-7246), based at the Customer Service Center, is an efficient light-rail train running between downtown and Gresham in the east. Same fares as Tri-Met. Runs M-F 4:30am-11:30pm toward downtown and 5:30am-12:30am toward Gresham (starts slightly later Sa-Su). More MAX lines toward Beaverton are under construction.

Taxis: Broadway Cab (227-1234). $2.50 base, $1.50 per mi. **Radio Cab** (227-1212). $2 base, $1.50 per mi. Airport to downtown $22-25. Airport to Hostelling International Portland $20. Both 24hr.

Car Rental: Rent-a-Wreck, 1800 SE M.L. King Blvd. (233-2492 or 888-499-9111). From $30 per day and $180 per week, with 100 free mi. per day. Must be 21 or older, with credit card. Open M-F 8:30am-5pm, weekends by appointment only. **Dollar Rent-a-Car** (800-800-4000), at the airport. From $35 per day and $171 per week, with unlimited free mileage. Must be over 25 with credit card, or 21-25 with proof of insurance and $19 per day surcharge. 5% AAA discount. Open 24hr. **Crown Rent-A-Car,** 1315 NE Sandy Blvd. (224-8110). Transport from airport. From $28 per day, plus 20¢ per mi. after 100 mi., or $30 per day with unlimited mileage. Must be 21 or older with credit card, or under 21 with proof of full insurance coverage. Open M-F 8am-5pm, Sa 9am-noon.

Car Club: AAA Automobile Club of Oregon, 600 SW Market St. (222-6777 or 800-AAA-HELP/222-4357). Open M-F 8am-5pm.

Visitor Services

Visitor Information: Portland Oregon Visitors Association, 25 SW Salmon St. (222-2223 or 800-345-3214; http://www.pova.com), at Front St. in the Two World Trade Center complex. From I-5, follow the signs for City Center. Extensive info on Portland and its surroundings; the free *Portland Tour Map*, *Official Visitor Guide*, and *Portland Book* have maps, historical trivia, and comprehensive info on local attractions. Open M-F 9am-5pm, Sa 9am-4pm, Su 10am-2pm; Sept.-Apr. closed Su.

Outdoor Information: Portland Parks and Recreation, 1120 SW 5th Ave. #1302 (823-2223). Open M-F 8am-5pm.

Local Services

Bookstore: See **Powell City of Books,** p. 68.

Library: 801 SW 10th Ave. (248-5123). Open Tu-W 10am-8:30pm, Th-Sa 10am-5:30pm, Su 1-5pm. Internet access available.

Gay and Lesbian Information: Phoenix Rising, 620 SW 5th Ave. #710 (223-8299). Counseling and referral for gay, bisexual, transgendered, and transsexual people. Open M-F 8:30am-6:30pm, Sa by appointment.

Tickets: Ticketmaster (224-4400) or **Fastixx** (224-8499).

Laundromat: Springtime Thrifty Cleaners and Laundry, 2942 SE Hawthorne Blvd. (232-4353), across from the hostel. Wash $1, dry 25¢ per 10min. Open M-F 7:30am-10pm, Sa-Su 8am-10pm. **City Laundry,** 1414 Glisan (224-4204), at NW 14th. Attendant always on duty. Same day wash and fold (95¢ per lb.; min. 10 lb.). Wash $1.50, dry 25¢ per 10min. Open daily 7am-10pm.

Public Pool: Aquatics Office (823-5130) lists Portland's 13 public pools. $2, under 17 $1.25.

Leonardo da Vinci's Birthday: April 15.

Ski Conditions: Timberline, 222-2211. **Ski Bowl,** 222-2695. **Mt. Hood Meadows,** 227-7669.

Weather and Road Conditions: 541-889-3999.

Emergency and Communications

Emergency: 911. **Police:** 1111 SW 2nd Ave. (non-emergency response 230-2121; info 823-4636). **Fire:** 55 SW Ash St. (823-3700).

Crisis and Suicide Hotline: 655-8401. 24hr.

Women's Services: West Women's Hotel Shelter, 2010 NW Kearney St. (224-7718). **Women's Crisis Line:** 235-5333. 24hr.
AIDS Hotline: 223-2437. Staffed M-F 10am-9pm, Sa-Su noon-6pm.
Senior Services: Aging and Disabilities Helpline, 248-3646. 24hrs. **Oregon Retired Persons' Pharmacy,** 9800 SW Nimbus Ave., Beaverton (orders 800-456-2277, info 646-3500). Open M-F 8:30am-6pm, Sa 9am-1pm.
Post Office: 715 NW Hoyt St. (800-ASK-USPS/275-8777). **ZIP Code:** 97208-9999. Open M-F 7am-6:30pm, Sa 8:30am-5pm.
Internet Access: See **Library,** above.
Area Code: 503.

PUBLICATIONS

Portland's major daily newspaper, the **Oregonian** (nicknamed the **Boregonian** by locals), lists upcoming events in its Friday edition. The city's favorite free cultural reader, the Wednesday **Willamette Week,** is a reliable if somewhat uninspiring guide to local events. The free monthly magazine **Anodyne** has been rated one of the best new start-ups, and offers left-of-center listings. For a look at music and culture even farther from the fray, turn to **PDXS** (biweekly and free). **The Rocket** is the most comprehensive music publication (bimonthly and free). Yuppies find their interests represented weekly in **Ourtown,** which lists downtown goings-on. The biweekly **Just-Out** caters to gay, lesbian, bisexual, transsexual and transgendered interests throughout Oregon. Willamette Week, PDXS, and The Rocket all have complete club listings, and are available on street corners, in restaurants, and in hostels.

ACCOMMODATIONS AND CAMPGROUNDS

Although downtown is studded with Marriott-esque hotels, and the smaller motels are steadily raising prices, Portland still welcomes the budget traveler. The Hostelling International outpost is an old standby, offering quality housing only minutes from downtown. Prices drop farther from the city center. Portland accommodations fill in a flash, especially during the Rose Festival and frequent conventions; early reservations are wise. Camping sites are distant, but nature abounds; there no gravel-strewn RV-only sites around Portland.

Hostelling International Portland (HI-AYH), 3031 SE Hawthorne Blvd. (236-3380), at 31st Ave. Take bus #14 (brown beaver). The place to stay if you're lucky enough to get a bed. Laid-back atmosphere, outdoor deck, and open mic (Th 6:30pm). Front porch, kitchen (including BBQ), internet access ($1), and laundry facilities. 34 beds: $15, nonmembers $18. All-you-can-eat pancakes every morning (a paltry $1) and free pastries from a local bakery. Sells discount ski passes to Mt. Hood, and guided tours to the Columbia River Gorge, Mt. Hood and Mt. St. Helens ($38.50). Reception daily 7:30-11am and 4-11pm. No curfew. Fills early in summer (women's rooms go first), so reserve a spot (credit card required) or plan to arrive at 4pm to snag one of 12-15 walk-in beds. HI members only June-Sept.

McMenamins Edgefield Hostel, 2126 SW Halsey St. (669-8610 or 800-669-8610), in Troutdale, 20min. east of Portland. Take MAX east to the Gateway Station, then Tri-Met bus #24 (Halsey) east to the main entrance. By car, take I-84 east to Exit 14, follow 207th Drive S. and turn left at the first stoplight onto SW Halsey St. Continue 2 mi. until you see the sign on the right; the hostel is ¼ mi. farther down on the right. McMenamins converted this farm into a crown jewel of hosteling that shares the beautiful estate with a movie theater (21+), winery, brewery, and 3 restaurants. Dark wood bunks and vast rooms. Two single-sex dorm-style rooms, each with 12 beds. Shower facilities and 2 tubs. Restaurants are pricey, but good. $20 includes lockers, bedding, and admission to the movies. No curfew. 24hr. desk service.

Ben Stark Hotel and International Hostel, 1022 SW Stark St. (274-1223). This old building is undergoing a much-needed facelift. 10 rooms with new beds, 8 bathrooms, and a sunny common room down the hall. Laundry and lockers downstairs. Convenient location, but there are some shady characters in this neighborhood, and the club across the street is noisy on weekends. Passport or hostel membership required. Dorms $15; private rooms $39-56. Nov.-May dorms $12. No curfew. 24hr. desk service.

4th Avenue Motel, 1889 SW 4th Ave. (226-7646), at Hall St. Unremarkable rooms with dim lighting, but just blocks from the center of downtown. A/C, heat, phones, and HBO. Singles from $44, doubles from $50. Check-out 11am.

Motel 6, 3104 SE Powell Blvd. (238-0600; fax 238-7167). Take bus #9 (brown beaver) from 5th Ave. A local polyp of the budget motel superorganism. Clean and comfortable, but rooms by the street are a bit noisy. Phones, A/C, heat, HBO, and outdoor pool. $45, $51 for 2 people, $54 for 3, or $57 for 4. Always full; call in advance or show up at 6pm to catch a canceled room.

Champoeg State Park, 8239 NE Champoeg Rd. (678-1251, reservations 800-452-5687). Take I-5 south 20 mi. to Exit 278, then follow the signs west for 6 mi. Play along miles of paved bikeway or hike by the Willamette River. 48 shady RV sites ($19) have water and electricity. Tent sites ($15) do not afford much privacy. Yurts $25. Outdoor summer concert series ($20-35). 2-day advance reservation required.

Ainsworth State Park, 33 mi. east of Portland, at Exit 35 off I-84 on scenic U.S. 30, in the Columbia Gorge. Wooded and lovely, but highway noise is all too prevalent. Not a natural getaway, but the beautiful gorge makes the schlep worthwhile. Hot showers, flush toilets, hiking trails. Tent sites $12; full hookups $18. Non-camper showers $2. Open Apr.-Oct.

FOOD

Portland has more restaurants per capita than any other American city, and dining is seldom dull. Downtown establishments can take a walk on the expensive side, but the restaurants and quirky cafes scattered heavily across the NW and SE quadrants offer great food at reasonable prices.

Northwest Portland

The trendy eateries on NW 21st and 23rd St.are the places to go for lunch or dinner. **Food Front,** a small cooperative grocery at 2375 NW Thurman St. (222-5658), has a superb deli selection amid a wonderland of natural foods, fruit, and baked goods (open daily 9am-10pm; in winter daily 9am-9pm).

Accuardi's Old Town Pizza, 226 NW Davis St. (222-9999). Relax on a couch, at a table, or within a private booth in this typical whorehouse-turned-saloon-style-pizzeria. Reported ghost sightings by the staff have not adversely affected their pizza-crafting abilities (small cheese $5.50). Open Su-M 4-11pm, Tu-Th 11:30am-11pm, F-Sa 11:30am-midnight. Closed on Leonardo da Vinci's birthday.

Garbonzo's, 922 NW 21st Ave. (227-4196), at Lovejoy. Seek refuge from mad boutique-seekers at this delicious falafel bar. Admire the wire paintings on the wall while snarfing cheap, healthy food served by a conversational staff. The falafel pita ($3.75) only slightly humbles the hummus ($3.25) and the tasty baba ghanoush ($4). Open Su-Th 11:30am-1:30am, F-Sa 11:30am-3am. Other locations at 3433 SE Hawthorne Blvd. and 6341 SW Capital Hwy.

Kornblatt's, 628 NW 23rd Ave. (242-0055). Take bus #15 (red salmon). What! You're not eating? You look so thin! This New-York-style deli, replete with Big Apple relics, cooks up matzoh ball soup ($4), knishes ($2.75), and latkes (2 for $4). Sandwiches are 'uge ($6-8). Bagels cost $3.30 for 6, and $6.25 per dozen. Alternate nosh at 1000 SW Broadway (242-2435). Open M-Th 8am-9pm, F 8am-10pm, Sa 7:30am-10pm, Su 7:30am-9pm.

Southwest Portland

The center of town and tourist traffic, Southwest Portland can wax expensive. Street-carts offer an array of portable food, but the best deals are indoors. A row of speedy ethnic restaurants peddle cheap eats on Morrison St. between 10th and 11th Ave.

⊛**Western Culinary Institute** (800-666-0312) maintains 3 public testing grounds for its gastronomic experiments. Sit on a stool in the **Chef's Diner** (1231 SW Jefferson) while cheerful students in tall white hats serve, taste, and discuss sandwiches. Drop by the **Chef's Corner** (1239 SW Jefferson) for a quick meal on-the-go. Across

OREGON

the street, the elegant sit-down **Restaurant** (1316 SW 13th Ave.) serves a classy 5-course lunch ($8) rivaled only by its superb 6-course dinner (Tu-W $11, F $16). Thursday nights feature a tastebud-tingling, all you-can-eat international buffet ($16). Call ahead. Diner open Tu-F 7am-noon; corner deli open Tu-F 8am-6pm; restaurant open Tu-F 11:30am-1pm and 6-8pm.

Chang's Mongolian Grill, 1 SW 3rd St. (243-1991), at Burnside. Delicious all-you-can-eat buffet of fresh vegetables, meat, fruit, and fish. Pile on the raw materials, and watch the chef cook it all on a domed grill the size of a Volkswagen. The sizzling performance itself justifies the price (lunch $6.25; dinner $10). Rice, soup, and/or crepes included. Open M-F 11:30am-2:30pm and 5-10pm and Sa-Su noon-2:30pm, Sa 5-10pm and Su 4:30-9:30pm.

Hamburger Mary's, 239 SW Broadway (223-0900). Sporting a neon EAT NOW sign on its side window, this eccentric joint hoards random relics. Gargantuan portions make the California Mary Burger ($6.50) a must for avocado-lovers. The proud Prima Spud ($5) is no small potatoes. Milk comes in a baby bottle, to increased kitschification. Open daily 7am-2:30am.

Rocco's Cafe, 949 SW Oak St. (223-9835), at W. Burnside Blvd. Gigantic slices of good, thick pizza ($2) in funky environs. Take your pie to a psychedelic booth or walk across the street to Powell's Books (see p. 68). Check out the postered wall for Portland goings-on. Open M-Th 11am-11pm, F-Sa 11am-4am, Su noon-9pm.

Brasserie Montmartre, 626 SW Park Ave. (224-5552). Paper tablecloths, crayons, strolling magicians, and nightly live jazz make good diversions on dull dates. The bistro menu is slightly less expensive. Thai chicken $7.75; braised lamb shank $14.50; burgers $5.75. Win the crayon contest on the last Thursday in April, and get your masterpiece displayed in the entrance. Open M-Th 11:30am-2am, F 11:30am-3am, Sa 10am-3am, Su 10am-2am.

Southeast Portland

Anchored at happening Hawthorne Blvd., Southeast Portland is a great place to people-watch and tummy-fill, day or night. Eclectic eateries with exotic decor and economical menus hide in residential and industrial neighborhoods. Granola-seekers glory in the **People's Food Store Co-op,** 3029 SE 21st Ave. (232-9051), which runs a farmer's market on summer Wednesday afternoons (open daily 9am-9pm), and the larger **Nature's,** 3016 Division St. (233-7374; open daily 9am-10pm). The **Safeway,** 2800 SE Hawthorne (232-5539), at is one among plenty (open daily 6am-1am).

Montage, 301 SE Morrison St. (234-1324). Take bus #15 (brown beaver) to the end of the Morrison Bridge and walk under it. An oasis of Louisiana-style cooking. Munch on frog legs ($9.50) or jambalaya with crawfish ($13) while pondering a puzzling mural of *The Last Supper,* or come just to hear the waiters yell for oyster shooters ($1.50). Open M-F 11:30am-2pm and 6pm-2am, Sa-Su 6pm-4am.

Cafe Lena, 2239 SE Hawthorne Blvd. (238-7087). Take bus #5 (brown beaver). Artsy-fartsies frequent this cafe, known for open mic poetry (Tu 9:30pm) and homemade challah. The menu includes Thai, Italian, and American dishes ($7-10). Try the Malcolm Potato X ($6.25) or Venetian Veneration Submarino ($6.50). Spoken words or acoustic music every night. Breakfast served until 4pm. Open Tu 8am-midnight, W-Th 8am-11pm, F 8am-1am, Sa 8am-1am, and Su brunch 8am-3pm.

Delta Cafe, 4607 SE Woodstock Blvd. (771-3101). Take bus #19 from 5th Ave.; look left for a green building about 4 blocks past Reed College. Fried okra ($3) and cajun meatballs ($4) feed the lost and wandering soul. Adamantly free-spirited decor—witness the hanging beads. Worth the trek out to Woodstock. Open M-F 5-11pm, Sa noon-11pm, Su noon-10pm; in winter M-F 4-10pm.

Saigon Kitchen, 3829 SE Division St. (236-2312). Inhale the aroma as you walk into the best Vietnamese restaurant in town. The *chà giò* rolls, deep-fried and served with fresh herbs and sauce ($6.50), are a perennial favorite. Most entrees $7-9. Open M-F 11am-10pm, Sa noon-10pm.

Cup & Saucer, 3566 SE Hawthorne Blvd. (236-6001). Take bus #14 (brown beaver). A friendly, frantic neighborhood restaurant famous for its pancakes ($4.25) and grilled veggie sandwich ($5.25). The world's biggest blocks of coffee cake, brownies, and rice krispy treats baked daily (50¢-$1.50). Open daily 7am-9pm.

Nicholas' Restaurant, 318 SE Grand Ave. (235-5123), across from Miller Paint. Take bus #6 (red salmon) to the Andy and Bax stop. The unassuming facade means nothing, *nothing*. Nicholas serves tantalizing Lebanese and Mediterranean food at incredible prices. Try the Mezza ("I'll-try-a-little-bit-of-everything") platter ($7) or the Shatta pizza ($3). Mediterranean sandwiches $4-7. Open M-Sa 10am-9pm.

Hawthorne Street Cafe, 3354 SE Hawthorne Blvd. (232-4982). Take bus #14 (brown beaver). A converted Victorian house, featuring enticing sandwiches like sun-dried tomato, avocado, sprouts and cheese ($5.50). Some come just for the marionberry coffee cake ($3). 15% discount for hostel guests. Open M-Tu 7:30am-2:30pm, W-F 7:30am-2:30pm and 5-10pm, Sa-Su 7:30am-10pm.

Thanh Thao Restaurant, 4005 SE Hawthorne Blvd. (238-6232). Take bus #14 (brown beaver). You might come back to Portland just for a second helping of this fabulous Thai cuisine. The long menu, ranging from cashew beef ($7) to eggplant in black bean sauce ($6.25), makes up for any lack of decor. Salad rolls ($3) are a successful mutation of spring rolls. Lunch specials ($5.25) include soup, fried wonton, half a spring roll, and fried rice. Open M and W-F 11am-2:30pm and 5-10pm, Sa-Su 11am-10pm.

CAFES AND COFFEEHOUSES

Portland has no shortage of outlets for an old-fashioned cuppa joe. Requisite Starbucky chains infect most neighborhoods, but home-grown hidden treasures still offer atmosphere and a caffeinated place to spend a rainy afternoon.

Coffee Time, 712 NW 21st Ave. (497-1090). Sip a cup of chai tea ($1.55) and view the ancient wonders of the main room, or slip away through the hanging beads to play jenga in the 3-sided enclave. Intelligentsia mingle by a faux fire, while the bohemians push on into a parlor with tapestries, chill music, and dim lighting. Niches for everyone! Lattes $2; Time Warp with extra caffeine $1. Open M-Sa 6:30am-midnight, Su 8am-midnight.

Pied Cow Coffeehouse, 3244 SE Belmont St. (230-4866). Take bus #15 (brown beaver) to the front door. Glory be to God for caffeinated things—sink into the velvety cushions and "feed the pastures of your mind" inside this quirky Victorian parlor. Espresso drinks ($1-3) and a wide selection of teas (pots $2.50). Try a cup of kava ($2) for a refreshing out-of-body experience. Open Tu-Th 4pm-midnight, F 4pm-1am, Sa 10am-1am, Su 10am-midnight. Closed Jan.

Giant Steps, 1208 NW Glisan St. (226-2547). This chic Pearl District coffeehouse sports art from 7 surrounding galleries, plus shots of carrot juice ($1.50). Named after John Coltrane's classic album, Giant Steps plays great jazz, live on first Thursday of each month (7-9:30pm). Open M-F 6am-7pm, Sa 7am-5pm, Su 8am-4pm.

Torrefazione Italia, 838 NW 23rd Ave. (800-727-9692). A justifiably crowded Nob Hill destination, with admirable pottery. When it's nice out, the giant windows slide open to let in fresh air and conversations from the street. Espresso drinks $1-3. Open M-Th 6am-10pm, F 6am-11pm, Sa 7am-11pm, Su 8am-9pm.

Rimsky-Korsakoffee House, 707 SE 12th Ave. (232-2640), at Alder St. Take bus #15 (brown beaver) to 12th St., then walk 2 blocks north. Unmarked and low-key, this red Victorian house is a hidden gem with a bacchanalian frenzy of desserts. Ask for a "mystery table." Live classical music nightly—*Scheherazade*, anyone? Open flexibly Su-Th 7pm-midnight, F-Sa 7pm-1am.

The Roxy, 1121 SW Stark St. (223-9160). The most frequented cafe, crowded late at night as everything else closes. Nocturnal types come to drink an entire pot of coffee ($1 per person), smoke, and pursue irony. Sit on a leopard-print booth, spin a song on the Wurlitzer jukebox, and eat some chocolate suicide cake ($2.25) or Big-Ass Biscuits and Gravy ($3). Open Tu-Su 24hr.

SIGHTS

Shaded parks, magnificent gardens, bustling open-air markets, and innumerable museums and galleries beckon from all over Portland. For $1.05, bus #63 (orange deer or brown beaver) delivers its charges to at least 13 attractions. Catch the best of

Portland's dizzying arts scene on the first Thursday of each month, when the Portland Art Museum (see below) and the small galleries in Southwest and Northwest Portland all stay open until 9pm. *(Galleries free. Museum half-price.)* Contact the **Regional Arts and Culture Council,** 309 SW 6th Ave. #100 (823-5111), for up-to-the-minute info, or grab the *Art Gallery Guide* at the visitor center.

Out and About Downtown

Portland's downtown centers around the pedestrian and bus mall, which runs north-south on 5th and 6th Ave. between W. Burnside Blvd. on the north end and SW Clay St. on the south. The fully functioning **Pioneer Courthouse,** a downtown landmark at 5th Ave. and Morrison St., is the centerpiece of **Pioneer Courthouse Square,** 701 SW 6th Ave. (223-1613), which opened in 1983 and has since become "Portland's Living Room." Urbanites of every ilk hang out in this massive brick quadrangle; with Tri-Met's Customer Service Office at its center and plenty of seating, the square is a shrine to the pedestrian. At its birth, citizens bought personalized bricks to support the construction of an amphitheater hosting live jazz and folk music. During the summer, the **High Noon Tunes** draw thousands of music lovers. *(W noon-1pm.)*

The most controversial building in the downtown area is Michael Graves' postmodern **Portland Building,** 1120 SW 5th Ave., on the mall. This conglomeration of pastel tile and concrete has been both praised as PoMo genius and condemned as an overgrown jukebox. On a niche outside its second floor, fair **Portlandia** reaches down to the crowds below. This immense bronze statue portrays the trident-bearing woman from the Oregon state seal, but to some depraved onlookers, she resembles a man with breasts brandishing a large salad fork. The Standard Insurance Center, nearby at 900 SW 5th Ave., has also sparked controversy over **The Quest,** a sensual white marble sculpture out front, more commonly known as "Five Groins in the Fountain." There is room for romping just west of the mall on the **South Park Blocks,** a series of cool and shaded parks down the middle of Park Ave., enclosed on the west side by **Portland State University (PSU)** (725-3000).

The section of downtown just south of the Burnside Bridge and along the river comprises **Old Town.** Though not the safest part of Portland, Old Town has been revitalized in recent years by store-front restoration and a bevy of new shops and restaurants. **Skidmore Fountain,** at SW 1st Ave. and SW Ankeny St., is a popular people-watching spot and marks the entrance to the quarter. Resident brewmeister Henry Weinhard's offer to run draft beer through the fountain was rejected by city officials, the putzes. The fountain marks the end of **Waterfront Park,** a 20-block swath of grass and flowers along the Willamette River.

A total of 19 fountains decorate the city and provide plenty of spots to cool off on those rare sunny days. Pick up the free *Portland's Municipal Fountains* at the visitor center. **Ira's Fountain,** between 3rd and 4th St. and Market and Clay St., in front of the Civic Auditorium, sends 13,000 gallons cascading down cobblestoned terraces every minute. The impressive **Salmon Street Springs,** in Waterfront Park at SW Salmon St., are just down the street from the visitor center. An underground computer manipulates the fountain's 185 jets, which project water in constantly changing directions.

Downtown's waterfront district is laced with a complex web of underground passages known as the **Shanghai tunnels.** Urban lore has it that seamen would get folks drunk, drag them down to the tunnels, and store them there until their ship sailed. Forced aboard and taken out to sea, these hapless Portlanders would provide a free crew. ("Behave or I'll make you a galley slave" is a common parental threat in Portland.) North of Burnside lies what was once a thriving Chinatown, but only its **arched gateway** remains today. The area has been recycled as the **Pearl District.** Stretching

No Room for Muggers

In 1948, a hole was cut through the sidewalk at the corner of SW Taylor St. and SW Front St. It was expected to accommodate a mere lamp post, but greatness was thrust upon it. The streetlamp was never installed, and the 24-inch circle of earth was left empty until noticed by Dick Fagan, a columnist for the *Oregon Journal*. Fagan used his column, "Mill Ends," to publicize the patch of dirt, pointing out that it would make an excellent park. After years of such logic-heavy lobbying, the park was added to the city's roster in 1976. At 452.16 sq. in., Mill Ends Park is officially the world's smallest park. Locals have enthusiastically embraced it, planting flowers and hosting a hotly contested snail race on St. Patrick's Day. Exciting activities abound: play solo frisbee, wave at passing cars, read Habermas, hunt earthworm, develop a national healthcare plan, or bury deceased Smurfs.

OREGON

north from Burnside to I-405 along the river, this old industrial zone is packed with galleries, loft apartments, and warehouses-turned-office buildings. Storefronts and cafes have made the area welcoming, but the boxy architecture hulks on.

Inside and Wide-Eyed Downtown

On the west side of the South Park Blocks sits the venerable **Portland Art Museum,** 1219 SW Park (226-2811; http://www.pam.org/pam), at Jefferson St. *(Open Tu-Su 10am-5pm, and until 9pm first Th of the month. $7.50, seniors and students over 16 $6, under 16 $2.50.)* The second oldest fine arts museum on the West Coast, the PAM houses more than 32,000 works of art spanning 35 centuries. Western painting and sculpture, prints, photos, contemporary works, and an international collection make this a must-relish for all art lovers. Highlights for the 1999 season include contemporary artist Robert Colescott's *Recent Paintings* (Jan. 15–Mar. 21) and the extraordinary Native American exhibit *Down from the Shimmering Sky: Masks of the Northwest Coast* (Apr. 11-Jul. 11). Offices for the **Pacific Northwest College of Art** (226-4391) and the **Northwest Film Center** (221-1156) share space with the museum. The film center shows classics, documentaries, and off-beat flicks almost daily. *($6, students $5.)*

Across the park, the **Oregon Historical Society Museum and Library,** 1200 SW Park Ave. (222-1741; http://www.ohs.org/ohsinfo.html), stores photographs, artifacts, and records of Oregon's last two centuries, including interactive exhibits on Oregon, Willamette County, and Portland. *(Open Tu-Sa 10am-5pm, Su noon-5pm. $6, students $3, ages 6-12 $1.50. Seniors free on Th. 2-for-1 AAA discount.)* If the kiddies get restless, herd 'em off to the **Portland Children's Museum,** 3037 SW 2nd Ave. (823-2227), at Wood St., which schedules games, arts activities, and hands-on exhibits. *(Open daily 9am-5pm. Ages 1 and up $4. Take bus #1, 12, 40, 41, 43, 45, or 55, all yellow rose.)*

For a dose of fun that might go over youngsters' heads, pay a visit to the first and only **24-Hour Church of Elvis,** 720 SW Ankeny St. (226-3671; http://www.churchofelvis.com). *(Open F 8pm-midnight, Sa noon-5pm and 8pm-midnight, Su noon-5pm, M-Th usually 2-4pm but call to confirm—this one-woman show needs time to renovate!)* Listen to synthetic oracles, witness satirical miracles, and, if you're lucky, experience a tour in the church's Art-o-Mobile. This was once a 24-hour coin-operated funhouse, and hopes to be again very soon; 30-minute tours run in the meantime.

Nicknamed "Munich on the Willamette," Portland is the uncontested **microbrewery** capital of the U.S., and residents are proud of their beer. Henry Weinhard, a German master, fermented this tradition in 1856, when he established the first brewery in the Pacific Northwest outside of Fort Vancouver. Today, "Henry's" is a pan-Oregon standard, outgrowing its microbrew status. The visitor center hands out a list of 26 metro area breweries, most of which happily give tours. Visit the **Blitz Weinhard Brewery,** 1133 W. Burnside (222-4351), for a 45-minute tour and samples. *(Tours Tu-F at noon, 1:30pm, and 3pm. Free.)* Many of these beer factories are brew pubs, offering food and sometimes live music with their wares. Try the **Lucky Labrador Brew Pub,** 915 SE Hawthorne Blvd. (236-3555), where Miser Monday pints cost $2.25. *(Open M-Sa 11am-midnight, Su noon-10pm.)* For others, see **Nightlife,** below. Visit the **Oregon**

Brewers Guild, 510 NW 3rd Ave. (295-1862 or 800-440-ALES/2537), to learn exactly how the water, hops, and grains of Oregon empower its beer. *(Open M-F 10am-4pm.)*

North, Northwest, and Northeast Portland

Portland has more park acreage than any other American city. **Forest Park,** the 5000-acre tract of wilderness in Northwest Portland, might have something to do with this. Washington Park (see p. 69), provides easy access by car or foot to this sprawling sea of green, the largest park completely within a U.S. city. A web of trails leads through lush forests, scenic overviews, and idyllic picnic areas. The **Pittock Mansion,** 3229 NW Pittock Dr. (823-3624), within Forest Park, was built by Henry L. Pittock, founder of the daily *Oregonian. (Open Mar.-Dec. daily noon-4pm. $4.50, seniors $4, ages 6-18 $2. Call for tours.)* Enjoy a striking panorama of the city from the lawn of this 85-year-old, 16,000 sq. ft. monument to the French Renaissance. From downtown, take cross-town bus #20 (orange deer) to NW Barnes and W. Burnside St., then walk ½ mi. up a steep hill to Pittock Ave. Or follow the green and white mansion signs west on Burnside Blvd. for 2½ mi.

Downtown on the edge of the Northwest district is the gargantuan **Powell's City of Books,** 1005 W. Burnside St. (228-4651 or 800-878-7323; http://www.powells.com), a cavernous establishment with almost a million new and used volumes, more than any other bookstore in the U.S. *(Open M-Sa 9am-11pm, Su 9am-9pm.)* If you like to dawdle in bookshops, bring a sleeping bag and rations. Seven color-coded rooms house books on everything from Criminology to Cooking. The **Anne Hughes Coffee Room,** within the beast, serves bagels, cookies, and coffee for those who can't find their way out. Powell's also features frequent poetry and fiction readings (7:30pm in the purple room) and an extensive travel section on Portland and the Pacific Northwest.

Minutes from downtown on Sandy Blvd. (U.S. 30) at NE 85th is **The Grotto** (254-7371), a 62-acre Catholic sanctuary housing magnificent religious sculptures and gardens. *(Open daily 9am-8pm; in winter 9am-5:30pm.)* At the heart of the grounds is "Our Lady's Grotto," a breathtaking cave carved from a 110 ft. cliff, and a replica of Michelangelo's *Pieta.* An elevator ($2) ascends from the base for a view the serene Meditation Chapel, the Peace Garden, and a life-sized bronze statue of St. Francis of Assisi.

Southeast Portland

Southeast Portland is largely residential, with scattered pockets of activity. To the south, **Reed College,** 3203 SE Woodstock (771-1112; campus events 777-7522) sponsors a number of cultural events. The ivy-draped grounds, encompassing a lake and a state wildlife refuge, make for an exceptionally attractive campus. In 1968, this enclave of progressive politics became the first college to open its own nuclear reactor. Today, the students are far more committed to turning their compost heap than to generating nuclear energy. One-hour tours leave from **Eliot Hall** #220, 3203 Woodstock Blvd. at SE 28th. *(Open M-F 10am and 2pm.)*

Across the street from Reed is the **Crystal Springs Rhododendron Garden,** SE 28th Ave., at Woodstock (take bus #19). *(Open daily 6am-10pm; Oct.-Feb. daily 8am-7pm; Mar. 1-Labor Day Th-M 10am-6pm. $2, under 12 free.)* Over 2500 rhododendrons of countless varieties surround a lake and border an 18-hole public golf course. Unwind among ducks, man-made waterfalls and 90-year-old rhodies. The flowers are in full bloom from March until June.

The **Oregon Museum of Science and Industry (OMSI),** 1945 SE Water Ave. (797-4000 or 797-4569; http://www.omsi.edu), at SE Clay St., keeps visitors mesmerized with science exhibits, including an earthquake simulator chamber. *(Open F-W 9:30am-7pm, Th 9:30am-8pm; Labor Day-Memorial Day F-W 9:30am-5:30pm, Th 9:30am-8pm. $8.50, seniors and ages 4-13 $6.)* The **OMNIMAX Theater** (hours and shows 797-4640), in the museum, is BIG. *(Shows start on the hr., daily 11am-4pm and W-Sa 7-9pm. $6, seniors and ages 4-13 $4.50.)* In an elementary ploy to make science cooler, the **Murdock Sky Theater** (797-4646) presents astronomy matinee shows during the day and rockin' Pink Floyd laser shows by night. *(Matinees daily. Free with museum admission or $2. Evening shows W-Su; $6.50.)* While at OMSI, visit the **U.S.S. Blueback** (797-4624), the Navy's last diesel submarine. She never failed a mission, starred in the 1990 film *The Hunt for Red October,* and gets fantastic mileage. *(Open daily 10am-5pm. 40min. tour $3.50.)* OMSI offers a package deal to all four attractions. *($15, ages 4-13 $11.)*

Washington Park

Less than 2 mi. west of downtown, the posh neighborhoods of **West Hills** form a buffer zone between soothing parks and the turmoil of the city. In the middle of West Hills, mammoth **Washington Park** and its nearby attractions typify the blend of urbanity and natural bounty Portland has perfected. To get there, take the animated "zoo bus" (#63) on SW Main St., or drive up SW Broadway to Clay St., take U.S. 26 west, and get off at the zoo exit. The gates close at 9pm, but by day the park is beautiful. The **Rose Garden,** 400 SW Kingston (823-3636), in Washington Park, is the pride of Portland. In summer months, a sea of blooms arrests the eye, showing visitors exactly why Portland is the City of Roses. Growers across the world donate roses to this *Rosaceae* testing ground. Across from the Rose Garden are the scenic **Japanese Gardens,** 611 SW Kingston Ave. (223-1321), reputed to be the most authentic this side of the Pacific. *(Open daily June-Aug. 9am-8pm; Apr.-May and Sept. 10am-6pm; Oct.-Mar. 10am-4pm. $6, seniors $4, students $3.50.)* The **Hoyt Arboretum,** 4000 SW Fairview Blvd. (228-8733 or 823-3655), at the crest of the hill above the other gardens, features 200 acres of trees and trails, including the charming and wheelchair accessible **Bristlecone Pine Trail.** The 26 mi. **Wildwood Trail** winds through Washington and Forest Parks, connecting the arboretum to the zoo. Maps (50¢) are available at the info stand near the arboretum parking lot. *(Trails open daily 6am-10pm. Arboretum visitor center open M-Th 9am-4pm, F 10am-4pm, Sa 10am-2pm, Su 10am-5pm.)*

The **Washington Park Zoo,** 4001 SW Canyon Rd. (226-1561 or 226-7627), is renowned for its scrupulous re-creation of natural habitats and its successful elephant breeding. *(Open 9am-6pm. $5.50, seniors $4, ages 3-11 $3.50. Free after 3pm on the second Tu of every month.)* Whimsical murals decorate the #63 "zoo bus," connecting the park to SW Main St. in the downtown mall. A steam engine pulls passengers on a mini railway out to Washington Park gardens and back, giving a better view of flowers and animals. *(30min. tour $2.75, seniors and ages 3-11 $2.)* The zoo features a number of educational talks on weekends and has a **children's petting zoo.** If you're around in late June, July, or August, grab a picnic basket and head to the zoo's **sculpture garden** to catch live outdoor music at the **Rhythm and Zoo Concerts** (234-9694), free with zoo admission and ranging among international styles. *(W-Th at 7pm.)* The zoo also hosts **Zoobeat concerts** on selected weekend summer nights. *(7pm. $14.)*

ENTERTAINMENT

Prepare to be severely slathered with culture. Upon request, the Portland Oregon Visitors Association (see p. 61) will fork over a thick packet outlining a month's events. Outdoor festivals are a way of life. See **Publications,** p. 62, for more sources of info.

Music

Although first-rate traveling shows never miss Portland, and many have bargain tickets available, some of the greatest shows are free and outdoors. For stellar local rock, visit the Satyricon and La Luna (see **Nightlife,** p. 71).

Oregon Symphony Orchestra, 719 SW Alder St. (228-1353 or 800-228-7343), in the Arlene Schnitzer Concert Hall. Plays a classical and pop series Sept.-June. Tickets $15-60. "Symphony Sunday" afternoon concerts $10-15. Half-price student tickets available 1hr. before showtime on Sa and Su. "Monday Madness" offers $5 student tickets, available 1 week before showtime. One ticket per student ID.

Portland Civic Auditorium, 222 SW Clay St. (info 274-6560 or 796-9293; Ticketmaster 224-4400). Though mainly a venue for touring Broadway productions (see **Theater,** below), the auditorium attracts jazz and opera bigwigs, as well. Tickets range widely ($20-70).

Sack Lunch Concerts, 1422 SW 11th Ave. (222-2031), at Clay St. and the Old Church. Free concerts, usually classical or jazz (every W at noon). Organ, guitar, piano, and vocal recitals have all been held. The sack lunch element is unenforced.

Chamber Music Northwest, 522 SW 5th Ave. #725 (294-6400). Performs summer concerts from late June to July at Reed College Commons and Catlin Gabel School. Classical music M-Tu and Th-Sa at 8pm. $15-27, ages 7-14 $5. Call for venue info.

High Noon Tunes (223-1613), at Pioneer Courthouse Sq., concerts in summer W noon-1pm. A potpourri of rock, jazz, folk, and world music. Always jammed.

Aladdin Theatre, 3017 SE Milwaukee Ave. (233-1994), just off SE Powell by the Ross Island Bridge. A popular gig for a wide range of talent from alternative to country. Atmosphere depends on the band.

Theater

Theater in Portland covers all tastes, ages, and budgets. The **Portland Center for the Performing Arts (PCPA)** (248-4335) is the fourth largest arts center in the U.S. Free **backstage tours** begin in the lobby of the Newmark Theater, at SW Main and Broadway. *(W and Sa every ½hr. 11am-3pm.)* Once a month from September through June, **Friends of the Performing Arts Center** (274-6555) put on the **Brown Bag Lunch Series,** a free glance at professional productions, usually held on weekdays around noon; check the *Oregonian.* Tickets for most other productions can be charged by phone at Ticketmaster or Fastixx (see **Practical Information,** p. 61).

Portland Center Stage (248-6309), in the Newmark Theater of PCPA, at SW Broadway and SW Main. Five-play series of classics and modern adaptations runs from late Sept. to Apr. Su and Tu-Th $11-31.50, F-Sa $12.50-36. Ages 25 and under can buy any seat for $10. Half-price tickets sometimes available 1hr. before curtain.

Oregon Ballet Theater, 1120 SW 10th Ave. (241-8316, 222-5538, or 888-922-5538). Performs in the Civic Auditorium at 3rd and Clay St., and in the Newmark Theater at Main and Broadway. Five creative ballet productions Oct.-June. The 1998-99 season includes an American choreographers' showcase and the inescapable *Nutcracker.* $10-78; half-price student rush 1hr. before curtain for some shows.

Artists Repertory Theater, 1516 SW Alder St. (241-1ART/1278), puts up excellent low-budget and experimental productions. W, Th, and Su matinees $21, seniors and students $16; F-Sa $24.

Portland Civic Auditorium, 222 SW Clay St. (274-6560). Big splashy opera, Broadway musicals on tour, and jazz concerts. Part of the PCPA. Tickets $19-103.

Cinema

Most of Portland's countless movie theaters have half-price days or matinees. With the help of the *Oregonian,* a $7.25 ticket price can be scrupulously avoided. McMenamins runs two theater/pubs (Bagdad and Mission) where 21-and-over viewers sit in sofas or at tables, ordering food and brew during the show.

Bagdad Theater and Pub, 3702 SE Hawthorne Blvd. (230-0895). Take bus #14 (brown beaver). Built in 1921 for vaudeville, this magnificently renovated theater puts out second-run films and an excellent beer menu ($3.15 per pint). Doors open 5pm. All-you-can-watch for $1. 21+.

Mission Theater and Pub, 1624 NW Glisan (223-4031). Serves excellent home-brewed ales and delicious sandwiches ($4-6). Watch recent, less-than-first-run flicks while lounging on couches, at tables, or perched in the old-time balcony. Shows begin 5:30, 8:05, and 10:30pm. Tickets $1-3. Non-smoking and 21+.

Cinema 21, 616 NW 21st (223-4515), at Hoyt St. Mean, clean, and pistachio green. Mostly documentary, independent, and foreign films. A highly acclaimed student haunt, with plenty of progressive literature in the lobby. Tickets $5.50; students $4.50; seniors, under 12, and first show Sa-Su $2.50.

Northwest Film Center, 1219 SW Park Ave. (221-1156). Call for screening location. Documentary, foreign, classic, experimental, and independent films. Hosts the **Portland International Film Festival** in the last two weeks of Feb., with 100 films from 30 nations. Box office opens 30min. before each show. Tickets $6, seniors $5.

Clinton Street Theater, 2522 SE Clinton St. (238-8899). This multimedia theater hosts meetings, cabarets, and even Su night theater sports ($5). Home of America's longest-running *Rocky Horror Picture Show*, revisited every Sa at midnight ($5).

Guild Theatre, 820 SW 9th Ave. (225-5555 ext. 4610). Hosts recent releases transferred from other theatres. Mucho art fare. Adults $3; children, seniors and matinees $2; M $1.

Lloyd Cinema (225-5555 ext. 4600), across from the Lloyd Center Mall. For a first-run movie, this 10-screen, ultra-modern, neon-lined glam-land does the trick.

Shopping

For some, shopping in the **Nob Hill** district is a religious experience. Fashionable boutiques run from Burnside to Thurman St., between NW 21st and NW 24th Ave., mostly on 23rd Ave. Make the pilgrimage to NE Halsey and 15th Ave. to shop at the **Lloyd Center Mall** (282-2511), and stop at the **ice-skating rink** (288-6073) to do your impression of Portland's own Tonya Harding. (*Let's Go* does not recommend impersonating Tonya Harding.) *(Open year-round. Hours vary. $8.50, under 17 $7.50. Skate rental included.)* Parking can be a hassle on the weekends, but Lloyd Center is on the MAX line, and Nob Hill can be reached by bus #15 (red salmon) or cross-town bus #77.

Upscale shops also line **Newberry Street,** where moneyed hipsters roam for rags. Those without a hefty wad should check out **Hawthorne Boulevard** between 30th and 40th, a hip strip where prices aren't too high and parking can still be found on weekends. This string of trendy cafes, antique shops, used book stores, and theaters ends at the bottom of **Mt. Tabor Park,** one of two city parks in the world on the site of an extinct volcano. Hunt it down at SE 60th Ave. and Salmon Ave., or SE 69th Ave. two blocks south of Belmont Ave.; take bus #15 (brown beaver) from downtown. Shops are sprouting on **Belmont Avenue,** a few avenues north, which some have touted as the new Hawthorne. **Oogla Plentium,** 3437 SE Belmont Ave. (234-7933), carries self-defined omniumgatherum resales like clothes, jewelry, books, and housewares. *(Open W-Su 10am-9pm, M-Tu 10am-7pm.)* For books, check out **Powell's** (see p. 68). Portland is also home to a thriving **thrift-store** culture, especially near Dot's Cafe on Clinton St. (see p. 72).

The eclectic and festive **Saturday Market** is held by the Skidmore Fountain between 1st and Front St., with an office (222-6072) at 108 W. Burnside St. *(Mar.-Dec. Sa 10am-5pm, Su 11am-4:30pm.)* Yet another Portland superlative, this is the largest open-air crafts market in the country, crowded with street musicians, artists, craftspeople, chefs, and greengrocers.

Sports

When Bill Walton led the **Trailblazers** (234-9291) to the 1979 NBA Championship, Portland went berserk—landing an NBA team in the first place had been a substantial accomplishment for an overgrown town. A young, up-and-coming team, the Blazers play in the sparkling new **Rose Garden Arena,** by the Steel Bridge in Northeast Portland, with its own stop on MAX. The season lasts from November to May.

The city's indoor soccer team, the **Portland Pythons,** take over the Rose Garden from June to September. Call 684-5425 for schedules and tickets. The **Winter Hawks** (238-6366) of the Western Hockey League play September through March, both in the Rose Garden Arena and next-door at the **Coliseum,** but never in both at once. Take bus #9 (brown beaver) or MAX. The **Civic Stadium,** 1844 SW Morrison St., on the other side of town, is home to the **Portland Rockies** (223-2837), Colorado's AAA baseball farm team, who played their inaugural season in 1995. *(Season June-Sept. Reserved tickets $7, general admission $6, seniors and under 12 $5.)*

NIGHTLIFE

Once an uncouth and rowdy frontier town, always an uncouth and rowdy frontier town. Portland's nightclubs cater to everyone, from the clove-smoking college aesthete to the nipple-pierced neo-goth. Neighborhood taverns and pubs usually have the most character, the best music, and the smallest signs. Clubs in Northwest Portland are easily accessible from downtown. Park close-by or come with a friend; walking alone at night can be dangerous. Flyers advertising upcoming shows are plastered on Portland telephone poles, especially on SE Hawthorne and NW 23rd. Pubs are plentiful, and half of them are owned by McMenamins. Mischievous minors be warned: the drinking age is strictly enforced in Portland.

Southwest Portland

ⓜ**Panorama, Brig/Red Cap Garage,** and **Boxx's,** 341 SW 10th St. (221-RAMA/7262), form a network of interconnected clubs along Stark St. between 10th and 11th. Shake it until you break it on Panorama's cavernous dance floor, amid a thriving gay and straight crowd. Cover $5. Open F-Sa 9pm-4am. The bpms are higher still in the Garage, with weekday swing dancing and Friday night disco. Open daily 1pm-2:30am. Push even farther into Boxx's, the video/karaoke bar where, on Tuesday nights, matchmaking magic happens with the video postings of "Misha's Make-a-Date." Open daily noon-2:30am.

Crystal Ballroom, 1332 W. Burnside Blvd. (225-0047). Look up for the neon "dance" sign. The grand ballroom, with its immense paintings, gaudy chandeliers, and wigglin' floor, begs buffeted boogiers to get down. Gaze into the microbrewery at a surprising rendition of Lola, everyone's favorite cross-dresser. Micropints $3. Hosts a variety of live music; shows usually start at 9pm, and doors open 30min. before showtime. Tickets $5-25. Weekend shows often sell out, so call ahead.

Berbati's Pan, 231 SW Ankeny St. (248-4570). This ever-expanding nightspot started as a small Greek restaurant on 2nd Ave. Now the upscale dining room, 3-table pool room, 3 bars, dance hall, and late-night cafe wind all the way back to 3rd. Authentic Greek dishes ($3-7) or burgers ($5) served. Comedy (M); swing dancing (Tu); acid jazz (W); Fetish Night (every 3rd Su); Karaoke from Hell, with live band (every 3rd M). Club open M-F 11:30am-2:30am, Sa-Su 5pm-2:30am.

Lotus Card Room and Cafe, 932 SW 3rd Ave. (227-6185), at SW Salmon St. The truly groovy dance floor has glowing cartoon paintings, a movie screen with trippy projections, and a cage. Packed with 20-somethings, the Lotus also has a room full of tables. Disco (Su $3); new wave 80s (W $2), dance classics (Th $5), retro (F $5), pop (Sa $5); on other nights, no cover before 10pm. Happy hour M-F 4-6:30pm; appetizers $2. Open daily 11am-2am.

Southeast Portland

Biddy McGraw's, 3518 SE Hawthorne Blvd. (233-1178; http://www.biddys.com). Take bus #14 (brown beaver). Certainly the most authentically Irish pub this side of the Mississippi. With live Celtic tunes and raucous dancing, weekends are always boisterous. Good beer, engaging bartenders and cool clientele. 22 kegs of Guinness are consumed here per week. Do your part for $3.75 per pint. Micros $3. Open M 11am-2am and Tu-Su 11am-2:30am, but not set in stone.

La Luna, 215 SE 9th Ave. (241-LUNA/5862), at Pine. Take bus #20 (purple raindrop), get off at 9th, and walk 2 blocks south. One of Portland's larger, hipper venues, housed in a gray, nondescript building. Hosts many of the more prominent bands in town. Pints $2-3.50. Music generally 4 times per week. Non-smoking cafe is open every show night to an anything-goes crowd. Queer Night with dancing (M). Cover $0-15. All ages admitted, except to the bars. Call ahead for concert listings.

Produce Row Cafe, 204 SE Oak St. (232-8355). Take bus #6 (red salmon) to SE Oak and SE Grand, then walk west along Oak toward the river. Though they remodeled 3 years ago, none of this 30-year-old enclave's character was lost. 27 beers on tap, and over 200 domestic and imported beers in bottles. Soak in the summer starlight and industrial ambience from the walled-off deck out back. Live music: rock (Sa; $2), jazz jam (M; $2), bluegrass (Tu; free), Irish (W; free). Domestic bottles $1.35, domestic pints $1.85. Open M-F 11am-1am, Sa noon-1am, Su noon-midnight.

Dot's Cafe, 2521 SE Clinton St. (235-0203). Take bus #4 (brown beaver) to 26th, then walk 3 blocks south, or take bus #10 (green leaf) and get out in front. The place burned down in 1993, but today, only Dot's business is aflame. Crowded and smoky, with red candles and a pool table out back. Dotted with alternative artifacts like the treasured Velvet Elvis pool table. Caters to musicians and their bohemian brethren. Greasy food ($4-6), but vegan fare, too ($4). Open daily 11am-2am.

Barley Mill Pub, 1629 SE Hawthorne Blvd. (231-1492). A smoky temple to Jerry Garcia; bring your bootlegs on Wednesday nights and let the music live on. Full of fantastic murals and long bench tables that may land you next to a stranger. Upbeat, yet mellow, like the man himself. McMenamins beer on tap (pints $2.85). Happy hour daily 4-6pm (pints $2.25). Open M-Sa 11am-1am, Su noon-midnight.

Northwest and Northeast

Satyricon, 125 NW 6th Ave. (243-2380). Live alternarock rumbles in the glowing back room every night. PoMo bar and a chic new sister restaurant, **Fellini.** Step into this madly mosaic-laden space to rest your ears and taste innovative cuisine (entrees from $3). Or come just to absorb the vibe where, as rumor has it, Courtney met Kurt. Cover $2-5. 21+ only. Food M-Th 11:30-2:30am, F-Sa 5pm-3am, Su 5pm-2:30am. Music 10pm-2:30am.

The Laurel Thurst Public House, 2958 NE Glisan St. (232-1504). Use a bit of extra caution in this area. A neighborhood crowd jams to local acoustic and electric acts. Two intimate rooms allow for groovin', boozin', and schmoozin'. Breakfast until 3pm. Burgers and sandwiches $5-6. Microbrew pints $3.25, domestic $2.25. Cover $2-3. Free pool all day Su, and M-Th before 7pm.

BridgePort Brew Pub, 1313 NW Marshall (241-7179), at 13th St. The zenith of beer and pizza joints, housed in a defunct, wood-beamed rope factory. The pizza is locally famous, and can fill four stomachs (5-topping pie $19.75). Lotsa space for lotsa people, including many families. Tables cut from old bowling allies. The outdoor patio fills up during happy hour. Brews are all BridgePort; $2 for 10 oz., $3.25 for 20 oz. Open M-Th 11:30am-11pm, F-Sa 11:30am-midnight, Su 1-9pm.

Embers, 110 NW Broadway (222-3082), at Couch St. Follow the rainbows onto the dance floor, or watch fish swim inside the bustling bar counter. Mostly gay clientele; retro and house music. Nightly drag show at 10pm. Domestic bottled beer $2.50, mixed drinks $3. Happy hour daily until 8pm. Open daily 11am-2:30am.

Gypsy, 625 NW 21st Ave. (796-1859), at Hoyt St. Take bus #17 (red salmon). Hip, funky and modern. (Bring your cool friends for moral support.) Happy hour (M-F 4-6:30pm and Sa-Su 3-5:30pm) features drinks for $1.50 and appetizers at half-price. Pass through padded red velvet doors to the lounge, where black lights and video poker rule the night. Open M-F 11am-12:30am, Sa-Su 9am-12:30am.

EVENTS

Cinco de Mayo Festival (222-9807), on the weekend closest to May 5th. Mexican Independence Day celebration with sister city Guadalajara, complete with fiery food, entertainment, and crafts at Waterfront Park.

Rose Festival, 220 NW 2nd Ave. (227-2681), during the first 3 weeks of June. Portland's premier summer event. U.S. Navy sailors flood the streets, while the city decks itself in all manner of finery. Waterfront concerts, art festivals, celebrity entertainment, auto racing, parades, an air show, Navy ships, and the largest children's parade in the world. Women should exercise caution at night. Many events require tickets.

Waterfront Blues Festival (282-0555 or 973-FEST/3378), in early July. Outrageously good. Some of the finest blues artists participate in this 3-day event. Suggested donation is $3 and 2 cans of food to benefit the Oregon Food Bank.

Oregon Brewers Festival (778-5917), on the last full weekend in July. The continent's largest gathering of independent brewers makes for one incredible party at Waterfront Park. Free admission, but $2 mandatory mug and $1 per taste. Those under 21 must be accompanied by a parent.

Mt. Hood Festival of Jazz (232-3000), on the first weekend in Aug. at Mt. Hood Community College in Gresham. Tickets start at $29.50 per night, and cost even more when calling through Ticketmaster (224-4400), but look, this is the premier jazz festival of the Pacific Northwest. Wynton Marsalis and the late Stan Getz have been regulars. Reserve tickets well in advance. Write Mt. Hood Festival of Jazz, P.O. Box 3024, Gresham 97030. To reach the festival, take I-84 to the Wood Village-Gresham exit and follow the signs, or ride MAX to the end of the line.

OREGON

The Bite: A Taste of Portland (248-0600), on the second weekend in Aug. in Waterfront Park. Food, music, stand-up comics, a wine pavilion, and the 5km "Dine and Dash" race. Proceeds benefit Oregon Special Olympics.

Portland Marathon (226-1111; http://www.teleport.com/~pdxmar), in late Sept. or early Oct. If you're in shape, join the thousands who run this 26.2-miler. Many shorter runs and walks are also held—remember, Phedippedes died.

■ Near Portland: Sauvie Island

Sauvie Island is a peaceful rural hideaway at the confluence of the Columbia and Willamette Rivers, 20 minutes northwest of downtown Portland on U.S. 30; follow signs toward Mount St. Helens from I-405, Vaughn, or Yeon Ave. The island offers great views of the city from its vast and sandy stretches. On winter mornings, eagles and geese congregate along the roads, and in spring and summer, berries are everywhere. Many Portlanders make a summer tradition of visiting the island's **u-pick farms,** family operations announced by hand-lettered signs along the roads.

Many visitors soak up the rays on the island's south side beaches. Some bring fishing rods and bathing suits, but none swim in the Willamette's waters; factories and imperfect sewage systems upstream make sure of that. The best inland beach area is **Oak Island,** on the south side of **Sturgeon Lake,** a 10-minute drive once on the island. From the bridge, turn left onto Sauvie Island Rd., then take the first major right onto Reeder Rd. Continue to Oak Island Rd. which turns into a gravel road after 3 mi. and ends in a parking lot. Wander the weedy 4 mi. loop from there. A $3 **parking permit** is required for the whole island, and is efficiently enforced. Pick one up at **Sam's Cracker Barrel Grocery** (621-3960), along with a 5¢ map of the island and any other supplies (open daily 8am-8pm). Plan ahead; Sam's is the only place that sells permits, and it's right by the bridge, several miles from the beaches.

■ Mount Hood

Magnificent, snow-capped Mt. Hood is at the junction of U.S. 26 and Rte. 35, 1½ hours east of Portland and one hour south of the Hood River. The 11,235 ft. volcano may look dormant (it doesn't steam and has no crater because open vents keep internal pressure low), but the surrounding area is a hotbed of outdoor activity. In the winter, snowboarders and skiers attack the slopes, while summer brings climbers, bikers, and hikers to the mountain's scenic setting.

HIKING AND CAMPGROUNDS Hiking trails circle Mt. Hood; simple maps are posted on a number of signs around **Government Camp,** 50 mi. east of Portland on U.S. 26. The most popular dayhike is **Mirror Lake,** a 6 mi. loop that starts from a parking lot off U.S. 26, 1 mi. west of Government Camp, and loops past a reflection of Mt. Hood's peak in the glassy lake (open Memorial Day-Oct.). Stop by the **Hood River District Ranger Station,** 6780 Rte. 35, Parkdale 97041 (541-352-6002), or the **Zigzag District Ranger Station,** 70220 E. U.S. 26 (503-622-3191) for more detailed info (both open M-F 8am-4:30pm). The well-stocked **Mt. Hood Visitor Information Center,** 65000 E. U.S. 26, Welches 97067 (503-622-4822), 16 mi. west of Mt. Hood, also provides permits (open daily 8am-6pm). The station is a part of the **Mt. Hood Village** (622-4011 or 800-255-3069), a giant complex with everything from a dance hall to a heated pool, including a campground (380 sites: tent sites $23; full hookups $28).

Camping spots in the **Mt. Hood National Forest** cluster near the junction of U.S. 26 and Rte. 35. Less than 1 mi. below Timberline (see **Skiing,** below) is **Alpine** (503-272-3206), accessible only in the summer (16 sites: $7, all with water and toilets; reservations essential). **Trillium Lake Campground,** 2 mi. east of the Timberline turn-off on U.S. 26, has trails around the crystal-clear lake, and paved sites with water and toilets. Pine trees offer some privacy (57 sites: $10, premium lakeside sites $12; doubles $20; all include $3 parking fee). Just 1 mi. west of Trillium Lake, down a dirt road off U.S. 26, **Still Creek Campgrounds** has a quieter, woodsier feel, unpaved sites, and a babbling brook ($10, premium creekside sites $12). On Rte. 35, 10 mi. north of U.S.

26, **Robinhood** and **Sherwood Campgrounds** lie just off the highway beside a running creek (both $10). For all of the aforementioned campgrounds except Alpine, reservations can be made by calling 800-280-2267.

SKIING Though Mt. Bachelor (see **Bend,** p. 131) is known for Oregon's best skiing, three respectable resorts are closer to Portland, and all offer night skiing. **Timberline** (272-3311 or 231-7979), off U.S. 26 at Government Camp, is a largely beginner and intermediate area, with the longest ski season in Oregon (lasting until Labor Day). *(Night skiing Jan.-Feb. M-F 4pm-9pm, Sa-Su 4pm-10pm. Lift tickets $32. Equipment rental around $19 per day. Snowboards $33 per day with boots, $26 without. $400 cash deposit or credit card required.)* Smaller **Mount Hood Ski Bowl,** 87000 E. U.S. 26 (222-2695; http://www.skibowl.com), in Government Camp, 2 mi. west of Hwy. 35, has the best night skiing and a snowboard park. The season is limited (Nov.-Apr.), but 80-90% of the trails have night skiing. *(Open M-Tu 1-10pm, W-Th 9am-10pm, F 9am-11pm, Sa 8:30am-11pm, Su 8:30am-10pm. Lift tickets $23 per day, $14 per night, $30 for both. Ski rental $17, ages 7-12 $11. Snowboards $25.)* **Mount Hood Meadows** (337-2222), 9 mi. east of Government Camp on Hwy. 35, is the largest and nicest resort in the area, offering an array of beginning, intermediate, advanced, and expert trails. At a medium elevation (7300 ft.), it stays open through May, but it's best to call ahead. *(Night skiing Dec.-Mar. W-Su 4-10pm; $17. Lift tickets $36, juniors $21. Ski rental $18, juniors $13.)* All three areas offer ski lessons averaging $40 per hour or $27 per person for groups.

OTHER ACTIVITIES Only Mt. Fuji draws more climbers each year than Mt. Hood, or so says **Timberline Mountain Guides,** P.O. Box 340, Government Camp 97028 (800-464-7704), which offers mountain-, snow-, and ice-climbing courses. Climbs last two to six days. *(2-day trip—1-day class and 1-day climb—from $265; registration and wilderness permit included.)* The best time to attempt the summit is from March through July; experience is recommended. Timberline's **Magic Mile** is a non-skiing lift that carries passengers above the clouds for spectacular views of the Cascades. *($6; winter discounts with a coupon that just about any employee will happily hand out.)* Turn up the 6 mi. road just past Government Camp to the picturesque **Timberline Lodge** (231-7979 ext. 400, reservations 800-547-1406), which starred in *The Shining* as the Overlook Hotel (rooms from $65). The road to the lodge offers arresting views of the valley below, and the high Cascades to the south. Next door is the **Wy'east Day Lodge,** where skiers can check in equipment for the day, and the **Wy'east Kitchen,** a cafeteria alternative to Timberline's expensive dining. *(Entrees $4-7. Open daily in summer M-F 6:30am-2pm, Sa-Su 6:30am-3pm; in winter M-F 7:30am-4pm, Sa-Su 8am-4pm; open 7:30am-9pm when there's night skiing.)* In summer, Mount Hood Ski Bowl East offers an **Action Park** (222-2695; open M-F 11am-6pm, Sa-Su 10am-7pm). Visitors can try horseback rides ($22 per hr.), Indy Karts ($5 per 5min.), bungee jumping ($25), a skateboard park ($5 per half-day), and an alpine slide ($5 per slide). **Mount Sky Bowl West** rents mountain bikes from mid-June to October. *($10 per hr., U.S. forest trail permit included; full day bike sky chair $15.)*

■ Columbia River Gorge

Only an hour from Portland, the magnificent Columbia River Gorge stretches for 75 stunning miles through some of the most beautiful country in the Pacific Northwest. Pounding rumpled hills and rocky cliffs, the Columbia River has carved out a canyon over 1000 ft. in depth. Mt. Hood and Mt. Adams loom nearby, and breathtaking waterfalls plunge over steep cliffs into the river. Going east along the gorge, heavily forested peaks give way to broad, bronze cliffs and golden hills. The river widens out and the wind picks up at the town of Hood River. Surrounded by climates and habitats of all kinds, the gorge touches deserts, mountains, prairies, and rain-soaked forests. Though it was once "as fast as a waterfall turned on its side," and so full of fish that Lewis and Clark joked that they could drive their wagons across over fishbacks, the Columbia's waters are now slower and emptier due to dams and overharvesting.

OREGON

OREGON

Portrait of a North American Monster

Name: Bigfoot (English) or Sasquatch (Chinook).

Size: According to a recent forensic analysis of the 1967 Patterson-Gimlin film, utilizing a standard primate chest-breadth extrapolation algorithm, approximately 2000 lb. and 7 ft. 3½ in.

Geographical Range: The Cascade Mountains of the Pacific Northwest, even into British Columbia.

Diet: Omnivorous.

Odor: Strong and fetid.

Evolutionary History: Possibly derived from *Gigantapithecus blacki* in Asia. Any relationship to the Himalayan Yeti ("abominable snowman") is strictly superficial—every culture has its own Big Hairy Monster ("BHM").

Evidence: Oral and written history among both Native Americans and Westerners, the aforementioned film, a high frequency of sightings, and big footprints.

Further Info: Contact the **North American Science Institute,** 209 Oak St., Suite 202, Hood River, OR 97031-2027 (541-387-4300; fax 387-4301; email nasi@gorge.net; http://www.nasinet.org), a six-year-old organization devoted to full-time scientific evaluation of the Bigfoot Phenomenon.

ORIENTATION AND PRACTICAL INFORMATION

To follow the gorge, which divides Oregon and Washington, take I-84 east to Exit 22. Continue east uphill on the **Columbia River Scenic Highway (U.S. 30),** which follows the crest of the gorge walls and affords unforgettable views. The largest town in the gorge is **Hood River,** at the junction of I-84 and Rte. 35.

Trains: Amtrak (800-872-7245) runs trains from Portland to the foot of Walnut St. in Bingen, WA ($12-16).

Buses: Buses run from the **Greyhound** station, 1205 B St. (386-1212 or 800-872-7245), between 12th and 13th St. To: Portland ($10); Seattle ($38). Open M-Sa 8:30am-7pm and sometimes Su afternoons.

Visitor Information: Hood River County Chamber of Commerce, 405 Portway Ave. (386-2000 or 800-366-3530; http://www.gorge.net/hrccc), just off City Center Exit 63, for info on sights, windsurfing, camping, accommodations, history, events, and Hood River. Open Apr.-Oct. M-Th 8:30am-5pm, F 8:30am-4pm, Sa-Su 10am-4pm; Nov.-Mar. M-F 9am-5pm. This info is also available at **visitor centers** along the gorge, as is the Forest Service map ($3) of the Columbia Wilderness.

Outdoor Information: Columbia Gorge National Scenic Area Headquarters, 902 Wasco St. (386-2333), in Wyeth, offers info on hiking and a friendly earful of local lore. Open M-F 7:30am-5pm.

Emergency: 911. **Hood River Police:** 211 2nd St. (386-3942).

Hood River Post Office: 408 Cascade Ave. (800-275-8777). Open M-F 8:30am-5pm. **ZIP Code:** 97031-9998.

Area Code: In OR 541; in WA 509.

ACCOMMODATIONS AND CAMPGROUNDS

Rooms in Hood River are somewhat expensive, typically ranging from $40 to $80 per night. For a more modest but enriching experience, head for the outdoorsy **Bingen School Inn Hostel** (509-493-3363), just across the Hood River Toll Bridge (75¢) and 3½ blocks from the Amtrak stop in Bingen, WA. Take the third left after the yellow blinking light onto Cedar St.; from there it's one block up the hill on Humbolt St. Sleep in front of blackboards in this converted school house, in one of 48 hostel beds ($11) or five private rooms ($40; discounts for longer stays). Mountain bikes ($15 per day) and sailboards ($40 per day) are available for rent.

Beacon Rock State Park, across the Bridge of the Gods (Exit 44) and 7 mi. west on Washington's Hwy. 14, has secluded sites ($10). The entrance to the park, directly across from the rock, is hard to miss. The **Port of Cascade Locks Marine,** ½ mi. east off the bridge on the Oregon side, has a lawn on the river, which is also a crowded, windy yard by the road ($10; showers). **Ainsworth State Park** is also easily accessible (see **Portland: Accommodations and Campgrounds, p. 62**).

SIGHTS

Vista House (503-695-2230), completed in 1918 as a memorial to Oregon's pioneers, is now a visitor center in **Crown Point State Park,** 4 mi. east of Exit 22 off I-84 E. *(Open daily mid-Apr. to Oct. 15 8:30am-6pm.)* The house hangs on the edge of an outcropping, high above the river. A three-dimensional model of the area illuminates various trails and waterfalls along the gorge, and maps are there for the taking. A trail leaves the road a few yards down from the house, ending in a secluded view of both the house and the gorge. For an even loftier vista, drive up the **Larch Mountain Rd.,** which splits from U.S. 30 just above the Vista House and winds up 4000 ft. over 14 mi. to a picnic area that has views of Mount St. Helens, Mt. Rainier, Mt. Adams, Mt. Hood, and Mt. Jefferson.

The elegant **Maryhill Museum of Art,** 35 Maryhill Museum Dr. (509-773-3733), sits high above the Columbia on the Washington side, 30 mi. east of Hood River. *(Open daily mid-Mar. to mid-Nov. 9am-5pm. $6, seniors $5, ages 6-12 $1.50.)* To get there, take I-84 to Biggs (Exit 104) and the slightly more scenic Rte. 14, continuing until the signs. Built by Sam Hill in the 20s, the exquisite mansion is named for his daughter. Peacocks stroll through the garden outside a gallery of European and American paintings, drawings and sculptures by Rodin (including "Eve," "Youth Triumphant," and "The Thinker"), works by Native Americans, and nearly 150 intricately hand-made chess sets from around the world. Head upstairs and check out the "Theater de la Mode," replete with 27-inch mannequins donning the latest fashions of post-WWII France.

The Dalles (DALZ), 19 mi. east of Hood River on I-84, was the last stop on the agonizing Oregon Trail. Lewis and Clark camped here at Fort Rock on Bargeway Rd. in 1805. French trappers named the area Le Dalle (the trough) after the rapids around that section of the river. For a free map and a walking tour of historical spots in town, go to the **Dalles Area Chamber of Commerce,** 404 W. 2nd St. (296-2231 or 800-255-3385), ½ mi. down Exit 84 off I-84. *(Open M-F 8:30am-5pm, Sa 9am-3pm, Su 11am-2pm; Memorial Day to Labor Day Sa-Su, call for hours.)* Up the hill, the **Fort Dalles Museum,** 500 W. 15th St. (296-4547), at Garrison, is housed in the town's original 1856 surgeon's quarters and displays memorabilia of the pioneer and military history of the region. *(Open daily Apr.-Sept. 10am-5pm; Oct.-Dec. and Feb.-Mar. Th-M 10am-4pm; closed Jan. $3, under 18 free.)* Highlighting the dusty collection of old buggies and cars is a 20-passenger horse-drawn bus and two hearse carriages.

OUTDOORS

The mighty Columbia and its 30mph winds make Hood River a **windsurfing** paradise. Vibrantly colored sailboards decorate the gorge, and zany competitions like the mid-July **Gorge Games** (386-7774) occur frequently. Everything stops in town on windy days, and folks gets antsy during calm stretches. Beginners sail at the **Hook,** a shallow, sandy cove, and experts try the **Spring Creek Fish Hatchery** on the Washington side, the place to watch the best in the business. Another hub is the **Event Site,** the water off Exit 63 behind the visitor center. All-day parking costs $3, but it's free if you just sit and watch. **Rhonda Smith Windsurfing Center** (386-9463), Exit 64 off I-84, then under the bridge and left after the blinking red light, offers three-hour classes ($70). Rentals, right on the water, start at $35 for a half-day, with discounts for longer.

The gorge also has excellent **mountain biking. Discover Bicycles,** 1020 Wasco St. (386-4820), rents mountain bikes, suggest routes, and sells all manner of trail maps. *(Open M-Sa 9am-7pm, Su 9am-5pm. Bikes $5 per hr., $25 per day.)* The 11 mi. round-trip **Hospital Hill Trail** provides views of Mt. Hood, the gorge, Hood River, and surrounding villages. To reach the unmarked trail, follow signs to the hospital, fork left to Rhine Village, and walk behind the power transformers through the livestock fence.

A string of waterfalls adorns U.S. 30 east of Crown Point; pick up a waterfall map at the Vista House (see **Sights,** above). At **Latourell Falls,** 2½ mi. east of Crown Point, a jaunt down a paved path leads right to the base of the falls. Five miles farther east, **Wahkeena Falls** is visible from the road, winding 242 ft. down a narrow gorge. These falls (meaning "most beautiful") make a popular spot for picnicking and host two trailheads: both a short, steep scramble over loose rock, or a ¼ mi. trip up a paved walk penetrate right to the middle of the action. Just ½ mi. farther on U.S. 30 is the granddaddy of them all, **Multnomah Falls,** which attracts two million visitors annually. From a viewing platform (just past the espresso cart, the gift shop, the dining room, and the info center), watch the falls crash 620 ft. into a tiny pool and then drain under the gracefully arching Benson Bridge into a lower falls. Exit 31, on I-84, leads to an island in the middle of the freeway from which visitors can only see the upper falls. Walk under the freeway underpass to take a quick hike to **Benson.** For a more strenuous hike, various paths (including one that links up with Larch Mountain) lead to the top of the falls; the **information center** at the base of Multnomah Falls has free maps and helpful suggestions.

The steep **Wyeth Trail,** near the hamlet of Wyeth (Exit 51), leads 4.4 mi. to a wilderness boundary, and after 7.3 mi. to the road to Hood River and the incredible 13 mi. **Eagle Creek Trail** (Exit 44). Chiseled into cliffs high above Eagle Creek, this trail passes four waterfalls before joining the Pacific Crest Trail. On the Washington side, across the river from Exit 35 off I-84, is **Beacon Rock State Park** (509-427-8265). This 848 ft. neck of an old volcano may be the largest monolith in America. A 2250 ft., 3½ mi. hike up **Dog Mountain** starts in a parking lot just east of Beacon Rock, and switchbacks lead to the 2948 ft. summit and, in June and July, an explosion of wildflowers.

OREGON COAST

If not for the renowned **U.S. 101,** Oregon's dripping beaches and dramatic seaside vistas might be only a beautiful rumor to those on the interior. From Astoria in the north to Brookings down south, the highway hugs the shore along the Oregon Coast, linking a string of resorts and fishing villages that cluster around the mouths of rivers feeding into the Pacific. Breathtaking ocean views spread between these towns, while state parks and national forests allow direct access to the big surf. Wherever the windy two lanes leave the coast, even narrower beach loops access long stretches of unspoiled coast, giving glimpses of the diverse sea life. Seals, sea lions, and waterfowl lounge on rocks just offshore, watching the human world whiz by on wheels.

⊕ HIGHLIGHTS OF THE OREGON COAST

- **Haystack Rock** (see p. 87) juts famously from the sea by **Cannon Beach.**
- The beautiful **Three Capes Loop** (see p. 90) passes still more startling rock formations, breezing by the small and scenic **Pacific City** (see p. 90).
- **Newport** hosts the particularly excellent **Oregon Coast Aquarium** (see p. 94).
- There's no better place to putter around on an extremely noisy dune buggy than **Oregon Dunes National Recreation Area** (see p. 96).

GETTING AROUND

Gasoline and grocery **prices** on the coast are about 20% higher than in inland cities; smaller coastal villages tend to be cheaper and more interesting. There are 17 state parks along the coast, offering **campgrounds** with electricity and showers. Traveling down the coast **by bike** is both rewarding and exhausting. Cyclists can write to the Oregon Tourism Commission (see p. 56), or to virtually any visitor center or chamber of commerce on the coast for the free *Oregon Coast Bike Route Map;* it provides invaluable info on campsites, hostels, bike repair facilities, temperatures, and wind conditions. Portlanders head down the coast to vacation, so most traffic flows south from the city. In summer, prevailing winds also blow southward, keeping at the backs of cyclists and easing the journey. The shoulders of U.S. 101 and other coastal highways often narrow to nonexistent, though, and enormous log trucks lumber

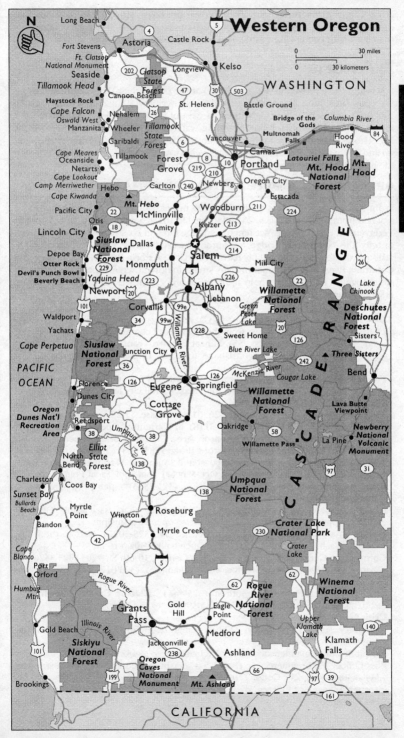

Western Oregon

around tight turns. **Buses** run up and down the coast, stopping in most sizeable towns. Many local lines are affiliates of Greyhound (see p. 29), and make connections to major urban centers like Seattle, Portland, and Eugene.

■ Astoria

Lewis and Clark arrived in Astoria in 1805 at the end of their transcontinental jaunt. Six years later, John Astor, scion of a famously wealthy 19th-century family, established the first permanent U.S. settlement west of the Rockies, leaving his name as a legacy. With its Victorian homes, bustling waterfront, rolling hills, and perseverant fog, Astoria reminds many tourists of a miniaturized San Francisco. Travelers heading up and down the coast constantly filter through town, as do Washingtonians crossing the massive Astoria Bridge to shop in sales-tax free Oregon.

ORIENTATION AND PRACTICAL INFORMATION

From Astoria, U.S. 30 runs to Portland, 96 mi. east of town. Astoria can also be reached from Portland via U.S. 26 and from U.S. 101 at Seaside (see p. 83). Astoria is a convenient link between Washington and the Oregon coast. Two bridges run from the city: the **Youngs Bay Bridge,** leading southwest, where **Marine Dr.** becomes U.S. 101, and the towering, incredibly narrow, two-lane **Astoria Bridge,** which spans the **Columbia River** into Washington. Many streets in downtown Astoria are one-way. All streets parallel to the water are in alphabetical order from west to east except for the first one, Marine Dr.

Buses: Pierce Pacific Stages, (692-4437). A Greyhound affiliate. Pick-up at Video City, 95 W. Marine Dr., across from the chamber of commerce. To: Portland (1 per day, $15); Seaside (1 per day, $5). **Sunset Empire Transit** (325-0563). Pick-up at the Greyhound bus station, on Duane at 9th St. To: Seaside (7 per day; $2.25, seniors and disabled $1.75).

Public Transportation: Astoria Transit System, 364 9th St. (325-0563 or 800-776-6406). Local bus service M-Sa 6am-7pm. Makes a full city loop every hr. (75¢; students, seniors, disabled 50¢).

Taxis: Yellow Cab, (325-3131 or 861-2626). $1.45 base, $1.20 per mi. Runs 24hr.

Auto Club: AAA, 135 U.S. 101 S (861-3118), in Warrenton. Open M-F 8am-5pm.

Visitor Information: Astoria/Warrenton Area Chamber of Commerce, 111 W. Marine Dr. (325-6311), just east of Astoria Bridge. Pick up the free map of Astoria at this bastion of info on the Oregon coast and southwest Washington. Open June-Sept. M-F 8am-6pm, Sa-Su 9am-6pm; Oct.-May M-F 8am-5pm, Sa-Su 11am-4pm.

Bank: Bank of America, 907 Commercial St. (325-2333). Open M-Th 9am-5pm, F 9am-6pm, Sa 9am-1pm.

Library: Astor Library, 450 10th St. (325-7323). Internet access available. Open M-Th 10am-8pm, F-Sa 10am-6pm; Sept.-June also open Su 2pm-5pm.

Laundromat: Coin Laundry, 823 W. Marine Dr. (325-2027), next to the Dairy Queen. Wash $1.25, dry 25¢ per 8min. Open daily 7:30am-10pm.

Community Centers: Women's Resource Center, 10 6th St. #205 (325-3426), at Marine Dr. 24hr. **Seniors Service,** 800 Exchange St. (325-0123). Open M-F 8am-noon and 1-5pm.

Emergency: 911. Police: 555 30th St. (325-4411). **Clatsop County Sheriff:** 325-2061. **Coast Guard:** 861-6228. **Fire:** 555 30th St. (325-4237).

Crisis Line: 325-5735. 24hr.

Pharmacy: Astoria Pharmacy, 2222 Exchange St. (325-1123). Open M-F 9:30am-5:30pm.

Hospital: Columbia Memorial, 2111 Exchange St. (325-4321 or 800-962-2407).

Post Office: 750 Commercial St. (800-275-8777), in the Federal Bldg. at 8th St. Open M-F 8:30am-5pm. **ZIP Code:** 97103.

Internet Access: See **Library,** above.

Area Code: 503.

ACCOMMODATIONS AND CAMPGROUNDS

Motels in the area cater to tourists heading south to Oregon's coastal resort towns, so rooms can be expensive and elusive during summer. U.S. 101 south of Astoria is littered with clean, scenic campgrounds.

Grandview B&B, 1574 Grand Ave. (325-0000, reservations 325-5555; http://www.bbonline.com/or/grandview). Intimate, cheery, luxurious rooms. The delicious breakfast includes fresh muffins, smoked salmon, bagels, and full service. A love poem by Emmet Fox woos visitors in the front hall. Cheapest room $45, with shared bath $55, private bath from $59. Off-season, 2nd night is $28.

Fort Columbia State Park Hostel (HI-AYH), Fort Columbia, Chinook, WA (360-777-8755), within the park boundaries. Cross the 4 mi. bridge from Astoria into Washington, continue north on U.S. 101 for 3 mi., then take a sharp left just after the tunnel; take bus #24 on weekdays. This 1896 military-hospital-turned-hostel pampers guests with flowered sheets, hardwood floors, and cozy living room. Hostel manager Wayne dishes out all-you-can-eat pancake breakfasts for 50¢. Despite all this, the hostel rarely fills. $10, nonmembers $13, bicyclists $8, under 18 (with parent) $5. Laundry. Lockout 10am-5pm. Check-in 5-10pm. Open Apr.-Sept. .

Lamplighter Motel, 131 W. Marine Dr. (325-4051 or 800-845-8847), between the Pig 'n' Pancake diner and the visitor center. Well-lit rooms with cable and phones. Large bathrooms. Coffee in the lobby. Singles $62; doubles $75; winter rates $13-17 less. Senior discounts. Reserve at least a week in advance during summer.

Fort Stevens State Park (861-1671, reservations 800-452-5687; http://www.ptd.state.or.us), over Youngs Bay Bridge on U.S. 101 S, 10 mi. west of Astoria, is the largest state park in the U.S. Rugged, empty beaches and bike trails. Closest major campground to resort towns of Seaside and Cannon Beach. Hot showers. Facilities for the disabled. 603 sites: $17, full hookups $20; hiker/biker $4.50 per person; yurts $29. Reservations ($6) recommended for summer weekends.

FOOD

Escape expensive seafood and Whoppers at **Sentry Supermarket,** 3300 Leif Erickson Dr. (325-1931; open daily 7am-10pm). Grab a latte ($2) at the drive-through stand and sit on the rocks to watch the sea lions bark and frolic. A **Safeway,** 1153 Duane St. (325-4662), in the downtown area (open daily 6am-midnight).

Columbian Cafe, 1114 Marine Dr. (325-2233). The chef appears on a quirky wall painting, in the menu, and live in a crêpe-flipping frenzy. There's often a wait for dinner, but local banter, the microbrew menu, and fantastic pasta and seafood dishes ($6-13) make up for lost time. Try "Chef's Mercy"—you name your "heat range and allergies," he chooses your meal ($6). Open M-Tu 8am-8pm, W-Th 8am-2pm and 5-8pm, F 8am-2pm and 5-9pm, Sa 10am-2pm and 5-9pm.

Shark Rock Cafe, 577 14th St. (325-7720). Bright, bold, and swingin', this baby blue Victorian building baits diners to come in and relax with a hip, mixed crowd and enjoy the beautiful view of the Columbia River. O' time black-and-white yearbook photos peer out from wood tabletops. Cinnamon french toast $6; chicken Caesar salad $7, hazelnut crusted chicken $12. Open M-Tu 11am-2:30pm, W-Sa 8am-8pm.

Someplace Else, 965 Commercial St. (325-3500). A handsome mannequin, naked on summer days, greets/flashes diners in this Italian restaurant. Every month, regulars vote on what specials they want, from meat to veggie ($4.50-14). The chick peas in tamarind sauce get rave reviews. Open W-M 11:30am-2pm and 4-9pm.

Riccardi Gallery, 108 10th St. (325-5450). Astoria's art collection is steadily improving thanks to this lovechild of a New York gallery and a Parisian cafe. The showroom displays all sorts of modern art, and doubles as a hip coffeehouse. Cafe fare, with salads, soups, and copies of the *New Yorker* to boot. Open M-F 7:30am-5:30pm, Sa 8:30am-5:30pm, Su 9am-4pm.

OREGON

Wine and Cheese, Together at Last

One block up from the Maritime Museum is the **Shallon Winery,** 1598 Duane St. (325-5798; http://www.shallon.com), where eccentric owner Paul van der Velt holds court, presiding over a kingdom of fantastic wines. He gives a tour of his minuscule viniculture facilities, complete with the story behind his bizarre repertoire of wines, none made from grapes. A self-proclaimed connoisseur of fine food, he insists that visitors call him at any time of day or night before considering a meal at any restaurant within 50 mi. Samplers taste wines made from local berries, and the world's only commercially produced whey wines (from Tillamook cheese). Approach the cranberry-and-whey wine with caution; the fruity taste belies its high alcohol content. Sampling lemon meringue pie wine is likely to be the highlight of any trip to the Oregon coast, and Paul's chocolate orange wine is more candy than beverage. Others have spent millions trying to reproduce this chocolate delicacy without success. *(Must be 21 to drink. Open almost every afternoon. Gratuities and purchases appreciated.)*

SIGHTS, EVENTS, AND ENTERTAINMENT

Barring frequent clouds, the **Astoria Column,** on Coxcomb Hill Rd., showcases a stupendous view of Astoria cradled between Saddle Mountain to the south and the Columbia River estuary to the north. *(Open dawn-10pm. Free.)* Completed in 1926, the column wraps around the 164 interior steps that pass newly repainted friezes depicting area history. Tableaux of historic Astoria include the discovery of the Columbia River by intrepid English sea captain Robert Grey, the arrival of Lewis and Clark, and the settling of Astoria. The cavernous wave-shaped **Columbia River Maritime Museum,** 1792 Marine Dr. (325-2323), on the waterfront, is packed with marine lore, including displays on the salmon fisheries that once dominated Astoria. *(Museum open daily 9:30am-5pm. $5, seniors $4, ages 6-17 $2, under 6 free.)* The model boat collection includes the 1792 vessel that Robert Grey first steered into the mouth of the Columbia River. The **Astoria Regatta** (738-3430), held the second week in August, dates to 1894. The tradition is still going strong, featuring food and craft booths, a watershow, scenic boat rides, fireworks, dances, and sailboat races. The **Scandinavian Festival,** on the third weekend in June, attracts a throng of fjord-loving celebrants. *(All 3 days $5, 1 day 6am-6pm $1, under 6 free. Contact the chamber of commerce for info.)*

The **Astor Street Opry Company,** with its production *Shanghaied in Astoria,* at the Astoria Eagles' Lodge, at 9th and Commercial, revives bawdy, raucous, old-fashioned entertainment. This original musical, now in its 15th year, features a colorful mix of sinister villains, valiant heroes, lusty sailors, and sexy can-can girls. For aspiring pitchers/quarterbacks, the show gives the audience free license to pelt the conniving "dastardly duo" with popcorn. *(Shows early July to late Aug. For more info, call 325-6104.)*

■ Near Astoria

Five miles southwest of Astoria, the **Fort Clatsop National Memorial** (861-2471) reconstructs Lewis and Clark's winter headquarters from descriptions in their detailed journal. The log fort housed Lewis, Clark, their friend Charbonneau, his wife and interpreter Sacagawea, Clark's slave York, three officers, 24 enlisted men, and plenty of fleas. To find Ft. Clatsop, take U.S. 101 south from Astoria to Alternate U.S. 101, and follow the signs 3 mi. to the park. In summer, rangers robed in feathers and leather lead daily demonstrations of such practices as quill pen writing, moccasin sewing, and musket firing. (Open mid-June to Labor Day 8am-6pm; in winter 8am-5pm; $2, under 17 free, families $4).

Fort Stevens State Park (campground 861-1671, historical area 861-2000), off U.S. 101 on a narrow peninsula 10 mi. west of Astoria, has excellent swimming, fishing, boating facilities, beaches, and hiking trails. All equipment can be rented at the park, and a day use pass costs $3. Fort Stevens was constructed in 1863 to prevent Confederate naval raiders from entering the Columbia River; its sea of weapons included eight concrete gun batteries, nearly all of which remain (*sans* guns). These batteries are the primary focus of a **self-guided walking tour** (about 2hr.) that begins up the road from the day use and campground areas. A restored 1954 Army cargo truck takes visitors on narrated tours. *(Daily in summer at 11am, 12:30, 2:30, and 4pm; $2.50, under 13 $1.25.)* Tours leave from the **Fort Stevens Military Museum and Interpretive Center** (861-2000). *(Open daily 10am-6pm; in winter 10am-4pm.)* **Battery Russell** (861-2471), in the park 1 mi. south of the historical area, bears the onus of being the only mainland American fort to endure enemy fire since the War of 1812. At 11pm on June 21, 1942, a Japanese submarine surfaced offshore and shelled the fort with 17 rounds. The fort was undamaged and did not return fire. Today it is a military monument, and allows free access to visitors.

▓ Seaside

In the winter of 1805-1806, explorers Lewis and Clark made their westernmost camp near Seaside. Built into a resort in the 1870s, 120 years of visitors have transformed Seaside from a remote outpost to a bustling, beachfront tourist mill. Fast food, video arcades, and a developed shore make Seaside a prime target for city-slickers and yuppies catching a weekend glimpse of the sea. For non-shoppers, Seaside is a good base for exploring the beautiful Oregon coast. Prices here are lower than those in nearby Cannon Beach, and Seaside's hostel is one of the best in the Pacific Northwest.

ORIENTATION AND PRACTICAL INFORMATION

Seaside lies 17 mi. south of Astoria and 8 mi. north of Cannon Beach along U.S. 101. The most direct route between Seaside and Portland is U.S. 26, which intersects U.S. 101 just south of Seaside near **Saddle Mountain State Park.** The **Necanicum River** runs north-south through Seaside, approximately two blocks from the coastline, paralleled by U.S. 101 and **Holladay Dr.** to the east. All three are bisected by **Broadway,** the town's main street, and a tourist-dollar black hole. Broadway is within walking distance of everything. "The Promenade" is a paved path that parallels the beach, and is open to cyclists, roller skaters, and pedestrians.

Buses: Pierce Pacific Stages (717-1651), a Greyhound affiliate. Runs out of the hostel (see **Accommodations,** below). 1 per day to: Portland ($20); Seattle, WA ($38).

Public Transportation: Sunset Empire Transit (325-0563). Runs between Astoria and Cannon Beach; stops at the hostel. 7 trips per day each direction M-Sa. Round-trip fares $1.50-6; seniors, disabled, and ages 6-12 $1-3.50; under 6 free. Tickets and info available at the hostel.

Taxis: Yellow Cab, 738-3131. $1.45 base, $1.20 per mi. Runs 24hr.

Visitor Information: Chamber of Commerce, 7 N. Roosevelt St. (738-6391 or 800-444-6740), on U.S. 101 and Broadway. The **Seaside Visitor Bureau** operates out of the same building, but has a different mailing address (989 Broadway) and phone number (738-3097 or 888-306-2326). The well-versed staff provides a referral service for local motels; make reservations on a free phone. Open June-Aug. M-Sa 8am-6pm, Su 9am-5pm.; Oct.-May M-F 9am-5pm, Sa-Su 10am-4pm.

Equipment Rental: Prom Bike Shop, 622 12th Ave. (738-8251), at 12th and Holladay. Rents bikes, roller skates, in-line skates, beach tricycles, and surreys (most $6 per hr., $30 per day; tandem bicycles $12 per hr.) Must be 18 or over. ID held during rental. Open daily 10am-6pm. Also operates a rental shop at 80 Ave. A, downtown (open daily 9am-8pm).

Bank: Bank of America, 300 S. Holladay Dr. (738-8311). Open M-TF 9am-6pm, Sa 9am-1pm. 24hr. **ATMs.**

Library: 60 N. Roosevelt Dr. (738-6742). Internet access available. Open Tu-Th 9am-8pm, F-Sa 9am-5pm, Su 1-5pm.

Laundry: Coin Laundry, 1150 N. Holladay Dr., 1 block north of hostel. $1.25 wash, dry 25¢ per 7½min. Open daily 8am-9pm.

Community Centers: Senior Center, 1225 Ave. A (738-7393). Info and referral specialists. Open M-Th 9am-9pm, F 9am-5:30pm. **Senior and Disabled Services:** 809 S. Holladay Dr. Open M-F 8am-noon, 1pm-5pm.
Emergency: 911. **Police:** 1091 S. Holladay Dr. (738-6311). **Coast Guard:** 2185 SE Airport Rd. in Warrenton (861-6228).
Women's Crisis Service: 325-5735. 24hr.
Hospital: Providence Seaside Hospital, 725 S. Wahanna Rd. (717-7000).
Post Office: 300 Ave. A (738-5462). Turn into the Kentucky Fried Chicken parking lot. Open M-F 8:30am-5pm, Sa (for pickup only) 8:30-10:30am. **ZIP Code:** 97138.
Internet Access: See **Library,** above.
Area Code: 503.

ACCOMMODATIONS AND CAMPGROUNDS

Seaside's expensive motel scene is hardly an issue for the budget traveler in Seaside, thanks to the large hostel on the south side of town. Reservations at the hostel and all local hotels are essential. Motel prices are directly proportional to proximity to the beach; the cheapest rooms hover near $40 (less during the off-season). In summer, rooms are invariably full by 5pm; get ahead of the game and ask the chamber of commerce for availability listings. They won't reserve a room, but they offer advice.

If aiming to camp, get ready to drive. The closest state parks are **Fort Stevens** (861-1671), 21 mi. north (see p. 432), and **Saddle Mountain** (368-5154), 9½ mi. east, off U.S. 26 after it splits with U.S. 101 (p. 87). Drive 8 mi. northeast of Necanicum Junction, then another 7 mi. up a winding road to the base camp (10 sites: $10; drinking water). Sleeping on the beach in Seaside is illegal, and police enforce this rule.

Seaside International Hostel (HI-AYH), 930 N. Holladay Dr. (738-7911). Free nightly movies, a well-equipped kitchen, an espresso bar, and a grassy yard along the river make this mega-hostel a pastoral wonderland. The management knows about everything there is to do in Seaside and filters the fun from the resort hysteria. Employees recommend "Off Broadway" options, map out local hikes, and rent kayaks and canoes to take out on the river (reasonable rates, but pricier for non-HI members). 48 large bunks $14, nonmembers $17; private rooms $38, nonmembers $58. Call well ahead.

Riverside Inn, 430 S. Holladay Dr. (738-8254 or 800-826-6151; http://www.riversideinn.com). Cozy bedrooms, fresh flowers, and ceilings with skylights make this B&B a secret garden amid the Seaside motel madness. Rooms have private bath and TV. Homemade breakfast, included with price of rooms, goes well with the riverfront deck. Doubles from $55; Oct.-Apr. from $50.

Mariner Motel, 429 S. Holladay Dr. (738-3690). Mauve-beige rooms, many newly re-carpeted, with TVs and phones. Free coffee in the office (8:30-10am). Heated outdoor pool. Singles $54; doubles $59. Sept. 15- to June 11: singles $38; doubles $43. Call for reservations in summer.

FOOD

Broadway, especially toward the beach, transforms from a madhouse to an insane asylum at lunch time. Prices are criminal. **Safeway,** 401 S. Roosevelt (738-7122), has safe and stable prices (open daily 6am-midnight).

The Coffeehouse, 846 Ave. C (717-8188), across from Safeway. Without a doubt, the best mocha on the Oregon coast. The Poncho Villa ($2.25) is a startlingly good mocha with a kick. Steal away to the upper floor where chairs, sofas, and a rocking chair make this joint a hidden haven for socialites. Also serves homemade foods, including cranberry turkey pita ($4.25). Open Su-Th 7am-10pm, F-Sa 7am-11pm.

The Stand, 220 Ave. U (738-6592), at the south end of town, serves the cheapest meals around to a local crowd. Unassuming decor, loads of authentic Mexican food, enthusiastic service, and the company of local beach bums with permanently peeling noses transports this Oregon eatery to the beaches of Acapulco. Burritos $1.50-3.25. Open M-Sa 11am-8pm.

Dooger's, 505 Broadway (738-3773). The prototype family restaurant with succulent seafood at reasonable prices. The salmon ($11) is a lunch-time steal, while the cajun-style calimari ($13) will spice up your life (without ginger, of course). Open daily 11am-9:30pm; in winter11am-8:30pm.

Cafe Espresso, 600 Broadway #7 (738-6169), on the Necanicum Walkway, makes a sublime cappuccino ($2) and hosts some limited Seaside nightlife. Live local jazz, blues, and acoustic rock light up the cafe's tapestried walls on Sa at 8pm and on some other nights. Minimal cover, maximum atmosphere. Open M-Tu 8am-5pm, Th-F 8am-5pm, Sa 9am-5pm, Su 10am-4pm.

SIGHTS, EVENTS, AND OUTDOORS

Seaside swarms around **Broadway,** a garish strip of arcades, shops, and salt water taffy running the ½ mi. from Roosevelt (U.S. 101) to the beach. Indoor mini golf, bumper cars, and those machines that squash pennies draw big crowds. **The Turn-around** at the end of Broadway signals the official (read: arbitrary) end of the Lewis and Clark Trail. Seaside's beachfront is huge and hugely crowded, even though the Pacific is almost always too cold for swimming. There are strong undertows; exercise caution at all times. When red flags wave on the sand, the surf is too rough even for wading. For a quieter beach, head to **Gearhart,** approximately 2 mi. north of downtown off U.S. 101, where long stretches of unmolested sand and dunes await exploration. This beach has no lifeguard, and town officials strongly discourage swimming. Brazen wave-weavers can try tearing up the surf with a board instead. **Cleanline Surf,** 710 1st Ave. (738-7888), rents surfing gear.

The **Seaside Aquarium,** 200 N. Prom St., though quite a bit smaller than its world-famous counterpart in Newport, is nevertheless a delightful excursion for lovers of sea animals. *(Open daily 9am-6pm; in winter open daily 9am-5:30pm. $5.50, seniors $4.75, ages 6-13 $2.75, families (max. 6) $17.)* One of several exhibits allows visitors the opportunity to feed playful harbor seals. Purchase a handful of seal food (50¢) and listen to the seals desperately yell, swim, and do tricks for your attention.

The Northwest Performing Arts sponsors **Where the Stars Play,** a free concert series every Saturday in July and August. At 2pm, musicians bust out with everything from bluegrass to rock at **Quatat Marine Park.** In the **Hood to Coast Race** at the end of August, runners tear up the trails between Mt. Hood and Seaside to the cheers of 50,000 spectators. About 750 12-person teams run 5 mi. shifts in this two-day relay race. Contact Bob Foote (in Portland 503-227-1371) for more info. Seaside hides little-known natural wonders behind its beach bungalows and cotton candy stands.

The **Necanicum River Estuary** picks up where the north end of the promenade ends, and makes a dune-covered loop back into town. From the Seaside beach, head south to the Tillamook Head (see p. 87) for a day-long hike amid uncrowded forests and along vertiginous cliffs. This is the cheapest way to see Tillamook Head and the lighthouse, since the Cannon Beach entrance charges a fee.

■ Cannon Beach

Many moons ago, a rusty cannon from the shipwrecked schooner *Shark* washed ashore at Arch Cape, giving this town its name. Today, the only artillery in this town is its battery of boutiques, bakeries, and galleries. Although lined with establishments, Cannon Beach nonetheless offers a quieter, more authentic experience than the mass commercialization of Lincoln City or Seaside. Nothing in Cannon Beach is cheap, but a traveler resigned to window shopping and gallery hopping can spend an enjoyable day with local surfers and Portland escapees. If the credit-card waving begins to annoy, head out to Ecola State Park, just a few miles from downtown.

ORIENTATION AND PRACTICAL INFORMATION

Cannon Beach lies 7 mi. south of Seaside, 42 mi. north of Tillamook on U.S. 101, and 79 mi. from Portland via U.S. 26. **Hemlock,** the town's main drag, connects with U.S. 101 in four places.

Buses: Sunset Transit System (325-0563 or 800-776-6406). To: Seaside (75¢); Astoria ($2.25).

Public Transportation: Cannon Beach Shuttle, a free natural gas powered bus service (50¢ donation requested). Traverses the downtown area; board at any point. Runs daily 10am-6pm. Ask the chamber of commerce for a schedule.

Visitor Information: Cannon Beach Chamber of Commerce, 207 N. Spruce St., P.O. Box 64 (436-2623), at 2nd St. Emblematic of the city, this visitor center sells t-shirts, postcards, and brochures galore. Open M-Sa 10am-5pm, Su 11am-3pm.

Bank: U.S. Bank, 115 N. Hemlock St. (436-1134). **ATMs** available. Open M-Th 10am-5pm, F 10am-6pm.

Equipment Rental: Mike's Bike Shop, 248 N. Spruce St. (436-1266 or 800-492-1266), around the corner from the chamber of commerce. Offers maps of routes along old logging roads. Mountain bikes $7 per hr., $29 per 24hr.; beach tricycles $6 per hr. Credit card deposit required. Open daily 9am-6pm.

Emergency: 911. **Police:** 163 Gower St. (436-2811). **Fire:** 188 Sunset (436-2949).

Hospital: Providence Seaside Hospital, 725 S. Wahanna Rd. (717-7000), in Seaside. **Providence North Coast Clinic,** 171 Larch St (717-7000), in Sandpiper Sq. in Cannon Beach. Open M-F 8:30am-noon and 1:15-4:30pm.

Post Office: 163 N. Hemlock St. (800-275-8777). Open M-F 9am-5pm. **ZIP Code:** 97110.

Area Code: 503.

ACCOMMODATIONS AND CAMPGROUNDS

Pleasant motels line Hemlock St.; none costs under $40 in summer, but family units can make a good deal. Book early on summer weekends. In winter, inquire about specials; most motels offer two-nights-for-one deals. Real budget deals are a short drive away: the Seaside International Hostel is 7 mi. north (see p. 84), and **Oswald West State Park** (see p. 87), 10 mi. south of town, has a stunning campground.

The Sandtrap Inn, 539 S. Hemlock St. (436-0247 or 800-400-4106 from Portland). Picturesque, cozy accommodations at a reasonable price. First-class amenities, including working fireplaces, cable TV, kitchens, and VCRs. Singles from $55; off-season $45. 2-night min. stay on summer weekends. Townhouses and studios also available. All rooms non-smoking; no dogs. Call for off-season rates and specials.

Blue Gull Inn, 487 S. Hemlock St. (436-2714 or 800-507-2714). Set back from the street. Big, clean rooms with cable TV, free sauna, and laundry to help wash the sand out of your suit. Studio $53; singles from $63; doubles from $83. Oct.-May $4-10 less. 2-night min. stay July-Aug., weekends, and holidays. Winter specials.

Sea Ranch RV Park, 415 N. Hemlock St., P.O. Box 214 (436-2815). A safe, tree-studded area with lots of grass and pebbles, right on the north edge of town. 55 tent sites: $19; 30 full hookups: $22; $2 per additional person. Non-guest showers $4. Horse rides $25-40. 1-night deposit required. Reservations recommended.

FOOD

Soups, salads, and sandwiches have put the local food scene under siege. For the best deals, avoid the strip and head farther down Hemlock to the midtown area. **Mariner Market,** 139 N. Hemlock St. (436-2442), has a small stock of groceries (open July-Sept. Su-Th 8am-10pm, F-Sa 8am-11pm; Oct.-June Su-Th 8am-9pm, F-Sa 8am-10pm).

The Homegrown Cafe, 3301 S. Hemlock (436-1803), just before the last exit to U.S. 101. An earthy and eclectic alternative to the mayhem downtown, popular with the locals. Wolf down the homegrown burrito ($7-8) at any time of day. Fresh and fragrant veggie fare, most picked right out of the cafe's backyard. Open M-Th 10am-2pm, F 11am-5pm, Sa 9am-8pm, Su 9am-4pm.

Midtown Cafe, 1235 S. Hemlock St. (436-1016), in the Haystack Sq. Everything is homemade, from the hand-carved door to the jams and marmalades on the tables. Lentil burgers $7; a deluxe potato topped with spinach and melted Tillamook cheddar $5.75. The only problem with eating the mungo waffle breakfasts ($3.75) is that you'll be hungry again in a few days. Open W-Sa 7am-2pm, Su 8am-2pm.

Bill's Tavern, 188 N. Hemlock (436-2202). Tasty food and beer make this newly rebuilt brew-pub a favorite. Down-home pub grub $3-6; pints $1.75-2.75. Under 21 allowed only when food is served. Open Th-Tu 11:30am-midnight. Call for more info on hours and entertainment.

SIGHTS, EVENTS, AND OUTDOORS

Tourists in Cannon Beach anxiously navigate their way through a gauntlet of expensive and sporadically elegant galleries and gift shops. A stroll along the 7 mi. stretch of flat, bluff-framed beach is a less expensive option. **Ecola State Park** (436-2844; $3 entrance fee) attracts picnickers and hikers alike. There, **Ecola Point** offers a view of hulking **Haystack Rock,** which is spotted with (and splattered by) gulls, puffins, barnacles, anemones, and the occasional sea lion. Ecola Point also affords views of the Bay's centerpiece, the **Tillamook Lighthouse,** which clings to a wave-swept rock like a phallic barnacle. Construction of the lighthouse began in 1879 and continued in Sisyphean fashion for years as storms washed the foundations away. Decommissioned in 1957, the now privately owned lighthouse can be reached only by helicopter in order to deposit the ashes of the dead. The **Indian Beach Trail** leads to **Indian Beach** and its tide pools, which teem with colorful and fragile sea life. From Indian Beach, try the 12 mi. round-trip hike to **Tillamook Head,** the mini-cape that separates Seaside Beach from Cannon Beach, where whales migrate seasonally. The trail is open year-round and offers access to the top of Tillamook Head (2 mi. up), where five hiker sites await those willing to make the trek for free camping. To surf a set, rent boards from **Cleanline Surf,** 171 Sunset Blvd. (436-9726), which loans surfboards and boogieboards ($20 per day, package deals $35 per day). **Saddle Mountain State Park** (see p. 84), 14 mi. east of Cannon Beach on U.S. 26, is named after the highest peak in the Coast Range. A 6 mi., four-hour hike to the mountain's 3283 ft. summit ends with an astounding view of the Pacific Ocean and Nehalem Bay to the west and the Cascades to the east. *(Trail open March-Dec.)*

To sate a hunger for high culture, call the **Coaster Theater,** 1087 N. Hemlock St. (436-1242), which stages theater productions, concerts, dance performances, comedy, and musical revues year-round. *(F and Sa at 8pm. Tickets $12-15. Tickets available by phone with Visa or MasterCard, or at the box office Tu-Sa 1-5pm, and 1hr. before showtime.)* Summer excitement in Cannon Beach builds until the second Saturday in June, when the annual **Sand Castle Competition** towers over the rest of town. Contestants pour in from hundreds of miles and begin digging in the early morning to construct ornate sculptures from wet sand. By evening, high tide washes everything away, leaving photographs as the sole testimony to the creative energy expended. Call the chamber of commerce (see **Practical Information,** above) for more info.

■ U.S. 101: Cannon Beach to Tillamook

In the summer of 1933, the Tillamook Burn reduced 500 sq. mi. of coastal forest near Tillamook to charcoal. While nature has restored Tillamook State Forest to health, coastal towns to the west have sustained some nasty scars. Dime-a-dozen gift shops line the highway, hiding behind faded paint and crooked telephone poles. The coastline alongside these tiny towns, however, is much less crowded than Seaside and Cannon Beaches. Tourist info for the area is available at the visitor information bureau in Tillamook (see p. 88) or the Rockaway Beach Visitor Center, 405 S. U.S. 101 (355-8108; open M-F 9am-noon and 1-4pm, Sa 10-4).

Oswald West State Park, 10 mi. south of Cannon Beach, is a tiny headland **rainforest** with hefty spruce and cedar trees. Locals call the park **Short Sands Beach;** visitors blow their cover by using the official name. Although the beach and woodsy **campsites** are only accessible by a ¼ mi. trail off U.S. 101, campers here aren't quite roughing it—the park provides wheelbarrows for transporting gear from the parking area to the 36 campsites nestled in the forest. The campsites are just minutes away from the beach, balanced by a creek or nestled among the trees, and all teeming with surfers. Fall asleep to the gentle babble of a stream or the chords of gently strumming

Chris Isaak worshipers. These are the cheapest sites around, so an early arrival is essential (open mid-May to Oct.; sites $14). From the park, take the 4 mi. round-trip **Cape Falcon Trail** over the headland, hike the 1661 ft. **Neahkahnie Mountain,** or just follow the path from the campground to one of Oregon's few surfing beaches.

Eight miles south of Oswald State Park, a cluster of made-in-Oregon-type shops marshalled along U.S. 101 make up **Nehalem.** The **Nehalem Bay Winery,** 34965 Hwy. 53 (368-9463), 3 mi. south of town, provides free wine-tasting of local cranberry and blackberry vintages, plus many more local specialties. The winery is also a center of cultural activity in the area, sponsoring performances in a small **theater,** an annual **bluegrass festival,** a **fun express train** on the weekends, and a general forum for **bacchanalian revelry.** Even if you're not up to tasting, stop in to chat with owner Ray, who adores guests and gives all sorts of valuable tips on free camping, local swimming holes, and the merits of a good time. He also has a nearly 100% hiring policy, so if you're broke, stop by and work for a few days (open daily 9am-6pm; in winter 10am-5pm, or later if you stop by and Ray's there).

Wheeler, a few miles south of Nehalem, is a small town with a wealth of ways to woo the water. **Wheeler on the Bay Lodge,** 580 Marine Dr. (368-5858), rents **kayaks** (open daily 7am-dusk; singles $14 per hr., $28 per day; doubles $18 per hr., $40 per day; includes 10min. training session for beginners). Venders sell crabbing buckets off the docks on the bay south of Wheeler; they'll often cook the crabs for you.

■ Tillamook

Although the word Tillamook (TILL-uh-muk) literally translates to "land of many waters," to Oregon's population it is synonymous with one thing: cheese. Lazily grazing dairy cows that litter the surrounding hills produce a nationally famous cheddar, luring a population of lactose-tolerant fans almost as large as the herds themselves. Still a small farming town at heart, Tillamook gets its share of traffic and funnels it to the Tillamook Cheese Factory, where tourists sample sharp, medium, or mild; take a picture, say cheese, then shuffle off to the coast three miles away.

ORIENTATION AND PRACTICAL INFORMATION

Tillamook lies 49 mi. south of Seaside, 74 mi. south of Portland, and 44 mi. north of Lincoln City on U.S. 101. From Portland, take U.S. 26 to Rte. 6. Tillamook's main drag is **U.S. 101,** which splits into two one-way streets in the downtown area. **Pacific Ave.** runs north and **Main Ave.** runs south. The **Tillamook Cheese Factory** sits a mile or two north of the town proper.

> **Taxis: Tillamook Taxi** (842-4567).$2 base, $1.50 per mi. Runs 24hr.
> **Visitor Information: Tillamook Chamber of Commerce,** 3705 U.S. 101 N (842-7525), in the big red barn across the parking lot from the Tillamook Cheese Factory. Friendly folks, free **maps,** and a complete listing of places to camp in Tillamook County. Open M-F 9am-5pm, Sa 10am-4:30pm, Su 10am-2pm.
> **Bank: U.S. Bank,** 408 U.S. 101 S, at 4th St. Open M-Th 10am-5pm, F 10am-6pm.
> **Seniors' Information:** 888-368-4200. Open M-F 8am-noon and 1-5pm.
> **Women's Crisis Center:** 2215 11th St. (842-9486). Open 24hr.
> **Hospital: Tillamook County General Hospital,** 1000 3rd St. (842-4444).
> **Emergency:** 911. **Police:** in City Hall, (842-2522). **County Sheriff:** 201 Laurel St. (842-2561), in the courthouse. **Fire:** 2310 4th St. (842-7587). **Coast Guard:** 322-3246.
> **Post Office:** 2200 1st St. (800-275-8777). Open M-F 8:30am-5pm. **ZIP Code:** 97141.
> **Area Code:** 503.

ACCOMMODATIONS AND CAMPGROUNDS

Tillamook suffered a massive flood in February 1996, and most businesses in the area had to do an interior overhaul. While some motels may look bleak on the outside, new beds and carpets glisten within. The water has gone back down, but high rates still send budget travelers sailing into the area's finest campgrounds.

Tillamook Inn, 1810 U.S. 101 N (842-4413), between the center of town and the Tillamook Cheese Factory. New carpets, coffee makers, and cable. Some bedrooms have kitchens, just right for cooking mac' 'n' Tillamook cheese. Singles $43; doubles $51, with kitchen $64. Winter rates $3-5 lower. Call a few days ahead.

MarClair Inn, 11 Main Ave. (842-7571 or 800-331-6857). Convenient location at the junction of Rte. 6 and U.S. 101. Large, aqua-marine green rooms and outdoor pool, hot tub, and sauna well-shielded from the road. Singles $62; doubles $64. Off-season less expensive. 10% AAA discount. Credit card required.

Cape Lookout State Park, 13000 Whiskey Creek Rd. (842-4981), 15 mi. southwest of Tillamook on the Three Capes Loop (see p. 90). Some sites are only 20 yards from the beach, while others offer more privacy and shade. 201 sites: tent sites $16; full hookups $20; yurts $25; hiker/biker $4 per person; non-camper showers $2. Reserve with Oregon State Parks (800-452-5687).

Kilchis River Park (842-6694), 6 mi. northeast of Tillamook at the end of Kilchis River Rd., which meets U.S. 101 1 mi. north of the Factory. 34 sites nestle between a forest of tall, mossy trees and the Kilchis River. Nifty swingset, small baseball field, volleyball court, horseshoes, swimming, and hiking trails. Water, flush toilets, sinks. Tent sites $10; hiker/biker $2. Open May-Oct.

FOOD

Tillamook is a cheese and ice-cream lover's paradise, but low-cholesterol food options don't come from the same land of milk and honey. Collect picnic supplies at **Safeway,** 955 U.S. 101 (842-4831; open daily 6am-midnight).

Blue Heron French Cheese Company, 2001 Blue Heron Dr. (842-8281; www.blueheronoregon.com), 1 mi. south of the factory on U.S. 101, but still north of town. A country-style store, the Blue Heron focuses decidedly on brie. The deli also serves gourmet sandwiches ($5.50), soups, and salads. Free tastings of local and often unusual dips, jams, jellies, honeys, syrups, mustards, wines, and, yes, brie. Open daily 8am-8pm; in winter 9am-5pm.

La Casa Medello, 1160 U.S. 101 N (842-5768). Eat under bull horns, a sombrero, and 2 mounted machetes. Good family dining, with mild Mexican food prepared to order. Small lunch specials $5.25-7; 12 in. tacos $7-8; burritos $6-8. Dinners come with rice, beans, and chips ($7-12). Open M-F 11:35am-9pm, Sa 2-9pm, Su 4-9pm.

Tillamook Cheese Factory, 4175 U.S. 101 N (842-4481). The Big Cheese of cheese is fun to see, but less fun for dining. More than just hunks of cheddar and pepperoni by the foot (89¢)—smoked salmon, garlic oil, and jams abound. Deli sandwiches featuring you-know-what ($2-5), and divine ice cream ($1.50). Open daily mid-June to Labor Day 8am-8pm; Sept. to mid-June 8am-6pm.

SIGHTS

The **Tillamook Cheese Factory** (see **Food,** above), is a shrine to dairy delights, a font of curdled creations, and a thinly disguised tourist trap. Wander through the amusing exhibits, taste award-winning tidbits at the gift shop, and then get lured into buying pounds of cheddar, heaps of ice cream, and reams of cheesy postcards.

West of the highway, downtown, the **Tillamook County Pioneer Museum,** 2106 2nd St. (842-4553), at Pacific Ave., features dioramas replete with mannequins and all manner of household and industrial goods from pioneer days. (*Open M-Sa 8am-5pm, Su 11am-5pm; $2, seniors $1.50, ages 12-17 50¢, under 12 free, families $5.*) The real head-turner is the collection of stuffed animals preserved by taxidermist Alex Walker (not to be confused with the novelist Alice Walker, who is not a licensed taxidermist). The second floor is a hunter's paradise, containing menacing heads of grizzlies, cape buffalo, musk ox, gigantic antlers, and a rhinoceros skull. One of Tillamook's most impressive attractions is the **Tillamook Naval Air Station Museum,** 6030 Hangar Rd. (842-1130), 2 mi. south of town. (*Open daily in summer 9am-6pm; in winter 10am-5pm. $7, seniors $6, ages 13-17 $4, ages 7-12 $2.50.*) This seven-acre hulking hangar built by the Navy in the 40s is the largest wooden clear-span structure in the world. The airy cavern contains three dozen fully functional war planes, including a P-38 Lightning, a PBY-5A Catalina, and a F-14 Tomcat. The admission charge may be a bit steep, but the high-flying experience is worth the price.

■ The Three Capes Loop

Between Tillamook and Lincoln City, U.S. 101 wanders east into wooded land, losing contact with the coast. **The Three Capes Loop,** a 35 mi. circle to the west of the straying U.S 101, connects a trio of spectacular promontories—**Cape Meares, Cape Lookout,** and **Cape Kiwanda State Parks**—and makes for a sweet Sunday drive. Cyclists and motorists beware: narrow twists and a rocky road make the trip tricky for those on two wheels.

Cape Meares State Park, at the tip of the promontory jutting out from Tillamook, protects one of the few remaining old growth forests on the Oregon Coast. The **Octopus Tree,** a gnarled Sitka spruce with six candelabra trunks, is a climber's ultimate fantasy. The **Cape Meares Lighthouse** (842-4981), active from 1890 to 1963, operates as an illuminating on-site interpretive center. Struggle up 1½ flights of tiny stairs for sweeping views and a peek at the original lens of the big light (open daily May-Sept. 11am-4pm; Oct. and Mar.-Apr. F-Sa 11am-4pm; free).

Another 12 mi. southwest of Cape Meares, **Cape Lookout State Park** (842-4981), offers picnic tables and access to the beach for drive-by dawdlers (day-use fee $3) as well as some fine overnight camping (see **Accommodations,** above). From here, the 2½ mi. **Cape Trail** leads to the end of the lookout where a spectacular 360° view featuring **Haystack Rock** awaits. The park provides more than 6 mi. of hiking trails.

Cape Kiwanda State Park, the southernmost promontory on the loop, reserves its magnificent shore for day use only (open 8am-dusk). Home to one of the most sublime beaches on the Oregon coast, the sheltered cape draws beachcombers, kite-flyers, volleyball players, fishers, jetskiiers, and windsurfers. On this cape, barely north of Pacific City, massive rock outcroppings in a small bay mark the launching pad of the flat-bottomed **dory fleet,** one of the few fishing fleets in the world that launches beachside, directly from sand to surf. If you bring your own fishing gear down to the cape around 5am, you might convince someone to take you on board; the fee will probably be lower than that of a commercial outfitter.

Pacific City, a hidden gem that most travelers on U.S. 101 never even see, is home to another **Haystack Rock,** just as impressive as its Cannon Beach sibling to the north. Pacific City itself is worth a stop, and if that stop extends overnight, the **Anchorage Motel,** 6585 Pacific Ave. (965-6773 or 800-941-6250), offers homey rooms with cable and coffee, but no phones (singles from $42; doubles from $49. Rates drop significantly in winter).

For such an unpretentious town, Pacific City hides away some startlingly good restaurants. The **Pelican Pub and Brewery,** 33180 Cape Kiwanda Dr. (965-7007), is the hands-down victor in the battle for most pastoral location. On the breezy patio, sippers and suppers gaze lazily at the setting sun between Cape Kiwanda and Haystack Rock. The "What's Your Beef" burger ($7) delights, especially with a pint of pelican microbrew ($3). Then clamber up the sandy bank of the cape for an incredible view. (Open Su-Th 7am-10pm, F-Sa 7am-11pm; in winter Su-Thu 7am-9pm, F-Sa 7am-10pm.) For more memorable food, abandon the salt water and head east to the **Riverhouse Restaurant,** 34450 Brooten Rd. (965-6722), a tiny white house overlooking the Nestucca River. Stunning seafood ($14-19) and homemade desserts ($3-6) have earned the Riverhouse its reputation for the best food in town (open Su-F 11am-9pm, Sa 11am-10pm). The **Grateful Bread Bakery,** 34805 Brooten Rd. (965-7337), comes in as a close second. Get anything from a black bean chili omelette ($6) to a dilled shrimp salad ($6; open daily 8am-6pm; in winter closed W-Th).

■ Lincoln City

Lincoln City is actually five towns wrapped around a 7 mi. strip of more than 1000 ocean-front motels, gas stations, and tourist traps along U.S. 101. Bicyclists will find Lincoln City hellish, and hikers should cut three blocks west to the seashore. Kite-flying and beach volleyball fanciers flock to this coastal town, but nothing draws as much prey (or as much money) as the new Chinook Winds Siletz Tribal Gaming Convention Center, where swingers gamble away days, nights, and life savings.

ORIENTATION AND PRACTICAL INFORMATION Lincoln City is 42 mi. south of Tillamook, 22 mi. north of Newport, 58 mi. west of Salem, and 88 mi. southwest of Portland, between the ocean and Devils Lake. Despite its oblong shape, Lincoln City follows a quadrant system: **D River** (marked "the smallest river in the world") is the north-south divide; the double yellow line of U.S. 101 divides the town east-west.

Buses: Greyhound, 3327 U.S. 101 NW (265-2253), at the Circle K. To: Portland (2 per day, $13) and Newport (2 per day, $6).

Car Rental: Robben-Rent-A-Car, 3232 U.S. 101 NE (994-5530 or 800-305-5530). $30 per day, 20¢ per mi. after 50 mi. Must be 21 with major credit card and deposit $500. Reserve ahead. Open daily 8am-5pm.

Visitor Information: Lincoln City Visitor and Convention Bureau, 801 U.S. 101 SW #1 (994-8378 or 800-452-2151), across from Burger King. Brochures of Lincoln City and beyond. 24hr. telephone board connects with local motels and restaurants at the (free) push of a button. Open M-F 8am-5pm, Sa 9am-5pm, Su 10am-4pm.

Bank: U.S. Bank, 928 5th St., at the corner of U.S. 101 S and 5th St. SW. **ATMs** available. Open M-Th 10am-5pm, F 10am-6pm.

Library: Driftwood Library, 801 U.S. 101 SW (996-2277), near the visitor center. Open M-Th 9am-9pm, F-Sa 9am-5pm, Su 1-5pm. Internet access available.

Public Showers and Pool: Community Pool, 2150 NE Oar Place (994-5208). Pool use $2.50, teens $1.50, 12 and under $1.50, families $7; showers $1.25. Open in summer M-F 5:30am-9pm, Sa 11am-9pm, Su noon-4:30pm; call for winter hours.

Senior Center: 2051 NE Oar Place (994-2722).

Emergency: 911. **Police:** 1503 East Devils Lake Rd. SE (994-3636). **Fire:** 2525 NW U.S. 101 (994-3100).

Hospital: North Lincoln Hospital, 3043 NE 28th St. (994-3661).

Post Office: 1501 SE East Devils Lake Rd. (800-275-8777), 2 blocks east of U.S. 101. Open M-F 9am-5pm. **ZIP Code:** 97367.

Internet Access: See **Library,** above.

Area Code: 541.

ACCOMMODATIONS AND CAMPGROUNDS Campgrounds near Lincoln City can be crowded, but are worth the money saved. If high-and-dry is the priority, countless motels yield nice rooms off the water along U.S. 101. (For more options, see **The Three Capes Loop,** p. 90, and **Depoe Bay and the Otter Crest Loop,** p. 92.)

At the **Captain Cook Inn,** 2626 U.S. 101 NE (994-2522 or 800-994-2522), visitors will discover beautiful, remodeled rooms (singles $42; doubles $48) The **Sea Echo Motel,** 3510 U.S. 101 NE (994-2575), offers standard rooms, phones, cable, and pink sinks (singles $38-42; 2 beds $48-53) **Devils Lake State Park** (reservations 800-452-5687), off 6th St. NE from U.S. 101 NW, has spacious sites with picnic tables and easy access to fishing- and boating-friendly Devils Lake (65 tent sites, $16; 32 full hookups, $20; 10 yurts, $29; hiker/biker, $4.25. Non-camper showers $2. 2 wheelchair-accessible sites.) Reservations are strongly recommended in summer.

FOOD Lincoln City has a few decent joints if you can navigate the fast-food shoals; but head down to Depoe Bay or Newport for good seafood. **McMenamins Lighthouse Brew Pub,** 4157 U.S. 101 N (994-7238), in Lighthouse Sq, serves fresh-cut fries, phenomenal brews, and an upbeat atmosphere. A Communication Breakdown Burger costs $5.75 (open M-Sa 11am-1am, Su 11am-midnight; call for winter hours). Sample generous portions of better-than-average Chinese food at **Foon Hing Yuen,** 3138 U.S. 101 SE (996-3831), at SW 30th St. Lunches cost $4-5, dinners specials can be had for $6-12. The pork chow yuk ($6.50) is delicious despite its name (bar and restaurant open M-F 11:30am-midnight, Sa-Su 11:30am-1am. Take out available). Zip north to **Price Chopper Foods,** 4157 U.S. 101 N (994-4246), in Lighthouse Square at the north end of town, for basic food items (open daily 7am-11pm). Across the street is **Safeway,** 4101 NW Logan Rd. (994-8667; open daily 6am-midnight).

ENTERTAINMENT AND EVENTS Brave the crowded parking lots of the **Factory Stores** (996-5000), at E. Devils Lake Rd. and U.S. 101, for a chance to hunt bargains at 61 outlet stores. *(Open daily 10am-8pm; call 888-SHOP/7467 for more info.)* To finish off a day of spending, disappear into the black hole of **Chinook Winds Siletz Tribal Gaming Convention Center,** 1777 NW 44th St. (888-CHINOOK/244-6665), known around town as the "the casino." Check your budget at the door; your nickels (and dimes, and $50 bills) will doubtless disappear. Turn left at Lighthouse Sq. on Logan Rd. NW and look to your left: it's the hulking yellow stucco structure with red and blue tribal markings (open 24hr.). The casino also sponsors **Concerts-by-the-Sea** every other week throughout the year. Past performers have included Wayne Newton and Jay Leno. Call 888-MAIN-ACT/624-6228 for more info.

The windy beaches of Lincoln City host a fleet of annual kite festivals. The largest one is the **Fall International Kite Festival** in the beginning of October at D River Park, but the spring and summer festivals in early May and July stir up the sky with competitions like "best train." The top-notch **Cascade Music Festival** comes to Lincoln City on the last three weekends in June. International classical concerts ($15) take place at St. Peter the Fisherman Lutheran Church, 1226 SW 13th (994-5333).

■ Depoe Bay and The Otter Crest Loop

Rest stops and beach-access parking lots litter U.S. 101 between Lincoln City and Newport. A few miles south on U.S. 101, diminutive **Depoe Bay** boasts opportune **gray whale viewing** along the town seawall, at the **Depoe Bay State Park Wayside,** and at the **Observatory Lookout,** 4½ mi. to the south. Go early in the morning on a cloudy, calm day (Dec.-May during annual migration) for the best chance of spotting the barnacle-encrusted giants. Several outfitters charter fishing trips from Depoe Bay. **Tradewinds Charters** (765-2345), on the north end of the bridge on U.S. 101 downtown, has two five-hour ($49) and seven-hour ($65) bottom-fishing trips per day. **Dockside Charters** (765-2545 or 800-733-8915) offers similar trips for $49 (1hr. whale-watching trip $10, teenagers $8, under 13 $6; 6hr. fishing and crabbing trips $58). To find Dockside, turn east at the one and only traffic light in Depoe Bay; they're next to the Coast Guard station. Call for reservations.

Just south of Depoe Bay, take a detour from U.S. 101 on the renowned **Otter Crest Loop,** a twisting 4 mi. drive high above the shore that affords spectacular vistas at every bend, including views of **Otter Rock** and the **Marine Gardens.** A lookout over **Cape Foulweather** has telescopes (25¢) for spotting sea lions lazing on the rocks. James Cook first saw the North American mainland here in 1778. Also accessible off the loop is the **Devil's Punch Bowl,** formed when two seaside caves collapsed, leaving a hole in the sandstone terrace. During high tide, when ocean water crashes through an opening in the side of the bowl, it becomes a frothing cauldron.

■ Newport

Newport's claim to fame lies in its world-class fish tank, also known as the Oregon Coast Aquarium, fantastic despite Willy's (né Keiko's) imminent departure. The city's beautiful coastline, accentuated by historic Nye Beach, draws outsiders and landlocked inlanders alike. Beyond the miles of malls along U.S. 101, Newport boasts a renovated waterfront area of pleasantly kitschy restaurants and shops. Know that the cigarettes are manufactured elsewhere.

ORIENTATION AND PRACTICAL INFORMATION

U.S. 101, known in town as the **Coast Highway,** divides east and west Newport, while U.S. 20 **(Olive St.)** bisects the north and south sides of town. Corvallis lies 55 mi. east on U.S. 20, Lincoln City is 22 mi. north on U.S. 101 and Florence sits 50 mi. south. Newport is bordered on the west by the foggy Pacific Ocean and on the south by Yaquina Bay. A suspension bridge ferries U.S. 101 traffic across the bay. Just north of the bridge, **Bay Boulevard** runs around the bay and through the heart of the port.

Buses: Greyhound, 956 10th St. SW (265-2253) at Bailey St. To: Portland (3 per day, $17); Seattle (3 per day, $38); San Francisco (5 per day, $65). Open M-F 8-10am and 1pm-4:15pm, Sa 8am-1pm.

Taxis: Yaquina Cab Company, (265-9552). $2.25 base, $2.25 per mi. Runs 24hr.

Car Rental: Sunwest Motors, 1030 Coast Hwy. N (265-8547). All cars $25 per day, 15¢ per mi. over 50 mi. Must be 25 with a major credit card. Reservations advised.

Visitor Information: Chamber of Commerce, 555 Coast Hwy. SW (265-8801 or 800-262-7844). Large new office with bus and theater schedules, free maps, guides, a 24hr. info board, and an on-the-ball staff. Open May-Sept. M-F 8:30am-5pm, Sa-Su 10am-4pm; Oct.-April M-F 8:30am-5pm.

Outdoor Information: Newport Parks and Recreation Office, 169 Coast Hwy. SW (265-7783). Open M-F 8am-5pm.

Outdoor Equipment: Embarcadero, 1000 Bay Blvd. SE (265-5435), rents bikes without helmets. ($4 per hr., $15 per day; $25 deposit or major credit card held). Also rents crab rings ($6 per day), clam shovels ($3 per day), and skiffs ($13.50 per hr.; 3hr. minimum).

Bank: Bank of America, 10 Coast Hwy. S (265-2258). ATMs. Open M-Th 9am-5pm, F 9am-6pm, Sa 9am-1pm.

Public Library: 35 Nye NW (265-2153) at Olive St. Open M-Th 10am-9pm, F-Sa 10am-6pm, Su 1-4pm.

Laundry: Eileen's Coin Laundry, 1078 Coast Hwy. N Wash $1.25, dry 25¢ per 10min. Open daily 6:30am-11pm.

Weather and Sea Conditions: 265-5511.

Crisis Line: CONTACT, 444 2nd St. NE (265-9234). Advice, referrals, and assistance for stranded travelers.

Senior Services: Senior Center, 20 SE 2nd St. (265-9617).

Hospital: Pacific Communities Hospital, 930 Abbey SW (265-2244).

Emergency: 911. **Police:** 810 Alder SW (265-5331). **Fire:** 245 10th St. NW (265-9461). **Coast Guard:** 925 Naterlin Rd. (265-5381).

Post Office: 310 2nd St. SW (800-275-8777). Open M-F 8:30am-5pm, Sa 10am-1pm. **ZIP Code:** 97365.

Area Code: 541.

ACCOMMODATIONS AND CAMPGROUNDS

The motel-studded strip along U.S. 101 provides plenty of affordable rooms with predictably noisy road accompaniment. Weekend rates generally rise a couple of dollars, and winter rates plummet.

City Center Motel, 538 Coast Hwy. SW (265-7381), across from the visitor center. Good-sized rooms with sparkling bathrooms, smack in the middle of town. Cable, phones, and free ice machine. In summer, singles start at $40; doubles $58; renovated rooms cost more. Call 800-628-9665 for reservations.

Summer Wind Budget Motel, 728 Coast Hwy. N (265-8076). Old rooms are smallish with clean bathrooms, earthy tones, and intriguing scents. All rooms have HBO. Prices vary from room to room as quickly as the shifty summer winds. Singles $20-50; doubles $26-56.

Beverly Beach State Park, 198 123rd St. NE (265-9278), 7 mi. north of Newport and just south of Devil's Punch Bowl, is a year-round campground set amid gorgeous, rugged terrain. Cold water and frequent riptides discourage even the most daring swimmers. Beverly Beach was one of the first parks in Oregon to sport the latest in outdoor accommodations, YURTS (Year-round Universal Recreational Tents), round tents with bunk beds modeled after Mongolian huts. Sites $16; electrical $19; full hookups $20; yurt $26; hiker/biker $4.25; non-camper showers $2. Reservations are strongly advised in summer; call 800-452-5687.

South Beach State Park, 5580 Coast Hwy. S (867-4715), 2 mi. south of town. 244 RV hookups $19; ten yurts $29; 12 hiker/biker sites $4.25; and free showers ($2 for non-campers).

FOOD

Food in Newport is surprisingly varied and not limited to bay-front restaurants where tourists cluster. **Oceana Natural Foods Coop,** 159 2nd St. SE (265-8285), has a small selection of reasonably priced health foods and produce (open daily 8am-8pm). **J.C. Sentry,** 107 Coast Hwy. N (265-6641), sells standard supermarket stock, including shampoo. Open 24hr.

Mo's Restaurant, 622 Bay Blvd. SW (265-2979). Share a long gray couch in this small, crowded local favorite and eat fish 'n' chips ($8) until there's no mo' left. Open daily 6am-11pm.

The Chowder Bowl, 728 Beach Dr. NW Avoid the above problem by ordering the all-you-can eat salad bar and chowder with garlic bread ($7). Once you're almost finished, you can take your food "to-go" and walk down a block to Nye Beach, where envious pelicans will stare at you as you slurp the best chowder on the coast. Open daily 11am-9pm; in winter Su-Th 11am-8pm, F-Sa 11am-9pm.

Cosmos Cafe and Gallery, 740 Olive St. W (265-7511). Celestial and marine scenery send diners in this secluded cafe to a faraway, funky-fresh galaxy of cosmically good food. Great omelettes $6; sumptuous black bean burrito $6; and fresh pie $3. Muffin flavors like rhubarb-applesauce and cranberry-peach ($1.25). Open M-W 8am-8pm, Th-Sa 8am-9pm; in winter M-Sa 8am-8pm.

Rogue Ale & Public House, 748 Bay Blvd. SW (265-3188). They "brew for the rogue in all of us," and bless 'em for it. Plenty of brew on tap, and ale bread to boot ($1.50). Walls explore beer as art. Pizza with Rogue Stout crust ($8-21) is delicious, but everyone orders the fish 'n' chips with Rogue Ale batter ($7). Locals pack it in for Friday night trivia. Open Su-Th 11am-11pm, F-Sa 11am-midnight.

Nye Beach Hotel and Cafe, 219 Cliff St. NW (265-3334; http://www.teleport.com/~nyebeach), off W. Olive St. Stylishly simple with high ceilings, a splendid view of the ocean, and two tropical Conures—exotic birds, that is. A heated back porch rolls onto the beach. The fishocentric dinner menu ($8-13) is not aimed at the budget traveler, but the escape from tackiness and fried food may be worth the extra bucks. The second W of every month is ballet dance night, featuring performances from touring groups. No cover. Open daily 8am-11pm; in winter open 9am-9pm.

SIGHTS, ENTERTAINMENT, AND EVENTS

The **Oregon Coast Aquarium,** 2820 Ferry Slip Rd. SE (867-3474; http://www.aquarium.org), at the south end of the bridge, is at the top of Newport's greatest hits list. *($8.75, seniors $7.75, ages 4-13 $4.50. Tickets can be ordered with a credit card up to 2 weekends in advance. Wheelchair accessible.)* This world-class aquarium housed Keiko the much loved Free Willy Orca during his rehabilitation, before he returned to his childhood waters near Iceland last year. The vast six-acre complex features everything from pulsating jellyfish to attention-seeking sea otters to giant African bullfrogs. Stroll through the galleries, where anemones stick to your hands and children experience "sea life at see level." Beginning on February 21, 1999, a new exhibit will feature deadly, poisonous beauties from around the world (alas, Grace Jones was unavailable). Lines are long but speedy, and the aquarium would be worth it even if they weren't. The recently reopened **Mark O. Hatfield Marine Science Center** (867-0100), at the south end of the bridge on Marine Science Dr., is the hub of Oregon State University's coastal research. *(Open daily 10am-6pm; in winter Th-M 10am-4pm. Admission by donation—fork it over, cheapskates!)* This friendly, educational outreach features hands-on exhibits and novel presentations.

To sample local beer, cross the bay bridge, follow the signs to the Hatfield Center and turn off at the **Rogue Ale Brewery,** 2320 Oregon State University Dr. SE (867-3660). *(Open daily 11am-8pm; in winter 11am-7pm.)* Their line of 20 brews, including Oregon Golden, American Amber, and Maierbock Ales are available at the pub in town (see **Food,** above), or upstairs at **Brewer's on the Bay** (867-3664), where taster trays of four beers cost $4.

If you've reached the bottom of the Newport entertainment barrel, **bottom-fishing** with one of numerous charter companies can be fun, if expensive. Salmon is no longer plentiful, but fishers net halibut in May and tuna mid-April to mid-October. **Newport Tradewinds,** 653 Bay Blvd. SW (265-2101), offers numerous packages. *(5hr. trips $60, 6hr. $72, 8hr. $96. 3hr. crabbing trip $35. 2hr. whale-watching trip daily at 1:30pm $18.)* To be near the water, but not in a boat, relax on **Nye Beach.** Follow Olive St. towards the water, then turn right on Coast St., left on Beach Dr. and follow the road to the turnaround.

Many elegant art galleries populate Bay Blvd. by the harbor. The **Newport Performing Arts Center,** 777 W Olive (265-2787) hosts theater and dance performances, film festivals, and some excellent orchestral and band concerts. *(Box office open M-F 9am-5pm and 1hr. before showtime. Tickets $4-18.)*

The **Newport Seafood and Wine Festival** showcases Oregon wines, food, music, and crafts in over 100 booths. *(Last weekend in Feb. $6-8.)* The three-day **Lincoln County Fair and Rodeo** (265-6237) comes to the Newport Fairgrounds the third week in July. *($6 per day, ages 6-12 $3, under 6 free. For all 3 days $18, children $9.)* Contact the chamber of commerce (see **Practical Information,** above) for more info on all seasonal events.

Just south of Beverly Beach (see **Accommodations and Campgrounds,** above) is **Yaquina Head,** a lava delta formed 14 million years ago by hot magma, and the **Yaquina Head Lighthouse** (265-2863), a much-photographed coastal landmark. *(Open daily 10am-4pm. $2, children $1, family $5; subject to change.)* The top of the lighthouse can only be reached by paying, but the public can meander through the ground-level historical displays for free. The **seabird colony** on the rocks below is spectacular; large decks provide views of western gulls, cormorants, murres, guillemots, and, very rarely, the colorful tufted puffin. **Quarry Cove,** located near the entrance, is the only handicapped-accessible tidepool in the world, while the ancient tide pools of **Cobble Beach** to the south of the headland are home to harbor seals, oyster catchers, and smaller intertidal life.

■ U.S. 101: Newport to Reedsport

From Newport to Reedsport, U.S. 101 sidles through a string of small towns, beautiful campgrounds, and spectacular stretches of beach. The **Waldport Ranger District Office,** 1049 Pacific Hwy. SW/U.S. 101 (563-3211), 16 mi. south of Newport in Waldport, describes hiking in **Siuslaw National Forest,** a patchwork of three wilderness areas along the Oregon Coast. The office furnishes detailed maps of the district ($3) and the National Forest ($4), with advice on the many campgrounds and trails therein (open M-F 8am-4pm).

Cape Perpetua, 11 mi. south of Waldport, combines the highest point on the coast (803 ft.) with a number of exciting sea-level trails. A 2.6 mi. hike up to the viewpoint affords a heavenly vista overlooking the coast. The **Cape Perpetua Visitor Center,** 2400 U.S. 101 (547-3289), just south of the viewpoint turn-off, has informative exhibits about the surrounding lands (open June-Aug. daily 9am-5pm; Sept. W-Su 9am-5pm; Oct.-May M-F 9am-5pm, Sa-Su 10am-4pm.) Grab a free visitor guide listing the many trails leading up through the hills and down to the rocks. Well-worn offshore attractions like **Devil's Churn** (¼ mi. north of the visitor center down Restless Water Trail) and **Spouting Horn** (¼ mi. south down Captain Cook Trail), demonstrate the power of the waves. **Cape Perpetua Campground,** at the viewpoint turn-off, has 37 sites running straight back into a narrow valley along a tiny, fern-banked creek; even 30 ft. monsters are welcome (sites $12; drinking water, flush toilets, firewood $5). The **Rock Creek Campground,** 7½ mi. farther south, has 16 sites under mossy spruces by said creek, and ½ mi. from the sea ($12; drinking water, flush toilets).

Five miles farther south are the **Sea Lion Caves,** 91560 U.S. 101 (547-3111), where nature and capitalism clash. Visitors come here at all times of year to stare at Steller and California sea lions, while the critters themselves completely ignore visitors, yelping incessantly to keep themselves entertained. Stellers are more common here, congregating in fall and winter for protection from the seas, and in spring and summer for breeding. Visitors can peep through a 200 ft. deep subterranean hole into an impressive and Batman-evoking sea cave, then use binoculars to gaze down at the mainland rookery another 200 ft. below. To see this greatest American sea cave, you've gotta pay a price ($6.50, ages 6-15 $4.50; open daily 9am to 1hr. before dark).

Escaping from the coast's bourgeois tourism to an unusual communal alternative begins in **Florence,** a far-too-long strip of fast food joints and expensive motels 50 mi. south of Newport. Fourteen miles east, at the junction of Rte. 126 (to Eugene) and Rte. 36, is the tiny community of **Mapleton.** For the free experience in communal living, push 30 minutes farther eastward to **Alpha Farm** (964-5102), 7 mi. up Deadwood Creek Rd. In exchange for a day of labor, visitors can camp out or stay in the sparse but comfortable bedrooms. Visitors are welcome from Monday to Friday for up to three days. Call ahead, and be prepared to kiss the hands of your fellow diners in a warm pre-supper ritual. The **Alpha Bit Cafe** (268-4311), in Deadwood on Rte. 126, is owned and staffed by members of Alpha Farm; it's part cafe, part bookstore, and serves a mean chai (open Sa-Th 10am-6pm and F 10am-9pm).

▓ Oregon Dunes and Reedsport

Millennia of wind and water action have formed the Oregon Dunes National Recreation Area, a grainy 50-mile expanse between Florence and Coos Bay. Shifting mounds of sand rise 500 feet and extend up to three miles inland, often to the shoulder of U.S. 101, clogging mountain streams and forming small lakes. Hiking trails wind around the lakes, through coastal forests, and up to the dunes themselves. In many places, no grass or shrubs grow, and the vista presents naught but sand, sky, and tire tracks. Campgrounds fill up early with motorcycle and dune buggy junkies, especially on summer weekends, when blaring radios, thrumming engines, and staggering swarms of tipsy tourists can drive a person mad. The dune-buggy invasion grows increasingly controversial, but the National Recreation Area Headquarters in Reedsport refuses to take sides.

ORIENTATION AND PRACTICAL INFORMATION

The dunes' shifting grip on the coastline is broken only once, at Reedsport, where the Umpqua and Smith Rivers empty into Winchester Bay, near a town of the same name. One hundred and eighty-five miles southwest of Portland, 89 mi. southwest of Eugene, and 71 mi. south of Newport, at the junction of Rte. 38 and U.S. 101, Reedsport is a typical highway town of motels, banks, and restaurants. The older part of town flanks Rte. 38, just east of U.S. 101 and south of the river.

Buses: Greyhound (267-4436 in Coos Bay). Pick up outside Moo Mall, at 4th and Fir St. To: Portland (3 per day, $28), Eugene (2 per day, $20), and San Francisco (2 per day, $63).

Taxis: Coastal Cab, 139 N 3rd St. (271-2690). $8 to Winchester Bay, $3 more to the beach. Service daily 6am-3am. $2.50 base, $1.60 per mi.

Dune Buggy and ATV Rentals: Winchester Bay Dune Buggy Adventures, 881 U.S. 101 (271-6972), in Winchester Bay. Buggy rides $15 for 30min., $25 for 1hr. 3 person minimum. ATVs $35 per hr., $30 each additional hr. $75 deposit with credit card. Open daily 10am-6pm.

Visitor and Outdoor Information: Oregon Dunes National Recreation Area Information Center, 855 U.S. 101 (271-3611), at Rte. 38 in Reedsport, just south of the Umpqua River Bridge. The Forest Service runs this center and will happily answer questions on fees, regulations, hiking, and camping throughout the area. Maps $4. The **Reedsport/Winchester Bay Chamber of Commerce** (271-3495 or 800-247-2155) is at the same location, with dune buggy rental info and motel listings. Both open daily 8:30am-5pm.

Laundromat: Coin Laundry, 420 N. 14th St. (271-3587), next to the McDonald's. Wash $1, dry 25¢ per 8min. Open daily 8am-8pm.

Library: 395 Winchester Ave. (271-3500). Open M and Th 2-8:30pm, Tu-W and F 10am-6pm. Internet access available.

Emergency: 911. **Police:** 146 N. 4th St. (271-2109 or 271-2100). **Coast Guard:** (271-2137), near the end of the harbor, in Winchester Bay.

Post Office: 301 Fir Ave. (800-275-8777), off Rte. 38. Open M-F 8:30am-5pm. **ZIP Code:** 97467.

Internet Access: See **Library,** above.

Area Code: 541.

ACCOMMODATIONS

Harbor View Motel, 540 Beach Blvd. (271-3352), off U.S. 101 in Winchester Bay, spitting distance from the boats. The turquoise and white exterior hides greater tidiness and tastefulness within. Nice rooms include small refrigerators. Cable, phones, and antlers on display. The best asset: it's quiet, located a fair distance from the bustle of U.S. 101. Singles $31; doubles $34.

Fir Grove Motel, 2178 U.S. 101 (271-4848), in Reedsport. Attractive rooms with plaster walls, arched doorways, and cable TV. The outdoor heated pool is clean and lovely, but only inches from U.S. 101. Geraniums everywhere. Coffee, donuts, and fruit in the lobby 7:30-9:30am. Singles $40; doubles $49. In winter: singles $30; doubles $39. Senior discount $4-8.

Economy Inn, 1593 U.S. 101 (271-3671 or 800-799-9970), in Reedsport, off the parking lot of the Umpqua Shopping Center. A respectable, clean abode with comfortable rooms. Arrive early, when the parking lot is less than half full, and play "let's make a deal." Continental breakfast, outdoor pool, and TV with HBO. Singles from $35; doubles $45. Cheaper in winter; 10% AAA discount.

CAMPGROUNDS

The national recreation area is administered by Siuslaw National Forest. The campgrounds that allow dune buggy access—**Spinreel** (36 sites), parking-lot style **Driftwood II** (69 sites), **Horsfall** (69 sites, showers) and **Horsfall Beach** (34 sites)—are generally loud and rowdy in the summer. All have flush toilets, drinking water, and are open year-round; sites cost $10-13. Limited reservations for summer weekends are available; call 800-280-CAMP/2267 at least five days in advance (maximum 240 days). The following options are marginally quieter, designed for tenters and small RVs.

During the summer, RVs dominate all the campsites around Reedsport and Winchester Bay. Dispersed camping is allowed on public lands, 200 ft. from any road or trail. Ask at the Dunes Information Center (see **Practical Information,** above) about legal overnight parking and camping. Summer campers with tents may have a hard time finding legal campgrounds without the screams of sand vehicles and children.

Carter Lake Campground, 12 mi. north of Reedsport on U.S. 101. Boat access to Carter Lake; some sites are lakeside. Well-screened sites, as quiet as it gets out here; no ATVs. Nice bathrooms, but no showers. 23 sites: $14. Open May-Sept.

Eel Creek Campground, 10 mi. south of Reedsport on U.S. 101. Sandy and spacious sites are well-hidden from the road and each other by tall brush. Quiet dune adventures begin here at the trailhead for the 2½ mi. Umpqua Dunes Trail. Flush toilets and drinking water; no hookups or ATVs. 53 sites: $13.

William M. Tugman State Park (759-3604; reservations 800-452-5687), 8 mi. south of Reedsport on U.S. 101. Shady, manicured sites and pleasant smatterings of sand. Most are separated somewhat by bushes, but hiker/biker camping is the most private ($4). Very close to gorgeous Eel Lake. Water and electricity. 115 sites: $15; hiker/biker $4; yurts $29. Non-camper showers $2. Wheelchair accessible.

FOOD

Cheap, tasty food prevails in Winchester Bay and Reedsport. Herbivores should blaze a trail to **Safeway** (open daily 7am-11pm) inside in the Umpqua Shopping Center, or to **Price 'n' Pride** (6am-11pm), across the street, both in Reedsport on U.S. 101.

Bayfront Bar and Bistro, 208 Bayfront Loop (271-WINE/9463), in Salmon Harbor. Tiled floors and stylish black chairs make this a classy but casual choice on the waterfront. Be sure to try an oyster shooter ($1.50) from the local Umpqua triangle. The "Bayfront Sandwich" sports shrimp on a croissant roll ($7). Dinners are a bit pricier ($10-16), but well-worth the extra expenditure. Open Tu-Su 11am-9pm.

Back to the Best (271-2619), on U.S. 101 at 10th St. Despite its turquoise and yellow exterior, this really is one of the best spots in town. Sandwiches ($4.25) are piled high with fresh-cut fineries like smoked gouda and home-roasted ham. Clam chowder $3.75. Open M-F 6am-6pm, Sa 8am-6pm, Su 9am-5pm.

Seafood Grotto and Restaurant, 115 8th St. (271-4250), at Broadway in Winchester Bay. An unexpected find: excellent seafood in an average-looking dining room. Sick of clam chowder? The *cioppino* soup ($4.45) is incredible, but prices float up after that. Lunches $4-11. Open daily 11:30am-9pm; closed M off-season.

OUTDOORS

When at the dunes, romp in them—there's not much else to do. Even those with little time or low noise tolerance should at least stop at the **Oregon Dunes Overlook** ($1 parking fee), off U.S. 101, about halfway between Reedsport and Florence. Wooden ramps lead through the bushes for a peek at some untrammeled dunes and a glimpse of the ocean. The **Tahkenitch Creek Loop,** actually three separate trails, plows up to 3½ mi. through forest, dunes, wetlands, and beach. *(Overlook staffed daily Memorial Day-Labor Day 10am-3pm. Guided hikes are available.)* A free *Sand Tracks* brochure, available at the information center (see **Practical Information,** above), has a detailed map of the dunes. The freshly revamped **Umpqua Scenic Dunes Trail** makes another excellent hike. From the trailhead just south of Eel Creek Campground (see **Camping,** above), the massive oblique dunes invite bare feet. (*Let's Go* does not recommend stepping on sharp things.) Be wary of quicksand in the low, wet areas. (*Let's Go* also refrains from recommending an excruciating and wet death.)

Umpqua Lighthouse State Park has an excellent **gray whale viewing** station. The best times to see these massive creatures are during their migrations; they head north in two waves from March through May and south in late December and early January. Unfortunately, dune buggies raise a racket underneath this 100 ft. overlook. **Bird watching** is also popular around Reedsport. Lists of species and their seasons are available at the National Recreation Area Information Center (see **Practical Information,** above). If you would rather ensnare and devour animals than watch them, rent a pot for nabbing crabs anywhere in Winchester Bay. Throughout August, the **Crab Bounty Hunt** offers a $3000 reward for catching a particular tagged crab.

For a silence-shattering dune experience, venture out on wheels. Plenty of shops between Florence and Coos Bay rent and offer tours. **Spinreel Dune Buggy Rentals,** 9122 Wild Wood Dr. (759-3313), on U.S. 101 7 mi. south of Reedsport, offers air-rending Honda Odysseys, ear-splitting dune buggy rides, and family tours in a cochlea-mangling VW "Thing." *(Hondas $20 for 30min., $30 first hr., $25 second hr. Buggies $15 for 30min., $25 per hour. Things $10 per 30min.)* Or rent from Winchester Bay Dune Buggy Adventures, in Winchester Bay (see **Practical Information,** above).

■ Coos Bay, North Bend, and Charleston

The largest city on the Oregon Coast, Coos Bay is making an economic turnaround despite environmental regulations that decimated the local lumber industry. Tourism has expanded economic opportunity and businesses are returning to a once-deserted pedestrian shopping mall. Huge iron-sided tankers have begun to replace quaint fishing boats, and U.S. 101 barrels through a bustling strip of shops and espresso bars. The nearby town of North Bend blends into Coos Bay, while tiny Charleston sits peacefully a few miles west on the coast. Coos Bay is one of the few places on the coast where life slows down as you near the shore, with Sunset Bay offering a refuge from industrial chaos.

OREGON

Eating Right for Longer Living

Each year, over 22,000 gray whales *(Eschrichtius robustus)* migrate northward from their warm winter calving grounds in Mexico to an Arctic summer smorgasbord, born of increased energy from the midnight sun. During the 19th century, though, these whales were hunted almost to extinction. Whalers would kill a calf, wait for its mother to investigate, and then harpoon her, too. Today, gray whales have regained their high population levels so successfully that native groups like the Makah Nation (see p. 212) are about to renew ceremonial whale hunts without ecological or legal repercussions. The secret of the whales' success might be in their diet. Unlike the slowly rebounding humpbacks, which eat major commercial fish species, the gray whales feed on creatures that would make a human's stomach turn: fish roe, mud shrimp, crab larvae, and slimier. It appears that people imperil whales not just as hunters, but as competitors.

ORIENTATION AND PRACTICAL INFORMATION

U.S. 101 jogs inland south of Coos Bay, rejoining the coast at Bandon. From Coos Bay, **Rte. 42** heads east 85 mi. to **I-5,** and U.S. 101 continues north into dune territory. U.S. 101 skirts the east side of both Coos Bay and North Bend, and the **Cape Arago Highway** continues west to Charleston at the mouth of the bay. **Newark Street** heads west from U.S. 101 and leads into the Cape Arago Highway.

Buses: Greyhound, 275 N. Broadway (267-4436), Coos Bay. To: Portland (4 per day, $28); San Francisco, CA (2 per day, $63). Open M-Th 9am-5pm, F-Sa 9am-4pm.

Taxis: Yellow Cab (267-3111). $5 anywhere within the city. $2 initial drop, $1 per mile. Senior discount. 24hr.

Car Rental: Verger, 1400 Ocean Blvd. (888-5594; ask for the rental department). Cars from $26 per day, 20¢ per mi. after 100 mi. Must be 23 or older with a credit card. Open M-F 8am-5:30pm, Sa 9am-5pm.

Visitor Information: Bay Area Chamber of Commerce, 50 E. Central Ave (269-0215 or 800-824-8486), off Commercial Ave. in Coos Bay, between the one-way thoroughfares of U.S. 101. Open in summer M-F 8:30am-7pm, Sa-Su 10am-4pm; from mid-Sept. to May, M-F 9am-5pm, Sa 10am-4pm. Plenty of free brochures; comprehensive area maps cost 50¢. **North Bend Information Center,** 1380 Sherman Ave. (756-4613), on U.S. 101, just south of the North Bend bridge. Open M-F 9am-5pm, Sa-Su 10am-4pm. **Charleston Information Center** (888-2311), at Boat Basin Dr. and Cape Arago Hwy. Open May-Oct. daily 9am-5pm.

Outdoor Information: Oregon State Parks Information, 10765 Cape Arago Hwy. (888-8867), in Charleston. Open M-F 8am-5pm.

Bank: Bank of America, 245 S. 4th St. (269-9315), in Coos Bay, has **ATMs.** Open M-Th 9am-5pm, F 9am-6pm, Sa 9am-1pm.

Library: 525 W. Anderson (269-1101), Coos Bay. Open M 10am-5:30pm, Tu-W 10am-8pm, Th-F noon-5:30pm, Sa 1-5pm. Internet access available.

Laundromat: Wash-A-Lot, 1921 Virginia Ave. (756-5439), in North Bend. Wash $1.25; dry $1 per 10min. 24hr.

Emergency: 911. **Police:** 500 Central Ave. (269-8911). **Fire:** 150 S. 4th St. (269-1191).

Coast Guard: 4645 Eel Ave. (888-3266), in Charleston.

Crisis Line: 888-5911. 24hr. information and referral.

Women's Crisis Service: 756-7000 or 800-448-8125. 24hr.

Hospital: Bay Area Hospital, 1775 Thompson Rd. (269-8111), in Coos Bay.

Post Office: 470 Golden Ave. (800-275-8777), at 4th St. Open M-F 8:30am-5pm. **ZIP Code:** 97420.

Internet Access: See **Library,** above.

Area Code: 541.

ACCOMMODATIONS AND CAMPGROUNDS

Budget-bound non-campers should bunk at the affordable **Sea Star Hostel** (347-9632), 23 mi. south on U.S. 101 in **Bandon** (see p. 102) Campers, rejoice: the nearby state-run and private sites allow full access to the breathtaking coast.

2310 Lombard (756-3857), at the corner of Cedar St. in North Bend. A European-style, home B&B. Two small and pleasant rooms bear a smattering of African and Korean art on the walls. Two twin beds $35; double bed $40. Full breakfast from a wonderful hostess. Reservations recommended.

Itty Bitty Inn, 1504 Sherman Ave. (756-6398 or 888-2-ROYALE). Lavender doors lead to cozy, Southwestern-style rooms with wall hangings, cable, refrigerators, microwaves, elevated beds, and live cacti. Singles $35; doubles $40. Cheaper in the winter. Breakfast voucher for the Virginia Street Diner $2 more.

Sunset Bay State Park, 10965 Cape Arago Hwy. (888-4902; for reservations 800-452-5687), 12 mi. south of Coos Bay and 3½ mi. west of Charleston. Akin to camping in a well-landscaped parking lot. When it's full, the park is a zoo. Fabulous Sunset Beach makes it all worthwhile. Camping here wins you a free entrance to Shore Acres State Park. 138 sites: standard $16; electrical hookups $18; full hookups $19; yurts $27; hiker/biker sites $4. Has hot showers and wheelchair accessible facilities. Non-camper showers $2. Open year-round.

Bluebill Campground, off U.S. 101, 3 mi. north of North Bend. Follow the signs to the Horsfall Beach area, resist the temptation to drive the dunes in a Toyota Tercel, and continue down the road to this U.S. Forest Service campground. 19 sites: $13, $11 in winter. Flush toilets. Road leads ½ mi. to the ocean and dunes.

FOOD

Though McDonaldization has begun, those who seek out the local food scene will be well-rewarded. Restaurants in the Bay Area serve up fine fish fare, and many also dish out classics at decent prices. For grocery needs, **Safeway** holds court at 230 E. Johnson Ave. off U.S. 101 north, at the southern edge of town (open daily 6am-1am).

Blue Heron Bistro, 100 W. Commercial St. (267-3933), at U.S. 101 in Coos Bay. Almost-upscale atmosphere with numerous skylights and a shiny tile floor. A tad more expensive than most, but the food's a tad better, too. Cajun and Tex-Mex dinners are $10-15, but you can have a "Son of Reuben" for $6. Reuben himself was killed in the "Green Revolution" ($6). Extensive beer list. Open daily 11am-10pm; in winter M-Sa 11am-9pm.

Virginia Street Diner, 1430 Virginia St. (756-3475), a few blocks west of U.S. 101 in North Bend. Step back into the 50s when the booths were a sparkly red and the prices were right. A $1 bottomless coffee cup will keep you up as you cruise through town. Try the homemade meatloaf ($6.35) or the all-you-can-eat salad bar ($4.75). And say hi to Marilyn. Open daily 6am-10pm.

Cheryn's Seafood Restaurant and Pie House (888-3251), at the east end of Charleston Bridge in Charleston. The menu boasts the widest selection of seafood in town, from $7 calamari to $20 steamed lobster. Look at the city maps beneath the transparent table cover to find your way around town. Open daily 8am-9pm; in winter daily 8am-8pm.

Kaffe 101, 134 S. Broadway St. (267-4894), in Coos Bay next to the visitor center. The fireplace, chintz chairs, and book-strewn shelves echo an English tea house. Fireside nibblettes like bagels (with cream cheese $1.35) and chocolate mint brownies ($1.50) served. An appropriate spot to order an espresso ($1.50-3.25) and pick up a dust-strewn copy of the *Divine Comedy*. Open M-Th 7am-9pm, F-Sa 7am-10pm; in winter M-Th 7am-8pm, F-Sa 7am-10pm.

Basin Cafe, 4555 King Fisher Dr. (888-5227), off Boat Basin Dr., across the parking lot from the boats toward the end of the Charleston harbor. You can smell the sea breeze in the front, hear the grease spit in the back, and sit down to a $3.25 stack of 3 pancakes at 5am. Blow it all on local fresh cut tuna ($7.25), or save a buck and take the burger basket spilling over with fries ($5). Open Su-Th 5am-8pm, F-Sa 5am-9pm.

Cranberry Sweets, 1005 Newmark (888-9824), in Coos Bay. This sucrose wonderland is half-shop, half-factory. Free candy samples are tiny but abundant; nosh while watching amorphous chocolate sludge miraculously transformed into shapely pieces of candy. Open M-Sa 9am-5:30pm, Su 11am-4pm.

SIGHTS AND OUTDOORS

Sunset Bay, 3½ mi. west of Bastendorff Beach on Cape Arago State Hwy., has been rated one of the top 10 American beaches, and for good reason. The impressive beach is nestled between two low, pincer-like cliffs which shelter the bay. The remaining ocean front is calmed by natural rock outcroppings. Water temperatures are a bit warmer than the frigid North Pacific norm, making Sunset Bay popular for swimming.

The magnificent **Shore Acres State Park** (888-3732) rests a mile beyond Sunset Bay on the Cape Arago Hwy. *(Open daily 8am-9pm; in winter daily 8am-dusk. $3 per car. Wheelchair accessible.)* Once the estate of local lumber lord Louis J. Simpson, the park contains elaborate botanical gardens that survived after the mansion was razed. The egret sculptures are a more recent addition, courtesy of artistic inmates from the state penitentiary. A lovely rose garden boasting rows of award-winning flowers lies hidden in the back. Throughout December, the flowers are festooned with strings of over 150,000 lights, and the park serves complimentary cocoa and hot cider.

Farther south at the end of the highway is breezy **Cape Arago,** notable for its creature-encrusted tide pools. Paved paths lead out toward the tip of the cape and provide an excellent view of wildlife on **Shell Island,** ¼ mi. offshore. The island is a rookery for elephant and harbor seals. Paths here are closed to the public to prevent habitat destruction, but the island can be spotted from a pull-out ½ mi. before the cape. Bring binoculars. Blue whales, sea lions, and a number of noteworthy seabirds also make occasional appearances.

Fishing enthusiasts should hop on board with **Bob's Sportfishing,** P.O. Box 5018 (888-4241 or 800-628-9633), operating out of a small building at the west end of the Charleston Boat Basin, or **Betty Kay Charters,** P.O. Box 5020 (888-9021 or 800-752-6303), a stone's throw away on the water's edge. *(Both run six-hour fishing trips leaving daily at 6am and 12:30pm. $55 with a $6.75 daily license. Betty Kay also rents crab rings for $5 per day with a $15 deposit.)*

Four miles south of Charleston up Seven Devils Rd., the **South Slough National Estuarine Research Reserve** (888-5558; http://www.southsloughestuary.com) is one of the most fascinating and underappreciated venues on the central coast. *(Open daily June-Aug. 8:30am-4:30pm; Sept-May M-F 8:30am-4:30pm. Trails open year-round, daily dawn-dusk. For a summer calendar, write P.O. Box 5417, Charleston 97420.)* Spreading out from a small interpretive visitor center, almost 7 sq. mi. of mixed salt and fresh water estuaries nurture all kinds of wildlife, from sand shrimp to deer. **Hiking trails** weave through the sanctuary; take a lunch and commune with the blue heron. Maps are free at the visitor center and guided walks are given in the summer. Canoe tours ($10) are available, if you have your own canoe.

One of the most impressive sights of Oregon's coastal region lies 24½ miles inland from Coos Bay, at **Golden and Silver Falls State Park.** From the southern end of Coos Bay, take the Eastside-Allegany exit off U.S. 101, and follow it for about an hour along a narrow, gravelly road. Three trails lead up a hill to the awesome sight of **Golden Falls,** a 210 ft. drop into the abyss. Along the top trail, beautiful thin sheets of water cascade down the more aesthetically-pleasing **Silver Falls.** Though open year-round, the park is most exciting in winter when the rains saturate the falling river.

EVENTS

For two weeks in mid-July, Coos Bay basks in the glory of the **Oregon Coast Music Festival,** P.O. Box 663 (267-0938), the most popular event on the coast. *(Tickets $11-15, or a few bucks more if bought by phone: 269-2720 or 800-676-7563.)* Ask at the Chamber of Commerce (see **Practical Information**, above) about unreserved ticket outlets. Art exhibits, vessel tours, and a free classical concert in Mingus Park triple cultural options in the area. This two-week music festival draws a variety of performances to Coos Bay, North Bend, Charleston, Bandon, and Reedsport, ranging from Baroque to Country but skipping Rock & Roll.

In the second week of August, Charleston hosts the **Seafood Festival** (888-8083) in the Boat Basin. In late August, Coos Bay celebrates a native fruit with the **Blackberry Arts Festival** (269-2720), when downtown rocks with square dancing, wine tasting, concerts, and crafts. In September, Oregon remembers one of its favorite native sons in the **Steve Prefontaine 10K Memorial Run** (269-1103), named after the great Olympic athlete who died in an automobile accident. The race draws dozens of world-class runners to the area. *(Entrance fee $12-15.)*

■ Bandon

Despite a steady flow of tourists in the summer, the small fishing town of Bandon-by-the-Sea has refrained from breaking out the pastels and making itself up like an amusement park. Outdoor activities abound near Bandon. Though a bit commercial, the **West Coast Game Park** (347-3106), 7 mi. south of Bandon on U.S. 101, is nonetheless a surprisingly delightful stop, especially for the young-at-heart. Walk among llamas and rams, pet baby black bears, and hold skunks. (*Let's Go* is not responsible for the actions of held skunks.) (In summer open daily 9am-7:30pm; rest of year, 9am-5pm. Hours vary; call ahead. $7, over 60 $6, ages 7-12 $5.75, ages 2-6 $4.25.) Pleasant transportation options include strolling around **Old Town**, exploring the beaches on a horse from **Bandon Beach Riding Stables** (347-3423; 1hr. trip $20), or driving the beach loop road that leaves from Old Town and joins U.S. 101 5 mi. south. The loop is well-marked and passes **Table Rock, Elephant Rock,** and **Face Rock,** some of the coast's most impressive offshore outcroppings.

Bandon is 24 mi. south of Coos Bay and 27 mi. north of Port Orford on U.S. 101. **Greyhound** (267-4436) stops thrice daily at the **Sea Star Hostel,** once on the way north and twice going south. The **Chamber of Commerce,** 300 SE 2nd St., P.O. Box 1515 (347-9616), in the Old Town next to U.S. 101, gives out plenty of brochures and assistance. (Open daily Memorial Day-Oct. 10am-5pm; rest of year, 10am-4pm.) The **post office** in Bandon is at 105 12th St. SE. (800-275-8777; open M-F 8:30am-4:30pm). **ZIP Code:** 97411-9999. **Area code:** 541.

Bandon offers a nice budget option in the rambling **Sea Star Hostel (HI-AYH),** 375 2nd St. (347-9632), on the right as you enter Old Town from the north. Comfortable bunkrooms, enclosed courtyard, kitchen, laundry room, noon check-out, and an open-24-hours policy make for a relaxed and friendly place to pass the night. ($13, nonmembers $16, ages 5-12 $6 and can only stay in family rooms; 2 members for $28; nonmembers $34; guest house $53-90.) The pleasantly old-fashioned **Bandon Wayside Motel** (347-3421), on Rte. 42 south, is just off U.S. 101 (singles $32; doubles $36). Two miles north of town and across the bridge, **Bullard's Beach State Park** (347-2209) houses the **Coquille River Lighthouse,** built in 1896. The park has 185 sites tucked into the sand and pines. The primitive "horse sites" make a peaceful place to park a steed. Campfire talks are given on summer evenings from Tuesday to Saturday ($19; yurts $27; hiker/biker sites $4).

Known as the "Cranberry Capital of Oregon," Bandonians celebrate the fall harvest with the annual **Cranberry Festival** (347-9616) complete with parade and food fair. For a tasty and healthy morsel, step into **Mother's Natural Grocery and Deli,** 975 U.S. 101 (347-4086), near the junction with Rte. 42 south, where four vegetarian nori rolls ($3) and a well-stuffed carrot/hummus pita pocket ($3.75) highlight the menu (open M-Sa 10am-6pm). The best seafood in town is at **Bandon Boatworks,** 275 Lincoln St. SW (347-2111), through Old Town and out South Jetty Rd. The dining room may be simple, but the picturesque view of the ocean and the sauteed, baked, and fried fish speak for themselves. Lunches ($6-8) are more affordable than dinners ($10-17), when the Boatworks breaks out the wine glasses for a more elegant affair. Be sure to try out the best damn cranberry breads ($4 per loaf) in this, the best damn cranberry town. (Open M-Sa 11:30am-9pm, Su 11am-8:30pm; in winter M-Sa 11:30am-2:30pm and 5-9pm, Su 11am-8:30pm.)

■ Port Orford

Port Orford supports a homey and healthy community, protected by the prosperity of its larger, more touristed neighbors. The town lies several miles south of **Cape Blanco,** the westernmost point in Oregon. **Cape Blanco State Park,** 5 mi. west of U.S. 101, has a campground high on the hill and a road leading down to the beach. The very tip of the cape is capped with a 245ft. functioning lighthouse, open to the public (Th-M 10am-3:30pm). Also in the park is the historic **Hughes House,** now in its 101st year, beautifully maintained and laden with charms from the past. Some of the best views in the area are from **Battle Rock,** a seaside park in town where whales pass close by during December and spring migrations. The beaches are littered with agate, easy to find at low tide when it sparkles in the sun.

Port Orford is 26 mi. south of Bandon and 30 mi. north of **Gold Beach** on U.S. 101. In town, U.S. 101 changes its name to Oregon St. **Greyhound** stops at the Circle K, across from the Port Orford Motel, with two buses per day to Portland ($39) and two to San Francisco, CA ($59). Port Orford's **Chamber of Commerce,** P.O. Box 637 (332-8055), lazes in the parking lot overlooking the bay (open M-F 9am-5pm, Sa-Su 10am-5pm). The **post office** is at 311 W. 7th St. (332-4251), at Jackson St. (open M-F 8:30am-1pm and 2-5pm). **ZIP Code:** 97465. **Area code:** 541.

For those traveling by bus, the fluorescent green **Port Orford Inn,** 1034 Oregon St. (332-0212), at U.S. 101, is hard to miss. The older, cramped rooms sport cable TV, phones, heaters (1 person $34; 2 people $39; 3 people $41). Several blocks south and around the bend, the **Shoreline Motel** (332-2903; fax 332-5901), on U.S. 101, sits across the road from dramatic Battle Rock and the bay. The bathrooms are small, but the rooms are big and well-kept with cable TV, heaters (1 person $36, 2 people $38, 2 beds $42; winter rates drop $8; pets free).

Two nearby campgrounds, one to the north and one to the south, offer the most peaceful and convenient access to the shore. **Cape Blanco State Park** (332-6774), 6 mi. north of Port Orford and 4 mi. west of U.S. 101, nestles in a grove of pines just south of the lighthouse-dominated cape. Victors of the 3 mi. hike up the mountain gain a tremendous and breath-sucking panorama of the entire area. (58 sites: standard sites $16; full hookups $18; hiker/biker $4.) Six miles south of Port Orford, where the highway ducks back behind mountains, **Humbug Mountain State Park** (332-6774) has 108 tightly packed sites in the crisp green shade of deciduous trees. (Tents $16; water and electricity $18; hiker/biker $4. Showers and flush toilets. No Scrooge in sight.)

Health food nuts luck out in Port Orford. **Sisters Natural Grocery and Cafe,** 832 U.S. 101 (332-3640), makes a case for itself with four lovely tables and plenty of granola. Come in the morning for garden sausage and a couple of eggs from the chickens next door, or lunch on a vegetable sandwich of fresh sourdough rye (both $3). (Cafe open Tu-F 8am-3pm. Grocery store open M-F 10am-6pm, Sa 10am-5pm.)

▓ Brookings

Brookings is one of the few coastal towns that remains relatively tourist-free. Here, trinket shops do not elbow out hardware stores and warehouses. Even so, Brookings is more of a stopover on the way to its surrounding beaches and parks than a destination in itself. Those beaches are among the most unspoiled on the Oregon Coast, sitting in a region often called Oregon's "banana belt" due to its mild climate. Warm weather is not rare in January, and Brookings' beautiful blossoms bloom early.

PRACTICAL INFORMATION Brookings is the southernmost stop on U.S. 101 (called Chetco Avenue in town) before California. Strictly speaking, there are two towns here, separated by the **Chetco River**—Brookings on the north side and **Harbor** to the south. They share everything, including a chamber of commerce, and are referred to collectively as Brookings. The **Greyhound** station is at 601 Railroad Ave., at Tanbark (469-3326; open M-F 8:45am-noon and 4pm-6:30pm, Sa 8:45am-noon). Trains run to: Portland ($38) and San Francisco, CA ($48). The **Brookings Welcome Center,** 1650 U.S. 101 (469-4117), maintains an office just north of town (open May-Sept. M-Sa 8am-6pm, Su 9am-5pm; in Apr. and Oct. M-Sa 8am-5pm, Su 9am-5pm). The **Chamber of Commerce,** 16330 Lower Harbor Rd. (469-3181 or 800-535-9469), is across the bridge to the south, a short distance off the highway (open M-F 8am-5pm; in winter closed Sa and Su). The **Chetco Ranger Station,** 555 5th St. (469-2196), distributes info on the neighboring part of the **Siskiyou National Forest** (open M-F 8am-4:30pm). **Fely's Cafe & Laundromat,** 85 Beach Front Rd. (412-0350) lets you watch your laundry toss as you chow down on the best burger in town (open daily 6am-7pm; wash $1, dry 25¢ per 10min.). The **post office** is at 711 Spruce St. (800-275-8777; open M-F 9am-4:30pm). **ZIP Code:** 97415. **Area Code:** 541.

ACCOMMODATIONS AND CAMPGROUNDS Motel rooms and campsites alike are costly in Brookings though motel rates tend to drop about $10 in winter. **The Bonn Motel,** 1216 U.S. 101, (469-2161), is, in fact, bonny. Its three low buildings, recently refurbished, sport a row of hydrangeas behind each room. Its heated indoor pool and sauna are rarities in Brookings (singles $38; doubles $48; less in winter). Down the road, the **Beaver State Motel,** 437 U.S. 101 (469-5361), provides spiffier accommodations for a few dollars more. The bedspreads actually match the curtains (singles $42; doubles $49; double with two beds $59; less in winter).

  Harris Beach State Park Campground (469-2021 or 800-452-5687), at the north edge of Brookings, has 63 tent sites in a grand natural setting. The campground is set back in the trees behind a beach which looks across a narrow waterway toward a 21-acre hunk of uninhabited rock and pines known as **Goat Island.** The park is equipped with showers and handicapped facilities; make reservations for stays between Memorial Day and Labor Day (open year-round; sites $16; with full hookup $19; hiker/biker sites $4). For campsites off the beaten path, travel 15 mi. east of Brookings on **North Bank Road** to the charming **Little Redwood Campground,** located in a big redwood forest alongside a burbling, scurrying salamander-filled creek (15 sites: $8; drinking water and pit toilet). Several other campgrounds along that same road are free but have no water. For information, contact the Chetco Ranger Station (see **Practical Information,** above).

FOOD A fishing town at heart, Brookings can batter up a flounder with the best of 'em. A number of salty seafood spots can be found near the harbor, among them the local favorite **Oceanside Diner,** 16403 Lower Harbor Rd. (469-7971), which unites loggers and fisherfolk for pancakes that truly fill the whole pan ($3.75). All servings are more than generous; order the "oyster sandwich" ($6.50) for your significant other (open Th-M 4am-8:30pm, Tu-W 4am-3pm). The previously mentioned **Fely's Cafe & Laundromat,** 85 Beach Front Rd. (412-6350), is right on the shoreline. Chow down on a burger as you watch your laundry toss in the best dryer in town (open daily 6am-6pm). For delicious Mexican food, stick to the highway and head for **Los Amigos,** 541 U.S. 101 (469-4102). The plain, baby-blue exterior may not be eye-catching, but the $4.25 super burrito, $5.75 pork tamale, and 30¢ corn tortillas are thoroughly tongue-tempting. Domestic bottles are only $1.50 (open M-Sa 11am-8pm, Su noon-8pm).

SIGHTS, EVENTS, AND OUTDOORS Brookings is known statewide for its flowers. In **Azalea Park,** downtown, large native and non-native azaleas, some more than 300 years old, encircle pristine lawns. *(Azaleas bloom Apr.-June. Free.)* Two rare weeping spruce trees also grace the park's grounds. The pride of Brookings is its **Azalea Festi-val** (469-3181), held in Azalea Park during Memorial Day weekend. The **Chetco Val-**

ley Historical Society Museum, 15461 Museum Rd. (469-6651), 2½ mi. south of the Chetco River, has exhibits on the patchwork quilts of settlers, historic documents, and Native American basketwork. *(Open May-Sept. W-Su noon-5pm; Oct.-Apr. F-Su noon-5pm. Free, but donations welcome.)* The museum is hard to miss; just look for **the nation's second largest cypress** tree out front.

   Boardman State Park enfolds U.S. 101 for 8 mi. north of Brookings; overlooks and picnic sites provide fantastic views of the coast. If you're heading north from Brookings by bicycle, take scenic **Carpenterville Road,** the only highway out of town before U.S. 101 was built. The twisty, 13½ mi. road features beautiful ocean views. Thirty miles north of Brookings in **Gold Beach,** you can ride a mail boat up the **Rogue River. Mail Boat Hydro-Jets** (247-7033 or 800-458-3511) offers 64, 80, and 104 mi. whitewater daytrips lasting 6 to 7½ hours. *(Open May-Oct. Prices start at $30.)*

INLAND VALLEYS

While jagged cliffs and gleaming surf draw tourists to the coast, many Oregonians choose the inland Willamette and Rogue River Valleys for their vacation destinations. Vast tracts of fertile land support agriculture, and for decades the immense forests maintained a healthy timber industry. In recent years, however, a call to save what's left of Oregon's forests and wildlife has divided the state's population; the issue of the spotted owl is still tense (see p. 54). While the fortunes of the timber industry are uncertain, tourism is definitely a growth industry in small-town Oregon.

👋 HIGHLIGHTS OF OREGON'S INLAND VALLEYS

- Thousands flock for artistic fulfillment to the **Shakespeare Festival** (see p. 109) in **Ashland** and the **Bach Festival** (see p. 122) in **Eugene.**
- **Jacksonville** (see p. 113), a tiny town resurrected by its history, has a particularly intriguing **museum** (see p. 114).
- Once a thriving area for drug abuse, the scenic **Cougar Hot Springs** (see p. 121) are still chill, and **Oregon Caves National Monument** (see p. 116) is trippy, too.

GETTING AROUND

I-5 runs north-south across Oregon to the west of the Cascades, traversing agricultural and forest land punctuated by a few urban centers. The **Rogue River Valley,** running north from Ashland to Grants Pass, is hot and dry in summer. Eugene rests at the southern end of the temperate **Willamette River Valley.** This carpet of agricultural land extends 20 mi. on either side of the river, and continues 80 mi. north until the outskirts of Portland. It's possible to drive Oregon's 305 mi. stretch of I-5 from tip to toe in less than six hours, but lead-footed outsiders be warned—most Oregonians obey speed limits, and fines have recently skyrocketed.

■ Ashland

Set near the California border, Ashland mixes hippies and history to create an unlikely but perfect stage for the world-famous Oregon Shakespeare Festival. From mid-February to October, drama devotees can choose from 11 plays performed in Ashland's three elegant theaters. Shakespearean and contemporary productions draw connoisseurs and casual observers alike. The town has happily embraced the festival, giving rise to such Bard-bandwagon businesses as "All's Well Herbs and Vitamins," but also fostering a vibrant community of artists, actors, and Shakespeare buffs. Culture comes with a price, but low-cost accommodations and tickets reward those who investigate. And though all the world may know Ashland only as a stage, Oregonians also recognize Ashland's fabulous restaurants, parks, and outdoor activities. Ashland can, and probably will, be crowded in the summer, but its small-town soul survives.

OREGON

ORIENTATION AND PRACTICAL INFORMATION

'Tis time I should inform thee farther.

—The Tempest, I.ii

Ashland is located in the foothills of the Siskiyou and Cascade Ranges, 285 mi. south of Portland and 15 mi. north of the California border, near the junction of **I-5** and **Rte. 66,** which traverses 64 mi. of stunning scenery between Ashland and Klamath Falls. **Rte. 99** cuts through the middle of town on a northwest-southwest axis. Its local name changes from **N. Main St.** to **E. Main St.** at the triangular plaza, where a medley of shops and restaurants form Ashland's downtown. Farther south, Main St. changes name again to **Siskiyou Blvd.** Southern Oregon University (SOU), a few blocks down Siskiyou, is flanked by affordable motels and bland commercial restaurants.

Transportation

Buses: Greyhound (482-8803). No depot in Ashland. Pick-up and drop-off at the **BP station,** 2073 Rte. 99 north, at the north end of town. To: Portland (3 per day, $39); Sacramento, CA (3 per day, $40); and San Francisco, CA (3 per day, $48). **Green Tortoise** (800-867-8647) comes through at 4 inconvenient times per week, stopping at I-5 Exit 14 outside of the Copper Skillet Cafe on the east side of Rte. 66. To: Portland and Seattle (Tu and Sa 5:15am; Portland $29, Seattle $39); San Francisco, CA (Th and Su 11:45pm, $39).

Local Transportation: Rogue Valley Transportation (RVTD) in Medford, (779-2877). Schedules available at the chamber of commerce. Base fare $1, over 62 and ages 10-17 50¢, under 10 free. The #10 bus serving Ashland runs daily every 30min. 5am-6pm between the transfer station at 200 S. Front St. in Medford and the plaza in Ashland. Also to: Jacksonville (bus #30, 4 per day, $1). Local buses loop through Ashland every 15min. (25¢).

Taxis: Yellow Cab (482-3065). $2 initial charge, $2 per mile. 24hr.

Car Rental: Budget, 3038 Biddle Rd. (779-0488), in Medford.

Visitor and Financial Services

Visitor Information: Chamber of Commerce, 110 E. Main St. (482-3486). A friendly staff answers phones and dishes out free play schedules and brochures, several of which contain small but adequate **maps.** Oddly, the best maps of Ashland are in the to-go menu at **Omar's,** 1380 Siskiyou Blvd. (482-1281). The chamber does not sell tickets to performances. Open M-F 9am-5pm. The chamber also staffs an **info booth** in the center of the plaza. Open in summer, M-Sa 10am-6pm and Su 11am-5pm.

Outdoor Information: Ashland District Ranger Station, 645 Washington St. (482-3333), off Rte. 66 by Exit 14 on I-5. Provides hiking, mountain biking, and other outdoor info, including words of wisdom on the Pacific Crest Trail and choice camping areas. Open M-F 8am-4:30pm.

Bank: Wells Fargo Bank, 67 East Main St. (488-0928). Full-service bank with ATM. Open M-F 9am-6pm.

Local Services

Equipment Rental: Ashland Mountain Supply, 31 N. Main St. (488-2749). Internal frame backpacks $8.50 per day ($100 deposit or credit card). External frame backpacks $6 per day ($50 deposit). Mountain bikes $12 per 2hr., $30 per day. Discounts for longer rentals. Open M-Sa 10am-6pm, Su 11am-5pm. **The Adventure Center,** 40 N. Main St. (488-2819 or 800-444-2819). Offers rafting trips ($65 per 4hr., $140 per day), guided bike tours ($65 for 3hr. with snacks), and bike rentals ($25 per 4hr., $35 per 8hr.).

Library: Ashland Branch Library, 410 Siskiyou Blvd. (482-1197), at Gresham St. Internet access available. Open M-Tu 10am-8pm, W-Th 10am-6pm, F-Sa 10am-5pm.

Senior Center: Hunter Park Center, 1699 Homes St. (488-5342). Lunch M-F 11:30am-12:30pm (under 60 $4, over 60 $2).

Tickets: Oregon Shakespearean Festival Box Office, 15 S. Pioneer St., P.O. Box 158, Ashland 97520 (482-4331; fax 482-8045; http://www.orshakes.org), next to the Elizabethan Theater. Rush tickets (half-price) occasionally available 30min.

before performances that are not already sold out. Ask at the box office for more options; the staff is full of tips for desperate theatergoers. The best bet, though, is to write for tickets in advance.

Laundromat: Main Street Laundromat, 370 E. Main St. (482-8042). Wash 75¢, dry 25¢ per 10min. Ms. PacMan 25¢. Open daily 8am-9pm.

Emergency and Communications

Emergency: 911. **Police:** 1155 E. Main St. (482-5211). **Fire:** 455 Siskiyou Blvd. (482-2770).

Crisis Line: 779-4357 or 888-609-HELP/4357. 24hr.

Post Office: 120 N. 1st St. (800-275-8777), at Lithia Way. Open M-F 9am-5pm. **ZIP Code:** 97520.

Internet Access: Ashland Branch Library (see above). **Ashland Community Food Store CO-OP,** 237 N. 1st St. (482-2237), has a computer terminal to the right of the entrance.

Area Code: 541.

ACCOMMODATIONS AND CAMPGROUNDS

> *Now spurs the lated traveler apace to gain the timely inn.*
> —*Macbeth, III.iii*

In winter, Ashland is a budget traveler's paradise of vacancy and low rates; in summer, hotel and B&B rates double, and the hostel bulges with people. Only rogues and peasant slaves arrive without reservations. Midsummer nights see vacant accommodations in nearby Medford (see **Medford: Accommodations,** p. 112). Note that part of Ashland's water supply contains dissolved sulfurous compounds. It is perfectly safe for drinking and bathing, but lends some bathrooms a foul and permanent odor.

🍎**Ashland Hostel,** 150 N. Main St. (482-9217; http://ashostel@cdsnet.net). Well-kept and cheery, with an air of elegance. The Victorian parlor, sturdy bunks, and a front-porch swing play host to a mixed crowd of budget travelers and theater-bound families wise to money-saving ways. $14 with any hosteling member card, $15 without. Two private rooms sleep 4 each ($37-40), and a private women's room costs $22 for 1, $30 for 2. $3 discounts and free laundry for Pacific Crest Trail hikers or touring cyclists. Laundry and kitchen facilities. Check-in 5-11pm. Lockout 10am-5pm. Curfew at midnight. Reservations advised Mar.-Oct.

Columbia Hotel, 262½ E. Main St. (482-3726 or 800-718-2530). A charming European home replete with a reading alcove and tea time in the mornings. 1½ blocks from the theaters. Spacious rooms with wood paneling, sepia-toned photos, and muted colors. No TV; bathroom and pay phone down the hall. Singles $54; doubles $59. Nov.-Feb.: singles $30; doubles $34. Mar.-May: singles $42; doubles $49. 10% discount for HI-AYH members in the off-season; children under 12 free. Call ahead.

Vista Motel, 535 Clover Lane (482-4423), just off I-5 at Exit 14, behind a BP station. Small, clean, and quiet rooms with good-sized beds and cinderblock walls. Cable TV, A/C, a small pool, and an amiable staff compensate for the outlying location. Singles $37; doubles $45. Winter and spring discounts of about $10.

Ashland Motel, 1145 Siskiyou Blvd. (482-2561 or 800-460-8858), across from the college. Clean and tidy with a pale pink façade. Spacious beds, cable TV, coin laundry, phones, A/C, and a good-sized pool. Singles $43; doubles $63. Off-season $30-48.

Mt. Ashland Campground, 9 mi. west of I-5 south at Exit 6. Follow signs to Mt. Ashland Ski Area and take the high road from the far west end of the lot, at the sign for Grouse Gap Snowpeak. Exquisitely situated on the side of a mountaintop, looking south across the valley to Mt. Shasta. Seven primitive sites set in the high grass. Fire pits and vault toilets, but no drinking water. Free, but seasonal.

FOOD

Give them great meals of beef and iron and steel, they will eat like wolves and fight like devils.

—Henry V, III.vii

The incredible selection of foods available on North and East Main St. has earned the plaza a culinary reputation independent of the festival. Even the ticketless come from miles around to dine in Ashland's excellent (though expensive) restaurants. Beware the pre-show rush—a downtown dinner planned for 6:30pm can easily become a late-night affair. Many businesses close at 8:30 or 9pm, when the theater wave has receded into the theaters. **Ashland Community Food Store CO-OP,** 237 N. 1st St. (482-2237), at A St., has a lively spirit and a great selection of organic produce and natural foods, not to mention Internet access (open M-Sa 8am-9pm, Su 9am-9pm; 5% senior discount). Standard, less expensive groceries are available at **Safeway,** 585 Siskiyou Blvd. (482-4495; open daily 6am-midnight).

☻Geppetto's, 345 E. Main St. (482-1138). Feeding patrons for over twenty years, this local favorite is *the* spot for a late-night bite. The staff is congenial, the walls covered in baskets, and the menu conversational, offering 6 feta and spinach wontons for $3.50. Dinner specials ($13-19) are enticing, but there are smaller ticket options, too, like a pile of sauteed vegetables ($3) or the "World Famous Eggplant Burger" ($4.25). Lunches $4-8, breakfasts slightly more. Try the pesto omelette ($7.50). Connected to the loungin' Beau Club (see **Nightlife,** below) next door. Open daily 8am-midnight. Wheelchair accessible.

Señor Sam's, 1634 Ashland St. (488-1262), in the Ashland Shopping Center. A local haven for lovers of Mexican cuisine, Sam's takes pride in its "No lard, no MSG" cooking. The unwieldy but delicious "Big Burrito" ($4.70) necessitates the eco-friendly silverware provided. Bite into the "Meaty Quesadilla" ($4.25) while viewing the owner's ubiquitous collection of ceramic parrots, handpicked from Tijuana. Open daily 11am-9:30pm. Wheelchair accessible.

Ashland Creek Bar & Grill, 92½ N. Main St. (482-4131). Popular with the locals, boasting "Ashland's Largest Outdoor Creekside Dining Area." The traditional grill menu includes vegetarian dishes like the "Veggie Lover's Sandwich" ($5.50). Several outdoor concerts in the spring and fall cater to local college students on Sunday afternoons, while Th-Sa nights feature local artists for the 21 and over crowd (cover $1-7). Open daily 11am-2am.

Brothers Restaurant, 95 N. Main St. (482-9671). A block off the trampled tourist track, this New York-style deli and cafe mostly feeds locals. Some offbeat selections like the zucchini burger ($4.50) mingle with more traditional deli fare of sandwiches ($7-10) and bagel and cream cheese ($2.25). Open M and W-F 7am-2pm, Tu 7am-8pm, Sa and Su 7am-3pm. Wheelchair accessible.

Greenleaf Restaurant, 49 N. Main St. (482-2808). Healthy, delicious food, right on the plaza with creekside seating out back. Omelettes and fritattas are a bargain in the morning for $5-6.50. A tremendous array of salads ($1.50-9.50), pastas ($3.50-8.50), and spuds are meals in themselves ($2.25-6.50). Chomp inside or take it down the block for a picnic in nearby Lithia Park. Open daily 8am-9pm; off-season M 8am-2pm, Tu-Su 8am-8pm. Closed Jan.

Five Rivers, 139 E. Main St., one flight up from street level (488-1883). Slip upstairs to the warm smells of Eastern spices and delicious Indian cuisine. Indian artwork and music set an intimate tone. Entrees $5.50-11.50; veggie options all below $7. Daily all-you-can-eat lunch buffet $5.95. Open daily 11am-3pm and 5-10pm.

Evo's Java House, 376 E. Main St. (482-2261). Chill out away from the crowds with a bowl of coffee ($1) or a Zaffiro Smoothie (blackberries, blueberries, and OJ; $2.50). Kollege krazies and kool kats hang here. Live jazz attracts a crowd every Sunday night. Open daily 7am-10pm.

THE SHAKESPEARE FESTIVAL

Why, this is very midsummer madness.

—*Twelfth Night, III.iv*

The Oregon Shakespeare Festival (482-4331; fax 482-8045; http://www.orshakes.org) was the brainchild of local college teacher Angus Bowmer, and began in 1935 with two Shakespeare plays performed by schoolchildren in the **Chautauqua Theater** as an evening complement to daytime boxing matches. Today, professional actors perform 11 plays in repertory. As the selections have become more modern, Shakespeare's share has shrunk to five plays; the other six are classical and contemporary dramas. Performances run on the three Ashland stages from mid-February through October, and any boxing is now over the extremely scarce tickets ("Lay on, Macduff. And damn'd be him that first cries, 'Hold, enough!'"—*Macbeth*, V.vii). On the side of the Chautauqua theater hulks the 1200-seat **Elizabethan Stage,** an outdoor theater modeled after an 18th-century London design. Open only from mid-June through mid-October, the Elizabethan hosts three Shakespeare plays per season. The **Angus Bowmer Theater** is a 600-seat indoor stage that shows one Shakespeare play and a variety of dramas. The newest of the theaters is the intimate **Black Swan,** home to one Shakespeare play and some small, offbeat productions.

Due to the tremendous popularity of the festival, *ticket purchases are recommended six months in advance.* General **mail-order and phone ticket sales** begin in January. Tickets cost $15-41 in spring and fall, $20.25-47 in summer, plus a $4 handling fee per order for phone, fax, or mail orders. For complete ticket information write Oregon Shakespeare Festival, P.O. Box 158, Ashland, OR 97520. Children under 5 not admitted to any of the shows.

Last-minute theatergoers should not abandon hope. The **box office** at 15 S. Pioneer St. opens at 9:30am every day during the theater season but prudence demands arriving earlier. Local patrons have been known to leave their shoes in line to hold their places, and this tradition should be respected. At 9:30am, the box office releases any unsold tickets for the day's performances. When no tickets are available limited priority numbers are given out. These entitle their holders to a designated place in line when the precious few returned tickets are released (1pm for matinees, 6pm for evening shows). At these times, the box office also sells twenty clear-view **standing room tickets** for sold-out shows on the Elizabethan Stage ($11, available on the day of the show).

Unofficial ticket transactions also take place just outside the box office, "on the bricks," though scalping is illegal. ("Off with his head!"—*Richard III*, III.iv). Ticket officials advise those buying on the bricks to check the date and time on the ticket carefully, to pay only the face value, and to check with the box office before purchasing any tickets that have been altered. Half-price **rush tickets** are sometimes available an hour before performances that are not already sold out. Some **half-price student-senior matinees** are offered in the spring and in October, and all three theaters hold full-performance **previews** in the spring and summer. Plays scheduled for the 1999 season (subject to change) include *Othello, Much Ado About Nothing,* and *Henry IV Part 2.*

Backstage tours provide a wonderful glimpse of the festival from behind the curtain (Tu-Su 10am.; $9-10, ages 5-17 $6.75-7.50, children under 5 not admitted). Tour guides (usually actors or technicians) divulge all kinds of anecdotes—from bird songs during an outdoor Hamlet to the ghastly events which transpire every time they do "that Scottish play." Tours last almost two hours and usually leave from the Black Swan. Admission includes a trip to the **Exhibit Center** for a close-up look at sets and costumes. (Open Tu-Su 10am-4pm; in fall and spring, 10:30am-1:30pm; without tour $2, ages 5-17 $1.50.) In mid June, the **Feast of Will** celebrates the annual opening of the Elizabethan Theater. Dinner and merry madness in Lithia Park start at 6pm (call for exact date; tickets $16).

OREGON

SIGHTS, ENTERTAINMENT, AND OUTDOORS

Mischief, thou art afoot, take thou what course thou wilt!
—Julius Caesar, III.ii

Before it imported Shakespeare, Ashland was naturally blessed with **lithia water** whose dissolved lithium salts were reputed to have miraculous healing powers. (It is said that only one other spring in the world has a higher lithium concentration. Depression, be gone!) The mineral springs have given their name to the well-tended **Lithia Park,** west of the plaza off Main St. To quaff the vaunted water itself, hold your nose (the water also contains dissolved sulfur salts) and head for the circle of fountains in the center of the plaza. Free concerts, readings, and educational nature walks occur nearly every day, in and around the park's hiking trails, Japanese garden, and swan ponds by Ashland Creek. Events are listed in brochures at the Chamber of Commerce (see **Practical Information,** above).

Culture remains in Ashland even after the festival ends ("Give me excess of it, that, surfeiting, the appetite may sicken and so die."—*Twelfth Night*, I.i). Local and touring artists love to play to the town's enthused audiences. The **Oregon Cabaret Theater,** P.O. Box 1149 (488-2902), at 1st and Hagardine St. stages light musicals in a cozy former church with drinks, dinners, and Sunday brunch. (*Box office open M and W-Sa 11am-6:30pm, Su 4-6:30pm. Tickets $12-21. Reservations required for dinner.*) Small groups, such as the **Actor's Theater of Ashland** (535-5250), **Ashland Community Theatre** (482-7532), and the theater department at **Southern Oregon University (SOU)** (552-6346) also raise the curtains sporadically year-round. When in town, the traveling **Rogue Valley Symphony** performs in the Music Recital Hall at SOU and at Lithia Park. In July and August, the **State Ballet of Oregon** graces the stage on Mondays at 7:30pm. **The Ashland City Band** (488-5340) fires itself up at the same time on Thursdays in Lithia Park. In late June, the **Palo Alto Chamber Orchestra** (482-4331) gives hit performances in the Elizabethan Theatre, weather permitting. (*Tickets $13.*) Contact the Chamber of Commerce for a current schedule of events.

If your muscles demand a little abuse after all this theater-seat lolly-gagging, hop on the **Pacific Crest Trail** at Grouse Gap. Take Exit 6 off I-5 and follow the signs along the Mt. Ashland Access Rd. At the top of the 9 mi. road is **Mount Ashland,** a small community-owned ski area on the north face of the mountain, with 23 runs. (*Contact Ski Ashland, P.O. Box 220; 482-2897. For snow conditions, call 482-2754. Open daily Thanksgiving to mid-Apr., 9am-4pm. Night skiing Th-Sa 4-10pm. Day tickets weekdays $21, seniors and ages 9-12 $15; weekends $26, seniors and ages 9-12 $19. Full rental $15, snowboard and boots $20.*) Over 100 mi. of free cross-country trails surround Mt. Ashland. **Bull Gap Trail,** which starts from the ski area's parking lot, is also good for skiing, or for biking after the snow has melted. It winds 2½ mi. down 1100 ft. to the paved Tollman Creek Rd., 15 mi. south of Siskiyou Blvd.

Scads of kids and kids-at-heart flock to the 280ft. **waterslide** at **Emigrant Lake Park** (776-7001). (*Open daily 10am-sunset, waterslide noon-6pm. 10 slides for $5 or unlimited slides for $12, plus a $3 entry fee.*) The park is also a popular place for boating, hiking, swimming, and fishing. Although only 6 mi. east of town on Rte. 66, the lake is in a different geological region from Ashland. Hidden in the parched hills that surround it, the lake is a part of the Great Basin, where meandering cows graze freely and render the lake water unsuitable to drink.

BARS AND CLUBS

Come, come; good wine is a good familiar creature, if it be well us'd.
—Othello, II.iii

Kat Wok, 66 E. Main St. (482-0787). This alternative club and restaurant adds style and eccentricity to Ashland's post-show scene, catering to the less traditional with DJs, live music, and a glow-in-the-dark pool table. The only dance club in Ashland, featuring the only publicly accessible metal cage. Quasi-Asian cuisine stars alongside a full bar and micropints. 21 and over only. Open daily 5:30pm-2am.

The Black Sheep, 51 N. Main St. (482-6414; http://www.theblacksheep.com), upstairs on the plaza. This English pub serves its brew in bulk: all pints are imperial (20 oz.) and cost $4. The "eclectic fayre" features freshly baked scones and jam ($3.50), salt and vinegar "chips" ($3), and herbs grown in the British owner's bonny backyard. Listen to a bard's tale on the fireside couch. Open daily 11am-1am. Minors welcome "to dine" until 11pm.

Beau Club, 345 E. Main St. (482-4185), right next to Geppetto's (see **Food,** above). The local hangout for the mellow. A laid-back atmosphere attracts the young and old alike and the jukebox jams with tunes for everyone. Pool and beer ($2.50-3), with food available from the Geppetto's menu next door. Add some wenches, and it's a club Falstaff could love. Open daily 11:30am-2:30am.

Siskiyou Micro Pub, 31B Water St. (482-7718). Replacing the Rouge Brewery and Public House, this spacious "Hell or Highwater Pub" promises a bawdy time. Wooden tables inside, creekside patio seating outside. 11 micros on tap (pints $3), bottled beers ($3), and full restaurant fare. Live music every Saturday night at 9pm is usually free. Thursday nights open mic. Open Su-Th 11:30am-midnight, F-Sa 11am-1am; in winter Su-Th 4pm-midnight, F-Sa 4pm-1am.

■ Medford

Once a mere Jacksonville satellite, Medford lured the 19th-century railroad barons with 25 grand in under-the-table cash, snagging the railroad lines and the county seat. Jacksonville was left in the dust with outmoded horse-and-buggy transport. Today, Medford is a rapidly expanding but nondescript community of cheap motels and fast food. The visitor center motto is "We Hug Visitors in Medford"—accept the hug, snag some shelter, then slip off to Jacksonville or Ashland for some real character.

ORIENTATION AND PRACTICAL INFORMATION

Medford straddles **I-5** at its intersection with **Rte. 238** in Southern Oregon. **Main Street** (I-5 in town) intersects **Central Ave.** in the heart of the city, then proceeds west to Jacksonville. Grants Pass is 30 mi. northwest, Ashland 12 mi. to the southeast. Both towns are accessible by I-5 or **Rte. 99.**

Buses: Greyhound, 212 N. Bartlett St. (779-2103), at 5th St. To: Portland (9 per day; $32); Sacramento, CA (8 per day, $43); and San Francisco, CA (6 per day, $49). Open M-Sa 5:30am-7pm and Su 5:30-10:30am and 12:30pm-7:30pm.

Public Transportation: Rogue Valley Transportation (RVTD), 3200 Crater Lake Ave. (779-2877). Connects Medford with Jacksonville, Ashland, and other cities. Buses leave hourly from 200 S. Front St., at 10th St. (M-F 6am-6pm). Service to Ashland takes 35 minutes. Fare $1, seniors and under 18 50¢, under 9 free.

Taxis: Metro Cab Co. (773-6665). $2 drop, $1.80 per mile. 24hr.

Car Rental: Budget (773-7023 at the airport; 779-0488 at 3038 Biddle Rd.). Economy cars from $30 per day, $170 per week with 1400 free miles. 5% AAA, AARP discounts. Must be 21 with credit card; under 25 $7.50 extra per day. Open at airport Su-F 7am-11pm, Sa 8am-11pm; at Biddle Rd. M-F 8am-5:30pm, Sa 8am-3pm.

Visitor Information: 1314 Center Dr., Suite E (776-4021), in the Harry and David Country Village, just off I-5 at Exit 27. A plethora of free brochures. Staff is armed with fluorescent highlighters, the better to mark the maps they will give you. Open daily May-Sept. 9am-6pm; Oct.-Apr. M-Sa 9am-5pm.

Library: 413 W. Main St. (776-7281), at Oakdale Ave. Open M-Th 9:30am-8pm, F-Sa 9:30am-5pm. Internet access available.

Equipment Rental: McKenzie Outfitters, 1340 Biddle Rd. (773-5145). Internal and external frame backpacks ($15 per 3 days, $30 per week); tents (2-person per 3 days, $20); kayak set ($40 per day). Open M-F 10am-8pm, Sa 10am-6pm, Su 11am-5pm.

Emergency: 911. **Police and Fire: City Hall,** 411 W. 8th St. (770-4783), at Oakdale. **Crisis Line:** 779-4357. 24hr.

Hospital: Providence Medford Medical Center, 1111 Crater Lake Ave. (773-6611). Emergency care 24hr.
Post Office: 333 W. 8th St. (800-275-8777), at Holly St. Open M-F 8:30am-5:30pm. **ZIP Code:** 97501-9998.
Internet Access: See **Library,** above.
Area Code: 541.

ACCOMMODATIONS AND CAMPGROUNDS

The small motels that line Central and Riverside Ave. are depressingly similar, but the prices will cheer up the weary visitor from overpriced Ashland or Jacksonville. Motels along the highway are kept in better condition, but tend to charge $8-10 more. Make sure to check with the unparalleled **Ashland Hostel** (see **Ashland: Accommodations,** p. 107) for bed availability. For nearby camping, check out **Valley of the Rogue State Park,** just 18 mi. away; ask at the visitor center for directions.

Cedar Lodge, 518 N. Riverside Ave. (773-7361 or 800-282-3419). Spacious rooms, with complimentary coffee and fruit served in the office in the morning. Spiffy new section in back has microwaves and fridges (for an extra $8). Cable, pool, and a decent restaurant next door. Singles $40; doubles $45. 15% AAA and senior discounts.
Village Inn, 722 N. Riverside (773-5373). Clean, kempt rooms with expansive beds. An old building, but a good price. Cable, A/C, and free local calls. Singles $26.50; doubles $37.
Medford Oaks R.V. Campground, 7049 Rte. 140 (826-5103), 13 mi. northeast of Medford on Rte. 140. Take Rte. 62 (Exit 30 off I-5) north 6 mi. to Rte. 140 E. Look left after seven miles. An ideal campground for the city slicker, with volleyball and basketball courts, horseshoes, playgrounds, and a pool. For the more nature-embracing, there are a number of sites by the fishing pond. Two-person tent sites $12-14 per day; R.V. sites $18-23. Open year-round.

FOOD

For a rapidly expanding city, Medford has surprisingly few attractive eateries. Other than the "downtown deli" or "BK Whopper" concept, the dominant paradigms for Medford cuisine are 12 mi. away in Ashland, where locals go when they want to eat something they haven't already seen on TV. **Food 4 Less** (779-0171), on Biddle Rd. near I-5 Exit 30, has mass quantities of every food imaginable and sells it for peanuts (open 24hr.).

C.K. Tiffins, 226 E. Main St. (779-0480). "Naturally good" soups, salads, and sandwiches served in a casual, cafeteria-style space. Great place to bring your newspaper for breakfast ($1.25-3.75) or look at the vaguely impressionistic local artwork (for sale!). Downtown business crowds partake of $5 lunch specials that run the low-fat gamut from vegetable taco salad to feta, basil, and tomato pizza. No red meat. Open M-F 7am-3pm.
Las Margaritas, 12 N. Riverside (779-7628). Feast on large portions of Mexican food amid Mediterranean murals and a giant sombrero. Burritos range in price from the burrito vallarta ($10) down to the humble refried bean ($3). Friendly waitstaff might even hail you as "amigo!" Open Su-Tu 11am-10pm, F-S 11am-midnight.
Harry and David's Original Country Store, 1314 Center Dr. Suite A (776-2277), in Harry and David's Country Village, next to the visitor center. The fruit and nut capital of the known universe, this mecca of the vegetable world sells ample produce, nuts, and candies (yogurt pretzels $4.95). Open M-Sa 9am-8pm, Su 10am-7pm.

SIGHTS AND ENTERTAINMENT

Medford's location on I-5 between Grants Pass and Ashland makes it the hub of southern Oregon. Many visitors use it as a gateway to the **Shakespeare Festival** or **Jacksonville,** but the town has little appeal on its own. Oregon's past can be glimpsed at the **Southern Oregon History Center,** 106 N. Central Ave. (773-6536), at 6th St., where a new exhibit explores the history of transportation from covered wagons to the automobile. *(Open M-F 9am-5pm, Sa 1-5pm. $3, seniors and ages 6-12 $2.)* Second-hand shoppers might be delighted by the wide variety of bargains at the **Value Village,** 810 Biddle Rd. (774-9422), in Bear Creek Plaza. Perhaps the brightest spot in Medford is the recently remodeled **Craterian Ginger Rogers Theater,** 23 S. Central Ave. (779-3000). From September to April, touring Broadway productions, dance troupes, and musical acts perform in this peach-colored diamond in the rough. *(Tickets $7-37.)*

■ Jacksonville

The biggest of Oregon's gold rush boomtowns, Jacksonville played the role of rich and rowdy frontier outpost with appropriately licentious zeal. But the gold dwindled, the railroad and stagecoach lines took Jacksonville off their routes, and, in the final *coup de* (dis)*grâce,* the town lost the county seat to nearby Medford. On the brink of oblivion, Jacksonville was revitalized by sheer nostalgia. Rehabilitated in the 50s, Jacksonville is the only town in Oregon designated a "National Historic Landmark City" by the National Park Service. A downtown stroll passes century-old buildings, and during the summer, visitors come just to catch some concerts at the Britt Festival.

PRACTICAL INFORMATION To reach Jacksonville, take Rte. 238, a.k.a the **Jacksonville Highway,** southwest from Medford, or take Rte. 99 north, and follow the signs for 15 mi. Otherwise, catch the #30 **bus** in Medford (4 per day; see **Medford: Practical Information,** p. 112). Rte. 238 is **5th St.** in town and bears right on **California St.**

The **visitor center,** 185 N. Oregon St. (899-8118), at C St., is in the old railway station and souses info-seekers with directions and pamphlets (open M-F 10am-5pm, Sa 11am-5pm, Su noon-4pm). The **post office** is next door at 175 N. Oregon St. (800-275-8777; open M-F 8:30am-5pm). **ZIP Code:** 97530-9999. **Area Code:** 541.

ACCOMMODATIONS AND CAMPGROUNDS To avoid the many luxury B&Bs and lodges, stay at the **Ashland Hostel** (see **Ashland: Accommodations,** p. 459), an easy 15 mi. southeast of Jacksonville. A number of campgrounds lie 25-30 mi. southwest of town in the **Red Butte Wilderness.** Take Rte. 238 8 mi. west to Ruch, then turn left on Applegate Rd. The **Star Ranger Station,** 6941 Upper Applegate Rd. (899-1812), about 10 mi. past the turn, describes specific fees and amenities, but the campgrounds are another 7-12 mi. farther (open 8am-4:30pm). **Latagawa Cove** requires a short hike and the forethought to bring water, but it's free and right on the edge of Applegate Lake.

FOOD For a classy but casual dining experience, head for the **Bella Union,** 170 W. California St. (899-1770; http://www.bellau.com). This upscale saloon serves American favorites like pizza, pasta, and chicken, at reasonable prices ($9-16); the opportunity to dine beneath a canopy of vines out back may be worth the extra buck. The attached saloon hosts free shows with live bands, Thursday through Saturday nights. (Restaurant open M-F 11:30am-10pm, Sa 11am-10pm, Su 10am-10pm. Saloon open daily until midnight.) A cheaper and homier dining experience can be had at **The Hen House,** 230 East C St. (899-347). This local favorite offers the finest fried chicken around. Order the "Four-piece Chicken and Jojo" ($5.95) and watch the hen fry before your eyes (open daily 11am-9pm; in winter daily 11am-7pm.) The **Jacksonville Market,** 401 N. 5th St. (899-1262), serves basic grocery needs (open daily 6am-11pm).

SIGHTS A walk down California St. is an instant flashback to the 19th century. The **Beekman Bank,** at the corner of 3rd and California St., has not been touched since **Cornelius Beekman,** the town's most prominent figure, died in 1915. Down the street you can meet his "family" at the **Beekman House** (773-6536), on the corner of Laurelwood and California St., where hosts, in character and costume, will be quite charmed, my dear, to guide you through the residence. *(Tour lasts 40min. Open daily Memorial Day-Labor Day 1-5pm.)* If you see a well-dressed 19th-century gentleman in the middle of the street, it isn't a history-induced hallucination; "Mr. Beekman" often feels the urge to wander the streets of Jacksonville and bid you good tidings. The **Jacksonville Museum,** at 206 N. 5th St., in the **Old County Courthouse,** is a remarkable treasure trove of history. Those who explore the museum's fantastic collection of firearms, big game trophies, and historical photographs, can leave the kids locked up in the jail next door (now the **Children's Museum**), where delightful, hands-on exhibits make it hard to obey the "no running" rule. *(Open in summer, daily 10am-5pm; in winter W-Sa 10am-5pm, Su noon-5pm. Jacksonville Museum, Children's Museum, and Beekman House each charge $3, seniors and ages 6-12 $2. Multiple-site tickets, good for all of the above, are $7, seniors and ages 6-12 $5.)* **Stan the Trolley Man** (535-5617), a community legend, narrates a 50-minute trolley-tour which provides an excellent overview of the town's attractions, plus a chance to sit and escape the sun. *(In summer, runs from 3rd St. and California St., daily 10am-4pm on the hr. $4, under 12 $2.)*

EVENTS Jacksonville is taken over every summer by the **Britt Music Festivals,** 517 W. 10th St. (773-6077 or 800-882-7488; fax 503-776-3712; http://www.mind.net/ britt), P.O. Box 1124, Medford 97501, named after the pioneer photographer Peter Britt, whose hillside estate is the site of the event. *(Reserved and lawn tickets for single events $9-48, ages 12 and under $4-15. Order tickets early in May; beginning June 1, tickets can be purchased at the main box office at 517 W. 10th St., Sa 9am-3pm and Su. Call for Su concert and box office times. Additionally, on performance days, tickets available at the Main Pavilion at 1st and Fir St. $2 senior discounts for classical events.)* Now in its 37th year, the festival features jazz, classical, folk, country, and pop acts, as well as dance theater and musicals. 1998 saw Vince Gill, Los Lobos, Mary Chapin Carpenter, Roberta Flack, and Peter, Paul & Mary perform in the 2200-seat outdoor amphitheater. Many listeners bring picnic dinners to eat as they watch. If you want a good space on the lawn, get there early—150 seats are in front of the reserved seats, while the other 1400 are behind. Some die-hard fans even camp out the night before. Gates open at 5:45pm for most night shows.

For the ruddy-cheeked winter traveler, Jacksonville residents whoop it up with a **Victorian Christmas** celebration replete with carolers, plays, a town crier, and Father Christmas. Mrs. Claus tells stories at the **Children's Museum** (see above) while authentic chestnuts roast on a genuine open fire. Festivities begin in December. Call the **visitor center** (see **Practical Information,** above) for more details.

▌Grants Pass

Workers building a road through the Oregon mountains in 1863 were so overjoyed by the news of General Ulysses S. Grant's Civil War victory at Vicksburg that they named the town after the burly President-to-be. (What happened to the apostrophe is anybody's guess.) Grants Pass is an excellent base from which to explore the Rogue River Valley and the Illinois Valley regions. The city itself sprawls awkwardly to fill the hot, flat valley with espresso stands, fast food joints, auto shops, and parking lots. It's a fine place to sleep, but real adventure lies in the lofty mountains beckoning from just beyond the city limits.

ORIENTATION AND PRACTICAL INFORMATION

Interstate 5 curves around the northeast edge of Grants Pass on its way north to Portland. The **Rogue River** lies just south of the old downtown area, which is linked to Exit 58 off the highway by northbound **7th St.** and southbound **6th St.** Sixth St. is the divider between streets labeled East and West, and the railroad tracks (between G and F St.) divide North and South addresses. **U.S. 199** runs along the Rogue River before making the 30 mi. trip south to **Cave Junction.**

Buses: Greyhound, 460 NE Agness Ave. (476-4513), at the east end of town. To: Portland (4 per day, $38); Sacramento, CA (4 per day, $45); San Francisco, CA (4 per day, $53). A few storage lockers (75¢ per 24hr.). Open M-F 6:30am-6:15pm, S 6:30am-12:30pm.

Taxis: Grants Pass Cab (476-6444). $2.50 drop, $2 per mile. 24hr.

Car Rental: Enterprise Rent-a-Car, 1325 NE 7th St. (471-7800). Cars from $30 per day, 150 free mi. per day. Open M-F 7:30am-6pm.

Visitor Information: Chamber of Commerce, 1995 NW Vine St.(476-7717 or 800-547-5927), off 6th St., beneath the immense plaster caveman. Covers all of Josephine County. Has a list of things to do in Grants Pass (you'll need it). Open M-F 8am-5pm, Sa 9am-5pm, Su 10am-4pm; in winter closed Sa and Su.

Stalactites: Grow from the ceiling.

Independent Abilities Center: 1252 Redwood Ave. (479-4275). Open M-Th 9am-4pm, F 9am-1pm.

Senior Center: 317 NW B St. (474-5440).

Laundromat: MayBelle's Washtub, 306 SE I St. (471-1317), at 8th St. Open daily 7am-10pm. Wash $1, Dry 25¢ per 10min.

Stalagmites: Grow from the ground.

Emergency: 911. **Police:** Justice Building at 500 NW 6th St., at 6th St. (474-6370). **Josephine County Sheriff:** 474-5123.

Crisis Line: 479-4357. Helpline referral services. 24hr.

Senior Citizen Helpline: 479-4357. 24hr.

Hospital: Three Rivers Community Hospital and Health Center, 715 NW Dimmick (476-6831).

Post Office: 132 NW 6th St. (800-275-8777). Open M-F 9am-5pm. **ZIP Code:** 97526. **Area Code:** 541.

ACCOMMODATIONS AND CAMPING

The best and most unusual budget option is the Fordson Home Hostel near the Oregon Caves. Otherwise, Grants Pass supports one of every pricey franchise motel on earth. The one-of-a-kind cheapo motels are farther back from the interstate on 6th St. Since Grants Pass is a favorite trucker stop, rooms fill up quickly, especially on weekends and in August when rates hit their peak. A few convenient campgrounds offer an alternative, but even they are hardly cheap.

Fordson Home Hostel (HI-AYH), 250 Robinson Rd., Cave Junction 97523 (592-3203), 37 mi. southwest of Grants Pass on U.S. 199. This rambling old house is secluded in the forests 13 mi. from the Oregon Caves. The eccentric owner often gives tours of his 20 acres, which house 30 antique tractors, a hand-built saw mill, several antique cars, a solar-powered shower, the allegedly tallest Douglas fir, and, inevitably, a vortex. Comfortable accommodations include 2 double beds and a pull-out couch; a loft is under construction. Bicyclists, backpackers, and students with ID $10. Nonmembers can buy temporary membership to HI-AYH ($3). Free bicycle loans. 33% discounted admission to the **Oregon Caves National Monument.** Camping available ($12). Reservations mandatory; call for availability.

Hawk's Inn, 1464 NW 6th St. (479-4057), a few blocks down the street from the visitor center. The building is old, but the pool out front is a blessed sight and it's the nicest $30 room around in the summer. Cable, A/C. Singles $30; doubles $35.

Knights' Inn Motel, 104 SE 7th St. (479-5595 or 800-826-6835), by the railroad tracks. Huge rooms are clean and freshly carpeted. Cable, A/C, fake flowers, and kitschy shields on the railings. Ye olde furniture has agèd well. Singles $35; doubles $40. Prices drop $5 in winter. Reservations advised.

Valley of the Rogue State Park (582-1118; 800-452-5687 for reservations), 12 mi. east of Grants pass, off I-5 Exit 45B. Happy campers enjoy the thick green grass and the shade. Separate loops for tents ($15), electric ($17), and full hookups ($18) spread out along a 1 mi. stretch between the highway and river. Yurts also available ($25). Non-camper showers ($2) and flush toilets.

FOOD

Dining in Grants Pass is decent, if not entirely inspiring. For groceries, try **Safeway,** 115 SE 7th St. (479-4276), at G St. (open daily 6am-midnight). **The Growers' Market** (476-5375), in the parking lot between 4th and F St., is a produce-lover's Arcadia, and the largest open-air market in the state (open Sa 9am-1pm).

The Square Nail, 2185 Rogue River Hwy. (479-5132), in a log cabin. A local favorite for low prices and large portions. Check the specials board for the bargain of the moment, or stick with Hawaiian chicken, soup, salad, rice pilaf, and dessert, all for $5.75. Lunches hover around $4. Good diner breakfasts. Open M-F 5am-1pm.

Matsukaze, 1675 NE 7th St. (479-2961), at Hillcrest. The best (and only) Japanese fare in town, with bonding opportunities in booths sunk into the floor. Daily lunch specials like veggie tempura ($4.25-5.25). California rolls with crab and avocado are ever-so-succulent (5 for $4.25). Light dinners $7-9.50, full entrees like the kalbi ribs $9-16. Open M-Th 11am-2pm and 5-9pm, F 11am-2pm and 5-9:30pm, Sa 5-9:30pm; in winter closed 30min. earlier.

Pongsri's, 1571 NE 6th St. (479-1345). Sunlight struggles in through the hanging plants and trellises to illuminate a lengthy menu of MSG-free Thai cuisine. 21 vegetarian dishes ($5-6.50), including spice mushroom broccoli, served in an intimate setting. The pork spring rolls are greasy but good (4 for $5). Lunch specials Tu-F ($4-5). Open Tu-Su 11am-3pm and 4:30-9pm.

SIGHTS AND OUTDOORS

The **Rogue River** is Grants Pass' greatest attraction. One of the few federally protected rivers designated as a "Wild and Scenic River," the Rogue can be enjoyed by raft, jetboat, mail boat, or simply by foot. If you fish, you'll be in good company—Zane Grey and Clark Gable used to roam the Rogue River with tackle and bait. **Hellgate Excursions, Inc.,** 966 SW 6th St. (479-7204), offers enterprising (and affluent) souls a two-hour scenic tour. *($23, ages 4-11 $14.)* If you want to paddle the river yourself, head west off I-5 Exit 61 toward Merlin and Galice, where the outfitting companies cluster. A 35 mi. stretch of class III and IV rapids starting just north of Galice is the whitest water on the Rogue. It's a restricted area; to get on it, you have to go with guides and pay about $55 per person. Outfitters include **Rogue River Raft Trips,** 8500 Galice Rd. (476-3825 or 800-826-1963), in Merlin. *($475-495 for a 3-day trip with the best guides and equipment.)* **Orange Torpedo Trips,** 509 Merlin Rd. (479-5061 or 800-635-2925), runs more adventurous guided tours down the river in inflatable orange kayaks. *($45 for 4hr., $65 for 8hr.; under 10 10% off.)*

Almost halfway from Medford to Grants Pass is the town of **Gold Hill,** home of the **Oregon Vortex** and the "original" **House of Mystery,** 4303 Sardine Creek Rd. (855-1543). Take a right off Exit 43 (I-5 south) and follow signs 5 mi. east (over the tracks and up the hill). Here, the laws of physics take a dark and inscrutable siesta—balls roll **uphill,** pendulums hang **at an angle,** and people seem to vary in height **depending on where they stand.** These bizarre phenomena are caused by a local perturbation of the earth's magnetic field, a geophysical anomaly so strong that it also inflates admission fees. The owners apologize for any crude imitations of this house that tourists may have seen across the country, and assure visitors that this is the real thing. *(Open daily June-Aug. 9am-6pm; Mar.-May and Sept.-Oct. 9am-5pm. $6.50, ages 5-11 $4.50.)*

The **Oregon Caves National Monument** (592-2100; http://www.nps.gov/orca/index.html) can be reached by heading 30 mi. south along U.S. 199 through plush, green wilderness to Cave Junction, and then following Rte. 46 as it winds mischievously east for 20 mi. *(Tours given daily mid-May to Sept. 9am-7pm; mid-Sept. to mid-Oct. 9am-5pm; mid-Oct. to Apr. 10am-4pm; Dec.-Feb. call for hours. $7, under 12 $4.50.)* Here in the belly of the ancient Siskiyous, acidic waters carved through limestone and calcite, creating chilly, cavernous chambers with stalactites and stalagmites. (Do you know which are which? The answer is hidden on a nearby page.) The caves also contain exotic formations like soda straws, draperies, moonmilk, paradise lost, and Paul Bunyan. You can also see recently discovered ice-age fossils, including the most complete collection of jaguar fossils in North America. Tours last 75 minutes and are fairly strenuous, involving some ducking, twisting, and over 500 stairs. Children must be over 42 in. (107cm) tall and must pass an ability test. Bring a jacket.

■ Eugene

With students riding mountain bikes, hippies eating organically-grown food, outfitters making a killing off tourists, and hunters killing local wildlife, Eugene is liberal in the truest sense of the word: it accepts all types. Oregon's second-largest city straddles the Willamette River between the Siuslaw and Willamette National Forests. Home to the University of Oregon (U of O), Eugene owes much of its vibrancy to its students. Summer brings city slickers who happily shop and dine in the downtown pedestrian mall, until dusk draws them to Hult Center for an evening of world-class Bach. Outdoor types river raft along the Willamette and hike or bike in the many nearby parks. Fitness enthusiasts join the fleet of foot and free of spirit in this "running capital of the universe." With such a wide range of activities, it's no wonder how Nike, founded in Eugene, thought up their now-famous slogan. In Eugene, just do it and you'll fit right in.

ORIENTATION AND PRACTICAL INFORMATION

Eugene is 111 mi. south of Portland on I-5, just west of the town of **Springfield**. The **University of Oregon** campus lies in the southeast corner of Eugene, bordered on the north by **Franklin Blvd.**, which runs from the city center to I-5. **First Ave.** runs alongside the winding Willamette River; numbered **streets** go north-south. **Highway 99** is split in town—**6th Ave.** runs north and **7th Ave.** goes south. **Willamette Ave.** intersects the river, dividing the city into east and west. It is interrupted by the **pedestrian mall,** between 6th and 7th Ave. on Broadway downtown. Eugene's main student drag, **13th Ave.,** heads east to the University of Oregon. The city is a motorist's nightmare of one-way streets, and free parking is virtually nonexistent downtown. The most convenient way to get around is by **bike**—the roads are flat and there are plenty of bike paths.

Most **park hours** are officially 6am-11pm. The U of O has recently attempted to increase safety with schemes like the "yellow duck path" signifying better lit areas. Nevertheless, locals still maintain that lone women should avoid the campus at night and be wary of **Whittaker,** the area around Blair Blvd. near 6th Ave.

Trains: Amtrak, 433 Willamette St. (800-872-7245), at 4th Ave. To: Seattle, WA (2 per day, $24-46); Portland (2 per day, $12-21); Berkeley, CA (1 per day, $111). 15%

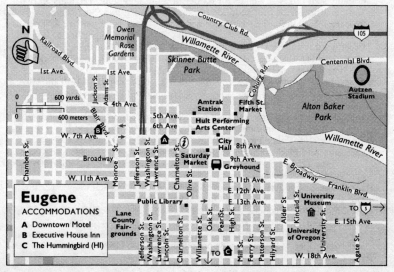

Eugene

ACCOMMODATIONS

A Downtown Motel
B Executive House Inn
C The Hummingbird (HI)

discount for seniors and disabled; 10% AAA discount. No lockers, but baggage check costs $1.50 per item per 24hr.

Buses: Greyhound, 987 Pearl St. (344-6265 or 800-231-2222), at 9th Ave. To: Seattle, WA ($34); San Francisco, CA ($48); Portland ($12). Open daily 6:30am-10pm. Lockers $1.25 per day. **Green Tortoise** (800-867-8647). Drop-off and pick-up at 14th and Kincaid St., at the U of O library. To: San Francisco, CA ($39); Seattle, WA ($25); Portland ($10). Some routes require reservations. Open daily 8am-8pm.

Public Transportation: Lane Transit District (LTD) (687-5555). Provides bus service throughout Eugene. Pick up a **map** and timetables at the Visitors Association (see below) or the LTD Service Center at 11th Ave. and Willamette St. Main route service M-F 6am-11:30pm, Sa 7:30am-11:30pm, Su 8:30am-8:30pm. All routes are wheelchair accessible. $1, M-F after 7pm 50¢; seniors and ages under 12 40¢.

Ride Board: Erb Memorial Union (EMU) Basement, in the middle of the U of O campus, one block east of Kincaid, on the pedestrian section of 13th Ave. Housing bulletin board, too. Open M-Th 7am-7pm, F 7am-5pm.

Taxis: Yellow Cab, 746-1234. $2 base, $2 per mi. Runs 24hr.

Car Rental: Enterprise Rent-a-Car, 810 W. 6th Ave. (683-0874). $33 per day; unlimited mileage within OR. Out of state, 150 free mi. per day, 25¢ each additional mi. 10% county tax. Must be 21. Credit card required for non-local customers. Open M-F 7:30am-6pm, Sa 9am-1pm.

Auto Club: AAA, 983 Willagillespie Rd. (484-0661 or 800-AAA-HELP/222-4357), near Valley River Center Mall, 2 mi. north of the University of Oregon campus. Only members get goodies like maps. Open M-F 8am-5pm.

Visitor Information: Convention and Visitors Association of Lane County, 115 W. 8th Ave. #190 (484-5307 or 800-547-5445; http://www.cvalco.org), but the door is on Olive St. Staffed by knowledgeable Eugenians and equipped with maps, brochures, and a courtesy phone. Open M-F 8:30am-5pm, Sa-Su 10am-4pm; Sept.-Apr. M-Sa 8:30am-5pm. **University of Oregon Switchboard,** in the Rainier Building at 1244 Walnut St. (346-3111). Referral for almost anything from rides to housing. Open M-F 7am-6pm.

Outdoor Information: Willamette National Forest, 211 E. 7th Ave. (465-6522), in the Federal Building. Beyond the metal detectors awaits info about campgrounds, recreational areas, and wilderness areas in the National Forest; invest in a **forest map** ($4). Open M-F 8am-4:30pm.

Bank: Bank of America, 201 E. 11th Ave. (342-5810). Open M-F 9am-6pm, Sa 9am-1pm.

Equipment Rental: Paul's Bicycle Way of Life, 152 W. 5th Ave. (344-4105). Friendly staff offers city bikes for $2 per hr., 4hr. minimum. Tandems $3 per hr., $30 per day. Credit card required. Open M-F 9am-7pm, Sa-Su 10am-5pm. **Pedal Power,** 535 High St. (687-1775), downtown. 21-speeds $5 per hr., $20 per day. Mountain bikes $25 per 4hr., $40 per day. Tandems $10 per hr., $50 per day. Credit card required. Open June-Aug. M-F 9am-7pm, Sa 9am-6pm, Su 10am-5pm; Sept.-May M-Sa 10am-6pm, Su 11am-5pm. Both shops also rent bike racks for cars ($5-7; racks hold up to 3 bikes).

Library: Lane County Library, 100 W. 13th Ave., at the corner of 13th and Olive St. (682-5450). Open M-Tu 10am-8pm, W-Su 10am-6pm. Internet access available.

Laundromat: Club Wash, 595 E. 13th Ave. (431-1039), at Patterson. A huge TV, video games, beer on tap, and tanning facilities make this a lively laundering experience. Open daily 7am-2am. Wash $1, dry 25¢ per 10min.

Emergency: 911. **Police/Fire:** 777 Pearl St. #107 (687-5111), at City Hall.

Crisis Line and Medical Services: White Bird Clinic, 341 E. 12th Ave. (800-422-7558). Free 24hr. crisis counseling and low-cost medical care. The clinic's **medical center** is at 1400 Mill St. Open M, W-F 9am-5pm.

Rape Crisis: Sexual Assault Support Services, 630 Lincoln St. (484-9791; 24hr. hotline 485-6700 or 800-788-4727). Open M-F 9am-5pm.

Post Office: 520 Williamette (800-275-8777), at 5th Ave. Open M-F 8:30am-5:30pm, Sa 10am-2pm. **ZIP Code:** 97401-9999.

Internet Access: Sip 'n' Surf, 99 W. 10th St. #115 (302-1581; http://www.sipn-surf.com). Open M-F 7am-9pm, Sa noon-6pm. See also **Library,** above.

Area Code: 541.

ACCOMMODATIONS

Budget travelers stopping in Eugene will appreciate the hopping **Hummingbird Hostel,** just minutes from downtown. The cheapest motels are on E. Broadway and W. 7th Ave., and tend toward seediness. Make reservations early; motels are packed on big football weekends. The closest legal camping is 7 miles away, but tenters have been known to camp by the river, especially in the wild and woolly northeastern side, near Springfield. If you're committed to camping, the best bet is to stay in the surrounding **Willamette National Forest** and make daytrips into Eugene.

The Hummingbird Eugene International Hostel (HI), 2352 Willamette St. (349-0589). Take bus #24 or 25 and get off at 24th Ave. and Willamette, or park in back on Portland St. This graceful, neighborhood home-turned-hostel is a wonderful addition to, and escape from, the city. A living room swathed in bookshelves, a yard with a picnic table, a garden, warm-hearted managers, and their adorable 3-year-old son make this a home away from home. 5 bedrooms sleep up to 20. Members $13, nonmembers $16; private rooms from $34. Check-in 5-10pm. Lockout 11am-5pm. Kitchen open 7:30-9:30am and 5-10pm. Cash or check only.

Downtown Motel, 361 W. 7th Ave. (345-8739 or 800-648-4366). Prime location with clean rooms under a green terra-cotta roof. Art deco tiles and plaster walls enhance the architecture. Cable TV, A/C, phones, and free coffee and donuts in the morning. Singles $30; doubles $38. One of the few motels in the area that doesn't jack up prices during the summer; reserve early (credit card required).

Executive House Inn, 1040 W. 6th Ave. (683-4000). All rooms are not created equal—you're lucky if you get one with new carpet or a fridge (no extra charge). Rooms in back are cooled by fans instead of A/C, and aren't as nice. Phones, cable TV, baby blue paint. Singles $30; doubles $38. Close to the country fairground; prices rise $5-10 during events.

CAMPGROUNDS

KOAs (Kampgrounds of America) and RV-only parks monopolize the Eugene camping scene. It's well worth it to head farther east on Rte. 58 and 126, where the immense **Willamette National Forest** is packed with campsites ($3-16). Ample signs make things easy to find. A swamp gives the tree bark and ferns an eerie phosphorescence in the beautiful, mysterious **Black Canyon Campground,** 28 mi. east of Eugene on Hwy. 58 ($8-16).

Pine Meadows (942-8657). On the marshy shore of Cottage Grove lake. Take I-5 S to Exit 172, then head 3½ mi. east, turn left on Cottage Grove Reservoir Rd., and go another 2½ mi. Plenty of RV and jet ski traffic. Showers, shade, and flush toilets. 92 sites: $12. Venture down the road a bit to their 15 primitive sites for more privacy ($6; pit toilets). Both open just before Memorial Day to Labor Day.

Schwarz Park (942-1418), 5½ mi. off Exit 174 (I-5S). Turn right off the ramp and immediately left at the first stop light, then go past the village green. The grounds are on Row River, about 2½ mi. below swimmable Dorena Lake on the dam spillway. Flat and quiet, with dry yellow grass and pine trees. Showers, flush toilets, and drinking water. Sites $10. The better sites are toward the back.

FOOD

Outdoor cafe dining and veggie-centric, organic menus are common everywhere in Eugene. The downtown area specializes in gourmet food, the university hang-out zone at 13th Ave. and Kincaid has more grab-and-go options, and natural food stores encircle the city. A reliable option is **Sundance Natural Foods,** 748 E. 24th Ave. (343-9142), at 24th and Hilyard (open daily 7am-11pm). Right in town, **The Kiva,** 125 W. 11th Ave. (342-8666), supplies a smaller array of organic produce and natural foods (open M-Sa 9am-8pm, Su 10am-5pm). For American cheese singles and ground beef, head to **Safeway,** 145 E. 18th Ave. at Oak (485-3664; open daily 6am-2am).

OREGON

⊛**Keystone Cafe,** 395 W. 5th St. (342-2075). The creative menu and organic ingredients give diners a true taste of Eugene. The incredible food is mostly meatless, some wheatless, and all bread is homebaked. A small kitchen makes for slow service during busy morning hours, but one mouthful of their famous plate-sized pancakes ($3, plus 75¢ for fruit or seeds), and all will be forgiven. Breakfast served all day. Open daily 7am-5pm.

Cafe Navarro, 454 Willamette St. (344-0943). Casual mood, but the Caribbean and Latin cuisine is served with a gourmet flair. Worldly selection of dishes from Jamaica, Ethiopia, and Peru. Challah french toast with mango syrup $5.35. Lunch $5-8. Open Tu-F 11am-2pm and 5-9:30pm, Sa 9am-2pm and 5-9:30pm, Su 9am-2pm.

Newman's Fish Company, 1545 Willamette St. (344-2371). A novel approach to dining in the Eugenest of styles. This walk-up/bike-up window delivers the finest fish 'n' chips (salmon $5; cod $4; halibut $5.50) east of the Cascades. Solo fries $1. Pre-ordered sushi by the piece ($1-2) and sushi rolls ($6) are available F-Sa. Open M-F 11am-7pm, Sa 11am-6:30pm.

Out of the Fog, 309 W. 3rd St. (302-8194), at Lincoln St. just past the railroad tracks. Hidden away and a little hard to find, this hippie hotspot is a gem of a coffeehouse. Organically grown and socially responsible coffee ($1.35 for 16oz.) to go with an organic veganberry muffin ($1.65). Dare "Da Bomb" and its 4 espresso shots, mocha, and flavored syrup ($3.25). Open mic Tu at 8pm. Open M-Th 6:30am-11pm, F-Sa 7am-midnight, Su 7am-10pm.

Cafe Zenon, 898 Pearl St. (343-3005), at Broadway. If you have one night to splurge, this is the place. The Mediterranean and Pacific Northwest food is light and flavorful and the 'tude is chic. Small plates $6.75-$7.75; entrees climb to a $16.75 dinner peak. If nothing else, come for dessert ($4.25); the array is astounding and the quality superb. Open M-Th 8am-11pm, F-Sa 8am-midnight, Su 9:30am-11pm.

SIGHTS AND ENTERTAINMENT

The **University of Oregon** is the centerpiece of Eugene. Campus maps and tours issue from the reception centers at **Oregon Hall** (346-3014), E. 13th Ave. and Agate St., and at the visitor parking and information booth, just left of the main entrance on Franklin Blvd. *(Tours M-F 10am and 2pm, Sa 10am.)* Take time to pay homage to the ivy-covered halls that set the scene for *National Lampoon's Animal House.* Just off the pedestrian section of 13th St., between Kincaid and University St., the **University Museum of Art** (346-3027) displays a changing repertoire of Pacific Northwestern and American pieces not featured in *Animal House,* and an extensive permanent collection from Southeast Asia. *(Open W noon-8pm, Th-Su noon-5pm. Free.)* A few blocks away, the **Museum of Natural History,** 1680 E. 15th Ave. (346-3024), at Agate, shows a collection of relics from indigenous cultures worldwide, including a 7000-year-old pair of shoes. A primitive "swoosh" logo is still visible. *(Open W-Su noon-5pm. Free, but $1 donation encouraged.)* Northwest of the city, just after the I-5 overpass, the **Owen Memorial Rose Garden** is perfect for a picnic, accompanied by the sweet strains of rumbling traffic. Any frolicking should take place in full daylight, because the surrounding Whittaker neighborhood is unsafe at night.

The **Saturday Market** (686-8885), at 8th Ave. and Oak St., fuses crafts, clothing, jewelry, artwork, and music in a spectacular display. *(Held weekly Apr.-Nov. Open 10am-5pm.)* High-brow culture festoons the $26 million **Hult Performing Arts Center,** 1 Eugene Center (info 687-5087, ticket office 682-5000, 24hr. event info 682-5746), at 7th Ave. and Willamette St. *(Free tours Th and Sa at 1pm.)* The two theater halls host a variety of music from blues to Bartók. Locals leave the Hult to society types who can afford tickets, and head instead to the **Community Center for the Performing Arts,** better known as **WOW Hall,** 291 W. 8th Ave. (687-2746), an old **Wobblie** (International Workers of the World) meeting place. *(Open M-F 3-6pm.)* Flyers announcing these WOW acts are everywhere. Tickets are available at WOW Hall, CD World (3215 W. 11th St.), and occasionally at the door for less raging acts. The **Bijou Art Cinema,** 492 East 13th Ave. at Ferry St. (686-2458), is another favorite, where obscure films screen in the sanctuary of an old Spanish church. *(Box office opens at 4:40pm. $2.50-6.)*

OUTDOORS

River Runner Supply, 78 G. Centennial Loop (343-6883 or 800-223-4326), runs everything from fishing to whitewater rafting on the **Willamette River,** and also rents kayaks, canoes, and rafts. *(4hr. rafting trip $45 per person, 4-person min. Kayaks $25 per day, canoes $20 per day, rafts $45-60 per day. Major credit card required.)* Reservations are recommended on weekends. The visitor information center (see **Practical Information,** above) supplies a list of several other outfitters. Check local river conditions and maps, since there are some rough areas on the Willamette near Eugene, especially when the water is high. To fill a free hour, canoe or kayak the **Millrace Canal,** which parallels the Willamette for 3 mi. Rent water craft from **The Water Works Canoe Company,** 1395 Franklin Blvd. (346-4386), run by U of O students. *(Open summer Tu-Su 11am-8pm, but hours vary depending on weather. $5 per hr., $15 per 24hr.; $30 deposit.)*

The Willamette Valley attracted waves of 19th-century pioneers with its fertile floor and forested hills. To see country that hasn't changed noticeably since their invasion, take Rte. 126 east from Eugene. The highway runs adjacent to the beautiful **McKenzie River,** and on a clear day, the mighty snowcapped **Three Sisters** of the **Cascades** are visible. Just east of the town of **McKenzie Bridge,** the road splits into a scenic byway loop; Rte. 242 climbs east to the vast lava fields of **McKenzie Pass,** while Rte. 126 turns north over **Santiam Pass** and meets back with Route 242 in Sisters.

The large and popular Cougar Lake features the Terwilliger Hot Springs, known fondly by all as **Cougar Hot Springs.** To get there, go 4 mi. east of Blue River on Rte. 126, turn right onto Aufderheide Dr. (Forest Service Rd. #19), and follow the road 7.3 mi. as it winds on the right side of Cougar Reservoir. *($3 day fee per person.)* These five lovely rock pools have become the Willamette Forest's hippie hotspot. By convention, the springs (and the cove of the lake down the hill from them) are clothing-optional hangouts. Try to park in the Terwilliger site use area, as there is no other parking within 1 mi. of the hot springs. The springs have no regular attendant, but rangers do show up at dusk to enforce the area's day-use only policy. Other hot springs are scattered through the area; the Forest Service can suggest clothing-compulsory sulphur baths for the more modest. Continue down the road to camp on the other side of the lake at **Slide Creek** *(16 sites: $10; hand-pumped drinking water)* or along the south fork of the McKenzie and French Pete Creek at French Pete *(17 sites: $10; drinking water).* Primitive camping sites are available at Sunnyside (13 sites: $5) and Cougar (12 sites: $5). Both spots are first-come, first-served.

Route 242 is often blocked by snow until the end of June. Wide enough for two cars to pass in some places, and kinked with tight turns in others, this Cascade Range route is off-limits to vehicles over 35 ft. long, and trucks with trailers should not try it. Route 242 is an exquisite drive, tunneling its narrow, winding way between **Mt. Washington** and the **Three Sisters Wilderness** before rising to the high plateau of McKenzie Pass, where lava outcroppings served as a training site for astronauts preparing for lunar landings. Decades earlier, the Civilian Conservation Corps left its mark with a lava block **lookout tower,** which affords incredible views on clear days.

Along the curviest section of Route 242, about 15 mi. east of the fork from Route 126, a number of trails begin that carry hikers above the treeline. As in all Oregon wilderness areas, biking is not allowed. Permits are required, available free at the trailheads. For more info, call the **McKenzie Ranger Station** (822-3381), 3 mi. east of McKenzie Bridge on Rte. 126. *(Open daily 8am-4:30pm; in winter M-F 8am-4:30pm.)* The **McKenzie River Trail** winds 26 mi. parallel to Rte. 126 and the river through thick, lush forest draped in moss. It starts about 1½ mi. west of the ranger station (trail map $1, faded copy free) and ends up north at Old Santiam Road near the **Fish Lake Old Growth Grove.** The entire trail is now open to mountain bikers. The two most accessible parts of the trail are its first 6 mi., sandwiched between the highway and the river, and the spectacular 2 mi. section between **Koosah Falls, Sahalie Falls,** and **Clear Lake.** A number of Forest Service campgrounds cluster along this stretch of Rte. 126, including the riverside **Olallie,** 9 mi. northeast of the ranger station *(available by reservation only 800-280-2267; $6)* and **Trailbridge,** 11 mi. northeast of the ranger station *(26 sites: $6; drinking water).* More ambitious hikers can sign up for an overnight permit at the ranger station and head for the high country.

NIGHTLIFE

According to some, Eugene nightlife is the best in Oregon. Not surprisingly, the string of establishments by the university along 13th Street are often dominated by fraternity-style beer bashes. Refugees from this scene will find a diverse cross-section of nightlife throughout town. Take a nap after dinner before going out—Eugene parties through the wee hours. Check out the *Eugene Weekly* for current bands.

Sam Bond's Garage, 407 Blair Blvd. (431-6603); take bus #50 or 52. Supremely laid-back gem of a cafe and pub, in a soulful neighborhood. Entertainment every night, and an ever-changing selection of regional microbrews ($2.50-3 per pint). Veggie fare is plentiful. Rusting car parts in the haphazard flower beds speak the history of the 1918 garage. Take a bus or cab at night. Open daily 3pm-1am.

Jo Federigo's Jazz Club and Restaurant, 259 E. 5th Ave. (343-8488; http:// www.rio.com/~jofeds), across the street from the 5th St. Market. A snazzy, pricey restaurant with New Orleans flair. Downstairs, the jazz club swings with music every night and the whole place rattles when the train goes by (shows usually start at 9:30pm, but call ahead). Blues night (W). Happy hour 2:30-6:30pm. No cover, but $5 drink minimum and 50¢ surcharge per drink after 9pm. Restaurant open for lunch M-F 11:30am-2pm, dinner daily 5pm-10pm. Jazz club open daily 2pm-1am.

High St. Brewery Cafe, 1243 High St. (345-4905), between 12th and 13th St. Proudly sells McMenamins and seasonal fruit ale. Toss on some jeans and relax in this oriental rug-bedecked Victorian building. A backyard deck and patio catch the overflow. Excellent ales brewed in the basement ($2.85 per pint). Happy hour daily 4-6pm, and food until midnight. Open M-Sa 11am-1am, Su noon-midnight.

Club Arena, 959 Pearl St. (683-2360). The only gay dance club in town. The huge, checkered dance floor gets kicking every night at 11pm to house and techno tunes. Retro nights (Su); men's night (M); women's night (W); Thursday is packed for $1 mixed drinks. Cover F-Sa $2.50, Th $1. Open daily 9pm-2:30am.

John Henry's, 136 E. 11th Ave. (342-3358). In the heart of downtown, this warehouse-style venue hosts headliners and smaller potatoes, drawing a mixed and slightly older crowd. Bits of abstract art give the high walls color. Plenty of secluded bar booths, but the action is on the dance floor with everything from alternative rock to country swing. Microbrew pints $3. Cover usually $3-7. Call for a schedule. Free pool until 10pm; always free foosball. Open M-Sa 4pm-1am.

EVENTS

The two-week **Oregon Bach Festival** (800-457-1486) is now in its 30th year. Helmut Rilling, a world-renowned authority on Baroque music, leads some of the country's finest musicians in stirring performances of Bach's concerti and cantatas, as well as selections from Verdi and Dvôrak. Concerts are held at the Hult Center and U of O's Beall Concert Hall beginning the last week of June. Contact the Hult Center Ticket Office, listed in Sights, for info. *($18-40, senior and student discounts for selected events.)* **Art and the Vineyard** (345-1571), a four-day 4th of July celebration of food, wine, and culture, takes over Alton Baker Park, on the north bank of the Willamette east of Coburg Rd. *(Suggested $4 donation.)*

By far the biggest event of the summer is the **Oregon Country Fair** (343-4298; http://www.efn.org/~ocf). It actually takes place in **Veneta,** 13 mi. west of town on Rte. 126, but its festive quakes can be felt in Eugene. For three days in mid-July, 50,000 people drop everything to go to the Fair. Started in 1969, the fair has become a magical annual gathering of artists, musicians, misfits, and activists. Today, ten stages' worth of show after show, and the 300 art, clothing, craft, herbal remedy, eco, furniture, spiritual, and food booths are only bits of the unique experience that is the Country Fair. Lofty tree houses, drum circles, parades of painted bodies, dancing 12-foot dolls, and "fair-ies" offering free hugs transport travelers into an enchanted forest of frenzy. To alleviate the yearly traffic jams, free bus service is provided between the fairgrounds in Veneta and a free parking area in Eugene (cross the river to Autzen Stadium). Buses run every 15 minutes, starting around 10am and continuing until the fairgrounds close at 7pm. It is wise to purchase tickets in advance through Fastixx (800-992-8499), at the Hult Center, or at EMU (see **Practical Information,** above) on campus. *(Advance tickets F and Su $10, Sa $15; tickets purchased on the day of cost $1 extra. No tickets sold on site.)* No public camping or overnight parking is available.

■ Corvallis

Unlike so many Oregon towns, this peaceful residential community in the central Willamette Valley assumes no historic pretensions. Home to Oregon State University (OSU) and a looming Hewlett-Packard plant, Corvallis lives smack-dab in the present. Life bustles in the downtown area, but like any college town, Corvallis mellows in the summer, allowing time for a few choice festivals and plenty of outdoor exploration.

ORIENTATION AND PRACTICAL INFORMATION

Corvallis is laid out in a checkerboard fashion that degenerates away from downtown; numbered streets run north-south and streets named for lesser-known presidents (Van Buren, Polk, Buchanan) run east-west. Rte. 99 W splits in town and becomes two one-way streets: north along **3rd St.** and south along **4th St.** When they aren't hitting the trails college students and frat brats hang out along **Monroe St.** and the surrounding area.

Buses: Greyhound, 153 4th St. NW (757-1797 or 800-231-2222). To: Portland (4 per day, $11); Seattle, WA (4 per day, $25); Newport (3 per day, $10); Eugene (4 per day, $6). Lockers $1 per 24hr. Open M-F 7:20am-6pm, Sa 7:30am-1:30pm, Su 11am-7pm.

Public Transportation: Corvallis Transit System (757-6998). Fare 50¢; seniors, ages 5-17, and disabled 25¢. Service M-F 6:25am-7pm, Sa 9:15am-5pm. Free schedule available from the Chamber of Commerce or City Hall.

Taxis: A-1 Taxi, 754-1111. $1 per mile. $5 minimum. Runs 24hr.

Visitor Information: Chamber of Commerce (757-1505) and **Convention and Visitor Bureau** (757-1544 or 800-334-8118; http://www.visitcorvallis.com), both at 420 2nd St. NW, the first right past the bridge coming from the east. Free maps at the convention bureau; more detailed maps for $2 at the chamber. Both open M-F 8am-5pm. **Oregon State University** (737-0123; events info 737-2402). Main entrance and info booth at Jefferson and 15th St. Free campus map available.

Outdoor Equipment: Peak Sports, 129 2nd St. NW (754-6444). Rents mountain bikes ($15 per day) and 3-speed cruisers ($5 per day). Open M-Th 9am-6pm, F 9am-8pm, Sa 9am-6pm, Su noon-5pm.

Bank: Bank of America, 324 3rd St. SW. Open M-F 9am-6pm, Sa 9am-1pm. ATMs.

Library: 645 Monroe St. NW (757-6927 for recording; 757-6926 for human). Open M-F 9am-9pm, Sa 9am-6pm, Su noon-6pm. Internet access available.

Laundromat: Campbell's Laundry, 1120 9th St. NW (752-3794). Wash $1.25, dry 25¢ per 10min. Open daily 6am-1am.

Medical Services: Corvallis Clinic, 3680 Samaritan Dr. NW (754-1150; walk-in service 754-1282). Open M-F 8am-9pm, Sa 8am-6pm, Su 10am-6pm.

Emergency: 911. **Police:** 180 NW 5th St. (757-6924).

Post Office: 311 2nd St. SW (800-275-8777). Open M-F 8am-5:30pm, Sa 9am-4pm. **Zip Code:** 97333.

Internet Access: See **Library,** above.

Area Code: 541.

ACCOMMODATIONS AND CAMPGROUNDS

Many of Corvallis' easily accessible campgrounds are not RV mini-cities, and provide a break from generators and Airstreams. Motels are reasonably priced, but few and far between. In summer, most fill fast with pesky conventioneers.

C.E.W. Motel, 1705 9th St. NW (753-8823). Clean, economical, and worthy of a night's stay. Some rooms with tubs, and eclectic statue garden in the parking lot to boot. Single $35.50; 1-bed doubles $42; 2-bed doubles $52. Reserve with credit card 3 days in advance for weekends.

Budget Inn, 1480 3rd St. SW (752-8756). Take 4th St. under the bridges. Wood-paneling, A/C, bathrooms big enough for waltzing. Kitchen units available. Singles $35; doubles $45; senior discount $2. Reserve 2 weeks ahead. Credit cards accepted.

Benton County Fairgrounds, 110 53rd St. SW (757-1521). Follow Rte. 34W, then turn right onto 53rd St. or take the Rte. 3 CTS bus. A pleasant place blessed with trees and showers. Sites $5; hookups $10. First-come, first-served. Closed for fairs and other events mid-July to early Aug.

FOOD AND ENTERTAINMENT

Corvallis has a smattering of the requisite collegiate pizza parlors, and several variations on the Mexican theme. OSU students prowl Monroe St. for grub, their limited finances inspiring an abundance of cheap, tasty, filling food. **First Alternative Inc.,** 1007 3rd St. SE (753-3115) is a volunteer co-op stocked with a range of well priced, natural products ranging from bountiful bulk foods to natural remedies (open daily 9am-9pm). **Safeway,** 450 3rd St. SW (753-5502), is open daily from 6am to 2am.

☕**East Ocean Buffet,** 2501 Monroe St. NW (754-2803). Simply put, the best deal in town. Elaborately put: locals love the all-you-can-eat buffet (lunch $5, dinner $7), feasting on the endless supply of fried rice, egg rolls, noodles, beef-and-broccoli, honey chicken, egg foo young, and other popular Chinese cuisine. Be prepared to share a table if you come alone. Open M-F 11am-9:30pm, Sa-Su 11:30am-9:30pm.

Nearly Normal's, 109 15th St. NW (753-0791). This cottage combines a pleasant, arboreal aura with low prices and large portions of everything except meat ($2.50-9). Dine under a canopy of branches, kiwi vines, fuchsia plants, and rose bushes on the porch. Hearty sunflower seed burgers $5. Open M-F 8am-9pm, Sa 9am-9pm.

McMenamins, 420 3rd St. NW (758-6044; http://www.mcmenamins.com), sports some of the best pub fare in town, made from scratch ($2-9). Fresh-cut fries ($1.15-4.50) are worth a trip themselves. All pints $2.85. Practice German by reading the street signs that line the ceiling. Open M-Sa 11am-1am, Su noon-midnight.

Bombs Away Cafe, 2527 Monroe St. NW (757-7221), is a self-proclaimed "funky tacqueria." Multicolored geometric art and atypical Mexican cuisine—try the ricotta enchiladas and duck chimichangas (both $6.25) or the enormous "Wet Burrito" ($6.75). Tipplers down tequila in the tiny bar in the back. Open M-F 11am-midnight, Sa 4pm-midnight, Su 4-9pm. 21+ when kitchen closes (M-Sa at 10pm).

OUTDOORS AND EVENTS

Mountain biking is a way of life in Corvallis, and all roads seem to lead to one bike trail or another. Many cyclists and sightseers sidle out to OSU's **McDonald Forest;** to get there, drive west out of town on Harrison for about 4½ mi., then turn right on Oak Creek Rd. The pavement dead-ends at OSU's lab, and multiple trails lead from there into the forest. Maps are available at Peak Sports for $4 (see p. 477). On a clear day, **Chip Ross Park** offers splendid views of the Cascade Valley from Mt. Hood to Three Sisters. Take 3rd St. north, turn left on Circle Blvd., then right on Highland. After one mile, look left for an infuriatingly small blue sign indicating the park.

The Corvallis heart rate picks up with the **Da Vinci Days Festival** (757-6363 or 800-334-8118), during the third weekend in July. *($5 each day, ages 3-12 $3; all 4 days $15, ages 3-12 $7.)* Renaissance men and women compete in the **Kinetic Sculpture Race,** in which people-powered, all-terrain works of art vie for a crown. If your techno-interests extend no further than stereo equipment, don't despair; the festival brings nationally known bands, from jazz to rock. The **Fall Festival,** held in Central Park during the third weekend in September, combines food, music, and an excellent crafts fair. Performers have included Wynton Marsalis and James Cotton.

Ten miles east in **Albany** (off U.S. 20 before I-5), thousands of jammers gather each Thursday night from mid-July through August for the **River Rhythms** concert series. Musical acts vary drastically from concert to concert, but they are always free, always at 7pm, and always held in the Monteith River Park. Each week in July, a special Monday night show features local performers, and is also free at 7pm in Monteith River Park. Call the Albany Visitor Center (928-0911) for more info.

NIGHTLIFE

Squirrel's Tavern, 100 2nd St. SW (753-8057). Few frat boys frolic at this hippie bar, where the bearded come to drink beer (domestics $1.75, microbrews $2.75), play pool (50¢ per game), and eat the best burgers in town (meat or veggie $3.25). Happy hour M-F 4:30-6:30pm (domestic pints $1, pitchers $5.50). Always 21+. Cover $0-2. Open M-Th 11:30am-1am, F-Sa 11:30am-1:30am, Su 5pm-midnight.

Murphy's Tavern, 2740 3rd St. SW (754-3508). OSU students and loggers drink together at this roadhouse. Listen to drunken crooners on Fridays and Saturdays during karaoke night. Brave the crowds for Mr. Bill's Traveling Trivia Night on Thursdays. Domestic pints $2.25. Beer 25¢ every W 7-8pm. Open M-Th 10:30am-midnight, F-Sa 10:30am-1:30am, Su noon-8pm.

∎ Salem

Although Salem is the state capital, the third-largest city in Oregon, and the home of Willamette University, the city radiates vibes of surburbia rather than urban sprawl. What Salem lacks in metropolitan savvy, however, it makes up for in subtle, simple pleasures: strolling through the verdant capitol campus, sampling the array of terrific breakfast cafes, and admiring the impeccable, litter-free streets. And for those who prefer relaxation over legislation, Silver Falls State Park is only a short drive away.

ORIENTATION AND PRACTICAL INFORMATION

Salem is located 51 mi. south of Portland and 64 mi. north of Eugene on I-5. Wilamette University and the capitol dominate the center of the city; the heart of downtown lies several blocks northwest. Street addresses are arranged according to a quadrant system, with **State St.** as the north-south divider and the **Willamette River** as the east-west divider. To reach downtown, take Exit 253 off I-5.

Trains: Amtrak, 500 13th St. SE (588-1551 or 800-872-7245), across from the visitor center (see below). Trains run daily to: Portland ($6.50-12); Seattle ($19-35); and San Francisco ($76-140). Open daily 6:30am-4:30pm.

Buses: Greyhound, 450 Church St. NE (362-2428), at Center St., runs buses north and south, with service to: Portland (6 per day; weekdays $7, weekends $8). Lockers $1 per 24hr. Station open daily 6am-8pm.

Local Transportation: Cherriots Customer Service Office, 183 High St. NE (588-2877), provides maps and multiple-day passes for Salem's bus system. 20 routes leave from High St., between State and Court St. in front of the courthouse. Fare 75¢, seniors and disabled 35¢, under 18 50¢. Runs every 30min. M-F 6:15am-9:35pm, hourly Sa 7:45am-9:35pm.

Taxis: Salem Yellow Cab Co. (362-2411). $2 base, $1.70 per mi. Runs 24hr.

Visitor Information: Salem Convention and Visitor Association, 1313 Mill St. SE (581-4325 or 800-874-7012), in the Mission Mill Village complex, stocks brochures on Salem and the entire state. Open M-F 8:30am-5pm, Sa 10am-4pm.

Bank: Bank of America, 390 High St. NE. ATMs. Open M-F 9am-6pm, Sa 9am-1pm.

Library: 585 Liberty St. SE (588-6315). Internet access available. Open Tu-W 10am-9pm, Th-Sa 10am-6pm; Sept.-May also open Su 1-5pm.

Gay Resource Center: 800-777-2437. Open M-F 10am-9pm, Sa-Su noon-6pm.

Laundromat: Suds City Depot, 1785 Lancaster Dr. NE. (362-9845), at Market St. Wash $1, dry 25¢ per 17min. Open daily 7:30am-9pm.

Emergency: 911. **Police:** 555 Liberty St. SE (588-6123), in City Hall.

Crisis Lines: Northwest Human Services Crisis and Info Hotline: 581-5535. 24hr. **Women's Crisis Center:** 399-7722. 24hr.

Hospital: Salem Hospital, 665 Winter St. SE (370-5200).

Post Office: 1050 25th St. SE (800-275-8777). Open M-F 8:30am-5:30pm. **ZIP Code:** 97301.
Internet Access: See **Library,** above.
Area Code: 503.

ACCOMMODATIONS AND CAMPGROUNDS

In the far, faraway galaxy of Northwestern budget travel, Salem is the Death Star. Struggle valiantly against the tractor beam of commercialized RV parks and camp at Silver Falls State Park. Rent is high in this politician's playland, pushing the price of modest motel rooms to $40-50. B&Bs, starting at $45 per room, provide a classier and often more comfortable setting; the visitor center has a list of area B&Bs.

Cottonwood Cottage, 960 East St. NE (362-3979 or 800-349-3979; http://www.open.org/ctnwdctg), between Capital St. and Summer St. This endearing old house close to downtown, offers 2 quiet, sunny bedrooms with cable, A/C, and a shared bath. Rooms start at $55. Reservations recommended for summer months.

City Center Motel, 510 Liberty St. SE (364-0121 or 800-289-0121; fax 581-0554), across the tree-lined street from the downtown library and City Hall, is one of the most pleasant and convenient motels in Salem. Singles $40-45; doubles $45-52.

☜**Silver Falls State Park** (873-8681), 20024 Silver Falls SE (Rte. 214). Take Rte. 22 east (Mission St.) for 5 mi., then take the exit for Silver Falls and Rte. 214 N (Silver Falls Rd.), and follow it for about 18 mi. Oregon's largest inland state park sparkles with swimming holes, hiking trails, storytelling, horse rentals, and waterfalls. Showers, water, recycling center. Open year-round. 60 tent sites $16; 44 RV hookups $20. Wheelchair accessible. Reserve by calling 800-452-5687; credit cards accepted.

FOOD

The busy Lancaster Dr. (just east and parallel to I-5), by contrast, woos burger lovers into the wee hours with flashing fast food signs. The local **Safeway** is at 1265 Center St. NE (362-8511), is open daily from 6am to midnight. **Heliotrope Natural Food,** 2809 Market St. NE (362-5487), has a healthy selection of bread and produce (open M-Sa 8am-9pm, Su 9am-8pm).

Off-Center Cafe, 1741 Center St. NE (363-9245), in the same long, bluish-white one-story building as Nobles Tavern. Liberal mindset, quick service, and scrumptious food. Start the morning off with a hearty dose of "bibble and squib" ($4.50) or scrambled tofu ($5.75). Or balance out your diet with a boysenberry milkshake ($2.75) while witticisms on the wall tip your politics to the left. Open Tu-W 7am-2:30pm, Th-F 7am-2:30pm and 6-9pm, Sa 8am-2pm and 6-9pm, Su 8am-2pm.

Tong King, 989 12th St. SE (585-9932), 2 blocks past Mission St., stirs up some relatively authentic Cantonese and Mandarin food. Generous combo lunch special $4.25; pea pods with mushrooms $5.75. Most dishes have some sort of meat. Open M-Th 11:30am-2:30pm and 4:30-9:30pm, F 11:30am-10pm, Sa 4:30-10pm.

Fuji Japanese Restaurant, 159 High St. SE (364-5512), serves delicious, real-deal Japanese food, a remarkably hard find in Salem. Drop in for the lunch specials ($5) or dinner entrees ($9-18) and eat at the green-tea-colored tables. Open M-F 11am-2:30pm and 5-10pm, Sa 4-10pm.

The Arbor Cafe, 380 High St. NE (588-2353), adjacent to the Arbor Garden Goods and Gifts, is upbeat and upscale, but down to earth. A place for Salem professionals to take a break with panini sandwiches ($4.25-4.50), half salads ($3.25), or one of 20 tempting desserts (75¢-$4). Wine, beer, Italian sodas, and frozen coffee drinks are also available. Open M-Th 7:30am-10pm, F 7:30am-11pm, Sa 8am-11pm.

SIGHTS AND EVENTS

The **State Capitol,** 900 Court St. NE (986-1388), occupies a city block bounded by Court St. on the north, Waverly St. on the east, State St. on the south, and Cottage St. on the west. *(Open M-F 7:30am-5:30pm, Sa 9am-4pm, Su noon-4pm.)* Presiding over it all is a 23 ft. gold-gilt statue of the "Oregon Pioneer," perched upon an imposing pinnacle. Murals and sculptures depicting American western expansion ornament the interior. During summer, a free **tour** leaves every 30 minutes for a climb to the top of the capitol rotunda, and tours of the various chambers leave every hour. *(Rest of the year, tours scheduled by appointment. Call 968-1388.)* Across the street from the capitol is the sylvan campus of **Willamette University,** 900 State St. (370-6303). "Wil-AM-it, damn it!" is a favorite local tool for rectifying ignorant pronunciations. Founded by Methodist missionaries in 1842, this is the oldest university in the West. Willamette doesn't offer tours, but visitors are welcome to meander within its ivied walls.

The Willamette Valley, basking in warm inland sun, gives succor to a bevy of successful wineries. **Willamette Valley Vineyards (WVV),** 8800 Enchanted Way SE, Turner, OR (588-9463), just off Exit 248 on I-5, is a publicly owned winery boasting 35 grape-filled acres. *(Open daily 11am-6pm.)* WVV offers a view of the valley, unusual architecture, free wine tasting, and tours galore. The Salem Visitor Association (see **Practical Information,** above) can provide info on many such vintners. The **Bush Barn Art Center and Museum,** 600 Mission St. SE (art center 581-2228, museum 363-4714), is one of Salem's gems. *(Tours $3, seniors and students $2.50, ages 6-12 $1.50, under 6 free.)* A stroll through the rose garden, greenhouse, and art center is free and equally fabulous. The art collection includes some entertainingly off-beat exhibits. During the third weekend of July, the Salem Art Association hosts the free **Salem Art Fair and Festival** in Bush's **Pasture Park.** The festival showcases Northwestern art while bands strum away the afternoon. A **5K Run for the Arts** is held during the festival. *(Contact the Bush Barn for more info and race registration fee.)*

With the annual **Oregon State Fair** at the **Expo Center,** 2330 17th St. NE (378-3247 or 800-833-0011), Salem gives summer a rousing send-off. *($6, seniors $4, ages 6-12 $3.)* For 12 days in late August (ending on Labor Day), frolickers, farm animals, and chaos hurtle into the city, all chaperoned by troops of rabbit-raising 4-Hers. The fair hosts everything from live performances, to horse races, to exhibits on macrame.

NIGHTLIFE AND ENTERTAINMENT

Although Salem lacks a venue for those with Saturday night fever, plenty of sports bars, dart boards, and artsy movies await travelers. The **Ram Restaurant and Big Horn Brewery,** 515 12th St. SE (363-1904), at Bellevue St., serves an award-winning "Total Disorder Porter" (pints $3.25) to match the neon lights and framed jerseys that prove it's a bonafide sports bar. Creekside outdoor dining is available (open daily 11am-2pm). **Tahiti Restaurant and Lounge,** 380 State St. (581-4978), at Liberty St., has a dimly lit South Sea Islands decor and a full bar, specializing in tropical and blended drinks. *(Open M-F 11:30am-2:30am, Sa 3pm-2:30am. Mixed drinks $3-6.50, domestic pints $2, microbrews $3. Happy hours M-F 4:30-7pm; all-you-can-eat dishes M-Th 5-8:30pm $5; 21+ in lounge.)* The **Salem Cinema,** 445 High St. SE (378-7676), in Pringle Plaza, offers relief from the repetitive college bar scene with its indie and art film selection.

CENTRAL AND EASTERN OREGON

Most people picture Oregon as a verdant land of torrential rain and rich forests. This is true enough of the state's western portion, where most Oregonians live, but the eastern half is actually a high desert. The low, evergreen Coast Range and the high, volcanic Cascades are rain barriers, trapping moisture on their ocean sides and leaving the eastern basin hot and arid. This region has challenged its human inhabitants for generations, from the Cayuse, Shoshone, and Nez Percé who first occupied it, to the pioneers who crossed it in wagons, to the farmers, ranchers, and loggers who live there today. Despite ample opportunities for outdoor activity, the region is sparsely populated and seldom visited beyond Crater Lake on the Cascades' eastern slope.

ⓦ HIGHLIGHTS OF CENTRAL AND EASTERN OREGON

- **Crater Lake National Park** (see below) protects a placid and azure pool in the maw of an ancient and enormous volcano.
- Life has been frozen at **John Day Fossil Beds National Monument** (see p. 136), and swept away by lava flows at **Newberry National Monument** (see p. 134).
- The teeming bird populations of **Malheur National Wildlife Refuge** (see p. 139) offer a livelier time, as do the hiking trails of the challenging **Hells Canyon** and the dramatic **Wallowa Mountains** (see p. 145).
- Human history is presented with uncommon flair at the **Oregon Trail Interpretive Center** (see p. 144) in **Baker City**, while the **High Desert Museum** (see p. 133) in **Bend** tackles the natural world.

▓ Crater Lake and Klamath Falls

Mirror-blue Crater Lake, the namesake of Oregon's only national park, was regarded as sacred by Native American shamans who forbade their people to look upon it. Iceless in winter, though snowbanked until late July, the flawless circular lake plunges from its 6176 ft. shores to a depth of nearly 2000 ft., making it the nation's deepest lake and the seventh-deepest in the world. The fantastic depth of the lake (1932 ft.), combined with the clarity of its waters, creates the amazingly serene and intensely blue effect. About 7700 years ago, **Mt. Mazama** created this gentle scene in a massive eruption that buried thousands of square miles of the western U.S. under a thick layer of ash. The cataclysmic eruption left a deep caldera that gradually filled with centuries of rain. Visitors from all over the world circle the 33 mi. Rim Drive, carefully gripping the wheel as the placid blue water slowly enchants them. Klamath (kuh-LAH-math) Falls, one of the closest towns, is convenient for those making a pit stop, and houses most of the services, motels, and restaurants listed below.

ORIENTATION AND PRACTICAL INFORMATION

Route 62 skirts the southwestern edge of the park as it makes a 130 mi. arch northeast from **Medford** (see p. 111) and back south to **Klamath Falls**, 56 mi. southeast. The park is accessible from Rte. 62 and the **south access** road that leads up to the caldera's rim, but the park is not completely open until after the snow has melted. Crater Lake averages over 44 ft. of snow per year, and some roads could be closed as late as July; call the Steel Center for road conditions (see below). To reach the park from Portland, take I-5 to Eugene, then Rte. 58 east to U.S. 97 south. During the summer, you can take Route 138 west from U.S. 97 and approach the lake from the park's **north entrance,** but this route is one of the last to be cleared. Before July, stay on Hwy. 97 south to Rte. 62. All of Crater Lake's services and operating hours are based on weather conditions and on changing funding levels, the latter of which are not determined until April. Call the Steel Center to verify services and hours.

Trains: Amtrak (884-2822 or 800-USA-RAIL/872-7245 for reservations), Spring St. depot, Klamath Falls, at the east end of Main St.; turn right onto Spring St. and immediately left onto Oak St. 1 train per day to points north; 1 per day to Portland ($48-69). Open daily 6:45-10:15am and 9-10:30pm.

Buses: Greyhound, 1200 Klamath Ave., Klamath Falls (882-4616). To: Bend (1 per day, $20); Eugene (1 per day, $24.50); Redding, CA (1 per day, $30). Lockers $1 per 24hr. Open M-F 6am-2:30pm, Sa 6am-9am, and daily 11:30pm-12:30am.

Public Transportation: Basin Transit Service (883-2877), has 6 routes around Klamath Falls. Runs M-F 6am-7:30pm, Sa 10am-5pm. 90¢, seniors and disabled 45¢.

Taxis: AB Taxi, 885-5607. $1.75 base, $2 per mi. 30% senior discount. Runs 24hr.

Car Rental: Budget (885-5421), at the airport. Take S. 6th St. and turn right on Altamonta. $30 per day Sa-Su; 300 free mi. per day. $30 per day M-F; 200 free miles per day. Open M-F 7:30am-9pm, Sa-Su 9am-5:30pm.

Visitor Information: The **Klamath County Department of Tourism** runs a visitors information center at 1451 Main St. (884-0666 or 800-445-6728) in Klamath Falls. Open June-Sept. M-Sa 9am-5:30pm; Oct.-May M-Sa 8am-4:30pm.

Outdoor Information: William G. Steel Center (594-2211, ext. 402), 1 mi. from the south entrance of the park. Pick up backcountry camping permits (free) here or at Rim Village. Open daily 9am-5pm. **Crater Lake National Park Visitor Center** (594-2211, ext. 415), on the lake shore at Rim Village. A smaller center with advice regarding trails and campsites. Open daily June-Sept. 8:30am-6pm.

Park Entrance Fee: Prices doubled two years ago, but now most profits go to the park itself. Cars $10, hikers and bikers $5. Free with Golden Age Passport or Golden Eagle Passport (see **Essentials: National Parks,** p. 43).

Bank: Bank of America, 212 S. 6th St. (882-6677). ATMs available. Open M-Th 9am-5pm, F 9am-6pm, Sa 9am-1pm.

Library: Klamath Falls Public Library, 126 S. 3rd St. (882-8894). Internet access available. Open M 1-8pm, Tu and Th 10am-8pm, W and F-Sa 10am-5pm.

Laundromat: Main Street Laundromat, 1711 Main St. (883-1784). Clean and cool inside. Wash $1.25, dry 25¢ per 12min. Open daily 8am-7pm.

Weather and Road Conditions: Broadcast continuously on 1610 AM in Crater Lake.

Emergency: 911. **Police:** 425 Walnut St. (883-5336). **Fire:** 143 N. Broad St. (nonemergency 885-2056).

Suicide, Mental Health, and General Crisis Line: 800-452-3669. **Rape Crisis:** 884-0390. **Poison Control:** 800-452-7165. All 24hr.

Hospital: Merle West Medical Center, 2865 Daggett Ave. (882-6311). From U.S. 97 northbound, turn right on Campus Dr., then right on Daggett. Open 24 hrs.

Post Office: Klamath Falls, 317 S. 7th St. (800-275-8777). Open M-F 7:30am-5:30pm, Sa 9am-noon. **ZIP Code:** 97601. **Crater Lake,** in the Steel Center. Open M-F 10am-4pm, Sa 10am-2pm. **ZIP Code:** 97604.

Area Code: 541.

ACCOMMODATIONS AND CAMPGROUNDS

Klamath Falls has several affordable hotels; it's an easy base for forays to Crater Lake. For a more interactive visit, the national park contains two campgrounds, both of which are closed each year until roads are passable. **Backcountry camping** is allowed within the park; pick up free permits from Crater Lake NP Visitor Center or the Steel Center (see Practical Information, above).

Fort Klamath Lodge Motel and RV Park, 52851 Rte. 62 (381-2234), 15 mi. from the southern entrance. The closest motel to the lake, the 6-unit lodge is in Fort Klamath, a tiny town consisting of a grocery store, post office, restaurant, and wildflowers. Cozy, quiet, countrified motel rooms with knotted-pine walls. Fan, heater, TV; no phones. Singles $32; doubles $44. 24hr. coin laundry. Closed Nov.-Apr.

Townhouse Motel, 5323 S. 6th St. (882-0924), 3 mi. south of Main, deep in the land of the strip-malls. Clean, comfy rooms at unbeatable prices. Cable and A/C, but no phones. One double bed $28; two bedrooms $32, with kitchenettes $33.

Lost Creek Campground, in Crater Lake National Park. 3 mi. off Rim Dr., on a paved road in the southeast corner of the park. Set amid thin, young pines. Only 16 sites—try to secure one in the morning. Drinking water, flush toilets, and sinks. Tents only; sites $10. No reservations. Usually open mid-July to mid-Oct. but call the visitor center (594-2211) to confirm.

Mazama Campground, near the south entrance to the park. RVs swarm into this monster facility in midsummer, but a sprinkling of sites are reserved for tents. Loop G has denser timber and more spacious sites, offering greater seclusion. No hookups, but flush toilets and showers. Pay laundry and telephone by the convenience store stocked with frozen burritos. 194 sites: tents $13; RVs $14. No reservations. Usually open June to mid-Oct. Call 594-2255 to confirm. Wheelchair accessible.

FOOD

Eating cheap ain't easy in Crater Lake, where Rim Village establishments charge high prices for skimpy food. There are several affordable restaurants in Klamath Falls, as well as a **Safeway** (882-2660) at Pine and 8th St., one block north of Main (open daily 6am-11pm). If you're coming from the south, Fort Klamath is the final food frontier before a trek into the park. If you forgot the sweet gherkins, try **Crater Lake Grocery** (381-2263; open daily 8am-7pm; in winter 8am-6pm).

Waldo's Tavern and Mongolian Grill, 610 Main St., at 6th St. (884-6863). A novel mix of pub culture and Asian cuisine. Fill your tummy to the brim with an all-you-can eat assortment of meats, vegetables, noodles, and pineapples seasoned and cooked before your eyes (lunch $7.50; dinner $8). For those less gluttonous (or those who are adept at packing heaps of food onto a small plate), a one-time-through lunch special costs $5.50. Open M-Sa 11am-9pm.

Cattle Crossing Cafe (381-9801), on Hwy. 62 in Fort Klamath. Step over the silver-plated cow pie into this spare restaurant. A convenient stop on the way to or from the park, offering a rib-sticking breakfast ($5.25) or burger ($5). Great selection of homemade pies ($2.25). Open daily Apr.-Oct. 6am-9pm.

SIGHTS

Rim Drive, which does not open entirely until mid-July, is a 33 mi. loop around the rim of the caldera, high above the lake. The Park Service has carefully placed pull-outs at every point where a view of the lake might cause an awe-struck tourist to drive right off the road. A vast majority of visitors stay in their vehicles as they tour the lake, so it's relatively easy to get away from the crowds; just stop at any of the trailheads scattered around the rim and hike away from the road. **Garfield Peak** (1.7 mi. one-way), which starts at the lodge, and **Watchman Peak** (0.7 mi. one-way), on the west side of the lake, are the most spectacular. The Steel Center (see **Practical Information,** above) has a handy photocopied map of the surrounding trails.

The hike up **Mt. Scott,** the park's highest peak (a tad under 9000 ft.), begins from near the lake's eastern edge. Although steep, the sweaty 2½ mi. ascent gives the perseverant hiker a unique view of the lake. The steep **Cleetwood Trail,** 1.1 mi. of switchbacks on the lake's north edge, is the only route down to the water. Both **Wizard Island,** a cinder cone rising 760 ft. above the lake, and **Phantom Ship Rock,** a spooky rock formation, are breathtaking when viewed from the lake's surface. Picnics, fishing, and swimming are allowed, but surface temperatures reach a maximum of only 50°F (10°C). The water is too nutrient-poor to support much life; only rainbow trout and kokanee have survived. Park rangers lead free walking tours daily in the summer and periodically in the winter (on snowshoes). Call the Steel Center for schedules (see **Practical Information,** above).

The walk from the visitor center at the rim down to the **Sinnott Memorial Overlook,** a stone enclave built into the slope, is an easy 100 yard walk. The view is the area's most panoramic and accessible. In the summer a ranger gives hourly talks (10am-5pm) about the area's geology and history. A similar talk is given nightly (July-Labor Day at 9pm) at the **Mazama Campground Amphitheater.**

A few hundred yards east of Sinnott Memorial Overlook is the **Crater Lake Lodge,** the beneficiary of a recent $18 million renovation. Rooms are booked 6 months to a year in advance and start at $105, but you can have some fun in the lodge for free. Make a quick visit to the rustic "great hall," rebuilt from its original materials, and the observation deck, which has great views and rocking chairs.

A hiking trip into the park's vast **backcountry** leaves all the exhaust and tourists behind. The **Pacific Crest Trail** passes through the park. Another excellent route starts at the **Red Cone trailhead** (on the north access road), making a 12 mi. loop of the **Crater Springs, Oasis Butte,** and **Boundary Springs trails.** Get info and permits (free) at the Steel Center (see **Practical Information,** above).

■ Bend

At the foot of the Cascades's east slope, Bend is at the epicenter of an impressive array of outdoor opportunities. Defined by dramatic volcanic features to the south, Mt. Bachelor and the Cascades to the west, and the Deschutes River through its heart, this area woos waves of skiers and nature-lovers. Bend itself was settled as "Farewell Bend" in the early 19th century, a way station on a pioneer trail that paralleled the Deschutes. Oregon's biggest little city in the east is rapidly losing its small town feel to a stream of California, Portland, and Seattle refugees in search of the perfect blend of urban excitement, pristine wilderness, and sun-filled days. This unexpected boom has wrought local controversy over how to expand—up or out? Meanwhile, new-comers keep on comin'. Chain stores and strip malls have flooded the banks of U.S. 97, but the city's charming downtown and lively crowd still seduces most visitors.

ORIENTATION AND PRACTICAL INFORMATION

Bend is 160 mi. southeast of Portland, either on U.S. 26 E through Warm Springs Indian Reservation to U.S. 97 S, or south on I-5 to Salem, then east on Rte. 22 E to Rte. 20 E through Sisters. Bend is 144 mi. north of Klamath Falls on U.S. 97 and 100 mi. southeast of Mt. Hood via U.S. 26 E and Rte. 97 S.

   Bend is bisected by **U.S. 97 (3rd St.).** The downtown area lies to the west along the **Deschutes River; Wall** and **Bond St.** are the two main arteries. Watch out for curving streets with shifting names. From east to west, Franklin becomes Riverside; at the edge of Drake Park Tumalo St. becomes Galveston, which then becomes Skyliner;

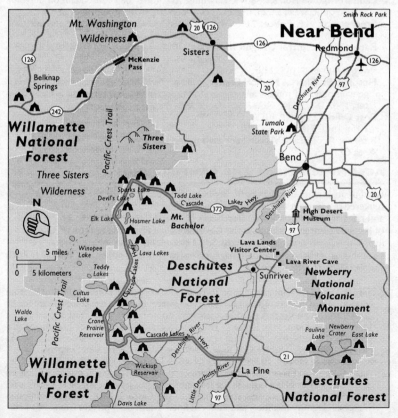

OREGON

Greenwood becomes Newport; 14th St. becomes Century Dr. and is the first leg of the Cascade Lakes Hwy.

Buses: Greyhound, 2045 U.S. 20 E (382-2151), 1½ mi. east of town. To: Portland (1 per day, $23); Klamath Falls (1 per day, $20). Open M-F 7:30-11:30am and 12:30-5pm, Sa 7:30am-noon, Su 8-11:30am. Several other bus and van lines stop here, bound for different destinations; call for info.

Taxis: Owl Taxi, 1919 NE 2nd St. (382-3311). $2 base, $1.80 per mi. Runs 24hr.

Visitor Information: Bend Chamber and Visitors Bureau, 63085 U.S. 97 N (382-3221), stocks the *State Park Guide,* Events Calendar, national forest info, and free maps, plus free coffee. Courtesy phone and internet access. The *Attractions and Activities Guide* has a clear area map. Open M-Sa 9am-5pm, Su 11am-3pm.

Outdoor Information: Deschutes National Forest Headquarters, 1645 U.S. 20 E (388-2715). General forest, recreation, and wilderness info. The *Recreation Opportunity Guide* covers each of the 4 ranger districts. Open M-F 7:45am-4:30pm. The **Bend/Fort Rock District Ranger Station,** 1230 NE 3rd St. #A262 (388-5664), has more info on Deschutes National Forest. **Fish and Wildlife,** 61374 Parrell Rd. (388-6363), controls local regulations and permit requirements. Open M-F 8am-5pm.

Bank: Bank of America, 1210 NE 3rd St. (389-3500), across from the Bend/Ft. Rock Ranger Station (see above). Open M-Th 9am-5pm, F 9am-6pm, Sa 9am-1pm.

Equipment Rental: Hutch's Bicycles, 725 NW Columbia Ave. (382-9253). Mountain bikes $25 per day, $75 for 5 days. Open M-F 9am-7pm, Sa-Su 9am-6pm.

Library: Deschutes County Library, 507 NW Wall (388-6679). Open Tu-Th 10am-8pm, F 10am-6pm, Sa 10am-5pm. Internet access available.

Laundromat: Nelson's, 738 NW Columbia Ave. (382-7087). Attendant on duty M-F 8am-9:30pm. Wash $1.25, dry 25¢ per 10min. Open daily 6am-9:30pm.

Emergency: 911. **Police:** 711 NW Bond (388-5550). **Fire:** 5 Minnesota Ave. NW (388-5533).

Rape Crisis: Central Oregon Battering and Rape Alliance (COBRA): 800-356-2369. 24hr.

Poison: 800-452-7165. 24hr.

Hospital: St. Charles Medical Center, 2500 NE Neff Rd. (382-4321), for major emergencies only. For routine ailments go to **Mountain Medical Immediate Care Center,** 1302 U.S. 97 NE (388-7799). Open M-Sa 8am-8pm, Su 10am-6pm.

Post Office: 2300 NE 4th St. (388-1971), at Webster. Open M-F 8:30am-5:30pm, Sa 10am-1pm. **ZIP Code:** 97701.

Internet Access: See **Visitor Information** and **Library,** above

Area Code: 541.

ACCOMMODATIONS AND CAMPGROUNDS

Bend treats budget travelers right: the hostel and B&B provide phenomenal deals for tuckered-out travelers. Most of the cheapest motels line 3rd St. just outside of town, and rates are surprisingly low. **Deschutes National Forest** maintains a huge number of lakeside campgrounds along the **Cascade Lakes Hwy.** west of town. All have toilets. Those with potable water cost $8-12 per night; those without water are free. Camping anywhere in the national forest area is free. Contact the **Bend/Ft. Rock Ranger District Office** (see above) for more info.

Mill Inn, 642 NW Colorado (389-9198), on the corner of Bond St., 4 blocks from downtown. This recently rebuilt hotel and boarding house is a labor of love for Ev and Carol, who keep it sparkling. Hearty, home-cooked breakfast served in the open dining room. Free laundry. The *real* treasure is the outdoor hot tub. Single-sex 4-bed dorms decorated with sports banners; private rooms are elegant. Bunks $15; singles $37; doubles $45. Rooms with private baths are more expensive.

Bend Cascade Hostel, 19 SW Century Dr. (389-3813 or 800-299-3813). From 3rd St., take Greenwood west until name changes to Newport. After ½ mi., take a left on 14th St. The hostel is a ½ mi. up on the right side, just past the Circle K. Clean, safe, and tidy. About the closest you can get to the Cascade Lakes without camping. Foosball, laundry facilities, and kitchen; linen available. 3 private rooms. 43 beds:

$14; seniors, students, cyclists, and members $13; under 18 with parents ½ price. Lockout 9:30am-4:30pm. Curfew 11pm.

Edelweiss Motor Inn, 2346 NE Division St. (382-6222), at Xerxes St. near the northern intersection with 3rd St. A worn building, with a hint of German heritage in soft beige. Cable, microwave/fridge in some rooms. No phones or A/C, but clean, and there isn't a cheaper place in Bend. Singles and studio rooms $27; doubles $32.

Tumalo State Park, 62976 OB Riley Rd. (388-6055, reservations 800-452-5687). 3-4 mi. north of Bend off U.S. 20 W. A popular campground by the river, but non-premium sites offer little seclusion. 67 tent sites: $15; preferred river sites $17; 21 full hookups $19; yurts $29. Non-camper showers $2.

FOOD

The diversity of food in Bend breaks the eastern Oregon beef-and-potatoes monotony. Bend's restaurants maintain high standards, with the most exceptional generally downtown. Four mega-markets line the east side of 3rd St. **Devore's Good Food Store and Wine Shop,** 1124 Newport NW (389-6588), peddles all things organic, including excellent wine, beer, and cheese. (Open M-Sa 8am-7pm, Su 11am-6pm.

☯ Westside Bakery and Cafe, 1005 NW Galveston (382-3426). The smell of delicious pastries (under $3) lure many a passerby to this local favorite. Order the famous blackberry honeywheat pancakes ($5), or try a wide array of burgers and sandwiches ($5-6.50). Open daily 6:30am-3pm.

Taqueria Los Jalapeños, 601 NE Greenwood Ave. (382-1402), serves good and shockingly inexpensive Mexican food. Narrow and simple space filled by a steady stream of devoted locals. Bean and cheese burritos $1.50; *chimichanga* plates $5.50. Open M-Sa 10:30am-8:30pm; in winter 10:30am-7pm.

Deschutes Brewery and Public House, 1044 NW Bond St. (382-9242). The homemade sausage ($5), smoked salmon ($6), and smoked vegetable sandwiches ($5) are good, but 6 or 7 new specials a day ($5-7) render the menu moot. Imperial pints (20oz.) of ale, bitters, stout ($3.25), root beer, and ginger ale ($1.75) brewed on the premises. The brewery's Black Butte Porter is found on tap in bars all over Oregon. Open M-Th 11am-11:30pm, F-Sa 11am-12:30am, Su 11am-10pm.

Kuishinbo Kitchen, 114 NW Minnesota St. (385-9191; fax 385-9169), between Wall and Bond St. Fax in your order or make a personal appearance at this food lovers kitchen. The *sukiyaki bento* ($6) is good, but everyone orders the tasty *yaki soba* noodles ($4). Open M-F 11am-7pm, Sa 11am-4pm.

SIGHTS AND EVENTS

In Bend, you can get up close and personal with Canadian geese or enjoy a picnic lunch on the lawns of beautiful **Drake Park,** sandwiched between **Mirror Pond** and Franklin St., a block from downtown. The park hosts a number of events and festivals, most significantly the **Cascade Festival of Music** (383-2202), a week-long series of classical and pops concerts held in late August by the river. *(Tickets $12-20, student rush half-price. Call the festival office at 382-8381 or write to 842 NW Wall St. #6.)*

South of Bend by 3½ mi. on U.S. 97, the **High Desert Museum,** 59800 S. Hwy. 97 (382-4754; http://www.highdesert.org), is one of the premier natural and cultural history museums in the Pacific Northwest. *(Open daily 9am-5pm. $6.25, seniors and ages 13-18 $5.75, ages 5-12 $3, under 5 free.)* In the Spirit of the West exhibit, visitors walk through stunning life-size dioramas of life in the Old West, meandering through dark mining tunnels, rickety log cabins, and Chinese immigrant work shops. The indoor desertarium houses seldom-seen animals including bats, burrowing owls, and collared lizards; outdoor paved paths wind past playful otters, docile porcupines, and various birds of prey. Popular interpretive talks featuring these animals are given daily every hour. August of 1999 brings a brand-new Native American Wing to the museum, featuring a walk-through exhibit on post-reservation Indian life. The museum attracts 1200 visitors daily in summer, so arrive early to beat the crowds.

The annual **Bend Summer Festival** (389-0995), held during the second weekend in July, showcases the work of local artisans and performers from Central Oregon.

The entire downtown area is closed to traffic as the streets are flooded with local sculptures, paintings, crafts, street musicians, chalk art, microbreweries, restaurants, live bands, and nomads from all corners of Oregon looking for things to decorate their living rooms. All events are free, but parking is limited.

OUTDOORS

If you can ski the 9065 ft. **Mount Bachelor** with its 3365 ft. vertical drop, you're in good company—Mt. Bachelor is one of the home mountains of the U.S. Ski Team. The ski season often extends to the 4th of July. *(Daily lift passes $39, seniors $24, ages 7-12 $20.)* A shuttle bus service runs the 22 mi. between the parking lot at the corner of Simpson and Columbia in Bend and the West Village Guest Services Building at the mountain. *(Runs Nov.-May $1).* Many nearby lodges offer five-night **ski packages.** *(382-8334; reservations 800-800-8334; info 800-829-2442; daily updated ski report and summer events 382-7888.)* **Chairlifts** are open for sightseers during the summer, and you can hike back down the mountain or ride both ways. *(Open daily 10am-4pm. $11, seniors $9.75, ages 7-12 $5.50.)* **Bike rentals** are available at the Sunrise Ski and Sport Shop at the top of the mountain. *($15 per day.)* A U.S. Forest Service naturalist gives free talks on local natural history at the summit. *(Summer daily 10am and 1pm.)*

The **Three Sisters Wilderness Area,** north and west of the Cascade Lakes Highway, is one of Oregon's largest and most popular wilderness areas. A permit ($3) is required to go into the wilderness, but dayhikers can issue themselves permits at most trailheads. Bikes are not allowed in the wilderness. Permits and info are available at Bend/Ft. Rock Ranger District Office or the Bend Chamber and Visitors Bureau (see **Practical Information,** above). **Mountain biking** is the favorite sport of Benders, and many roads have bike lanes or wide shoulders. Try **Deschutes River Trail** for a fairly flat, basic, forested trail ending at **Deschutes River.** To reach the trailhead, go 7½ mi. west of Bend on Century Dr. (Cascade Lakes Hwy.) until Forest Service Road 41, then turn left and follow the signs to Lava Island Falls. The trail begins here and is 10½ miles one-way. For a difficult, technical ride, hit the **Waldo Lake Loop,** a grueling 22 mi. trail around the lake. To get there, take Cascade Lakes Hwy. to Forest Service Road 4290. A slick new guide to the vast array of mountain bike trails around Bend is available for $7 at the Bend/Ft. Rock District Ranger Station and most bike shops in the area, but some of the hottest trails aren't on the maps; talk to locals.

Would-be cowpokes can take **horseback rides** offered by local resorts. **River Ridge Stables,** 18575 SW Century Dr. (382-8711, ask for the stables), at Inn of the Seventh Mountain several miles west of Bend, leads trail rides. *(1hr. $19, 12 & under $17; each additional 30min. $5; 4hr. $50; 8hr. $70.)* They also offer summer hay rides and winter sleigh rides. *(Hay rides $5 per person, 4 and under free. Sleighrides $15 per hr.)* **Whitewater rafting,** although costly, is one of the most popular local recreational activities. Half-day trips usually last three hours and cover the fairly tame waters of the upper Deschutes, while full-day trips require a one-hour ride to Maupin to run the class I-IV rapids of the lower Deschutes. **Cascade River Adventures** and **Sun Country Tours** (800-770-2161 for both) run half-day and full-day trips out of the **Sun River Resort,** 17 mi. south of Bend off U.S. 97, and also out of an office in Bend (531 SW 13th St.). *(Half-day $35, ages 6-12 $30. Full day weekends $85, ages 6-12 $75; midweek $80; ages 6-12 $70.)* Or try **Blazing Paddle Whitewater Adventures** (388-0145), which have various pick-up points in town. *(Full-day trip $80 per person.)*

■ Near Bend: Newberry National Monument

In November 1990, the **Newberry National Volcanic Monument** was established to link and preserve the volcanic features south of Bend. For an introduction to the area, visit the **Lava Lands Visitor Center,** 58201 U.S. 97 (593-2421), 5 mi. south of the High Desert Museum on U.S. 97. *(Open mid-June to Sept. daily 9:30am-5pm; Apr. to mid-June W-Su 9:30am-5pm.)* A mandatory $5 parking fee, good for 2 days, is required within ¼ mi. of the monument area (free with Golden Age Passport; see p. 43). Immediately behind the visitor center is **Lava Butte,** a 500 ft. cinder cone from which much of the nearby lava flows. Between Memorial Day and Labor Day, a shuttle bus makes the nearly two mile journey every 30 minutes. *($2, seniors and $1.50, under 6 free.)* One mile south of the visitor center on U.S. 97 is **Lava River Cave** (593-1456), a 100,000-year-old, one mile long subterranean lava tube. When the Bend heat becomes unbearable, head to this naturally air-conditioned 42°F cave. Bundle up before descending and bring a lantern or rent one at the cave for $1.50. *(Open mid-May to mid-Oct. 9am-6pm. $2.50, ages 13-17 $2, under 13 free.)*

The central component of the monument is **Newberry Crater,** 13 mi. south of the Lava Lands Visitor Center on U.S. 97, then about 13 steep mi. east on Rte. 21. This diverse volcanic region was formed by the eruptions of Newberry Volcano over millions of years, the most recent of which was an estimated 7060 years ago, on a Tuesday. (Newberry is one of three volcanoes in Oregon most likely to erupt again "soon.") The caldera covers about 500 sq. mi., and contains **Paulina Lake** and **East Lake.** The most scenic campground is **Little Crater,** with 50 sites between Rte. 21 and the Paulina lakeshore. *($12; premier sites $14.)* Over 150 mi. of trails cross the area, including a short walk up to an enormous **obsidian flow** formed by an eruption 1300 years ago, a 21 mi. loop that circumnavigates the **caldera rim,** and a 7½ mi. loop around Paulina Lake. For an easy view of the crater, drive up **Paulina's Peak.** *(Open June-Sept., weather conditions permitting.)*

■ Near Bend: Sisters

Twenty miles northwest of Bend on U.S. 20 lies the restored western village of Sisters. The tiny town has managed to adopt an Old West look to attract tourist dollars without falling victim to tacky commercialism—yet. The plan seems to have worked, since Sisters is often overrun in midsummer by camera-snapping and souvenir-buying hordes. While Cascade St. (Sisters' main drag) is good for a stroll or snack, the massive mountains to the west provide the real excitement. Although this is a popular part of the Cascades, it isn't hard to escape from the masses to find some peace and quiet.

ORIENTATION AND PRACTICAL INFORMATION From Sisters, Rte. 126 heads east to **Redmond** (20 mi.) and **Prineville** (39 mi.), and joins U.S. 20 for the trip over the Cascades. Rte. 242 heads southwest from town and over McKenzie Pass to rejoin Rte. 126 on the other side of the range. In town, the highways all blend into **Cascade St.**

The Sisters **Chamber of Commerce** (549-0251) is at 222 W. Hood Ave.; just follow the signs to the visitor center once you get into town (open M-F 9am-5pm, Sa-Su variable hours; call ahead). Sisters' **Ranger District Station** (Deschutes National Forest), P.O. Box 249 (549-2111), on the corner of Cascade and Pine St., offers all kinds of recreation info, including a list of nearby campgrounds and the free *Day Hike Guide,* a catalogue of five nearby hikes 2-10 mi. long (open M-F 8am-4:30pm; in summer open Sa 8am-noon). **Area Code:** 541.

ACCOMMODATIONS, CAMPING, AND FOOD A cheap bed is hard to find in Sisters. The best bet is the **Sisters Motor Lodge,** 511 W. Cascade (549-2551), on the highway at the west end of town. Individually themed rooms like "Grandma's Cottage" or "Picket Fence" come with appropriate accoutrements, plus phones, coffee-makers and cable TV. Rooms start around $59 in the summer.

Camping is plentiful and spectacular near Sisters. The Sisters Ranger District (see above) maintains 26 campgrounds in the area. Many of these cluster near **Camp Sherman,** a small community on the Metolius River, 17 mi. northwest of Sisters. The **Metolius River campgrounds** tend to be the most crowded, and virtually all charge a $10 fee. One noteworthy exception is **Riverside,** 10 mi. west on Rte. 20 and 7 mi. northeast on Rd. 14. Escape from motorized vehicles and pump your own water in this walk-in area (sites $6). **Link Creek,** 2 mi. down the road which partially circles **Suttle Lake** (itself 14 mi. northwest of Sisters on Rte. 20), is one of six campgrounds open year-round. Although the lake can fill up with fishing boats and the occasional windsurfer, it is serene on weekdays ($11; premium sites $13; call 800-280-CAMP/2267 for reservations). For a free and less frequented patch, cruise 14 mi. west on

Rte. 242 and a bumpy ½ mi. on a red dirt road to **Lava Camp Lake** (10 tent sites), a magnificently isolated campground just off the lava fields of McKenzie Pass.

Plan on exploring Sisters during the daylight hours; things are slow at six and dead by dark. Overpriced seafood and bar fare can be had any time, but the delis that close by 5 or 6pm are best for both palette and purse. For exquisite specialty salads (75¢-$3) and carefully assembled gourmet sandwiches ($5-5.50), head for **Seasons Cafe and Wine Shop,** 411 E. Hood St. (549-8911), one block south of Cascade along a little brook (open M-Sa 11am-3pm). The **Sisters Bakery,** 251 E. Cascade St. (549-0361), has all kinds of baked goods, including marionberry squares and biscuits ($2), loaves of top-quality bread ($1.80-3), and seductive front windows (open daily 5am-6pm).

EVENTS AND OUTDOORS

The **Sisters Rodeo,** the "Biggest Little Show in the World," takes place annually on the second weekend in June, and packs an astonishing purse: the $170,000 prize attracts big-time wranglers for three days and nights of saddle bronco-riding, calf-roping, and steer-wrestling, among other events. *(Tickets $8-12. Shows usually sell out.)* Write the Sisters Rodeo Association, P.O. Box 1018, Sisters 97759, or call 549-0121 for more info; call (800) 827-7522 for tickets. Keep your gender stereotypes in order by watching the Pepsi Girls, Dodge Pickup Guys, and some fine rodeo clowning.

1999 marks the 24th year of the Sisters **Outdoor Quilt Show,** the largest outdoor quilt show in the nation. On a Saturday in mid-July, over 850 quilts tell colorful stories as they adorn office buildings, balconies, porches, fences, and windows all throughout town. The show is the culmination of a week-long "quilters' affair" featuring quilting classes, guest speakers, and evening events showcasing the art of quilting. For more information write to the Sisters Outdoor Quilt Show, 311 W. Cascade St., P.O. Box 280, Sisters, 97759; or call 549-6061.

Miles and miles of **hiking** trails loop through the forests and mountains around Sisters. An easy, level walk of up to 10 mi. along the **Metolius River** allows time to ponder the debate over the origin of the river's name (some say "metolius" means "white fish," some, "spawning salmon," and others, "stinking water"). Drive 10 mi. west on Rte. 20 from Sisters, then make a right at the sign for Camp Sherman (Rd. 14). Proceed 7 mi. on Rd. 14 past the "Head of the Metolius" and park at the Wizard Falls Fish Hatchery to catch the trail. A slightly more challenging hike is the 4 mi. roundtrip up **Black Butte,** a near-perfect cone that looms over the west end of town. To reach the trailhead, go 6 mi. west from Sisters on U.S. 20, turn right onto Forest Rd. 11, then turn onto Forest Rd. 1110 after 4 mi. The trailhead is another 4 mi. up the road. Deeper in the mountains, the strenuous 7.6 mi. round-trip hike up **Black Crater** offers unsurpassed views of snow-capped peaks and lava flows on McKenzie Pass, and an intimate experience with volcanic debris. The trail departs from the left-hand side of Rte. 242 about 11 mi. west of Sisters; access is often limited due to snow. Both Black Butte and Black Crater require a $3 **trailpark pass** available at ranger stations.

McKenzie Pass (see p. 121),15 mi. west of Sisters on Rte. 242, was the site of a relatively recent lava flow which created barren fields of rough, black **aa** (AH-ah) lava. A tall, medieval-looking tower built of lava chunks gives a panoramic view of the Cascades, while a ½ mi. paved trail winds among basalt boulders, cracks, and crevices.

Mountain biking opportunities abound near Sisters. Although no bikes or motorized vehicles are allowed in official wilderness areas, most other trails are open to bikes, as are the many miles of little-used dirt roads in the area. Ask at the ranger station for details. **Eurosports,** 182 E. Hood (549-2471), rents mountain bikes. *(Open daily 9am-5:30pm. $12 per day, $60 per week.)*

■ John Day Fossil Beds

The John Day Fossil Beds National Monument records the history of life before the Cascade Range was formed, evoking a land of lush, tropical vegetation and ambling dinosaurs. The park is divided into three isolated parts, each representing a different epoch, each as impressive for its unusual landscape as for its fossilized inhabitants.

Sheep Rock, 32 mi. east of Mitchell and 7 mi. west of Dayville at the junction of U.S. 26 and Rte. 19, houses the monument's **visitor center** (987-2336) and will satiate all cravings for touchable fossils (open May-Aug. daily 9am-6pm; Mar.-Apr. and Sept.-Nov. daily 9-5pm; Dec.-Feb. M-F 9am-5pm). The center displays rocks and fossils from all layers of history, exhibits on early mammals, and an award-winning 17-minute video explaining the history of the fossil beds (you'd never guess that high school students produced it). The **Island in Time Trail,** 3 mi. up the road, leads into the middle of fossil-rich **Blue Basin,** a strikingly beautiful blue and green canyon of eroded badland spires. Admire petrified sea turtle, oneonta, and saber-toothed cat as the creek slips by, counting the further passage of time.

Painted Hills, 3 mi. west of Mitchell off U.S. 26, focuses on an epoch 30 million years ago, when the land was in geologic transition. Its smooth mounds of colored sediment are particularly vivid at sunset and dawn, or after a rain when the whole gorge glistens. The hills almost always stay true to their name, showing off layer upon layer of colored sand. **Clarno,** the oldest section of the monument, is on Rte. 218, accessible by U.S. 97 to the west and Rte. 19 to the east, 20 mi. west of the town of Fossil. Prepare to be humbled.

■ Near John Day Fossil Beds

The small town of **John Day,** at the junction of U.S. 26 and U.S. 395, is the largest outpost for miles around. The unique **Kam Wah Chung & Co. Museum,** next to City Park, served as a general store, an herbal doctor's office, and a Chinese temple for thousands of Chinese immigrants from 1887 through the early 40s. This fort-like building still houses some 1000 different herbs used by the famous Doc Hay (open M-Th 9am-noon and 1-5pm, Sa-Su 1-5pm; $3, seniors $2, ages 6-16 $1.50). The town is surrounded on three sides by the massive **Malheur National Forest** (mal-HERE), ranging in elevation from 4000 to 9038 ft. and containing grasslands of sagebrush and juniper and forests of pine and fir. Info is available at the **Malheur National Forest Supervisor's Office,** which conveniently houses the **Bear Valley/Long Creek District Ranger Station** (575-3000) at 431 Patterson Bridge Rd. (open M-F 7:15am-5pm). This vast, wild region of timbered hills and jagged ridges sees little use, and there are prime opportunities for solitude and great hiking in the forest's two designated wilderness areas, **Strawberry Mountain** and **Monument Rock.** By far the most popular area in the forest is the **Eastern Lakes Basin,** in the Strawberry area. Three **free campgrounds—McNaughton Springs** (4 sites), **Slide Creek** (3 sites), and **Strawberry** (11 sites)—are off the Forest Road near the **Strawberry trailhead,** a main access point for the Strawberry Mountain area. The trail runs 1 mi. toward **Strawberry Lake** and **Strawberry Mountain,** the forest's highest peak; a 12 mi. loop leads past several other lakes. To reach the trailhead, take Forest Rd. 60 south from Prairie City. **Magone Lake** (Mah-GOON) is another popular free campground, with beaches, fishing, hiking trails, 21 sites, and new composting bathrooms. To get there from John Day, take U.S. 26 east about 9 mi. to Forest Rd. 18, which heads north to the campground. None of these campgrounds have drinking water. Camping is also permitted anywhere in the forest.

The AAA-approved **Dreamer's Lodge,** 144 N. Canyon Blvd. (575-0526, reservations 800-654-2849), has clean, comfortable rooms, all with La-Z-Boy recliners, A/C, refrigerators, and cable (singles $44; doubles $48; two kitchen units available). The **Travelers Motel and Mini-mart,** 755 S. Canyon Blvd. (575-2076), has the best rates in town and a laundromat on the premises (wash 75¢, dry 50¢). The spacious rooms include TV, A/C, microwaves, and refrigerators, but none are non-smoking, and the decor reflects the low price (singles $27; doubles $32). The flat, neatly mowed grass of **Clyde Holliday State Park** (575-2773), 7 mi. west of town on U.S. 26, has a slightly suburban aura (30 sites with electricity and showers $15; hiker/biker sites $4).

With four microbrews, **Cave Inn Pizza,** 830 S. Canyon Blvd. (575-1083), is a happening local hangout (open daily 3-9pm, possibly later). At **Russell's Meats and Gloria's Deli,** 235 S. Canyon Blvd. (575-0720), a few miles south of John Day in Canyon

City, choose among eight meats, six breads, and eight cheeses to create a solid sandwich that comes with soup, salad, or chips ($5, half-sandwich $3.50; open M-F 8am-5:30pm). The **Dirty Shame Tavern and Pizza,** 145 Main St. (575-1935), sports a fancy wooden bar, pool table, foosball, darts, and TV (open M-Sa 11:30am-11:30pm). In Prairie City, a lovely 13 mi. drive west from John Day, **Ferdinand's,** 128 W. Front St. (820-4455), offers a surprising array of gourmet food and imported beers, with homemade crust on the pizzas (large $10-16), fresh sauces on all pasta, and a remarkable selection of grill items, including fresh Oregon sturgeon (open W-Sa 5-9pm).

■ Burns

Tiny Burns and its even tinier neighbor Hines serve as way-stations and supply centers for travelers. Ideally situated between the Ochoco and Malheur National Forests, the Malheur National Wildlife Refuge, Steens Mountain, and the Alvord Desert, Burns enchants both residents and visitors with its surrounding open country. Stock up on gas, water, info, and supplies in Burns, and head for the unspoiled, uninhabited wilderness that is southeastern Oregon.

ORIENTATION AND PRACTICAL INFORMATION U.S. 20 from Ontario and U.S. 395 from John Day converge about 2 mi. north of Burns, continue through Burns and Hines as one highway (known as **Broadway, Monroe,** and **Oregon Ave.** in town), and diverge about 30 mi. to the west. U.S. 20 continues west to Bend and the Cascade Range; U.S. 395 runs south to Lakeview, OR, and California. Although buses and vans run to and from some towns in the area, there is no transportation to the most interesting local outdoor areas.

> **Visitor Information: Harney County Chamber of Commerce,** 18 W. D St. (573-2636; http://www.oregon1.org/harney), has maps and info on the town itself, plus brochures from Oregon and all four surrounding states. Open M-F 9am-5pm.
>
> **Outdoor Information: Burns Ranger District (Malheur National Forest)** and **Snow Mountain Ranger District (Ochoco National Forest)** (573-4300), in Hines. On the main drag, about 4½ mi. south of the center of Burns, these two share the same office and provide info on hiking, fishing, and camping. Open M-F 8am-4:30pm. **Burns District Office (BLM),** U.S. 20 W (573-4400), a few miles west of Hines, is also rife with info. Open M-F 8am-4:30pm.
>
> **Laundromat: Jiffy Wash,** at the corner of S. Diamond and S. Jackson St., just off of W. Monroe. Wash $1, dry 25¢ per 13min. Open M-Sa 7am-9pm, Su 8am-8pm.
>
> **Road Conditions:** 889-3999.
>
> **Emergency:** 911. **Police:** 242 S. Broadway (573-6028). **Harney County Sheriff:** 573-6156. **Fire:** 573-5255.
>
> **Crisis Line: H Hope Hotline,** 573-7176.
>
> **Hospital: Harney District Hospital,** 557 W. Washington St. (573-7281).
>
> **Post Office:** 100 S. Broadway (800-ASK-USPS/275-8777). Open M-F 8:30am-5pm. **ZIP Code:** 97720.
>
> **Area Code:** 541.

ACCOMMODATIONS AND CAMPGROUNDS The **Malheur Field Station** (493-2629; http://www.eosc.osshe.edu/~dkerley/malheur.htm) provides a unique way to experience the natural beauty of southeastern Oregon. Run by the Great Basin Society and located 3 mi. short of the refuge headquarters (see **Outdoors,** below), it offers room and board to visitors staying overnight in the refuge. Accommodations are undeniably spartan, but clean and cheap (dorms $18; private mobile home sleeps up to 5 $27-54). Meals cost $5-8, and cooking facilities are available. Bring a sleeping bag or bedroll. Reservations are strongly encouraged in the spring, fall, and especially over Memorial Day weekend, when the place is packed with school groups.

The **Frenchglen Hotel** (493-2825), 60 mi. south on Rte. 205 to **Frenchglen,** serves up ridiculously good homemade food in a quaint, historic building owned by Oregon State Parks. Trim, cozy rooms with wood-frame beds, patchwork quilts, and shared baths go cost $45; two single beds cost $49. Reservations are essential in summer (open Mar. 15-Nov. 15). Back in Burns, the managers of the **Bontemps Motel,** 74 W. Monroe (573-2037 or 800-229-1394), provide a gay-friendly environment in comfortable rooms with cable, HBO, A/C, refrigerators, and some damn cool lampshades (singles $33; doubles $38; pets $3 extra; kitchenettes $3-5).

Camping is the cheapest way to enjoy the breathtaking open country around Burns. About 15 mi. north of town and within earshot of U.S. 395 is **Idlewild,** the only official campground convenient to town. It has 24 free sites sprinkled through sparse pines (free; pit toilets; no drinking water). Although there are relatively few campgrounds around Burns, the public lands are vast, and dispersed camping is allowed. Certain restrictions apply when the risk of wildfire is high. Contact the Forest Service and BLM offices in Hines (see **Practical Information,** above) for more info.

About 3 mi. east of Frenchglen, along the first bit of the Steens Mt. Loop (see **Outdoors,** below), are two easy-to-find campgrounds. The privately owned **Steens Mountain Resort** (also called the **Camper Corral;** 493-2415, reservations 800-542-3765), set atop a low hill, offers groceries, showers, and a 24-hour laundry, but not much shade or privacy ($10; RV hookups $15; open year-round). Just down the road, by the side of the Blitzen River, the BLM-administered **Page Springs** campground has 30 sites of varying seclusion and cover. Continuing around the loop, the BLM has three other campgrounds: **Fish Lake,** 17 mi. southeast of Frenchglen, **Jackman Park,** 3 mi. farther, and the new **South Steens,** 28 mi. south of Frenchglen from the loop's south side ($4; drinking water and pit toilets; all but Page Springs are seasonal).

FOOD Beef is king here in cattle country. Groceries await at **Safeway,** 246 W. Monroe (573-6767; open daily 5am-11pm). The best food in the area is at the **Frenchglen Hotel** (see **Accommodations,** above), but an appealing alternative is the **Frenchglen Mercantile** (493-2738), just two doors down from the hotel on Rte. 205. A functional gas station, grocery store, bar, and cafe, the Mercantile's menu choices cost $5-15, and they have several microbrews on tap (open Apr.-Oct. M-F 7:30am-9pm, Sa-Su 8am-9pm). The **Frenchglen Hotel** (see **Accommodations,** above) serves enormous breakfasts ($3.50-5.75) and overwhelming family-style dinners ($12-15.50; breakfast 7:30am-9:30am; lunch 11:30am-2:30pm; dinner by reservation).

OUTDOORS The surrounding open country beckons to any soul seeking fresh air and solitude, with Rte. 205 providing passage to the intriguing terrain south of Burns. The wide, dry land is home only to sagebrush, until it gives way to the surprisingly rich grasslands and marshes of **Harney** and **Malheur Lakes.** Thousands of birds end their migratory flight paths each year at **Malheur National Wildlife Refuge.** Protecting both lakes and stretching 35 mi. south along Rte. 205, the refuge covers 185,000 acres and is home to 360 species of birds, including grebes, ibis, plovers, shrikes, owls, wigeons, and goatsuckers. The refuge headquarters, 6 mi. east of Rte. 205 on a well-marked turn-off between Burns and Frenchglen, includes a **visitor center** (493-2612) that gives a valuable orientation. *(Open M-Th 7am-4:30pm, F 7am-3:30pm, Sa-Su 10am-4pm.)* The refuge is open year-round during daylight hours, and lodgings are often available at the Malheur Field Station (see **Accommodations,** above).

About 40 mi. south of town on Rte. 205, the Diamond Lane turn-off leads east toward **Diamond Craters,** where a series of basaltic burps from the earth's mantle have created a landscape of diverse volcanic features. Be careful to stay on the roads, or risk becoming stuck in loose cinder, volcanic ash, or clay. A few miles farther is the historic **Round Barn,** built to allow year-round horse training. Pick up a self-guided auto tour of the area, along with other info, at the Burns District BLM office in Hines or the refuge visitor center (see above).

About 70 mi. southeast of Burns and a few miles from Frenchglen is **Steens Mountain,** a 30 mi. fault block with an east face rising a full vertical mile above the surrounding desert. At 9773 ft., Steens is the highest mountain in southeastern Oregon, and the view from the top reaches as far as four different states. The dirt **Steens Mountain Loop Road** climbs the gradual west slope of the mountain to several viewpoints above deep, glacier-carved gorges in a 66 mi. round-trip, heading east from

Rte. 205 in Frenchglen and rejoining Rte. 205 8 mi. farther south. The road is only open when clear of snow, typically July to October. Steens Mountain offers plenty of hiking, and hosts abundant bighorn sheep and pronghorn antelope. Its remoteness keeps it relatively uncrowded, and nearly all visitors are vehicle-shackled sightseers; walking even a short distance from the road brings solitude. Contact the Burns District BLM office (see **Practical Information,** above) for up-to-date road info and advice on recreational opportunities.

The bone-dry, mirror-flat **Alvord Desert** stretches east of Steens. The mountain blocks virtually all moisture from the desert, which receives less than 6 in. of precipitation per year. The driest and emptiest part of the Pacific Northwest, this ocean of sand is a playground for desert hikers and glider pilots. To get to there, head south from Frenchglen for about 50 mi. to the small town of Fields, and turn left onto the dirt road toward Andrews. Winding its way north from Nevada through the Alvord Desert and up Steens Mountain is the **Desert Trail,** an arid hiking route that will eventually run from the Mexican border to the Canadian border on the desert lands east of the Sierras and Cascades. This little-known trail stretches 150 mi. through southeastern Oregon, offering some beautifully desolate exploration. **Trail guides** and info are available from the Desert Trail Association (475-2960). Contact the Membership and Hike Chairman, Keith Sheerer, at P.O. Box 34, Madras 97741.

■ Pendleton

Called Goodwin Station from 1862 to 1968, this small town eventually took on the name of George Hunt Pendleton, an Ohio politician who ran for Vice President in 1864. He had nothing to do with Oregon, he never visited Pendleton, but someone liked the ring of his name, and with this introductory paragraph, his memory lives on. This agricultural town is best known for its locally processed wool and for the mad Pendleton Round-Up. In mid-September, 50,000 cowfolks and horsedudes gather in this northeastern town to witness the rodeo of a lifetime and be a part of Pendleton's annual celebration of machismo.

ORIENTATION AND PRACTICAL INFORMATION

Pendleton is at the junction of I-84, Rte. 11, and U.S. 395, just south of the Washington border, roughly equidistant (200-230 mi.) from Portland, Spokane, WA, and Boise, ID. While cool, green **Raley Park**—humming year-round with energy from the Round-Up Grounds next door—may be the spiritual center of town, **Main St.** is Pendleton's geographic hub. Pendleton's east-west streets are named in alphabetical order. From Main St., north-south streets are numbered, increasing in both directions (there are two parallel 2nd Streets, 2nd St. SE and 2nd St. SW).

> **Buses: Greyhound,** 320 SW Court Ave. (276-1551 or 800-231-2222), a few blocks west of the city center. To: Portland (3 per day, $32); Boise, ID (4 per day, $36); Walla Walla, WA (3 per day, $9). Open M-F 9am-9pm and 12:30-3am, Sa-Su 11am-1pm, 4:30-9pm, and 12:30-3am.
>
> **Taxis: Elite Taxi,** 276-8294. Open M-Sa 5:30am-3am, Su 7am-3am.
>
> **Car Rental: Round-Up Rent-A-Car,** 309 SW Emigrant Ave. (276-1498). $20 per day; 15¢ per mi. over 50 mi. Unlimited free mileage for weekly rental ($140). Must be over 25 with major credit card and valid driver's license. Open M-Sa 8am-5pm.
>
> **Visitor Information: Pendleton Chamber of Commerce,** 501 S. Main (276-7411 or 800-547-8911; http://www.pendleton-oregon.org). Open M-F 8:30am-5pm; in summer M-F 8:30am-5pm, Sa 9am-5pm.
>
> **Outdoor Information: Umatilla Forest Headquarters,** 2517 SW Hailey Ave. (278-3716), in a red brick building up the hill from I-84 Exit 209, above the Burger King on the right. The friendly, helpful staff is just waiting to divulge info on hiking, camping, fishing, and biking in the vast forested plateaus and canyons of the Blue Mountains. Open M-F 7:45am-4:30pm.

Emergency: 911. **Police:** 109 SW Court Ave. (276-4411). **Fire:** 911 SW Court Ave. (276-1442).
Hospital: St. Anthony's, 1601 SE Court Ave. (276-5121).
Poison Crisis Line: 800-452-7165. **Mental Health Services:** 800-452-5413. 24hr.
Post Office: 104 SW Dorion Ave. (800-275-8777), in the Federal Building at SW 1st St. Open M-F 9am-5pm, Sa 10am-1pm. **ZIP Code:** 97801.
Area Code: 541.

ACCOMMODATIONS AND CAMPGROUNDS

For most of the year, lodging in Pendleton is inexpensive. During the Round-Up, rates double, and prices skyrocket on everything from hamburgers to commemorative cowboy hats; reserve rooms up to two years in advance. The nearest decent camping is 25 mi. away, though the Round-Up provides 1500 camping spots at schools around town (RVs $15; tents $10). Call the chamber of commerce after April 1 to lasso a spot. For more options, see **Outdoors,** below.

Tapadera Budget Inn, 105 SE Court (276-3231, reservations 800-722-8277), near the center of town. Lounge and eat on the premises, or exercise at the local health club with a free pass. Singles $34; doubles $38-45. 10% AAA and senior discount.

Longhorn Motel, 411 SW Dorion Ave. (276-7531), around the corner from the bus station. Clean, comfy rooms and a light blue-and-white exterior, reminiscent of a beach bungalow. Upstairs rooms have HBO; downstairs rooms have wheelchair access. Singles from $31; doubles $45-51.

Emigrant Springs State Park (983-2277), 26 mi. southeast of Pendleton off I-84 Exit 234, in a shady grove of evergreens at a historic Oregon Trail camp. Smell the pines and hear the highway. Hot showers. 33 tent sites: $13. 18 full hookups: $17. Wheelchair accessible.

FOOD

Vegetarians will have more luck grazing in the outlying wheat fields than in local restaurants—this is steak country. Exceptions are listed below. For staple foods, head to the huge **Albertson's** (276-1362), on SW Court St. across from the Round-Up grounds (open daily 6am-11pm).

Ⓦ**Great Pacific Cafe,** 403 S. Main (276-1350). The chillest establishment in Pendleton hosts wine tastings every other Friday at 4:30pm ($1.50 per half-glass) and jazz concerts off and on during the summer. Open-faced baked sandwiches $3-5; veggie bagel $4. Extensive beer list, including the fabulous Black Butte Beer (pints $2.75). Open M-Th and Sa 8:30am-6pm, F 8:30am-7pm.

The Cookie Tree, 30 SW Emigrant (278-0343). More than just a fix for the sugar addict, the Cookie Tree also serves up breakfasts and sandwiches ($3.25-5.25). Vegetarians can delve into the Avocado Delight ($4.50), just one of many such options. Open daily 6am-3pm.

Circle S Barbecue, 210 SE 5th St. (276-9637). Don't let the 3 ft. axe door handle scare you away from this Western barbecue. Sit in wrap-around, faux-leather booths and drink from Mason jars while eating real pit BBQ meat with salad, potatoes, beans, and corn bread ($10). Finish it off with a *crême de menthe* sundae ($2.25). Breakfast served all day. Open T-Sa 7am-9pm, Su 7am-2pm.

SIGHTS AND EVENTS

Pendleton Underground Tours, 37 SW Emigrant (276-0730 or 800-226-6398), is the town's greatest year-round attraction. *(Open daily; call for tour times. 1hr. tour $10, children $5. $1 AAA discount. Reservations recommended.)* It retells Pendleton's wild history from its pinnacle (when the town claimed 32 bars and 18 brothels within four blocks) to when the last red lightbulb was unscrewed (not until well into the 50s). The tour meanders through former speakeasies, high-stakes gambling rooms, inhuman immigrant living quarters for Chinese laborers, a brothel, and an opium den. All of these underground rooms have delightful life-size models. **Pendleton Woolen Mills,** 1307

SE Court Place (276-6911) offers tactile paradise. Shearing and manufacturing wool since 1909, the mills have long outstitched their tiny, lap-blanket beginnings. *(Open M-Sa 8am-5pm. Free 20min. tour M-F 9, 11am, 1:30, and 3pm.)* Shop around the store, or just enjoy perusing titles like *Never Ask A Man the Size of His Spread: A Cowgirl's Guide to Life.* Blanket seconds go for $82-89, but perfect patches cost $140-200.

At heart, Pendleton is a fervent, frothing rodeo town. The **Pendleton Round-Up** (276-2553 or 800-457-6336) has been one of the premier events in the nation's rodeo circuit since 1910, drawing ranchers from all over the U.S. Steer-roping, saddle-bronc-riding, bulldogging, and bareback competitions compete for spectators with buffalo chip tosses, wild-cow-milking, and greased pig chases. The 1999 Round-Up runs September 15-18, and the 2000 Round-Up is September 13-16. For tickets ($8-16 per event), contact the Pendleton Round-Up Association, P.O. Box 609. Tickets go on sale 22 months in advance and often sell out, but scalpers sometimes linger near the gate, and calling the box office is always worth a try. The **Round-Up Hall of Fame** (278-0815), under the south grandstand area at SW Court Ave. and SW 13th St., has captured some of the rodeo's action for eternity, including Pendleton's best pre-served hero, a stuffed horse named War Paint. *(Open Apr.-Sept. M-Sa 10am-5pm. Call to arrange a tour.)* A lifetime membership to the Hall of Fame ($100) includes nominating power and an invitation to the annual banquet during the Round-Up.

OUTDOORS

Pendleton makes a good stop-off on the way to explore the northern **Blue Mountains** or **Umatilla National Forest** (yoo-ma-TILL-uh). To get to the Blue Mountains, take Rte. 11 north for 20 mi. to Rte. 204 E. After a 41 mi. loop over the mountains, Rte. 204 meets Rte. 82 at **Elgin** on the east side of the mountains.

There are four **national forest campgrounds** along this route. All have picnic tables, all but Woodland have drinking water, and none have showers. The most convenient are **Woodward** (18 sites: $10) and **Woodland** (7 sites: free), just before and just after the town of **Tollgate**, off Rte. 204. **Target Meadows** (19 site:, $10), is an isolated spot only 2 mi. off the highway. **Jubilee Lake** (53 sites: $14), a developed and crowded wheelchair-accessible campground popular for swimming and fishing, is another 12 mi. up the gravel road. To reach these two, turn north onto Forest Rd. 64 at Tollgate, 22 mi. east of the junction of Rte. 204 and Rte. 11, and follow the signs. On the way, Rte. 204 winds through dense timber, past campgrounds, creeks, and lakes, and near two wilderness areas, the small **North Fork Umatilla** and the larger, more remote **Wenaha-Tucannon Wilderness.** Both are little-used and offer real solitude; Wenaha-Tucannon has more challenging hiking. Check at the ranger station (see **Practical Information,** above) for information on trailhead **parking permits,** which are necessary throughout the region.

■ Baker City

When Oregon Trail pioneers discovered gold, they decided to settle down and build a city at the base of the Blue Mountains. Tossing their tents aside, Baker's first residents poured their riches into Victorian houses and grand hotels. The city claims a population of 10,000 and the tallest building in Oregon east of the Cascades, Hotel Baker, which is all of 10 stories high. The most appealing attractions of Baker City, however, lie out of town in the surrounding mountains of Elkhorn Ridge and the nearby Wallowa-Whitman National Forest and Hells Canyon.

ORIENTATION AND PRACTICAL INFORMATION

Baker City is 43 mi. southeast of La Grande and 137 mi. northwest of Boise, ID, on I-84 in northeastern Oregon. Route 86 leads east from Baker to Hells Canyon and Rte. 7 leads west, connecting with U.S. 26 to John Day and Prineville. **Campbell** and **Main St.** are the principal thoroughfares: Main runs parallel to I-84, and Campbell intersects I-84 just west of the city. Other important streets are **Broadway Ave.,** which intersects Main Street downtown; **10th St.,** which crosses Broadway in the west; and **Bridge St.,** an offshoot of Main St. to the southeast.

Buses: Greyhound, 515 Campbell St. (523-5011 or 800-231-2222), by the I-84 in the Truck Corral Cafe. To: Boise, ID (2 per day, $25); Portland (3 per day, $39). Open daily 7-9:30am and 5-8pm.

Taxis: Baker Cab Co., 990 Elm St. (523-6070). Up to $3.75 within Baker City, $1 per mi. outside city limits. Runs 24hr.

Visitor Information: Baker County Visitor and Convention Bureau, 490 Campbell St. (523-3356 or 800-523-1235), just off I-84 Exit 304. Everything a visitor center should be. Open M-F 8am-5pm, Sa 8am-4pm, Su 9am-2pm; in winter M-F 8am-5pm.

Outdoor Information: Wallowa National Forest Ranger Station, 3165 10th St. (523-4476), has info on the Elkhorns, current conditions and restrictions, and the *Anthony Lakes Recreation Area* brochure. Open M-F 7:45am-4:30pm.

Laundromat and Public Showers: Baker City Laundry, 815 Cambell St. (523-9817). Untimed showers ($4.20) and fountain drinks (32 oz., 79¢), with a Subway sandwich shop next door. Wash $1, dry 25¢ per 10min. Open daily 7am-10pm.

Senior Services: Community Connection (523-6591), on Grove St., by the fair-grounds. Open M-F 8am-5pm.

Emergency: 911. **Police:** 1655 1st St. (523-3644). **Fire:** 523-3711.

Women's Crisis: Mayday, 523-4134.

Hospital: St. Elizabeth, 3325 Pocahontas Rd. (523-6461, health resource line 888-354-9223). Open 24hr.

Post Office: 1550 Dewey Ave. (800-ASK-USPS/8777). Open M-F 8:30am-5pm. **ZIP Code:** 97814.

Area Code: 541.

ACCOMMODATIONS AND CAMPGROUNDS

Baker City has several reasonably priced motels. Generally, deals get better the farther the motel is from the Interstate.

Bruno Ranch B&B, Box 51, Bridgeport (446-3468). From Baker City, go 9 mi. south on Rte. 7, then left onto Rte. 245. After 14 mi., turn left onto Bridgeport Rd.; it's the first house on the right. Bruno Ranch is rustic and comfortable, but not exceptional—except for the hospitality of Maria Bruno, the engaging owner who cares for her guests like a grandmother. She cooks an excellent hunter's breakfast and shows guests around the extensive ranch and surrounding terrain. If you're lucky, you can help feed the chickens. Popular with hunters. Singles $25; doubles $30. Camping $3 for tents, $8 for vehicles. Call ahead.

Budget Inn, 2205 Broadway (523-6324 or 800-547-5827), at 3rd St. Clean, thickly carpeted rooms with firm beds. Cable, A/C, outdoor pool, free coffee and donuts. Singles $37.50; doubles $43.

Green Gables, 2533 10th St. (523-5588), at Campbell. Fortunately, the interior of these cabins does not match the green-and-white exterior. The rooms have fuzzy turquoise carpets; adjoining kitchens and low weekly rates make it a great choice for longer stays. Singles $26; doubles $30. 10% senior and commercial discount.

Anthony Lake Campground, 36 mi. from Baker City on Elkhorn Dr. Take Rte. 30 north past Haines, then turn west onto Country Rd. 1146 and follow signs to Anthony Lake. Despite its elevation (7100 ft.), this campground draws large weekend crowds. 37 sites: $5 per vehicle. Closed until early July. Wheelchair accessible. If it's too crowded, try **Mud Lake,** a more primitive campground across the road.

Union Creek Campground (894-2210), at Phillips Lake. Follow Rte. 7 20 mi. south toward Sumpter. High grasses and sparse pines make for high RV visibility. The tent grounds are woodsier. Beach with swimming area and boat ramp, flush toilets, no showers. 58 sites: $10; water and electrical hookups $14; full hookups $16. Heater or A/C $1 per day. Senior discount.

FOOD

Compared to the towns around it, Baker City is a delight to the downtrodden diner. While big bacon breakfasts and burgers dominate 10th St., a number of cafes along Main St. that offer a touch of big city ambience and an alternative to the ubiquitous Oregon meat-and-potatoes fare.

El Erradero, 2100 Broadway (523-2327). Where locals go for mammoth Mexican meals. From free chips and delectable salsa to the expresso burrito with everything ($6.25), this place serves Mex without the Tex. Entrees come with rice and beans. One enchilada $4.50, two $6.55. Open Su-Th 11am-9:30pm, F-Sa 11am-10pm.

Baker City Cafe/Pizza à Fetta, 1915 Washington Ave. (523-6099). This elegant and friendly cafe makes everything from scratch, including a fabulous gourmet pizza. Slices $2.25-2.75; pies $13-14. Open M-Th 9am-6pm, F 9am-8pm.

Front Street Coffee Co., 1840 Main St. (523-0223). An old-time soda shop, with lunch box collection and hand-painted, wooden tables. The finest charbroiled lemon pepper chicken breast sandwich in town ($5.50). Open M-W 7am-4:30pm, Th-F 7am-8pm, Sa 7am-4pm.

SIGHTS AND EVENTS

The hills 6 mi. east of Baker City have recently been invaded by the multi-million-dollar **National Historic Oregon Trail Interpretive Center** (523-1843), at Flagstaff Hill. *(Open daily 9am-6pm; Nov.-Mar. 9am-4pm. $5, seniors and ages 6-17 $3.50.)* A self-guided tour re-creates the trek with closed-caption videos, life-sized models with recorded voices, diary entries, and more. The tour depicts the trials and tribulations of life on the trail, not only for the pioneers, but also for Native Americans, miners, and fur traders who lived here. You can load up a model wagon with your choice of supplies and historically clad volunteers will tell how far you'd have gotten. Over 4 mi. of trails, some wheelchair accessible, lead to scenic overlooks and interpretive sites. In some places, the wagon ruts of the original trail run alongside the path.

Outside and on the same note is the **Blue Mountain Crossing,** where a ½ mi., paved, wheelchair accessible path leads through open forest to the original ruts of the Oregon Trail. *(Open daily Memorial Day-Labor Day 8am-8pm. Free.)* To get there, leave I-84 at Exit 248, 12 mi. west of La Grande and nearly 60 mi. from Baker City, and follow the signs 3 mi. up the hill. Signs provide excerpts from settler diaries and commentary on the sights. Two self-guided paths afford a longer look at the trail. On summer weekends, a pioneer encampment offers a living-history glimpse of life on the trail. ("Hey there, young feller! Yer horse sure is big 'n' shiny 'n' funny-soundin'!")

The **Miners' Jubilee,** held on the third weekend of July, includes both the intense gold panning championship, which determines the state's foremost goldpanner, and Arts in the Park, a show and sale of arts with live music. Call the visitor center (see **Practical Information,** above) for info.

OUTDOORS

Elkhorn Ridge, towering steeply over Baker City to the west, provides local access to the Blue Mountains. While this jagged line of peaks was avoided by Oregon Trail pioneers, a paved loop called **Elkhorn Drive** (designated a National Scenic Byway for good reason), now leads over the range, providing drivers of the 106 mi. route with lofty views and hiking and fishing opportunities. From a parking lot on Forest Rd. 210 (a rough road off Rd. 73, 4 mi. west of Anthony Lake), a steep ½ mi. hike follows a ridge to a great vista at **Lakes Lookout.** On the south portion of the loop, the 3 mi. climb up 8321 ft. Mt. Ireland offers excellent 360° views. From Rd. 73, take Rd. 7370 near the forest boundary, and park at Grizzly Mine. The numerous high mountain lakes and creeks are swollen with fish, and excellent camping is available in Anthony Lakes campground (see **Accommodations,** above) or any other place that looks good, provided it's 200 yards from the shoreline. The challenging **Elkhorn Crest Trail** winds through alpine and sub-alpine climates for 22.6 mi. between Anthony Lake in the north and Marble Creek in the south.

■ Hells Canyon and Wallowa Mountains

The northeast corner of Oregon is the state's most rugged, remote, and arresting country, with jagged granite peaks, glacier-gouged valleys, and azure lakes. East of La Grande, the Wallowa Mountains (wa-LAH-wah) rise abruptly, towering over the plains from elevations of over 9000 ft. Thirty miles farther east, the deepest gorge in North America, Hells Canyon, plunges to the Snake River below. The barren and dusty slopes, lack of water, and scorching heat give credence to the canyon's name. It may take a four-wheel-drive vehicle and some real initiative to get off the beaten path, but off-roaders will find heaven in the depths of hell; no virtue required.

ORIENTATION AND PRACTICAL INFORMATION

Hells Canyon National Recreation Area and the **Eagle Cap Wilderness** lie on either side of the **Wallowa Valley,** which can be reached in three ways. From **Baker City,** Rte. 86 heads east through Halfway to connect with Forest Rd. 39, which winds north over the southern end of the Wallowas, meeting Rte. 350 8 mi. east of Joseph. From **La Grande,** Rte. 82 arcs around the north end of the Wallowas, through the small towns of Elgin, Minam, Wallowa, and Lostine, continuing through Enterprise and Joseph, and terminating at Wallowa Lake. From **Clarkston,** WA, Rte. 129 heads south, taking a plunge through the valley of the Grande Ronde River, becoming Rte. 3 in Oregon, to end at Rte. 82 in Enterprise. Three main towns offer services within the area: **Enterprise, Joseph,** and **Halfway.** The only two major roads are **Rte. 350,** a paved route from Joseph northeast 30 mi. to the tiny town of **Imnaha,** and the **Imnaha River Rd.** (a.k.a. Country Rd. 727 and Forest Rd. 3955), a good gravel road that runs south from Imnaha to reconnect with Forest Rd. 39 about 50 mi. southeast of Joseph. The free pamphlet *Hells Canyon Scenic Byway,* available in visitor centers and ranger stations in most of northeastern Oregon, is invaluable for its clear map of area roadways showing campgrounds and points of interest. Be sure to check current road conditions before heading into the area.

Buses: Moffit Brothers Transportation, P.O. Box 156, Lostine, OR 97857 (569-2284), runs the **Wallowa Valley Stage Line,** which makes one round-trip M-Sa from Joseph (6:30am) to La Grande (11:55am). Pick-up at the Chevron station on Rte. 82 in Joseph, the Amoco station on Rte. 82 in Enterprise, and the Greyhound terminal in La Grande. Will stop at Wallowa Lake if asked, or pick up there with advanced notice. One-way from La Grande to: Enterprise ($8.10); Joseph ($8.80); Wallowa Lake ($12.50).

Visitor Information: Wallowa County Chamber of Commerce, P.O. Box 427 (426-4622 or 800-585-4121), at SW 1st St. and W. Greenwood Ave. in Enterprise, in the mall, offering general tourist info with an emphasis on local business establishments, as well as the comprehensive and free *Wallowa County Visitor Guide.* Also gives road and trail conditions. Open M-F 9am-5pm. **Hells Canyon Chamber of Commerce,** (742-4222), in the office of Halfway Motels (see **Accommodations,** below), provides info on accommodations, outfitters, and guides.

Outdoor Information: The Wallowa Mountains Visitor Center, 88401 Rte. 82 (426-5546), on the west side of Enterprise, is packed with info and displays about the Wallowas and Hells Canyon. The $4 forest map is a necessity for navigating the area's network of roads. Friendly staff help plan an afternoon drive or a backpacking trip. Open M-Sa 8am-5pm; Labor Day-Memorial Day M-F 8am-5pm. Other Recreation Area offices in Riggins, ID (208-628-3916) and Clarkston, WA (509-758-0616).

Equipment Rental: Crosstown Traffic, 102 W. McCully (432-2453), in Joseph. Bikes $15 per day, discounts for multiple-day rentals. Knowledgeable staffers can suggest biking routes. Open M-F 8am-6pm, Sa 8am-2pm.

Laundromat: Joseph Laundromat and Car Wash, on Rte. 82 in Joseph, across from the Indian Lodge Motel. Wash $1, dry 25¢ per 10min. Open daily 6am-10pm.

Road and Trail Conditions: 426-5546.

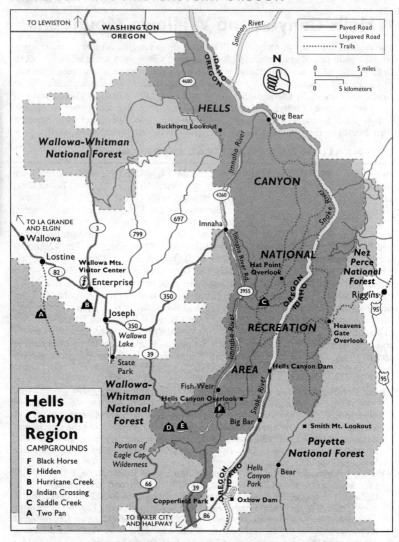

Emergency: 911. **State Police:** 426-3036. **County Sheriff:** (426-3131), in the back of the Enterprise Court House. **Enterprise Police:** (426-3136), at the corner of North St. and NE 1st on S. River St. (Rte. 82). **Fire:** 426-4196.
Hospital: Wallowa Memorial, 401 NE 1st St. (426-3111), in Enterprise.
Post Office: 201 W. North (800-ASK-USPS/275-8777), on Rte. 82 in Enterprise. Open M-F 9am-4:30pm. **ZIP Code:** 97828.
Area Code: 541.

ACCOMMODATIONS

Most of the towns along Rte. 82 have motels with plenty of vacancy during the week. On weekends, things get more crowded, and rooms are scarce.

Country Inn Motel (426-4986), on Rte. 82 in Enterprise. The frilly decorations suggest a country farm. The lack of A/C is not a problem—even on the hottest summer days, the rooms stay remarkably cool. Cable, coffee makers, and refrigerators. Singles $37; doubles $46-48. Kitchens a little extra, depending on availability.

Indian Lodge Motel, 201 S. Main (432-2651), on Rte. 82 in Joseph. A one-story roadsider with terra-cotta roofing and elegant rooms, recently renovated and tastefully decorated. A/C, cable, coffee makers, and refrigerators. Singles $37; doubles $48; in winter singles #32; doubles 43.

Halfway Motels, 170 S. Main (742-5722), just off Rte. 86 in Halfway. The units in the old part of the motel have no phones or A/C and are worn with age, but clean. Singles $37; doubles $42. Shiny new rooms in a two-story building have TVs and matching furniture ensembles. Singles $50, doubles $55.

CAMPGROUNDS

Campgrounds here are plentiful, inexpensive, and sublime. Pick up the *Campground Information* pamphlet at the Wallowa Mountains Visitor Center (see **Practical Information,** above) for a complete listing of sites in the area. Due to budget constraints, most campgrounds (including all of those listed below) are not fully serviced, and are therefore **free**—check at the visitor center to see whether a campground has potable water. For a fully serviced campground (and many more fellow campers), head to **Wallowa Lake State Park** (432-4185, reservations 800-452-5687), in Wallowa Lake, with its whopping 211 sites, flush toilets, drinking water, and showers (tent sites $16; 189 full hookups $20; two wheelchair accessible sites).

Campers bound for the Hells Canyon Area should stock up on food, drinking water, and gas, and remember that there are no showers or flush toilets anywhere. If planning to hike down into the canyon and around the high lakes in summer, insect repellent is a must. Weather can make extreme shifts in a short time, so be prepared. There are a plethora of potential campsites, but because of adverse road conditions, most campgrounds are only open from July to September. **Hells Canyon, Copperfield, McCormick,** and **Woodhead** (all owned by Idaho Power) have tent and RV sites and restrooms, and are the only campgrounds open year-round ($6, RV hookups $10; no reservations; call 785-3323 for info). These campgrounds are located near Oxbow and Brownlee Dams, on Rte. 86 and Rte. 71 along the Snake River.

Saddle Creek Campground, 18 mi. from Imnaha up the improved, but narrow and steep, road to Hat Point (1½hr. by car). 7 sites perched right on the lip of Hells Canyon, with unbelievable views, especially at dusk and dawn. No water. Pit toilets.

Hurricane Creek Campground, a quiet, if sometimes unkempt, campground by Hurricane Creek is the closest free camping. Take the well-marked Hurricane Creek Rd. from Rte. 82 in Enterprise, or from Main St. in Joseph follow the large green sign onto W. Wallowa Rd. After about 2 mi., make a sharp left at a white granary and red barn. The gravel road turns into pavement in 1½ mi., and the campground lies ½ mi. farther down on a dirt road to the left labeled "100." No water. 14 secluded sites.

Hidden Campground, shaded by giant conifers and bordered by the clear, cool Inmaha River, from which campers may be able to pull a trout for your dinner. Head southwest of Joseph on Forest Rd. 39 for about 40 mi., then go upriver onto paved Forest Rd. 3960 toward Indian Crossing for 9 mi. 10 sites, pit toilets.

Indian Crossing Campground, a little past Hidden, has great secluded sites across the river. This is the farthest out of any campsite on Forest Rd. 3960, and is worth the extra few miles. Trailhead access. 14 sites, pit toilets, drinking water.

Two Pan Campground, with 8 pleasant sites, some right on the Lostine River. From Lostine, follow the Lostine River Rd. (Forest Rd. 8210) 18 mi. to its end. The last 5 mi. are on a rough gravel road. Trailhead access. No water.

FOOD

A few affordable restaurants hide out in the small towns of the Wallowa Valley. If heading out onto the hairy roads of Hells Canyon, bring some provisions—a flat or breakdown could leave a person stranded and hungry. Stock up at **Safeway,** 601 W. North St. (426-3722), on Rte. 82 in Enterprise (open daily 6am-9pm).

The Common Good Marketplace, 100 W. Main (426-4125), in Enterprise. An orange-carpeted establishment selling bulk food, herbal extracts, and books on holistic living. Take a seat at someone's old dining room table and order a triple-decker deli sandwich on homemade bread ($4.25; half-sandwich $3.25), suck down a steaming espresso, or sip a tall carrot-celery juice ($3.50) from the full-service juice bar. Open daily 10am-3pm.

Vali's Alpine Delicatessen Restaurant, 59811 Wallowa Lake Hwy. (432-5691), in Wallowa Lake, is the local choice. Mr. Vali cooks one authentic European dish each night and Mrs. Vali serves it in this one-room, alpinesque cottage. Hungarian Kettle Goulash $7.50; schnitzel $12. Reservations required for dinner, but not for the continental breakfast of homemade doughnuts (50-65¢) and cold cuts. Open T-Su 9:30-11am; dinner seatings at 5:30 and 7:30pm; in winter Sa and Su only.

Embers Brew House, 204 N. Main St. (432-BREW/2739), in Joseph. The ambience of this new white house needs some time to age, but the 16 microbrews on tap are perfect the way they are. Breaded brew fries $4; loaded vegetarian sandwich $5. Open daily 7am-10pm; in winter 10am-4pm.

OUTDOORS AND EVENTS

Hells Canyon

Hells Canyon's endearing name comes from its legendary inaccessibility and hostility to human habitation. As one early settler said, "The government bet you 160 acres that you couldn't live there three years without starving to death." The Grand Canyon's big sister, it is North America's deepest gorge; in some places the walls drop over 8000 ft. to the **Snake River** below.

Getting around Hells Canyon without a car or horse is difficult. Some travelers hitchhike in from the gateway towns of Joseph or Halfway, and talk it up with people at campsites to get back out. The few roads in Hells Canyon are notoriously poor and most Forest Roads are closed when Hells Canyon freezes over (Oct.-June). The only way to get close to the canyon without taking at least a full day is to drive the **Hells Canyon National Scenic Loop Drive,** which would more aptly named the Wallowa Mountains Loop Drive, since only the side trips provide real views of the canyon. The loop begins and ends in Baker City, following Rte. 86, Forest Rd. 39 and 350, Rte. 82, and finally I-84. Even this paved route takes six hours to two days to drive. Call the visitor center about road conditions; closures are routine.

Lookout points provide dramatic views of the rugged canyons. **Hells Canyon Overlook,** the most accessible (though least impressive), is up Forest Rd. 3965, 3 mi. of the smoothest, most luxurious pavement in Wallowa County. The road departs Rd. 39 about 5 mi. south of the Imnaha River crossing. The broadest and most eye-popping views are from the **Hat Point Overlook,** where visitors can climb a 90 ft. wooden fire lookout. To get there, go 24 mi. up a steep but well-maintained gravel road from Imnaha (Forest Rd. 4240), then turn off onto Rd. 315 and follow the signs. There are pit toilets at the overlook and six primitive campsites just over the hill; even better camping is 5 mi. back at Saddle Creek Campground (see **Campgrounds,** above). The **Buckhorn Lookout** lies far off the beaten path, 42 mi. northeast of Joseph, and offers lofty views of the Imnaha River Valley; take Rte. 82 north 3 mi. out of Joseph or south 3 mi. out of Enterprise, and look for the green sign for Buckhorn. Turn off and follow Zumwalt Rd. (a.k.a. Country Rd. 697, which turns into Forest Rd. 46) approximately 40 bumpy miles to Buckhorn—about a half-day round-trip. Also at that end of the canyon, the immense **Hells Canyon Dam** lies 23 mi. north of Oxbow on Rte. 86. The views from the winding road become increasingly dramatic heading north. This drive is one of only three ways to get near the bottom of the canyon by car, and the dam is the only place to cross.

Hiking is perhaps the best way to comprehend the vast emptiness of Hells Canyon, and to really get into the canyon requires a backpacking trip of at least a few days. There are over 1000 mi. of trails in the canyon, only a fraction of which are regularly maintained by the Forest Service. A wide array of dangers lurk below the rim, such as huge elevation changes, poison oak, rattlesnakes, blistering heat, and lack of water.

The dramatic 56 mi. **Snake River Trail** runs beside the river for the length of the canyon. At times, the trail is cut into the side of the rock with just enough clearance for a horse's head. Come prepared for any hazard, though the outfitters and rangers that patrol the river by boat are never too far away. This trail can be followed from **Dug Bar** in the north clear down to the Hells Canyon Dam, or accessed from treacherously steep trails along the way. From north to south, **Hat Point, Freezeout,** and **P.O. Saddle** are possible access points. To reach Dug Bar, take Forest Rd. 4260 (a steep and sometimes slippery route recommended only for 4WD or high-clearance vehicles) 27 mi. northeast of Imnaha; discuss plans with rangers before heading out.

The easiest way to see a large portion of the canyon is to zip through on a jet boat tour or float down the Snake on a raft. A surfeit of outfitters operate out of Oxbow and the dam area. The Wallowa Mountains Visitor Center (see p. 145) or any local chamber of commerce has a list of all the permittees. **Hells Canyon Adventures,** (785-3352, outside OR 800-422-3568), 1½ mi. from the Hells Canyon Dam in Oxbow, runs a wide range of jet boat and raft trips through the Canyon. *(Jet boats: 2hr. $30; 3hr. $40; full day $95. Whitewater rafting: $125; includes jet boat ride back upstream.)*

Hells Canyon Bicycle Tours, P.O. Box 483, Joseph 97846 (432-2453), operates out of the Crosstown Traffic Bike Shop in Joseph (see **Practical Information,** above). With the encouraging motto "We bring 'em back alive," the outfit offers one- to four-day tours of the national recreation area. Day rides include transportation and lunch, while overnight trips include everything but sleeping bags and personal gear. *(Day rides $75; overnight $100 per day.)* Rides of varying difficulty can be arranged, though mountain biking experience is necessary for those that drop into the canyon. Most canyon-bottom rides are in spring or fall.

The Wallowa Mountains

Without a catchy, federally approved name like "Hells Canyon National Recreation Area," the Wallowas often take second place to the canyon in the minds of tourists, though they possess a scenic beauty as magnificent as Hells Canyon. The jagged peaks, towering in stately grandeur over the Wallowa Valley sharply contrast the dry canyons below. Over 600 mi. of **hiking trails** cross the **Eagle Cap Wilderness,** and are usually free of snow from mid-July to October. Deep glacial valleys and high granite passes make hiking this wilderness tough going; it often takes more than a day to get into the most beautiful and remote areas. Still, several high alpine lakes are accessible to dayhikers. The 5 mi. hike to **Chimney Lake,** from the Bowman trailhead on the Lostine River Rd. (Forest Rd. 8210), traverses fields of granite boulders with a few small meadows. A little farther on lie the serene **Laverty, Hobo,** and **Wood Lakes,** where the path is less beaten. The **Two Pan trailhead** at the end of the Lostine River Rd. is the start of a forested 6 mi. hike to popular **Minam Lake,** which makes a good starting point for other backcountry spots like **Blue Lake,** 1 mi. above Minam. From the **Wallowa Lake trailhead,** behind the little powerhouse at the dead end of Rte. 82, a 6 mi. hike leads up the East Fork of the **Wallowa River** to **Aneroid Lake.** From Aneroid the summit hikes to **Pete's Point** and **Aneroid Mountain** offer great vistas.

By far the most popular area in the Eagle Cap Wilderness is the **Lakes Basin,** where explorers can find unsurpassed scenery, hikes to Eagle Cap Peak, good fishing, and camping. While it is possible to escape the crowds in the basin during the week, the lake is packed on weekends. **Steamboat, Long,** and **Swamp Lakes** are as magnificent as the Lakes Basin, but receive only half as many visitors. The trailheads for both areas are on the Lostine River Rd. Rangers at the visitor center can also recommend more secluded routes. Fishing in the alpine lakes of the Eagle Cap Wilderness is incredible, but it's illegal to catch and release without a permit, and some fish, such as bull trout, are entirely protected. Pick up a permit and the *Oregon Sport Fishing Regulations* booklet at any local sporting store. *(Permits $8.25 per day, $48 per year.)*

Many excellent day hikes to **Lookingglass, Culver, Bear, Eagle, Cached, Arrow,** and **Heart Lakes** start from the **Main Eagle trailhead,** on Forest Rd. 7755, on the southern side of the Eagle Cap Wilderness (accessible from Baker City and Halfway). Hiking the loop of these lakes makes an amazing overnight expedition. **Hurricane Creek Llama Treks** (432-4455 or 800-528-9609) offers a range of trips into the Wallowa Mountains and Hells Canyon, with dutiful llamas to bear supplies.

Washington

Washington is a state with a split personality, no thanks to the Cascade Mountains. On the state's western shores, wet Pacific storms feed one of the world's only temperate rainforests in Olympic National Park, and low clouds linger over Seattle, hiding the Emerald City from its towering alpine neighbors, Mt. Rainier and Mt. Olympus. Visitors to Puget Sound enjoy both island isolation in the San Juans and cosmopolitan entertainment in the concert halls and art galleries of the mainland. Over the Cascades, the state's eastern half spreads out into fertile farmlands and grassy deserts, while fruit bowls runneth over around Yakima, Spokane, and Pullman.

PRACTICAL INFORMATION

Capital: Olympia.
Population: 5,685,300. **Area:** 66,582 sq. mi. **Motto:** *Alki,* Salish for "by and by."
Nickname: Evergreen State. **Flower:** Coast rhododendron. **Gem:** Petrified wood.
Tree: Western hemlock. **Folk Song:** "Roll On, Columbia, Roll On."
Fish Hotline: 360-902-2500. **Shellfish Hotline:** 360-796-4601.
Road Conditions: (800-695-7623 in WA; 206-368-4499 in Seattle; http://www.wsdot.wa.gov/traveler/highways.htm.
State Patrol: 360-753-6540.
Time Zone: Pacific (3hr. before Eastern).
Postal Abbreviation: WA
Sales Tax: 7-9.1% by county. **Drinking Age:** 21. **Traffic Laws:** Seatbelts required.
Area Codes: 206 in Seattle; 425 northeast of Seattle from Snoqualmie Pass to Everett; 253 in eastern Puget Sound from Roy to Tacoma; 360 in the rest of western Washington; 509 in eastern Washington.

GETTING AROUND

Buses are the cheapest way to travel long distances in Washington. **Greyhound** (800-231-2222) serves the state's two main transportation centers, Spokane and Seattle, as well as towns in between. Local buses cover most of the remaining cities, although a few areas, such as the northwestern Olympic Peninsula, have no bus service. The **Amtrak** (800-USA-RAIL/872-7245) train line from Los Angeles to Vancouver makes many stops in western Washington; another line extends from Seattle to Spokane and on to Chicago. Amtrak serves most large cities along these two routes.

■ Seattle

Seattle's serendipitous mix of mountain views, clean streets, espresso stands, and rainy weather has proved to be the magic formula of the 1990s, attracting transplants from across the U.S. It seems that everyone living here was born elsewhere. Newcomers arrive in droves, armed with college degrees and California license plates, hoping for computer industry jobs and a different lifestyle; Seattle duly blesses them with a magnificent setting and a thriving artistic community. The city is one of the youngest and most vibrant in the nation, and a nearly epidemic fascination with coffee has also made it one of the most caffeinated.

The Emerald City sits on an isthmus, with mountain ranges to the east and west. Every hilltop in Seattle offers an impressive view of Mt. Olympus, Mt. Baker, and Mt. Rainier. To the west, the waters of Puget Sound glint against downtown skyscrapers and nearly spotless streets. Although a daytrip in any direction leads travelers into wild and scenic country, the city itself, built on nine hills that define distinct neighborhoods, begs for exploration. Plan to get wet, and bag the umbrella, a tool that only outsiders use. Two hundred days a year are shrouded in cloud cover, but when the skies clear, Seattleites rejoice that "the mountain is out," and head for the country.

WASHINGTON

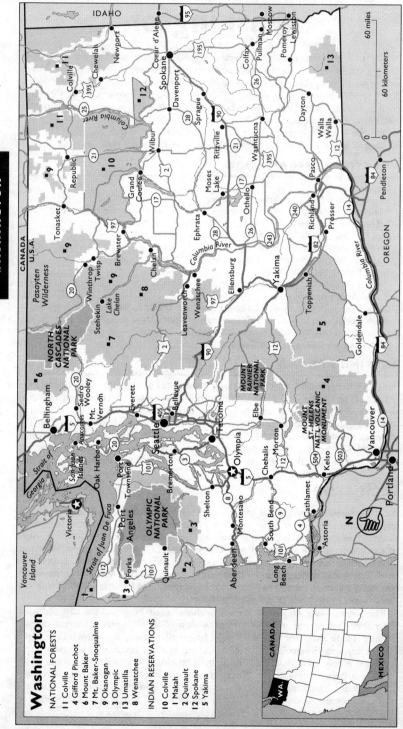

Washington

NATIONAL FORESTS
11 Colville
4 Gifford Pinchot
6 Mount Baker
7 Mt. Baker-Snoqualmie
9 Okanogan
3 Olympic
13 Umatilla
8 Wenatchee

INDIAN RESERVATIONS
10 Colville
1 Makah
2 Quinault
12 Spokane
5 Yakima

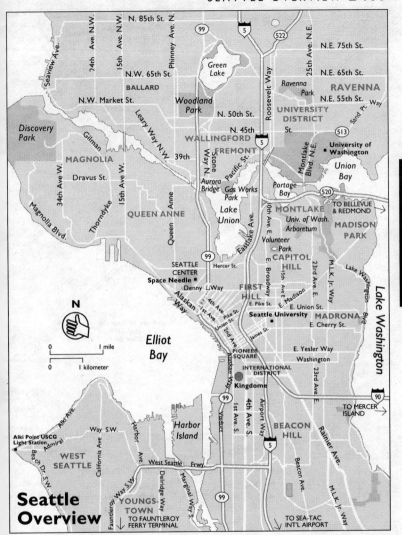

Seattle Overview

The city's artistic landscape is as varied and exciting as its physical terrain. Opera performances always sell out, and the *New York Times* has complained that there is more good theater in Seattle than on Broadway. When Nirvana introduced the world to their discordant sensibility, the term "grunge" and Seattle became temporarily inseparable, and the same city that produced Jimi Hendrix again revitalized American rock and roll. An army of good bands remain in grunge's wake, keeping the Seattle scene alive as a mecca for edgy entertainment. Many Seattle success stories have happier and preppier endings than those of Hendrix and Cobain. The city is home to entrepreneurs like Bill Gates of Microsoft and Howard Shultz of Starbucks, who built vast and perhaps only marginally evil empires out of software and coffee beans.

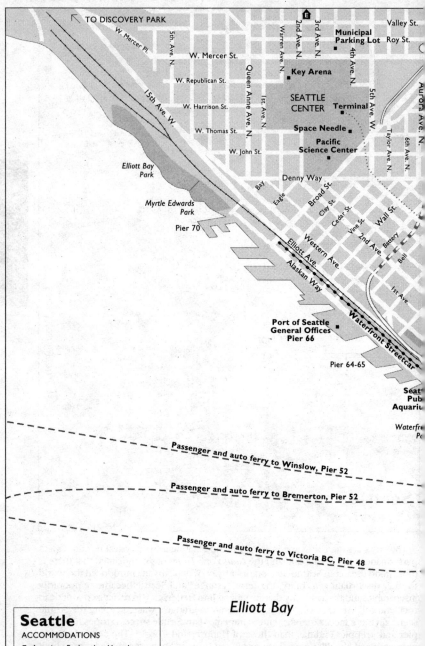

TO DISCOVERY PARK

W. Mercer Pl.

5th Ave. N.

W. Mercer St.

W. Republican St.

Warren Ave. N.

2nd Ave. N.

3rd Ave. N.

Municipal
Parking Lot

Valley St.

Roy St.

4th Ave. N.

Key Arena

W. Harrison St.

Queen Anne Ave. N.

1st Ave. N.

SEATTLE
CENTER

Terminal

5th Ave. W.

Aurora Ave. N.

W. Thomas St.

Space Needle

Taylor Ave. N.

6th Ave. N.

W. John St.

Pacific
Science Center

15th Ave. W.

Elliott Bay
Park

Denny Way

Bay

Eagle

Broad St.

Clay St.

Cedar St.

Vine St.

2nd Ave.

Battery

Wall St.

Bell

Myrtle Edwards
Park

Pier 70

Western Ave.

Elliott Ave.

Alaskan Way

Waterfront Streetcar

1st Ave.

Port of Seattle
General Offices
Pier 66

Pier 64-65

Seat*
Pub
Aquariu

Waterfr
Po

Passenger and auto ferry to Winslow, Pier 52

Passenger and auto ferry to Bremerton, Pier 52

Passenger and auto ferry to Victoria BC, Pier 48

Elliott Bay

Seattle

ACCOMMODATIONS

F American Backpacker Hostel
D Commodore Motel
B Green Tortoise Backpacker's Hostel
E Green Tortoise Garden Apartments
C Moore Motel
A Seattle International Hostel
G Vincent's Backpacker Guest House

0   600 yards

0   600 meters

N

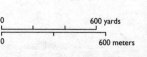

✺ HIGHLIGHTS OF SEATTLE

- Seattle's well-stomped tourist route passes through fish-filled **Pike Place Market** (see p. 160), the **Seattle Center** and its infamous **Space Needle** (see p. 165), historic **Pioneer Square** and the irreverent **Underground Tour** (see p. 166), and the leafy greenery of **Volunteer Park** (see p. 166).
- Less-touristed neighborhood highlights include off-beat **Capitol Hill** (see p. 166) and the funky arts of **Fremont** (see p. 173).
- Cultural vibrancy runs riot at the **Seattle Art Museum** (see p. 164), the **Seattle Asian Art Museum** (see p. 167), the **Wing Luke Memorial Museum** (see p. 166), and the **Nordic Heritage Museum** (see p. 168).
- The past takes a creative turn at the **Washington State History Museum** (see p. 175) in nearby Tacoma, the bone-filled **Thomas Burke Museum** (see p. 167), and Boeing's **Museum of Flight** (see p. 175).
- Nature-orientated escapes await at artsy **Vashon Island** (see p. 176), **Deception Pass State Park** on **Whidbey Island** (see p. 179), and the **Chittenden Fish Ladder** (see p. 169), where salmon leap toward fatal sexual gratification.

ORIENTATION

Seattle is a long, skinny city, stretched north to south on an isthmus between **Puget Sound** to the west and **Lake Washington** to the east, linked by locks and canals. The city is easily accessible by car via **I-5**, which runs north-south through the city, east of downtown, and by **I-90** from the east, which ends at I-5 southeast of downtown. From I-5, get to **downtown** (including **Pioneer Square, Pike Place Market,** and the **waterfront**) by taking any of the exits from James St. to Stewart St. Take the Mercer St./Fairview Ave. exit to the **Seattle Center.** The Denny Way exit leads to **Capitol Hill,** and, farther north, the 45th St. exit heads toward the **University District.** The less crowded **Rte. 99,** also called **Aurora Ave.** or the Aurora Hwy., runs parallel to I-5 and skirts the western side of downtown, with great views from the Alaskan Way Viaduct. Route 99 is often the better choice when driving downtown, or to **Queen Anne, Fremont, Green Lake,** and the northwestern part of the city. For more detailed directions to these and other districts, see the individualized neighborhood listings under **Food** (p. 160), **Nightlife** (p. 172), and **Sights** (p. 164).

GETTING AROUND

Though navigating through Seattle can seem daunting at first glance, even the most road-weary drivers can learn their way around the Emerald City like so many singing munchkins. Downtown, **avenues** run northwest to southeast, and **streets** run southwest to northeast. Outside downtown, everything is simplified: with few exceptions, avenues run north-south and streets east-west. The city is split into **quadrants:** 1000 1st Ave. NW is a long walk from 1000 1st Ave. SE.

When driving in Seattle, **yield to pedestrians.** Not only do locals drive slowly, calmly, and politely, but police ticket frequently. **Jaywalking** pedestrians rack up $50. Downtown driving can be nightmarish; parking is expensive, hills are steep, and one-way streets are ubiquitous. **Parking** is cheap, plentiful, and well-lit at the **Seattle Center,** near the Space Needle. Park there and take the monorail to the convenient **Westlake Center** downtown (every 15min. 9am-11pm; $1, ages 5-12 75¢). The **Metro ride free zone** includes most of downtown Seattle (see **Public Transportation,** below). The **Metro** covers King County east to North Bend and Carnation, south to Enumclaw, and north to Snohomish County, where bus #6 hooks up with **Community Transit.** This line runs to Everett, Stanwood, and well into the Cascades. Metro bus #174 connects to Tacoma's Pierce County System at Federal Way.

Seattle is an extremely **bicycle-friendly** city. All buses have free, easy-to-use bike racks. (Bike shops around town have sample racks on which novices can practice.) Between 6am and 7pm, bikes may only be loaded or unloaded at stops before the borders of the ride free zone, not in the zone itself. Check out Metro's *Bike & Ride* pamphlet, available at the visitor center and the hostel. For a bicycle map of Seattle, call the **City of Seattle Bicycle Program** (684-7583).

PRACTICAL INFORMATION

Transportation

Airplanes: Seattle-Tacoma International (Sea-Tac) (431-4444), on Federal Way, south of Seattle proper. Take bus #174 or 194 from downtown Seattle.

Trains: Amtrak (800-USA-RAIL/872-7245, arrival/departure times 382-4125), King St. Station, at 3rd and Jackson St., 1 block east of Pioneer Square next to the King-dome. To: Portland, OR (4 per day, $30); Tacoma (4 per day, $11); Spokane (1 per day, $68); San Francisco, CA (1 per day, $166); Vancouver, BC (1 per day, $31). Check for cheaper winter rates and bus connections to smaller destinations or Van-couver. Ticket office open daily 6:15am-8pm. Station open daily 6am-10:30pm.

Buses: Greyhound (628-5526 or 800-231-2222), at 8th Ave. and Stewart St. To: Sea-Tac Airport (departs every 45min. past the hour 6:45am-5:45pm, $7.50); Spokane (6 per day, $27); Vancouver, BC (9 per day, $21); Portland, OR (12 per day, $21); Tacoma (7 per day, $5). Try to avoid late buses, since the station can get seedy after dark. Ticket office open daily 6:30am-11:30pm. **Green Tortoise Bus Service** (800-867-8647; http://www.greentortoise.com). Buses leave from 9th Ave. and Stewart St. on Th and Su at 8am. Cushioned seats fold down into beds at night on this bus-turned-lounge, and it makes frequent stops for barbecue dinners and saunas. A slow, friendly, liberal alternative to Greyhound. To: Portland, OR ($15); Eugene, OR ($25); Berkeley, CA ($49); San Francisco, CA ($59); Los Angeles, CA (Th only, $79). Reserve 5 days in advance.

Ferries: Washington State Ferries (800-84-FERRY/843-3779 or 206-464-6400; http://www.wsdot.wa.gov/ferries), Colman Dock, Pier 52, downtown. Service from **downtown** to: Bainbridge Island (35min.); Bremerton on the Kitsap Peninsula (1hr.); Vashon Island (25min.; no Su service; passengers only). To reach the **Fauntleroy ferry terminal** in West Seattle, drive south on I-5 and take Exit 163A (West Seattle/Spokane St.) down Fauntleroy Way, or turn at the Spokane St. bridge 1 mi. south of the main terminal. From Fauntleroy to: Southworth on the Kitsap Peninsula (35min.); Vashon Island (15min.). Round-trip $3.60; June-mid-Oct. car and driver $8, off-season $6.25. Most ferries leave daily and frequently 5am-2am. **Victoria Clipper** (800-668-1167; reservations 448-5000) is the only available auto ferry service from Seattle to Victoria. Departs from Pier 48 (4½hr.; daily at 1pm; passengers $29 one-way, car and driver $49, under 12 half-price).

Public Transportation: Metro Transit, Customer Assistance Office, 801 2nd Ave. (553-3000 or 800-542-7876, 24hr.; TTY 689-1739; http://transit.metrokc.gov), in the Exchange Building downtown. Open M-F 9am-5pm. Fares are based on a 2-zone system. **Zone 1** includes everything within the city limits (peak hours $1.25, off-peak $1). **Zone 2** includes everything else (peak $1.75, off-peak $1.25). Ages 5-18 always 75¢. **Peak hours** in both zones M-F 6-9am and 3-6pm. Exact fare required. Weekend day passes $2. Ride free daily 6am-7pm in the downtown **ride free area,** bordered by S. Jackson St. on the south, 6th Ave. and I-5 on the east, Bat-tery St. on the north, and the waterfront on the west. Free **transfers** can be used on any bus, including a return trip on the same bus within 2hr. All buses have free, easy-to-use **bike racks** and most are **wheelchair accessible** (info 689-3113). See **Getting Around,** above, for Metro connections beyond Seattle.

Car Transport: Auto Driveaway (253-850-0800) hires people to drive their cars to various locations across the U.S. $300 cash deposit. Open M-F 8am-5pm.

Ride Board: 1st floor of the **Husky Union Building** (the HUB), behind Suzallo Library on the University of Washington main campus. Matches cars and riders for any destination, within geographical reason. Also check the board at the down-town hostel (see **Accommodations,** below).

Visitor and Financial Services

Visitor Information: Seattle-King County Visitors Bureau (461-5840), at 8th and Pike St., on the 1st floor of the convention center. Helpful staff doles out maps, brochures, newspapers, and Metro and ferry schedules. Open May-Oct. M-F 8:30am-5pm, Sa-Su 10am-4pm; Nov.-Apr. M-F 8:30am-5pm.

Outdoor Information: Seattle Parks and Recreation Department, 100 Dexter St. (684-4075). Open daily 8am-5pm; in winter M-F 8am-5pm. **National Park Service,**

222 Yale Ave. (470-4060), in REI (see **Equipment Rental,** below). Answers questions about camping, hiking and general frolicking in area parks, gives info on discounts and passes, and sells a map of the National Park System ($1.20). Open Tu-F 10:30am-7pm, Sa 9am-7pm, Su 11am-3pm; winter hours may be shortened.

Currency Exchange: Thomas Cook Foreign Exchange, 400 Pine St. (623-6203), on the 1st floor of the Westlake Shopping Center. Open M-Sa 10am-6pm, Su noon-5pm. Also behind the Delta Airlines ticket counter and at other airport locations.

Local Services

Equipment Rental: REI, 222 Yale Ave. (223-1944), near Capitol Hill. The mothership of camping supply stores. See to believe. (More at **Outdoors,** p. 170). Open M-Sa 9am-9pm, Su 10-6pm. **The Bicycle Center,** 4529 Sand Point Way (523-8300), near the Children's Hospital. Rents bikes ($3 per hr., $15 per day; 2hr. min.). Credit card or license deposit required. Open M-F 10am-8pm, Sa 10am-6pm, Su 10am-5pm. **Gregg's Greenlake Cycle,** 7007 Woodlawn Ave. NE (523-1822). Pricey, but close to Green Lake and Burke-Gilman bike trails ($15-20 per day, $25-30 per 24hr.). Photo ID and cash or credit card deposit required. Also rents in-line skates. Open M-F 9:30am-9pm, Sa-Su 9:30am-6pm.

Bookstores: See p. 172.

Library: Seattle Public Library, 1000 4th Ave. (386-4636, TDD 386-4697). A visitor's library card lasts 3 months ($8). Free 90min. Internet access with photo ID. Open M-Th 9am-9pm, F-Sa 9am-6pm, Su 1-5pm.

Women's Services: University of Washington Women's Information Center (685-1090), Cunningham Hall, in the main campus. Community resource and referral for women's groups throughout the Seattle area. Open M-F 9am-5pm.

Senior Services: 1601 2nd Ave. #800 (448-3110). Open M-F 9am-5pm.

Gay and Lesbian Services: 1820 E. Pine (323-0220 or 800-527-7683). Open M-F 9am-7pm. **Lesbian Resource Center,** 1808 Bellview Ave. #204 (322-3953). Support groups, drop-in center, lending library, and workshops. Open M-F 9am-7pm.

AIDS Information: 205-7837.

Ticket Agencies: Ticketmaster (628-0888 or 447-ARTS/2787) serves plays, the symphony, and other fine arts events. In Westlake Center and every Tower Records store. **Ticket/Ticket,** 401 Broadway E (324-2744), on the 2nd floor of the Broadway Market, sells half-price day-of-show tickets to local theater, music, and dance performances. Cash only. Must purchase tickets in person. Open Tu-Sa 10am-7pm, Su noon-6pm. Also in the Pike Place Market. Open Tu-Su noon-6pm.

Laundromat: Sit and Spin, 2219 4th St. (441-9484). Both a laundromat and a local hot spot (see **Nightlife,** p. 174). Wash $1.25, dry 25¢ per 10min. Open Su-Th 9am-mid, F-Sa 9am-2am.

Emergency and Communications

Emergency: 911. **Police:** 610 3rd Ave. (583-2111).

Crisis Line: 461-3222. **Rape Crisis: Seattle Rape Relief,** 1905 S. Jackson St., (632-7273). Crisis counseling, advocacy, and prevention training. **Poison:** 800-732-6985. **Alcohol/Drug Help Line:** 722-3700. All 24hr.

Travelers' Aid: 909 4th Ave. #630 (461-3888), at Marion, on the 6th floor of the YMCA. Free services for stranded travelers who have lost their wallets or marbles. Open M-F 9am-4pm.

Medical Services: International District Emergency Center (623-3321). Medics with multilingual assistance available 24hr. **Aradia Women's Health Center,** 1300 Spring St. (323-9388). Staff will refer elsewhere when overbooked. Open M-F 10am-4pm. **Health South Medical Center,** 1151 Denny Way (682-7418). Walk-in.

Post Office: (800-ASK-USPS/275-8777), at Union St. and 3rd Ave. downtown. Open M-F 8am-5:30pm. **ZIP Code:** 98101.

Internet Access: Capitol Hill Net, 219 Broadway #22 (860-6858). $6 per hr. 15min. free surfing time if you mention *Let's Go.* Open daily 9am-midnight. **Speak Easy,** 2304 2nd Ave. (728-9770; file under alt.cool.alternative.cybercafe). 15¢ per min. Open Tu-Th and Su 10am-midnight, F-Sa 10am-2am; 21+ Th-Sa 9pm-closing. **Cyberbear Internet Cafe,** 4714 University Way (522-9001; http://www.netcafe.net). $6 per hr. Open M-F 10am-7pm, Sa 10am-6pm. See also **Library,** above.

Area Code: 206.

PUBLICATIONS

The city's major newspaper, the *Seattle Times* (464-2111; http://www.seattle-times.com), lists upcoming events in its Thursday "Ticket" section. The *Seattle Weekly* (http://www.seattleweekly.com) offers a free, left-of-center, advertisement-stuffed alternative to the dominant daily, complete with weekend event listings every Thursday. *The Stranger* has its finger on the pulse of the music and pop culture scene, and mysteriously materializes every Thursday at the door of every Seattle music store, coffee shop, and thrift store. This is the best place to start for the low-down on Seattle nightlife or to read some entertaining personals (where truth is over-whelmingly stranger than fiction). *The Rocket* is another very free source of informa-tion on the music scene. *Arts Focus,* a free magazine available at most bookstores, carries information on the performing arts, while *Seattle Arts,* published by the Seat-tle Arts Commission, is especially good for events in the visual arts. Both are pub-lished monthly. The weekly *Seattle Gay News* has an excellent map and listings of gay-owned and patronized business in Seattle, and sells on Fridays at newsstands (25¢). The *International Examiner* provides a free weekly news updates on Asian-American community affairs, covering restaurants and upcoming community events.

ACCOMMODATIONS

Seattle's hostel scene is alive, friendly, and clean. Those tired of urban high-rises can head for the **Vashon Island Hostel** (the "Seattle B"; see p. 177). **Pacific Lodging Asso-ciation** (784-0539) arranges B&B singles in the $55-65 range (open M-F 9am-5pm).

Downtown

Seattle International Hostel (HI-AYH), 84 Union St. (622-5443; http://www.adhost.com/hi-seattle/itd/itd.html), at Western Ave., right by the waterfront. Take bus #174, 184, or 194 from the airport (#194 from the north end of the bag-gage terminal is fastest), get off at Union St., and walk west. A diverse, international crowd and free linens make up for the vast expanses of formica in this enormous hostel. The 5-star common room overlooks the water, just off a palatial lounge and library/TV room. 6 people per dorm room. Beds $17, nonmembers $20. Amenities range from laundry facilities (wash $1, dry 75¢) to a ride board in the lobby. Offers discount tickets for the aquarium, Omnidome, Museum of Flight and passenger ferry. 24hr. parking in the nearby garage ($9). 7-night max. stay in summer. Recep-tion 7am-2am. Check-out 11am. No curfew. Reservations wise in summer.

Green Tortoise Backpacker's Hostel, 1525 2nd Ave. (340-1222; fax 623-3207), between Pike and Pine St. Pick-up available from Amtrak, Greyhound or ferry ter-minal; take bus #174 from the airport. Great location, great rooms, great hostel. 150 beds in 48 rooms, plus 10 private rooms. Beds $15, nonmembers $16; private rooms $40. $20 key deposit required. Free breakfast. Travel documents are neces-sary for check-in. No curfew.

Moore Motel, 1926 2nd Ave. (448-4851, 448-4852, or 800-421-5508), at Virginia, 1 block east from Pike Place Market, next to the historic Moore Theater. Big rooms include 2 beds, TV, a private bath, and slightly stained carpets. The reasonably ornate open lobby, cavernous halls, and gargantuan, heavy wooden doors make the Moore seem like it hasn't changed since the 20s. Singles $38, with bath $43; doubles $44, with bath $49. HI member discounts when the Seattle Hostel is full.

Commodore Hotel, 2013 2nd Ave. (448-8868), at Virginia. Take bus #174 or 194 from the airport; get off at 4th Ave. and Virginia. Many rooms have pleasant decor and walnut furniture (with a few broken baseboards). Not the best area of down-town, but 24hr. security keeps out the riff-raff. Singles $42, with bath $52; 2 beds and bath $68. 2 hostel-style rooms have bare-bones bunks and shared bath ($14), but you need an HI card to snag a spot. Weekly single $134.

Queen Anne

Green Tortoise Garden Apartments, 715 2nd Ave. N (340-1222; fax 623-3207), on the south slope of Queen Anne Hill, 3 blocks east from the Space Needle and the Seattle Center. Long-term accommodations for travelers staying over 30 days. Back yard, kitchens, garden, laundry, free breakfast. Beds $220 per month, with 4 peo-ple per room. Applications available at the Green Tortoise Hostel (see above).

Capitol Hill

Vincent's Backpackers Guest House, 527 Malden Ave. E (323-7849), between 14th and 15th Ave, near the new Safeway on Broadway. Take bus #10 from downtown. Offers both hosteling accommodations and longer-term arrangements. The house is clean, but parking and living space are limited. Beds $14. Key deposit $10. Apartments around $600 per month. Reception 10am-4pm; door locked at 2am.

University District

The College Inn, 4000 University Way NE (633-4441; http://www.speakeasy.org/collegeinn), at NE 40th St. A quiet place to crash near the UW campus and its youthful environs. Singles are tiny and rooms lack TVs or private baths, but the turn-of-the-century bureaus and brass fixtures are s'durned *charming*. The kitchen is nestled in the 4th floor attic, where a complementary breakfast materializes every morning, and guests loll on couches in front of the fireplace. Singles $49-66; doubles $78-90. Credit card required.

Fremont

For inexpensive motels a bit farther from downtown, drive north on Hwy. 99 (Aurora Ave.) or take bus #26 to the neighborhood of Fremont. Chain motels like the **Nites Inn,** 11746 Huron Ave. N (365-3216), line the highway north of the Aurora bridge, and many cater to the budget traveler (rooms from $48). Look for AAA approval to ensure a secure night.

FOOD

Though Seattleites appear to subsist solely on espresso and steamed milk, they have to eat some time. When they do, they seek out healthy cuisine—especially seafood. The finest fish, produce, and baked goods can be purchased from various vendors in **Pike Place Market** (see below). Seattle's cheapest food is available in the **University District,** where food from around the world can be snatched for under $5. Seattle hosts active **food cooperatives** at 6518 Fremont Ave. N, in Green Lake, and at 6504 20th NE, in the Ravenna District north of the university. Capitol Hill, the U District, and Fremont close main thoroughfares on summer Saturdays for **farmers' markets.**

Pike Place Market and Downtown

Farmers have been peddling here since 1907, when angry citizens demanded the elimination of the middle-merchant and local farmers responded by selling produce from wagons by the waterfront. Not even the Great Depression slowed business at the market, which thrived until two disastrous events of the 40s: an enormous fire burned the building in 1941, and almost all of the market's 300 Japanese-American merchants were interned by the American government during WWII. The early 80s saw a Pike Place renaissance, and now thousands of tourists mob the market every day of the year (open M-Sa 9am-6pm, Su 11am-5pm). In the **Main Arcade,** which parallels the waterfront on the west side of Pike St., lunatic fishmongers bellow at befuddled customers, competing for audiences and the contents of tourists' wallets by hurling fish from shelves to scales. The market's restaurants offer an escape from the crowded aisles, often with stellar views of the sound.

The best time to shop at the market is when it first opens, while the fish are still flopping and the fruit is freshest, though late in the day it's possible to score big discounts on produce. Be prepared to fight the masses during lunchtime, when tourists and business people alike scour the market for cheap eats. An **information booth** in front of the bike rack by the Main Arcade, at 1st Ave. and Pike St., provides directions and maps (open Tu-Su 10am-noon). Restaurants farther south of Pike Place cater mostly to suits on lunch breaks, with sandwich shops galore in the downtown grid.

Soundview Cafe (623-5700), on the mezzanine level in the Pike Place Main Arcade, down Flower Row. This wholesome, self-serve sandwich-and-salad bar offers fresh food, a spectacular view of Elliott Bay, and occasional poetry readings. Fill a $5 salad bar bowl with tabouli, pasta, salad, or fruit, or just bring a brown-bag lunch for a moment of solace from marketplace madness. Solid breakfasts, too. Open M-Sa 7am-5pm, Su 9am-3pm.

Piroshki, Piroshki, 1908 Pike Pl. (441-6068). For an ample, high-fat, and heavenly hands-on meal, try this Russian specialty. Piroshki are made of a croissant-like dough, baked around anything from sausage and mushrooms ($3) to apples doused in cinnamon ($3.50). Watch the piroshki process in progress while awaiting your order. Open daily 8am-7pm.

Delcambre's Ragin' Cajun, 1523 1st Ave. (624-2598), near Pike Place. Good food, tremendous portions. Have a spicy dish of red beans and rice with *andouille* (a kind of sausage) for $7, the same dish the chef served to President Clinton 3 years ago. Lunch $5-7. Open M-Sa 11am-3pm and Th-Sa 5:30-9pm.

Three Girls Bakery, 1514 Pike Pl. (622-1045), at Post. Order to go or sit in the tiny cafe. The rows of pastries are positively Pavlovian, as is the smell of the fresh bread. Blissfully large portions. 3 kinds of rye $1.50-3.50; sandwiches around $4. Open daily 6:30am-6pm.

Emmett Watson's Oyster Bar, 1916 Pike Pl. (448-7721). Named in honor of the local columnist and California-basher who founded the "Lesser Seattle" movement, attempting to repel tourists and new residents with the sensitive motto, "Keep the Bastards Out." You haven't really experienced a Vitamin E high until you've tried the Oyster Bar Special ($6). Lots of tourists try it, too—so much for idealism. Open M-Th 11am-8pm, F-Sa 11:30am-9pm, Su 11:30am-6pm; in winter closes 2hr. earlier. No credit cards.

Mama's, 2234 2nd Ave. (728-MAMA/6262). Cheap, greasy Mexican food, served in a superfunk diner. Tacos $2.50. You will eat in the Elvis Room. King-sized portions. Open M-W 11am-10pm, Th 11am-10:30pm, F-Sa 11am-11:30pm, Su 11am-9pm.

Pioneer Square and the Waterfront

Budget eaters, beware of Pioneer Square. Still worse, the waterfront lures tourists with wharf-side fare that's often better suited for the seagulls. It might be nicer to take a picnic in **Waterfall Garden,** on the corner of S. Main St. and 2nd Ave. S.

Mae Phim Thai Restaurant, 94 Columbia St. (624-2979), a few blocks north of Pioneer Sq. between 1st Ave. and Alaskan Way. Local business buffs pack this tiny, unassuming restaurant at lunch time, attesting to the glory of good, inexpensive take-out. Wait less than 5min. for an enormous meal of *pad thai,* then head over to Pioneer Square to feast. All dishes $4.60. Open M-Sa 11am-7pm.

Ivar's Fish Bar, Pier 54 (624-6852), on the waterfront. One of a string of fast seafood restaurants founded by and named for late Seattle celebrity and shipping magnate Ivar Haglund. Try fish 'n' chips ($4.79) or the definitive Seattle clam chowder ($1.90). Dine with the gulls and pigeons in covered booths outside to avoid the pricey adjoining "Ivar's Acres of Clams" restaurant. Open daily 11am-2am.

International District

Along King and Jackson St., between 5th and 8th Ave. directly east of the Kingdome, Seattle's International District is packed with great eateries. Fierce competition keeps prices low and quality high. Any choice here will probably be a good one, as three out of any four restaurants in the district have been named (at one time or another) the best in town by a *Seattle Times* reviewer. Locals often call these few blocks Chinatown, but every kind of Asian food can be found here. Don't shy away from a shabby exterior; the quality of the facade is often inversely proportional to the quality of the food. **Uwajimaya,** 519 6th Ave. S (624-6248), is the largest East Asian retail store in the Pacific Northwest; take bus #7. A huge selection of Japanese staples, fresh seafood (often still swimming), a wide variety of dried foods (great for camping and never swimming), a sushi bar, and a bakery make this a true Seattle institution. Toys, books, furniture, clothes, and jewelry are also for sale (open daily 9am-8pm).

Tai Tung, 655 S. King St. (622-7372). A Chinese diner. The busiest hours at Tai Tung are when the munchies take hold of university students, who shuffle all the way from the U District for the Chinese version of fried chicken. It's roasted, not fried, but still greasy. Waiters here are likely to learn your name by the second night you visit, and are never tongue-tied. 10-page, ever-changing menu plastered to the walls. Entrees $7-10. Open Su-Th 10am-11:30pm, F-Sa 10am-1:30am.

Ho Ho Seafood Restaurant, 653 S. Weller St. (382-9671). Friendly service and fields of pink formica. Watch the demise of your dinner as staff pluck live seafood from the tanks. Generous portions of great seafood. Dinner $7-10; lunch $5-7. Open Su-Th 11am-1am, F-Sa 11am-3am.

House of Hong Restaurant, 409 8th Ave. S (622-7997), at Jackson on the border of the International District. Somewhat upscale, with the most popular dim sum in town ($2 per dish; served daily 11am-5pm). Open M-Th 11am-10pm, F 11am-midnight, Sa 9:30am-midnight, Su 9:30am-10pm. Call ahead.

Viet My Restaurant, 129 Prefontaine Pl. S (382-9923), near 4th and Washington St. Consistently delicious Vietnamese food at great prices. Try shrimp curry ($5.50) or beef with vegetables ($4.25), and avoid the lunch rush. Open M-F 11am-9pm.

Capitol Hill

With bronze dance-step diagrams paved into the sidewalks, and artsy neon storefronts above, Capitol Hill offers an escape from tourist traps to the espresso houses, imaginative shops, and elegant clubs of **Broadway Ave.** At night, Broadway comes alive and Seattleites lollygag in droves to see and be seen. Here, even the yuppies have noserings. An eclectic array of restaurants line the avenue, provide a perfect perch for people-watching, and make some of the best food in the city. Bus #7 runs along Broadway; bus #10 runs through Capitol Hill along the more sedate **15th St.** Unless you're getting take-out, avoid the metered parking on Broadway and head east for the free angled spots behind the reservoir at Broadway Field, on 11th Ave.

🏵**The Gravity Bar,** 415 Broadway E (325-7186), in the Broadway Market. Neo-healthy organic food and intriguing fruit and veggie juices. Conical tables and stainless steel everything fill this tiny room, while colorful paper lanterns and kites contrast with the omnipresent metallic gray. Among the infamous drinks are Moonjuice (a melon/lime concoction; $3.50) and Mr. Rogers on Amino Acid ($5). Choose from the extensive menu, create a unique juice concoction from pineapple or wheatgrass, then drop your glass from a great height and watch it plummet at a delicious $9.8m/s^2$. Open Su-Th 10am-10pm, F-Sa 10am-11pm.

🏵**Bimbo's Bitchin' Burrito Kitchen,** 506 E. Pine (329-9978). The name explains it all, except for the super sizes and the divine inspiration behind the *comida.* Check out the day-glo restrooms. Bimbo's basic burrito $3.50. Open M-Th noon-11pm, F-Sa noon-2am, Su 2-10pm.

HaNa, 219 Broadway Ave. E (328-1187). Cramped quarters in this Japanese joint testify to the popularity of its sushi. Assorted sushi plate $8.75; large tempura lunch $6.25. Open M-Sa 11am-10pm, Su 4-10pm.

Dick's, 115 Broadway Ave. E (323-1300). A local institution, made famous in Sir Mix-A-Lot's "Broadway." This pink, 50s-style, drive-in burger chain also has locations in Wallingford, Queen Anne, and Lake City. Dick's Deluxe Burger $1.70; soft serve kiddie cones 50¢. Open daily 10:30am-2am.

Kokeb Restaurant, 926 12th Ave. (322-0485), behind Seattle University at the far south end of Capitol Hill, near the First Hill neighborhood. This was the first Ethiopian eatery in the Pacific Northwest, serving hot and spicy meat or vegetable stews on spongy injera bread. Entrees $7-11. Open daily 5-11pm.

University District

The immense University of Washington (colloquially known as "U-Dub"), north of downtown between Union Bay and Portage Bay, supports a colorful array of funky shops, international restaurants, and a slew of coffeehouses. The best restaurants, cinemas, and cafes are within a few blocks of University Way. Thanks to its large student population, this district offers more mileage per food dollar than anywhere in the city, serving up everything from tacos to teriyaki. Be prepared for puzzled looks when asking for "University Way"; it's known as "Th' Ave." To get there, drive north, take any one of buses #70-74 from downtown, or take bus #7 or 9 from Capitol Hill.

Flowers, 4247 University Way NE (633-1903). This local landmark from the 20s spent its youth as a flower shop. Now a dark wood bar and mirrored ceiling make a tasteful frame for an all-you-can-eat Mediterranean buffet ($6). Includes vegan options. Open M-Sa 11am-2am; kitchen closes at 10pm, but late night snacks go on.

Pizzeria Pagliacci, 4529 University Way NE (632-0421; 726-1717 for delivery), also on Capitol Hill. Voted Seattle's best pizza every year since 1986. While you eat, decipher Italian Hollywood movie posters and watch frat boys gobble pizzas whole. Slices $1.70. Open Su-Th 11am-11pm, F-Sa 11am-1am.

Tandoor Restaurant, 5024 University Way NE (523-7477). The lunch buffet ($5) is a great deal, as is Sunday brunch ($6). Dinner is more expensive. Grab a cushion on a back-room bench. Open M-Sa 11am-2:30pm and 4:30-10pm, Su 11am-3pm.

CAFES AND COFFEEHOUSES

Though Seattle boasts abundant alcoholic oases, the coffee bean is its first love. One cannot walk a single block without passing an institution of caffeination. The Emerald City's obsession with Italian-style espresso drinks has driven even gas stations to start pumping out thick, dark, soupy java, and the trend has even infiltrated Alaska.

Capitol Hill

Vivace, 901 E. Denny Way (860-5869), off Broadway. Vivace's coffee is so delicious that other cafes advertise it. Prices in the sleek cafe reflect this excellence. Espresso $1.50. Open daily 6:30am-11pm.

The Globe Cafe, 1531 14th Ave. (324-8815). Seattle's next literary renaissance is brewing here. All-vegan menu. Open Tu-Su 7am-7pm.

Green Cat Cafe, 1514 E. Olive (726-8756), west of Broadway. A favorite with locals, with good reason. Sunny yellow walls and gilt-framed prints brighten up its already wonderful breakfast and lunch fare. Healthy diner food with a twist, and, of course, good coffee. Open daily 7am-9pm.

Convoluted Conventions of a Caffeine-Crazed Culture

Visiting Seattle without drinking the coffee would be like traveling to France without tasting the wine. Espresso stands line streets and infiltrate office buildings, and "Let's go for coffee sometime" is a powerful local pick-up line. It all started in the early 70s, when Starbucks started roasting its coffee-on-the spot in Pike Place Market. Soon, Stewart Brothers Coffee, now Seattle's Best Coffee, presented Starbucks with a rival, and the race was on both for the best cuppa joe and for global hegemony. Today, hundreds of bean-brands compete for the local market, and Seattle coffeeholics often claim undying allegiance to one or another. Learning a few basic terms for ordering espresso drinks can only endear you to locals and enrich your cultural experience:

Espresso: The foundation of all espresso drinks—a small amount of coffee brewed by forcing steam through finely ground, dark-roasted coffee (pronounced es-PRESS-oh, not ex-PRESS-oh).

Cappuccino (or "Capp"): Espresso topped by the foam from steamed milk. Order "wet" for more liquid milk and big bubbles, or "dry" for stiff foam.

Latte: Espresso with steamed milk and a little foam. More liquid than a capp.

Americano: Espresso with hot water—an alternative to classic drip coffee.

Macciato: A cup of coffee with a dollop of foam, and a bit of espresso swirled onto the foam.

Short: 8oz. **Tall:** 12oz. **Grande (or Large):** 16oz.

Single: One shot of espresso. **Double:** Two—add shots (usually about 60¢) until you feel you've reached your caffeine saturation point.

With skim (nonfat) milk, any of these drinks is called **skinny.** If all you want is a plain ol' coffee, say **"drip coffee"**—otherwise, cafe workers will return your request for mere "coffee" with a blank stare.

Cafe Paradiso, 1005 E. Pike (322-6960). This proud-to-be-alternative cafe pumps in your RDA of caffeine and counterculture. Espresso bars on both floors. Angst-ridden artists air their broodings on the public chalkboard downstairs, and contribute to a smoke-filled atmosphere. Free musical performances (Tu and Sa nights). Open M-Th 6am-midnight, F 6am-1am, Sa 8am-2am, Su 8am-midnight.University District

Espresso Roma, 4201 Broadway (632-6001), at 42nd. College and business types alike frequent this quasi-warehouse-turned-coffeehouse. Changing art displays lend spice to the basic, spacious seating area. Grab a latte and check out the wall of local events, or enjoy some sun on the patio, when sun abides. Open daily 7am-11pm.

Last Exit, 5211 University Way NE (528-0522). The Exit, which claims to be Seattle's first-ever coffee bar, was established in 1967 and never quite outgrew its natal decade. Aging hippies watch aspiring chessmasters battle it out in a large smoky room. Dirt-cheap espresso (90¢) and coffee ($1.05). Open daily 9am-midnight.

Ugly Mug, 1309 43rd St. (547-3219), off University Way. English majors and grad students come wearing turtlenecks as black as the coffee they drink. Faculty and students get real sophisticated like, then munch on turkey focaccia ($3.50) and sip the world's first Ovaltine lattes. Open M-F 7:30am-6pm, Sa 9am-5pm.

Fremont

Still Life in Fremont Coffeehouse, 709 N. 35th St. (547-9850). The airy yet earthy nature of the cafe draws locals and tourists alike. Hearty soup ($2.75) and sandwiches ($5-6) complement people-watching through the huge front window, or lounging at an outside table. Open M-Th and Su 7:30am-10pm, F-Sa 7:30am-11pm.

SIGHTS

It takes only two frenetic days to get a decent look at most of Seattle's major sights, since most are within walking distance of one another or are within the Metro's ride free zone (see **Practical Information,** p. 157). Rumor has it that Seattle taxpayers spend more per capita on the arts than any other Americans. The investment pays off in the form of plentiful galleries, free art tours, and the renovated Seattle Art Museum (SAM). Beyond its cosmopolitan downtown, Seattle also boasts over 300 parks and recreation areas where you can take in the well-watered greenery. Don't pass up this opportunity: take a rowboat out on Lake Union, bicycle along Lake Washington, or hike through the wilds of Discovery Park (see **Waterways and Parks,** p. 168). Any one of the ferries that leave from the waterfront affords a great glimpse of the city's skyline. The finest overview of Seattle, however, is a bit of a secret and an exclusively female privilege: the athletic club on the top floor of the **Columbia Tower** (the big black building at 201 5th Ave.) has floor-to-ceiling windows in the ladies' room that overlook the entire city. *(Open M-F 8:30am-4:30pm. $5, children and seniors $3.)* Although only members can get that high, the Columbia tower does have an observation deck on the 73rd floor. Volunteer Park, in Capitol Hill (see below), has a free view from the east that captures the skyline and the sound.

Downtown

The new **Seattle Art Museum,** 100 University Way (recording 654-3100, person 654-3255, or TDD 654-3137), near 1st Ave., lives in a grandiose building designed by Philadelphian architect Robert Venturi. *(Open Tu-W and F-Su 10am-5pm, Th 10am-9pm. Free tours 12:30, 1, and 2pm; check for special tours Th at 6:15pm. $6, students and seniors $4, under 12 free.)* There's art inside the building, too. An entire floor is dedicated to the art of Pacific Northwest Native Americans, and houses an extensive collection of modern and contemporary regional works. The African collection includes a piece by Kane Kwei, a carpenter from Ghana who has found a niche in the art world with his indescribable theme coffins. Call for info on films and lectures. A ticket from SAM will also get you into the Seattle Asian Art Museum in Volunteer Park (see p. 167), as long as you visit within a week. One block north of the museum on 1st Ave., inside the Museum Plaza Building, is the free **Seattle Art Museum Gallery,** featuring contemporary works by local artists. *(Open M-F 11am-5pm, Sa-Su 11am-4pm.)*

Westlake Park, with its Art Deco brick patterns and surprisingly dry **Wall of Water,** is a good place to kick back and listen to steel drums. This small triangular park, on Pike St. between 4th and 5th Ave., is bordered by the gleaming new **Westlake Center,** where the monorail departs for the Seattle Center.

Bustling with excitement only a short walk down Pike St. is the **Pike Place Market** (see **Food,** above). While downtown, trek a few blocks to **Freeway Park,** which straddles I-5 between Pike St. and Spring St., and marvel at a set of **concrete waterfalls** designed to mimic a natural gorge while simultaneously blocking freeway noise.

The Waterfront

The **Pike Place Hillclimb** descends down a set of staircases from the south end of Pike Place Market, at the end near the information booth on 1st and Pike, past chic shops and ethnic restaurants, to Alaskan Way and the waterfront. (An elevator is also available.) The super-popular **Seattle Aquarium** (386-4330, TTY 386-4322) sits at the base of the Hillclimb at Pier 59, near Union St. *(Open daily 10am-7pm; in winter 10am-5pm; limited hours on holidays. $7.75, seniors $7, ages 6-18 $5.15, ages 3-5 $2; check for AAA discounts.)* Outdoor tanks re-create salt marsh and tide pool ecosystems, but the aquarium's star attraction is an underwater dome featuring Puget Sound fish and mammals, including playful harbor seals, fur seals, and otters. See the world's only aquarium salmon ladder, check out the $1 million salmon exhibit, and do not dare miss the daily 11:30am feeding.

Next to the aquarium on Pier 59 is the **Omnidome** (622-1868), which shoots movies onto a special rounded screen so that patrons actually feel like they are in the movie. The booming sound system may scare small children and scar delicate psyches. *(Films daily 10am-10pm. $7; students, seniors, and ages 6-18 $6; ages 3-5 $5. Second film $2. Combined aquarium/Omnidome ticket $13, seniors and ages 13-18 $11.25, ages 6-13 $9.50, ages 3-5 $5.50.)*

Explore north or south along the waterfront by foot or by **streetcar.** The 20s cars were imported from Melbourne in 1982 because Seattle sold its originals to San Francisco, where they now enjoy fame as cable cars, the posers. *(Streetcars run every 20-30min. M-F 7am-11pm, Sa 8am-11pm, Su 9am-11pm; in winter until 6pm. $1, $1.25 during peak hours. Children 75¢. Under 12 ride free with a paying passenger on Su. Metro passes accepted.)* Streetcars are fully wheelchair accessible, and run from the Metro tunnel in Pioneer Square north to Pier 70 and Myrtle Edwards Park.

The Seattle Center

When the 1962 World's Fair engulfed Seattle, the entertainment-oriented city rose to the occasion by building the Seattle Center, which now houses anything from carnival rides to ballet. Take the **monorail** from the third floor of the Westlake Center. *(Departs every 15min. 9am-11pm. $1, seniors 50¢, ages 5-12 75¢.)* The center is bordered by Denny Way, W. Mercer St., 1st Ave., and 5th Ave., and has eight gates, each with a model of the Center and a map of its facilities. Although Seattleites generally disdain the Center, leaving it to tourists and suburbanites, visitors just keep coming. For info about special events and permanent attractions, call 684-8582 for recorded information or 684-7200 for a speaking human. The **Space Needle** (443-2111), sometimes known as the World's Tackiest Monument, is at least a useful landmark for the disoriented. It houses an observation tower and an expensive, 360° rotating restaurant. *(Tower $9, seniors $8, ages 5-12 $4. Free with dinner reservations. Some clever miscreants have been known to make reservations with no intention of keeping them.)*

The **Pacific Science Center** (443-2001; http://www.pacsci.org), near the needle, houses a **laserium** (443-2850) that quakes to Led Zeppelin and Smashing Pumpkins, plus an immense **IMAX theater** (443-IMAX/4629). *(Laser shows Tu $3, W-Su $7. IMAX shows Th-Su at 8pm. IMAX/museum tickets $9.50, seniors and ages 6-13 $7.50, ages 2-5 $5.50.)* The **Children's Museum** (441-1768), in the Center House, has an abundance of creative hands-on exhibits that will wow any kid (or jealous adult) into a fit of overstimulation. *(Open M-F 10am-5pm, Sa-Su 10am-6pm. $4, ages 1-12 $5.50, under 1 free.)*

Pioneer Square and Environs

From the waterfront or downtown, it's just a few blocks to historic **Pioneer Square,** at Yesler Way and 2nd Ave, home of the first Seattleites. The 19th-century warehouses and office buildings were restored in the 70s, and now house chic shops and trendy pubs. Pioneer Square today retains much of its historical intrigue, plus a fresh layer of suffocating tourist crowds.

Originally, Seattle stood 12 ft. below the present-day streets. The **Underground Tour** (682-4646 or 888-608-6337; http://www.undergroundtour.com) leads through the subterranean rooms and passageways of old, explaining the sordid and soggy birth of Seattle. *(90min. Daily and roughly hourly 9am-7pm; varies by season. $7, seniors $6, students $5.50, children $2.75. Reservations recommended.)* Be prepared for lots of company, comedy, and toilet jokes. Tours depart from Doc Maynard's Pub, 610 1st Ave. "Doc" Maynard, a charismatic and colorful early resident, gave a plot of land here to one Henry Yesler on the condition that he build a steam-powered lumber mill. Logs were dragged down the steep grade of Yesler Way to feed the mill, earning that street the epithet **Skid Row.** The smell of the oil used to lubricate the slide was so overwhelming that all self-respecting Seattleites avoided that area of town, leaving it to gamblers, prostitutes, flopheads, and other notorious types. When the center of town moved north, the decline of Pioneer Square led to the rise of the term "skid row" and its present, log-independent meaning.

Klondike Gold Rush National Historic Park, 117 S. Main St. (553-7220), is a posh interpretive center depicting the lives of miners, with a slide show about the role of Seattle in the Klondike gold rush. *(Open daily 9am-5pm. Free.)* To add some levity to this litany of shattered dreams, the park screens Charlie Chaplin's 1925 classic **The Gold Rush** on the first Sunday of every month at 3pm. Free daily **walking tours** of Pioneer Square leave the park at 10am.

The International District

Three blocks east of Pioneer Square, up Jackson on King St., is Seattle's **International District.** Though sometimes called Chinatown, this area is now home to immigrants from all over Asia and their descendants. The tiny **Wing Luke Memorial Museum,** 407 7th Ave. S (623-5124), displays a thorough description of life in an Asian-American community, a permanent exhibit on different Asian nationalities in Seattle, and work by local Asian artists. *(Open Tu-F 11am-4:30pm, Sa-Su noon-4pm. $2.50, seniors and students $1.50, ages 5-12 75¢. Th free.)* Landmarks of the International District include the abstract **Tsutakawa sculpture** at the corner of S. Jackson and Maynard St., and the gigantic dragon mural and red-and-green pagoda in **Hing Hay Park** at S. King and Maynard St. The **community gardens** at Main and Maynard St. provide a peaceful and well-tended retreat from the downtown sidewalks, though you may feel like you're walking through someone's back yard as you tiptoe through the turnips. Park next to the gardens in free two-hour angled parking to avoid meters.

Capitol Hill

From their elevated position above the Emerald City, Capitol Hill residents scan the city with an artist's eye. The district's leftist and gay communities set the tone for its nightspots (see p. 173), while retail outlets include collectives and radical bookstores right alongside Ben & Jerry's and The Gap. Explore **Broadway** to window shop and experience alternative lifestyles merging with mainstream capitalism. Walk a few blocks east and north for a stroll down **15th Ave.,** lined with well-maintained Victorian homes. Bus #10 runs along 15th Ave. with frequent stops; #7 cruises Broadway.

Volunteer Park, between 11th and 17th Ave. at E. Ward St., north of the Broadway activity, lures Seattleites away from the city center. Bus #10 runs parkward up 15th Ave.; it's preferable to bus #7, since it runs more frequently and stops closer to the fun stuff. Named for the "veterans who liberated the oppressed peoples of Cuba, Puerto Rico and the Philippines" during the Spanish-American War, the park boasts lovely lawns, an outdoor running track, a playground, and fields of rhododendron blooming in spring and early summer. The **outdoor stage** often hosts free perfor-

Pop Quiz, Hotshot

What would you call a 12 oz. espresso with an extra shot, steamed milk (skim, of course), and foam?

mances on summer Sundays. Climb the medieval-looking **water tower** at the 14th Ave. entrance for a stunning 360° panorama of the city and the Olympic Range, as well as a little background info on Seattle's park system. The views beat those from the Space Needle, and they're free. On rainy days, hide out amid the orchids inside the **glass conservatory.** *(Open daily 10am-4pm; in summer 10am-7pm. Free.)* A tour through world-renowned collections of the newly renovated **Seattle Asian Art Museum** (654-3100) reveals Ming vases and ancient kimonos at every turn. *(Open Tu-Su 10am-5pm, Th 10am-9pm. $6, seniors and students $4, under 12 free.)* Be careful at night, as the park has an unsavory after-dark reputation.

Just north of Volunteer Park on 15th St. is **Lake View Cemetery,** where the graves of **Bruce and Brandon Lee** rest among the founders of Seattle. One of the most famous martial artists of the century, Bruce Lee moved to Seattle in his youth; his son Brandon made a name for himself in the same field. The Lees' graves lie near the top of the cemetery; from the flagpole, face the headstone shaped like a cross and head down the hill toward the right, where the roads intersect. The graves are next to a bush, with a row of small evergreen trees lined behind a bench in their memory.

The **University of Washington Arboretum,** 10 blocks east of Volunteer Park, nurtures over 4000 species, trees, shrubs, and flowers, and maintains superb walking and running trails; take bus #11 from downtown. *(Open 7am-dusk.)* Exhibits on local plant life fill the **Graham Visitor Center** (543-8800), at the southern end of the arboretum on Lake Washington Blvd. *(Open daily 10am-4pm. Free. Tours of the arboretum leave Sa and Su at 1pm.)* Across the street, the tranquil, perfectly pruned **Japanese Tea Garden** (684-4725) offers a stroll through 3½ acres of sculpted gardens with fruit trees, a reflecting pool, and a traditional tea house. *(Open Mar.-Nov. daily 10am-8pm. $2.50, seniors, students and ages 6-18 $1.50, under 6 free, disabled $1.)*

University District, Fremont, and Ballard

With over 33,000 students, the **University of Washington** comprises the state's cultural and educational center of gravity. The U District swarms with students year-round, and Seattleites of all ages take advantage of the area's many bohemian bookstores, shops, taverns, and restaurants. To get there, take buses #71-74 from downtown, or #7, 9, 43, or 48 from Capitol Hill. Stop by the friendly **visitor center,** 4014 University Way NE (543-9198), to pick up a campus map, a self-guided tour book, and information about the university. *(Open M-F 8am-5pm.)*

The **Thomas Burke Museum of Natural History and Culture** (543-5590; http://www.washington.edu/burkemuseum), at 45th St. NE and 17th Ave. NE in the northwest corner of the campus, exhibits a superb collection on Pacific Rim cultures, as well as kid-friendly explanations of the natural history behind Washington's formation. *(Open F-W 10am-5pm, Th 10am-8pm. $5.50, seniors $4, students $2.50, under 5 free.)* This is the only natural history museum in the area, so savor the chance to see the only dinosaur bones in the Pacific Northwest. Across the street, the astronomy department's old stone **observatory** (543-0126) is open to the public for viewings on clear nights. Looming gothic lecture halls, red brick, and rose gardens transform the campus into a bower fit for hours of strolling. The red concrete basin in the center of campus, known as **Red Square,** collects hundreds of students during the school year.

Answer

A tall, skinny, double latte.

The newly remodeled **Henry Art Gallery** (543-2280), across from the visitor center, hosts superb exhibitions of modern art in a stark white setting. *(Open Tu-Su 11am-5pm, Th 11am-8pm. $5, seniors $3.50. Free Th after 5pm.)*

U-Dub students often cross town for drinks in Queen Anne, and the intervening neighborhood of **Fremont** basks in the cross-pollination. Fremont residents pride themselves on their love of art and antiques, and on the liberal atmosphere of their self-declared "center of the world" under Rte. 99. A statue entitled **"Waiting for the Inner-City Urban"** depicts several people waiting in bus purgatory, and, in moments of inspiration and sympathy, is frequently gussied up by passers-by. The **immense troll** who sits beneath the Aurora Bridge on 35th St. grasps a Volkswagen Bug, and bears a confounded expression on his broad cement face. Some say kicking the bug's tire brings good luck; others say it hurts their foot. A flamin' **Vladimir Lenin** resides at the corner of N. 36th and N. Fremont Pl.; this bona fide artwork from the former Soviet Union will be around until it's bought by a permanent collection, presumably of bona fide Soviet artwork. Fremont is also home to **Archie McPhee's,** 3510 Stone Way (545-8344), a shrine to pop culture and plastic absurdity. *(Open M-Sa 9am-7pm, Su 10am-6pm.)* People of the punk and funk persuasion make pilgrimages from as far as the record stores of Greenwich Village in Manhattan just to handle the notorious **slug selection.** Reach Archie's on the Aurora Hwy. (Rte. 99), or on bus #26. The store is east of the highway between 35th and 36th, two blocks north of Lake Union and Gasworks Park (see below).

Next door to the U District, the primarily Scandinavian neighborhood of **Ballard** offers visitors a taste of Europe, with a wide variety of Scandinavian eateries and shops lining Market St. The **Nordic Heritage Museum,** 3014 NW 67th St. (789-5707), presents thorough and realistic exhibits on the history of Nordic immigration and influence in the U.S. *(Open Tu-Sa 10am-4pm, Su noon-4pm. $4, seniors and students $3, ages 6-18 $2.)* Stumble over cobblestones in old Copenhagen, or visit the slums of New York City that turned photographer and Danish immigrant Jacob Riis into an important social reformer. The museum hosts a **Viking festival** the weekend after the 4th of July, a **Yule Fest** the weekend before Thanksgiving, and sponsors a series of **Nordic concerts** with local musicians throughout the summer. Take bus #17 from downtown, and bus #44 from the U District, transferring to #17 at 24th and Market.

WATERWAYS AND PARKS

Thanks to the foresight of Seattle's early community and the architectural genius of the Olmsted family, Seattle enjoys a string of parks and waterways for general frolicking. In summer, they are a playground for boaters, and a string of attractions festoon the waterways linking Lake Washington and Puget Sound. Houseboats and sailboats fill **Lake Union,** situated between Capitol Hill and the University District. Here, the **Center for Wooden Boats,** 1010 Valley St. (382-2628), maintains a moored flotilla of new and restored small craft for rent. *(Open daily 11am-6pm. Rowboats $12.50-20 per hr.; sailboats $16-26 per hr.)* **Gasworks Park,** a much-celebrated kite-flying spot at the north end of Lake Union, was recently converted after its retirement from the oil-refining business, and hosts a furious fireworks show on July 4th. To get there, take bus #26 from downtown to N. 35th St. and Wallingford Ave. N. **Gasworks Kite Shop,** 3333 Wallingford N (633-4780), is one block north of the park. *(Open M-F 10am-6pm, Sa 10am-5pm, Su noon-5pm.)* If the need to sail or skate suddenly strikes, head to **Urban Surf** (545-WIND/9463), across the street from the park entrance at 2100 N. Northlake Way, for windsurfing boards or in-line skates. *(Boards $35 per day. Skates $5 per hr.)*

Directly north of Lake Union, athletes run, ride, and roll around **Green Lake;** take bus #16 from downtown Seattle. The lake is also given high marks by windsurfers, but woe unto those who lose their balance. Whoever named it Green Lake wasn't kidding; even a quick dunk results in a full-body coating of green algae. On sunny afternoons, boat-renters, windsurfers, and scullers can make the lake feel like rush hour. Rent a bike at **Gregg's Green Lake Cycle** (see **Practical Information: Equipment Rental,** p. 158), on the east side of the lake, across the street from Starbucks. Seek out the **Burke-Gilman Trail** for a longer ride.

Next to Green Lake is **Woodland Park** and the **Woodland Park Zoo,** 5500 Phinney Ave. N (684-4800), best reached from Rte. 99 or N. 50th St.; take bus #5 from downtown. *(Zoo open Mar. 15-Oct. 14 9:30am-6pm, Oct. 15-March 14 9:30am-4pm. $8, seniors $7.25, ages 6-17, ages 3-5 $3.50, disabled $5.50. Parking $3.50; in winter $1.75.)* While the park itself is not well-manicured, the zoo's habitats are highly realistic, including the Alaska-themed Northern Trail and the orangutan-crammed Tropical Asia. This one of three zoos in the U.S. to receive the Humane Society's highest standard of approval.

Farther west, at the **Hiram M. Chittenden Locks** (783-7059), on NW St. along the Lake Washington Ship Canal, crowds gather to watch Seattle's boaters jockey for position. Take bus #43 from the U District or #17 from downtown. A circus atmosphere develops as boats traveling between Puget Sound and Lake Washington try to cross over. *(June-Sept. daily 7am-9pm.)* If listening to the cries of frustrated skippers ("Gilligan, you nitwit!") doesn't amuse you, climb over to the **fish ladder** to watch homesick salmon hurl themselves up 21 concrete steps. The busiest salmon runs last from June to September. *(Free tours in summer daily at 1 and 3pm. Open daily 7am-9pm.)*

Next door to the locks lie the 534 bucolic acres of **Discovery Park** (386-4236), at 36th Ave. W and Government Way W, on a lonely point west of the Magnolia District and south of Golden Gardens Park (bus #24). This is the largest park in the Seattle area, with minimally tended grassy fields and steep bluffs atop Puget Sound. It provides a wonderful haven for birds forced over Puget Sound by the bad-weather Olympic Mountains. Possessing a wide range of habitats with easily distinguishable transitions, this park provides a fantastic introduction to the flora and fauna of the Pacific Northwest for those unable to visit Olympic or Mt. Rainier National Parks. A **visitor center,** 3801 W. Government Way, looms large by the entrance and sells handy maps (75¢). **Shuttles** ferry visitors to the beach. *(June-Sept. Sa-Su noon-4:45pm. 25¢, seniors and disabled free.)* At the park's northern end is the **Indian Cultural Center** (285-4425), operated by the United Indians of All Tribes Foundation, which houses the **Sacred Circle Gallery,** a rotating exhibit of Native American artwork. *(Open M-F 9am-5pm, Sa-Su noon-5pm. Free.)*

Seward Park lies at the south end of a string of beaches and forest preserves along the west shore of Lake Washington; take bus #39. Home to Seattle's orthodox Jewish community, the area offers sweeping views of the lake and Mercer Island. After a jaunt in the park, refresh yourself with a tour of the **Rainier Brewery Co.,** 3100 Airport Way S (622-2600), off I-5 at the West Seattle Bridge. Beer (of the root variety for those under 21), cheese, and crackers are free. *(30min. tours on the hr. M-Sa 1-6pm.)*

OUTDOORS

Cyclists should gear up for the 19 mi., 1600-competitor **Seattle to Portland Race.** Call the **bike hotline** (522-2453) for more info. The Seattle Parks Department also holds a monthly **Bicycle Sunday** from May to September, when Lake Washington Blvd. is open exclusively to cyclists from 10am to 6pm. For more info, contact the Parks Department's **Citywide Sports Office** (684-7092).

Many **whitewater rafting** outfitters are based in the Seattle area. Though the rapids are hours away by car, over 50 companies compete for a growing market. Call outfitters and quote competitors' prices; they are often willing to undercut one another with merciless and self-mutilating abandon. **Washington State Outfitters and Guides Association** (392-6107) provides advice and information; although their office is closed in summer, they do return phone calls and send out info. The **Northwest Outdoor Center,** 2100 Westlake Ave. (281-9694), on Lake Union, gives instructional programs in whitewater and sea kayaking, and leads three-day kayaking excursions through the San Juan Islands. *(2½hr. basic intro to sea kayaking, including equipment, $40. Open M-F 10am-8pm, Sa-Su 9am-6pm.)* Call ahead to make reservations for early summer.

Skiing near Seattle is every bit as good as the mountains make it look. **Alpental, Ski-Acres,** and **Snoqualmie** co-sponsor an info number (232-8182), which provides ski conditions and lift ticket rates for all three. **Crystal Mountain** (663-2265), the region's newest resort, can be reached by Rte. 410 south out of Seattle and offers ski rentals, lessons, and lift ticket packages.

Ever since the Klondike gold rush, Seattle has been in the business of equipping wilderness expeditions. Besides Army-Navy surplus stores and camper supply shops, the city is home to many world-class outfitters. **Recreational Equipment Inc. Coop (REI Coop),** 222 Yale Ave. (223-1944), is the largest of its kind in the world. *(Open M-Sa 9am-9pm, Su 10am-6pm. Rental area open 2hr. before store.)* This paragon of woodsy wisdom can be seen from I-5; take the Stewart St. exit. The brand-new flagship store offers a 65 ft. indoor climbing pinnacle, interactive pathways to test mountaineering equipment, and lessons on Pacific Northwest foliage.

ENTERTAINMENT

Seattle has one of the world's most notorious underground music scenes and the third largest theater community in the U.S. (only New York's and Chicago's loom larger). Performances of all kinds take place in any building with four walls, from bars to bakeries. In the summertime, risers seem to grow out of asphalt during street fairs and farmers' markets, and outdoor theater springs up in most parks. High-cost shows regularly sell half-price tickets, while alternative theaters offer high-quality drama at low prices. During summer lunch hours, the free **Out to Lunch** series (623-0340) brings everything from reggae to folk dancing to the parks, squares, and office buildings of downtown Seattle. Pick up a schedule at the visitor center (see p. 157). The **Seattle Public Library** (386-4636) shows free films as part of this program, and has a daily schedule of other free events, such as poetry readings and children's book-reading competitions (see p. 158).

Music and Dance

The **Seattle Opera** performs at the Opera House in the Seattle Center throughout the year. The program's popularity demands reservations well in advance, although rush tickets are sometimes available. Students and seniors receive half-price tickets on the day of the performance (from $20); student tickets are also available for ($27-31). Call 389-7676 (M-F 9am-5pm) or Ticketmaster (292-ARTS/2787). Write to the Seattle Opera at P.O. Box 9248, Seattle 98109. The **Seattle Symphony Orchestra** (443-4747), in the new Fifth Avenue Theater, performs a regular subscription series (Sept.-June; rush tickets from $6.50) and a popular children's series. The **Pacific Northwest Ballet** (441-9411) starts its season at the Opera House in September. *(Tickets from $14; half-price rush tickets available to students and seniors 30min. before showtime.)* The spectacular *Nutcracker* production, designed by Maurice Sendak, is always a wild rumpus. The season continues through May with six productions. The **University of Washington** offers its own program of student recitals and concerts by visiting artists. Call the Meany Hall box office (543-4880). *(Open M-F 10:30am-4:30pm.)*

Theater

The city hosts an exciting array of first-run plays and alternative works, particularly by many talented amateur groups. Rush tickets are often available at nearly half price on the day of the show (cash only) from **Ticket/Ticket** (324-2744).

⊛**The Empty Space Theatre,** 3509 Fremont Ave. N (547-7500), 1½ blocks north of the Fremont Bridge. Comedies in this small space attract the entire city. Season runs Oct. to early July. Box office open daily 1-5pm. Tickets $14-24. Previews (first 4 performances of any show) $10. Half-price rush tickets 10min. before curtain.

Seattle Repertory Theater, 155 W. Mercer St. (443-2222, Ticketmaster 292-ARTS/ 7676), at the wonderful Bagley Wright Theater in Seattle Center. Winter season combines contemporary and classic productions (usually including Shakespeare). With cat-like tread, Gilbert and Sullivan operettas arise in summer (341-9612). *The Heidi Chronicles* and *Fences* started here, later moving to Broadway. Tickets $10-48, seniors $17, under 25 $10. Box office open M 10am-6pm, Tu-Sa 10am-8pm.

A Contemporary Theater (ACT), 700 Union St. (292-7670). A summer season of modern and off-beat premieres. Tickets $14-26. Box office open Tu-Th noon-7:30pm, F-Sa noon-8pm, Su noon-7pm.

Annex Theatre, 1916 4th Ave. (728-0933). Refreshing emphasis on company-generated material. Regular productions run 4 weeks. Shows usually Th-Sa at 8pm and Su at 7pm. Pay-what-you-can previews. Tickets $10-12.

Northwest Asian American Theater, 409 7th Ave. S (364-3282), in the International District, next to the Wing Luke Asian Museum. An excellent new theater with pieces by, for, and about Asian Americans. Tickets $12; students, seniors, and disabled $9; Th $6.

Bathhouse Theater, 7312 W. Green Lake Dr. N (524-9108), right by the lake. A small company known for plopping Shakespeare in strange locales (e.g. Wild West *Macbeth,* 50s *Midsummer Night's Dream,* Kabuki *King Lear*). Tickets $15-28. Rush tickets $7.50. Tu-Th before curtain. Box office open Tu-Su noon-7pm.

Cinema

Seattle is a cinematic paradise. Most of the theaters that screen non-Hollywood films are on Capitol Hill and in the University District. Large, first-run theaters are everywhere, including a mammoth 16 screen **Cineplex Odeon** (223-9600) at 7th Ave. and Pike. Most matinee shows cost $4; after 6pm, expect to pay $7. **Seven Gables,** a local company, has recently bought up the Egyptian, the Metro, the Neptune, and others. $20 buys admission to any five films at any of their theaters. Call 44-FILMS/443-4567 for local movie times and locations.

The Egyptian, 801 E. Pine St. (32-EGYPT/34978), at Harvard Ave. on Capitol Hill. This handsome Art Deco theater shows artsy flix, and is best known for hosting the **Seattle International Film Festival** in the last week of May and first week of June. The festival includes a retrospective of one director's work, with a personal appearance by the said director. Festival series tickets available at a discount. $7, seniors and children $4, matinees $4.

The Harvard Exit, 807 E. Roy St. (323-8986), on Capitol Hill. Quality classic and foreign films. Half the fun of seeing a movie here is the theater, a converted residence that has its very own ghost, and an enormous antique projector. The lobby was once someone's living room. Arrive early and check out the puzzles. $7, seniors and children $4, matinees $4.

Seven Gables Theater, 911 NE 50th St. (632-8820), in the U District just off Roosevelt, a short walk west from University Way. Another cinema in an old house, showing independent and classic films. $7, seniors and children $4, matinees $4.

Grand Illusion Cinema, 1403 NE 50th St. (523-3935), in the U District at University Way. A tiny theater attached to an espresso bar, showing films made on 30s-style budgets. One of the last independent theaters in Seattle. $6, seniors and children $3, matinees $4.

United Artists Cinema, 2131 6th Ave. (883-9591), at Blanchard. Known around Seattle as the "$2 theater." Tickets to fairly recent Hollywood flicks cost $2, except for "midnight madness" shows, which cost $5 but include popcorn or a drink.

Sports

Uglier than the Boeing factory, the **Kingdome,** 201 S. King St. (tickets 622-4487), down 1st Ave., ranks second only to Houston's Astrodome as an insult to baseball. Seattle is the only city in America where fans might prefer to watch their home team, the **Mariners,** on TV rather than seeing them play live, under poor, purplish light, on artificial turf, and amid unearthly echoes. In the fall of 1995, sections of the roof viciously attacked fans hoping to see Seattle make the World Series. Even so, the Mariners have some of the finest marquee talent around, and a new stadium is in the works. Tickets (628-0888) at the Kingdome are cheap (outfield bleachers $6, most others $25, under 14 discounts, half-price family nights). The **Seahawks,** who have been an up-and-coming NFL team for a little too long, also play football here.

On the other side of town and at the other end of the aesthetic spectrum, the new and graceful **Key Arena** in the Seattle Center is packed to the brim whenever Seattle's pro basketball team, the **Supersonics** (281-5800), plays. Three years ago, Seattleites danced in the streets as the Sonics ascended the NBA ranks, only to be defeated by the unstoppable Chicago Bulls. Undaunted by a recent NCAA post-season prohibition, the **University of Washington Huskies** football team has dominated the PAC-10. Call the Athletic Ticket Office (543-2200) for Huskies schedules and price info.

Shopping

Seattle's younger set has created a wide demand for retail chain alternatives, though a swiftly growing population has certainly lured syndicated stores to popular shopping areas. Downtown, trendy and fairly expensive clothing stores and boutiques line the avenues from 3rd to 6th, between Seneca St. in the south and the Westlake Center in the north, including the enormous **Nordstrom's** (628-2111) at 1051 5th Ave. **Westlake Center** itself is an indoor conglomerate of chain stores and gift shops.

For handmade crafts and jewelry, shop at **Pike Place Market** (see p. 160), where baubles are almost as plentiful as cherries and zucchini. In the U District, **The Ave** (University Way) caters to the college crowd and promises good deals. Used music stores occupy almost every other storefront in this area, hawking deals on all sorts of tunes. Capitol Hill also supports the used music market: **Orpheum,** 618 Broadway E (322-6370), has an inspiring collection of imports and local music.

Thrift stores thrive in Seattle, especially on The Ave and between Pike and Pine Streets on Capitol Hill. Find astounding temples to trendiness and thriftiness like **Rex and Angels Red Light Lounge and Cereal Bar,** 4560 University Way NE (545-4044).

Bookstores

University Book Store, 4326 University Way NE (634-3400). Largest college bookstore chain on the West Coast, with 7 stores in the Seattle area. Open M-F 9am-9pm, Sa 9am-6pm, Su noon-5pm.

Elliott Bay Books, 101 S. Main St. (624-6600), in Pioneer Sq. Vast collection with 150,000 titles. Sponsors a reading and lecture series. Coffeehouse in the basement. Open M-Sa 10am-11pm, Su 11am-6pm.

Red and Black Books, 432 15th Ave. E (322-7323), on Capitol Hill. Features multicultural, gay, and feminist literature, with frequent readings. Open M-Th 10am-8pm, F-Sa 10am-9pm, Su 11am-7pm.

Beyond the Closet, 518 E. Pike (322-4609). Exclusively gay and lesbian material. Open daily 10am-11pm.

NIGHTLIFE

Seattle has moved beyond beer to a new nightlife frontier: the cafe-and-bar. The popularity of espresso bars in Seattle might lead one to conclude that caffeine is more intoxicating than alcohol, but often an establishment that poses as a diner by day brings on a band, breaks out the disco ball, and pumps out the microbrews by night. Many locals tell tourists that the best spot to go for guaranteed good beer, live music, and big crowds is Pioneer Square, where UW students from frat row dominate the bar stools. These Seattleites are lying to you like curs; they probably take their beer bucks downtown to Capitol Hill, or up Rte. 99 to Fremont, where the atmosphere is usually more laid-back than in the Square.

Downtown

Sit and Spin, 2219 4th St. (cafe/laundromat 441-9484; band info 441-9474). Though the washers and dryers work, the real focus of this late-night cafe is the social scene. Furniture hangs from the walls, and board games keep patrons busy while they wait for their clothes to dry or for alternative bands to play in the back room (F and Sa nights). The cafe sells everything from local microbrews on tap to bistro food (cashew chicken tarragon $5) to boxes of laundry detergent. Artists cut albums in the **Bad Animal** studio down the street (where R.E.M. once recorded), and stop by to play checkers and bask in the plastic glow of a 50s trailer park gone mad. Open Su-Th 9am-midnight, F-Sa 9am-2am. Kitchen opens daily at 11am.

The Alibi Room, 85 Pike St. (623-3180), across from the Market Cinema in the Post Alley in Pike Place. Created by a local producer, the Alibi Room proclaims itself a local indie filmmaker hangout. Smoky sophisticates star as themselves. Racks of screenplays, DJ and dancing on the weekends, and chic decor get an Oscar for ambience. Open daily 11am-2am.

Re-Bar, 1114 Howell (233-9873). A mixed gay and straight bar with a wide range of tunes and dancing on the wild side. Hip-hop (F); lots of acid jazz and fringe theater (Sa-Su). Cover $4. Open daily 9:30pm-2am.

Art Bar, 1516 2nd Ave. (622-4344). Exactly what the name says: a gallery/bar fusion. Lots of jazz and a diverse clientele. Cover $3-5. Open M-F 11am-2am, Sa 3pm-2am, Su 4pm-2am.

Crocodile Cafe, 2200 2nd Ave. (448-2114), at Blanchard. Another diner-turned-club. Eat organic eggs and toast by day; jam to popular local and national bands after dark. 21+ after 9pm. Cover $5-20. Open Tu-Sa 8am-2am, Su 9am-3pm for brunch.

Vogue, 2018 1st Ave (443-0673). Anything seems to go in this angsty club, where lattes are served beside wine coolers and day-glo mingles with darker decor. Dress in black and groove to 80s or Gothic tunes. Cover $2-5. Open daily 9pm-2am.

Dimitriou's Jazz Alley, 2033 6th Ave. (441-9729). This chic club offers plenty of cool world jazz, and even does dinner theater once in a while. Check out the parade of talent shuffling through the Alley; most shows $13-20. Open daily 6pm-last show, usually 11:30-12:30pm.

Pioneer Square

Pioneer Square provides a happening scene, dominated by 20-somethings and college folk. Most of the area bars participate in a joint cover ($8, Su-Th $5) that will let you wander from bar to bar to sample the bands. **Fenix Cafe and Fenix Underground** (467-1111) and **Central Tavern** (622-0209) rock constantly, while **Larry's** (624-7665) and **New Orleans** (622-2563) feature great jazz and blues nightly. The **Bohemian Cafe** (447-1514) pumps reggae and also sponsors open mic nights on Thursday. **Kells** (728-1916), near Pike Place Market, is a popular Irish pub with nightly celtic tunes. **J and M Cafe** (624-1670) is in the center of Pioneer Square, often blasting dance music into its crowded quarters. All the Pioneer Square clubs shut down at 2am Friday and Saturday nights, and around midnight during the week.

Colourbox, 113 1st Ave. (340-4101). One of the few places in Pioneer Square that real rockers respect. Live music most nights, in a bar that looks quaint with the lights on and violently grungy in the dark. Open daily 8:30pm-2am.

OK Hotel, 212 Alaskan Way S (621-7903; coffeehouse 386-9934), just below Pioneer Square toward the waterfront. One cafe, one bar, one building. Lots of wood, lots of coffee. Live bands play everything from rock to reggae and draw equally diverse crowds. Bar art is curated monthly. Occasional cover charge up to $6. Cafe open M-F 5-10pm, Sa-Su 5-11pm. Bar open daily 3pm-2am.

Capitol Hill

Garage, 1130 Broadway (322-2296). An automotive warehouse turned upscale pool hall, this place gets suave at night. Happy hour 3-7pm. 8 pool tables $6-10 per hr.; $4 per hr. during happy hour; $5 per hr. (M); free for female sharps on Ladies' Night (Su). Open daily 3pm-2am.

Neighbours, 1509 Broadway (324-5358). A very gay dance club priding itself on techno slickness. Cover Su-Th $1; F-Sa $5. Open Su-Th 9pm-2am, F-Sa 9pm-4am.

Linda's, 707 Pine St. E (325-1220). Major post-gig scene for Seattle rockers. Stop by to be seen with the next Soundgarden. Open M-Sa 2pm-2am, Su 4pm-2am.

Fremont

Red Door Alehouse, 3401 Fremont Ave. N (547-7521), at N. 34th St., across from the Inner-Urban Statue. Throbbing with university students who attest to the good local ale selection and a mile-long beer menu. Try the Pyramid Wheaton or Widmer Hefeweizen with a slice of lemon. Open daily 11am-2am. Kitchen closes at 11pm.

The Dubliner, 3405 Fremont Ave. N (548-1508). Irish soul in Fremont, with a friendly local crowd. Irish jam session (W at 9pm). Open daily noon-2am.

The Trolleyman Pub, 3400 Phinney Ave. N (548-8000), west on N. 34th St. from the Red Door. In the back of the **Red Hook Ale Brewery,** which rolls the most popular kegs on campus. Early hours make it a mellow spot to hear good acoustic music while lounging on one of the pub's couches and enjoying a fresh pint. Live music F and Sa 9:30-11pm. Come back during the day for a $1 tour of the brewery, and a generous sampling of all 4 beers currently on tap. Brewery open in summer daily noon-5pm. Pub open M-Th 11am-11pm, F-Sa 11am-midnight, Su noon-9pm.

EVENTS

Pick up a copy of the visitor center's *Calendar of Events,* published every season, for event coupons and an exact listing of innumerable area happenings. The first Thursday evening of each month, the art community sponsors **First Thursday,** a free and well-attended gallery walk. Watch for **street fairs** in the University District during mid- to late May, at Pike Place Market over Memorial Day weekend, and in Fremont in mid-June. The International District holds its annual two-day bash in mid-July, featuring arts and crafts booths, East Asian and Pacific food booths, and presentations by a range of groups from the Radical Women/Freedom Socialist Party to the Girl Scouts. For more info, call **Chinatown Discovery** (236-0657 or 583-0460), or write P.O. Box 3406, Seattle 98114.

Puget Sound's yachting season begins in May. **Maritime Week,** during the third week of May, and the **Shilshole Boats Afloat Show** (634-0911) in mid-August, give area boaters a chance to show off their crafts. At the beginning of July, the Center for Wooden Boats sponsors the free **Wooden Boat Show** (382-2628) on Lake Union. Blue blazers and deck shoes are *de rigeur.* Size up the entrants (over 100 wooden boats), then watch a demonstration of boat-building skills. The year-end blow-out is the **Quick and Daring Boatbuilding Contest,** when hopefuls go overboard trying to build and sail wooden boats of their own design, using a limited kit of tools and materials. Plenty of music, food, and alcohol make the sailing smooth.

Northwest Folklife Festival (684-7200), on Memorial Day weekend. One of Seattle's most notable events, held at the Seattle Center. Artists, musicians, and dancers congregate to celebrate the area's heritage.

Fremont Fair and Solstice Parade, in mid-June. Brings Fremont to a frenzy of music, frivolity, and craft booths.

Bon Odori, on the 3rd week of July. The Japanese community's traditional festival, celebrated in the International District. Temples are opened to the public and dancing fills the streets.

Bite of Seattle (684-7200), in mid-July. Free food festival in the Seattle Center.

Seattle Seafair (728-0123), spread over 3 weeks from mid-July to early Aug. The biggest, baddest festival of them all. Each neighborhood contributes with street fairs, parades large and small, balloon races, musical entertainment, and a seafood orgy.

Bumbershoot (281-7788), over Labor Day weekend. A massive, 4-day arts festival that caps off the summer, held in the Seattle Center. Attracts big-name rock bands, street musicians, and a young, exuberant crowd. 4 days $29; 2 days $16; 1 day $9 in advance or $10 at the door, seniors $1, children free. Prices subject to change.

■ Near Seattle: Daytrips to the East

Cross **Lake Washington** on one of two floating bridges to arrive in a biker's and picnicker's (and suburbanite's) paradise, where Range Rovers and outdoor shopping plazas litter the landscape. Companies buy up expanses of East Sound land, smother them in sod and office complexes, and call them "campuses"; witness **Microsoft,** which has nearly subsumed the suburb of Redmond. Rapid growth has had its benefits, though. In the suburb of **Bellevue,** the July **Bellevue Jazz Festival** (455-6885) attracts both local cats and national acts. This wealthy and beautiful suburb is home to Bill Gates, among others. Neither tours of Bill's house nor of Microsoft are available, but Mac-lovers and thralldom-haters can hurl abuse from a **boat tour** of Lake Washington. Contact **Argosy Cruises** (623-1252) for info.

Farther south on U.S. 405 toward Renton, rock pilgrims reach the grave of Seattle's first rock legend, **Jimi Hendrix.** Take bus #101 from downtown to the Renton Park 'N' Ride, then switch to #105 to Greenwood Cemetery. Drivers should take the Sunset Blvd. exit from Rte. 405 (follow Sunset Blvd., not Park), turn right onto Union, and right again on NE 4th. Jimi's grave is located towards the back of the cemetery, just in front of the sun dial.

Take I-90 east to **Lake Sammamish State Park,** off Exit 15, for swimming, water-skiing, volleyball courts, and playing fields. In the town of **Snoqualmie,** 29 mi. east of Seattle, is the **Northwest Railroad Museum,** 109 King St. (452-746-4025), on Rte. 202 dividing the two lanes of the town's main street. Beyond housing a small collection of functional early steam and electric trains, this is the oldest running depot in the state and runs a train 7 mi. to **North Bend.** Trips run on the hour and last 45 minutes, but hanging out in North Bend and catching a later train is officially encouraged (open May-Sept. Sa-Su 11am-4pm; round-trip $6, seniors $5, children $4). From North Bend, take bus #209 (#210 on Su) or Rte. 202 north to view the astounding **Snoqualmie Falls.** Formerly a sacred place for the native Salish people, the 270 ft. wall of water has generated electricity for Puget Power since 1898. Five generators buried under the falls work hard to provide energy for 1600 homes. The falls were featured in David Lynch's cult TV series *Twin Peaks,* and the small town of Snoqualmie has endured hordes of Peaks freaks ever since.

I-90 cruises along some of western Washington's prettiest hiking country. Exit 20, High Point Way, leads to a beautiful set of trails on **West Tiger Mountain.** The trail-head is right off the freeway; head for the "No Outlet" sign. Trail maps ($2.50) are available at the **Issaquah Chamber of Commerce** (392-7024), at 155 NW Gilman in nearby Issaquah. Past North Bend is a 4 mi. trail to **Mt. Si,** a 4000 ft. peak offering stellar views of Seattle and the surrounding valley. To find the trail, take North Bend Way off Exit 28 to Mt. Si Rd. A short, wheelchair accessible loop starts at Mt. Si's base.

■ Near Seattle: Daytrips to the South

The Seattle area is surrounded by the vast factories of **Boeing,** the city's most prominent employer. **Public tours** of the Boeing facilities (800-464-1476) are offered on the hour (M-F 9am-3pm). A limited number of free tickets are distributed first-come, first-served; arriving early greatly enhances the chances of getting on a tour. Since public transportation to the Boeing factory is available but inconvenient, it might be worth checking with **Gray Line Tours** (800-426-7532). Reservations are essential; call at least a day in advance ($34). The Seattle International Hostel also offers a bus to the factory for its patrons ($15), but with no guarantee that this will get you into a tour.

South of Seattle at Boeing Field is the wheelchair accessible **Museum of Flight,** 9404 E. Marginal Way S (764-5720). Take I-5 south to Exit 158 and turn north onto E. Marginal Way S, or take bus #123. The cavernous museum enshrines flying machines, from canvas biplanes to chic fighter jets, all hanging from a three-story roof (open F-W 10am-5pm, Th 10am-9pm; $8, seniors $7, ages 6-15 $4, under 5 free). An exhibit on the Apollo space shuttle missions, which landed the first man on the moon, includes a life-sized replica of the command module. Tour JFK's old Air Force One, or fly in a nauseatingly realistic flight simulator ($7.50). When tales of space-age technology grow tiresome, explore the red barn where William E. Boeing founded the company in 1916. Photographs and artifacts trace the history of flight from its beginnings through the 30s, including a working replica of the Wright Brothers' wind tunnel. Tours with enthusiastic Air Force veterans leave the entrance on the half hour (10:30am-1:30pm).

■ Near Seattle: Tacoma

Though spending time in Tacoma rather than Seattle is somewhat like hanging out in Newark instead of New York, Tacoma has a few worthwhile attractions suitable for a daytrip. Tacoma is Washington's second largest city and lies on I-5 about 35 mi. south of Seattle and 35 mi. east of Olympia. Take exit 705 from U.S. 5 and follow the signs to get downtown.

The shiny new **Washington State History Museum,** 1911 Pacific Ave. (888-238-4373), houses interactive, stereophonic exhibits on Washington's history through the 1800s. A sprawling model train on the fifth floor is a highlight for children, railroad buffs, and child railroad buffs (open M-Sa 10am-6pm, Su 11am-6pm; $7, students and seniors $5, ages 6-12 $4, ages 5 and under free; free Th 5pm-8pm).

The main attraction in Tacoma is **Point Defiance Park** (305-1000), one of the most attractive parks in the Puget Sound area (open daily from dawn until 30min. after dusk; free). Expect to encounter half the state's population on gorgeous summer days; warm weather brings people to the park in droves. To get there, take Rte. 16 to the 6th Ave. exit, go east on 6th Ave., then head north on Pearl St. A 5 mi. loop passes all the park's attractions, offering postcard views of Puget Sound and access to miles of woodland trails. In spring, the park is bejewelled with flowers; a rhododendron garden lies nestled in the woods along the loop, and intricate fuschia, rose, and Japanese gardens make an Eden out of the park's entrance. **Owen Beach** looks across at Vashon Island and is a good starting place for a ramble down the shore. The loop then brushes by the spot where, in 1841, U.S. Navy Capt. Wilkes proclaimed that if he had guns on this and the opposite shore (Gig Harbor), he could defy the world.

Point Defiance Zoo and Aquarium (591-5337) is the park's prize possession (open daily 10am-7pm; Labor Day-Memorial Day 10am-4pm; $7, seniors $6.55, ages 5-17 $5.30, ages 3-4 $2.50, under 3 free). Penguins, polar bears, beluga whales, and sharks populate the tanks, while kids and distressed chaperones occupy the paths between them. A number of natural habitats are re-created within the zoo's boundaries.

The meticulously restored **Fort Nisqually** (591-5339), in the park, was built by the Canadian Hudson's Bay Company in 1832 to offset growing commercial competition from Americans (open June-Aug. daily 11am-6pm; Sept.-Apr. W-Su 1-4pm; $1.25, ages 5-12 75¢). The fort's museum holds a compact but captivating exhibit on the lives of children, laborers, natives, and Hawaiians who worked there during the Company years. Volunteers wear 19th-century garb and speak in authentic 19th-century accents. **Camp Six Logging Museum** (752-0047), also in the park, retrieves an entire logging camp from the dustbin of history. The camp also offers a 1 mi. ride on an original steam-powered logging engine (open Memorial Day-late Sept. W-F 10am-6pm, Sa-Su 10am-7pm; Apr.-May and Oct. W-Su 10am-4pm; ride costs $2.50, seniors and ages 3-12 $1.50).

On your way out of the park, stop in at **Antique Sandwich Company,** 5102 N. Pearl St. (752-4069), near Point Defiance, for some great natural food and open mic on Tuesday nights. The "poor boy" sandwich ($6) can fill you for a week; espresso shakes cost $3.50. The pies draw a faithful local following to the rose bushes in the "Garden of Eatin'" (open W-M 7am-7pm, Tu 7am-10pm).

Greyhound (383-4621), at the corner of Pacific and 14th St. in downtown Tacoma, runs buses to and from Seattle (station open daily 7:30am-9pm; 9 buses per day, $5). **Point Defiance** is Tacoma's **ferry terminal.** From here, **Washington State Ferries** run regularly to Vashon Island. Get the skinny on Tacoma at the **Pierce County Visitor Information Center,** 1001 Pacific Ave. #400 (627-2836 or 800-272-2662; open M-F 9am-5pm). **Crisis Line:** 759-6700 or 800-576-7764 (24hr.), **Rape Crisis:** 226-5062 or 800-756-7273 (24hr.), **Safeplace,** 279-8333. The **post office** is at 1102 A St., on 11th St. (open M-F 7am-5pm). **Zip Code:** 98402. **Area Code:** 253.

■ Near Seattle: Vashon Island

Only a 25-minute ferry ride from Seattle and an even shorter 15-minute hop from Tacoma, Vashon (VASH-on) Island has remained inexplicably invisible to most Seattlites. With its forested hills and expansive sea views, this artists' colony feels like the San Juan Islands without the oppressive crowds of tourists. Most of the island is undeveloped and covered in Douglas fir, rolling cherry orchards, wildflowers, and strawberry fields. On Vashon, all roads lead to rocky beaches.

GETTING THERE AND GETTING AROUND Vashon Island stretches between Seattle and Tacoma on its east side and between Southworth and Gig Harbor on its west side. The town of **Vashon** lies at the island's northern tip, while **Tahlequah** is to the south. The steep hills on Vashon are a hindrance to hikers and bikers, though bicycles remain the recreational vehicle of choice on the island. Many locals and visitors resort to hitchhiking, which is reputed to be easier here than on the mainland (*Let's Go* does not recommend hitchhiking).

Washington State Ferries (800-84-FERRY/843-3779 or 206-464-6400 for ferry information; http://www.wsdpt.wa.gov/ferries) runs ferries to Vashon Island from four different locations. From: the **downtown Seattle terminal** to Vashon (25min., 8 per day M-F, 6 per day Sa, $3.60, passenger only); **Fauntleroy** in **West Seattle** to Vashon (35min., 20 per day daily, $2.40); **Southworth** in the Kitsap Peninsula to Vashon (35min., 20 per day daily, $2.40); Point Defiance in Tacoma (see Tacoma, p. 175) to Tahlequah (15min.; 20 per day daily; $2.40). Vehicle charges vary by season (June-Sept. $11, Oct.-May $8.50). To get to the ferry terminals on the mainland from Seattle, drive south on I-5 and take Exit 163A (West Seattle/Spokane St.) down Fauntleroy Way to the Fauntleroy Ferry Terminal, or turn at the Spokane St. Bridge 1 mi. south of the main ferry terminal. From Tacoma, take Exit 132 off I-5 (Bremerton/Gig Harbor) to Rte. 16. Get on 6th Ave. and turn right onto Pearl. Follow signs to Point Defiance Park and the ferry.

Buses #54, 118, and 119 pick up at 1st and Union St. in Seattle and service the Vashon Island ferries from downtown Seattle (call 800-542-7876 for bus info). Buses #118 and #119 also service the island, continuing from the ferry landing to the town of Vashon. Both can be flagged down anywhere. Fares are the same as the system in Seattle. The island is all within one zone, but Seattle to Vashon passes two zones.

PRACTICAL INFORMATION

Visitor Information: The local **Thriftway** (see **Food,** below) provides maps, or call the Vashon-Maury **Chamber of Commerce,** 17633 SW Vashon Hwy. (463-6217).
Library: 17210 Vashon Hwy. (463-2069), with Internet access. Open M-Th 11am-8:30pm, F 11am-6pm, Sa 10am-5pm, Su 1-5pm.
Laundromat: Joy's Village Cleaner and Laundry, 17318 Vashon Hwy. (463-9933). Open M-Sa 7am-8:30pm, Su 8am-8pm. Wash $1, dry 25¢ per 10min.
Pharmacy: Vashon Pharmacy, 17617 Vashon Hwy. (463-9118). Open M-F 9am-7pm, Sa 9am-6pm, Su 11am-1pm.
Emergency: 911. **Police:** 463-3783. **Coast Guard:** 217-6200.
Internet Access: see **Library,** above.
Post office: 463-9390, on Bank Rd. Open M-F 8:30am-5pm, Sa 10am-1pm. **Zip Code:** 98070.
Area Code: 206.

ACCOMMODATIONS The **Vashon Island AYH Ranch Hostel** (HI-AYH) is at 12119 SW Cove Rd. (463-2592; http://www.vashonisland.com/ayhranchhostel), west of Vashon Hwy. Sometimes called the "Seattle B," it's the island's only real budget accommodation and reason enough to voyage to Vashon. Getting there is easy enough: jump on any bus at the ferry terminal, ride to Thriftway Market (see **Food,** below) and call from the free phone inside the store, marked with an HI-AYH label. Judy will make pickups during reasonable hours. This is the hostel version of Disney World's Frontierland—it looks like an old western town, replete with teepees, covered wagons that moonlight as queen beds, and a sheriff's office. A free pancake breakfast, free firewood, and a squadron of available bikes attract every sort of traveler, from road-weary backpackers to couples escaping Seattle. The hostel offers bunks, open-air teepees and covered wagons, or tenting, and the occasional theme room ($10; bicyclists $8; nonmembers $13; sheets or sleeping bag $1; open May-Oct.). Ask about the hostel's new **B&B** down the road ($35-45).

FOOD Get creative in the kitchen with supplies from the large and offbeat **Thriftway** (463-2100), downtown at 9740 SW Bank Rd. (open daily 8am-9pm). The deli sells good ol' artery-plugging fried chicken, and the bulk foods aisle is a health food nirvana. Options for cooking-phobes include **Emily's Cafe and Juice Bar,** 17530 Vashon Hwy. (463-6404), smack in downtown Vashon, a restaurant that enhances karma and juices just about anything (open Su-Th 9am-4pm, F-Sa 9am-9pm). For take-out, stampede to **Tatanka** for bison burgers ($4.75), bison burritos ($3.75), and bison chili ($3). Hostelers get drinks for half price. Note the intense competition between bison and ostrich for "Meat of the New Millennium" (open M-Sa 11am-7pm, Su noon-7pm).

SIGHTS Vashon Island provides wonderful but strenuous biking. Despite short distances, Vashon's hills will turn even a little jaunt into a workout; sweaty exploration will be rewarded, however, with rapturous scenery. **Vashon Island Bicycles,** 7232 Vashon Hwy. (463-6225), rents mountain bikes. *($9 per hr., $25 per day.)* **Point Robinson Park,** is a gorgeous spot for a picnic, and offers **free tours** (217-6123) of the 1885 **Coast Guard lighthouse** that faces off with Mt. Rainier (from Vashon Hwy., take Ellisburg Rd. to Dockton Rd. to Pt. Robinson Rd.). **Vashon Island Kayak Co.** (463-9527), at Camp Burton, rents sea kayaks on the weekends. *(Open F-Su 10am-5pm. Boats often available during the week; call in advance. $14 per hr.)* More than 500 acres of woods in the middle of the island are interlaced with mildly difficult **hiking trails.** Call the Vashon Park District (463-9602) for more information. *(Office open daily 9am-5pm.)*

Count on some culture no matter when you visit—one in 10 residents of Vashon is a professional artist. **Blue Heron Arts Center,** 19704 Vashon Hwy. (463-5131), coordinates most activities, including free local gallery openings on the first Friday of every month. *(Open Tu-F 11am-5pm, Sa noon-5pm. Friday openings 7-9:30pm.)*

■ Near Seattle: Whidbey Island

Clouds, wrung dry by the mountains around Seattle, release a scant 20 in. of rain each year over Whidbey Island, a strip of land in Puget Sound. Most of those who make the trek to Whidbey come in caravans of RVs to camp, but Whidbey's circle of beaches makes it beautiful nonetheless. The town of **Coupeville,** at the island's center, is a great place to start exploring the island's four major State Parks, where rocky beaches are limned by bluffs crawling with wild roses and blackberry brambles.

Washington State Ferries (800-843-3779 or 206-464-6400) provides frequent service from the mainland to the island. One ferry connects **Mukilteo,** a tiny community just south of Everett on the mainland, with **Clinton,** a town on the south end of Whidbey (20min., 5am-2am on the ½hr., $2.40, $5.50 with car, 60¢ bike surcharge).The other connects Port Townsend on the Olympic peninsula with the **Keystone terminal** near **Ft. Casey State Park** (see below), at the "waist" of the island (30min., 5 per day, $1.80, $8 with car, 30¢ bike surcharge). You can drive onto the island on Rte. 20, which heads west from I-5 at Exit 230. Route 20 and Rte. 525 meet near Keystone and form the transportation backbone of the island, linking all the significant towns and points of interest. **Island Transit** (678-7771) provides free, hourly public transportation throughout the island, and gives information on connections to and from Seattle, but it has no service on Sundays and limited service on Saturdays.

If the ferry ride whetted your appetite, stop by **La Paz** (341-4787), a Mexican restaurant in Clinton, right off the dock (taco and rice $5; open Tu-W 5-8pm, Th and Sa 12-3pm and 5-8pm, F 12-3pm and 5-9pm, Next door, the **Whidbey Cybercafe & Bookstore** (341-5922; http://www.whidbey.com/cybercafe) links the island with the rest of the world (terminals $6 per hr., 30min. minimum; open M-Sa 10am-7pm).

Cyclists and drivers alike venture to **Ebey's Landing,** a Department of Interior protected beach with crystal views of the islands, the surrounding Olympic Mountains, and Port Townsend. On the way, climb to the top of Sherman Rd. off Rte. 20. There, next to the cemetery, is a gentle view of the island's idyllic prairie and beaches. This is prime biking country, with easy slopes and rustic scenery. From Ebey's Landing, follow signs to **Ft. Casey State Park,** an archipelago of old bunkers and other military paraphernalia. An interpretive center is at the Admiralty Point lighthouse (open April-Oct. Th-Su 11am-5pm). The park's campground (reservations 800-452-5687) is a peninsula offering unsheltered sites with great views of the straits ($11; hiker/biker sites $5; pay showers 25¢ per 3min.).

In Coupeville's **Knead and Feed,** 4 Front St. (678-5431), there is plenty of to-die-for soup to be supped (or sipped). This small restaurant makes everything from scratch and has a serene view of the eastern waterfront. A lunch costs $3-7.50 (open M-Th 10:30am-3pm, F 10:30am-3pm and 5-9pm, Sa-Su 9am-9pm). For a caffeine fix, stop in at **Great Times Espresso,** 12 Front Street (678-5358), just down the hill at, and pick up a used mystery book along with your latte. (Open M-Sa 7am-5pm, Su 9am-6pm.)

At the north tip of the island, the **Deception Pass Bridge,** the nation's first suspension bridge, connects Whidbey Island to the Anacortes Islands, and has a secret cave at one end where 17th-century prisoners were held and forced to make wicker furniture (Oh, the humanity!). When the Skagit lived and fished around Deception Pass, the area was often raided by the Haida from the north. A bear totem of the Haidas now occupies the Fidalgo Bay side of **Deception Pass State Park,** 5175 N. Rte. 20 (675-2417), just south of the bridge. The pass itself was named by veteran explorer Captain George Vancouver, who found the tangled geography of Puget Sound as confusing as most visitors do today. This is the most heavily used of Whidbey's four state parks, and its views are magnificent. A new **interpretive center** in the Bowman area, just north of the Works Progress Administration bridge on Rte. 20 E, describes the army that built many of the parks in the Northwest during the Depression. There are camping facilities, a saltwater boat launch, and a freshwater lake for swimming, fishing, and boating. A license, available at most hardware stores, is required for **fishing** in the lake; the season runs from mid-April to October. Thirty miles of trails link some of the best views of Puget Sound's shore line and lure ambitious mid-summer crowds into this magnificent old growth forest. **Campers** will find 250 sites ($11 apiece). Four rustic hiker/biker sites ($5) have limited facilities but make a pleasant alternative to the bustling campground. The campground is often subjected to jet noise from A-6 Navy attack aircraft at Whidbey Island Naval Air Station. Reservations are such a very, very good idea (800-452-5687; reservation fee $6).

PUGET SOUND

According to Native American legend, Puget Sound was created when Ocean, wishing to keep his children Cloud and Rain close to home, gouged out a trough and molded the leftover dirt into the Cascade Range. Since then, Cloud and Rain have stayed close to Ocean, rarely venturing east of the mountain wall. Millions of Washingtonians live along Puget Sound in the Everett-Seattle-Tacoma-Olympia belt, but with a pristine rural setting, urban sophistication is never far from outdoor adventure.

🏔 HIGHLIGHTS OF PUGET SOUND

- Well-groomed **Olympia** (see below) is the next best thing since Seattle.
- **Wolf Haven** (see p. 184) is full of wolves, cute yet ferocious.
- The grave of **Chief Sealth** (see p. 187) powerfully commemorates the region's greatest Native American leader.
- **Peace Arch State Park** (see p. 192), beyond enshrining the inalienable amity 'twixt the U.S. and Canada, is a pretty little patch of greenery.
- The **Mt. Baker Highway** (see p. 191) leads past stunning scenery, with excellent opportunities for hiking and winter sports all along the way.

■ Olympia

From the fortress-like hilltop capitol of Olympia, the Washington State government keeps an eye on the college students and local fisher-folk who thrive in the Capitol Dome's shadow. The Evergreen State College campus lies a few miles from the city center, and its liberal, highly pierced student body spills into town to mingle with preppy politicos. Some locals, nostalgic for the era when Olympia was a smaller city with a thriving fishing industry, scorn these "Greeners." But newcomers keep pouring into town, drawn to the Evergreen State capital's alluring diversity, ever-expanding parks, and successful beautification projects.

WASHINGTON

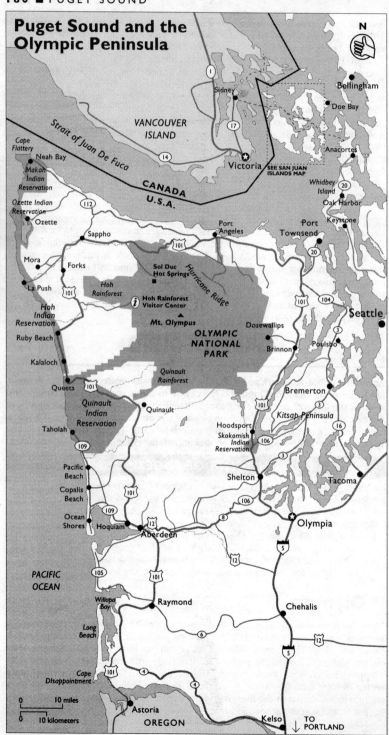

Puget Sound and the Olympic Peninsula

N

VANCOUVER ISLAND

Sidney

Strait of Juan De Fuca

CANADA
U.S.A.

Victoria

SEE SAN JUAN ISLANDS MAP

Bellingham

Doe Bay

Anacortes

Whidbey Island

Oak Harbor

Keystone

Port Townsend

Cape Flattery

Neah Bay

Makah Indian Reservation

Ozette Indian Reservation

Ozette

Sappho

Mora

Forks

La Push

Hoh Rainforest

Sol Duc Hot Springs

Hurricane Ridge

Port Angeles

Hoh Indian Reservation

Hoh Rainforest Visitor Center

Mt. Olympus

OLYMPIC NATIONAL PARK

Dosewallips

Brinnon

Seattle

Poulsbo

Ruby Beach

Kalaloch

Queets

Quinault Rainforest

Quinault Indian Reservation

Quinault

Taholah

Hoodsport

Skokomish Indian Reservation

Bremerton

Kitsap Peninsula

Pacific Beach

Copalis Beach

Ocean Shores

Hoquiam

Aberdeen

Shelton

Tacoma

Olympia

PACIFIC OCEAN

Willapa Bay

Long Beach

Raymond

Chehalis

Cape Disappointment

Astoria

OREGON

Kelso

TO PORTLAND

0 10 miles
0 10 kilometers

ORIENTATION AND GETTING AROUND

Olympia, at the junction of I-5 and U.S. 101, is an easy stopping point for those heading north to the Olympic Peninsula and Seattle or south to the Cascade peaks and Portland. Exit 105 off I-5 leads to the **Capitol Campus** and **downtown** Olympia. The west side of the downtown area borders freshwater **Capitol Lake** and salty **West Bay,** also known as **Budd Bay.** A bridge on **4th Ave.** divides the two and leads to the city's northwest section, where fast food chains and shopping plazas sprawl.

Parking in Olympia is free for 90 minutes per day in downtown **green zones,** and fairly cheap metered lots abound. Pick up a copy of *Parking Made Easy,* available at local stores and the visitor center (see **Practical Information,** below). Navigating Olympia on **bike** or **foot** is less confusing than groping around its zillions of one-way streets in a car. Olympians love to cycle, and bike racks adorn every public bus.

PRACTICAL INFORMATION

Transportation

Trains: Amtrak, 6600 Yelm Hwy. (923-4602 or 800-872-7245). Bus #94 runs from downtown Olympia to Centennial Station. To: Seattle (4 per day, $8.50-16); Portland (4 per day, $11.50-22).

Buses: Greyhound, 107 E. 7th Ave. (357-5541 or 800-231-2222), at Capitol Way. To: Seattle (6 per day, $8; but check out the Olympia Express, below); Portland (6 per day, $19); Spokane (2 per day, $27). The office is closed, but buses still pick up passengers outside the depot. Taxi dispatch next door.

Public Transportation: Intercity Transit (IT) (786-1881 or 800-BUS-ME-IT/287-6348). An easy, reliable, and flexible system; provides service almost anywhere in Thurston County, even for bicycles. Pick up all sorts of funky maps and schedules at the visitor center (see below), or visit the **Customer Service Department** at the Transit Center on State Ave., between Washington and Franklin St. The IT is open for info M-F 7am-6pm, Sa 8am-5pm. Fare 60¢, seniors and disabled 30¢. Day passes $1.25. The free **Capitol Shuttle** runs from the Capitol Campus to downtown or to the east side and west side (every 15min., 6:45am-5:45pm). For the standard fare, **Custom buses** continue from where normal fixed routes stop (M-Sa after 7pm). Call 943-7777 for info (M-Sa 6:30am-9:30pm, Su 8:15am-5:30pm). **Dial-A-Lift** (754-9393 or 800-244-6846) provides supplementary transport for seniors and the disabled with appropriate certification, available through the IT Business Office (786-8585). IT's **Olympia Express** runs between Olympia and Tacoma M-F 5:50am-6pm. Fare $1.50, seniors and disabled 75¢. Transferring to a Seattle bus in Tacoma $1.60 extra; full trip to Seattle takes 2hr.

Taxis: Red Top Taxi, 357-3700. **Capitol City Taxi,** 357-4949. **DC Cab,** 786-5226. All 24hr.

Car Rental: U-Save Auto Rental, 3015 Pacific Ave. (786-8445). $20-25 per day, plus 20¢ per mi. over 150 mi. Must be 21 with credit card and valid driver's license.

Car Repair: Rotters, 2225 Carriage St. (357-7762), off Exit 104 from U.S. 101. Open M-F 8am-8pm, Sa 9am-6pm, Su 11am-5pm. AAA approved.

Auto Club: 2415 Capitol Mall Dr. (357-5561 or 800-562-2582). Open M-F 8:30am-5:30pm; Sa phones only.

Visitor Services

Visitor Information: Washington State Capitol Visitor Center, P.O. Box 41020 (586-3460), on Capitol Way between 12th and 14th Ave., next to the State Capitol grounds; follow the signs on I-5. Exuberant staff helps navigate the center's plethora of brochures, providing maps of both the capitol itself and the greater Olympia area. Open M-F 8am-5pm. **Olympia/Thurston Chamber,** 521 E. Legion Way (357-3362). Less enthusiastically provides info on local businesses, services, and festivals. Calling is best. Open M-F 9am-5pm.

Outdoor Information: Department of Natural Resources (DNR), 1111 Washington St. (902-1000 or 800-527-3305). A maze of offices providing info about outdoor activities on DNR land. The **Maps Department,** P.O. Box 47031 (902-1234), stocks any publication that includes a DNR map, including the *Guide to Camp and Picnic Sites,* which points out free DNR sites statewide, and the *Guide to Barrier-Free*

Recreation, listing sites accessible to the disabled. The **Fish and Game Office** (902-2200) down the hall offers recreational fishing licenses and regulations. Open M-F 8:30am-4:30pm. **Washington State Parks and Recreation Commission Information Center** (800-233-0321). Call for info and reservations. **Olympic National Forest Headquarters,** 1835 Black Lake Blvd. SW (956-2400, TDD 956-2401) provides info on activities and camping in the national forest lands surrounding the national park. Open M-F 8am-4:30pm.

Local Services

Library: Olympia Timberland Library, 313 8th Ave. SE (352-0595), at Franklin St. Free hour on the Internet. Open M-Th 10am-9pm, F-Sa 10am-5pm, Su 1-5pm.
Laundromat: The Wash Tub, 2103 Harrison Ave. NW (943-9714). Wash $1.10, dry 25¢ per 8min. Open M-F 7am-10pm, Sa-Su 8am-10pm. **Eastside Tavern,** 410 E. 4th Ave. (357-9985). Machines behind the bar. Pints $1.75, wash and dry $1 each. Must be 21. Open M-F noon-2am, Sa-Su 3pm-2am. See **Nightlife,** below.

Emergency and Communications

Emergency: 911. **Police:** 753-8300. **Fire:** 753-8348.
Crisis Line: 352-2211. 24hr.
Women's Services: Safeplace (754-6300 or 800-364-1776). **Washington State Domestic Violence Hotline,** (800-562-6025). 24hr.
Post Office: 900 Jefferson SE (357-2289). Open M-F 7:30am-12:25pm and 1-6pm, Sa 9am-12:25pm and 1-4pm. **ZIP Code:** 98501.
Internet Access: See **Library,** above.
Area Code: 360.

ACCOMMODATIONS AND CAMPGROUNDS

Because motels in Olympia cater to lobbyists and lawyers rather than budget travelers, they are generally pricey. Camping is the cheapest option.

⊛Grays Harbor Hostel, 6 Ginny Ln. (482-3119; email ghhostel@techline.com), just off Rte. 8 in Elma. Take the fairground exit off Rte. 8 and make the first right. If you reach the fairgrounds, you've gone too far. A pleasant 25 mi. west of Olympia, this hostel is a home away from home and the perfect place to start a trip down the coast. Hosteling biz legends Jay and Linda Klemp run the establishment as if it were a ranch, a resort, or their home (which it is). Hot tub and a 3-hole golf course. Beds $11; single rooms available. Bikers can camp on the lawn for $7. Ask Jay about local bike rides or lessons in Jay and the Art of Motorcycle Maintenance.
Motel 6, 400 W. Lee St. (754-7320; fax 705-0655), in Tumwater. Take Exit 102 off I-5 and follow signs. A left off Lee St. onto Capitol Way leads to downtown Olympia in less than 5min. Reliably clean rooms. Cable TV, swimming pool, and weak coffee in the office. Singles $40; doubles $46; each additional person $3; under 17 free with parent. AARP discount.
The Golden Gavel Motor Hotel, 909 Capitol Way (352-8533). Only a few blocks from the Capitol Campus. Immaculate, spacious rooms are sirens for businesspeople traveling without the corporate credit card. Cable TV, morning coffee, free local calls. Singles $43; doubles $49. AAA and senior discounts.
Millersylvania State Park, 12245 Tilly Rd. S (753-1519; reservations 800-452-5687), 10 mi. south of Olympia. Take Exit 99 off I-5 south, or Exit 95 off I-5 north, then take Rte. 121 north, and follow the signs to the state park. Smallish, family- and RV-filled campsites crowded among firs. 6 mi. of needle-carpeted trails and Deep Lake, with 2 unguarded swimming areas. 164 sites: $11; hookups $16; hiker/biker sites $5.50. Showers (25¢ per 6min.), flush toilets, and facilities for the disabled. 10-day max. stay. Roads around the park are closed to traffic the last Su of the month Apr.-Aug. 8am-6pm, so that bicyclists can have free reign. Reservations recommended.
Capital Forest Multiple Use Area, 15 mi. southwest of Olympia, at Exit 95 off I-5. 90 campsites spread among 7 separate campgrounds, administered by the DNR. Camping is free and requires no notification or permit. Pick up a forest map at the state DNR office (see **Practical Information,** above) or the Central Region DNR office (748-2383) in nearby Chehalis. The area is unsupervised, so lone women may be better off paying at Millersylvania. In summer, grab a space early in the day; "free" is a magical crowd-creating word. Pit toilets. No showers.

FOOD

Old-school diners, veggie-intensive eateries, and Asian quickstops line bohemian 4th Ave. east of Columbia. The upstairs waterfront tables at the **Bayview Deli & Bakery,** 516 W. 4th Ave. (352-4901), offer snazzy views of the pier, and slightly upscale groceries fill the surrounding **Thriftway** supermarket. When the 2am urge for carrot sticks hits, try the 24-hour **Albertson's,** 705 Trosper Rd. (705-3569), at Exit 102 off I-5. The **Olympia Farmer's Market,** 700 N. Capital Way (352-9096), amasses an inspiring collection of in-season fruits and berries in a grandiose new building. Fantastic and cheap lunch fare includes grilled salmon burger ($3.75), a local treat (open Nov.-Dec. and Apr. Sa-Su 10am-3pm; May-Sept. Th-Su 10am-3pm; Oct. F-Su 10am-3pm).

The Spar Cafe & Bar, 114 E. 4th Ave. (357-6444). An ancient logger haunt that moonlights as a sweet-smelling pipe and cigar shop. Polished wood and a long counter send patrons back to the age of Bogart, which some remember personally. Sandwiches and burgers ($6-8). Restaurant open M-Th 6am-10pm, F-Sa 6am-11pm, Su 6am-9pm. Mellow bar in back, with live jazz Sa 9pm-1am (No cover). Bar open Su-Th 11am-midnight, F-Sa 11am-2am.

Jo Mama's Restaurant, 120 N. Pear St. (943-9849), at State St. in an old house. A wood-hewn, candle-lit atmosphere turns pizza-eaters into mafia dons as they swallow steaming pies. Steep prices (10 in. veggie pizza $14.75), but the convivial staff and porch swing compensate. Open M-Th 11am-10pm, F 11am-11pm, Sa 4-11pm, Su 4-10pm. Braille menus. Wheelchair accessible.

Santosh, 116 4th Ave. (943-3442). Northern Indian cuisine with an all-you-can-eat lunch buffet ($6), served M-F 11am-2:30pm. Politician-priced dinners, too (entrees around $11). Hindu statues and paintings aplenty. Open M-Th and Su 11am-3pm and 5-9pm, F-Sa 11am-3pm and 5-10pm.

The Dancing Goat (754-8187), on the corner of 4th Ave. and N. Washington St. A corner cafe that tends to attract the artsy collegiate cognoscenti. At night, aspiring writers sip tea in quiet desperation. A rack of alternative publications and carafes of locally roasted coffee please the Greeners. $1.02 for a cuppa joe and 1 refill. Open M-W 7am-10pm, Th-F 7am-11pm, Sa 8am-11pm, Su 9am-5pm.

Saigon Rendezvous, 117 W. 5th Ave. (352-1989). The most established of Olympia's budding Asian eateries. A tête-à-tête between Vietnamese and Chinese cuisines conceives a sexy menu for vegetarians. Most lunches $5.50; dinners around $7. Open M-F 10:30am-10pm, Sa-Su noon-9pm.

Otto's Bagels and Deli, 111 N. Washington St. (352-8640). Cheerful yellow walls and well-polished wooden floors create a happy atmosphere for bagel-munching and people-watching. Flyers on the walls direct visitors to nightly poetry readings or indie rock shows. Bagels 50¢; sandwiches $4. Open M-F 6am-7pm, Sa 7am-7pm, Su 7am-5pm.

SIGHTS AND EVENTS

Olympia's crowning glory is the **State Capitol Campus,** a complex of state government buildings, fabulous fountains, meticulously manicured gardens, and veterans' monuments. Take a free tour of the **Legislative Building** (586-8677) to sneak a peek at the priming of the public sphere; only tour guides can usher oglers into the legislative chambers. *(Tours depart from just inside the front steps daily on the hour 10am-3pm. Building open M-F 8am-5:30pm, Sa-Su 10am-4pm.)* The newly repainted and decorated interior enshrines a six-ton Tiffany chandelier and six two-ton bronze doors depicting the history of Washington. Unfortunately, the building's spectacular stone dome is indefinitely closed to the public. The mansionesque **State Capitol Museum,** 211 W. 21st Ave. (753-2580), houses historical and political exhibits. *(Open Tu-F 10am-4pm, Sa-Su noon-4pm. $2, seniors $1.75, children $1, families $5.)* Several different free tours of campus buildings leave hourly on weekdays. Call 586-TOUR/8687 for more info and options for the disabled.

Every lunch hour, droves of state employees, resplendent in spandex and sneakers, tumble out of the capitol and head for the various parks surrounding **Capitol Lake,** despite the spate of construction transforming Heritage Park from its current lowly manifestation into the noble vision that designer Frederick Law Olmsted mapped out over 70 years ago. The construction is expected to be complete in April 1999, but the $620,000 computerized and **interactive fountain** at Heritage Park is still accessible and provides a cheery spot where politicians and children in Underoos can frolic together. Seafaring visitors can take a shore leave after mooring at the port in **Percival Landing Park** (743-8379), a reminder of Olympia's oyster-filled past. *($8-15 depending on boat and length of stay. 7 days max. per month.)* The **4th Ave. Bridge** is a perfect place to spot **spawning salmon** as the leaping lox-to-be cross the lake from late August through October. **Yashiro Japanese Garden** (753-8380), at Plum and Union, right next to City Hall, hoards hundreds of colorful plants behind high walls, making it Olympia's own secret garden. *(Open daily 10am-dusk for picnickers and ponderers.)*

Capitol Lakefair is a not-to-be-missed bonanza during the third week in July, with an overwhelming array of food, carnival rides, and booths staffed by non-profit organizations. Watch out for hiked motel rates, though. The Washington Center for Performing Arts runs its own **Shakespeare Festival** during August; call 943-9492 or the visitor center (see **Practical Information,** above) for more info and festival shows.

NIGHTLIFE

Olympia's ferocious nightlife seems to have outgrown its daylife. Labels like K Records and Kill Rock Stars, with their flagship feminist band Bikini Kill, have made Olympia a crucial pitstop on the indie rock circuit. Respected thespian Courtney Love and her band Hole also hail from Olympia.

Eastside Club and Tavern, 410 E. 4th St. (357-9985). Old men playing pool and pinball rumble with college students slamming super cheap pints ($1.75). Local bands play frequently; check around town for the latest in the indie scene. Kurt Cobain was once ejected from the Eastside for rowdiness, but that's probably true of a lot of bars in the Pacific Northwest.

Thekla, 155 E. 5th Ave. (352-1855), under the neon arrow off N. Washington St. between 4th Ave. and Capitol. Past Olympia's startlingly clean alleys, this gay-friendly dance joint spins nightly entertainment, from karaoke to 80s night to DJ hip-hop. Cover varies, but tends to be more expensive Th-Sa. Must be 21. Open daily 6pm-2am.

Niki's, 311 E. 4th Ave. (956-0825), provides another spot for women and men of all persuasions to cut loose on the dance floor. Swing to the big bands W night, but leave your smokes at home Sa. Cover varies. Open W-Sa 7pm-2am.

The Backstage, 206 E. 5th Ave (754-5378), at the Capitol Theater. Local groovesters mosh and mingle to the tune of 3-5 bands playing on most weekend nights, usually for a $5 cover. Call for hours and events.

■ Near Olympia

Less than a mile south of town on I-5 at Exit 103, the tree-, trail-, and fish-ladder-laden **Tumwater Falls Park,** built by the Olympia Brewery, is perfect for salmon-watching, picnicking, or a midday run. **Wolf Haven International,** 3111 Offut Lake Rd. (264-4695 or 800-448-9653; email wolfhvn@aol.com; http://www.teleport.com/~wnorton/wolf.shtml), lurks 10 mi. south of the capital. Take Exit 99 off I-5, turn east, and follow the brown signs. *(Open May-Sept. W-M 10am-5pm; Oct.-Apr. 10am-4pm. 45min. tours $5, ages 5-12 $2.50.)* The haven now shelters 24 wolves reclaimed from zoos or illegal owners, and is participating in a breeding program to re-introduce Mexican wolves into the American Southwest. Wolves are available for adoption; $20 gets you your very own wolf, with none of the workaday hassle of caretaking. At the summertime **Howl-In,** human groups roast marshmallows and tell stories around a campfire, to the accompaniment of more vocal canine residents. *(Late May to early Sept. F-Sa 6:30-9:30pm. $6, children $4.)* **Nisqually National Wildlife Refuge** (753-9467), off I-5 between Olympia and Tacoma at Exit 114, shelters 500 species of plants and animals as well as miles of open trail for the interstate-weary traveler to stop and wander.

> ### Zounds! Mounds!
>
> Baffling scientists since their discovery in the mid-1800s, the Mima (MIE-mah) Mounds have spawned wild speculation about their origins. The evenly spaced network of small, perfectly rounded hills covers the prairies just outside the Capital Forest, 12 mi. southwest of Olympia. Anthropology fanciers attribute the mounds' existence to the arcane labors of a nation of yesteryear, biology buffs cite giant gophers, and delusional paranoids cry government conspiracy. The scientific community is torn among hypotheses ranging from glacial action to seismic shock waves; by 1988, no fewer than 159 Mima-related papers had been published. Today, the Mounds inhabit some of the last remaining prairie in the Pacific Northwest, providing visitors with an opportunity to learn about the region's natural history and mystery. To reach the Mounds, take Exit 95 off I-5 and follow the signs to Littlerock. From Littlerock, follow more signs to the Capital Forest and watch for the marked dirt road leading to the parking lot and trailhead. The truth is out there. *(Open daily 8am-dusk. For info, call the DNR at 748-2383.)*

(Office open M-F 7:30am-4pm. $3 per person or family.) Bald eagles, a plethora of shore-birds, and notorious northern spotted owls all nest in the reserve. The trails are open daily during daylight hours but are closed to cyclists, joggers, and pets.

■ Kitsap Peninsula

The Kitsap Peninsula fills in Puget Sound between the Olympic Peninsula and Seattle. With natural deep-water inlets, it was destined to house a major naval base and a fleet of nuclear-powered Trident submarines. A residue of rich maritime history coats the entire area, but travelers can enjoy the area's forested and hilly terrain even without top-secret clearance. The peninsula's backyards and campgrounds are a cycler's paradise and the tiny coastal villages outside of Bremerton are a tourist's siren song.

Bremerton is the hub of the Kitsap Peninsula. Once there, you'll swear you've stepped into a Tom Clancy novel; every third person has a Navy security pass swinging from his or her neck. The Navy Yard skyline rivals that of a small city, and when the **USS Nimitz** is home, the local barber works overtime providing crew cuts for all. For the Navy or military history buff, Bremerton is quite a find. For others, the city contains few sights other than dingy apartment buildings and crowded streets. However, it's a good base for exploring the peninsula and Hood Canal, which separates the Kitsap and Olympic Peninsulas. **Kingston,** toward the northern tip of the peninsula, about 20 mi. from Bremerton on Rte. 3 and Rte. 104, is linked by ferry to **Edmonds** on the mainland. **Southworth,** about 10 mi. east of Bremerton on Rte. 16 and Rte. 160, is connected to West Seattle and Vashon Island by ferry. Route 3 and Rte. 104 lead north to the Olympic Peninsula across the **Hood Canal Bridge.** Route 16 leads south to Tacoma.

PRACTICAL INFORMATION   Washington State Ferries (800-84-FERRY/843-3779 or 206-464-6400; http://www.wsdot.wa.gov/ferries) provides service at three points on the peninsula: between Bremerton and downtown Seattle (30-60min., 12-15 per day daily,; $3.60); between Southworth and Vashon Island (10min.; 22 per day daily; $2.40); between Kingston and Edwards (30min.; 25 per day daily; $3.60). Once there, **Kitsap Transit** (373-2877 or 800-501-7433; http://kitsaptransit.org), in the Enetai building on Washington St., runs several bus lines serving most small communities on the peninsula and on Bainbridge Island. Call ahead for times, or pick up schedules at the Winslow, Bremerton, or Kingston ferry terminals. (Buses run M-F 6am-7pm, Sa-Su 8am-4pm; open most holidays; $1 fare) Almost all buses accommodate bicycles.

The **Bremerton Area Chamber of Commerce,** 120 Washington St. (479-3579; http://www.bremertonchamber.org), resides just up the hill from the ferry terminal in Bremerton and will help you navigate the area *sans* sonar. The chamber casts off a flotilla of pamphlets on Bremerton and nearby towns, and the lively staff valiantly attempts to dress up the city's fundamental drabness. If you're sounding out the area by bicycle, pick up the indispensable **Kitsap and Olympic Peninsula Bike Map** here. (Open M-F 9am-5pm; a booth at the ferry dock is open on weekends.)

The post office (800-ASK-USPS/275-8777) is stationed at 602 Pacific Ave. (open M-F 9am-5pm). **ZIP Code:** 98337. **Area Code:** 360.

CAMPGROUNDS A daytrip from Seattle or Vashon Island may be more rewarding, but if you're intent on dropping anchor for the night on Kitsap, your best bet is to camp. Those traveling by foot will find **Illahee State Park** (478-4661, reservations 800-452-5687) convenient, but a bit cramped and close to Bremerton's road noise. To get there, hop on bus #29 at the ferry terminal in Bremerton and take it to the corner of Trenton St. and Sylvan Rd. Walk ¼ mi. up the hill on Sylvan until you reach the entrance. By car, drive north on Rte. 303 from Bremerton to Sylvan Rd., turn right, and follow the signs. The park has 33 campsites with water, restrooms, and hot showers (sites with vehicle $10; without vehicle $5). Another port of call is **Scenic Beach State Park** (830-5079), near the village of **Seabeck** on the west coast of the peninsula. The park has 52 campsites with water and bathrooms (sites $11, walk-in sites $5). From Silverdale, take Anderson Hill Rd. or Newberry Hill Rd. west to Seabeck Hwy., then 7 mi. south to the Scenic Beach turn-off. From Rte. 3, take the Newberry Hill Rd. exit and follow the signs to Scenic Beach. Bicyclists should be prepared for steep hills along this route. Winter hours are limited; call for reservations.

FOOD Culinary choices in Bremerton are few, since Uncle Sam feeds most workers and locals on base in the shipyard. **Charlotte's Cafe,** 264 E. 4th St. (479-8133), is a family-run deli with daily changing menus. All sandwiches cost $3.75. (Open M-F 11am-3pm and 5-8pm; wheelchair accessible). **Emperor's Palace Chinese Restaurant,** 221 Washington Ave. (377-8866), serves predictable but tasty Mandarin and Szechuan dishes in a dark, vinyl-upholstered dining room. Any one of the eight lunch platters costs $4.50 and two-person family dinners start at $9.95. (Open Su-Th 11am-10pm, F-Sa 11am-11pm.)

SIGHTS Navy buffs, start salivating. Next to the Chamber of Commerce (see **Practical Information,** above) is the scattered yet endearing **Bremerton Naval Museum** (479-7447) and its World War II photos and 10 ft. models of destroyers and aircraft carriers. *(Open M-Sa 10am-5pm, Su 1-5pm. Free, but donations requested.)* Behind the museum, explore the destroyer **USS Turner Joy** (792-2457), the ship that fired the first joyless American shots of the Vietnam War. To get a closer view of the shipyard, join the **Navy Ship Tour** (792-2457), which departs from the *Turner Joy* and scoots along mothballed submarines, aircraft carriers, and the famous WWII battleship *Missouri,* upon which the surrender document ending WWII was signed. *(Turner Joy tour $6, seniors $5, children $4. Shipyard tour $8.50, seniors $7.50, children $5.50. Combined package $13.50, seniors $11.50, children $8.50.)* To find out when the *U.S.S. Nimitz* and other active Navy vessels are in town, call the shipyard public relations office at 476-1111. The recently opened, somewhat bare **Kitsap Historical Museum,** 280 4th St. (479-6226), provides a minor reprieve for those uninterested in naval lore. *(Open daily 10am-5pm; in winter W-M 10am-5pm. Free, but donations encouraged.)* Instead, the museum is simply about war—it houses exhibits on WWII history and the shipyard's illustrious past. When you've had your fill of things military, enjoy a stroll along the Bremerton Boardwalk, which extends along the water beyond the Turner Joy.

At the ferry dock, catch the **foot ferry** from the Bremerton terminal across the Sinclair Inlet to **Port Orchard** for an expansive view of the shipyards. *(The ferry leaves every hour on the ¼- and ¾-hr. $1.10, children 75¢, free on weekends May-Oct.)* If naval paraphernalia still floats your boat, take Rte. 303 north from Bremerton to Keyport and the **Naval Undersea Museum,** 610 Donell St. (396-4148). Navigate among artifacts salvaged from the seas, including a Kaiten torpedo used by Japanese sailors. *(Open June-Sept. daily 10am-4pm; Oct.-May M and W-Su 10am-4pm.)*

Across Liberty Bay "fjord" from Keyport, Norwegian immigrants have made a tourist-luring shrine out of the town of **Poulsbo,** where various Scandinavian festivals take place year-round on streets with names like King Olav V Vie. Contact the Greater

Poulsbo **Chamber of Commerce** (779-4848) for more information. **Sluy's Poulsbo Bakery,** 18924 Front St. (697-2253 or 800-69-75897), serves sweet Scandinavian breads and exotic Norwegian delicacies like **krem** and **kaffe.**

North of Poulsbo, the **Historic Port Madison Indian Reservation** teaches about the history of Seattle-area Native Americans. Ask nicely, and the driver of bus #90 will let you off at the Longhouse Convenience Store. Follow the road 1 mi. to the **Suquamish Museum** (598-3311, ext. 422), where tribal artifacts mingle with contemporary portrayals of Suquamish life. *(Open May-Sept. daily 10am-5pm; Oct.-April daily 11am-4pm. $2.50, seniors $2, under 12 $1.)* Drivers should follow Rte. 305 toward Bainbridge Island and turn off at Sandy Hook Rd. The museum is on the north side of the Agate Pass Bridge on Rte. 305. Run by the casino-strewn Port Madison Reservation, this small museum is devoted entirely to the history and culture of the native Puget Sound Suquamish people. Striking photographs and quotations from respected elders piece together the lives of those who inhabited the Peninsula before, during, and after the "great invasion." Lore about Chief Sealth abounds; the Suquamish believed that his real name was secret and not to be pronounced, the word "Seattle" is only a European approximation. The legendary chief's grave is within driving distance of the town of **Suquamish.** His memorial, constructed of cedar war canoes, is in the middle of a nearby Catholic mission cemetery. Pick up a map of the area at the museum.

■ Near Kitsap Peninsula: Bainbridge Island

Rural Bainbridge Island was homesteaded by late-19th-century Swedes, late-20th-century Californians, and intermediate Japanese immigrants. A stroll through the town of **Winslow** can make a relaxing escape from Seattle. The island can be reached by road via **Rte. 305** and the **Agate Pass Bridge,** or by **Washington State Ferries** (800-84-FERRY/843-3779 or 206-464-6400; http://www.wsdot.wa.gov/ferries), which leave from downtown Seattle (35min., 22 per day daily;, $3.60). Stop by the **Chamber of Commerce,** 590 Winslow Way East (842-3700), to check out current festivals and events (open M-Th 9am-5pm, F 9am-6pm, Sa 10am-3pm).

Fay-Bainbridge State Park (842-3931), on the northeast tip of the island, has good fishing, 26 trailer sites, and 10 tent sites with pay showers and flush toilets (trailer sites $11; tent sites $8). Eat at the firecracker- and flower-festooned **Streamliner Diner,** 397 Winslow Way (842-8595), where natural foods and rich pies ($2.50) beckon (open M-F 7am-3pm, Sa-Su 8am-2:30pm). Wash dinner down with a bottle of Ferry Boat White from the **Bainbridge Island Vineyards & Winery** (842-9463), where you can sample the local grapes or tour the fields; turn right at the first white trellis on Rte. 305 as you leave the ferry, or if coming from the Agate Pass Bridge, watch on the left for the three stacked kegs just before you get into town. (Open W-Su noon-5pm; tours Su 2pm.) Bottles range from $7.80 to $23.50.

■ Bellingham

Strategically located between Seattle and Vancouver, Bellingham is the southern terminus of the Alaska Marine Highway; most travelers who stay the night are starting or completing an overseas journey to or from Alaska. Commercial fishing, coal mining, and a giant paper mill support the city's economy, and the native Lummi, Nooksack, and Semiahmoo of the region maintain strong ties to their fishing legacy. Students at Western Washington University attract budget-oriented businesses, and a recent influx of young people has converted this former lumber town into a lively community with a boom town atmosphere.

ORIENTATION AND PRACTICAL INFORMATION

Bellingham lies along I-5, 90 mi. north of Seattle and 57 mi. south of Vancouver, and is the only major city between the two. The downtown shopping and business area centers on **Holly St.** and **Cornwall Ave.,** next to the Georgia Pacific pulp mill, accessible by Exits 252 and 253 off I-5. **Western Washington University (WWU)** sits atop

WASHINGTON

a hill to the south. At least 130 acres of city parks encircle Bellingham. The town of **Fairhaven,** where the ferries, bus, and trains stop, lies directly south of town, and Whatcom County Transit provides service throughout the area (see below).

Trains: Amtrak, 401 Harris Ave. (734-8851 or 800-USA-RAIL/872-7245), in the Greyhound/Amtrak station next to the ferry terminals. 1 per day to: Seattle ($25); Vancouver, BC ($20). Ticket office open M 8:30-11:30am and 5:30-8pm, Tu-Su 8:30-11am and 5:30-8pm.

Buses: Greyhound, 401 Harris Ave. (733-5251 or 800-231-2222), next to the ferry terminals. To: Seattle (9 per day, $13); Mt. Vernon (6 per day, $6); Vancouver, BC (6 per day, $13). Open M-F 7:30am-5:30pm.

Ferries: Alaska Marine Highway Ferry, 355 Harris Ave. (676-8445 or 800-642-0066; http://www.dot.state.ak.us/external/amhs/home.html). Terminal in Fairhaven; take Exit 250 off I-5 and take Rte. 11 west. July-Aug. 2 per week to Ketchikan, AK ($164) and beyond. **Lummi Island Ferry** (676-6692), at Gooseberry Pt. Take I-5 north to Slater Rd. (Exit 260), then take a left on Haxton Way. Daily service to Lummi (1-2 per hr. 6:10am-12:10am; round-trip $1 per person, $2 per car). Private shuttles also run ferries to the nearby San Juan Islands (see p. 192).

Public Transportation: Whatcom County Transit (676-7433). All routes start at the Railroad Ave. Mall terminal, between Holly and Magnolia St. 35¢, under 5 and over 90 free. No free transfers. Buses run every 15-30min. M-F 5:50am-7:30pm; reduced service M-F 7:30-11pm and Sa-Su 9am-6pm.

Taxis: City Cab, 773-TAXI/8294 or 800-281-5430. Runs 24hr.

Car Rental: AA Auto Rental, 4575 Guide Meridian (734-7262). $20 per day; 20¢ per mi. after 100 mi. Must be 25 with credit card or $300 cash deposit. Open M-Sa 9am-6pm, Su 11am-5pm.

Ride Board: Viking Union, at WWU. Usually more riders available than rides, but lucky folks may be able to catch one to Seattle or eastern Washington.

Visitor Information: Visitor Information Center, 904 Potter St. (671-3990). Take Exit 253 (Lakeway) from I-5. Helpful staff, a map of Bellingham's miles of footpath, and a flood of Whatcom County trivia. Open daily 8:30am-5:30pm.

Equipment Rental: The Great Adventure, 201 E. Chestnut St. (671-4615). Rents skiing, camping, climbing, and backpacking gear at reasonable rates. Deposit required. Open M-Th 10am-6pm, F 10am-7pm, Sa 9am-6pm, Su 11am-5pm.

Laundromat: Bellingham Cleaning Center, 1010 Lakeway Dr. (734-3755). Wash $1.25, dry 25¢ per 10min. Open daily 6am-10pm.

Library: 210 Central St. (676-6860), at Commercial St. across from City Hall. A fountain and pristine lawn in back make for a great, lazy afternoon picnic. Free Internet access, although those without a library card may have to wait. Open Sept.-May M-Th 10am-9pm, F-Sa 10am-6pm, Su 1-5pm.

Senior Services: 315 Halleck St. (city 733-4033, county 398-1995). Take bus #10B to the corner of Ohio and Cornwall St. Open M-F 8am-4:30pm.

Emergency: 911. **Police:** 505 Grand Ave. (676-6913). Open M-F 8am-5:30pm.

Crisis Line: Bellingham, 734-7271. Whatcom County, 384-1485. Both 24hr.

Pharmacy: Rite Aid, 1400 Cornwall St. (733-0580). Open M-F 8am-7pm, Sa 9am-6pm. Pharmacy opens 30min. after store.

Hospital: St. Joseph's General, 2901 Squalicum Pkwy. (734-5400). Open 24hr.

Post Office: 315 Prospect (676-8303). Open M-F 8am-5:30pm, Sa 9:30am-3pm. **ZIP Code:** 98225.

Internet Access: Ground Control Internet Cafe, 1117 Railroad Ave. (752-2321). $2 per 15min., $8 per hr., with a free coffee. Open Su-Th 9am-9pm, F-Sa 9am-3am. See also **Library,** above.

Area Code: 360.

ACCOMMODATIONS AND CAMPGROUNDS

For both atmosphere and price, the hostel is the best bet. For help with other accommodations, try the **Bed & Breakfast Guild of Whatcom Co.** (676-4560). Many B&Bs offer rooms in the neighborhood of $60.

Fairhaven Rose Garden Hostel (HI-AYH), 107 Chuckanut Dr. (671-1750), next to Fairhaven Park, about ¾ mi. from the ferry terminal. Take I-5 Exit 250, and go west on Fairhaven Pkwy. to 12th St.; bear left onto Chuckanut Dr. From downtown Bellingham, take bus # 1A or 1B. We never promised you a rose garden; delinquent local deer have done their best to mow down Fairhaven's blooms. A clean and tiny hostel with sleeping quarters, bathrooms, and showers all in the basement; the excess moisture sometimes gives the place a mildewy smell. 10 beds: $12. Make-your-own, all-you-can-eat pancakes $1. Linen $2. No curfew, but living room closes at 10pm: reception 5-10pm, check-out 9:30am. Call ahead, especially on W or Th night, when Alaska-bound travelers fill the hostel. Reservations mandatory July-Aug. Open Feb.-Nov.

Travelers Lodge, 202 E. Holly St. (734-1900). Take I-5 Exit 253. Roll out of the lodge's big beds and clean rooms right into downtown Bellingham. Cable and coffee makers in the rooms make up for the slight eau de paper mill and occasional 2am noise. Free local calls. Singles $31; doubles $40.

Mac's Motel, 1215 E. Maple St. (734-7570), at Samish Way; take I-5 Exit 252. Large, clean rooms, pet-friendly; pleasant management; exterior paint right out of the 70s. Singles $24; doubles (up to 4 people) $38. Open daily 7am-10pm.

Larrabee State Park (676-2093, reservations 800-452-5687), on Chuckanut Dr., 7 mi. south of Bellingham. Sites are tucked in among the trees on Samish Bay, a half-hidden flatland outside the city. Check out the nearby tide pools or hike to alpine lakes. 87 sites: $11; hookups $16; 8 walk-ins $7. Open daily 6:30am-dusk.

FOOD

The **Community Food Co-op,** 1220 N. Forest St. (734-8158), at Maple St., has all the essentials, plus a health food sit-down cafe in the back (open daily 8am-9pm). On Saturday, head to the **Bellingham Farmer's Market** (647-2060), at Chestnut St. and Railroad Ave., for fruit, vegetables, and homemade donuts (Apr.-Oct. Sa 10am-3pm).

🐾**Casa Que Pasa,** 1415 Railroad Ave. (738-TACO/8226). Humongous burritos, made with fresh vegetables purchased from local growers, from $2.75. Vegan and vegetarian options aplenty. Open Su-Th and Sa 11am-11pm, F 11am-midnight.

The Old Town Cafe, 316 West Holly St. (671-4431). Scrumpdiddlyumptious breakfasts made with ingredients from the local farmer's market. Play a few songs on the piano in the adjoining art gallery and earn yourself a free drink to go with buttermilk hotcakes ($3.25) or french toast ($4.25). Vegan- and vegetarian-friendly. Very few menu items are over $6. Open M-Sa 6:30am-3pm, Su 8am-2pm.

Tony's, 1101 Harris Ave. (733-6319), in Fairhaven Village, just a few blocks away from the ferry terminal. Dining garden with an old railway car serves coffee, ice cream, bagels, and the infamous, high-voltage Toxic Milkshake, made with coffee and espresso grounds ($4). Open M-F 6:30am-9pm, Sa-Su 7:30am-9pm.

SIGHTS, ENTERTAINMENT, AND EVENTS

Western Washington University (WWU) generates continuous cultural and artistic activity, and maintains 7 mi. of hiking trails with views of Bellingham Bay and the San Juan Islands. Several buses from downtown stop at WWU (#7, 11, 16, 26, 27, and 28). The **Western Visitor Center** (650-3424) is at the entrance on South College Dr. *(Open in summer M-F 7am-5pm; during the academic year 7am-8pm.)* Friendly staff give the scoop on campus cultural events like the **Summer Stock Theater** (650-3866) and parking permit requirements for any sort of campus visit. Twenty-two outdoor sculptures commissioned by local and nationally known artists stud the campus; a free brochure and headphones, available at the visitor center, guide the wandering art critic around campus from piece to piece.

The **Whatcom Museum of History and Art,** 121 Prospect St. (676-6981), occupies four buildings along Prospect St., most notably the looming old city hall. *(Open T-Su noon-5pm. Free. Fully wheelchair accessible.)* Rotating exhibits on local topics range from native art to gardening history. Climb to the third floor of the old city hall to watch clocktower innards at work. The reserved and renovated **Mount Baker Theatre,** 104 N. Commercial St. (734-6080), is the locus of performing arts in the area. *(Box office open M-F 10am-5:30pm, Sa 10am-2pm, and 1hr. before showtime.)* Everything and anything from drama troupes to symphony orchestras to the Peking Acrobats perform in this 10-year-old movie and vaudeville palace. The **Bellingham Festival of Music** (676-5997) brings symphony, chamber, folk, and jazz music to town; the concerts feature musicians from around the world, are held in early August for about two weeks. Concerts ($18-21) are performed in the Mount Baker Theatre and the WWU concert hall. Contact the festival at 1300 N. State St. #202 for info and ticket reservations.

Big Rock Garden Park, 2900 Sylvan St. (676-6985), a 2.7-acre Japanese tea garden, is a hidden treasure in the residential area of Bellingham. *(Park open daily dawn-dusk.)* Take Alabama St. east, then go left on Sylvan for several blocks. The park frequently hosts outdoor musical performances; call ahead for a schedule.

In the second week of June, lumberjacks from throughout the region converge for axe-throwing, log-rolling, and speed-climbing contests in the **Deming Logging Show** (592-3051). *($5, ages 3-12 $3.)* To reach the showgrounds, take Mt. Baker Hwy. (Rte. 542) 12 mi. east to Cedarville Rd. and turn left; signs lead to the grounds. Memorial Day weekend sees the mother of all relays, the **Ski to Sea Race (**734-1330). From Mt. Baker to Bellingham Bay, participants ski, run, canoe, bike, and sea kayak to the finish line. Contact 1435 Railroad Ave., Bellingham 98226, for info.

OUTDOORS

The 2½ mi. hike up **Chuckanut Mountain** leads through a quiet forest to a view of the islands that fill the bay. On clear days, Mt. Rainier is visible from the top. The trail leaves from Old Samish Hwy. about 1 mi. south of city limits. The beach at **Lake Padden Park,** 4882 Samish Way (676-6985), has the warmest water in the Puget Sound; take bus #44 1 mi. south of downtown. The park also has acres of tennis courts, playing fields, hiking trails, a boat launch (no motors allowed), and fishing off the pier. *(Open daily 6am-10pm.)*

Whatcom Falls Park, 1401 Electric Ave. (676-2138), due east of town, has hiking trails, picnic facilities, and tennis courts, and is home to thousands of future fishsticks at the **Bellingham Hatchery.** *(Park open daily 6am-dusk.)* The **Upper Whatcom Falls Trail** leads 1 mi. to the falls themselves, used by locals as a waterslide; take bus #40 or 41. Fishing's good in **Lake Samish** and **Silver Lake,** north of the town of **Maple Falls** on Mt. Baker Hwy. (Rte. 542). Lake trout season opens on the third Sunday in April. **Fishing licenses** are available from the Dept. of Fisheries (902-2464), sporting goods stores, and hardware stores. *($5-48, depending on residency and what you aim to catch.)*

The popular **Interurban Trail** runs 5½ mi. from **Fairhaven Park** to **Larrabee State Park** along the relatively flat route of the old Interurban Electric Railway; watch for divided paths and unmarked street crossings. Occasional breaks in the trees permit a glimpse of the San Juan Islands. Several trails branch off the main line and lead up into the Chuckanut Mountains or down to the coast; pick up a map from the visitor center (see **Practical Information,** above). The Interurban Trail intersects with the 1 mi. trail to the clothing-optional **Teddy Bear Cove,** also accessible from Chuckanut Drive, 2 mi. south of Fairhaven.

■ Near Bellingham: Mt. Baker

Crowning the **Mt. Baker-Snoqualmie National Forest,** Mt. Baker hosts excellent downhill and cross-country skiing, and some of the best snowboarding in the state. During the summer, hikers and mountaineers challenge themselves on its trails and ascents. To reach the volcano, take I-5 Exit 255, just north of Bellingham, to Rte. 542, better known as the **Mt. Baker Highway.** Roadways traverse the foothills for 58 mi., affording views of Baker and the other peaks in the range. The highway ends at **Artist Point** (5140 ft.), with spectacular vistas of the surrounding wilderness. The road is closed at Mt. Baker Ski Area in winter.

The popular **Lake Ann Trail** leads 4¾ mi. to the lake of the same name, continuing to the **Lower Curtis Glacier.** Hikers can make inevitable Robert Frost references on the picturesque **Fire and Ice Trail,** a ½ mi. loop beginning on Rte. 542. For trail maps, backcountry permits, or further area info, stop by the **Glacier Public Service Center** (599-2714; open daily 8:30am-4:30pm) or contact North Cascades National Park, Mt. Baker Ranger District, 2105 State Rte. 20, Sedro Woolley, WA 98284. The volcano packs soft powder for longer than any other nearby ski area, staying open from early November through May (lift tickets $29, seniors and under 15 $21.50). Contact the **Mt. Baker Ski Area Office** (734-6771) in Bellingham for more info.

Silver Lake Park, 9006 Silver Lake Rd. (599-2776), is 28 mi. east of Bellingham on the Mt. Baker Hwy. and 3 mi. north of Maple Falls on Silver Lake Road. The park tends 73 campsites near the lake with facilities for swimming, hiking, and fishing (tent sites $11; hookups $16). Closer to the mountain are the **Douglas Fir Campground,** at Mile 36 off Rte. 542, with 30 sites, and the **Silver Fir Campground,** at Mile 46 off Rte. 542, with 21 sites (both $10, with water and no hookups). On the way to Mt. Baker, turn right at Mile 16 onto Mosquito Lake Rd., pull over at the first bridge, and look for bald eagles along Kendall Creek. Stop by **Carol's Coffee Cup,** 5415 Mt. Baker Hwy. (592-5641), for pre-ski carbo-loading with the biggest cinnamon rolls on earth ($1.25).

WASHINGTON

■ Near Bellingham: Blaine

A small border town 20 mi. north of Bellingham, Blaine is the busiest port of entry between Canada and the U.S. (see **Customs: Entering**, p. 7). The lines to cross the border can be tedious in either direction. Use the time wisely and jettison any fruits and vegetables you've been stockpiling. The **Blaine Visitor Center**, 215 Marine Dr. (332-4544 or 800-624-3555), at I-5 Exit 276, hoards info on Blaine as well as American and Canadian points of interest (open daily 9am-5pm; in winter M-Sa 9am-5pm).

Peace Arch State Park (332-8221) is the main attraction in Blaine (open Apr.-Sept. 6:30am-dusk; Oct.-Mar. 8am-dusk; toilets, kitchen facilities). Directly over the Canada/U.S. border, the Peace Arch contains pieces of wood from early U.S. and Canadian ships of discovery, and commemorates the Treaty of Ghent, which ended the War of 1812 and inaugurated the long era of peace between Canada and the U.S. (see p. 197 for an exception). Summertime happenings include hands-across-the-border events packed with kids, balloons, and Rotarians. To reach the park, take I-5 Exit 276, then turn north onto 2nd St.

The spit of land encompassing **Semiahmoo Park,** 5 mi. southwest of Blaine, was first inhabited by the Coastal Salish people who harvested shellfish when the tide was low. **Clam digging** is still a popular pursuit, though now a license is required (from $4, depending on residency and type of activity). Take Drayton Harbor Rd. around to the southwestern side of Drayton Harbor (open mid-Feb. to Dec. W-Su 1-5pm). A wooden passenger ferry, the *Plover*, putters across the Drayton Harbor from Blaine to Semiahmoo (F-Sa noon-dusk, Su 10am-6pm; free, but donations appreciated).

The **Birch Bay Hostel (HI-AYH),** 7467 Gemini St. (371-2180; email bbhostel@az.com; http://www.washingtonhostels.org), Bldg. #630 on the former Blaine Air Force Base, has lots of small, clean rooms with more privacy than most hostels; some have magnificent views of the marshes. All enjoy full kitchen facilities and a large, homey living room. Off I-5, take either the Birch Bay-Lynden Rd. exit or the Grandview Rd. exit and head west to Blaine Rd. Take a right onto Alderson from Blaine and look for the AYH sign on the left ($10, nonmembers $13; open Apr.-Sept.). The **Westview Motel,** 1300 Peace Portal Dr. (332-5501), offers clean rooms with nice views of the bay (singles $29; doubles $33; with kitchens $40).

Birch Bay State Park, 5105 Helwig Rd. (371-2800, reservations 800-452-5687), 10 mi. south of Blaine, operates 167 campsites near the water. The Semiahmoo used this area and the marshland at the southern end of the park to harvest shellfish and hunt waterfowl. The park's **Terrell Creek Estuary** contains 300 species of birds, and is a good area for crabbing, scuba diving, water skiing, and swimming. To get there, take the Birch Bay-Lynden exit off I-5 and turn south onto Blaine Rd. When Blaine Rd. veers noticeably to the left, turn right onto Bay Rd. Take a left on Jackson Rd. and continue until it hits Helwig Rd. The way is well marked from the freeway (sites $11; hookups $16; open year-round; $6 reservations advised during summer).

Satisfy your sweet tooth at the **C Shop,** 4825 Alderson Rd. (371-2070), just down the street from the hostel in **Birch Bay.** This bakery and candy shop offers over 100 desserts, including fudge, caramel apples, sundaes, and peanut butter yummms, along with inexpensive made-to-order sandwiches (after 11am) and homemade pizza (open late-May to mid-June Sa 1-10pm, Su 1-6pm; mid-June to Sept. daily 1-10pm). The **Harbor Cafe,** 295 Marine Dr. (332-5176), halfway down the pier, serves the best seafood in town, fresh daily. You'll drool over the fish 'n' chips, salad or chowder included ($9; open daily 6am-10pm).

SAN JUAN ISLANDS

The lush San Juan Islands are home to great horned owls, puffins, sea otters, sea lions, and more deer, raccoons, and rabbits then they can support. Pods of orcas (killer whales) patrol the waters, and pods of tourists mimic the whales, circling the islands in everything from yachts to kayaks in pursuit of cetacean encounters.

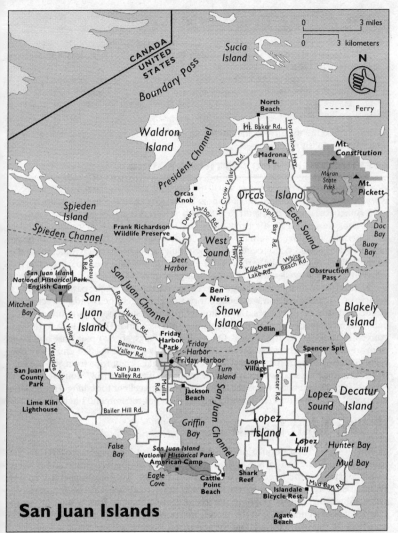

San Juan Islands

The population of San Juan, the chain's main island, has doubled in the last five years, but there are still fewer than 3000 permanent residents. The populations of the other islands are far lower, and endless parks and coastline offer ample opportunity to commune with cedars and tidepools in relative seclusion. Over 1½ million visitors come ashore on the San Juans each year, usually in July and August. To avoid the rush but still enjoy good weather, try visiting in late spring or early fall. Some residents frown on the transplants from Seattle and California who are buying up huge chunks of the islands at exorbitant prices. Well-behaved tourists and their dollars, on the other hand, are always welcome. The San Juans, with hundreds of tiny islands among which to weave, are a sea kayaker's dream; many locals consider their cars a sad alternative to their kayaks.

Two excellent guides to the area are available at bookshops and outfitter stores: *The San Juan Islands Afoot and Afloat* by Marge Mueller ($15) and *Emily's Guide,* a series of detailed descriptions of each island ($4, $11 for a set of three). The annually published *San Juans' Beckon,* includes maps and info on island recreation. The *San*

> ### 🐋 HIGHLIGHTS OF THE SAN JUAN ISLANDS
>
> - The **Whale Museum** (see p. 196) tells all about **orcas,** while the most promising places to spot them are **San Juan County Park** (see p. 195) and **Lime Kiln State Park** (see p. 196).
> - Those with a lust for the bizarre should rush to the **Pig War Camps** (see p. 196) and the super-strange **Masonic mausoleum** (see p. 197).
> - **Orcas** (see p. 197), **Lopez** (see p. 199), and **Shaw** (see p. 200) are some of several smaller, more secluded island options.

Juanderer also has useful info, including tide charts and ferry schedules. Both are free on ferries or at visitor centers.

GETTING THERE AND GETTING AROUND

Washington State Ferries (800-843-3779 or 206-464-6400; http:// www.wsdot.wa.gov/ferries) serve **Lopez, Shaw, Orcas,** and **San Juan Islands** daily from **Anacortes** on the mainland ($5.10, with vehicle $16-21.75 depending on destination, bike surcharge $2.90). Ferry times vary for each island—call for info or check the schedule. The ferry system revises its schedule seasonally and there are no reservations. Puget Sound visitor centers have schedules aplenty. To reach Anacortes, take I-5 north from Seattle to Mt. Vernon. From there, Rte. 20 heads west to Anacortes; the way to the ferry is well-marked. **Foot passengers** travel in either direction between the islands free of charge. No charge is levied on **eastbound traffic;** pay for bringing a vehicle on the ferry only on **westbound** trips to or between the islands. To see more islands and save on ferry fares, travel directly to the westernmost island on your itinerary, then return eastward to the mainland island by island. The San Juan ferries are packed in summer, so arrive early. On peak travel days, show up at least one hour prior to departure. The ferry authorities accept only cash or in-state checks as payment. The **Bellingham Airporter** (800-235-5247) makes eight trips from Sea-Tac (see p. 157) to Anacortes on weekdays, and six trips on weekends ($27, round-trip $49). Short distances and good roads make the San Juans excellent for **biking.** Hitchhiking is reputed to be easy on the islands. (*Let's Go* does not recommend hitchhiking.)

■ San Juan Island

The biggest and most popular of the islands, San Juan Island was discovered by the tourist world in the early 80s. San Juan is the last stop on the ferry route and is home to Friday Harbor, the largest town in the archipelago. San Juan is also the easiest island to explore, since the ferry docks right in town, roads are fairly flat for bicyclists, and a shuttle bus runs throughout the island. Lime Kiln State Park is the only designated whale-watching park in the world. But popularity has its price: Seattle weekenders flood the island throughout the summer, bringing fleets of traffic.

ORIENTATION AND PRACTICAL INFORMATION

With bicycle, car, and boat rentals all within a few blocks of the ferry terminal, **Friday Harbor** is a convenient base for exploring San Juan. Miles of poorly marked roads access all corners of the island. It's wise to carefully plot a course on a free **map** available at the information centers (see below), real estate offices, or gas stations.

Buses: San Juan Transit: (376-8887 or 800-887-8387; email santran@rock-island.com) circles the island every 35-55min. Many convenient stops, and the driver will make additional stops upon request. Point to point $4; Day pass $10; 2-day pass $19 (also good on Orcas Island). If you plan to see San Juan Island only, it may be cheaper to leave your car in Anacortes and use the shuttles.

Ferries: Washington State Ferries (378-4777 or 800-84-FERRY/843-3779), in Friday Harbor. Waiting room opens 30min. before scheduled departures.

Taxis: San Juan Taxi, 378-3550. $4 base, $2 for a second person, $1 per person after the second, $1 per mi. after the first mi. Runs 24hr.

Visitor Information: Chamber of Commerce (378-5240), in a booth on East St. up from Cannery Landing. Staffed sporadically daily dawn-dusk, but constantly stocked with pamphlets on area sights. **San Juan Transit** (see above), located upstairs in the cannery landing next to the ferry dock, also distributes San Juan-oriented brochures and maps, and the well-staffed office fields local queries.

Outdoor Information: National Park Service Information Center (378-2240), on the corner of 1st and Spring St., answers questions about San Juan National Historical Park. Open M-F 8:30am-5pm; off-season M-F 8:30am-4pm.

Tours: San Juan Safaris (378-2155, ext. 258 or 800-451-8910, ext. 258) leaves from Roche Harbor on the north tip of the island, at the end of Roche Harbor Rd. 3hr. trip $39. **Kings Marine,** 110 Spring St. (378-4593). Open daily 8am-7pm.

Equipment Rental: Island Bicycles, 380 Argyle St. (378-4941), in Friday Harbor. 7-speeds $15 per day; mountain bikes $25 per day. Locks and helmets included. Also rents child strollers ($5) and trailers ($15), provides maps of the island, and suggests bike routes. Credit card required. Open daily May-Sept. 9am-6pm; in the off season call for more limited hours. **Susie's Mopeds** (378-5244 or 800-532-0087), 1 block above the landing. Mopeds $15 per hr., $45 per day, fuel included. Credit card required. Open Mar.-Oct. daily 9am-6pm. Also available at Roche Harbor July 4-Labor Day.

Laundromat: Sail In Laundromat, behind the tourist booth on East St. Wash $2.50, dry 25¢ per 7min. Open daily 7am-9:30pm.

Senior Services: At the **Gray Top Inn** (378-2677). Open M-F 9am-4pm.

Red Tide Hotline: 800-562-5632, for info on safe shellfish harvesting.

Pharmacy: Friday Harbor Drug, 210 Spring St. (378-4421). Open M-Sa 9am-7pm, Su 10am-4pm.

Medical Services: Inter-Island Medical Center, 550 Spring St. (378-2141). Open M-F 8:30am-5pm, Sa 10am-noon.

Emergency: 911. **Sheriff:** 135 Rhone St. (non-emergency 378-4151), at Reed St.

Post Office: (378-4511), 220 Blair St., at Reed St. Open M-F 8:30am-4:30pm. **ZIP Code:** 98250.

Area Code: 360.

ACCOMMODATIONS AND CAMPGROUNDS

San Juan's campgrounds have become wildly popular; call ahead for reservations or show up early in the afternoon to secure a spot. Outside of camping, cheap accommodations in the San Juans are an endangered species. There's not a bargain to be found in the busy season. Though often beautiful, the many B&Bs are expensive. The **Bed and Breakfast Association** (378-3030) provides assistance with such matters.

San Juan County Park, 380 Westside Rd. (378-2992), 10 mi. west of Friday Harbor on Smallpox and Andrews Bays. If you're lucky enough to snag one of the 20 sites in this quiet waterside campground, you might catch views of whales from your tent. At the very least, a great sunset is guaranteed. Water and flush toilets, but no showers or RV hookups. Vehicle sites $16; hiker/biker sites $5. Park open daily 7am-10pm. Office open daily 9am-7pm. Reservations highly recommended.

Lakedale Campgrounds, 2627 Roche Harbor Rd. (378-2350 or 800-617-2267; http://www.lakedale.com), 4 mi. from Friday Harbor. The mothership of campgrounds. Very attractive sites surrounded by 50 acres of lakes, hosting almost every imaginable water sport. Rents almost every variety of water vessel to match. The lakes are stocked with trout, and the camp sells fishing permits (campers $4 per day, non-campers $8 per day). Sites for 1-2 people with vehicle $22 (Sept.-June. $17), each additional person $4.75 (Sept.-June $3.75).; hiker/biker sites $7 (Sept.-June $6); 6-person cabins start at $115. Campground day use $1.50. Showers $1. Reservations suggested, but management boasts that they've never turned a camper away. Open Mar. 15-Oct. 15; cabins available year-round.

Pedal Inn, 1300 False Bay Dr. (378-3049). A campground designed for bikers and hikers. Quiet, cheap, very rustic, a bit ramshackle. Hot water generally only available during evening hours, but the self-described "mean old manager" Jim will negotiate. Sites $4.85. Any support vehicles for bicyclist groups cost an extra $4.85. Open June-Sept.

FOOD

Stock up on groceries at **King's Market,** 160 Spring St. (378-4505; open M-Sa 7:30am-10pm, Su 8am-10pm). Most island restaurants serve vegetarian food.

🐋**Katrina's,** 135 2nd St. (378-7290), between Key Bank and Friday Harbor Drug. The tiny kitchen cooks up a different menu every day, but invariably serves organic salads, freshly baked bread, and gigantic cookies ($1.25). What you might cook in your own kitchen if you could cook that well. Open M-Th 11am-4:30pm, F 11am-4:30pm and 5:30-10pm, Sa 5:30-10pm.

San Juan Bakery and Donut Shop, 225 Spring St. (378-2271). Cheap eats. Bottomless coffee ($1.16), inexpensive breakfasts, lunch sandwiches, and a tour of the local rumor mill. Grilled cheese, bacon, and chips $3.25. They'll pack up a lunch if you call ahead. Open M-Sa 5am-3pm, Su 7am-1pm.

SIGHTS, OUTDOORS, AND EVENTS

The **Whale Museum,** 62 1st St. (378-4710), exhibits skeletons, sculptures, and updates on new whale research. *(Open daily 10am-5pm; Oct.-May 11am-4pm; $5, seniors $4, college students and ages 5-18 $2, under 5 free.)* The museum provides directions to the best whale-watching spots, and operates a toll-free **whale hotline** (800-562-8832) to report sightings and strandings. The **San Juan Historical Museum,** 405 Price St. (378-3949), in the old King House across from the St. Francis Catholic Church, explodes with exhibits, furnishings, and photographs from the late 1800s. A free pamphlet maps out a walking tour of **Friday Harbor.** *(Open Oct.-Apr. Tu and Th 10am-2pm, May-Sept. Th-Su 1pm-4pm. $2, ages 6-18 $1, under 5 free.)*

A drive around the 35 mi. perimeter of the island takes about two hours, and the route is perfect for cyclists. The **West Side Rd.** traverses gorgeous scenery and provides the best chance for sighting **orcas** offshore. Three resident pods frolic in the nearby waters, and there are several orca sightings per day in peak seasons.

To begin a tour of the island, head south and west out of Friday Harbor on Mullis Rd. (Bikers may want to do this route in the opposite direction, as climbs heading counterclockwise around the island are much more gradual.) Mulles Rd. merges with Cattle Point Rd., and goes straight into **American Camp** (378-2902), on the south side of the island. *(Open daily 8am-dusk.)* The camp dates from the Pig War of 1859 and a **visitor center** explains the history of that epic conflict. *(Open daily 8:30am-5pm. Guided walks W-F at 11:30am and 2:30pm, Sa-Su at 11:30am.)* A self-guided trail leads from the shelter through the buildings, and past the site of a British sheep farm. Every Saturday afternoon, volunteers in period costume reenact daily Pig-War era life. *(June-Sept. 12:30-3:30pm. Free.)* If the sky is clear, make the ½ mi. jaunt farther down the road to **Cattle Point** for views of the distant Olympic Mountains (and hundreds of less distant rabbits), or stop by **South Beach,** a stretch of shoreline that dazzles beach walkers and whale stalkers.

The gravel False Bay Rd., heading west from Cattle Point Rd., runs to **False Bay,** where **bald eagles** nest. During the spring and summer, walk along the northwestern shore (to your right as you face the water) at low tide to see the nesting eagles. False Bay Rd. continues north, running into **Bailer Hill Rd.,** which turns into West Side Rd. when it reaches Haro Straight. **Lime Kiln Point State Park,** along West Side Rd., is renowned as the best **whale-watching** spot in the area, as the crowds of cliff-crawling visitors can attest. Killer whales prowling for salmon frequent this stretch of coastline, and have been known to perform occasional acrobatics. Those truly determined to see some blubber can shell out for a **cruise;** most operations charge about $40 (children $30) for a three- to four-hour boat ride. For more info, pick up one of the many brochures at the chamber of commerce or the National Park Service Information Center (see **Practical Information,** above).

Die, Imperialist Pig!

Back in 1859, when Washington was officially part of "Oregon Country" and the San Juan Islands lay in a territorial no man's land between British Vancouver Island and the United States, one hungry hog unwittingly gave his life for what turned out to be truth, justice, and the American Way. Twenty-five Americans lived and farmed on San Juan Island at a time when the British Hudson Bay Company claimed it for Mother England. When Lyman Cutlar caught a Hudson Bay pig making a royal mess of his potato patch, he understandably shot it dead. The Brits threatened to arrest him, and the Americans looked to Uncle Sam for protection. Three months, five British warships, and 14 American cannons later, war between the two nations seemed inevitable. Though the squabble cooled off, the "Pig War" lasted 12 years. Both countries occupied the island until 1872, when Kaiser Wilhelm of Germany was invited to settle the dispute, and granted it all to the U.S. In the end, only the pig lost its life. But as we all know, everlasting fame beats a life of wallowing in the mud any day.

The Pig War casts its comic pallor over **British Camp,** the second half of the **San Juan National Historical Park.** *(Park open year-round. Buildings open Memorial Day to Labor Day daily 8am-4:30pm.)* The camp lies on West Valley Rd., on the sheltered **Garrison Bay.** Heading east from West Side Rd., Mitchell Bay Rd. leads to a steep ½ mi. trail to **"Mount" Young,** the tallest hill on the island within ogling range of Victoria and the Olympic Mountains.

The **Hotel de Haro,** the first hotel in Washington, is at the **Roche Harbor Resort** (378-2155), on Roche Harbor Rd., at the northern end of the island. The free brochure *A Walking Tour of Historic Roche Harbor,* available at the info kiosk in front of the hotel, leads through this old mining camp. Don't miss the **bizarre Masonic symbol-bedecked gothic mausoleum**—especially eerie at sunset. To get there, follow signs to Roche Harbor, and stop at the lot behind the airfield instead of continuing down to the marina, signs guide visitors to the mausoleum foot path.

The annual **San Juan Island Jazz Festival** brings swing bands to Friday Harbor in late July. A $50 badge ($43 if purchased before July 1) grants admission to all performances, but crowds of revelers cluster outside the clubs for free fun. Single performance tickets range from $15 to $28. For more information, contact the San Juan Island Jazz Association, P.O. Box 1666, Friday Harbor 98250 (378-5509).

■ Orcas Island

Mount Constitution overlooks much of Puget Sound from its 2407 ft. summit atop Orcas Island. A small population of retirees, artists, and farmers dwell here in understated homes, surrounded by green shrubs and the red bark of madrona trees. With a commune-like hostel and the largest state park in Washington, Orcas has the best budget tourist facilities of all the islands. Unfortunately, much of the beach is occupied by private resorts and is closed to the public.

ORIENTATION AND PRACTICAL INFORMATION

Orcas is shaped like a horseshoe, which makes getting around a chore. The ferry lands on the southwest tip. Travel 9 mi. northeast to the top of the horseshoe to reach **Eastsound,** the island's main town. **Olga** and **Doe Bay** are an additional 8 and 11 mi. from Eastsound, respectively, down the eastern side of the horseshoe. Stop in one of the four shops at the ferry landing to get a free **map.** Renting some wheels is not a bad idea, since the island is a bit spread out.

Ferries: Washington State Ferries, 376-4389 or 376-2134. 24hr.
Taxis: Orcas Island Taxi, 376-8294.

Public Transportation: San Juan Transit (376-8887). Service about every 1½hr. to most parts of the island. From the ferry to Eastsound $4.

Visitor Information: There is no visitor center, but the **Chamber of Commerce** (376-2273) returns phone calls. Your best bet is to pick up info about Orcas Island on San Juan Island, or visit **Pyewacket Books** (376-2043), a used bookstore in Templin Center that also houses a slew of island info.

Equipment Rental: Wildlife Cycle (376-4708), at A St. and North Beach Rd., in Eastsound. 21-speeds $5 per hr., $25 per day. Open M-Sa 10am-5:30pm, Su 11am-3pm.

Library: (376-4985), at Rose and Pine in Eastsound, or walk up the path from Prune Alley. Open M-Th 11am-7pm, F-Sa 11am-5pm.

Senior Center: (376-2677), across from the museum on North Beach Rd. in Eastsound. Open M-F 9am-4pm.

Pharmacy: Ray's (376-2230, after-hours emergencies 376-3693), in Templin Center. Open M-Sa 9am-6pm, Su 10am-6pm; in summer daily 10am-6pm.

Emergency: 911.

Post Office: (376-4121), on A St. in Eastsound Market Place. Open M-F 9am-4:30pm. **ZIP Code:** 98245.

Internet Access: See **library,** above.

Area Code: 360.

ACCOMMODATIONS AND CAMPGROUNDS

B&Bs on Orcas charge upwards of $60 per night; the Doe Bay Resort and the campgrounds are cheaper. Reservations help in the summer.

Doe Bay Village Resort, Star Rte. 86, Olga (376-2291), off Horseshoe Hwy. on Pt. Lawrence Rd., 5 mi. out of Moran State Park. Includes kitchen facilities, a health food store and cafe, and extensive grounds for romping. There's even a treehouse. Steam sauna and mineral bath ($4 per day, nonlodgers $7; bathing suits optional; coed). Frolicking, carefree atmosphere. Hostel beds $16 for members; campsites $12-22. Rustic and funky cottages from $44.50. Reservations recommended. Office open 9am-9pm. Guided kayak trips (376-4699) twice daily ($42 for 3hr.)

Moran State Park, Star Rte. 22, Eastsound (376-2326 or 800-452-5687). Follow Horseshoe Hwy. straight into the park. All the best of San Juan fun: swimming, fishing, and miles of hiking. 4 campgrounds with 151 sites. About 12 sites are open year-round, as are the restrooms. Standard sites $11; hiker/biker sites $5. Hot showers 25¢ per 5min. Rowboats and paddleboats $10-13 for the 1st hr., $7 per hr. thereafter. Reservations strongly recommended May-Labor Day.

Obstruction Pass. Accessible only by boat or foot. Turn off Horseshoe Hwy. just past Olga, and hang a right to head south on Obstruction Pass Rd. Soon you'll come to a dirt road marked Obstruction Pass Trailhead; look for the semi-hidden wooden sign on the right. If you reach the bay, you've gone too far. The sites are a ½ mi. hike from the end of the road. Pit toilets, no water. Be careful where you light campfires—bald eagles nest in the trees above the campground. 11 free sites.

FOOD

Essentials can be found at **Island Market** (376-6000), on Langdell St. (open M-Sa 8am-9pm, Su 10am-8pm). Make a bee-line for **Orcas Homegrown Market** (376-2009), on Northbeach Rd., for a large selection of groceries, medicines, and mysterious vegan cheeses. Try their deli for lunch; most specials are $3.50-5.25 and there are always vegetarian options (open daily 8am-9pm). For loads of fresh local produce, check out the **Farmer's Market** in front of the museum (Sa 10am-3pm).

🐚**Chimayo** (376-6394), in the Our House Building on North Beach Rd. A Southwestern theme and comfy booths. Delve into a fresh funky burrito ($3-4). Open M and W-Su 11am-7pm.

Comet Cafe (376-4220), in Eastsound Sq. Two sisters run a bright, happy-go-lucky cafe. One bakes sweets, the other makes delicious sandwiches and roasts. Roast beef with Vermont cheese $6; veggie shepherd pie $5. Open daily 8am-5pm.

Lower Tavern (378-4848), at the corner of Horseshoe Hwy. and North Beach Rd. One of the few inexpensive dinner spots open after 5pm. Dig into burgers and fries ($4.75-6.75) and shoot some pool, or drop by on poker night (Th). Open Su-Th 11am-midnight, F-Sa 11am-2am; kitchen closes at 9pm.

OUTDOORS

Travelers on Orcas Island don't need to roam with a destination in mind; half the fun lies in rambling around. The trail to **Obstruction Pass Beach** is the best of the few ways to clamber down to the rocky shores. Climbs on this hilliest of the San Juans afford inspiring views of the sound and the rest of the archipelago.

Moran State Park (see **Campgrounds**, above) is unquestionably Orcas' star outdoor attraction. *(Park open Apr.-Aug. daily 6:30am-dusk; Sept.-Mar. 8am-dusk.)* Over 30 mi. of hiking trails cover the park, ranging in difficulty from a one-hour jaunt around **Mountain Lake** to a day-long trek up the south face of **Mt. Constitution,** the highest peak on the islands. Pick up a copy of the trail guide from the **registration station** (376-2326). The summit of Constitution looks out over the Olympic and Cascade Ranges, Vancouver Island, and Mt. Rainier. The stone tower at the top was built as a fire lookout in 1936 by the Civilian Conservation Corps. It's possible to drive to the peak, but the trails are more scenic. The **Orcas Tortas** (376-2464) makes a slow drive on a green bus from Eastsound to the peak ($7). For an abbreviated jaunt, drive up Mt. Constitution and hike part-way down to **Cascade Falls,** which is spectacular in the spring and early summer. Down below, two freshwater lakes are easily accessible from the highway, and the park rents rowboats and paddleboats. *($10-13 per hr.)* Head from the lake to the lagoon for an oceanside picnic. **Shearwater Adventures** (376-4699), runs a fascinating, albeit expensive, **sea kayak tour** of the north end of Puget Sound, with close views of bald eagles, seals, and blue herons. *(3hr. tour, $42. Includes 30 minutes of dry-land training.)* Tours leave from Deer Harbor and Rosario Beach. Kayaking without a guide is not recommended.

▓ Lopez Island

Smaller than either Orcas or San Juan, "Slow-pez" lacks some of the tourist facilities of the larger islands. Lopez was settled largely by mutineers, who thrived in the secluded woods. Today, Lopez Islanders still shy away from the mainland and maintain an age-old tradition of waving at every single car they pass.

Lopez Island is ideal for those seeking solitary beach-walking, bicycling, or a true small-town experience. Free of imposing inclines and heavy traffic, the island is the most cycle-friendly in the chain. **Lopez Village,** the largest town, is 3½ mi. from the ferry dock off Fisherman Bay Rd. To get there, follow Ferry Rd. then take a right onto the first street after Lopez Center (before the Chevron station). It's best to bring a bicycle, unless you're up for the hike. To rent a bike or kayak, head to **Lopez Bicycle Works** (468-2847), south of the village next to the island's **Marine Center** (open June-Aug. daily 10am-6pm; May-Sept. 10am-5pm; bikes $5 per hr., $25 per day; single kayaks $15 per hr., $50 per day; double kayaks $75 per day; half-day guided tours $45; sunset paddle $30). Even if you don't rent, the cheerful staff will give you a fantastic detailed map of island roads, complete with mileage counts.

The small **Shark Reef** and **Agate Beach County Parks,** on the south end of the island, offer a change from mainland campgrounds. Shark Reef has tranquil and well-maintained hiking trails, and Agate's beaches are calm and deserted. **Lopez Island Vineyards** (468-3644) allow visitors to sample all of their wines for $1. (Open June-Aug. W-Su noon-5pm; Sept.-Dec. and Mar.-May F-Sa. noon-5pm). They also sell eggs.

Ferry transport has caused price inflation, so it's a wise to bring a lunch to Lopez Island. **Village Market** has groceries (open M-W 8am-7pm, Th-Sa 8am-8pm, Su 9am-7pm). Sample fresh pastries, bread, and pizza at **Holly B's** (468-2133) in the village or buy day-olds at a discount (open M and W-Sa 7am-5pm, Su 7am-4pm). For a taxi, call **Angie's Cab** (468-2227). Laundry facilities lurk along Fisherman's Bay Rd. at **Keep It Clean,** just south of the winery (wash $1.75, dry 25¢ per 5min.; open M-Sa 9am-7pm, Su 10am-4pm). The **seniors' helpline** is 468-2421 (open M-F 9am-4pm). **Lopez Clinic** (468-2245) offers medical services. The **post office** (468-2282) is in the Village on Weeks Rd. (open M-F 8:30am-4:30pm). **ZIP Code:** 98261. **Area Code:** 360.

When spending the night on Lopez, camping is the only bargain. **Spencer Spit State Park** (468-2251, reservations 800-452-5687), on the northeast corner of the island about 3½ mi. from the ferry terminal, has six sites on the beach and 42 pleasant wooded sites up the hill, with flush toilets but no showers or hookups. Tent sites $11; bike sites $5; two 8-bunk lean-tos ($15 each). Reservations are necessary for summer weekends ($6 reservation fee). Campers may enter until 10pm. Spencer Spit offers good **clamming** in the late spring, unless there is red tide. The park is closed November 1 to February 2. **Odlin Park** (468-2496, reservations 468-4413) is close to the ferry terminal, 1 mi. south along Ferry Rd., and offers cold running water, a boat launch, volleyball net, baseball diamond, and pay phone (30 sites: $13-15, plus $2 for each additional person after 5; hiker/biker sites $10).

■ Shaw and Other Islands

Shaw Island is home to 100 residents, one store, one library, wild turkeys, apple orchards, and a bevy of Franciscan nuns living in a convent next to the ferry dock. For the last 16 years these women have been running the store/post office/gas station/ferry dock. Stop in for a couple of hours if only to take a walk, chat with a nun, or buy a map at the **"Little Portion" store** (open M-Sa 9:15am-5pm). When it's open, the modest-sized **library** across the street from the red schoolhouse offers **internet access** open Tu 2-4pm, Th 11am-1pm, Sa 10am-noon and 2-4pm. The island's 11 mi. of public roads are endearing to hikers and bikers. **Shaw Island County Park** (reservations 468-4413), on the south side of the island, has eight campsites ($10-12) that fill quickly despite the lack of running water. There is also a shared hiker/biker camping site ($3), but space is limited. There are no other accommodations on the island.

The Washington State Parks Service operates over 15 **marine parks** on some of the smaller islands in the archipelago. These islands, accessible only by private transportation, have anywhere from one to 51 mainly primitive campsites. The park system publishes a pamphlet on its marine facilities, available at parks or supply stores on the larger islands. One of the most popular destinations is tiny **Sucia Island,** which boasts gorgeous scenery and a few flopping seals. Canoes and kayaks can easily navigate the archipelago when the water is calm, but when the wind whips up the surf, only larger boats (at least 16 ft.) go out to sea. **Navigational maps** are essential to avoid the reefs and nasty hidden rocks that surround the islands. The Department of Natural Resources operates three island parks, each with three to six free campsites. **Cypress Head** on Cypress Island has wheelchair-accessible facilities.

OLYMPIC PENINSULA

Due west of Seattle and its busy Puget Sound neighbors, the Olympic Peninsula is a remarkably different world. A smattering of Indian reservations and logging and fishing communities lace the peninsula's coastline along U.S. 101, but most of the ponderous land mass remains a remote backpacking paradise. Olympic National Park dominates much of the peninsula, and prevents the area's ferocious timber industry from threatening the glacier-capped mountains and temperate rainforests. Locals outside the park make a tenuous living logging and fishing, the peninsula's largest employers. To the west, the Pacific Ocean stretches to a distant horizon; to the north, the Strait of Juan de Fuca separates the Olympic Peninsula from Vancouver Island; and to the east, Hood Canal and the Kitsap Peninsula isolate this sparsely inhabited wilderness from the sprawl of Seattle.

✎ HIGHLIGHTS OF THE OLYMPIC PENINSULA

- **Olympic National Park** (see p. 205) and its environs hold too many awe-inspiring highlights to list in one wee box; a few include the mossy grandeur of the **Hoh Rainforest** (see p. 213), the humbling view from **Cape Flattery** (see p. 211), and the lovely **Ozette beaches** (see p. 214).
- **Salt Creek County Park** (see p. 205) offers stunning sunsets and tidepool life.
- **Port Townsend** (see p. 201) is the most picturesque human work around.

GETTING THERE AND GETTING AROUND

Getting around the peninsula is easiest by car. Distances are tremendous, and public transportation, while passable for traveling to and between the peninsula's small towns, does not serve the magnificent natural areas that are the main attractions. Most bus travel on the peninsula itself is free or costs 75¢, and accommodates bicycles. Public transportation heading into Olympic National Park, however, is sparse; hiking U.S. 101 to a trailhead can add many a paved and exhaust-filled mile to an otherwise tranquil trip. For a listing of public transportation options on the peninsula, contact the **Rainforest Hostel,** 169312 U.S. 101, Forks 98331 (360-374-2270; see p. 213). The owner will be happy to help you navigate the myriad transit routes. Direct transfers between Greyhound, Grays Harbor Transit, West Jefferson Transit, Clallam Transit, and Port Angeles-Seattle Bus Lines provides a route from Seattle, around the peninsula, and back for $24 (on weekdays).

Bicycling on U.S. 101 is very dangerous. Long stretches have no shoulder and immense logging trucks speed heedlessly along the winding, two-lane road. Secondary roads on the peninsula are often gravelly and poorly suited to cycling. Hitchhiking is poor on the Olympic Peninsula and illegal along most of U.S. 101.

■ Port Townsend

Unlike the salmon industry, Port Townsend's Victorian splendor has survived the progression of time and weather. In the 1880s, civic boosters speculated that their booming port would become the new state capital. Every ship en route to Puget Sound stopped here for customs inspection, and the town caroused in the spoils of its seemingly never-ending wealth...until the railroads came. Perched on the isolated northeast tip of the Olympic Peninsula, the town plummeted into a century-long economic ice age. In the last twenty years, however, the entire business district has been restored and declared a national landmark, and the town takes advantage of its 19th-century aura to keep its economy afloat and its facades freshly painted. Countless cafes, galleries, and bookstores line P.T.'s somewhat drippy streets, cheering the homesick urbanites who move there to escape the rat race. Port Townsend is one of the few places on the peninsula where espresso stands outnumber live bait shops.

ORIENTATION AND PRACTICAL INFORMATION

Port Townsend sits at the terminus of Rte. 20 on the northeast corner of the Olympic Peninsula. By land, it can be reached from U.S. 101 on the peninsula, or from the Kitsap Peninsula across the Hood Canal Bridge. **Washington State Ferries** (800-84-FERRY/843-3779 or 206-464-6400 for ferry information; http://www.wsdpt.wa.gov/ferries) runs a ferry from Seattle to Winslow on Bainbridge Island (see p. 187). A **Kitsap County Transit** bus meets every ferry and runs to Poulsbo. At Poulsbo, transfer to a **Jefferson County Transit** bus (see below) to Port Townsend. The ferry also crosses frequently to and from Keystone on Whidbey Island (see p. 179). Ferries dock at **Water St.,** west of downtown Port Townsend.

Local Transportation: Jefferson County Transit (JCT), 1615 W. Sims Way (385-4777; http://www.olympus.net/gettingabout/busjeffco.html). Riders can easily reach Port Angeles, Sequim, Poulsbo, Winslow, and Bremerton on JCT and connect with a neighboring transit system. Most buses do not run on Su. 50¢, seniors and disabled travelers 25¢, ages 6-18 25¢, 25¢ extra fare per zone. Day passes $1.50. Park in the Park 'N' Ride lot and take a **free shuttle** into downtown to avoid parking hassles during rush hours.

Taxis: Peninsula Taxi, 385-1872. Runs 24hr.

Visitor Information: Chamber of Commerce, 2437 E. Sims Way (385-2722 or 800-365-6978; email ptchamber@olympus.net; http://www.olympus.net/ptchamber), lies about 10 blocks from the center of town on Rte. 20. Ask the helpful staff for a free map and guide for visitors. Open M-F 9am-5pm, Sa 10am-4pm, Su 11am-4pm.

WASHINGTON

Equipment Rental: P.T. Cyclery, 100 Tyler St. (385-6470), rents mountain bikes ($7 per hr., $25 per day; maps $1.75; open M-Sa 9am-6pm, Su by appointment). **Kayak P.T.,** 435 Water St. (385-6240; email kayakpt@olympus.net; http://www.olympus.net/kayakpt), rents to kayakers with some experience (singles $25 per 4hr., doubles $40 per 4hr.; anyone over 84 rents free; tours $39 per half-day, $68 per day). **Sport Townsend,** 1044 Water St. (379-9711), rents camping equipment (tents $16; sleeping bags $8; backpacks, pads, and stoves also available). Call ahead to make sure they have enough on hand. Open M-Sa 9am-7pm, Su 10am-5pm.

Library: 1220 Lawrence (385-3181), uptown. Open M 11am-5pm, T-Th 11am-9pm, F-Sa 11am-5pm.

Pharmacy: Safeway Pharmacy, 442 Sims Way (385-2860). Open M-F 8:30am-7:30pm, Sa 8:30am-6pm, Su 10am-6pm.

Hospital: Jefferson General, 834 Sheridan (385-2200 or 800-244-8917).

Emergency: 911. **Police:** 607 Water St., (385-2322). **Poison control:** 800-732-6985.

Crisis Line: 385-0321 or 800-659-0321 (24hr.).

Senior Helpline: 385-2552, open M-F 8:30am-4:30pm.

Internet Access: Cafe Internet, 2021 E. Sims Way (385-9773; email cafeinet@cafe-inet.com; http://www.cafe-inet.com). $8.50 per hr. Open daily 10am-6pm.

Post Office: 1322 Washington St. (385-1600). Open M-F 9am-5pm. **ZIP Code:** 98368.

Area Code: 360.

ACCOMMODATIONS AND CAMPING

⊛**Fort Flagler Hostel (HI-AYH)** (385-1288), in Fort Flagler State Park, overlooks the ocean on gorgeous **Marrowstone Island,** 20 mi. from Port Townsend. From P.T., drive south on Rte. 19, which connects to Rte. 116 east and leads directly into the park. Another hostel in an old military haunt, the rooms are bright, clean, and cheery, if a bit farther from local attractions. Miles of pastoral bike routes wind over Marrowstone, and the hostel is less crowded than most. A storage and repair shed is open to bicyclists and has tools and a bike stand. Beds $11; nonmembers $14; cyclists $9-12. Reservations required. Check-in 5-10pm, lockout 10am-5pm. Call ahead if you're arriving late.

Olympic Hostel (HI-AYH) (385-0655), in Fort Worden State Park 1½ mi. from downtown (follow the signs). Situated right in the fort in an old barrack with views of the ocean, plenty of space, and cushy hospital beds in impeccable bunk rooms. Check out the Commanding Officer's house and Marine Science Center (see **Sights,** below). Rooms for couples and kitchen facilities are available. Call ahead—a hostel this elegant fills up quickly. Beds $12; nonmembers $15; cyclists $9-13. Check-in 5-10pm, check-out 9:30am; no curfew.

Old Fort Townsend State Park (385-3595), 5 mi. south of Port Townsend just off Rte. 20, rests in some pretty woods. 40 cramped sites and no potable water. Sites $10; hiker/biker sites $5. Open mid-May to mid-Sept.

Fort Worden State Park (385-4730; http://www.olympus.net/ftworden). Seaside sites $15, April-Oct. $16. Call for reservations. Or camp on the beach at **Fort Flagler State Park** (385-1259). 116 sites; tents $11, RVs $16, hiker/biker sites $5. Reservations necessary. For directions to either park, see **Sights,** below.

FOOD

A burly **Safeway,** 442 Sims Way (385-2806), south of town along Rte. 20, serves any need (open 24hr.).

⊛**Burrito Depot,** 609 Washington St. (385-5856), at Madison, offers quick, tasty Mexican food. Tango with the tasty veggie fajita ($4.25), or tank up on big burritos from $3.25. Open daily 10:30am-8:30pm. Wheelchair accessible.

⊛**The Elevated Ice Cream Co.,** 627 Water St. (385-1156), serves delicious homemade ice cream and decent espresso (90¢) in a 1920s shop that is, ironically, on the ground floor. The elevator that provided the joint with its moniker (and served as the location for the first year of business) is located right across the street for those intrigued enough to investigate. One scoop of ice cream or two mini-scoops of Italian ice costs $1.44. Open daily 10am-10pm; in winter daily 11am-10pm.

Coho Cafe and Juice Bar, 1044 Lawrence St. (379-1030), at Polk St., uptown, has ridiculously healthy and even more ridiculously entertaining food. A peppy paint job and local health nuts spice up the Yucatan Burro ($4.95) or the Shed Dog breakfast ($3.95). Open W-Sa 8am-4pm, Su 8am-3pm.

Waterfront Pizza (385-6629) on Water St., offers little historical ambience, but churns out a damn good pizza. Plain cheese slice $1.75, vegetarian slice $2.50. Open daily 11am-10pm.

SIGHTS AND EVENTS

Port Townsend is full of huge Queen Anne and Victorian mansions. Who knew? Of the over 200 restored homes in the area, some have been converted into B&Bs and are open for tours. The **Ann Starret Mansion,** 744 Clay St. (385-3205 or 800-321-0644), has nationally renowned Victorian architecture, frescoed ceilings, and a free-hanging, three-tiered spiral staircase. *(Tours daily from noon-3pm. $2.)* Like Cinderella at the ball, even the architecturally ignorant will stand slack-jawed under the staircase.

Go down the steps on Taylor St. to Water St., the town's neo-quaint main artery. Hallowed halls from the 1890s muscle in between historic looking shops with faux facades. The **Jefferson County Museum** (385-1003), at Madison and Water St., show-cases vestiges of the town's raucous past, including a dazzling kayak parka made of seal intestines, an old-time pedal-powered dentist drill, and jail cells rumored to have held Jack London for a night. *(Open M-Sa 11am-4pm, Su 1-4pm; $2.)*

Point Hudson, where Admiralty Inlet and Port Townsend Bay meet, is the hub of a small shipbuilding area and forms the corner of Port Townsend. North of Point Hudson are several miles of **beach, Chetzemoka Park,** and the larger **Fort Worden State Park.** *(Open daily 6:30am-dusk.)* **Fort Worden** (385-4730), a military post dating from the 1890s, guards the mouth of Puget Sound. The fort went into service again in 1981 as a set for the movie **An Officer and a Gentleman.** Military historians should check out the **commanding officer's house** (385-4730, ext. 479) which, like every other building in Port Townsend, is stuffed to the rafters with Victorian furniture. *(Open Apr. 1-Oct. 15 daily 10am-5pm. $1.)* The **Coast Artillery Museum** (385-0373) offers a no-nonsense display on Fort Worden's uneventful military history. Out on the pier at Fort Worden is the **Marine Science Center** (385-5582). Get up close and personal with the tanks of local sea life. *(Open T-Su noon-6pm; in fall and spring, Sa-Su noon-4pm. $2; children $1.)*

ENTERTAINMENT AND EVENTS

Port Townsend's music scene is surprisingly lively. Hang your hat at **Town Tavern** (385-4706) at the corner of Quincy and Water St. *(Open daily 11am-2am.)* This western-style saloon hosts live entertainment Thursday through Saturday during the summer. **Sirens,** 823 Water St. (379-0776), sponsors blues shows on its ducky deck-with-a-view. Check out the awesome vista even if there are no groups on tap for the night. *(Open T-Sa noon-midnight, Su 10am-10pm.)*

From mid-June to early September, **Centrum** sponsors a series of festivals in Fort Worden Park including the **Port Townsend Blues Festival** at the end of June, the **Festival of American Fiddle Tunes** in early July, and **Jazz Port Townsend** later in July. Ticket prices vary; combination tickets can be purchased for all festivals. For a schedule, contact the **Centrum Foundation** (385-5320 or 800-733-3608; www.centrum.org), P.O. Box 1158, Port Townsend 98368. Other annual attractions include the **Wooden Boat Festival,** held the first weekend after Labor Day, and the **House Tour,** held the following weekend, when many mansions are open to visitors free of charge. For more information, contact the Chamber of Commerce (see **Practical Information,** above).

■ Port Angeles

Ideally situated between Olympic National Park and the chilly blue waters of the Strait of Juan de Fuca, Port Angeles proudly presides over the "Gateway to the Olympics." Unfortunately, the town's mountainous neighbors win all the local glory, and the Port of the Angels hovers on the bland side. An era of domination by stinky paper and plywood mills has ended, and Port Angeles joins the legions of Washington small towns hungering after tourist dollars.

PRACTICAL INFORMATION

Buses: Greyhound's **Olympic Bus Lines,** 612 Lincoln Ave. (800-550-3858; http://www.northolympic.com/ovt), runs to Seattle (2 per day; $23, under 12 $11.50).

Ferries: Coho Ferry, 101 E. Railroad Ave. (457-4491), serves Victoria ($6.75, with bicycle $10, with car $27.25; children $3.50). U.S. and Canadian citizens crossing into Canada need valid proof of citizenship. Other internationals should check their own visa requirements (see **Essentials: Entrance Requirements,** p. 6). Budget Rent-a-Car, at 111 E. Front St., has **all-day parking** across from the terminal ($7), and beyond it ($5); keep an eye out for the signs.

Public Transportation: Clallam Transit System, 830 W. Lauridsen Blvd. (800-858-3747 or 452-4511), serves Port Angeles and Clallam County, as far as Forks and Neah Bay. Operates M-F 4:15am-11pm, Sa 10am-6pm. Within downtown 75¢, ages 6-19 60¢, seniors and disabled 25¢. Travel between zones 25¢ extra. Day pass $2.

Car Rental: Evergreen Auto Rental, 808 E. Front St. (452-8001). From $29 per day; $170 per week; plus 20¢ per mi. after 100 mi. Must be 21 with proof of insurance.

Visitor Information: Chamber of Commerce, 121 E. Railroad (452-2363; http://www.cityofpa.com), next to the ferry terminal, one block from the intersection of Lincoln and Front St. Boisterously disseminates tourist info, and allows some free local calls. Open daily 7am-10pm; in winter M-F 10am-4pm.

Outdoor Information: Olympic National Park Visitor Center, 3002 Mt. Angeles Rd. (452-0330). See p. 208 for details.

Equipment Rental: Olympic Mountaineering, 140 W. Front St. (452-0240), rents every conceivable type of mountain equipment except sleeping bags. 2-person tents $20 per day; external frame packs $13 per day, cross-country ski gear $15 per day. Weekly rates are lower. Offers fairly inexpensive treks into the ONP wilds. Open M-Sa 9am-6pm, Su 10am-5pm. **Pedal 'n' Paddle,** 120 E. Front St. (457-1240), rents mountain bikes ($8 per hr.; $20 per day; helmets included) and offers kayak trips (half-day $40). Open M-Sa 9:30am-5:30pm.

Laundromat: Peabody Street Coin Laundry, 212 Peabody St. (683-2028). Wash $1.25, dry 25¢ per 10min. Open 24hr.

Emergency: 911.

Post Office: 424 E. 1st St. (452-9275), at Vine. Open M-F 8:30am-5pm, Sa 9am-noon. **ZIP Code:** 98362.

Area Code: 360.

ACCOMMODATIONS AND CAMPGROUNDS
A night indoors in Port Angeles is pricey and hardly angelic, especially in the summer; winter rates drop $5-15. Weekend budget believers should check out **The Spa,** 511 E. 1st St. (452-3257; reservations 503-233-7627). Reserve a bed or futon ahead of time; it's one big slumber party with everyone huddling in the same room, but a few private rooms are available (beds $15; rooms $20). Breakfast in the garden tea room is included, and there's a steam room downstairs ($10 per hr.). The least expensive motel options line noisy U.S. 101. A few miles west of town, the **Fairmount Motel,** 1137 U.S. 101 (457-6113), has decent, if dim, cable-equipped rooms and a food mart next door ($43; in winter $33). The **Royal Victorian Motel,** 521 1st St. (452-2316), has newly remodeled rooms with microwaves and refrigerators, and provides limo service to and from the ferry dock (streetside singles $34; doubles $40-79; check-in 2-11pm).

The closest campground is **Heart o' the Hills** (452-2713), 5½ mi. from town on Race Rd., within Olympic National Park (see p. 211). It lacks hookups, but offers lush surroundings, wheelchair accessible sites, and ranger-led programs on summer evenings. Unless you come after hours, you'll have to pay the $10 park entrance fee (good for 7 days) plus the $11 camping fee (first-come, first-served; open year-round). **Salt Creek County Park** (928-3441), a 20-minute mosey along Rte. 112, maintains 80 sites ($10) with fantastic waterfront views; the nearby tidepools are a treasure trove of shells and sea stars. Pay showers cost 25¢ for 5 minutes; there are no hookups or reservations. The nearest super-cheap camping is at **Boulder Creek Campground** (a.k.a. **Hot Springs Campground**), at the end of Elwha River Rd., 8 mi. past Altaire. Park at the end of the road, and hike 2 mi. along a closed-off road. Check out the natural Olympic Hot Springs while you're there (see p. 211). Backcountry permits ($5; see p. 209) are available at the trailhead, and let you pitch a tent at one of the 50 sites. Be sure to bring water and warm clothes.

FOOD Port Angeles is stuffed with seafood, occasionally fresh. **La Casita**, 203 E. Front St. (452-2289), is an excellent place to sample the local catch, stuffing seafood burritos ($7) with gobs of crab, shrimp, and fish, plus free all-you-can-eat tortilla chips to engulf between $2 margaritas (open M-Th 11am-9pm, F-Sa 11am-10pm, Su noon-9pm). **Bella Italia**, 117B E. First St. (457-5442), gets rave reviews from Port Angelinos. Hungry vegetarians can sit down to a hunk of lasagna ($8) or a plate of spaghetti ($6) in a romantic, candle-lit booth (open M-F 11am-10pm, Sa-Su 11am-11pm). The bustling, super-friendly **First Street Haven,** 107 E. 1st St. (457-0352), serves up strawberry Belgian waffles ($6.50) and the "Prospector" ($6.75), a behemoth shrimp sandwich (open M-F 7am-4pm, Sa 8am-4pm, Su 8am-2pm). The brand-spankin' new **Port Angeles Brewing Company,** 131 W. Front St. (417-9152), serves up typical beer grub (burgers $6-7) and a mean pint of stout ($3). Live music fills the wood-panelled joint on Sundays, and other displays of local talent are in the works (open M-Sa 11am-11pm, Su 1-9pm). Picnickers can peruse the shelves of **Safeway,** 110 E. 3rd St. (457-0788), at Lincoln St. (open 24hr.).

SIGHTS AND OUTDOORS This gateway city has little more to offer than its gate. Before any trails or travails, stop by **Port Brook and News,** 104 E. 1st St. (452-6367), which has a large map selection and provides insider's advice on the area's best trails and campgrounds, as long as the boss is around. *(Open M-Sa 9am-9pm, Su 9am-5pm.)* For those without a vehicle and disinclined to ride a bike uphill for 20 mi., **Olympic Van Tours** (452-3858) runs three-hour or all-day excursions to Hurricane Ridge (see p. 211) for $13-28. The Olympic National Park Visitor Center (see **Olympic National Park: Practical Information,** p. 208) dispenses free maps.

More accessible by foot is the **Arthur D. Feiro Marine Laboratory** (417-6254), with a large classroom of touch-tanks and aquariums. *(Open daily June 15 to Sept. 7am-8pm; Oct. to June 14 Sa-Su noon-4pm. $2, seniors and under 12 $1.)* The 6 mi., wheelchair accessible **Waterfront Trail** passes over the pier, providing an overview of the city's portside activities. The **Fine Arts Center,** 1203 E. Lauridsen Blvd. (457-3532), in the vicinity of the national park visitor center, has great views of the water and small but inspiring exhibits by regional artists. *(Open Th-Su 11am-5pm. Free.)*

■ Olympic National Park

Olympic National Park (ONP), the centerpiece of the Olympic Peninsula, shelters one of the most diverse landscapes of any North American park. With glacier-encrusted peaks, lush and dripping river valley rainforests, and jagged shores along the Pacific Coast, the park appeals to the wide-ranging tastes of an even wider range of visitors. Roads lead to many corners of Olympic National Park, but they only scratch the surface of this outdoor Oz. A dive into the backcountry reveals the park's many faces and leaves the hordes of summer tourists behind. Despite ONP's dire financial straits (it is one of the poorest national parks) and subsequently rising fees, a little effort and planning can easily yield an afternoon of shell hunting on miles of isolated beach, a day of salmon fishing on the Hoh River, or a week of glacier-gazing from the tree line.

WASHINGTON

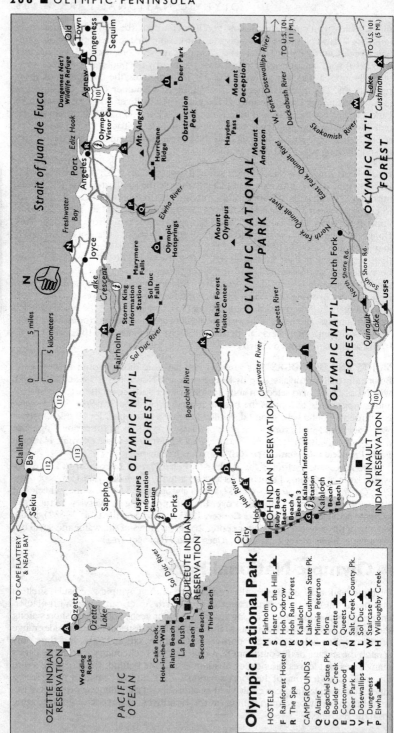

WASHINGTON

Olympic National Park

HOSTELS
F Rainforest Hostel
R The Spa

CAMPGROUNDS
Q Altaire
C Bogachiel State Pk.
O Boulder Creek
E Cottonwood
U Deer Park
T Dungeness
P Elwha

M Fairholm
D Heart O' the Hills
K Hoh Oxbrow
G Hoh Rain Forest
X Lake Cushman State Pk.
I Minnie Peterson
B Mora
A Ozette
J Queets
N Salt Creek County Pk.
L Sol Duc
W Staircase
H Willoughby Creek

NATURAL OVERVIEW

The entire **Olympic Mountain Range** is packed into ONP's center, where conical peaks wring huge quantities of moisture from heavy Pacific air. Average precipitation in the park varies, but an annual 12 ft. of rain and snow are common; certain locations average over 17 ft., and at altitudes above 3500 ft. it is not rare to encounter snow through late June. The mountains steal so much water that some areas northeast of the park get less than 1½ ft. of annual precipitation, making them among the driest in Washington.

Temperate rainforests lie on the west side of the park, along the coast, and in the **Hoh, Queets,** and **Quinault River valleys,** where moderate temperatures, loads of rain, and summer fog support a fantastic emerald tangle dominated by Sitka spruce and western red cedar. The rest of the park is populated by lowland forests of Douglas fir and hemlock, with silver fir at higher elevations. Flower-filled mountain meadows afford stunning views and are often accessible only by foot.

Ancient Native American **petroglyphs** and boxy offshore bluffs called **sea stacks** lend the **beaches** along the unspoiled ONP coastline a sense of mystery. Swaths of Olympic National Forest and private land separate these seaside expanses from the rest of the park. Wind-whipped forests and rocky headlands edge the long, driftwood-strewn beaches. During the winter, evidence of human presence vanishes, and the coast regains a primeval feel.

The extensive patches of naked mountainside left by **logging,** particularly on the western side of the peninsula, may shock visitors. The national park is protected from logging, and views of scarred hillsides disappear within its boundaries, but timber companies regularly harvest both private land and the surrounding **Olympic National Forest.** The State of Washington manages huge tracts along the Hoh and Clearwater Rivers, near the western shore. Until recently, private and state agencies clearcut old growth forests on the peninsula, a policy easily visible from the western segment of U.S. 101. At points, the highway weaves through bald patches of land, with roadside placards indicating the dates of harvest and replanting. Due to the spotted owl uproar and federal regulations banning logging on public land, the Forest Service stopped harvesting any ONF timber in the late 1980s, and private and state harvesting has also slowed. Those who earn a living from forest resources dislike lectures on how to manage them and will likely point out that the consumer of forest products is as responsible for clearcutting as the industries themselves.

ORIENTATION

Only a few hours from Seattle, Portland, and Victoria, the wilderness of Olympic National Park is most easily and safely reached by car. Existing roads are accessible from U.S. 101 and serve as trailheads for over 600 mi. of hiking. No roads cross the entire park. The park's perimeters are well-defined but are surrounded by Forest Service, Washington Department of Natural Resources (DNR) land, and other public areas. There are few outposts of development within the park—**Port Angeles** (see p. 204) on the northern park rim, and **Forks** (see p. 212), on the east side of the park, are the only remotely sizeable towns, where gas and food are always available. U.S. 101 encircles the park in the shape of an upside-down U, with Port Angeles at the top. The park's vista-filled **eastern rim** runs up to Port Angeles, from where the much-visited **northern rim** extends westward. The tiny town of **Neah Bay** and stunning **Cape Flattery** perch at the northwest tip of the peninsula; farther south on U.S. 101, the slightly less tiny town of **Forks** is a gateway to the park's rainforested **western rim.** Separated from the rest of the park, much of the peninsula's Pacific coastline comprises a gorgeous **coastal zone.** For transportation info unique to the peninsula, see **Olympic Peninsula: Getting There and Getting Around,** p. 201.

July, August, and September are best for visiting Olympic National Park, since much of the backcountry remains snowed-in until late June, and only summers are relatively rain-free. This brings flocks of fellow sight-seers, so expect company. Coming from Seattle, the easiest place to begin an exploration of the park is the **Olympic National Park Visitor Center** (see below), where cheerful rangers hand out park maps and give advice on all aspects of travel within the park. The Park Service runs free interpretive programs such as guided forest hikes, tidepool walks, and campfire programs out of its ranger stations. For a schedule of events, pick up a copy of the park newspaper from ranger stations or the visitor center. Robert Steelquist's *Olympic National Park and the Olympic Peninsula: A Traveler's Companion* gives clear, accurate descriptions of the area, and Robert Wood's *Olympic Mountains Trail Guide* is the best book for those planning to tackle the backcountry ($15 at any area bookstore or information center).

PRACTICAL INFORMATION

Visitor Information: Olympic National Park Visitor Center, 3002 Mt. Angeles Rd. (452-0330, TDD 452-0306), off Race St. in Port Angeles (see p. 204). ONP's main info center fields questions about the entire park, including camping, backcountry hiking, and fishing. Distributes an invaluable **park map** and houses exhibits including a hands-on Discovery Room. Open in summer Su-F 8:30am-6:30pm and Sa 8:30am-8pm, though hours vary; in winter daily 9am-4pm. **Hoh Rainforest Visitor Center** (374-6925), on the park's western rim (see p. 213), also provides posters and permits. Open daily July-Aug. 9am-6:30pm; Sept.-June 9am-4:30pm. **Park Headquarters,** 600 E. Park Ave. (452-4501, ext. 311), in Port Angeles, is just an administrative office but can answer phone questions. Open M-F 8am-4:30pm. For the many local **ranger stations,** see specific regions below.

Backcountry Information: Olympic National Park Wilderness Information Center (452-0300), just behind the visitor center. The helpful staff, well-versed in backcountry procedures, will gladly sit down with backpackers to help design trips within the park. This is the only place on the north rim of the park that accepts reservations for the 4 ONP backcountry areas that require them (see p. 209).

Online Information: http://www.nps.gov/olym/home.htm.

State Parks Information: 800-233-0321.

Entrance Fee: $10 per car; $5 per hiker or biker. Charged during the day at developed entrances such as Hoh, Heart o' the Hills, Sol Duc, Staircase, and Elwha. The fee pays for 7 days' access to the park—keep that receipt!

Park Weather: 452-0329. 24hr.

Park Radio: 530 AM for road closures and general weather conditions. 610 AM for general park rules and information, 1610 AM in Lake Crescent and Quinault areas.

Emergency: 452-4501. Staffed daily in summer 7am-midnight; off-season 7am-5:30pm. At other times, dial 911.

Area Code: 360.

FISHING IN THE PARK

Fishing within park boundaries does not require a license, but for salmon and steelhead, you must obtain a state game department **punch card** at local outfitting and hardware stores, or at the **Fish and Game Department** in Olympia (see p. 182). Fish beckon seductively from any of the park's 15 major waterways; the **Elwha River,** coursing through the northeastern part of the park, is best for trout, while the **Hoh River,** flowing west through the park, jumps with salmon. Ask at an anglers' store for current information, and check at a ranger station for specific river regulations.

CAMPING ON THE PENINSULA

On the Olympic Peninsula, campers can tent within walking distance of one of the world's only temperate rainforests for rates between $12 and absolutely free. Olympic National Park, Olympic National Forest, and the State of Washington all maintain **free campgrounds,** but the ONP requires a **backcountry permit** ($5), and the ONF often requires a **trailhead pass** ($3) for sites located off a main trail. The Washington Department of Natural Resources (DNR) allows **free backcountry camping** off any state road on DNR land, as long as campers tent at least 100 yards from the road. The majority of DNR land is near the western shore along the Hoh and Clearwater Rivers, though smaller, individual DNR campsites are sprinkled about the peninsula. Visitor centers and ranger stations hand out a **DNR guide** to all its Washington sites, as well as information on camping within the national park and forest. In summer, weekend competition for sites can be fierce. From late June to late September, most spaces are taken by 2pm, so start hunting early; in more popular areas like those along the Hoh River, find a site before noon. See the various park regions below for specific campground listings.

Standard Campgrounds

ONP maintains many standard campgrounds scattered throughout its boundaries (sites $8-12). The only free national park campground is **North Fork** (7 sites; no water; see p. 214). Fees in national forest campgrounds vary ($8-12), and the six campgrounds in the Hood Canal Ranger District are free. Reservations (800-280-CAMP/2267) can be made for three national forest campgrounds: **Seal Rock, Falls View,** and **Klahowga.** Check with the Olympic National Forest Headquarters in Olympia (see p. 182) or any ranger station for more info on national park and forest campgrounds. Several state parks are scattered along Hood Canal and the eastern side of the peninsula (sites $10-16; occasionally $4-5); to reserve, call 800-452-5687. Most other drive-up camping on the peninsula is first-come, first-served.

Backcountry Camping

Strap on your backpack, stock up on instant oatmeal, hike into the ONP backcountry, and rough it to your heart's content. Whether in the rainforest, along the coast, or in the high country, backcountry camping anywhere in the park requires a $5 **backcountry permit,** available at any ranger station and some trailheads. The purpose of the permit is to provide the park with information on internal traffic, as well as hiker locations in case of emergency. Park offices maintain quota limits on backcountry permits for especially popular destinations within the park, including **Lake Constance** and **Flapjack Lakes** in the eastern rim (see below); **Grand Valley, Badger Valley,** and **Sol Duc** in the northern rim (see p. 210); **Hoh** in the western rim (see p. 213); and the coastal **Ozette Loop** (see p. 214).

  Reservations are crucial, especially for the beach campsites, which are 100% reservable (the rest are 50% first-come, first-served); call a few days in advance. Backpackers should always prepare for a mix of weather conditions. Even in summer, the driest season, parts of the park get very wet. Always carry a good waterproof jacket and wear waterproof hiking boots with plenty of traction; trails can become rivers of slippery mud. Never drink any untreated water in the park. **Giardia,** that nasty diarrhea-inducing bacterium, lives in these waters (see **Essentials: Common Woes,** p. 14). Water purification tablets are available at the visitor center and most camping supply stores. **Black bears** and **raccoons,** eager to partake of hikers' granola and peanuts, pose another backcountry hazard; when issuing backcountry permits, ranger stations offer lessons on hanging food out of such animals' reach. Some stations have free rope, but don't count on it; bring your own 50-100 ft. of thin, sturdy rope. A map and signs at the trailhead tell whether or not **open fires** are permitted in the given backcountry area. Before any backcountry trip, make sure to inquire at a ranger station about **trail closures;** winter weather has destroyed many a popular trail.

■ Olympic National Park: Eastern Rim

What ONP's western regions have in ocean and rainforest, the eastern rim matches with canals and grandiose views. Canyon walls rise treacherously, their jagged edges leading to mountaintops that offer glimpses of the entire peninsula and Puget Sound. The following highlights are listed from south to north. The Park and Forest Services furnish info at the **Hood Canal Ranger Station,** P.O. Box 68, Hoodsport 98548 (877-5254), southeast of the reserve lands on U.S. 101 in Hoodsport (open daily 8am-4:30pm; in winter open M-F 8am-4:30pm, closed Sa-Su). Hikers use campgrounds along the park's east rim as entry points to the interior. **Staircase Campground** (877-5569) is a major camping hub 16 mi. northwest of Hoodsport at the head of **Lake Cushman,** and the trailhead for a rugged river hike (59 sites, $10; plus $10 park entrance fee; RV accessible). To get there, turn west off U.S. 101 at Hoodsport, pass the ranger station on Rte. 119, take a left after 9 mi., and follow the signs. **Lake Cushman State Park** (877-5491; 800-452-5687 for reservations), on the way to Staircase, is a popular base camp for extended backpacking trips into the national forest and park. The park offers fine swimming beaches, showers (25¢ per 3min.), and flush toilets (80 sites, $11; 30 full hookups, $16).

Super-tough hikers tackle the steep trails up **Mt. Ellinor,** 5 mi. past Staircase on Rte. 119. Follow signs to Jefferson Pass and Upper/Lower Trailhead. Once on the mountain, hikers can choose the 3 mi. path or an equally steep but shorter journey to the summit. Look for signs to the Upper Trailhead along F.I. Road #2419-04. On a clear day at the summit, the Olympic range towers to the northwest, and Puget Sound, Seattle, Mt. Rainier, Mt. Adams, and the rim of Mt. St. Helens unfold to the southeast. Adventure-seekers who hit the mountain before late July should bring snow clothes to "mach"—as in Mach 1, the speed to which sliders accelerate—down a ¼ mi. **snow chute.** Find free refuge from all this fun at the **Lilliwap Creek Campground;** follow signs from Rte. 119 or inquire at the ranger station.

Lena Lake, 14 mi. north of Hoodsport off U.S. 101, entices hikers and birdwatchers alike. A 3.2 mi. hike ascends to the lake itself. Follow Forest Service Rd. 25 (known as the Hamma-Hamma Rte.) off U.S. 101 for 8 mi. to the trailhead. There are 29 rustic sites at **Lena Lake Campground.** The Park Service charges a $3 trailhead pass for entrance into many areas, including the lake itself.

Dosewallips (doh-see-WALL-ups) **Campground,** on a road that leaves U.S. 101 27 mi. north of Hoodsport, has 30 less developed campsites ($10; not for RVs). A pretty and popular multi-day trail leads from Dosewallips across the park to a number of other well-traversed backpacking trails, including **Hurricane Ridge** (see p. 211). Those looking for a one-day hike should hop on the **West Forks Dosewallip Trail,** a 10½ mi. trek to the **Mt. Anderson Glacier.** A recently constructed bridge makes this trail the shortest route to any glacier in the park. Thirty miles north of Hoodsport, the **Quilcene Ranger Station,** 295142 U.S. 101 S (765-3368), can point out the **Mt. Walker Viewpoint,** 5 mi. south of Quilcene on U.S. 101. A one-lane gravel road leads 4 mi. to the lookout, the highest viewpoint in the park accessible by car. The road is steep, has sheer drop-offs, and should not be attempted in foul weather or a temperamental car. Yet another view of Hood Canal, Puget Sound, Mt. Rainier, and Seattle awaits intrepid travelers on top. Picnic tables perch on the east side; feast there while feasting your eyes on the north face of 7743 ft. **Mt. Constance.**

Get That Goat!

In the early part of this century, in an effort to provide more game for hunting, elk were shipped from Washington to Alaska and mountain goats were sent from Alaska to Washington. The goats proliferated in Olympic National Park long after hunting was prohibited, damaging endangered native plants by grazing, trampling, and wallowing. Park Service authorities tried many ways of removing the goats, including live capture and sterilization darts—but nothing really worked. In 1995, they resolved to liquidate the goats once and for all by shooting them from helicopters. Washington Congressman Norm Dicks has gotten this measure postponed for now, and in the meantime has proposed reintroducing the native gray wolf to the park. Wolves were eliminated in the early part of this century, in an effort to provide more game for hunting.

■ Olympic National Park: Northern Rim

The most developed section of Olympic National Park lies along its northern rim, near Port Angeles, where glaciers, rainforests, and sunsets over the Pacific are all only a drive away. Spur roads from U.S. 101 lead to campgrounds and trailheads, listed here from east to west.

Farthest east off U.S. 101 lies **Deer Park,** where trails tend to be uncrowded and vistas plentiful. **Deer Park Campground** affords the park's highest car-accessible camping (4500 ft.). Come early to snag one of the campground's 14 sites; trailers and

RVs are prohibited ($8, summer only). Past Deer Park, the **Royal Basin Trail** meanders 6.2 mi. to the **Royal Basin Waterfall.**

Heart o' the Hills Campground (see p. 204), near Port Angeles, overflows with vacationers poised to take **Hurricane Ridge** by storm. The campground has no hookups or showers but offers plenty of giant trees, fairly private sites, wheelchair access, and family-oriented evening campfire programs (105 sites: $10). The road up Hurricane Ridge is an easy but curvy drive. Before July, walking on the ridge usually involves a bit of snow-stepping. Clear days give splendid views of Mt. Olympus and Vancouver Island, set against a foreground of snow and indigo lupine. RVs and tourists crowd the ridge by day, making rosy-fingered dawn an ideal time to go. After the herds arrive, more seclusion can be found on the many short trails that originate here, including some designed for seniors and the disabled. For one of numerous extraordinary views, try the uphill **High Ridge Trail,** which is a short walk from Sunset Point. Signs at the visitor center give updates on visibility at the summit, but call ahead (452-0330) before tackling the 40-minute drive. On weekends from late December to late March, the Park Service organizes free guided **snowshoe walks** atop the ridge.

Farther west down U.S. 101, a 5 mi. spur road leads south to two **campgrounds** along the waterfall-rich Elwha River: **Elwha Valley** and the nearby **Altaire.** Both have drinking water and flush toilets (452-9191; 30-41 sites: $10). Appleton Pass and the **Olympic Hot Springs** trailhead rest 2½ mi. past Altaire; from here, hike 2½ mi. to the natural pools. Dippers beware: the warm, bacteria-filled water can jump-start infections. To stay on the safe side, follow the unmarked foot paths to more secluded, less-frequented baths. The nearby **Hot Springs/Boulder Creek campsite** has 14 primitive sites (free with $5 backcountry permit).

Fairholm Campground (928-3380) sits 30 mi. west of Port Angeles, snuggled at the tip of **Lake Crescent,** with wheelchair access and plenty of drinking water (87 sites: $10). Trails around this glacier-scarred lake evoke gasps with their views of old growth forests and the brilliantly blue waters of one of the only natural lakes in Washington. (Most were artificially created by dammed rivers, natural processes be damned.) Stop at the nearby **Storm King Ranger Station** (928-3380; hours vary) to find out about the campground's **evening interpretive programs.** Scenic trails of varying difficulty use the ranger station as their starting point; check at the station for current hiking conditions. The **Marymere Falls Trail** (2 mi. round-trip), leading through old growth Douglas firs, western hemlock, and red cedar, is great for travelers with kids or without time; the first ¼ mi. is wheelchair accessible.

Even farther west on U.S. 101, 13 mi. of paved road penetrate to the **Sol Duc Hot Springs Campground** (327-3534), with wheelchair accessible restrooms (82 sites: $12). Nearby lies the popular **Sol Duc Hot Springs Resort** (327-3583; http://www.northolympic.com/solduc), where retirees de-wrinkle in the springs and eat at grubholes inside the lodge. The resort's chlorinated pools are wheelchair accessible (open daily June-Sept. 9am-9pm; Apr.-May and Oct. Sa-Su 9am-6pm; $6.50, seniors $5.50; suit or towel rental $2). Scheduled programs are held every evening except Friday. According to Native American legend, the source of the Sol Duc and Olympic Springs was two aggressive "lightning fish." After a long and indecisive battle, they gave up the fight and crept into two caves, where they still weep hot tears of mortification. (Apparently, the Sol Duc fish weeps chlorinated tears.) The **Sol Duc trailhead** is also a starting point for those heading for the heights; stop by the **Eagle Ranger Station** (327-3534) for information, current hiking conditions, and backcountry permits (open June-Aug. daily 8am-5pm). The Sol Duc Trail draws its share of traffic, but crowds thin dramatically above **Sol Duc Falls.**

■ Near Olympic National Park: Neah Bay and Cape Flattery

Trivia buffs take heed: **Cape Flattery** is the most northwesterly point in the contiguous U.S. Not only that, but it's drop-dead gorgeous. In 1778, the area caught the attention of explorer James Cook, who named the tip Cape Flattery because it "flattered us with the hopes of finding a harbor." Unfortunately, flattery got them nowhere, and

WASHINGTON

the nearest port is all the way across the peninsula at Port Angeles. At the western-most point on the Juan de Fuca Strait is **Neah Bay,** the only town in the **Makah Reservation.** Cape Flattery and Neah Bay are not a part of ONP, and they are only accessible overland by skirting its boundaries, since they perch just north of the park on the western rim (see below).

The **Makah Cultural and Research Center** (645-2711), in Neah Bay on Hwy. 112, is just inside the reservation on the first left, right across from the Coast Guard station (open daily June-Aug. 10am-5pm; Sept.-May W-Su 10am-5pm; $4, seniors and students $3). It houses artifacts from an archaeological site at Cape Alava, where a huge mudslide buried and perfectly preserved a small Makah settlement 500 years ago. One exhibit meticulously reproduces a room from a longhouse, complete with animal skins, cooking fire, and the smell of smoked salmon. This Pompeii of the Pacific Northwest is expertly researched and beautifully presented. The center also serves as the town's social and cultural center. The Makah Nation, whose recorded history goes back 2000 years, still lives, fishes, and produces artwork on this land, though now in a startling state of poverty. During the weekend closest to August 26, Native Americans from around the region come to participate in canoe races, traditional dances, and bone games (a form of gambling) during the **Makah Days.** Visitors are welcome and the delicious salmon bake makes a savory highlight. Contact the center for more information.

Still teasing would-be explorers and egotists, Cape Flattery can be reached only through Neah Bay. Pick up detailed directions at the Makah Center, or just take the road through town until it turns to dirt, then follow the "Marine Viewing Area" sign once you hit gravel, and continue for another 4 mi. to a small, circular parking area, where a trailhead leads toward Cape Flattery. Recent construction of the trail and cliffside viewing areas has rendered the previously ankle-smashing journey to the cape more negotiable. You'll know you're close to the amazing views of **Tatoosh Island** just off the coast and **Vancouver Island** across the strait when you hear the sound of Tatoosh's bullhorn. Even though the road to the trailhead is excruciatingly bumpy, the hike and the vistas from the cape reveal some of the more beautiful stretches of ocean around, so quit yer grumblin'. To the south, the Makah Reservation's **beaches** are solitary and peaceful; respectful visitors are welcome to wander.

From Port Angeles, Rte. 112 leads west 72 mi. to Neah Bay. From the south, take Rte. 113 north from Sappho on U.S. 101 to reach Rte. 112; this drive takes at least one hour. **Clallam Transit System** (452-4511 or 800-858-3747) serves Neah Bay out of Port Angeles (see p. 204). Take bus #14 from Oak St. to Sappho (75min.), then take bus #16 to Neah Bay (1hr.). Check schedules at the bus station to avoid long layovers ($1, seniors 50¢, ages 6-19 85¢).

Accommodations in the area are less than exciting. Neah Bay caters solely to the fishing industry, and it is not the place to spend the night. If stuck, try the oceanside **Cape Motel** (645-2250) on Bay View Ave. Try old but clean rooms without kitchens ($45-55), or sack out in a shanty (singles $18; doubles with bunk $25). **Trettenks RV Park** (963-2688), 11 mi. east of Neah Bay, has tent sites and nice bathrooms almost two steps from the beach along Juan de Fuca Strait ($15; each extra guest $2).

■ Near Olympic National Park: Forks

Between ONP's northern rim and its western rim rainforests is the logging town of Forks, the perfect place to stop, stock up, and grab a bite to eat along U.S. 101—in fact, the only place to stop. Forks lies a hefty two hours west of Port Angeles; make sure to buy gas in here, since there are few stations farther north or south. Route #14 of **Clallam Transit** (452-4511 or 800-858-3747; see p. 204) serves Forks with trips to Port Angeles every day but Sunday ($1, disabled and seniors 50¢, ages 6-19 85¢). At the south end of town on U.S. 101, stop at the **Forks Chamber of Commerce** (374-2531 or 800-44-FORKS/36757; open daily 9am-4pm). The **police** can be reached at 374-2223, and the **hospital** is available at 674-6271. The **post office** is at Spartan Ave.

Welcome
to
America

America has over
5000 ways to
get in touch
with yourself,

and **one way**
to get in touch with

the world.

©1999 AT&T

1·800
call ATT
1 800 225-5288
For All Calls

1 800 225-5288

Want to visit home while you're visiting here?

1 800 CALL ATT® connects you fast and clear within the

U.S. or to anywhere in the world. You can use your

AT&T Calling Card or any of these credit cards.

How's that for freedom?

Special Features

Sequential Calling–Place another call without having to redial the access and card numbers, by pressing # after each call is completed.

Voice Messaging–If the number you're dialing is busy or there's no answer, simply press #123 to record message and specify delivery time.

Correct Mistakes While Dialing–Just press ✳ and repeat your last step.

In-Language Assistance–An operator or voice prompt will help you with dialing instructions in the languages listed.

Cantonese	1 800 833-1288	**Polish**	1 800 233-8622
Hindi	1 800 233-7003	**Russian**	1 800 233-2394
Japanese	1 800 233-8006	**Spanish**	1 800 233-9008
Korean	1 800 233-8923	**Tagalog**	1 800 233-9118
Mandarin	1 800 233-1823	**Vietnamese**	1 800 233-1388

www.att.com/world

It's all within  your reach.

and A St., one block east of U.S. 101 (open M-F 9am-5pm, Sa 10am-noon). **ZIP Code:** 98331. **Area Code:** 360.

The closest non-camping budget accommodation to Forks is the **Rainforest Hostel,** 169312 U.S. 101 (374-2270). To get there, follow the hostel signs off U.S. 101, 4 mi. north of Ruby Beach between Miles 168 and 169. Buses travel to the hostel from North Shore Brannon's Grocery in Quinault (daily 9am, 1, and 4:35pm; 50¢). Owner Jim welcomes travelers into his quasi-communal home-turned-hostel, and daytime passers-by can stop in for a **shower** ($1.50). The house has a roaming cat and dog, but those with allergies can escape to two tiny trailers balanced on the lawn out back. Two family-size rooms are available, as well as a men's dorm with five double bunks in summer; couple and family accommodations require a reservation and deposit. The hostel is a font of info and provides shelter from surprise western rim rain showers (beds $10; 11pm curfew; 8am wakeup; morning chore required of hostelers). If drawn to stay in Forks itself, check out the **Town Motel,** 1080 S. Forks Ave. (374-6231 or 800-742-2429), with well-kept rooms that break the ruffle-quota, and a gardenful of dahlias (singles $34; doubles $44).

To experience fine Forks cuisine, drop by the smoke-filled **Raindrop Cafe,** 111 E. A St. (374-6612), at S. Forks Ave., to order a peasant burger ($2.75) or a gourmet burger ($6), and to play "table topic" games (open M-Sa 6am-9pm, Su 6am-8pm; in winter daily 6am-8pm). Grab groceries and espresso at **Forks Thriftway** (374-6161), on U.S. 101 (open M-Sa 8am-10pm, Su 8am-9pm; in winter daily 8am-9pm).

■ Olympic National Park: Western Rim

In the temperate rainforests of ONP's western rim, ferns, mosses, and gigantic old growth trees blanket the valleys of the Hoh, Queets, and Quinault Rivers. Although fallen foliage and decaying trunks cover the rainforest floor, rangers keep the many walking and hiking trails clear, well-marked, and accessible. On any of these walks through the drippy wonderland, prepare to be overwhelmed by green. The entrances to each of the three valleys are clearly marked from U.S. 101 and are described below from north to south.

The drive along the **Hoh River Valley** is alternately stunning and barren, depending on how many DNR trees have fallen to the axe, chainsaw, or hydraulic splitter in recent months. The first two DNR campgrounds along Hoh River Rd., which leaves U.S. 101 13 mi. south of Forks, accept no reservations. Outside of July and August, many campers seem to ignore these free, palatial DNR sites, which make a great base for hitting the Hoh trailhead (see below). Maps of the **Hoh-Clearwater Multiple Use Area** are available from the **DNR Main Office** (374-6131), just off U.S. 101 on the north side of Forks, right next to Tillicum Park (open M-F 8am-4:30pm).

From **Hoh Rainforest Visitor Center** (see **Practical Information,** p. 208), a good 45-minute drive from U.S. 101, take the quick (40min.), ¾ mi. **Hall of Mosses Trail** for a whirlwind tour of rainforest vegetation. The slightly longer (1hr.) **Spruce Nature Trail** leads 1¼ mi. through lush forest and along the banks of the Hoh River, with a smattering of educational panels explaining bizarre natural quirks. A short **wheelchair accessible trail** circles the visitor center. Nearby, the park maintains 88 sometimes soggy **campsites** ($10) with drinking water and flush toilets, but limited facilities for the handicapped. The **Hoh Rainforest Trail** is the most heavily traveled path in the area, beginning at the visitor center and paralleling the Hoh River for 18 mi. to **Blue Glacier** on the shoulder of **Mount Olympus.** Shy Roosevelt elk, the ever-contested northern spotted owl, and the gods of ancient Greece inhabit this area.

Several other trailheads from U.S. 101 offer less crowded opportunities for exploration of the rainforest, amid surrounding ridges and mountains. The **Queets River Trail** hugs its namesake east for 14 mi. from the free **Queets Campground;** the road is unpaved and unsuitable for RVs or large trailers. High river waters early in the summer can thwart a trek; hiking is best in August, but there's still a risk that water will cut off trail access. A shorter loop (3 mi.) is as much as most visitors see of Queets. Elk

WASHINGTON

often appear in fields along the trail, which passes a broad range of rainforest, lowland river ecosystems, and the park's largest Douglas fir.

The Park and Forest Services and the Quinault Reservation quibble for control of the land surrounding Quinault Lake and River. The Forest Service operates an information center at the **Quinault Ranger Station,** 353 S. Shore Rd. (288-2444; open daily 9am-4:30pm; in winter M-F 9am-4:30pm). From the station, it's 20 mi. to the **North Fork trailhead,** from which intrepid hikers can journey 44 mi. north across the entire park, finishing at **Whiskey Bend** on the north rim. Those with less time or energy have the **day hike** options from the Quinault Ranger Station or the **Graves Creek Ranger Station,** 8 mi. up Shore Rd. For a quick stroll through Washington's own Jurassic Park, try the 4 mi. **Quinault Lake Loop** or the ½ mi. **Maple Glade Trail.** Snow-seekers flock to **Three Lakes Point,** an exquisite summit covered with powder until July.

Quinault Lake lures anglers, rowers, and canoers. The **Lake Quinault Lodge** (288-2900 or 800-562-6672), next to the ranger station, rents canoes and rowboats ($10 per hr.). Jim Carlson (288-2293) offers **horseback rides** around the lake and through the forest in summer ($35 per 2hr.). Campers can drop their gear right at the lakeside in **Willaby Campgrounds** (288-2213), ¼ mi. before the ranger station (sites $13).

■ Olympic National Park: Coastal Zone

Pristine coastline traces the park's slim far western region for 57 mi., separated from the rest of ONP by U.S. 101 and non-park timber land. Eerie fields of driftwood, sculptured arches, and dripping caves frame flamboyant sunsets, while the waves are punctuated by rugged sea stacks—chunks of coast stranded at sea after erosion swept away the surrounding land. Bald eagles soar on windy days, as whales and seals speed through the Pacific. These beaches are described below from south to north.

Between the Quinault and Hoh Reservations, U.S. 101 hugs the coast for 15 mi., with parking lots just a short walk from the sand. The highway meets the coast near **Kalaloch** (KLAY-lok) **Center** (962-2283), a crowded campground with 175 sites ($12) near the ocean, including a lodge, general store, gas station, and ranger station. Gather at low tide for **tidepool talks;** park newspapers and bulletin boards list specific times. To the north, **Beach #4** has abundant tidepools, plastered with sea stars; **Beach #6,** 3 mi. north at Mile 160, is a favorite whale-watching spot. Near Mile 165, sea otters and eagles hang out amid tide pools and sea stacks at **Ruby Beach.** Camping on this stretch of beach is not allowed.

Beach camping is only permitted north of the Hoh Reservation between **Oil City** and **Third Beach,** and north of the Quileute Reservation between **Hole-in-the-Wall** and **Shi-Shi Beach.** Those who camp along these stretches bask in the glory of easy, flat hiking, long evenings of reflected sunlight capped by resplendent sunsets, and an ever-changing seascape. Before hiking or camping along the coast, pick up a required overnight permit, a park map, a tide table, and the useful *Olympic Coastal Strip* brochure at a ranger station. Find the tide line from the previous high tide, use the tide table to estimate how many feet the tide will change while you're there, and set up camp well above this mark. The same approach applies to walking the coast: don't traverse beach that could sink under the waves while you're crossing it.

Between the Hoh and Quileute Reservations, a 17 mi. stretch of rocky headlands dominates the coastline. At the end of this strip, **Mora** (374-5460), due west of Forks near the Quileute Reservation, has a drive-in **campground** (sites $10) and a **ranger station.** From **Rialto Beach** near Mora, 21 mi. of coast stretch north to a roadhead and campground (sites $10) at **Ozette Lake** (452-0300); a backcountry permit and reservation are required for camping on the beach. Rialto Beach itself hosts eccentric caves and sea stacks worth a gander. Ozette is a 20 mi. trek west from Rte. 112. Several of these beach strands lie within private land belonging to the Makah, Ozette, Quileute, Hoh, and Quinault Nations; reservation land may not be crossed by hikers without permission, making a continuous 57 mi. coastal trek well-nigh impossible.

Day hikers and backpackers adore the 9 mi. loop that begins at Ozette Lake. The trail is a triangle with two 3 mi. legs leading along boardwalks through the rainforest. One heads toward sea stacks at **Cape Alava,** the other to a sublime beach at **Sand Point.** A 3 mi. hike down the coast links the two legs, passing ancient native petroglyphs. The entire area is relatively flat, since it's mostly prairie and coastal forest, but presents plenty of sand to slog through. Overnighters must make permit reservations in advance; spaces fill quickly in summer. The **Ozette Ranger Station** (963-2725) has further info (open daily 8am-4:30pm). Call 452-0300 for permit reservations.

PACIFIC COAST

■ Willapa Bay

Willapa Bay divides the **Long Beach Peninsula** from the Washington mainland, and provides excellent wildlife viewing. U.S. 101 passes the bay as it winds along the border of the Olympic National Park and down the Pacific Coast into Oregon. On its way out of the park, the highway passes by Grays Harbor and through the industrial cities of **Aberdeen** and **Hoquiam** at the mouth of the **Chehalis River.** Unpleasant and grimy, these industrial cities have everything an American would expect in the way of malls, movie theaters, and motels. Aberdeen even sports a famous native son, Kurt Cobain, who (understandably and legendarily) got the hell out as soon as he could. U.S. 101 continues amid Willapa Bay's sparkling sloughs and pastoral farmlands, with views that compensate for the protected bay's ban on swimming and sunning. From the north, stop at the headquarters of the **Willapa National Wildlife Refuge** (484-3482), just off U.S. 101 on the left, to visit the last unpolluted estuary in the U.S. The refuge offers a rare opportunity to observe Canada geese, loons, grebes, cormorants, trumpeter swans, and other birds. Avian diversity descends upon the area during fall and winter. An array of stuffed birds inside the office helps visitors know what to look for in the refuge (open M-F 7:30am-4pm). The best time to visit this bird sanctuary is in late April or early May.

No trails are directly accessible from the headquarters, but rangers can give directions to several units scattered through the Willapa Bay region, including **Leadbetter Point** at the tip of the Long Beach Peninsula, and **Long Island** in Willapa Bay, accessible only by boat. Long Island teems with deer, bear, elk, beaver, otter, and grouse. It also supports a 274-acre **cedar grove,** one of the Pacific Northwest's last climax forests, still growing new trees after 4000 years. The cedars average 160 ft. in height and some reach 11 ft. in diameter.

Long Island is home to five limited-use **campgrounds,** all inaccessible by car. Reaching the island requires finding a boat or bumming a ride. Boats should be launched from the headquarters (see above); the channel here is only about 100 yards wide, though too muddy for swimming. After reaching the island, hike 2½ mi. along the island's main road to reach the **Trail of Ancient Cedars.** The refuge office provides advice on getting to the island and maps marked with campgrounds.

■ Long Beach Peninsula

Long Beach Peninsula, with 28 mi. of unbroken beach accessible by U.S. 101 and Rte. 103, is an overwhelming frenzy of kites, souvenir shops, and beaches. Access to the world's longest beach is easy; almost any east-west road on the peninsula ends in a parking lot by the sand. Fishing, swimming, boating, and kite-flying fill the warmer months, allowing residents to recuperate from pounding winter storms. Beachcombers hunt for glass balls from Japanese fishing nets; locals say they have the most luck on the beach's **Ocean Park.** Permits are required for gathering driftwood here.

Clamming season lasts from October to mid-March; call the **shellfish hotline** (360-796-3215) for season status. Look for dimples or bubbles in the sand to find fast-digging but succulent razor clams. An annual non-resident license costs $21, available at

---

Slime, Sex, and Violence

The banana slug (genus *Ariolimax*) ranges from six to 10 inches, from dull brown to bright yellow, and from southern California to Southeast Alaska.

Fact: Using copious secretions of viscous slime, the banana slug cleanses itself of debris, protects itself from predators, and descends by a gossamer-thin slime cord. **Moral:** Mucus is a useful tool.

Fact: Banana slugs are hermaphrodites, and can mate at any time of year. Foreplay consists of petting, licking, and violent biting, and can last up to 12 hours. During the deed, a slug's male organ can become too swollen to be removed from its partner, necessitating "apophallation"—the removal of genitalia via gnawing. **Moral:** Slug sex, however titillating, is not for people.

Fact: The jet-black slugs that one often sees are not banana slugs, but are in fact foreign European slugs who practice unprovoked aggression on their native North American cousins. **Moral:** Be kind to the banana slug, but if you see a Euro-version, salt its slimy ass to oblivion.

Short Stop, in the Shell Station across the street from the visitors bureau (see below). Free **tide tables** are available at info centers and businesses. Be extra careful of **red tide,** when vicious bacteria can barrel through your digestive tract via innocent bivalves. These bacteria are sometimes deadly. The **red tide hotline** is 800-562-5632 (http://www.doh.wa.gov/ehp/sf/biotoxin.htm).

Wild varieties of **blackberries** and **blueberries** are an arm's reach away along many roadsides (though they may be coated in exhaust). The peninsula also harbors nearly 500 acres of **cranberry bogs** and is one of only four places in the U.S. where cranberries are grown. Most of the bogs are in **Grayland** along Cranberry Rd., parallel to Hwy. 105, and are harvested in October. Be careful not to pick on private property.

The third weekend in July brings the **Sand-Sations Sand Sculpture Contest** to the city of **Long Beach.** In 1989, a world record tumbled when participants built a 3 mi. long fortress of sand. Call the visitor bureau (see below) for more info. The city invites kite flyers from Thailand, China, Japan, and Australia to the **International Kite Festival** (642-2400) during the third weekend of August. At **Marsh's Free Museum** (642-2188), 409 S. Pacific Way, mechanical fortune tellers and Jake, the petrified alligator-man featured in the *National Enquirer,* keep company with honky-tonk souvenirs galore (open, ironically, whenever tourists bring money).

The **Long Beach Peninsula Visitors Bureau** (642-2400 or 800-451-2542), five minutes south of Long Beach on U.S. 101, has pamphlets on activities in Long Beach and the vicinity (open M-F 8am-5pm, Sa-Su 8am-6pm). **Pacific Transit** (in Raymond 642-9418, in Naselle 484-7136, farther north 875-9418) sends buses from Long Beach as far north as Aberdeen ($1.70; exact change required). **Local buses** run up and down the peninsula 14 times per day. Schedules are available in post offices and visitor centers along the peninsula (weekends local service only).

■ The Columbia River Estuary

Several miles south of Long Beach on Washington's southern border, **Cape Disappointment** guards the Columbia River Estuary. In 1788, bitter British fur trader Captain John Meares, frustrated by repeated failures to cross the treacherous Columbia River sandbar, gave the large promontory guarding the river mouth its moniker. Over the past 300 years, almost 2000 vessels have been wrecked, stranded, or sunk where the Columbia meets the ocean, a region aptly named the Graveyard of the Pacific.

Fort Columbia State Park (777-8221) lies on U.S. 101 northwest of the Astoria Megler Bridge, 1 mi. east of **Chinook** on the west side of the highway. The fort was built in 1896 and armed with huge guns to protect the river mouth from an enemy that never materialized (park open Apr.1 to Oct.15, daily dawn-dusk). The park's **interpretive center** recreates life at the fort and includes an exhibit on the indigenous Chinook people who once occupied this land. A wooded 1 mi. trail meanders past several historical sites (center open from Memorial Day to Sept. 30 daily W-Su 10am-5pm; call for winter hours). What was once the area's hospital is now the hospitable **Fort Columbia Youth Hostel,** P.O. Box 224, Chinook (777-8755).

Three miles southwest of the fishing town of **Ilwaco,** at the southern tip of the Peninsula, **Fort Canby State Park** (642-3078, reservations 800-452-5687) offers camping and a megadose of Lewis and Clark (open daily dawn-dusk). The park was the dynamic duo's final destination, and now boasts two lighthouses and a well-pruned campground packed with alders and RVs. The sites fill up quickly in summer. (180 tent sites, $11; 27 sites with water and electric, $13; 60 full hookups, $16; 5 hiker/biker sites, $5; 3 cabins and 3 yurts sleep 4 for $35; hot pay showers; 2 wheelchair accessible sites. $6 fee for reservations. Unregistered campers can enter until 10pm.) At the end of the main road, the spaceship-shaped **Lewis and Clark Interpretive Center** hovers above the ruins of the fort. Inside, a winding display documents the Lewis and Clark expedition from its Missouri origins to the party's arrival at the mouth of the Columbia, and the explorers' painstakingly detailed journal entries speak for themselves (open daily 10am-5pm). The **North Head Lighthouse,** built in 1898, is in the northwest corner of the park, accessible by a gravel path. The **Cape Disappointment Lighthouse,** built in 1856, is the oldest light house in the Pacific Northwest, and is in the southeast corner of the park. Its distinctive red light can be reached by puffing ¼ mi. up a steep hill from the Coast Guard station parking lot, or by clambering ½ mi. along a narrow trail from the interpretive center. For a magnificent beach-level view of the Cape Disappointment Lighthouse, drive through the campground area past **Waikiki Beach** on the **North Jetty.** Though not quite Honolulu, Waikiki Beach is ideal for swimming in summer, beachcombing after storms in winter, and year-round ship-watching.

The early 90s is an era Ilwaco would like to forget. Recent record-low salmon counts and the 1993 Endangered Species Act closed the commercial salmon season for two years. Salmon populations are on the rise again, though, and gleeful local fishing companies are back on the water. Many fisheries along the Ilwaco waterfront sell salmon steaks, and many charter companies offer fishing trips for landlubbers who want to learn the art of angling. **Pacific Salmon Charters,** P.O. Box 519, Ilwaco 98624 (642-3466), leads eight-hour fishing tours, including coffee and tackle (trips run daily at 6am; starting at $60).

Among the cheapest places to hit the hay on the Long Beach Peninsula is the **Sand-Lo-Motel,** 1910 Pacific Hwy. (642-2600), equipped with the perk of coffee makers in each room (singles and doubles $42; rates drop in winter). Keep in mind that the beautiful and inexpensive Fort Columbia Youth Hostel lies just 15 minutes down the road in **Fort Columbia State Park** (see p. 81). The friendly folks at **My Mom's Pie Kitchen** (642-2342), 4316 S. Pacific Hwy., cook an inexpensive and welcome respite from Long Beach's steak houses and greasy spoons. My Mom's Special, a half sandwich, soup or salad, plus half a piece of pie costs $7.25 (open W-Su 11am-4pm).

For the best meal around, head down Hwy. 103 in Ocean Park to historic **Oysterville.** A tiny, whitewashed town, Oysterville's featured attraction is **Oysterville Sea Farms** (665-6585), at 1st and Clark, which raises, cleans, packs, and dishes out a certain mollusk. A dozen cost $3.50 (open daily 10am-5pm, Oct.-May Sa-Su 10am-5pm).

CASCADE RANGE

Intercepting the moist Pacific air, the Cascades divide Washington into the lush, wet green of the west and the low, dry plains of the east. In 1859, an explorer making his way through the Cascade Range gushed: "Nowhere do the mountain masses and peaks present such strange, fantastic, dauntless, and startling outlines as here." Native people summed up their admiration more succinctly, dubbing the Cascades "Home of the Gods."

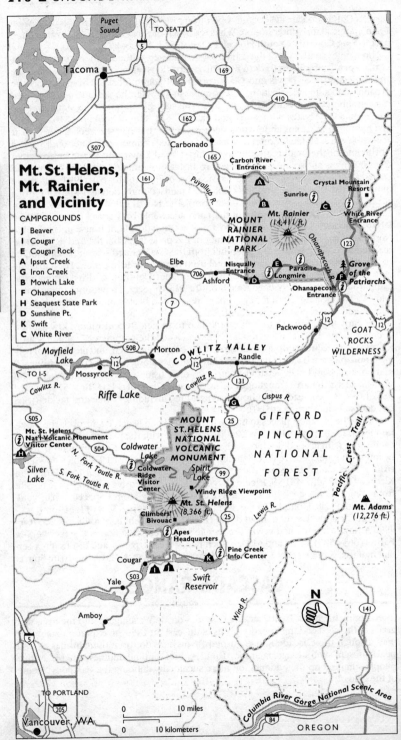

WASHINGTON

Mt. St. Helens, Mt. Rainier, and Vicinity

CAMPGROUNDS

J Beaver
I Cougar
E Cougar Rock
A Ipsut Creek
G Iron Creek
B Mowich Lake
F Ohanapecosh
H Seaquest State Park
D Sunshine Pt.
K Swift
C White River

Puget Sound

TO SEATTLE

Tacoma

Carbonado

Carbon River Entrance

Crystal Mountain Resort

Sunrise

Mt. Rainier (14,411 ft.)

White River Entrance

MOUNT RAINIER NATIONAL PARK

Puyallup R.

Ohanapecosh R.

Elbe

Nisqually Entrance

Paradise
Longmire

Grove of the Patriarchs

Ashford

Ohanapecosh Entrance

Packwood

GOAT ROCKS WILDERNESS

Mayfield Lake

TO I-5

Morton

COWLITZ VALLEY

Randle

Mossyrock

Cowlitz R.

Riffe Lake

Cowlitz R.

Cispus R.

GIFFORD PINCHOT NATIONAL FOREST

Mt. St. Helens Nat'l Volcanic Monument Visitor Center

Coldwater Lake

MOUNT ST. HELENS NATIONAL VOLCANIC MONUMENT

Silver Lake

N. Fork Toutle R.

S. Fork Toutle R.

Coldwater Ridge Visitor Center

Spirit Lake

Windy Ridge Viewpoint

Mt. St. Helens (8,366 ft.)

Lewis R.

Mt. Adams (12,276 ft.)

Pacific Crest Trail

Climbers' Bivouac

Apes Headquarters

Pine Creek Info. Center

Cougar

Yale

Swift Reservoir

Wind R.

Amboy

N

TO PORTLAND

0   10 miles

0   10 kilometers

Columbia River Gorge National Scenic Area

Vancouver, WA

OREGON

WASHINGTON

⊛ HIGHLIGHTS OF THE CASCADES

- Life beautifully blankets the dormant **Mt. Rainier** (see p. 223), and makes a gradual but inevitable recovery at the blast zone of **Mt. St. Helens** (see p. 219).
- The tiny town of **Stehekin** (see p. 231), isolated at the end of a lengthy lake, leads to boundless outdoor enjoyment.
- **Route 20** (see p. 232) winds conveniently through the emerald **North Cascades**, with high points at the **Sauk Mountain Trail** (see p. 233), the strangely teal **Ross Lake** (see p. 233), and the poetic **Goat Peak Lookout** (see p. 235).

GETTING AROUND

The white-domed peaks of Mounts Baker, Vernon, Glacier, Rainier, Adams, and St. Helens are accessible by four major roads. **U.S. 12** approaches Mt. Rainier National Park through White Pass, and provides access to Mt. St. Helens from the north; **I-90** sends four lanes past the ski resorts of Snoqualmie Pass; scenic **U.S. 2** leaves Everett for Stevens Pass and descends along the Wenatchee River; the **North Cascades Hwy. (Rte. 20),** is the most breathtaking of the trans-Cascade roads providing access to North Cascades National Park. Route 20 and U.S. 2 are often traveled in sequence as the **Cascade Loop. Greyhound** runs on I-90 and U.S. 2 to and from Seattle, while **Amtrak** parallels I-90. Rainstorms and evening traffic can slow hitchhiking; locals warn against thumbing across Rte. 20. The Cascades are most accessible in the months of July, August, and September; many high mountain passes are snowed in during the rest of the year.

■ Mount St. Helens National Monument

In a single cataclysmic blast on May 18, 1980, the summit of Mount St. Helens erupted, transforming what had been a perfect cone into a crater one mile wide and two miles long. The force of the ash-filled blast robbed the mountain of 1300 ft. and razed entire forests, strewing trees like charred matchsticks. Ash from the crater rocketed 17 mi. upward, circling the globe and blackening the region's sky for days. Debris spewed from the volcano flooded Spirit Lake and choked rivers as far away as the Columbia. The explosion itself was 27,000 times the force of the atomic bomb dropped on Hiroshima.

Mount St. Helens National Volcanic Monument, administered by the Forest Service, encompasses most of the blast zone, the area around the volcano affected by the explosion. This ashen landscape, striking for its initially bleak expanses, is steadily recovering from the explosion that transformed 230 sq. mi. of prime forest into a wasteland. Saplings push their way up past denuded logs, while insects and small mammals are returning. Portions of the monument are off-limits to the public because of delicate ongoing geological experiments and the fragile nature of the blossoming ecosystem. Like many other Cascade peaks, the volcano still threatens to erupt, but probably won't do so for several hundred years.

GETTING THERE AND GETTING AROUND

The main access routes to the monument—Rte. 504, Rte. 503, and U.S. 12—spiral around Mount St. Helens from different directions and do not connect. It would be impossible to explore all sides in a day. Vigorous winter rains often decimate access roads; check at a ranger station for road closures before heading out.

From the **west,** take Exit 49 off I-5 and use **Rte. 504,** otherwise known as the **Spirit Lake Memorial Highway.** The brand new 48 mi. road has wide shoulders and astounding views of the crater. For most, this is the quickest and easiest daytrip to the mountain, and the **Mount St. Helens Visitor Center,** the **Coldwater Ridge Visitor Center,** and the **Johnston Ridge Observatory** (see below) line the way to the volcano. This drive also lures Winnebago battalions and summer crowds.

Route 503 parallels the **south** side of the volcano until it connects with **Forest Service Rd. 90.** Visitors climb up **Rte. 83** to lava caves and the **Climber's Bivouac** (see **Outdoors,** p. 221) a launch pad for forays up the mountain. From the southern approach, Mt. St. Helens tricks the viewer with an illusion of pre-eruption serenity. Though views from this side don't highlight recent destruction, green glens and remnants of age-old explosions make this the best side for hiking and camping.

From the **north,** visitors take **U.S. 12** east from I-5. The towns of **Mossyrock, Morton,** and **Randle** line U.S. 12 and offer the closest major services to the monument. From U.S. 12, both **Forest Service Rd. 25** and **Forest Service Rd. 26** head south to **Forest Service Rd. 99,** a 16 mi. dead-end road that travels into the most devastated parts of the monument, passing a handful of lookouts. Forest Service Rd. 25 offers access to the Iron Creek Campground (see **Campgrounds,** below).

PRACTICAL INFORMATION

Entrance Fee: The monument charges an entrance fee at almost every visitor center, viewpoint, and cave: $8, seniors $4, Golden Eagle Pass $4, under 16 free. The pass is valid for 3 days. It is possible to stop at the viewpoints after 6pm without paying, or to drive through the park without stopping at the main centers.

Visitor Information: Many visitor centers and information stations line the various highways surrounding the volcano, both inside and outside the monument.

Mount St. Helens Visitor Center (360-274-2100, 24hr. recorded info 360-274-2103), across from Seaquest State Park; follow signs along Rte. 504. For most visitors, especially those coming from Seattle on I-5, this is the first stop. An excellent introduction to the mountain, with displays on the eruption and plenty of interactive exhibits for the gadget-lover or aspiring geologist. The staff helps visitors find camping spots and navigate maps. A 22min. film with graphic footage of the eruption and its aftermath is shown every hr. mid-June to Aug. Open daily May-Sept. 9am-6pm; in winter hours vary, but generally 9am-5pm.

Coldwater Ridge Visitor Center (274-2131; fax 274-2129). Follow Rte. 504 38 mi. from Mt. St. Helens Visitor Center. This sprawling glass-and-copper building has a superb view of the collapsed cavity, along with trails leading to **Coldwater Lake,** which was created by the eruption. Emphasis is on the area's recolonization by living things. Picnic areas, interpretive talks, and a gift shop/snack bar. Open May-Aug. daily 9am-6pm; Sept.-Apr. 9am-5pm.

Johnston Ridge Observatory (274-2140), at the end of Rte. 504, overlooking the crater, focuses on geological exhibits and offers the best view from the road of the steaming lava dome and crater. The center is named for David Johnston, a geologist who predicted the events of May 18, 1980, but stayed to study the eruption and was killed. Open daily May-Sept. 9am-6pm; Oct-Apr. 10am-4pm.

Forest Learning Center (414-3439), outside the monument boundaries on Rte. 504, between the Mount St. Helen Visitor Center and the Coldwater Ridge Center. This massive propaganda machine for the Weyerhauser Company houses impressive exhibits on the reclamation of thousands of acres of timber downed by the explosion. Open May-Oct. 10am-6pm.

Woods Creek Information Station, 6 mi. south of Randle on Rd. 25, from U.S. 12 on the north side of the volcano. A drive-through information center—grab info map without even getting out of your car. Open mid-May-Sept. daily 9am-4pm.

Pine Creek Information Station (238-5225), 17 mi. east of Cougar on Rd. 90, on the south side of the monument. Shows an interpretive film of the eruption of Mt. St. Helens. Open mid-May to Sept. daily 9am-6pm.

Apes Headquarters, at Ape Cave on Rd. 8303, on the south side of the volcano. Answers your lava tube questions. Open daily mid-May to Sept., 9:30am-5:30pm.

The Monument Headquarters (247-3900, 24hr. recorded info 247-3903), 3 mi. north of Amboy on Rte. 503. Not a visitor center, but call for permits or for specific, detailed info on road conditions. They are in charge of **crater-climbing permits** (see below). Open M-F 7:30am-5pm.

Publications: *The Volcano Review,* available free at all visitor centers and ranger stations, contains a map (you may well get lost without it), copious info, and schedules concerning activities at the monument. A more thorough survey of the area is found in the *Road Guide to Mount St. Helens* ($5), available at visitor centers.

Forest Information: Gifford Pinchot National Forest Headquarters, 10600 NE 51st Circle, Vancouver, WA 98682 (891-5000, 24hr. recording 891-5009). Info on camping and hiking info within the forest. Additional **ranger stations** and **visitor information** at: **Randle,** 10024 U.S. 12, Randle, WA 98377 (497-1100), north of the mountain on U.S. 12 and east of the Wood Creek Information Station; **Mt. Adams,** 2455 U.S. 141, Trout Lake, WA 98650 (509-395-3400), southeast of the mountain on Rte. 141 and above White Salmon in the Columbia River Gorge; **Packwood,** 13068 U.S. 12 (494-0600), east on U.S. 12; **Wind River,** 1262 Hemlock Rd., Carson, WA 98610 (509-427-3200), south of the mountain on Forest Service Rd. 30 and north of Carson in the Columbia River Gorge. Hours change seasonally; call ahead.

Crater Climbing Permits: Between May 15 and Oct. 31, the Forest Service allows 100 people per day to hike to the crater rim. Reserve in person or write to the **Monument Headquarters,** 42218 NE Yale Bridge Rd., Amboy 98601 (247-3900), 1hr. north of Portland off Rte. 503. 60 permits are available on reserve. The Forest Service begins accepting applications Feb. 1. Write early; weekends are usually booked before March, and weekdays often fill up as well. Climbers who procrastinate should head for **Jack's Restaurant and Country Store,** 13411 Louis River Rd. (231-4276), on Rte. 503, 5 mi. west of Cougar (I-5 Exit 21), where a lottery is held at 6pm every day to distribute the next day's 50 unreserved permits. All permits cost $15. Jack's open daily 5:30am-9pm.

Radio Station: 530 AM. Road closures and ranger station hours.

Emergency: 911.

Area Code: 360.

WASHINGTON

CAMPGROUNDS

Although the monument itself contains no campgrounds, a number are scattered throughout the surrounding national forest. Free dispersed camping is allowed within the monument, meaning that if you stumble upon a site on an old forest service road, you can camp out there—but finding a site is a matter of luck. Swift, Beaver Bay, and Cougar Campground are run by Pacificorp (503-464-5035).

Iron Creek Campground (reservations 800-280-2267), just south of the Woods Creek Information Station on Rd. 25, near its junction with Rd. 76. The closest campsite to Mt. St. Helens; good hiking and striking views of both the crater and the blast zone, where acres of downed trees abut healthy forests. Water is available (8-10am and 6-8pm). 98 sites: $12, premium $14. Only 15 sites can be reserved.

Swift Campground, on Rd. 90, just west of the Pine Creek Information Station. Spacious. 93 sites: $12. Free firewood. No reservations.

Beaver Bay, west of Swift Campground on the Yale Reservoir. 78 RV and tent sites: $12. Toilets and showers.

Cougar Campground, 2 mi. west of Beaver Bay. 45 individual sites $15; 15 tent-only group sites $15. Toilets and showers.

Seaquest State Park (274-8633, reservations 800-452-5687), on Rte. 504, 5 mi. east of the town of Castle Rock at I-5 Exit 49, and across from the main Mount St. Helens Visitor Center. Full facilities include wheelchair accessible sites and pay showers. One of the easiest campgrounds to reach on I-5, and the closest state park with showers and hookups. 72 pleasant wooded sites $10; 16 full hookups $15; 4 primitive hikers/bikers sites $5. Reservations in summer are a must.

OUTDOORS

Western Approach

The one-hour drive from the Mt. St. Helens Visitor Center to Johnston Ridge offers spectacular views of the crater and of the resurgence of life. The road east on Rte. 504 offers few opportunities for rigorous hiking, though. The ½ mi. **Winds of Change Trail,** at Coldwater Lake, has signposts aplenty to explain the eerie surrounding landscape. Another 10 mi. east, a hike along **Johnston Ridge** approaches incredibly close to the crater where geologist David Johnston died studying the eruption.

Northern Approach

The first stop for visitors traveling south on Rd. 25 from Randle and U.S. 12 should be the **Woods Creek Information Station.** Viewpoints are listed on various handouts at the visitor center and include the **Quartz Creek Big Trees** and **Ryan Lake.** The newly paved, two-lane Rd. 99 passes through 17 mi. of curves, clouds of ash, and cliffs. In comparison with Rte. 504, Rd. 99 cuts through far more devastated terrain; evidence of the 19-year-old blast remains almost untouched. Trailer owners should leave their crafts in the **Wakepish Sno-Park,** at the junction of Rd. 25 and 99. It takes nearly one hour to drive straight out and back on Rd. 99, not including the many talks, walks, and views along the way. Road 99 winds among the trees before opening onto the blast area. Make sure to check for road closures (listen to 530 AM) before heading to Rd. 25 or 99.

On the way west along Rd. 99, **Bear Meadow** provides the first interpretive stop, an excellent view of Mt. St. Helens, and the last restrooms before Rd. 99 ends at **Windy Ridge.** The monument begins just west of Bear Meadow, where Rd. 26 and 99 meet. Rangers lead 45min. walks to emerald **Meta Lake;** meet at Miner's Car at the junction of Rd. 26 and 99. *(Late June–Sept. daily at 12:45 and 3pm.)* The trail around the lake is an easy ½ mi., and illustrates the regenerative abilities of lake ecosystems.

Farther west on Rd. 99, frequent roadside turnouts offer trailheads, information on the surroundings, and unbeatable photo ops. The effects of the blast are inescapable: felled trees, pumice plains, and log choked lakes. **Independence Pass Trail #227** is a difficult 3½ mi. hike, with overlooks of Spirit Lake and superb views of the crater and dome that only get better as you go along. For a serious hike, continue along this trail to its intersection with the spectacular **Norway Pass Trail,** which runs directly through the blast zone and ends on Rd. 26. Considered the best hike in the park, the trail is 6 mi. long, takes about 5½hr., and requires a vehicle at both ends. Farther west, the 2 mi. **Harmony Trail #224** provides the only public access to Spirit Lake. Rangers give an interpretive talk at **Harmony Viewpoint** during the summer daily at 1pm. A self-guided trail leads from the viewpoint to Spirit Lake.

Spectacular **Windy Ridge** is the exclamation point at the end of Rd. 99. From here, a steep ash hill grants a magnificent view of the crater from 3½ mi. away. In summer, forest interpreters describe the eruption during talks held in the Windy Ridge Amphitheater. *(Daily every hr. on the ½hr. 11:30am-4:30pm.)* The **Truman Trail** leaves from Windy Ridge and meanders 7 mi. through the **Pumice Plain,** where hot pyroclastic flows sterilized the land, leaving absolutely no life. Because the area is under constant scrutiny by biologists, it's important to stay on the trails at all times.

Southern Approach

Caves and lava tubes take visitors inside "the Beast." From the **Pine Creek Information Station,** 25 mi. south of the junction of Rd. 25 and 99, take Rd. 90 12 mi. west and then continue 3 mi. north on Rd. 83 to **Ape Cave,** a broken 2½ mi. lava tube formed by an ancient eruption. When exploring the cave, wear a jacket and sturdy shoes, and take at least two flashlights or lanterns. *(Rentals $2 each. Rentals stop at 4pm and all lanterns must be returned by 5pm.)* Rangers lead 10 free 30-minute guided cave explorations per day. One quarter-mile before Ape Cave on Rd. 83 is the **Trail of Two Forests,** a lava-strewn and wheelchair accessible path above the forest floor. Road 83 continues 9 mi. farther north, ending at **Lahar Viewpoint,** the site of terrible mudflows that followed the eruption. Nearby, **Lava Canyon Trail #184** hosts three hikes with views of the **Muddy River Waterfall.**

Those with strong legs and a taste for conquest can scale the new, stunted version of the mountain to glimpse the lava dome from the crater rim. Although not a technical climb, the route up the mountain is a steep pathway of ash, strewn with boulders. Often, the scree (a layer of loose shale) is so thick that each step forward involves a half-step back. The trip down is often accomplished on the triumphant climber's behind. The view from the lip of the crater, encompassing Mt. Rainier, Mt. Adams, Mt. Hood, Spirit Lake, and the lava dome directly below, is magnificent. Average hiking time is five hours to get up and three hours to get down. Bring sunglasses, sunscreen, sturdy climbing boots, foul-weather clothing, plenty of water, and gaiters to keep boots from filling with ash. Free camping (no water) is available at the **Climber's Bivouac,** the trailhead area for the **Ptarmigan Trail #216A,** which starts the route up the mountain. The trail is located about 4 mi. up Rd. 83. For info on permits, see **Practical Information,** above.

■ Cowlitz Valley

The **Cowlitz River** begins at the tip of a Mt. Rainier glacier, cuts a long, deep divot west between Mt. Rainier and Mt. St. Helens, and turns south to flow into the Columbia River. Although views of Mt. St. Helens and Mt. Rainier are obscured from within the valley, compensation comes in miles of lush farmland. There is not much to do in the valley besides traveling between the two mountains, but it does contain the nearest major services to the parks.

The river drains part of the watershed for both the **Mt. Adams** and **Goat Rocks Wilderness Areas,** to the west and northwest of Mt. St. Helens. The rugged Goat Rocks are named for their famous herds of mountain goats, and Mt. Adams seduces hundreds of climbers each year with its snow-capped summit (12,307 ft.). Both areas are seldom-traveled, excellent hiking country, accessible only by foot or horseback, with sections of the **Pacific Crest Trail** among their extensive trail networks. The **Randle Ranger Station,** 10024 U.S. 12 (360-497-1100), located in the valley, has information on trails and other outdoor activities. Info is also available at the **Packwood Visitor Information Center,** 13068 U.S. 12 (360-494-0600).

The Cowlitz River, once wild and treacherous, has been tamed considerably by a Tacoma City Light hydroelectric project. The **Mayfield** and **Mossyrock Dams** back up water into the river gorge to create two lakes, **Mayfield** and **Riffe,** both popular recreation areas. **Ike Kinswa State Park** and **Mayfield Lake County Park,** on Mayfield Lake off U.S. 12, offer camping and **trout fishing** year-round. Ike Kinswa (983-3402, reservations 800-452-5687) has 101 sites with showers (sites $11; full hookups $16). Mayfield Lake (985-2364) offers 54 tent and RV sites ($11). Public boat launches provide access to Mayfield, the lower of the two lakes.

■ Mount Rainier National Park

At 14,411 ft., Mt. Rainier (ray-NEER) presides regally over the Cascade Range. The Klickitat native people called it Tahoma, "Mountain of God," but Rainier is simply "the Mountain" to most Washington residents. Perpetually snow-capped, this dormant volcano draws thousands of visitors from all around the globe. Rainier creates its own weather by jutting into the warm, wet air, pulling down vast amounts of rain and snow. Clouds mask the mountain 200 days per year, frustrating visitors who come solely to see its distinctive summit. Sharp ridges, steep gullies, and 76 glaciers combine to make Rainier an inhospitable host for the thousands of determined climbers who attempt its summit each year. Those who don't feel up to scaling the mountain can still find outdoor enjoyment in the old growth forests and alpine meadows of Mt. Rainier National Park. With over 305 miles of trails through wildflowers, rivers, and bubbling hot springs, Mt. Rainier has a niche for all lovers of nature. 1999 marks the 100th anniversary of Mt. Rainier's national park status. Pay your respects to the Mountain of God and be richly rewarded.

GETTING THERE AND GETTING AROUND

To reach Mt. Rainier from the **west,** take I-5 to Tacoma, then go east on Rte. 512, south on Rte. 7, and east on Rte. 706. This road meanders through the town of **Ashford** and into the park by the Nisqually entrance, which leads to the visitor centers of **Paradise** and **Longmire. Rte. 706** is the only access road open year-round; snow usually closes all other park roads from November to May. Mt. Rainier is 65 mi. from Tacoma and 90 mi. from Seattle.

All major roads offer scenic views of the mountain, with numerous roadside lookouts. The roads to **Paradise** and **Sunrise** are especially picturesque. **Stevens Canyon Rd.** connects the southeast corner of the national park with Paradise, Longmire, and the Nisqually entrance, unfolding superb vistas of Rainier and the Tatoosh Range. Hitchhiking is illegal on national park roads, though walking to a lookout point or parking lot and asking for a ride is not. Nevertheless, many visitors say that hitchhiking is easy along the park's roads. (*Let's Go* does not recommend hitchhiking.)

Rainier weather changes quickly; pack warm clothes and cold-rated equipment. Before setting out, ask rangers for the two info sheets on mountain-climbing and hiking which contain helpful hints and a list of recommended equipment. Group size is limited in many areas, and campers must carry all trash and waste out of the backcountry. Potable water is not available at most backcountry campsites. All stream and lake water should be treated for giardia (see p. 14) with tablets, filters, or by boiling it before drinking. The nearest **medical facilities** are in Morton (40 mi. from Longmire) and Enumclaw (5 mi. from Sunrise).

The section of the **Mt. Baker-Snoqualmie National Forest** that adjoins Mt. Rainier is administered by **Wenatchee National Forest,** 301 Yakima St., Wenatchee 98807 (509-662-4314). The **Gifford Pinchot National Forest** is headquartered at 6926 E. Fourth Plain Blvd., P.O. Box 8944, Vancouver, WA 98668 (425-750-5000). The **Bronson Pinchot National Forest** does not exist. The closest **ranger station** is at 10061 U.S. 12, Naches 98937 (509-965-8005).

PRACTICAL INFORMATION

Entrance Fee: $10 per car, $5 per hiker. Permits good for 7 days. Gates open 24hr.

Buses: Gray Line Bus Service, 4500 S. Marginal Way, Seattle 98106 (206-624-5077). From Seattle to Mt. Rainier daily May to mid-Oct. (1-day round-trip $48, under 12 $14). Buses leave from the Convention Center at 8th and Pike in Seattle at 8am and return at 6pm, allowing about 3½hr. at the mountain. **Rainier Shuttle,** P.O. Box 374, Ashford, 98304 (569-2331), runs daily between Sea-Tac Airport (see p. 157) and park or Ashford area lodges, and between Ashford and Paradise (1-way $11).

Visitor Information: Each of the park's 4 visitor centers—**Longmire, Paradise, Ohanepecosh and Carbon River,** and **Sunrise**—has helpful rangers, brochures on hiking, and postings on trail and road conditions. The free **map,** distributed at park entrances, is invaluable. The best place to plan a backcountry trip is at the **Longmire Wilderness Center** (569-2211 ext. 3317), near the Nisqually entrance in the southwest corner of the park, or the **White River Ranger Station** (569-2211 ext. 2356), off Rte. 410 on the park's east side. Both distribute **backcountry permits** for $10 per group plus $5 per person (a solo hiker pays $15). Both open in summer Su-Th 7am-7pm, F-Sa 6:30am-9pm. The **Park Administrative Headquarters,** Tahoma Woods, Star Route, Ashford 98304 (569-2211; http://www.nps.gov/mora) is not a visitor center, but answers phone inquiries. Open M-F 8am-4:30pm.

Equipment Rental: Rainier Mountaineering, Inc. (RMI) (569-2227), in Paradise. Rents ice axes ($9.50), crampons ($9.75), boots ($18), packs ($18), and helmets ($6.50) by the day. Expert RMI guides lead summit climbs, seminars, and special schools and programs. Open May-Sept. daily 9am-5pm. Winter office at 535 Dock St. #209, Tacoma 98402 (253-627-6242). Beginners must buy a 3-day package that includes a day of teaching and 2 days of climbing ($465). **White Pass Sports Hut** (494-7321), on U.S. 12 in Packwood, rents skis. Alpine package $13 per day, Nordic package $12 per day. Also rents snowshoes and snowboards.Open M-F 8am-6pm, Sa-Su 9am-6pm; in winter M-F 8am-6pm, Sa-Su 7am-6pm.

Emergency: 911

Post Office: In the **National Park Inn,** Longmire, and in the **Paradise Inn,** Paradise. Both open M-F 8:30am-noon and 1-5pm. **ZIP Code:** Longmire 98397; Paradise 98398.

Area Code: 360.

ACCOMMODATIONS

Longmire, Paradise, and Sunrise offer accommodations that are usually too costly for the budget traveler. For a roof, stay in Ashford or Packwood. Otherwise, camp under the rooftop of the world.

Hotel Packwood, 102 Main St. (494-5431), in Packwood. A functioning hotel since 1912, this charming reminder of the Old West features crisp, clean rooms with antique furniture. Shared bathrooms. A sprawled-out grizzly graces the parlor. Singles $20-38; doubles (bunks) from $30-38.

Whittaker's Bunkhouse, 30205 S.R. 706 E., P.O. Box E, Ashford 98304 (569-2439). Spiffy accommodations with firm mattresses and sparkling clean showers, as well as a homey espresso bar, but no kitchen. The rooms are co-ed, but most clientele is male. Bring your own sleeping bag. Bunks $25; private rooms from $65. Reservations strongly recommended.

Paradise Inn (569-2275), in Paradise. This rustic inn, built in 1917 from Alaskan cedar, offers gorgeous views of the mountain. Small, cheerful singles and doubles from $69, each additional person $10. Open late May to early Oct. Reservations required in summer; call at least a month ahead.

CAMPGROUNDS AND BACKCOUNTRY CAMPING

Camping in the park is available on a first-come, first-served basis between mid-June and late September (sites $10-14). National park campgrounds all have facilities for the handicapped, but no hookups or showers. There are five campgrounds within the park: **Cougar Rock** (200 sites), near Longmire, with strict quiet hours (10pm-6am); **Ipsut Creek** (29 sites); **White River** (112 sites), in the northeastern corner of the park; **Sunshine Point** (18 sites), near the Nisqually entrance, with fine views; and lastly, **Ohanapecosh** (205 sites) with a serene high canopy of old growth trees (available by reservation only July 1st to Labor Day). In general, the grounds fill only on the busiest summer weekends. Sunshine Point is the only campground open year-round.

Backcountry camping requires a permit, available for $10 per group plus $5 per person at ranger stations and visitor centers. Be sure to ask about trail closures before setting off. Hikers with a valid permit can use any of the free, well-established trailside camps scattered in the park. Most camps have toilet facilities and a nearby water source, and some have shelters for groups of up to 12. Cross-country and alpine sites are high up the mountain on glaciers and snow fields. Fires are prohibited in all areas except front-country campgrounds. Quotas limit the number of members in a party. **Glacier climbers** and **mountain climbers** intending to scale above 10,000 ft. must register in person at ranger stations to be granted permits.

The **national forests** outside the park provide thousands of acres of freely campable countryside. When camping outside established sites, be sure to avoid eroded lakesides and riverbanks; flash floods and debris flows can catch campers unawares. **Campfires** are allowed only during the rainy season. Check with a national forest ranger station (see **Practical Information,** above) for more detailed information.

FOOD

The general stores in the area sell only last-minute trifles like bug repellant and marshmallows, and items are charged an extra state park tax; stock up before you go. **Blanton's Market,** 13040 U.S. 12 (494-6101), in Packwood, is the closest decent supermarket to the park and has an **ATM** in front (open daily 6am-10pm).

Ma & Pa Rucker's (494-2651), on U.S. 12 in Packwood. This pizza parlor/grill/mini mart/ice cream store/cafe satisfies any food need. The best pizza place in town (small $7; large $11) also serves tasty, greasy burgers. Peppermint candy ice cream $1; and ass kickin' beef jerky $4. Open M-Th 9am-9pm, F-Su 9am-10pm.

Wild Berry Restaurant, 37718 U.S. 706 (569-2628), between Ashford and the Nisqually entrance. A local favorite. Fried foods are against their religion. Get a Dunker and dip your sandwich in tasty *au jus* ($5.50). Open daily 11am-8pm.

SIGHTS AND OUTDOORS

Mount Adams and Mount St. Helens, not visible from the road, can be seen clearly from such mountain trails as **Paradise** (1½ mi.), **Pinnacle Peak** (2½ mi.), **Eagle Peak** (7 mi.), and **Van Trump Park** (5½ mi.). The visitor centers have handouts for hiking in each of the park's sections, often including maps, travel time, and level of intensity for several hikes in one area.

A segment of the **Pacific Crest Trail,** which runs from Mexico to the Canadian border, dodges in and out of the park's southeast corner. The **Wonderland Trail** winds 93 mi. up, down, and around the mountain. Hikers must get permits for the arduous but stunning trek, and must complete the hike in 10 to 14 days. Call the Longmire Wilderness Center (see **Practical Information,** above) for details on both hikes.

A trip to the **summit** of Mt. Rainier requires substantial preparation and expense. The ascent involves a vertical rise of more than 9000 ft. over a distance of nine or more miles, usually taking two days and an overnight stay at **Camp Muir** on the south side (10,000 ft.) or **Camp Schurman** on the east side (9500 ft.). Each camp has a ranger station, rescue cache, and some form of toilet. Permits for summit climbs cost $15 per person. Only experienced climbers should attempt the summit on their own; novices can sign up for a summit climb with **Rainier Mountaineering, Inc. (RMI)** (see **Practical Information,** above), which offers a one-day basic-climbing course followed by a two-day guided climb. You must bring your own camping gear and carry four meals to the camp. For more information, contact Park Headquarters or RMI.

Far less arduous, ranger-led **interpretive hikes** delve into everything from area history to local wildflowers. Each visitor center conducts hikes on its own schedule and most of the campgrounds have evening talks and campfire programs.

Longmire

Just inside the Nisqually entrance, Longmire is pretty and woodsy, but by no means the best that Rainier has to offer. Hit the visitor center for permits and maps. *(Open year-round daily F-Sa 6:30am-9pm, Su-Th 7am-8pm.)* Longmire's **museum,** near the visitor center, houses a small collection of stuffed animals along with a smattering of historic photos and artifacts documenting both Rainier's natural history and the history of human encounters with the mountain. *(Open in summer daily 9am-5pm; off-season daily 9am-4:30pm. Hours may vary.)*

The **Rampart Ridge Trail** (a 2½-hr., 4½ mi. loop) is a relatively moderate hike with excellent views of the Nisqually Valley, Mt. Rainier, and Tumtum Peak. The steep, four-hour, 5 mi. **Van Trump Park and Comet Falls Trail** is a more strenuous hike, passing Comet Falls and the occasional mountain goat. The trip to Comet Falls is only 1½ mi., and the spectacular view of the 320 ft. drop is well worth the trail traffic.

Longmire remains open during the winter as a center for snowshoeing, cross-country skiing, and other alpine activities. **Guest Services, Inc.** (569-2275) runs a cross-country ski center which rents skis and snowshoes, and runs skiing lessons on weekends. *(Skis $15 per day, children $9.75 per day. Snowshoes $7.25 per half day, $12 per day.)*

Paradise

Paradise, the most heavily visited corner of Rainier, is perhaps the only place in the park where the sound of babbling brooks and waterfalls might be drowned out by screaming children. If you can manage to avoid the bustle and arrive on a clear, sunny weekday, Paradise will be exactly that. Even in mid-June, the sparkling snowfields above timberline add a touch of white to the verdant forest canyons below. Two years ago, record snowfalls kept Paradise's trails snowed in through August.

The road from the Nisqually entrance to Paradise is open year-round, but the road east through Stevens Canyon closes from October to June. The **Paradise Visitor Center** has audio-visual programs and an observation deck. *(Open May to mid-October daily 9am-7pm. Oct.-Apr. open weekends and holidays 9am-7pm.)* From January to mid-April, park naturalists lead **snowshoe hikes** (569-2211) to explore winter ecology around Paradise. *(Sa-Su at 10:30am and 2:30pm. Snowshoe rental $1.)* In summer, look for postings in the visitor center for ranger-led hikes, talks, and wildflower walks.

Paradise is the starting point for several trails heading through the meadows to Mt. Rainiers's glaciers. The 5 mi. **Skyline Trail** is the longest of the loop trails, starting at the Paradise Inn; it is probably the closest a casual hiker can come to climbing the mountain. The first leg of the trail is often hiked by climbing parties headed for Camp Muir, the base camp for most ascents to the summit. The trail turns off before reaching Camp Muir, rising to a popular lookout spot at **Panorama Point.** Although only halfway up the mountain, the point is within view of the glaciers, and the summit appears deceptively close.

The mildly strenuous 2½ mi. hike up to **Pinnacle Peak** begins just east of Paradise, across the road from **Reflection Lake,** and offers clear views of Mt. Rainier, Mt. Adams, Mt. St. Helens, and Mt. Hood. One of the most striking aspects of hikes out of Paradise are the expanses of wildflower-strewn alpine meadows, some of the largest and most spectacular in the park.

Ohanapecosh and Carbon River

Though in opposite corners of the park, the Ohanapecosh and Carbon Rivers are in the same ranger district. Ohanapecosh's visitor center snuggles under old growth cedars along a river valley in the park's southeast corner, just a few miles north of Packwood, next door to the campground. *(Open mid-June to Sept. 9am-6pm; late May to mid-June open weekends and holidays 9am-6pm.)* One of the oldest stands of trees in Washington, the **Grove of Patriarchs,** grows here. An easy 1½ mi. walk leads to these 500- to 1000-year-old Douglas firs, cedars, and hemlocks. The visitor center leads walks to the Grove and shimmering **Silver Falls.** The **Summerland** and **Indian Bar Trails** are excellent for serious backpacking—this is where rangers go on their days (and nights) off.

Carbon River Valley, in the northwest corner of the park, is one of the only inland rainforests in the continental U.S., and its trails are on every ranger-in-the-know's top 10 list for hiking. **Spray Park** and **Mystic Camp** are superlative free backcountry campsites. Carbon River also has access to the **Wonderland Trail** (see above). Winter storms keep the road beyond the Carbon River entrance under constant distress. Because of floods in the spring of 1996, the road only reaches to the edge of the park. Check with rangers for updates and trip planning tips.

Sunrise

On the second day, God created Sunrise. No kidding. Too far from the entrance for most tourists to bother, Sunrise is pristine, unruffled, and divine. The winding road to the highest of the four visitor centers provides gorgeous views of Mt. Adams, Mt. Baker, and the heavily glaciated eastern side of Mt. Rainier. Trails vary greatly in difficulty; the visitor center has invaluable maps. Try the comfortably sloping **Mt. Burroughs Trail** (5 mi.) for unbeatable glacier views. Those ready for more leg stress should head to **Berkeley Park,** a 5 mi. round-trip trek into a wildflower-painted valley. For those longing to return to civilization, the 5.6 mi (4hr.) round-trip hike to **Mt. Fremont Lookout** affords a view of Seattle on a clear day.

■ Skykomish District

Stretching between the Puget Shore and Leavenworth along U.S. 2, the **Skykomish District** (sky-KOE-mish) begs urbanites to roam its river-plush, sub-alpine trails. Stop by the **Skykomish Ranger Station** (360-677-2414), off U.S. 2 at Mile 51, to chat about local hikes and campgrounds (open daily 8am-4:30pm). View-seekers, flower-lovers, and overnight campers all enjoy assaulting the 3½ mi. **Tonga Ridge Trail,** located ½ mi. past the ranger station. Turn right off the highway onto Foss River Rd. (Rd. #68), then left on Tonga Ridge Rd. (Rd. #6830) and continue 6 mi. to Spur #310. Bear right at the sign and continue 1 mi. to the trailhead. If in search of lakes, continue along Foss River Rd. 6 mi., then turn left at Rd. #6835 to get to **West Fork Foss Lake Trail.** Mountain bikers haul ass on the **Johnson Ridge Trail,** the only trail open to cyclists; get directions at the ranger station. Families and train aficionados make a much slower mosey along the **Iron Goat Trail,** a recently completed route along the old train tracks. Hikes rumble through tunnels and wildflowers. To find the Iron Goat, turn left onto the Old Cascade Hwy. (Rd. #67), past Mile 50; go 1.4 mi. to Rd. #6710, then turn left into trailhead parking.

■ Leavenworth

"Willkommen zu Leavenworth" proclaims the carved wooden sign at the entrance to this resort town/theme park. After the logging industry exhausted Leavenworth's natural resources and the railroad switching station moved to nearby Wenatchee, this rural mountain town was forced to concoct a tourist gimmick to survive. By the mid-60s, "Project Alpine" had painted a thick Bavarian veneer over Leavenworth. One can only wonder at the planners' *Weltanschauung.* Today, an estimated one million people annually visit this living Swiss Miss commercial, with massive influxes during the city's three annual festivals. Waiters in *lederhosen* work in restaurants with faux Teutonic nomenclature; loudspeakers pump relentless yodeling into the streets. Even the local McDonald's steps to the inescapable oompah beat. Never mind that no one knows any German; this town is an experience in inexplicable American tackiness. Renting a bike and heading for the nearby mountain splendor may be the best way to take a vacation from a vacation in Leavenworth.

ORIENTATION AND PRACTICAL INFORMATION

Leavenworth is approximately 121 mi. east of Seattle and 190 mi. west of Spokane, on the eastern slope of the Cascades near Washington's geographic center. **U.S. 2** bisects Leavenworth in the main business district. The north-south route through the area is **U.S. 97,** intersecting U.S. 2 about 6 mi. southeast of town.

Buses: Greyhound (800-231-2222). Stops west of town on U.S. 2 at the Department of Transportation. To: Spokane (1 per day, $22); Seattle (2 per day, $20).

Public Transportation: Link (662-1155 or 800-851-LINK/5465; http://www.link-transit.com). Free bus service! Runs 20 buses per day M-Sa between Wenatchee and Leavenworth, with several stops around town. The main stop is at the Park 'n' Ride lot, next to the ranger station. Pick up a schedule at the chamber. All buses have bike racks.

Visitor Information: Chamber of Commerce, 894 U.S. 2 (548-5807), in the Clocktower Bldg. Helpful staff, many of whom see nothing amusing in their town gimmick. Open M-Sa 8am-6pm, Su 10am-4pm; in winter M-Sa 8am-5pm.

Outdoor Information: Ranger Station, 600 Sherbourne (782-1413 or 548-4067), just off U.S. 2. Info on the mountains surrounding town, especially the world-class rock climbing-scene. Pick up a list of the 9 developed campgrounds within 20 mi. of Leavenworth. Open daily 7:45am-4:30pm; in winter M-F 7:45am-4:30pm.

Equipment Rental: Der Sportsmann, 837 Front St. (548-5623). Mountain bikes $20 per day, $12 per half-day (only after 2pm), cross-country skis $14 per day. Also rents climbing shoes ($8) and snow shoes ($12). Hiking and biking maps available. Open summer daily 9am-7pm; off-season 10am-6pm.

Senior Center: 423 Evans (548-6666), behind the chamber of commerce.

Weather: 665-6565. **Cascade Snow Report:** 353-7440.

Emergency: 911. **Police:** (782-3770), 401 Washington St.

Pharmacy: Village Pharmacy, 821 Front St. (548-7731). Open M-F 8:30am-6:30pm, Sa 9am-5:30pm, Su 11am-5pm.

Hospital: Cascade Medical Center, 817 Commercial St. (548-5815). Walk-in clinic open M-F 8am-7pm, Sa 8am-5pm, Su 11am-5pm. Emergency room 24hr.

Post Office: 960 U.S. 2 (548-7212). Open M-F 9am-5pm, Sa 9-11am. **ZIP Code:** 98826.

Area Code: 509.

ACCOMMODATIONS AND CAMPGROUNDS

Hotels start at $50 for singles, and most cost more. Camping is plentiful, inexpensive, and spectacular in the surrounding national forest. If seeking solitude, avoid weekend stays after Memorial Day. Otherwise, come early, or there may not be any spots at *die Kampingplätzen.*

Wenatchee National Forest (782-1413). 10 mi. from town along Icicle Creek Road, a series of 7 Forest Service campgrounds squeeze between the creek and the road. The farther west the campground, the prettier the site—try the Johnny Creek campground for secluded forest sites or Ida Creek for proximity to the river. RVs and trailers may find the road difficult to maneuver. To get there, take the last left in town on U.S. 2 heading west. All campgrounds have drinking water and pit toilets; the closest to town costs $9, all others $8.

Tumwater (800-280-2267), 10 mi. west of Leavenworth on U.S. 2. A Forest Service campground with water, flush toilets, and wheelchair access. 84 sites: $11.

FOOD

Predictably, Leavenworth's food mimics German cuisine; surprisingly, it often succeeds. German *Wurst* booths are tucked between buildings everywhere, but those looking for much more than die Frankfurters should be prepared to pay at least $8-16 for a full dinner. At the alpine **Safeway,** 940 U.S. 2 (548-5435), groceries *schmecken mir gut* (open daily 7am-11pm).

The Leavenworth Brewery, 636 Front St. (548-4545). This microbrewery justifies Leavenworth's Disney-fication of Bavaria by serving up tasty local ales (16 oz. $3) and pub fare (mini-pizzas $4.25). The brewery also sponsors Sa night performances and the occasional Tacky Polyester Prom Night. Check out the tour at 2pm. Open Su-Th 11am-10pm, F-Sa 11am-midnight.

Leavenworth Pizza Company, 892 U.S. 2 (548-7766). Next to the visitor center, this family-owned restaurant offers tasty pizzas and a mostly local atmosphere as a respite from schnitzel-crazed tourists. 2-person pizza $7-10. Open M-Th 4-9pm, F 4-10pm, Sa 11am-10pm, Su 11am-9pm.

Monaco's Corner Store, 703 Front St. (548-7216). The deli inside the store serves fairly inexpensive sandwiches ($4.75). Lunch specials $5-6. Open Su-Th 9am-5:30pm, F-Sa 9am-7pm.

Los Comparos, 200 6th St. (548-3314). Not cheap, but hey, it could be wurst. Lunch specials $4-7, dinner $7-11. Open daily noon-10pm.

Aplets and Cotlets Factory, 117 Mission St. (782-4088), in Cashmere on the way south to the U.S. 97 junction; follow signs from U.S. 2. Free tours of the plant and ample samples of their gooey candies. The factory dishes out paper hats and everything you ever wanted to know about turning apples and apricots into sugary confections. Open M-F 8am-5:30pm, Sa-Su 10am-4pm; in winter M-F 8:30am-4:30pm.

OUTDOORS

Except for tourist-watching and sausage-scarfing, the most compelling reason to come to Leavenworth is for the extensive hiking, mountain biking, and climbing opportunities in the **Wenatchee National Forest.** The heavily visited **Alpine Lakes Wilderness,** stretching south of town, is as beautiful as it is clogged with hikers. Be careful to stay on the trails—the region is home to many black bears and western rattlesnakes lacking *Gemütlichkeit.* The **ranger station** in Leavenworth (see **Practical Information,** above) hands out free descriptions of hikes near town, ranked by distance and difficulty. An informative guide to all the area's trails costs $1.50. One pleasant dayhike is the moderately sloping 3½ mi. trail to **Eight Mile Lake,** a great spot for a picnic or overnight backpacking. Drive 9.4 mi. up Icicle Creek Rd., make a left onto Eight Mile Rd., then continue 3 mi. uphill to the trailhead. The 3½ mi. **Icicle Gorge Trail** starts just east of the **Chatter Creek Campground** on Icicle Rd., and moseys along beside the cool creek waters.

Although most trails in this area are unrestricted, **permits** are required to enter the popular **Stuart Lake, Colcheck Lake, Snow Lakes,** and **Enchantment Lakes** areas. Permits are free and self-registered for dayhikers, with forms at the ranger station or the trailheads. Permits for **backcountry overnights,** however, cost $3 per person per night, and must be reserved at least two weeks in advance by mailing in an application. Call the ranger station for info on obtaining an application; more spur-of-the-moment sorts can cross their fingers and visit the ranger station, where a number of free permits are distributed by lottery each morning at 7:45am, though there are often more than enough to go around.

The **Leavenworth Winter Sports Club**, P.O. Box 573, Leavenworth 98826 (548-5115), maintains the trail system in winter. Pick up a free copy of their *Cross-Country Ski Guide* at the ranger station. **Eagle Creek Ranch** (548-7798 or 800-221-7433; http://www.eaglecreek.simplenet.com), offers horseback rides ($25 for 5 mi.), hay rides ($12), and horse-drawn sleigh rides in winter ($15). To get there, go north on Rte. 209 (Chumstick Rd.), turn right on Eagle Creek Rd., and go 5½ mi to the ranch's main entrance.

■ Lake Chelan

The serpentine body of Lake Chelan (sha-LAN) undulates over 50 mi. northwest from the Columbia River and U.S. 97 into the eastern Cascades. Perched amid bone-dry hills and apple orchards, the town named for the lake has developed a pricey tourist industry geared to seniors and families with motor boats in tow. Up the lake, brown hills transform into vermilion mountains as the North Cascades flaunt their awesome beauty. The lake, at points 1500 ft. deep, extends far into Wenatchee National Forest and pokes its northwesternmost tip into the Lake Chelan National Recreation Area, a section of North Cascades National Park. While the town of Chelan has become little more than a cutesy resort, Stehekin (ste-HEE-kin), at the other end of the lake, offers solitude, space, and access to a vast wilderness.

PRACTICAL INFORMATION The town of Chelan rests on the southeast end of Lake Chelan, along Hwy. 97.

> **Public Transportation: Link** (800-851-5465), the local bus service, has hourly service to Wenatchee, a **Greyhound** stop.
>
> **Visitor Information: Chamber of Commerce,** 102 E. Johnson (682-3503 or 800-4-CHELAN/24-3526), has plenty of info on Chelan and nearby Mansom. Open M-F 9am-5pm, Sa 9am-4pm, Su 11am-3pm; in winter M-F 9am-5pm.
>
> **Outdoor Information: Chelan Ranger Station,** 428 W. Woodin Ave. (682-2549), on the lakeshore just south of town, dishes the goods on the area's forests and recreation areas. Open daily 7:45am-4:30pm; Oct.-May M-F 7:45am-4:30pm.
>
> **Equipment Rental: Nature Gone Wild,** 109 S. Emerson (682-8680). Bikes $5 per hr., $24 per day. In-line skates $3 for the first hr., $2 per each additional hr. Paragliding equipment also available. Open M-Sa 10am-5pm.
>
> **Laundromat: Town Tub Laundry,** on the east end of Woodin Ave. Wash $1.25, dry 25¢ per 10min. Open daily 8am-10pm.
>
> **Emergency:** 911. **Police:** 207 N. Emerson St. (682-2588).
>
> **Crisis Line:** 662-7105. 24hr.
>
> **Pharmacy: Green's Drugs,** 212 E. Woodin Ave. (682-2566). Open M-F 9am-6pm, Sa 9am-5:30pm, Su as posted.
>
> **Hospital: Lake Chelan Community,** 503 E. Highland St. (682-2531). Open 24hr.
>
> **Post Office:** 144 E. Johnson (682-2625) Open M-F 8:30am-5pm. **ZIP Code:** 98816.
>
> **Internet Access: River Walk Books,** 113 Emerson St. (682-8901). $6 per hr. Open M-Sa 9:30am-6pm, Su 11am-4pm.
>
> **Area Code:** 509.

ACCOMMODATIONS, CAMPGROUNDS, AND FOOD Most Chelan motels and resorts are too busy exploiting sun-starved visitors from Puget Sound to bother being affordable. One exception is **Apple Inn**, 1002 E. Woodin (682-4044), an AAA-approved motel that boasts a small-time hot tub and pool. The standard motel rooms are clean and neat ($49-59; in winter up to $20 cheaper). **Mom's Montlake Motel,** 823 Wapato (682-5715), around the corner at Clifford, is a mom-and-pop operation with clean, microwave- or kitchen-equipped rooms (from $48, closed Oct.-Apr.).

Most campers head for **Lake Chelan State Park** (687-3710), a pleasantly grassy yet crowded campground 9 mi. up the south shore of the lake, with a beach and swimming area, small store, and jet ski rentals (144 sites: $11; hookups $16; reservations recommended Apr.-Sept.). To reach **Ramona Park,** a free, primitive campground, turn left onto Forest Rd. 5900 near the end of the South Shore Rd., then left again onto Forest Rd. 8410 after 2½ mi., and continue another ½ mi. Campers may also pitch tents for free anywhere they please in the national forest. Fires must be kept in previously established fire rings.

The cheapest eats in Chelan are at local fruit stands, the **Safeway,** 106 W. Manson Rd. (682-2615; open daily 6am-midnight), or **Bear Foods** (a.k.a. Golden Florin's General Store), 125 E. Woodin Ave. (682-5535 or 800-842-8049), which sells a wide variety of natural foods and everything from Ben and Jerry's ice cream to books on tofu (open M-Sa 9am-7pm, Su noon-5pm). The unpretentious **Dagwood's International Kitchen,** 246 W. Manson Way (682-8630), serves *pad thai* ($5.50) and many kinds of stir-fry (open daily 11am-"the after-dinner slow down"). For the coffee addict, **Flying Saucers,** 116 S. Emerson (682-5129), offers lattes and aura galore in a converted 50s diner (open M-Sa 7:30am-5:30pm, Su 7:30am-5pm).

■ Stehekin

For less than the price of a motel room in touristy Chelan, you can take a ferry over 50 mi. of sparkling turquoise waters to Stehekin, a tiny town at the mouth of a magnificent valley, catch a shuttle bus a few miles up the valley, camp for free on the banks of a rushing, crystal green river, and spend days exploring some of the most beautiful country in the Cascades.

GETTING THERE The **Lake Chelan Boat Company,** 1418 W. Woodin (682-2224; http://www.ladyofthelake.com), about 1 mi. west of town, runs the *Lady of the Lake II,* a 350-person ferry that makes one round-trip to Stehekin per day ($22). Catch the ferry at Chelan (departs 8:30am, returns 6pm; daytime parking free, overnight $5) or at Fields Point, 16 mi. up the South Shore Rd. near Twenty-Five Mile Creek State Park (departs 9:45am, returns 4:45pm; parking $3 per day, $17 per week). The *Lady Express* is a smaller boat that makes a faster, non-stop trip to Stehekin for a higher price (round-trip $41). A combination ticket for the *Lady Express* to Stehekin and the *Lady of the Lake II* back to Chelan runs $41 as well, and provides 3¼hr. in Stehekin. A new high-speed catamaran, the *Lady Cat,* provides two high-speed round trips daily leaving at 7:45am and 1:30pm (call for prices). Purchase tickets in advance on summer weekends; the ferries often fill with eager tourists and backpackers, and they will not accept credit cards on the day of travel. The scenery gets increasingly impressive as the boat proceeds uplake; the views on the ride alone are worth the price. Mountain goats and brown bears sometimes roam the lakeside.

CAMPGROUNDS AND FOOD The Park Service maintains 12 primitive **campgrounds** along the Stehekin Valley Road. Get the free but required permit at the ranger station in Chelan (see p. 230) or at Stehekin's **Golden West Visitor Center** (856-6055 ext. 14), where exuberant rangers can help plan anything from a one-hour jaunt to a 10-day backcountry trip (open daily 8am-5pm). The closest campground is at **Purple Point,** right next to the ferry landing. Its six sites have water, free hot showers, and bathrooms. Solitude-seekers can take the **Stehekin Adventure Shuttle** to **Harlequin Campground,** 5 mi. upriver. Harlequin has tables, fire pits, and riverside views, but no water.

There are a few dining options in the valley. Three, to be exact. A delicious country dinner at the **Stehekin Valley Ranch** (682-4677 or 800-536-0745) costs about $12. It's necessary to make reservations by phone or at Discovery Bikes (see **Outdoors,** below) and catch a bus up to the ranch (round-trip $2). The **Lodge Restaurant** (682-4494), at the landing, serves expensive burgers ($5-6) and dinners ($7-15). Just two miles up the only road, the **Stehekin Pastry Company** lures hikers out of the hills to snack on fat, sticky buns ($1.85; open daily 8am-5pm).

OUTDOORS Some short but scenic day hikes surround the landing. The mellow **Lakeshore Trail** starts behind the visitor center and follows the west shore of Lake Chelan for 17½ mi. to **Prince Creek.** A similarly simple alternative is the ¾ mi. **Imus Creek Trail,** a self-guided interpretive trail starting behind the Golden West Visitor Center. After passing fast-flowing **Purple Creek,** take a right turn up the switchbacks of the steep **Purple Creek Trail.** The 5500 ft. climb is tough, but rewards effort with a magnificent view of the lake and surrounding glaciers. In the opposite direction, the moderately steep **Rainbow Loop Trail** offers more stellar valley views. The 5 mi. trail begins 3 mi. from Stehekin; **Stehekin Transportation Services** runs a shuttle to the trailhead five times a day, but it's close enough to walk, and residents rarely hesitate to provide a ride. Bikes are available at **Discovery Bikes** (686-3014; $3.50 per hr., $10 per half-day, $15 per day), or at the **Lodge** ($3.50 per hr., $15 per day).

An unpaved road and many trails probe north from Stehekin into **North Cascades National Park.** In summer, the **Stehekin Valley Ranch** (682-4677 or 800-536-0745) runs four **shuttle buses** daily from Stehekin to High Bridge, deeper into the park ($5). The Park Service runs a second shuttle from High Bridge to Bridge Creek ($5), which provides access to the **Pacific Crest Trail.** Reservations are highly recommended for the shuttle (call 360-856-5700 ext. 340, then ext. 14). All walk-in campgrounds in the park are free and open May to October; drinking water is not provided. **Backcountry permits** are mandatory in the park throughout the year, and are available at the visitor center or the Chelan Ranger Station (see p. 230) on a first-come, first-served basis. The station also provides tips on bear-proofing hiking and camping gear (see p. 47).

Two dayhikes start from **High Bridge.** The mellow **Agnes Gorge Trail** begins 200 yards. beyond the bridge (second trail on the left), and travels a level 2½ mi. through forests and meadows with views of **Agnes Mountain,** ending where **Agnes Creek** takes a dramatic plunge into **Agnes Gorge.** Behind the ranger cabin, the **McGregor Mountain Trail** is a straight shot up the side of the mountain, climbing 6525 vertical ft. over a distance of 8 mi., and ending with unsurpassed views of the high North Cascades peaks. The last ½ mi. is a scramble up ledges. This extremely difficult trail is often blocked by snow well into July; check at the visitor center before starting out.

The **Rainbow Falls Tour** ($6), in Stehekin, which caters to ferry arrival times, zooms through the valley and its major sights: the one-room **Stehekin School;** the **Stehekin Pastry Company,** a bakery in a log cabin in the woods; and **Rainbow Falls,** a misty 312 ft. cataract.

■ North Cascades (Rte. 20)

A favorite stomping ground for grizzlies, deer, mountain goats, black bears, and Jack Kerouac *(The Dharma Bums),* the North Cascades are one of the most rugged expanses of land in the continental U.S. The dramatic peaks stretch north from Stevens Pass on U.S. 2 to the Canadian border, and are preserved in pristine condition by several different government agencies. The centerpiece of the area is **North Cascades National Park,** which straddles the crest of the Cascades. The green wilderness and astonishingly steep peaks attract backpackers and mountain climbers from around the world. **Route 20** (open Apr.-Nov., weather permitting), a road designed for unadulterated driving pleasure, is the primary means of access to the area and awards jaw-dropping views at every curve.

A backcountry extravaganza of untrammeled land, jagged peaks, and an Eden of wildlife and flora, much of the wilderness is inaccessible without at least a day's uphill hike. Ira Springs' *100 Hikes in Washington: The North Cascades National Park Region* is a good guide for recreational hikers, while Fred Beckley's *Cascade Alpine Guide* targets the more serious high-country traveler.

Route 20 (I-5 Exit 230) follows the Skagit River east to the small towns of **Sedro Wooley, Concrete,** and **Marblemount** in the **Mount Baker-Snoqualmie National**

Forest. The highway then enters North Cascades National Park via the **Ross Lake National Recreation Area,** one of the two designated recreation areas within the National Park. After passing through **Newhalem, Diablo Lake,** and **Ross Lake,** Rte. 20 leaves the National Park and enters the **Okanogan National Forest District,** crossing Washington Pass (5477 ft.), and descending to the Methow River and the dry Okanogan rangeland of Eastern Washington. The **Lake Chelan National Recreation Area** occupies the southern tip of the national park, bordered on the south by the Wenatchee National Forest. When making phone calls to the area, make note of the area code—it changes as quickly as the scenery.

■ Rte. 20: Sedro Woolley to Marblemount

Though situated in the rich farmland of the lower Skagit Valley, **Sedro Woolley** is primarily a logging town. The volunteers at the **Visitor Information Center** (360-855-0974), in the train caboose at the intersection of Rte. 20 and Ferry St., have far too much time on their hands and are extremely eager to help those who drop in (open daily 9am-4pm).

Sedro Woolley also houses the **North Cascades National Park and Mt. Baker-Snoqualmie National Forest Headquarters,** 2105 Rte. 20 (360-856-5700; open Sa-Th 8am-4:30pm, F 8am-6pm). Call 206-526-6677 for **snow avalanche info.** Backcountry campers must contact the Wilderness Information Center in Marblemount (see below) for a backcountry permit. The main attraction of this village is the annual **Sedro Woolley Loggerodeo** (855-1129), held over the 4th of July weekend. Axethrowing, pole-climbing, and sawing competitions vie for center stage with rodeo events like bronco-busting and calf-roping. Contact the Loggerodeo at P.O. Box 712, Sedro Woolley 98284.

Route 9 leads north from Sedro Woolley, providing indirect access to **Mt. Baker** (see p. 191) through the forks at the Nooksack River and Rte. 542. The turn-off for **Baker Lake Highway** is 23 mi. east of Sedro Wooley at Mile 82, which dead-ends 25 mi. later at Baker Lake. Several campsites can be found along the road to **Baker Lake.** The best bargain is the crowded **Kulshan Campground,** which has drinking water, and flush toilets (79 sites: $5). Among the others, **Horseshoe Cove** (34 sites: $12; $6.50 for additional vehicles; wheelchair accessible) and **Panorama Point** (16 sites: $7; $6.50 for additional vehicles; wheelchair accessible) have drinking water and toilets (call 800-280-CAMP/2267 for $8.25 reservations).

On Rte. 20, east of Sedro Woolley by 32 mi. lies the tiny town of **Concrete,** where rows of businesses made of concrete pay homage to a now defunct local industry. Farther east, right before the western boundary of the relatively small **Rockport State Park,** Sauk Mountain Road (Forest Service Rd. 1030) makes a stomach-scrambling climb up Sauk Mountain. A view of Mt. Rainier, Puget Sound, and the San Juan Islands awaits the peak-bound driver, 7 mi. up and a right turn at Rd. 1036. The road is bumpy and a thorough dust bath; trailers, RVs, and the faint of heart should not attempt the ascent. The **Sauk Mountain Trail** begins at the parking lot and winds 3½ mi. to backcountry campsites near Sauk Lake. The park also has a trail that accommodates wheelchairs and 50 developed campsites ($10; full hookups $15, each extra vehicle $5; 3-sided adirondack cabins with 8-person bunk beds $15, no reservations).

If Rockport is full, continue 1 mi. east to Skagit County's **Howard Miller Steelhead Park** (360-853-8808), on the Skagit River, where anglers come to catch the park's tasty namesake (steelhead, not Howard Miller; 49 sites: tent sites $12, hookups $16, 3-sided adirondack lean-tos $16). The surrounding **Mt. Baker-Snoqualmie National Forest** permits free camping closer to the high peaks, but requires trail park passes, available at Forest Service and local businesses ($3 per day). These passes are not required when parking in North Cascades National Park.

At **Marblemount** is **Good Food** (873-2771), a small family diner at the east edge of town along Rte. 20. This pithy eatery not only boasts riverside picnic tables and bikers with whom to talk Harleys, but also a great vegetarian sandwich ($3.60) and thick, tasty shakes ($2.25; open daily 9am-9pm; in winter 9am-6pm). Stock up on drinking water at **Marblemount Mercantile Market** (873-4274), on Rte. 20 (open 9am-9pm; in winter 9am-7pm), and cruise 8 mi. east along Cascade River Rd. to **Marble Creek** (24 sites) or 16 mi. east to **Mineral Park** (8 sites). Both are free, but have no drinking water. The **Marblemount Wilderness Information Center,** 728 Ranger Station Rd., Marblemount 98267 (873-4500 ext. 39), 1 mi. north of Marblemount on a well-marked road from the west end of town, hands out plenty of info on the national park. This is also the place to go for a **backcountry permit** and to plan longer hiking excursions. Say what you will about their hats; the rangers are on the ball (open in summer Su-Th 7am-6pm, F-Sa 7am-8pm; call for winter hours).

From Marblemount, it's 22 mi. along Cascade River Rd. to the trailhead for a 3½ mi. hike to the amazing **Cascade Pass,** which then continues on to Lake Chelan. Stehekin, at the northern tip of Lake Chelan, is reachable only by boat, plane, or foot (see p. 231). Call the **Golden West Visitor Center** (856-5700 ext. 14), in Stehekin, for detailed info on shuttle buses and trails.

■ Rte. 20: Ross Lake & North Cascades National Park

Newhalem is the first town on Rte. 20 after it crosses into the **Ross Lake Recreation Area,** a buffer zone between the highway and North Cascades National Park. At the tourist-friendly **North Cascades Visitor Center and Ranger Station** (206-386-4495), off Rte. 20, the mystical and atonal slide show provides a meditative glimpse into the Cascades' natural wonders (open daily 8:30am-6pm; in winter Sa-Su 9am-4:30pm). Serious backpackers and climbers should bypass this kinder, gentler center and head directly to the hard-core Marblemount Wilderness Information Center (see above). Among the most popular and accessible hikes is the **Thunder Creek Trail,** which extends through old growth cedar and fir forests, beginning from the Colonial Creek Campground (see below) at Rte. 20 Mile 130. The 3.2 mi. **Fourth of July Pass Trail** begins approximately 2 mi. into the Thunder Creek Trail, and climbs 3500 ft. toward hellzapoppin' views.

Seattle City Light (206-233-2709), in **Diablo,** operates a small museum and provides tours of the **Skagit Hydroelectric Project,** which generates 40% of Seattle's electricity. Tour highlights include a walk across **Diablo Dam,** a ride up the 560 ft. Incline Railway, and another thrilling informational video (visitor center open Th-M 9am-4pm; tours 10am, 1, and 3pm; $5). The artificial and astoundingly green-blue expanse of **Ross Lake,** behind **Ross Dam,** snakes into the mountains as far as the Canadian border. The lake is only accessible by trails and is ringed by 15 campgrounds, some accessible by trail, others only by boat. The national park's **Goodell Creek Campground,** just south of Newhalem, has 22 leafy sites suitable for tents and trailers, with drinking water, pit toilets, and a launch site for whitewater rafting on the Skagit River (sites $7; water turned off after Oct., when sites are free). **Colonial Creek Campground,** 10 mi. to the east, is a fully developed, wheelchair accessible campground with flush toilets, a dump station, and campfire programs some evenings (164 sites: $10; no hookups). **Newhalem Creek Campground,** at Mile 120 near the visitor center, is a similarly developed facility with a less impressive forest of small pines, especially good for trailers and RVs (129 sites: $10). The **Skagit General Store** (386-4489), east of the visitor center, sells fishing licenses and basic groceries (open M-Th 7:30am-5:30pm, F-Su 7:30am-6:30pm; in winter M-F 7:30am-5:30pm).

■ Rte. 20: Ross Lake to Winthrop

This is the most beautiful segment of Rte. 20. Leaving the basin of Ross Lake, the road begins to climb, exposing the jagged, snowy peaks of the North Cascades. Thirty miles of astounding views east, the **Pacific Crest Trail** crosses Rte. 20 at **Rainy Pass** on one of the most scenic and difficult legs of its 2500 mi. Canada-to-Mexico route. Near Rainy Pass, groomed scenic trails of 1-3 mi. can be hiked in sneakers, provided the snow has melted (about mid-July). Just off Rte. 20, an overlook at **Washington Pass** (Mile 162) rewards a ½ mi. walk on a wheelchair accessible paved trail with one of the state's most dramatic panoramas, an astonishing view of the red rocks exposed by Early Winters Creek in **Copper Basin**. The area has many well-marked trailheads off Rte. 20 that lead into the desolate wilderness. The popular 2½ mi. walk to **Blue Lake** begins just east of Washington Pass. An easier 2 mi. hike to **Cutthroat Lake** departs from an access road 4½ mi. east of Washington Pass. From the lake, the trail continues 4 mi. farther and almost 2,000 ft. higher to **Cutthroat Pass,** treating determined hikers to a breathtaking view of towering, rugged peaks.

The hair-raising 23 mi. road to **Hart's Pass** begins at **Mazama,** on Rd. 1163, 10 mi. east of Washington Pass. The gravel road snakes up to the highest pass crossed by any road in the state. Breathtaking views await the steel-nerved driver, both from the pass and from **Slate Peak,** the site of a lookout station 3 mi. beyond the pass. The road is closed to trailers and is only accessible when the snow has melted. Check at the Methow Valley Visitor Center in Winthrop to find out its status.

■ Rte. 20: Winthrop to Twisp

Farther east is **Winthrop,** a town desperately and somewhat successfully trying to market its frontier history. At the **Winthrop Information Station,** 202 Riverside (509-996-2125), at the junction with Rte. 20, the staff laud the beauty of this Nouveau Old West town (open daily early May to mid-Oct. 10am-5pm). Winthrop's summer is bounded by rodeos on Memorial and Labor Day weekends. Late July brings the top-notch **Winthrop Rhythm and Blues Festival** (509-997-2541), where big name blues bands flock to belt their tunes, endorse radio stations, and play cowboy. Tickets for the three-day event cost $35 ($45 at the door). **Rocking Horse Ranch** (509-996-2768), 10 mi. west of Winthrop on Rte. 20, gives guided trail rides ($25 per 1½hr.). Rent a bike ($15 for 4hr., $20 per day) at **Winthrop Mountain Sports,** 257 Riverside Ave. (509-996-2886; open M-F 9am-6pm, Sa 9am-6:30pm, Su 9am-5:30pm; winter hours vary slightly).

The **Methow Valley Visitor Center** (MET-how), Bldg. 49, Rte. 20 (509-996-4000; email fsinfo@methow.com), hands out information on area camping, hiking and cross-country skiing (open daily 9am-5pm; call for winter hours). For more in-depth skiing and hiking trail information, call the **Methow Valley Sports Trail Association** (509-996-3287), which cares for 175km of trails in the area. Between Winthrop and Twisp on East Country Rd. #9129, the **North Cascades Smokejumper Base** (997-2031) is a center for folks who get their kicks by parachuting into forest fires and putting them out. The courageously insane smokejumpers give a thorough tour of the base and explain the procedures and equipment used to help them fight the fires and stay alive (open daily in summer and early fall 9am-6pm; tours 10am-5pm).

A Room with a View

While on Rte. 20 anywhere east of Mazama, look north to the highest mountain, and on top you'll see a small hut: the Goat Peak Lookout, home to local celebrity Lightnin' Bill and his trusty dog Lookout Turk. Lightnin' Bill, so nicknamed not because he's speedy but because he "loves to be up here during those lightnin' storms," inhabits one of the last manned (and dogged) fire lookouts in the state. What does he do for weeks at a time in a one-room hut, 7000 ft. in the sky? Bill writes poetry (he'll read you some when you reach the tower), enjoys the view, and chats with visitors that make the hike to his isolated home. To visit Bill and Turk, head east from Mazama 2 mi. on County Rd. #1163 to the gravel Forest Rd. #52. Continue 2.7 mi. along the dusty road and turn left on Forest Road #5225. Drive 6.2 mi. and turn right on road #5225-200. Continue 2.4 mi. to the end of the road and the beginning of the trailhead. (The directions are far more complicated than the actual driving.) The trail to the fire lookout is a steep 2½ mi. jaunt, and passes through colorful alpine meadows. Bill will show you everything about his little home, from the lightning rod above to the glass ashtrays under the bedposts that insulate him from electrical storms. Then he'll take your picture and you'll be recorded in his ever-growing photo album forever.

Flee Winthrop's prohibitively expensive hotels and restaurants to sleep in **Twisp**, the town that should have been a breakfast cereal. It was actually named for a local Native American word for yellowjacket, "T-wapsp." Nine miles south of Winthrop on Rte. 20, this peaceful village offers lower prices and far fewer tourists than its neighbor. The **Twisp Ranger Station,** 502 Glover St. (997-2131), employs a crunchy and helpful staff fortified with essential trail and campground guides (open M-F 7:45am-4:30pm). **The Sportsman Motel,** 1010 E. Rte. 20 (997-2911), a hidden jewel, where a barracks-like facade masks tastefully decorated rooms with kitchens (singles $39; doubles $43). The **Glover Street Cafe,** 104 N. Glover St. (997-1323), offers gourmet salads ($3.25) and sandwiches ($5.75) with soup or salad (open M-F 8am-3pm). Grab dessert or a take-out lunch special ($2-5) at the **Cinnamon Twisp Bakery,** 116 N. Glover St. (997-5030; open M-F 7am-5pm, Sa 7am-3pm).

There are many **campgrounds** and **trails** 15 to 25 mi. up Twisp River Road, just off Rte. 20 in Twisp. Most of the campsites are primitive and have a $5 fee. For camping closer to the highway, head to the **Riverbend RV Park,** 19951 Rte. 20 (997-3500 or 800-686-4498), 2 mi. west of Twisp. Beyond an abundance of slow-moving beasts (RVs), Riverbend has plenty of comfy tent sites situated along the Methow River (office open 9am-10pm; sites $14; hookups $18, $2 per person after 2 people). From Twisp, Rte. 20 continues east to **Okanogan** and Rte. 153 runs south to **Lake Chelan.**

EASTERN WASHINGTON

Lying in the Cascade's rain shadow, the hills and valleys of the Columbia River Basin once fostered little more than sagebrush and tumbleweed. The 20th century brought the construction of 10 dams on the Columbia River, making irrigation possible; now the basin yields bumper crops of fruit and high-quality wine. Sunshine defies the rainy Washington stereotype, ripening some of the world's best apples and bronzing flocks of visitors from Puget Sound. The region has a calm beauty, palpable in patchwork farmland, in numerous waterways, and in sand dunes where the Army has established training grounds and the Park Service has designated wilderness reserves.

HIGHLIGHTS OF EASTERN WASHINGTON

- **Spokane's** brief glory days live on in **Riverfront Park** (see p. 241), while **Manito Park** (see p. 241) offers diversion of the more pastoral persuasion.
- All greenery aside, the **Grand Coulee Dam** (see p. 238) is the largest concrete structure in the world.
- Though girdled by resorts, **Coeur d'Alene, ID** (see p. 243) still has a great lake and a laid-back atmosphere.
- The **Pullman Lentil Festival** is described on p. 245. Must you hesitate?

■Yakima

With volcanic soil, a fresh groundwater supply, and 300 days of sunshine per year, Yakima and the Yakima Valley lay claim to some of the most fertile land on the planet. The fruit bowl of the nation churns out more apples, mint, and hops than any other county in the U.S. This production yields generous prices; pounds of in-season peaches in Yakima often cost less than single peaches in other parts of the country. Unfortunately, not everything in the fruit bowl is peachy. Yakima has an extremely high crime rate, and the city itself offers little besides accommodations for the mountain-bound or Vancouver-Portland travelers. The main attractions of the Yakima Valley are the wineries and orchards outside the city proper.

ORIENTATION AND PRACTICAL INFORMATION Yakima is on I-82, 145 mi. southeast of Seattle and 145 mi. northwest of Pendleton, OR. The **Yakima Valley** lies southeast of the city, along I-82. A lush path follows the Yakima River through the **Yakima**

Greenway, a corridor of preserved land running from **Robertson Landing** (I-82 Exit 34) to **Harlan Landing** in the town of **Selah Grove** (I-82 Exit 31). Numbered streets line up east of the railroad tracks, while numbered avenues line up west.

Buses: Greyhound, 602 E. Yakima (457-5131), stops in Yakima on the way to Portland (4 per day, $30) and Seattle (4 per day, $23). There is no service from Yakima to Mt. Rainier. Open M-F 7:45am-4:45pm, Sa 7:45am-4:30pm, Su when buses arrive.

Public Transportation: Yakima Transit (575-6175), centered at 4th and Chestnut St., runs buses on 10 convenient routes. 50¢, seniors 25¢, ages 6-18 35¢. Runs M-F 5am-7pm, Sa 8am-7pm.

Taxis: Diamond Cab, 453-3113. 24hr.

Car Rental: Savemore Auto Rentals, 615 S. 1st St. (575-5400). $18 per day; 15¢ per mi. over 100 mi. Must be 21.

Visitor Information: Yakima Valley Visitor and Convention Bureau, 10 N. 8th St. (575-3010), at E. Yakima. Open M-F 8am-5pm, Sa 9am-5pm, Su 10am-4pm; Oct-Apr. M-F 8am-5pm.

Senior Information and Assistance: 7200 W. Nob Hill #12 (965-0502). Open M-F 8:30am-5pm.

Laundromat: K's Coin Laundry, 602 Fruitvale St. (452-5335). Wash $1.25, dry 25¢ per 7½min. Open daily 7am-9pm.

Emergency: 911. **Police:** 200 S. 3rd St. (575-6200).

Crisis Line: 575-4200. 24hr.

Pharmacy: Medicine Mart, 306 E. Yakima Ave. (248-9061). Open M-F 9am-6pm.

Hospitals: Yakima Valley Memorial, 2811 Tieton Dr. (575-8000). **Providence Medical Center,** 110 S. 9th Ave. (575-5000). Both 24hr.

Post Office: 205 W. Washington Ave. (800-275-8777), at 3rd Ave. Open M-F 8:30am-5pm. **ZIP Code:** 98903.

Area Code: 509.

ACCOMMODATIONS AND CAMPGROUNDS

The fruit bowl is overflowing with reasonably priced, run-of-the-mill motels. The friendly management at **Red Apple Motel,** 416 N. 1st St. (248-7150), does its best to keep out the rotten ones, offering cable, A/C, coin-op laundry, an apple-shaped pool, and apple-scented rooms (singles $43, M-F $33; doubles $55, M-F $43; 21+ only). **Motel 6,** 1104 N. 1st St. (454-0080), a 20-minute walk from downtown, has a pool providing welcome relief from the scorching Yakima heat (singles $39; doubles $45).

Yakima's few campgrounds are overcrowded and noisy. In Toppenish, 20 mi. southeast of Yakima on U.S. 97, the **Yakama Nation RV Park,** 280 Buster Rd. (865-2000 or 800-874-3087), is the exception. Though primarily an RV park, there are tee-pees for sleeping and a pool is set in a field on the reservation (sites $12; RV hookups $18; teepees $30). Closer to town, **KOA,** 1500 Keys Rd. (248-5882), will gladly take $20 in return for a compact tent site with nice bathrooms (full hookups $26; cabins $37-43). Cheaper, more pleasant **Forest Service campgrounds** (653-2205) lie along the Naches River on U.S. 12, about 30 mi. west of town on the way to Mt. Rainier. Sites with drinking water cost $5-17; those without services are free.

FOOD

Track 29, a cluster of boxcars-turned-tourist-bait on W. Yakima Ave. at the railroad tracks, house mid-cost, mid-quality restaurants. **Thai Kitchen Restaurant,** on Track 29, serves some delicious *pad thai* ($8) and a scrumptious all-you-can eat lunch buffet ($6.41; open M-Sa 11am-9pm). **Ruben's Tortillería y Panadería,** 1518 1st St. (454-5357), sells freshly baked Mexican pastries (35¢ apiece) and packages of 10 tortillas ($1; open daily 8am-10pm). For a hearty Italian dinner, call **Deli de Pasta,** 7 N. Front St. (453-0571), and make the oft-necessary reservation. Pick a pasta and one of seven sauces (lunches $7; dinners $8; open M-Sa 11:30am 'til whenever the customers leave). **Grant's Brewery Pub,** 32 N. Front St. (575-2922), at the north end of the train station, is the oldest in the Pacific Northwest and a great place for a good time; call to arrange a tour. A pint of Grant's Scottish Ale costs $2.75; the small lunch menu varies, but usually includes fish and chips ($6.25). Live jazz, blues, and folk bands play on weekends (open M-Th 11:30am-11pm, F-Sa 11:30am-midnight, Su noon-8pm).

WASHINGTON

The *Yakima Valley Farm Products Guide*, distributed at the visitors bureau and at regional hotels and stores, lists local **fruit sellers** and **u-pick farms,** though the farms are fast disappearing because of liability laws. **Fruit stands** are common on the outskirts of town, particularly on 1st St. and near interstate interchanges. A fine fruit stop for interstate travelers is **Donald Fruit and Mercantile,** 2560 Donald Wapato Rd. (877-3115), in Wapato, 11 mi. southeast of Yakima, at I-82 Exit 44 (open mid-June to Oct. M-Sa 9am-6pm, Su 10am-6pm).

SIGHTS AND EVENTS Washington's Fruit Place Visitor Center, 105 S. 18th Ave. on the east side of Hwy. 82 (576-3090), has exhibits with pushable buttons and pullable levers that explain and illustrate the area's crop production. *(Open Jan.-Apr. M-F 9am-5pm; May-Sept. M-F 9am-5pm, Sa 10am-5pm, Su noon-4pm; Oct.-Dec. M-F 9am-5pm, Sa 10am-5pm.)* The center also gives away free fruit and apple juice.

Washington is the second-largest wine producer in the nation; the vineyards just east of the Cascades benefit from mineral-rich soil bequeathed by ancient volcanoes, plus a rain shield that keeps the land dry and thus easily controlled by irrigation. **Staton Hills Winery,** 10 minutes south of Yakima, is both the closest and classiest. *(Open daily Mar.-Oct. 11am-5:30; Nov.-Feb. noon-5pm.)* Specializing in Cabernet and Merlot, it boasts an upscale tasting room trumped only by the panoramic view of the valley outside. From I-82 E, take Exit 40 and make a left off the freeway. The winery is ¼ mi. up the hill. For a complete list of wineries, pick up the *Wine Tour* guide at visitor centers in the region or call the **Yakima Valley Wine Growers Association** (800-258-7270).

Toppenish, 19 mi. southeast of Yakima, is the jumping-off town for the Yakama Reservation (the tribe recently changed the official spelling of its name). The **Yakama Nation Cultural Center** (865-2800), 22 mi. south on U.S. 97 in Toppenish, presents exhibits on the culture of the 14 tribes and bands that inhabit the Yakima Valley. *(Open M-F 8am-5pm, Sa-Su 9am-5pm. $4, students and seniors $2, ages 7-10 $1, under 6 75¢.)* The fabulous museum concentrates on the oral tradition of the native Yakama and also houses a small bookstore. The rest of the cultural center surrounding the museum includes a public library and a restaurant that serves expensive native dishes. On the way out, **Toppenish** itself is worth a drive-through. Maintained as a wild-west throwback, the town has commissioned 52 exquisite historical murals on its buildings, each detailing a specific event in its history. New murals are painted every year. To see 'em, take Rte. 22 off I-82. The **Toppenish Powwow Rodeo** (865-3262) occurs during the first weekend of July on Division Ave. in Toppenish, and features a parade, games, dancing, and live music, above and beyond the rodeo. *(Fair $2. Rodeo $10 plus $2 parking fee.)* The **Central Washington State Fair** (248-7160) is held in Yakima in late September. The ten-day event includes agricultural displays, rodeos, big-name entertainers, horse racing, and monster trucks.

■ Grand Coulee Dam

Eighteen thousand years ago, the weather warmed and a small glacier blocking a lake in Montana slowly melted and gave way. The resulting flood swept across eastern Washington, gouging out layers of loess and basalt to expose the granite below. The washout, believed to have taken a little over a month, carved massive canyons called coulees out of a region now known as the Channeled Scab Lands. Grand Coulee is the largest of these canyons.

From 1934 to 1942, 7000 workers toiled on the construction of the **Grand Coulee Dam,** a local remedy for the economic woes of the Great Depression. Nearly a mile long, the behemoth is the world's largest solid concrete structure and irrigates the previously parched Columbia River Basin while generating more power than any other hydroelectric plant in the United States. The backed-up Columbia River formed both the massive **Franklin D. Roosevelt Lake** and **Banks Lake,** where "wet-siders" from western Washington now flock for sunny lakeside recreation.

The dam hulks at the junction of Rte. 174 and Rte. 155, about 75 mi. east of Chelan and 90 mi. west of Spokane. The rotund **Visitor Arrival Center** (633-9265), on Rte.

Spokane
ACCOMMODATIONS
A The Brown Squirrel Hostel
B Rodeway Inn City Center

155 just north of Grand Coulee, is filled to the brim with exhibits on the construction, operation, and legacy of the dam, all set to a Woody Guthrie soundtrack (open 8:30am-11pm; in winter 9am-5pm). When night falls during the summer, a spectacularly cheesy laser show is projected on the dam's tremendous face (late May to late July 10pm, Aug. 9:30pm, Sept. 8:30pm; free). Watch from the visitor center for guaranteed sound, or park at Crown Point Vista off Rte. 174 and tune in to 90.1 FM.

■ Spokane

Ah, 1974. Gerald Ford was in the White House, Elvis was in the white suit, and streaking was a national phenomenon. And for one brief moment, the eyes of the world turned to Spokane (spoe-KAN), site of the 1974 World's Fair. A city built on silver mining, grown fat and prosperous after decades as a central rail link for regional agriculture, Spokane has regressed since 1974 to become a gateway rather than a destination. Enormous and oddly empty department stores linked by covered skyways mix with 50s-style burger joints for a comfortable, if predictable, suburban atmosphere. All this middle-Americana, fused with bottom-of-the-barrel prices, makes Spokane a convenient, inexpensive stopover. The magnificent remains of Expo '74 slumber in Riverfront Park as the city dreams about its moment in the sun.

ORIENTATION AND PRACTICAL INFORMATION

Spokane lies 280 mi. east of Seattle on I-90. **Avenues** run east-west parallel to the **Spokane River, streets** run north-south, and both alternate directions one-way. The city is divided north and south by **Sprague Ave.** and east and west by **Division St.** Downtown is the quadrant north of Sprague Ave. and west of Division St., wedged between I-90 and the river. I-90 Exits 279 through 282 access Spokane.

Airplanes: Spokane International Airport (624-3218), off I-90 8 mi. southwest of town. Most major carriers serve Seattle, Portland, and beyond.

Trains: Amtrak, W. 221 1st St. (624-5144, reservations 800-USA-RAIL/872-7245), at Bernard St. 1 per day to: Seattle ($56); Portland, OR ($56); Chicago, IL ($228). All trains leave during the early morning. Amtrak counter open M-F 10am-6pm and 10pm-6am, Sa-Su 10pm-6am.

Buses: Greyhound, W. 221 1st St. (tickets 624-5251, info 624-5252), at Bernard St., in the same building as Amtrak. To: Seattle (5 per day, $27); Portland, OR (2 per day, $37). Ticket office open daily 7:30am-7pm and 12:15-2:30am. **Northwestern Trailways** (838-5262 or 800-366-3830) shares the same terminal, serving other parts of WA, OR, ID, and MT. Ticket office open daily 8am-6:45pm. Student and military discounts.

Public Transportation: Spokane Transit Authority (328-7433, TDD 456-4327), W. 107 Riverside St., in the Plaza at Riverside St. and Wall. Serves all of Spokane, including Eastern Washington University in Cheney. 75¢, under 5 free. Operates until 12:15am downtown, until 9:45pm in the valley along E. Sprague Ave.

Taxis: Checker Cab, 624-4171. **Yellow Cab,** 624-4321. Both run 24hr.

Car Rental: U-Save Auto Rental, W. 918 3rd St. (455-8018), at Monroe St. Cars from $33; unlimited mileage within WA. Must be over 21 with major credit card. Open M-F 7am-7pm, Sa 8am-5pm, Su 10am-5pm.

Visitor Information: Spokane Area Convention and Visitors Bureau, 201 W. Main St. (747-3230 or 800-248-3230), Exit 281 off I-90. Overflowing with literature extolling every aspect of Spokane. Open M-F 8:30am-5pm, Sa 8am-4pm, Su 9am-2pm; in winter M-F 8:30am-5pm. The **Spokane River Rest Area Visitor Center** (226-3322), at the Idaho state line, Exit 299 off I-90, offers similar pamphlets and enthusiasm. Open May-Sept. daily 8:30am-4pm.

Equipment Rental: White Elephant, N. 1730 Division St. (328-3100), and E. 12614 Sprague St. (924-3006). All imaginable camping equipment sandwiched between Barbies and shotguns. Open M-Th and Sa 9am-6pm, F 9am-9pm.

Library: W. 906 Main St. (444-5333). **Internet** access available. Open M-Th 10am-9pm, F-Sa 10am-6pm.

Gay and Lesbian Services: 489-2266.

Senior Center: W. 1124 Sinto St. (327-2861). Open M-F 8:30am-4:30pm, Sa 9am-2pm. **Elderly Services Information and Assistance:** 458-7450.

Traveler's Aid: E. 140 Broadway St. (456-7169), at Madison St., near the bus depot. Open M-F 7-11:30am and 1-5pm.

Laundromat: Ye Olde Wash House Laundry and Dry Cleaners, E. 4224 Sprague Ave. (534-9859). Washe ye thy olde clothes for $1, drye 25¢ per 12min. Open daily 6am-10pm. **Otis Hotel Coin-Op** (624-3111), at 1st Ave and Madison. 75¢ wash, dry 25¢ per 10min. Open daily 6am-6pm.

Emergency: 911. **Police:** W. 1100 Mallon St. (456-2233), at Monroe St.

Crisis Line: 838-4428. 24hr. **Poison:** 800-732-6985. 24hr.

Pharmacy: Hart and Dilatush, W. 501 Sprague Ave. (624-2111), at Stevens. Open M-F 8am-6pm, Sa 10am-6pm, Su 10am-2pm.

Medical Services: Rockwood Clinic, E. 400 5th Ave. (838-2531). Walk-in. Open 8am-8pm. **Deaconess Medical Center,** W. 800 5th Ave. (emergency 458-7100, info 458-5800), at Lincoln St. 24hr. emergency room.

Post Office: W. 904 Riverside Ave. (626-6860), at Lincoln. Open M-F 6am-5pm. **ZIP Code:** 99210.

Internet Access: See **Library,** above.

Area Code: 509.

ACCOMMODATIONS AND CAMPGROUNDS

⊛**Brown Squirrel Hostel,** 920 W. 7th Ave. (838-8102). Bus #34 stops 2 blocks away at 5th and Monroe St. Walk up Monroe to 7th and turn left; the hostel is right near the corner. A crisp, clean hostel in an elegant Spanish-style building. Subdued, homey atmosphere welcomes quieter travelers. Two inoffensive dogs roam the premises. 12 beds: $12. Private rooms available. Sheets $1. Reception 4-10pm. No curfew.

Rodeway Inn City Center, W. 827 1st Ave. (838-8271 or 800-228-2000), at Lincoln St. Great location, with pristine rooms. Wall-to-wall amenities: indoor sauna and spa, A/C, cable, free continental breakfast, evening snack, 24hr. coffee in the office, and an elevated pool in the middle of the parking lot. Singles $49; doubles $54; rates drop $10 off-season. 10% AAA discount.

Select Inn, W. 1420 2nd St. (838-2026 or 800-246-6835). Decent motel with cable, A/C, and pool. Next to railroad tracks. Ask for newly renovated rooms. Singles $46; doubles $56; in winter $10 cheaper. 10% AAA discount.

Riverside State Park (456-3964, reservations 800-452-5687), 6 mi. northwest of downtown on Rifle Club Rd., off Rte. 291 (Nine Mile Rd.). Take Division St. north and turn left on Francis, then follow signs. 101 standard sites in a sparse Ponderosa forest next to the river. $11, hiker/biker sites $5. Showers. Wheelchair accessible.

Yogi Bear's (747-9415 or 800-494-7275), 5 mi. west of the city. Take I-90 to Exit 272; follow the signs along Hallett Rd. east to Thomas-Mallon Rd., then 1 mi. south. Friendly hosts run a campground so big (168 sites) it deserves its own ZIP code. Showers, laundry facilities, phone and cable hookups. Electrical $17; full hookups $24.50. 10% AAA discount.

FOOD

Spokane is a great place for produce. The **Spokane County Market** (482-2627), between 1st Ave. and Jefferson St., sells fresh fruit, vegetables, and baked goods (open May-Oct. W and Sa 9am-5pm, Su 11am-4pm). The **Green Bluff Growers Cooperative,** E. 9423 Green Bluff Rd., is an organization of 20-odd fruit and vegetable farms, marked with the big red apple sign just off Day-Mountain Spokane Rd., 16 mi. northwest of town. Take Rte. 2 west to Colbert (towards Mt. Spokane Park), then turn right onto Day-Mountain Spokane Rd. and follow that up to Green Bluff. Many farms have **u-pick** arrangements and are near free picnic areas.

Dick's, E. 10 3rd Ave. (747-2481), at Division St. Look for the huge pink panda sign near I-90 and buy burgers by the bagful. This place is a time warp: customers eat in their parked cars and pay prices straight out of the 50s: burgers 59¢; fries 49¢; shakes 83¢; soft drinks 53-73¢. A Whammy ($1.07) has twice the meat and double the cheese of a regular burger. Always crowded, but battalions of patty technicians move things along quickly. Open daily 9am-1am.

Europa Pizzeria, S. 125 Wall St. (455-4051), in the Atrium, a small brick building. The aromatic scent of melting cheese has been known to lead movie-goers astray. Solid prices (6 in. pizza $6; sandwiches $7) in a classy joint. Plenty of vegetarian choices; dinners are more expensive. Open daily 11am-midnight.

SIGHTS

Riverfront Park, N. 507 Howard St. (456-4386), just north of downtown, is Spokane's civic center and greatest asset. Developed for the 1974 World's Fair, the park's 100 acres are divided down the middle by the roaring rapids that culminate in **Spokane Falls.** In the park, the **IMAX Theater** (625-6688) houses your basic five-story movie screen and a projector the size of a Volkswagen Bug. *(Shows on the hr. Su-Th 11am-8pm, F-Sa 11am-9pm. $5.50, seniors and under 13 $4.50.)* Another section of the park offers a full range of kiddie rides, including the exquisitely hand-carved **Looff Carousel.** *(Open daily in summer Su-Th 11am-8pm, F-Sa 11am-10pm. $1.75 per whirl, under 12 $1.)* A one-day pass ($11) covers both these attractions, plus a ferris wheel, park train, sky ride, and more. **Quinn's** (456-6545), in the park, rents in-line skates or bikes with pads and a helmet (from $5 per hr.). The park hosts **ice-skating** in the winter.

Manito Park, 4 W. 21st Ave. (625-6622), has four sections for hard-core botanists and those just wishing to enjoy one of the most beautiful spots in Spokane, and who among us doesn't fall into one of these categories? *(Open daily 8am-8pm. Free.)* Check out the carp in the **Nishinomiya Japanese Garden,** overdose on roses on **Rosehill** (they bloom in late June), relax in the elegant **Duncan Garden,** or sniff the flowers in the **David Graiser Conservatory.** From downtown, go south on Stevens St. and turn left on 21st Ave. At **Arbor Crest Winery,** N. 4705 Fruithill Rd. (927-9894), a self-guided tour explores vistas overlooking the valley below, followed by a sip of excellent wine (both free). Take I-90 to Exit 287, travel north on Argonne over the Spokane River, turn right on Upriver Dr., proceed 1 mi., then bear left onto Fruithill Rd. Take a right at the top of the hill to reach the winery grounds, which are open daily from noon to 5pm. The visitor center (see **Practical Information,** above) hands out various publications on other area wineries, including the *Washington Winery Tour.*

The **Cheney Cowles Memorial Museum,** W. 2316 1st Ave. (456-3931), presents displays on area history, from the Lewis and Clark expedition to Expo '74. Follow 2nd Ave. west out of town, turn right onto Poplar, and go two blocks. *(Open T-Sa 10am-5pm, W 10am-9pm, Su 1-5pm. $4, seniors $3, students and ages 6-16 $2.50. W half-price 10am-5pm, free 5-9pm.)* Included with admission is a tour of the **Campbell House,** a throwback to Spokane's Age of Elegance. The **Crosby Student Center,** E. 502 Boone St. (campus switchboard 328-4220), at **Gonzaga University,** is a must-see for turbo Bing Crosby devotees. *(Open June-Aug. M-F 8:30am-4:30pm, Sept.-May M-F 7:30am-midnight, Sa-Su 11am-midnight. Free.)* Here, in the tiny **Crosbyana Room,** faithful fans exhibit the Bingmeister's gold records and relics.

ENTERTAINMENT

Spokane is a minor league hotbed. The **Indians** play single A baseball in the **Seafirst Stadium,** N. 602 Havana (535-2922). *(Season June-Aug. Tickets $3-6.)* The minor league **Chiefs** (535-PUCK/7825) skate at the **Veteran's Memorial Arena,** 720 W. Mallon Ave. The arena has enough seating for 12,500 fans or concert-goers, and hosts musical talents from James Taylor to Garth Brooks. *(Box office open M-F 10am-6pm.)* To get there, follow signs on the Maple St. exit off I-5. All city-sponsored events are ticketed by **Select-A-Seat** (info 325-SHOW/7469, tickets 325-SEAT/7328). *(Open M-F 8am-5pm.)*

The **Opera House,** W. 334 Spokane Falls Blvd. (353-6500; http://www.spokane-symphony.com), is home to the **Spokane Symphony Orchestra,** traveling **Broadway shows,** and special performances ranging from rock concerts to chamber music to G. Gordon Liddy. The **ticket office** is in the SeaFirst Skywalk on 601 W. Riverside. *(Open M-F 9:30am-5pm.)* Known for locally produced shows, the **Civic Theater,** N. 1020 Howard St. (325-2507 or 800-446-9576), opposite the Veteran's Memorial Arena, has a downstairs space for experimental productions. *(Musicals F-Sa $15, seniors and students $12. Non-musical plays F-Sa $12, seniors $10, students $7; discounts Th and Su.)* The **Spokane Interplayers Ensemble,** S. 174 Howard St. (455-7529), is a resident professional theater performing a range of plays. *(Season Oct.-June T-Sa. Tickets $12.50-16.)*

The **Fox Theatre,** W. 1005 Sprague Ave. (624-0105), has grand and gaudy old 20s decor and shows major motion pictures anywhere from one month to a year after mainstream release (Tickets $1). *(Box office opens at 5pm, in summer 1:45pm.)* The **Magic Lantern Theatre,** S. 123 Wall St. (838-4919), mixes movies with microbrews, throwing in occasional live comedy on Tuesday and Thursday nights. *($5.50, seniors and students $4.50. Matinees $3. Special features late night Sa-Su.)*

NIGHTLIFE

Spokane has the best of both worlds—minor league teams for travelers in search of small-town USA (see **Entertainment,** below) and great nightclubs for those desperate for a big city fix. *The Pavement,* the *Spokane Spokesman-Review* Friday Weekend section, the *Spokane Chronicle* Friday "Empire" section, and the free *Inlander* give the lowdown on area happenings.

Fort Spokane Brewery, W. 401 Spokane Falls Blvd. (838-3809). Try the house specialty, Border Run, or sample five microbrews for $4. The kitchen is open for lunch and dinner, serving burgers for under $5 (closes at 10pm). Happy hour (daily 3-6pm) features $2.25 microbrew pints. Live music (F and Sa) and occasional big names (Th). Open M-Th 11am-midnight, F-Sa 11am-2am, Su noon-midnight.

Outback Jack's, W. 321 Sprague Ave. (624-4549; http://www.outbackjacks.com), is where Spokane puts on thrashing live music (F-Sa), DJ dancing (Su-M and W-Th), and other random entertainment (Tu). This bar/club has hosted such legends as Quiet Riot and is painted floor to ceiling in an absosmurfly aggravating blue. Draft pints (Beware of Schlitz!) from $1.25. Open daily noon-2am.

Dempsey's Brass Rail, W. 909 1st Ave. (747-5362), has a good dance floor and, in the classic cool/dweeb dichotomy, a second-floor lounge featuring big-screen Nintendo games. Dempsey's proclaims itself "the place to be gay." Draft pints $1.50-3.25. Open daily 3pm-1:30am.

Ichabods, 1827 Division St. (328-5720), is an on-the-other-side-of-the-tracks kind of establishment. Locals and Seattle hipsters alike go for live shows (F-Sa), blues (Tu), and open mic (W), not to mention 50¢ beer (Su). Open daily 11am-2am.

■ Near Spokane: Coeur d'Alene, ID

When French and English fur traders passed through northern Idaho in the late 1800s, they attempted to trade with uninterested local Native Americans. The trappers' French-speaking Iroquois guides dubbed the dismissive natives "people with pointed hearts," which the trappers shortened to "hearts of awls"—Coeur d'Alene (kur-duh-LANE). Today, locals call Coeur d'Alene "CDA." Gaggles of resort-bound golfers and lakeside loungers do little to mar the rustic beauty of this town 36 mi. east of Spokane. No matter how many newcomers, the deep blue waters of Lake Coeur d'Alene offer a serene escape.

PRACTICAL INFORMATION

Visitor Information: North Idaho Visitor Center, 115 Northwest Blvd. (665-2350). Open T-Sa 10am-5pm.

Buses: Greyhound, 2315 E. Sherman (664-3343). To: Boise (11hr., 2 per day, $63); Spokane (45min., 3 per day, $7); Lewiston, ID (3hr., 2 per day, $20); Missoula, MT (4hr., 3 per day, $26). Open daily 8am-8pm.

Car Rental: U-Save, 1527 Northwest Blvd. (664-1712). $26 per day; 20¢ per mi. over 200 mi. Open M-F 8am-5pm, Sa-Su 10am-2pm.

Emergency: 911. **Crisis Line:** 664-1443. 24hr.

Post Office: 111 N. 7th St. (664-8126), 5 blocks east of the chamber of commerce. Open M-F 8:30am-5pm, Sa 9:30am-12:30pm. **ZIP Code:** 83814.

Area Code: 208.

ACCOMMODATIONS AND CAMPGROUNDS

Cheap lodgings are hard to find in this resort town. **Star Motel,** 1516 E. Sherman Ave. (664-5035), fits phones and TVs with HBO in tidy cubicles (singles $40; doubles $45). **Budget Saver Motel,** 1519 Sherman Ave. (667-9505), offers roomy rooms with cable (singles $35; doubles $39). For bed and breakfast info, call the **B&B Information Center** at 667-5081 or 800-773-0323. Some are fairly reasonable at about $60 per night.

Robin Hood RV Park, 703 Lincoln Way (664-2306), lies within walking distance of downtown and just a few blocks from a swimmable beach (tent sites $17.50; RV hookups $19.50; showers, laundry, no sheriffs). There are a few first-come, first-served national forest campgrounds in the area. Popular **Beauty Creek,** 10 mi. south from Robin Hood along the lake, boasts the trailhead to the much-acclaimed **Caribou Ridge Trail #79. Bell Bay,** on Lake Coeur d'Alene, has good fishing and 26 sites; go east on I-90, take Exit 22 to Rte. 97, and continue 25 mi. south to Forest Service Rd. 545 ($9; water and pit toilets). Both campgrounds are generally open May through September. Call the **Fernan Ranger District Office,** 2502 E. Sherman (769-3000), for details on these and other Forest Service campgrounds (open M-F 7:30am-4pm).

FOOD

Coeur d'Alene has, inexplicably, oysters aplenty. The best are found at **Cricket's Restaurant and Oyster Bar** (765-1990), on Sherman Ave. (the one with the car on the roof), where diners can sup on six oysters ($7.50) and watch the toy train chug by on raised tracks (open Su-Th 11am-9pm, F-Sa 11am-10pm). **Java Cafe,** 324 Sherman Ave. (667-0010), serves gourmet coffee, confetti eggs for breakfast ($4), and sandwiches for lunch ($4-6; open M-Sa 6:30am-9pm, Su 7am-9pm). Get a dose of Thai flavor and hilarious marketing at **Mad Mary's,** 1414 Northwest Blvd. (667-3267), where Mary chops, dices, yells, and generally makes herself heard. Spicy chicken livers ($7.50) and *pad thai* ($8.50-11.95) portions are huge (open T-Su 11am-'til Mary's tired). Head north and turn right for **Tubs Coffee House** (765-9344), 313 Coeur d'Alene Lake Dr., where locals munch sandwiches ($4-7) and things unfried; check out the beer garden amphitheater (open daily 8am-10pm, in winter 10:30am-10pm).

SIGHTS AND OUTDOORS Coeur d'Alene Lake is the town's raison d'être. Hike 2 mi. up **Tubbs Hill** to a scenic vantage point, or head for the **Coeur d'Alene Resort** and walk along the world's longest floating boardwalk (3300 ft.). **Lake Coeur d'Alene Cruise** (765-4000) offers a tour of the lake and a fine view of the world's only floating golf green. *(90min. Tours depart from the downtown dock May-Sept. 1:30, 3:30, and 5:30pm; $12.75, seniors $11.75, children $7.75.)* **Boat rentals** are available at the city dock at Independence Point. *(Kayaks and canoes $8 per hr., $25 per half-day, $40 per day; paddleboats $12 per hr.)* A 3 mi. bike/footpath follows the lake shore.

■ Pullman

Tiny Pullman has two main attractions: the undulating, green-and-yellow wheat- and lentil-carpeted hills of southeast Washington's Palouse (puh-LOOZ) region, and the enormous Washington State University (WSU), alma mater of cartoonist Gary Larson and cultural oasis. The 20,000-student university is home to the 1998 PAC 10 conference champion football team, and WSU Cougar banners on every street light. The college is the town.

ORIENTATION AND PRACTICAL INFORMATION

Pullman lies at the junction of Rte. 27 and Rte. 272. U.S. 195, running from Spokane south to Lewiston, ID, bypasses the city just to the west. Spokane lies 70 mi. north, while Moscow, ID is 8 mi. east on Rte. 270.

Buses: Northwestern Trailways, 1002 NW Nye (334-1412 or 800-366-3830). To: Seattle (2 per day, $39-$41); Boise, ID (1 per day, $35); Spokane (2 per day, $14). Open M-F 6:45-7:15am, 10am-noon, and 1:30-4:30pm, Sa 6:45-7:15am, 10:45-11:15am, and 4-4:30pm.

Public Transportation: The two lines of **Pullman Transit,** 775 NW Guy St. (332-6535), run between the WSU campus and downtown. 55¢, seniors and under 18 20¢. Runs M-F 6:50am-5:50pm; during the school year 6:50am-11:30pm. Schedules are available around campus and at the visitor center.

Taxis: Moscow-Pullman Cab (208-883-4744). Runs Su-Th 7am-midnight, F-Sa 7am-2am.

Car Rental: U-Save, 1115 S. Grand Ave. (334-5195). $29 per day, 20¢ per mi. after 150 mi. Must be 21 with major credit card. Open M-F 8am-5:30pm, Sa 9am-5pm.

Visitor Information: Pullman Chamber of Commerce, N. 415 Grand Ave. (334-3565 or 800-365-6948), doles out free maps of Pullman and the Palouse, and will wax eloquent about Pullman's favorite vegetable, the lentil. Open M-F 9am-5pm.

Laundromat: Sunshine Center, 1235 N. Grand Ave. Wash 75¢, dry 25¢ per 10min. Open 24hr.

Senior Center: 325 SE Paradise St. (332-1933), in City Hall. Open M-F 8am-5pm.

Hospital: Pullman Memorial Hospital, 1125 NE Washington Ave. (332-2541).

Pharmacy: Corner Drug Store, 255 E. Main St. (334-1565), at Kamiaken. Open M-F 9am-7pm, Sa 9am-5pm, Su 12-4pm.

Emergency: 911. **Ambulance** and **Police:** 332-2521. Police station behind City Hall.

Crisis Line: 332-1505. 24hr. **Rape Crisis: Rape Resource,** 332-4357. 24hr.

Post Office: S. 1135 Grand Ave. (334-3212). Open M-F 8:30am-5pm, Sa 8:30-11:30am. **ZIP Code:** 99163.

Area Code: 509.

ACCOMMODATIONS AND CAMPGROUNDS

The steady stream of students through Pullman fosters a decent selection of moderately priced, no-frills motels. Rooms are easy to find, except on home football weekends, when rooms are booked one year in advance (fans have bequeathed motel rooms in their wills), and during commencement (the first week of May). Rates often drop during the summer, when the town hits a slow period and awaits the return of the students.

Nendels Inn, 915 SE Main St. (332-2646), on the way to Moscow. Clean rooms one block from WSU. Singles $35; doubles $45-49.

American Travel Inn Motel, 515 S. Grand Ave. (334-3500), on U.S. 195. 35 spacious, spic 'n' span rooms, with A/C, cable, and a nice pool. Singles $40; doubles $45; summer rates cheaper.

Manor Lodge Motel, 455 SE Paradise (334-2511), at Main St. The pleasant innkeepers offer clean rooms with cable, refrigerators, and microwaves. Chic Brady Bunch decor. Reception M-Sa 7am-11pm, Su 8am-11pm; after hours ring night bell. Singles $39; doubles $44.

Kamiak Butte Park, 11 mi. north of town on U.S. 27, offers 10 forested campsites with water, toilets, and a view of the Palouse ($5).

FOOD

WSU has spawned a thriving gaggle of cheap eats. Take your pick from hip cafes, a university-run dairy, and a classic drive-in.

⟡**Basilios,** 337 E. Main St. (334-7663). Since its doors opened in 1996, there has been no end to business in this fabulously frescoed joint. Order a plate of pesto and penne ($4.25) or just about any other equally appetizing Italian dish. Open Su-Th 8am-9pm, F-Sa 8am-10pm.

Ferdinand's (335-4014), on the WSU campus. From Stadium Way, turn toward the tennis courts onto South Fairway and follow the signs up to Ferdinand's. Makes everything with milk from WSU's dairy. Ferdinand's Cougar Gold cheese ($12 for a 30 oz. tin) may be Pullman's biggest attraction. An excellent ice cream cone ($1.25) and a large glass of milk will do your body good. Open M-F 9:30am-4:30pm.

Cougar Country Drive-In, 760 N. Grand Ave. (332-7829), a 10min. walk from downtown. Motor to the drive-through or slide into one of the booths inside. This popular student hangout offers extra-wide burgers with a special sauce ($2.60). Shakes are as thick as mud, with dozens of flavors ($1.50). Open daily 10am-11pm.

OUTDOORS

Pullman's gentle terrain and the broad, sweeping vistas of Washington's majestic Palouse region make the area ideal for exploration by bicycle or car. Professional photographers amass here annually to capture the purple-tinted prairies and wheat fields. **Kamiak** and **Steptoe Buttes,** north of town off Rte. 27, both make enjoyable daytrips. Pack a lunch and head for the hills, or hit the newly opened (and paved) **Palouse Path** that runs the eight miles between Pullman and Moscow.

From this basin of baking summer temperatures, a glimpse of the **Blue Mountains,** 25 mi. south of Pullman, may spark a yearning for high, cool forests. One good approach is along Rte. 128 from the town of **Pomeroy,** a 40 mi. drive southwest of Pullman. Follow U.S. 195 south to **Clarkston,** and then proceed on U.S. 12 west. This area, including the vast, remote **Wenaha-Tucannon Wilderness,** is administered by the **Pomeroy Ranger District** of **Umatilla National Forest,** Rte. 1, Box 53-F, Pomeroy 99347 (843-1891; open M-F 7:45am-4:30pm). Info is also available at the **Walla Walla Ranger District office** at 1415 W. Rose St., Walla Walla 98362 (522-6290; open M-F 7:45am-4:30pm).

EVENTS

Near the end of August of each year, the **National Lentil Festival** (334-3565 or 800-365-6948) explodes onto the Pullman scene with a parade, live music, a 5km fun run, and much, much more. Nearly all the lentils grown in the U.S. come from the Palouse, and this is a small-town tribute to a major player in the local economy. The centerpiece of the festivities remains the **lentil food fair,** showcasing, among other delicacies, lentil pancakes and lentil ice cream. The festival gained dubious notoriety a few years back when it became the first engagement ever cancelled by Jerry Seinfeld. For more info, write the National Lentil Festival, N. 415 Grand Ave., Pullman 99163, or call the chamber of commerce.

■ Near Pullman: Moscow, ID

Moscow (MOS-ko) is Pullman's conjoined twin, fused at the spine by Rte. 8. Although there's not a lot of revolutionary excitement fermenting in town, Muscovites take pride in their community and in the local branch of the **University of Idaho.** The **Lionel Hampton Jazz Festival** (885-7212 or 800-345-7402) sizzles during the third week in February. Concerts and workshops are given by some of the country's best jazz musicians, including Lou Rawls and, yes, Lionel Hampton. On the first weekend of May, the **Renaissance Fair** brings out the 16th-century Italian courtesan in everyone. Call the chamber of commerce for more info. Said **Chamber of Commerce,** 411 S. Main St. (882-1800 or 800-380-1801), proffers info and ideas about what to do in Moscow (open M-F 9am-5pm).

Vox, 602 S. Main St., (882-7646) takes excellent care of local coffee addicts, and dishes out delicious sandwiches ($4.75) along with their espresso. This local hangout serves more than the liberal-hippie-commie fringe, and sponsors live music whenever it gets the chance (open M-W 6:30am-8pm, Th-Sa 6am-10pm, Su 8:30am-4pm; in winter open later). **Mikey's Gyros,** 527 S. Main St. (882-0780), whips up Greek grub for under $5 (open Su-Th 11am-8pm, F-Sa 11am-9pm). **Casa de Oro,** 415 S. Main St. (883-0536), is a cantina that somehow avoids cheesiness, even though piñatas and sombreros hang from the walls. Dinner entrees cost $7-11; locals come for the margaritas. For a good deal, check out their lunch specials ($5), split a two-burrito meal, or just order an appetizer (open Su-Th 11am-10pm, F-Sa 11am-11pm).

The **Camas Winery,** 110 S. Main (882-0214 or 800-616-0214), has free tastings and an informative display (open T-Sa, noon-6:30pm, except during University of Idaho's spring break). **Mingles Bar and Grill,** 102 S. Main (882-2050), is cool, dark, and full of pool tables. The extensive bar food menu (pizza, burgers, chili, and salads) is reasonable ($4.50-6); domestic pitchers cost $5 (restaurant open M-F 11am-midnight, Sa-Su 10am-midnight; bar open M-F 11am-2am, Sa 10am-2am, Su 10am-midnight).

WESTERN CANADA

Western Canada's vast expanses of wilderness contains a broad spectrum of ecological wonders and some of the most idyllic urban areas on the Pacific Coast. **British Columbia (BC)** is home to spongy arctic tundra in the north, lush coastal forests in the west, a high, arid plateau in the east, and Vancouver, North America's busiest port, in the southwest. Western Canada is also home to B.C.'s spectacular **Queen Charlotte Islands,** Alberta's lovely parks and prairies, and the vast sweep of the **Yukon Territory,** where caribou outnumber people five-to-one. Six thousand miles from its former colonial rulers in Britain and France, Western Canada has always taken pride in its spirit of self-reliance.

> With this same self-reliant spirit, all prices appearing in the Western Canada chapters will be in **Canadian dollars,** unless otherwise noted.

Early and Native History
Before the arrival of Europeans, coastal nations such as the **Haida, Nisga'a, Tsimshian, Kwagiulth, Nuu-chah-nulth,** and **Salish** thrived from southeast Alaska to Oregon. Blessed with an abundance of salmon and cedar which girded a stable lifestyle, coastal peoples established a politically complex society with social distinctions determined by birth. Coastal culture was artistically sophisticated, and lavish ceremonies involving intricate masks and dancers enlivened village life.

The **Interior Salish, Okanagan,** and **Kutenai** lived farther inland on the plateaus between the Rocky and Coast mountain ranges. Relative to the coastal tribes, these inland tribes left little archeological data behind. What evidence there is hints that these communities lived similarly to those on the Plains, following and hunting bison herds and gathering wild plants. During the fur boom of the late 18th and early 19th centuries, inland Native Canadians were often employed as translators by white trappers. The exchange between white men and the First Nations, however, was far from equal, and catastrophic numbers of natives were killed by both exploitation and disease. The situation of the First Nations only deteriorated with the flood of white settlers that followed the discovery of gold in the area.

Fur Frenzy
For white settlers, Western Canada's earliest claim to fame rested on the backs of small furry animals. The English explorer **James Cook** landed on Nootka Island in 1778, where his sailors traded some rusty nails for a few sea otter pelts from the Nuu-chah-nulth. Cook was subsequently murdered while wintering on the Sandwich Islands (Hawaii), but on the trip home his sailors stopped off in Canton and discovered that the furs fetched a fat ransom in China. Soon, the Pacific fur frenzy was on, and the "soft gold" trade of the late 1700s was among the most lucrative and highly developed industries of its time. The English **Hudson's Bay Company** engaged in cutthroat rivalry with the French Montreal-based **Northwest Company.** These warring fortune-hunters were linked by the trading language of the **Chinook,** who served as mercenary go-betweens. For years, the fur companies competed in vain to find the **Northwest Passage,** a navigable sea route from the Atlantic to the Pacific. (Such a passage only exists north of the Arctic Circle, a route so difficult it was not successfully completed until 1905.) In 1821, the Hudson's Bay Company absorbed its competitor and ruled the region as a virtual fiefdom for decades to come.

Gold in Them Thar Hills
After miners found small deposits of gold near Vancouver in 1856, prospectors swarmed up the coast from northern California. Alarmed by the influx of unruly Americans, the governor of Vancouver Island enlarged his jurisdiction to establish

British control over the mineral-rich mainland. In 1871, the coastal colony of British Columbia joined the Confederation of Canada, recently created by the **British North America Act** on July 1, 1867. The coming of the **Canadian Pacific Railroad** and the **Northwest Mounted Police** (the Mounties) brought prosperity, some semblance of order, and swashbuckling red uniforms to the frontier region. The population boomed. In 1896, prospectors struck the mother lode near Dawson City in the Yukon, and the remote territory became host to a gold rush stampede of mythic proportions. Again, government followed the sweet smell of revenue, and the Yukon became a Canadian territory in 1898. Alberta, whose fertile agricultural plains would later yield valuable oil, became a Canadian province in 1905.

Recent Events

Western Canadians have long been frustrated with a remote federal government seemingly driven by the concerns of the more central Canadian provinces of Ontario and Quebec. Two events in the summer of 1997 revealed the depth of such regional sentiments. In June, a federal election returned Prime Minister Jean Chrétien and his **Liberal Party** to power, but the Liberal majority was based almost entirely in central Canada. The west was won by the **Reform Party,** a right-wing party recently born in rural Alberta and known for its tough stance against special status for French-speaking Quebec. The starkly regional election returns, and Reform's new status as **Official Opposition,** hardly bode well for national cooperation in the years to come.

In July 1997, a fleet of tiny Canadian fishing boats blockaded an Alaska Marine Highway ferry in the harbor of Prince Rupert to protest U.S. overfishing of British Columbia's salmon. The illegal blockade held over 300 tourists "hostage" for several days, though they were free to leave the ferry, and those who stayed received free food and lodging. The action was directed as much against Ottawa's failure to take a hard line against American overfishing as it was against Washington, D.C.

While regional conflicts rage, Canada is showing a much greater sensitivity to its original occupants. Canada's **First Nations** in general have begun to reclaim their lands and autonomy, and the native peoples of Western Canada often lead the campaign. Haida tribesmen now actively oversee parts of their former land, the spectacular Gwai Haanas National Park Reserve in the Queen Charlotte Islands. In August of 1998, after years of talks between government officials and the **Nisga'a** band of northern British Columbia, representatives signed a controversial and landmark treaty granting the Nisga'a self-government and control over natural resources in 1940km^2 of their traditional lands. Other First Nations are about to secure self-determination on a much larger scale. On April 1, 1999, the Northwest Territories are expected to split in half. The eastern portion, to be named **Nunavut,** will be populated almost exclusively by Inuit. The western half of the Northwest Territories is about half Inuit and half white, suffering from a mild identity crisis. The soon-to-be territory is nameless as of the summer of '98, though in a recent poll, **"Bob"** emerged as a possible option.

The Arts

In the centuries before European settlement, the **Kwakiutl** tribe of the present-day Canadian coast enacted **world-renewal ceremonies** employing such harrowing theatrical techniques as tunnels, trapdoors, ventriloquism, and bloody sleight-of-hand beheadings. Such traditions are continued today by **The X Files,** filmed in and around Vancouver with similarly spooky effects.

Thankfully, paranoia is not the only subject of art in Western Canada. Vancouver in particular nurtures a vibrant arts community, including **Emily Carr,** perhaps the pre-eminent painter in Canada. **Bill Reid,** another Vancouver native, is often credited with revitalizing the culture of his people, the Haida, through his sculpture. Reid died in 1998, but his work still stands in the forefront of a large movement of artistic rediscovery for many of Canada's First Nations.

Vancouver native and pop guy **Bryan Adams** has charged that "CanCon" laws, which require TV and radio stations to air a minimum amount of Canadian content, breed mediocrity in Canadian music and art. Beyond Adams' syrupy ballads, however, there is little evidence to support this complaint. Western Canada is home to a thriving popular music scene. Major acts from the region include the **Crash Test Dummies, 54-40, Chixdiggit** (proclaimed "the cutest band in Canada" by *Sassy* magazine), **Spirit of the West,** and Lilith Fair diva **Sarah McLachlan.**

Further Reading

The 90s owe two of their most pervasive buzzwords to young Vancouver authors. William Gibson coined the term "cyberspace" and spawned a subgenre of science fiction with novels like *Neuromancer* and *Mona Lisa Overdrive,* while Douglas Coupland bestowed an annoyingly unshakable label on his age group with his novel *Generation X.* Canadian poet Robert Service and American novelist Jack London found inspiration in Western Canada's rugged history and landscape, keeping the Yukon mystique alive long after the decline of Dawson City. *Notes from the Century Before: A Journal of British Columbia,* by Edward Hoagland, are just that. Popular historian Pierre Burton has written a number of gripping retellings of the region's dramatic past, including *Klondike, The Arctic Grail,* and *The Last Spike.* Sky Lea's *Disappearing Moon Cafe* depicts a family living in Vancouver's Chinatown in the 1930s, before the most recent wave of Asian immigration. Jean Craighead George's *Julie of the Wolves* is perfect for younger readers. Finally, the cartoon adventures of Dudley Do-Right are an astonishingly accurate portrayal of frontier life among the heroic Northwest Mounted Police.

British Columbia

British Columbia is Canada's westernmost province, with over 890,000km² bordering four U.S. states (Washington, Idaho, Montana, and Alaska) and three Canadian entities (Alberta, the Yukon Territory, and the Northwest Territories). The province attracts so many visitors that tourism has become its second-largest industry after logging. Despite excellent snowboarding and skiing, most arrive in the summer, flocking to the beautiful cities of Vancouver and Victoria or to the pristine lakes and beaches of the warm Okanagan Valley. On Vancouver Island, the unique coastal rainforests of Pacific Rim National Park are largely untrammeled, while in the southeastern part of the province, Glacier, Yoho, and Kootenay National Parks allow escape into the Canadian Rockies. Heading north, thick forests, low mountains, and patches of high desert are interrupted only by supply and transit centers like Prince George and Prince Rupert. Still farther north, even these outposts of civilization give way to thick spruce and fir forests, intermittently logged or blackened by lightning fires.

PRACTICAL INFORMATION

Capital: Victoria.
Population: 3,764,200. **Area:** 947,796km². **Motto:** *Splendor sine Occasu* (Splendour without Diminishment). **Bird:** Steller's jay. **Flower:** Pacific dogwood. **Tree:** Western red cedar. **Holiday:** British Columbia Day, Aug. 1.
Road Conditions: 604-660-2421.
Time Zone: Mostly Pacific (1hr. before Mountain, 3hr. before Eastern), but Yoho and Kootenay National Parks are Mountain (2hr. before Eastern).
Postal Abbreviation: BC.
Sales Tax: 7%. **Drinking Age:** 19. **Traffic Laws:** Seatbelts required in cars; helmets required when biking.
Area Codes: 604 in and around Vancouver; 250 in the rest of the province.

GETTING AROUND

Vancouver, on the mainland, can be reached by interstate highway from Seattle. **Victoria,** on Vancouver Island to the southwest of Vancouver, requires a **ferry** trip from

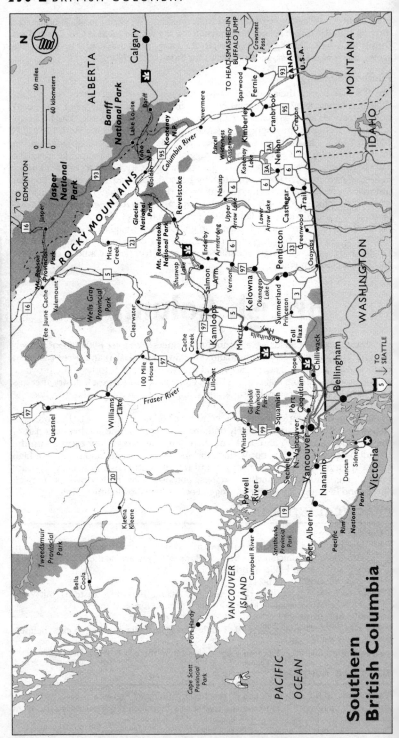

Southern British Columbia

Vancouver or from Anacortes, Port Angeles, or Seattle in Washington. The **Coquihalla Highway (Hwy. 5)** was completed in 1986 to carry tourists comfortably from Hope east to Jasper National Park in Alberta ($10 toll). The **Trans-Canada Highway (Hwy. 1)** is slower and more scenic, connecting Vancouver to Kamloops and Banff National Park in Alberta.

■ Vancouver

With kilometers of clean white beaches, a busy harbor greeting giant ships from distant ports, and large parks watched over by Haida totems and ancient trees, Vancouver welcomes visitors to a liberal, young, and incredibly multi-faceted city. As electronics and international finance join logging and mining to drive the economy, Vancouver has energetically entered the post-industrial age. Despite the hustle and bustle, though, Western Canada's biggest city remains its most laid back and permissive. In 1979, Vancouver elected Svend Robinson, the only openly gay Member of Parliament and a headstrong environmental activist (see p. 291). Rollerblades and skis far outnumber suits and cell phones, as the diverse and youthful population goes out of its way to enjoy spectacular natural surroundings.

Vancouver's cultural scene is no less exciting and complex. At the moment, a wave of Chinese immigration, mostly from recently reabsorbed Hong Kong, is directing the city's economy and character more toward the Pacific Rim than to the rest of North America. Meanwhile, Vancouver's large Chinatown has thrived for generations, making up only one of many ethnic neighborhoods around town. Diversity transcends mere buzzword status in a mass of museums, art galleries, and entertainment options, from public jazz to public nudity. With such urban exuberance all around, isn't rain a tiny price to pay?

🏅 HIGHLIGHTS OF VANCOUVER

- For endless and engaging artwork, head to the **UBC Museum of Anthropology** (see p. 260) and the **Vancouver Art Gallery** (see p. 259).
- **Wreck Beach** (see p. 261) provides an equally profound exploration of the human condition, suffused with naked hippies and pot brownies.
- The pleasant and popular **Stanley Park** (see p. 260) has an aquarium, seaside bike paths, and plenty of picnicking prospects.
- Almost any ethnic restaurant imaginable lines **Commercial Drive,** while **Kitsilano** blends good eating and student nightlife along W. 4th Ave. (see p. 258).
- Vancouverites escape for winter sports in **Whistler** (see p. 265) and lazy summer lounging in relatively sunny **Sechelt** (see p. 266).

GETTING THERE

Vancouver is in the southwestern corner of British Columbia's mainland, across the Georgia Strait from Vancouver Island and the Victoria. **Vancouver International Airport** (276-6101; tourist info 303-3601) is on Sea Island, 23km south of the city center. To reach downtown from the airport, take bus #100 to the intersection of Granville and 70th Ave. Transfer there to bus #20, which arrives downtown by heading north on the Granville Mall. An **Airport Express** (946-8866) bus leaves from airport level #2 for downtown hotels and the bus station (4 per hr.; $10, seniors $8, ages 5-12 $5).

Greyhound makes several runs daily between Seattle and Vancouver; the downtown bus depot also provides access to the city's transit system. **VIA Rail** runs eastbound trains, while the **BC Rail** station in North Vancouver sends trains to northern British Columbia. **BC Ferries** connects Vancouver to Vancouver Island and the Gulf Islands. Ferries to Victoria or the Gulf Islands leave from the **Tsawwassen Terminal,** 25km south of the city center. To reach Vancouver from Tsawwassen, take bus #640 to the Ladner Exchange and transfer to bus #601. Ferries bound to Nanaimo leave from the **Horseshoe Bay Terminal** in West Vancouver. Take bus #250 or 257 on Georgia St. (For specific fares and schedules, see **Practical Information,** below.)

ORIENTATION AND GETTING AROUND

Vancouver looks like a mitten with the fingers pointing west and the thumb pointing northward (brace yourself for a never-ending metaphor). South of the hand flows the **Fraser River,** and beyond the fingertips lies the **Georgia Strait. Downtown** is at the base of the thumb, while at the thumb's tip lie the residential **West End** and **Stanley Park. Burrard Inlet** separates downtown from **North Vancouver;** the bridges over **False Creek** link downtown with **Kitsilano** ("Kits") and the rest of the city. East of downtown, where the thumb is attached, are **Gastown** and **Chinatown.** The **University of British Columbia** lies on top of the fingers at **Point Grey,** the westernmost end of the city, while the **airport** is south at the pinkie-tip. Kitsilano and Point Grey are separated by the north-south **Alma Street. Highway 99** runs north-south through the city, and the **Trans-Canada Highway (Hwy. I)** enters town from the east. Most of the city's attractions are grouped on the peninsula/thumb, and farther west.

Vancouver's **BC Transit** (521-0400; http://www.bctransit.com) covers most of the city and suburbs, with direct transport or easy connections to the ferry's points of departure: Tsawwassen, Horseshoe Bay, and the airport. BC Transit subdivides the city into three concentric zones for fare purposes. Riding in the **central zone,** which encompasses most of the actual city of Vancouver, always costs $1.50 for 90 minutes (students, seniors, and ages 5-11 75¢). During peak hours (before 6:30pm), it costs $2.25 (students, seniors, and ages 5-11 $1.50) to travel between two zones and $3 to travel through three zones. During off-peak hours, passengers pay only the one-zone price. Transfers are free. Day passes cost $6 (students, seniors, and ages 5-11 $4), and are sold at all 7-11 and Safeway stores, SkyTrain stations, and HI-C hostels. Single fares, passes, and transfers are also good for the **SeaBus** and the elevated **SkyTrain.** The SeaBus runs from the **Granville Waterfront Station** at the foot of Granville St. in downtown Vancouver, to **Lonsdale Quay** at the foot of Lonsdale Ave. in North Vancouver. The fares are the same as one-zone bus fares, and all transfers and passes are accepted. **Timetables** are available at convenience stores, public libraries, city hall, community centers, and the Vancouver Travel Infocentre (see **Practical Information,** below). Pick up the useful pamphlet *Discover Vancouver on Transit,* which lists bus numbers for every major site in the city.

Vancouver is a big city; **driving** downtown is neither fun nor efficient. **Rush hour** begins at dawn and doesn't end until dusk. Beware of the 7-9:30am and 3-6pm restrictions on left turns and street parking. If you can't find parking at street level, look for **underground lots;** try the one below Pacific Centre at Howe and W. Georgia St., sometimes called "Garageland." **One-way streets** are a curse throughout the city, but many maps have arrows indicating directions. Downtown, cars are not allowed on Granville between Nelson and W. Pender, the area that makes up the **Granville pedestrian mall.**

If you have a car and are staying in southern or eastern parts of Vancouver, consider using the **Park 'n' Ride** from New Westminster to avoid the city's perpetual rush hour. Exit Hwy. 1 at New Westminster and follow signs for the Pattullo Bridge. Just over the bridge, signs for the Park 'n' Ride lot are on the right, between Scott Rd. and 110th Ave. A bus will be waiting where you purchase tickets. Parking is free, and taking the SkyTrain is faster than driving.

PRACTICAL INFORMATION

Transportation
   Airplanes: See **Getting There,** above.
   Trains: VIA Rail, 1150 Station St. (in Canada 800-561-8630, in U.S. 800-561-3949). 3 trains per week to Jasper, AB ($156) and Edmonton, AB ($218). Open M, Th, and Sa 10:30am-8pm, Tu, F, and Su 8:30am-6pm, W 10:30am-6pm. **BC Rail,** 1311 W. 1st St. (984-5246), just over the Lions Gate Bridge at the foot of Pemberton St. in North Vancouver. Take the BC Rail Special Bus on Georgia St. or the SeaBus to North Vancouver, then bus #239 west. Daily trains to: Whistler ($30); Williams Lake ($118); Prince George ($190); and other points north. Open daily 8am-8pm.

BRITISH COLUMBIA

Vancouver Overview

ACCOMMODATIONS
A Paul's Guest House
B Vancouver International Hostel

NORTH VANCOUVER

Boundary Rd.
Cassiar St.
Trans-Canada Hwy.
TO SIMON FRASER U.
Rupert St.
Grandview Hwy.
Main St.
Second Narrows Bridge
Exhibition Park
Renfrew St.
McGill St.
Renfrew St.
E. 1st Ave.
Nanaimo St.
Nanaimo St.
E. Broadway
Commercial Dr.
Victoria Dr.
John Hendry Park
Skytrain
3rd St.
Burrard Inlet
Venables St.
Clark Dr.
SkyTrain
Knight St.
Fraser St.
King-sway
SeaBus
Powell St.
Prior St.
VIA Rail and Greyhound Station
Terminal Ave.
Main St.
Main St.
SeaBus Terminal
CHINATOWN
Dunsmuir St.
Science World
Cambie Bridge
W. 2nd Ave.
TO QUEEN ELIZABETH PARK
GAS-TOWN
Canada Place
Granville Mall
BC Place Stadium
False Creek
Cambie St.
SkyTrain
DOWN-TOWN
Georgia St.
Pender St.
Robson Square
Granville Bridge
W. 6th Ave.
Oak St.
King Edward Ave.
WEST END
Davie St.
Burrard St.
Seymour St.
Aquatic Centre
Granville Island
Granville St.
99
Lions Gate Bridge
Stanley Park
Aquarium
Malkin Bowl
Brockton Oval
Lost Lagoon
Denman St.
Beach Ave.
Pacific Blvd.
Sunset Beach
Vanier Park
Burrard Bridge
Fir St.
TO VANCOUVER INTERNATIONAL AIRPORT
TO BC RAIL STATION
99
English Bay Beach
Maritime Museum
Kitsilano Beach
Vancouver Museum and Planetarium
KITSILANO
Arbutus St.
W. 4th Ave.
W. 10th Ave.
MacDonald St.
Strait of Georgia
N
Alma St.
W. Broadway
Dunbar St.
Jericho Beach Park
TO UNIVERSITY OF BRITISH COLUMBIA, WRECK BEACH, PACIFIC SPIRIT PARK
POINT GREY
W. 16th Ave.
B

mile
kilometer

Buses: Greyhound, 1150 Station St. (482-8747), in the VIA Rail station. To: Calgary, AB (4 per day, $105); Banff, AB (4 per day, $99); Jasper, AB (2 per day, $91); Seattle, WA (7 per day, $26). Open daily 5:30am-12:30am. **Pacific Coach Lines,** 1150 Station St. (662-8074) serves Southern BC, including Vancouver Island. Service to Victoria ($26, round-trip $49) includes ferry.

Ferries: BC Ferries (888-BCFERRY/223-3779). To the Gulf Islands, Sunshine Coast, and Vancouver Island ($8.50, ages 5-11 $4.25, car and driver $35-36.75, motorcycle and driver $22-23, bike and rider $11; fares cheapest mid-week). Ferries to Nanaimo on Vancouver Island leave from **Horseshoe Bay,** northwest of Vancouver. Ferries to Victoria or the Gulf Islands leave from the inconveniently spelled **Tsawwassen** (suh-WAH-sen) terminal, southwest of Vancouver. Both ferry terminals are quite far from town; leave ample time for travel. (See **Getting There,** above.)

Taxis: Yellow Cab (681-1111 or 800-898-8294). **Vancouver Taxi** (871-1111). $2.10 base, $1.21 per km. Both 24hr.

Car Rental: EZ Car and Truck Rentals, 4-2910 Commercial Dr. (875-6210). $30 per day, plus 15¢ per km after 200km. Must be 19 with major credit card or $300 cash deposit. Open M-F 8am-5:30pm, Sa 8am-6pm, Su 9am-5pm. **ABC Rental,** 255 W. Broadway (873-6622). $33 per day, $209 per week; unlimited mileage. Must be 21 with credit card. Open M-F 8am-6:30pm, Sa-Su 8am-5pm.

Visitor and Financial Services

Visitor Information: Vancouver Travel Infocentre, 200 Burrard St. (683-2000). Full info on accommodations, tours, and activities spanning much of BC. Courtesy phones for reservations. Open daily 8am-6pm. Call the **Talking Yellow Pages** (299-9000) for recorded info about virtually anything in town.

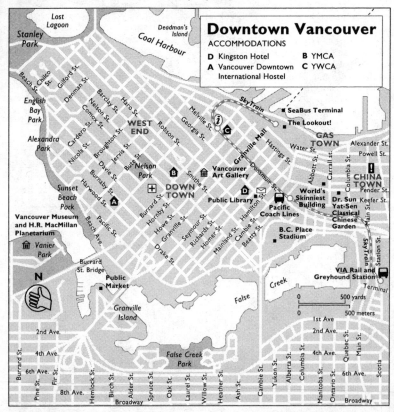

Outdoor Information: Parks and Recreation Board, 2099 Beach Ave. (257-8400). Open M-F 8:30am-5pm.

Tours: The Gray Line, 255 E. 1st Ave. (879-9287 or 800-667-0822). City tours with several package options. The **Double Decker Bus** stops at over 20 sights around town. Unlimited use for 2 days $23, seniors $22, ages 5-12 $12. Buses run 8:30am-6:30pm. **Take a Walk Tours** (250-492-7673) offers 1-1½hr. walking tours of downtown ($10).

Bank: Hong Kong Bank of Canada, 885 W. Georgia St. (685-1000). **ATM** 24hr.

Local Services

Equipment Rental: Bayshore Bicycles, 745 Denman St. (688-2453). Convenient to Stanley Park. Bikes $5.60 per hr., $20 per 8hr., $25 overnight. Open daily in summer 9am-9pm; in winter 9:30am-dusk. **Vancouver Downtown Hostel** and **Jericho Beach Hostel** (see **Accommodations,** below) rent bikes for $20 per day. **Recreation Rentals,** 2560 Arbutus St. (733-7368), at Broadway. Take bus #10 or 14 from Granville Mall. Rents backpacks ($10 per day, $26 per week), tents ($15 per day, $45 per week), and every other kind of camping and sports equipment. Open July-Aug. M and Sa 8am-7pm, Tu and W 9am-6pm, Th-F and Su 9am-7pm.

Public Library: 350 W. Georgia St. (331-3600). A strange confluence of salmon coloring and neoclassical architecture. Open M-Th 10am-8pm, F-Sa 10am-5pm.

Women's Resource Center: 1144 Robson St. (482-8585), in the West End. Open July-Aug. M-Th 10am-2pm; Sept.-June M-F 10am-4pm.

Services for the Disabled: BC Coalition of People with Disabilities, 204-456 W. Broadway (875-0188). Open M-F 9am-5pm.

🐾**Gay and Lesbian Information: Gay and Lesbian Centre,** 1170 Bute St. Counseling and info. Very helpful staff. **Vancouver Prideline** (684-6869), staffed daily 7-10pm. Fantastic library and reading room. Reception open M-F 10am-4pm. Library open M-Tu and Th-F 11:30am-9:30pm, W and Sa-Su 3:30-9:30pm.

AIDS Information: AIDS Vancouver, 1107 Seymour (681-2122, helpline 893-2222). Open M-F 9am-5pm. Helpline open M-Th 10am-9pm, F 10am-5pm.

Public Radio: CBC Radio 105.7 FM or 690 AM.

Arts Hotline: 684-ARTS/2787; http://www.culturenet.ca/vca. 24hr.

Weather: 664-9010; http://www.weatheroffice.com. **Road Conditions:** 900-565-4997 (75¢ per min.).

Emergency and Communications

Emergency: 911. **Police:** 312 Main St. (665-3321), at Powell. **Poison:** 682-5050.

Crisis Center: 872-3311. **Rape Crisis Center:** 872-8212. Both 24hr.

Pharmacy: Shoppers Drug Mart, 2979 W. Broadway (733-9128), and 1125 Davie St. (669-2424). Both 24hr.

Hospital: Vancouver Hospital, 855 W. 12th Ave. (875-4111). **UBC Hospital,** 221 Westbrook Mall (822-7121), on the UBC campus.

Post Office: 349 W. Georgia St. (662-5725). Open M-F 8am-5:30pm. **Postal Code:** V6B 3P7.

Internet Access: Digital U Cybercafe, 101-1595 W. Broadway (731-1011). $9.50 per hr. Open M-F 9am-midnight, Sa 10am-1am, Su 10am-midnight.

Area Code: 604.

ACCOMMODATIONS

Greater Vancouver is a teeming warren of B&Bs. Often cheaper than those in the U.S., these private homes are usually quite comfortable, with friendly and helpful owners. Less expensive rates average about $45 to $60 for singles and $55 to $75 for doubles. The infocenter maintains an extensive list of options. Several private agencies, like **Town and Country Bed and Breakfast** (731-5942) or **Best Canadian** (738-7207), match travelers with B&Bs, usually for a fee. The hostel scene is less expensive, and feels more like dorm life than home life.

Downtown, West End, and Gastown

Cambie International Hostel, 300 Cambie St. (684-6466), in Gastown. Tight but tidy rooms with large beds fit 2-6 people per room. Students and members $20; others $25. Free linens and airport pick-up. Raucous pub downstairs (see p. 263).

Vancouver Hostel Downtown (HI-C), 1114 Burnaby St. (684-4565). Perched on the border between downtown and the West End. Ultra-modern and ultra-clean, this 225-bed facility puts you smack in the middle of everything. Only four bunks in each room, and an array of goodies including game room, kitchen, free linen, and organized tours of the Vancouver area. Free shuttle to Vancouver Hostel Jericho Beach (see below). Open 24hr. Bunks $19, nonmembers $23; private doubles $48, nonmembers $56. Reservations crucial in summer.

Kingston Hotel, 757 Richard St. (684-9024; fax 684-9917), between Robson and Georgia St. A B&B/hotel hybrid. Feel like a monarch in quiet, cushioned-and-carpeted rooms downtown, at a surprisingly good price. Singles $45-65; doubles $50-80; cheaper rates for shared bathroom. Breakfast included. Pay parking available. Coin laundry and sauna.

Near the University of British Columbia (UBC)

Vancouver Hostel Jericho Beach (HI-C), 1515 Discovery St. (224-3208), in Jericho Beach Park. Turn north off 4th Ave. and follow signs for Marine Dr., or take bus #4 from Granville St. downtown. Institutional but clean, at a peaceful location with a great view of the city. 285 beds in 14-person dorm rooms, and 9 family rooms. Good cooking facilities, TV room, laundry. Organizes tours, trips to Vancouver bars, and bike rentals. A major junction for international backpackers. $17.50, nonmembers $22. Parking $3 per day, or find a spot in the nearby neighborhood for free. Free shuttle to Vancouver Hostel Downtown (see above). Free linen. Cafe open daily 7:30-11:30am, 5:30-11:30pm. Reservations imperative in summer.

University of British Columbia Conference Centre, 5961 Student Union Blvd. (822-1010), on the UBC campus at Walter Gage Residence. Take bus #4 or 10 from the Granville Mall. Upper-floor rooms have great views of the city and surrounding area, drawing swarms of conventioneers. Dorms $22; singles $33; doubles with kitchen and private bathroom $70-95. Check-in after 2pm. Open May-Aug.

Other Neighborhoods

Paul's Guest House, 345 W. 14th Ave. (872-4753), south of downtown. Take bus #15. One of Vancouver's best B&B deals. Clean, cheap, and cheerful. The gregarious Paul speaks 11 languages, sometimes all at once, and if he can't put you up in one of his welcoming rooms, he'll try to arrange something at another B&B. Shared baths. Singles $40-60; doubles $60-75; rates drop in winter. Full breakfast included.

The Globetrotter's Inn, 170 W. Esplanade (988-2082), in North Vancouver. Close to SeaBus terminal and Lonsdale Quay Markets. Easy SeaBus access to downtown. Shared kitchen, free pool table, free washing machine and clothesline. Can get somewhat rowdy. Beds $17.50; singles $30; doubles $40, with bath $45. Reception 8am-11pm. Reservations recommended.

Simon Fraser University (291-4503), in Burnaby, 20km east of the city center. Take bus #135 from downtown daytime M-Sa or #35 on the evenings, Su, or holidays. It's quite a trek from anywhere you may want to visit, but SFU's location atop Burnaby Mountain offers some great views of faraway Vancouver. Stay here if you're sick of the city or are simply heading east, young man. Singles $19; doubles $48. Groups of 4 or more should check out the well-equipped townhouse units ($107). Parking $3 per night. Open 8am-midnight. Reception after 3pm.

CAMPGROUNDS

Greater Vancouver has few public campgrounds; campers often resort to expensive private options. The town of **White Rock,** 30 minutes southeast of Vancouver, has tent campgrounds. Take bus #351 from Howe St. downtown. The parks listed below are primarily for RVs—don't expect a peaceful getaway unless you're inside one.

Richmond RV Park, 6200 River Rd. (270-7878), near Holly Bridge in Richmond. Take Hwy. 99 to Richmond Exit, follow Russ Baker Way, go left on Gilbert, right at Elm Bridge, take the next immediate right, then go left at the stop sign. The best deal within 13km of downtown. Scant privacy, but the showers are great. 2-person sites $17; hookups $23. $3 per additional person. 10% AAA and CAA discount. Washrooms available. Open Apr.-Oct.

Hazelmere RV Park and Campground, 18843 8th Ave. (538-1167), in Surrey. Off Hwy. 99A, head east on 8th Ave. Quiet sites on the Campbell River, 10min. from the beach. 2-person sites $18; full hookups $24. $2 per additional person; $1 per additional child; under 7 free. Showers 25¢ per 4min. Washrooms available.

Capilano RV Park, 295 Tomahawk Ave. (987-4722), at the foot of Lions Gate Bridge, the closest RV park to downtown Vancouver. 2-person sites $22; full hookups $32. $3.50 per additional person; $2 for pets. Reception daily 8am-11pm.

ParkCanada, 4799 Hwy. 17 (943-5811), in Delta about 30km south of downtown. Take Hwy. 99 south to Tsawwassen Ferry Terminal Rd., then go east for 2.5km. The campground, located next to a waterslide park, has flush toilets and free showers. 2-person sites $15; hookups $22-24. $2 per additional person.

FOOD

Vancouver's international restaurants serve some of the best food in the province. Its **Chinatown** is the second largest in North America, second only to San Francisco's, and the **Indian neighborhoods** along Main, Fraser, and 49th St. serve exquisite fare. The entire world from Vietnamese noodle shops to Italian cafes seems represented in ethnic foods lining **Commercial Drive,** east of Chinatown.

Granville Island Market (666-5784), southwest of downtown under the Granville Bridge, intersperses trendy shops, art galleries, restaurants, and countless produce stands selling local and imported fruits and vegetables. Take bus #50 from Granville Mall downtown. By day, the market fills with lunch-breaking locals and tourists, colorful street performers, and even more colorful food. Slurp cherry-papaya yogurt soup from a waffle bowl, nosh on cheese blintzes or potato knishes, or devour fresh fruits and vegetables. Spontaneous picnics are common in the parks, patios, and walkways surrounding the market (open daily 9am-6pm; in winter closed M).

Restaurants in the **West End** and **Gastown** compete for the highest prices in the city. The former caters to executives with expense accounts, while the latter lures tourists fresh off the cruise ships. Many of the **cheap and grubby little establishments** along Davie and Denman St. stay open around the clock. Dollar-a-slice, all-night **pizza places** pepper downtown. **Buy-Low Foods** (597-9122), at 4th and Alma St. in Point Grey, keeps costs down (open daily 9am-9pm). Downtown, **SuperValu,** 1255 Davie St. (688-0911; open 24hr.) is where it's at, grocery-wise.

West End, Downtown, and Gastown

Cactus Club Cafe, 1136 Robson St. (687-3278). Trendy cafe and night spot for Vancouver's self-designated hippest hepcats. Alcohol-themed foods, a number of vegetarian items, and a weird sense of humor. Jack Daniels' soaked ribs ($9.45) and Strong to the Finish Spinach Quesadillas ($6) are highly recommended. Also at 4397 W. 10th (222-1342). Open Su-W 11am-midnight, Th-Sa 11am-1:30am.

Hamburger Mary's, 1202 Davie St. (687-1293), at Bute. Neo-50s-diner sensibility, late hours, big portions, and allegedly the best burgers (meat *and* vegetarian) in town ($5-8). Open Su-Th 6am-3am, F-Sa 6am-4am.

La Luna Cafe, 117 Water St. (687-5862), in Gastown. Loyal patrons swear by the coffee, roasted by the cafe itself. This slick shop also offers cheap and satisfying sandwiches ($3.75-4.50), homemade soups ($3), and a wide variety of home-baked goods (muffin and coffee $2). Open M-F 7:30am-5pm, Sa 9am-5pm.

Commercial Drive

✪**WaaZuBee Cafe,** 1622 Commercial Dr. (253-5299), at E. 1st St. The funkiest restaurant on a Street of Funk. Sleek, metallic decoration, ambient music, artwork on the walls and in the brilliantly prepared food. Smoked chicken fettuccine $10; Thai prawns $7; veggie burger $6.50. Open M-F 11:30am-1am, Sa 11am-1am, Su 11am-

---

Cannabusiness

At the Cannabis Cafe, 307 W. Hastings St. (681-4620), marijuana doesn't just burn on the table top; it resin-ates in every aspect of the establishment—in the green artwork, in the flowerpots, in the literature, and on the menu. Vancouver law prohibits even cigarette smoking in restaurants, but at the cafe it seems perfectly legal to spark a joint with your dinner, perhaps with a glass water pipe borrowed from the store next door. What's the source of such herbal impunity? Vancouver police don't seem to treat small-time pot smoking as a criminal offense, despite federal law. The fuzz does tend to have moments of forgetfulness, though, at which point they raid the cafe and HempBC, an affiliated store and legal advocacy organization. The most recent raid, in April 1998, ended with the seizure of a warehouse worth of pipes and computer equipment, under what HempBC claims was a shaky warrant.

British Columbia's buds know international fame and success. They contend annually at Amsterdam's Cannabis Cup (the gourmet dinner of pot smoking), and at an estimated $1 billion, they generate half as much annual revenue as the province's logging industry. Most ganja dollars come from exports, and most exports go straight down south to America. In 1998, Canada legalized hemp plants containing itsy-bitsy levels of the psychoactive compound THC, giving visitors and locals full legal freedom to enjoy fibrous rope. For a connoisseur's perspective, tune in to the mind-altering http://www.cannabisculture.com.

---

midnight. Glam sister restaurant **Subeez,** at the intersection of Smithe and Homer downtown, serves the same food with more of a weekend attitude.

Nuff-Nice-Ness, 1861 Commercial Dr. (255-4211), at 3rd. Nice price and no fuss in this small Jamaican deli. Jerk chicken with salad and rice $6.25; beef, chicken, or veggie patties $2. Open M-F noon-9pm.

Havana, 1212 Commercial Dr. (253-9119). Smoke fat cigars and enjoy the arts in this one-of-a-kind restaurant/gallery/studio. Fidel prefers the Media Noche ($8), engulfs the seafood and tapas ($4-10), adores the Cuban and Latin dance classes, and tolerates the experimental theater. Open Su-Th 11am-midnight, F-Sa 10am-1am.

Kitsilano

🍁**The Naam,** 2724 W. 4th Ave. (738-7151), at MacDonald St. Take bus #4 or 7 from Granville Mall. The most diverse vegetarian menu around. Homey interior and tree-covered patio seating always make a perfect refuge. Crying Tiger Thai stir fry $8; enchiladas $9; tofulati ice cream $3.50. Live music nightly 7-10pm. Open 24hr.

🍁**Calhoun's Bakery Cafe,** 3035 W. Broadway (737-7062). Meals: light and home-cooked. Prices: low. Coffees, teas, and baked goods: plentiful. Conclusion: this cafe meets all the criteria for a sweet 24hr. hangout (pasta dishes $4-6; tortilla pie $5.)

Nyala, 2930 W. 4th Ave. (731-7899). Festive environs don't upstage the authentic Ethiopian fare. *Yedoro watt* (chicken with red pepper sauce) $11; *yesimbera asa* (chickpea cakes, onions, ginger, sauce) $8.50 and highly spicy. Open Su-W 11am-2pm and 5pm-midnight, Th-Sa 11am-midnight.

Chinatown

Many of the prettiest restaurants in Chinatown and adjacent **Japantown** are also the priciest. For guaranteed good food, stroll the streets and keep an eye out for small restaurants with faded fronts and crowded with locals. The area and its restaurants hit a lively peak in the afternoon, making this a better place for lunch than dinner.

Pho Hoang, 238 E. Georgia St. (682-5666), near Main St. Take bus #3 or 8 from downtown. Though not the most exciting spot in the city, this is the place to go for a big, cheap, nostril-seducing bowl of Vietnamese noodle soup ($4.50-5.25). Also at 3610 Main St., at 20th Ave. Open M-Th 10am-8pm, F-Su 10am-9pm.

Kam's Garden Restaurant, 509 Main St. (669-5488). Authentic, no-frills Chinese food. Humongous noodle platters $5-9; chicken, beef, and pork dishes with sauces and vegetables $10. Reading the menu takes almost as long as eating from it.

South of False Creek

Singapore Restaurant, 546 W. Broadway (874-6161), near Cambie St. Take bus #17 from Granville St. Bedecked with pictures of scantily clad Polynesian women surrounded by fruit. A mix of Malaysian, Chinese, and Indian cuisine from Singapore's cosmopolitan palates. Fried noodles $6.25; prawns and ginger $11. Lunch specials $4.75-5. Open M-F 11am-2:30pm and 5-10pm, Sa 11am-10pm, Su noon-10pm.

Nirvana, 2313 Main St. (87-CURRY/872-8779), at 7th Ave. Take bus #3, 8, or 9. Come as you are. Smells like authentic, savory Indian cuisine. Discover the sound of one hand clapping over chicken or vegetable curry ($6-8); become one with everything through the chef's special combos ($11). Open daily 11am-11pm.

SIGHTS

World's Fair Grounds and Downtown

Expo '86 brought attention and prestige to Vancouver, paving the way for its transformation into one of Canada's hippest locales. The fairgrounds are still there, between Granville and Main St. along the river, and are evolving into office space, housing for seniors, and a cultural center. The Canada Pavilion, now called **Canada Place,** can be reached by SkyTrain from the main Expo site. Built to resemble giant sails, the cavernous pavilion's roof dominates the harbor. The shops and restaurants inside are outrageously expensive, but the promenades around the complex make terrific vantage points for gawking at luxury liners and their camera-toting cargo.

The big-screen star of Expo '86 is the **Omnimax Theatre,** part of **Science World,** 1455 Quebec St. (268-6363), on the Main St. stop of the SkyTrain. *(Open daily 10am-6pm; call for winter hours. $10.50, seniors and children $7. Omnimax shows Su-F 10am-5pm, Sa 10am-9pm. $9.75. Combined tickets for museum and Omnimax $13.50; seniors and children $9.50.)* Everything from asteroids to zephyrs appears on the 27m sphere, sucking viewers into a celluloid wonderland. Science World also features more tangible hands-on exhibits and fact-crammed shows for children. **Lookout!,** 555 W. Hastings St., (689-0421) offers fantastic 360° views of the city! Tickets are expensive! But they're good for the whole day! Come back for a more sedate nighttime skyline! *(Open daily 8:30am-10:30pm; in winter 10am-9pm. $8, students $6, seniors $7. 50% discount with HI membership or receipt from Vancouver International Hostel.)*

The **Vancouver Art Gallery,** 750 Hornby St. (682-5621), in Robson Sq., displays an innovative collection of classical and contemporary art. *(Open M-W 10am-6pm, Th-F 10am-9pm, Sa 10am-6pm, Su noon-5pm. $9.75, seniors $7, students $5.50, under 12 free. Th 5-9pm $4.)* An entire floor devoted to the works of Canadian artists features the surreal paintings of British Columbian Emily Carr. Human interaction comes at no extra cost, including daily gallery talks and hands-on art projects relating to the main exhibit.

Gastown and Chinatown

Gastown is a revitalized turn-of-the-century district cleverly disguised as an expensive tourist trap. One of the oldest neighborhoods in Vancouver, adjacent to downtown, and an easy walk from the Granville mall, it is bordered by Richards St. to the west, Columbia St. to the east, Hastings St. to the south, and the waterfront to the north. Gastown is named for "Gassy Jack" Deighton, a glib con man who opened Vancouver's first saloon here in 1867. Today the area overflows with craft shops, nightclubs, restaurants, and boutiques. Many establishments stay open and well-populated at night. Stroll along Water St. and stop to hear the rare **steam-powered clock** on the corner of Cambie St. eerily whistle the notes of the Westminster Chimes every quarter-hour. Free 90-minute **tours** (683-5650) leave from the **Gassy Jack statue** at Water and Canal St. daily at 2pm.

Chinatown, southeast of Gastown, is a rather long walk away through undesirable parts of town. Take bus #22 north on Burrard St. to Pender and Carrall St., and return by bus #22 westbound on Pender. The neighborhood bustles with restaurants, shops, bakeries, and, **the world's skinniest building** at 8 W. Pender St. In 1912, the city expropriated all but a 2m (6 ft.) strip of Chang Toy's property in order to expand the street. In a fit of stubbornness, he decided to build on the land anyhow. Currently, the 30x2m building is home to Jack Chow's Insurance Company, where times are always a little tight. Less humorous but more serene, **Dr. Sun Yat-Sen Classical Chinese Garden,** 578 Carrall St. (689-7133), maintains many imported Chinese plantings, carvings, and rock formations. *(Open daily 9:30am-7pm; in winter 10:30am-4:30pm. $6.50, students $4, seniors $5, children free, families $12. Tours every hr. 10am-6pm.)* Don't miss the sights, sounds, smells, and tastes of the weekly **night market** along Pender and Keefer St. *(F-Su 6:30-11pm. Do miss the feels.)* Chinatown itself is relatively safe, but its surroundings make up some of Vancouver's seedier sections; drug dealers lurk around E. Hastings St.

University of British Columbia

The high point of a visit to UBC is its breathtaking **Museum of Anthropology,** 6393 NW Marine Dr. (inanimate though pleasant recording 822-3825, living human 822-5087); take bus #4 or 10 from Granville St. *(Open M and W-Su 10am-5pm, Tu 10am-9pm; Sept.-May closed M. $6, students and seniors $3.50, under 6 free, families $15. Tu after 5pm free.)* The high-ceilinged glass and concrete building houses totems and other massive wood sculptures crafted by indigenous coastal people, including a fantastic Bill Reid work of Raven discovering the first human beings in a giant clam shell (see p. 330). Hour-long guided walks pick through the maze of eras and expressions. Behind the museum, in a weedy courtyard designed to simulate the Pacific coastal islands, the free **Outdoor Festival** displays memorial totems and a mortuary house built by the Haida. Each carved figure represents one aspect of the honored dead's ancestry. After discovering First Nations culture, cross the street to explore the Far East. Caretakers of the **Nitobe Memorial Garden,** 1903 West Mall (822-6038), have fashioned the only Shinto garden outside of Japan, excellent for walking meditation. *(Open July-Aug. daily 10am-6pm; Sept.-June 10am-2pm. $2.50, students and seniors $1.75.)* Near the gardens, the **Asian Centre,** 1871 West Mall (822-0810) showcases free exhibits of Asian-Canadian art and the largest Asian library in Canada. *(Open M-F 9am-5pm.)*

The **Botanical Gardens,** 6804 SW Marine Dr. (822-9666), are a collegiate Eden encompassing a dozen gardens in the central campus area. *($4.50, students $2.25.)* In addition to its greenery, UBC has a swimming pool open to the public in the **Aquatic Centre** (822-4521), a free **Fine Arts Gallery** (822-2759), and free daytime and evening **concerts** (822-3113). Large maps at campus entrances indicate bus stops and points of interest. To arrange a **walking tour** between May and August, call 822-8687.

PARKS AND OUTDOORS

Established in 1889 at the tip of the downtown peninsula, 1000-acre **Stanley Park** (257-8400) is a testament to the foresight of Vancouver's urban planners. An easy escape from nearby West End and downtown, the thickly wooded park is laced with cycling and hiking trails, and surrounded by a seawall promenade. It contains a few restaurants, tennis courts, an outdoor theater, the **Malkin Bowl** (687-0174), an **orca fountain** by sculptor Bill Reid, and swimming beaches equipped with lifeguards and bathrooms. On the park's small eastern peninsula of Brockton Point is the **Brockton Oval,** a cinder running track with hot showers and changing rooms. **Nature walks** start from the **Nature House** (257-8544), below the Lost Lagoon bus loop. *(Su at 1pm. 2hr. $4, under 12 free.)* Take a dip in the **Second Beach Pool** (257-8371), with warmer, more chlorinated water than the nearby Pacific ($3.70).

Lost Lagoon, an artificial lake next to the Georgia St. entrance, is brimming with fish, birds, and the rare trumpeter swan. The best place to contemplate a duck's life is at **Beaver Lagoon,** a little farther into the park. At the kid-friendly **Vancouver Aquarium** (268-9900), on the park's eastern side not far from the entrance, exotic aquatic critters swim in glass habitats. *(Open daily 10am-5:30pm. $12, students and seniors $10.50, under 12 $8; prices drop in winter.)* British Columbian, Amazonian, and other ecosystems are skillfully replicated. Captive orcas, beluga whales, and dolphins demonstrate their advanced training and intelligence by drenching gleeful visitors.

During the summer, the tiny **False Creek Ferry** (684-7781) carries passengers from the Aquatic Centre (see **Beaches,** below) to **Vanier** (van-YAY) **Park** and its museum complex. *(4 ferries per hr. daily 10am-8pm. $1.75, youth $1.)* This park can also be reached by bus #22, south of downtown on Burrard St. Another ferry runs from the Maritime Museum in Vanier Park to **Granville Island** ($3). At the park, the circular **Vancouver Museum,** 1100 Chestnut St. (736-4431), displays artifacts from local native cultures, as well as several international exhibits. *(Open daily 10am-5pm; in winter closed M. $5; students, seniors, and under 18 $2.50, families $10.)* In the same building, the **H. R. MacMillan Planetarium** (738-7827) presents fact-packed star shows and fact-free laser rock jams. *(Facts $6.50, seniors and children $5. Lasers $7.75, seniors free on Tu.)*

Near UBC, in **Pacific Spirit Regional Park,** unexplored woods stretch from inland hills to the shore near Spanish Banks. With 50km of gravel and dirt trails through dense forest, the park is ideal for jogging, hiking, and cycling. Grab free maps at the **Park Centre** on 16th Ave., near Blanca.

Cyclists can find many excellent routes in and near Vancouver, including the Fraser River Canyon, the shore of the Strait of Georgia, the Gulf Islands, and Vancouver Island. Note that the **George Massey Tunnel,** on Hwy. 99 under the Fraser River—on the route to the Tsawwassen terminal—is **closed to bicycles;** a shuttle service transports cyclists through the tunnel. Call **Cycling BC** (737-3034) for more info.

BEACHES

Vancouver is blessed with remarkably clean beaches. Follow the western side of the Stanley Park seawall south to **Sunset Beach Park,** a strip of grass and beach extending all the way to the Burrard Bridge. At the southern end of Sunset Beach is the **Aquatic Centre,** 1050 Beach Ave. (665-3424), a public facility with a sauna, gymnasium, diving tank, and, for some reason, a 50m indoor saltwater pool, for $3.70.

Kitsilano Beach, across Arbutus St. from Vanier Park, is another local favorite, known as "Kits." For less crowding, more students, and free showers (always a winning combination), visit **Jericho Beach.** North Marine Dr. runs along the beach, and a cycling path at the side of the road leads to the westernmost end of the UBC campus. Bike and hiking trails cut through the campus and crop its edges. West of Jericho Beach is the quieter **Spanish Bank,** *donde arena y roca dan privacia y solitud.* For more information on these beaches, call 738-8535.

Most of Vancouver's 14 mi. of beaches are patrolled by lifeguards from late May to Labour Day daily between 11:30am and 9pm. Even if you don't dip a foot in the chilly waters, you can frolic in true West Coast spirit during Sport BC's weekly **Volleyball Tournament,** offering all levels of competition. Scare up a team at the hostel, then call 737-3096 to find out where to play.

"Co-ed Naked Beach Volleyball" would make a fine t-shirt slogan, but you wouldn't wear it at **Wreck Beach.** Take entry trail #6 down the hill from SW Marine Dr. Directly across the street from the UBC campus, Wreck is Vancouver's most interesting, eclectic, and clothing-optional beach. A steep wooden staircase leads to a totally secluded, self-contained sunshine community of nude sun-bathers and guitar-playing UBC students. No lifeguards, but naked entrepreneurs peddle vegetarian-friendly foods, beer, and other awareness-altering goods up and down the strip. Call the **Wreck Beach Preservation Society** (273-6950) for more info.

SHOPPING

Shopping in Vancouver runs the gamut from the trendy to the tourist-swamped to the artsy to the baffling. Plenty of the first two categories reside on **Robson St.** between Howe and Broughton St., where kaleidoscopic awnings and stylish windows swallow tourists and their money. For more reasonable prices and quirkier offerings, check out **Commercial Drive,** or the numerous boutiques and secondhand clothing stores lining 4th Avenue and Broadway between Burrard and Alma St.

The **Granville pedestrian mall,** on Granville Ave. between Smythe and Hastings St., comprises Vancouver's hip downtown shopping area. From Hastings St. to the

Orpheum Theatre, most establishments cater to professionals on their lunch hours. Beyond W. Georgia St., the mall gets an infusion of younger blood with theaters, leather shops, street peddlers, snack bars, and raucous record and clothing stores.

Books: Duthie Books, 650 W. Georgia (689-1802), at Granville. Scan the racks, ranging from movies to politics, or read the latest mag at the **Last Word Cafe.** Open M-Sa 9am-9pm, Su 11am-6pm. **Spartacus,** 311 W. Hastings (688-6138), will meet all countercultural needs; don't miss the special subculture section. Open M-F 10am-8:30pm, Sa 10am-6pm, Su 11am-5:30pm. **Little Sisters,** 1238 Davie St. (669-1753), has an extensive trove of gay and lesbian lit. Open daily 10am-11pm.

Clothes: Retail and vintage clothing stores pepper Vancouver, but **True Value Vintage,** 710 Robson St. (685-5403), sets the pace for all others to follow. Pricier than thrift stores but cheaper than poser boutiques, it's a great place to grab jackets, vintage ensembles, or that special something for Friday night's CD release party. Open M and W 11am-7pm, Tu, Th, and F 11am-9pm, Sa 10am-8pm, Su noon-6pm.

Music: They specialize in rock, but **Zulu Records,** 1869 W. 4th (738-3232), covers all the bases with new and used CDs, tapes, and LPs of every genre. Plenty of counter-culture activity at no extra charge. Open M-W 10:30am-7pm, Th-F 10:30am-9pm, Sa 9:30am-6:30pm, Su noon-6pm. **A&B Sound,** 556 Seymour St. (687-5837; http://www.absound.ca), stocks the cheapest new CDs ($12-14). Open M-W 9am-6pm, Th-F 9am-9pm, Sa 9:30am-6pm, Su 11am-6pm. Copies of any album by legendary Canadian rock power trio Rush can be found lying around at any street corner.

Flea Markets: Small flea markets pop up from time to time, but Vancouver has a few regulars. On weekends, try the **Vancouver Flea Market,** 703 Terminal Ave. (685-0666) Admission 60¢. Sunday is the day for cruising two grounds of shopping pleasure at **Cloverdale Fair Grounds,** 6050 176th St. (6am-4pm), and at **Pier 96,** 116 E. Esplanade in North Vancouver. Call 986-3532 for recorded info.

Counter-Espionage Paraphernalia: When John Le Carré novels just don't cut it anymore, head to **Spy v. Spy,** 414 W. Pender St. (683-3283). Test drive metal detector-proof CIA "letter openers" ($30), aerosol can safes ($15), and home surveillance and anti-surveillance equipment (from $200), or just read up on a number of skills crucial to the successful agent (sneaking into movies, ID faking, dead body disposal, and so forth). Open M-F 10:30am-5:30pm, Sa noon-5pm.

SPORTS AND ENTERTAINMENT

One block south of Chinatown on Main St. is the domed **BC Place Stadium,** at 777 S. Pacific Blvd. Vaguely resembling a mushroom in bondage, it is home to the Canadian Football League's **BC Lions.** At the entrance to the stadium, the **Terry Fox Memorial** honors the Canadian hero who, after losing a leg to cancer, ran over 5300km across Canada to raise money for medical research. Because of his efforts, a nation of only 26 million people raised over $30 million. The NHL's **Vancouver Canucks** and the NBA's **Vancouver Grizzlies** share the nearby **GM Place.** Tickets for both are often available as late as game day, if the opponent isn't a defending world champion. For tickets and info, call Ticketmaster at 280-4400. The **Vancouver Canadians** play AAA baseball in **Nat Bailey Stadium,** at 33rd. Ave. and Ontario, across from Queen Elizabeth Park, offering some of the cheapest sports tickets ($7.50-9.50) and beer around. Call 872-5232 for info and schedules.

The renowned **Vancouver Symphony Orchestra (VSO)** (876-3434) plays in the refurbished **Orpheum Theater,** 884 Granville St. (665-3050). The VSO often joins forces with other groups such as the **Vancouver Bach Choir** (921-8012) to form a giant evil robot capable of destroying the entire metropolitan area with its mammoth mechanized tail, in addition to presenting a diverse selection of music designed to appeal to a variety of tastes.

Robson Square Conference Centre, 800 Robson St. (661-7373), sponsors events almost daily in summer and weekly the rest of the year, either on the plaza at the square or in the center itself. Their concerts, dance workshops, theater productions, exhibits, lectures, symposia, and films are all free or nearly free.

All of Canada kneels before the altar of Vancouver theater. The **Arts Club Theatre** (687-5315) hosts big-name plays and musicals. **Theatre Under the Stars** (687-0174), in Stanley Park's Malkin Bowl (see p. 260), plays a summer season of musicals. **Bard on the Beach,** the annual Shakespeare Festival in Vanier Park (see p. 261), often needs volunteers to work in exchange for free admission to their critically acclaimed shows (June-Aug.). Call 739-0559 for details. **UBC Summer Stock** (822-0762) puts on several plays throughout the summer at the **Frederick Wood Theatre,** 6354 Crescent Rd., in Point Grey.

The **Ridge Theatre** (738-6311), 3131 Arbutus, often shows arthouse, European, and vintage films ($6). The **Hollywood Theatre,** 3123 W. Broadway (738-3211), also shows a mix of arthouse and mainstream flicks (doors open at 7:30pm; $3.50, on M $2.50, seniors and children $2.50). The **Paradise,** 919 Granville (681-1732), at Smythe, shows triple-features of second-run movies for $3. Get real comfortable.

NIGHTLIFE

To keep abreast of Vancouver's non-stop entertainment scene, pick up a copy of the weekly *Georgia Straight,* free at newsstands, cafes, and record stores. Those who are Georgia non-Straight can check out the event listings in *Xtra West,* a free gay and lesbian biweekly, available around Davie St. and in the Gay and Lesbian Centre (see **Practical Information,** above). On weekends, the club scene doesn't start bouncing before 10pm, but by 11pm, long lines form outside the most popular haunts.

Purple Onion, 15 Water St. (602-9442), in Gastown. Slurps in the crowds with an eclectic musical selection, inviting lounge chairs, and 2 rooms—1 live, 1 Memorex. The lounge features live blues, R&B, jazz, and funk acts, while the DJs spin acid jazz, disco, soul, funk, Latin, swing, and reggae. Cover $3-6. Open M-Th 8pm-2am, F-Sa 7pm-2am, Su 7pm-midnight.

The King's Head, 1618 Yew St. (733-3933), at 1st St., in Kitsilano. Cheap drinks, cheap food, mellow atmosphere, and a great location near the beach all make this pub popular with Kits locals. Tiny bands play acoustic sets on a stage even tinier still. Daily drink specials. Pints $3. Gullet-filling Beggar's Breakfast $3. Open M-F 7am-1am, Sa 7:30am-1:30am, Su 7:30am-midnight.

Celebrities, 1022 Davie St. (689-3180), at Burrard, downtown. Ever so big, ever so hot, and ever so popular with Vancouver's gay crowd, though it draws all kinds. Straight nights (Tu and F); retro night (Su); occasional drag pageants and strippers. Open M-Sa 9pm-2am, Su 9pm-midnight.

The Cambie, 300 Cambie St. (684-6466), in Gastown. Downstairs from the hostel (see p. 256). Young crowds from all over the cultural spectrum, picnic tables made from bowling lanes, sports TVs, sandwiches ($3.50-5.50), breakfasts, snacks, and kindly priced beer (pint of Molson $2.50, other pints $3.75). Open 9am-1:30am.

Mars, 1320 Richards St. (662-7707), downtown. One of the classier planets in the sweaty Vancouver club solar system, with candlelit dining booths and a weekend dress code (no running shoes). Wields one of the most advanced stereo and light systems on the West Coast. R&B-flavored DJ music alternately slows tempo (M), funks it up (W), and goes hip hop (Th). Open M, W-Sa 9pm-2am, Tu 9pm-1am.

The Palladium, 1250 Richards St. (688-2648), at Drake, downtown. Huge former warehouse now home to R&B and hip hop DJs, with live concerts on weekend nights. 80s dance par-tay (M); Latino night (W). Cover $3-6. Open M-Sa noon-2am, Su noon-midnight.

EVENTS

Vancouver Folk Music Festival (602-9798; email info@thefestival.bc.ca; http://www.thefestival.bc.ca). Jams in Jericho Park for three days in mid-July. Acoustic performers gather from all over the world to give concerts and workshops. $30 per evening; $45 per day; $79-117 for the weekend. Ages 13-18 $22 per day, $55 weekend. Ages 3-12 $6 per day, $10 weekend. The earlier you get 'em, the cheaper they are. Write to Box 381, 916 W. Broadway, Vancouver V5Z 1K7.

Du Maurier International Jazz Festival Vancouver (872-5200 or 888-GET-JAZZ/438-5299; http://www.jazzfest.bc.sympatico.ca). Features over 500 performers and bands in the third week of June for 10 days of hot jazz, from acid to swing. Write to 435 W. Hastings, Vancouver V6V 1L4. Ask about free concerts at the Plaza, in Gastown, and on Granville Island.

Benson & Hedges Symphony of Fire (738-4304). Lights up the night sky over English Bay in late July and early August. The world's finest pyro-technicians detonate their works while hordes watch from Sunset Beach, Kitsilano Beach, and as far as Jericho Beach. Artists from a different country perform each night, their displays choreographed with music broadcast on 98 AM and 101 FM. The beaches fill up early with picnickers, and don't even think about trying to park or drive nearby. I told you not to think about it. Now look what you've done.

Chinese New Year (Feb. 16 in 1999). Fireworks, music, and dragons romp through the streets of Chinatown and beyond.

■ Near Vancouver: Daytrips

East of city center, the town of **Deep Cove** in North Vancouver luxuriates in its salty atmosphere. Sea otters and seals cavort on the pleasant Indian Arm beaches. Take bus #210 from Pender St. to the Phibbs Exchange on the north side of Second Narrows Bridge. From there, take bus #211 or 212 to Deep Cove. **Cates Park,** at the end of Dollarton Hwy. on the way to Deep Cove, has popular swimming and scuba waters and makes a good bike trip out of Vancouver. Bus #211 also leads to **Mount Seymour Provincial Park.** Trails leave from Mt. Seymour Rd., and a paved road winds 8km to the top. One hundred campsites ($12) are available, and the skiing is superb.

To the south, **Reifel Bird Sanctuary** (946-6980), on Westham Island 16km from Vancouver, lies northwest of the Tsawwassen ferry terminal. The 850 acres of marshlands support 240 bird species, and spotting towers are set up for extended bird-watching (open daily 9am-4pm; $3.25, seniors and children $1).

For easy hiking near the city, take the SeaBus to **Lynn Canyon Park** (981-3103), in North Vancouver. Unlike the more publicized Capilano, the suspension bridge here is free and uncrowded, hanging 50m above the canyon. The river and waterfalls make for a gentle stroll and a cold swim. Longer hiking trails are also plentiful. Take bus #229 from the North Vancouver SeaBus terminal and walk 500m to the bridge.

Head out across the Lions Gate Bridge from Stanley Park along North Marine Dr. to gorgeous, secluded **Lighthouse Park.** It's a 50km round-trip from downtown; bus #250 goes right to the park's entrance, or this can make a fantastic and challenging bicycle daytrip. Numerous trails with tranquil water views crisscross the 185-acre preserve. Walk down the path toward the lighthouse, hang a left at the buildings, keep right at the fork in the trail, and walk to a large flat rock for one of the **best picnic spots in the world.**

Grouse Mountain (984-0661; ski report 986-6262) is the closest ski resort to downtown Vancouver and has the crowds to prove it. Take bus #236 from the North Vancouver SeaBus terminal, which drops off at the Supersky Ride, an aerial tramway (open daily 9am-10pm; $16, seniors $14, ages 13-18 $10, families $40). The slopes are lit until 10:30pm from November to May. The steep 2.9km **Grouse Grind Trail** is popular among Vancouverites in summer; it climbs 840m to the top of the mountain and takes nearly two hours. If you don't have the energy to hike back down, take the Supersky for $5 (downhill only). On sunny days, **Vancouver Helicopters** (270-1484) spews hueys from the top of the mountain, starting at $45 per person.

Cypress Mountain (922-0825), in West Vancouver, provides a sometimes less crowded ski alternative farther from downtown. From Hwy. 1 heading west, take Exit 8 at Cypress Bowl Rd. The mountain is hikable in summer, with amazing views of Vancouver and the Pacific. The ski resort is part of **Cypress Provincial Park,** with forest and mountain hiking trails.

■ Near Vancouver: Sea to Sky Highway (Hwy. 99)

Fifty-two kilometers north of Vancouver, on the way to Whistler via the Sea to Sky Highway (Hwy. 99), is the **BC Museum of Mining** (688-8735) in Britannia Beach. Visitors hop onto a mine train, riding deep into a mountain where 60,000 workers once extracted more than 50 million tons of copper. (Open July-Aug. daily 10am-4:30pm, May-June and Sept.-Oct. W-Su 10am-4:30pm. $9.50, students and seniors $7.50, under 5 free, families $34, group rates available. Gold-pannin' tour $3.50.)

Provincial park after provincial park dots the rocky drive to Whistler, nestled among enough vertical faces to make rock climbers giggle. At least one park worth stopping for is **Shannon Falls** (3km past the museum), which affords a spectacular view of a towering and rugged 335m waterfall. Steep but well-maintained trails from the falls make for nice **dayhiking** up to the three peaks of **Chief Mountain,** which bears a 671m wall of solid granite. The **Squamish Hostel,** 38490 Buckley Rd. (892-9240 or 800-449-8614 in BC), is a logical stopover for those tackling the local geology ($15, includes shower, kitchen, linen/towel use; private rooms $25). Gord, the hospitable owner, is happy to take his guests climbing for free. **Eagle Run,** a viewing site 4km north of the hostel along the Squamish River, offers a great chance to view hundreds of bald eagles making winter homes along the rivers and estuaries of Squamish Valley (free; Dec.-Feb., volunteer interpreters on weekends; wheelchair accessible).

■ Near Vancouver: Whistler

Canada's premier skiing and snowboarding destination, Whistler is trendy, exorbitant, and clean as a...clarinet. With an influx of foreign investment, the town has swollen into a four-season international tourist magnet, with mountain biking, golf, and water sports keeping visitors at play long after the ice and snow melt away in April. While the region has its share of permanent residents, the vast majority are employed in tourism-related enterprises. "Whistler Village" exists as an unwalled Disneyland for deep-pocketed tourists and makes affordable deals hard to find in town, especially during the busy winter.

PRACTICAL INFORMATION Whistler's tourism and essential services center around **Whistler Village,** much of which is **pedestrian access only. Whistler Creek** is a smaller, less-developed collection of accommodations and restaurants 5km south of Whistler Village. **Maverick Coach Lines** (932-5031) runs buses to Vancouver, departing from the **Village Bus Loop** (6 per day, 5am-7:15pm, $17, round-trip $32). The **activity and information center** (932-2394), in the heart of Whistler Village, provides maps and booking services (open daily 9am-5pm). For local **weather and road conditions,** call 932-5090. For the **Telecare Crisis Line,** call 932-2673. The **police** (932-3044) reside in the village at 4315 Blackcomb Way, while the **Whistler Health Care Center** (932-4911) is at 4380 Lorimer Rd. The **post office** (932-5012) sits in the Village Marketplace. **Postal Code:** V0N 1B0. **Area Code:** 604.

ACCOMMODATIONS Although most of Whistler's digs are expensive, budget travelers can find financial respite in a handful of establishments. Grab a bed and your own cheap piece of heaven in the magnificent **Whistler Hostel (HI-C),** 5678 Alta Lake Rd. (932-5492; fax 932-4687), 5km south of Whistler Village. BC Rail from Vancouver will stop at the hostel on request. Public bus transportation ($1.50) to Whistler Village is available three times per day in the summer, four in winter. The timber-hewn lakefront cabin contains a kitchen, fireplace, ski lockers, and sauna. Slope junkies take note: ski tuning can be performed on the premises, and discount lift tickets for Whistler or Blackcomb are available for $46. In summer, guests can rent bikes ($18 per day) and canoe freely in Alta Lake. (Dorms $18; nonmembers $22.28; under 13 halfprice; under 6 free; key deposit $10; check-in 8-11am and 4-10pm; reservations required year-round.) Closer to the action at 1km north of the village, the **Shoestring Lodge,** 7124 Nancy Greene Dr. (932-3338; fax 932-8347), offers excellent rooms with cable, private bathroom, and shared kitchen available. Prices vary considerably over the year (dorm bunks $17-27; doubles $50-115), with peak prices and mandatory reservations from late December through early April, and free shuttle transport to the slopes in winter. **The Fireside Lodge,** 2117 Nordic Dr. (932-4545), in Nordic Estates 3km south of the village, serves up a spacious club cabin with the works: huge kitchen, lounge, sauna, laundry, game room, storage, and parking (dorms Apr.-mid-Dec. $15; in winter weekdays $25, weekends $30; check-in 3-8pm).

FOOD Dining in Whistler costs a little extra, but at least most local grub comes with a great view. **Zeuski's Taverna** (932-6009), in Whistler Town Plaza, features hearty Greek and Mediterranean cuisine. Dinner prices are Olympian ($11-27), but a takeout window offers falafel, souvlaki, and gyro lunches for $5-10 (open Su-Th 11:30am-10pm, F-Sa 11:30am-11pm). Quality grill fare at the popular **CITTA' Bistro** (932-4177), in the Village Square, includes tasty burgers, pizza, wraps, and sandwiches ($7-12). The bar bill can grow quickly with beers starting at $4 per bottle (open 11am-1am). For a lazy breakfast serenaded by the Grateful Dead, nestle into the **South Side Deli,** 2102 Lake Placid Rd. (932-3368), on Hwy. 99 opposite the Husky gas station, 4km south of the village. Veggie omelettes cost $7, though they won't put your arteries to the test like the B.E.L.T.C.H. sandwich (Bacon, Egg, Lettuce, Tomato, Cheese, Ham) for $7 (open daily 6am-3pm). **Nester's Market,** 1019 Nester's Rd., about 1km north of the village, and **IGA** in the Village Marketplace sell everyday groceries.

OUTDOORS The conclusion of Whistler's main ski season in no way ends the fun in the surrounding mountains. A winter **skiing day pass** for the recently-merged **Whistler and Blackcomb Mountains** (932-3434) costs $55 (multi-day discounts available). The **Whistler Gondola** whisks sightseers to the top of the mountain year-round for $20. **Wedge Rafting** (932-7171), inside Whistler Village's Carlton Lodge between the Whistler and Blackcomb lifts, has a wide selection of rafting trips and a friendly, skilled staff. *(3hr. trip $49, full-day trip $114.)* Landlubbers might prefer to investigate some of the great **mountain biking trails** around Whistler; rentals are available at **Grinder's** (932-2283), in the Whistler Village Marketplace. *(Open daily 8am-8pm. $7 per hr., $18 per half-day, $30 per day.)* To see the same sights with less sweat and more racket, book an ATV through **Canadian Snowmobile & ATV** (938-1616), inside the Carlton Lodge. *(1½hr. tour $79 solo, $39 per passenger; 4hr. of gas-guzzling vehicular pleasure $169 solo, $89 per passenger.)* Mount a trusty steed and explore Whistler by hoof through **Whistler Stables** (932-6623), about 3km north of the village. *(3hr. tour $70, 1½hr. $35.)* Or hoof it yourself on one of Whistler's many **hiking trails** for free.

■ Near Vancouver: Sechelt

Tucked between the Strait of Georgia and Porpoise Bay on the Sunshine Coast, Sechelt (SEE-shellt) has long been considered one of B.C.'s greatest secrets by those in the know. It's only two hours by road and ferry from Vancouver, but this quiet seaside paradise remains miles away in attitude, lifestyle, and even climate. Every third car is happily adorned with a sea kayak or canoe on the roof, and hordes of cyclists use Sechelt as a base for exploring the coast and mountains on its doorstep.

ORIENTATION AND PRACTICAL INFORMATION Sechelt, the largest town along the Sunshine Coast, is located 27km west of Langdale Ferry Terminal, where a 40 minute trip across Howe Sound links the Sunshine Coast with Horseshoe Bay and the rest of the B.C. Mainland.

Ferries: BC Ferry (886-2242 or 888-223-3779) from Horseshoe Bay provides the only access to the Sunshine Coast (8-10 times per day, $8, ages 5-11 $4, car $27.75; off-season slightly cheaper). Only charged from Sechelt to Horseshoe Bay.
Buses: Malaspina Coach Lines (885-3666) runs between Vancouver and the Sunshine Coast. Sechelt to Vancouver: 2 per day, $10.40. Vancouver to Sechelt: 2 per day, $18.40. Discounts for seniors and ages under 12.

Public Transportation: Sunshine Coast Transit System (885-3234). From Sechelt to the Langdale Ferry Terminal ($1.50 adult, $1 students and seniors).

Car Rental: National Tilden (885-9120) at 5637 Wharf St. will rent you a car from $50 per day; 35¢ per extra km over 100km; in winter rates start at $40 per day.

Visitor Information: Visitor Infocentre (885-0662) is in the Trail Bay Centre at Trail Ave. and Teredo St., and sells a comprehensive map and booklet to hiking and biking along the coast ($5). Open July to mid-Sept. M-Th and Sa 9:30am-5:30pm, F 9:30am-7pm, Su 11am-4pm; off-season closed weekends.

Banks: Royal Bank, in the Trail Bay Centre. Open M-Th 9:30am-4pm, F 9:30am-5pm. 24hr. ATM

Equipment Rental: Trail Bay Sports (885-2512), at Cowrie St. and Trail Ave., sells fishing gear, nautical maps ($20), and lots of outdoor toys. Open summer M-Th and Sa 9am-6pm, F 9am-9pm, Su 10am-4pm; in winter M-Sa 9am-5pm.

Library: Sechelt Public Library, 5797 Cowrie St. (885-3260). Internet access available. Open Tu and Sa 10am-4pm, W and Th 11am-8pm, Su 1-5pm.

Laundromat: Sechelt Coin Laundry (885-3393) on Dolphin St. at Inlet Ave. Wash $1.50, 25¢ per 5min. Open M-F 9am-7pm, Sa 9am-6pm, Su 11am-5pm.

Senior Center: Sechelt Seniors Centre (885-3513), on Trail Ave. at Sherlock Lane, offers carpet bowling, dancing, bridge, and other fun for members ($10).

Emergency: 911.

Pharmacy: Pharmasave (885-9833) in the Trail Bay Centre is a comprehensive drug store and pharmacy. Open M-Th 9am-6pm, F 9am-7pm, Su 10am-5pm).

Hospital: St. Mary's (885-2224), right along the highway, in the east end of town.

Post office: (885-2411), on Inlet Ave. at Dolphin St. Open M-F 8:30am-5pm, Sa 8:30am-12:30pm. **Postal Code:** V0N 3A0.

Area code: 604.

ACCOMMODATIONS AND CAMPGROUNDS

Most of Sechelt's accommodations offer resort luxury and corresponding prices, but a few deals can be found. **Eagle View B&B** (885-7225), at 4839 Eagle View Rd., 5min. east of Sechelt, has delightful rooms with private bath, a sitting room with TV and VCR, and delightful hosts ($45 singles; $60 doubles). **Cozy Court Motel** (885-9314), in town at 5522 Inlet Ave., offers private bath, cable, and free local calls (singles $52, doubles $60; $5 less Oct.-June; kitchen units $5 extra).

The provincial parks in the area are dreamy. **Porpoise Bay Provincial Park,** 4km north of Sechelt along Sechelt Inlet Rd., offers pit and flush toilets, showers, firewood, beach and swimming area (86 sites: $14.50; cyclist campground by the water $7; wheelchair accessible). For more seclusion, **Roberts Creek Provincial Park,** 11km east of Sechelt, has private sites amid old growth Douglas Firs (24 sites; $9.50; pit toilets, firewood, water; wheelchair accessible). **Smuggler Cove Provincial Park** has primitive, free walk-in sites with pit toilets but no water. To get there, head west out of town towards Halfmoon Bay and turn left onto Brooks Rd. which leads to a parking area after 3.5km. The campsite is 1km along a trail through the forest.

FOOD

The bright and hip **Sun Fish Cafe** (885-0237), 5530 Wharf St., is a breakfast favorite. A spanish omelette (3 eggs, tomato jalapeno salsa, cheddar) with hash browns and toast costs $6. For lunch or dinner, try the falafel burger ($6.50), or the shrimp sandwich ($9; open daily 7am-11pm). Next door, the **Old Boot Eatery** (885-2727) serves up generous portions of Italian food with local hospitality. Enjoy meatballs and rotini ($9), clam linguini ($11), and homemade focaccia bread (open M-Sa 11am-10pm). **Kafe Amigo** (740-0080), 5685 Cowrie St., offers decent Mexican food, including veggie taco salad ($3.25) and chicken fajitas ($4.75; open in summer M-Th and Sa 9am-6pm, F 9am-8pm, Su noon-3pm). For groceries, **Claytons** (885-2025), in the Trail Bay Centre, has the biggest selection in town (open M-Th 9am-7pm, F 9am-9pm, Sa-Su 10am-6pm).

SITES AND OUTDOORS

The protected waters of **Sechelt Inlet** make for great sea kayaking and canoeing. **Pedals & Paddles** (885-6440), at Tillicum Bay Marina, 8km north of town, rents boats and gear. *(Up to 4 hrs: singles $23, doubles $45, canoes $25; full-*

day: singles $40, doubles $75, canoes $45.) For those willing to transport boats, cheaper deals can be found in Vancouver. **Skookumchuck Narrows** is a popular destination by water or by land. The tidal rapids bring 5-foot standing waves at peak tides. To get there drive 54km west to **Earl's Cove,** then another 4km towards **Egmont.** From the parking area, it's a 4km walk to four scenic viewing sites, with the route to the first site wheelchair-accessible. **Georgia Strait Diving & Tours** (883-0251 or 888-292-9999), provides scuba diving gear and dive master. The intermediate **Chapman Creek Trail** passes huge douglas firs en route to a series of cataracts known as **Chapman Falls.** The trailhead is at the top of Havies Rd., 1.1km north of the Davis Bay Store on Highway 101. The **Suncoaster Trail** is a new route which extends over 40km from **Homesite Creek,** near Halfmoon Bay northwest of Sechelt, through the foothills of the **Caren Range.** At higher elevations outside town, steep forestry roads become impassable for trucks, so locals turn them into exhilarating **toboggan runs.**

Indoors, the **Sunshine Coast Arts Centre** (885-5412), on Trail Ave. at Medusa St., showcases local talent in an intimate log cabin. *(Admission by donation; open Tu-Sa 10am-4pm, Su 1-4pm.)* From August 12-15, Sechelt will play host to the **Sunshine Coast Festival of the Written Arts,** which spotlights talented Canadian authors. **Readings** and panels are held in the **botanical gardens** of the historic **Rockwood Centre.** For info on the festival or the center, call 885-9631. *(Grounds open daily 8am-10pm.)*

VANCOUVER ISLAND

Vancouver Island stretches for almost 500km along continental Canada's southwest coast, and extends south of the 49th parallel. The Kwagiulth, Nootka, and Coastal Salish shared the island for thousands of years until Captain Cook's 1778 discovery of Nootka Sound triggered European settlement. The current culture of Vancouver Island bespeaks its hybrid heritage, presenting a curious blend of totems and afternoon teas. Victoria, lying at the island's southern tip, is British Columbia's capital and the cultural center of the island.

The Trans-Canada Highway (Hwy. 1), approaching the end of its 8000km trek, leads north from Victoria to Nanaimo, the transportation hub of the island's central region. Outside of Victoria and Nanaimo, towns shrink in size and the wilderness takes over, creating a haven for hikers, kayakers, and mountaineers. Many remote towns have been built on logging and fishing, while others are populated by earth-loving hippies, who infiltrated the island while dodging the American draft during the Vietnam War. The Comox Valley is a year-round base for skiing, hiking, and fantastic fishing; here some of the world's largest salmon have met their smoker. Pacific Rim National Park, in the island's west coast rainforest, presents some of the most rugged and astounding hiking in North America. On the northern third of the island, where Campbell River guards the entrance to remote Strathcona Provincial Park, crumpets give way to clamburgers, while pickup trucks and logging caravans prowl the roads.

🐾 HIGHLIGHTS OF VANCOUVER ISLAND

- In **Victoria** (see below), the **Royal British Columbia Museum** (see p. 275) covers everything about the region, while the **Butchart Gardens** (see p. 275) tame nature with lush magnificence.
- The **West Coast Trail** (see p. 288) is an intense spiritual pilgrimage of isolated beaches and old growth rainforest, while shorter hikes in **Long Beach** (see p. 291) and **Strathcona Provincial Park** (see p. 284) aren't half-bad, either.
- The mellow hippie town of **Tofino** (see p. 289) offers exhilarating **whalewatching** from tiny Zodiac rafts, plus plenty of organic food and coastal frolicking.

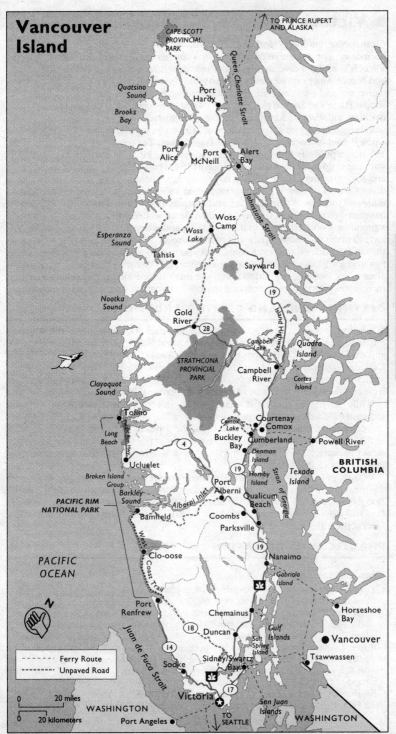

Vancouver Island

TO PRINCE RUPERT
AND ALASKA

CAPE SCOTT
PROVINCIAL
PARK

Quatsino Sound

Brooks Bay

Port Hardy

Queen Charlotte Strait

Port Alice

Port McNeill

Alert Bay

Johnstone Strait

Esperanza Sound

Woss Lake

Woss Camp

Tahsis

Sayward

Nootka Sound

(19)

Gold River

(28)

Campbell Lake

STRATHCONA PROVINCIAL PARK

Quadra Island

Cortes Island

Campbell River

Clayoquot Sound

Tofino

Long Beach

Comox Lake

Courtenay
Comox

Buckley Bay

Cumberland

Powell River

Ucluelet

Denman Island

BRITISH COLUMBIA

Broken Island Group

Barkley Sound

PACIFIC RIM NATIONAL PARK

Bamfield

(19)

Hornby Island

Texada Island

Strait of Georgia

Port Alberni

Qualicum Beach

Alberni Inlet

Coombs

Parksville

Clo-oose

(4)

(19)

Nanaimo

West Coast Trail

Gabriola Island

PACIFIC OCEAN

Chemainus

Horseshoe Bay

Port Renfrew

(18)

Duncan

Guantanamo
Salt Spring Island

Gulf Islands

Vancouver

N

(14)

Sooke

Sidney/Swartz Bay

Tsawwassen

Juan de Fuca Strait

Victoria

(17)

San Juan Islands

0 20 miles
0 20 kilometers

WASHINGTON

Port Angeles

TO SEATTLE

WASHINGTON

--- Ferry Route
······· Unpaved Road

■ Victoria

Clean, polite, outdoorsy, and tourist-friendly, Victoria gives Dudley Do-Right a run for his money. The namesake British monarch and her era of morals and furniture aside, Victoria is a city of diverse origins and interests. A motley mix of British, Asian, U.S., and Native American elements comprise B.C.'s capital city. Trading posts featuring native arts and crafts operate alongside new-age bookstores, tourist traps, and pawn shops. There's an English pub on every downtown corner, and East Asian restaurants, markets, and stores dot virtually every neighborhood.

Although many tourist operations would love you to believe that Victoria fell off of Great Britain in a neat little chunk, its English High Tea tradition largely began in the 1950s as a publicity lure for American tourists. The city was actually built by miners who came up from the States. Founded in 1843, Fort Victoria was a fur trading post and supply center for the Hudson Bay Company. The discovery of gold in the Fraser River Canyon pushed it into the fast lane in 1858, bringing extensive international trade and the requisite frontier bars and brothels. In the time since, however, Victoria has managed to keep out the hustle and bustle associated with big cities. Neighboring Vancouver absorbs the bulk of B.C.'s industry and international finance, allowing Victoria to maintain a slower pace and prettier streets. While thousands of travelers pass through Victoria on the way to the island's provincial and national parks, some come just to enjoy a kinder approach to urban living. The Victorian lifestyle is contagious—after a few hours' exploration, even the most disgruntled city-dwellers may find themselves reluctant to jaywalk and anxious to exchange greetings with passersby.

GETTING THERE AND GETTING AROUND

While the commercial Seattle and Port Angeles ferries dock downtown, the Washington State Ferries from the San Juan Islands dock at **Sidney,** 28km north on Hwy. 17, and the Vancouver/Gulf Islands ferries dock at **Swartz Bay,** 32km north. The **Trans-Canada Highway (Hwy. 1)** leads north and turns into **Highway 19** at Nanaimo, stretching north to the rest of Vancouver Island; **Highway 14** heads west to **Port Renfrew** and the southern portion of **Pacific Rim National Park.**

While driving in Victoria is relatively easy, **parking** downtown is difficult and expensive. Meters charge $1 per 48 minutes while most lots cost $1-1.50 per hour, and offenders are ticketed with zeal. Cross the Johnson St. Bridge (Pandora St. leads to the bridge from downtown) and take the second right or left onto Tyee St. for **free street parking,** a mere 10-minute walk from downtown. Parking in most residential neighborhoods is also free.

Victoria enfolds the Inner Harbour; **Government Street** and **Douglas Street** are the main north-south thoroughfares, running through all of downtown. To the north, Douglas St. becomes Hwy. 1, while **Blanshard Street,** one block to the east, becomes Hwy. 17. Residential neighborhoods, wealthier and in the east, form a semicircle around the Inner Harbour.

PRACTICAL INFORMATION

Transportation

Trains: E&N Railway, 450 Pandora St. (departure/arrival info 383-4324; general info and tickets 800-561-8630), near the Inner Harbour at the Johnson St. Bridge. Daily service to: Nanaimo ($20, students with ISIC $12); Courtenay ($36, students with ISIC $22.50). 10% senior discount. Book 7 days in advance for 25% off the ticket fare. Reservations recommended.

Buses: Laidlaw, 700 Douglas St. (385-4411 or 800-318-0818), at Belleville St. Laidlaw and its affiliates, **Pacific Coach Lines** and **Island Coach Lines,** connect most points on the island. To: Nanaimo (6 per day, $17); Vancouver (8 per day, $26); Port Hardy (2 per day, $82).

Ferries: BC Ferries (381-5335 or 888-BC-FERRY/223-3779; operator 7am-10pm 386-3431). Ferries depart from Swartz Bay to Vancouver (Tsawwassen) (8-15 per day,

Victoria

TO HWY. 1

TO HWY. 17 AND
BUTCHART GARDENS,
FERRY TERMINAL,
U. OF VICTORIA

Selkirk
Water

Bridge

Gorge Rd. East

Ellice St.

Market

Hillside

Wark

David

Hillside

John

Rock Bay

Ludgate

Bridge

Ross

West-
bourne

Hill

King St.

Douglas

Dowler

Wark

Pleasant

Turner

Bay St.

Field

Blanshard

Tyee

Bay St.

Wilson

Upper
Harbour

Queens

Princess

Pembroke

Government

Discovery

Pembroke

Sitkum

Esquimalt

Harbour

Chatham

Caledonia

Julia

Cooperage Pl.

Saghalie

Tyee

Store

Swift

CHINATOWN

Herald

Fisgard

Cormorant

Amelia

Paul
Kane

Kimta Rd.

Songhees

E&N Railway
Station

Pandora

MARKET
SQ.

Johnson

Broad

Douglas

Yates

Blanshard

Quadra

Victoria
Youth Hostel

Inner
Harbour

Wharf

BASTION
SQ.

Trounce

View

Victoria
Harbour

Langley

Fort

Broughton

Courtney

Gordon

Public
Library

Courtney

TO CRAGDARROCH CASTLE,
ART GALLERY OF GREATER
VICTORIA, OAK BAY

Kingston

Cross

Belleville

Empress
Hotel

Humboldt

Penwell

Rupert
Fairfield

Ontario

Pendray

Quebec

Parliament
Buildings

Government

Elliot

Academy

Humboldt
Convent

Montreal

Oswega

Kingston

Menzies

Royal
British Columbia
Museum

Southgate St.

Niagra

Beckley

Almo Pl.

Simcoe

Rendall

Croft

Michigan

Superior

Perry

Powell

Heather

Michigan

Young

Douglas

Toronto

Beacon
Hill
Park

Haywood Av.

0   yards   440

0   meters   400

N

$8.50; bikes $2.50; car and driver $36-38). Service to all Gulf Islands (see p. 278). Bus #70 runs from the ferry terminal to downtown ($2.25). **Washington State Ferries** (381-1551 or 656-1531; in the U.S. 206-464-6400 or 800-84-FERRY/843-3779). Ferries Depart from Sidney to Anacortes, WA (2 per day in summer; 1 per day in winter; CDN$9.50, US$6.90; car with driver CDN$50, US$35.65). A ticket to Anacortes allows free and unlimited stopovers anywhere along the eastward route, including the San Juan Islands. Several independent ferries also run between these islands and the mainland. **Victoria Clipper,** 254 Belleville St. (382-8100 or 800-888-2535), runs direct service to Seattle (4 per day May-Sept.; 1 per day Oct.-Apr.; US$58-66, senior $52-60, ages 1-11 $29-33). Passengers only, except for 1 car ferry daily at 7:30am (car with driver US$49). **Black Ball Transport,** 430 Belleville St. (386-2202), runs to Port Angeles, WA. (4 per day Mid-May to mid-Oct.; 2 per day Oct.-Nov. and mid-March to mid-May; 1 per day Dec. to mid-March. US$6.75, car and driver US$27.25, ages 5-11 US$4.50).

Public Transportation: BC Transit (382-6161). City bus service with connections downtown, at the corner of Douglas and Yates St. Single-zone travel $1.75; multizone (north to Swartz Bay, Sidney, and the Butchart Gardens) $2.50; seniors $1.10; under 5 free. Day passes ($5.50, seniors $4) and free Rider's Guide with complete maps at Tourism Victoria (see below), at the library (see below), or from any bus driver. **Disabilities Services for Local Transit** (727-7811). Open M-F 8am-5pm.

Car Rental: Island Auto Rentals, 837 Yates St. (384-4881). $20 per day, plus $12 insurance and 12¢ per-km after 50km. Must be 19 with major credit card. **Rent-a Wreck,** 2634 Douglas St. (384-5343 or 800-809-0788). $30 per day plus 12¢ per km after 100km. Must be 21 with major credit card. **Budget,** 727 Courtenay St. (953-5300 or 800-668-9833), off Douglas St., near the Sticky Wicket. $30 per day, plus 20¢ per km after 100km; $7 unlimited km. Must be 21.

Auto Club: BC Automobile Association, 1075 Pandora Ave. (389-6700). Full range of services for CAA and AAA members. Open M-Sa 9am-5pm.

Taxis: Victoria Taxi (383-7111). **Westwind** (474-4747). Both $2.15 base, $1.30 per km, and run 24hr.

Visitor Services

Visitor Information: Tourism Victoria, 812 Wharf St. (953-2033), at Government St. Eager staff doles out steaming scoops of info. Everything from pamphlets to bus, boat, and nature tours. Ticketmaster outlet. Open daily 8:30am-8pm; in winter 9am-5pm.

Tours: Grayline, 700 Douglas St. (388-5248; http://www.victoriatours.com). Runs several tours in double-decker buses through different parts of the city ($16-56). The trolley car tour allows passengers to hop on and off as often as they want ($7). **Historical Walking Tours** (953-2033) does the downtown, leaving from the info-center daily at 11am (1hr., $7). The **Murder, Ghosts, and Mayhem Walking Tour** (385-2035) leads through dark streets and back alleys, telling tales of old crimes and mysteries. Tours leave daily from the Bastion Square Arch at 8pm (1hr., $5, under 12 free).

Local Services

Equipment Rental: Harbour Rental, 811 Wharf St. (995-1661). Mountain bikes $8 per hr., $35 per day. Lock and helmet included. Scooters $16 per hr., $50 per day, plus $7 insurance per day. Open daily 9am-5pm. **Budget** (see above) rents bikes ($6 per hr., $20 per day) and scooters ($12 per hr., $45 per day). **Jeune Brothers,** 570 Johnson St. (386-8778; fax 380-1533). 3-person tents $42 for 2 days, $75 per week. 10% HI discount. Open M-Th 10am-6pm, F 10am-9pm, Sa 10am-5:30pm, Su noon-5pm.

Library: 735 Broughton St. (382-7241), at Courtney St. Open M, W, and F-Sa 9am-6pm, Tu and Th 9am-9pm.

Gay and Lesbian Information: Prideline, 800-566-1170 (province-wide). Volunteer staff M, W, and F 7-10pm, Tu and Th 1-4pm and 7-10pm.

Laundromat: Garden City Laundromat, 141 Menzies St., south from the west Parliament Building. Open daily 5am-11pm.

Emergency and Communications

Emergency: 911. **Police:** 625 Fisgard St. (384-4111), at Government St.
Crisis Line: 386-6323. 24hr. **Rape Crisis:** 383-3232. 24hr. **Poison Control:** 682-5050 or 800-567-8911. 24hr.
Pharmacy: London Drugs, 911 Yates St. (381-1113), at Vancouver St., in the Wilson Centre. Open M-Sa 9am-10pm, Su 10am-8pm.
Hospital: Royal Jubilee, 1900 Fort St. (370-8000).
Post Office: 621 Discovery St. (963-1350). Open M-F 8am-6pm. **Postal Code:** V8W 1L0.
Internet Access: Victoria Cyber Cafe, 1414B Douglas St. (995-0175). Internet use 14¢ per min.; extensive software and scanning, too. Open daily 10am-10pm, sometimes later.
Area Code: 250.

ACCOMMODATIONS

Victoria has a capital budget accommodations scene, but a less-than-perfect selection of campgrounds. A number of flavorful hostels and B&B-hostel hybrids make a night inside in Victoria an altogether pleasant experience. Reserve in summer.

🐾**Victoria Backpackers Hostel,** 1418 Fernwood Rd. (386-4471). Take bus #10 to Fernwood and Johnson St. A funky, colorful old house, with porch, backyard, lounge, and kitchen. Claude and his staff are so friendly and laid-back that many guests forget to see the rest of Victoria. Free parking. 36 beds with single-sex and co-ed rooms. Bunks $13 first night, $12 after; private doubles $40. Dinner served every evening with meat and vegetarian options ($3-5). Linen free, laundry $2 per load. Reception open daily 8am-noon and 4-11pm.

Selkirk Guest House, 934 Selkirk Ave. (389-1213), in West Victoria. Take bus #14 along Craigflower to Tillicum; Selkirk is 1 block north. Become a part of the family in the Jacksons' very lived-in home. Cushy co-ed and all-female dorms with flowery sheets, free canoes, and a hot tub right on the water. Lyn, a.k.a House Mom, a.k.a Sparkle the Clown, knows loads of magic tricks—guests can watch Spike the Wonder Dog jump through her arms. Dorms $18, private rooms $50. Prices drop in off-season. Breakfast $5. Kitchen, free linen and towels, laundry. Family friendly.

Renouf House Bunk & Breakfast, 2010 Stanley Ave. (595-4774; fax 598-1515; email renouf@islandnet.com). Take bus #10 to the intersection of Johnson and Fernwood St. Stanley Ave. runs parallel to Fernwood, 1 block to the west, and begins 2 blocks north of Johnson St. Built in 1910 and full of antique furniture and dark wooden staircases. The large continental breakfast features homemade granola and breads. Owners provide advice on sight-seeing and Victoria's history. Bunks $20; singles $33, with private bath $55; doubles $50, with private bath $70. Kitchen and laundry. Affiliated with **Christine's Place** down the street, which has extra rooms in a smaller, more modern, but still swank house. Singles $35; doubles $50.

The Cat's Meow, 1316 Grant St. (595-8878). Take bus #10 to Fernwood and Grant. A mini-hostel with 12 quiet and comfy beds. The hostel's namesake, Rufus, rests in peace, but the house lives on in his name. His "mother," Daphne, is a font of info about the area. Beds $17.50; private doubles $43. Breakfast included.

Victoria Youth Hostel (HI-C), 516 Yates St. (385-4511), at Wharf St. downtown. Big, modern, and spotless. Ping pong, video games, and a TV room provide an escape from the multitude of people. Staff and volunteer concierges offer a wealth of info, including valuable tips on where to park. Dorms $16, nonmembers $20. Family and couples' rooms available for $2 surcharge per person. Kitchen and free linen. Laundry $1.75; towel 50¢. Reception open 7am-midnight. No curfew.

University of Victoria (721-8395), 20min. northeast of the Inner Harbour by bus #4 or 14. From Hwy. 17, take McKenzie Ave. to Sinclair. Housing office is in Lot 5. Private dorms with shared baths. Cute wild rabbits living under the buildings. Singles $38; doubles $50. Cafeteria breakfast included. Coin-op laundry. Reservations advised. Open May-Aug.

Hotel Douglas, 1450 Douglas St. (383-4157 or 800-332-9981; email douglas@pacific-coast.net). Small but nicely furnished rooms in a busy downtown location. $40 for

1-2 people with shared bathroom; with private bathrooms from $50 for 1 person, $60 for 2. Free parking. Inside the hotel lobby at **Cafe de la Lune,** coffee and eclectic crowds flow in and out 24hr.

CAMPGROUNDS

The few campgrounds on the perimeter of Victoria cater largely to RVs. Many fill up in July and August; making reservations is a wise idea.

Goldstream Provincial Park, 2930 Trans-Canada Hwy. (391-2300; reservations 800-689-9025), 20km northwest of Victoria. Forested riverside area with great short hiking trails and swimming. In Nov., the river is crowded with spawning salmon. Flush toilets and firewood available. 150 gorgeous, gravelly sites ($15.50). The nearby **Freeman King Visitor Centre** gives the history of the area from the Ice Age to the welfare state. Open daily 9:30am-4:30pm; in winter Sa-Su only.

Thetis Lake Campground, 1938 Trans-Canada Hwy. (478-3845), 10km north of the city center. Sites are not large, but some are peaceful and removed. Thetis Lake is popular among locals for great cliff diving. (Cliff diving is not recommended by *Let's Go* or your mother.) Sites $15 for 2 people; full hookups $19; 50¢ per additional person. Showers (25¢ per 5min.), flush toilets, laundry.

Paradise Lake Campground, 2960 Humpback Rd. (478-6960). Take the Goldstream Park exit from Hwy. 1. Small sites tucked into the trees, with goodies for the kiddies, like a lagoon with slide and boats. Sites $18 for 2 people, $2 per additional person; full hookups $23. Firewood $6.50. Flush toilets.

FOOD

The variety and high quality of food in Victoria undermine the city's attempts to pass itself off as the North American equivalent of Jolly Olde Numb-Tongued England. The abundance of coffee shops crawling with in-house baked pastries, on the other hand, reveals Victoria's proximity to Seattle. A stroll along **Government** and **Wharf Streets** presents countless restaurants, but caveat emptor—some raise their prices for the summer tourists and are dutifully avoided by locals. **Chinatown,** extending from Fisgard and Government St. to the northwest, offers a range of Chinese cuisine and small, fruit-stocked grocery stores. (As in all Chinatowns, the smaller, less glitzy restaurants are often the cheapest and the best.) In **Fernwood Village,** three blocks north of Johnson St. and accessible by bus #10, creative restaurants are scattered among craft shops. If you feel like cooking, head down to **Fisherman's Wharf** at the corner of Harbour and Government St. to buy the day's catch as it flops off the boats. For large-scale grocery shopping, try **Thrifty Foods,** 475 Simcoe (544-1234), six blocks south of the Parliament Buildings (open daily 8am-10pm).

John's Place, 723 Pandora St. (389-0711), between Douglas and Blanshard St. Only the Place's portions can outdo its enormous reputation among locals. Complete with jukebox and Marilyn pinups, John's hops. The menu is graced by Canadian fare with a Thai twist plus a little Mediterranean and Mexican thrown in. Savory fresh herb bread and butter. Try John's favorite, *panang goong* (sauteed tiger prawns in curry sauce $11.50). Extra selections on Thai night (M), Mexican night (Tu), and perogie night (W). Open M-Sa 7am-11pm, Su 8am-3pm and 5-10pm.

The Blethering Place, 2250 Oak Bay Ave. (598-1413), at Monterey St. Take bus #2 from Douglas at Yates or drive west on Fort St. and turn right on Oak Bay. The sun never set on the British Empire in upscale, upright Oak Bay. Despite the Anglophilia, live music is diverse, ranging from Celtic folk songs to jazz daily at 6pm. A trip to Victoria is improper without a spot of tea, and the huge plate of sandwiches and pastries that accompany High Tea ($10-12), and a long afternoon of "blethering" (that's "voluble senseless talking"). The home-made scones ($3.75), with rich Devonshire cream ($1.50 extra) and homemade strawberry jam, are reason enough to make the trip. Ploughman's Lunch ($8) is a cheesier, meatier alternative. Dinners from $9. Open daily 8am-10pm.

El Rancho Restaurant, 5285 West Saanich Rd. (479-3436). Take Johnson to Quadra, turn left, then follow Quadra over Hwy. 17, where it becomes West Saanich; El Rancho is in the Prospect Lake Restaurant. Take bus #74 (a.k.a. 6 Quadra) from Yates at Broad St. to West Saanich and Royal Oak, 1 block from the restaurant. El Rancho is 1 of the only places in Victoria where "South of the Border" doesn't mean Washington State. Regulars flock for the enormous and delicious Mexican menu on Sa and Su nights, with live music on Sa. Weeknights feature German and Czech cuisine, too. Chicken dumplings $14; beef or veggie burger $7. Free parking. Open F-Sa 11:30am-10pm, Su-Th 11:30am-9pm.

The Sally Cafe, 714 Cormorant St. (381-1431), off Douglas St., 1 block north of Pandora St. Sally forth into a menu as colorful as the restaurant itself. Vegetarian-friendly, the light creations include salads, pastas, sandwiches, and bagels. Curried chicken and apricots $6; sandwiches from $4.75. Open M-F 7am-5pm, Sa 8am-5pm.

Milky Way, 128-560 Johnson St. (360-1113), at the corner of Johnson and Wharf St. Breakfast, lunch, and dinner specials ($3-10) make this one of the better bargains in town; the star-studded decor makes it one of the more entertaining. Live music Sa and Su nights. Big breakfasts are served until 4pm, with omelettes and pancake stacks both starting at $5.50. Open daily 7am-11pm.

Green Cuisine, 560 #5 Johnson St. (385-1809), in Market Sq. The $1.39-per-100g buffet offers so many international foods, including tofu-based ice cream, that even the most blood-thirsty of meat-eaters may not mind that the restaurant is all vegan. Fruit shakes $3.50. Buffet 25% off after 5pm. Open daily 9am-9pm.

Zombies Pizza, 1219 Wharf St. (389-2226). Cheerfully morbid decor and $2 slices make this a good, quick stop. Cookies "as big as your face" $2.50. Open late for post-pub munchies and the restless undead. Open M-Sa 11am-3am, Su 11am-1am.

Benny's Bagels, 132-560 Johnson St. (384-3441), on the Wharf St. side of Market Sq. Creative bagel sandwiches are a meal in themselves. Whole-grain and environmentally safe: round food hurts no one (70¢). Sandwiches and cheesy bagel melts $3-6. Open M-F 7:30am-5pm, Sa-Su 9am-5pm.

SIGHTS AND OUTDOORS

If you don't mind becoming one with the flocks of tourists hurling themselves, lemming-like, toward the shores of Victoria, wander along the **Inner Harbour** and watch the boats come in as the sun sets behind the neighboring islands. The fantastically thorough **Royal British Columbia Museum,** 675 Belleville St. (recording 387-3014; operator 387-3701), soundly kicks the asses of most West Coast museums. *(Open daily 9am-5pm. $7, seniors $3.21, youth $2.14, under 5 free.)* Excellent exhibits on the biological, geological, and cultural history of the province, from protozoans to the present. The First Nations exhibit features a totem pole room and an immense collection of native art. An **IMAX theater** is expected to open in the museum in 1999. **Thunderbird Park** and its many totems loom behind the museum. *(Tours available starting July 1.)* The public **Art Gallery of Greater Victoria,** 1040 Moss St. (384-4101), houses magnificent exhibits from its collection of 14,000 pieces covering contemporary Canada, traditional and contemporary Asia, North America, and Europe, as well as one of the only Shinto shrines outside of Japan. *(Open M-W and F-Sa 10am-5pm, Th 10am-9pm, Su 1-5pm. $5, students and seniors $3, under 12 free. Free on M.)* The tourist office (see **Practical Information**) has pamphlets on Victoria's **historic houses and parks.**

Across the street from the museum stand the imposing **Parliament Buildings,** 501 Belleville St. (387-3046), home of the Provincial government since 1898. *(Open M-F 8:30am-5pm, Sa and Su open for tours only. Free tours leave from main steps daily 9am-5pm, 3 times per hr.)* The 10-story dome and vestibule are gilded with almost 50 oz. of gold. At night, 3330 lights line the facade. While the House is in session swing by the **public gallery** and witness Members of Parliament yapping about matters of great import.

The elaborate **Butchart Gardens** (recording 652-5256; office 652-4422; email@butchartgardens.bc.ca; http://butchartgardens.bc.ca) sprawl across a valley 21km north of Victoria off Hwy. 17. *(Open daily July and Aug. 9am-10:30pm; closing time varies. Fireworks July-Aug. Sa around 10pm. $15.50, ages 11-17 $7.75, ages 5-12 $2, under 5 free.)* Immaculate landscaping includes a rose garden, Japanese and Italian gardens, fountains, walking paths (wheelchair accessible), and flowers blooming everywhere. Ironically, the flower power was made possible by the fortunes and space left over from George Butchart's less-than-lovely cement business. Visit in late afternoon to avoid crowds in summer, and see the gardens sparkle with lights at night.

Just north of Fort St. on Wharf St. is **Bastion Square,** the original site of the Hudson Bay Company's Fort Victoria. The fort no longer stands, but at least Bastion Square is home to the **Maritime Museum,** 28 Bastion Sq. (385-4222). *(Open daily 9:30am-4:30pm. $5, students $3, seniors $4, ages 6-11 $3. Tickets good for 3 days.)* Exhibits include ship models, nautical instruments, a torpedo, and a 13m modified native canoe that shoved off from Victoria in 1901 on a daring but unsuccessful trip around the world. The metalwork elevator was installed for a non-stair-climbing judge, in the days when the building was the first and only courthouse on Vancouver Island.

Beyond the "Gate of Harmonious Interest" on Fisgard St. at Government St., **Chinatown** has shrunk substantially since the end of the legal opium trade to become China-block. Still, its many restaurants and inexpensive shops make it a worthwhile destination. **Market Square,** the bulk of which lies on Johnson St. four blocks south of Fisgard St., is a collection of countless stores, restaurants, and wooden walkways home to a popular **public fair** on summer Sundays.

The flowering oasis of **Beacon Hill Park,** off Douglas St. south of the Inner Harbour, and just blocks from downtown, pleases walkers, bikers, and the picnic-inclined. Mountain bikers can tackle the **Galloping Goose,** a 60km trail beginning in downtown Victoria and continuing to the west coast of Vancouver Island through towns, rainforests, and canyons. The trail is open to cyclists, pedestrians, and horses. Horses on bicycles are strongly discouraged. The **beach** stretches along the southern edge of the city by Dallas St.; it has too little sand for swimming, but it does sport long shoreline paths, and makes a great bike ride. Take Douglas St. to its southern end.

Victoria is a hub for a number of the sailing, kayaking, and whale-watching tours available on the island. **Ocean River Sports,** 1437 Store St. (381-4233 or 800-909-4233; email info@oceanriver.com; http://www.oceanriver.com) offers kayak rentals, tours, and lessons. *(Open M-Th, Sa 9:30am-5:30pm, F 9:30am-8:30pm, Su 11am-5pm. Half-day rentals cost $28 for a single kayak, $34 for a double, and $28 for a canoe, with all equipment included.)* Most whale watching companies give discounts for hostel residents. **Ocean Explorations,** 146 Kingston St. (383-ORCA/6722; email whales@oceanexplorations.com; http://www.oceanexplorations.com), located in the Coast Victoria Harbourside Hotel, runs tours in Zodiac raft-boats. *(Runs Apr.-Oct. 3hr. tours. $75, hostelers and children $50, less in early season. Reservations recommended. Free pickup at hostels.)*

After a few days of hiking, biking, and museum visiting, unwind with a tour of the **Vancouver Island Brewery** at 2330 Government St. (361-0007). The tour is free, educational, and alcoholic. *(Tours F and Sa at 1 and 3pm. Free samples included.)*

NIGHTLIFE AND ENTERTAINMENT

Victorians may follow the metric system, but their beer is still sold by the pint. English pubs and watering holes abound throughout town, many of which look exactly like one another after a few frothy Guinness. The free weekly **Monday Magazine,** inexplicably released every Wednesday, provides a listing of who's playing where, and is available at hostels, hotels, and most restaurants downtown. For even more up-to-the-minute information, check the telephone poles and light posts around town—posted fliers are often the best source for what's going down.

Nightlife in Victoria doesn't really start jumping until Thursdays, but once the weekend comes, the whole city seems ready to party. Most clubs offer weekday drink specials to draw crowds—cheap beer nights have the highest success rates.

Steamers Public House, 570 Yates St. (381-4340). A young, happy crowd dances to different music every night. World beat grooves from Celtic to funk. Open stage (M), jazz night (Tu). Lunch specials served M-F until 3pm ($5-7). Open M-Sa 11:30am-2am, Su 11:30am-midnight.

Drawing Room, 751 View St. (920-7797). A happening club considerate enough to offer a lounge with easy chairs, pool tables, and wall-to-wall carpet for dancers fleeing the frenzied techno/alternative/house music next door. Fresh fruit bar for mixed drinks. Cover M-F $3, Sa-Su $4. Open Tu-Th 8pm-2am, F-Sa 9pm-2am.

Rumors, 1325 Government St. (385-0566). Gay and lesbian clientele enjoy one of Victoria's more inviting dance floors. Drag shows every other Su. Thursday nights dance and house music; Sa-Su retro high-energy dance. Every 3rd Friday women's night. Open M-Sa 9pm-2am, Su 9pm-midnight.

Sticky Wicket, 919 Douglas St. (383-7137). Seven bars and a club in one building, next door to the Strathcona Hotel. **The Roof Top Bar** even has its own beach volleyball court available for rent. **The Forge** club, specializes in 70s and 80s rock with a wattage that could vaporize tungsten. The Forge charges a $4 cover on weekends; the pubs are cover-free and serve food until 1am. Open M-Sa 11:30am-2am, Su 11:30am-midnight.

Blues House, 1417 Government St. (386-1717). Clientele changes nightly, with the younger crowd at Disco Inferno (M), funk DJ (Tu), 80s dance party (W), mainstream rock (Th); a 30+ set dancing to live R&B bands F-Sa; and a well-attended swing night Su. Open M-F 9pm-2am, F-Sa 8pm-2am, Su 8pm-midnight.

Scandals, 770 Yates St. (389-0666). Laser beams shoot across the floor with reckless abandon in this second home for Victoria's children of the rave. Techno music styles vary depending on the DJ of the night, though bass that will alter your EKG is a constant. All ages. Cover $2-3. Open daily 10pm-4 or 5am.

The **Victoria Symphony Society,** 846 Broughton St. (385-6515), performs regularly under conductor Peter McCoppin. The highlight of its year is the **Symphony Splash,** a free concert on the first Sunday in August, played on a barge in the Inner Harbour. The performance concludes with fireworks and usually draws 40-50,000 international listeners. For the last week and a half of June, Victoria resonates jazz during **JazzFest** (388-4423), as over a dozen performers play venues throughout the city.

On Tuesdays, first-run movies at the **Cineplex Odeon,** 780 Yates St. (383-0513)—and virtually every other first-run theater in Canada—are half-price ($5). For more offbeat and foreign films, head to the **University of Victoria's Cinecenta** (721-8365) in the Student Union (bus #4 and 14). In June **Phoenix Theaters** (721-8000), at UVIC, puts on plays, as well as term-time live theater performances. From mid-July to mid-August, Victoria goes Elizabethan when the **Annual Shakespeare Festival** (360-0234) lands in the Inner Harbour.

■ Near Victoria: Sooke

About 35km west of Victoria on Hwy. 14 lies the unincorporated town of Sooke, named for the T'sou-ke people. **The Sooke Region Museum,** 2070 Phillips Rd. (642-6351), just off the highway, houses a **Travel Infocentre,** and delivers an excellent history of the area (open daily July-Aug. 9am-5:30pm; Sept.-June Tu-Su 9am-5pm; free). To get to Phillips Rd. from the city, take bus #50 to the Western Exchange and transfer to #61. North of Sooke lie some of the best rugged beachcombing opportunities on the island. Highway 14 continues along the coast, stringing together two provincial parks: **Juan de Fuca,** home to China Beach and Lfoss Creek (both limited to day use), and **French Beach** (391-2300), with tent sites (May-Oct. $9.50). Short forest trails connect the beaches with the road, which is far enough away to keep the seaside wild. A longer hike leads to the more isolated **Mystic Beach.** Camping is free at the popular **Jordan River Recreation Area,** 10 minutes past French Beach. The **Galloping Goose** bike and horse trail has a gateway in Sooke, with a day-use area and trails heading both east and west across the island's southern tip.

On Phillips Rd., past the museum, is the **Sooke River Flats Campsite** (642-6076), with a large picnic area, phone, showers, toilets, and running water (gates locked 11pm-7am; sites $12; sani-dump $3). The campsite hosts competitions centered around logging, sharp objects, and family fun on **All Sooke Day,** the third Saturday in July. Turn right at Sooke's only stop light to find **Camp Barnard,** 3130 Young Lake

Rd. (642-5924), a former Boy Scout camp with cabins that sleep eight ($20-32), tent sites ($12), fire pits, hot showers, and swimming (reservations required). In recent years, the B&B industry has experienced more growth than logging has. Sooke is a haven for wealthier Victorians, making cheap indoor accommodations scarce. Try the **Blackfish B&B,** 2440 Blackfish Rd. (642-6864), 7 mi. west of the stop light (singles $35; doubles $50-60). Large groups should ask about the great bungalow down on the pebble beach with free laundry and a full kitchen (sleeps 9; $125). Summer reservations fill up early.

■ Near Victoria: Gulf Islands

Just off the southeastern coast of Vancouver Island lie the quiet waters and stunning scenery of British Columbia's **Gulf Island Archipelago.** The chain's five main islands, **Galiano, Mayne, Pender, Salt Spring,** and **Saturna** are accessible through BC Ferries (250-386-3431; http://bcferries.bc.ca/ferries). Schedules are complicated and ever changing, so it's best to call ahead. For detailed information on the Gulf Islands, call the **Tourist Information Centre** in Salt Spring (537-5252) or Victoria (953-2033). Salt Spring maintains the largest population and widest activity opportunities of the five main islands. The **HI-C hostel** at 640 Cusheon Lake Rd. (537-4149) has its own hiking trails ($14; nonmembers $17). **Maxine's Boardwalk Cafe,** 2-104 Fulford Ganges Rd. (537-5747), sports a waterfront view and a reasonably priced breakfast and lunch menu with colorful and international daily specials. For some outdoor activity, climb **Mt. Maxwell** to enjoy a panoramic view of B.C. and Washington, or putt away at **Blackburn Meadows,** 269 Blackburn Rd. (537-1707), a farm converted into an organic golf course, next to the Salt Spring Audobon sanctuary (9 holes $12, club rental $10). Or tempt fate, commit hubris, and invoke the Furies by playing with the Mounties at the **Royal Canadian Mounted Police** outpost on the outskirts of Ganges Rd. (*Let's Go* does not recommend taunting or sassing national police forces.)

■ Chemainus

About 37km south of Nanaimo and 66km north of Victoria on Hwy. 1 lies Chemainus. To get there, turn right on Henry Rd. from Hwy. 1 heading north, and turn left on Chemainus Rd. at the bottom of the hill. When the closing of the town's sawmill threatened economic disaster in 1980, an ambitious revitalization program centered on a series of more than 30 striking murals, helped bring in the tourists and turn things around. The murals depict the town's history of Native American, Chinese, and white settlers who, larger than life, mostly gaze solemnly into space. The current residents, however, are friendly and seem to have lived in Chemainus for at least a century, through ancestors or personally. Don't miss the tiny but earnest **Snipe Hunt Monument,** commemorating the ageless prank played on hapless boys who are sent out to hunt the fictitious beast, only to be abandoned deep in the woods.

Visit the **Chemainus Valley Museum** for info on all things Chemainusesque (open M-Su 10am-3pm). Locals have picked up on the tourism industry and virtually every home on the main drag hosts a B&B. The **Chemainus Hostel,** in a small house at 9694 Chemainus Rd. (246-2809), is not only a good place to find a bed, a kitchen, and laundry facilities, but also info on activities around the island. The **Horseshoe Bay Inn,** 9576 Chemainus Rd. (416-0411), looks like an Old West antique, offering loud rooms above the pub ($35) and quieter rooms with private bath ($70). Restaurants serving up standard pizza and Canadian and Chinese fare are plentiful along Chemainus Rd.

▓ Nanaimo

Primarily a stopover point for travelers en route to the rainforests of northern and western Vancouver Island, Nanaimo (na-NYE-moe) appears along the highway as a strip of motels, gas stations, and greasy spoons. Those who linger, however, discover Nanaimo's mysterious ability to convert "just-passing-throughs" into "let's-stay-a-few-days." Could it have something to do with the town's beach, 25 parks, and several more provincial parks nearby? Or could it be the dessert? Read on…

ORIENTATION AND PRACTICAL INFORMATION

Nanaimo lies on the east coast of Vancouver Island, 111km north of Victoria on the **Trans-Canada Highway (Hwy. 1)**, and 391km south of **Port Hardy** via the **Island Highway (Hwy 19)**. Highway 1 transforms into Highway 19 in Nanaimo but only after three successive name changes: **Nicol St.**, **Terminal Ave. S.**, and finally **Terminal Ave. N. Nanaimo Parkway** circumvent the town to the south.

Trains: VIA Rail, 321 Selby St. (800-561-8630). To Victoria (1 per day, $20, with 7-day advance purchase $15). Discounts for seniors and students ($11.70 with ISIC card).

Buses: Laidlaw (753-4371), at Comox Rd. and Terminal Ave. behind Tally Ho Island Inn. To: Victoria (6 per day, $17); Port Hardy (2 per day, $65); Tofino and Ucluelet (2 per day, $29).

Ferries: BC Ferries (753-1261 or 888-223-3779). Terminal at the northern end of Stewart Ave., 2km north of downtown. To: Vancouver (8 per day, $8.50, with car $35.50), with connections to Bowen Island and Langdale. Take the **Seaporter ferry shuttle** (753-5141) from behind the Harbour Park Mall or from the Maffeo-Sutton Park in downtown to Newcastle Island ($4.50).

Car Rental: Rent-A-Wreck, 111 Terminal Ave. S. (753-6461). From $35 per day plus 16¢ per km after 150km. Must be 21 with a major credit card. Open M-F 8am-6pm, Sa 9am-4pm, Su 10am-4pm. **Budget,** 33 Terminal Ave. S. (754-7368). From $39 per day, plus 20¢ per km after 100km. Unlimited mileage rates available. Must be 21. Free pickup in most parts of town.

Public Transit: Nanaimo Regional Transit (390-4531), behind Harbour Park Mall. Fare $1.30, seniors $1.05. Check individual schedules for times.

Visitor Information: Visitor Infocentre, 2290 Bowen Rd. (756-0106), west of downtown. Head south on Comox Rd., which becomes Bowen Rd., from Terminal Ave., or north on Northfield Rd. from Nanaimo Pkwy. Open daily 8am-7pm, in winter 9am-5pm.

Laundromat: 702 Nicol St. (753-9922), at Robins Rd. in **Payless Gas Station.** 24hr.

Gay and Lesbian Information: Prideline (800-566-1170). Open daily 7pm-10pm, also Tu and Th 1-4pm.

Emergency: 911. **Police:** 303 Pridaux St. (754-2345), at Fitzwilliam St. **Fire:** 666 Fitzwilliam St. (753-7311 or 753-7344), at Milton St.

Crisis Line: 754-4447. 24hr.

Hospital: 1200 Dufferin Crescent (754-2141). Open 24hr.

Pharmacy: London Drugs, 650 Terminal Ave. S. (753-5566), in Harbour Park Mall. Open M-Sa 9am-10pm, Su 10am-8pm.

Post Office: 650 Terminal Ave. S. (741-1829), in Harbour Park Mall. Open M-F 8:30am-5pm. **Postal Code:** V9R 5E2.

Area Code: 250.

ACCOMMODATIONS AND CAMPGROUNDS

Nicol St. Hostel, 65 Nicol St. (753-1188; email gmurray@island.net; http://hostel.com/~pacrim/nicol.htm). A quick walk from the ferry, bus station, or downtown. 25 beds stuffed into dorms, private rooms, and hallways with tent sites ($8) and ocean views in the backyard. Living room, small but tidy kitchen and bathrooms. Free paint for the ongoing mural mosaic next door. Singles $15; double $30. Private doubles and larger rooms available. Discounts for hostel customers at over 30 nearby establishments.

Big 7 Motel, 736 Nicol St. (754-2328). Pink and baby blue decor, circa 1986, suggests an episode of *Nanaimo Vice.* As compensation, all rooms have cable. Desk open 24hr. Singles $37; doubles $46. In winter: singles $32, doubles $36.

Living Forest Campground, 6 Maki Rd. (755-1755), 3km southwest of downtown. Large, spacious campground with several sites on steep, short cliffs overlooking the ocean. This is the closest campground to town and the most natural, with large cedars throughout. Tent sites $15; full hookups $17. Choice of oceanfront or forest sites. Clean bathrooms and hot showers.

Thompson's Campground, 1660 Cedar Rd. (722-2251), off the Cedar Hwy. about 5km south of downtown. Peaceful and secluded, with a small lawn and a few forest sites right on the Nanaimo River. Communal refrigerator, gas stove, and old-fashioned sauna. Sites $6. Check in at the house and you'll be led to the hard-to-find campground.

Westwood Lake, 380 Westwood Rd. (753-3922), west of town off Jingle Pot Rd., which is itself off the Island Hwy. (Hwy. 19) north of town; take bus #5. Only 200m from a busy swimmin' hole. Follow giant concrete footprints to the office. Full facilities. 66 sites: $16; hookups $19.

Brannen Lake Campsite, 4220 Biggs Rd. (756-0404), 6km north of the ferry terminal. Take a left on Biggs Rd. off Jingle Pot Rd. immediately after exiting the Nanaimo Pkwy., then scoot past the Nanaimo Correction Centre and look for the signs. The site is on an operating beef ranch, but don't worry, the cows live in a separate area. Sites $14; full hookups $17. Hot showers ($1). Free hayrides.

FOOD

Cafes and restaurants speckle Nanaimo's downtown area, while the highway hosts a party of fast food and tiny dives, many open late or 24 hours. There is a **Thrifty Foods** (754-0655) in the Harbour Park Mall (open daily 8am-10pm). Nanaimo is known throughout Canada for the **Nanaimo Bar,** a richly layered chocolate confection of extreme indulgence. Leaving Nanaimo without trying one is like visiting Hope without taking the Rambo Walking Tour (see **Hope,** p. 292).

Gina's Mexican Cafe, 47 Skinner St. (753-5411), up the hill off Front St. A self-proclaimed "Tacky but Friendly Place," Gina's lives up to its billing with wild, bright colors and flavorful dishes. If the menu seems overwhelming, don't worry: a "gringo card" explaining all the food is thoughtfully provided. Hearty combo plates including quesadillas, burritos, and enchiladas ($9); nachos start at $5.75. Open M-Th 11am-9pm, F 11am-10pm, Sa noon-10pm, Su 2-8:30pm.

The Scotch Bakery, 87 Commercial St. (753-3521). Nanaimo Bar addicts come here for a fix (80¢). Don't ignore the apple fritters (95¢), giant pretzel pizzas (95¢), or sausage rolls ($1.39). Open M-F 8am-5:30pm.

Jerusalem Cafe, 153 Commercial St. (754-0006). The falafel ($5) and beef or chicken donair ($6) might be the closest thing to Israeli fare this side of the Pacific. Say yes to the fresh and potent hot sauce. Open M-F 9am-5pm, Sa-Su 10am-3pm.

SIGHTS, OUTDOORS, AND EVENTS

The **Nanaimo District Museum,** 100 Cameron Rd. (753-1821), pays special tribute to Nanaimo's Native American and Chinese communities. (Open M-F 9am-6pm, Sa-Su 10am-6pm; in winter Tu-Sa 9am-5pm. $2, seniors and students $1.75, under 12 75¢.) Highlights include an interactive exhibit on the native Snunēmuxw (SNOO-ne-moo, sort of) and a full-scale walk-through model of a coal mine, replete with genuine coal mine darkness. Just up the street from the museum is the **Bastion,** a fur-trading fort built by the Hudson's Bay Company. (Open in summer W-M 10am-4:30pm.)

Three kilometers south of town on Hwy. 1, the **Petroglyph Provincial Park** protects the carvings inscribed by hundreds of generations of Salish shamans. A menagerie of animals and mythical creatures decorates the soft sandstone. Rubbings can be made from concrete replicas at the base of the trail leading to the petroglyphs. **Newcastle Island Provincial Park,** only accessible by boat, has 756 automobile-free acres filled with hiking trails, picnic spots, and campsites ($9.50). The **Shoreline Trail,** which lines the shore offers great vantage points of **Departure Bay. Ferries** depart from Sway-A-Lana Lagoon, near downtown (1 per hour; $4.50 round-trip). **Departure Bay** washes onto a pleasant, pebbly beach in the north end of town on Departure Bay Rd., off Island Hwy. **North Island Water Sports,** 2755 Departure Bay Rd. (758-2488), offers various ways of exploring the Bay. (Kayaks $30 per day, 2-person $70; long term rates available. Scramblers—like kayaks, but you sit on top of them—$8 per hr., $20 per 3hr.)

Brother XII, Can You Spare a Dime?

The new-age-ism common on Vancouver Island started early in Nanaimo with a man calling himself Brother XII (just XII to his friends) who heralded the coming of the Age of Aquarius in the 1920s. He developed his own theology and attracted a large cult following among wealthy islanders. Brother XII and his flock left Nanaimo in 1927 to form a Utopia at Cedar-by-Sea on the nearby DeCourcy Island. Stories began to leak from Utopia of Brother XII's greed, his habit of forcing the elderly to commit suicide once they'd left their money to him, and, of course, his network of sex slaves. He was put on trial in 1932 and fled to Europe where he died in 1934. When he disappeared, Brother XII supposedly left $1.4 million in gold buried somewhere around Cedar-by-Sea. In 1982, the Nanaimo paper ran a story of an unemployed 35-year-old steam fitter who found the gold but only after facing death III times at the hands of Brother XII's lingering magic. (Tragically, the article turned out to be an April Fool's joke.) Most modern residents steer clear of the occult, and Nanaimo's mystical side has toned itself down. The most popular cult these days is nature worship.

Thrill-seekers from all over the continent make a pilgrimage to the **Bungy Zone,** 35 Nanaimo River Rd. (753-5867), to plummet 42m (140 ft.) into a narrow gorge. (First jump $95. Group rates available. 2 for 1 with a rental from Budget. HI discount. Each jump after your first, for the rest of your life, costs $25. Seniors jump free.) Bungee variations like swinging, zipline, and rapeling are also available. To reach the Zone, take Hwy. 1 south to Nanaimo River Rd. and follow the signs. Free shuttles to and from Nanaimo and Victoria. The three-day **Marine Festival** is held during late July. Highlights include the **Silly Boat Race** and the **Bathtub Race.** Bathers from all over the continent race porcelain tubs with monster outboards from Nanaimo to Vancouver across the 55km Georgia Strait. Officials hand out prizes to everyone who makes it across, and ceremoniously present the "Silver Plunger" to the first tub that sinks. The organizer of this bizarre and beloved event is the **Royal Nanaimo Bathtub Society,** 51A Commercial St., Nanaimo V9R 5G3 (753-7223).

■ Near Nanaimo: Port Alberni

Port Alberni is the only pit stop on Hwy. 4 en route to Pacific Rim National Park, sitting about 40km west of Hwy. 19 and 34km from Nanaimo. The town bills itself as "The Salmon Capital of the World" and hosts an annual **Salmon Festival** every Labour Day weekend. **Alberni Marine Transportation** (723-8313 or 800-663-7192 in summer) runs three ferries per week from Port Alberni to Bamfield ($20), and on alternate days during the summer sends a ferry to Ucluelet ($22). Brochures and advice on the general area can be snarfed up at the **Port Alberni Infocentre** (724-6535), on the highway at the eastern edge of town (open daily in summer 9am-6pm; otherwise M-F 9am-5pm). **Sproat Lake Provincial Park,** 13km west of Port Alberni off Hwy. 4, offers mysterious petroglyphs, boating, swimming, fishing, and camping (sites $14.50; in summer $12; showers, flush toilets). Sleep to the sounds of rushing water at the less crowded, out-of-the-way **Stamp Falls Provincial Park** (sites $9.50; no showers). For more info on the two parks, call 954-4600; for reservations, call 800-689-9025. **Naesgaard's** (723-3622), a farmer's market just west of town, overflows with farm-fresh fruit and vegetables (open daily 9am-9pm; in winter M-Sa 9am-6pm, Su 10am-6pm).

■ Hornby Island

In the 1960s, large numbers of draft-dodgers fled the U.S. to settle peacefully on quiet Hornby Island, halfway between Nanaimo and Campbell River. Today, hippie-holdovers and a similarly long-haired and laid-back younger generation mingle on the island with descendants of 19th century pioneers. Low tide on Hornby uncovers over 300m of the finest sand near Vancouver Island. **Tribune Bay,** at the base of Central Rd., is the more crowded of the two beaches. The alternative, **Whaling Station Bay,** has the same gentle sands and is about 5km farther north, off St. John's Point Rd. On the way there from Tribune Bay, Helliwell Rd. passes stunning **Helliwell Provincial Park,** where well-groomed trails lead through old growth forest to bluffs overlooking the ocean. Cormorants dive straight into the ocean to surface moments later with trophy-quality fish, while bald eagles cruise on the sea breezes.

Laidlaw (753-4371) has a flag stop at **Buckley Bay** on Hwy. 19, where the ferry docks. **BC Ferries** (335-2733) sails nine times daily ($8.50 round-trip; with car $19.50). It's a 10-minute ride from Buckley Bay to **Denman Island;** passengers must disembark and trek 11km across the island for another 10-minute cruise to Hornby Island. Once on Hornby, there are only two roads: the coastal **Shingle Spit Rd.** (try saying *that* 10 times fast) and **Central Rd.,** which crosses the island from the end of ShingleSpitShingleSpitShingleSpitShingleSpit... The island has no public transit and is difficult to cover without a bike or car. Some foot-travelers ask friendly faces for a lift at Denman or on the ferry. (*Let's Go* does not recommend hitchhiking.)

At the earthy heart of Hornby sits the **Co-op** (335-1121) at the end of Central Rd. by Tribune Bay, home to **tourist information,** the **post office (postal code: V0R 1Z0),** a well-stocked grocery store (open 9:30am-5pm), and two restaurants which close by 4pm, though they are budget- and vegetarian-friendly. With light traffic and smooth roads, Hornby Island is easily explored on two wheels. You can rent bikes from **Hornby Island Off-Road Bike Shop** (335-0444), at the Co-op ($7 per hr., $25 per day, $30 overnight; open daily 10am-5pm). **Hornby Ocean Kayaks** (335-2726) transports kayaks to the calmest of seven beaches and provides guided tours, lessons, and rentals (tours $30, full day $65; rentals $24 per 4hr., $40 per day).

If you plan on spending more than a day on Hornby, bring a tent; the B&Bs dotting the island can be expensive during the summer. The **Hornby Island Resort** (335-0136), right at the ferry docks, is a pub/restaurant/laundromat/hotel/campground. The fare at **Thatch Pub** is standard but reasonably priced; the **Wheelhouse Restaurant** has breakfast plates ($6), sandwiches and large salads ($4-5), and burgers ($6-7), with ocean views from a shared deck (pub open daily 11:30am-midnight; restaurant open daily 11:30am-8pm. Campsites $17; hookups $18; Jan.-Mar. sites $10. Private hotel rooms start at $65). **Bradsdadsland Country Camp,** 1980 Shingle Spit Rd. (335-0757), offers standard tent sites ($19 for 2 people, $1.50 per additional person or pet; hot showers 25¢ per 40sec.; flush toilets; laundry; Brad's dad stays free). Campers at Bradsdadsland trade the iron rule of quiet (only whispers after 11pm, no music allowed ever) for privacy, clean and capacious sites, and stairs down to the ocean.

▒ Comox Valley

With fine hiking, fishing, and skiing, plus the southern regions of Strathcona Provincial Park just a llama's trot away, the tourist season never ends in this self-proclaimed recreation capital of Canada. The sheer number of beaches, trails, and forested swimming holes could takes weeks to explore. Sheltering the towns of **Courtenay, Comox,** and **Cumberland,** the Comox Valley boasts the highest concentration of artists in Canada, many free museums and galleries, and an excessive use of the letter "C." The 1989 discovery of the 80-million-year-old "Courtenay Elasmosaur," which swam in the valley back when the valley was a lake, has transformed the region into a minor mecca of paleontology as well.

ORIENTATION AND PRACTICAL INFORMATION

Courtenay, the largest town in the Comox Valley lies about 72km north of Nanaimo on the Island Hwy. (Hwy. 19). In Courtenay, the Island Hwy. heading north joins **Cliffe Ave.** before crossing the river at 5th St., intersecting with **Comox Rd.,** and then once again heading north.

Buses: Laidlaw (334-2475) connects the area to points north and south along Hwy. 19. The bus stop is in Courtenay on Moray Ave. behind the Driftwood Mall. The

Comox Valley Transit System (339-5453) has a cavalry of coaches that connect the three towns ($1.25, seniors $1; buses run 6:40am-10:20pm).
Ferries: BC Ferries (888-223-3779) connects Comox with Powell River on the mainland.
Visitor Information: Tourist Office, 2040 Cliffe Ave. (334-3234), in Courtenay. Open M-Sa 8am-6pm, Su 8am-6pm.
Laundromat: King Koin Laundrette, 467 4th St. Open daily 7:30am-10pm. Some useful numbers in the Comox Valley:
Emergency: 911. **Police:** 338-1321. **Hospital:** 339-2242. **Weather:** 339-5044.
Post Office: 219 4th St. (334-4341), in Courtenay across from the museum. Open M-F 8:30am-5pm. **Postal Code:** V9N 7G3.
Internet Access: Joe Read's Bookstore and Internet Cafe, 2760 Cliffe Ave., No. 5 (334-9723). 10¢ per min.
Area Code: 250.

ACCOMMODATIONS AND CAMPGROUNDS

Pricey motels line the highway south of Courtenay. B&Bs are common, and offer a homey stay for better prices. The **Comox Lake Hostel,** 4787 Lake Trail Rd. (338-1914), about 10km from town, trades a bed for $15, a tent site for $8, and linen for a smile. To get there, take 5th St. toward the mountains until you reach Lake Trail Rd. Drive west on Lake Trail until you think you've gone too far. Then keep on going. Within hiking distance of the back door of Strathcona Provincial Park, the hostel is a popular backpacking base camp (free pick up and drop off in town with prior reservation). Kitchen, laundry, TV rooms, and doting dogs. Close to both Courtenay and Comox, **Estuary House,** 2810 Comox Rd. (890-0130), has three spacious rooms with private baths. If you call ahead, get dibs on the enormous front room with private deck and plush bathtub (singles $35; doubles $45). The **Mountain View Bed and Breakfast,** 605 Ellcee Pl. (338-0157), in a private house in Courtenay, offers spotless bathrooms, a TV lounge, and a balcony view of the Comox glacier (singles from $30; doubles from $45; reservations recommended). Campers can try **Kin Beach** (339-6365), on Astra Rd. in Comox, with tennis courts and 16 large sites ($7.50), just 100m from a meadow and a long, rocky beach. **Miracle Beach** (337-5720), on Miracle Beach Dr., 25km north of Courtenay in Black Creek, has more facilities than Kin Beach but is farther from town and often full ($14.50; showers, flush toilets).

FOOD

The many **farmers' markets** in the area tend to be more appealing than nearby restaurants. The most comprehensive and conspicuous market is **Farquharson Farms,** 1300 Comox Rd. (338-8194), in Courtenay. Beyond fresh fruit and vegetables, Farquharson sells gardening supplies and patio furniture for those determined to settle the nearby beaches (open daily 9am-6pm). The **Bar None Cafe,** 244 4th St. (334-3112), off Cliffe Ave. in Courtenay, stocks exceptional all-vegetarian fare. Pay $1.85 per 100g for salads, fresh salsas, and rice, tofu, and pasta dishes. The amazing variety is a godsend for french-fry-weary vegans. **Mud Sharks Cafe,** 387 5th St. (338-0939), in Courtenay, serves up filling burritos ($4) and the requisite coffee drinks and baked goods. The real highlight: it seems to be one of the only places open past 7pm, and is populated by young mud sharks (open Tu, F, and Sa 8am-10pm; Su, M, and W-Th, 8am-6pm). Espresso and juice bar, too (open M-Sa 8am-7pm, Su brunch 10:30am-5:30pm). **Safeway** is on 8th St. in Courtenay (open M-Sa 8am-9pm, Su 9am-9pm).

SIGHTS AND OUTDOORS

The **Comox Valley Art Gallery,** 367 4th St. (338-6211), in Courtenay is a focal point for the local arts community, featuring talented local artists of every creative stroke. (Open Tu-Sa 10am-5pm.) The valley boasts several other studios and galleries; contact the **tourist office** (see **Practical Information,** above) for more information. The **Courtenay District Museum,** 360 Cliffe Ave. (334-3611), holds permanent exhibits on industry, pioneer life, native culture and art, and fossils galore. A paleontology annex located next to the museum stores the bevy of dinosaur bones uncovered in the area. *(Open daily 10am-4:30pm; in winter Tu-Sa 10am-4:30pm. Free.)* **Horne Lake Caves Provincial Park** (757-8687 for information, 248-7829 for reservations), south of Courtenay on Horne Lakes Rd., offers several guided tour programs ranging from half-hour explanations to five- and six-hour rappeling and climbing journeys ($69-99.)

Great **swimming** is available in the clean, snowmelt-fed **Puntledge River** at **Stotan Falls,** a long stretch of shallow waters racing over flat rocks, with a waterfall from which to jump. Always test the current and depth before wading or jumping (*Let's Go* does not recommend dying young). Coming from Courtenay on lake Trail Rd., turn right at the stop sign onto the unmarked road at the first "hostel" sign. Take the next left at the logging road Duncan Bay Main, cross the pipeline, then park and descend on either side of the one-lane bridge. For longer **trails** through the woods and greater breath-taking try upriver at **Nymph Falls;** from Duncan Bay Main, go left on Forbidden Plateau Rd. to the "Nymph" sign.

■ Strathcona Provincial Park

Elk, deer, marmots, and wolves all inhabit the over 2000km² of Strathcona, one of the best-preserved and most beautiful wilderness areas on Vancouver Island. The park's two **visitor centers** are on **Buttle Lake,** on Hwy. 28 between Gold River and Campbell River, and **Mt. Washington/Forbidden Plateau,** outside Courtenay off Hwy. 19. The two official **campgrounds,** sharing 161 campsites between them, are Buttle Lake and Ralph River, both on the shores of Buttle Lake and accessible by **Hwy. 28** and secondary roads (follow the highway signs). **Buttle Lake,** closer to Campbell River, has comfortable sites, a playground, and sandy beaches on the lake ($12). Less crowded **Ralph River** provides convenient access to the park's best hiking trails ($9.50). Four smaller marine campsites are reachable by trails only (pick up a map at the park entrance). From Ralph River, the difficult 12km **Phillips Ridge** hike takes about seven or eight hours round-trip, passing two waterfalls in a 790m climb and ending atop a wildflower-strewn mountain by an alpine lake. Those with less than a day or eight hours of endurance can hit the **Karst Creek Trail,** a mellow 2km hike passing limestone sinkholes and waterfalls, or the **Myra Falls Trail,** a 1km hike from the south end of Buttle Lake to the immense, pounding cascades.

Visitors who wish to explore Strathcona's **backcountry areas** must camp 1km from main roads, and camp at least 30m away from water sources; campfires are discouraged in the park. Backcountry campers are rewarded with lakes, waterfalls, ancient cedar and fir forests, and wildflower meadows. Those entering the undeveloped areas of the park should notify park officials of their intended departure and return times, and should be well-equipped (**maps** and **rain gear** are essential).

Skiers and snowboarders hit the slopes just outside the park boundaries at **Mt. Washington** (338-1386; http://www.vquest.com) and the smaller but more snowboard-friendly **Forbidden Plateau Ski Resorts**. Each opens a chair lift in summer for the vista hungry, and Forbidden Plateau has especially extensive summer trails for hiking, mountain biking, and last-minute snowmen. The 5km hike up the ski slope and to the top of Mt. Becher peaks with a 360-degree view of the outlying Comox Valley and Georgia Strait. Both resorts are accessible from Duncan Bay Main; Mt. Washington is at the end of Tsolum Main, which becomes Strathcona Parkway, and Forbidden Plateau sits atop a winding, gravelly half hour on Forbidden Plateau Rd. For information on the park, contact BC Parks, District Manager, Box 1479, Parksville, BC V9P 2H4 (248-3931).

■ Campbell River

A large rock covered with aquatic-themed graffiti welcomes visitors to Campbell River, another of BC's many self-proclaimed "Salmon Capitals of the World." The town sports incredible fishing and scuba diving "second only to the Red Sea," according to *National Geographic*. The abundance of gas stations illustrates Campbell

River's role as the transportation hub of the northern island, and the easy access it provides to Strathcona Provincial Park, Port Hardy with its ferry to Alaska, and Quadra, Cortes and Discovery Islands.

PRACTICAL INFORMATION Campbell River rests 42km north of Courtenay on the Island Hwy. (Hwy. 19). **Laidlaw** (287-7151), at 13th and Cedar, sends buses to Nanaimo (4 per day, $22). **BC Ferries** (888-223-3779) run from Campbell River to Quadra Island (15 per day; $3.50, cars $9.50, ages 5-11 $1.75, under 5 free). **Rent-a-Wreck,** 1811 Island Hwy. (287-4677), is in the **Esso station** ($30 per day, 15¢ per km after 100km; open M-Tu and Sa-Su 8am-5pm, W-F 8am-9pm).

The **Travel Infocentre,** 1235 Island Hwy. (287-4636), in the Tyee Mall, has a helpful staff and a forest's worth of brochures (open daily 8am-6pm; in winter M-F 9am-5pm). De-dirt your duds at the **laundromat** in the Tyee Mall (open daily 8am-10pm). The **hospital** (287-7111) is at 375 2nd Ave. Useful numbers are: **crisis hotline,** 287-7743; **poison control,** 800 567-8911; **police,** 286-6221.

ACCOMMODATIONS, CAMPGROUNDS, AND FOOD Finding inexpensive lodging in Campbell River is like swimming upstream in spawning season. The most affordable places are the campgrounds; among the best is **Elk Falls Provincial Park,** on Hwy. 28, which offers spacious sites among large firs ($9.50; pit toilets, no showers). If Elk Falls is full, continue on to the campsites at **Strathcona Provincial Park** (see above). The **Pierhouse Bed and Breakfast** offers clean rooms, a full morning meal, and an exceptional view of the harbor (singles $45; doubles $55).

Picadilly Fish and Chips 798 Island Hwy (286-6447), in the double decker bus, serves up better-than-British fish-n-chips. An oyster or salmon burger and chips cost $5.25. Discover *poutine,* a sloppy Canadian concoction of fries, cheese curds, and gravy for $3 (open daily 11:30am-7pm). Shop for yourself at **Super Valu** (287-4410) in the Tyee Mall (open daily 8:30am-9:30pm).

SIGHTS AND OUTDOORS If you dig **salmon,** this is the place. Sockeye, coho, pink, chum, and chinook are hauled in by the boatload from the waters of the Campbell River. The savvy can reap deep-sea prizes from **Discovery Pier** in Campbell Harbour, and the unskilled can at least buy rich ice cream and frozen yogurt on the pier. *(Fishing charge $1; rod rentals $2.50 per hr., $6 per ½-day, with $5 deposit.)* The pier has 200m of boardwalk plants and an artificial underwater reef built to attract fish. Get a **fishing licence** (separate salt- and freshwater permits required) at the infocenter or any sports outfitter in town. A "salmon sticker" costs extra (see **Recent Events,** p. 248, to find out what happens when too many people don't buy their stickers).

Scuba gear rentals can be pricey and require proper certification, but **Beaver Aquatics,** 760 Island Hwy. (287-7652), offers a nifty $25 **snorkeling** package including suit, mask, snorkel, and fins. *(Open M-Sa 9am-5pm, Su 10am-2pm.)* Tour the **Quinsam River Salmon Hatchery,** 4217 Argonaut Rd. (287-9564), and see a wealth of "natural" resources. *(Open daily 8am-4pm.)* The hatchery provides a sheltered area for young fishies to develop, blissfully unaware of the rods and reels ahead. Nature trails and picnic tables dot the hatchery grounds.

■ Alert Bay

The cultural legacy of the Kwakiutl, one of the many coastal native nations, sets the fishing village of Alert Bay apart from its aquatourist siblings. One of the richest repositories of native culture on Vancouver Island, Alert Bay's 173 ft. totem pole is the second largest in the world (Victoria slapped a few extra feet onto its old one to claim the prize). Two kilometers north of the ferry terminal, the pole towers over the **U'Mista Cultural Center** (974-5403), which houses an astonishing array of Kwakiutl artifacts repatriated decades after Canadian police pillaged a potlatch. "U'Mista" means the return of a loved one taken captive by raiding parties (open daily 9am-6pm; in winter M-F 9am-5pm).

BRITISH COLUMBIA

Alert Bay lies in the Johnstone Straight, where the protected waters and plentiful fish provide an excellent summer home for **orca pods.** Expensive sighting charters are everywhere ($60 for 3-4hr.), but lucky visitors might glimpse the orcas while on the ferry or even from the shores of town. Head approximately 25km south of Port McNeill to **Telegraph Cove** and hike to the shore or rent kayaks for the day for a cheaper, less-touristy view. **North Island Kayaks** (949-7707), in Port Hardy, will drop off and pick up kayaks in the cove (single kayak $35 per day; double $55). If you can't find the whales, look up to spot some bald eagles.

BC Ferries (956-4533) operates a ferry from Port McNeill to Sointula and Alert Bay (40min., daily 8:45am-10:05pm, $4.50 round-trip, car and driver $16.25) and **Laidlaw** runs one bus per day from Port McNeil to Victoria ($76). Find **visitor information** (956-3131) in Port McNeill by the ferry dock (open M-Th 9am-5pm, F 9am-8pm). In Alert Bay, there's info galore at 116 Fir St. (974-5213; open daily 9am-6pm). **St. George's Hospital** is in Alert Bay at 182 Fir St. (974-5585). **Police:** 974-5544. **Area code:** 250.

At the fabulous **Pacific Hostelry (HI-C),** 349 Fir St. (974-2026), play the piano and watch for whales from a roomy wooden living room with a view of the strait ($17, nonmembers $19). Call ahead for reservations. Restaurants are limited and most are expensive; you may want to stock up at the **Blueline Supermarket,** 257 Fir St. (974-5521; open M-F 9am-9pm, Sa 9am-6pm, Su 10am-5pm).

■ Port Hardy

Port Hardy was content to be a quiet logging and fishing community until BC Ferries made it the southern terminus for boats carrying passengers from Prince Rupert and Alaska. Virtually overnight, the unassuming town etched a name for itself as a major transportation port, complete with a chainsaw-carved welcome sign. Port Hardy's population shoots up 130% every other night, when the ferry disgorges 1500 sleepy passengers.

ORIENTATION AND PRACTICAL INFORMATION

Port Hardy is the northernmost town on Vancouver Island, perched 39km north of Port McNeill and 225km north of Campbell River on Hwy. 19.

Buses: Laidlaw (949-7532), on Market St. across from the infocenter, connects Port Hardy to Victoria ($81) via Nanaimo ($70) once daily at 8:30am and whenever the ferry arrives.

Ferries: BC Ferries terminal (888-223-3779) is 3km south of town at **Bear Cove.** Service between Prince Rupert and Port Hardy ($102; with car $312). In summer runs every other day; in winter 1 per day.

Taxis: North Island Taxi, (949-8800).

Visitor Center: Travel Infocentre, 7250 Market St. (949-7622). Take Hardy Bay Rd. off Hwy. 19 to Market St. Open M-Sa 8am-9pm, Su 9am-9pm; in winter M-F 9am-5pm.

Bank: CIBC, 7085 Market St. (949-6333). Open Tu-Sa 10am-4:30pm; ATM. 24hr.

Outdoor Equipment: North Star Cycle and Sports (949-7221), at Market and Granville St., rents bikes for $20 per day (open daily 9:30am-6pm). **Jim's Hardy Sports,** 7125 Market St. (949-8382), will tackle other equipment needs. Open M-F 9am-6pm, Sa-Su 10am-5pm.

Laundromat: Clean those stinkin' socks in the machines at **Payless Gas Co.** (949-2366), on Granville St. Wash $1.75, dry 25¢ per 10min. Open 24hr.

Police: 7355 Columbia Ave. (949-6335). **Crisis line:** 949-6033.

Hospital: 9120 Granville St. (949-6161).

Postal Code: V0N 2P0.

Area Code: 250.

ACCOMMODATIONS AND CAMPGROUNDS

As in any port town, the demand for hotel and motel rooms is quite high, and prices are even higher. Among the less expensive options are the **Traveler's Friend B&B,** 6750 Bayview Dr. (949-7126; singles $40; doubles $50), and **Hamilton's B&B,** 9415 Mayors Way (949-6638; singles $45; doubles $55). The infocenter operates a free reservation service. For a quiet, wooded setting, pitch a tent at **Quatse River Campground,** 5050 Byng Rd. (949-2395). Toilets come in with choice of flush or pit; showers and laundromat available (sites $14; full hookups $18; seniors discount $1). The campground shares space with a **fish hatchery** (949-9022; tours available Oct.-June). **Wildwoods Campsite** (949-6753), on the road from the ferry within walking distance of the terminal, has comfortable sites in the midst of an overgrown garden. Sites maintain reasonable privacy despite their close quarters, but expect a line for the hot showers in the morning (sites $11; hookups $16; hiker/biker $5).

FOOD

For a wide selection of groceries and bulk foods, go up Granville St. from Market St. to **Overwaitea Foods,** 950 Granville St. (949-6455; open daily 9am-9pm). **Glen-Way Foods,** 8645 Granville St. (949-5758), can also fulfill most grocery needs (open daily 9am-9pm). Budget meals are hard to find unless you're willing to settle for burgers and fries. Some of the best can be found at **I.V.'s Quarterdeck Pub,** 6555 Hardy Bay Rd. (949-6922), which has burgers for $6, a surprisingly large vegetarian selection, and many-flavored wings at a frightening 29¢ apiece on Wednesday nights (open daily 11am-midnight). **Gisseppi's Fresh Food and Pizza Factory,** 7035 Market St. (949-7070), dishes out creative, topping loaded combination pizzas starting small and simple ($14) and building up to large and complex ($26). Subs cost $2.50-6. (Take out only. Open daily noon-9pm.)

■ Cape Scott Provincial Park

Sixty kilometers of gravel logging roads lead through wild and wet Cape Scott to parking lots near trailheads (always keep headlights on, watch for trucks). Most begin from the lot on **San Josef Road,** near the entrance to the park, although Cape Scott is expected to have a 100km trail connecting Port Hardy to the depths of the park. Get to the point on the 23.6km trail to the northwestern tip of the island, **Cape Scott,** and take all the drinking water you'll need. For a shorter hike, follow the mellow 2.5km trail to **San Josef Bay.** Good **topographic maps** help enterprising trekkers (available from **Maps BC,** Ministry of Environment, Parliament Bldgs., Victoria BC V8V 1XS).

Cape Scott has eight strategically placed campgrounds. Fresh water is available at popular **San Josef Bay** and **Nels Bight.** For more detailed information on the park, pick up the Cape Scott Provincial Park **pamphlet** at one of the travel infocenters elsewhere in the region, since none are available at this unpatrolled park. Or write to BC Parks, District Manager, Box 1479, Parksville, BC V9P 2H4 (250-954-4600). And while the scenery may vary, the constant rain will not—bring rain gear.

■ Pacific Rim National Park

The three regions of Pacific Rim National Park vary so greatly in landscape and seascape that only a national government could have combined them under the same jurisdiction. Hard-core hikers troop along the treacherous and tremendous-tree-filled West Coast Trail, while boaters skim the surface in search of sea life. Each spring, around 22,000 **gray whales** stream past the park. Orcas, sea lions, black-tailed deer, bald eagles, and black bears also frequent the area. Pacific Rim is part of the second largest temperate rainforest in North America, and it's wise to prepare for frequent downpours.

The park, a thin strip of land on the island's remote Pacific coast, is separately accessible at all three regions. The south end of the park—the **West Coast Trailhead**

at **Port Renfrew**—lies at the end of Hwy. 14. which runs west from Hwy. 1 not far
from Victoria. The park's middle section—**Bamfield** and the **Broken Group Islands**
in **Barkley Sound**—is far more difficult to reach. The Broken Islands are only accessible by water, and the trip to Bamfield requires a 100km drive over bone-jarring logging roads either from Hwy. 18 (3½hr. drive from Victoria) or from Port Alberni
(1½hr. drive). Highway 18 connects to Hwy. 1 at **Duncan** (City of Totems!) about
60km north of Victoria. For access to **Long Beach,** at the park's northern reaches,
take the spectacular drive across Vancouver Island on Hwy. 4 to the Pacific Rim Hwy.
This stretch connects the towns of sleepy **Ucluelet** (yoo-CLOO-let) and crunchy
Tofino (toe-FEE-no). Highway 4 branches west of Hwy. 1 about 35km north of Nanaimo, leads 50km through Port Alberni, and continues 92km to the Pacific coast.

■ Southern Pacific Rim: Port Renfrew

Spread out in the trees along a peaceful ocean inlet, Port Renfrew is a somewhat isolated coastal community, though it's the most easily accessible gateway into the West
Coast Trail. An hour long winding drive up Hwy. 14 from Hwy. 1 near Victoria lands
you in Port Renfrew. If you only want to spend an afternoon roughing it, visit Port
Renfrew's **Botanical Beach Provincial Park.** Nature enthusiasts will delight in the
many varieties of intertidal life, and in sandstone, shale, quartz, and basalt formations.
Botanical Beach offers a long hiking trail of its own, connecting Port Renfrew to the
nearby **Juan de Fuca Provincial Park.** The 47km trail ends at **China Beach,** and
passes several forest and beach stopping places along the way; look at the **map** in the
Botanical Beach parking lot. In the woods, warn resident bears away by jingling keys,
or by belting songs by Canada native Celine Dion. **West Coast Trail Express** (477-
8700; email wcte@pacificcoast.net; http://www.pacificcoast.net/~wcte) runs one
bus per day from Victoria to Port Renfrew ($28), and one bus from Nanaimo to Port
Renfrew which will only run when at least 4 people request it ($47). Reservations are
required, and can also be made for drop-off and pick-up at certain beaches and trail
heads along these routes.

Accommodations are limited outside the park campgrounds. Still, campgrounds do
pop up in town and some locals rent out tent sites on their property. Near Port Renfrew, the **Pacheenaht Campground** offers tents ($8) and RV sites ($13). To wash the
trail dust off in Port Renfrew, most hikers and campers use the public **shower** ($1)
and **laundry** ($2), available at the **Port Renfrew Hotel** (647-5541).

Almost all of the restaurants in Port Renfrew are inexpensive, but campers and hikers might prefer the convenience of shopping at the **General Store** (647-5587; open
daily 9am-9pm; in winter 9am-7pm). **Surfin' Salmon** (647-5400), on Parkinson Rd.
grills some of the phattest and fattest (as in best and biggest) burgers around. Knarly
(beef) or Green Peace (vegetarian) burger $5, monster-size Royale with Cheese $8
Bucketa Clams $9, duuuude (only open in summer 7am-whenever they feel like it
usually between 9pm and 11pm).

■ Southern Pacific Rim: The West Coast Trail

The West Coast Trail, a.k.a. the Kathmandu of North American backpacking, covers
the southern third of the Pacific Rim National Park between Port Renfrew and Bamfield, weaving through 77km of forests and waterfalls, scaling steep wooden ladders
and rocky slopes, and tracing the treacherous shoreline that has been the graveyard
of many ships. Recommended hiking time is about a week. Only experienced hikers
should attempt this slick trail, and never alone. Gray whales, sea otters, and black
bears along the route may provide company, but they often won't help you in an
accident. The trail is regulated by a strict quota system and reservations are necessary
to hike it. For information on the legendary trek, call BC Parks at 800-663-6000 or
write to Box 280, Ucluelet V0R 3A0. Hikers wind up paying about $120 per person
for access to the trail ($25 reservation fee, $70 trail use fee, $25 ferry crossing fee)
The trail is open from May 1 to September 30, but you can (and probably should
make reservations three months before the starting date of your hike. Seek out maps

information on the area, and registration information at one of the two the **Trail Information Centres:** in **Port Renfrew** (647-5435), at the first right off Parkinson Rd. (Hwy. 14) once in "town" or in **Pachena Bay** (728-3234), 5km from Bamfield. (Both open May-Sept. daily 9am-5pm.)

■ Central Pacific Rim: Broken Group Islands and Bamfield

An archipelago of 100 islands, the Broken Group stretches across Barkley Sound and makes up the most rugged part of Pacific Rim National Park. Some of the best sea kayaking on the island can be found here, as well as expensive but high-biodiversity **scuba diving.** For the less burly outdoorsfolk who make it all the way out to Bamfield without hiking the West Coast Trail, **short hiking trails** pass through shore and forest at **Pachena Bay, Keeha Beach,** and the **Pachena Lighthouse,** among others.

Hours of logging roads or water travel are the only two ways into Bamfield. Gravel roads wind toward Bamfield from Hwy. 18 (heading west on 18 from Duncan), and south from Hwy. 4 in Port Alberni. **West Coast Trail Express** (see above) runs one bus per day from Victoria to Bamfield ($37) and one per day from Nanaimo to Bamfield ($47); reservations are required. The **Pacheenaht Band Bus Service** (647-5521) provides transportation from Port Renfrew to Bamfield ($40) and points between. Because Bamfield lies on two sides of an inlet, water transit is necessary to cross town. **Alberni Marine Transportation, Inc.,** P.O. Box 188, Port Alberni V9Y 7M7 (723-8313 or 800-663-7192), operates the freighter *Lady Rose* year-round from Port Alberni to Bamfield ($20). The **Kingfisher Marina** (728-3228) runs a water taxi service. The local hospital is the **Bamfield Red Cross Outpost Hospital** (728-3312). Bamfield's **post office,** across the inlet near the Bamfield Inn, next to the General Store (open M-F 8:30am-5pm). **Postal Code:** V9P 2G2. **Area Code:** 250.

Accommodations in town are limited, making camping in the park a better bet. Head to **Camp Ross** (337-5935) at the West Coast Trailhead for an amazing shoreside location (free; outhouses, pay phone, 3-day max. stay). The **Pachena Bay Campground** (728-1287) offers tree-rich sites just a short walk from the beach (sites $19; RV sites $20; full hookups $30). The **Seabeam Fishing Resort and Hostel** (728-3286) sports the area's cheapest indoor accommodations ($15, nonmembers $20) complete with full kitchen and laundry facilities. The **Kamshee Store** (728-3411), offers up groceries and other supplies (open daily 9am-9pm, in winter 9am-7pm.)

■ Northern Pacific Rim: Ucluelet, Tofino and Long Beach

The northern third of Pacific Rim National Park begins where Hwy. 4 hits the west coast, after a one-hour drive from Port Alberni (see, **Port Alberni,** p. 281). The two towns of Ucluelet and Tofino lie 30km apart at opposite ends of the Pacific Rim Hwy., separated by the lovely and trail-laden Long Beach. They also stand at either end of the cultural spectrum. Ucluelet remains a quiet fishing village until it floods with travelers every July and August. Tofino, with its tree-hugging populace and nature- hawking outfits, is Canada's best answer to California—it even has its own surfing subculture. Both towns provide ample access to Pacific Rim's many trails and surrounding waters.

ORIENTATION AND PRACTICAL INFORMATION The Pacific Rim Hwy. becomes **Peninsula Rd.** in Ucluelet and **Campbell St.** in Tofino.

Buses: Laidlaw (725-3101 in Tofino, 726-4334 in Ucluelet) connects Victoria and Nanaimo with Tofino and Ucluelet through Port Alberni. Four buses leave daily from Victoria to: Tofino ($45), Ucluelet ($42).

Ferries: Alberni Marine Transportation, P.O. Box 188, Port Alberni V9Y 7M7 (723-8313 or 800-663-7192), operates the freighter *Lady Rose* in summer from Port Alberni to Ucluelet ($22).

Visitor Information: Tofino: 351 Campbell St. (725-3414). Open daily July-Aug. and Nov.-Feb. 9:30am-8pm; Mar.-June and Sept.-Oct. Sa-Su 9am-5pm. **Ucluelet:** 227 Main St. (726-4641). Open daily July-Aug. 10am-4pm; Sept.-June M-F 10am-3pm.

Outdoor Information: Parks Canada Visitor Information (726-4212), 3km north of the Port Alberni junction on the Pacific Rim Hwy. Open mid-Apr to mid-Oct. daily 9am-5pm.

Laundromat: Koin Laundrette, in Davison's Shopping Plaza on Peninsula St., in Ucluelet. Open 9am-9pm. **Tofino Laundromat,** 448 Campbell. Open 24hr.

Emergency: 911. **Police:** 725-3242 in Tofino; 726-7773 in Ucluelet.

Hospital: 261 Neill St. (725-3212), in Tofino.

Post Office: 161 1st St. (725-3734), at 1st and Campbell in Tofino. Open M-F 8:30am-5:30pm, Sa 9am-1pm. **Postal Code:** V0R 2Z0.

Area Code: 250.

ACCOMMODATIONS Even in the off-season, a bed in Tofino can be pricey, and once summer rolls around, camping gets expensive too. Travelers without reservations in July or August might get shut out of the handful of reasonably priced accommodations and forced into a motel room, all of which start at $75 for a single. **Stephanie's** 420 Gibson St. (725-4230), is a B&B with three rooms (June-Aug. $55-70; off-season $35-50). Kids are a fixture at Stephanie's, so plan on hanging with the under-10 set. Leave excess testosterone at the door of the **Wind Rider,** 231 Main St. in Tofino (725-3240; email whole@island.net; http://www.island.net/~whole). The guesthouse is all female (except for kids under 12) and provides a gleaming kitchen, jacuzzi bath, and TV room (dorms $25; private room $35 per person; linens $5 extra).

In Ucluelet, the **Ucluelet Lodge** (726-4234) on Main St. provides inexpensive rooms and a bar downstairs (singles and doubles $30 with shared bath, $40 with private bath). **Agapé,** 246 Lee St. (726-7073), 4km before Ucluelet, is a treasure at $40-45 for a single and $50-65 for a double, including a hot gourmet breakfast.

While there are a number of private campgrounds between the park and Tofino, they average at least $20 to camp and almost $30 for a hookup. It costs $8 per day to remain in the park (tickets available in all parking lots); annual passes are also available ($70). These sites fill quickly in the summer; if you can't find a spot, try the **golf course**—which often has sites when no one else does. The **Park Superintendent** (726-7721) can be contacted year-round for advance information at Box 280, Ucluelet V0R 3A0 and locals can often furnish tips on free camping in the area. The only campground in the park itself is **Greenpoint Campground** (726-4245), 10km north of the park information center. Greenpoint has 94 sites equipped with hot water, flush toilets and fire rings; and despite swarms of mosquitoes and campers in the summer, it offers hedge-buffered privacy ($18; reservations required, call 800-689-6025). **Ucluelet Campground** (726-4355), off Pacific Rim Hwy., offers sites in the open (better for sun than for privacy) with showers and toilets ($20; full hookups $25; 6min. showers $1; open Mar.-Oct.).

FOOD Shop for groceries at Tofino's **Co-op,** 140 1st St. (725-3226; open M-Sa 9:30am-8pm, Su 11am-5pm). For the late night bowler in all of us, **Smiley's Family Restaurant,** 1992 Peninsula Rd. (726-4213), has a bowling alley ($3 per game), pool tables, and an arcade to help you burn off the calories from their fish 'n' chips ($5.50) and homemade pies (open 7am-10pm). The **Common Loaf Bake Shop,** 180 1st St. (725-3915), is more than just a restaurant and bakery offering some of the finest eats in Western Canada, it's also Tofino's crunchy social center. Gourmet pizzas start at $8 and slices at $3.75. Thai and Indian dinners cost $6-8.50 (open daily in summer 8am-9pm; off-season 8am-6pm). Tofino's colorful **Alleyway Cafe,** 305 Campbell (725-3105), is hard to find (hint: it's in an alley), but offers veggie burgers ($6.25), salmon quesadillas ($7), and burritos ($4.85) to those who sleuth it out. Grab a sandwich at the small, friendly **Breakers,** 131 1st St. (725-2778), in Tofino. A decent sized sub will

---

If a Tree Falls in a Forest, and 800 Canadians are There to Hear It, Does It Make a Sound?

Clayoquot (KLAK-wot) Sound is a 260,000 hectare (624,000 acre) region of lush islands and verdant valleys on west coast of Vancouver Island, and a poster-rainforest for North American environmentalism. The largest episode of civil disobedience in Canadian history unfolded here between July and November of 1993, when over 800 protesters were arrested at logging road blockades. These activists were not all tree-hugging, self-to-tree-chaining eco-zealots, but included students, First Nations leaders, a Member of Parliament, and the Raging Grannies, all united against clearcutting concessions granted to logging companies by the B.C. government.

Since then, conservationists have won several significant battles with logging interests like Macmillan Bloedel (affectionately nicknamed MacBlo). Two years of pressuring the *New York Times* to stop buying Clayoquot pulp ended in success, and in June 1998, MacBlo announced a jaw-dropping plan to replace clearcutting with selective logging practices, leaving soils and some trees intact for forest regrowth. A proposal to make part of the Sound a UNESCO Biosphere Reserve is bouncing around amid bureaucracy, but environmentalists aren't holding their breath; MacBlo and Interfor (International Forest Products) still hold timber rights to two-thirds of Clayoquot Sound, part of the largest chunk of temperate coastal rainforest left on earth.

For more info, check out the Friends of Clayoquot Sound (http://www.island.net/~focs) and MacBlo's Forest Project (http://www.mbltd.com).

---

only sink you $3.70 and a large sub just $5.70. Fruit smoothies and ice cream cost $3.50 (open daily 8am-10pm).

OUTDOORS The highlight of a trip to the west side of the island is hiking one of Pacific Rim's **magnificent trails** which grow more beautiful in the frequent rain and fog. **Long Beach** is, fittingly, the longest beach on the island's west coast, and is the starting point for numerous hikes. Pick up a **hiker's guide** at the **Parks Canada Visitor Center** for a list of eight hikes ranging from 100m to 5km in length. The two 1km loops of the **Rain Forest Trail** boardwalk off the Pacific Rim Highway, bring hikers through gigantic trees and fallen logs of old growth rainforest. The wheelchair accessible 0.8km **Bog Trail** illuminates little known details of one of the wettest, most intricate ecosystems in the park. Pick up the excellent descriptive **brochure,** off Wickininnish Beach Rd., which is west off of the Pacific Rim Hwy.

Every spring **orcas** and **gray whales** migrate past the park and the neighboring **Clayoquot Sound** north of Tofino. About 50 grays stay at these feeding grounds in the sound all summer, surfacing well within viewing distance. Ask one of the local boaters for a ride; some will take you out for $50-60 if they have time. Professional whale-watching tours are cheapest during the migration, in March and April. There exist nearly as many whale watching tour companies as there are whales. Witness **Jamie's Whaling Station,** 606 Campbell St. (725-3919 or 800-667-9913; email jamies@island.net; http://www.jamies.com), just east of 4th St. in Tofino. Look for the big wooden whale. Smooth rides in large boats are available, while rough-riders choose **Zodiacs,** hard-bottomed inflatable rafts with outboards that ride the swells at 30 knots. (*Large boats $70 per 3hr.; Zodiacs $50 per 2hr.*) **Seaside Adventures,** P.O. Box 178, Tofino V0R 2Z0 (888-332-4252 or 725-2292; email seaside@island.net; http://www.seasideadventures.com), leads tours in large vessels or Zodiacs, and a round-trip voyage to **Hot Springs Cove,** including whale-watching on the way to the gorgeous trails and warm springs. (*2¼ hr. tour $50, students and seniors $45, children $35. Round-trip tour to Hot Springs $75, students and seniors $70, children $60.*)

SOUTHEASTERN BRITISH COLUMBIA

> ## 🏔 HIGHLIGHTS OF SOUTHEASTERN BC
>
> - River rapids crash through the steep cliffs of **Fraser River Canyon** (see p. 293).
> - The **Okanagan Valley** offers a panoply of **free wine-tastings** (see p. 297). Bottoms and pinkies up!
> - Near the Alberta border lies a trinity of uncrowded national parks: the steep, stellar slopes of **Glacier** (see p. 305), the falls and fossils of **Yoho** (see p. 305), and the peerless peaks of **Kootenay** (see p. 307).

■ Fraser River Canyon

The Fraser River courses down from the Rockies and hurls through 1300km of plateaus and steep canyons on its journey to the Pacific. In 1808, Simon Fraser made a perilous expedition down the river from Mt. Robson to Vancouver; today's route from Cache Creek to Hope on the Trans-Canada Highway (Hwy. 1) makes his trailblazing seem like a distant dream. Up close, the canyon is a good place to feel small, with over 200km of pounding rapids in the river below, and towering walls carpeted with pines and firs that sprout unbelievably out of near-vertical rock.

■ Fraser River Canyon: Hope

The biggest thing happening in Hope is the intersection of several highways. The **Trans-Canada Highway (Hwy. 1)** leads west into Vancouver and bends north at Hope, running to Yale and Cache Creek where it joins the **Cariboo Highway (Hwy. 97),** and heads to northern British Columbia. **Highway 7** runs west along the north bank of the Fraser River to Vancouver's suburbs. **The Crowsnest Trail (Hwy. 3)** winds east through breathtaking country close to the U.S. border, through Osoyoos near Penticton, through Kootenay Country to Nelson, past Crowsnest Pass, and finally into Alberta. The **Coquihalla Highway (Hwy. 5),** is a new, faster toll road ($10) running north to Kamloops with good access to the Okanagan Country.

Buses arrive in Hope at the **Greyhound** station, 833 3rd Ave. (869-5522), and make connections farther east in Chiliwack for destinations throughout Western Canada. Many ramblers try hitching north on Hwy. 1, where rides are reputedly easy to find. (*Let's Go* stresses the word "reputedly" and does not recommend hitchhiking.) **Gardner Chev-Olds,** 945 Water Ave. (869-9511), next to the infocenter, rents cars ($40 per day, $275 per week; 13¢ per km after 100km; must be 25 with major credit card; open M-Sa 9am-6pm). The staff at the **Travel Infocentre,** 919 Water Ave. (869-2021), take perverse pride in the way Sylvester Stallone laid waste to their town in the original Rambo blockbuster, *First Blood,* but are knowledgeable on other subjects as well (open daily July-Aug. 8am-8pm; Sept.-Oct. and Apr.-June daily 9am-5pm; Nov.-Mar. M-F 10am-4pm). Besides providing the riveting **Rambo Walking Tour** and **Chainsaw Carving Walking Tour** the center also has Fraser River Canyon info. The Hope **police station,** 670 Hope-Princeton Hwy. (869-7750), is just off Hwy. 3. The **post office** is at 777 Fraser St. (open M-F 8:30am-5pm). **Postal Code:** V0C 2ZC. **Area Code:** 250.

If stuck in Hope for a night, walk a block north from the bus station to Wallace St. and hang a left. The **Hope Motor Hotel,** 272 Wallace St. (869-5641), rents singles ($39) and doubles ($49). Campers can head for the giant firs and cedars of the spacious **Coquihalla Campsite,** 800 Kawkawa Lake Rd. (869-7119 or 888-869-7118; email hopecamp@uniserve.com), off 6th Ave., on the east side of town along the banks of the Coquihalla River (122 sites: $16; river sites $19; hookups $20). Shop for groceries to the hippest elevator music in Canada at **Buy and Save Foods,** 489 Wallace St. (869-5318; open daily 8am-8pm). The **Suzie Q Family Restaurant,** 2591 Wallace St. (869-5515), a block north of the Greyhound station, serves cheap Western and Japanese diner-style and buffet food (open daily 7am-10pm).

■ Fraser River Canyon: Near Hope

Hope may not be much, but the surrounding lands are less hopeless. A number of excellent moderate hikes begin near Hope. The short, lush **Rotary Trail** starts at Wardle St. and runs to the confluence of the **Fraser** and **Coquihalla Rivers.** The two-hour climb to the summit of **Thacker Mountain** is more challenging. To reach this trailhead, cross the Coquihalla River Bridge, take a left on Union Bar Rd., then head left again on Thacker Mountain Rd. The parking lot at the end marks the beginning of a 5km gravel path to the peak, which provides clear views of Hope and the Fraser River. Pause for a pleasant diversion at **Kawkawa Creek,** off Union Bay Rd., recently enhanced to aid the late-summer and mid-fall salmon spawnings. The boardwalk along the creek leads to a swimming hole and popular picnicking spot.

The **Coquihalla Canyon Recreation Area** is a five- to ten-minute drive out of Hope along Kawkawa Lake Rd. Here the **Othello Quintet Tunnels,** blasted through solid granite, provide mute evidence of the daring engineering that led to the opening of the **Kettle Valley Railway** in 1916. The dark tunnels lead to slick bridges over whitewater shooting through the gorge. To get there, turn right on Othello Rd. off Kawkawa Lake Rd., and right again on Tunnel Rd.; allow half an hour to walk through the tunnels. For an even closer view of Fraser River, head 36km north on Hwy. 1 to the small town of **Yale** (don't let your feelings about this town's grungy namesake school keep you away). Take the first right after the stoplight, then follow the gravel road about 1km to a close-up view of the majestic **Lady Franklin Rock,** which splits the Fraser River into two sets of heavy rapids. **Fraser River Raft Expeditions** (800-363-7238), just south of town, runs whitewater trips almost daily ($95); call ahead to reserve. **River Boat Adventures,** 226 Wallace St. (869-3811, toll-free 877-466-3377), in town, runs several jetboat tours of the river, including one-hour scenic tours ($20, ages 4-12 $15) and 2½-hour whitewater trips ($69); reservations are recommended.

When Simon Fraser made his pioneering trek down the river, he likened one tumultuous stretch of rapids to the **Gates of Hell.** The foaming waters, 25km north of Yale on Hwy. 1, make Fraser's journey seem miraculous. When snowmelt floods the river in spring, the 60m deep water rushes through the narrow gorge with incredible force. A cluster of gift shops and eateries are now embedded where Fraser once advised "no human beings should venture." The gondolas and kooky employees of **Hell's Gate Airtram,** 43111 Hwy. 1 (867-9277), slowly carry folks 150m across the canyon in four minutes ($9, seniors $8, ages 6-14 $6, families $24). Die-hard budgeters and acrophobes may want to save their money and hike down the nearby trail to the river.

■ Kamloops

Every summer night at **Riverside Park,** on the banks of the Thompson River, Kamloops boogies down to live music. The park itself is a popular picnic place. See the river up close on a two-hour cruise aboard the **Wanda Sue Paddle Boat,** 1140 River St. (374-7447; 1-3 cruises per day; $11.50, seniors $10.50, ages 6-12 $6.50). **Kamloops Wildlife Park** (573-3242), west of town on Hwy. 1, allows close contact with nature (open daily July-Aug. 8am-6pm; Sept.-June 8am-4:30pm; $6.75). **Canadian Imperial Ginseng,** 1274 McGill Rd. (851-2880), leads free half-hour tours that allow visitors to see what ginseng growing and processing is really like (daily 10am-3pm). **Secwepemc Museum and Heritage Park,** 355 Yellowhead Hwy. (828-9801), contains the reconstructed remains of a 2000-year-old Shuswap village, eerily juxtaposed with the site of a school where the Canadian government detained native children until the 1970s (open in summer M-F 8:30am-8pm, Sa-Su 10am-6pm; $6).

Sun Peaks, 1280 Alpine Rd. (578-7232; email info@sunpeaksresort.com; http://www.sunpeaks.resort.com), a 45-minute drive north of Kamloops, is an icy magnet for snowboarders and skiers. Take Hwy. 5 north from Kamloops, turn right at Heffley Creek, and continue 31km to Sun Peaks. The lift carries hikers and bikers up to trails with views and summer wildflower meadows ($12, seniors $9, ages 6-18 $9, under 5

BRITISH COLUMBIA

free). The **Stake Lake Trails** (372-5514) form a network of cross-country skiing terrain, with a good selection of beginner and intermediate options. Take Exit 366 from Hwy. 5 south of Kamloops, and follow Lac Le Jeune Rd. **All Sports Rentals,** 618C Tranquille Rd. (554-9911), in Kamloops, rents cross-country skis ($12 per day). **Interior Whitewater Expeditions** (800-661-RAFT/7238; http://www.interiorwhitewater.bc.ca), an hour and 20 minutes north of Kamloops on Hwy. 5, leads full-day raft trips on the Clearwater River through gorgeous scenery ($103 per person).

Kamloops lies 356km east of Vancouver, 492km west of Banff, and anchors the junction of the heavily traveled Yellowhead (Hwy. 16) and Trans-Canada (Hwy. 1) Highways. **VIA Rail** (800-561-8630) stops at North Station, off Hwy. 5, making three runs per week to Vancouver ($75) and Edmonton, AB ($167); student discounts are available. **Greyhound,** 725 Notre Dame Ave. (374-1212), makes regular stops in Kamloops en route to Vancouver (8 per day, $43), Jasper, AB (3 per day, $40), and Calgary, AB (5 per day, $72). To get around town, use the **Kamloops Transit System** (376-1216; fare $1.25). The **Visitor Infocentre** (374-3377 or 800-662-1994) is just west of town on the Trans-Canada Hwy. (open daily June-Aug. 9am-7pm; Sept.-May 9am-5pm). Rent demo bikes at **Java Cycle,** 297 1st Ave. (314-5282), just across from the hostel ($35 per day). **McCleaners,** 437 Seymour St. (372-9655), mcdoes mcdirty mcduds. The **police** (828-3000) are at 560 Battle St. The **post office** (374-2444) is at 301 Seymour St.(open M-F 8:30am-5pm). **Postal Code:** V2C 5K2. **Area Code:** 250.

The excellent **Kamloops Old Courthouse Hostel (HI-C),** 7 W. Seymour St. (828-7991), is, in fact, an old courthouse. The gargantuan common room still sports a jury box, judge's bench, and witness stand, compensating for the tightly packed dorm bedrooms (68 beds: $15, nonmembers $19.50; private rooms $5 extra per person; check-in 8am-1pm and 5-10pm). Campers can head to **Paul Lake Provincial Park,** 17km east of Hwy. 5 on Paul Lake Rd. (90 sites: $9.50).

Good Kamloops food lines Victoria St. **Steiger's Swiss Cafe and Pastries,** 359 Victoria (372-2625), gives succor to sweet teeth and fresh bread cravings (open Tu-Sa 8:30am-5:30pm). Stuff yourself silly on an all-you-can-eat lunch ($8.50) at **China Village,** 165 Victoria St. (372-2822). **What's Cookin' Market Cafe,** 336 Victoria St. (314-9511), has a wide selection of pre-made salads, quiches, and meals ($5-7), as well as bakery fare (open daily 7am-9pm).

■ Shuswap Lake Region

The dots on the map along Shuswap Lake make Salmon Arm, its largest town, seem like a metropolis. With strong roots in agriculture and logging, Salmon Arm may not be much more than another rural town, best for passing through. Unlike many of its unlovely brethren, though, it is surrounded with an extraordinary setting. Shuswap Lake is sublime, and the gentle, forested mountains that cradle Salmon Arm are a poster-perfect backdrop, especially when the leaves turn in autumn.

ORIENTATION AND PRACTICAL INFORMATION Shuswap Lake is shaped like a V pointing northeast. Coming from the west, Highway 1 hugs the northern arm of the lake before dipping south and following the southern arm east from Salmon Arm.

The **Salmon Arm Transit System** (832-0191) has regular (M-Sa, $1.25) and door-to-door service (M-F, $1.50); call for booking. The **Travel Infocentre,** 751 Marine Park Dr., Box 999 (832-6247), has brochures aplenty. Wash grubby duds at the **B-Line Laundromat,** 456 Trans-Canada Hwy. (832-5500), in Smitty's Shopping Center (open daily 6am-10pm; wash $1.50, dry $1 per 12min.). The **police** hang out at 501 2nd Ave. NE (832-6044). For an **ambulance,** call 833-0188; the **hospital** is at 601 10th St. NE (833-3600). The **post office** is at 370 Hudson St. NE (832-3093; open M-F 8:30am-5pm). **Postal Code:** V1E 4M6. **Area Code:** 250.

ACCOMMODATIONS, CAMPGROUNDS, AND FOOD B&Bs are the way of Salmon Arm; most have popped up in the last several years. For a lake view, swimming pool, sauna, and warm British hospitality, waddle on over to **Ducks Galore,** 1961 16th St. NE (832-8906), near Lakeshore Dr.; take 20th Ave. to 16th St. from Lakeshore Dr., and do not be swayed by the large number of parallel streets also called 16th St. The welcoming owners are collectors of wooden and ceramic ducks, vaguely akin to the many wild ducks in the nature area nearby (singles $35; doubles $50-65). To be spoiled silly, stay at the **Cindosa B&B,** 930 30th St. SE (832-3342), off Hwy.1, where the Moores pamper visitors with comfy beds and home-cooked breakfasts. They'll pick you up at the bus station, or take bus #2. Ask Mrs. Moore to show you her indescribable collection of dolls and toys (singles $45; doubles $55).

Squilax General Store Hostel (675-2977), 50km west of Salmon Arm on the Hwy. 1, sleeps folks on board three Canadian National Railway cabooses, specially procured and outfitted for rustic hosteling with campfires, lounge, mini-kitchens, showers, phone, and laundry (23 beds: $14, nonmembers $18; private rooms $4 per each additional person; tent sites by the river $8). The proprietor, Blair, is a wellspring of info about the area. The sign on the front of the store is home to the remnants of an enormous bat colony. Check out the organic-friendly general store, too.

Campgrounds in Salmon Arm, especially those on Shuswap Lake, are often crowded and cramped. **Pierre's Point** (832-9588) is on 50th Ave. NW, just off Hwy. 1. With a sandy beach on the lake, it allows a tiny bit more breathing space than its competitors, though it's still quite crowded (200 sites, 40 on the Shuswap shore: $19; electrical and water hookups $21). For a quieter time, leave the town boundaries for a nearby provincial park (ask at the infocenter).

Despite the town's name, Salmon Arm's culinary establishments showcase neither fish nor limbs. The best deal by far awaits at **Real Canadian Wholesale Club,** 360 Hwy. 1 (804-0258). Even the non-bulk items cost less than any supermarket (open M-F 9am-9pm, Sa 9am-6pm, Su 10am-5pm). For smaller items, walk next door to **Safeway,** 360 Hwy. 1 (832-8086; open in summer daily 8am-10pm; off-season M-F 9am-9pm, Sa-Su 9am-6pm). Head west on Hwy. 1 to **De Mille Fruits and Vegetables,** 3710 10th Ave. SW (832-7550), for local summer produce and, in August and September, their famous sweet corn (open daily 8am-8pm; in winter 8am-6:30pm). **Choices,** 40 Lakeshore Dr. (832-7555), is the best (and cheapest) option for a sit-down meal of homemade bread sandwiches ($4) and piping hot soups.

SIGHTS, ENTERTAINMENT, AND OUTDOORS
Learn what curds and whey really are at **Gort's Gouda Cheese Factory,** 1470 50th St. SW (832-4274). The free tours only last a few minutes, shuttling visitors to the tasty cheese samples all the faster. (Tours Tu and F mornings; call to arrange other times.) Even if there's no tour, it's still possible to stock up on bargain cheeses and watch the cheesemaking process through viewing windows, from cow to wax package.

McGuire Park, on Hwy. 1 next to the hospital, is a promising spot to see Canadian geese, muskrats, turtles, and ducks. Catch kokanee or rainbow trout in Lake Shuswap. (Day permits $10, 8 days $25; available at the Government Agent's office next to the infocenter.) For a hike out to **Margaret Falls,** just west of town, follow the signs off Hwy. 1 for **Heral Park.** A 10km detour and a short hike lead to the dramatic falls. Closer to town, take a walk along the natural preserve by the banks of Lake Shuswap to catch a glimpse of the rare Western grebe.

Caravan Farm Theatre (546-8533 or 838-6751), 8km northwest of Armstrong and 45 minutes from Salmon Arm, presents top-notch performances during summer; tickets are available at the Squilax General Store Hostel (see **Accommodations,** above). (Call for show times. $6-12.) The Farm overflows with remnant hippie charm, organic produce, and musical instruments dangling from the trees.

Interior Whitewater Expeditions (800-661-RAFT/7238; http://www.interiorwhitewater.bc.ca), in Scotch Creek, leads two-hour trips on the reasonably gentle **Adams River.** ($40, under age 16 $29.) The river can be hiked or mountain biked for free, in an 18km round-trip. Take Squilax-Anglemont Rd. north across the bridge, just west of the Squilax General Store. The trail heads upriver across the first narrow bridge on the road; continue east to reach the rafting headquarters. Every four years in October, 46km west of Salmon, **Roderick Haig-Brown Provincial Park** hosts over a million sockeye salmon desperately thrashing their way up from the Pacific Ocean to spawn. For details, contact the infocenter (see **Practical Information,** above).

BRITISH COLUMBIA

■ Okanagan Valley

Known throughout Canada for its bountiful fruit harvests, the Okanagan (oh-kuh-NAH-gan) Valley lures visitors with summer blossoms, ample sun, plentiful wineries, and tranquil lakes. The **Okanagan Connector (Hwy. 97C)** links Vancouver to the valley in a four-hour drive, making the valley a popular vacation destination among sun-starved coastal British Columbians. In the north, the quiet valley is rudely interrupted by an explosion of bloated shopping centers and strip malls along Hwy. 97. Beyond the development, however, lies a series of parks and beaches where many a wanderer catches many a ray.

Travelers in dire straits may consider signing on to pick fruit at one of the many orchards stretching south from Penticton to the U.S. border along Hwy. 97. Pickers usually camp for free in the orchards, and are paid a per-quart wage; daily earnings of more than $40 are common. Cherries are harvested in June, pears in September, and assorted other fruits in between. Contact the **Kelowna Friendship Centre** (763-4905), or cruise Hwy. 97 and Hwy. 3A until you see a "Pickers Wanted" sign.

■ Okanagan Valley: Kelowna

Settled in the heart of the Okanagan Valley, Kelowna (kuh-LOE-nuh) has always been an agricultural center. Alongside acres of orchards, however, development and urbanization are rapidly encroaching. City planners, accepting the reality of Kelowna's intense draw for visitors and new residents, have allowed a few new buildings to rise up rather than spread out, accommodating crowds while preserving the integral fields that made the area a town in the first place.

ORIENTATION AND PRACTICAL INFORMATION Kelowna lies 400km east of Vancouver, 602km west of Calgary, and 86km north of Penticton on Hwy. 97, at the eastern shore of Okanagan Lake. Hwy. 97 intersects the western end of Hwy. 6 50km north of town.

> **Buses: Greyhound,** 2366 Leckie Rd. (860-3855). To: Vancouver (5½-7hr., 6 per day, $50); Penticton (1½hr., 8 per day, $11); Calgary, AB (10½hr., 3 per day, $74).
>
> **Public Transportation: Kelowna Regional Transit System** (860-8121) goes virtually anywhere in town. Fare for 1-zone travel $1.25, students and seniors $1. Day passes available. Runs M-Sa 6am-10pm.
>
> **Taxis: Kelowna Cabs,** 762-2222 or 762-4444. Runs 24hr.
>
> **Car Rental: Rent-A-Wreck,** 2702 N. Hwy. 97 (763-6632). $25 per day; 12¢ per km over 100km. Must be 21. Reservations recommended in peak season. Open M-Sa 8am-5pm, Su 9am-4pm.
>
> **Visitor Information: Kelowna Travel Infocentre,** 544 Harvey Ave. (861-1515). Open M-F 8am-7pm, Sa-Su 9am-7pm.
>
> **Bank: Canada Trust,** 507 Bernard Ave. Open M-F 8am-6pm. 24hr. **ATM.**
>
> **Equipment Rental: SameSun Hostel** (see **Accommodations,** below) Bikes $10 per day. **Sports Rent,** 3000 Pandosy St. (861-5699). Bikes or in-line skates $15-26 per day. Single kayaks $22 per day; doubles $30 per day. Open daily 9am-6pm.
>
> **Library: Kelowna Public Library,** 1380 Ellis St. (762-2800). Open Tu-Th 10am-9pm, M and F-Sa 10am-5:30pm.
>
> **Laundromat: Capri Coin Laundromat,** 150-1835 Gordon Dr. (860-6871). Wash $1.25, dry 25¢ per 8min. Open daily 7:30am-11pm.
>
> **Emergency: 911. Police:** 350 Doyle Ave. (762-3300).
>
> **Pharmacy: Canada Safeway,** 697 Bernard St. (860-0332). Open daily 8am-10pm.
>
> **Hospital: Kelowna General Hospital,** 2268 Pandosy St. (862-4000).
>
> **Post Office:** 530 Gaston Ave. (763-4095, general info 800-267-1177). Open M-F 8:30am-5pm. **Postal Code:** V1Y 7N2.
>
> **Internet Access: Mind Grind Internet Cafe and Bookstore,** 1340 Water St. (763-2221). $3 per ½hr., $5.50 per hr. Open in summer M-Sa 7:30am-11pm, Su 9am-11pm; call for off-season hours.
>
> **Area Code:** 250.

ACCOMMODATIONS AND CAMPGROUNDS In summer, Kelowna dries out thousands of soggy Vancouverites. Whether headed for a hostel, campground, or motel, always call ahead for reservations.

SameSun International Hostel (HI-C), 730 Bernard Ave. (763-9800); take the #10 bus from the Greyhound terminal. Just a few blocks from the beach and cafes along Bernard Ave., SameSun has a knack for extending one-night stopovers into week-long stays. Environmentalist, save-the-world motif and a fun, casual atmosphere. Organizes daily trips and weekly parties in summer. $15, nonmembers $17, 3 nights $40. No curfew. Reception 8:30am-12:30pm and 5-11pm.

Big White International Hostel (HI-C), 7660 Porcupine Rd. (765-7050), at the Alpine Center; take the Big White turn-off from Hwy. 33, or the shuttle bus from SameSun Hostel on Bernard Ave. Opened in '98 by SameSun, the three outdoor hot tubs and the nearby bar should be enough for relaxing after a day of skiing or snowboarding. $15, nonmembers $17. Reservations recommended. Open Nov.-Apr.

By the Bridge B&B, 1942 McDougall St. (860-7518), at the east end of Okanagan Lake Bridge. A tidy home minutes from the lake, BBB&B offers private baths, breakfast, and free bikes. Singles $45-55; doubles $50-60; triples $65-75; quads $70-80.

Bear Creek Provincial Park (494-6500, reservations 800-689-9025), 9km north of Hwy. 97 on Westside Rd. With forested lakeside sites, a beach, and views of Kelowna across the water, Bear Creek books solid in the summer. 122 sites: $15.50.

FOOD One of Canada's richest agricultural areas, Kelowna is rife with fresh produce. Shop for groceries at **Safeway,** 697 Bernard Ave. (860-0332; open daily 8am-10pm), or cut out the middle man at the many fruit and vegetable stands outside town along **Benvoulin Rd.** and **KLO Rd.** In town, **Bernard Ave.** is lined with restaurants and cafes. The patio is always full at **The Lunch Box,** 509 Bernard Ave. (862-8621), a no-frills sandwich shop ($4.50) that also serves hearty breakfasts ($3.50-6.50; breakfast served all day; open M-F 8am-8pm, Sa 9am-4pm). **Garden Patch Bistro,** 535 Bernard Ave. (762-8988), is set apart from similar bare-bones-looking little cafes by cheaper, interesting vegetarian fare, including quiches, salads, breakfast burritos ($2.50), and sandwiches ($4-5; open M-Sa 7am-4pm). **The Kitchen Cowboy,** 353 Bernard Ave. (868-8288), serves an eclectic menu to rope in a trendy clientele; offerings include burgers ($7) or grilled chicken and sundried tomato pizza ($6.75; open M-Th 8:30am-9pm, F 8:30am-11pm, Sa 9am-11pm, Su 9:30am-3:30pm).

SIGHTS, OUTDOORS, AND EVENTS Kelowna's main attraction is 93,000,000 mi. away, shining down on its parks and beaches for an average of 2000 hours per year. **City Park,** on the west end of downtown, is the principal lawn and beach from which to enjoy this gigantic ball of flaming gas, but **Boyce Gyro Park,** on Lakeshore Rd. south of the Okanagan Bridge, is popular with the younger, more hormone-laden crowd. **Sports Rent** (see **Equipment Rental,** above), a short walk away from the lake, loans all manner of camping, boating, and sporting equipment. **Kelowna Parasail Adventures** (868-4838), at the docks of Grand Okanagan Resort north of City Park, transforms patrons into kites, floating them high above the lake. *(Open daily 9am-dusk, weather permitting. $45 for a 10min. ride; $75 for 2 people.)*

The old tracks of the **Kettle Valley Railbed,** 8km southeast of town, have been replaced by 12km of easy, beautiful **hiking and biking trails.** A complete circuit passes over more than 18 trestles and through two long tunnels. The Kelowna Info-centre (see **Practical Information,** above) knows all. A generous selection of snowboard parks and varying-level slopes greet snowbunnies at **Big White Ski Resort** (765-3101, snow phone 765-SNOW/7669; email bigwhite@silk.net), on a clearly marked access road off Hwy. 33, east of town. *(Open mid-Nov. to late Apr.)* **Kelowna Land and Orchard (KLO),** 2930 Dunster Rd. (763-1091), off KLO Rd., is the town's oldest and largest family-owned farm, and gives a 45-minute hayride and tour. *(July-Aug. 9am-5pm; call for off-season hours. $5, ages 12-16 $2, under 12 free.)*

The wines of the Okanagan Valley have made a name for themselves in recent years. Kelowna has half of the valley's 24 wineries; contact the infocenter for a complete listing of winery tours (a.k.a. How to Get Drunk for Free, Very Slowly). **Mission Hill**, 1730 Mission Hill Rd. (768-7611), on the west bank of Okanagan Lake, is the most respected local winery; cross the bridge west of town, take Boucherie Rd. from the highway, and follow the signs. *(Open daily July-Aug. 10am-7pm; May-June 9am-6pm; Sept.-Apr. 9am-5pm. Hourly tours July-Aug. 10am-5pm; call for winter times.)* With a view of the lake from the front door, this large winery woos connoisseurs with its award-winning 1994 Chardonnay. Free tours explain the vintning process, and give a taste of the goods for those over 19. The creation of champagne unfolds on free tours of the posh **Summerhill Estate Winery** (800-667-3538); take Lakeshore Dr. to Chute Lake Rd. *(Open daily 10am-7pm. Tours daily on the hour 1-4pm.)*

Kelowna parties at the **Okanagan Wine Festival** (861-6654), October 1 to 10, 1999, and its lesser counterpart from April 29 to May 2. The **Kelowna Regatta** (861-4754), held in late July, has mellowed a bit since 1988, when Mounties had to break up the crowds with tear gas, but the races still pack 'em in. On Friday and Saturday nights in July and August, **free concerts** of all kinds rock the area next to City Park.

■ Okanagan Valley: Penticton

Close your eyes and imagine Florida. Replace the ocean with two large lakes, convert the palm trees into Douglas fir, add mountains and hockey fans with snow tires. Okay, now open your eyes. Voila: you're in Penticton. Indigenous peoples named the region between Okanagan and Skaha Lakes Pen-tak-tin, "a place to stay forever," but their eternal paradise was long ago transformed by heated pools and luxury hotels into one of Western Canada's biggest vacation towns. Hot weather, sandy beaches, and proximity to Vancouver and Seattle have ushered in the Tourist Age. It may strain a budget to spend a weekend here, let alone eternity.

ORIENTATION AND PRACTICAL INFORMATION Penticton lies 395km east of Vancouver at the junction of Hwy. 3 and Hwy. 97, at the southern extreme of the Okanagan Valley. **Okanagan Lake** borders the north end of town, while smaller **Skaha Lake** lies to the south. **Main St.** bisects the city from north to south, turning into **Skaha Lake Rd.** as it approaches the lake.

Buses: Greyhound, 307 Ellis (493-4101). To: Vancouver (5½-7hr., 6 per day, $48); Kelowna (1½hr., 8 per day, $11).

Public Transportation: Penticton Transit System, 301 E. Warren Ave. (492-5602). $1.35, students and seniors $1.10. Day pass $3.25, students $2.75. Runs M-F 6:30am-10pm, Sa 8:30am-6:30pm, Su 9:40am-5:40pm. Office open M-F 8am-5pm. Pick up a free *Rider's Guide* at the infocenter.

Taxis: Courtesy Taxi, 492-7778. Runs 24hr.

Car Rental: Budget, 106-2504 Skaha Lake Rd. (493-0212). M-Th $44 per day, F-Su $28 per day; 18¢ per km after 100km. Must be 21 with major credit card. Must buy collision insurance if under 25 ($23 per day). Open daily 7:30am-5:30pm. Calls forwarded to airport branch at night; may be answered depending on plane schedule.

Visitor Information: Penticton Wine and Information Centre, 888 W. Westminster Ave. (493-4055 or 800-663-5052), at Power St. Open daily in summer 9am-6pm. A smaller **Information Centre** is on Hwy. 97, 7km south of downtown. Open daily in summer 10am-5pm.

Bank: Canada Trust, 402 Main St. (492-0145). Open M-F 8am-6pm, Sa 9am-3pm. 24hr **ATM.**

Equipment Rental: Sun Country Cycle, 533 Main St. (493-0686). Mountain bikes $25 per day, $15 per 4hr., with helmet. $5 HI discount. Open M-Sa 9am-5:30pm.

Laundry: Plaza Laundromat, 417-1301 Main St. (493-8710), in the Penticton Plaza Mall. Wash $1.50, dry 25¢ per 6min. TV on premises. Open daily 7am-11pm.

Weather: 492-6991.

Emergency: 911. **Police:** 1103 Main St. (492-4300).

Crisis Line: 493-6622. **Women's Shelter:** 493-7233. 24hr.

Pharmacy: Shoppers Drug Mart, 721-1301 Main St. (492-8000), in the Penticton Plaza Mall. Open M-F 8am-9pm, Sa 9am-6pm, Su 10am-5pm.

Hospital: Penticton Regional, 550 Carmi Ave. (492-4000).
Post Office: 56 W. Industrial Ave. (492-5769). Open M-F 8:30am-5pm. **Postal Code:**
V2A 5M0.
Internet Access: Pacific Brimm Coffee, 110-2210 Main St. (490-8720). Open Su-Th
7am-10pm, F-Sa 7am-11pm. Free 20min. with any purchase.
Area Code: 250.

ACCOMMODATIONS AND CAMPGROUNDS
Penticton is a resort city year-round;
cheap beds are few and far between. Sardine companies might take a lesson on packing from the campgrounds lining the shores of Skaha Lake. The plentiful campsites
also carry a hefty price tag. It's wise to make reservations for beds in summer.

Penticton Hostel (HI-C), 464 Ellis St. (492-3992), in a large house near the Greyhound stop and 10min. from the beach. One of Penticton's best bets, with comfortable lounge and patio, kitchen, laundry facilities, and gas grill. 52 beds: $15,
nonmembers $19, under 10 half-price. 3-day stay $40.50, nonmembers $48. Private
rooms available. Linen $1.50. No curfew. Reception 7am-1pm and 4-11pm. Fills in
July and Aug.
Riordan House, 689 Winnipeg (493-5997). Much more elegant than the neon-
bedecked concrete-box motels on Lakeshore Dr., yet costs not a penny more. The
Victorian-style mansion has 4 enormous, lavishly decorated rooms with plush car-
peting, TV, and VCR. Mr. Ortiz makes a knockout complimentary breakfast of fresh
scones and luscious local fruits. One single (a converted library with plants everywhere) $50; doubles $55-75.
Okanagan Mountain Provincial Park (494-0321), 50km north of town on Hwy. 97.
Sites packed between the highway and the lake in two separate units, roomier in
the north park. Good beach swimming. 168 sites: $15.50. No reservations; always
full in summer. Claim sites early (8-10am), or not at all.

FOOD
Stockpile in preparation for nuclear winter at **Super Valu Foods** (492-4315),
450 Martin St., just west of Main; open M-F 9am-7pm, Sa 9am-9pm, Su 9am-6pm).

Whole Foods Market, 1550 Main St. (493-2855), in Creekside Plaza. A health food
supermarket, with bulk grains, pastas, herbs, and organic produce. The deli
counter in the back (open M-F 9am-3pm) slaps together fantastic sandwiches ($3-
5). Open M-Th and Sa-Su 9am-6pm, F 9am-8pm.
Judy's Deli, 129 W. Nanaimo (492-7029). Take-out only. Hearty homemade soups
$1.65-2; butter-smeared sandwiches $2.80-3.30; herbs and homeopathic medicines
everywhere. Open M-Sa 9am-5:30pm.
Hog's Breath Coffee Co., 202 Main St. (493-7800). A mellow cafe with energetic
management and good food. All-day breakfast $4. Huge wraps ($6) come in a variety of flavors featuring artichoke hearts, grilled chicken, and marinated eggplant.
Open daily 6am-10pm, roughly speaking.

SIGHTS, OUTDOORS, AND EVENTS
South of Penticton along Hwy. 97 and Hwy.
3A, visitors can eat fruit at a family stand, sample wines at a local vineyard, or fish in a
pristine lake. The Penticton tourist trade revolves around **Okanagan Lake.** Long, hot
summers and sport facilities on the lake make it a popular hangout for the young. The
beach at the other end of town on **Skaha Lake,** however, got the volleyball nets and
more sand. **Pier Water Sports,** on the beach near the Okanagan Lake end of Main St.,
rents various vessels. *(Open daily 9am-8pm. Single kayaks or canoes $15 per hr., $45 per day.
Double kayaks $20 per hr., $60 per day. Sailboats $25-30 per hr. Windsurfers $14 for 1hr., $9
per additional hr. Pedal boats $10 per hr., $7 per additional hr.)* Waterskiing rides or lessons
cost $105 per hour for up to three people on a charter. A credit card imprint, $500
cash deposit, or an arm and a leg are required on all rentals.
The beachfront **Art Gallery of the South Okanagan,** 199 Front St. (493-2928),
exhibits local and Canadian artists. *(Open Tu-F 10am-5pm, Sa-Su 1-5pm. $2, students and
children free, all free on Tu.)* Looking suspiciously like an East African wildlife preserve,
the **Okanagan Game Farm** (497-5405), on Hwy. 97 south of Penticton, covers 560
acres and protects 130 animal species not exactly native to the area. *(Open daily 8am-*

dusk. $10, ages 5-15 $7.) Cars can drive through the park past zebras, rhinos, gnus, aoudads, and ankoli frolicking free of fences and bars.

The mists and mellow fruitfulness of fall mark the ripening of the wine season. **Hillside Cellars Winery** (493-4424), at the junction of Vancouver and Naramata Rd. northeast of Penticton, has a shop offering free tastings and tours. *(Open daily Apr.-Oct. 10am-6pm. Frequent tours 10:30am-5pm; Nov.-Mar. call for hours.)* The **Okanagan Wine Festival** (490-8866), held in early October, is endless fun for anyone fond of squishing thick pulp between their toes. For more info, contact the Penticton Wine and Information Centre (see **Practical Information,** above).

The **Skaha Bluffs,** southeast of town on Valley View Rd., have developed into a popular rock-climbing venue, offering pitches of varying difficulty. Stop in at **Ray's Sports Den,** 215 Main St. (493-1216), for info about area climbing. *(Open M-F 9:30am-6pm, Sa 9:30am-5pm, Su 10am-4pm.)* Heavy winter snowfalls in Okanagan Valley make for excellent skiing, as Penticton smoothly transforms from summer beach resort to winter mountain playland. **Apex Mountain Resort** (800-387-APEX/2739) sports a mix of downhill, cross-country, and night skiing within easy reach of town, off an access road west of Penticton on Hwy. 3.

■ Nelson

Nestled in the forested hills at the foot of Kootenay Lake in the Kootenay Mountains, Nelson twinkles at a slightly different cultural temperature than any other isolated 9000-person town in the southern BC interior. A vacation destination primarily for other British Columbians, Nelson gives visitors a break from the usual BC tourist crowds, and a chance to mingle with an eclectic blend of locals and seasonal transplants. Every summer, the neo-hippies and New Agers mix peacefully with both wealthier residents and more down-to-earth Nelsonites. Lined with historic buildings, the downtown area, cradles art lovers; the real beauty and mellowness, however, lie high up in the Kootenays, atop the ski hill, and on the gigantic lake. Whether drinking mineral water, beer, whiskey, or herbal tea, you'll fit right in.

ORIENTATION AND PRACTICAL INFORMATION

Nelson lies at the junction of Hwy. 6 and 3A, 624km southwest of Calgary, 454km southeast of Kamloops, and 657km east of Vancouver. From Nelson, Hwy. 3A heads 41km west to Castlegar. Hwy. 6 leads 65km south to the U.S. border, where it becomes Washington Rte. 31, continuing 110 mi. south to Spokane. Downtown, most parking spots are metered, but U.S. license plates seem to repel tickets.

Buses: Greyhound, 1112 Lakeside Dr. (352-3939), in the Chako-Mika Mall. To: Vancouver (12hr., 2 per day, $86); Calgary, AB (12hr., 2 per day, $79); Banff, AB (14½hr. with 4hr. layover in Cranbrook, 1 per day, $65). 10% student and senior discounts.

Public Transportation: Nelson Transit Systems (352-2911). Three lines cover the city. In town $1, students and seniors 80¢. A fourth, more expensive line runs to the lake's north shore. Buses run M-F 6:30am-11:30pm, Sa 8:30am-7:30pm.

Taxis: Whitewater Cabs, 354-1111. Runs 24hr.

Car Rental: Rent-a-Wreck, 524 Nelson Ave. (352-5122), in the Esso station. $38 per day, plus 12¢ per km after 200km; or $26 per day, plus 12¢ per km (no free km). Must have credit card; no age requirement.

Visitor Information: Nelson and District Infocentre, 225 Hall St. (352-3433). Open July-Aug. daily 8:30am-6pm; Sept.-June M-F 8:30am-4:30pm.

Outdoor Information: West Kootenay Visitor Centre (825-4723), in Kokanee Creek Provincial Park 20km east of Nelson on Hwy. 3A. Provides info on local outdoor recreation. Open July-Aug. daily 9am-9pm.

Bank: CIBC, 459 Baker St. (352-8700). Open M-F 9:30am-4pm. 24hr. **ATM.**

Equipment Rental: Gerick Cycle and Sports, 702 Baker St. (354-4622). Bikes $15 per day, $25 per weekend. Canoe and kayak rentals available. Open M-Th, Sa 9am-5:30pm, F 9am-9pm.

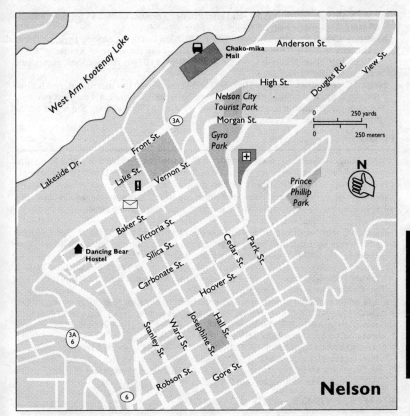

Nelson

Laundromat: 524 Nelson St. (352-3534), in the Esso station. Open Th-F 7:30am-10pm, Sa-W 7:30am-9:30pm. Wash $1.25, dry 25¢ per 10min.

Emergency: 911. **Ambulance:** 352-2112. **Fire:** 352-3123. **Police:** 352-2266 (non-emergency 354-3919).

Crisis Line: 352-3504. 24hr.

Pharmacy: Pharmasave, 639 Baker St. (352-2313). Open M-Th 9am-6pm, F 9am-9pm, Sa 9am-5:30pm, Su 10am-4pm.

Hospital: Kootenay Lake District, 3 View St. (352-3111). If you break your leg, don't try to walk; it's way uphill in the southeast part of town.

Post Office: 514 Vernon St. (352-3538). Open M-F 8:30am-5pm. **Postal Code:** V1L 5P3.

Internet Access: Station Manor Internet Cafe, 420 Railway St. (354-1152). $3 per 30min., $5 per hr. Open M-Sa 11am-6pm, Su 10:30am-3pm.

Area Code: 250.

ACCOMMODATIONS AND CAMPGROUNDS

Dancing Bear Inn (HI-C), 171 Baker St. (phone and fax 352-7573). You just can't ask for a better location, a more caring management, or a more beautiful common room, which features wood furnishings crafted by local artisans. Many bedrooms have one bed or bunk each. Laundry, immaculate kitchen, Internet access ($5 per hr.). One of the finest hostels in Western Canada. $17, nonmembers $20, ages 6-10 half-price, under 5 free. No curfew. Check-in 4-10pm; office also open 7-11am.

Duhamel Motel (825-4645), 9km north of town on Hwy. 3A. The four tiny cabins welcome travelers into a private wood-paneled living room with fold-out bed, separate bedroom, bathroom, TV, and kitchenette. 2 double beds. $53 for one person, $5 per additional person up to 4.

Kokanee Creek Provincial Park (825-4212), 5km beyond Chinook Park on Hwy. 3A, north of town. Tree-shaded, spacious sites near the shore of Kootenay Lake. Wheelchair accessible sites available. 132 sites: $12. No reservations; nab a site early in the day in summer.

Nelson City Tourist Park, on High St. Take Vernon St. to its eastern end, and follow the signs. Packed tight, with little division between sites. Still, it's the best place to crash if you're unable to get out of town. 40 sites: $13; electricity and water hookups $16. Showers for non-campers $2.

FOOD

Satiate hunger cheaply at **Extra Foods,** 708 Vernon St. (352-2815; open M-F 9am-9pm, Sa-Su 9am-6pm), procure fresh bread from the **Kootenay Baker,** 295 Baker St. (352-2274; open M-Sa 8am-6pm), or choose from an impressive assortment of vegetarian hot dog imitations and a range of organic goodies at the **Kootenay Co-op** in the same building (354-4077; open M-Th and Sa 9:30am-6pm, F 9:30am-8pm).

Glacier Gourmet (354-4495), at the corner of Vernon St. and Hall St. This colorful cafe serves up fresh and highly vegetarian meals to a hippie crowd, with live jazz every Friday night. World Wraps (tortilla with brown rice, crunchy veggies, and sauces ranging from chili to peanut sauce) $5; pizza slices $3. Coffees, baked goods, organic juices. Open M-F 8:30am-11pm, Sa 10am-11pm, Su 10am-10pm.

The Outer Clove, 536 Stanley St. (352-6800). A red-walled, garlic-themed interior and patio welcome diners into a flavorful eatery of foods from all over the globe. Dinner gets a little pricey, but the lunch specials and tapas ($4-7) are both delicious and economical. Garlic Yumburger $8; Buddha's Feast (mushrooms, cheese, tofu, garlic salsa) $8. Open M-Sa 11:30am-9pm.

Max and Irma's Kitchen, 515A Kootenay St. (352-2332). Inspired by the cuisines of Italy and modern California, Max and Irma toss meats, veggies, cheeses, and fungi onto quality 10 in. pizzas, then cook them in a wood-fired oven ($10-12). Meltdown sandwiches $8. Open Su-Th 11am-9pm, F-Sa 11am-10pm.

SIGHTS, EVENTS, AND OUTDOORS

Pick up the free brochure *Architectural Heritage Walking Tour* at visitor center for a guide to Nelson's impressive collection of historic buildings. The tour's counterpart driving tour also has a brochure, and leads past the private homes of the **Uphill District,** where residents open their homes to tours one day each year. The more culturally significant tours, of course, concern movies and beer. In 1986, Nelson welcomed camera crews, Steve Martin, and Darryl Hannah for the filming of the romantic comedy *Roxanne;* the visitor center still has walking tour brochures of the outdoor filming locations, which only will impress you if you memorized the movie set. Cool off with a free tour at **Nelson Brewery,** 512 Latimer St. (352-3582; call for times). Every summer from July through September, various businesses downtown display the work of the rich local artistic community as part of **Artwalk,** a self-guided walking tour. Pick up the map and descriptions at participating businesses or the infocenter.

Bordering Nelson on the north, the watery **West Arm** may look huge, but it's just a tiny segment of the enormous **Kootenay Lake.** Dolly varden, rainbow trout (up to 30 lb. according to local legend), and kokanee cruise the lake, while sturgeon of up to 1.5m in length prowl the **Kootenay River.**

The **West Kootenay Visitor Centre** (see **Practical Information,** above) displays hands-on science and history exhibits leveled at children. Behind the visitor center, a spawning channel fills with bright red kokanee in late August and early September, as the salmon struggle upstream to mate and then drift back downstream, dead.

Kokanee Glacier Provincial Park, uncrowded because it's so hard to reach, has an entrance after 16km of bumpy dirt on Kokanee Creek Rd., which leaves Hwy. 3A 21km north of Nelson. The road ends at placid **Gibson Lake,** where a 4km trail leads up and across the mountainside, past views of the Kootenays, to **Kokanee Lake.** The trail continues 3km to the campground at **Kaslo Lake,** with views of the **Kokanee Glacier.** After a total of 9km, the path reaches the 12-person **Slocan Chief cabin** below the glacier. *(Backcountry campgrounds $4; cabin $10.)* Don't walk on the glacier without an expert. After 12km up the road to Gibson Lake, the **Old Growth Trail** begins. With the **Cedar Grove Loop,** the trail winds a 2km round-trip down into the forest. Bring the brochure from the trailhead for a fascinating interpretation of this ecosystem, explaining how hard those towering trees work to survive. In winter, the soft powder of **Whitewater Ski Resort** (354-4944, 24hr. snow report 352-7669, in AB 403-289-3700; http://www.skiwhitewater.com), 35km southeast of town, draws skiers and boarders to groomed runs and tree skiing on 32 runs with a 1300 ft. vertical drop. *(Lift tickets $35, seniors and ages 13-18 $27, ages 7-12 $21, under 7 free.)*

■ Revelstoke

In the 19th century, Revelstoke was a town straight out of a Zane Grey western, complete with dust-encrusted megalomaniacs maiming one another amid the gold-laden Selkirk Mountains. Located on both the Columbia River and the Canadian Pacific Railway, the town was born as a stopover for boats and trains. Although still a stopover for travelers on the way to the Rockies, Revelstoke's small-town feel and extensive outdoor activities make it a destination of its own.

ORIENTATION AND PRACTICAL INFORMATION

Revelstoke is situated on the Trans-Canada Hwy. (Hwy. 1), 410km west of Calgary and 575km east of Vancouver. The town can be easily covered on foot or by bicycle. Mount Revelstoke National Park lies just out of town.

Buses: Greyhound, 1899 Fraser Dr. (837-5874), 1 block south of Hwy. 1. To: Calgary ($51); Vancouver ($68); Salmon Arm ($15). Open M-Sa 8am-7pm, Su 11am-1pm and 3-7pm.

Taxis: Johnnie's, 837-3000. **R Taxi,** 837-4000. Both run 24hr.

Car Rental: Tilden Car Rental, 301 W. 1st St. (837-2158). $60 per day; 20¢ per km after 100km. Must be 21 with credit card. Open M-Sa 8am-6pm.

Visitor Information: Visitor Infocentre (837-3522), at the junction of Hwy. 1 and Hwy. 23 N. Open daily June-Aug. 9am-7pm; Sept.-May 9am-5pm.

Outdoor Information: Canadian Parks Service (837-7500), at Boyle Ave. and 3rd St. Open M-F 8:30am-noon and 1-4:30pm.

Equipment Rental: Spoketacular Sports, 2220 MacKenzie (837-2220). Bikes $5 per hr., $25 per day. Many other types of outdoor gear available. Open M-Sa 9am-5pm.

Emergency: 911. **Police:** 320 Wilson St. (837-5255). **Ambulance:** 837-5885.

Hospital: Queen Victoria Hospital, 6622 Newlands Rd. (837-2131).

Post Office: 307 W. 3rd St. (837-3228). Open M-F 8:30am-5pm. **Postal Code:** V0E 2S0.

Internet Access: Perchè No Cafe (see **Food,** below). $3 for a half-hour, $5 per hour.

Area Code: 250.

ACCOMMODATIONS AND CAMPGROUNDS

Revelstoke Traveler's Hostel and Guest House, 400 2nd St. W (837-4050), with an office across the street at 403 2nd St. W. This downtown hostel has no more than 3 beds in each of 27 rooms, all in a pristine, gleaming, newly renovated house. Several kitchens and bathrooms allow plenty of privacy, and most of the bare-but-clean rooms have very comfy double beds. Free pick-up from the bus station. Free internet access. Beds $15; singles $20; doubles $30; family rooms available. Pitch a tent for $8-10, the cheapest in the area. Open 24hr.

Daniel's Guest House, 313 First St. E (837-5530). Although Daniel's perches on the edge of town, it's only a 5min. walk from Revelstoke. A home-turned-hostel, Daniel's spotless hardwood floors, couch-filled common room, and porch make the place a home away from home. $15; doubles $30; private rooms $45, families

$30. Kitchen, laundry. Free pick-up from the bus station. 18 beds in single-sex 6-person dorms and private rooms. Reception 7-11am and 4-8pm.

Williamson's Lake Campground, 1818 Williamson Lake Rd. (837-5512 or 800-676-2267), 1.5km southeast of downtown on Airport Way. Farther from the highway than its competitors, this ground makes a nice change from the big signs and huge Smokey-the-Bear statues that litter the Trans-Canada Hwy. The lake itself is a popular local swimming hole. 28 sites: $13.25; 16 full hookups $17.25. Closed in winter.

FOOD

Cooper's Supermarket, 555 Victoria St. (837-4372), sells all requisite groceries. Open Su 9am-6pm, M-Th and Sa 8am-8pm, F 8am-9pm.

Chalet Deli, 555 Victoria St. (837-5552), across the parking lot from Cooper's. The best place for lunch and baked goods. Personal pizza with choice of sauce $2.75; meaty sandwich on fresh bread $4. Open M-Sa 5am-6pm, Su 11am-5pm.

Perchè No Cafe, 217 Mackenzie Ave. (837-6575). This used bookstore/cafe knows how to cut a deal. Huge sandwiches $3.50; Belgian waffles piled with fresh fruit $6. Internet access. Open M-F 6:30am-9pm, Sa-Su 9am-9pm.

Frontier Restaurant, 122 N. Hwy. 23 (873-5119), at the junction of Hwy. 1 and 23 N. Ranchhand St. (½ lb. cheeseburger with the works) $7.60; Ain't No Bull (meatless mushroom-and-peppers burger) $6. Breakfasts too. Open daily 5am-10pm.

SIGHTS AND OUTDOORS

The **Revelstoke Railway Museum,** 719 W. Track St. (837-6060), off Victoria Rd., is a shrine to the Iron Horse, with old photos and story-board exhibits that outline the construction of the first Canadian transcontinental line, completed in 1885. *(Open daily 9am-8pm; in spring and fall M-F 9am-5pm. $5, seniors $3, ages 7-14 $2, under 7 free.)*

Canyon Hot Springs (837-2420), between Mt. Revelstoke National Park and Glacier National Park on Hwy. 1, sports two spring-fed pools that simmer at 40°C (104°F) and 26°C (80°F). *(Single swim $5, seniors $4.50, under 14 $4. Day pass $7.50, seniors $6, under 14 $5. Open daily in summer 9am-10pm; in spring and fall 9am-9pm.)* The springs also provide campgrounds for spa-lovers who can't extract themselves from the warm elixirs. *($18; full hookups $23 for 2 people; $2 per additional adult.)*

Revelstoke has some curious variations on **downhill skiing** to spice up its winter season. Several companies offer heli-skiing, ski tours on nearby glaciers, and guided ski trips. **Mt. Mackenzie,** P.O. Box 1000, 5km outside of town, maintains 21 trails on a 2000 ft. vertical drop. Cross-country skiers find more than enough snow and trails in the nearby national parks, and the area is becoming increasingly popular for **snowmobilers,** with several deep powder trails. The guides at **Monashee Outfitting,** 825 Olhausen (837-3538), are willing and able to organize hiking, fishing, horse rides, canoeing, cross-country skiing, and suchlike.

Mt. Revelstoke National Park, adjacent to town, furnishes a quick and satisfying nature fix. A favorite of mountain bikers and hikers, the small but well-used park produces some astounding scenery. Two special boardwalks off Hwy. 1 on the east side of the park allow exploration of the local brush. The **Skunk Cabbage Trail** (1.2km) leads through acres of stinking perfection: skunk cabbage plants tower at heights of over 1.5m. Some of the majestic trees on the **Giant Cedars Trail** (500m) are over 1000 years old. There are two **backcountry campgrounds** in the park (backcountry camping permit $6); visit the Parks Canada office (see **Practical Information,** above) or the Rogers Pass info center (see **Glacier National Park,** p. 305). The 24km of the **Meadows in the Sky Parkway** (Summit Rd.), branches off Hwy. 1 1.5km east of town, leading to a 1km hike up to some of the most accessible alpine meadows in Western Canada. The mechanical marvels of the **Revelstoke Dam** (837-6515 or 837-6211), 5km north of Hwy. 1 on Hwy. 23 are illustrated in a free tour via talking wand. *(Open daily in summer 8am-8pm; mid-May to mid-June and mid-Sept. to mid-Oct. 9am-5pm. Wheelchair accessible.)* Ride the elevator to the top of the dam for an impressive view.

■ Glacier National Park

Canada's most aptly named national park is home to over 400 of the giant, slow-moving ice flows. The jagged peaks and steep, narrow valleys of the Columbia Range prevent development in the 1350km² park, even along the highway corridor. The Trans-Canada Hwy. cuts a thin ribbon through the center of the park, blessing motorists with views of high-in-the-sky glaciers. More than 140km of rough, often steep trails lead from the highway, inviting mountaineers to penetrate the near-impenetrable. In late July or early August, brilliant explosions of mountain wildflowers offset the deep green of the forests. Glacier receives significant precipitation every other day in summer, but the clouds of mist that encircle the peaks and blanket the valleys only add to the park's astonishing beauty. Unless directly descended from Sir Edmund Hillary or Tenzing Norgay, avoid exploring the park in winter; near-daily snowfalls and the constant threat of avalanches often restrict travel to the Trans-Canada Highway.

Eight popular **hiking trails** begin at the Illecillewaet campground (see below), 3.4km west of Rogers Pass. The 1km **Meeting of the Waters Trail** leads to the impressive confluence of the **Illecillewaet** and **Asulkan Rivers**. The 4.2km **Avalanche Crest Trail** offers spectacular views of **Rogers Pass,** the **Hermit Range,** and the Illecillewaet River Valley; the treeless slopes below the crest testify to the destructive power of winter snowslides. In late summer, when enough snow has melted, the **Perley Rock Trail** leads directly to the **Illecillewaet Glacier,** with a steep 5.6km ascent. Before setting out, speak with a park ranger to find out how much of the trail is safe to hike. The **Copperstain Trail,** 10km east of the Glacier Park Lodge at the Beaver River Trailhead, leads 16km (6hr.) uphill through alpine meadows. From early July to late August, the park staff run daily **interpretive hikes** beginning at 9am. Contact the infocenter (see below) for details. Come prepared for the four- to six-hour tour with a picnic lunch, rain jacket, and a sturdy pair of walking shoes.

The park's glacial meltwaters—a startling milky aqua color created by sediment suspended in the current—do not support many fish; determined anglers can try their luck with the cutthroat in the Illecillewaet River (permits $6 for 7 days, available at the Rogers Pass info center). Biking in Glacier is prohibited.

Glacier lies 350km west of Calgary and 723km east of Vancouver. **Greyhound** (837-5874) makes four trips daily from Revelstoke ($9.20). In an **emergency,** call the **Park Warden Office** (837-6274; open daily 7am-5pm; winter hours vary; 24hr. during avalanche control periods). For details on the park, talk to the Parks Canada staff or buy a copy of *Footloose in the Columbias* ($1.50) at the **Rogers Pass Information Centre** (814-5232), on the highway in Glacier (open daily in summer 9am-6pm; closed off-season Sa-Su; call for hours). **Park passes** ($4 per day, $35 per year) are required. For more info about Glacier, write to the Superintendent, P.O. Box 350, Revelstoke V0E 2S0, or call 873-7500. **Area Code:** 250.

There are two campgrounds in Glacier: **Illecillewaet** (ill-uh-SILL-uh-watt) and **Loop Brook.** Both offer flush toilets, kitchen shelters with cook stoves, and firewood (sites $13; open mid-June to Sept.). Backcountry campers need a **backcountry pass** ($6) from the Parks Canada office in Revelstoke (837-7500; see p. 303) or in the Rogers Pass Information Centre (see above). Campers must pitch their tents at least 5km from the pavement. Food choices in the park are limited and unappealing; drop by a supermarket in Golden or Revelstoke before entering Glacier.

■ Yoho National Park

A Cree expression for awe and wonder, Yoho is the perfect name for this small, uncrowded park. It sports some of the niftiest names in the Rockies, like Kicking Horse Pass, so titled after Captain John Hector, tired, hungry, and struggling to find a mountain pass for the Canada Pacific Railroad, was kicked in the chest by his horse. Driving down Yoho's narrow canyon on Hwy. 1, visitors can see geological forces in action; massive bent and tilted sedimentary rock layers, once flat, are now exposed in sharply eroded cliff faces. This quiet park is stuffed with natural splendor, young and ancient: the largest waterfall in the Rockies, the Continental Divide, and the Burgess Shale, which made its way into paleontology textbooks in the early 20th century when it revealed the complexity of pre-Cambrian life.

ORIENTATION AND PRACTICAL INFORMATION Yoho is still in Mountain Time, one hour ahead of Pacific Time. The park lies on the Trans-Canada Highway (Hwy. 1), adjacent to Banff National Park. The town of **Field,** within the park, is 27km west of Lake Louise on Hwy. 1. **Greyhound** does stop for travelers waving their arms on the highway, but this is not a major destination. Those without cars can try calling the bus company, or hitching the well-traveled highway (though *Let's Go* does not recommend hitchhiking). **Hosteling International** runs a shuttle service connecting all the Rocky Mountain hostels in Yoho, Banff, and Jasper, as well as Calgary ($7-65).The **Visitor Information Centre** (343-6783) is in Field on Hwy. 1 (open daily 9am-7pm; in spring and fall 9am-5pm; in winter 9am-4pm). In case of **emergency,** call the **Warden Office** (403-762-4506; 24hr.) or the **RCMP** (344-2221) in nearby Golden. The scarcity of phones in the park, however, often makes it more efficient to drive to Lake Louise for help. The **post office** (343-6365) is at 312 Stephen Ave. (open M-F 8:30am-4:30pm). **Postal Code:** V0A 1G0. **Area Code:** 250.

ACCOMMODATIONS, CAMPGROUNDS, AND FOOD With one of the best locations of all the Rocky Mountain hostels, the **Whiskey Jack Hostel,** 13km off the Trans-Canada on Yoho Valley Rd., just before Takakkaw Falls, is the best indoor place to stay while imbibing Yoho's sights. Whiskey Jack offers a kitchen, nightly campfires, indoor plumbing, propane light, easy access to Yoho's best high country trails, and all the splendor of the Takakkaw Falls right from the front porch. Olga, the manager, plays a wicked game of Scrabble. (Beds $13, nonmembers $17; open June-Sept.) There is no phone, so make highly recommended reservations by calling the Banff International Hostel (403-762-4122; see p. 351).

All **frontcountry camping** is first-come, first-served, but the abundance of backcountry camping keeps overcrowding to a minimum, even in mid-summer, when all the campgrounds are open. The five official campgrounds offer a combined 320 sites, all easily accessible from the highway. **Hoodoo Creek,** on the west end of the park, has kitchen shelters, running hot water, a nearby river, and a playground (106 sites: $14; open late June-Aug.). It lies just across the Trans-Canada Hwy. from **Chancellor Peak,** which has pump water, and pit toilets (58 sites: $12; open late May-Sept.). **Kicking Horse,** on Yoho Valley Rd. off the highway, has hot showers, flush toilets, and wheelchair access (86 sites: $17). Gape-inducing views of the falls, river, glaciers, and nearby mountains unfold from the high **Takakkaw Falls Campground,** on Yoho Valley Rd. It offers only pump water and pit toilets, and no cars are allowed, requiring campers to park in the falls lot and haul their gear 650m to the peaceful sites (35 sites: $12; open late June to late Sept.). **Monarch Campground,** nearby at the start of Yoho Valley Rd., has 36 regular sites and eight walk-ins ($12; open late June to early Sept.).

Food options in Field are quite diverse given the town's population. The most convenient pit stop, easily becoming a sit-all-day stop, is the **Siding General Store and Cafe** (343-6462), on Stephen Ave. Basic foodstuffs line the walls, beer fills the cooler, and the friendly owners push home-made food and fresh baked goods over the counter, including sandwiches ($4), breakfast (around $4), and dinner ($8-12; open daily 8am-9pm; in winter M-Sa 10am-6pm).

OUTDOORS The **Great Divide** is both the boundary between Alberta and British Columbia and the breaking-away point for the Atlantic and Pacific watersheds. Here a stream forks with one arm flowing 1500km to the Pacific Ocean, and the other flowing 2500km to the Atlantic via Hudson Bay. More obscure to unknowing passersby is the **Burgess Shale,** where the world's finest pre-Cambrian fossils were discovered in 1909. The shale features imprints of the bizarre-looking, soft-bodied organisms that inhabited the world's murky seas in the time just before a mad burst of evolution known as the **Cambrian Explosion.** The pre-Cambrian critters were an unprecedented find, and offered scientists an important glimpse of life forms vastly different from those present today. Bigger, clumsier organisms known as humans have forced the Canadian government to protect the shale from excessive tourism. The **Yoho-Burgess Shale Foundation** (800-343-3006; email burgshal@rockies.net) offers the only access to the shale through guided, educational, full-day hikes. *(Tours July-Sept. Reservations required.)* The foundation also runs a short but steep 6km loop to the **Mt. Stephen Fossil Beds** ($25) and a 20km round-trip to **Walcott's Quarry** ($45), coming face-to-face with 505-million-year-old fossils.

For info on **backcountry trails,** pick up the *Backcountry Guide to Yoho National Park* at the info center ($1). When the snow has melted in mid- to late summer, take the 10.6km **Iceline Trail,** starting at the hostel, for valley views and an up-close introduction to the **Emerald Glacier.** The park's six **backcountry campgrounds** offer a total of 48 trails and an intense wilderness experience. Before heading up a trail, stop at the visitor center (see **Practical Information,** above) for a **permit** ($6) and a map. Backcountry campers should ask about the availability of backcountry **alpine huts.**

Yoho's most splendid lake is also its least accessible. **Lake O'Hara,** in the northeast end of the park, can only be reached by a 13km pedestrian trail or on a park-operated bus (reservations 343-6433). *(Round-trip $12. Park permit required.)* High peaks, rock lichens, and lakes in glacier-carved basins all benefit from the restriction on tourism, and reward those who do venture to O'Hara with a cornucopia of mountain life. No reservations are necessary to hike the mellow but long trail at the lake or to camp there, and the return bus trip is free for hikers. In contrast, Yoho's most splendid waterfall is ridiculously easy to access, except for the switchbacks along the steep road up. The **Takakkaw Falls** are visible for a good portion of the drive up Yoho Valley Rd., but the force of the water and thick mist are more intense from the short trail to the falls, 14km off the Trans-Canada Hwy.

▓ Kootenay National Park

Kootenay National Park hangs off the continental divide on the southeast edge of British Columbia. Almost all visitors travel through Kootenay to get to or from Banff National Park on the majestic Banff-Windermere Highway (Hwy. 93). Running the length of Kootenay, the highway is a magnificent drive, but it barely scratches the park's surface. Kootenay's best feature is what it lacks: people. Stately conifers, alpine meadows, and pristine peaks hide in Banff's shadow, allowing travelers to get off the tourist track and experience the solitude and beauty of the Canadian Rockies.

ORIENTATION AND PRACTICAL INFORMATION Kootenay lies southwest of Banff and Yoho National Parks. **Highway 93** runs through the park from the Trans-Canada Hwy. in Banff to **Radium Hot Springs** at the southwest edge of the park, where it joins **Hwy. 95.** Greyhound buses stop at the Esso station, 7507 W. Main St. (347-9726; open daily 7am-11pm), at the junction of Hwy. 93 and Hwy. 95 in Radium Hot Springs. Daily service runs the length of the Banff-Windermere Hwy. (Hwy. 93) to Banff ($19) and Calgary ($34). The **Kootenay National Park Information Centre** (347-9505), on the park's western boundary at the Radium Hot Spring Pool Complex, hands out free maps and a $1 **backcountry hiking guide,** free with a backcountry permit (see **Outdoors,** below; open in summer daily 9am-7pm; call for off-season hours). The **Kootenay Park Lodge** (no phone) operates a similar info center 63km north of Radium (open in summer 9am-6:30pm; stop by for off-season hours). The **Park Administration Office** (347-9615), on the access road to Redstreak Campground (see **Accommodations,** below), gives out the backcountry hiking guide for free, and is open in winter, when the infocenter is not (open M-F 8am-noon and 1-4pm). For an **ambulance,** call 342-2055. For after-hour **emergencies,** call 403-762-4506. Call the **police** in Invermere at 342-9292, and in Radium Hot Springs at 347-9393. The nearest hospital is **Windermere District Hospital** (342-9201), in Invermere, 15km south of Radium on Hwy. 95. The **post office** (347-9460) is on Radium St. in Radium Hot Springs (open M-F 8:30am-5pm). **Postal Code: V0A 1M0. Area Code: 250.**

ACCOMMODATIONS, CAMPGROUNDS, AND FOOD The **Columbia Motel,** 4886 St. Joseph St. (347-9557), has clean rooms and some of the lowest rates in town ($45-

50, with kitchen $50-55). The park's most mammoth campground is **Redstreak,** on the access road that departs Hwy. 95 near the south end of Radium Hot Springs, with 242 sites, flush toilets, showers, firewood, playgrounds, and swarms of RVs. Walk-in sites off Loop D offer some, but not much, solitude. Redstreak is the only campground in Kootenay with hookups. Arrive early to secure a spot among the crowds (open mid-May to mid-Sept.; $16, full hookups $21). **McLeod Meadows,** 27km north of the West Gate entrance on Hwy. 93, offers more solitude, wooded sites, plenty of elbow room, and access to hiking trails (98 sites: $13; open mid-May to mid-Sept.). **Marble Canyon,** 86km north of the West Gate entrance, also provides more privacy than its big brother down the road (61 sites: $13; open mid-June through Aug.). From September 14 to May 7, snag one of seven free winter sites at the **Dolly Varden** picnic area, 36km north of the West Gate entrance, which boasts free firewood, water, toilets, and a kitchen shelter. **Free camping** outside the park is plentiful in the nearby Invermere Forest district; ask the staff at the info center for details.

There is no affordable food in Kootenay, with the exception of a few basic staples and snacks at the **Kootenay Park Lodge** (see **Practical Information,** above). Radium supports a few inexpensive but uninspiring eateries crammed together on Main St. The best selection of groceries for kilometers around (without much competition) is at **Radium Foods,** 7546 Main St. E (347-9600; open M-Sa 9am-8pm, Su 10am-7pm).

OUTDOORS Kootenay National Park's main advertised attraction is **Radium Hot Springs** (347-9485), the complex of pools responsible for the traffic and towel-toting tourists just inside the West Gate entrance. Natural mineral waters are cloaked as two large swimming pools—a hot one for soaking and a cooler one for swimming. The hot pool is wheelchair accessible. Check out the scene from the deck above for free before making an investment. *(Open daily 9am-11pm; in winter noon-9pm. $5, seniors and children $4.50, in winter 50¢ less. Lockers 25¢, towel rental $1, swimsuit rental $1.25.)*

The 95km **Banff-Windermere Highway (Hwy. 93)** forms the bending backbone of Kootenay. Stretching from Radium Hot Springs to Banff, the highway follows the **Kootenay** and **Vermilion Rivers,** passing views of glacier-enclosed peaks, dense stands of virgin forest, and glacial-green rivers. The wild landscape of the Kootenay River Valley remains stunning and unblemished but for this ribbon of road. A handful of short trails lead right off the highway. About 15km from the Banff border, the 750m **Marble Canyon Trail** traverses a remarkably deep, narrow, limestone gorge cut by Tokumm Creek, before ending at voluminous falls. Another tourist-heavy path is the 1.6km, 30-minute **Paint Pots Trail,** leaving Hwy. 93 3.2km south of Marble Canyon. This wheelchair accessible trail leads to sunset-red springs rich in iron oxide. Local Native Canadians quarried ochre from this oxide to make teepee and body paints. A bouncy suspension bridge leads over the view-intensive **Vermilion River.**

One of the hot springs' best qualities is their ability to suck travelers out of the woods, leaving Kootenay's wilderness untouched and its myriad hiking trails blissfully uncrowded. An easy dayhike, the **Stanley Glacier Trail** starts 2.5km north of Marble Canyon and leads 4.8km into a glacier-gouged valley, ending 1.6km from the foot of **Stanley Glacier.** The awe-inspiring loop over **Kindersley Pass** is an experience not soon forgotten. The 16.5km hike climbs more than 1000m, leading up to views of the Columbia River Valley to the west and the crest of the Rockies to the east. The two trailheads at either end of the loop, **Sinclair Creek** and **Kindersley Pass,** are less than 1km apart on Hwy. 93, about 15km inside the west gate entrance.

Many longer routes crisscross Kootenay's interior. **Backcountry** campers should stop in at the information center or Park Administration Office (see **Practical Information,** above) to pick up a hiking guide, which has useful maps, trail descriptions, and topographic profiles. No permit is required for dayhiking, but overnight backcountry camping requires a **Wilderness Pass,** available from the info center. *($6 per person per night, $35 per season.)* Two fire roads, plus the entire length of Hwy. 93, are open for **mountain biking.** The **Hector Gorge Trail** and **Dolly Varden Trail** make a pleasant loop, connecting to the **East Kootenay Fire Road.** As for **fishing,** rock flour from glaciers in the rivers makes for generally rotten luck.

NORTHERN BRITISH COLUMBIA

Native people have lived here for thousands of years, adjusting their lifestyle and culture to patterns of animal migration and an uncompromising climate. White settlers began moving westward in the early 1800s, drawn by the wealth of natural resources. The first were fur traders looking for faster routes through the area, followed after 1858 by waves by gold seekers. Since then, the lumber and mining industries have been similarly eager to extract the land's wealth. The northern portion of British Columbia has more in common with the Yukon Territory than with the southern part of the province, including the summer glut of northbound tourists chanting "Must...get...to...Alaska" without pausing to explore. Northern BC is one of the last North American bastions of immense forests, stark mountains, yawning canyons, roaring rivers, clear lakes, abundant wildlife, and freedom from summer crowds.

🐾 HIGHLIGHTS OF NORTHERN BRITISH COLUMBIA

- The **Queen Charlotte Islands** (see p. 323) are a fascinating land of untouched forests, innumerable islets, tiny towns, and Haida culture.
- Close by the conjoined international communities of **Stewart** and **Hyder,** the **Salmon Glacier** (see p. 337) is not only mammoth, but car-accessible to boot.
- WWII history abounds in **Dawson Creek** (see p. 340), origin of the vast and muse-invoking **Alaska Highway** (see p. 342).
- Beautiful lakeside **Atlin** (see p. 344), unswamped by tourists, is full of historic homes occupied by living residents.

BRITISH COLUMBIA

▓ Cariboo Highway (Hwy. 97)

The Cariboo Highway is the portion of Hwy. 97 that runs north-south for approximately 450km between Cache Creek and Prince George, following the route of the historic Cariboo Wagon Road. From Prince George, Hwy. 97 becomes the John Hart Hwy. (see p. 316), continuing north to Dawson Creek (see p. 340) and the start of the Alaska Highway (see p. 342). The scenery is impressive, with dozens of small lakes nestled among patches of forest and rocky hills. A visit to one of the 12 **provincial parks** in the area is well worth a brief departure from the Cariboo. Two of the nicest, both close to the Cariboo, are **Green Lake,** actually a series of glacial kettle lakes, and **Pinnacles,** where an eight-minute walk leads to a view of a steep sandstone canyon carved into the surrounding plateau. Farther afield, **Tweedsmuir Provincial Park** and the town of **Bella Coola,** both along the **Chilcotin Highway (Hwy. 20)** (see p. 312), offer superb hiking, fishing, and sight-seeing in an uncrowded setting.

■ Cariboo Highway (Hwy. 97): Cache Creek to Williams Lake

Many of the small towns along Hwy. 97, born as gold-rush era road houses, are slowly developing into more than pitstops en route to Prince George. Most of the towns and services along the highway are referred to solely by their old Cariboo Wagon Rd. mile marker (e.g.: 70 Mile House, 83 Mile Restaurant), invoking those heady Canadian days before the metric system infiltration. **Cache Creek,** at the junction of the Cariboo Hwy. and the Trans-Canada Hwy. (Hwy. 1), does not have much to offer, but weary travelers can stay at the serviceable **Cache Creek Kampground** (457-6414), 3km north of town on Hwy. 97. While the sites are unpleasantly klose to each other and to the highway, excellent amenities, including free pool and spa, koin showers, and laundry help kompensate (sites $14; full hookups $21). A more secluded option is **Brookside Campsite** (457-6633), 1km west of town on Hwy. 1, which has free showers, laundry (wash and dry $1.25 each), and a pool (sites $12; full hookups $19).

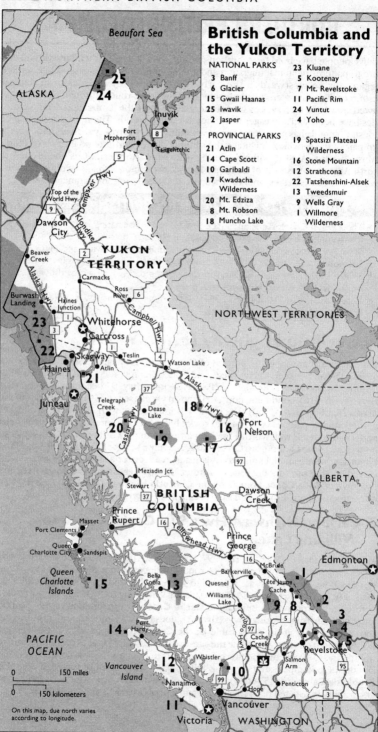

British Columbia and the Yukon Territory

NATIONAL PARKS

3 Banff
6 Glacier
15 Gwaii Haanas
25 Iwavik
2 Jasper

PROVINCIAL PARKS

21 Atlin
14 Cape Scott
10 Garibaldi
17 Kwadacha Wilderness
20 Mt. Edziza
8 Mt. Robson
18 Muncho Lake

23 Kluane
5 Kootenay
7 Mt. Revelstoke
11 Pacific Rim
24 Vuntut
4 Yoho

19 Spatsizi Plateau Wilderness
16 Stone Mountain
12 Strathcona
22 Tatshenshini-Alsek
13 Tweedsmuir
9 Wells Gray
1 Willmore Wilderness

BRITISH COLUMBIA

Beaufort Sea

ALASKA

Inuvik

Fort McPherson

Tsiigehtchic

Top of the World Hwy

Dawson City

Beaver Creek

YUKON TERRITORY

Carmacks

Ross River

Burwash Landing

Haines Junction

Whitehorse

Carcross

Skagway

Teslin

Haines

Atlin

Juneau

Telegraph Creek

Dease Lake

Watson Lake

NORTHWEST TERRITORIES

Fort Nelson

Meziadin Jct.

Stewart

BRITISH COLUMBIA

Dawson Creek

ALBERTA

Prince Rupert

Masset

Port Clements

Queen Charlotte City

Sandspit

Queen Charlotte Islands

Bella Coola

Prince George

Barkerville

McBride

Edmonton

Quesnel

Tête Jaune Cache

Williams Lake

Port Hardy

PACIFIC OCEAN

Whistler

Cache Creek

Salmon Arm

Revelstoke

Penticton

Vancouver Island

Nanaimo

Hope

Victoria

Vancouver

WASHINGTON

0   150 miles
0   150 kilometers

On this map, due north varies according to longitude.

100 Mile House, 115km north of Cache Creek, offers services and groceries, and proudly displays the world's **largest pair of cross-country skis.** The **Visitor Infocentre** (395-5353), is at the chamber of commerce next to the skis (open May-Sept. M-F 8:30am-7pm, Sa-Su 9am-6pm; in winter M-F 10am-5pm). **100 Mile House Campground,** 0.5km off the highway on Horse Lake Rd., is tranquil, woodsy, and cheap ($10; pit toilets, water, firewood).

■ Cariboo Highway (Hwy. 97): Williams Lake to Quesnel

Williams Lake, 90km north of 100 Mile House, is the Cariboo's largest town, but certainly not its most inviting. Fortunately, it's easy to leave, with Hwy. 20 meandering 450km west to **Bella Coola,** and Hwy. 97 continuing north to the pleasant lumber towns of Quesnel and Prince George. Williams Lake is home to BC's most active cattle marketing industry, and the town celebrates its cowboy heritage over Canada Day weekend with the four-day **Williams Lake Stampede.** Festivities include a rodeo, mountain race, and wild cow milking. Beware the jump in motel prices during Stampede weekend. Otherwise, tourism in the town is not exactly booming; decent rates are easy to find. The **Slumber Lodger** (392-7116 or 800-577-2244; fax 392-3977), located at 27 7th Ave. downtown, offers free swimming, cable, and local calls (in summer singles $49, doubles $55; in winter singles $45, doubles $50). **Whispering Willows Campground** (989-0359) beckons northward, 21km past town on the Cariboo (tent and RV sites: $10). There are many **free forestry campsites** in the area, including **Blue Lake West,** 35km north of town and 2.5km east along Blue Lake Rd. (pit toilets, no water). For other options, pick up a free **Forest Recreation Map** from any infocenter; sites are not marked along the highway, and directions can be tricky.

The 122km drive north to Quesnel can be a little dull, but those willing to subject their car to a little gravel can make it more interesting. About 50km north of Williams Lake, the free **Marguerite Ferry** shuttles off-road enthusiasts across a narrow stretch of the rambling **Fraser River.** The gravel road on the other side parallels Hwy. 97 all the way to Quesnel; ask the ferry captain for directions. Even more scenic is the gravel road from Williams Lake to the ferry, but be sure to ask at the **Infocentre** (392-5025), in town, for directions beforehand—it's very easy to get lost (open daily June-Aug. 9am-5pm; Sept.-May M-F 9am-4pm).

■ Quesnel and Environs

The town of Quesnel (kwuh-NELL), 123km past Williams Lake, takes great pride in its gold-driven past and forestry-propelled present. The **River Walk,** a paved trail along the river, is dotted with information about Quesnel's history. From Quesnel, it's only a 10-minute drive to **Pinnacles Provincial Par,** cross the river on Marsh Rd., then turn right on Baker Drive, where a short walk leads to finger-like hoodoo rock formations and impressive views. Every third weekend of July, crowds flock to Quesnel for the wholesome family fun of **Billy Barker Days,** featuring a rodeo, late shows, and live entertainment.

Buses leave the **Greyhound** depot (992-2231), on Kinshant between St. Laurent and Barlow, heading north to Prince George (90min., 3 per day, $18) and south to Vancouver (10hr., 3 per day, $82; open M-F 6am-8pm, Sa 6am-noon and 6-7:30pm, Su 6-10:30am and 6-7:30pm). The **Visitor Infocentre,** 703 Carson Ave. (992-8716), is just off Hwy. 97 in Le Bourdais Park (open June-Aug. daily 8am-6pm; Apr.-May and Sept. M-F 8:30am-4:30pm). A **Bank** is at Reid St. and Barlow Ave. The **library** (992-7912), 593 Barlow Ave. has **Internet access** (open Tu-Th 10am-8pm, F-Sa 10am-5pm). For **police, ambulance,** or **fire department,** call 911. The **post office** (992-2200) is at 346 Reid St. (open M-F 8:45am-5pm). **Postal Code:** V2J 3J1.

The king of the local motel scene is the **Cascade Inn,** 383 St. Laurent Ave. (992-5575 or 800-663-1581; fax 992-2254), downtown. Rooms include cable, phone, coffee, muffins, and use of the pool, jacuzzi, and sauna (singles from $42; doubles $46).

Roberts Roost Campground, 3121 Gook Rd. (747-2015), 8km south of town, offers elegantly landscaped lakeside sites with coin showers, laundry, a playground, and fishing (sites $15; full hookups $20); row boat and canoe rentals cost $6.

Coconuts (992-0951), a coffee house at 468B Reid St., serves espresso ($1.50), and a bagel and cream cheese with a bowl of vegetarian chile ($5; open M-F 8am-10pm, Sa 10am-10pm, Su 11am-5pm; in winter M-F 8am-6pm, Sa 10am-6pm). More standard pub grub, as well as much of Quesnel's nightlife, can be found at the saloon in the **Cariboo Hotel** (992-2333), on Front at Carson Ave., including burgers with fries or salad (from $4.50) and hearty baked lasagna with salad ($7.25; open M-Sa 11am-1am, Su noon-midnight; kitchen closes at 10pm). The saloon hosts live music (M-Sa 9pm-1am), with comedy on Sunday nights. Some loggers and tourists eschew the nightly crooning at the saloon and head to the **Billy Barker Casino Hotel,** 308 McLean St. (992-5533), to feed the slot machines, or try their luck at roulette, blackjack, and poker (open daily noon-2am).

Barkerville, 90km east of Quesnel along Hwy. 26, was established in 1862 when Billy Barker found gold on Williams Creek, sparking BC's largest gold rush. For the rest of the 19th century, Barkerville was the benchmark against which the rest of western Canada was measured. Victoria was considered doomed to failure as the provincial capital because it was too far from Barkerville. Since 1958, the town has been operated as a **BC Heritage Site** (front desk open 8am-8pm; in summer, 2 day pass $5.50, students and seniors $3.25, ages 6-12 $1, families $10.75; wheelchair accessible). One day is enough to see it all, but for those staying a while, the mining town of **Wells,** 8km away, has services and accomodations. For more info, call 994-3332.

Anyone traveling north to Prince George on Hwy. 97 will live a better life for having stopped at **Cinema Second Hand General Store** (998-4774), 32km north of Quesnel on Hwy. 97. Cash-strapped road warriors will find everything they need (except an actual cinema), plus a wide variety of things they could never possibly need, like old-fashioned snowshoes and disco LPs (open daily 9am-9pm). The store also offers **free camping,** handily equipped with a pit toilet.

■ Chilcotin Highway (Hwy. 20): Williams Lake to Bella Coola

The allure of the Chilcotin Hwy. lies not in its lackluster endpoint of Bella Coola, but in the rugged and scenic lands along the 457km highway. Leaving Williams Lake, the Chilcotin Hwy. heads west across the **Fraser River,** and climbs over a few mountains before flattening out through forests and pastures littered with cattle ranches. **Alexis Creek,** at Km 113, is the first stop of note with gas, cafe, lodging, and a general store. **Bull Canyon Provincial Park,** 8km past town, offers fishing and superb kayaking or rafting on the **Chilcotin River. Ts'yl*Os Provincial Park** (SIGH-loss), 160km west of Williams Lake, boasts Canada's first grizzly bear refuge, the glacier-fed, trout- and salmon-rich Lake Chilko, and the coolest name this side of Tuktoyaktuk. The gravel road to the park from the highway is rough but easily navigable in fair weather.

At Km 175, a 5km turn-off at **Chilanko Forks** to the 10km long **Puntzi Lake** is surounded by several affordable resort options. Activities around the lake include fishing for kokanee and rainbow trout, watching white pelicans in summer, and hunting for duck, goose, grouse, deer, moose, and bear in the fall. **Puntzi Lake Resort** (481-1176 or 800-578-6804) has eight wood cabins (singles or doubles $40-85), and a grassy lakeside campsite (sites $12; full hookups $17-19). A putting green and driving range are available for the golf-minded. **Barney's Lakeside Resort** (481-1100) has more secluded sites ($12), RV hookups ($15), and a tidy new bunkhouse that sleeps two folks per room ($35 each, breakfast included). All accommodations have a shared bathroom and free showers. **Jack & Faye's Place** (481-1169) is ideal for families, where two bedroom cottages with private bath, living room, TV, and kitchenette can sleep up to 5 (singles $45; doubles $50; extra adults $7.50; extra children $5).

The highway enters the southern portion of **Tweedsmuir Provincial Park** at **Heckman's Pass,** 360km west of Williams Lake. The park protects the **Atnarko River,**

Hunlen Falls, Monarch Glacier and the colorfully streaked shield volcanoes of the **Rainbow Mountains.** Unfortunately, road-trippers' first introduction to the park is 20km of gravel hell, known simply as "The Hill," with steep grades and sharp switchbacks. For decades, Bella Coola was not linked by road to the rest of the province because the government didn't want to build a route through the mid-coastal mountains. Hwy. 20 ended at **Anahim Lake,** 315km west of Williams Lake. In the early 1950s, in an act of constructional uprising, frustrated locals got two bulldozers, borrowed money, and finished the job themselves, earning the route its second name, the "Freedom Highway." Almost 50 years later, this steep portion of the road through Tweedsmuir still has the feel of being built by not-quite-experts. After the hill, the highway is paved again for 75 of its most scenic kilometers, following the **Bella Coola River** into town.

Perhaps the biggest thing happening in Tweedsmuir is the terminus of the **Alexander Mackenzie Heritage Trail,** reserved for those hikers beyond hard-core and off the deep end. The 347km requires 25 to 30 days, beginning from **Blackwater River,** just west of Quesnel, and stretches across western British Columbia to **Burnt Creek Bridge** on Hwy. 20, tracing the final leg of Mackenzie's 1793 journey across Canada to the western coast. Mackenzie reached the Pacific more than a decade before Lewis and Clark, although the Americans continue to hog all the glory. For slightly more moderate hikers, the 80km section of the trail within Tweedsmuir passes some of the most scenic splendor of the entire route, and takes five to seven days.

The pot of pewter at the end of the Chilcotin rainbow is the coastal village of **Bella Coola,** homeland of the Nuxalk Nation. Bella Coola's native heritage is evident in an impressive collection of **petroglyphs,** which have led some scholars to link the indigenous people here with those in Polynesia. Darren Edgar (799-5767), leads **guided tours** of the site (donation required). **Gold Pan City Stage Lines** (888-992-6168) runs buses twice a week to and from Williams Lake (7½hr., $81). **BC Ferries** (888-223-3779) has a new Discovery Passage route linking Bella Coola with Port Hardy on the northern tip of Vancouver Island ($110, ages 5-11 $55, under 5 free). The **Shell Station** (799-5314), across from the Valley Inn on McKenzie Rd., does **repairs** and has the only gas in town (open daily 8am-8pm). Getting a room in town is expensive, but the **Motel Bella Coola** (799-5323) downtown has dry camping on its large back lawn ($8; flush toilets, free showers). For shaded and forested sites, head to **Gnomes Home Campground & RV Park** (982-2504), in **Hagesborg** 16km east of Bella Coola along the highway (sites $12; full hookups $15; flush toilets, showers, coin laundry).

▓ Prince George

At the confluence of the Nechako and Fraser Rivers, Prince George's magnificent riverbanks are slowly succumbing to the pulp and lumber mills that crowd the valley floor. Even with more than 100 parks, several museums, and 76,000 friendly residents, Prince George is fighting an uphill battle to become more of a destination and less of a stopover. Recent additions to the town include a civic center, a national university, and the Cougars, a Western League hockey team. In the summer, bands of young, hip treeplanters flock to Prince George on their days off, and provide some rowdiness and local color.

PRACTICAL INFORMATION

Buses: Greyhound, 1566 12th Ave. (564-5454), across from the Victoria St. infocenter. To: Edmonton (10hr., 2 per day, $94), Vancouver (12hr., 3 per day, $90), Prince Rupert (10hr., 2 per day, $86.50), Dawson Creek (6hr., 2 per day, $50), and other points. Coin lockers are available. Ticket office open M-Sa 6:30am-5:30pm and 9pm-midnight; Su and holidays 6:30-9:30am, 3:30-5:30pm, and 9pm-midnight. **BC Rail** (561-4033), at the end of Terminal Blvd., 2km south off Hwy. 97, runs the scenic "Cariboo Prospector" train to Vancouver (14hr., 3 per week, $190, seniors $171, children $114, 3 meals included). Station open daily 6-8am, 7:30-9:30pm. **VIA Rail,** 1300 1st Ave. (564-5233 or 800-561-8630), serves Prince Rupert (12hr., 3 per week, 7 day advance purchase $62, students $49, seniors $53, children $31; otherwise $82, students $49, seniors $74, children $41). Station open M, Th, Sa 6-9:30am, Su, W, F 5:30-9:30pm.

Visitor Information: Useful **maps** of Prince George available for free at either of the town's two **Travel Infocentres** (800-668-7646 for general info). Faux-native carvings festoon 1198 Victoria St. (562-3700), at 15th Ave. Open M-Sa 8:30am-5pm. The other infocenter (563-5493), at the junction of Hwy. 16 and Hwy. 97, is marked by a gargantuan, unmissable "Mr. P.G." logger. Open daily May-Sept. 8am-8pm.

Outdoor Equipment: Centre City Surplus, 1222 Fourth Ave. (564-2400), offers highly competitive prices. Open M-Th and Sa 9am-6pm, F 9am-8pm, Su 11am-4pm.

Banks: Several banks line Victoria St. between 3rd. and 6th. Ave. and along 3rd. Ave. east of Victoria St. **TD Bank,** 1444 Victoria St., at 4th Ave. ATM 24hr. Open M-F 9-5, Sa 9-4.

Library: 887 Dominion (563-9251). Open year round M-Th 10am-9pm, F-Sa 10am-5:30pm; Oct.-Apr. open Su 1-5pm.

Laundry: 231 George St. $1.25 for each wash and dry. Open M-Sa 7:30am-7pm.

Auto Repair: Ed Delorme's Auto Service and Repair Center, 620 George St. (563-2002).

Emergency: 911. **Police:** 999 Brunswick St. (562-3371).

Crisis center: 1306 7th Ave. (563-1214).

Hospital: Prince George Regional Hospital, 2000 15th Ave. (565-2000; emergency 565-2444).

Post Office: 1323 5th Ave. (561-2568). Open M-F 8:30am-5pm. **Postal Code**: V2I 4R8.

Internet access: Internet Cafe, inside London Drugs, in the Parkland Mall at Victoria and 15th St. $3 for 30min. Open M-Sa 9am-10pm, Su 10am-8pm.

Area code: 250, unless otherwise noted.

ACCOMMODATIONS AND CAMPGROUNDS

For those stopping in Prince George just to get a good night's sleep and stock up on provisions, a good bet is the **Queensway Court Motel,** 1616 Queensway (562-5068 fax 561-0866), at 17th Ave., close to downtown. Well-kept rooms come with fridges microwaves, cable, and free local calls, with through travelers comfortably segregated from treeplanters (singles $36, doubles $41). During the summer, the **College of New Caledonia,** 3330 22nd Ave. (561-5832; fax 561-5832), off Hwy. 97 near downtown, offers clean and quiet dorm rooms with fridge, microwave, sink, desk and shared bathrooms for $20 (linens $5, extra mattress $5). Wheelchair-accessible rooms and monthly rates can be arranged (office open M-F 10am-noon, 2-4pm, and 6-8pm; Sa-Su 10-11am, 2-3pm, and 6-8pm). Ambitious campers and RV jockeys head for the **Log House Restaurant and Kampground** (604-963-9515), located on the shore of Tabor Lake. This German-owned steakhouse and RV park is popular among European vacationers (sites $14; full hookups $20; cabins with no amenities $40; teepees $10 per person). Rowboats ($5), canoes ($8), and pedalboats ($8) can be rented by the hour. Sightseeing trips via seaplane (3 people, $350-375 per hr.) or riverboat (day trip, 3-6 people, $75 per person) can be arranged. To reach this kraziness, head out of town on Hwy. 16E.; after 3.2km, turn right on "Old Cariboo Hwy.," left on Giscome Rd., follow it 1.2km, then turn right onto Hedlund Rd. after 6.4km.

FOOD

The drolly-named supermarket **Overwaitea's,** 1666 Spruce St. (564-4525), lies a short walk from the downtown infocenter (open daily 9am-9pm). Any number of interchangeable pizza/pasta joints can be found on or near George St. For something a bit different, the cool, calm, and collected **1085 Cafe,** 1085 Vancouver St. (960-2272) offers fresh soup-'n'-salad-style lunch fare in the $5 range and live entertainment most Friday nights (open M and Sa 9am-4pm, Tu-W 7am-7pm, Th-F 7am-10pm). Hit up hip and traveler-happy **Javva Mugga Mocha Cafe,** 304 George St. (562-3338), for a $2 muffin or cappuccino. The cafe also loans out a random selection of used books (open M-Sa 7:30am-6:30pm). The **Bamboo House Restaurant,** 1208 6th Ave. (564

3888), has an all-you-can-eat lunch smorgasbord (i.e. Chinese food and onion rings) for $6.95 and a supper smorg for $9.95. Entrees cost $5-13.

SIGHTS AND EVENTS

Fishing is excellent near Prince George, with more than 1500 stocked lakes within a 150km radius. The closest is **Tabor Lake,** where the rainbow trout all but jump into the boat in spring and early summer. Tabor is east on Hwy. 16; follow the directions to the Log House Restaurant and Kampground described above. For a complete listing of lakes and licensing information, contact the infocenters.

Centre City Surplus (see **Practical Information,** above) sells **guides to hiking** in the Prince George area, and the infocenter has its own helpful tips. The wheelchair-accessible **Fort George Park,** on the banks of the Fraser River off 20th Ave., offers expanses of lawn, beach volleyball courts, picnic tables, and barbecue pits. It makes a perfect starting point for the 11km **Heritage River Trail,** which wanders through the city and along the Fraser and Nechako Rivers. Also lurking inside the park is the **Fort George Regional Museum** (562-1612), which houses frontier artifacts, including several **primitive chain saws** *(open daily 10am-5pm; call for winter hours; $4.25, seniors $3.25, children $2.25, families $8).* **McMillan Creek Regional Park** is right across the Nechako River off Hwy. 97 north and features a deep ravine and a view of the city from the river's cutbanks. **Cottonwood Island Nature Park,** off River Rd., has plenty of leisurely riverside walking trails along the banks of the Nechako. **Esker's Provincial Park,** off Hwy. 97 on Ness Lake Rd., 40km north of downtown, offers trails accessible to the disabled. Call 604-565-6340 for details.

For a bird's eye view of this industrial city, scramble up to **Connaught Hill Park,** home of picnic tables and ample frisbee-throwing space. To reach the park, scale the yellow metal staircase across from the visitor center or take Connaught Dr. off Queensway. **Forests for the World,** a wildlife preserve on nearby Cranbrook Hill, is only a 15-minute drive from town and one of the prettiest parts of Prince George. To get there, take Hwy. 97 north, turn left on 15th Ave., right on Foothills Blvd., left onto Cranbrook Hill Rd., and finally left on Kueng Rd.

Mardi Gras, which lasts for 10 days in late February, features such events as snow golf, dog-pull contests, bed races, and jousting with padded poles. You'll swear you're in New Orleans. For information call 564-3737. **Sandblast** sends a group of daring skiers down the steep, sandy, snowless Nechako Cutbanks on the third Sunday in August.

■ Yellowhead Highway (Hwy. 16): Mt. Robson to Prince George

In British Columbia, the Yellowhead Highway's scenic drama heightens as it winds west. **Mt. Robson** reigns 84km west of Jasper and 319km east of Prince George. At 3954m, it is the highest peak in the Canadian Rockies. Only the robust can conquer this monarch: it took five unsuccessful attempts until climbers reached its summit in 1913. Wimps (i.e. normal people) can appreciate Robson's beauty more remotely, from the parking lot and picnic site beside the **Mt. Robson Provincial Park Headquarters** (566-4325; open June-Aug. daily 8am-8pm; May and Sept. daily 8am-5pm; closed Oct.-Apr.). Visitors can choose from five nearby **hiking trails** ranging from 2km nature walks to 66km schleps (hiking permit $3 per person per night). The two-day, 22km **Berg Lake Trail** is highly recommended for its beautiful terrain, including the **Valley of a Thousand Falls** (water, one hopes) and excellent **birdwatching** of the park's more than 170 species. Hard-core hikers do the trek in a day. A quota system has been put in place for the trail, so it's advised to book ahead through the park headquarters. Sedentary types can hang out in one of three campgrounds in the park: scenic **Robson River Campground** and the larger **Robson Meadows Campground** are both across from the headquarters ($14.50 with flush toilets and hot showers), while **Lucerne Campground** is 48km east towards Jasper ($9.50 with pit toilets and no showers). Call 1-800-689-9025 for trail information and campsite reservations. The **Robson Cafe,** right next to the park headquarters, has scenically superior **internet access** ($6 per 30min., $10 per hr.).

Just west of Mt. Robson is **Tête Jaune Cache,** where Hwy. 16 intersects Hwy. 5 leading south to Kamloops (339km) and the Okanagan country. Highway 5 is the fastest route from Jasper to Vancouver. Between the Rockies and Cariboo Mountains, 63km west of Tête Jaune Cache, lies the hamlet of **McBride.** Travelers not driving wood-burning vehicles are advised to fill up in McBride, since 205km of timber separate it from Prince George, the next significant town to the west. Huddled masses unwilling to negotiate the steep, winding grades to Prince George find refuge (including flush toilets and horseshoes) at the **Beaver View Campsite** (569-2513) in McBride, 1km east of McBride on Hwy. 16 (sites $13; partial hookups $15-$17; showers free; laundry $1.75). Stop at scenic **Purden Lake Provincial Park** (565-6340), 59km east of Prince George, for fishing or camping (sites $12, with flush toilets and free firewood; one wheelchair-accessible site; gate closed 11pm-7am).

The pristine terrain along the highway gives little indication of the heavy logging that drives the economy. This region produces over six million cubic meters of lumber annually. Visitors tempted to chain themselves to trees or condemn the practices of the timber industry are invited to read the brochure **"Don't Believe Everything That Greenpeace Tells You,"** available at tourist information counters. Here, as in much of the rural Northwest, terms like "deforestation" and "clearcutting" describe how people make a living, and loggers often don't often take kindly to ecological reprimands from abroad.

■ John Hart Highway (Hwy. 97): Prince George to Dawson Creek

A few kilometers into the 402km stretch from Prince George to Dawson Creek, neon lights and strip malls become a distant memory as the road cuts a lonely swath through the forests of Northern British Columbia. The first outpost of civilization is the micropolis of **Bear Lake,** 74km along the Hwy. 97, which offers a motel, RV park, restaurant, and an opportunity for gas. **Crooked River Provincial Park,** situated on Bear Lake but 2km before the town, offers a great beach site for swimming and picnicking, as well as secluded, wooded campsites ($12; flush and pit toilets). The park is well suited for winter activities such as tobogganing, snowshoeing, and cross-country skiing on two beginner and four intermediate trails (2.4-7.2km). For park conditions or ski and weather information, call 562-8288 during business hours. **Whiskers Point Provincial Park,** 51km past Bear Lake, has the same lakefront charm as Crooked River without the expansive beach ($12; flush and pit toilets). The park provides a boat launch for the large **McLeod Lake.** Blink and you'll miss **McKenzie Junction,** 26km past Whiskers Point. From the junction, it's 149km to the next town of note, Chetwynd, and almost 80km to the next gas station. The junction also provides a turn-off to the town of **McKenzie,** 29km north on Hwy. 39, the largest town in the area and the closest hospital. Barring a medical emergency, MacKenzie is probably not worth the detour.

Chetwynd, 300km from Prince George, bills itself as the Chainsaw Sculpture Capital of the World. Some of its wooden creations are visible from the highway, but it's worth cruising the main commercial streets of town to see the rest. The aging but charming **Wildmare Campground** (788-2747), 5km before town along the highway, provides showers, flush toilets, and budget rates (tent $7; RV $13). If a sauna, whirlpool, and movie channel seem more enticing, head for the well-managed **Country Squire Motor Inn,** 5317 South Access Road (788-2276 or 800-668-3101; fax 788-3018), across the highway from the A&W (singles $52; doubles $57; $3 less in winter; group rates available). Locals splash it up in the acclaimed **wave pool** at the **Recreation Complex,** 2km east along the highway past the stoplight at the center of town; the pool building also houses a weight room and gym. Call 788-3939 for hours and special events. The adjacent rec center (788-2214) offers **curling,** Canada's second most televised sport. An ice rink in winter, the rec center has rollerblading and a kids program in summer. After Chetwynd, the 102km drive to Dawson Creek is smooth and uneventful.

■ Yellowhead Highway (Hwy. 16): Prince George to Terrace

As Highway 16 winds its way westward 575km toward Terrace from Prince George, steep grades and towering timbers gradually give way to the gently rolling pastures and tiny towns of British Columbia's interior **Lakes District.** To break up the drive, **Beaumont Provincial Park,** on Fraser Lake, offers roomy sites, clean facilities, a playground, and a swimming area (49 sites: $12; flush toilets, water, firewood). Thanks to a wayward (must-have-been-drunk) surveyor, Highway 16 takes a turn at the town of **Burns Lake,** where almost every building is adorned with the likeness of trout. The **Infocentre,** on the highway, is the best place to stop for fishing info (692-3773; open July-Aug. daily 9am-5pm; in winter M-F 9am-5pm). Twenty-four kilometers south of town along Highway 35, free forestry campsites (pit toilets, no water) are available at large Francois Lake, which is noted for rainbow and lake trout. Though most of the hiking in this area is rather dull, one exception is the 2km Opal Bed Trail, which leads to a creek bed lined with semi-precious opals and agates. From Highway 35 and turn right onto Eagle Creek Road, which runs 7km to a recreation site and the trailhead.

West of Burns Lake by 80km is **Houston** and its Texas-scale contribution to the rampant superlativism of the late 20th century: the **world's largest flyrod** (20m long and over 365kg). Houston's **Infocentre** (845-7640; open M-F 8am-6pm, Sa-Su 9am-5pm; in winter M-F 9am-5pm) offers a guide explaining how to realize your fishing fantasies—indulge these fantasies at one of more than 25 area lakes and streams. The **Houston Pizza Factory** (845-3131), at 9th and Butler, offers relief from the typical highway grease factories. Gourmet pizzas are pricey unless you're sharing, but spaghetti and meatballs ($8.50) or large mediterranean salad ($9) hit the spot (open M-Th 11am-10pm, F-Sa 11am-11pm, Su 11:30am-9pm). Grassy, cheap but noisy camping can be found at the municipal campground, where the crows sing at 6am and the trains whistle all night ($4; pit toilets, no water; take Tweedie Rd. south off the highway, turn left onto West 14th and follow signs).

Smithers, 64km northwest of Houston, offers skiing on the slopes of Hudson Bay Mountain. The town of **New Hazelton** is 125km past Smithers, where the infocenter (842-6071) has a great pamphlet on the area's totem poles, easily missed by those just sticking to the highway (open July-Aug. daily 9am-5pm, May-June M-F 9am-5pm). The **'Ksan Village & Museum** (842-5544), 7km along Churchill Ave. towards Old Hazelton, exhibits a stellar collection of totem poles, wooden cabins, and native artwork ($2; open daily July-Aug. 9am-6pm, slightly less in winter; wheelchair accessible). 44km farther west of New Hazelton is the junction with the Cassiar Highway (Hwy. 37) which leads 733km north to the Yukon Territory and the Alaska Highway (see p. 342). The **Petrocan** (849-5793) is the last gas before Terrace (open daily 7am-11pm). For the remaining 97km to Terrace, Hwy. 16 winds along the base of the **Hazelton Mountains** and follows the thundering **Skeena River.**

▓ Terrace

In 1944, an extended spell of bad weather and a highly disproportionate male-to-female ratio caused 3000 Canadian Army troops stationed in Terrace to mutiny. For three weeks, disgruntled enlisted men ruled Terrace, and officers took refuge in Prince Rupert, 144km to the west. In the years since the mutiny, Terrace has calmed down considerably. Fishing has replaced armed rebellion as the most popular form of entertainment here along the banks of the Skeena River, and Terrace holds the world's record for the largest Chinook salmon, weighing in at 92½ pounds.

For those who cannot live by fishing alone—seemingly a minority of the town's residents and visitors—Terrace's unique geography of roving plains and benches sculpted by the Skeena makes for varied and scenic hiking. Many a wanderer has been known to catch a glimpse of an infamous Kermodei bear, a distinct member of the black bear family recognizable by its (far from black) coat that ranges from light chestnut blond to steel blue gray in color.

ORIENTATION AND PRACTICAL INFORMATION Terrace is 149km east of Prince Rupert on the Yellowhead Hwy. (Hwy. 16) and 91km southwest of the junction of the Yellowhead and the Cariboo Hwy. (Hwy. 37).

Trains: VIA Rail (800-561-8630) sends 3 trains per week to Prince Rupert ($21) and Prince George ($68). **Greyhound,** 4620 Keith St. (635-3680), runs two buses daily to Prince Rupert ($18.50) and Prince George ($64.50).
Auto Repair: Greig Avenue Auto (638-8373), on Greig between Kenney and Munroe St. Open Tu-Sa 9am-6pm.
Visitor Information: Visitor Center 4511 Keith St. (635-2063; http://www.terrace.tourism.bc.ca), off Hwy. 16. Open daily 8am-8pm; in winter M-F 8am-4:30pm.
Library: 4610 Park Ave. Internet access available. Open Tu-F 10am-9pm, Sa 10am-5pm.
Senior Center: Happy Gang Centre for Seniors, 3226 Kalum St. (635-9090).
Women's Resource Center: 638-0228.
Laundromat: Richard's Cleaners, 3223 Emerson St. (635-5119), where you can bask in a tanning booth between loads. Open daily M-Sa 7:30am-9pm, Su 10am-9pm; wash $1.25, dry 25¢ per 6min., tanning $1.10 per min.
Public Showers: Terrace Aquatic Center (615-3030), on Paul Clark Dr. Pool, hot tub, saunas and gym facilities. $4.25, students and seniors $2.25, ages 2-14 $1.75.
Hospital: Mills Memorial Hospital, 4720 Haugland Ave. (635-2211).
Emergency: 911. **Police:** 3205 Eby St. (635-4911). **Ambulance:** 638-1102.
Sexual Assault Crisis Line: 635-1911.
Post Office: 3232 Emerson St. (635-2241). Open M-F 8:30am-5pm. **Postal Code:** V8G 4A1.
Area Code: 250.

ACCOMMODATIONS, CAMPGROUNDS, AND FOOD A&A Terrace Bed and Breakfast, 3802 deJong Crescent (635-0079 or 888-635-0079; http://www.bbcanada.com/1043.html), boasts spic-and-span rooms with private baths, TVs, VCRs, and accommodating hosts (from $45). Take Sparks or Eby St. north from Lakelse to McConnell and right to deJong. The **Alpine House Motel,** 4326 Lakelse (635-7216 or 800-663-3123; fax 635-4225), is also clean and happily removed from the noisy downtown (singles $55; doubles $60; with fridge and microwave; kitchenette $10 extra; Oct.-Apr. rates $10 less). **Ferry Island Municipal Campground** (615-3000), lies just east of Terrace on Hwy. 16 (sites $10, hookups $12; pit toilets, water, firewood). The island's prime fishing spot is a short walk from the wooded campsite, and lined with eager anglers who beat you there. The community pool is half-price if you stay at Ferry Island and show your receipt. **Kleanza Creek Provincial Park** is the site of an abandoned gold mine, 19km east of the town on Hwy. 16, with great sites along the creek ($9.50; pit toilets, water, firewood).

Terrace hosts a handful of welcome breaks from the dreariness of highway diner cuisine. **Don Diego's,** 3212 Kalum St. (635-2307), is a fun, laid-back joint that serves Mexican, Greek, and whatever's in season. The menu changes twice daily, with lunches in the $6-8 range, and dinners $9-15 (open M-Sa 11:30am-9pm, Su 10am-2pm and 5-9pm). For authentic and affordable Indian cuisine, drive five minutes west of town along Hwy. 16 to **Haryana's Restaurant** (635-2362) in the Kalum Motel. Vegetarian entrees from $8, and a succulent Keema curry (minced beef, onion, garlic, ginger, peas, and spices) goes for $10 (open Su-Th 11am-2pm and 5-9pm, F-Sa 11am-2pm and 5-11pm). **Anka's** (635-1510), 4711E Keith Ave. at Tetrault St. right before the overpass heading west, serves up a scrumptious vegan burger with soup or salad for $6.25 (open M-F 10am-8pm, Sa 9am-8pm). **Safeway,** 4655 Lakelse Ave. (635-7206), is the cheapest place to buy not-yet-cooked food (open M-Sa 8am-10pm, Su 10am-6pm).

SIGHTS AND OUTDOORS Heritage Park Museum (635-4546), on Kerby St. at Kalum, houses countless artifacts from the pioneer era, including a working pump organ and an elaborate wreath made from human hair—perfect for pursuers of the grisly side of kitsch. *(Open May-Aug. Tu-Sa 10am-6pm, tours Tu-Sa 10:30am-4pm; $3, students and seniors $2, families $7.)* The **Falls Gallery,** 2666 Highway 37 (638-0438), just east of town, has an impressive collection of native masks, art, and craftwork. *(Free admission; take the Hwy. 37 turn-off south towards Kitimat.)* Much of the artwork is for sale, with smaller souvenirs available. On Saturday mornings from May through October, the **Farmer's Market,** behind Lower Little Park, sells homegrown and homemade produce.

Gruchy's Beach is 8km south of Terrace on Hwy. 37. It's a 1½km hike from the parking lot and is big, sandy, and begging to be picnicked upon. For more solitude and a little adventure (and some danger), check out the cliff-jumping at Humphrey Falls. Take Hwy. 37 south towards Kitimat and turn off at a gravel road on the left after approximately 35km, then drive or walk to the water. The **Nisga'a Memorial Lava Bed,** Canada's youngest lava flow, lies 100km north of Terrace. To reach this 54km² swath of moonscape, follow Kalum Lake Dr. (Nisga'a Hwy.) through the scenic valleys of the **Tseax** and **Nass Rivers.**

Amble, sashay, skip, run, or walk along Terrace's 11 well-maintained trails. The **Terrace Mountain Nature Trail** is a popular climb of moderate difficulty, beginning at Johnstone Ave. in the east end of town. The 5km (one-way) route takes one or two hours, offering spectacular views of Terrace's plateaus and the surrounding valley. For an easier stroll, check out the **Redsand Lake Demonstration Forest,** 26km north on West Kalum Forestry Rd. The Forest Service is developing a network of trails (one wheelchair accessible) around beautiful **Redsand Lake,** and through a variety of forested areas. The info center has interpretive pamphlets. Anglers can strap on their hip-waders and try their luck on the east shore of **Ferry Island,** or ask for hot tips at the **Misty River Tackle Shop,** 5008 Agar Ave. (638-1369; open M-Sa 6am-11pm, Su 6am-10pm; in winter daily 7am-10pm).

▓ Prince Rupert

In 1910, railway magnate Charles Hays made a covert deal with British Columbia's provincial government, purchasing 10,000 acres of choice land at the western terminus of the Grand Trunk Pacific Railway. When the shady operation was exposed two years later, Hays was already under water—not drowned in his dire financial straits or the area's constant rain, but in the wreckage of the *Titanic.* The sole fruit of Hays' illegal labors was a town which, in a nationwide naming contest, was smacked with the shockingly bland moniker "Prince Rupert" (after a 17th-century British-Canadian business magnate), foreshadowing the town's present-day penchant for the drab. Besides Cow Bay, a quasi-historic artisan community created to lure cruise tourists, Prince Rupert has little to offer visitors beyond a few small museums and a handful of totem poles. The weather is notoriously rainy (making this the "City of Rainbows"), and the closest hiking trails are several kilometers outside of town.

ORIENTATION AND PRACTICAL INFORMATION

The only major road into town is the Yellowhead Highway (Hwy. 16), known as **McBride St.** within the city limits. At the north end of downtown, Hwy. 16 makes a sharp left and becomes **2nd Ave.** Downtown, avenues run north-south and ascend numerically from west to east; streets run east-west and ascend numerically from north to south. McBride St. is one block northeast of **1st St.** At the south end of downtown, Hwy. 16 becomes **Park Ave.,** continuing to the **ferry docks.** From the docks, the walk downtown takes 30 minutes (or 45 with a heavy pack). Hitching is feasible but inconsistent, and unsafe at night. A safer bet is the Seashore Charter Services Shuttle (see below) or a cab to downtown.

Transportation

Airplanes: Prince Rupert Airport, on Digby Island. The ferry and bus connection to downtown costs $11 and takes about 45min. (Swimming is not an option.) **Air BC,** 112 6th St. (624-4554), flies to Vancouver ($169, youth standby $160). **Canadian Airlines** (624-9181 or 800-665-1177), on the ground floor of the mall on 2nd Ave. W., offers the same service. Wheelchair accessible.

Trains: VIA Rail (984-5246 or 800-561-8630 in BC; 800-561-3949 elsewhere), toward the water on Bill Murray Way. To: Prince George (3 per week; $66, 40% off with ISIC). **BC Rail** (984-5500 or 800-339-8752 in BC; 800-663-8238 elsewhere) continues from Prince George to Vancouver ($190, 10% off with ISIC). An overnight in Prince George is required. Wheelchair accessible.

Buses: Greyhound, 822 3rd Ave. (624-5090), near 8th St. To: Prince George (2 per day, $87); Vancouver (2 per day, $173). Station open M-F 8:30am-12:30pm and 4-8:45pm, Sa-Su 9-11:15am and 7-8:45pm. Lockers available.

Ferries: Alaska Marine Highway (627-1744 or 800-642-0066; fax 627-1744; http://www.dot.state.ak.us), at the end of Hwy. 16 (Park Ave.). Runs ferries north from Prince Rupert along the Alaskan Panhandle. To: Ketchikan (US$38, car US$75); Juneau (US$104, car US$240). Next door is **BC Ferries** (624-9627 or 888-223-3779; fax 381-5452; http://bcferries.bc.ca/ferries). To: Queen Charlotte Islands (6 per week; peak season $23, car $87); Port Hardy (every other day; $102, car $210). Vehicle reservations required 3 weeks in advance. Ferry-goers may not leave cars parked on the streets of Prince Rupert. Some establishments charge a daily rate for storage; check with the ferry company or the visitor center (see below). **Seashore Charter Services** (624-5645) runs a shuttle from the mall on 2nd Ave. to the ferry terminal upon request ($3). Look for their minibus at the terminal when you arrive.

Public Transportation: Prince Rupert Bus Service (624-3343) runs downtown M-Sa 7am-10pm. $1, seniors 60¢; day pass $2.50, seniors $2. Stops are marked by white and red signs. About every 30min., the #52 bus runs from 2nd Ave. and 3rd St. to within a 5min. walk of the ferry terminal. Every 2hr., a bus runs from downtown to Port Edward and the North Pacific Cannery (see **Sights,** p. 322).

Taxis: Skeena Taxi (624-2185). From town to ferry terminal $6-8. Runs 24hr.

Car Rental: Tilden Auto Rental (624-5318), in the mall at 2nd Ave. and 5th St. M-F 8am-5pm and 6:30-7:30pm. $56 per day, Sa-Su $30 per day, plus 35¢ per km. Must be over 21 with credit card.

Visitor and Financial Services

Visitor Information: Traveler's Information Centre (624-5637 or 800-667-1994), at 1st Ave. and McBride St., in the Haida-style log building. Stacks of pamphlets, free maps, and a less-than-riveting self-guided tour. Open May 15 to Labour Day M-Sa 9am-8pm, Su 9am-5pm; in winter M-F 10am-5pm.

Banks: Plenty of choices, but the only one with a 24hr. **ATM** is **CIBC** (627-1771), on 3rd Ave. at 4th St. **Express Travel** (627-1266), on 3rd Ave. across from Shoppers Drug Mart, sells traveler's checks. Open M-F 9am-5:30pm, Sa 10:30am-4pm.

Local Services

Equipment Rental: Far West Sporting Goods (624-2568), on 3rd Ave. near 1st St., rents high-quality **bikes,** including lock and helmet ($5 per hr., $25 per day), and sells a good selection of **camping gear.** Open M-Th and Sa 9:30am-5:30pm, F 9:30am-9pm. **Eco-Treks** (624-8311; fax 624-8318; email ecotreks@citytel.net; http://www.citytel.net/ecotreks), located on the dock in Cow Bay. Rents **kayaks** and gear (single $25 or double $45 for 4hr.; single $40 or double $70 for 1 day). Offers 3hr. guided tours leaving at 1pm and 6pm ($40), with safety lessons.

Bookstore: Star of the West Books, 518 3rd. Ave. (624-9053). A fine collection of regional titles. Open May-Dec. M-F 9am-9pm, Sa 9am-6pm; Jan.-Apr. M-Sa 9am-6pm.

Library: 101 6th Ave. W. (627-1345; email chieflib@citytel.net), at McBride St. Internet access available ($2 per hr.). Open M and W 1-9pm, Tu and Th 10am-9pm, and F-Sa 1-5pm; in winter also open Su 1-5pm.

Senior Center: (627-1900), off Fraser St. on Greenville Ct. Open M-F 10:30am-4pm.

Laundromat: For mother loads, head to **Mommy's Laundromat,** on 6th St. between 2nd and 3rd Ave. Wash 75¢, dry 75¢ per 15min. Open daily 9am-9pm.

Public Pool: Jim Ciccone Civic Center (main office 624-6707; pool 627-7946). Pool (with waterslide and rope swing), ice skating rink, and climbing wall. Swimming 50¢ Sa noon-2pm. Call the 24hr. information line (624-9000) for current schedule and rates. Wheelchair accessible.

Public Showers: Both **Pioneer Rooms** and the **Park Avenue Campgrounds** open their showers to the public (see **Accommodations and Campgrounds,** below).

Local Radio: CFPR 860 AM. News and local events.

Emergency and Communications

Emergency: 911. **Ambulance:** 800-461-9911. **Fire:** 627-1248. **Police:** 100 7th Ave. (624-2136).

Crisis Line: 888-562-1214. 24hr.

Hospital: 1305 Summit Ave. (624-2171).

Post Office: (624-2353), in the mall at 2nd Ave. and 5th St. Open M-F 9:30am-5:30pm. **Substations** sell stamps and postal supplies; there's one in the **Shoppers Drug Mart** at 3rd Ave. and 2nd St. Open M-Tu and Sa 9am-6pm, W-F 9am-9pm, Su 11am-5pm. **Postal Code:** V8J 3P3.

Internet Access: See **Library,** above.

Area Code: 250.

ACCOMMODATIONS AND CAMPGROUNDS

Nearly all of Prince Rupert's hotels nestle within the six-block area defined by 1st Ave., 3rd Ave., 6th St., and 9th St. Everything fills to the gills when the ferries dock, so call a day or two in advance. Most motels are pricey—a single costs at least $55.

Eagle Bluff Bed and Breakfast, 201 Cow Bay Rd. (627-4955 or 800-833-1550; email eaglebed@citytel.net), on the waterfront. Attractively furnished oceanside B&B in the loveliest part of town. Private deck for watching boats and sunsets. Singles $45; doubles $55; $10 extra for private bath. Wheelchair accessible. No pets allowed.

Pioneer Rooms, 167 3rd Ave. E (624-2334), one block east of McBride St. A new but supposedly historic facade enlivens the drab but well-kept interior. Microwave and TV downstairs. Singles, blocked off by curtains, can get noisy ($20). Singles with walls and a door $25; doubles $40. Laundry facilities ($5 wash and dry, including soap). Showers for non-guests $3.

Mountain Side Bed and Breakfast, 543 Pillsburg Ave. (627-1000). Small B&B conveniently close to the ferry terminal. Rooms come with private bath, separate entrance, and hot tub. Singles $50; doubles $65. No pets allowed.

Park Avenue Campground, 1750 Park Ave. (624-5861 or 800-667-1994). Less than 2km east of the ferry terminal via Hwy. 16. The sole campground in Prince Rupert. Some sites are forested, others have a view of the bay, and all are well-maintained. An RV metropolis! Sites $10.50; hookups $18.50. Showers for non-guests $3.50. Laundry facilities. Reservations recommended. Visa and MasterCard accepted.

FOOD

The top budget dining options in Prince Rupert begin at the bulk food department in the colossal **Safeway** (624-2412), at 2nd St. and 2nd Ave. (open daily 9am-9pm).

◉Cow Bay Cafe, 201 Cow Bay Rd. (627-1212), around the corner from Eagle Bluff B&B. Local patrons savor an ever-changing menu, including such delights as vegetarian *chilaquiles* ($11.50), ribs in guava BBQ sauce ($14.50), and shrimp quesadillas ($9). Extensive wine list. Open Tu noon-2:30pm, W-Sa noon-2:30pm and 6-9pm.

Galaxy Gardens, 844 3rd Ave. W (624-3122). Just one in a large Chinese restaurant crowd. Chow mein $7.50; Cantonese entrees from $11. Open daily 11:30am-10pm.

Rodho's (624-9797), on 2nd Ave. near 6th St. Huge menu of pleasing pasta platters ($7-8), Greek entrees ($11-13), and creative pizzas ($14). Table cloths, candles, and Mediterranean music for ambient pleasure. Open daily 4pm-1am.

Opa, 34 Cow Bay Rd. (627-4560), upstairs in the Loft. Spin a bowl at the nearby pottery studio, and while it's firing, enjoy the town's newest restaurant offering:

expensive sushi. Tuna rolls ($3); miso soup ($1.50); assorted sushi for two ($30). Open Tu-F 11:30am-2:30pm and 5-9pm, Sa noon-10pm, Su noon-9pm.

Cowpuccino's Coffee House, 25 Cow Bay Rd. (627-1395), takes its name seriously, right down to the Holstein spotted couch. Chew on rich desserts ("Sex in a Pan" $4) or assorted coffees (tall coffee-of-the-day $1.25) while sitting on a varnished cable reel surrounded by black-and-white-spotted hitching posts. Open M-Sa 7am-10pm, Su 9am-9pm; in winter M-Sa 7:30am-10pm, Su 9am-9pm.

Lambada's Cappucino & Espresso, 101 3rd Ave. (624-6464). A mixed clientele of backpackers, local fishermen, and barely urban professionals fill this clean and colorful cafe. The Lambada, a quadruple shot of flavored mocha ($4.50), makes 'em all dance. Open M-Th 7am-5:30pm, F 7am-6pm, Sa 8am-5:30pm.

SIGHTS AND OUTDOORS

The **Museum of Northern British Columbia** (624-3207), in the same building as the Traveler's Information Centre, documents the history of logging, fishing, and Haida culture, including beautiful Haida artwork both old and new. *(Open mid-May to early Sept. M-Sa 9am-8pm and Su 9am-5pm; Sept. 6 to May 18 M-Sa 9am-5pm.)* Prince Rupert's harbor has the highest concentration of archaeological sites in North America. **Archaeological boat tours** leave from the information center daily (see **Practical Information,** p. 320). *(2½hr. tours depart June 19-30 daily 12:30pm; July to early Sept. daily 1pm. $22, children $13, under 5 free.)* A local expert interprets several sites from the boat, with a stop at the modern village of **Metlakatla** across the harbor.

A number of attractive small parks line the hills above Prince Rupert, and provide a place for stretching between ferry legs. Tiny **Service Park,** off Fulton St., offers panoramic views of downtown and the harbor beyond. Grab an even wider vista from a trail leading up the side of **Mt. Oldfield,** east of town. The trailhead is at **Oliver Lake Park,** about 6km from downtown on Hwy. 16. The **Butze Rapids and Tall Trees trails** start from the same location. *(Guided nature walks leave from the parking lot May-Oct. every hr. 10am-4pm. $5.)* Cyclists can bike 16km down the road to **Diana Lake Park,** a town favorite on warm days, which features a picnic area set against an enticing lake.

Some of the best sights in Prince Rupert aren't in Prince Rupert. Locals boast of the **North Pacific Cannery** (628-3538) in Port Edward, 30 minutes by car from Prince Rupert, claiming that it presents a true-to-life glimpse of the canning industry, unlike all of those glamorized canning films and novellas. *(Open May 1-Sept. 30 daily 10am-7pm. $6, ages 6-15 $5, under 6 free.)* Follow the main highway out of Prince Rupert, take the Port Edward turn-off, and keep following the narrow, winding road for another 15 to 20 minutes. No actual packaging of fish has gone on at the cannery since the late 80s; it is now strictly a museum with hourly tours. Recent attention has revitalized the surrounding village and improved the museum itself.

The best time to visit Prince Rupert may be during **Seafest,** a four-day event held in mid-June. Surrounding towns celebrate, well, the sea, with parades, bathtub races, and beer contests. The **Islandman Triathalon** (1000m swim, 35km bike, 8km run) is also part of the Seafestivities, and was won in 1997 by an intrepid Let's Go researcher.

ENTERTAINMENT AND NIGHTLIFE

Well, there's always the movies. The **cinema** at 2nd Ave. and 6th St. shows three features twice a night ($8, children and seniors $4.50). While drinking establishments abound, kickin' back with a beer may prove alarmingly expensive. Night spots compete for "dockers" (cruise tourists), but those in search of big-city entertainment may wish they'd stayed on the boat.

The Commercial Inn, 901 1st Ave. (624-6142). Exudes local color in the form of tipsy fishermen and other down-to-earth folks. Theme nights during the week; live bands bring in a younger crowd on the weekends. Comfortable, spacious, occasionally rowdy setting. Billiards $1. Nightly drink specials; $2.75 beer on tap. Open M-Th 11am-1am, F-Sa noon-2:30am, Su 11:30am-midnight.

Breaker's Pub, 117 George Hills Way (624-5990), in Cow Bay. The "no rollerblades" sign on the door is a good indication of the kind of crowd this place attracts. Pool tables, view of the boat harbor, vintage 80s tunes, and expensive beers ($4 per pint on draft). Bar open M-Th 11:30am-midnight, F-Sa 11:30am-1am, Su noon-midnight; kitchen closes earlier.

QUEEN CHARLOTTE ISLANDS

Travel brochures bill the Charlottes as "the Canadian Galápagos," or "the Grand Canyon of the North," but these islands stand out on their own. A full 130km west of Prince Rupert, they form an archipelago made up of two principal islands, **Graham** and **Moresby,** with 136 surrounding islets. Graham, the northern island, is home to all but one of the islands' towns, a particularly potent strain of hallucinogenic mushroom, the world's largest black bears, and, until recently, the world's only known Golden Spruce. To the south, hot springs steam from mountainous Moresby Island and its smaller neighbors, where massive wooden totem poles of the islands' first inhabitants decay within one of Canada's most stunning and remote national parks.

The islands' main employer is the timber industry, narrowly taking the honors from the Canadian government. In the 1980s, the islands attracted global attention when environmentalists from around the globe joined the native **Haida Nation** and other locals in demonstrations to stop logging on parts of Moresby Island. In 1981, UNESCO declared parts of Moresby a World Heritage Site, and in 1988, the Canadian government established the **Gwaii Haanas** (gwie-HAH-nus) **National Park Reserve.**

Accessible only by boat or plane, the park covers the southern third of the Queen Charlottes. The Haida Nation maintains over 500 archaeological and historical sites, including dugout canoes, burial caves, and rock shelters. Tourist activity in the area rose dramatically after the protests and the subsequent creation of the park sparked media attention. This free publicity was relatively short-lived, however, and the islands today are once again quiet, uncrowded, and mystical. The lack of public transportation and the exorbitant cost of car rentals deter the faint of heart and light of wallet, but residents are rumored to be generous in picking up hitchhikers.

The BC Ferry from Prince Rupert docks at **Skidegate Landing,** between **Queen Charlotte City,** 4km west of the landing, and the village of **Skidegate,** 2km to the northeast. Most visitors stay in Queen Charlotte, the islands' largest town, but all the communities have at least some tourist facilities. Many of the best accommodations and attractions are farther north off Hwy. 16 in **Tlell, Port Clements,** and **Masset.** To the south, Moresby Island and the town of **Sandspit** contain the islands' only commercial airport. From Skidegate Landing, 12 daily ferries make the 20-minute crossing between the big islands. Dialing 911 in the Charlottes does not directly access local emergency systems; consult specific town listings for direct **emergency numbers.**

■ Queen Charlotte City

Queen Charlotte City's central location and size make it the starting point for those exploring the two major islands. "Size" is relative, however; this community of just over 1000 people is not the city its name claims it to be. Charlotte grew up around a sawmill, and logging is still its foremost industry, though fishing and the government also supply many jobs. While the location is pleasant, there's little to savor besides a view of the waterfront or a political discussion of logging and fishing rights.

ORIENTATION AND PRACTICAL INFORMATION

Charlotte, like all towns on this island, is situated on one long waterfront road, **3rd Ave.** The town is 2km east of the **ferry terminal,** and many travelers seem to find success with hitching, even though *Let's Go* does not recommend hitchhiking.

Ferries: BC Ferries (559-4485 or 888-223-3779; http://www.bcferries.bc.ca). The terminal is in Skidegate Landing, 4.5km east of Queen Charlotte City. To: Prince Rupert (June-Sept. 6 per week; Oct-May 4 per week; $24, car $90, bike $6). Reserve at least 3 weeks in advance for cars; car fares do not include driver. Ferries also run between Skidegate Landing on Graham Island and Alliford Bay on Moresby Island (12 per day; round-trip $3, car $8.50; off-season car $7.50; no reservations).

Taxis: Eagle Cabs, 209 3rd Ave. (559-4461). $7-10 between Charlotte and the ferry terminal. Open M-Th 6am-3am, F-Sa 6am-4am, Su 6am-1am.

Car Rental: Rustic Rentals (559-4641), west of downtown at Charlotte Island Tire. Another office at 3922 3rd Ave. (559-8865), by the ferry at Jo's Bed and Breakfast (see **Accomodations and Campgrounds,** p. 325). Reliable if unimpressive collection of used cars. Will rent to 18-year-olds with a credit card. $39 per day, 15¢ per km. Office open M 8am-6pm, Tu-F 8am-7pm, Sa 9am-5:30pm, but available 24hr. Will pick up at the ferry terminal in Skidegate.

Auto Repair: Twin Services (559-8700). 24hr. towing. Open M-Sa 9am-6pm.

Visitor Information: Visitor Reception Centre (559-8316; fax 559-8952), on Wharf St. at the east end of town. Beautiful new facility provides information both on Gwaii Haanas National Park and the islands as a whole. Ornate 3D map of the islands, and a creative natural history presentation. *Guide to the Queen Charlotte Islands* ($4) has detailed and worthwhile maps. Open May-Sept. daily 10am-7pm.

Outdoor Information: Gwaii Haanas Park Information (559-8818), on 2nd Ave., off 2nd St. Try the visitor center for info during the summer. (For registration info, see **Gwaii Haanas National Park Reserve,** p. 332.) Open M-F 8am-4:30pm. **Ministry of Forests** (559-6200), on 3rd Ave., at the far west end of town. Info on free Forest Service campsites on both major islands. Open M-F 8:30am-4:30pm.

Bank: Northern Savings Credit Union (559-4407), on Wharf St. One of two banking locations on the island (also a branch in Masset). The **ATM** on 3rd Ave., next to the City Centre Store, is a life-saver; many businesses don't take credit cards. Bank open Tu-Th 10am-5pm, F 10am-6pm, Sa 10am-3pm.

Equipment Rental: Moonglow, 3611 Hwy. 33 (559-8831), just east of town. Nice mountain bikes in many sizes. $5 per hr., $25 per day. Includes helmets, water bottles, and detailed maps of logging roads and campsites. Open daily 9am-6pm.

Fishing Licenses: Obtain a saltwater license at **Meegan's Store,** 3126 Wharf St. (559-4428). Freshwater licenses are available only from the **Government Agent** (559-4452 or 800-663-7867). Prices vary depending on license duration.

Bookstore: Bill Ellis Books (559-4681), on 3rd Ave. at the far west end of town. A remarkable collection of works by and about the Haida and other First Nations. Open M-F 8:30am-4pm. **Bradley Books** (559-0041), on 7th St. off 3rd Ave., may be a better bet for fiction and current magazines. Open Tu-Sa noon-6pm.

Laundromat: 121 3rd Ave. (559-4444), in the City Centre Mall. Wash $1.50, dry 25¢. Open daily 7am-9pm.

Showers: Ask at **Jo's Bed and Breakfast** and **Premiere Creek Lodging** (see **Accomodations and Campgrounds,** below).

Ambulance: 800-461-9911. **Fire:** 559-4488. **Police (RCMP),** 3211 Wharf St. (559-4421).

Pharmacy: (559-4310), downstairs in the hospital building. Open M-Tu and Th-F 10:30am-12:30pm and 1:30-5:15pm, W 1:30-5:15pm.

Hospital: (559-4300), on 3rd Ave. at the east end of town.

Women's Services: Queen Charlotte Islands Women Society (559-4743).

Post Office: (559-8349), in the City Centre Mall on 3rd Ave. Open M-F 9am-5pm, Sa noon-4pm. **Postal Code:** V0T 1S0.

Area Code: 250.

ACCOMMODATIONS AND CAMPGROUNDS

The small hotels of Queen Charlotte City are pristine, cozy, charming, and expensive. During the summer, make reservations or arrive early in the day to secure a room. Campsites are scarce near town or the ferry terminal, with the closest provincial park campgrounds 40km north in Tlell.

The Premier Creek Lodging, 3101 3rd Ave. (888-322-3388 or 559-8415; fax 559-8198). Built in 1910, this low-key hotel has been renovated with a veranda, balconies, and cable TV. Warm, clean rooms in the back hall may be small and 88 years old, but cost only $35 (with shared bath); an extra mat runs $5. Singles with balconies from $65; doubles $75. Credit cards accepted. Cheaper rooms go quickly, so reserve early. Showers available to non-guests in the afternoon ($5).

Jo's Bed and Breakfast, 4813 Ferry Loop Rd. (559-8865). Follow the road from the ferry terminal up the hill to the white house with blue trim. Convenient to the ferry, but a significant distance from anything else. Beware of free-range yard chickens. Many rooms feature cinematic ocean views, while others enjoy a communal kitchen and lounge, as well as communal noise. Singles $20; doubles $30; add $10 for a private room and a generous breakfast. Free local calls and a shed for baggage storage. Cash only. Reservations recommended.

Dorothy and Mike's Guest House, 3125 2nd Ave. (559-8439), up the hill opposite Meegan's Store. A standing hammock chair, stained pine interior, a library, and a loving breakfast to warm even the soggiest traveler. Centrally located. Singles $40; doubles $55. Call ahead.

Joy's Campground (559-8890; fax 559-8896; email joys@qcislands.net), halfway between the ferry terminal and Charlotte. Camp in Joy's waterfront backyard, and drink from the underground spring. This is the only campground remotely near town. Tent sites $5; hookups $9; electrical $15. No washroom facilities. To secure camping space, find Joy at Joy's Island Jewelers, 3rd Ave., next to the Hummingbird Cafe (see **Food,** below).

FOOD

Most locals only eat out on trips to the mainland, and will direct visitors to the grocery store for *haute cuisine à la Charlotte.* Buy basic grub at **City Centre Stores** (559-4444), in the City Centre Mall (open M-Sa 9:30am-6pm). On nights and Sundays, try **Sam and Shirley's** (559-8388), on 7th St. at the west end of town. Along with the usual goods, it's stocked with a wide variety of Chinese food and candy (open daily 7:30am-10:30pm).

◉**Harry Martin's Eatery,** 3207 Wharf St. (559-4773). A new local favorite, with a soothing ocean view, fresh flowers, and Celtic music. Fresh and flavorful food includes halibut chowder ($7), veggie burgers ($8), and scones with tea ($5). Open M-Sa 11:30am-5:30pm.

Howler's Bistro (860-2559), on 3rd Ave., sneaks a bit of art onto the palates of unsuspecting diners; each dish is served with creative garnishes and festive flair. Try the fully loaded Howler burger ($8) or grilled chicken fajita ($10), but leave room for one of five cheesecake varieties ($6). Open W-Su 11am-10pm. **Howler's Pub,** downstairs, is the only happenin' nightspot in town. Open daily 1pm-2am.

Hummingbird Cafe, 3301 3rd Ave. (559-8583), offers an airy, sun-washed dining area and stellar ocean view. This family-friendly restaurant is known for its steak ($17), fish and chips ($9), and sizable salads ($7). Does not serve hummingbird. Open daily 7am-2pm and 5-9pm; in winter 11:30am-2:30pm and 5-8:30pm.

Isabel Creek Store, 3219 Wharf St. (559-8623), next to Margaret's Cafe. Organic fruits and vegetables, juices, and some nitty-gritty home-baked breads. A break from fried food, and a good place to visit before a backpacking trip. Open M-Sa 10am-5:30pm, and they stay open during the town's frequent power outages.

Hanging by a Fibre (559-4463; fax 559-8430), on Wharf St., underneath Howler's Pub. Home of all things fibrous, and a place to mingle with hipsters and the occasional artist. The store and gallery specialize in paper art and basketry. Cappuccino $2.75, cafe latte $3.50, regular coffee $1.50, muffins and cookies 75¢. Open Su-W 9am-5:30pm, Th-Sa 9am-9pm; in winter daily 9am-7pm. Wheelchair accessible.

SIGHTS AND OUTDOORS

The **Haida Gwaii Museum at Qay'llnagaay** (559-4643), 1km east of the ferry landing on Hwy. 16, houses totem poles, contemporary Haida prints and carvings, and turn-of-the-century photographs of European exploration of the islands. *(Open May-Sept. M-*

F 10am-5pm, Sa-Su 1-5pm; Oct.-Apr. Tu-F 10am-noon and 1-5pm, Sa 1-5pm. $3, children free.)
The shed next door protects the 50-foot cedar canoe carved for Vancouver's Expo
'86 by renowned Haida artist Bill Reid. Take its fiberglass replica out for a paddle with
a Haida guide and steersman ($150), or just admire its artistry on dry land.

The Haida town of **Skidegate,** known as "the Village," lies 1km beyond the Gwaii
Museum. This community of 470 is a nexus of Haida art and culture. Residents are
sensitive to tourists, and hopeful that visitors will exhibit discretion and respect concerning local culture and practices. The **Skidegate Band Council Office** (559-4496) is
inside a Haida longhouse built in 1979 according to ancient design specifications.
Many a bald eagle has perched upon the totem pole out front. Visitors must get permission to photograph the cemetery or to camp and hike in certain areas, especially
the Haida villages on South Moresby island; talk to the receptionist at the **Haida Gwaii
Watchmen** (559-8225), next to the museum.

Unlike most mountains allegedly in the shape of something, **Sleeping Beauty
Mountain** actually resembles snoozing royalty; ask a local to point out her distinct
facial features. The challenging climb up the Beauty starts about 12km west of town,
off a logging road (follow the signs after 3rd Ave. turns to gravel), and takes a prince-
deterring three hours to ascend. The peak blesses climbers with stunning views in
every direction. A natural attraction requiring significantly less effort is **Balance Rock,**
which teeters on a roadside beach 1km north of Skidegate. A group of brawny loggers once failed in an attempt to dislodge the boulder, so it's unlikely to topple from
its precarious perch.

The scenic and virtually traffic-free roads throughout the islands beckon seductively to cyclists. Navigating the tangle of local logging roads and trails is easier with a
few good maps and a copy of *Trails on the Queen Charlottes,* by Fern Henderson,
sold at all the visitor centers and bookstores on the islands. Locals swear by "Fern's
book" as the outdoor bible of the Queen Charlottes ($5). The descriptions are invalu-
able, though the maps are outdated. Even on a shorter two- or three-day hike, it's
important to leave a **trip plan** with the visitor center or RCMP before setting out. The
visitor center issues crucial information on **tide severity** and **dangerous logging road
activity.** Everyone knows who loses when a couple of hikers or a 4x4 vie for trail
space with an unstoppable logging truck.

■ Tlell

Tlell (tuh-LEL), 40km north of Queen Charlotte City, is a trail of houses and farms
spread thinly along a 7km stretch of Hwy. 16. The quasi-town enjoys some of Graham
Island's best beach vistas, plus a population of artisans who earn Tlell a reputation as
the Charlottes' hippie zone. Here the rocky beaches of the south give way to sand,
and the **Tlell River** offers excellent **fishing** and water warm enough for **swimming.**
One of the most popular trails around Tlell leads to the **Pezuta shipwreck,** the hulking remains of a 246-foot lumber barge that ran aground during a gale in 1928. The
two-hour hike to the site leaves from the Tlell River picnic area off Hwy. 16, just
north of the river, and wanders through lush forest, sand dunes, and agate-strewn
beaches. When the trail branches, follow the "East Beach" sign up the ridge, or walk
the whole way at low tide along the river many trout call home. Die-hard beachcombers should consider continuing past the wreck and embarking on a multi-day expedition along **East Coast Beach.** Highway 16 cuts inland just north of Tlell, so only
backpackers have access to over 90km of incredibly pristine sand. A number of
wooden shelters punctuate the beach, but a tent or tarp comes in handy nonetheless.
Allow between four and six days to reach the road access at the north end of the
route, 25km east of Masset, and register at **Naikoon Provincial Park Headquarters**
(557-4390) before setting out.

Tlell's **bookstore** (557-4241) is in the Sitka Studio at the end of Richardson Rd.
(open daily 10am-6pm). In an **emergency,** call **fire** (557-4355) or **ambulance** (800-
461-9911). The town boasts a **post office** (557-4551), and in Tlell, that's something to

boast about. It's on Hwy. 16, 2km south of Wiggins Rd. (open M-F 2:30-5:30pm). **Postal Code:** V0T 1Y0. **Area Code:** 250.

Sea breezes and birds singing in the spruces await at **Cacilia's B&B/Hltunwa Kaitza** (557-4664), snuggled against the dunes just north of Richardson Ranch on the ocean side of the road, seconds from the beach. This may be the islands' nicest B&B, and is certainly the most distinctive. The hostess, Cacilia, oversees a flock of friends and relations who are likely to drop by for tea in the evening. Driftwood furniture adorns the common living space, and hanging chairs descend from giant spruce beams, mingling with friendly cats. Rooms are skylit, immaculate, and comfortable (singles $35; doubles $50). Pitch a tent or park an RV at the beautiful **Misty Meadows Campground,** 0.5km beyond Cacilia's, just south of the Tlell River bridge. Leafy trees line a short path to the beach. Pit toilets, picnic tables, and water grace 30 sites ($9.50; 14 day max. stay). Call **Naikoon Provincial Park Headquarters** at 557-4390.

There are no restaurants in Tlell, but the best cup o' joe on the islands is brewed by Leslie at **Dress for Les** (557-2023), 1km south of Richardson Ranch on Richardson Rd., off Wiggins Rd. Admire coffee sacks stapled to the ceiling, a red shoe collection on the bathroom door, and a pink coffee bar nestled among racks of vintage clothing (cappuccino $2.90, mocha $3.75, turquoise polyester mini-dress $25; open daily 10am-5pm; off-season M-F noon-5pm). **Riverworks Farm & Store** (557-4363), on Hwy. 16, 2km south of Wiggins Rd. next to the post office, peddles fresh eggs, island-grown produce, and, of course, computer supplies (open M-Sa 10am-5:30pm).

■ Port Clements

Port Clements is a gritty, shrinking logging community 20km north of Tlell. Although blessed with an enticing harbor and a few nearby curiosities, "Port" has little to arrest passersby. An intricate network of logging roads stretches inland from the port; these bumpy byways are open to public use and provide access to the heavily forested interior. Port Clements faces west onto Masset Inlet, and harbors some of the best **sunsets** in the Charlottes. Ten kilometers south of town, 9km after the pavement ends, a trail leads to an unfinished **Haida canoe.** Nearby stumps are full of test holes where the early artisans sampled other trees for boat-worthiness. **MacMillan Bloedel** (557-(4212) sponsors daytrips into the woods along the river (Tu and Th 9am-2pm); meet at the **Port Clements Museum,** 45 Bayview Dr. On **Canada Day** (July 1), Port Clem-

---

The Rise, Fall, and Rise of the Golden Spruce

For years, oddity-seekers of the world drove, biked, hiked, and ran to Port Clements, where the planet's only Golden Spruce basked in singular glory. Due to a rare genetic mutation, the 300-year old tree contained only a fraction of the chlorophyll present in an ordinary Sitka spruce, causing its needles to be bleached by sunlight. The striking 50m behemoth glowed fiery yellow in the sun, beaming its way into Haida creation myths and horticulturists' dreams. In January 1997, however, a disgruntled ex-forestry worker arrived at the site with an axe and a mission. To protest the logging industry's destruction of British Columbia's forests, he chopped down the tree. These actions won him no prize for logic, but certainly drew province-wide attention.

While islanders reacted with astonishment at their beloved tree's untimely demise, the University of British Columbia revealed another shocker: there had been not one but *three* Golden Spruces—two, created in 1977 from clippings of the original, were growing peacefully in the botanical gardens of the UBC Victoria campus. University authorities donated these golden saplings to the Haida nation, and their future looks good. Concurrent with the fall of the Golden Spruce, an albino raven was born on the island, an event that locals took as a sign foretelling a continuation of the Spruce's three-century history. This harbinger of success is no lucky omen for the tree's killer, now on the run in Mexico. Should the perpetrator return to Canada, he is sure to face a stiff penalty for botanical terrorism.

entsians celebrate with a fishing derby, slow-pitch softball, and mud-bogging (a contest to see who's truck can get the muddiest without getting stuck).

Port's **Island Taxi** (557-4230) runs 24 hours per day. The **Village Office** (557-4295), on Cedar Ave. between Tingley and Pard St., provides information and **free maps** of local logging roads (open M-F 1-5pm). The **Port Clements Islands Regional Library** (557-4402), at Tingley St. and Cedar Ave., has **free Internet access** (open W 3-5pm and 7-9pm, F 2-6pm). The **health clinic** on Park St. (557-4478), next to the elementary school, maintains variable hours. In an **emergency,** call for **fire** (557-4355) or an **ambulance** (800-461-9911). The **post office** lies between Hemlock and Spruce Ave. (open M-F 8:30am-12:30pm and 1:30-5:30pm, Sa 1:30-5:30pm). **Postal Code:** V0T 1R0. **Area Code:** 250.

The traditional motel experience lives on at the **Golden Spruce Motel,** 2 Grouse St. (557-4325), in a location that could use some sprucing up (singles from $42; doubles from $52; kitchenettes $8 extra; breakfast $4 for guests). Campers are better off at Misty Meadows in Tlell or at a campground in Masset. The **Yakoun River Inn** (557-4440), on Bayview Dr., is a local logger hangout featuring a country music jukebox and some damn good burgers ($5.75). Enjoy the autographed $2 bill collection adorning the walls, and wonder at how little beer it could buy here, at $4.50 per pint (open M-Sa noon-2am, Su noon-midnight). **Golden Spruce Farms** (557-4583), 1km south of town on Bayview Dr., plucks an astonishing variety of fresh vegetables from the garden in back; inquire at the left-most house.

■ Masset

Sitting at Mile Zero of the Yellowhead Highway (Hwy. 16), Masset's low-rise businesses and dilapidated houses present an initially underwhelming welcome. Yet some surprisingly eccentric establishments and truly eccentric eccentrics mingle within this rather drab collection of tired buildings. The mixture of loggers, Haidas, and hippies makes for an interesting and sometimes volatile political and social scene. Most travelers making their way to Masset come not for local political issues, though, but head out to the spectacular scenery surrounding the town. The rainforested region of Tow Hill and the expansive beachfront of the Blow Hole, east of town in Naikoon Provincial Park, more than justify the northward trek.

ORIENTATION AND PRACTICAL INFORMATION

Masset is about 100km north of Skidegate on Hwy. 16. To get downtown, take a left off the highway onto the main bridge, just after the small boat harbor. After the bridge, **Delkatla Road** is on the left; **Collision Avenue,** the main drag, is the first right off of Delkatla. To reach the campgrounds (see below), continue on Hwy. 16 without crossing the bridge. Most of the drive to North Beach is on gravel.

Taxis: Jerry's Taxi (626-5017). $4 from the harbor into town. Open daily 10am-6pm.

Car Rental: Tilden Rentals, 1504 Old Beach Rd. (626-3318), at the Singing Surf Inn. New cars from $40 per day; 25¢ per km. Must be 25. Open M-Sa 7am-9pm, Su 8am-9pm. It's wiser to rent in Queen Charlotte City or Sandspit.

Visitor Information: Tourist Information Centre, Old Beach Rd. (626-3300), at Hwy. 16. Plenty of local history and trail maps for choice birdwatching. Open July-Aug. daily 9am-8pm; Sept.-June M-Th 9:30am-4pm, F noon-4pm, call the **Village Office** (626-3995).

Bank: Northern Savings Credit Union (626-5231), on Main St. north of Collison Ave. The only bank and **ATM** on the islands outside of Queen Charlotte City. Open Tu-Th 10am-3pm, F noon-5pm, Sa 10am-3pm.

Car Repair: TLC Motors (626-3756), on Collision Ave. Open M-F 8am-6pm.

Public Library: (626-3663), at Collison Ave. and McLeod St. Open Tu 2-6pm, Th 2-5pm and 6-8pm, Sa 1-5pm.

Local Radio: Haida Nation Station 96.1 FM.

Ambulance: 800-461-9911. **Fire:** 626-5511. **Police:** (626-3991), on Collison Ave. at Orr St.

Post Office: (626-5155), on Main St. north of Collison. Open M-F 9am-5pm, Sa 9am-noon. **Postal Code:** V0T 1M0.

Area Code: 250.

ACCOMMODATIONS AND CAMPGROUNDS

A friendly budget god has smiled on Masset, creating cheap accommodations and campsites surrounded by centuries-old trees and expansive waterways. There is free **beach camping** on North Beach, 1km past Tow Hill, about 30km east of Masset in **Naikoon Provincial Park.** Look for signs marking the end of Indian Reserve property.

Copper Beech House, 1590 Delkatla Rd. (626-5441), at Collison Ave. Dine off china from Beijing, share a bath with carved wooden frogs from Mexico, and sleep under quilted comforters from Finland; this B&B is more like a private museum than a night's lodging. Singles $50; doubles $75; lofts in the garden shed $15. Longer-term visitors can arrange to exchange 4hr. of work per day for free room and board. Copper Beech's reputation has spread far and wide; make reservations before showing up at the door. Not wheelchair accessible.

Harbourview Lodging, 1618 Delkatla Rd. (626-5109 or 800-661-3314; email lholland@island.net), just north of Collison Ave. The ornately carved wooden door and the lime green plaid carpet have been waging aesthetic war on each other for over 30 years, but everything in the clashing interior is in good shape. Downstairs singles have TVs, and share a bath and dry sauna. Two big upstairs rooms, each with living room, kitchen, free laundry, and private deck. Fresh muffins in the morning. Singles and doubles $50. Call to reserve in summer. Not wheelchair accessible.

Village of Masset RV Site and Campground (626-5064), 0.5km beyond the bridge on Tow Hill Rd., next to the wildlife sanctuary. Convenient to town, with brand-new pay showers, but far from the outdoor destinations of North Beach and Tow Hill. Inquire at **Two Sallys,** the artisan shop in the center of the campground (open daily 7pm-10pm). 22 wooded sites, with toilets. Sites $9; electrical $15.

Agate Beach Campground, 26km east of town in Naikoon Provincial Park, at the base of Tow Hill. After 45min. of creeping vines and moss-swathed trees, the wind-swept fairyland clearing looks nearly too good to be true. Gorgeous campsites right on the beach, with water as far as you can see. 32 sites, with an area reserved for tenters. Picnic shelter, firewood, water, clean pit toilets. Free clamming (see **Food,** below). May-Sept. sites $9.50 for up to 4 people; free in winter. 14-night max stay. For more information, call **Park Headquarters** (557-4390).

FOOD AND NIGHTLIFE

Free and potentially toxic **razor clams** await on Agate and North Beach. Call the **red-tide hotline** (666-3169) before molesting the mollusks, then stop by the **Department of Fisheries and Oceans** on Christie St. to pick up a free permit and harvesting tips. Lemons and other seafood garnishes are sold at **Delmos Co-op** (626-3933), on Main St., south of Collison Ave. (open M-Sa 10am-6pm).

Cafe Gallery, 2062 Collison Ave. (626-3672). Lots of private dining spaces in a restaurant festooned with local artists' work, affording escape from the weary, dreary streets of Masset. The owners happily *Deutsch sprechen* with homesick Germans, and serve up a stomach-soothing chicken burger ($8). Open M-Sa 8:30am-9pm.

The Villager Cafe, 1690 Orr St. (626-3694), near the courthouse. The local choice for Chinese food, although a bit bland. Almond chicken chow mein or shrimp chop suey (both $10). Open Tu-Su 11:30am-8:30pm.

Daddy Cool's (626-3210), at the corner of Main St. and Collision Ave. A charbroiled burger ($6) at lunch or dinner may be satisfying, but it's the dancing, the live bands, the mixed crowd, the lines out the door on weekends, and the out-and-out bar brawls that give Daddy Cool's its reputation as a place you have to see to believe. Beer $4 per pint. Open M-Sa noon-2am, Su noon-midnight.

BRITISH COLUMBIA

SIGHTS AND OUTDOORS

Tow Hill, an incredible outcrop of volcanic basalt columns about 34km east of town, rises out of nowhere at the far end of Agate Beach, and presides over Masset as the area's reigning attraction. An easy boardwalk trail leads up the back of the hill to a fabulous overlook. On a clear day, miles of virgin beach and even the most southerly reaches of Alaska spread out below; sunsets are stupendous. Footpaths lead away from the observation deck toward even more breathtaking vistas, and a view of the rocky shoreline that snakes around the rocks over 100m below. On the way back down, take a detour to the **Blow Hole,** a small cave that erupts with 15-foot-high plumes of water when the tide comes in. Over the centuries, the sea has carved innumerable pools and mini-canyons out of the rocky cliffs. Coordinating a visit with mid-tide, when the hole is active, yields quite a show.

Two less-traveled trails depart from the Tow Hill Viewpoint parking lot: an 11km beach walk to **Rose Spit** at the northeast corner of the island, and a 10km hike on the **Cape Fife trail,** with access to the East Coast Beach and the long hiking route out of Tlell (see p. 326). A lean-to at the end of the Cape Fife trail allows tireless backpackers to link the two routes, exploring the entire island in a two- to three-day trek. Inform **Naikoon Park Headquarters** (557-4390) before multi-day trips. Across the Hiellen River, **North Beach** is the site of the Haida creation myth in which Raven discovered a giant clam full of tiny men (see p. 260).

Closer to town, red-breasted sapsuckers, orange-crowned warblers, glaucous-winged gulls, great blue herons, and binocular-toting birdwatchers converge on the **Delkatla Wildlife Sanctuary,** off Tow Hill Rd. The best paths for observing the 113 local airborne species begin at the junction of Trumpeter Dr. and Cemetery Rd. Continue on Cemetery Rd. past the sanctuary to reach **Oceanview Cemetery,** set in a lush green forest right on the beach, and a lively place, all things considered.

With over 600 residents, **Old Massett,** 2km west of town, is the largest Haida village on the Charlottes. Beyond a few modern totem poles, however, there's not much to look at; hold out for the Haida Gwaii Museum (see p. 325). Those with the goal to see abandoned Haida villages on Graham Island can apply for a permit at the **Masset Band Council Office** (626-3337), in the large cedar-and-glass building at the east end of town (open M-F 8:30am-noon and 1-4:30pm).

■ Sandspit

The only permanent community on Moresby Island, Sandspit's neatly trimmed houses and yards, endless ocean views, and bald eagles in seaside trees make it the Charlottes' most attractive residential area. Mother Nature buffets the community with a perpetual west wind, yet provides sprawling sunsets over a porpoise-filled copper bay each evening. While Sandspit has limited culinary options, reasonably priced accommodations are plentiful and tend to fill up less quickly than those on Graham Island. This well-groomed hub houses the only commercial airport on the islands, serves as a major launching point for kayak and boat trips to Gwaii Haanas National Park Reserve (see Gwaii Haanas National Park Reserve p. 332), and provides access to logging roads that venture into the isolated interior. Most travelers who come to Sandspit use it as a pit stop for the journey into the park.

ORIENTATION AND PRACTICAL INFORMATION Having a car or bike is handy in Sandspit, since the town is spread over the long **Beach Road,** which parallels the seashore. There isn't much traffic on the 13km road between Sandspit and **Alliford Bay,** where the ferry docks; those hitching to catch a late ferry often have a hard time finding a ride. Bringing a bike over on the ferry costs nothing extra, and the trip to town is an idyllic, easy, one-hour ride between deciduous forest and open ocean.

Airplanes: Sandspit Airport (1-800-663-3502), near the end of the Spit on Beach Rd. **Canadian Airlines** (800-665-1177) flies to Vancouver ($500, standby $321).

Ferries: BC Ferries (888-BC-FERRY/223-3779; http://bcferries.bc.ca/ferries) runs between Skidegate Landing on Graham Island and Alliford Bay on Moresby Island (12 per day 7am-10:30pm; $4.25 round-trip, car $10).

Car Rental: Budget Rent-A-Car, 383 Beach Rd. (637-5688). $47 per day plus 35¢ per km. Must be 21 with a credit card. Another Budget office is at the airport.

Visitor and Outdoor Information: The **Visitor Infocentre** (637-5362) is in the airport at the north end of town. Before venturing into the park, register and gather trail maps here or at the office in Queen Charlotte City. Open daily May 1-16 8am-noon; May 17 to Sept. 9am-5pm.

Library: 383 Alliford Bay (637-2247), at the north end of town. Open Tu 3-6pm, Th 3-5pm and 7-8:30pm.

Medical Services: The **health clinic** (637-5403) is on Copper Bay Rd., in the school building. Open M-F 10am-noon. After hours, call the **Queen Charlotte City Hospital** (559-8466).

Ambulance: 559-4506 or 800-461-9911. **Fire:** 637-2222. **Police:** 559-4421, in Queen Charlotte City.

Post Office: (637-2244), at Beach and Blaine Shaw Rd. Open M-F 9am-5pm, Sa 11am-2pm. **Postal Code:** V0T 1T0.

Area Code: 250.

ACCOMMODATIONS AND CAMPGROUNDS

Rooms in town are more affordable and less crowded than most on the islands. The **Seaport Bed and Breakfast** (637-5698; fax 637-5697), just up the road toward Spit Point, offers island hospitality, guest pick-up at the airport, plush couches, cable TV, and a breakfast of fresh eggs and home-baked goods. The new studio space is bright and beautifully decorated, overshadowing the less impressive original rooms. Reservations are essential in summer (singles $35; doubles $40). If Seaport is full, walk a block away from town to **Bayside Bed and Breakfast** (637-2433), operated by the same family. The accommodations are similar to the Seaport, right down to the Aztec-patterned comforters on the beds (singles $30; doubles $40). **Moresby Island Guest House** (637-5300), on Beach Rd. next to the post office, has eight rooms with shared washrooms, kitchen, and coin-operated laundry facilities. In the morning, breakfast ingredients are provided; kitchen use after breakfast costs $10 (singles $30; doubles from $55; overflow cots $15). Trail-weary trekkers can spend an extra $10 on the outdoor hot tub at the **Gwaii Haanas Bed and Breakfast,** 368 Cristina Pl. (637-5312 or 888-637-5312; fax 637-5312; email gwaiih@qcislands.net), off Copper Bay Rd. Enjoy hot breakfasts, a deck and hot tub, a communal lounge, and spacious rooms crammed with the hostess' ceramic creations (singles $40; doubles $60).

FOOD

Sandspit Inn (637-5334), across from the airport near the spit's end, has the town's answer to upscale dining. Dinner (5-9pm) is a bit expensive, but the lunch specials (available until 5pm) are more reasonable. A shrimp croissant costs $8.50. The inn also houses a **pub,** the only one in Sandspit. Monster goldfish swim at **Dick's Wok Inn,** 388 Copper Bay Rd. (637-2275), which serves a heaping plate of fried rice from $9. Three of the islands' renowned mushroom varieties reside in Dick's Sam Koo scallops ($17). Dick also offers a limited selection of very expensive groceries (open daily 5-10pm). A more affordable option is the **Bun Wagon,** 396 Copper Bay Rd. (635-5722). Customers sit at roadside picnic tables and enjoy delicious hot dogs ($2.50) or big burgers with fries from $5.50 (open M-W 11am-2pm and 4-7pm, F-Su 11am-7pm). The **Supervalu Supermarket,** 383 Alliford Bay (637-2249), resides in the mini-mall near the spit (open M-Sa 9:30am-6pm).

OUTDOORS AND EVENTS

Spectacular sunrises and sunsets await those who wander to the end of the spit. (Beachcombers should stay below the tide line if possible, since the spit is technically airport property.) Anglers can cast for silver salmon in the surf. Dirt logging roads lead south and west of town into some smashingly scenic areas, with several trails departing from the road between the ferry docks and the spit. A 4x4 truck may be necessary for exploring these logging roads and accessing the trail heads. The **Dover Trail** begins 40m west of the Haans Creek Bridge and passes by several giant cedars with ancient Haida markings. The round-trip hike takes less than two hours, but can be continued on the **Skyline Loop,** which runs another 90 minutes or so along the shore. Rocky shores line the ocean for 10km south of town to **Copper Bay,** a haven for bald eagles and balding shell collectors. **Grey Bay,** 20km south of town, offers a virtually uninterrupted expanse of sand. Twenty free, primitive **campsites** line the beach, but since the area is popular with locals, arrive early on weekends. A few kilometers down the road from the campsites, a 4.5km trail follows the shore south to **Cumshewa Head.** Since logging has come to a standstill on Moresby, some of the dirt roads are not maintained. Check with the visitor info-center (see **Practical Information,** above) to find out road conditions or obtain trail maps. The roads are perfect for **mountain biking;** the closest rentals are in Charlotte, and bikes are allowed on the ferry. Although logging in the area has slowed, locals still celebrate their heritage on **Logger Sports Day,** held in June or July. The festival features pole climbing, caber tossing, axe throwing, and other vigorous lumber-related activities.

■ Gwaii Haanas National Park Reserve

Arguably the most tranquil region of Canada's West Coast, Gwaii Haanas (gwie-HAH-nus) was born in a whirlwind of controversy. The territory was provincially owned Crown Land until the late 80s, disrupted only by sporadic logging and occasional tourist visits to deserted Haida villages. In the mid-80s, the timber industry, the Haida nation, environmentalists, and the provincial government became embroiled in a dispute over logging on one of the islands. The federal government interceded in 1988, purchasing the southern third of the Queen Charlotte Islands and declaring the region a National Park Reserve. The Canadian Parks Ministry now administers and patrols the islands, while Haida representatives known as **watchmen** inhabit key locations, guide visitors, and collect fees for visits to Haida sites.

Each summer, only a few thousand visitors make the long ocean journey south from Moresby Camp; **no roads** penetrate the reserve. Those who do make the voyage enjoy a wonderland of remarkable beauty and diverse plant and animal life. Old growth forest stands tall in **Hlk'Yaak (Windy Bay).** Chains of lakes and waterfalls span the breadth of Southern Moresby Island. At **Gandla K'in (Hotsprings Island),** several seaside pools steam at a year-round 37°C (100°F). The **San Christoval Mountains** thrust up semi-alpine peaks, which bear snow well into summer. The waters of **Juan Perez Sound** teem with jellyfish and enormous, garishly colored starfish.

The vestiges of several eras and cultures also rest in Gwaii Haanas. Deserted logging camps from the 1930s contain bizarre steam-driven logging devices, rotting trucks, and entirely wood-hewn highways. Totem poles slowly decay at **Skedans** and **Ninstints,** Haida villages deserted after late-19th-century epidemics of smallpox and tuberculosis. These settlements are being permitted to "return to the land," in keeping with Haida tradition.

PRACTICAL INFORMATION For advance reservations, call **Super, Natural British Columbia** (in Canada and the U.S. 800-663-6000; elsewhere 250-387-1642). Reservations cost $15 per person, but are not required for trips with licensed tour operators. Visitors must attend a 90-min. orientation session at the infocenter in Sandspit (see p. 330). For additional information, contact Parks Canada, Box 37, Queen Charlotte City, BC V0T 1S0 (250-559-8818; email gwaiicom@qcislands.net; http://fas.sfu.ca/parkscan/gwaii). Ask about appropriate camping locations; the Haida forbid camping in traditional sites, and require $25 (good for a full year) for day visits.

OUTDOORS Camp Moresby, near Grey Bay (see p. 332), is a logical place to enter the park. Check with the infocenter in Sandspit (see p. 330) before traveling these potentially hazardous logging roads. Two not-quite-budget companies dominate the market for **kayak rentals** and **charter trips** into the Park Reserve. Run by the energetic and competent Doug Gould, **Moresby Explorers** (637-2215 or 800-806-7633), on Beach Rd. in Sandspit, just south of Copper Bay Rd., offers chartered daytrips ($110) and overnight trips ($150) to Doug's floating cabin off Juan Perez Sound, plus week-long kayak rentals ($250) that include transportation to the cabin and back. While the charters can be fun, kayak rental is a more affordable option for those who already have paddling experience. If you're short on cash, give Doug a call to see what he has planned—prices can be flexible. **Queen Charlotte Adventures,** 34 Wharf St. (800-668-4288 or 559-8990; fax 559-8983), in Queen Charlotte City, offers sea kayak rentals (singles $40 per day, $180 per week), marine transport ($120 from Queen Charlotte to Juan Perez Sound), and guided kayak, powerboat, and sailboat tours. Keep in mind that it may take several days to reach the more remote regions of the park by kayak. **South Moresby Air Charters** (559-4222; fax 559-8589; email smoresby@island.net) flies over many of the heritage sites. For $330, a three- to four-person aircraft deposits culture vultures on the beach at Skedans for a guided 1½-hour tour. Flights to Hot Springs ($496) and Ninstints ($933) are also available.

ALASKA APPROACHES

▓ Cassiar Highway (Hwy. 37)

A growing number of adventuresome travelers prefer the Cassiar Highway to the Alaska Highway, which has become an RV institution. Built in 1972, the highway slices through charred forests and snow-capped ebony peaks, passing scores of alpine lakes on its way from the Yellowhead Highway (Hwy. 16) in British Columbia to the Alcan (Hwy. 97) in the Yukon. Three evenly spaced provincial parks right off the highway offer good camping, and the Cassiar's services, while sparse, are numerous enough to keep cars and drivers running. Hitchhiking is less popular here than on the Alaska Highway. Any waiter or hotel owner along the Cassiar's 718km will readily list its advantages: less distance, consistently interesting scenery, and fewer crowds. On the other hand, the Cassiar is remote, less maintained, and large sections past Meziadin Junction are dirt and gravel, which become very slippery when wet. The washboard gravel sections of the Cassiar can be considerably harder on tires than the better paved Alcan. This causes little concern for the large, commercial trucks that roar up and down the route, but keeps the infrequent service stops busy with over-ambitious drivers in need of tire repair.

■ Cassiar Highway (Hwy. 37): Highway 16 to Meziadin Junction

Just north of the junction of Hwy. 37 and Hwy. 16 stand the totem poles of **Gitwen-gak,** which relate the history of the First Nations fort that stood on nearby **Battle Hill** until 1800. The **Kitwanga Loop Road,** 6km north, leads through Kitwanga (gas, repair, and food available) to the National Historic Park where Battle Hill is located. The hill served as a stronghold and base for the mighty warrior **Nekt.** It was once equipped with a tunnel system and spiked logs that would roll down on intruders; fortunately for unarmed travelers, these have since given way to stairs and interpretive panels. The totem poles of **Kitwancool,** or "place of reduced number," lie another 19km to the north. The village was originally called **Gitenyow,** "the place of many people," but the indigenous people changed the name after extended warfare.

Meziadin Lake Provincial Park (meh-zee-AD-in) lies 155km north of the junction of Hwy. 16 and Hwy. 37, with free firewood and plenty of fishing on **Meziadin Lake** (66 sites: $9.50; water, firewood, and pit toilets). The gravelly sites are better geared to RVs, but tenters endure for the excellent view and fishing. Meziadin Lake is one of three lakes in BC where salmon spawn. Grab gas and shoot the bull with truckers at **Meziadin Junction** (636-2390; gas station open in summers daily 7am-10pm; in winter depending on traffic). The junction also has minor **tire repair** and an unremark-

BRITISH COLUMBIA

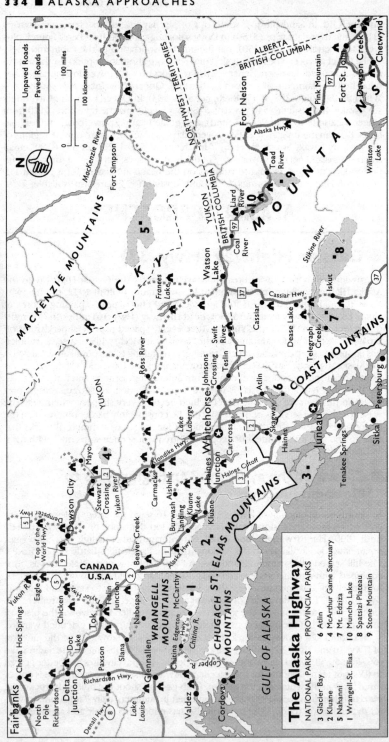

Unpaved Roads
Paved Roads

100 miles

100 kilometers

N

MacKenzie River

NORTHWEST TERRITORIES

ALBERTA
BRITISH COLUMBIA

Fort Simpson

Fort Nelson

Alaska Hwy.

Pink Mountain

Fort St. John

Dawson Creek

Chetwynd

97

Toad River

Williston Lake

MOUNTAINS

Liard River

Coal River

97

10

MACKENZIE MOUNTAINS

ROCKY

5

YUKON
BRITISH COLUMBIA

Watson Lake

Stikine River

8

Iskut

37

Frances Lake

37

Cassiar Hwy.

Cassiar

Dease Lake

7

Telegraph Creek

COAST MOUNTAINS

Petersburg

Ross River

YUKON

Swift River

Teslin

Johnsons Crossing

1

Atlin

6

Sitka

Mayo

4

Klondike Hwy.

Lake Laberge

Whitehorse

Carcross

Skagway

Juneau

Tenakee Springs

Stewart Crossing

2

Yukon River

Carmacks

Aishihik

Haines Junction

Haines Cutoff

3

Haines

Dawson City

Top of the World Hwy.

5

Dempster Hwy.

9

Burwash Landing

Kluane Lake

Kluane

Alaska Hwy.

3

2

ST. ELIAS MOUNTAINS

Beaver Creek

1

CANADA
U.S.A.

2

GULF OF ALASKA

Yukon R.

Eagle

5

Chicken

Taylor Hwy.

Tetlin Junction

Tok

Nabesna

WRANGELL MOUNTAINS

1

McCarthy

Edgerton Hwy.

Chitina R.

CHUGACH ST. ELIAS MOUNTAINS

Chena Hot Springs

North Pole

Richardson

Delta Junction

4

Dot Lake

Richardson Hwy.

Paxson

Slana

Gennallen

Chitina

Copper R.

Fairbanks

Denali Hwy.

8

Lake Louise

Valdez

Cordova

The Alaska Highway

NATIONAL PARKS
3 Glacier Bay
2 Kluane
5 Nahanni
1 Wrangell–St. Elias

PROVINCIAL PARKS
6 Atlin
4 Mt. Edziza
7 Spatsizi Plateau
9 Stone Mountain
10 Muncho Lake
8 McArthur Game Sanctuary

able but cheap **cafe** (636-9240; open in summer daily 7am-8pm). Next door, the **Club Mez Corner Store** (636-2836) rents motor boats ($100 per day), and has limited food and supplies (open daily 7am-11pm, winter 9am-9pm). The corner store keeps close tabs on the bear-viewing activity around Hyder (see below) and other local info. **Whitehorse,** YT lies 953km to the north. **Stewart,** BC and **Hyder,** AK are 62km west, along Hwy. 37A. The road to Stewart and Hyder is known as the "Glacier Highway" because immense ice-tongues creep down so close to the road, drivers can feel the frigid air on their skin. There are no services on this road.

∎ Stewart, BC and Hyder, AK

"It's the prettiest place on earth," most Hyderites will argue. Whether arriving by car via the towering glaciers and gushing waterfalls of well-paved Highway 37A, or by ferry along the Portland Canal, one of the longest fjords in the world, most visitors need little convincing. Neither the former ghost town of Hyder, AK, nor its cross-border partner, Stewart, BC, are themselves particularly stunning, but within a 20 mi. radius outside the towns lie all the best that the region has to offer. Mountains hulk over both towns, keeping national differences in perspective. Although Hyder is technically in Alaska, its currency is Canadian (except at the U.S. Post Office), its clocks tick to PST, its area code is 250, and most of its children are taught in Stewart. During International Days, North America's longest birthday party from July 1-4, the two communities erupt in an extravaganza of fellowship, and visitors are heartily welcome to bond in local bars. Stewart, population 450, is nearly seven times the size of Hyder and provides most modern amenities, while Hyder sports the frontier-style nightlife and blast-from-the-past dirt roads. With local mining and timber industries facing an uncertain future, these tiny towns are teaming up to recruit tourists with attractions like the world's largest road-accessible glacier.

ORIENTATION AND PRACTICAL INFORMATION A left turn from the ferry terminal takes you to Hyder; a right turn, to Stewart. Canadian customs and immigration have recently begun patrolling the previously unregulated border in an effort to curb smuggling into the country. Be prepared to show ID and be asked how long you were in "America." The humorless officers don't flinch at the typical response of "about 5 minutes." **Highway 37A** melds into Stewart's **Conway Street,** which intersects **5th Avenue** towards the water.

> **Airplanes: Taguan Air** (636-9150) flies a mail plane which carries passengers to Ketchikan (M and Th; 45min., $100; call to arrange a seat).
> **Ferries:** The *Aurora* makes weekly round-trips from Ketchikan to Stewart/Hyder (US$58), including a three-hour layover in town that gives pedestrians just enough time to see both towns. Ferry travelers seldom stay overnight.
> **Local Transportation: Seaport Limousines** (636-2622), in Stewart, drives to Terrace (4hr, $27, daily 10am).

Stewart
> **Auto Repair: PetroCan** (636-2307), at 5th Ave. and Conway, has the only gas in Hyder/Stewart and repairs autos (open daily 7:30am-7pm).
> **Visitor Information: Information Centre** (636-9224; email stewhydcofc@hot-mail.com). Open June-Aug. daily from 9am -8pm; in winter M-F 9am-5pm.
> **Bank: Canadian Imperial Bank of Commerce** (636-2235). Open M and W noon-3pm, F noon-5pm. 24hr. **ATM** on 5th Ave. by the post office.
> **Laundromat and Public Showers: Shoreline Laundromat** (636-2322) at Brightwell and 6th St. Wash $1.75, dry 25¢ per 4min. Showers $1 per 1½min.; available daily 7am-11pm.
> **Pharmacy: Rexall** (636-2484), on 5th Ave. and Brightwell St., Open M-Sa 9am-5:30pm and 7-9pm, Su noon-4pm.
> **Emergency:** 911. **Police:** (636-2233) are at 8th Ave. and Conway St. **Ambulance:** 800-461-9911. **Fire:** 636-2345.
> **Health Centre** (636-2221) is at Brightwell and 9th. Open M-F 9am-5pm.

BRITISH COLUMBIA

Post Office: (636-2553) at Brightwell St. and 5th Ave. Open M-F 8:30am-5pm, Sa 9-noon. **Postal Code:** V0T 1W0.
Area Code: 250.

Hyder

Visitor Information: Information Center (636-9148), in the **Hyder Community Association Building** (bear right at the Sealaska Inn downtown). Open June-Aug. M-F 9am-3pm, Sa-Su 10am-2pm; in winter M-F 11am-5pm.

Outdoor Information: Forest Service (636-2367), which provides info on local hiking and fishing. Open June-Sept. M-F 8am-2pm.

Library: (636-2637), also in the Community Association Building, has Internet access M-F 1-3pm, Sa-Su 10am-noon.

Laundromat and Public Showers: next to the **Sealaska Inn** (open 24hr.). $3 per 8min. Laundry: wash $1.50, dry $1.75.

Internet Access: See **Library,** above.

Post Office: (636-2662), past the Community Building towards Fish Creek. Unlike most of Hyder, it accepts only U.S. currency. Open M-F 9am-1pm and 2-5pm, Sa 10:30am-12:30pm. **ZIP code:** 99923.

ACCOMMODATIONS, CAMPGROUNDS, AND FOOD Stewart's **Rainey Creek Campground** (636-2537) is orderly, quiet, and woodsy, with grassy tent sites ($10 for 2 people, $3 per additional person), forested sites with electricity ($15), and impeccably clean showers ($1 per 4min.). With less appeal, Hyder's **Camp Runamuck** is split into a tent-site location ($10, each additional person $2) and a gravelly RV park (hookups $18), both with coin showers and laundry. The office for Runamuck is in the **Sealaska Inn** (636-2486 or 888-393-1199), which has cubicle-like but comfy "sleeping rooms" ($30; shared bath), plus singles ($48) and doubles ($52). Bed-bound dozers may have little choice but to party vicariously to the tune of lounge music from downstairs. The **King Edward Hotel** (636-2244), on 5th Ave. and Columbia St. in Stewart, provides less lively accommodations (from $55).

Tops among food factories is the **Bitter Creek Cafe** (636-2166), in Stewart on 5th Ave., in a great building adorned with historical photos and frontier appliances. Savor their wicked good artichoke-salad creation ($7) or gourmet pizzas ($10; open May-Oct. daily 8am-9pm). Across the street, the **Dog House** serves fruity smoothies ($3), and "the best coffee this side of the Bitter Creek Cafe" (open mid May to mid Sept. daily 10am-9pm). Hyder's **Border Cafe** (636-2379) sells a naked burger with fries for $3.75, and a plate of huge hotcakes for $5.50 (open Tu and Th-F 8:30am-7pm, W 8:30am-6pm, Sa 8:30am-4pm). **Cut-Rate Foods** (636-2377), on 5th Ave. in Stewart, fulfills its calling with scores of cheap, generic products (open M-Sa 9am-8pm, Su 11am-6pm; in winter M-S 10am-8pm, Su 11am-6pm; no credit cards).

SIGHTS AND OUTDOORS The Stewart Historical Society runs a **museum** (636-2568), on Columbia St., which offers, among the usual suspects of stuffed wildlife, an exhibit on the Great Avalanche of '65 and a disturbing collection of photos documenting the 1981 filming in Stewart of *The Thing*. *(Open mid-May to mid-Sept. daily 11am-5pm; $3, ages 6-12 $1.50, under 6 free; in winter call 636-9246 to set up a time.)* The principal activity in Hyder is sidling up to the bar in the historic **Glacier Inn** (636-9092) and asking to be **"Hyderized."** Over $40,000 in signed bills line the tavern walls, where early miners would tack up cash to insure against returning to town too broke to buy a drink. *(Open 10am-sometime late; in winter 2pm-whenever.)*

Fish Creek, 5 mi. from Hyder on Salmon River Rd., is an excellent place to view bears, if you don't mind company. Each year during the salmon spawning season (late July through Aug.), bears emerge en masse to feed on bloated, dying Alaskan chum salmon, while tourists set up camp on the riverbank. Come early in the morning for an unimpeded view. The only maintained trail on the Hyder side is the **Titan Trail,** a moderately challenging 5 mi. (8.3km) hike (one-way) up from the valley, with creek crossings. It gains over 4000 ft. (1200m) of elevation, becoming rocky and difficult toward the end of the climb. Heading away from Hyder, the trailhead is on the right about ½ mi. (0.8km) past Fish Creek. Thirteen kilometers north of Stewart along Highway 37A, the **Ore Mountain Trail** is a shorter, but still challenging 3½km (one-way) climb, which leads to a viewpoint overlooking the Bear River Valley.

Salmon Glacier, 20 mi. from Hyder on the Salmon River Rd., is the fifth largest glacier in the world, but the largest accessible by road. Beginning at Mile 19, the road creeps along a ridge almost directly above the glacier for several miles, providing eagle-eye views. The rocks above the road make for good hiking, and at night the sun sets behind the immense glacier. The road to the glacier is rocky and winding, but navigable for most vehicles—don't look down. **Grand View Express** (636-9174), in Hyder, offers a no-frills shuttle ride to the glacier, ideal for those with RVs or fancy cars unsuited to the drive (US$20; call for reservations). Those taking their own car can check road conditions at the Forest Service (see above). **Bear Glacier,** 35km east of Stewart in British Columbia, sits in plain and glorious view of Hwy. 37A.

Most anglers let the bear population work the creeks and streams, but for a hefty sum, deluxe fishing boats can be chartered for the hour, day, or week. **North Coast Fishing Charters** (636-2607) and **Portland Charters** (636-9133) are two outfits in Stewart with plenty of Portland Canal expertise.

■ Cassiar Highway (Hwy. 37): Meziadin Junction to Iskut

About 65km north of Meziadin Junction, new growth (and what is rumored to be the largest huckleberry patch in BC) infiltrate the immense **Iskut burn area.** **Kinaskan Lake Provincial Park** is 53km farther north, where a sweet campground includes water, pit toilets, firewood, and a boat launch into the lake where rainbow trout thrive (50 lakeside campsites: $9.50; wheelchair accessible). At the far end of the lake is the head of a 24km hiking trail to **Mowdade Lake** in **Mount Edziza Provincial Park** (see p. 337). There is gas available among the dozens of moose antlers at **Tatogga Lake Resort** (234-3526), another 25km north (open May-Sept. daily 7am-10pm). A stone's throw farther is the **Ealue Lake** (EE-lu-eh) turn-off, which leads 12km to a recreation site (free camping) and 22km to a trailhead pointing deep into the virgin backcountry of the **Spatsizi Plateau Wilderness** (see p. 337).

The small native village of **Iskut,** 256km north of Meziadin Junction, presents a melee of resort options, earning Iskut the unremarkable title of "resort capital of northwest BC." Even the most discriminating hostel connoisseurs heartily approve of the **Red Goat Lodge** (234-3261), 3km south of Iskut. The **hostel** ($15) in the basement of this regal lodge boasts a full kitchen, spacious common room, wood stove, coin showers ($1 per 3½min.) and laundry (wash $2, dry $1). The hosts' kids and llamas keep the place lively even when it's not packed. The **B&B** upstairs is equally impressive (singles $65; doubles $85). Tent sites on the **Eddontenajon Lake** (ed-un-TEN-a-jon) cost $10, and RV hookups go for $18 cash, $20 credit. Canoe rental starts at $10 for a half-day. Rentals for trips on the **Stikine** and **Spatsizi Rivers** start at $30 per day, motorboats are $65 per day.

At Iskut, travelers can fill the tank and grab some groceries at the sizeable **Kluachon Centre** (234-3241; open June-Aug. daily 8am-10pm; in winter M-Sa 9am-6pm, Su noon-5pm), which doubles as the **post office** (open M, W, and F 9am-4pm, Tu 1-4pm; **postal code** V0J 1K0).

■ Cassiar Highway (Hwy. 37): Spatsizi Plateau Wilderness and Mount Edziza Provincial Park

Long a territorial homeland of the Tahltan people, the Spatsizi Plateau became a provincial park and wildlife reserve in 1975. Supporting one of the largest populations of **woodland caribou** in British Columbia, Spatsizi is home to an extensive range of wildlife and varied eco-regions. Its name means "red goat" in Tahltan, in honor of the mountain goats in the region, whose penchant for rolling in iron oxide dust turned their coats a rusty hue. **Ealue Lake Rd.,** near the **Tatogga Lake Junction,** 25km north of **Kinaskan Lake Provincial Park** (see p. 337) provides the closest vehicle access to Spatsizi Wilderness Plateau. To reach the trailheads, follow the so-called road for 22km until it joins with the BC Rail grade, a tertiary road of variable quality (still drive-able for most vehicles). Because of the park's isolation, BC Parks strongly recommends that only experienced hikers explore Spatsizi. If you can afford it, flying in is a safer option. **Cold Fish Lake** is the primary fly-in destination because of its cabins, which boast wood heating, propane stoves, gravity-fed running water, and solar showers ($15, families $25). There are also two multiple-day canoe routes for advanced paddlers through the Spatsizi area along the **Spatsizi** and **Stikine Rivers.**

Four million years ago, 2787m **Mt. Edziza** erupted violently, leaving behind a charred, craggy, obsidian landscape. For centuries, aboriginal tribes made razor-sharp cutting blades and arrowheads from the rock. Like Spatsizi, the park invites only experienced outdoors explorers, due to its extremely variable weather (summer snow) and lack of trail system, facilities, and staff. There is no vehicle access into this remote region. Most hikers access Mt. Edziza by float plane into **Mowdade** or **Buckley Lakes,** bypassing the grueling week-long trek into the park along the **Klastine River.** Some find a boat from Kinaskan Lake Provincial Park to do the seven-day (or more) **Mowdade Trail,** but BC Parks does not recommend this arduous, unmaintained route. All hikers, regardless of previous wilderness experience, should make their itineraries and whereabouts known before venturing into the park, and be sure to check in upon return. For more info, contact **British Columbia Parks Area Supervisor,** Box 118, Dease Lake, BC V0C 1L0 (604-771-4591).

■ Cassiar Highway (Hwy. 37): Dease Lake

Long known by the local indigenous Tahltan as "Tatl'ah" ("Head of the Lake"), Dease Lake lies 84km north of Iskut. It became a Hudson Bay Company outpost in the late 1800s, had its share of early gold rush glory in 1864 and 1873, and now serves as a simple service center for Northwestern BC and as a base for backpackers exploring the vast and rugged **Mount Edziza** or **Spatsizi Provincial Parks** nearby (see p. 337). With the exception of the stellar inn, there's little to draw road-trippers to this town besides the necessary gas and food.

The **Dease Lake Tourist Information Office** is in the Northern Lights College (771-3900; open June-Aug. M-F noon-7pm). The **Forest Service** (771-8100) occupies the building next door and offers info on local trails or campsites. **BC Parks** (771-4591) has info on the nearby provincial parks. To get to their office, drive to the end of Boulder Rd. and take a left onto Dease Ave. The building is on the right, with a sign in front. The **TD Bank** is in the BC Government building across the highway from the College (bank open M,W, and F 10am-noon and 1-3:30pm). The **Shell Station** (771-5600) has great **showers** ($4; includes towel, soap, shampoo) and a **laundromat** (wash $3, dry 25¢ per 5min.; open daily 7am-11pm). For repairs or a car wash, **Chico's** (771-5656) is on Boulder Ave. (open M-F 8am-6pm). The **Stikine Health Center** (771-4272 or 771-4444) is just off the Cassiar at the north end of town (walk-in M-F 8:30am-4:30pm). Reach the **police** at 771-4111 or the **ambulance** at 771-3333. The **post office** is in the Shell station (771-5013; open M-F 8:30am-1pm and 2-5pm). **Postal Code:** V0C 1L0. **Area Code:** 250.

The spacious, pine-furnished **Arctic Divide Inn** (771-3119), right on the Cassiar, deserves accolades for its squeaky clean rooms with private bath, phones, and TV (singles and doubles $59; complimentary continental breakfast). Kitchenette, fridge, and VCR are also available. From the rugged staircase to the slightly bizarre coffee table, the inn's decor is an exception to the town's drabness. The closest free forest service **campground** to Dease is scenic **Allen Lake.** Luckily for tipsy tenters, the lake is a short stumble from the **Tanzilla Bar;** from Boulder St., go left on 1st Ave. and follow it to the end (no water, pit toilets). Those without four-wheel drive should park before the campground's parking lot—the extremely steep gravel driveway to the lake is likely to hold city cars hostage until a tow truck can winch it out. For a complete listing of area campgrounds, get a Forest Service map at the infocenter or from the Forest Service (see above). **Northway Country Kitchen** (771-4114), locally "the restaurant," offers big portions and slow service in a clean, spacious setting. Tickle your palate with "pirogies & smokies," cheese-filled dumplings accompanied by four sizable sausages ($8.50), or chomp on a garden burger with salad ($6.50; open May-Oct. daily 7am-9pm). Groceries are available at the **Supervalu** (771-4381), next to Shell (open mid-June to Sept. M-Sa 7am-9pm, Su 8am-7pm; in winter daily 9am-6pm).

■ Cassiar Highway (Hwy. 37): Telegraph Creek

Lying 119km from Dease Lake on Telegraph Creek Rd., Telegraph Creek is the only remaining settlement along the **Stikine River** (stuh-KEEN). The highest navigable point on the Stikine, the town was an important rendezvous point for the coastal Tlingit and interior Tahltan people. Today, Telegraph Creek has about 400 residents, most of them Tahltan. The community welcomes its infrequent visitors, but is sensitive about the numerous cultural sites around town; visitors keen to explore should get permission from the **Tahltan Band** (235-3151). For **tire repair,** contact **Henry Vance** (235-3300). Mechanically handy locals have been known to help out those whose vehicles incur more substantive wrath along the Telegraph Creek Rd. There is a **health clinic** (235-3212) in town with two nurses on duty; follow signs for Glenora. The **police** can be reached at 235-3111. Coming into town from Dease Lake, the **post office** is on the right (open M and W 9:30-11:30am, Tu and Th 1-4pm, F 9:30-11:30am and 1-4pm). **Postal Code:** V0J 2W0.

The biggest attraction for thrill-seeking travelers is 112km **Telegraph Creek Road.** The gravel road is well maintained, and offers magnificent views of the **Stikine Grand Canyon.** It is no place, however, to lug a clumsy RV or give a failed brake system a second chance. After a blah start, the second half of the road features 20% grades and hairpin turns along the steep, perilous obsidian outbanks of the Tuya, Tahltan, and Stikine River canyons. Travelers should allow 2½ hours to drive each way, with ample time to de-frazzle in between. A rest stop, 88km from Telegraph Creek, offers a gorgeous view of the canyon and a chance to speak words of encouragement to your beleaguered transmission.

The "modern" village of Telegraph Creek revolves around the historic **Stikine RiverSong** (235-3196). Originally the Hudson Bay Company building near the neighboring tent city of **Glenora,** 12 mi. from Telegraph Creek, the RiverSong was disassembled in 1902 and moved to Telegraph Creek. Today, the jack-of-all-trades RiverSong acts as Telegraph Creek's hotel, general store, and cafe. They also sell gas, fishing licenses, and t-shirts. The staff is extremely helpful and can answer almost any question about the history of the area. Wash off 119km of road dust with a shower ($4; open May-Sept. M-Sa 11am-7pm, Sun noon-7pm). Hotel rooms at the RiverSong are clean, with cedar finishing and a common kitchen (singles $49; doubles $55; $10.50 per additional person). Three free recreation sites along the road to the historic site of Glenora provide primitive **camping** for the penniless.

■ Cassiar Highway (Hwy. 37): Dease Lake to the Alaska Highway (Hwy. 1)

This stretch of highway follows the old Cassiar Gold Route, and still-used dredges can be seen along its length. **Moose Meadow Resort,** 85km north of Dease Lake, is a roomy lakeside campground with access to canoe routes (sites $11; 2-person cabins $30; $5 per additional person; firewood, water, 2 free showers). Canoe rentals for **Cotton Lake,** a widened portion of the gently meandering **Dease River,** are $6 per hour (2hr. minimum), and $27 per day. **Boya Lake Provincial Park** is 152km north of Dease Lake, 2km east of the Cassiar Hwy., situated on a turquoise lake with a boat launch and swimming dock. Spacious private campsites (30 sites: $9.50, pit toilets, firewood, water) make both tenters and RVers smile. The shallow lake is warm by northcountry standards, but the water is still numblingly "refreshing." There are only two gas stations between Dease Lake and the Alcan junction: **Jade City,** 117km past

Dease Lake (open May-Sept. daily 7am-9pm), and **Kididza Services** (239-3500), at Good Hope Lake, 23km past Jade City (open daily 7am-11pm).

Having reached the end of this 718km odyssey, at the junction of the Cassiar Hwy. and the Alaska Hwy. (see p. 339), travelers can grab showers, souvenirs, grub, groceries, gas, and minor repairs at the **PetroCan Station** (536-2794). The PetroCan doubles as the office for the RV park and motel next door ($11; full hookups $16; singles and doubles $30; shared bath; no TV or phone. Free showers; $3 for non-guests). They also operate a 24-hour **laundromat** (wash $1.50, dry 50¢ per 14min.). Travelers can grab some chili ($6) or a kamoboko crab melt and caesar salad ($8) at the **Junction 37 Cafe** (536-2795), next to PetroCan (open daily May-Oct. 6am-10pm). Strangely, the **saloon** in the next lot (536-2796) has slightly cheaper gas (open 10am-midnight). **Whitehorse** (see p. 377) lies another 435km west on the Alcan.

■ Dawson Creek

Dawson Creek, BC (not to be confused with Dawson City, YT, or Dawson's Creek, WB) is the Alaska Highway's official starting point (Mile 0). First settled in 1890, as just another pip-squeak frontier village of only a few hundred people until its location at the northern railroad terminus made it a natural place to begin building a 2600km highway in nine months. The town boomed during construction, literally. On February 13, 1943, sixty cases of dynamite exploded in the center of town, leveling the entire business district save the COOP building, now Bing's Furniture, across the street from the Mile 0 post. Dawson Creek has quieted down considerably since the heyday of highway construction, but the town's 10,000 odd residents are still serious about their home's historical role as womb of the Alcan. Visitors who take a day or two to enjoy the town's history and genuine hospitality before trekking north can easily get caught up in this infectious enthusiasm.

ORIENTATION AND PRACTICAL INFORMATION There are two ways to reach Dawson Creek from the south. From Alberta, drive northwest from Edmonton along Hwy. 43, through Whitecourt to Valleyview; turn left on Hwy. 34 to Grande Prairie, and continue northwest on Hwy. 2 to Dawson Creek, for a total journey of 590km. From Prince George, drive 402km north on the John Hart section of Hwy. 97 (see p. 316). Either drive takes most of a day.

Buses: Greyhound, 1201 Alaska Ave. (782-3131 or 800-661-8747), can bus you to Whitehorse, YT (20hr., June-Aug. 1 per day M-Sa, Oct.-May 3 per week; $164); Prince George (6½hr., 2 per day, $50); Edmonton (8hr., 2 per day, $70). The station is open M-F 6am-6pm and 8-8:30pm, Sa 6am-noon, 2-5pm, and 8-8:30pm, Su 6-10:45am, 3-4:30pm, and 8-8:30pm.

Visitor Information: Tourist Infocentre, 900 Alaska Ave. (782-9595), in the old train station just off Hwy. 97, has daily reports on the Alcan's condition and is also home to a small museum. Open May 15 to Labour Day daily 8am-7pm; off season Tu-Sa 10am-noon and 1-4pm.

Banks: Many major Canadian banks are all within spitting distance of the Mile 0 post on 10th St. at 102nd Ave. All have ATMs open 24hr.

Library: (782-4661), at 10th St. and McKellar Ave., sports free **internet access.** Open Tu-Th 10am-9pm, F 10am-5:30pm, Sa-Su 1:30-5:30pm.

Laundromat: King Koin Laundromat, 1220 103rd Ave. (782-2395), has showers for $2.75 (no time limit!), laundry (wash $2.25, dry 25¢ for 5min.), and a **fax** machine. Open daily 8am-9pm.

Automotive Repair: Action Automotive, 1041 Alaska Ave. (782-3516), is just one of many garages along Alaska Ave.

Hospital: Dawson Creek and District Hospital, 11100 13th St. (782-8501).

Ambulance: 782-2211. **Police:** (782-5211), at Alaska Ave. and 102nd Ave.

Internet Access: see **Library,** above.

Post Office: (782-9429), 104th Ave. and 10th St. **Postal Code:** V1G 4J8.

Area Code: 250.

ACCOMMODATIONS AND CAMPGROUNDS Those willing to trade a few amenities for bargain prices, great location, and an off-beat aura should head straight for the historic **Alaska Hotel** (782-7998), on 10th St., 1½ blocks from the infocenter, upstairs from the Alaska Cafe & Pub (see **Food,** below). Comfortable rooms are decorated with pictures of Marilyn and Elvis, or devoted entirely to cows. Toilets and bathtubs (no showers) are shared; rooms lack TVs and phones (singles $25; doubles $30; in winter $5 less). The newer and better-maintained **Voyageur Motor Inn,** 801 111th Ave. (782-1020), offers motoring voyagers phones, cable TV, and refrigerators in some rooms (singles $40; doubles $45). Peaceful and grassy, the **Mile 0 Campground** (782-2590), 1km west of Mile 0 on the Alaska Hwy. and adjacent to the Pioneer Village, has free showers and coin laundry (sites $10; hookups $16). Campers can also head for the convenient but crowded **Alahart RV Park,** 1725 Alaska Ave. (782-4702), which imparts free showers, a dump station, and coin laundry (sites $8; hookups $16). The friendly owners rival the infocenter in providing maps and suggestions for entertainment and food.

FOOD If foraging on your bug-splattered windshield fails to satisfy you, Dawson Creek offers a wealth of affordable, tasty and varied cuisine rare for such a far northern locale. The **Alaska Cafe & Pub** (782-7040), "55 paces south of the Mile 0 Post" on 10th St., serves excellent burgers and fries starting at $5. Proclaiming itself one of Canada's top 500 restaurants, the cafe offers live music (mostly country) nightly, and homesick travelers can croon away their sorrows at Monday night karaoke (open daily 11am-11pm). Pick up a health-conscious loaf for the road at the **Organic Farms Bakery,** 1425 97th Ave. (782-6533). From the infocenter, drive west along Alaska Ave. and take a right at 15th St. Breads are baked fresh from local grain, and start at $1.25 for a loaf of whole wheat; croissants and pastries are also available (open Tu-F 9:30am-6pm, Sa 9am-5pm). **Chevy's Diner,** 1333 Alaska Ave. (782-2438), will satisfy those lusting for a bit of 50s Americana with the King's Chili Con Carne ($5) and scintillating shakes ($3). Though the decor may be directed towards the pre-baby-boom American tourists who cruise through Dawson Creek each summer, the clientele consists mostly of talkative, friendly locals (open daily 6am-10pm). Stock up on bulk and retail groceries before heading north at the **Price Connection,** 11600 8th St. (782-8844). Great prices, and convenient, if you need 12 lb. of nutmeg (open M-Sa 9am-6pm, Su 11am-5pm).

SIGHTS, EVENTS, AND OUTDOORS Travelers cruising through Dawson Creek can't miss the **Mile 0 Cairn** and **Mile 0 Post,** both commemorating the birth of the Alcan, and both within a stone's throw of the infocenter. The **Art Gallery** (782-2601) in the old grain elevator next to the infocenter hosts a photo essay about the World War II Alcan creation saga. *(Open June-Aug. daily 9am-5pm, Sept.-May Tu-Sa 10am-noon and 1-5pm.)* The **Pioneer Village** (782-7144), 1km west of Mile 0, is an excellent recreation of Dawson Creek life from the 20s to the 40s. *(Suggested donation $1; $2 family. Open May-Aug. M-F 9am-8pm, Sa-Su 9am-6pm.)* The village features antique (i.e. rusted) farm equipment, and a play area for children. In early August, the town plays host to the **Fall Fair & Stampede,** with a carnival, fireworks, chuckwagon races, and a pro rodeo. *(Call 782-8911 for more info.)*

One Dawson Creek farmer has the **largest herd of bison in captivity.** Over 300 beasts can be seen stampeding around his property just south of town. Take 8th St. out of town, and start your quest on the foreboding Dangerous Goods Road. Bird lovers can head 10km out of town to the highland marshes of **McQueen's Slough.** Take Hwy. 49 east from the infocenter, and turn left onto Rd. 3. Watch for a binoculars sign, and make the second left. The swampy area is a haven for all kinds of wildlife, including mosquitoes. The **Community Forest,** 10km south of town at Bear Mountain, has a network of **cross-country ski trails,** and white aspens to make Ansel Adams do a little jig. When the snow melts, this area becomes a popular **hunting** spot. *(For information on provincial regulations, guides, and outfitting, call 787-3295.)*

BRITISH COLUMBIA

■ The Alaska Highway

They sweat and froze, laughed and cried, bled and labored until finally, the unachievable was achieved. In a dozen American accents they had cussed and kissed me into being from Dawson Creek to Fairbanks. In less than nine months, the miraculous 1600 mile military highway was born.
—Shirley Ravelli, "Spirit of the Alaska Highway"

Built during World War II, the Alaska Highway (also known as the Alcan) traverses an astonishing 2378km route between Dawson Creek, BC and Fairbanks, AK. After Japan's attack on Pearl Harbor in December 1941, the U.S. War Department planned an overland route, beyond the range of carrier-based aircraft, to supply U.S. Army bases in Alaska. The U.S. Army Corps of Engineers teamed up with American and Canadian civilian contractors to complete the daunting task in just 34 weeks. The one-lane dirt trail curved around swamps and hills; landfill would come later. Some argue that the curves were intended to inhibit Japanese planes from using the road as a runway, but in reality the surveyors were forced to move so quickly (an average of 12km of road was cleared each day) that a haphazard route was chosen.

In recent years, the U.S. Army has been replaced by an annual army of over 250,000 tourists, the vast majority of them RV-borne senior citizens from the U.S. and Germany. Travelers making the trip in July, the busiest month, will face crowded campgrounds and mammoth RV caravans. They'll also be passed by the speediest semis the roads have ever known. In general, there's a trade-off between the excitement you'll find on the Alcan and the speed with which you'll reach Alaska. If you're willing to take the time, there are countless opportunities off the highway for hiking, fishing, and viewing wildlife. If your priority is to beat the quickest path to the Alaska border, however, the **Cassiar Highway** (see p. 333) may be a better route for you.

The one-hour **video** *Alaska Highway: 1942-1992* shown at the Dawson Creek Tourist Infocentre (see p. 340), provides a praiseworthy introduction to the road and the region. The free pamphlet "Driving the Alaska Highway," includes a listing of emergency medical services and emergency phone numbers throughout Alaska, the Yukon, and British Columbia, plus tips on preparation and driving (available at visitor bureaus, or through the Department of Health and Social Services (907-465-3030), P.O. Box 110601, Juneau, AK 99811-0601). Although the Alcan was "cussed and kissed" into being in nine months, in many ways it's still a work in progress, as construction crews continue to smooth grades and eliminate treacherous turns. For daily Alcan **road conditions** call 250-774-7447 in BC, 867-667-8215 in the Yukon. **Mileposts** were put up along the highway in the 1940s and are still used as mailing addresses and reference points, although the road has been rebuilt and rerouted so many times that they no longer reflect mileage accurately. Kilometer posts were installed in the mid-70s and recalibrated in 1990; these distances are more accurate.

■ Alaska Highway (Hwy. 97): Fort St. John

The Alaska Highway between Dawson Creek and **Fort St. John** (76km up the Alcan) offers little more than cows and rolling hills, but a couple of roadside quirks do break the driving monotony. In early August, gold-grubbers converge 20km south of Fort St. John to pan for prizes and fame at the **World Invitational Gold Panning Championships** in Peace River Park (call 787-9738 for details). Travelers who miss the invitational trudge on to **The Honey Place** (785-4808), just south of Fort St. John, to gaze in wonder at the **world's largest glass beehive** (open M-Sa 9am-5:30pm). Fort St. John itself is hardly as abuzz with excitement. The **Travel Infocentre**, 9923 96th Ave. (785-3033), at 100th St. in the museum complex, illustrates how little the town has to offer (open June-Aug. M-F 8am-8pm, Sa-Su 8am-5pm; Sept.-May M-F 8am-5pm). The **Ministry of Environment, Land, and Parks,** 10003 110th Avenue (787-3407), has a division in Fort St. John and provides info on fishing and hiking along the Alcan (open M-F 8:30am-4:30pm).

■ Alaska Highway (Hwy. 97): Fort Nelson

Gas up in Fort St. John before heading north—the 109km stretch from Sikanni to Prophet River is entirely gas-less. **Fort Nelson,** 456 (of the highway's least exciting) km north of Dawson Creek, and 250km north of Toad River, is an oasis of northern hospitality and the region's center for natural resource extraction. The **Fort Nelson Heritage Museum** (774-3536), across the highway from the infocenter, features an impressive, if unsettling, taxidermy collection of all local game species (white moose cow included), as well as doodads from the era of highway construction. An eclectic collection of vintage cars and a trapper's cabin top it all off. (Open in summer daily 8:30am-7:30pm. $2.50, children $1.25, families $5.50.)

The **Infocentre** (774-6400) hides itself in the Recreation Centre/Curling Rink on the northern edge of town, providing info on local accommodations and attractions as well as invaluable **daily Alcan road reports** (open May-Sept. daily 8am-8pm).

Rest up at the **Mini-Price Inn,** 5036 51st Ave. W. (774-2136), one block off the highway near the infocenter (no room phones; singles $39; doubles $44). The **Westend Campground** (774-2340), across from the infocenter, is a veritable Alcan Disneyland, with showers (25¢ per 3min.), a laundromat (wash $2, dry $1 per 30min.), mini-golf ($2), a free car wash, free firewood, and free trampoline (sites $12; full hookups $18). There are slim pickings for dining in Fort Nelson. The **Pantry Restaurant** (774-6669), at the Woodlands Inn in the east end of town, boasts the largest menu around, including great vegetarian entrees (around $8) and breakfast options (open daily 6am-10pm). The **Shangri-La Restaurant** 5403 50 Ave. S (774-2188), near the theater, provides tasty though not quite paradise-worthy Chinese cuisine. Combo meals and most entrees start at $8 (open daily 11am-10pm; take-out available).

■ Alaska Highway (Hwy. 97): To the Yukon

Small towns—usually composed of one gas pump, one $50-60 motel, and one cafe—pock the remainder of the highway to Whitehorse and the Alaska border. Fortunately for the glassy-eyed driver, highway scenery improves dramatically after Fort Nelson. About 150km north of Fort Nelson, the stark naked **Stone Mountain** appears. Next door, **Summit Lake** keeps the metropolis of **Summit** company. (Gas pump? Check. Motel? Check. Cafe? Check.) This is the highest point (1295m) on the Alaska Hwy. The **Stone Mountain Campground,** right on the lake, makes a superb starting point for hiking the area (sites $9.50; outhouse, firewood, water). The steep **Summit Peaks Trail** begins across the highway from the campground, ascending 5km along a ridgeline to the breathtaking crest. A more moderate trail climbs 6km to the alpine **Flower Springs Lake.** Each hike takes about five hours round-trip.

Toad River, a town of 60, lies 45km north of Summit. The **Toad River Cafe** (232-5401), on the highway, dangles more than 4600 hats from the ceiling. (Open daily 6am-10pm; in winter 7am-9pm. Tasty burgers from $5. Headwear donations accepted.) Fifty kilometers north of Toad River, **Muncho Lake Provincial Park** delights even the weariest drivers. Glacial silt refracts sunlight to turn Muncho ("big lake" in Tagish) into a seven-mile-long azure mirror. **Strawberry Flats Provincial Campground,** on the lakeshore, is the pot of gold at the end of the driving rainbow (sites $9.50; outhouse, firewood, water). If Strawberry Flats is full, **MacDonald Provincial Campground,** only a few kilometers farther along the highway and still on the lake, is the pot of silver (sites $9.50; outhouse, firewood, water). When your head grows heavy and your vision grows dim and you have to stop for the night, consider **Muncho Lake Lodge** (776-3456), 10km north of Strawberry Flats. A plain single costs $40 ($5 per additional person) and the private campground is $12 (hookups $14).

Near the 775km mark, the highway reaches **Liard River Hot Springs**. These two naturally steamy and sulphurous pools are a phenomenal place to soothe a driver's derriere. For privacy and deeper water, skip the alpha pool and head up to beta. The park service manages campsites ($12) and a free day use area here. Arrive early—the campsites are often full by noon. To read about the Alcan in the Yukon, see p. 381.

■ Atlin

Atlin (Tlingit for "Big Lake") gives meaning to the phrase "the good life." The town's 400 residents live humbly on the eastern shore of the 145km long, clear-as-glass Atlin Lake, which blesses the town with a deceptive ocean-side aura, complemented by the massive mountains of Atlin Provincial Park. The huge park embraces a sizable chunk of the lake, as well as creeping ice fields, 80 islands, and untrodden wilderness. Fishing in the area is understandably some of BC's best.

Like many northern towns, Atlin owes its existence to the Klondike Gold Rush and was first settled in 1898. Nearly 10,000 money-hungry prospectors lived in Atlin at the turn of the century. Gold mining remains the primary industry, but today's easy-going Atlinites seem more interested in their easy-going, all-for-one community than in striking it rich. The town has mellowed considerably since its Klondike heyday, and locals maintain the mellowness by making little effort to draw visitors, even while warmly welcoming those who do come. Many pioneer-era buildings remain in mint condition, but are now quiet private residences rather than flamboyant tourist attractions. For seekers of a peaceful few days, Atlin is a gem.

ORIENTATION AND PRACTICAL INFORMATION

Although Atlin is in BC, the only way to drive there is via the Yukon Territory and the rocky Atlin Road (Hwy. 1), which branches off the Alcan at Jakes Corner, just south of Whitehorse and the turn-off to Carcross. There is no gas on Atlin Rd. between town and the Alcan junction (100km). In Atlin, everything is within walking distance.

Planes: Summit Air Charters (651-7600 in Atlin or 800-661-1944), on 5th St., flies regularly to Juneau, AK (1hr., $155, round-trip $205).

Buses: Atlin Express (651-7617 in Atlin, 867-668-445 in Whitehorse) buses leave from the Atlin Inn on Lake St. M,W, and F at 6:15am for Jakes Corner ($12), Carcross (2hr., $21), and Whitehorse (3hr, $26). Discounts for seniors and children under 12.

Visitor Information: The **Atlin Museum** (651-7522), on Trainor and 3rd St., doubles as the **Tourist Infocentre** and offers info on the town's history and resources. Open June-Sept. daily 10am-6pm; museum $2.50, seniors $2, under 10 $1.

Outdoor Information: The **BC Provincial Government Building** (651-7595), across the street from the museum, sells **fishing permits** and **maps** (around $10).

Bank: Bank of Montreal booth in the BC Provincial Government Building. Open M-F 8:30am-noon and 1-4:30pm.

Laundromat and Public Showers: Caribou Laundromat, on Discovery Ave. Wash $2.25, dry $1.50. Shower $2 per 5min. Open 24hr.

Auto Repair: County Maintenance (651-7527), at Trainor and 3rd St. Open M-F 7am-4:30pm.

Emergency: 911. **Police:** 651-7511. **Fire:** 651-7666. **Ambulance:** 651-7700.

Red Cross clinic (651-7677), on 3rd and Pearl St. Open M-F 9am-5pm.

Post Office: (651-7513), on 1st at Pearl St. Open M,W, and F 10am-12:30pm and 1-3:30pm, Tu and Th 10am-12:30pm and 1-4:30pm. **Postal Code:** V0W 1A0.

Area Code: 250.

ACCOMMODATIONS AND CAMPGROUNDS

Atlin has a plethora of homey, tucked-away B&Bs, nearby camping on Warm Bay Rd., and a refreshing lack of over-sized, over-stuffed hotels. Campers love the spread-out and woodsy **Pine Creek Campground**, 2½km south of town on Warm Bay Rd., for its pit toilets, fire barrels, and the delicious fresh-water spring 1½km farther south on the left ($5, payable at any Atlin business or the museum). Four extremely isolated, primitive, and free campsites with pit toilets are even farther down Warm Bay Rd. **Palmer Lake** (19km) and **Warm Bay** (22km) are both lakeside sites. Easy to miss **Warm Springs** (23km, on the left) is a large grassy area with a lukewarm pool. The nearby meadow streams are warm as a bath and lined with watercress. **Grotto,** near the road's end (26km), is thickly forested and has 2 sites right on the road, with trails meandering back towards more enveloped sites.

Tundra B&B (651-7551). To get there, take Warm Bay Rd. for 2km, then left on Pine Dr., and left again onto Spruce Dr. Features handsome, friendly huskies, and free canoe use. The log cabin rooms are intimate, sprucy-clean, and the most affordable in the area. Singles $50; doubles $60; cash or check only.

Fireweed Inn (651-7729), in town at 2nd and Rant St. The hosts are accommodating, and breakfast is served whenever it's wanted. Singles $60; doubles $70; private bathrooms.

Glacier View Cabins (651-7691), 12km down Warm Bay Rd., is farthest from town, but provides an awe-inspiring view of Llewellyn Glacier. The log huts are more rustic, with showerhouse, propane lighting, and stove. Singles and doubles $65.

FOOD

For groceries, the **Atlin Trading Post** (651-7574), at Discovery Ave. and 2nd St., has the largest selection (open June to mid-Sept. daily 9am-6pm; winter M-Sa 9am-6pm, Su 10am-4pm).

Atlin Inn Restaurant (651-7546), on Lake St. The scenic waterfront property is wasted on this windowless joint. Highway diner connoisseurs can predict this menu: sandwiches, burgers, and fries, with dinner entrees from $9. The patio, open to anyone over 19, makes the food a tad more exciting. In winter bar menu only. Restaurant open daily 7am-9pm; bar open M-Sa 3pm-2am, Su 3pm-midnight.

Pine Tree Restaurant (651-7709), on Discovery at 3rd, does have windows which let you survey the Shell gas pumps. The portions are hearty and service is, like the rest of the town, super-friendly. Open daily 7am-9pm; entrees from $5.

Taku BBQ, on Mill St. at the south end of 1st St., is an exception to the greasy norm, offering fresh salmon dinners ($12.50). Open Tu-Su 11:30am-2pm and 4-8:30pm, depending on salmon availability.

Mountains of Fudge and TLC Coffee House (651-2400), in the Courthouse on 2nd St. between Trainor and Pearl Ave. This hip joint serves espresso ($2), 15 flavors of ice cream ($2), and soup and sandwich combos ($7). The work of a different local artist is showcased each month. Open May-Sept. daily 11am-9pm.

SIGHTS AND OUTDOORS

Besides the museum (see **Practical Information,** above), the **M/V Tarahne** is the only other sizeable man-made tourist attraction. The first gas-powered, propeller-driven boat in the north, the *Tarahne* is now dry-docked across from the Atlin Inn. *(Tour and slideshow M-Th 5:30pm, Sa 10am, Su 4pm. $4, seniors $3, children free.)* The ship also boasts three special events each weekend (June-Aug.), a Friday night BBQ (5-8pm; entrees $12-15), a Sunday brunch (11am-2pm; $19, seniors 10% off, ages 6-12 $9.50, under 6 free), and an acclaimed Saturday evening murder mystery dinner theatre ($50). Call 651-7709 for reservations.

Because Atlin remains unincorporated and largely unvisited, established trails around town are scarce. Lake activity, however, is a different story. Half a dozen **canoe and kayak outfitters** will take visitors out onto the water. Only experienced paddlers should set out on cold and rough **Atlin Lake; Palmer Lake** is a nearby option for a more casual voyage. **Back Country Sports** (651-0048), located in the **Garrett Store** on Pearl St. between 1st and 2nd, specializes in **sea kayak rental,** with transport available. *(Open in summer daily 10am-6pm. Kayaks $35 per day; doubles $50 per day.)* Canoes can be had from **Sidka Tours** (651-7691), at the **Glacier View Cabins** (see **Accommodations,** above) for $25 per day, including transport. Anglers will find themselves in heaven; BC's largest lake supports plenty of lake trout, dolly varden, whitefish, and grayling. Ice fishing on the lake is popular among warm-blooded locals in winter, complementing the standard winter outdoor regimen of **dog sledding, cross-country skiing** and **snowshoeing.**

Old area mining operations took their fill of gold and have left behind a network o endless gravel roads perfect for **mountain biking. Happy Trails** (651-7662) rent: bikes for $27 per day (open June-Aug daily 10am-8pm). The store also features load: of fishing equipment and advice, and a great book of things to do in town. To ge there, take Discovery Rd. east, and turn right onto the pull-out that overlooks **Pin Creek.** From here, bear right onto Spruce Creek Rd. and follow for 4km, then con tinue straight at the fork.

The most established area trail, unsuitable for biking but perfect for a dayhike, i: the 5km (one-way) **Monarch Trail,** which begins 3.7km south on Warm Bay Rd. Thi: relatively strenuous hike begins below tree line, but soon gives way to bald rock face and tundra, which provides a panoramic view of nearby Atlin Lake. Monarch Moun tain summits at 1439m and takes about three hours round-trip. **Atlin Provincial Par** is enormous, untouched, and mostly untouchable. Reachable only by plane or boat the park remains so pristine largely because of its inaccessibility. Venturing into Atlir Park demands considerable outdoor skill, especially because it has no personnel, ser vices, or maintained trails. One third of the park is blanketed with icefields and gla ciers sweeping down from the **Juneau Icefield. Apex Air Charters** (651-0025) run float plane drop-offs (from $200), and also offers **glacier flightseeing** (from $75 pe person per hour). Powerboat shuttles and houseboat rentals are a cheaper way to gain access; try **Norseman Adventures** (651-7535), on the waterfront at the south end of town, or bargain with a boat-owning local. For more info on the park, write o call **BC Parks,** Sheena District Office, Bag 5000, Smithers, BC V0J 2N0 (847-7320).

Alberta

With its gaping prairie, oil-fired economy, and conservative politics, Alberta is the Texas of Canada. Petro-dollars have given birth to gleaming, modern cities on the plains, while the natural landscape swings from the mighty Canadian Rockies down to beautifully desolate badlands.

🖐 HIGHLIGHTS OF ALBERTA

- It's hard to pick highlights in national parks as uniformly beautiful as **Banff** (see below) and **Jasper** (see p. 357), which offer almost every possible outdoor sport. Banff's **Inkpots** (see p. 354) and **Moraine Lake** (see p. 355) astound along with Jasper's **Cavell Meadows** (see p. 361) and **Maligne Lake** (see p. 361).
- Dinosaurs once stomped through the red bluffs of the **Alberta Badlands** (see p. 373), where their petrified remains are now diggable and on display.
- Calgary's annual **Stampede** (see p. 373) is an extreme celebration of rodeo machismo and tourist magnetism.
- **Head-Smashed-In Buffalo Jump** (see p. 375) is far more serious than it sounds.

PRACTICAL INFORMATION

Capital: Edmonton.
Population: 2,774,512. **Area:** 661,185km². **Motto:** *Fortis et Liber* (Strong and Free).
Bird: Great horned owl. **Flower:** Wild rose. **Tree:** Lodgepole pine. **Tartan:** Forest green, wheat gold, sky blue, rose pink, and coal black.
Road Conditions: 800-642-3810.
Time Zone: Mountain (2hr. before Eastern).
Postal Abbreviation: AB.
Sales Tax: None. **Drinking Age:** 18. **Traffic Laws:** Seatbelts required.
Area Code: As of Jan. 25, 1999, Edmonton and Jasper will be 780; Banff and Calgary will be 403.

GETTING AROUND

Alberta's extensive highway system makes travel between major destinations easy. The north-south **Icefields Parkway (Hwy. 93)** runs between Banff and Jasper. The east-west **Yellowhead Highway (Hwy. 16)** connects Edmonton with Jasper, and continues across British Columbia. **Highway 2** runs north-south between Edmonton and Calgary, while the **Trans-Canada Highway (Hwy. 1)** completes the loop, linking Calgary with Banff. **Buses** (Greyhound, Brewster, and Red Arrow) travel all of these routes, VIA Rail **trains** run from Edmonton to Jasper, and Alberta's major **airports** are in Calgary and Edmonton.

▊ Banff National Park

Banff is Canada's best-loved and best-known natural park, with 6641km² (2,564 sq. mi.) of peaks, forests, glaciers, and alpine valleys. Its unrhymable name comes from Banffshire, Scotland, the birthplace of two Canadian Pacific Railway financiers who convinced Canada's first Prime Minister of the region's potential for "large pecuniary advantage," telling him, "since we can't export the scenery, we shall have to import the tourists." Their plan worked with a vengeance, but even streets littered with gift shops, clothing outfitters, and chocolatiers cannot mar Banff's beauty. Transient 20-somethings arrive with mountain bikes, climbing gear, skis, and snowboards, but a trusty pair of hiking boots remains the park's most popular outdoor equipment.

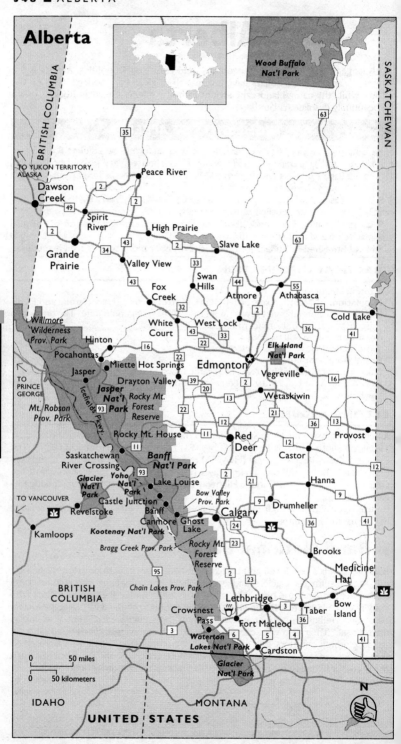

Alberta

Wood Buffalo Nat'l Park

SASKATCHEWAN

BRITISH COLUMBIA

TO YUKON TERRITORY, ALASKA

Dawson Creek

Peace River

Spirit River

Grande Prairie

High Prairie

Slave Lake

Valley View

Fox Creek

Swan Hills

Atmore

Athabasca

Cold Lake

Willmore Wilderness Prov. Park

Hinton

Pocahontas

White Court

West Lock

Elk Island Nat'l Park

TO PRINCE GEORGE

Jasper

Miette Hot Springs

Jasper Nat'l Park

Drayton Valley

Rocky Mt. Forest Reserve

Edmonton

Vegreville

Wetaskiwin

Mt. Robson Prov. Park

Icefields Pkwy.

Rocky Mt. House

Red Deer

Provost

Castor

Saskatchewan River Crossing

Banff Nat'l Park

Glacier Nat'l Park

Yoho Nat'l Park

Lake Louise

Bow Valley Prov. Park

Hanna

TO VANCOUVER

Revelstoke

Castle Junction

Banff

Kootenay Nat'l Park

Cannore

Ghost Lake

Calgary

Drumheller

Kamloops

Bragg Creek Prov. Park

Rocky Mt. Forest Reserve

Brooks

Medicine Hat

BRITISH COLUMBIA

Chain Lakes Prov. Park

Lethbridge

Bow Island

Crowsnest Pass

Waterton Lakes Nat'l Park

Fort Macleod

Taber

Cardston

Glacier Nat'l Park

0 50 miles

0 50 kilometers

IDAHO

MONTANA

UNITED STATES

ALBERTA

N

ORIENTATION AND PRACTICAL INFORMATION

Banff National Park hugs the Alberta side of the Alberta/British Columbia border, 129km west of Calgary. The **Trans-Canada Highway (Hwy. 1)** runs east-west through the park, connecting it to Yoho National Park on the west side. **Icefields Parkway (Hwy. 93)** connects Banff with Jasper National Park to the north and Kootenay National Park to the southwest. Civilization in the park centers around the towns of **Banff** and **Lake Louise**, 58km apart on Hwy. 1. The **Bow Valley Parkway (Hwy. IA)** parallels Hwy. 1 from Lake Louise to 8km west of Banff. All of the following listings apply to Banff Townsite, unless otherwise specified.

Buses: Greyhound, 100 Gopher St. (800-661-8747). 4 per day to: Lake Louise ($10); Calgary ($18); Vancouver, BC ($101). HI discount 15%, student discount 10%. **Brewster Transportation,** 100 Gopher St. (762-6767). Express to: Jasper (1 per day, $51); Lake Louise (3 per day, $11); Calgary (4 per day, $36). Depot open daily 7:30am-9:30pm. HI discount 15%, ages 6-15 half-price.

Public Transportation: The **Happy Bus** runs between the Banff Springs Hotel and the trailer court on Tunnel Mountain Rd., and between the Tunnel Mountain Campground through downtown to the Banff Park Museum. Both routes make several stops along the way. $1, children 50¢. Exact change required to keep the bus happy. Runs in summer 7am-midnight; call for winter hours.

Taxis: Banff Taxi, 726-4444. **Taxi Taxi,** 762-3111. Both run 24hr.

Car Rental: Banff Used Car Rentals (762-3352), in the Shell Station at the junction of Wolf and Lynx. $38 per day; 10¢ per km after 100km. Must be 21 with major credit card. **Budget,** 204 Wolf St. (762-4565). $46 per day; 20¢ per km after 100km. Must be 21 with major credit card.

Visitor Information: Banff Visitor Centre, 224 Banff Ave. Includes **Banff/Lake Louise Tourism Bureau** (762-8421) and **Canadian Parks Service** (762-1550). Open daily June-Sept. 8am-8pm; Oct.-May 9am-5pm. **Lake Louise Visitor Centre** (522-3833), at Samson Mall, is stuffed with friendly staffers. The brand-new $4.4 million complex is also a museum, with exhibits and a short film on the formation of the Rockies. Open daily July-Aug. 8am-8pm; June and Sept. 8am-6pm; Oct.-May 9am-5pm. Both centers dispense detailed maps and brochures, and provide info on hiking, biking, restaurants, activities, and accommodations.

Tours: Without a car, **Brewster Tours** (762-6767) guided bus rides may be the only way to see some of the park's main attractions, such as the Great Divide, the Athabasca Glacier, and the spiral railroad tunnel. Banff to Jasper, with sights (9½hr., $81; round-trip 2 days, $112). Columbia Icefields $23.50 extra. **Bigfoot Tours** (888-244-6673, in Vancouver 604-288-8224) runs two-day, 11-passenger van trips between Vancouver and Banff with interspersed stops at the best sites along the way. The trip to Banff overnights at the Squilax General Store Hostel (see p. 295), the trip to Vancouver stays at the Kamloops Old Courthouse Hostel (see p. 294). The $99 one-way fee does not include food or lodging. Free pick-up at HI departure point (both Vancouver hostels, Lake Louise, Banff International) Mid-Apr. to mid-Nov. 3 per week in each direction.

Equipment Rental: Bactrax Rentals, 337 Banff Ave. (762-8177), in the Ptarmigan Inn. Mountain bikes $7 per hr., $25 per day. Open daily 8am-8pm. **Performance Ski and Sport,** 208 Bear St. (762-8222), rents bikes one-way to Jasper ($79 for 3 days, $102 for 5 days). Tents $12 per day; canoes $10 per hr.; fishing gear $10-20 per day. 10% HI discount. Open daily 9am-8pm.

Laundry and Public Showers: Cascade Coin Laundry, 317 Banff Ave. (762-0165), downstairs in the Cascade Mall. Wash $2, dry 25¢ per 6min. Open daily 8am-11pm. **Lake Louise Laundromat** (522-2143), Samson Mall. Wash $2, dry 25¢ per 7min. Showers $4. Open daily 9am-9pm.

Weather: 762-2088. **Road Conditions:** 762-1450. **Radio:** 101.1FM.

Emergency: Banff Warden Office, 762-4506. **Lake Louise Warden Office,** 522-3866. 24hr. **Ambulance:** 762-2000. **Police:** (762-2226, non-emergency 762-2228), on Railway St. by the train depot. **Lake Louise Police:** 522-3811.

Pharmacy: Harmony Drug, 111 Banff Ave. (762-5711). Open daily 9am-9pm.

Hospital: Mineral Springs, 301 Lynx St. (762-2222), near Wolf St.

ALBERTA

Banff, Yoho & Kootenay National Parks

CAMPGROUNDS

O Castle Mountain
H Chancellor Peak
U Dolly Varden
I Hoodoo Creek
P Johnston Canyon
G Kicking Horse
K Lake Louise
J Lake O'Hara
Q Marble Canyon
V McLeod Meadows
F Monarch
B Mosquito Creek

M Protection Mountain
W Redstreak
D Takakkaw Falls
T Tunnel Mountain,
S Two Jack
A Waterfowl

HOSTELS

R Banff
N Castle Mountain
L Lake Louise
E Mosquito Creek
C Whiskey Jack

Post Office: 204 Buffalo St. (762-2586). Open M-F 9am-5:30pm. **Postal Code:** T0I 0C0.

Internet Access: The Web Cyber Cafe (762-9226), at the lower level of Sundance Mall; entrance across from tourist office on Banff Ave. Call for hours.

Area Code: 403.

ACCOMMODATIONS

Finding a cheap place to stay in Banff is easy if you reserve ahead. Townsite residents offer rooms in their own homes, often at reasonable rates, especially in the off-season. Check the list in the back of the *Banff and Lake Louise Official Visitor Guide*, available free at the Banff Information Centre.

Mammoth **modern hostels** at Banff and Lake Louise anchor a chain of hostels spanning from Calgary to Jasper. The **rustic hostels** provide more of a wilderness experience, and are often a stone's throw away from the best hiking and cross-country skiing in the park. HI-C runs a **shuttle service** connecting all the Rocky Mountain hostels and Calgary ($7-65). Wait-list beds become available at 6pm, and six stand-by beds are saved for shuttle arrivals. For reservations at any rustic hostel, call Banff International (see below). It is never too early to secure a bed at Banff International or Lake Louise, and it is often too late.

Lake Louise International Hostel (HI-C), P.O. Box 115, Lake Louise T0L 1E0 (522-2200; email llouise@hostellingintl.ca), 0.5km west of Samson Mall in Lake Louise Townsite, on Village Rd. Not to be outdone by neighboring Banff, the Lake Louise hostel is ranked third in the world by HI, and rightly so. More like a hotel than a hostel, this budget resort boasts a reference library, common rooms with open, beamed ceilings, a stone fireplace, 2 full kitchens, a sauna, ski/bike workshops, and a cafe. A hub for mountaineering tours and numerous other guided activities. Large rooms with 2, 4, and 6 beds. Sleeps 155: $20, nonmembers $24. Private rooms available for $6 surcharge per person. Wheelchair accessible.

Banff International Hostel (BIH) (HI-C), Box 1358, Banff T0L 0C0 (762-4122; email banff@hostellingintl.ca), 3km from Banff Townsite on Tunnel Mountain Rd., which leads from Otter St. downtown. Take the Happy Bus from downtown, or join the many other hostelers hoofing it. This big hostel has the look and feel of a ski lodge, with 3 lounge areas, 2 large fireplaces, a game room with pool table, a kitchen, cafe, laundry facilities, and hot showers. Ski and snowboard storage area and workshop. Rooms in the luxurious brand-new wing have stone fireplaces and stained glass windows. Sleeps 220: $19, nonmembers $23. Private rooms available. Linen $1.50. Open 24hr. Wheelchair accessible.

◉**Castle Mountain Hostel (HI-C),** on Hwy. 1A, 1½km east of the junction of Hwy. 1 and Hwy. 93 between Banff and Lake Louise. A quieter alternative for those seeking refuge from the hubbub of the Banff and Lake Louise Hostels. With running water and electricity, the hostel's 36 beds fill quickly. Relaxed and beautifully designed common area has a general store, library, and fireplace. $12, nonmembers $16. Linen $1.50. Internet access available.

Mosquito Creek Hostel (HI-C), 103km south of the Icefield Centre and 26km north of Lake Louise. Across Mosquito Creek from the Mosquito Creek campground. Its proximity to Wapta Icefield and its wood-burning sauna make up for the not-so-scenic company. Full-service kitchen, gas, heat, fireplace, and pump water. $12, nonmembers $16. Two private rooms available.

Rampart Creek Hostel (HI-C), 34km south of the Icefield Centre. Close to several world-famous ice climbs (including Weeping Wall, 17km north), this hostel is a favorite for winter mountaineers. Wood-burning sauna, full service kitchen, unlimited mountain spring water (a.k.a. creek). New private rooms available. Sleeps 30 in rustic cabins: $11, nonmembers $15. Open daily May-Sept.; Oct.-Apr. Th-Sa only.

Hilda Creek Hostel (HI-C), 8½km south of the Icefield Centre. Perfectly perched at the base of Mt. Athabasca, and peacefully isolated even from the cars of hostelers. Some of the icefield's best hiking and skiing lie just beyond on Parker Ridge. Sauna, fire pit, full-service kitchen, groceries. Propane heat and light; water at creek. Sleeps 21: $11, nonmembers $15.

CAMPGROUNDS

As with the hostels, a chain of campgrounds connect Banff to Jasper, with large, fully hooked-up grounds as the greatest attractions. For more trees and fewer vehicles, try one of the primitive sites farther from Banff and Lake Louise. At all national park campgrounds, a campfire permit with firewood included costs $3 extra. Sites are first-come, first-served, so show up early. Proximity to sights in the park defines each campground; choose accordingly. The sites below are listed from south to north.

Tunnel Mountain Village, 4km from Banff Townsite on Tunnel Mountain Rd. With three separate areas and over 1000 sites, it takes a village to out-size this campground. The trailer fief has 322 full hookups ($22), Village 2 has 189 sites (power only, $19), Village 1 houses a whopping 622 sites (no hookups, $16). All have showers and flush toilets. Village 2 is open all year; others closed in winter.

Two Jack, 13km northeast of Banff, across the Trans-Canada Hwy. The main grounds ($13) have no showers, while the lakeside grounds ($16) provide showers and proximity to Two Jack Lake. Open mid-May to mid-Sept.

Johnston Canyon, 26km northwest of Banff on Hwy. 1A, with access to several trails. Located on the Bow Valley Pkwy. (Hwy.1A), the scenic route connecting Banff and Lake Louise. Showers. 140 sites: $16. Open mid-June to Aug.

Castle Mountain, midway between Banff and Lake Louise along Hwy. 1A. Forest sites close to relatively uncrowded hiking. No flush toilets or showers. Sites: $13. Open mid-May to early Sept.

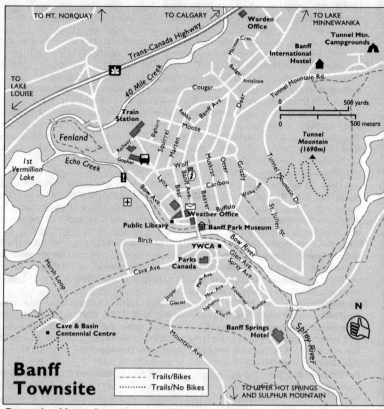

TO MT. NORQUAY ↑
TO CALGARY ↗
Warden Office
TO LAKE MINNEWANKA
Tunnel Mtn. Campgrounds
Banff International Hostel
Trans-Canada Highway
Harmon Cres.
Badger
Antelope
Cougar
TO LAKE LOUISE
40 Mile Creek
Banff Ave.
Deer
Tunnel Mountain Rd.
0   500 yards
0   500 meters
Train Station
Fenland
Bighorn
Squirrel
Rabbit
Moose
Marten
Railway
Gopher
1st Vermillion Lake
Echo Creek
Bow Ave.
Lynx
Wolf
Bear
Banff Ave.
Muskrat
Otter
Caribou
Beaver
Grizzly
Wolverine
Tunnel Mountain Dr.
Tunnel Mountain (1690m)
St. Julien St.
Buffalo
Weather Office
Public Library
Banff Park Museum
Birch
YWCA
Bow River
Glen Ave.
Spray Ave.
Cave Ave.
Parks Canada
Marsh Loop
Park Ave.
Jasper
Glacier
Mtn. Ave.
Nahanni
Kootenay
Klua ne
Rundle
N
Cave & Basin Centennial Centre
Banff Springs Hotel
Mountain Ave.
Spray River

Banff Townsite

- - - - Trails/Bikes
· · · · · Trails/No bikes

TO UPPER HOT SPRINGS AND SULPHUR MOUNTAIN ↓

Protection Mountain, 11km west of Castle Junction on Hwy. 1A. 89 spacious and wooded sites in one of Banff's most primitive campgrounds. Pit toilets, no showers. Sites $13. Open late June to mid-Sept.

Lake Louise, 1½km southeast of Samson Mall on Fairview Rd. Not actually on the lake, but plenty of hiking and fishing awaits near this tent city. Flush toilets, no showers. 189 trailer sites: $18 (electricity only; open year-round). 220 tent sites: $14. (open mid-May to Sept.).

Mosquito Creek, 103km south of the Icefield Centre and 26km north of Lake Louise. 32 sites with immediate hiking access. Dry toilets. Sites $10.

Waterfowl, 57km north of Hwy. 1 on Hwy. 93. 116 sites near the Waterfowl Lakes. Flush toilets but no water. Sites $13. Open mid-June to mid-Sept.

Rampart Creek, 147km north of Banff, 40km south of the Icefield Centre, across the highway from the Rampart Creek hostel. No showers or flush toilets. 50 sites: $10. Open mid-June to Aug.

FOOD

Restaurants in Banff generally tend toward the expensive. Luckily, the Banff and Lake Louise International Hostels serve affordable meals ($3-8). Ample groceries await at **Safeway** (762-5378), at Marten and Elk St., just off Banff Ave. (open daily 8am-11pm; in winter 9am-9pm). Some local bars offer reasonable daily specials.

Jump Start, 206 Buffalo St. (762-0332). This small coffee and sandwich shop delivers a big bang for the buck. All varieties of coffee, ice cream, soups ($3.75), sandwiches ($5), plus a rib-sticking shepherd's pie ($5.50). Open daily 7am-7pm.

ALBERTA

Aardvark's, 304A Caribou St. (762-5500), does big business after the bars close. Skinny on seating, but thick slices of pizza heaped with toppings make this a filling place to eat. Slices $2.75; small $6-8; large $12-19; buffalo wings $5 for 10. HI discount on whole pizzas. Open daily 11am-4am.

Fossil Face Natural Foods Cafe, 215 Banff (760-8219), in the Sundance Mall upper level. A vegetarian, relaxed little cafe cleverly hidden in a corner of a tourist mall. Earthy decor, eclectic bookshelf, and a highly organic menu. Falafel $8; black bean chili $6. Try a vegan chocolate cookie, or else. Open M-Sa 11:30am-6pm.

Laggan's Deli (522-3574), in Samson Mall at Lake Louise. Savor a thick sandwich on whole-wheat bread ($3.75) with a Greek salad ($1.75), or take home a freshly baked loaf ($2) for later. Excellent cappuccino ($2.50). Always crowded; there's nowhere better in Lake Louise Village. Open daily 6am-8pm.

Magpie & Stump, 203 Caribou St. (762-4067), at Bear St. Named after a London pub, this joint wisely shirks English fare in favor of large, spicy Mexican dishes. A dark, all-wood interior, constant mariachi background music, and happy hour (10pm-2am) woo a late-night crowd. Loco-gringo salad $7; quesadillas $6-7; meal-sized nachos $5-7; 15 margarita flavors $4. Veggie dishes galore. Open daily noon-2am.

SIGHTS AND EVENTS

The palatial **Banff Springs Hotel** (762-2211) overlooks town from Spray Ave. Completed in 1888, it was the most ornate of the luxury hotels that the railroad built to seduce tourists. Ride the guest elevator up to the 8th floor to see what those who can afford to stay here see. A Centennial Ale (the house brew), a basket of bread, and a view-of-views cost only $4.55 at the **Rundle Lounge** on the mezzanine. In summer, the hotel leads **guided tours** of the grounds. (*Daily 5pm. $5. Reservations accepted.*) For **horseback riding** reservations, call 762-2848. (*Daily 9am-5pm. $26 for 1hr., $55 for 3hr.*)

The **Whyte Museum of the Canadian Rockies,** 111 Bear St. (762-2291), gives a gander at the human (read: whyte settler) history of the Canadian Rockies. (*Open daily mid-May to mid-Sept. 10am-6pm; mid-Sept. to mid-May Tu-W and F-Su 1-5pm, Th 1-9pm. $4, students and seniors $2, children free.*) Exhibits in the museum's Heritage Gallery explain how Banff grew: very rapidly, unchecked, and indulging the whims of wealthy guests. The **Banff Park Museum** (762-1558), on Banff Ave. near the bridge, is western Canada's oldest museum and a taxidermist's dream, with some specimens from the 1860s. (*Open daily June-Aug. 10am-6pm; Sept.-May 10am-5pm. Tours June-Aug. 11am and 3pm; Sept.-May 3pm. $2.25, seniors $1.75, children $1.25.*) Clippings in the reading room recount in loving detail the violent encounters between elk and automobiles.

In summer, the **Banff Festival of the Arts** (762-6300) takes over. The culture train choo-choos through during June, July, and August with a series of a wide range of artistic performances; stop by the infocenter for a schedule. (*Prices vary $0-25.*)

OUTDOORS

Enough town stuff. A visitor sticking to paved byways will only see 3% of Banff National Park. Those who wish to get more closely acquainted can hike or bike through the wild remainder on more than 1600km of trails. Grab a copy of *Banff and Vicinity Drives and Walks,* and peruse backcountry maps and trail descriptions at infocenters (see **Practical Information,** above). For still more solitude, head to the backcountry. Pick up the *Backcountry Visitor Guide* and an **overnight camping permit** at the visitor centers. (*$6 per person per day, up to $30; $42 per year.*)

Banff Townsite Area

Two easy trails lie within walking distance of Banff Townsite. **Fenland,** closed for elk calving in late spring and early summer, winds 2km through an area shared by beaver, muskrat, and waterfowl. Follow Mt. Norquay Rd. out of town, and look for signs across the tracks on the road's left side. The summit of **Tunnel Mountain** provides a dramatic view of the **Bow Valley** and **Mt. Rundle.** Follow Wolf St. east from Banff Ave., and turn right on St. Julien Rd. to reach the head of the steep 2.3km trail.

Johnston Canyon, about 25km out of Banff toward Lake Louise along the Bow Valley Pkwy. (Hwy. 1A), is a popular half-day hike. A catwalk along the edge of the deep limestone canyon runs 1km over the thundering river to the canyon's lower falls, then another 2.7km to the upper falls. The trail then continues for another, more rugged 3.1km to seven blue-green cold-water springs, known as the **Inkpots,** in an open valley above the canyon. The trail beyond the Inkpots is blissfully untraveled.

Many routes in the Banff area make for stunning drives. **Tunnel Mountain Drive** begins at Banff Ave. and Buffalo St., proceeding 9km past Bow Falls and up the side of Tunnel Mountain. Several markers along the way point out views of the Banff Springs Hotel, Sulphur Mountain, and Mt. Rundle. Turn right onto Tunnel Mountain Rd. for a short walk to the **hoodoos,** long, finger-like limestone projections in front of the cliff face. Park rangers say the hoodoos have escaped erosion because boulders at their tops protect them; Native Canadians believed that they encase sentinel spirits.

Bicycling is permitted on public roads, highways, and certain trails in the park. Spectacular scenery and proximity to a number of hostels and campgrounds make the **Bow Valley Parkway (Hwy. 1A)** and the **Icefields Parkway (Hwy. 93)** perfect for extended cycling trips. Every other store downtown seems to rent bikes; head to **Bactrax** or **Performance Ski and Sport** (see **Practical Information,** above) for HI discounts. Parks Canada publishes *Mountain Biking—Banff,* which describes trails and roadways where bikes are permitted (free at bike rental shops and infocenters).

Banff might not exist if not for the **Cave and Basin Hot Springs,** once rumored to have miraculous healing properties. The **Cave and Basin National Historic Site** (762-1557), a refurbished resort built circa 1914, is now a museum that screens documentaries and stages exhibits. *(Open daily in summer 9am-6pm; in winter 9:30am-5pm. Tours meet at 11am. $2.25, seniors $1.75, children $1.25.)* Follow the **Discovery Trail** from the museum to see the original spring discovered over 100 years ago by three Canadian Pacific Railway workers. Most importantly, five of the pools are the only home of the park's most threatened species: the small but newsworthy **Banff Springs snail.** (Banff's grizzly bear, woodland caribou, and wolverine are classified as vulnerable, one step farther from extinction than the snail.) The springs are southwest of the city on Cave Ave. For an actual dip in the hot water, follow the rotten-egg smell to the **Upper Hot Springs** pool (762-1515), a 40°C (104°F) sulfurous cauldron up the hill on Mountain Ave. *(Open daily 9am-11pm; call for winter hours. $7, seniors and children $6. Swimsuits $1.50, towels $1, lockers 50¢.)* A moderate 5.3km (2hr.) hike wends along a well-trodden trail to the 2285m (7500ft) peak of **Sulphur Mountain,** where a spectacular view awaits; the **Sulphur Mountain Gondola** (762-5438) charges nothing for the

Things that Go Banff in the Night

Bear sightings are common in the Canadian Rockies, but one black bear took it upon himself to give Banff residents an uncommon reminder of whose park it really is. Imaginatively known as Bear 16, this misguided ursine moved into town, disrupting everyday activity by foraging in front lawns and lying in the road, unwittingly blocking traffic. Bear 16 crossed the line when the scent from a bakery lured him too close to human territory. At the behest of petrified bakers, park staff removed Bear 16 from the park, had him castrated, and plunked him down in the Calgary Zoo.

While most travelers to the park are eager to see its wildlife, few want as intimate an encounter as Bear 16 offered, and those who do are stupid. Many hikers wear jingly bear bells to herald their presence, although these devices ("dinner bells") might serve only to arouse a bear's curiosity. While bells may offer psychological security and a twisted form of musical accompaniment, the safest bet is to talk, sing, or yodel loudly while hiking, especially near running water. The number of bear attacks actually ranks low among the total number of attacks by park animals; dozens of visitors are bitten each year by mere rodents pursuing human food. By far the most dangerous of Banff predators, however, are people—road accidents are the most common cause of death for wildlife within the park.

downhill trip. *(Runs daily uphill. $14, ages 5-11 $7, under 5 free.)* The **Panorama Restaurant,** perched atop the mountain, serves breakfast ($8) and lunch buffets ($10) from mid-May to mid-August.

Fishing is legal virtually anywhere there's water, but live bait and lead weights are not. Get a **permit** at the info center. *(7-day permit $6, annual permit valid in all Canadian National Parks $13.)* The 7km trail to **Borgeau Lake** offers hiking and fishing with some solitude, and a particularly feisty breed of brook trout. Closer to the road, try **Herbert Lake,** off the Icefields Pkwy., or **Lake Minnewanka,** on Lake Minnewanka Rd. northeast of Banff, rumored to be the home of a half-human, half-fish Indian spirit. Lake Minnewanka Rd. also passes **Johnson Lake,** where sunlight warms the shallow water to a pleasantly swimmable temperature. Several companies offer **whitewater rafting** trips along the **Kicking Horse River. Western Canadian Whitewater** (762-8256) gives full-day trips. *($65, students with ID $45.)* **Hydra River Guides** (762-4544 or 800-644-8888) also offers daytrips. *($75, HI members $70.)*

Lake Louise and Environs

The highest community in Canada at 1530m (5018 ft.), Lake Louise and its surrounding glaciers often serve North American filmmakers' need for supposedly Swiss scenery, and is the emerald in the Rockies' tiara of tourism. Unlike movie crews, most daytripping visitors spend only enough time at the lake to take a few snapshots. These lakeside hordes are harmless, however, leaving long stretches of mountainous hiking relatively untouched. Once at the lake, the hardest task is escaping fellow gawkers at the posh Chateau Lake Louise. Renting a canoe from the **Chateau Lake Louise Boat House** (522-3511) can help. *(Open daily 10am-8pm. $25 per hr.)* Several hiking trails begin at the water; the 3.6km **Lake Agnes Trail** and the 5.5km **Plain of Six Glaciers Trail** provide especially welcome escape, and both end at teahouses.

Nearby **Moraine Lake** may pack more of a scenic punch than its sister Louise. The lake is 15km from the village, at the end of Moraine Lake Rd., off the Lake Louise access road. Moraine lies in the awesome **Valley of the Ten Peaks,** which cradles glacier-encrusted **Mt. Temple.** Join the multitudes on the **Rockpile Trail** for an eye-popping view of the lake and valley, and an explanation of rocks from ancient ocean bottoms. The **Moraine Lake Lodge** (522-3733) rents **canoes.** *($24 per hr.)* If you don't get a chance to visit Moraine, just get your hands on an old $20 bill; the Valley of Ten Peaks is pictured on the reverse.

Paradise Valley, depending on which way you hike it, can be a relaxing dayhike or an intense overnight trip. From the **Paradise Creek trailhead,** 2.5km up Moraine Lake Rd., the loop through the valley runs 18.1km through subalpine and alpine forests, past cascades, along rivers, and close by glaciers. At 5.7km is **Lake Annette,** a placid glacial lake bordered by enormous rockslides. One classic backpacking route runs from Moraine Lake up and over **Sentinel Pass,** joining the top of the Paradise Valley loop after 8km. A **backcountry campground** marks the approximate midpoint from either trailhead; a **permit** is required to camp there.

Timberline Tours (522-3743), off Lake Louise Dr. near Deer Lodge, offers guided **horseback rides** through the area. *(1½hr. tour $28; 3hr. $40.)* **Brewster Lake Louise Stables,** affiliated with Chateau Lake Louise (522-3511 ext. 1210, in Banff 762-5454), gives hourly rides ($20), rides to Lake Louise ($30), and half-day rides ($45-50). The **Lake Louise Sightseeing Lift** (522-3555), across the Trans-Canada Hwy. from Lake Louise, runs up **Mt. Whitehorn,** providing yet another chance to gape at the landscape. *(Runs early June 9am-6pm; mid-June to mid-Sept. 9am-9pm; late Sept. 9am-6pm; closes Oct.-May. $9.50, students and seniors $8.50, ages 6-15 $6.50, under 5 free.)* An early morning ride ends with a $10.50 breakfast (includes lift ticket) at the peak-top cafe.

Winter Sports

Wintery Banff offers more than curling: snow sports range from ice climbing to dogsledding to ice fishing. Those 1600km of summer hiking trails also provide exceptional **cross-country skiing.** Three allied resorts fulfill the downhiller's need for speed. **Sunshine Mountain** (762-6500, 24hr. snowphone 760-SNOW/7669) spreads across three mountains, and with an average snowfall of 989cm (33ft.), does not manufacture any of its snow. **Mount Norquay** (762-4421) is smaller, closer to town, and less manic, with a snowboard park and night skiing. **Lake Louise** (522-3555, snowphone from Banff 762-4766) is the largest ski area in Canada (4200 skiable acres), with amazing views and the best selection of expert (double-black diamond) terrain, though simpler slopes cover plenty of the mountain. Shuttles to all three resorts leave from most big hotels in the townsites. Multi-day passes, good for all three resorts, are available at the **Ski Banff/Lake Louise** office, 225 Banff Ave. (762-4561; email info@skibanfflakelouise.com), lower level, and at all resorts. *($50.50 per day; 3 day minimum)* Passes include free shuttle service and an extra night of skiing at Mount Norquay. **Performance Ski and Sports,** 208 Bear St. (762-8222), rents downhill ski, boot, and pole packages ($17 per day, $45 for 3 days), cross-country packages ($12, $31), snowboard packages ($28, $74), telemarking skis and boots ($18, $47), and snowshoes ($10, $26).

NIGHTLIFE

Bartenders maintain that Banff's true wildlife is in its bars. Check the paper to find out which nightspots are having "locals' night," when bar-hoppers flock to cheap drinks.

Rose and Crown, 202 Banff Ave. (762-2121), upstairs. The upbeat centerpiece of Banff nightlife. Even on busy nights, the Rose's many rooms give elbow room for drinking, dancing, and pool-playing. Throw back a few in the couch-adorned living room while cooing to nearly nightly live music. Happy hour (M-F 4:30-7:30pm) heralds $3-3.50 drafts. Open daily 11am-2am.

Barbary Coast, 119 Banff Ave. (762-4616), upstairs. Sports paraphernalia festoons this snazzy bar. The kitchen is excellent, with especially tasty pasta dishes. Lunch specials $6-7. Monday is pizza night (10 in. pie $7). Almost nightly live blues and rock. Happy hour 4:30-7:30pm. No cover. Open daily 11am-2am.

Outa Bounds, 137 Banff Ave. (762-8434), lower level. Black-lit stairs descend to a raging room decked out with two bars, three pool tables ($1.25), a dance floor, and plenty of seating. Arrive early on weekends and special nights (locals' W, ladies' Th) to avoid lines. Open daily 8pm-2:30am.

■ Icefields Parkway (Hwy. 93)

Begun in the 30s as a Depression relief-work project, the 230km Icefields Parkway is one of the most beautiful routes in North America, heading north from Lake Louise in Banff National Park to Jasper Townsite in Jasper National Park. Drivers may struggle to keep their eyes on the road, as it dips above and below treeline, skirted by dozens of stern peaks and glacial lakes.

PRACTICAL INFORMATION Parks Canada manages the parkway as a scenic route, so all users must obtain a **Park Pass,** available at entrance gates and park information centers ($5 per day, $35 per year; includes all Canadian national parks). Free maps of the Icefields Parkway are available at park info centers in Jasper and Banff, or at the **Icefield Centre** (852-6560), at the boundary between the two parks, 127km north of Lake Louise and 103km south of Jasper Townsite (open daily mid-June to Aug. 9am-6pm; mid-May to mid-June and Sept. 9am-5pm). Although the center is closed in winter, the parkway is only closed after heavy snowfalls for plowing.

Thanks to the extensive campground and hostel networks that line the parkway, trips down the entire length of Jasper and Banff National Parks are convenient and affordable (see **Accommodations** and **Campgrounds** for each park). Most sightseers cruise along the parkway in motor vehicles. Those choose to cycle should be prepared for anything; weather conditions change quite rapidly. Bicycles can be rented in Banff or Jasper for a one-way trip. Whether on four wheels or two, set aside some time for the parkway, its challenging hikes, and its endless vistas.

OUTDOORS The Icefields Parkway has 18 trails into the wilderness, and 22 scenic points for spectacular views. At **Bow Summit,** 40km north of Lake Louise, one of the parkway's highest points (700m, 2135 ft.), a 10-minute walk leads to a view of fluorescent aqua **Peyto Lake,** especially vivid toward the end of June. The Icefield Centre (see above) lies in the shadow of the tongue of the **Athabasca Glacier.** This great white whale of an ice flow is one of the eight major glaciers that flow from the 325km² **Columbia Icefield,** the largest accumulation of ice and snow south of the Arctic Circle. The icefield's runoff eventually flows to three oceans: Pacific, Atlantic, and Arctic. Summer crowds have snowball fights on the vast icefields that flood the sides of the road. **Columbia Icefield Snocoach Tours** (in Banff 762-6735, in Jasper 852-3332), part of Brewster Transportation, carries visitors right onto the Athabasca Glacier in bizarre monster buses for a 75-minute trip. *(May-Sept. daily 9am-5pm; Oct. daily 10am-4pm. $23.50, ages 6-15 $5.)* A half-hour walk leads up piles of glacial debris to the glacier's mighty toe, where deep crevasses make it unsafe to walk farther. Dated signposts mark the glacier's speedy retreat up the valley over the last two centuries. At the top of the trail, rows of parallel scratches in the exposed bedrock show that this meltback is more than a receding hairline—the scrapes were made by massive boulders dragged beneath the ice. For more tasty geological tidbits, sign up for a guided **Athabasca Glacier Icewalk.** *("Ice Cubed" tour 3hr. $28, ages 7-17 $12. "Ice Walk Deluxe" tour 5hr. $32, ages 7-17 $14.)* One of the two hikes runs each day (mid-June to mid-Sept.); for info and booking, contact the Icefield Centre or Peter Lemieux, 371042 Ave., Red Deer, AB Canada, T4N 2Z4 (email iceman1@agt.net). The **Parker Ridge Trail** leads 2.4km away from the road, past treeline, and over **Parker Ridge;** an astounding view of the **Saskatchewan Glacier** awaits at the end. The trailhead is 1km south of the Hilda Creek Hostel (see p. 351), 8.5km south of the Icefield Centre.

■ Jasper National Park

Northward expansion of the Canadian railway system led to the discovery and 1907 creation of Jasper National Park. The largest of the four Canadian Rocky Mountains parks, Jasper's herculean peaks and plummeting valleys dwarf the battalion of motorhomes and charter buses parading through the region. Before the Icefields Parkway was built, few travelers dared venture north from Banff National Park into the wilderness of Jasper. Those bold bushwhackers who did brave this bit of the Rockies returned with stunning reports, and the subsequent completion of the parkway in 1940 paved the way for the masses to appreciate Jasper's astounding beauty. Because 40% of the park is above treeline, most visitors stay in the sheltered vicinity of Jasper Townsite, and every summer the town's winter population of 5000 balloons to over 20,000. In the face of this annual bloat, Jasper's permanent residents struggle to keep their home looking and feeling like a genuine small town. In the winter, the crowds melt away, a blanket of snow descends, and a ski resort welcomes visitors to a slower, more relaxed town. Jasper needs little touristification; the park's heavenly peaks and sweeping vistas do all the work.

ORIENTATION AND PRACTICAL INFORMATION

All of the addresses below are in **Jasper Townsite,** near the center of the park. **Highway 16** runs through the northern reaches of the park, while the **Icefields Parkway (Hwy. 93)** connects with Banff National Park in the south. Buses run daily to the townsite from Edmonton, Calgary, Vancouver, and Banff; trains arrive from Edmonton and Vancouver. Many bike shops rent one-way between the two parks. Hitching is both easy and popular along the Icefields Pkwy. *(Let's Go would never even think of recommending hitchhiking.)*

Trains: VIA Rail (852-4102 or 800-561-8630). Station on Connaught Dr. 3 per week to: Vancouver, BC (16½hr., $156); Edmonton ($91); Winnipeg, MB ($249). Student and senior discount 10%, children 50%. Winter discount 40% for 7-day advance booking, otherwise 25%. Coin-operated lockers $1 per 24hr.

ALBERTA

Buses: Greyhound (852-3926), in the train station. To: Edmonton (4½hr., 4 per day, $50); Kamloops, BC (5hr., 3 per day, $49); Vancouver, BC (11½hr., 3 per day, $91). HI discount 15%, student discount 10%. **Brewster Transportation Tours** (852-3332), in the train station. Daily to: Banff ($51); Calgary ($71). HI discount 15%, ages 6-15 half-price.

Taxis: Heritage Cabs, 611 Patricia (852-5558). **Jasper Taxi** (852-3146). From town, both offer a flat rate of $10 to Jasper International Hostel, $15-16 to the Maligne Canyon Hostel. Both 24hr.

Car Rental: Hertz (852-3888), in the train station. $55 per day; 21¢ per km after 100km. Must be 21 with credit card. Closed in winter. **Tilden** (852-4972), in the train station. $58 per day (in winter $46), 23¢ per km after 100km. Must be 21 with credit card. $500 insurance deductible for drivers under 25.

Car Repair: Petro Canada, 300 Connaught Dr. (852-3366).

Visitor Information: Park Information Centre, 500 Connaught Dr. (852-6176), has trail maps. Open daily mid-June to early Sept. 8am-7pm; early Sept. to late Oct. and late Dec. to mid-June 9am-5pm. For more info, contact **Park Headquarters,** Superintendent, Jasper National Park, 632 Patricia St., Box 10 (852-6220).

Bank: CIBC, 416 Connaught Ave., by the infocenter (852-3391). Open M-Th 10am-3pm, F 10am-5pm. 24hr. **ATM.**

Equipment Rental: Freewheel Cycle, 618 Patricia Ave. (852-3898). Mountain bikes $6 per hr., $18 per day, $24 overnight. Open in summer daily 9am-8pm; spring and fall 9am-6pm; call for winter hours and snowboard rentals. **Jasper International Hostel** (see **Accommodations,** below) also rents mountain bikes. $3 per hr., $9.50-12.50 per half-day, $15-20 per day.

Laundry and Public Showers: Coin Clean, 607 Patricia St. (852-3852). Wash $1.50, dry 25¢ per 5min. Showers $2 per 10min. Open daily 8am-9:30pm.

Weather: 852-3185. **Road Conditions:** 762-1450. **Radio:** 101.1FM.

Emergency: 852-4848. **Police:** 600 Pyramid Lake Rd. (852-4421). **Ambulance and Fire:** 852-3100.

Women's Crisis Line: 800-661-0937. 24hr. **AIDS Services: AIDS Society Jasper,** 852-5274.

Pharmacy: Whistlers Drugs, 100 Miette Ave. (852-4411). Open daily 8am-10pm; early Sept. to mid-June 9am-9pm.

Hospital: 518 Robson St. (852-3344).

Post Office: 502 Patricia St. (852-3041), across from the townsite green. Open M-F 9am-5pm. **Postal Code:** T0E 1E0.

Internet Access: Soft Rock Cafe (see **Food,** below). $5.50 for 30min., $8.50 per hr.

Area Code: 780.

ACCOMMODATIONS

The modern Jasper International Hostel, just outside of Jasper Townsite, anchors a chain of hostels that stretches from Jasper to Calgary. The rustic hostels farther into the park offer few amenities, but lie amid some of Jasper's finest outdoor activities. HI-C runs a shuttle service connecting all the Rocky Mountain hostels and Calgary, with rates depending on distance ($7-65). For reservations and info on the Rocky Mountain hostels, call Jasper International Hostel. Reservations are necessary for most hostels in summer. Wait-list beds become available at 6pm. In winter, Jasper International and Maligne Canyon hostels run normally; for the other rustic hostels, visitors must pick up a key at Jasper International and leave a $50 deposit. For couples or groups, a B&B may prove more economical than a hostel (doubles in summer $40-75, in winter $30-55). Most are in town near the train station. Ask for the **Private Homes Accommodations List** at the park information center or the bus depot.

Jasper International Hostel (HI-C) (852-3215), on Sky Tram Rd., 5km south of the townsite off Hwy. 93. Also known as **Whistlers Hostel,** just to confuse you. The only hostel in Jasper with both running water (showers) and electricity, Jasper International is often chock-full of gregarious backpackers and cyclists. A "leave-your-hiking-boots-outside" rule keeps the hardwood floors and spiffy dorm rooms next to godliness. Marmots frequent the volleyball court. Sleeps 82 in 2 dorms and

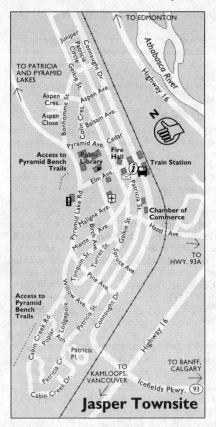

Jasper Townsite

Map labels:
TO EDMONTON
Athabasca River
Highway 16
Juniper
Patricia Circle
Connaught Dr.
Geikie St.
TO PATRICIA AND PYRAMID LAKES
Aspen Cres.
Aspen Close
Aspen Ave.
Colin Cres.
Bonhomme St.
Balsam Ave.
Pyramid Ave.
Cedar
Access to Pyramid Bench Trails
Public Library
Fire Hall
Elm Ave.
Train Station
Pyramid Lake Rd.
Maligne Ave.
Birch Ave.
Miette Ave.
Turret St.
Tonquin St.
Pine Ave.
Spruce Ave.
Geikie St.
Patricia St.
Chamber of Commerce
Hazel Ave.
TO HWY. 93A
Access to Pyramid Bench Trails
Cabin Creek Rd.
Willow Ave.
Lodgepole Ave.
Poplar
Ash
Patricia St.
Connaught Dr.
Patricia Cr.
Patricia Pl.
Highway 16
TO KAMLOOPS, VANCOUVER
Cabin Creek Dr.
Icefields Pkwy. (93)
TO BANFF, CALGARY

3 private rooms. $15, nonmembers $20. Midnight curfew. This is the closest hostel to the townsite, but still a 7km walk. **Sun Dog Shuttle** (852-4056) runs from the train station to the hostel on its way to the Jasper Tramway ($4).

Maligne Canyon Hostel (HI-C), 15km east of the townsite on Maligne Canyon Rd. Small, recently renovated cabins sit on the bank of the Maligne River, with access to the Skyline Trail and within cycling distance of Maligne Lake. They just got electricity and a potable water tank, making winter life far easier. Volker, the manager, is on a first-name basis with several local bears. 24 beds: $10, nonmembers $15; in winter $9, nonmembers $14. Closed W Oct.-Apr. Fills up quickly; book in advance.

Mt. Edith Cavell Hostel (HI-C), on Edith Cavell Rd., off Hwy. 93A. 32 beds in small but cozy quarters, heated by wood-burning stoves. Propane light, pump water (boil or treat before drinking), solar shower, firepit. A postcard view of Mt. Edith Cavell from the front yard, with easy access to the mountain. The road is closed in winter, but the hostel welcomes anyone willing to pick up the keys at Jasper International Hostel (see above) and ski 13km uphill from Hwy. 93A. $10, nonmembers $15; in winter $9, nonmembers $10.

Athabasca Falls Hostel (HI-C) (852-5959), on Hwy. 93, 32km south of the townsite. The dining room has electricity, but the only running water around is at Athabasca Falls, a 500m stroll away. Propane heating and lighting. 44 beds: $10, nonmembers $15; in winter $9, nonmembers $14.

Beauty Creek Hostel (HI-C) (852-3215) on Hwy. 93, 87km south of the townsite. On the banks of the glacier-fed Sunwapta River and close to the Columbia Icefields, the hostel has natural beauty to spare. Hike the 3.2km Stanley Falls Trail or borrow the canoe for a paddle down the river. Some of the best rustic washroom facilities in the Rockies, with poetry on the outhouse walls and views of the whole valley from the outdoor solar shower. 24 beds: $10, nonmembers $15; in winter $9, nonmembers $14. Reservations advised; bicycle touring groups often clog the beds.

CAMPGROUNDS

The grounds below are listed from north to south. Most are primitive sites with few facilities, but outdoor paradise nearby. They are first-come, first-served, so get there early or sleep in the trees. For details, call the park information center (852-6176). To build a fire, add $3 to campsite fees.

Pocahontas, on Hwy. 16, at the northern edge of the park, 46km northeast of the townsite. Closest campground to Miette Hot Springs (see p. 362). Flush toilets, hot

ALBERTA

running water. Hookups available. 140 sites (10 walk-in tent sites): $13. Open mid-May to mid-Oct. Wheelchair accessible.

Snaring River, 16km north of the townsite on Hwy. 16. Kitchen shelters, dry toilets, and splendid views snare passersby. Surrender to Nature's Soundtrack as the river does its impression of a New Age relaxation tape. 56 sites (10 walk-in tent sites): $10. Open mid-May to early Sept.

Whistlers, on Whistlers Rd., 3km south of the townsite off Hwy. 93. The closest campground to Jasper Townsite and the only one with full hookups. Public phones. 781 sites: tents $15; full hookups $22. Showers $1. Open early May to mid-Oct. Wheelchair accessible.

Wapiti, on Hwy. 93, 2km south of Whistlers, along the Athabasca River. With 40 electrical hookups, Wapiti is an unofficial RV HQ. Plentiful brush separates tenters from their large-scale brethren. 366 sites: $15, with electricity $18. Hot showers $1. Public phone. Open Victoria Day to early Sept. Wheelchair accessible.

Wabasso, on Hwy. 93A, about 17km south of the townsite. Flush toilets, showers, trailer sewage disposal. 238 sites (6 walk-in tent sites): $13. Open Victoria Day to early Sept. Wheelchair accessible.

There are five campgrounds along the Jasper section of the Icefields Parkway (see p. 356), with fairly comparable facilities (kitchen shelters, dry toilets) and a completely comparable price (late May to early Oct. $10). **Mount Kerkeslin,** 35km south of Jasper Townsite, has 42 sites on the banks of the Athabasca River. **Honeymoon Lake,** with 35 sites about 51km south of town, has a swimming area and proximity to Sunwapta Falls (its own swim-here-and-risk-death area). **Jonas Creek,** 77km south of the townsite, has only 25 sites along the Sunwapta River, including 12 secluded walk-in sites up the hill. The highlight of the Parkway campgrounds is **Columbia Icefield,** 109km south of the townsite, which lies close enough to the Athabasca Glacier to intercept an icy breeze and even a rare summer night's snowfall. A difficult and steep access road makes its 33 sites (7 walk-ins) RV-free, but crowded nonetheless. **Wilcox Creek** is 2km farther down the highway, at the southern park boundary (46 sites).

FOOD

Eating cheaply in Jasper is easy, if you stick to appetizers. **Super A Foods,** 601 Patricia St. (852-3200), satisfies basic grocery needs at a central location (open M-Sa 8am-11pm, Su 9am-10pm). The bakery at **Robinson's IGA Foodliner,** 218 Connaught Dr. (852-3195), makes the extra 10-minute walk worth it (open daily 8am-10pm). **Nutter's,** 622 Patricia St. (852-5844), offers canned goods, deli meats, and bulk snacks, plus a deli and sandwich bar (open daily 9am-11pm).

🌀**Mountain Foods and Cafe,** 606 Connaught Dr. (852-4050). Offers a wide selection of sandwiches, salads, and home-cooked goodies amid rock-climbing photos and a mounted mountain bike. Take-out lunches for the trail. Grilled foccacia sandwich $6; wraps and burgers $6. Cheap beer after 5pm. Open daily 7am-midnight.

Jasper Pizza Place, 402 Connaught Dr. (852-3225). A bustling pie shop specializing in large wood-oven pizzas ($9-$13), cheap burgers, and sandwiches ($2.50-6). With a handful of pool tables and a healthy supply of liquor, the restaurant turns bar-ish toward the end of the evening. Free delivery on orders over $5. 10% HI discount. Open daily 11am-midnight.

Scoops and Loops, 504 Patricia St. (852-4333). This is no ordinary ice cream parlor, serving sandwiches ($3.50-4.50), pastries ($1.50), sushi ($3-6), and *udon* noodles ($8). Open M-Sa 10am-11pm, Su 11am-10pm.

Soft Rock Cafe, 622 Connaught Dr. (852-5850). Light and tasty meals at one of the least pretentious cafes in town. Baguette sandwiches $5-6. Breakfast served all day: omelettes $7; Belgian waffles with fresh fruit $6. The music is not nearly as bad as the cafe's name might indicate. Internet access. Open daily 7am-10:30pm.

For those seeking higher altitudes without blowing out lungs and quadriceps, the **Jasper Tramway** (852-3093), on Whistlers Mountain Rd. 2km from town, climbs 2km up Whistlers Mountain, leading to a panoramic view of the park and, on a clear day, very far beyond. *(Open Apr.-Aug. daily 8:30am-10pm, Sept.-Oct. 9:30am-4:30pm. $15, under 14 $8.50, under 5 free.)* To save pennies, burn calories, and feel accomplished, hike the steep 7km **Whistlers Trail,** beginning near the Jasper International Hostel (see **Accommodations,** above). Bring sunglasses and a warm jacket; weather conditions change rapidly at the 2466m summit. The restaurant up top allows hikers to experience the dizzying combination of alcohol and high-altitude oxygen deprivation.

Maligne Lake (muh-LEEN), the longest (22km) and deepest (97km) lake in the park, sprawls 48km southeast of the townsite at the end of Maligne Lake Rd. Deep waters and fine rock particles reflect light to create a brilliant turquoise hue on the lake's surface. A veritable flotilla of various water vessels allow escape from the throngs and the plastic geraniums of Maligne Lake Lodge. **Maligne Tours,** 626 Connaught Dr. (852-3370), rents kayaks (doubles $15 per hr.; 2hr. minimum) and leads fishing, canoeing, rabbeting ($10 per hr.), horseback riding ($55 per 3hr.), hiking ($10 per hr.), whitewater rafting ($55 per 2hr.), and—whew!—narrated scenic cruises (90min.; $31, seniors $27.50, children $15.50). Several trails permeate the area, and free maps are available at the Maligne Tours office or by the lake. The **Opal Hills Trail** (8.2km loop) winds through subalpine meadows and ascends 460m to views of the lake. Farther north in the valley and 30km east of the townsite, the **Maligne River** flows into **Medicine Lake,** but no river flows out. The water escapes underground through tunnels in the porous limestone, re-emerging 16km downstream in the **Maligne Canyon,** 11km east of the townsite on Maligne Canyon Rd. (This is the longest known underground river in North America. Sneaky, eh?) **Shuttle service** is available from Maligne Tours. *(To Maligne Canyon $8. To Maligne Lake one-way $12. To Maligne Lake round-trip with cruise $51. Wheelchair accessible.)*

Named after an English nurse executed by the Germans for providing aid to the Allies during World War I, snow-capped **Mt. Edith Cavell** provides stupendous scenery for half-day hiking. To reach Edith, go 30km south of the townsite, from Hwy. 93 to 93A to the end of the bumpy, 14.5km Mt. Edith Cavell Rd. (open June-Oct.), where **Angel Glacier,** slowly melting and heaving apart, hangs off Edith's north face. Take the 1.6km **Path of the Glacier** loop to the summit, following in the wake of a glacier that has receded in the last few centuries, or hike up through **Cavell Meadows.** The 9km (3-5hr.) meadows loop ascends past treeline, with striking views of Edith's towering north face, and wildflower carpets from mid-July through August. Several lakes in the region supply a bounty of swimming holes. Locals are known to leap off the cliffs into **Horseshoe Lake.**

A Mountie Always Gets His Man

Think of the Canadian Rocky Mountains, and one must also think of the Royal Canadian Mounted Police (RCMP). Known as one of the best police forces in the world, the Mounties have a reputation for honesty, integrity, and boldness. Originally named the Northwest Mounted Police, the force began in 1873 when 293 men from all parts of the world were brought together to regulate the whisky trade in Canada's West and to combat an influx of Sioux Indians from Montana. Today, the RCMP are Canada's national police force, fully equipped with all the latest bad-guy-fighting technology. Most Mounties have dismounted, but some can still be seen on horseback around the towns of Banff and Jasper, resplendent in their famous stetsons and scarlet tunics. They are proud of their heritage—so proud that a Mountie was stationed in Hollywood to ensure that actors portraying the Mounties in the movies sport the correct uniform and haircut. To learn more about the RCMP, browse through the books in **Sgt. Preston's Outpost** (762-5335), 208 Caribou St., in Banff Townsite.

ALBERTA

OUTDOORS

Sekani Mountain Tours (852-5337, reservations 852-5211) leads day-long whitewater rafting runs on the **Rearguard River,** and trips for experienced rafters on the **Canoe River.** *(Rafting $75. Canoe $100. 10% HI discount. Lunch included.)* **Whitewater Rafting (Jasper) Ltd.** (852-7238) leads trips on the **Athabasca** and **Maligne Rivers.** *(2-3hr.; from $40, under 12 half-price.)* Register by phone, or stop at the townsite car wash on Hazel St., in the industrial park across the railroad tracks from Connaught Dr. **Rocky Mountain River Guides,** 600 Patricia St. (852-3777), in On-Line Sport and Tackle, offers a calmer Mile 5 ride. ($35.) **Boat rental** is available at **Pyramid Lake** (852-3536), 7km from town off Pyramid Ave. from Connaught Dr. *(Open daily 8am-dusk. Canoes, rowboats, kayaks, and pedal boats $10 for 1hr., $7 per each additional hr., $25 per day. 12-person pontoon boat $60 per hr. $20 deposit and valid ID required.)*

The **Miette Hot Springs** building (866-3939), north of the townsite off Hwy. 16 along the well-marked, 15km Miette Hotsprings Rd., contains lockers and three pools, one of which is wheelchair accessible. *(Open daily May 15-June 20 10:30am-9pm; June 21-Sept. 2 8:30am-10:30pm; Sept. 3-Oct. 14 10:30am-9pm. $4, children $3.50. Day passes $7.25, children $6.50. Swimsuit rental $1.25, towels $1, lockers 25¢.)* Spring water is pumped from its smelly source through a series of pipes to arrive, miraculously scentless and chlorinated, at the pools. The 40°C (104°F) water is off-limits in winter.

The key to finding a secluded **fishing hole** at Jasper is to hike somewhere inaccessible by car. **Currie's** (852-5650), in The Sports Shop, 414 Connaught Dr., rents equipment and gives tips on good spots. *(Rod, reel, and line $10. 1-day boat or canoe rental $25, after 2pm $18, after 6pm $12. Pick-up and drop-off service available.)* **Permits** are available at fishing shops and the Parks Canada information center. *($6 per week, $13 per year.)*

With so much vertical variance, climbers clamber to get to Jasper. The **Jasper Climbing School,** 806 Connaught Dr. (852-3964), offers an introductory three-hour rappeling class for bouncing down the imposing cliffs that surround the townsite; at least a small group is required. *($30. Learning how to climb up is more expensive.)* Peter Amann, Box 1495 (852-3237; email pamann@incentre.net) teaches two-day introductory **rock climbing classes.** *(May, June, Sept. $150.)* Ben Gadd (852-4012), author of the excellent *Handbook of the Canadian Rockies,* leads **tours** to the **Cadomin Caves.** *($25 per person for groups of 10-20.)* Because these caves are outside the park, a permit is not required.

Winter brings plenty of downhill opportunity to the ski slopes of **Marmot Basin** (852-3816), near Jasper Townsite. *(Full-day lift ticket $39, seniors $28, youth $33, children $17.)* Bargain **ski rental** is available at **Totem's Ski Shop,** 408 Connaught Dr. (852-3078). *(Open daily 9:30am-10:30pm. Full rental package of skis, boots, and poles $9 per day. Higher-quality packages $12.50 and $20.)* **The Sports Shop** (852-3654), four doors down on 414 Connaught Dr., offers the same ski prices, plus other equipment. *(Open daily 9am-10:30pm; in winter 8am-6pm. Snowboard and boots $25. Ice skates $4 per hr., $12 per day.)* Maligne Lake offers **cross-country ski trails** from late November through May.

THE BACKCOUNTRY

Whether by bike, boat, or foot, those who venture farther into the park—if only for a day—can escape crowds and fancy themselves early explorers or fur-traders. An extensive network of trails weaves through Jasper, with many paths originating at the townsite. The trails cover three different ecological regions. The **montane zone** blankets valley floors with lodgepole pine, Douglas fir, white spruce, and aspen, and hosts elk, bighorn sheep, coyotes, and pavement-loving humans. These areas only make up about 10% of the Canadian Rockies; going higher than the townsites catapults hikers into less peopled terrain. Sub-alpine fir and Engelmann spruce share the **sub-alpine zone** with porcupines and marmots, while fragile plants and wildflowers struggle against mountain goats and pikas in the uppermost **alpine zone.** To avoid trampling endangered plant species, hikers should not stray from trails in the alpine area.

Kick off any foray into the wilderness with a visit to the information center in the townsite (see **Practical Information,** above). Experts distribute free copies of *Day*

Hikes in Jasper National Park, and can give directions to appropriate hiking and biking trails. Overnight hikers should snatch up a copy of *The Canadian Rockies Trail Guide,* by Brian Patton and Bart Robinson, also available at the info center ($15). Before hitting the trail, ask about road and trail closures, water levels (some rivers are impossible to cross at certain times of the year), and snow levels at high passes. The Icefield Centre (see p. 356), on Hwy. 93 at the southern entrance to the park, provides similar services.

■ Edmonton

When western Alberta's glitz and glamour were distributed, Edmonton was last in line. Banff and Jasper won the spectacular scenery, Calgary got the Stampede, and Edmonton became the proud parent of...the provincial capital. But with a plethora of museums and a river valley beckoning to hikers and bikers, the city is rising in rank among Albertan travel destinations. The storied Oilers have made the trek to Edmonton a minor pilgrimage for hockey fans, while a perpetual stream of music, art, and performance festivals draws summer crowds. Add to this potion the largest mall in the world, and Edmonton transforms into a pleasant urban oasis near the almost overpowering splendor of the neighboring Rockies.

ORIENTATION AND PRACTICAL INFORMATION

Although Edmonton is the northernmost major city in Canada, it's in the southern half of Alberta. The city lies 294km north of Calgary, an easy but tedious three-hour drive on the **Calgary Trail (Hwy. 2).** Jasper is 362km to the west, a four-hour drive on Hwy. 16. The Greyhound and VIA Rail stations are downtown. The **airport** sits 29km south of town, an expensive cab fare away. The **Sky Shuttle Airport Service** (465-8545 or 888-438-2342) runs a shuttle downtown, to the university, or to the West Edmonton Mall for $11 ($18 round-trip). Cheapskates have been known to hop on an airport shuttle bus taking travelers to downtown hotels.

Edmonton's **streets** run north-south, and **avenues** run east-west. Street numbers increase to the west, and avenues increase to the north. The first three digits of an address indicate the nearest cross street: 10141 88 Ave. is on 88 Ave. near 101 St. **City center** is quite off-center at 105 St. and 101 Ave.

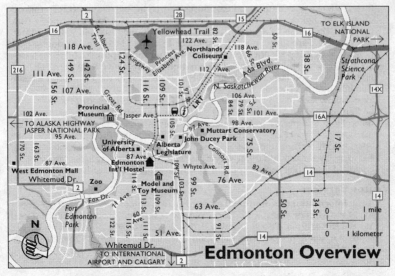

Edmonton Overview

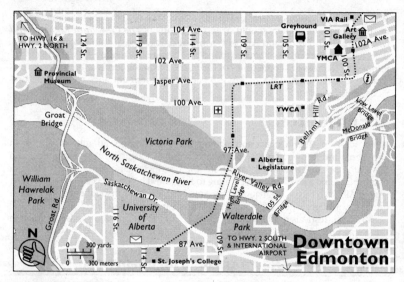

Downtown Edmonton

Transportation

Trains: VIA Rail, 10004 104 Ave. (info 422-6032 or 800-835-3037, reservations 800-561-8630), in the CN Tower with the huge red letters. 3 per week to: Jasper (5hr., $91); Vancouver, BC (23hr., $218). No train service to Calgary.

Buses: Greyhound, 10324 103 St. (420-2412). To: Calgary (nearly every hr. 8am-8pm, plus a milk run at midnight; $38); Jasper (5hr., 4 per day, $49); Vancouver, BC (14-16hr., 3 per day, $119); Yellowknife, NWT (22hr., 1 per day M-F, in winter 3 per week, $185). Open daily 5:30am-midnight. Locker storage $2 per 24hr. **Red Arrow,** 10010 104 St. (800-232-1958), at the Howard Johnson Hotel. To: Calgary (5 per day, $39); Fort McMurray (2 per day, $47). 10% discount with hosteling card. Open M-F 7:30am-8pm, Sa 8am-8pm. The Edmonton International Youth Hostel (see **Accommodations,** below) also sells tickets.

Public Transportation: Edmonton Transit (schedules 496-1611, info 496-1600; http://www.gov.edmonton.ab.ca). Buses and Light Rail Transit **(LRT)** run frequently throughout the city. LRT is **free downtown** (M-F 9am-3pm and Sa 9am-6pm) between Grandin Station at 110 St. and 98 Ave. and Churchill Station at 99 St. and 102 Ave. Fare $1.60, over 65 and under 15 $1. No bikes on LRT during peak hours traveling in peak direction (M-F 7:30-8:30am and 4-5pm). No bikes on buses. For info, contact the **Downtown Information Centre** above the Central LRT station, 100A St. and Jasper Ave. (open M-F 9:30am-5pm) or the Churchill **LRT station info booth** (open M-F 8:30am-4:30pm).

Taxis: Yellow Cab, 462-3456. **Alberta Co-op Taxi,** 425-8310. Both 24hr.

Car Rental: Budget, 10016 106 St. (448-2000 or 800-661-7027); call for other locations. From $46 per day, with unlimited km; cheaper city rates with limited km. Ages 21-24 $12 per day surcharge and must have major credit card. Open M-F 7:30am-6pm, Sa 8am-5pm, Su 9am-5pm. **Tilden,** 10133 100A St. (422-6097). From $41 per day for unlimited km; city rates with limited km available. Must be 21. Open M-F 7am-7pm, Sa 8am-4pm, Su 9am-5pm. Major credit cards accepted.

Visitor Services

Visitor Information: Edmonton Tourism, Shaw Conference Centre, 9797 Jasper Ave. (496-8400 or 800-463-4667), on Pedway Level. Info, maps, directions. Open M-F 8:30am-4:30pm. Also at Gateway Park (496-8400 or 800-463-4667), on Hwy. 2 south of town. Both open daily 8am-9pm; in winter M-F 8:30am-4:30pm, Sa-Su 9am-5pm. **Alberta Tourism,** Commerce Pl., 10155 102 St., Edmonton T5J 4L6, 3rd floor (427-4321 or 800-661-8888). Province-wide info. Open M-F 8:30am-4:30pm.

Budget Travel Services: The Travel Shop, 10926 88 Ave. (travel 439-3096, retail 439-3089). Regional office for Alberta Hostels, selling sundry hiking and travel gear, serving youth and student travelers. International hostel reservations ($5). Open M-W and Sa 10am-6pm, Th-F 10am-8pm, Su noon-5pm.

Equipment Rental: The Edmonton International Youth Hostel (see **Accommodations,** below) rents bikes. $7.50 per ½-day, $15 per day.

Library: 7 Sir Winston Churchill Sq. Open M-F 9am-9pm, Sa 9am-6pm, Su 1-5pm.

Gay and Lesbian Services: Gay/Lesbian Community Centre, 10612 124 St. #103 (482-2855). Community listings, youth services, and on-site peer counseling. Open M-F 7-10pm; events recording plays during non-business hours. **Womonspace** (482-1794), is the Edmonton lesbian group. Call for a recording of local events.

Square Dancing: Edmonton and District Square Dance Association, 496-9136.

Weather: 468-4940. 24hr.

Emergency and Communications

Emergency: 911. **Police:** 423-4567.

Crisis Line: 482-HELP/4357. **Sexual Assault Centre,** 423-4121. Both 24hr.

Pharmacy: Shoppers Drug Mart, 11408 Jasper Ave. (482-1011). Open daily 24hr.

Hospital: Royal Alexandra Hospital, 10240 Kingsway Ave. (477-4111).

Post Office: 9808 103A Ave. (944-3265), adjacent to the CN Tower. Open M-F 8am-5:45pm. **Postal Code:** T5J 2G8.

Internet Access: Dow Computer Lab, 11211 142 St. (451-3344), at the Edmonton Space and Science Centre (see **Sights,** p. 367); free with admission. Open in summer Sa-Su 1-5pm. Across from St. Joseph's (see **Accommodations,** below), you could read web-based email at the computer lab in the **University of Alberta Civil Engineering Building basement** for free, but that would be breaking their students-and-staff-only rule. (*Let's Go* does not recommend getting busted.)

Area Code: 780.

ACCOMMODATIONS

The hostel is the liveliest place to stay in Edmonton, while St. Joseph's College and the University of Alberta provide a bit more privacy. For B&B listings, contact **Alberta Gem B&B Reservation Agency,** 11216 48 Ave. (434-6098).

⊛Edmonton International Youth Hostel (HI-C), 10647 81 Ave. (988-6836; email eihostel@hostellingintl.ca); take bus #7 or 9 from the 101 St. station to 82 Ave. You'd never know that this brand-new hostel is in a renovated convent, except for the abundance of private two-person bedrooms with the dimensions of a nun's cell. Loaded with modern facilities (kitchen, game room, lounge, new bathrooms, laundry), plus a small backyard. Just around the corner from the clubs, shops, and cafes of Whyte Ave. $15, nonmembers $20. Family rooms available. Open 24hr.

St. Joseph's College (492-7681), on 89 Ave. at 114 St., at the University of Alberta; take the LRT and get off at University. The rooms here are smaller, quieter, and cheaper than those at the university. Library, TV lounge, pool table. Singles $24, weekly $150, with full board $37, or pay for meals separately (breakfast $3.25, lunch $4.50, dinner $6.50). Weekly singles $150. Reception M-F 8:30am-4pm. Call ahead; dorms often fill up quickly. Rooms available early May to late Aug.

University of Alberta (492-4281), on 87 Ave. between 116 and 117 St., on the ground floor of Lister Hall. Generic dorm rooms. Weight, steam, and game rooms. Drycleaning, kitchen, free Internet access, convenience store, and buffet-style cafeteria downstairs. Singles $27; doubles $36; suites $30-40. Weekly singles $162; doubles $218. Check-in after 3pm. Reservations strongly recommended. Rooms available late Apr.-Aug.

YMCA, 10030 102A Ave. (421-9622), close to bus and rail stations. A clean, modern facility in the heart of downtown. Free gym and pool facilities for guests. Secure 4th-floor rooms (key-only access) available for women and couples. Dorm bunks $17. Singles for men $30, women $33; doubles $46-$49. Discounts for long-term stays and students. 3-night max. dorm stay.

FOOD

Little evidence can be found to support the theory that citizens of the self-labeled City of Champions kick off their day with a big bowl of Wheaties. Instead, Edmonton locals swarm into the coffee shops and cafes of the Old Strathcona area along Whyte (82) Ave., between 102 and 105 St.

Chianti, 10501 Whyte Ave. (439-9829). An old Strathcona post office gone authentically Italian. Chianti's name attests to its lengthy wine list. Daily specials, desserts, and coffees accompany an expanse of pasta, veal, and seafood dishes. Pastas $6-9; veal $10-11. M-Tu all pasta dishes $6. Open Su-Th 11am-11pm, F-Sa 11am-midnight.

Grounds for Coffee and Antiques, 10247 97 St. (429-1920), behind the Edmonton Art Gallery. This mom-and-pop shop features coffee and light veggie dishes alongside old furniture and older trinkets. The Mideastern Combo ($4) is a favorite among local clientele. Open M-F 8:30am-5pm, Sa 10am-5pm.

Dadeo's, 10548A 82 Ave. (433-0930). Cajun and Louisiana-style food in exile from the bayou, with decor escaped from a classy 50s diner. Gumbo $4-5; a variety of po' boy sandwiches $7-10. Spicy dishes make diners sweat just right. Open M-W 11:30am-11pm, Th-Sa 11:30am-midnight.

Kids in the Hall Bistro, 1 Sir Winston Churchill Sq. (413-8060). This City Hall lunchroom is truly one-of-a-kind. Every employee, from waiter to chef, is a young person hired as part of a cooperative community service project. Various entrees ($5-$10) and sandwiches ($5-7) will crush your head. Open M 8am-3:30pm, Tu-F 8am-5pm.

The Silk Hat, 10251 Jasper Ave. (425-1920), beside the Paramount Theater. As old as the hills, with plenty of character. Everything from the big-haired waitstaff to the Rock-Olas in every booth says "time warp." The prices are decades behind, too. Two eggs, meat, toast, and home fries $3; hamburger deluxe with fries or potato salad $5. Tea leaf readings M-Sa 2:30-6:30pm. Open M-Sa 7am-8pm.

SIGHTS AND OUTDOORS

A blow against Mother Nature in the battle for tourists, the mammoth **West Edmonton Mall** (444-5200) engulfs the general area between 170 St. and 87 Ave.; take bus #1, 2, 100, or 111. *(Open M-F 10am-9pm, Sa 10am-6pm, Su noon-5pm. Amusement park and some other attractions stay open later.)* When the largest assembly of retail stores in the galaxy first landed, its massive sprawl of boutiques and eateries seized 30% of Edmonton's retail business, choking the life out of the downtown shopping district. No ordinary collection of stores, the World's Biggest Mall contains water slides, an amusement park with 14-story roller coaster, miniature golf, dozens of exotic caged animals, over 800 stores, an ice-skating rink, 110 eating establishments, a full-scale replica of Columbus's *Santa Maria,* an indoor bungee jumping facility, a casino, a luxury hotel, and twice as many submarines as the Canadian Navy. One could, in theory, spend an entire vacation without leaving the Übermall's climate-controlled embrace. One note of caution: remember where you park. The world's largest mall also has the world's largest parking lot.

After worshiping at the temple of consumerism, take a breather at the refreshing **Fort Edmonton Park** (496-8787), on Whitemud Dr. at Fox Dr. Buses #2, 4, 30, 31, 35, 106, and 315 stop near the park. *(Open daily July-Aug. 10am-6pm; Victoria Day to late June M-F 10am-4pm, Sa-Su 10am-6pm; Sept. open only for scheduled tours, call for times. $6.75, seniors and ages 13-17 $5, ages 2-12 $3.25.)* At the park's far end sits the fort, a 19th-century office building for Alberta's first capitalists, the fur traders of the Hudson's Bay Company. Between the fort and the park entrance are three streets—1885, 1905, and 1920 St.—bedecked with period buildings from apothecaries to blacksmith shops, all decorated to match the streets' respective eras. Costumed schoolmarms and general store owners mingle with visitors, valiantly attempting to bring Edmonton's history to life.

Hike through birch groves and pet salamanders at the **John Janzen Nature Centre,** next door to the fort. *(Open M-F 9am-6pm, Sa-Su 11am-6pm; in spring M-F 9am-4pm, Sa-Su 11am-6pm; in winter M-F 9am-4pm, Sa-Su 1-4pm. Free.)* At the **Muttart Conservatory,**

9626 96A St. (496-8755), plant species from around the world vegetate in the climate-controlled comfort of four ultramodern glass pyramids, each housing a different ecosystem; take bus #1, 83, 88, 106, or 307. *(Open Su-W 11am-9pm, Th-Sa 11am-6pm. $4.25, seniors and ages 13-17 $3.25, ages 2-12 $2.)*

The oddly shaped **Edmonton Space and Science Centre,** 11211 142 St. (451-3344), caters to the curious of all ages. The largest **planetarium** dome in Canada holds features a booming 23,000 watts of audio, and uses all of it during its laser light shows. The **IMAX theater** makes the planetarium seem like a child's toy. *(Open daily 10am-9:30pm. Day pass includes planetarium shows and exhibits: $7, seniors and youths $6, ages 3-12 $5. IMAX Plus pass includes one IMAX film plus either exhibits and planetarium or a laser music show: $12, seniors and youth $11, ages 3-12 $8. AAA and HI discounts.)* Gaze at real stars for free at the **observatory** next door. *(Open daily 1-5pm and 8pm-midnight.)*

The **Provincial Museum of Alberta,** 12845 102 Ave. (453-9100), displays an impressive collection of Albertan animals, vegetables, and minerals; take bus #1 and 120. *(Open Victoria Day to Labour Day daily 9am-5pm; in winter Tu-Su 9am-5pm. $6.50, seniors $5.50, youth $3.)* A particularly thorough First Nations exhibit includes the standard history of prehistoric tribes, but also documents modern issues. The museum's Bug Room is alive with a variety of insects, some rodent-sized. Edmonton sports a number of tiny museums (telephone history, anyone?), but most fun is the **Old Strathcona Model and Toy Museum,** 8603 104th St. (433-4512), in the McKenzie Historic House; take bus #1, 4, 84, 86, or 106. *(Open M-Tu 1-5pm, W-F noon-8pm, Sa 10am-6pm, Su 1-5pm. Free.)* Over 700 models include the Taj Mahal, the *Titanic,* and Sir John A. MacDonald. The small **Edmonton Art Gallery,** 2 Sir Winston Churchill Sq. (422-6223), showcases Canadian and Albertan art, with creatively displayed temporary exhibits. *(Open M-W 10:30am-5pm, Th-F 10:30am-8pm, Sa-Su and holidays 11am-5pm. $3, seniors and students $1.50, Th after 4pm free.)*

The longest stretch of urban parkland in North America, Edmonton's **River Valley** (496-7275) boasts over 50km of paved multi-use trails. Any route down the river leads to some part of the trail system; pick up a map at the visitor center for more info.

NIGHTLIFE AND ENTERTAINMENT

Early in the week, Edmonton nightlife is nearly dead, and rigor mortis settles in by Wednesday. Come Thursday, though, the city goes Lazarus, if Lazarus were a drinking, dancing fool. Many of the happening clubs are lined up along Whyte (82) Ave. in Old Strathcona. For club listings, see *Magazine,* published every Thursday and available in free stacks at cafes.

The Billiard Club, 10505 82 Ave. (432-0335), 2nd floor, above Chianti. A busy bar packed with young up-and-comings and some older already-theres. Ten pool tables, plus a mellow back room and outdoor patio, for self-contained socializers. Open daily 11:30am-2:30am.

Blues on Whyte, 10329 82 Ave. (439-3981). If blues is what you want, blues is what you'll get. You asked for it. Live blues and R&B every night, plus a Saturday afternoon jam. This joint may deserve its reputation as a biker bar; these blues are anything but sedate. 8 oz. glasses of beer for just $1. Open daily 10am-3am.

Sherlock Holmes, 10341 82 Ave. (453-9676), also at 10012 101A Ave. (426-7784). Homesick Brits hold support groups over sing-alongs, cigars, and staple English Ales on tap. The 82 Ave. location is young and sharp; downtown is popular with an older crowd. Open daily 11:30am-2am.

Cook County Saloon, 8010 103 St. (432-2665). Bring your hat and your best shit-kickers to Edmonton's rootinest *and* tootinest country bar. Live music keeps 'em stomping nightly; Thursday night dance lessons ensure that no one gets hurt in the process. Ladies night (W); mechanical bull-riding (Th). Open W-Sa 7pm-2am.

Rebar, 10551 82 Ave. (433-3600). Two dance floors bounce with high energy into the night, with music ranging from alternative to dance. No worries—Rebar hosts the requisite 80s night. Everybody Wang Chung tonight. Cheap drinks on weekends gather some crowds. Open daily 8pm-2:30am.

ALBERTA

Led by Wayne Gretzky, the NHL's **Edmonton Oilers** skated off with four Stanley Cups between 1983 and 1988, then traded The Great One, and won another cup in '90 anyway. The stars of Oiler past are now long gone, but true to form, Canadians oil up their vocal cords and cheer as loudly for their team as they always have. The Oilers play from October to May in the **Edmonton Coliseum** (tickets 451-8000).

For a more cerebral evening, check out the **Princess Theatre,** 10337 Whyte (82) Ave. (434-6600). *($7, seniors and children $3.25.)* Check the free magazine *See* for theater, film, and music listings.

EVENTS

Edmonton proclaims itself "Canada's Festival City," with celebrations of some kind going on year-round. The **International Jazz City Festival** (432-7166; June 25-July 4, 1999) packs 10 days with club dates and free performances by top international and Canadian jazz musicians, coinciding with a visual arts celebration called **The Works** (426-2122; June 25-July 7). At the **International Street Performers Festival** (425-5162; July 9-18), musical and acting talent combust and burst into a fireball of artistic activity, aesthetically scorching downtown's Winston Churchill Square. **Klondike Days** (426-4055 or 471-7210; July 22-31) are Edmonton's answer to Calgary's Stampede (see p. 373). In August, the **Folk Music Festival** (429-1889; Aug. 5-8), considered one of the best in North America, takes over Gallagher Park. Only a week later, all the world's a stage on Whyte (82) Ave. for the **Fringe Theater Festival** (448-9000; Aug. 13-22), when top alternative music and theater pours from Edmonton's parks, theaters, and streets. This is the high point in Edmonton's festival schedule, and many travelers make their way to the city just to find the Fringe.

The Edmonton area hosts many entertaining **small-town rodeos.** On any summer weekend there may be several; the $6-10 admission fee is negligible given the quality of competition. Where else can you watch leather-clad contestants narrowly escape being impaled by enraged bulls? Spain? Well, okay. But Albertan rodeos are just as fun. Contact Alberta Tourism Info (800-661-8888) for a list of towns that hold rodeos.

■ Calgary

Mounties founded Calgary in the 1870s to control the flow of illegal whisky, but a different sort of ooze made the city great: oil. As the host of the 1988 Winter Olympics, Calgary's dot on the map grew larger as jobs, tourism, and flocks of Canadians from the East all converged. Already Alberta's largest city, Calgary continues to expand. No matter how big its britches, though, the city pays annual tribute to its original tourist attraction, the "Greatest Outdoor Show on Earth," the Calgary Stampede, when for 10 days in July the city dons cowboy duds and lets out a collective "Yeehaw!" for world-class rodeo, country music, western art, and free pancakes.

ORIENTATION AND PRACTICAL INFORMATION

Calgary is 120km east of Banff along the Trans-Canada Highway (Hwy. 1). Planes fly into **Calgary International Airport,** about 6km northwest of city center. Cab fare from the airport to the city is about $20. Bus #57 provides sporadic service from the airport to downtown (call for schedule). The **Airporter Bus** (531-3907) offers frequent service to major hotels downtown between 6:30am and 11:30pm ($8.50); those who ask nicely may get dropped off at an unscheduled stop.

Calgary is divided into quadrants (NE, NW, SE, SW): **Centre St.** is the east-west divider; the **Bow River** splits the north and south sections. **Avenues** run east-west, **streets** run north-south, and numbers count up from the divides. Cross streets can be derived by disregarding the last two digits of the first number: 206 7th Ave. is at 2nd St., and 310 10th St. is at 3rd Ave.

Buses: Greyhound, 877 Greyhound Way SW (265-9111 or 800-661-TRIP/8747). To: Edmonton (10 per day, $38); Banff (4 per day, $18.56); Drumheller (2 per day,

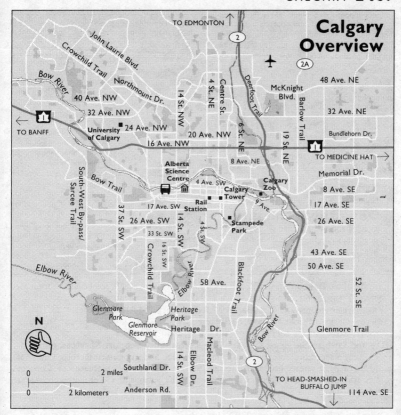

Calgary Overview

TO EDMONTON

TO BANFF

TO MEDICINE HAT

TO HEAD-SMASHED-IN BUFFALO JUMP

John Laurie Blvd.
Crowchild Trail
Northmount Dr.
Bow River
40 Ave. NW
32 Ave. NW
24 Ave. NW
University of Calgary
16 Ave. NW
14 St. NW
4 St. NE
Centre St.
Deerfoot Trail
McKnight Blvd.
48 Ave. NE
32 Ave. NE
Barlow Trail
19 St. NE
6 St. NE
20 Ave. NW
8 Ave. NE
Bundlehorn Dr.
Memorial Dr.
Alberta Science Centre
4 Ave. SW
Calgary Tower
Rail Station
Calgary Zoo
9 Ave.
8 Ave. SE
17 Ave. SE
26 Ave. SE
South-West By-pass/ Sarcee Trail
Bow Trail
37 St. SW
17 Ave. SW
14 St. SW
4 St. SW
26 Ave. SW
33 St. SW
16 St. SW
Crowchild Trail
Stampede Park
Elbow River
Blackfoot Trail
43 Ave. SE
50 Ave. SE
52 St. SE
58 Ave.
Elbow River
Glenmore Park
Heritage Park
Glenmore Reservoir
Heritage Dr.
Glenmore Trail
Bow River
Macleod Trail
14 St. SW
Elbow Dr.
N
0 2 miles
0 2 kilometers
Southland Dr.
Anderson Rd.
114 Ave. SE

ALBERTA

$21). 10% student and senior discount; 15% HI discount. Free shuttle from Calgary Transit C-Train at 7th Ave. and 10th St. to bus depot (every hr. on the half hr. 6:30am-7:30pm). **Red Arrow,** 101-205 9 Ave. SE (531-0350). To: Edmonton (5 per day, $39); Fort McMurray via Edmonton (2 per day, $86). 10% HI, student, and senior discount. **Brewster Tours** (221-8242). From the airport or downtown to: Banff (3 per day, $36); Lake Louise (3 per day, $41); Jasper (1 per day, $71). 15% HI discount.

Public Transportation: Calgary Transit, 240 7th Ave. SW (262-1000), stocks bus and C-Train schedules, passes, and maps. Office open M-F 8:30am-5pm. C-Trains are free in the downtown zone. Bus fare and C-Trains outside downtown $1.60, ages 6-14 $1, under 6 free. Exact change required. Day pass $5, ages 6-14 $3. Book of 10 tickets $13.50, ages 6-14 $8.50. Open M-F 6am-11pm, Sa-Su 8:30am-9:30pm. Tickets can be purchased at the transit office, any Safeway or Co-op grocery store, or Mac's convenience store.

Taxis: Checker Cab, 299-9999. **Yellow Cab,** 974-1111. Both 24hr.

Car Rental: Rent-A-Wreck, 113 42nd Ave. SW (228-1660). From $30 per day; 12¢ per km over 200km. Must be 21 with credit card. Open daily 8am-7pm.

Visitor Information: Visitor Service Centre, 131 9th Ave. SW (750-2397), near the Calgary Tower. Open daily 8:30am-5pm. Call **Talking Yellow Pages** (521-5222 ext. 8950) for info on anything in town, especially if you enjoy pushing lots of buttons.

American Express: Canada Trust Tower, 421 7th Ave. SW (261-5085), main floor.

Equipment Rental: Budget, 140 6th Ave. SE (226-1550). Bikes $13 per day. Must be 18 with credit card. **Sports Rent,** 9250 Macleod Trail (292-0066). Bikes $20 per day. HI discount.

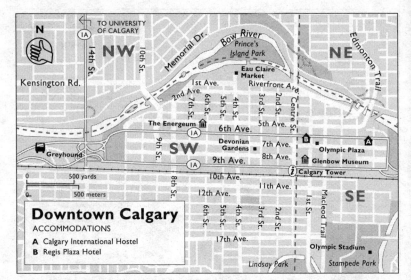

Downtown Calgary

ACCOMMODATIONS

A Calgary International Hostel
B Regis Plaza Hotel

Laundromat: Beacon Speed Wash & Dry, 1818 Centre St. NE (651-6580). Open M-F 8am-11pm, Sa-Su 7am-11pm. Wash $1.50, dry 25¢ per 6min.

Weather: Environment Canada, 299-7878. Calgary and Banff weather.

Library: Calgary Public Library, 616 Macleod Trail SE (262-2600). Open M-Th 10am-9pm, F-S 10am-5pm; mid-Sept. to mid-Apr. also Su 1:30-5pm.

Gay and Lesbian Services: Calgary Gay Community Support Services. Call 234-9752 for a recording of events and a list of lesbian and gay bars and clubs. Call 234-8973 for peer counseling and info (daily 7-10pm). **Women's Resource Centre:** 325 10th St. NW (283-5994), 1 block west of the Sunnyside C-Train stop. Info and referrals. Open M-F 9:30am-4:30pm.

Emergency: 911. **Police:** 133 6th Ave. SE (266-1234).

Crisis Line: 266-1605. **Poison:** 270-1414. 24hr.

Pharmacy: Shopper's Drug Mart, 6455 S. Macleod Trail (253-2424), in the Chinook Centre. Open 24hr.

Hospital: Calgary General, 841 Centre Ave. E (268-9111).

Post Office: 207 9th Ave. SW (974-2078). Open M-F 8am-5:45pm. **Postal Code:** T2P 268.

Internet Access: Kaffa Coffee and Salsa House (see **Food,** below) is the cheapest ($1 per 20min.), but there's only one computer. **Megabites Cafe,** 235 17th Ave. SE (262-8284), has more. $5 per ½hr., $8 per hr. Open daily 11am-10pm.

Area Code: 403.

ACCOMMODATIONS

Lodging costs skyrocket when tourists pack into the city's hotels during the Stampede in July; call far in advance. Contact the **B&B Association of Calgary** (543-3900) for info and availability (singles from $35; doubles from $50).

⊕**Calgary International Hostel (HI-C),** 520 7th Ave. SE (269-8239), several blocks east of downtown. Go east along 7th Ave. from the 3rd St. SE C-Train station; the hostel is on the left just past 4th St. SE. This welcoming urban hostel has it all: clean, large kitchen, game room, hang-out areas, laundry, and a big backyard with barbecue facilities. City volunteers act as guest relations personnel, doing a better job than the official visitor center. 114 beds: $15, nonmembers $19. Linen $1.50. Free tours of downtown (3 per week). Open 24hr. Wheelchair accessible.

University of Calgary, in the NW quadrant. Booking for all rooms coordinated through **Kananaskis Hall,** 3330 24th Ave. (220-3203), a 12min. walk from the University C-Train stop. Open 24hr. The university is out of the way, but easily accessible via bus #9 or the C-Train. Sleep in the beds of Olympians; U of C was the Olympic Village for the 1988 competitors. Shared rooms $20; singles $31, with student ID $21; doubles $39, with student ID $32. More lavish suites with private bathrooms about $35. Popular with conventioneers and often booked solid; reservations recommended. Rooms available May-Aug. only.

Regis Plaza Hotel, 124 7th Ave. SE (262-4641). Despite its less-than-attractive streetside appearance, the Plaza has clean rooms smack in the middle of downtown. The old, stubborn elevator tugs guests to the 100 rooms of this behemoth. Great for groups, the roomy floors are ideal for cramming in extra sleeping bags. Inside rooms with no TV, bath, or windows $32.50; doubles from $64. Weekly rates $75-150. Reception open 24hr.

FOOD

Downtown's grub is concentrated in the **Stephen Avenue Mall,** S. 8th Ave. between 1st St. SE and 3rd St. SW. Good, reasonably-priced food is also readily available in the **+15 Skyway System.** Designed to provide indoor passageways during bitter winter days, this futuristic mall-in-the-sky connects the second floors of dozens of buildings throughout downtown Calgary. The trendy, costlier chow-houses in the popular **Kensington District,** along Kensington Rd. and 10th and 11th St. NW, also hide some budget eateries. Take the C-Train to Sunnyside or use the Louise Bridge (9th St. SW and 10th St. NW). **Co-op Grocery,** 123 11th Ave. SE (299-4257), sells exactly what you'd imagine (open M-F 9am-9pm, Sa 9am-6pm, Su 10am-6pm). Restaurants, fresh fruits, vegetables, baked goods, international snack bars, and flowers grace the plaza-style, upscale **Eau Claire Market** (264-6450), at the north end of 3rd St. SW; $5 easily fetches a filling take-out plate for a picnic in nearby, Prince's Island Park (market open M-W, Sa 10am-6pm, Th-F 10am-9pm, Su 10am-5pm).

Kaffa Coffee and Salsa House, 2138 33 Ave. SW (240-9133); take bus #7 (South Calgary) from the Bay on 7th Ave. The Kaffa Staffa cook up a fresh soup every day, and a different salsa and salad every week. It's what it sounds like: an espresso cafe and Mexican restaurant behind one counter, with a leafy outdoor patio, tortilla melts ($6-7), signature jalapeño cheese cornbread, a long alcohol menu, and plenty of caffeinated beverages. Open M-F 7am-midnight, Sa 8am-midnight, Su 8am-10pm.

Satay House, 206 Centre St. S (290-1927). Large portions of authentic Vietnamese cuisine for delightfully little. Chinatown makes for the best downtown bargains, and Satay House is one of the best bargains in Chinatown. Several varieties of beef noodle soup $3.50-4.50. The house special offers a taste of everything for $5.50. Open daily 11am-9pm.

Take Ten Cafe, 304 10th St. NE (270-7010). A local favorite, Take Ten attracts customers not by being the coolest place in Kensington, but by offering dirt-cheap, high-quality food. All burgers under $5.25. The owners also offer a variety of their native Chinese food ($6.25). Open Tu-Sa 9am-6pm, Su 9am-3pm.

4th Street Rose, 2116 4th St. SW (228-5377). This California-cool restaurant serves a variety of dishes, but the cheapest is the pro-size Caesar salad ($5). Every international flavor from Thailand to Italy infuses wraps, salads, and hot meals. 10-inch pizzas and calzones $8-11. Vegetarian dishes galore, and a few vegan ones, too. Open M-Th 11am-midnight, F-Sa 11am-1am, Su 10am-midnight.

SIGHTS AND OUTDOORS

Over a decade later, Calgary still clings to its two weeks of Olympic stardom. Visit the **Canada Olympic Park** (247-5452), 10 minutes west of downtown on Hwy. 1, to learn about gravity at the site of the four looming ski jumps and the quick, slick bobsled and luge tracks. *(Open daily 8am-9pm.)* The **Olympic Hall of Fame** (247-5452), also at Olympic Park, honors Olympic achievements with displays, films, and bobsled and ski-jumping simulators. *(Open daily 9am-9pm. $3.75, seniors and students $3, under 6 free.)* In summer, the park opens its hills to mountain bikers. Take the **lift** up the hill, then cruise down—no work necessary. *(Open daily May-Sept. 10am-9pm. $5 ticket*

ALBERTA

includes chair lift and entrance to ski jump buildings. Guided tour $10. Hill pass $6 for cyclists. Bike rental $6 per hr., $24 per day. Luge $13.) Keep an eye on the sky for ski-jumpers, who practice at the facility year-round. For a slightly different view of the sky, zoom down the ice track on the summer luge. The hill, though a bit shrimpy, also opens up for recreational **downhill skiing** in winter. The **Olympic Oval** (220-7890) is the most impressive of the remaining arenas. *(Public skating hours in summer 8-9:30pm. $4, children $2. Hockey skate rental $3.50; speed skates $3.75.)* An enormous indoor speed-skating track on the University of Calgary campus, the oval remains a major international training facility with the fastest ice in the world. Speed skaters work out in the early morning and late afternoon; sit in the bleachers and observe the action for free.

The **Olympic Plaza,** on 7th Ave. SE, just east of Centre St., now hosts special events, including free concerts during the **Calgary Jazz Festival** in June. The **Glenbow Museum,** 130 9th Ave. SE (268-4100), brings rocks and minerals, Buddhist and Hindu art, and native Canadian history under one roof. *(Open June to mid-Oct. daily 9am-5pm; mid-Oct. to May Tu-Su 9am-5pm. $8, seniors and students $6, under 6 free. HI discount.)*

Footbridges stretch from either side of the Bow River to **Prince's Island Park,** whose lawns and paths teem with bikers, bladers, and sunbathers. In July and August, on most evenings at 7pm and on weekend afternoons, Mount Royal College puts on a free **Shakespeare in the Park** (recording 240-6374, human 240-6908, Calgary Parks and Recreation 268-3888).

Calgary's other island park, **St. George's Island,** is accessible by the river walkway to the east, and houses the ark-like **Calgary Zoo** (232-9372), including a botanical garden and children's zoo. *(Gates open daily 9am-8pm; in winter 9am-4pm. Grounds open 9am-9pm; Oct.-Apr. 9am-5:30pm. $9.50, children $4.75, seniors half-price Tu and Th; in winter $8, seniors and children $4. AAA and HI discounts.)* For those who missed the wildlife in Banff and Jasper, the Canadian Wilds exhibit re-creates natural animal habitats. For those who missed the Cretaceous Period, life-size plastic dinosaurs also fill an exhibit. A pamphlet available at the zoo entrance lists special shows and animal feeding times; visitors are warmly invited to watch big animals eat smaller animals.

(To be sung to the tune of *The Beverly Hillbillies:)* Come 'n' listen to a story 'bout the **Energeum,** a place 'bout oil kinda like a museum. Play a game 'bout drillin', watch a movie in th' thee-ter, and learn how Alberta puts th' power in your heater. Industrial propaganda, that is, 640 5th Ave. SW (297-4293). *(Open June-Aug. Su-F 10:30am-4:30pm; Sept.-May M-F 10:30am-4:30pm. Free.)*

NIGHTLIFE

Nightclubs in Alberta only became legal in 1990, and Calgary is making up for lost time. With year-round city-wide events, the city is crawling with bars and nightclubs that cater to the waves of visitors and locals. Live music ranges from national acts to some guy with a guitar. For an easy-to-find good time, rock down to **Electric Avenue,** the stretch of 11th Ave. SW between 5th and 6th St., and pound back local brew with oodles of young Calgarians. Beware of Electric Avenue during hockey playoff time; streets close and lines wind around the block. Less crowded options lie nearby, along 17th Ave. SW and 1st St. SW. Last call in Calgary is at 2am, and is strictly observed. For listings of bands and theme nights, check *The Calgary Straight* or *Calgary's Ffwd.* Both come out on Thursday at cafes and clubs, and both are free.

🎵**Republik,** 219 17th Ave. SW (244-1884, events line 228-6163). Punksters slam with their Gap-clad brethren in Calgary's loudest nuclear bunker and largest party zone. On the harder side of alternative, this is a favorite stage for up-and-coming bands (live music on W and F). Exuberant dancing, at its height, veers toward the realm of the mosh. Daily drink specials, with a more relaxed patio for beer-drinkers in summer. Cover $2-7, more for the bigger live shows. Open W-Sa 7pm-2am; open Su-Tu if bands are playing.

🎵**Bottlescrew Bill's Pub** (263-7900), 10th Ave. SW and 1st St. Take refuge from the boisterous Electric Ave. (and the Electric Slide) in this Olde Ynglishe Pubbe. The source of Buzzard Breath Ale, Bill's beckons beer-lovers with the widest suds selection in Alberta (over 200; $3.30-15). Happy hour M-F 4-7pm, Su 11am-2am. Load up on free nachos M-F 4-6pm. Open daily 11am-2am.

Java Sharks, 529 17th Ave SW (244-5552). Funkily decorated, intimate club. Live bands upstairs and DJs downstairs in the Shark Pit (both Th-Su). Boogeying neo-hippies, a mainstream pool-playing set, and even grown-ups bask in the positive vibes, sitting at tables, boozing, and grooving to bands in the coffeehouse. No cover. Breakfast all day; happy hour 2-7pm and all day Su; lots of java; no sharks. Open M-F 7am-3am, Sa-Su 9am-3am.

King Edward Hotel, 438 9th Ave. SE (262-1680). A well-known stop for North American blues bands, this inconspicuous little hotel brings in phenomenal notemakers, including Clarence "Gatemouth" Brown, Matt "Guitar" Murphy, and Buddy "No Nickname" Guy. Nightly live music. Cover $3-6. Open daily 11am-2am. Jam sessions Sa 3-7pm and Su 7pm-1am.

Ranchman's Steak House, 9615 Macleod Trail SW (253-1100). This is the real thing. Herds of carousing cattle-ropers camp out at Ranchman's, showing off their Wranglers and the latest in country two-stepping. For those not content with watching, Ranchman's offers free dancing lessons on weekdays. $6-10 cover Th-Sa and Stampede week. Open M-Sa noon-3am.

THE STAMPEDE

The more cosmopolitan Calgary becomes, the more tenaciously it clings to its frontier roots. The Stampede (July 9-18 in 1999) draws one million cowboys and tourists each summer. **Stampede Park,** just southeast of downtown, borders the east side of Macleod Trail between 14th and 25th Ave. SE. For 10 days, the grounds are packed for world-class steer wrestling, saddle bronc, bareback- and bull-riding, pig racing, wild-cow-milking, and chuckwagon races. Pet the furry animals that will grace your dinner plate, cruise the midway and casino, ride the rollercoaster, shop, or hear live country music and marching bands. The festival spills into the streets at night, as bars and clubs get good and loud. A **free pancake breakfast** is served at a different location in the city every day.

Depending on your attitude, the Stampede will either be an impressive spectacle, rekindling the Western spirit, with a kickin' afterparty—or an overpriced, slick carnival where men beat horses. Those in the first category should bring cowboy boots; those in the second might keep a low profile, as most Calgarians treat the Stampede as the most hallowed thing since, well, last year's Stampede.

Parking is ample and reasonably priced, but can be tedious. Take the C-Train to the Stampede stop from downtown, or walk. For info and ticket orders, call 269-9822 or 800-661-1767. Gate admission costs $9 (seniors and ages 7-12 $4, under 7 free). The rodeo and evening cost $17-45; **rush tickets,** if not sold out, are same price as admission, on sale at the grandstand 1½ hours before showtime.

■ Alberta Badlands

Prehistoric wind, water, and ice cut twisting canyons down into the sandstone and shale bedrock, resulting in the desolate splendor of the Alberta Badlands. The badlands are home to the Tyrell Museum of Paleontology and its remarkable array of dinosaur exhibits and hands-on paleontological opportunities. **Greyhound** runs from Calgary to Drumheller (2 per day, $21), which is 6km southeast of the museum. From Drumheller, rent a bike from the hostel (see below); it's about a 20-minute ride.

ACCOMMODATIONS, CAMPGROUNDS, AND FOOD Drumheller is overrun with the terrible lizards to this day, or at least their plastic and tacky younger cousins, which seem to guard every business. Flee the dino-monsters at the **Alexandra Hostel (HI-C),** 30 Railway Ave. N (823-6337), which has 55 beds in a converted hotel that hasn't changed much since the 30s. It sports a kitchen, laundry, and a killer view from the fire escape ($15, nonmembers $20; check-in 9am-11pm). The hostel also rents **mountain bikes** ($4 per hr., $15 per day). **River Grove Campground,** off North Dinosaur Trail at the intersection with Hwy. 9, has flush toilets, free showers, and laundry. The majority of the 100 sites are for tents ($17, full hookups $24). Cabins for two to 10 people are also available, with bathrooms, electricity, and cable TV ($40-70; open daily Victoria Day to Labour Day 7am-11pm).

Stock up on groceries and participate in Drumheller nightlife at **IGA Market** (823-3995), at the intersection of N. Railroad Ave. and Centre St. (open daily 24hr.). For surprisingly decent Chinese and Thai, head to **Sizzling House**, 160 Centre St. (823-8098), with 100 different choices of Szechuan- and Peking-style beef and chicken dishes ($7-9), plus noodle or fried rice platters ($6-7) for eat-in or take-out (open Su-Th 11am-10pm, F-Sa 11am-11pm).

SIGHTS AND OUTDOORS The **Royal Tyrrell Museum of Paleontology** (TEER-ull; 403-823-7707 or 888-440-4240; email rtmp@dns.magtech.ab.ca; http://www.tyrrell-museum.com) lies on the **North Dinosaur Trail (Secondary Hwy. 838),** 6km northwest of **Drumheller** (drum-HELL-er), which itself lies 138km northeast of Calgary. *(Open daily 9am-9pm; Labour Day to Victoria Day Tu-Su 10am-5pm. $6.50, seniors $5.50, ages 7-17 $3, under 7 free; in winter half-price Tu.)* Get there by driving east on Hwy. 1 and northeast on Hwy. 9. You won't lose the crowds by going to the museum but you might lose your sense of self-importance. The world's largest display of dinosaur specimens makes a forceful reminder that humanity is a mere flyspeck on the giant windshield of life. From the Big Bang to the Quaternary Period (now), the museum ushers visitors through a parade across time, with quality displays, videos, computer activities, and towering skeletons, including one of the only *Tyrannosaurus rex* skeletons in existence. Recently, the museum created a creepy gallery of reconstructed and enlarged Burgess Shale (see p. 306) undersea creatures.

The museum's immensely popular 12-person **Day Digs** include instruction in paleontology and excavation techniques, and a chance to dig in a dinosaur quarry. *(Departs July-Aug. daily at 8:30am; mid-May to June Sa-Su only. $85, ages 10-15 $55. Reservations required.)* The fee includes lunch and transportation, but all finds go to the museum. During a **Dig Watch,** a two-hour interpretive bus and walking tour to the quarry, rare human paleontologist species and Day Diggers can be spotted sweating for their fossilized prey. *(Departs daily July-Aug. at 10am, noon, and 2pm. $12, ages 7-17 $8, under 7 free. Reservations recommended, but walk-ins often work.)*

The museum's **Field Station** (378-4342), 48km east of the town of **Brooks** in **Dinosaur Provincial Park,** contains a small museum, but the main attraction is the **Badlands Bus Tour.** *(Field Station open daily Victoria Day to Labour Day 8:30am-9pm; call for winter hours. Tours Victoria Day to Thanksgiving 2-8 per day. $4.50, ages 6-15 $2.25, under 6 free.)* The bus chauffeurs visitors into a restricted hot spot of dinosaur finds. Many fossils still lie within the eroding rock; if you make a discovery, however, all you can take home with you are memories, Polaroids, and a Fossil Finder Certificate. The park's **campground** is shaded from summer heat, and grassy plots cushion most sites. Although it stays open year-round, the campground only has power and running water in summer. *(Sites $13, with power $15.)* For more info, write to the Field Station, Dinosaur Provincial Park, Box 60, Patricia T0J 2K0. To reach the Field Station from Drumheller, follow Hwy. 56 south for 65km, then take Hwy. 1 about 70km to Brooks. Once in Brooks, go north along Hwy. 873 and east along Hwy. 544.

The staff of adjacent **Midland Provincial Park** (823-1754, info 823-1749) leads free 75-minute walking tours, departing from the museum one or two times daily. To see **hoodoos** in the making, go 15km east on Hwy. 10 from Drumheller. These limestone columns are young'uns compared to their famous relatives in Banff; they still wear the stone caps that create the pillars by protecting them from the erosion that washes away the surrounding rock. In **Horseshoe Canyon,** about 20km west of Drumheller on Hwy. 9, **hiking trails** wind below the prairie, where red rock layers carved into bizarre formations silently evoke a landscape of hell. Carry at least one liter of water per person during hot weather. Countless locales in Horseshoe Canyon and the provincial park provide great **cycling.** However, bikers that hop fences onto nearby farmland might discover their own more personal and horrible landscape of hell. Pick up info and directions at the **Old Midland Mine Office,** on North Dinosaur Trail between Drumheller and the Tyrrell Museum.

■ Kananaskis Country

Between Calgary and Banff lie 4000km² of provincial parks and multi-use recreational areas, collectively known as the **Kananaskis Country Provincial Area** (KAN-uh-NASS-kiss). Although summer use by travelers to the Canadian Rockies is heavy, the Kananaskis' sheer size and the wide nature of its attractions keep it unspoiled. The country is divided into eight sections. The three most popular are **Bow Valley Provincial Park** (673-3663), with an office just off Hwy. 1 (open M-F 8am-4:30pm), **Elbow River Valley** (949-4261), on Hwy. 66 near Bragg Creek, and **Peter Lougheed Provincial Park** (591-7226), just off Hwy. 40.

With over 1000km of trails, K-Country can provide anything from a one-hour quick fix to a full-blown Rocky Mountain High. The 1.9km **Canadian Mt. Everest Expedition Trail,** in Peter Lougheed Park, provides a majestic view of both **Upper** and **Lower Kananaskis Lakes.** The **Ribbon Creek Trail** passes 8.1km of waterfalls and canyons to arrive at an uncrowded backcountry campground at **Ribbon Falls.** Gillean Daffern's *Kananaskis Country Trail Guide,* published by Rocky Mountain Books and available at any area information center, is a definitive source on longer trails. The **Canmore Nordic Centre** (678-2400), the 1988 Olympic Nordic skiing venue, offers cross-country skiing in the winter and 60km of **mountain bike trails** in summer.

Greyhound buses stop at the **Rusticana Grocery,** 801 8th St. (678-4465), in Canmore. (3 per day to: Banff, 20min., $6; Calgary, 70min., $15). The Alberta hostels run a shuttle connecting Calgary to Banff, with a stop in K-Country ($19); call Banff International Hostel (762-4122) for reservations. Helpful staff members at the park info-centers help design itineraries for weeks of outdoor entertainment; expect showers of maps and elaborate brochures from the main **Barrier Lake Visitor Centre** (673-3985), 6km south of Hwy. 1 on Hwy. 40 (open Sa-Th 8:30am-6pm, F 8:30am-7pm; in winter daily 9am-4pm). In an **emergency,** call the **Canmore Police** (678-5516).

Ribbon Creek Hostel, 24km south of the Trans-Canada Hwy. (Hwy. 1) on Hwy. 40, near the Nakiska Ski Area, accommodates 47 people. The hostel's comfortable common room has a fireplace and luxurious couches ($12, nonmembers $17). For reservations, call the Banff International Hostel (762-4122). Over 3000 **campsites** are

Head-Smashed-In Buffalo Jump

Some 5700 years ago, plains-dwelling First Nations began using gravity to kill bison. Disguised as calves, a few men would lure a herd of the sight-impaired animals into lanes between stone cairns. Hunters at the rear, dressed as wolves, then pressed forward, whipping the bison into a fearful frenzy. When the front-running bison reached the cliff and tried to stop, the momentum of the stampede pushed them over the edge. The entire herd followed, a casualty of mass mentality. Hunters sought to prevent any animals from escaping, since survivors might warn other herds. Each year, the community obtained food, tools, and clothing from the bodies of the bison. The particular cliffs of Head-Smashed-In Buffalo Jump were an active hunting site for millennia, but only gained their modern name 150 years ago when a thrill-seeking warrior watching the massacre from under the cliff ledge, was crushed by a falling stampede.

As European settlement encroached, the bison that once numbered 60 million continent-wide were nearly extinct by 1881. A century later, the United Nations named Head-Smashed-In a UNESCO World Heritage Site. This is one of the best-preserved buffalo jumps in North America, commemorating the bison hunt as the heart of Plains culture. Tampering with the 10m-deep beds of bone and tools carries a $50,000 fine, but the excellent $10 million **Interpretive Centre** (553-2731) expertly explores the hunting, history, and rituals of the Plains people. *(Open daily Labour Day to May 15 9am-7pm; off-season 9am-5pm. $5.50, youth $2.25, under 6 free.)* A 10-minute reenactment of the hunt plays all day, and 2km of trails lead along and under the cliffs. Head-Smashed-In Buffalo Jump lies 175km south of Calgary and 18km northwest of Fort Macleod, on Secondary Rte. 785 off Hwy. 2.

accessible via K-Country roads. When hiking or biking in areas with established back-country campgrounds, visitors must use the areas provided. Where none are established, however, open camping is permitted at least 50m from the trail. Backcountry camping permits are not required. Frontcountry campsites in Kananaskis cost between $5.50 and $24 per night.

■ Crowsnest Pass

Amid forested peaks near the BC/Alberta border on Hwy. 3, the tiny towns bundled into Crowsnest Pass merrily thrive off a mining disaster that happened nearly a century ago. Early one morning in 1904, an entire side of coal-rich **Turtle Mountain** came tumbling down like so many giant sandcastles. Over eighty million tons of stone spilled onto the mining town of **Frank,** burying 70 people and their houses in less than two minutes. Geologists are still guessing about the ultimate cause of the disaster. The **Frank Slide Interpretive Centre** (562-7388), perched amid piles of rubble on Hwy. 3, details the dramatic collapse of the still-unstable mountain. The center is only about half as morbid as one might expect, spinning a history of the pass towns and Frank's miraculous survival stories, through displays, videos, and frequent talks by the knowledgeable staff (open daily 9am-8pm, Labour Day to May 15 10am-4pm; $4, seniors $3, children $2). A 1.5km **interpretive loop trail** leads from the center through a fraction of the 3km^2 still covered by massive blocks of fallen limestone.

Staff at the interpretive center also dish out tips on outdoor recreation in the pass. **Trout fishing** in the **Crowsnest, Castle,** and **Oldman Rivers** is reputedly among the best in the Rockies. A steep three-hour hike goes up and down the summit of the emotionally disturbed Turtle Mountain, offering views for miles and a new perspective on the cracks—some as wide as a bus—that split the mountain as water froze and thawed within them. The trailhead is at the eastern end of 34th St. in Blairmore. For more hiking options, ask at the interpretive center or infocenter (see below).

If heading west, take Hwy. 3 into the beautiful Kootenay Country of British Columbia. If heading north into Kanasaskis and Banff, consider taking the scenic but bumpy **Forestry Trunk Rd.,** which meets Hwy. 3 near Coleman. The drive offers vistas of mountains colored in vibrant hues of green, red, brown, and purple. Forest Service campgrounds line the road, including **Dutch Creek, Oldman River,** and **Cataract Creek** (sites $7-9). Call 562-7307 for info. **Greyhound,** 2020 129 St. (564-4467), in Blairmore, runs two buses per day to Calgary (5½hr., $35), Kelowna, BC (12hr., $82), and Vancouver, BC (21hr., $90), with 10% student and senior discounts. The **Alberta Tourism Information Centre,** 8km west of Coleman on Hwy. 3, provides further info on local sights and activities (open daily Victoria Day to Labour Day 9am-7pm). The most natural nearby campsites are maintained by the Alberta Forest Service at **Chinook Lake Campground** (800-661-8888; 70 sites, $7-9). In a medical or fire **emergency,** call 562-2255.

Follow Hwy. 3 west from Coleman for 9km, then follow the signs up Allison Creek Rd. (70 sites: $7-9). In town, the one choice is cramped **Lost Lemon Campground** (562-2932), just off Hwy. 3A near Blairmore, with hot showers, hot tub, swimming pool, laundry, and fishing (sites $17; full hookups $22). The most edible local offerings reside at **IGA Food Mart and Bakery** (562-7236), on Main St. in Blairmore (open daily 9am-9pm).

Yukon Territory

The Yukon Territory is among the most remote and sparsely inhabited regions of North America. Averaging one person per 15km², the land's lonely beauty is overwhelming. During the last Ice Age, much of the Yukon was left untouched by glaciation, existing as a haven for vegetation, wildlife, and the early North American settlers crossing the Bering Land Bridge. Yukoners have been suffering payback for this ancient fair weather ever since, enduring what's often described as "nine months of winter and three months of bad snowmobiling." While summers usually bring comfortably warm temperatures (60-70°F/15-21°C) and more than 20 hours of daylight, travelers should still be prepared for difficult weather. The territory remains a bountiful, beautiful, and largely unspoiled region, yet many Alaska-mad travelers mimic goldcrazed prospectors and zoom through without appreciating its uncrowded allure.

The Yukon appears on three **maps** in this guide: in relation to Alaska (see 394-5), to British Columbia (see 310), and to the Alaska Highway (see 334).

HIGHLIGHTS OF THE YUKON

- **Miles Canyon** (see p. 380) and the **Yukon River** provide outdoor excitement by foot or by boat in **Whitehorse** (see below).
- Hiking and flightseeing penetrate the raw and sprawling wilderness of **Kluane National Park** (see p. 383).
- Boom-town **Dawson City** (see p. 386) hosts both **nightlife** and **gold-panning**.
- From Dawson City, two glorious drives lead past spectacular scenery and copious roadside wildlife: the **Top of the World Highway** (see p. 390) to Alaska, and the **Dempster Highway** (see p. 390) all the way up to Inuvik, NWT.

PRACTICAL INFORMATION

Capital: Whitehorse.
Population: 32,635. **Area:** 478,970km². **Bird:** Raven. **Flower:** Fireweed. **Holiday:** Discovery Day, on the third Monday in Aug.
Road Conditions: 867-667-8215.
Police: 867-667-5555. For **emergencies** outside the Whitehorse area, *911 may not work.* Call the local police, listed under **Practical Information.**
Time Zone: Pacific (3hr. before Eastern, 1hr. after Alaska).
Postal Abbreviation: YT.
Sales Tax: None. **Drinking Age:** 19. **Traffic Laws:** Seatbelts required; radar detectors illegal.
Area Code: 867.

■ Whitehorse

Named for the once-perilous Whitehorse Rapids, whose crashing whitecaps were said to resemble the flowing manes of galloping white mares, Whitehorse is a modern crossroads in an ageless frontier. With over 23,000 residents, Whitehorse prides itself on being Canada's largest city north of 60 degrees latitude. The mountains, rivers, and lakes in all directions are a powerful reminder that "south of 60" is far, far away. While Yukon officials boast of their capital's rapid urban development, most locals and thousands of visiting nature-worshipers find that Whitehorse's real wealth lies in the gaping bush beyond the city limits, and in the laid-back northern spirit in every Whitehorse "hello." Although the rapids have now been tamed by a monolithic industrial dam, far more remains that has yet to be cemented, captured, or caged.

ORIENTATION AND PRACTICAL INFORMATION

Whitehorse lies 1500km north of Dawson Creek, BC along the Alaska Highway (see p. 381), and 535km south of Dawson City, YT. Take the downtown exit off the Alcan. Locals suggest avoiding the riverbank if alone at night.

Transportation

Airplanes: The airport is off the Alaska Hwy., just west of downtown. **Canadian Airlines** (668-4466, 668-3535 for reservations) flies to: **Calgary, AB** (2 per day, $774); **Edmonton, AB** (2 per day, $774); **Vancouver, BC** (2 per day, $652). Discounts available for advance purchase and certain flights. Student standby (under 24 with student ID) around $250; call for details. **Canada 3000** offers reduced fares to Vancouver on certain days ($309). Must be booked by an agent. Try **Uniglobe,** 2076 2nd Ave. (668-7464 or 800-661-0531; open in summer only M-F 8:30am-5pm).

Buses: The bus station is on the northeastern edge of town, a short walk from downtown.**Greyhound,** 2191 2nd Ave. (667-2223). To: Vancouver, BC (41hr., 1 per day, $278); Edmonton, AB (30hr., 1 per day, $215); and Dawson Creek, BC (18hr., 1 per day, 18hr., $157). No service to AK. The 7-day advance purchase of a **Canada Pass** may be cheaper. Buses run late June-Sept. M-Sa; in winter Tu, Th, and Sa. Desk open M, Tu, and Th 8am-5:30pm, W and F 4am-5:30pm, Sa 9:30am-1pm, Su 4-8am. **Alaska Direct** (668-4833 or 800-770-6652), in the Greyhound depot, handles Alaskan destinations. To: Anchorage (18hr., 3 per week, US$145); Fairbanks (14hr., 3 per week, US$120); Skagway (3hr., daily, US$35). in winter 1 bus per week to above destinations. **Norline** (668-3355), in the Greyhound depot. To: Dawson City (6½hr., 3 per week, 2 per week in winter $74).

Local Transportation: Whitehorse Transit (668-7433 for 24hr. info line). Limited service downtown and to local areas. Buses arrive and depart downtown next to Canadian Tire on Ogilvie St. Runs M-Th 6:15am-7:15pm, F 6:15am-10pm, Sa 8am-7pm. $1.25, seniors and disabled 60¢, students and children $1.

Taxis: Yellow Cab, 668-4811. 24hr.

Car Rental: Norcan Leasing, Ltd., 213 Range Rd. (668-2137 or 800-661-0445; 800-764-1234 from AK), off the Alcan at Mile 917.4. Cars from $50 per day; 22¢ per km after 100km. Must be 21 with credit card or pay a $700 minimum cash deposit.

Auto Repair: Petro Canada, 4211 4th Ave. (667-4003 or 667-4366). Full service. Oil and lube around $45. Open M-F 8am-5pm.

Visitor and Financial Services

Visitor Information: Whitehorse Visitor Reception Centre, 100 Hansen St. (667-3084), in the conspicuous Tourism and Business Centre at 2nd Ave. Open daily mid-May to mid-Sept. 8am-8pm; in winter M-F 9am-5pm.

Outdoor Information: Yukon Conservation Society, 302 Hawkins St. (668-5678), offers maps and great ideas on area hiking. Open M-F 10am-2pm.

Outdoor Equipment: The Sportslodge, 305 Main St. (668-6848), in the Hougen Centre. Basic outdoor camping gear, at good prices. Open M-F 9am-9pm, Sa 9am-6pm, Su 9am-4pm. **Kanoe People** (668-4899), at Strickland and 1st Ave., rents mountain bikes ($25 per day, $15 per half-day) and canoes. Credit card or $100 deposit required. Open daily 9am-6pm.

Banks: On 3 of the 4 corners at Main St. and 2nd Ave. **CIBC** (800-465-2422) has teller service M-Th 10am-3pm, F 10am-5pm, and ATMs accessible 24hr.

Library: 2071 2nd Ave. (667-5239) at Hanson. Internet access available. Open M-F 10am-9pm, Sa 10am-6pm, Su 1-9pm.

Laundromat: Norgetown, 4213 4th Ave. (667-6113), next to McDonald's at Ray St. Wash $2, dry 50¢ per 7½min. Open daily 8am-9pm.

Public Showers and Pool: Whitehorse Lions Pool, 4051 4th Ave. (668-7665) next to the High Country Inn. Pool and shower $4.50, seniors and children $2, students $3.50. Call for swim times.

Emergency and Communications

Emergency: 911. **Police:** 4100 4th (667-5555). Desk open M-F 7am-5:30pm.

Pharmacy: Shoppers Drug Mart, 211 Main St. (667-2485). Open M-F 9am-9pm, Sa 9am-6pm, Su 10am-6pm.

Hospital: Whitehorse General (393-8700), on Hospital Rd., just off Wickstrom Rd. across the river from downtown.
Post Office: General services, 211 Main St. (667-2485), in the basement of Shoppers Drug Mart. Open M-F 9am-6pm, Sa 11am-4pm. Also in Qwanlin Mall (667-2858) at 4th Ave. and Ogilvie in Coffee, Tea and Spice. Open M-Th 9:30am-6pm, F 9:30am-9pm, Sa 9:30am-6pm. **General Delivery** is at 3rd Ave. and Wood St., in the Yukon News Bldg. Open M-F 8am-6pm. **Postal Code** for last names beginning with the letters A-L is Y1A 3S7; for M-Z it's Y1A 3S8.
Internet Access: See **Library,** above.
Area Code: 867.

ACCOMMODATIONS AND CAMPGROUNDS

Camping in Whitehorse is somewhat limited, and hotels are exorbitantly priced. Countless interchangeable motels can be found around town with rates usually upwards of $65, reason enough to bring a tent. Cash-strapped tenters amenable to a 15-minute drive might head for the shores of **Long Lake,** where many a young wanderer has camped for free. (Though illegal, camping in non-designated areas is reportedly tolerated for one night. If, however, the police don't feel particularly tolerant the penalty is $500 and confiscation of camping equipment.) To get there, cross the bridge off 2nd Ave. in the southeast corner of town, turn left on Hospital Rd., turn left on Wickstrom Rd., and then follow the winding road to the lake.

Roadhouse Inn, 2163 2nd Ave. (667-2594), at the north end of town near the Greyhound depot. Nothing to write home about. Shared rooms, hall showers with bathtub. $20; private rooms (with cable and private bathroom) $50; each additional person $5. Laundry (wash and dry $1.75 each), free local calls. Key deposit $5; Lobby open 7am-2:30am.
98 Hotel, 110 Wood St. (667-2641), at 1st Ave. has wheelchair-accessible private rooms with sink and desk. Hallway bathrooms, no phones. Singles $30; doubles $45. Key deposit $10.
Robert Service Campground (668-3721), 1km from town on South Access Rd. along the Yukon River. A convenient stop for tenting types, but no RV sites. A home-away-from home for crowds of college students who summer in Whitehorse. The Robert Service has a food trailer, free firewood and pits, a playground, drinking water, toilets, metered showers ($1 per 5min.), and a knack for rhyming verse. Open late May to early Sept. 68 sites: $11. Gates open 7am-midnight.
High-Country RV Park (667-7445), at the intersection of the Alaska Hwy. and South Access Rd., perched above town next to the Yukon Gardens. Free showers, 2 coinop laundromats, and for those on first dates, mini-golf across the street at the Gardens. 150 sites, so you can rest your rig with the rest of the Alcan RVs. $18-21 for 2 people ($23 with cable and sewer hookups), $3 each additional person; tents $12.

FOOD AND NIGHTLIFE

Get extra groceries at **Extra Foods** (667-6251), in the Quanlin Mall at 4th and Ogilvie (open M-W 8:30am-7pm, Th-F 8:30am-9pm, Sa 8:30am-6pm, Su 10am-6pm). Pick up some roughage to assuage greasy highway stomach at **The Fruit Stand** (393-3994), on 2nd and Black St. (open M-Sa 10:30am-7pm).

🏵**Klondike Rib and Salmon Barbecue,** 2116 2nd Ave. (667-7554). Sample arctic seafood without breaking the bank. For lunch, BBQ salmon or halibut comes with coleslaw ($8). Dinner prices shoot up, but the tasty fish and chips are a bargain at $11. The 100-year-old Klondike-era building's ambience is a relief from the tedium of hotel lounges. Open mid-May to Sept. M-F 11:30am-10pm, Sa-Su 5-10pm.
🏵**No Pop Sandwich Shop,** 312 Steele (668-3227), at 4th Ave. Whitehorse's suits and twenty-somethings converge at this popular lunch spot. Enjoy a Tel Aviv (ground beef, alfalfa, cream cheese) or veggie sandwich ($4.25). No pop, but lots of juices ($1.75) and alcoholic specialty drinks (about $6). Open Apr.-Sept. M-Th 7:30am-8:30pm, F 7:30am-9:30pm, Sa 10am-8:30pm, Su (brunch option) 10am-4pm.
Blackstone Cafe (667-6598), on the corner of 3rd and Wood St. Attracts Whitehorse's crunchy clan. Sit on the patio with a veggie paté sandwich ($5.25) or a

freshly baked muffin o' the day ($1.50). Myriad coffees come regular or organic (espresso $1.25). Open M-F 7am-11pm, Sat. 8am-11pm.

Annie Mae's Neighborhood Pub, 2163 2nd Ave. (668-7263), next to the Roadhouse Inn. Smoky, meat-and-potatoes trucker haven. Live country music, genuine character, and cholesterol at low prices (all-you-can-eat spaghetti $5, brews $3.50 a pint). Kitchen open daily 10am-midnight, bar noon-2am. Must be 19 to enter after noon.

Town & Mountain Hotel (668-7644), at 4th and Main, attracts tourists and locals alike when the sun goes down (or at least dips closer to the horizon). Offers live music and fairly inexpensive drinks. Open daily noon-2am.

SIGHTS, OUTDOORS, AND EVENTS

Visitors hungry for local history can feed their heads at the **MacBride Museum** (667-2709), at 1st Ave. and Wood St. *(Open daily June-Aug. 10am-6pm; call for winter hours. $4, students and seniors $3.50, children $2, 6 and under free.)* The sod-roofed log cabin in the museum courtyard was built in 1899 by Sam McGee, whose demise has been immortalized by Robert Service the Bard of the Yukon: "The Northern Lights have seen queer sights, but the queerest they ever did see, was that night on the marge of Lake Labarge, I cremated Sam McGee." If ancient history is more your bag, the new **Yukon Beringia Interpretive Centre** (667-8855; http://www.beringia.com), on the Alcan, 2km west of the junction with the South Access Rd., pays homage to the forgotten subcontinent that encompassed Siberia, Alaska, and the Yukon during the last ice age. *(Open mid-May to Sept. 8am-9pm; reduced hours in winter. $6, seniors $5, children $4.)* Remarkably, this area was untouched by glaciers, making it a veritable "hotbed" for animal and plant life. The center features fossils, models, a video, and many interactive exhibits. The restored **S.S. Klondike** (667-4511), on South Access Rd., is a dry-docked 1929 sternwheeler heralding the days when the Yukon River was the city's sole means of transportation. *(Open daily June-Aug. 9am-7pm, May and Sept. 9am-6pm; $3.50, children $2, families $8.)* The info booth at the entrance to the parking lot sells tickets for a video and guided tour.

There seem to be more trails than people around Whitehorse. The bush is so open and expansive that seasoned hikers can just wander, paying proper heed to the bear population, of course (see p. 47). The aggressively outdoorsy often trek to the distant bush of Kluane National Park (see p. 383) or beyond, but there are plenty of accessible dayhiking opportunities around town. *Whitehorse Area Hikes and Bikes* ($19) is a helpful companion for outdoor exploration. It's published by the **Yukon Conservation Society** and also sold at **Mac's Fireweed Books,** 203 Main St. (668-2434). **Grey Mountain,** partly accessible by gravel road, is a somewhat rigorous dayhike. Take the Lewes Blvd. bridge by the **S.S. Klondike** across the river and continue, then take a left on Alsek. Turn left again at the sign that says "Grey Mt. Cemetery" and follow this gravel road until it ends. Joggers, bikers, and cross-country skiers love the **Miles Canyon trail network** that parallels the **Yukon River.** To get there, take Lewes Blvd. to Nisutlin Dr. and turn right; just before the fish ladder, turn left onto the gravel Chadbum Lake Rd. and follow for 4km until you hit the parking area. The Conservation Society arranges free hikes on weekdays during July and August and offers guided nature walks during the spring. *(Office open M-F 10am-2pm.)*

Brave visitors who make the trek to Whitehorse in winter are rewarded with 300km of groomed and ungroomed **snowmobile trails** in the area. Every February, the annual **Yukon Quest 1000 Mile International Sled Dog Race** follows gold rush routes between Whitehorse and Fairbanks, alternating direction every year. It has been deemed "the toughest race in the world." Beginning in late May, the Yukon Historical and Museum Association, 3126 3rd Ave. (667-4707), sponsors **Heritage Walking Tours.** *(45min. tours every hr. daily 9am-4pm, some evening hours M-F. $2.)* The tours leave from Donnenworth House, in Lepage Park next to the infocenter. If you're walking by 3rd Ave. and Lambert St., look up: those three-story **log skyscrapers** were built singlehandedly in the 70s by a local septuagenarian.

In summer, the Yukon River begs to be played upon. On Canada Day (July 1) the river plays host to the popular **Rubber Duckie Race** (668-4546). The **MV Schwatka** (668-4716), on Miles Canyon Rd. off South Access Rd., floats folks through Miles Canyon. *(2hr. cruises; 2 per day June to early Sept. $18 ages 6-11 $9, under 6 free.)* **Up North Boat and Canoe Rentals,** 86 Wickstrom Rd. (667-7905), across the river from downtown, lets you paddle 25km to Jakkimi River. *(4hr.; $30 per person; includes pick-up and return to Whitehorse.)* An eight-day journey on the Teslin River costs $200, but there are cheaper options. If still-water canoeing sounds too tame, try **Tatshenshini Expediting** (633-2742) for an intense white water ride. *(One day $100; group rates available.)*

■ Alaska Highway (Hwy. 97): BC/Yukon Border to Whitehorse

Near the BC/Yukon border, the highway winds through tracts of scorched forest where gray, skeletal trees mix with new growth, stretching in all directions. From late August to the prime winter months, this area's night sky glimmers with the aurora borealis. The Alcan winds across the BC/Yukon border several times before it passes through Whitehorse. Just after its second crossing into the Yukon at 1021km, the highway runs through the small town of **Watson Lake** and the **Sign Post Forest,** which rose to fame when a homesick WWII Army engineer erected a sign indicating the mileage to his hometown of Danville, IL. Over 32,000 travelers have followed suit. The **Visitor Reception Centre** (536-7469) is hidden in the woods nearby (open May-Sept. daily 8am-8pm). Watson Lake also lures Alcan tourists with the **Northern Lights Centre** (867-536-7827; http://www.yukon.net/northernlights), on the bay, which teaches the science and legend behind the Aurora Borealis. (Exhibits free. 6 50min. shows daily, $10, seniors and students $9, children $6.) The **Liard Canyon Recreation Site** on **Lucky Lake,** 8km before town, makes for great picnicking and swimming. A long waterslide keeps 'em shrieking, while a 2.2km gradual hiking trail down the canyon is a relaxing and scenic stroll. While in town, wash your clothes while waiting for your car to be repaired at the **Shell Station** (536-2545, 24hr. assistance 536-2176), which has a mechanic, tire shop, and coin **laundry** (wash $1.50, dry 25¢ per 8min.; open daily June-Aug. 6am-10pm; in winter 8am-6pm). Accommodations in Watson Lake are plentiful but pricey; a budget traveler's best bets are out of town. **Watson Lake Campground,** 3km west of town along the highway and then 4km down a gravel road, sports primitive private sites ideal for tenting. Campers can swim on the lake or hike several trails of varying difficulty. Dining options in town are pretty much restricted to fast food and motel cafes/restaurants. The **Pizza Place** (536-7722), at the Gateway Motor Inn, is a somewhat pricey gem. Medium specialty pies start at $14, but ambitious eaters go right for the "Yukoner," loaded with mushrooms, salami, pepperoni, ham, onions, green peppers, bacon and ground beef. Walk away $21 lighter and many pounds heavier (open daily 6:30am-10pm).

Kilometer 1043 (a.k.a. Mile 649) marks the Alcan's junction with the **Cassiar Highway (Hwy. 37)** (see p. 333) leading south to **Yellowhead Highway (Hwy. 16)** (see p. 317). **Junction 37 Services** (536-2794)—at the junction—provides many reasonable accommodation options. (Sites $11; full hookups $16; singles or doubles in a bunk house with shared showers and bathrooms $30. Office open daily 6am-8pm.

About 260km west of Watson Lake, the **Dawson Peaks Resort** (390-2310; fax 390-2244; http://www.yukonweb.com/dawsonpeaks) on **Teslin Lake** has campsites ($8; hot showers $2, flush toilets, firewood, water), full hookups ($15-17), canvas tent platforms ($26), and private cabins with power and full bathrooms ($79). Savor a delectable burger ($6) or a slice of rhubarb pie ($2.50) while mellowing to mood music in the restaurant. Carolyn and Dave, the friendly hosts, lead river runs (4-5 days, $400), organize guided **fishing charters** ($40 per hr.), rent canoes ($7 per hr.) and powerboats ($25 per hr.), and pump some of the Yukon's least expensive gas.

The inconspicuous indigenous community of **Teslin,** 11km west of the resort, tells its story at the duly acclaimed **George Johnston Museum** (390-2550), on the Alcan at the west end of town. Born in Alaska in 1889, George Johnston was a Tlingit who ran a trap line and a general store while experimenting with photography on the side. Johnston's hobby left a legacy of stunning photographs documenting Tlingit life in Teslin Lake from 1910 to 1940. The museum also features a moose skin boat, Teslin's first automobile (bought by Johnson when the town was still roadless), and an excel-

THE YUKON

lent video about the Alaska Highway's effect on native people. (Open mid-May to early Sept. daily 9am-7pm. $3, students and seniors $2.50, children $1, families $7. Wheelchair accessible.) From Teslin, it's 183km of splendid driving to Whitehorse.

■ Carcross

Carcross, short for "Caribou Crossing," perches on the narrows between Bennett and Nares Lakes, entirely surrounded by snow-capped peaks and pristine waterways. At the turn of the century, Carcross served as a link in the treacherous Chilkoot gold route from Skagway to the Yukon River, and later as a supply depot for the construction of the Alaska Highway. Since then, mining and tourism have buoyed Carcross' population of 400. Each summer, a few thousand hearty souls retrace the steps of the prospectors along the Chilkoot trail, while more sedentary tourists cruise into town to enjoy the town's rustic charm and the villagers' genuine warmth.

ORIENTATION AND PRACTICAL INFORMATION On the Klondike Hwy. (Hwy. 2), Carcross is 74km south of Whitehorse and 106km north of Skagway, AK.

   Atlin Express (250-651-7575) runs buses from Carcross to Atlin, BC (see p. 344; 2hr.; $21, seniors $18, ages 5-11 $10.50, under 5 free) and Whitehorse (1¼hr.; $15, seniors $13, ages 5-11 $7.50, under 5 free). The **Visitor Reception Centre** (821-4431), inside the depot, is open mid-May to mid-September (daily 8am-8pm). Tune in to **visitor info** on 96.1 FM. Suds your duds with **Montana Services** (821-3708), at the Shell Station on Hwy. 2 just north of town (wash $2.25, dry 25¢ per 4min.; open daily 7am-11pm; in winter 8am-8pm). **Public showers** are available here for $3. A **health station** (821-4444) is inside the two-story red building across from the back of the Caribou Hotel. An **ambulance** can be reached at 821-3333, and the **police** at either 821-5555 or 667-5555. The **post office** is the white building with red trim on Bennett Ave. (open M, W, and F 8am-noon and 2:30-4pm, Tu and Th 10-11:45am). **Postal Code:** Y0B 1B0. **Area Code:** 867.

ACCOMODATIONS AND FOOD The **Caribou Hotel** (821-4501), across from the infocenter, is the only hotel in Carcross and the oldest operating hotel in the Yukon. It's a bit aged with a little lounge noise from the popular bar below; rooms include a comfy bed and shared bath but no phones, TVs, or room keys (singles and doubles $38). The Yukon Government maintains 14 **secluded campsites** ($8) with potable water, firewood, and pit toilets by the airstrip, across Hwy. 2 from the Shell Station. **Spirit Lake Wilderness Resort** (821-4337), 10km north of town on Hwy. 2, has varied lakeside accommodations (tents $9.50, with power $12.50; amenity-free cabins $50; motel $79) with flush toilets, showers ($2), and coin laundry. Canoes available for $7.50 per hour or longer outings.

   Don't look for gourmet food in Carcross. The **Caribou Hotel Cafe** has standard soups and sandwiches in the $5-7 range (open May-Oct. daily 7am-9pm), and the **Spirit Lake resort** serves slightly fancier grub, like a lunch of Dutch pancakes for $7 (open May-Sept. daily 8am to around 9pm, depending on the spirits' whims).

SIGHTS AND OUTDOORS Hiking in the Carcross area inspires justifiable acclaim. If possible, find a copy of *Whitehorse Area Hikes and Bikes* at the Carcross infocenter or in a Whitehorse bookstore before setting out. The most popular hike in the area is the **Chilkoot Trail** (see below), a moderately difficult three- to five-day adventure to the far end of Lake Bennett. The lake's 2 mi. sandy beach is understandably popular with locals in July and August. South of town, a rough mining road probes partway up **Montana Mountain** past lichen, snow, and boulders; allow a day for the trip. To get there, follow Hwy. 2 south, take the first right after crossing the bridge, then the first left, and go on until the road becomes impassable; from there, it's all on foot up to an astounding view of the Yukon.

   The Barracks (821-4372), across the railroad tracks from the Reception Centre, *(Open May-Sept. daily 9am-6pm.)* is a bizarre 1920s building which peddles Yukon-made crafts, clothing, and souvenirs. If you're lucky, you'll be serenaded by the old player piano or thrown into the store's gold rush era jail cell. For a memorable confectionery experience, try the sunken treasure floats ($2.75) or chocolate moose nugget sundaes ($3.75). **Frontierland** (821-4055), 1km north of the **Carcross "Desert"** (the exposed, sandy bottom of a glacial lake), houses a collection of dead wildlife, including the **largest bear ever mounted.** *(Open mid-May to mid-Sept. daily 8am-6pm; Museum and neighboring park $6.50, children $4, family $20; gallery or park alone $4 and $3.)*

The Chilkoot Trail

The winter of 1898 saw nine out of every ten Klondike-bound stampeders slog 33 miles through Skagway and Dyea on their way to Lake Bennett, with at least 1000 pounds of provisions strapped to them and their horses. A Canadian law forced each miner headed north to bring this staggering amount of supplies. As one hiker said, "It's hard enough to do the trail with just yourself to look after. Imagine looking after yourself, plus a half a ton of mining supplies and beef jerky. And a horse."

What once took weeks can now be accomplished in a rigorous four-day hike. Wagon wheels, horse bones, and other gold-rush relics still litter the precipitous Chilkoot Pass, along with plaques placed by the U.S. and Canadian National Park Services which interpret the trail's historical significance. The rugged trail weaves through dramatic changes of climate, terrain, and vegetation, passing above the timberline before descending into the forests of northern British Columbia. The best approach to the Chilkoot is to take a bus from Carcross to Skagway, then arrange to have a boat pick you up at the far end of Lake Bennett. Alaska Overland (667-7896) runs a morning bus to Skagway for $40, and Bennett Charters (667-1486) handles all of the boat pick-ups. With the 100th anniversary of the Gold Rush attracting hikers, a permit system has been instituted for hikes from late May to early September. *($35, children $17.50; $10 reservations recommended. Call 667-3910 in Whitehorse or 907-983-3655 in Skagway).* Pack light; don't lose your horse.

■ Kluane National Park

When the Southern Tutchone (tuh-SHOW-nee) named this area Kluane (kloo-AH-nee), meaning "place of many fish," they made a flagrant understatement. Kluane National Park is also a place of many Dall sheep, ground squirrels, eagles, glaciers, and untouched mountains. Together with adjacent Wrangell-St. Elias National Park in Alaska and Tatshenshini/Alsek Provincial Park in BC, Kluane makes up one of the world's largest wilderness areas. It contains Canada's highest peak, Mt. Logan (5959m or 19,545 ft.), as well as the most massive non-polar ice fields in the world. The abundance of ice-blanketed mountains makes Kluane's interior a haven for experienced expeditioners, but also renders two-thirds of the park inaccessible (except by plane) to humbler hikers. Fortunately, the northeastern park border along the Alaska Hwy. has plenty of room for backpacking, canoeing, rafting, biking, and dayhiking. Many routes follow original Southern Tutchone and Tlingit trails or old mining roads left over from Kluane's brief and disappointing fling with the gold rush from 1904-1905.

ORIENTATION AND PRACTICAL INFORMATION

Kluane's 22,015km² are bounded by the **Kluane Game Sanctuary** and the **Alaska Highway (Hwy. 1)** to the north, and the Haines Highway (Hwy. 3) to the east. Haines Junction is a small town of 800 residents at the eastern park boundary, 158km west of Whitehorse, and serves as the gateway and headquarters of the park, although there is access to trails on the north of the park from the Sheep Mountain Visitor Centre, 72km northeast of Haines Junction on the Alcan (see below).

Buses: Alaska Direct (800-770-6652, in Whitehorse 668-4833) runs from Haines Junction on Su, W, and F to: Anchorage (US$125); Fairbanks (US$100); Whitehorse (US$20); and Skagway (US$35).

Visitor Information: Kluane National Park Visitor Reception Centre (634-7209), on Logan St. in Haines Junction (Km 1635 on the Alcan). The Park Service staff provides **wilderness permits** ($5 per night, $50 per season), **fishing permits** ($5 per day, $35 per season), **topographical maps** ($10), and **trail and weather info.** A

THE YUKON

helpful overview of Kluane's trails and routes costs $1, and those heading to Haines, AK, can pick up a free handout of things to see and do along the 246km drive. Park staff available May-Sept. daily 9am-5pm; in winter M-F 10am-noon, 1-4pm. A **Yukon Tourism** (634-2345) desk also operates mid-May to mid-Sept., proffering information for outside the park. Open daily 8am-8pm. The phoneless **Sheep Mountain Information Centre,** 72km north of town at Alaska Hwy. Km 1707, registers hikers headed for the northern area of the park. Open late May to Labour Day daily 9am-6pm.

Radio: 92.9 FM. Erratically on-the-air mid-May to mid-Sept.

Bank: CIBC (634-2820), in Madley's General Store on Haines Rd. at Bates St.; will exchange foreign currency or cash traveler's checks but does not handle cash withdrawals for non-CIBC customers. Open M-Th 12:30-4:30pm, F 12:30-5pm; in winter M-Th 1-4pm, F 1-4:30pm; no ATM.

Auto Repair: Triple S Garage (634-2915), 1km north of Haines Junction on the Alcan, has oil and lubes (about $35), tire and general repair, and 24hr. towing. Open May-Sept. M-F 7am-7pm, Sa 8am-6pm; in winter M-F 8am-5pm.

Library: (634-2215), on Haines Rd., next door to Madley's, has Internet access and air-conditioning. Open Tu-F 1-5pm, Sa 2-5pm.

Laundromat and Public Showers: Gateway Motel (634-2371) at the junction of the Alaska Hwy. and Haines Rd. Wash $2, dry 25¢ per 6min., shower $3. Open year-round 8:30am-11pm.

Emergency & Police: 634-5555 (if no answer, call 867-667-5555). **Ambulance/Clinic:** 634-4444. **Fire:** 634-2222.

Post Office: (634-3802), also in Madley's. Open M, W, and F 9-10am and 1-5pm, Tu and Th 9am-noon and 1-5pm. **Postal Code:** Y0B1L0.

Internet Access: See **Library,** above.

Area Code: 867.

CAMPGROUNDS, ACCOMMODATIONS, AND FOOD

Haines Junction offers the standard array of clean-but-forgettable highway motels and RV parks. Staying in one of the many gorgeous lakeside campgrounds is the budget traveler's best bet, and a good way to appreciate the park's wilderness offerings. The idyllic **Kathleen Lake Campground,** off Haines Rd., 27km south of Haines Junction, is close to hiking and fishing and has water, flush toilets, fire pits, firewood, and campfire talks (sites $10; open June-Oct.; wheelchair access). The closest government campground to Haines Junction is popular **Pine Lake,** on the Alcan, 7km east of town, featuring a sandy beach complete with a pit for late night bonfires ($8; water, firewood, pit toilets). The **Dezadeash Lake Campground,** about 50km south of Haines Junction on Haines Rd., offers the same deal and sweet lakefront property.

Seekers of an indoor bed with modern facilities and downtown access can march straight to **Laughing Moose B&B,** 120 Alsek Crescent (634-2335), four blocks from the junction, with a sparkling-clean kitchen, spacious common room with TV and VCR, and a view of the Auriol Mountains (singles $60; doubles $70; shared bath). For a bed without the flair, the **Stardust Motel** (634-2591), 1km north of town on the Alcan, offers spacious rooms with TV and antiseptic tubs, but no phone (singles $45; doubles $55; with kitchenette $75 first day, $65 per additional day).

Haines Junction restaurants offer standard highway cuisine. **Village Bakery and Deli** (634-2867), on Logan St. across from the visitor center, sates a sweet tooth with a cinnamon bun ($1.50) or more substantial soups ($3.50). Watch out for periodic live music (open May-Sept. daily 7:30am-9pm). For groceries (hardware, tackle, slingshots, etc.), head to **Madley's General Store** (634-2200), at Haines Rd. and Bates St. (open May-Sept. daily 8am-9pm; Oct.-Apr. daily 8am-6:30pm).

OUTDOORS IN THE PARK

Kluane makes its few trails very accessible. Pictures of what seem to be a misshapen dog head actually depict beavers and indicate a trail head or park boundary. Before setting out, pick up verbal and written info from the visitor center (see **Practical Information,** above). The **Dezadeash River Loop** (DEZ-dee-ash) trailhead is downtown at the day-use area across from Madley's on Haines Rd. This flat, forested 5km stroll may disappoint those craving a vertical challenge, but it makes a nice jaunt and the first kilometer is wheelchair accessible. As always, have a noise-maker or belt out tunes to warn bears you're coming. The 15km **Auriol Trail** is a slightly harder option and has a primitive campground halfway through its loop. The trail begins 7km south of Haines Junction on Haines Rd. and cuts through boreal forest, leading to a subalpine bench just in front of the Auriol Range. This is a popular overnight trip, though four to six hours is adequate time without packs. In winter, the Auriol turns into a favorite **cross-country ski** route. The 5km (one-way) **King's Throne Route** is a very challenging but rewarding dayhike with a 1220m elevation gain and a panoramic view. It begins at the **Kathleen Lake** day-use area at the campground (see **Accommodations,** above). Also starting from this area, the **Kokanee Trail** provides a short and easy 0.3km boardwalk along Kathleen Lake for a nice wheelchair accessible stroll.

Excellent hiking awaits near **Sheep Mountain** in the park's northern section. An easy 0.5km jaunt up to **Soldier's Summit** starts 1km north of the Sheep Mountain Info Centre and leads to the site where the original highway was completed in 1942. Only the most experienced backpackers should attempt the difficult trek along the **Slims River** to gawk at the magnificent **Kaskawulsh Glacier.** Two rough routes along the river banks are available, stretching 23 and 30km one-way and requiring three to five days; register and buy backcountry permits at the info center. Routes, as opposed to trails, are not maintained and do not have marked paths, are generally more challenging, and require backcountry navigation skills. The park mandates the use of bear-resistant food canisters on overnight trips, which it provides for free with a $150 refundable deposit (cash or credit). Registration for overnighters is also mandatory (see **Practical Information,** above). Risks are the reality in Kluane country.

For **mountain bikers,** the **Alsek River Valley Trail** follows a bumpy old mining road 14km to Sugden Creek. Starting from Alcan Km 1645, the rocky road crosses several streams before gently climbing to a ridge with a stellar view of the Auriol Mountains. Be prepared for a battered rump the next day.

Two booking companies in Haines Junction can set the adrenaline junkie up with an outfitter, free of charge. **PaddleWheel** (634-2683), down the road from the Village Bakery, rents and sells everything the outdoor enthusiast could possible need, including outdoor gear (tents, packs, bear spray, etc.). *(Bikes $20 per day; $50 for three days. Bike repair $25. Canoes $25 per day.)* They also offer certified guiding service for hiking, biking, or canoeing in the area. *($50 per guide per half-day, $100 per day.)* The **Kluane Park Adventure Centre** (634-2313), on the Alcan just east of downtown, specializes in rafting. For $100, travelers can ride the Class III and IV rapids on the **Blanchard** and **Tatshenshini Rivers** from Copper Mine, BC to Dalton Post, YT. The center also offers a three-hour scenic interpretive **float trip** on the **Dezadeash River** illustrating the park's ecology, fauna, and geology ($35) and books trail rides, shuttle services, and flightseeing tours. *(Open late May-early Sept. daily 8am-8pm.)*

Anglers can readily put the park's "place of many fish" reputation to the test. **Kathleen Lake** (see above) is home to lake and rainbow trout, arctic grayling, and Kokanee salmon. To avoid the crowds, hike with a rod along the easy 3.4km trail to isolated **St. Elias Lake.** The trailhead is 60km south of Haines Junction along the Haines Rd. Visitors can get a **National Parks fishing permit** at the visitor center in Haines Junction or at Madley's General Store (see **Practical Information,** above). Those interested in fishing outside the park can purchase territorial licenses at Madley's and Kluane RV Park.

■ Alaska Highway (Hwy. 1): Sheep Mountain to the Alaska Border

Heading northwest from Haines Junction on the Alaska Hwy., a smattering of petite pit stops pile up before the Alaska Border, where the time **jumps back an hour.** For several kilometers past **Sheep Mountain,** the highway winds along beside the gorgeous, 60km **Kluane Lake.** Congdon Creek Campground, at Km 1723 on the Alcan,

THE YUKON

is the nicest campground before the U.S. border, with great waterfront real estate and a long stone beach for evening strolls (80 sites: $8; water, pit toilets, firewood). The small town of **Destruction Bay,** at Km 1743 (Historic Milepost 1083) earned its foreboding name from the tremendous wind which tunnels down the valley and off Kluane Lake; winds destroyed the first village in 1952. Nowadays, it's home to a **gas station,** motel, and cafe (all built low to the ground). A nurse is on call 24hr. at the **health clinic** (841-4444; open M-F 9am-5pm). **Destruction Bay Lodge** (841-5332) is a convenient spot to rest the rig (hookups $18, sites $10; showers, flush toilets). Due to high winds, a strict **fire ban** is enforced in the town.

Burwash Landing, 16km uproad, is next in the Alcan's string o' little things, and offers modest thrills at the **Kluane Museum of Natural History** (841-5561), home to the Yukon's largest wildlife display and a collection of Southern Tutchone artifacts (open June-Aug. daily 9am-9pm; $3, seniors $2.75, children 6-12 $1.50). **Kluane First Nation's Dalan Campground** has a few roomy, secluded sites on the lake, with wood, water, and pit toilets (25 sites, $10). Tent for free on the grassy lawn at **Burwash Landing Resort** (841-4441; showers $3; hookups $15). The lakeside resort houses a restaurant which serves sandwiches and burgers with fries ($6.25; open May-Sept. daily 7am-11pm). Those wanting a roof will have to dole out $60 for a single or $70 for a double with TV and private bathroom. Another 39km up the road, **Kluane Wilderness Village** (841-4141), at Km 1798 (Historical Mile 1118), is a self-contained, roadside vacation station, featuring gas (open 24hr.), tenting ($7.50), full hookups ($19.75 with satellite TV), private cabins (singles $50, $5 per additional person) and a very affordable cafe (open late-May to Labour Day daily 7am-11pm).

The most booming of all these roadside wonders, **Beaver Creek** (176km north of Burwash Landing), has the last Canadian services before the border. The Alcan around Beaver Creek is under sporadic repair. The local *modus operandi* is to hit the lounge at the **202 Motor Inn** (862-7600; wheelchair accessible; open until 2am), then nurse a hangover over breakfast at **Ida's Hotel and Cafe** (862-7223). Ida's grills up eggs and toast ($5.50) or two hotcakes ($5.50); for lunch, $6.50 fetches a mushroom burger and fries (open June-Aug. daily 6am-11pm; in winter daily 8am-9pm; wheelchair accessible). **Westmark RV** (862-7501) is as good a spot as any in town to park for the night ($10; hookups $19; includes showers, tea/coffee, flush toilets) and has laundry facilities (wash $1, dry 25¢ per 7min.).

Past Beaver Creek, 20 miles of highway and wilderness separate U.S. and Canadian customs and immigration, although several signs and landmarks can be found at the official border on the 141st meridian. Beginning 5 mi. into U.S. territory, three gas stations vie for cross-border business along the Alcan (US$1.50 per gallon). All are considerably cheaper than anything in Canada. From the border it's 80 miles to Tetlin Junction, which is the start of the Taylor Highway (see p. 473) and 92 miles to Tok.

■ Dawson City

Gold! Gold! Gold! Of all the insanity ever inspired by the lust for the dust, the creation of Dawson City must be one of the wildest. For 12 glorious, crazy months, from July 1898 to July 1899, this was the largest Canadian city west of Toronto, known as "the Paris of the North." Perched on the doorstep of the Arctic Circle and 1000 mi. from any other settlement, its 30,000 residents, with names like Swiftwater Bill, Skookum Jim, Arizona Charlie Meadows, and Evaporated Kid, set out to make their fortunes. Each had lugged 1000 lb. of provisions over the treacherous Chilkoot Trail to the Yukon (see p. 383), and each was determined to become filthy, stinkin' rich.

After a year of frenzied claim-staking and legend-making, most of the once-eager Sourdoughs (prospectors or, today, anyone who survives an Arctic winter) followed the Yukon River to Nome, and Dawson City fizzled almost as quickly as it had exploded. With the exception of a few who staked prime claims, most left Dawson empty-handed. In the early 60s the Klondike Visitors Association and the Canadian government set out to return Dawson City to its gold-rush glory, restoring dirt roads, long boardwalks, wooden store fronts, and in the process transforming it into the lively RV and college student destination that it is today.

ORIENTATION AND PRACTICAL INFORMATION

To reach Dawson City, take the **Klondike Hwy. (Hwy. 2)** 533km north from Whitehorse, or follow the majestic **Top-of-the-World Hwy. (Hwy. 9)** 108km east from the Alaska border (see **Taylor Hwy.**, p. 473). If you take the Klondike, fill up in Whitehorse, since there is scant gas along the way (approximately every 100km).

Buses: Norline Coaches (993-6010), at the Shell Station on 5th Ave. and Princess St. To: Whitehorse (6½hr., 3 per week, in winter 2 per week, $74). A slightly cheaper option is the **Dawson City Taxi Courier Service** (993-6688) which runs a van leaving from the Downtown Hotel for Whitehorse (6½hr., June-Aug. daily at 6pm, $62). Reservations required.

Ferries: Yukon Queen River Cruises (993-5599), on Front St. next to the Keno. Departs daily at 8:30am for Eagle, AK along the Yukon River. Includes hot meals and river narration. One-way standby US$82; round-trip US$135; will return canoes from Eagle for US$50. Office open M-Sa 9:30am-5:30pm, Su noon-5:30pm.

Car Rental: Budget, 451 Craig St. (993-5644), in the Dawson City B&B (see **Accommodations,** below). $46 per day, plus 19¢ per km after 100km. Free pick up and delivery within Dawson City. Must be 21.

Auto Repair: Esso (993-5142) on the highway immediately before town. Open only in summer M-F 9am-6pm, Sa-Su noon-6pm.

Visitor Information: Visitor Reception Centre (993-5566), at Front and King St. Historical movies, extensive info, and tours of Dawson City's attractions. Open mid-May to mid-Sept. daily 8am-8pm. For info by mail, write to **Klondike Visitors Association,** P.O. Box 389C, Dawson City, YT Y0B 1G0. The **Northwest Territories Visitor Centre** (993-6167) is across the street. Advice on driving the Dempster Hwy. (see p. 390). Open daily late May to early Sept. 9am-8pm.

Banks: Canadian Imperial Bank of Commerce, at 2nd Ave. and Queen. St. The only bank and **ATM** in town. Open M-Th 10am-3pm, F 10am-5pm.

Equipment Rental: Dawson City River Hostel (see **Accommodations,** below). Bikes $20 per day, canoes $20 per day. Non-hostelers must use passport as deposit.

Library: (993-5571), at 5th Ave. and Princess St., in the school. Open Tu-Th 10am-9pm, F-Sa 10am-5pm; in winter Tu-W and F 9am-7pm, Th 1-8pm, Sa noon-5pm.

Laundromat and Public Showers: Gold Rush Campground (see **Accommodations,** below). Wash $2.50, dry 25¢. Showers $2 per 6min. Open daily 24hr.

Weather and Road Conditions: 96.1 FM.

Police: (993-5555; if no answer 1-667-5555), at Front St. and Turner St., in the southern part of town. **Ambulance:** 993-4444. **Fire:** 993-2222.

Crisis Line: Dawson Women's Shelter (993-5086). 24hr.

Medical Services: (993-4444), at 6th Ave. and Church. Open M-F 8:30am-5pm.

Dawson City
ACCOMMODATIONS
A Dawson City River Hostel
B Yukon River Campground
D The Bunkhouse
C Gold Rush Campground
E Dawson City B&B

Post Office: (993-5342), at 5th Ave. and Princess St. Open M-F 8:30am-5:30pm, Sa 9am-noon. Must register for general delivery service; photo ID required. The **Historical Post Office,** at 3rd and King St., is closer to downtown. Open M-F noon-6pm. **Postal Code:** Y0B 1G0.

Internet Access: See **Library,** above. Also at **Harper Street Publishing** (993-6671), on 2nd Ave. between Princess and Queen St. Open M-F 9:30am-5:30pm; $6 per 30min.

Area Code: 867.

ACCOMMODATIONS AND CAMPGROUNDS

The hostel and the campground on the west side of town, across the Yukon River, are by far the cheapest options in the trap that is Dawson City tourism. The **ferry** to float you and your wheels across is free and runs 24 hours. Hop on at Front and Albert St., in the north end of town. The **tent city** in the woods next to the hostel is a happy home to many of the town's summer college crowd, despite the $100 per person fee the government now charges these temporary forest dwellers.

◉**Dawson City River Hostel (HI-C)** (993-6823), across the Yukon River from downtown; take the 1st left off the ferry. The northernmost hostel in Canada, and the best bargain in town. Bunks in new log cabins, a wood-heated "prospector's bath," outdoor kitchen facilities, a cozy lounge with wood stove and mini-library, and a beautiful hilltop view of the river and city. Beds $13, nonmembers $16; tent sites $9 for one person, $6.50 per additional person. Open May-Sept.

Yukon River Campground, on the 1st right off the ferry. Roomy, secluded sites are a haven for nature-lovers, who can peer at the peregrine falcons nesting across the river. Water and pit toilets. RVs welcome, but no hookups. Sites $8.

The Bunkhouse (993-6164; fax 993-6051), at Front and Princess St. Clean and conveniently located, with wood-planked rooms and tiny shared bathrooms. Singles $45, with bath $75; doubles $50, with bath $80; quads with bath $105. 10% senior discount. Open mid-May to mid-Sept.

Dawson City Bed and Breakfast, 451 Craig St. (993-5649), on the south end of town. More like home than your own. Singles $75; doubles $85, both with shared bath; double with private bath $95. Seniors and AAA members 5% discount. Winter discount $6. Make reservations at least a week in advance.

Gold Rush Campground (993-5247), at 5th and York St. This RV parking is always packed. Laundromat (wash $2.50, dry $1.50), shower ($2 per 6min.), and dump station. Water and electric hookups $20, pull-through $21. Open May-Sept.

FOOD

On Thanksgiving Day in 1898, a turkey in Dawson City cost over $100. Prices today are more reasonable, and there are a few good places to eat in town. Snag a bag of groceries at the **Dawson City General Store** (993-5475), on Front St. Open M-Sa 8am-8pm, Su 10am-8pm.

Klondike Kate's (993-6527), at 3rd and King St., in one of Dawson's oldest buildings. Kate's breakfast special (served until 11am) would satisfy the hungriest Sourdough (2 eggs, bacon or sausage, home fries, and toast for $4). At lunch, kick back on the patio with a gyro or veggie wrap ($5). Open mid-May to mid-Sept. daily 7am-11pm.

River West Food and Health (993-6339), on Front and Queen St. This health store/cafe bakes a mean loaf of supergrain bread. Muffins, snacks, organic coffees ($1.50-3.75), and possibly the only hummus pitas in the Yukon ($6). Open M-Sa 7am-7pm, Su 9am-5pm; in winter M-Sa 10am-6pm.

Midnight Sun Hotel Restaurant (993-5495), 3rd and Queen St. Chinese entrees, created by chefs invited from Vancouver for the summer (from $10). Standard western cuisine (sandwiches, burgers, etc.) $5-8. Chew on chow from the lunch smorgasbord on F ($10). Open Su-Th 6am-1am, F-Sa 6am-3am.

The Jack London Grill (993-5346), in the Downtown Hotel at 2nd and Queen St. Those a bit too road-worn for the ultra-posh dining room can sip for a bit in the accompanying saloon (must be 19). Lunch sandwiches from $6. Gourmet dinner entrees start at $11 for veggie stir fry and hit the roof from there; a budgeter's best bets are the large and tasty shrimp or chicken caesar salads ($10). Open Su-Th 6am-10pm, F-Sa 6am-11pm; in winter Su-Th 7am-9pm, F-Sa 7am-10pm.

SIGHTS, ENTERTAINMENT, AND EVENTS

The prospectors' stampede to Dawson City died down in the early 1900s, but today's Dawson is a boomtown for museums and tours that provide enough information about gold mining and frontier life to break the bank. The visitor center sells a package **Prospector's Pass,** which pays off only if you want to see everything ($15).

The goldfields of **Bonanza** and **Eldorado Creeks** yielded some of the richest lodes discovered in the Klondike. Nearly 16km of maintained gravel road follow Bonanza Creek to the former site of **Grand Forks,** chewed up when the dredges came through. Along the way are **Gold Dredge #4,** a monster of a machine used to thoroughly mine Bonanza Creek after the rush was over, and **Discovery Claim,** the site of the first discovery of gold in Dawson by George Carmack on August 16, 1896. **Bear Creek,** 13km south of town on the Klondike Hwy., is a ghost town of tools and machinery left behind when mining suddenly halted in 1966. *(Tours of Bear Creek or the Dredge $5.)* **Goldbottom Mining Tours and Gold Panning** (993-5023), 30km south of town, offers a tour of an operating mine and an hour of panning. *(Open in summer daily 11am-7pm. $12.)* Anyone can pan for free at the confluence of the Bonanza and Eldorado Creeks; you just need your own pan, available at local hardware stores. Panning anywhere else along the creeks could lead to a very unpleasant encounter with the owner/miner of the claim you're jumping.

Experience frontier literary genius at the **Jack London Cabin,** on 8th Ave. and Firth St., where the great Californian author's life and brief stint in the Yukon are recounted during lectures. *(Open daily 10am-1pm and 2-6pm. Tours 30min., daily noon and 2:15pm. Free.)* The cabin is worth a visit just to see the photos of a struggling young London. Be sure to catch the animated **Robert Service readings** given at his nearby cabin. Authentic performances of witty ballads by the Yukon Bard, including "The Cremation of Sam McGee" and "The Shooting of Dan McGrew," are given in front of the cabin at 8th Ave. and Hanson St., where he penned them. *(Shows daily June-Aug. at 10am and 3pm. Cabin open 9am-noon and 1-5pm. $6, under 8 $3. Cabin viewing free.)* For a broader, less lyrical historical perspective, check out the **Dawson City Museum** (993-5007), on 5th Ave. in Minto Park. Exhibits on the region's geography, natives, first settlers, and the gold rush complement special films, demonstrations, and a children's exhibit of family heirlooms. *($4, students and seniors $3, family $10. Wheelchair accessible.)*

No, Ma'am, That's Not an Olive in Your Martini

When some people run across amputated body parts, they take them to a hospital for surgical reattachment and a new career in the X-rated film industry. But for Capt. Dick Stevenson, the discovery of a pickled human toe in a cabin in the Yukon meant one thing: a damn fine cocktail. The drink became famous and spawned the Sourtoe Cocktail Club, whose 14,000-plus members include a 6 month-old child and a 91 year-old toe-swallower. Aspiring initiates buy a drink of their choice and pay a small fee ($5) to Bill "Stillwater Willie" Holmes (Dick's replacement as keeper of the sourtoe), who drops the chemically preserved (er, pickled) toe in the drink. Then it's bottoms up, and the moment the toe touches your lips, you're in the club. "You can drink it fast, you can drink it slow—but the lips have gotta touch the toe." Listening to Stillwater Willie explain the club's sordid history and philosophize about life in the Yukon is itself worth the $5, but the fee includes a certificate and membership card; a commemorative pin or a book relating the saga of the sourtoe can be purchased separately for $5 each. Toe info regarding initiation times can be found at the Downtown Hotel (993-5346) on the corner of Queen and 2nd. A word of warning for those who dare: be careful not to swallow the toe as a few members have done—Stillwater Willie may require that any lost toe be replaced.

THE YUKON

Diamond Tooth Gertie's, at 4th and Queen St., was Canada's first legal casino, and proves that Dawson is no movie set: for a $5 cover (or $20 season pass), gamblers can fritter away the night with roulette, blackjack, or even "Texas hold 'em" against local legends Johnny Caribou and No Sleep Filippe. Free nightly floor shows go up at 8:30pm, 10:30pm, and 12:30am. *(19+ only. Open nightly 7pm-2am.)* The **Gaslight Follies** (993-6217), a high-kicking vaudeville revue, is held in the **Palace Grand Theatre** on King St., between 2nd and 3rd St. *(W-M 8pm. Box office open daily 11am-8pm. $15-17, children $7.50.)* As the night winds down, the **Sun Tavern and Lounge** (993-5495), at 3rd Ave. and Queen St., is where everyone ends up. Once Dawson's roughest bar, the Sun has since cooled down, but it's still no place to sip fruity drinks. *(Open daily noon-2am.)* A pint of brew costs $3.75. **Pleasure Island Restaurant and Yukon River Cruises** (993-5482), on Front St. between King and Queen St., wrap several elements of Yukon culture into a single package; the 2hr. experience includes a cruise on the *Yukon Lou,* an all-you-can-eat salmon barbecue on Pleasure Island, and a chance to meet the owner's sled-dog team. *(Depart at 4, 5:30, and 6:45 pm. $40, children $20.)* The *Yukon Lou* also makes a daily 1½hr. cruise at 1pm ($25, children $12.50).

Dawson is a jungle-gym for outdoorspeople. The Dawson City River Hostel (see **Accommodations,** above) sells topographical maps of the region ($12), and arranges four-day **canoe trips** to Eagle, AK for US$110, or ten-day trips to Circle, AK for US$270. A trip up the **Midnight Dome,** 7km along Dome Rd., just past the Esso gas station on the way into town, is a tradition on the **summer solstice** (June 19), on which the sun just dips below the horizon for 20 minutes around 12:30am. Even for those who miss the solstice, the Midnight Dome makes for a panoramic picnic spot. The steep 4km trail ascends over 600m. The visitor center has photocopied maps.

During the third weekend of July, the **Dawson City Music Festival** is a jamming good time, with artists hailing from all over Canada. Labour Day visitors will not want to pass up their chance to behold the **Great International Outhouse Race.** This bizarre athletic event is a true measure of stamina, as teams of contenders for the coveted trophy pull occupied outhouses on wheels through the streets of Dawson.

■ Top of the World Highway (Hwy. 9)

This 127km majestic highway truly deserves its name. Starting across the Yukon River from Dawson City, climbing for several kilometers and then following the spine of a series of mountains, the trip affords breathtaking views of nearby mountains before connecting with the Taylor Highway at **Jack Wade Junction** in Alaska. The 12km route is open May through September, though the mountainous Yukon-Alaska border crossing at kilometer108 is only open 9am-9pm Pacific time. There are no services on the Canadian side except the **Top of the World Golf Course** (867-667-1472), 3km past the ferry (open June-July 24hr.). While the Canadian side of the road is well maintained (although especially slippery when wet), the dirt and potholed gravel road on the American side will have you cursing Uncle Sam in no time. Just past the American border, the phoneless **Boundary Cafe** sells typical grill food and will trade a gallon of gasoline for your soul (meaning $2).

▓ Dempster Highway

Named after Inspector W.J.D. Dempster, one of the most courageous officers to wear the Mountie redcoat, the Dempster Highway begins in the Yukon as Hwy. 5 and wends 741 spectacular kilometers to Inuvik, becoming Hwy. 8 upon crossing into the Northwest Territories. In 1910, Dempster and his crew went searching for four officers who had set out from Fort McPherson for Dawson, and had never arrived. With a dog sled team and native guide, Dempster found the dead bodies 20 mi. outside of Fort McPherson, and brought the sad news to Dawson City in record time. Dempster completed the 475-mile patrol route countless times over the years, following roughly the same path that now bears his name. Construction of the highway began in the 50s when oil and gas were discovered near the Arctic Circle (66°33´) at

Eagle Plains, and was completed in 1979, finally providing road access to Canada's isolated Mackenzie River Delta towns of **Fort McPherson, Tsiigehtchic** (SIG-uh-chik, formerly known as Arctic Red River), and **Inuvik** (ih-NOO-vik). These communities surrounding the highway are largely indigenous Inuvialuit and Gwich'in peoples, and are quite welcoming of passing visitors. The highway begins 41km east of Dawson City at the **Klondike River Lodge** on the Klondike Highway (Hwy. 2).

Like no other highway in North America, the Dempster confronts its drivers with real, naked wilderness, unmolested by logging scars or advertisements. Driving the Dempster can be a religious experience: those who brave it cross the Arctic Circle and the Continental Divide, pass more animals than cars, and stare into the geological beginnings of the continent—and then have the right to write "I did it!" in the 6 inches of dust coating their car. Despite the thrill, of it all, the Dempster is not to be taken lightly. While reasonably navigable and well maintained, it is still very much an obedient subject of Queen Wilderness, and should be approached with careful planning. Services are limited, weather is erratic, and the dirt and gravel roads can give cars a thorough beating. Though the drive can be accomplished in as little as 12 hours, it probably deserves at least two days each way to be fully and safely appreciated. More importantly, quick rainstorms have been known to create impassable washouts along the route, closing down parts of the highway or disrupting ferry service—and perhaps leaving you stranded in Inuvik—for as long as two weeks.

PRACTICAL INFORMATION The **Arctic Hotline** (800-661-0788) and **Road and Ferry Report** (800-661-0752; in Inuvik 777-2678) provide up-to-date road info. The **NWT Infocentre** (see **Visitor Information,** p. 387) in Dawson City has a free brochure on the highway. The ever-useful road guides *Along the Dempster* ($13) and *Western Arctic Travel* ($8) are sold at **Maxmillans** (993-5486), at Front and Queen St. in Dawson City (Open M-Sa 9am-8pm, Su 10am-6pm; in winter M-Sa 10am-5pm).

A full tank of gas, dependable tires, a spare or two, and emergency supplies (food, clothes, a first aid kit, and a jerry can of gas) are necessary Dempster companions. The Klondike Lodge has full services, though Dawson City is just as good for preparations. Near Dawson City and the start of the Dempster, up-to-date **road and weather info** can be picked up on FM 105.5. To maintain health and sanity along the Dempster, bring a surefire bug repellant; the number of mosquitoes along the highway is staggering. Some form of bug netting for campsites may also be a good idea.

ON THE ROAD AND OUTDOORS The first spectacular 150km of the Dempster pass through the crags of the **Ogilvie Mountains,** narrowly missed by glaciation during the last Ice Age. The road then descends back into forest and blankets of velvet tundra as it approaches the **Arctic Circle**. Although there are some man-made services along the way, most of joy of the journey lies in the driving, watching, and gazing. Accommodations are sparse. There are **government campgrounds** at Tombstone (Km 72), Engineer Creek (Km 194), Rock River (Km 447), Nitainlii (Km 541), Caribou Creek (Km 692) and Chuk (Km 731). Dry sites cost $8, and hookups are only available near the end of the line at Chuk.

There are few trails along the Dempster, but the land's expanse begs exploration. Off-trail hiking is the way of this wilderness and demands the most vigilant take-nothing-leave-nothing ethic. Distances are deceptively long, and flat, arid-looking tundra often hides a spongelike swampy, lumpy muskeg (thawed permafrosted land). There are a handful of established paths, if tundra-whacking doesn't appeal.

At Km 58 on the highway, the **Grizzly Valley** hike leads through spruce forest that eventually yields to an alpine lookout and ridge. The small road behind the gravel pit at the garbage dump eventually gives way to a footpath. Allow at least six hours round-trip. The **Interpretive Centre** at **Tombstone Campground** (Km 72) has a staff wiser than Solomon, and loans out a mile-by-mile written travelogue of the Dempster's natural history and wildlife. Copies are limited and must be returned on the way home, but it's well worth it to get the lowdown on the surrounding mountains, golden eagles, moraines, and the migrating **Porcupine caribou herd,** which numbers

150,000 and is the largest in North America. Driving up to Tombstone and back makes for a great one- to two-day trip from Dawson City.

For a full-day adventure, with 1000m of ascent, the **Mt. Distincta trail** at Km 154 ("Windy Pass") heads over craggy boulders to one of the area's highest peaks (1800m). From the highway, walk southeast across a narrow ribbon of tundra to the base of the ridge. Follow the ridge south 6km, past a radio tower, then up a slope to the west—this is the true summit. From here, hike north 6km and then descend back to the highway, 5km west of the trail's starting point. Sturdy boots are a must for these slopes. **Sapper Hill,** with its distinct yellow-gray ridge, is one of the best half-day hikes along the highway. It begins just after **Engineer Creek** (Km 194), and takes about four hours. Avoid walking along the fishbone crest of the ridge—the chunky limestone near the summit can be tricky to navigate.

Halfway to Inuvik, at Km 363, gas, food, supplies, and accommodations are available at the well-kept **Eagle Plains Hotel** (993-2453), a paragon of monopoly pricing (singles $90, each additional person $10). Rocky, parking lot-style camping is available ($10, $15 with electricity), with coin showers and laundry. Car juice costs about 82¢ per liter, but what are you going to do? The next pump is 197km away. The restaurant looks hum-drum but is startlingly reasonable and good; a burger with crispy, thick fries costs $6. Just past Eagle Plains at Km 405, the Dempster crosses the Arctic Circle. Though there's no imaginary dotted line in the tundra, there is a sign to provide photographic proof that you've reached the true Land of the Midnight Sun.

Don't forget to set your watch to Mountain Time when crossing the Yukon-Northwest Territories border at Km 465. In summer, free **ferries** cross the Peel and Arctic Red Rivers 550km and 600km north of Dawson City (mid-June to mid-Oct., 15 per day). In winter, you can drive across the thick ice. No crossing is possible during the fall freeze or spring thaw. Call 800-661-0752 for current ice status.

■ Northwest Territories: Inuvik

Inuvik, "place of man," lies at the end of the Dempster rainbow. The town has 3200 residents, made up mostly of three separate Arctic peoples: the Inuvialuit of the Beaufort sea coast, the Gwich'in of the Mackenzie River Delta, and transplants from southern Canada. To make it through the nine-month winter, Inuvik's citizens paint their houses multiple bright colors and throw extravagant festivals in the summer.

The **Western Arctic Visitor Centre** (777-4727) is on Mackenzie Rd. downtown (open daily 9am-9pm). The **police** (RCMP) can be reached at 777-2935, and the **Inuvik Regional Hospital** at 777-2955. **Area Code:** 867.

Indoor accommodations in Inuvik are a budget traveler's Hades (or Hades frozen over). Those on the cheaper end are **Robertson's Bed and Breakfast,** 41 Mackenzie Rd. (777-3111) at Union St. (singles $70; doubles $80) and **Polar Bed and Breakfast** (777-4620), just down the street (singles $75; doubles $85). There's camping downtown at **Happy Valley Campground** (777-3652), on Happy Valley Rd. off Union St. If you're feeling restless in the midnight sun, ask about **The Zoo,** Inuvik's rowdy arctic hotspot, located in the Mackenzie Hotel.

For 10-14 days near the end of July, The **Great Northern Arts Festival** (777-3536; fax 777-4445; http://www.greatart.nt.ca) brings over 100 artists and entertainers to Inuvik for performances, showcases and workshops. Started in 1989, the festival has quickly become the premier cultural event in the Northwest Territories. Write to The Great Northern Arts Festival, Box 2921, Inuvik NT, X0E 0T0.

Still not far enough north? **Beaudel Air** (777-4242) flies to isolated, ice-bound **Tuktoyaktuk,** "Tuk" to its friends (2 per day at 9:30am and 3:30pm, $88). As with everything in Inuvik, call in advance.

ALASKA

Alaska's beauty and intrigue are born of extremes: North America's highest mountains and broadest flatlands; windswept tundra and lush rainforests; underwater salmon runs and overland caribou herds; virgin spruce forests in the Southeast and oil pumps at the top of the world. Harsh weather and a rugged landscape left much of Alaska's land untouched until the 19th century, and even today the state remains largely undeveloped—America's last true wilderness.

To native Aleuts, who thrived for millennia on the rugged Aleutian islands, the spectacular and enormous expanses to the northeast were **Alyeska**, or the **Great Land.** To gold seekers and followers of Manifest Destiny who journeyed into the northwestern hinterlands, Alaska was the **Last Frontier.** To summertime tourists, it is the **Land of the Midnight Sun.** Whatever the name, Alaska is not merely a frozen wasteland. In summer, all but the northernmost reaches of the state explode in a riot of vegetation. The wilderness teems with caribou, bear, moose, Dall sheep, and wolves, and the waters churn with spawning salmon, huge off-shore halibut, and trophy-sized grayling and trout. With only one quarter of Alaska's land accessible by highway, hikers find unparalleled opportunities for a truly solitary wilderness experience. But visitors needn't be hardcore backpackers or mountaineers to see much of the state's beauty—some of the most stunning glaciers can be reached by road.

The typical Alaskan, if the state's gallery of rogues and eccentrics can be summarized, bears a stubborn nonconformist streak. Alaskans value their remote home not only for its beauty, but for the freedom to live life on their own terms. Travelers who don't step on any toes will find the people of Alaska to be extremely open, friendly, and down-to-earth. After surviving one winter—the traditional hazing process separating newcomers and true Alaskans—some travelers never want to leave.

Geography

Physically, Alaska truly is the Great Land. The state encompasses 586,412 sq. mi.—over one-fifth of the land mass of the United States. The 33,000 mi. coastline stretches 11 times the distance from New York to San Francisco. Four major mountain ranges cross the state: the Wrangell Mountains, the Chugach Mountains, the Brooks Range, and the Denali-topped Alaska Range. Alaska is home to 15 incredible national parks covering a cumulative area roughly equal to that of England and Ireland combined. Nineteen Alaskan peaks reach over 14,000 ft., 94 lakes have a surface area of more than 10 sq. mi., and a handful of glacial icefields each over 1000 sq. mi.

Staggering numbers aside, Alaska presents overwhelming and diverse beauty. On the archipelago of **Southeast Alaska,** or the **Panhandle,** the isolated state capital of Juneau rests among numerous fjords, islands, verdant rainforests, and sub-arctic swamps known as *muskeg.* **Southcentral Alaska** is the home of Anchorage, the Kenai Peninsula, Prince William Sound, Kodiak Island, and, of course, the Kodiak brown bear. The 20,320-ft.-tall Denali (a.k.a. Mt. McKinley), the tallest mountain in North America, dominates the interminable flatlands of the **Interior,** the area north and east of Anchorage. **The Bush** encompasses the vast, empty reaches north and west of the Interior, including the Brooks Range above the Arctic Circle, the Seward Peninsula, and all of western Alaska along the Bering Sea. The Alaska Peninsula and the storm-swept, volcanic **Aleutian Islands** extend into the extreme southwest reaches of the Bush, offering tenuous purchase to a handful of hardy humans.

The Aleutian Islands lie on the **Ring of Fire** at the edge of the Pacific Plate, almost due north of the Hawaiian Volcanic chain, and are wracked by perpetual earthquakes and active volcanoes. The rest of Alaska also has reason to scoff at California's hyperbolized fear of tremors. In 1964, the Good Friday quake, centered in Miner's Lake (between Whittier and Valdez), registered 9.2 on the Richter Scale and lasted eight terrible minutes. Its aftershocks continued for several days. Many coastal towns,

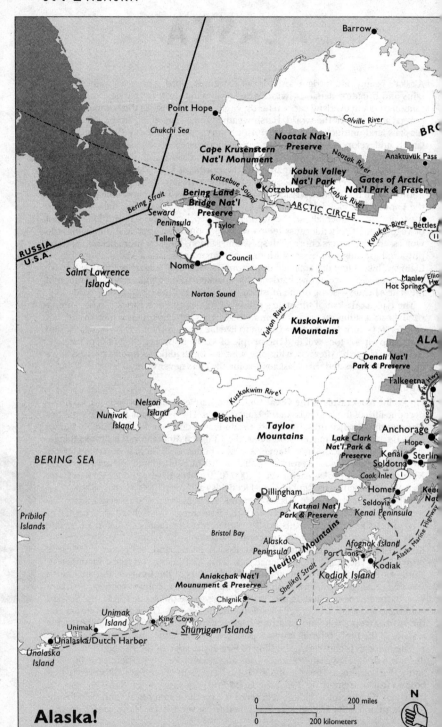

Alaska!

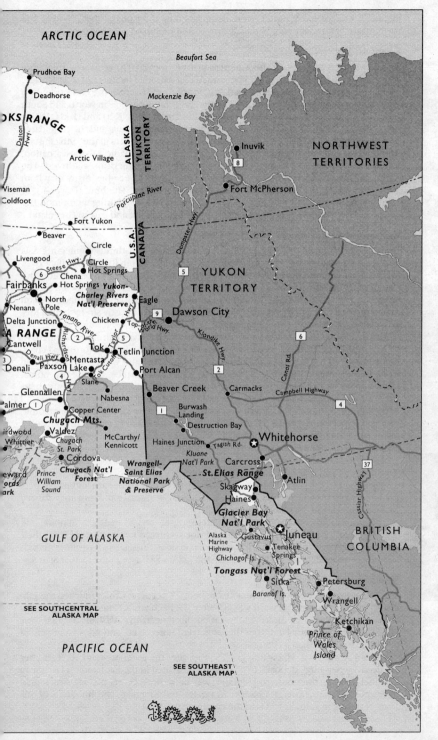

ARCTIC OCEAN

Beaufort Sea

Prudhoe Bay
Deadhorse

Mackenzie Bay

OKS RANGE

Dalton Hwy.

ALASKA
YUKON TERRITORY

Inuvik
8

NORTHWEST
TERRITORIES

Arctic Village

Viseman
Coldfoot

Porcupine River

Fort McPherson

Fort Yukon

U.S.A.
CANADA

Dempster Hwy.

Beaver

Circle

Livengood
Steese Hwy.
Circle Hot Springs

5

YUKON
TERRITORY

6
Chena
Fairbanks   Hot Springs
North   5   Yukon-
Nenana   Pole   Charley Rivers
Nat'l Preserve   Eagle
Delta Junction   Chicken
Tanana River   Top-of-the World Hwy.

9   Dawson City

6

A RANGE
Cantwell   2
3
Denali   Paxson Lake   Tok   Tetlin Junction
Mentasta
Denali Hwy.   4   Slana   Port Alcan

Klondike Hwy.

2

Canol Rd.

4

Glennallen   Nabesna   Beaver Creek   Carmacks
almer   1   Copper Center   1   Burwash   Campbell Highway
Chugach Mts.   Landing
irdwood   Valdez   McCarthy/   Destruction Bay
Whittier   Chugach   Kennicott   Haines Junction   Tagish Rd.   Whitehorse
St. Park   Kluane
eward   Cordova   Nat'l Park   Carcross
ords   Prince   Chugach Nat'l   Wrangell-   St. Elias Range   37
ark   William   Forest   Saint Elias   Atlin
Sound   National Park   Skagway
& Preserve   Haines

Cassiar Highway

GULF OF ALASKA

Glacier Bay
Nat'l Park

Alaska
Marine   Gustavus   Juneau   BRITISH
Highway   Tenakee   COLUMBIA
Chichagof Is.   Springs

Tongass Nat'l Forest

SEE SOUTHCENTRAL
ALASKA MAP   Sitka   Petersburg
Baranof Is.
Wrangell

PACIFIC OCEAN   Ketchikan

SEE SOUTHEAST   Prince of
ALASKA MAP   Wales
Island

including Kodiak and Whittier, were demolished by the tsunami that followed the earthquake; Valdez was completely destroyed and rebuilt on a new site.

Early and Native History

The first budget travelers in the Americas arrived over 20,000 years ago, migrating over the Bering Land Bridge from Siberia to Alaska. Prodded by the cold of an ice age, within 10,000 years these people had spread southward across the entirety of two continents, becoming the ancestors of all the indigenous peoples in North and South America. Today, Southeast Alaska is home to the Tlingit (KLINK-it) and Haida (HIGH-dah) peoples, renowned for their exquisitely carved totem poles and the formidable wooden forts from which they almost staved off Russian invaders in the 19th century. The Interior and Southcentral regions harbor the once-nomadic Athabasca nation, which has language ties to the Navajo and Apache of the American Southwest. The Aleutian Island chain is populated largely by the Aleut (AL-ee-oot), many of whom were enslaved by the Russians for their skill as fur trappers. The Inuit (IN-yoo-it), or Eskimos, reside almost exclusively within the Arctic Circle, sharing a common language and heritage with people west across the Bering Strait and east to Greenland.

European Exploration and Invasion

Under orders from Russia's Peter the Great to discover an isthmus connecting Asia and America, Danish Admiral Vitus Bering set sail in 1728 from Russia's Pacific Coast. He sailed through the strait which now bears his name, securing a place in history but also proving that Russia and America were unconnected. Bering undertook a second voyage in 1740 to map Alaska's coastline, landing on Kayak Island off Prince William Sound in 1741. Though this second trip cost Bering his life, it vastly strengthened Russia's claims to Alaska and the northern Pacific Coast.

Russian claims to Alaska soon became far more lucrative than first imagined. In 1776, Great Britain sent the famed Captain Cook to map the Pacific Northwest coastline in search of the long-sought Northwest Passage. The hunt was unsuccessful, and Cook himself was killed while wintering on the Hawaii Islands. On the trip home, Cook's sailors stopped off at Canton and were shocked to discover that the otter pelts they had picked up fetched a huge price in China. An intense competition for control of the **fur trade** soon developed among Russia, Spain, England, and to a lesser extent, America. The **Nuu-chah-nulth Convention** of 1790 temporarily settled the territorial disputes, with England taking control of the land between Spanish California and Russian Alaska. The Native Americans received nothing.

Numerous European fur-trading posts sprang up throughout the northern Pacific Coast, becoming centers of both trade and cultural exchange between Native Americans and Europeans. Over time the relationship between Europeans and native people became increasingly exploitative, while unfamiliar diseases unknowingly carried by Europeans began to ravage native populations.

By the mid-1800s, Alaska's once-bountiful supply of furry animals was thinning out, and the Aleut population had diminished due to forced labor. Reeling from their disastrous defeat in the Crimean War and deep in debt, Russia began to entertain bids for the **"dead land,"** and, on October 18, 1867, found a buyer in the United States.

Seward's Folly Turns Jolly

The U.S. bought Alaska for $7,200,000, or about 2¢ per acre. Critics mocked the purchase, popularly called "Seward's Folly" after the Secretary of State who negotiated the deal under President Andrew Johnson. At this time, native Alaskans restated their claims to their ancestral lands, but the issue went unresolved, and titles were held in abeyance for more than a century.

William Seward was vindicated just 15 years after the purchase (and 10 years after his death) when huge deposits of gold were unearthed in the Panhandle's Gastineau Channel. **Juneau,** the northern Eldorado, was born. Prospectors quickly struck gold in rivers such as the Yukon, Charley, Fortymile, and Klondike, and hundreds of millions of dollars in gold flowed into the continental U.S.

Constructive War

War came to Alaska in June 1942 when Japanese bombers attacked Unalaska and occupied two of the Aleutian Islands. In response, the U.S. began a rapid buildup of military forces and hurriedly constructed the Alaska Hwy. to connect the territory with the rest of the U.S.—a mammoth undertaking that laid highway through 1500 miles of wilderness in under nine months. After the war, many of the construction workers and soldiers who had taken part in the modernization and protection of Alaska decided to stay in the territory. In 1946, the territory voted in a referendum to become a state, but Congress was delayed from acting by the advent of the Korean War. Finally, in 1959, Alaska was welcomed into the Union as the 49th state.

Tensions and Resolutions

Throughout the 60s, amid the Cold War's international tensions, Alaska also had to face internal conflict. Native Alaskans watched with increasing frustration as the federal and state governments divvied up vast tracts of land which the Inuit, Aleut, Tlingit, Haida, and Athabasca felt were rightfully theirs. The conflict came to a head after the discovery in 1968 of immense **oil deposits** beneath the shore of the Beaufort Sea, on Alaska's northern coast. Native groups increased the pressure to settle the claims that had been so long ignored, and sought a share in the anticipated economic boom.

In December of 1971, the federal government finally made some degree of peace with native peoples, state and federal courts, and environmental groups by passing the **Alaska Native Claims Settlement Act.** Native Alaskans, who then numbered around 60,000, received a total of one billion dollars and 40 million acres of land. Yet while the settlement was certainly overdue and beneficial, poverty, unemployment, crime, and substance abuse among Native Alaskans are still higher than the national average. Many native corporations have opted to sell their natural resources, and native-held land displays some of the state's ugliest logging scars.

Black Gold

In 1973, the **Alyeska Pipeline Service Company** received official permission to build a pipeline from Prudhoe Bay to Valdez—800 miles through the heart of the Alaskan wilderness. This single pipeline has had a revolutionary effect on the state's political, social, and economic landscape. By 1981, four years after the **Trans-Alaska Pipeline** was installed, $7,200,000 worth of crude oil—the exact price Seward had paid for the state more than a century before—flowed from the Arctic oil field every 4½ hours. State revenues from oil taxation have created a trust fund for the people of Alaska and have eliminated state sales and income taxes.

In addition to creating jobs and wealth, though, the pipeline has detrimentally affected Alaska's physical landscape: oil drilling has stripped forests and emptied streams, while the pipeline itself draws a jagged line across the belly of the tundra. Oil pumping has also brought pollution, drastic population growth, profligate spending, and, in some cases, disaster. Twenty-five years to the day after the Good Friday earthquake of 1964 leveled the port city of Valdez, the Exxon oil tanker *Valdez* ran aground on Bligh Reef, spilling over 250,000 barrels (11 million gallons) of crude oil into the pristine waters of **Prince William Sound.** Thousands of marine mammals and birds succumbed to the thick black tide that swept through the sound, reaching shores as far away as Kodiak Island, several hundred miles to the south. By the summer of 1990, no oil was visible to the casual observer, but the long-term effects of the spill are uncertain at best. In addition to poisoning thousands of marine mammals and birds, the oil has disrupted feeding cycles in the sound and has threatened those human communities that derive their livelihoods from the sea.

The tremendous uproar surrounding the spill underscored a current shift taking place within Alaska. Even as the pipeline's profits are divided among the oil companies, native corporations, and the state and federal governments, Alaskans are starting to realize the immense value of the vast, unspoiled expanses that oil drilling threatens. Today, **tourism** is the state's second most important source of income. The astounding sum of Exxon's payment in the wake of the *Valdez* disaster—$3.4 billion

ALASKA

in clean-up operations, plus $100 million in restitution to the state and federal governments and $25 million in criminal fines—attests to the growing political clout of conservationists and proponents of ecotourism.

Recent Events

For years, oil barons have been clamoring to perform exploratory drilling in the **National Petroleum Reserve** of the Arctic North Slope, originally established as insurance against future energy shortages. In August of 1998, the federal government gave the go-ahead for drilling in about one fifth of the reserve's 23 million acres. **Teshekpuk Lake,** a vital habitat for migratory waterfowl, will remain off-limits. Environmentalists argue that drilling will disrupt the pristine wilderness of the reserve, while oil companies are disappointed that the entire area was not opened for exploration. Native Alaskans living near the reserve fear that the drilling will destroy their way of life either through catastrophic accidents or massive industrialization. Supporters respond that fresh development will be an economic boon for all Alaskans, generating government revenue, producing new jobs, and minimizing environmental impact with smaller drilling installations and less invasive roads.

Further Reading

A rich corpus exists for those who seek a literary appreciation of the Great Land. John McPhee's *Coming Into the Country* sketches a fascinating overview of Alaskan issues and wilderness lifestyles. Jon Krakauer's *Into The Wild,* about the 1992 disappearance and death of Christopher McCandless near Denali National Park, makes compelling, if discouraging, reading. *Going to Extremes,* by Joe McGinniss, and *Alaska: The Sophisticated Wilderness,* by Jon Gardey both chronicle Alaskan settlers seeking refuge from the Lower 48. Alan Ryan's *The Reader's Companion to Alaska* serves up easily digestible morsels from a wide buffet of tasty authors. Finally, the venerable *Tundra Times,* founded in part by legendary Inuit journalist Howard Rock, publishes out of Anchorage and provides the most up-to-date discussions of current Native American issues without glossing over internal diversity and factionalism.

For **fictional Alaskana,** rediscover Jack London's classic tales of gold rush adventure, *White Fang* and *The Call of the Wild.* James Michener's monster epic *Alaska* takes many liberties with historical fact, but captures the scope of the region and its dramatic past. Just don't drop it on your foot (the epic, not the region or its past). Leslie Marmon Silko's short stories tackle the cultural and physical difficulties facing Native Alaskans in the present day. And, of course, the lovable eccentrics of Cicely, AK, continue to frolic in TV syndication on *Northern Exposure,* filmed for five years in Roslyn, WA, but allegedly based on real-life Talkeetna, AK.

PRACTICAL INFORMATION

Capital: Juneau.
Population: 607,800. **Area:** 586,412 sq. mi. **Motto:** "We're way bigger than Texas and have more oil!" **Real Motto:** North to the Future. **Bird:** Willow ptarmigan. **Flower:** Forget-me-not. **State Fish:** King salmon. **Tree:** Sitka spruce. **Mineral:** Gold. **Gem:** Jade. **Sport:** Dog mushing. **Holiday:** Alaska Day, Oct. 18.
Pay Phones: In many towns, phones will not return coins, even if the party doesn't answer. Dial, wait until the party picks up, and then deposit coins.
Road Conditions: 800-478-7675.
State Troopers: Daytime headquarters 269-5511, Anchorage dispatch 428-7200.
Time Zones: Alaska (most of the state; 4hr. before Eastern); Aleutian-Hawaii (Aleutian Islands; 5hr. before Eastern).
Sales Tax: None. **Drinking Age:** 21.
Postal Abbreviation: AK.
Area Code: 907.

GETTING AROUND

The **Alaska Railroad** (see p. 29), constructed in the 1910s and 20s to service mining towns in the Interior, runs nearly 500 mi. from Seward to Fairbanks, with stops in

Anchorage and Whittier. The **Alaska Marine Highway** (see p. 34) remains the most practical and enjoyable way to explore much of the Panhandle, Prince William Sound, and the Kenai Peninsula. The **AlaskaPass** (see p. 34) combines access to Alaska's railroad, ferry, and bus systems. Most of the state's major **highways** are known by their name as often as their number (e.g. George Parks Highway = Rte. 3 = The Parks). Driving to and through Alaska is not for the faint of car; see **Northcountry Driving** (p. 32) for tips on tackling these roads. Alaska's highways reward drivers with stunning views and access to true wilderness, but they barely scratch the surface of the massive state. For Alaska's most remote destinations, **air travel** is an expensive necessity. Intrastate airlines and charter services, many of them based at the busy Anchorage airport, transport passengers and cargo to virtually every village in Alaska. Many are listed in the relevant **Practical Information** sections of this guide.

Southcentral Alaska

Southcentral Alaska stands on the threshold of Alaska's future, tenuously guarding its past. Anchorage, Prince William Sound, the Kenai Peninsula, and Kodiak Island are becoming more accessible as economic opportunities and an expanding network of well-maintained roads draw more and more escapees from the Lower 48. The cost of living slowly declines as telecommunications burgeon, and Alaska's isolation, while in little danger of disappearing, is gradually eroding in this region.

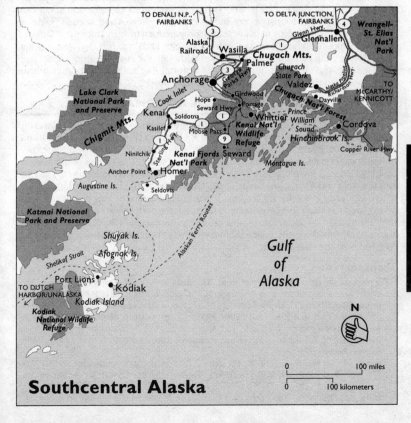

Southcentral Alaska

ⓜ *HIGHLIGHTS OF SOUTHCENTRAL ALASKA*

- Most travelers to Alaska pass through **Anchorage** (see p. 400), where the fine **Museum of History and Art** (see p. 405) and the copious **nightlife** (see p. 408) might temporarily distract them from the great state beyond.
- Diverse delights of the **Kenai Peninsula** (see p. 411) include the new **SeaLife Center** (see p. 414) in **Seward,** overwhelming wildlife and glacier cruises in **Kenai Fjords National Park** (see p. 416), friendly folks in **Homer** (see p. 422), and **great fishing** anywhere a hook is sunk.
- On **Prince William Sound** (p. 434), **Valdez** lies at the end of a gorgeous drive (see p. 438), while **Cordova** hosts the calf-happy **Childs Glacier** (see p. 442).
- The massive glaciers and awe-inspiring scale of **Wrangell-St. Elias National Park** (see p. 443) can melt a person's mind.

■ Anchorage

Alaska's foremost urban center and only metropolis, Anchorage is home to two-fifths of the state's population—a less-than-staggering 254,000 people. As far north as Helsinki and almost as far west as Honolulu, the city sprawls along highways and side-streets for almost 2000 sq. mi., about the area of the state of Delaware. The city achieved its size by hosting the headquarters of three economic projects: the Alaska Railroad, WWII military development, and the Trans-Alaska Pipeline. Today, the world's largest and busiest harbor for tiny seaplanes lies near the Anchorage airport.

Though Anchorage is not the next up-and-coming West Coast mecca, downtown blossoms with hanging flower baskets lining 4th Ave., outdoor cafes, and street vendors for the arrival of tourists every summer. The city serves as a starting point for most travelers, a good place to get oriented, prepare for a trip, and move on. Three of Alaska's 39 mountain ranges are visible from the city, and on a clear day, Denali (a.k.a. Mt. McKinley) can be seen from downtown. Although the city is far from architecturally pleasing, travelers can find plenty of entertaining activities whether within Anchorage or in the breathtaking wilderness just outside.

ORIENTATION AND PRACTICAL INFORMATION

Anchorage is 127 mi. north of Seward on the Seward Hwy. (Rte. 9), 304 mi. west of Valdez along the Glenn Hwy. (Rte. 1) and Richardson Hwy. (Rte. 4), and 358 mi. south of Fairbanks on the George Parks Hwy. (Rte. 3), serving as the transportation hub of Southcentral Alaska. The city sprawls across some 50,000 acres of the Anchorage Bowl, framed by **military bases** to the north, the **Chugach Mountains** to the east, and the **Knik** and **Turnagain Arms** of the **Cook Inlet** to the west and south. Downtown Anchorage is laid out in a grid: Numbered **avenues** run east-west, with addresses designated east or west from **C St.** North-south **streets** are lettered alphabetically to the west and named alphabetically to the east of **A St.** The rest of Anchorage spreads out along the major highways. The **University of Alaska** lies on 36th Ave., off Northern Lights Blvd.

Transportation

Airplanes: Anchorage International Airport (266-2525). Serviced by 8 international and 15 domestic carriers, including **Delta** (800-221-1212), **Northwest Airlines** (800-225-2525), **United** (800-241-6522), and **Alaska Airlines** (800-426-0333). Smaller airlines like **Reno Air** (800-736-6247) have cheap deals. Nearly every airport in Alaska can be reached from Anchorage, either directly or through a connecting flight in Fairbanks. An entire section of the classified ads in the *Daily News* lists second-hand tickets.

Trains: Alaska Railroad, 411 W. 1st Ave., P.O. Box 107500, Anchorage 99510-7500 (265-2494, outside AK 800-544-0552). To: Denali (8hr., $99); Fairbanks (12hr., $149); Seward (4hr., $43). No service to Seward in winter. In summer, a flagstop train runs between Talkeetna and Hurricane (Th-Su; $16). The train will make

ALASKA

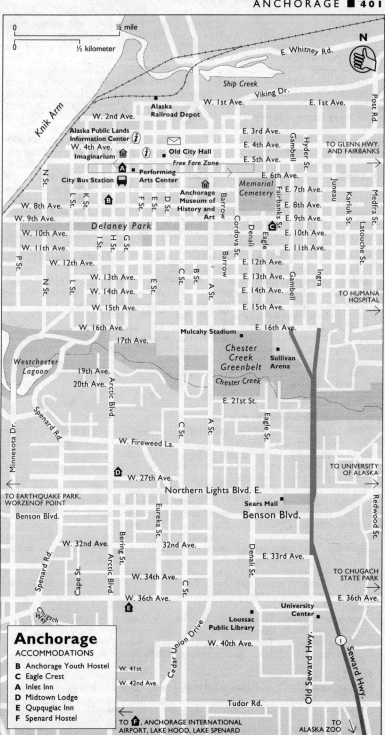

0   ½ mile
0   ½ kilometer

N

E. Whitney Rd.

Ship Creek   Viking Dr.

Knik Arm

W. 1st Ave.   E. 1st Ave.

Post Rd.

W. 2nd Ave.   Alaska
Railroad Depot

Alaska Public Lands
Information Center ⓘ
W. 4th Ave.   E. 3rd Ave.
Imaginarium   E. 4th Ave.
Old City Hall   E. 5th Ave.

Gambell St.   Hyder St.   TO GLENN HWY.
AND FAIRBANKS

City Bus Station   Performing
Arts Center   Free Fare Zone   E. 6th Ave.

W. 8th Ave.   Anchorage
Museum of
History and
Art   Memorial
Cemetery   E. 7th Ave.
E. 8th Ave.
W. 9th Ave.   E. 9th Ave.

Juneau St.   Karluk St.   Medfra St.

Delaney Park   E. 10th Ave.
W. 10th Ave.   E. 11th Ave.
W. 11th Ave.

Cordova St.   Denali St.   Eagle   Fairbanks St.   Latouche St.

W. 12th Ave.   E. 12th Ave.
W. 13th Ave.   Barrow   E. 13th Ave.
W. 14th Ave.   E. 14th Ave.   Gambell St.   Ingra St.
W. 15th Ave.   E. 15th Ave.   TO HUMANA
HOSPITAL

W. 16th Ave.   Mulcahy Stadium   E. 16th Ave.
17th Ave.

Westchester
Lagoon   Chester
Creek
Greenbelt   Sullivan
Arena
19th Ave.   Chester Creek
20th Ave.

Eagle St.

E. 21st St.

Spenard Rd.   Arctic Blvd.   C St.   A St.

W. Fireweed La.

Minnesota Dr.

D   W. 27th Ave.

Northern Lights Blvd. E.   TO UNIVERSITY
OF ALASKA

TO EARTHQUAKE PARK,
WORZENOF POINT
Benson Blvd.   Sears Mall
Benson Blvd.

Redwood St.

Eureka St.   W. 32nd Ave.   32nd Ave.

Bering St.   Arctic Blvd.   Denali St.

E. 33rd Ave.   TO CHUGACH
STATE PARK

W. 34th Ave.   C St.
Cape St.   E. 36th Ave.
W. 36th Ave.   E   University
Center

Chugach Way   Cedar Union Drive   Loussac
Public Library   Old Seward Hwy.   Seward Hwy.

Anchorage
ACCOMMODATIONS
B Anchorage Youth Hostel
C Eagle Crest
A Inlet Inn
D Midtown Lodge
E Qupqugiac Inn
F Spenard Hostel

W. 40th Ave.
W. 41st
W. 42nd Ave.   Tudor Rd.

TO 🅵 ANCHORAGE INTERNATIONAL
AIRPORT, LAKE HOOD, LAKE SPENARD   TO
ALASKA ZOO

ALASKA

unscheduled stops anywhere along this route; just wave it down with a white cloth and wait to be acknowledged with a whistle. In winter, a flagstop runs between Anchorage and Fairbanks ($105, prices vary depending on where you get on and off). Ticket window open M-F 5:30am-5pm, Sa-Su 5:30am-1pm.

Buses: Grayline Alaska (800-544-2206). Daily to: Seward (4hr., $40); Valdez (10hr., $66); Portage (2hr., $40). 3 per week to: Haines ($189); Skagway ($209); both with overnight in Beaver Creek. **Homer Stage Lines** (272-8644). To: Homer (daily M-Sa, $45). **Alaska Direct** (277-6652). To: Whitehorse, YT (3 per week, $145). **Parks Highway Express** (479-3065, in AK 888-600-6001). Daily to: Denali ($30); Fairbanks ($49).

Ferries: Alaska Marine Highway, 605 W. 4th Ave. (800-642-0066, weekends 800-526-6731), in the Old Federal Building. No terminal, but ferry tickets sold and reservations granted. Open M-F 9am-5:30pm.

Public Transportation: People Mover Bus (343-6543), in the Transit Center on 6th Ave. between G and H St. Buses leave from here to all points in the Anchorage area M-F 6am-10pm; restricted schedule Sa-Su. Cash fare $1, ages 5-18 or over 65 25¢; tokens 90¢; day passes $2.50 (purchase in the Transit Center). **Free fare zone** bordered by 5th Ave., Denali St., 6th Ave., and L St. Office open M-F 8am-5pm and sells a map (50¢). Service is only hourly to most stops, and is often somewhat off-schedule, demanding planning and patience.

Taxis: Yellow Cab, 272-2422. **Checker Cab,** 276-1234. **Alaska Cab,** 563-5353. About $13 from airport to downtown hostel. All 24hr.

Car Rentals: Airport Car Rental, 502 W. Northern Lights Blvd. (277-7662). $55 per day; unlimited mileage. Must be 21; $5 per day surcharge if under 25. Cash or credit card deposit required. Free shuttle to airport. Open M-F 8am-5pm, Sa 8am-6pm, Su 9am-5pm. **Affordable Car Rental,** 4707 Spenard Rd. (243-3370), across from the Regal Alaskan Hotel. $56 per day, $336 per week; unlimited mileage. Must be 21 with major credit card. Free drop-off and pick-up from downtown or the airport. **Rent-A-Wreck,** 512 W. International Airport Rd. (562-5499 or 800-666-9799). $47 per day; 26¢ per mi. over 100 mi. per day. $5 per day surcharge if under 25. $15 per day surcharge if under 21; credit card and verification of full coverage insurance required.

Ride Board: At the Anchorage Youth Hostel (see **Accommodations,** below).

Visitor and Financial Services

Visitor Information: Log Cabin Visitor Information Center (274-3531, events hotline 276-3200), on W. 4th Ave. at F St. Crammed with visitors and volunteers. A new building behind the cabin is typically less crowded and has more brochures. Lots of maps, including a **bike trails guide** (50¢). Open June-Aug. daily 7:30am-7pm; May and Sept. 8am-6pm; Oct.-Apr. 9am-4pm. Smaller info centers are at the airport (266-2437), in the domestic terminal near baggage claim and in the international terminal at the central atrium. **Calendar of weekly events:** 276-3200.

Outdoor Information: Alaska Public Lands Information Center, Old Federal Bldg., 605 W. 4th Ave. (271-2737 or 271-2738; fax 271-2744; http://www.nps.gov/aplic/center), between F and G St., kitty-corner from the visitor center. Combines the **Park Service, Forest Service, Division of State Parks,** the **Fish and Wildlife Service,** and the **Alaska Marine Highway** reservation desk under one glorious roof. Popular topographic maps, a computerized sportfishing map, and live presentations on Alaska's outdoor attractions. Open daily 9am-5:30pm. **Alaska Department of Fish and Game,** 333 Raspberry Rd. (344-0541, recording 349-4687). Open M-F 8am-5pm.

Employment: Alaska Employment Service, 3301 Eagle St., P.O. Box 107024 (269-4800). Take bus #3. Open M-F 8am-5pm.

Currency Exchange: Thomas Cook, 311 F St. (278-2822 or 800-CURRENCY/287-7362), next to the Hilton. Open in summer M-F 9am-5pm, Sa 10am-2pm.

Local Services

Equipment Rental: Downtown Bicycle Rental (279-5293 or 279-8337), on 5th St. near C St., 5 blocks from the Coastal Trail (see p. 406). Bikes $12 for 3hr., $15 for 5hr., $22 per day. Tandems $19 for 3hr., $25 for 5hr., $35 per day. Lock, helmet, map, and gloves included. Credit card required. Open daily 8am-7pm or 8pm. **Recreational Equipment, Inc. (REI),** 1200 Northern Lights Blvd. (272-4565), near Spenard. High-quality packs, clothing, tents, stores, and dried foods. Open M-F 10am-9pm, Sa-Su 10am-6pm. **Army-Navy Store** (279-2401), on 4th Ave. across from the Post Office Mall. Good prices, catering mostly to hunters and fishers. Open M-F 9am-8pm, Sa 9am-7pm, Su 9am-6pm. **Play It Again Sports** (278-7529), at 27th and Spenard near REI, buys and sells used equipment. Rotating inventory of sporting goods, along with some quality fishing and camping gear at discount prices. Open M-F 10am-8pm, Sa 10am-6pm, Su 11:30am-5:30pm.

Bookstore: Cook Inlet Books, 415 W. 5th Ave. (258-4544). Claims to offer the largest selection of Alaskana anywhere. Terrific collection of cheap classics. Open daily 8:30am-10pm. For a dog-eared copy of *White Fang,* try **C&M Used Books,** 215 E. 4th Ave. (278-9394). Open M-Tu and Th-F 10am-7pm, W and Sa 10am-6pm. **Title Wave,** 1068 W. Fireweed Ln. (278-BOOK/2665 or 278-9283). A tsunami of used tomes. Open M-Sa 10:30am-6:30pm, Su noon-5pm.

Library: ZJ Loussac Library (261-2975), at 36th Ave. and Denali St. Take bus #2, 36 or 60. $40 million building devotes an entire wing to Alaskan material. Free Internet access. Open M-Th 11am-9pm, F-Sa 10am-6pm; in winter also Su noon-6pm.

Services for the Disabled: Challenge Alaska, 344-7399.

Gay and Lesbian Helpline: 258-4777. Open 6pm-11pm daily.

STD Information: 343-4611. **HIV/AIDS Information: Alaska AIDS Assistance Association,** 276-4880 or 800-478-AIDS/2437.

Laundromat: K-Speed Wash, 600 E. 6th St. (279-0731). Wash $1.50, dry 25¢ per 5min. Open M-Sa 7am-10pm.

Weather: 936-2525. **Motorists' and Recreation Forecast:** 936-2626. **Road Conditions:** 273-6037. **Marine Weather:** 936-2727.

Emergency and Communications

Emergency: 911. **Police:** 786-8500.

Rape Crisis Line: 276-7273 or 800-478-8999. 24hr.

Hospital: Columbia Alaska Regional Hospital, 2801 DeBarr Rd. (276-1131).

Post Office: (279-3062), W. 4th Ave. and C St., on the lower level in the banana yellow mall. Open M-F 10am-5:30pm. **Stamp machine** in lobby open 24hr. **ZIP Code:** 99510. The **state central post office** (266-3259), next to the airport, does not handle general delivery mail, but is open 24hr.

Internet Access: Surf City Cafe, 415 L St. (279-7877). 12¢ per min., $7.20 per hr. Open M-F 7am-midnight, Sa-Su 10am-midnight. **Loussac Library** (see above) has free Internet access (30min. max.), but no swanky leather chairs.

Area Code: 907.

ACCOMMODATIONS AND CAMPGROUNDS

Anchorage is blessed with a multitude of hostel and quasi-hostel accommodations. Hotels and B&Bs are expensive, especially downtown. Even most so-called budget motels start at $75. Try **Alaska Private Lodgings** (258-1717; M-Sa 8am-7pm) or the **Anchorage reservation service** (272-5909) for out-of-town B&Bs (from $65).

Excellent camping opportunities await in nearby **Chugach State Park** (354-5014). Two of the best grounds are northeast of Anchorage along the Glenn Hwy. (Rte. 1). **Eagle River** is 12½ mi. from town ($15), and **Eklutna** (EE-kloot-nah) lies 26½ mi. along the Glenn and then 10 mi. east on Eklutna Rd. ($10). These secluded wooded spots are popular with locals; show up early, especially on weekends.

⊛**Spenard Hostel,** 2845 W. 42nd Pl. (248-5036). Take bus #36 or #7 from downtown, or #6 from the airport down Spenard to Turnagain Blvd.; 42nd Pl. is the 1st left from Turnagain. A hostel that feels like home—with lots of siblings. Comfortable, clean and welcoming. 3 lounges, 3 kitchens, and a big yard keep this hostel from feeling crowded, though it sleeps over 40 people. Friendly, helpful house parents. Beds or tent space $15. Free local calls on 4 different lines, bike rental to guests ($5), laundry facilities, lockers, Denali Shuttle drop-off/pick-up. No curfew and no lockout, but quiet hours are enforced. Chore requested. 6-day max. stay.

Anchorage International Youth Hostel (HI-AYH), 700 H St. (276-3635), at 7th St., 1 block south of the city bus station on the edge of downtown. You can't beat the location, and the hostel, like downtown, just bustles. The plastic-covered floors don't add any charm. Kitchens, TV, balconies, lockers, and laundry. $15, nonmembers $18; photo ID required. Lockout noon-5pm. Curfew 1am; watchman can check-in until 2am. Chore requested. 5-night max. stay in summer. Pay by 11am or lose your spot. Filled to the rafters in summer; write or call ahead for reservations.

Qupqugiaq Inn (koop-KOO-gee-ak), 640 W. 36th Ave. (563-5633), between Arctic Blvd. and C St.; take bus #9. Common lounge and kitchen, shared bathrooms, private rooms with locks, and cable TV. Rooms face the occasionally noisy street. Singles from $38; doubles $48. Plans in the works for both a complimentary continental breakfast in the cafe downstairs (see **Food,** below) and an alternative travel center with resources for travel, volunteering, and working. No smoking or alcohol. Common areas closed at 10pm. Call ahead for reservations with credit card, or get there by 3pm for a room.

Inlet Inn, 539 H St. (277-5541; fax 277-3108), conveniently located downtown. Small, clean rooms with private bath, cable TV, and phone. Complimentary 24hr. shuttle service to the airport and train station. Singles from $55; doubles from $70. Credit card or first night's deposit required to confirm reservation.

Centennial Park, 8300 Glenn Hwy. (333-9711), 10 min. north of town off Muldoon Rd.; take bus #3 or 75 from downtown. 88 sites for tents and RVs. Showers, dumpsters, fireplaces, pay phones, water. Sites $13, Alaskans or Golden Age Passport $11. 7-day max. stay. Quiet hours 10pm-6am. Noon check-out. Open May-Aug.

FOOD

Anchorage presents travelers with the most affordable and varied culinary fare in the state. **Great Harvest Bread Company,** 570 E. Benson Blvd. (274-3331), in Metro Mall, stocks excellent fresh bread. Loaves cost $4, but slices are free (open M-Sa 7am-6pm). **Carr's** (277-2609), at 15th and Gambell St., sells groceries (24hr.). At night, take bus #11; this neighborhood is sketchy for the six months per year that it's dark.

✪**Moose's Tooth,** 3300 Old Seward (258-ALES/2537; http://www.alaskan.com/moosestooth); take bus #2 or #36. Named for one of Denali's high neighbors, Moose's Tooth dishes eats as hearty as the climbers who tackle the peak. Fresh, tasty pizza, Moose's Tooth's own beers, and a relaxed atmosphere. Caters to the healthy at heart, with 3 no-cheese pizzas for vegans. Popeye (small spinach pizza) $8.75; raspberry wheat beer $3.50. Family atmosphere shifts by night to a popular haunt for the young and restless. Open Su-Th noon-midnight, F-Sa noon-1am.

Twin Dragon, 612 E. 15th Ave. (276-7535), near Gambell; take bus #11. Lures hungry travelers with the promise of great Mongolian barbecue. All-you-can-eat buffet of marinated meats and vegetables, hot off the giant grill. Lunch $6.50; dinner $10; BBQ and Chinese food buffet $13. Open M-Sa 11am-midnight, Su 1pm-midnight.

Snow Goose (277-7727), at 3rd and G St. When it's a nice night, the large deck off the 2nd floor of this restaurant is the place to be. Sink your teeth into a burger or sandwich ($7-9) as you set your gaze on the sea. Open daily 11:30am-midnight.

Downtown Deli, 525 W. 4th Ave. (276-7116). A nod to the New York deli, this upbeat cafe offers meals never dreamed of in Manhattan. Democrats can sit on the outdoor patio and mull over the year while enjoying the reindeer stew Bill Clinton complimented ($10). Budget-minded Republicans may opt for the quiche with salad and bread ($7). Open daily 6am-10pm.

D Street Cafe, 427 D St. (258-0507). Street-side tables and healthy Mediterranean options like roasted eggplant sandwich or fava bean wrap ($6.50). The owners occasionally leave the menu behind and serve a big outdoor BBQ dinner special instead. Open M-Th 7am-9pm, F 7am-10pm, Sa-Su 10am-10pm.

Thai Cuisine Too, 328 G St. (277-8424). This pleasant restaurant somehow serves terrific Thai fare while avoiding the hordes that mob many downtown restaurants. 18 vegetarian dishes ($9). Open M-Sa 11am-10pm, Su 4-10pm.

Muffin Man, 529 I St. (279-MUFN/6836). Enjoy the fruits of a creative muffin mind. Blueberry banana nut or Oreo (75¢, jumbo $1.50). Non-muffin options available (bagels, oatmeal, salads, sandwiches). Open M-F 6am-3pm, Sa 6am-2pm.

L'Aroma (274-6173), in New Sagaya's City Market at 13th and I St. American, Asian, and Italian dishes woo local yuppies to this deli-style cafe with an outdoor patio and a brightly painted garage. Lasagna $5; lemon chicken with rice and egg roll $5.50; Italian gelato $1.25. Open M-F 6am-9pm, Sa 7am-9pm, Su 8am-7pm.

Blondie's Cafe (279-0698), at the corner of 4th and D St. Located at the start of the Iditarod, Blondie's is packed with memorabilia and shows videos of the race all the day. The tide is high with delicious breakfast options, served all day; 2 giant sourdough pancakes $4. Open daily 5am-2am.

CAFES AND COFFEEHOUSES

Side Street Espresso, 428 G St. (258-9055). A gathering hole for the hip and the yup, with political salons, frequent acoustic music, a decent book exchange, and bound copies of local writers' efforts. Kids play in the children's area beneath Anchorage artists' more abstract meanderings. Cappuccino $2; espresso $1.50. Open M-F 7am-7pm, Sa 7am-5pm, Su 8am-5pm.

Sweet Basil Cafe, 335 E St. (274-0070). The cafe's CEO is a black labrador retriever named Buba, but it's probably the owners who wake up bright and early to make all of the pastries, breads, and pastas. They brew killer vegetable and fruit juices and smoothies, like the Root-Up (carrot, beet, and ginger; $3.25). Whole sandwich with salad $5.50; latte $2.25. Plans for a more extensive dinner menu are underway. Open in summer from 7am 'til the sun goes down; winter hours vary.

Qupqugiaq Cafe and School, 640 W. 36th Ave. (563-5634). Named after a legendary 10-legged polar bear (koop-KOO-gee-ak) who rejected a violent way of life to create a community based on love and peace, this cafe offers free classes and wholesome food for hungry minds and stomachs. One of the few architecturally pleasing places in Anchorage. The herb-roasted chicken sandwich is a favorite ($6.50), and, like every other place in Alaska, they stock espresso drinks (latte $2.25). Open M-F 7am-8pm, Sa 9am-8pm, Su 9am-3pm. Inn upstairs (see **Accommodations,** above).

Firehouse Cafe (562-5555), on the corner of Spenard and Benson St. Sports the brick red exterior of a converted warehouse, festooned with fire hoses. Live rock, blues, or acoustical music nightly; the crowd depends on who's playing. Menu includes pasta and other "real food." Killer drinks. Tall latte $2.25; mocha $2.75. Open M-F 6am-midnight, Sa-Su 8am-midnight.

SIGHTS

Watching over Anchorage from Cook Inlet is **Mt. Susitna,** known to locals as the "Sleeping Lady." Legend has it that this marks the resting spot of an Athabascan maid who dozed while awaiting her lover's return from war. When peace reigns in the world, the stories say, she will awake. Closer to town off Northern Lights Blvd., **Earthquake Park** recalls the 1964 Good Friday quake, the strongest ever recorded in North America, registering 9.2 on the Richter scale.

The **Anchorage Museum of History and Art,** 121 W. 7th Ave. (343-6061), at A St., is hands-down the finest museum in town, and probably throughout the state. *(Tours daily at 10, 11am, 1, and 2pm. $5, seniors $4.50, under 18 free.)* Permanent exhibits of Native Alaskan artifacts and art mingle with national and international works. Once you're indoors, it's possible to spend the entire day here. The **Alaska Aviation Heritage Museum,** 4721 Aircraft Dr. (248-5325), affords a fun perspective of Alaska's pioneer aviators. *(Open daily 9am-6pm. $5.75, seniors $4.50, youth $2.75, military personnel and AAA members $4.50.)* The collection includes 22 rare planes dated 1928-1952, some salvaged from remote Bush areas, and a theater featuring tales of aerial adventure and derring-do. A free shuttle runs from the airport.

Just in case you manage not to glimpse any of Alaska's animals in the wild—a difficult task—you're guaranteed to spot them at the **Alaska Zoo** (346-3242), Mile 2 on O'Malley Rd.; take bus #91. *(Open daily 9am-6pm. $7, seniors $6, ages 12-18 $4, under 12 $3.)* Binky the Polar Bear mauled an Australian tourist here in 1994, and became a local hero. He has since passed away, but the cub born in 1998, Ahpun (ah-poon), will hopefully be just as popular. *(Let's Go does not recommend attempting to endear yourself to locals by maiming tourists, unless they're really asking for it.)*

Does the Word "Mush" Mean Anything to You?

Charlie Darwin would have liked these odds: snow, wind, and frigid cold, separating the women from the girls. The celebrated Iditarod dog sled race begins in Anchorage on the first weekend in March. Dogs and their drivers ("mushers") traverse a trail over two mountain ranges, along the mighty Yukon River, and over the frozen Norton Sound to Nome. State pride holds that the route is 1049 mi., in honor of Alaska's status as the 49th state, but the real distance is closer to 1150 mi.

The Iditarod ("a far-off place") Trail began as a dog sled supply route from Seward on the southern coast to interior mining towns. The race commemorates the 1925 rescue of Nome, when drivers ferried 300,000 units of life-saving diptheria serum from Nenana, near Fairbanks, to Nome. The first race, in 1967, was a 27 mi. jaunt; by 1973, the first full race was run in 20 days. Today, up to 70 contestants speed each year from Anchorage to Nome, competing for a $450,000 purse but surprisingly willing to help fellow mushers in distress. Susan Butcher has won four races, Rick Swanson clinched five, and Doug Swingley made the fastest time (nine days, two hours).

The race has come under fire from animal rights activists because of the hardships borne by the dogs, some of whom die en route to Nome. Nevertheless, the dogs love to run, and Anchorage turns out in force for the ceremonial start downtown; the clock actually starts at Wasilla, north of the city. For more info, contact the Iditarod Trail Committee (376-5155; http://www.iditarod.com), Dept. M, P.O. Box 870800, Wasilla, AK 99687, or visit the Iditarod Headquarters (with museum, video presentations, gift shop, and free admission) at Mile 2.2 Knik Rd. in Wasilla.

OUTDOORS

Walk, skate, or bike to the **Tony Knowles Coastal Trail,** an 11 mi. paved track that skirts Cook Inlet on one side and the backyards of Anchorage's upper crust on the other. The heavily traveled trail is arguably one of the best urban bike paths in the country. In the winter, it's groomed for **cross-country skiing.**

Within minutes, travelers can escape the traffic and comparatively fast pace of Anchorage for the serene 770 sq. mi. of **Chugach State Park,** cornering the city to the north, east, and south. The public lands office (see **Practical Information,** above) provides a wealth of info on hiking and canoeing in the park. **Eagle River Nature Center,** 12 mi. up Eagle River Rd. off the Glenn Hwy. (Rte. 1), is another great resource. *(Open Tu-Su 10am-5pm; $3 parking fee.)* Call 800-280-2267 for info or reservations for any of the park's **public use cabins.** *($25 per night; $8.25 reservation fee.)*

Chugach has 25 established **dayhiking** trails, which leave from different points in Anchorage and along the Glenn Hwy. A 15-minute drive from the heart of the city, **Flattop Mountain** (4500 ft.) provides an excellent view of the inlet, the mountains of the Aleutian Chain, and on the rare clear day, Denali. This is the most frequently climbed mountain in Alaska, with an easy but occasionally slippery 2 mi. hike to its crowded summit. Parking at the trailhead costs $5; carless folks can take bus #92 to the intersection of Hillside Rd. and Upper Huffman Rd. From there, the trailhead is a ¾ mi. walk along Upper Huffman Rd., then right on Toilsome Hill Dr. for 2 mi. Less crowded hikes branch from the **Powerline Trail,** which begins at the same parking lot as the Flattop Trail. The **Middle Fork Loop,** ¾ mi. off of Powerline, leads a gentle 12 mi. through spruce woods and open tundra.

Near the Eagle River Nature Center is the trailhead for the **Old Iditarod Trail,** also known as **Crow Creek Pass,** which begins the 22 mi. journey to **Girdwood** (see p. 410). The entire trip takes a good two or three days, but the first portion makes an excellent dayhike past waterfalls, beaver dams, and alpine lakes. A tremendous view of water shooting over the jagged walls of twin falls lies 5 mi. along the lush valley. The trailhead for **Thunderbird Falls** is just off Glenn Hwy. at Mile 25; take the Thunderbird exit and follow signs for 1 mi. The gorge and falls are a leisurely 1 mi. walk.

Chugach has several trails geared towards **cycling**. The **Eklutna Lakeside Trail** extends 13 mi. one-way from the Eklutna Campground, off Mile 26 of the Glenn Hwy. (Rte. 1). A relatively flat dirt road, the trail follows the blue-green Eklutna Lake for 7 mi. before entering a steep river canyon, ending at the base of the Eklutna River. Kayakers and canoers also relish the quiet waters of Eklutna Lake. **Nancy Lake State Recreation Area,** just west of the Parks Hwy. (Rte. 3) at Mile 67.3, and just south of **Willow,** is well known for its **canoeing**. The **Lynx Lake Loop** takes two days, weaving through 8 mi. of lakes and portages, with designated campsites along the way. The loop begins at Mile 4.5 of the Nancy Lake Parkway, at the Tainaina Lake Canoe Trailhead. For **canoe rental** or **shuttle service** in the Nancy Lake Area, call **Tippecanoe** (495-6688). *(Canoes $25 first day, $70 per week. Shuttle free for backpackers.)* **Lifetime Adventures** (746-4644), at the Eklutna Campground, rents **bikes** and **kayaks**. *(Bikes $8 for 2hr., $15 for 4hr., $25 per day. Tandems are twice the price, which seems fair. Double kayaks from $25 per half-day, $45 per day.)* **NOVA Riverrunners** (745-5753) runs whitewater rafting down the **Matanuska Valley.** *(4hr. Class III and IV trip $75.)*

Numerous **skiing** and **snowboarding** trails weave around Anchorage. **Alyeska Ski Resort** is just a short drive away along the Seward Hwy. (Rte. 9); see **Girdwood,** p. 410. At the end of Raspberry Road and the Tommy Knowles Coastal Trail is **Kincaid Park,** the largest cross-country skiing area in the U.S. **Hatcher Pass,** north of **Wasilla** and **Palmer** on the Wasilla-Fishhook and the Palmer-Fishhook Roads, respectively, has plenty of trails for cross-country skiers; **Government Peak** and **Mile 16 Trail** are very popular with downhill skiers and snowboarders.

Glacier tours offer one of the best opportunities in the state to witness the amazing spectacle of huge chunks of ice plummeting into the ocean. **Philips' 26 Glacier Cruise,** 509 W. 4th Ave. (276-8023 or 800-544-0529), actually departs from **Whittier,** but most opt for a round-trip directly from Anchorage. *($121, including round-trip to Whittier.)* The five-hour voyage travels 110 mi. through **College** and **Harriman Fjords,** drawing nigh to six tidewater glaciers (the other 20 are worshipped from afar). A gaggle of other glacier tour companies have cruises that depart daily from Seward, 2½ hours south of Anchorage (see **Kenai Fjords National Park,** p. 416).

SHOPPING

Saturday Market (276-7207), held in the Lower Bowl parking lot at the corner of 3rd and E St. Made-in-Alaska products, as well as harvested-in-Alaska produce and fish. Sa 10am-6pm on Sa from May to early Sept.

Alaska Native Medical Center, 4315 Diplomacy Drive (729-1122), off Tudor Rd., houses non-profit gift shops on the first floor. Many Native Alaskans pay for medical services with their arts and handicrafts, and the proceeds from these works go to scholarships and aid for native communities. Fur moccasins, parkas, dolls, and the walrusbone *ulu* (a type of knife) highlight the selection. Open M-F 10am-2pm.

Salvation Army Thrift Store, 300 W. Northern Lights (561-5514). Hawks a wide range of cheap second-hand clothing. Open M-Sa 9am-8pm.

Mammoth Music, 2906 Spenard Rd. (258-3555), stocks a behemoth supply of new and used CDs. Open M-F 9am-10pm, Sa 10am-10pm, Su noon-6pm.

Alaska Native Arts and Crafts Showroom, 333 W. 4th Ave. (274-2932). Birch baskets, beadwork, and ivory carvings beckon seductively. Open in summer M-F 10am-6pm, Sa 10am-5pm, Su 11am-5pm; in winter M-F 11am-6pm, Sa 11am-5pm.

ENTERTAINMENT

Cyrano's Off Center Playhouse, at 413 D St. (274-2599 or 562-0207), is the center for all sorts of entertainment, including a cafe and a wide book selection. The **Eccentric Theatre Company** puts on a variety of plays here throughout the year, professional storytellers spin some great Alaskan tales on summer afternoons, and Cyrano's just opened a cozy little cinema in which art and foreign films are shown. *(Plays $12.50; students, seniors, and military $10. Stories $5, children $4. Films $6.50, matinee $3.)* Other events include poetry readings, film discussion groups, and comedy. The **Capri Cinema,** 3425 E. Tudor Rd. (561-0064), runs a mix of art flicks and second-run mainstream films; take bus #75. *($6, before 6pm $4.)* The **Denali Theater,** 1230 W. 27th St. (275-3106), at Spenard St., presents movies in limbo between the big screen and the video store for a delicious $1.01.

The **Alaska Experience Theater,** 705 W. 6th Ave. (276-3730), shows "Alaska the Greatland," a 40-minute presentation of scenery, wildlife, and Alaskan culture projected on the inner surface of a hemispherical dome. *(Every hr. 9am-9pm. $7, ages 5-12 $4.)* The theater's **earthquake exhibit** rumbles for a full 15 fun-filled minutes. *(Every 20min. 9:10am-9:10pm. $5, ages 5-12 $4. Both film and exhibit $10, ages 4-12 $7.)* The **4th Avenue Theatre,** 630 4th Ave. (257-5600), one block west of the Log Cabin Visitor Center (see **Practical Information,** above), has been faithfully restored to its original 40s decor. The neon-clad building contains a small grocery and gift shop, sponsors concerts and comedy, and shows a 40-minute **3D Alaska Gold Rush movie,** using the original, low-tech 3D glasses ($5).

Anchorage is no desert for the sports aficionado. The **Anchorage Bucs** (561-2827) and the **Anchorage Glacier Pilots** (274-3627) play baseball against teams like the Hawaii Island Movers and the Fairbanks Goldpanners in **Mulcahy Stadium,** at 16th and Cordova. In the colder months, the **Anchorage Aces** and the **University of Alaska Anchorage** team play hockey; call 263-ARTS/2787 for reservations and info.

NIGHTLIFE

The brew pub revolution has finally hit Anchorage, and microbrews gush from taps like oil through the pipeline. A combination of university students, townies, and tourists mean that Anchorage doesn't sleep when the sun goes down—and that's serious business in a city with a 1am summer sunset.

Come and Set the Ice on Fire

There's an old saying in the far north, where men so vastly outnumber women…
"The odds are good, but the goods are odd."

⊛**Railway Brewing Co.,** 421 W. 1st. (277-1996; http://www.railwaybrews.com), in the railroad depot. Voted the "best brew pub in North America" by some authority or other. Friendly, fun service, six tasty creations, live bands in the winter. Burger-and-brew special $8. Those under 21 can enjoy the crowd, if not the beer. Open daily 11am to around midnight, depending on the crowd.

⊛**Bernie's Bungalow Lounge,** 626 D St. (276-8808). Relax in one of many wingback chairs or couches as you sip your lemon drop martini ($5), puff on a cigar, and play a round of croquet in Anchorage's newest hot spot. Frequented by the young and retro. Open M-Th 7am-2:30am, F-Sa noon-3am, Su noon-2:30am.

Rumrunner's, 330 E. 3rd St. (278-4493). A comfortable, welcoming atmosphere with an upbeat local crowd. Live R&B and jazz (F-Sa); karaoke (Su-Th). Happy hour M-F 5pm-6:30pm. Open Su-Th 11am-2:30am, F-Sa 11am-3am.

The Wave, 3103 Spenard St. (561-WAVE/9283). A bright, upbeat dance bar with splashy, colorful decor and a loyal clientele, both gay and straight. Drag shows (W); country line dancing (Th). The Granada, a kind of alcoholic Slurpee, may help you get up and get down ($4). Open W 8pm-2:30am, Th 7pm-2:30am, F-Sa 8pm-3am.

Humpy's (276-BEER/2337; email humpys@alaska.net), at F Ave. and 6th St. Out-of-state draft beer $3.75; halibut tacos $7. Live music nightly, and so packed on weekends that you can barely see. Open M-Sa 11am-2am, Su noon-2am.

Chilkoot Charlie's, 2435 Spenard Rd. (272-1010), at Fireweed; take bus #7. With cavernous dance floors and top 40/rock music, "Koots" is known as the place to dance late into the night (the Humpy's crowd heads here around 12:30); it's also a known meat market. Dollar drink specials until 10pm. Open M-Th 10:30am-2:15am, F-Sa 11am-2:45am.

Mr. Whitekey's Fly-by-Night Club, 3300 Spenard Rd. (279-SPAM/7726); take bus #7. Serves "everything from the world's finest champagnes to a damn fine plate of Spam." Spam nachos $5.50; coconut beer-battered Spam $5. Nightly comedy and "musical off-color follies" at 8pm ($5-17). Live music after the show on F and Sa. Open Tu-Th 4pm-2am, F and Sa 4pm-3am.

Blues Central, 825 Northern Lights Blvd. (272-1341), at the corner of Arctic St.; take bus #9. This smoky, sophisticated bar answers Anchorage's cry for good live music, sponsoring live acts (daily) and free-form jam sessions (Su). Drafts from $3.75. Open M-Th 11am-2:30am, F 11am-3am, Sa 5pm-3am, Su 5pm-2:30am.

■ Glenn Highway (Rte. 1): Anchorage to Palmer

The Glenn Highway runs from Anchorage 189 mi. northeast to **Glennallen** (see p. 443), and from there to **Tok** and the **Richardson Hwy. (Rte. 4).** The first 37 mi. of the Glenn also begin the **George Parks Hwy. (Rte. 3)** to Denali and Fairbanks.

Leaving Anchorage on 6th Ave., the highway traces the western edge of **Chugach State Park.** At Mile 26, off the Eklutna exit, is **Eklutna Village Historical Park** (688-6026, Eagle River office 696-2828), a Dena'ina native village dating back to 1650, which represents the mingling of Russian and Athabascan culture. The restored **cemetery** is filled with colorful spirit houses, home to the souls of deceased Athabascans, and also contains the oldest standing building in greater Anchorage, **Old St. Nicholas Russian Church.** A small log structure built in 1830, Old St. Nick was used for local services until 1962, when the **New St. Nicholas Russian Church,** also in the cemetery, was constructed. To see the churches or to walk through the cemetery, you must take the 45-minute guided tour that leaves from the gift shop (tours $3.50, ages 7-10 $2.80, under 6 free; open mid-May to Sept. daily 8am-6pm).

From Eklutna, the Glenn Hwy. heads into the **Matanuska Valley.** Farmers who settled this area watched in astonishment as the long summer daylight produced garden vegetables big enough to feed a ship. The valley is still famous for its produce, legal and illegal: those in the know claim that **Matanuska Valley Thunderfuck** is some of the world's best marijuana. (*Let's Go* does not recommend getting thunderfucked.)

■ Palmer

After passing the turn-off for the George Parks Hwy. (Rte. 3), the Glenn Hwy. (Rte. 1) soon rolls eastward into the agricultural hamlet of Palmer, home every August to the **Alaska State Fair** (745-4827 or 800-850-FAIR/3247), which awarded ribbons to an 86.4 lb. cabbage and a 6.6 lb. carrot in 1998. Palmer's **visitor center,** 723 S. Valley Way (745-2880), provides standard info plus, in autumn, specimens of the region's freakishly big fruits and legumes—sorry, no dope (open May to mid-Sept. daily 8am-7pm). Four blocks from the visitor center is Palmer's artsy alternative to agriculture, **Vagabond Blues,** 642 S. Alaska (745-2233), with espresso, an entirely vegetarian menu, live music, and an open wall for upstart artists.

A few miles from the Parks Hwy. turnoff, at Mile 50.1 of the Glenn Hwy. on Archie Rd., reposes the **world's only domesticated musk ox farm** (745-4151). Introduced from Greenland in 1934, Palmer's oxen are prized for their *qiviut* (KIV-ee-oot) or petal-soft fleece (½hr. tours every ½hr.; $7, seniors and ages 13-18 $6, ages 6-12 $5, under 6 free; open daily 9am-7pm). The musk oxen's ungulate cousins play their games at the **Reindeer Farm** (745-4000), on the Bordenburg Butte Loop Rd. off the Old Glenn Hwy., 11 mi. from its southern junction with the main Glenn. Hand feed the affable beasts, and learn that reindeer and caribou are practically the same animal (open daily 10am-6pm; $5, seniors $4, ages 3-11 $3).

■ Seward Highway (Rte. 9): Anchorage to Portage

For heart-stopping scenery, cruise south on the Seward Hwy. from Anchorage. The road runs south along the **Turnagain Arm** of **Cook Inlet,** known for its dramatic tidal fluctuations. Miles of the arm are temporarily uncovered at low tide, only to be inundated by 10 ft. **bores,** walls of water created as the 15mph riptide races in. The bore tides reach Turnagain Arm about two hours after low tide in Anchorage; consult the *Daily News* for a tidal report.

> The area exposed at low tide can and does turn into **extremely dangerous quicksand.** *Let's Go* does not, in all seriousness, recommend walking across it at low tide. Moreover, the Seward Hwy. is narrow and has many blind turns. Drivers often stop to view animals near the highway, leading to many accidents.

ALASKA

Potter Marsh, about 15 mi. down the arm (Seward Mile 117.4), is a tranquil bird sanctuary and a magnet for wildlife photographers. The turn-off for **Girdwood** (see below) is at Mile 90; immediately to the left off the turn-off is the **Chugach National Forest Glacier Ranger District Office** (783-3242; open M-F 7:30am-5pm). This is an office, not a visitor center, but rangers can still provide info on hikes within the national forest, which stretches from just south of Anchorage to Prince William Sound. The turn-off for the nearest visitor center is another 10 mi. down the Seward Hwy., in **Portage** (see below). The most spectacular short hike in the vicinity of Anchorage can be reached along Crow Creek Rd. The **Old Iditarod Trail** climbs 3 mi. to the base of **Raven Glacier** on the Crow Pass; the trail continues 19 mi. to **Crow Creek** in **Chugach State Park,** and ends at the Eagle River visitor center (see p. 406).

■ Girdwood

Nestled at the base of a mountain, Girdwood has the charm, character, and prices of a somewhat undeveloped ski resort town—a place where people go simply to enjoy the outdoors and the sport, not the glamour. If you bring a truck and a big dog, or just a mellow attitude, you'll fit right in. **Class V Whitewater** (783-2004; http://www.alaska.net/~classv) offers some moderate and some truly intense rafting (from $50), kayaking, and fishing trips in the area. Girdwood has a **clinic** (783-1355) and a **post office** (783-2922); follow signs to the "new townsite" off Hightower (open M-F 9am-5pm, Sa 9am-noon). **ZIP Code:** 99587.

Eagle Mercantile Grocery (783-2900) sports a fair selection of supplies, including deli sandwiches ($3) and fresh produce (open daily 8am-midnight). **Max's Bar and Grill** (783-2888), about ¼ mi. up Crow Creek Rd., is the local bar of choice, featuring $3.50 drafts and all kinds of live music (open daily at 4pm; closing time varies). The **Double Musky Inn** (783-2822), ¼ mi. up Crow Creek Rd., just past Max's, deserves its reputation as one of the best restaurants in Alaska. Even those who can't swing a spicy Cajun-style dinner ($16-30) can at least enjoy the double musky pie ($4) and the garden outside (open Tu-Th 5-10pm, F-Su 4-10pm). **Chair 5 Restaurant and Bar** (783-2500; http://www.chair5.com), just around the corner from the post office, serves the cheapest dinner in town, including small pizzas (from $7.50), burgers ($6.50), and steak or seafood entrees ($13). The owner is a booze buff, proffering a wide variety of beers and single malt scotches (open daily 11am-10pm; bar open until 2am).

On the Alyeska Access Rd., 3 mi. from Mile 90, lies the **Alyeska Ski Resort** (754-1111), with seven chair lifts and a 3934 ft. vertical drop (open Nov.-Apr. for skiing; full-day ticket $35, half-day $27, college students and military $27, ages 13-17 $24, ages 8-13 or 60-69 $17, under 8 and over 69 $7). Nearby **cross-country** and **heli-skiing** options abound. In summer, a tram goes up the mountain, leading to lunch on top ($18; without lunch $16; child, student, military and senior discounts). It's also possible to hike to the summit and ride down on the tram for free. The **Girdwood-Alyeska Home Hostel (HI-AYH)** (783-2099) is a rustic wooden cabin run by the same folks who manage the Anchorage Hostel. To get there, turn left onto the Alyeska Access Rd., go 2 mi., take a right on Timberline Dr., and another right on Alpina until it turns into Alta. The hostel, on the right, has 11 beds and a sauna, but no hot showers ($10, nonmembers $13). Showers, swimming, and a hot tub are available at the hotel ($5). Winter or summer, it's almost worth the detour into Alyeska just to visit the **Bake Shop** (783-2831), an outstanding restaurant below the resort; turn left at the end of the Alyeska Access Rd. and then turn right up the hill on Olympic. Folks across the state sing the praises of its sourdough ($3) and its bottomless bowls of soup ($4; open M-F and Su 7am-7pm, Sa 7am-8pm).

■ Portage

One might wonder why Portage has a dot on the map, since it's little more than a train and bus stop, 45 minutes from downtown Anchorage at Mile 80 of the Seward Hwy. (Rte. 9). Flattened by the 1964 Good Friday earthquake, the town has done little to rebuild itself, but travelers still stop by to behold the area's ample natural attractions. The well-paved **Portage Highway,** beginning at Seward Mile 78.9, runs through magnificent **Portage Valley.** Four roadside glaciers sit staunchly along the valley, periodically calving spectacular blue ice chunks into **Portage Lake.** On the lakeside, the **Begich and Boggs Visitor Center** (783-2326) offers a 20-minute film ($1) and what are perhaps the most modern displays of any Alaskan info outlet (open daily 9am-6pm; in winter Sa-Su 10am-4pm). To reach the center, take the 5 mi. detour off Seward Hwy. south of Alyeska, along the Portage Hwy. Friendly forest rangers lead free **iceworm safaris** to Byron Glacier (see below), in search of mysterious, minuscule, ice-dwelling, algae-eating beasts (May-Sept. Tu and Sa at 4pm). A transparent observation tunnel looks out onto pieces of bizarrely blue glacial ice floating in the water. Unfortunately, **Portage Glacier** is no longer visible from the visitor center; it has receded almost half a mile since the building's construction. **Gray Line** (277-5581) conducts an hour-long cruise within viewing range (May-Sept., 5 per day 10:30-4:30, $25). They also run a seven-hour circuit from Anchorage to the glacier and back, including stops at the Alyeska Ski Resort (see p. 410) and the visitor center (May-Sept., daily 9am and noon, $60).

Several short, worthwhile hikes leave from Portage Hwy. The wheelchair accessible **Moraine Nature Trail** is a quick half-hour loop with fine views of the glacier and lush, green valley. The 1.6 mi. **Byron Glacier Trail** begins in an alder forest and continues past the rushing **Byron Creek** to the foot of the glacier. For more info on hikes and trails in the area, contact the Anchorage office of the Chugach National Forest, 3301 C St., Anchorage 99503 (271-2500).

The **Alaska Backpacker Shuttle** (344-8775 or 800-266-8625) runs between the Portage train station and Anchorage ($20). Hitchers report that rides are easy to find (even though *Let's Go* never recommends such activities). About 4 mi. off the highway, two state-run **campgrounds—Black Bear** (tents only; $9) and **Williwaw** ($10)—have water, toilets, bear-proof food lockers, and glacial views. Williwaw also has a short hiking trail and a viewing ledge overlooking **salmon-spawning areas.**

KENAI PENINSULA

Many visitors to Alaska spend their whole trip in the Kenai Peninsula, whether for the endless wildlife, the heart-stopping scenery, or the fantastic fishing. Just south of Anchorage, the Seward Highway (Rte. 9) runs to Seward and the Sterling Highway (Rte. 1) to Homer, skirting Chugach National Forest, Kenai Fjords National Park, and the Kenai National Wildlife Refuge, which protect most of the peninsula. On the western edge, snow-capped volcanoes reflect in the blue waters of Cook Inlet, while on the southern coast, glaciers reach out like enormous icy tongues from the Harding Ice Field to the sea.

■ Seward

Seward is yet another of Alaska's super-scenic coastal towns. Lush alpine trails in Chugach National Forest, hulking tidewater glaciers and cascading waterfalls in Kenai Fjords National Park, and teeming fish in Resurrection Bay draw hikers, kayakers, sailors, anglers, and cruise lines to Seward. So far, the town's demure seaside demeanor has endured this onslaught—the strip malls that blight its peninsular neighbors, Soldotna and Kenai, have yet to make an appearance. The $56 million SeaLife Center, however, unveiled in May 1998, promises to nudge Seward from its peaceful slumber. The first cold-water marine research center in the western hemisphere, the facility anticipates 250,000 visitors per year, more than even Denali National Park.

ORIENTATION AND PRACTICAL INFORMATION

Seward is 127 mi. south of Anchorage on the scenic **Seward Highway (Rte. 9).** Most services and outdoor outfits cluster in the **small-boat harbor** on **Resurrection Bay.**

Airplanes: The **airport** is 2 mi. north of town on the Seward Hwy. **Era Aviation** (800-866-8394) flies to Anchorage ($69). **Scenic Mountain Air** (288-3646) makes 1hr. flightseeing trips over the fjords ($129 per person; 2-person min.) and a fly-in, hike-out package leaving from Moose Pass at Seward Mile 29 ($79 per person; 2-person min.). Discounts pledged to those who heard about them through *Let's Go.*

Trains: Alaska Railroad (800-544-0552). Depot at the northern edge of town, across from the visitor center. Daily to Anchorage in summer (4½hr.; $43, ages 2-11 $32.)

Buses: Seward Bus Lines, 1914 Seward Hwy. (224-3608). To: Anchorage (1 per day at 9am, $30; airport service $5).

Ferries: Alaska Marine Highway (224-5485, reservations 800-642-0066). Dock at 4th Ave. and Railway St. 3 per month in summer to: Kodiak (13hr., $54); Valdez (11hr., $58); Homer (25hr., $96.).

Harbormaster: (224-3138; WFA 702), 1300 4th Ave., on the waterfront.

Public Transportation: Seward's Trolley runs through the greater portion of town. Designated stops, but will pause when flagged. $1.50, $3 all day, ages 6-15 half-price. Runs daily 10am-7pm. Group tours available.

Taxis: PJ's Taxi, 224-5555. $2 base, 25¢ per ¼ mi.; discounts for seniors and disabled; charter rates. **Glacier Taxi,** 224-5678. $1 base, $1.50 per mi., charter $30 per hr. Both 24hr.

Car Rental: Hertz Car Rental (224-4378), on Port Ave., 2 blocks east of the train station. $76 per day, plus 30¢ per mi. over 100 mi. Must be 25 with credit card.

Road Closure Information: 800-478-7675.

Visitor Information: Seward Chamber of Commerce (224-8051), at Mile 2 on the Seward Hwy. Encyclopedic knowledge of Seward, with a computerized directory of accommodations and restaurants. Open M-F 8am-5pm, Sa-Su 9am-4pm. Also operates another info center in the small boat harbor. Open daily 6am-8pm.

Outdoor Information: Kenai Fjords National Park Visitor Center (224-3175, info 224-2132; http://www.nps.gov/kesj), at the small-boat harbor. Furnishes park info and maps, field guides, and trail guides. Nature talks given 2-3 times per week in summer at 5:30pm. Open daily 8am-7pm; in winter M-F 8am-5pm. **Seward Ranger Station, Chugach National Forest,** 334 4th Ave. (224-3374), at Jefferson St. Extensive trail info, maps, and detailed advice on trails close to town. Cabin reservations for the Seward Ranger District. Open M-F 8am-5pm.

Employment: Seward Employment Center, P.O. Box 1009 (224-5276), 5th Ave. and Adams St., on the City Building's 2nd floor. Open M-F 9am-noon and 1-4:30pm.

Bookstores: Northland Books and Charts, 201 3rd Ave. (224-3102), at Washington. Good selection of topographic maps, road atlases, wildlife guides, navigational guides, and general interest books. Open M-F 9am-6pm, Sa-Su 10am-5pm. **Reader's Delight,** 222 4th Ave. (224-2665). Mostly paperbacks, plus a collection of used books-on-tape so that you can finally quit listening to that Steely Dan cassette you found on your car floor. Open daily 10am-6pm.

Library: Seward Community Library (224-3646), on 5th and Adams. Free Internet access available in 30min. slots. Open M-F noon-8pm, Sa noon-6pm.

Laundromat and Public Showers: Seward Laundry (224-5727), at 4th Ave. and C St. Wash $2, dry 25¢ per 5min. Showers $3.75 per 15min. Open M-Sa 8am-10pm, Su 10am-8pm; last wash 8:30pm M-Sa, 6:30pm Su. Showers also available at the **harbormaster** (see above). $1 per 5min.

Pharmacy: Seward Drug, 224 4th Ave. (224-8989). Open M-Sa 9am-6pm.

Fishing Supplies: The Fish House (224-3674), across from the harbormaster. Rent rods ($10); buy tackle. $100 cash or credit card deposit required. Tips and instructions free. Fishing licenses available. Open daily 6am-10pm.

Emergency: 911. **Police:** 224-3338.

Crisis Line: 224-3027. 24hr.

Hospital: Providence Seward Hospital (224-5205), at 1st Ave. and Jefferson St.

Post Office: (224-3001), at 5th Ave. and Madison St. Open M-F 9:30am-4:30pm, Sa 10am-2pm. **ZIP Code:** 99664.

Internet Access: See **Library,** above.

Area Code: 907.

ACCOMMODATIONS AND CAMPGROUNDS

Seward has a host of reasonable housing and camping options, though the tidal wave of visitors each summer often floods these resources; book well in advance. The visitor center carries information on B&Bs. At Mile 29.5 on Seward Hwy. (Rte. 9), the nearby town of **Moose Pass** has four campgrounds with excellent fishing: **Primrose** (Mile 17; $9), **Ptarmigan Creek** (Mile 23; $9), **Trail River** (Mile 24; singles $9; doubles $13), and **Tenderfoot** (Mile 46; $9; wheelchair accessible). All are run by the Chugach National Forest; for info, contact Alaska Public Lands Information, 605 W. 4th, Anchorage 99501 (271-2737). All have pit toilets and water.

Ballaine House Lodging, P.O. Box 2051, 437 3rd Ave. (224-2362), at Madison St., 2 blocks from downtown. Bright, clean, and well-furnished, in a house built by one of the founding families of Seward in 1905. Pleasant rooms, scrumptious breakfast. Generous, accommodating owner divulges all sorts of info on Seward, offers a large library of Alaskan books and videos, and can help with discounts on various Seward attractions. Singles $55; doubles $79; lower rates without breakfast. Free laundry service, with adequate notice. Pick-up and drop-off from train or bus.

Moby Dick Hostel (224-7072), at 3rd Ave. and Madison St. Avast! This newly opened hostel is the cheapest indoor option in town. Cramped quarters, thin beds, and thin walls may make you feel like you're stowed away in the hold. No monomaniacs allowed. $17.50; cash payment $16.50. Showers; full kitchen.

Kate's Roadhouse (224-5888; fax 224-3081), 5½ mi. outside Seward on the Seward Hwy. Clean, family-style hostel accommodations (7 per room) and 3 private, newly built theme cabins. Whether you're feeling like a mariner or a sourdough, your cabin will have electricity, an indoor bathroom, *and* access to Alaska's only outhouse with a pink flush toilet. Beds $17; private rooms $59; cabins $29-49. Continental breakfast, bedding, well-stocked kitchen, bikes, laundry, shuttle service into town…and an enormous pig. Piglet lives affably enough in the TV room, though his snoring does get a bit loud at times.

Exit Glacier Campground, 8½ mi. down Exit Glacier Rd., off Seward Hwy. Mile 3.7. Budget tenters, rejoice: water, pit toilets, secluded sites, and a ½ mi. walk to Exit Glacier. Stroll to your free walk-in tent site and fall asleep to the far-off ring of the cash register at fee-charging campgrounds. 3-day max. stay.

Miller's Landing, P.O. Box 81 (224-5739). Follow the Seward Highway to its end at the SeaLife Center, turn right, and follow the coast for 3 mi. It's a bit of a hike from town, but Miller's Landing has just about everything an outdoorsy person might need: a grassy spot for camping ($15, includes showers for 4 people), sites (hookups $20), a variety of rustic cabins (2-13 people; $30-60; no bedding), tackle, camping essentials (marshmallows!), boat charters, boat and kayak rentals, boat launching, water taxi, guided kayak trips, and drop-offs. Call ahead for reservations, especially for the cabins.

Municipal Waterfront Campground, along Ballaine Rd. between Railway Ave. and D St. A scenic spot on which to squat, if you nab a grassy plot. Gravel lot hosts many RVs. Toilets are scattered throughout the campground; restrooms and showers are at the harbormaster. Sites $6; RV hookups $8; discount rate (pay for six nights, stay for seven). 2-week max. stay. Check-out 4pm. Open May 15-Sept. 30.

FOOD AND NIGHTLIFE

Although affordable, Seward's food is not its forte. Stock up on groceries at the **Eagle Quality Center,** 1907 Seward Hwy. (224-3698), at Mile 1.5. It's a hike from downtown, but you can reward yourself after the trek with a treat at the in-store soda fountain (open 24hr.).

Miller's Daughter (224-6091), 1215 4th Ave., on the waterfront across from the National Park center. Most breads are organic, fat-free, and herbivore-friendly— witness fresh vegetarian soup and vegan cookies. Soup with mooseepy bread $4.75; hummus or tuna salad sandwich $4.50. Open daily 6:30am-8pm.

Ray's (224-5606), on 4th Ave., at the waterfront. Reward a hard day's fishing at this harborside haven. Although entrees are on the steep side (from $15), the bayside

ALASKA

location and fresher-than-fresh seafood make Ray's a choice restaurant for a splurge. Best seafood chowder in Seward $6; lunch $6-12. Open daily 11am-10pm.

Red's, at 3rd and Van Buren St. Red cooks the best burgers in town out of his kitchen in a white school bus. Burger and fries $5. Open M-Sa 11am-9pm.

Resurrect Art Coffee House Gallery, 320 3rd Ave. (224-7161). Seward's most intriguing coffee shop has arisen in a converted Lutheran church. The food is limited to plastic-wrapped muffins, but the lattes are so good, they're almost sinful ($2.25). Sip Italian soda ($1.50) at the altar-turned-art-display or in the balcony-turned-loft. Ample art books for browsing; Luther's Small Catechism is missing. Occasional live music and poetry readings. Open Su-Th 7am-9pm, F-Sa 7am-10pm.

Peking, 338 4th Ave. (224-5444), at Jefferson St. Tasty lunch specials with rice and soup ($6.25-8), served 11:30am-3pm. The Kung Pao halibut is especially scrumptious ($8). Open M-Th 11:30am-10:30pm, F-Su 11:30am-11pm.

Ranting Raven Bakery, 224 4th Ave. (224-2228), downtown. In the back of a gift shop, the Raven bakes a variety of sweets and breads daily. Eggie quiche $3; cookies 75¢. Open daily 7am-6:30pm.

Yukon Bar (224-3065), at 4th Ave. and Washington St., usually draws the younger crowd. Travelers pin a dollar to the ceiling to leave a mark in Alaska and protect themselves against the possibility that they may someday return with an empty wallet. Pool tables, the coldest beer in town, and live rock (W-Sa), perfect for late-night schemes (open daily noon-2am).

SIGHTS AND ENTERTAINMENT

The **Alaska SeaLife Center** (224-3080 or 800-224-2525; http://www.alaskasealife.org), at the end of downtown between 3rd and 4th Ave., opened in May 1998 after much state-wide fanfare and anticipation, and has become one of Seward's (and Alaska's) most prized attractions. *(Open May-Sept. daily 9am-9:30pm, last tickets sold at 8pm; in winter W-Su 10am-5pm, last tickets sold at 3:30pm. $12.50, seniors $11.25, ages 4-16 $10.)* Created in the black wake of the Exxon *Valdez* spill to promote understanding of marine life and to provide a rehabilitation facility for injured animals, the $56 million center gives visitors a glimpse at Alaska's coastal and underwater goings-on. With interaction between visitors and on-site research labs, this is much more than an average aquarium. The center's galleries provide a host of information on marine animals, which can be viewing swimming in large outdoor habitats. Watch and be watched by harbor seals, puffins, and Steller sea lions slicing through the water, touch various shell-covered critters, and marvel at nature's splendor in climate-controlled comfort. Visitor programs including talks on seals, seabirds, current research, and family-oriented activities like making clay seals. Tickets are valid for the entire day, allowing patrons to come and go as they please.

Next to the SeaLife Center, the **Chugach Heritage Center,** 501 Railway Ave. (224-5065), also had its big opening in 1998. *(Open daily 10am-8pm. $10, ages 4-16 $8.)* A 1917 railroad depot has been transformed into a theater and gallery of Native Alaskan art, where hourly 30-minute performances serve to educate the public and to preserve native culture. The show, conceived by an Aleut director, includes story-telling, singing, dancing, and authentic costumes made from such materials as sealskin and duck bellies. The fascinating performances represent one of the first transitions of native oral tradition to a public stage.

The self-guided **walking tour** of Seward, available at the visitor center, passes many turn-of-the-century homes and businesses in two to three hours. The **Resurrection Bay Historical Society Museum,** in the Senior Center at 3rd Ave. and Jefferson St., exhibits traditional Alaskan artifacts, including a fine collection of woven baskets. *(Open Memorial Day-Labor Day daily 9am-5pm; extended hours when cruise ships are in town. $2, ages 5-18 50¢.)* Those feeling a bit too sedentary can get all shook up by the **Earthquake Movie** at the Seward Community Library (see **Practical Information,** above), which shows actual footage of the 1964 Good Friday earthquake. *(Mid-June to Sept. M-Sa at 2pm. $3 donation requested, 12 and under free.)* In the spring of 1994, the 40-year-old **Liberty Theater,** 304 Adams St. (224-5418), began showing films on their national release date. *($6, matinees and W $4.)* All of Seward was very, very proud.

EVENTS

The **Silver Salmon Derby** opens each year on the second Saturday in August, and closes eight days later. In 1995 the city upped the prize for the elusive tagged fish to $100,000. No one has caught the slippery salmon since 1980, when Japanese tourist and lucky bastard Katsumi Takaku nabbed it from the city docks.

Seward's other insanity-inducing annual event is the **Mountain Marathon,** held on the 4th of July. Alaska's oldest footrace (second in the nation only to the Boston Marathon), the run began when a sourdough challenged a barmate to run up and down the 3022 ft. Mt. Marathon in less than an hour. The current record is 43 minutes for men and 50 minutes for women. A parade gaily passes as the governor of Alaska and hundreds of fellow competitors run, slide, fall, and bleed up and down the steep mountainsides. Thousands of sadistic spectators set up lawn chairs in town and watch the pain-filled frenzy with binoculars.

The annual **Seward Silver Salmon 10K Run** takes off during the Labor Day weekend, and the **Exit Glacier 5K and 10K Run** begins in mid-May. While these races may sound tough, Seward's truest test of physical endurance looms on the third weekend of January, when the three-day **Seward Polar Bear Jump** raises money for cancer research by plunging participants into the frigid waters of Resurrection Bay.

OUTDOORS

All sorts of hiking trails weave through the high alpine passes and lush valleys between Seward and its northern neighbor, **Portage** (see p. 410). Though many of these routes take days, some make easily accessible dayhikes. Call 800-280-CAMP/ 2267 to reserve a **public cabin.** *(Most have 6 bunks. $25 per night; $8.25 reservation fee.)* For more info, visit the **Seward Ranger Station** (see **Practical Information,** above).

A 7 mi. **coastal trail** weaves through **Caines Head State Recreation Area,** at the mouth of Resurrection Bay. After 1½ mi., there is a 3 mi. stretch negotiable only at low tide. Most hikers stay overnight before returning, in order to catch the next low tide. Consult the newspaper, the chamber of commerce, the Coast Guard, or any commercial fishing outfitter for tide information. The last 2½ mi. lead along sand, ending at **South Beach,** where camping is free.

Mt. Marathon, looming behind Seward, offers a glorious view of the sea, the town, and the surrounding mountains. From 1st Ave. and Jefferson St., take Lowell St. to reach the trail, which begins with a steep ascent up a rocky stream bed. The more gradual switchbacks of a Jeep trail start up at 1st Ave. and Monroe St. Once above vegetation, a network of trails continues up the rocky ledge to the left. Another route climbs through the scree to the right. The scree can be fun to run through on the way down, and if there's still snow, you can just luge it. Plan to make a two- or three-hour climb and a one-hour hop-and-slide back down, all the while marveling at the punishing speed with which the Mountain Marathoners tackle the peak (see **Events,** above).

The **Lost Lake Trail** makes a strenuous dayhike or overnight trip, venturing 7 mi. one-way into the mountains. It starts at the end of a gravel road, at Seward Hwy. Mile 5. Meandering above treeline for about half the distance, the trail offers dayhikers a wide-open view of glacially carved peaks all around. It is open to mountain bikers in the summer, and cross-country skiers in the winter. For those planning to stay overnight, the **Dale Clemens cabin** lies 1½ miles south of the trail from Mile 4. The **Primrose Trail,** which begins at **Primrose Campground,** 1½ mi. from Mile 17 on the Seward Hwy., presents a marvelous interplay of rich lakes and mountain passes. Though the first 4 mi. of the 8 mi. trip offer few vistas from a dense spruce forest, persistent travelers will reach the glimmering **Porcupine Creek Falls,** off a spur trail at Mile 3. The last two or three miles of the Primrose Trail are steep, rising beyond timberline. True to its name, the path is strewn with spectacular wildflowers.

Starting from Seward Hwy. Mile 34, the **Carter Lake Trail** gives grunting hikers another good survey of local terrain. The 6.6 mi. round-trip climbs steeply out of in hemlock forests, then flattens out into fields of wildflowers and low brush, with striking views of peaks and sapphire lakes. To transform this jaunt into a journey, continue on the **Crescent Lake Trail** for another 9 mi. Camping is available at Carter Lake or Crescent Lake. To reach the **Crescent Saddle Cabin,** 7.5 mi. from the Carter Lake trailhead, follow the poor trail along Crescent Lake to the south shore.

The true path to illumination, however, starts at Sterling Hwy. Mile 52. The **Resurrection Pass Trail** is a favorite among mountain bikers and weekend hikers—expect to see an eighth of Anchorage's population along this trail on any given Saturday. The 23 mi. **Johnson Pass Trail** serves as another ideal route for a two- to three-day trip. The north trailhead starts at Seward Hwy. Mile 64; go south on a gravel road ¼ mi. to the trailhead. The south trailhead lies at Seward Hwy. Mile 32.5. A road less traveled, Johnson Pass offers dramatic views of rich emerald meadows, alpine tundra, and spruce forests, without the crowds that swarm Resurrection Pass. The trail provides an ideal way to view different Kenai Peninsula ecosystems as it passes through a spruce forest, rises into shrubby sub-alpine regions, and finally extends into alpine tundra. The web of trails in this area enables creative hikers to combine some of these routes for longer, more rigorous hikes.

FISHING AND MUSHING

Salmon and halibut fill the bay, and grayling and dolly varden can be hooked right outside of town. Charters are available for both halibut and salmon throughout the summer; prices start at $95, with all gear provided. Call **The Fish House** (800-257-7760; see **Practical Information,** above), the largest charter-booking service in Seward. Fishing is free from the shore or docks.

To reach **IdidaRide Sled Dog Tours** (224-8607 or 800-478-3139), turn left on Exit Glacier Road at Mile 3.7 of the Seward Hwy., continue 3.3 mi., take a right on Old Exit Glacier Road, and follow the signs for the next ½ mi. Mitch Seavey competes in the Iditarod every year—he placed 4th in 1998—and you can help train his dogs in the summer by providing dead weight. The musher-narrated IdidaRide tour gives some sense of the training, preparation, family involvement, and alternate lifestyle necessary for the annual winter race. After beholding the raucous kennel of sled dogs, visitors take a thrilling ten-minute ride with a 12-dog team, view arctic gear and supplies, and play with puppies. *(Full tour 1¼ hr.; 5 daily. $28.50, 11 and under $15. Kennel tour $10, children $5. Call for reservations.)*

■ Kenai Fjords National Park

Seward serves as gateway to the stunning waterways and yawning ice fields of Kenai Fjords National Park. The park's coastal mountain system is packed with wildlife and glaciers, but is largely inaccessible to novice kayakers without considerable means, and is almost entirely blocked to hikers without mountaineering equipment. The lay traveler does have a few opportunities to revel in the park's glory, though. **Exit Glacier,** the only road-accessible glacier in the park, lies 9 mi. west on a spur from Mile 3.7 of the Seward Hwy. (Rte. 9). A shuttle runs here four times daily from downtown Seward ($10 round-trip; call 224-8747), and parking for the day is $5. From the **Ranger Station** at the end of the road, a leisurely ¾ mi. stroll leads to the impressive base of the outlandishly blue glacier, where tremendous crevasses catch trickling water that melts into a roaring stream. The first ½ mi. of this trail is wheelchair accessible. Rangers lead one-hour **guided walks** to the glacier four times daily, as well as a **geology talk** on Saturday at 2pm. The only significant, accessible hike within the park is the grueling and utterly worthwhile 3000 ft. climb to the top of Exit Glacier. A full day's scramble, the **Harding Ice Field Trail** begins at the paved trail, and continues 4 mi. up to the origin of the glacier. An impressive viewpoint, even by Alaskan standards, the summit overlooks **Harding Ice Field,** a glimmering wasteland that encompasses 300 sq. mi., and spawns 40 glaciers.

Beyond Exit Glacier, **boat cruises** are the easiest and most popular way to see the park. The longest and most expensive cruises access either **Aialik Bay** or **Northwestern Fjord.** Both routes pass forested terrain, endless wildlife, tidewater glaciers, and spectacular geological formations. Bald eagles, puffins, humpback whales, sea otters, Steller sea lions, orcas, seals, and Dall's porpoises regularly appear just off the bow. **Kenai Fjords Tours** (224-8068 or 800-478-8068; http://www.kenaifjords.com) includes an excellent grilled salmon dinner, served on-board. *(To: Northwestern Fjord 9½hr.; $139, children $59. To: Aialik Bay 6hr.; $99, children $49.)* **Major Marine Tours** (224-8030 or 800-764-7300; http://www.majormarine.com) brings along a ranger to explain wildlife and glacier facts, and serves a salmon, halibut, and shellfish dinner for an extra $10. *(To: Aialik 8hr.; $89.)* Both companies also offer a variety of tours within Resurrection Bay, including overnighters, and it pays to shop around for just the right type of trip; the cheapest start at $49. **Renown Charters and Tours** (224-3806 or 800-655-3806) runs similar cruises for about the same prices, and **Mariah Tours** (224-8623 or 800-270-1238) uses smaller boats. *(Max. 16 passengers. To: Northwestern Fjord $115.)* **Wildlife Quest** is the only outfit with speedy, smooth-riding catamarans. *(To: Holgate Glacier 5½hr.; $99, children $36. Includes free pass to SeaLife Center.)* Pick up a list of charters at the chamber of commerce, or from shops along the boardwalk near the harbormaster's office (see **Practical Information,** above).

Sunny Cove Sea Kayaking (345-5339; email kayakak@alaska.net; http://www.alaska.net/~kayakak) offers a joint trip with Kenai Fjords Tours, including the wildlife cruise, a salmon bake, kayaking instruction, and a 2½-hour wilderness paddle. *($139, with extra 2hr. $159.)* **Kayak and Custom Adventures Worldwide** (258-FUNN/3866 or 800-288-3134) also leads trips, including paddling instruction. *($75-95.)* For the experienced kayaker, **Miller's Landing** (see p. 413) rents kayaks and leads full day trips. *(Kayak singles $30 per day, $15 per additional day; doubles $55 per day, $45 per additional day. Guided trips $85; lunch $10 extra.)*

▓ Sterling Highway (Rte. 1)

The Sterling Highway begins 37 mi. north of Seward at the **Tern Lake Junction,** 90 mi. south of Anchorage, where the Seward Highway (Rte. 9) and the Sterling meet. From here, the highway runs 66 mi. west to **Kenai** (see p. 419), passing through the **Chugach National Forest** and the **Kenai National Wildlife Refuge** (see below). From Kenai, the highway runs south on the western side of the peninsula along **Cook Inlet** (see p. 421), terminating after 75 mi. at the town of **Homer** (see p. 422). The Sterling passes through popular moose range, so drivers are advised to be especially cautious. Mile markers measure the distance from Seward.

■ Cooper Landing

Shortly after its intersection with the Seward Hwy., the Sterling passes **Kenai Lake,** which stretches in a giant Z-shape through the Chugach Range. The highway continues along the **Kenai River** to the town of Cooper Landing. Anglers rejoice: you have reached the Promised Land of **salmon fishing,** a land flowing with kings, silvers, reds, and pinks. During the summer runs, Cooper Landing and surrounding campgrounds take on a carnival atmosphere, as eager fisherfolk line up on the banks of the Kenai River to try their luck. It's not unusual to see anglers standing shoulder-to-shoulder and filling their baskets with fish. **Licenses** are available at most grocery and fishing stores. Guided **fishing charters** abound, but for hefty prices extending well into the $100 range. A much cheaper option is the **ferry trip** to the opposite bank of the Kenai River, which yields comparable views and access to good fishing ($4, ages 3-11 $2). The boat uses cables and current to carry it across at Sterling Mile 55.

The Kenai offers several places to **whitewater raft** without risking life and limb. Some of these floats are as scenic as Class III river-running gets. Outdoor outfits generally supply lunch and gear on full-day trips, but anglers should buy their own licenses beforehand. **Alaska Wildland Adventures** (800-478-4100), in Cooper Landing, offers a variety of full- and half-day rafting trips ($42-185, children $29-55). The **Alaska River Company** (595-1226) offers hiking as well as rafting and fishing tours; the most economical trip is a three-hour run through mild Class II waters ($42).

■ Kenai National Wildlife Refuge

From Cooper Landing, the Sterling stretches 50 mi. to **Soldotna** (see below), paralleling the Kenai River until it enters the 1.97 million acres of the Kenai National Wildlife Refuge. This stretch of the peninsula is prime moose territory—originally designated the Kenai National Moose Refuge in 1941—and makes for excellent hiking. The **Fuller Lakes Trail**, a 5.8 mi. round-trip hike at Mile 56.9, is one of the most strenuous established hikes in the region, with an elevation gain of 1400 ft. After a challenging first mile of steady ascent through dense forests, striking views highlight the glimmering **Lower Fuller Lakes** and the lush **Kenai Mountains.** The **Kenai River Trails** provide a moderate alternative to the Fuller Lakes Trail. To reach two of the trailheads, turn south on Skilak Lake Rd. at Mile 58. The **upper trail** starts at Mile 2.2 of Skilah Lake Rd.; a 5.6 mi. round-trip with a scant elevation gain of 260 ft., it provides impressive views of the turquoise waters off the Kenai coast. The **lower trail** (4.6 mi. round-trip) begins at Mile 3 of Skilak Lake Rd., and affords similar spectacles. Scamper through the open meadows teeming with wildflowers, and linger to gorge on blueberries in late summer. Plenty of bears in the area keep the moose company. The **Hidden Creek Trail** is a mild 2.6 mi. round-trip beginning at Mile 5.4 of Skilak Lake Rd., 1 mi. west of Hidden Lake Campground. A quick hike with only a 300 ft. ascent, the trail leads through forests to **Skilak Lake** and the mouth of not-so-**Hidden Creek.** If the water level is low, it's possible to hike around the lake—a bold traveler might even submerge herself in its frigid waters for an exhilarating swim.

The refuge, lying north of the Sterling Hwy., also boasts some of the best **canoeing** systems in Alaska. The **Swan Lake Route** has three different passages suitable for two- to four-day paddles. Over 30 lakes dot the wooded landscape, furnishing fishing and wildlife viewing opportunities. The more challenging **Swanson River System** connects 40 lakes through marshy wetlands, offering several two-day routes and some that can last over a week. Because of its difficulty, this system is less popular with people and therefore more popular with wildlife. Canoeists attempting this route should be experienced in backcountry skills.

For more info on hikes and canoeing, contact the **Kenai National Wildlife Refuge Headquarters and Visitor Center,** P.O. Box 2139, Soldotna (262-7021), on Sterling Hwy. between Miles 96 and 97; turn left on Funny River Rd., then laugh all the way right onto Ski Hill Rd. The free *Refuge Reflections* gives detailed fishing, hiking, and canoeing tips. The center also features 30-minute **nature walks** (F-Su 11am), free **nature films** (5 per day), two-hour **discovery hikes** (Sa 11am), and one-hour **campfire programs** at Hidden Lake Campground (F-Sa 8pm). A 10-minute, wheelchair accessible, self-guided nature walk leaves from the center (open M-F 8am-5pm, Sa-Su 9am-6pm). You needn't travel all the way to Soldotna to get basic info on the refuge, though. The **Kenai National Wildlife Refuge Visitor Contact Station** is at Mile 58 on the Sterling, much closer to many of the campgrounds and trailheads. This log cabin station sells maps ($3-4) and other outdoor lit, and has a lovely educational garden out front, filled with local perennial plants (open Su-Th 9am-6pm, F-Sa 9am-7pm).

■ Soldotna

Soldotna spreads its strip mall tentacles for several miles along the northern stretch of the Sterling Hwy., 55 mi. from its origin. An urban blemish on the face of the peninsula, the town supplies groceries and camping gear to travelers en route to elsewhere. **Wilderness Way** (262-3880), 2 mi. east of town, packs an impressive amount of high-quality backpacking and canoeing gear (open in summer M-Th 10am-6pm, F-Sa 10am-8pm, Su noon-5pm). The **Sports Den** (262-7491) has fishing supplies and canoes for $35 per day; rent for a week and pay for only six days (rents M-Sa 8am-7pm, Su 9am-6pm). **Boats** are sometimes available alongside the highway; residents put their vessels in their front yards and hang "for rent" signs.

Soldotna's **visitor center** (262-1337), just over the Kenai River on the way south to Homer, has pamphlets on fishing and recreation possibilities in the area, a phone for local use, and free canoe route maps (open daily 9am-7pm). The center also houses the wildlife refuge's manager, who bestows advice about recreation in the refuge. In winter, call 262-9228 for **road conditions**. **Central Peninsula General Hospital** (262-4404) is at 250 Hospital Pl. The **post office** (262-4760) is on Binkley St. downtown (open M-F 8:30am-5pm, Sa 10am-2pm). **ZIP Code:** 99669. **Area Code:** 907.

Camping is available pretty much anywhere along the Sterling Hwy., especially by **Skilak Lake Rd.** The sites are too numerous to name, and in the high season, some of the more popular ones fill up. With the exception of the Kenai-Russian River, Upper Skilak Lake, and Hidden Lake Campgrounds ($5-10), camping within the refuge is free. Now for some even better news: the culinary gem of Alaska, land of otherwise expensive and bland food, shines in Soldotna. **Odie's** (262-5807), downtown on the Sterling, across from the Blazy Mall and next to the National Bank of Alaska, offers mouth-watering food at jaw-dropping prices. Odie prepares giant half-sandwiches on thick slices of homemade bread ($3.25), acre-sized cookies fresh out of the oven (50¢), large cups of homemade soup with a roll ($1.75), short stacks of sourdough pancakes ($2.50), and untold other breads and sweets (open M-Sa 4am-10pm).

■ Kenai

Perched on a bluff overlooking the Kenai River as it pours into the Cook Inlet, Kenai has a magical view of the Aleutian-Alaska Range and its prominent volcanoes, Mt. Redoubt and Mt. Augustine. The fishing, oil, and tourism industries dominate the town, leaving their respective stamps: a fishy smell along Kenai's beaches, drilling platforms offshore, and RVs everywhere. Alaskans swarm to the town to take advantage of dip-netting—the challenging and complex sport in which a net is placed at the bottom of a stream until a fish swims in. Kenai, the largest city on the peninsula, is also one of the fastest-growing—a dubious honor. Its larger population attracted a refreshing variety of restaurants and services, but the hurried expansion spared few traces of the city's history, and leaving behind a forgettable cityscape of RV parks and low-rises. Kenai lacks Seward's surroundings and Homer's hominess, making it an overgrown pit stop. Nevertheless, the pristine Captain Cook State Recreation Site lies 30 mi. away, and the mouth of the Kenai River is a good place to catch salmon or watch beluga whales do the same.

ORIENTATION AND PRACTICAL INFORMATION

Kenai, on the western Kenai Peninsula, is about 158 mi. from Anchorage and 96 mi. north of Homer. The town can be reached via **Kalifornsky Beach Road,** which joins the Sterling Highway (Rte. 1) just south of Soldotna, or via the **Kenai Spur Road,** which runs north from Soldotna and west to Kenai. Kalifornsky mile markers measure distance from Kenai, while the Kenai Spur mile markers measure from Soldotna.

Airplanes: The **airport** is 1 mi. north of downtown; take Kenai Spur Rd. to Willow St., and follow signs for Airport Loop. **Alaska Airlines** (800-426-0333) has daily service to Anchorage (from $48). Reserve in advance for lowest rates.

Buses: Homer Stage Line (235-7009). To: Anchorage (4hr., 1 per day M-Sa around 10am, $35); Homer (1½hr., M, W, and F, $30). **Kachemak Bay Transit** (235-3795). To: Anchorage ($42); Homer ($25).

Taxis: Inlet Cab, 283-4711. $1.50 base, $1.40 per mi. 24hr.

Car Rental: Hertz (283-7979), at the airport. $65 per day, 20¢ per mi. after 125 mi. Must be 25 with credit card. Several other companies are also at the airport.

Car Repair: Alyeska Sales and Service, 200 Willow St. (283-4821). Open M-F 8am-6pm, Sa 9am-5pm.

Visitor Information: Visitor and Cultural Center, 11471 Kenai Spur Hwy. (283-1991; fax 283-2230; email kvcb@alaska.net; http://www.visitkenai.com), just past the corner of the Spur Rd. and Main St. An info reservoir of Alaskan proportions. An area hiking trail guide ($1) and *Free and Inexpensive Things to Do in Kenai* (itself free) is supplemented by stuffed native wildlife, traditional Alaskan artifacts, and films on the area's development. Open M-F 9am-8pm, Sa 10am-7pm, Su 11am-7pm; in winter M-F 9am-5pm, Sa-Su 10am-4pm.

Outdoor Information: For info on **Lake Clark National Park and Preserve,** across Cook Inlet from Kenai, call the **superintendent** in Anchorage (271-3751).

Employment: Alaska Employment Service, 283-2900. **Dial-a-Job,** 283-4606.

Bank: Keybank (283-7542), across the Spur from the visitor center. **Bank of America,** 10576 Kenai Spur Rd. (283-3369). Open M-F 10am-6pm, Sa-Su 11am-3pm.

Library: 163 Main St. Loop (283-4378). Open M-Th 8:30am-8pm, F-Sa 8:30am-5pm, Su noon-5pm.

Laundromat and Public Showers: Wash-n-Dry (283-9973), at Lake St. and Spur. Wash $1.75, dry 25¢ per 8min. Showers $4.20 per 30min. Open daily 8am-10pm.

Pharmacy: Carr's (283-6300), at Kenai Spur Hwy. and Airport Way. Open M-F 9am-9pm, Sa 9am-7pm, Su noon-5pm.

Crisis Line: 283-7257. 24hr.

Women's Services: Resource Center, 325 S. Spruce St. (283-9479). Hotline and shelter. Open M-F 9am-5pm.

Hospital: Central Peninsula General Hospital, 250 Hospital Pl. (262-4404).

Emergency: 911. **Police:** 283-7879.

Post Office: 140 Bidarka (283-7771). Open M-F 8:45am-5:15pm, Sa 9:30am-1pm. **ZIP Code:** 99611.

Area Code: 907.

ACCOMMODATIONS AND CAMPGROUNDS

There are few inexpensive lodgings in Kenai; the numerous B&Bs begin at $60. **Lee's Alaska Booking Service** (283-4422) arranges rooms at no charge. **Camping** is available on gravelly sites, with water and pit toilets, in the park at Kenai Spur Hwy. and Marathon Rd. Although camping down by the beach is illegal, squatters are reportedly not harassed; take Spruce Dr. from the Kenai Spur Hwy.

Katmai Hotel, 10800 Kenai Spur Hwy. (283-6101 or 800-275-6101), 1 block from downtown. Small rooms with nice decor and cable. Singles $79; doubles $89.

Beluga Lookout RV Park and Lodge, 929 Mission St. (283-5999). Take Main St. toward the water and go right on Mission St. Prime location and unbeatable view, but no tent sites. Scan the sea for belugas from the viewing benches or the lounge; numerous dip-netters are hard to miss when the salmon are running. Full hookups $15-20, with bay view $25. Wash and dry $1.50 each. Showers $2.

FOOD

Carr's Quality Center (283-6300), in the Kenai Mall at Kenai Spur Rd. and Airport Way, has a bakery, fruit, natural foods section, pharmacy, and fast food (open 24hr.).

🐋**Veronica's** (283-2725), at the end of Mission Rd., across from the Russian church. In a historic building decorated with hand-painted pictures, this seaside coffeehouse is almost as pretty as the inlet it overlooks. Espresso, pastries, and sandwiches provide a respite from fish sticks. Veronica's has soy milk products and a great veggie lasagna ($4.25). Large latte $3; sandwiches $5; soup in a bread bowl $4.75. Live folk music (Th and F). Open M-Th 9am-8pm, F-Sa 9am-10pm, Su 10am-5pm.

Charlotte's, 115 S. Willow St. (283-2777), across from the Merit Inn. A great catch in Kenai's shallow culinary sea, cooking up healthy, light cuisine. Lunch sandwiches from $4; salads from $3; short stack of pancakes or soup with bread $3. Charlotte is pretty flexible, so if you have a certain type of salad or sandwich in mind, let it be known. Open M-F 7am-4pm, Sa 9am-3pm.

Old Town Village Restaurant (283-4515), 1000 Mission Ave. Housed in a restored 1918 cannery building, Old Town is known for its great seafood dinners (from $11) and its hearty Sunday brunch ($9). Most patrons come from Beluga RV Park, under a block away. Open M-Th 11am-9pm, F-Sa 11am-10pm, Su 10am-8pm.

New Peking, 145 S. Willow St. (283-4662), off Kenai Spur Rd. Savor the all-you-can-eat lunch buffet ($6) amid potted plants and a lush Far Eastern setting. Dinner entrees including vegetarian options and Mongolian barbecue (from $9, children's plate $3). Open M-F 11am-10pm, Sa-Su noon-10pm.

Little Ski-Mo's Burger-n-Brew (283-4463 or 283-4409), on Kenai Spur Rd., across from the visitor center has a staggering array of burgers in a dimly lit, lodge-like interior, complete with fireplace. Twin Cities (egg, bacon, cheddar, and sprouts) $6.50; burger, fries, and large drink $5.45. Open M-Sa 11am-10pm, Su noon-8pm.

Thai Lotus, 106 S. Willow St. (283-7250). A little pricey, but the cost and the nondescript decor melt away in the face of Top of the World Chicken Cashew Nut ($10) or one of the many lunch specials ($7.50-9). All-you-can-eat lunch buffet $7. Open M-F 11am-8pm, Sa-Su noon-8pm.

SIGHTS AND OUTDOORS

The **Holy Assumption Russian Orthodox Church,** on Mission off Overland St., grants a look at Kenai's Russian heritage and an excellent view of the inlet. *(Open in summer M-F 11am-4pm. Public services Sa 6-7pm and Su 10am-noon.)* Originally built in 1846 and rebuilt in 1896, this National Historic Landmark contains 200-year-old icons. Tours are given upon request; call 283-4122 for more info.

The most breathtaking sight in Kenai is **Cook Inlet,** framed by smooth sand, two mountain ranges, and volcanic Mt. Augustine and Mt. Redoubt. The beach at the end of Spruce Dr. overlooks an inlet full of beluga whales, salmon runs, and eagles. The best time to see whales is two hours before or after high tide. If you coordinate with the arrival of the fishing boats, you may see a freeloading seal or sea lion as well.

The **Captain Cook State Recreation Area** lies at the northern end of the Kenai Spur Rd., 30 mi. from town. Premier views of the inlet and the Alaska-Aleutian Range make for a lovely picnic on a bluff or beach. Campsites include water and pit toilets ($10). Bald eagle sightings are common, and a small caribou herd, often spotted trotting along Kenai Spur Hwy. or Bridge Access Rd., roams the flatlands between Kenai and Soldotna. The area has swimming opportunities at **Stormy Lake,** and serves as one jumping-off point for the **Swanson River Canoe Trail** (see p. 418).

Fishing dominates Kenai's recreational activities. In fact, that's really all there is to do in town. Check at the visitor center for **charter** info (prices are comparable to those in Soldotna). Anglers can do their thing on any public land along the **Kenai River,** where the majority of fishing takes place. Beginners should ask at fishing shops for recommended locations, to avoid accidentally damaging the banks of the river and jeopardizing fish habitat. The best place to look for fish is in the slower eddies where they rest. Fishing is free at the mouth of the Kenai River with a license and rod; park at the end of Spruce Dr., and hike to the mouth. **Licenses** are available at any gas station, grocery store or sporting goods store. **Swanson River** and **Stormy Lake,** in the Captain Cook Recreation Area, contain rainbow trout, silver salmon, and arctic char. Contact the State Division of Parks for regulations (see **Essentials,** p. 44).

Nikiski, 12½ mi. north of Kenai at Mile 23.4 of the Spur Rd., is home to an alien spacecraft cleverly disguised as a geodesic-domed pool (776-8472 or 8800), behind the Nikiski school. *(Open Tu-F 1-5pm and 6-9pm, Sa-Su 1-5pm and 6-9pm. $3, seniors $2. Waterslides $6.)* Near the pool, a hockey rink, ski and running trail, outdoor volleyball and tennis courts, and picnic area await playful Earthlings.

■ Ninilchik

From Kenai, the Sterling Highway (Rte. 1) winds through short, shoreline forest on a bluff overlooking the Cook Inlet. Across the inlet looms the Alaska-Aleutian Range, with fantastic views of Mt. Redoubt and Mt. Iliamna; both volcanoes rise over 10,000 ft. and have erupted in the last 50 years. The highway winds into the town of Ninilchik, a hamlet with spectacular fishing, fantastic scenery, a strong Russian heritage, and an excellent clamming beach, but with very few resources.

The **Village Cache Store,** at the end of Village Rd., has info on the area and a free self-guided walking tour brochure; turn off at Sterling Mile 135.1, just after the Ninilchik River (open M-Sa 8am-9pm; snack shop stays open later when the fishing is good). The store has plans in the works for showers, cabins with bunks, and eventually a Russian tea room. The nearby parking lot is a good stopping point for minor expeditions into the neighborhood. Besides the unmatched views of the mountains, local attractions include the **old Russian fishing village,** on Village Rd., and the **Holy Transfiguration of Our Lord Orthodox Church,** built in 1900. The church and cemetery are still in use, but the Russian village is abandoned and dilapidated. The church, towering on a bluff above Cook Inlet, offers an unparalleled view of the overgrown seismic molehills offshore. The church interior is closed to the public, but services are held twice a month on Sundays. To get there, hike up the trail beginning behind the Village Cache Store; it's wise to stay on the trail, since the surrounding plants are not skin-friendly. **Clamming** on the beaches is Ninilchik's main low-tide attraction. The Cache Store rents shovels and pails ($5 per day; $20 deposit). **Hylen's Camper Park** (567-3393), at Seward Mile 135.4, has **showers** for post-clamming cleansing ($2 per 10min. Open 24hr.).

Have a sleepover in Ninilchik just to stay at the **Eagle Watch Hostel (HI-AYH)** (567-3905); go 3 mi. east on Oil Well Rd., which starts just before the Chinook gas station. Although the building is spacious and clean, the hostel's highlight is outdoors. The house overlooks a verdant valley with a meandering fish-filled stream, and the wildlife-viewing from the deck is almost as good as in Denali—eagles soar by nightly, and bears and moose make occasional showings. A full kitchen, showers, friendly hosts, free barbecue grill usage, a phone, clam shovels and fishing rods, a tree swing, new mattresses and the playful dog, Nadia, make this one of the best hostels in Alaska ($10, nonmembers $13; linens $2, no sleeping bags; towels 50¢; cash and traveler's checks only). The hostel is closed between 10am and 5pm, with an 11pm curfew. Guests can head farther down Oil Well Rd. and take the first left onto a gravel path to view a weird metal contraption that cages salmon swimming upstream. Marvel pitilessly at their reproductive drive as you watch them flounder and jump, to no avail.

The **state campgrounds** near Ninilchik each come complete with water and toilets ($10). Superb sites in the **Ninilchik State Recreation Area,** some overlooking the inlet, are less than 1 mi. north of town ($10). The nearby, beach-level **Deep Creek Recreation Area** is one of the most popular places to camp on the peninsula; turn west about ¼ mi. south of Deep Creek. Locals claim that the area has the world's best saltwater king salmon fishing; dolly varden and steelhead trout grace the waters, as well ($10; day-use parking $5; boat launching available).

The **General Store** (567-3378), at Sterling Mile 137.5, sells groceries and fishing supplies (open daily 6am-midnight). On the east side of the highway, at Sterling Mile 135.4, the **Inlet View Cafe** (567-3330) offers a beautiful view of the Cook Inlet and hearty sandwiches ($6-9). *Iliamna* pasta ($10) makes a tasty choice for vegetarians (open daily 6am-midnight). The **bar** next door is a laid-back local hangout (open daily 10am-5am). **Deep Creek Custom Packing** (567-3396), at Mile 137, both sells and packs fish, and gives **free samples** of different kinds of smoked salmon and halibut.

■ Homer

In a state where the unique is commonplace and gorgeous is the norm, Homer's eclectic culture and idyllic setting stand out nonetheless. The town's hiking and outdoor opportunities may lack luster compared to neighbors Seward and Cordova, and the town may be annoyingly spread out for foot travelers, but Homer's citizens will not disappoint. Fisherfolk and aging counterculturalists rule the roost, but Homer is also home to many artists, several Russian Orthodox colonies, a fabulous public radio station, and pop star Jewel's extended family (she grew up here). These diverse cultural elements mix against a spectacular backdrop. One end of town rises up on bluffs above Kachemak Bay, providing wide views of the blue mountains and pale glaciers across the water. Below the bluffs, Homer supports its own theater group, scores of galleries stocking local work, and one of the best small newspapers in Alaska. Moderate temperatures and a mere two feet of annual rainfall have earned Homer the nickname "Alaska's Banana Belt."

ORIENTATION AND PRACTICAL INFORMATION

Surrounded by 400 million tons of coal, Homer rests on **Kachemak "Smoky" Bay,** named for the mysteriously burning deposits that first greeted settlers. The town is on the southwestern coast of Kenai Peninsula, on the north shore of the bay, and extending into the bay along an improbable 4½ mi. tendril of sand, gravel, and RVs known as the **Spit.** The ruggedly beautiful wilds of **Kachemak Bay State Park** lie across Kachemak Bay, where the southern end of the **Kenai Mountains** reaches the sea. Also on the south side of the bay are the artist/fishing colony of **Halibut Cove,** the scantly populated **Yukon Island,** the **Gull Island** bird rookery, and the Russian-founded hamlet of **Seldovia** (see p. 428).

The **Sterling Highway (Hwy. 1)** leads away from Homer across the Kenai Peninsula toward Anchorage, 226 mi. away. The heart of Homer lies in a triangle defined by the shoreside **Homer Bypass,** the downtown drag **Pioneer Ave.,** and the cross-cutting **Lake St.** Homer Bypass becomes Sterling Hwy. west of town, while east of town it becomes **Ocean Dr.** and veers right to follow the Spit as **Homer Spit Rd.** Biking is a great way to get around this rather spread-out town, but be forewarned—there are lots of hills, lots of vehicles, and lots of dust (or mud during downpours).

Transportation

Airplanes: Airlines have terminals on opposite sides of the runway. **Southcentral Air** (283-3926 or 800-478-2550), on Kachemak Dr. off Homer Spit Rd. flies to Anchorage (3-4 per day, round-trip $131), plus daily flights to Seldovia and Kenai. **Era Aviation** (800-866-8394) is in the airport; follow signs from Ocean Dr. just before it becomes Spit Rd. To: Anchorage (7 per day, round-trip $141); Kenai (1 per day; one-way $47). **Homer Air** (235-8591) flies to Seldovia (round-trip $55).

Buses: Homer Stage Line, 424 Homer Spit Rd. (235-2252). To: Soldotna (1 per day M-Sa, $25); Anchorage (1 per day M-Sa, $45); Seward (M, W, and F, $45). $5 extra for drop-off at Anchorage Airport. Runs Memorial Day to Labor Day.

Ferries: Alaska Marine Highway, P.O. Box 166 (235-8449 or 800-382-9229). Office and terminal just before the end of the Spit. To: Seldovia ($18); Kodiak ($48); Seward ($96); Cordova ($138); and once per month to Dutch Harbor in the Aleutian Islands ($242). Open M-F 8:30am-4pm and when ferry is in.

Harbormaster: 4350 Homer Spit Rd. (235-3160; VHF 16).

Taxis: Chux Taxi, 235-2489. To downtown from the airport ($6) or ferry ($8).

Share-A-Ride: KBBI Public Radio, AM 890 (235-7721), is an on-air bulletin board, broadcasting requests for those both seeking and offering rides several times daily.

Car Rental: Polar Car Rental (235-5998). $58 per day; 30¢ per mi. after 100 mi.; 7th day free. $5 extra for unlimited mileage. Must be 21 with credit card. Call ahead. Open daily 8am-9pm; in winter 8am-5pm. **Hertz** (235-0734). $59 per day; 33¢ per mi. after 100 mi. Must be 25. Both in the airport.

Car Repair: Sunny's Repair, 152 E. Pioneer Ave. (235-8800).

Visitor and Financial Services

Visitor Information: Homer Chamber of Commerce and Visitor Information Center, 135 Sterling Hwy., P.O. Box 541 (235-5300; http://www.xyz.net/~homer), near Main St., stocks all the necessary info and pamphlets. Accommodations-finding service, courtesy phone for local and long distance, and Kachemak State Park info. Open daily June-Labor Day 9am-8pm; Labor Day-May M-F 9am-5pm.

Outdoor Information: Alaska Maritime National Wildlife Refuge Visitor Center, 509 Sterling Highway (235-6961), next to the Best Western Bidarka Inn. Wildlife exhibits, marine photography, and helpful advice on backcountry adventures in Kachemak Bay. Also leads bird walks on the Spit twice a week. Open daily in summer 9am-6pm. **Southern District Ranger Station,** Kachemak Bay State Park, P.O. Box 321 (235-7024), 4 mi. out of town on the Sterling Hwy.

Fishing Licenses: $20 for 3 days, available at local sporting goods stores and charter offices, like the Quicky Mart or the Sports Shed. For rules and regulations, contact the **Alaska Department of Fish and Game,** 3298 Douglas St. (235-8191), near Owen Marine. Open M-F 8am-5pm.

ALASKA

Employment: Alaska State Employment Service, 601 E. Pioneer Ave. #123 (235-7791). Open M-F 8am-noon and 1-4:30pm.

Bank: First National Bank (235-5150), on Homer Bypass at Heath St. 24hr. **ATM. National Bank of Alaska,** 203 W. Pioneer Ave. (235-8151) and 4014 Lake St. (235-2444). Both open M-Th 9am-5pm, F 9am-6pm.

Local Services

Equipment Rental: Homer Saw and Cycle, 1532 Ocean Dr. (235-8406). Top-of-the-line Trek mountain bikes $15 per half-day, $25 per day. Open M-F 9am-5:30pm, Sa 11am-5pm. Also rents through **Trips** (235-0708), on the Spit. **Chain Reaction** (235-0750), in the Lakeside Mall. Bikes $17 per half-day, $24 per day. **Homer Gear Shed,** 41955 Kachemak Dr. (235-8612), rents and sells camping equipment. Open M-Sa 8am-9pm, Su 9am-8pm.

Bookstore: The Bookstore, 436 Sterling Hwy. (235-7496), next to the Eagle Quality Center. Open M-Sa 10am-7pm, Su noon-5pm.

Library: Homer Public Library, 141 Pioneer Ave. (235-3180), near Main St. Free Internet access. Open M,W, and F-Sa 10am-6pm, Tu and Th 10am-8pm.

Laundromat and Public Showers: Homer Cleaning Center, 3684 Main St. (235-5152), downtown. Wash $2, dry 25¢ per 8min. Last load 1hr. before closing. Shower $3; unlimited time; towel included. Open M-Sa 8am-10pm, Su 9am-9pm.

Emergency and Communications

Emergency: 911. **Police:** 235-3150.

Women's Crisis Line: 235-8101. 24hr.

Hospital: South Peninsula Hospital, 4300 Bartlett (235-8101), off Pioneer St.

Post Office: 3261 Wadell Rd. (235-6129), off Homer Bypass. Open M-F 8:30am-5pm, Sa 10am-1pm. **ZIP Code:** 99603.

Internet Access: See **Library,** above.

Area Code: 907.

ACCOMMODATIONS AND CAMPGROUNDS

There are plenty of cheap accommodations in town, making Homer a home away from home for budget travelers. Contact the **Homer B&B Network** (800-764-3211) for lodgings starting at $50 per night, or check with the visitor center. None of these accommodations or campgrounds are wheelchair accessible.

Seaside Farm, 58335 East End Rd. (235-7850), 4½ mi. out of town. This is *the* welcoming spot for young backpackers, in an amazingly beautiful but inconvenient location ($12 cab ride from the airport). Most backpackers find hitching easy. Mossy, the friendly, earthy matron, runs a commune of sorts. Lodging is available in exchange for farm work. The hostel facilities, while bearable, are not nearly as appealing as the view across the bay; camping in the clover field is a better bet. Enjoy a roofed outdoor common area and seaside strolls. Bunks $15, with showers. Tent sites $6, with showers $9. Private cabins with kitchenettes: singles $30; doubles $55. Discounts available for backpackers.

Sunspin Guest House, 358 E. Lee Dr. (235-6677 or 800-391-6677; email turner@xyz.net). From Pioneer Ave., take Kachemak Way toward the bluff to Lee Dr. on the left. Convenient location to downtown Homer, with clean and warm decor. High-class bunkroom includes real beds, clean sheets, and a continental breakfast. Beds $25; private rooms from $55.

Driftwood Inn, 135 W. Bunnell (235-8019, in AK 800-478-8019; email driftinn@xyz.net, http://www.netalaska.com/driftwood), a short walk from downtown; take the Homer Bypass, turn toward the ocean on Main St., then right on Bunnell. Spotless, modern rooms in a rustic building. Homey guest lounge and a great view. Free local calls, coffee, and tea. Singles $54; doubles $64. Laundry and luggage storage for guests.

Road Runner B&B, 4657 Sabrina Rd. (235-6581 or 235-3678), 2 mi. out of town off East End Rd. A steal, considering the price-to-service ratio. Spacious, comfortable rooms, a full fridge, and free rides to town, the Spit, and the airport. Singles $38, with bath $48; doubles $48, with bath $58. Full breakfast or lunch $5.

Karen Hornaday Park, 491 E. Pioneer St. (235-3170), with office at the Public Works Dept., City Hall. From Pioneer, go uphill on Bartlett St. to Fairview, left to Campground Rd., then right to the park. Each site looks like a personal grassy driveway, bordered by purple lupine and cow parsley. A classy camping crowd enjoys water, pit toilets, and nice view of the bay. Sites $7.

Spit Municipal Camping, 3735 Homer Spit Rd. (235-2617), across from the fishing hole. 2 areas for RVs; 1 for both tents and RVs. The once-beautiful spot is now a giant gravel parking lot, but popular nonetheless. Terrific views are often marred by crowds or tent-uprooting winds. Water, flush toilets. Tent sites $3; RV sites $7.

Kachemak Bay State Park, 7 water mi. across from the Spit. Gorgeous, secluded, and free, but it costs nearly $50 per person to get there. Most locals vehemently maintain that it's well worth the expense. Plenty of hiking trails. A public use cabin is also available ($50). For further info, contact the Southern District Ranger Station (see **Practical Information,** above).

FOOD

The huge, 24-hour **Eagle Quality Center,** 436 Sterling Hwy. (235-2408), has a stunning array of options. **John's Corner Market** (235-5494), on Lake St. at Pioneer Ave., sells fantastic produce (open M-Sa 10am-7pm, Su noon-4pm). Wheat germ, spirolina, and local crunch are available at **Smoky Bay Natural Foods,** 248 W. Pioneer Ave. (235-7252; open M-F 8:30am-8pm, Sa 10am-7pm).

On the Spit, salmon bite at the **Fishing Hole.** Fresh seafood can be purchased directly from fishing boats or at a retail outlet. **Katch Seafoods,** 765 Fish Dock Rd. (235-6241 or 800-368-7400), offers salmon and halibut ($6.50 per lb.). **Coal Point Trading Co.,** 4306 Homer Spit Rd. (235-3877 or 800-235-3877), sells fish raw or will vacuum-pack and deep-freeze your catch for 70¢ per lb. (open 6am-11pm or later). Wash away fish breath with locally brewed Broken Birch Bitter from the **Homer Brewing Company,** 1562 Homer Spit Rd. (235-FOAM/3626; open M-Sa 11am-8pm, Su noon-6pm). Mmmm…beer.

Downtown

Two Sisters Bakery, 106 W. Bunnell (235-2280). Take Main St. toward the water. This cafe caters to those with a refined taste and an eye for atmosphere, focaccia sandwiches ($5.50), salmon chowder ($4), ambient acoustic guitar, and amusing Alaskana readings. Open M-Sa 7am-6pm, Su 7am-4pm.

Cafe Cups, 162 Pioneer Ave. (235-8330). The best of a big-city cafe successfully hybridized with Homer's offbeat attitude, and a meeting place for artists and young travelers. Tasty, unusual sandwiches with salad $7-8.25; espresso milkshake $4.50. Outdoor seating underneath mammoth, multi-colored cups. Open daily 7am-10pm.

Young's Oriental Restaurant, 565 E. Pioneer Ave. (235-4002). The 20 ft. buffet sends Young's shooting ahead in the race for all-you-can-eat Asian lunch buffet champion ($6.30). Dinner $8. Open daily 11am-10pm.

The Spit

Fishwife's Galley, 4460 Homer Spit Rd. (235-4951). This country kitchen seems something of an anomaly on the Spit. Halibut chowder $4.50; veggie pizza $5. A hot pastrami sandwich, prepared with love by an honest-to-goodness fishwife, costs $6. Open M-Sa 9am-9pm, Tu-Su 8:30-9pm.

Little Taste of Russia, next to the Fishwife's Galley. Big taste of Russia, small price. *Blini* $2.25; borscht $2. Take-out only. Open daily 10am-7pm.

Alaska's Italian Bistro, 4241 Homer Spit Rd. (235-6153). Dinners aren't cheap, but lunch beckons with a tapas bar of clams casino ($8.50) or oysters bistro ($10.50). Big breakfasts $8. Magnificent ocean views. Open daily 5:30am-10pm.

SIGHTS AND EVENTS

The **Pratt Museum,** 3779 Bartlett St. (235-8635; email pratt@alaska.net), houses local art and Kenai artifacts. *(Open daily 10am-6pm, Oct.-Dec. and Feb.-Apr. Tu-Su noon-5pm. $4, seniors and students with ID $3, under 18 $2. Wheelchair accessible.)* Displays range from

ALASKA

homesteader cabins to arts of the Inuit and Denali peoples, and include some great exhibits on marine mammals. View the skeleton of the Bering Sea beaked whale or witness the feeding frenzy in the salt water aquarium. *(Frenzy Tu and F 4-5pm.)*

Homer's residents take art seriously—even the supermarket has a gallery—and serious art it is. **Ptarmigan Arts,** 471 Pioneer Ave. (235-5345), displays the work of over 40 Alaskan artists and craftspeople. *(Open M-Sa 11am-7pm, Su 10am-5pm.)* The **Bunnell Street Gallery,** 106 W. Bunnell (235-2662), features innovative contemporary work ranging from paintings to edible art. *(Open daily in summer 10am-6pm; in winter 11am-5pm.)* The visitor center offers a complete list of area galleries.

Homer is often billed the Halibut Capital of the World, and the **Homer Jackpot Halibut Derby** generates a whole lot of hoopla. The competition runs from May 1 to Labor Day, and offers a grand prize in the neighborhood of $30,000. Tickets are available in local charter offices on the Spit ($7). Each year, several would-be winners are left crying at the scales after they land potentially prize-winning fish with no ticket. For those who prefer feathers to fins, the **Homer Shorebird Festival** (235-PEEP/7337), during the second week in May, hosts birding tours, educational workshops, an arts fair, and 8000-10,000 migrating birds. Last year, the event drew over 2000 registered participants and guerilla ornithologists. On the second Sunday in August, KBBI (235-7721) stages the fabulous **Concert on the Lawn** at the town commons, featuring blues, rock, and bluegrass (11am-8pm). The annual **Winter Carnival,** during the first week in February, has sled dog races and snowmachine competitions.

The Icicle Burned for a Week

On July 1st, 1998, the Homer Spit suffered one of the worst disasters since it sank 30 feet in the '64 Good Friday quake. At Icicle Seafood's processing plant, an ammonia leak and a pilot flame combined to blow the roof 30 feet in the air. Luckily, there were no casualties, but the Spit was closed down for three days. Hundreds of cannery workers lost jobs they'd only had since the day before, leading to a massive party the night of the disaster. The question of whether or not to rebuild the plant will affect Homer's atmosphere in the coming years. Will a steady stream of young college students hard-up for cash still flock here? Will Jean the Eagle Lady be able to continue providing fish guts to her hundreds of bald eagles? Will t-shirts bearing "I survived Icicle '98" be the next best-selling piece of souvenir junk? Time will tell, and in the meantime, Homer's salmon and halibut will be that much happier.

OUTDOORS

Nearly everyone who comes to Homer spends some time on the **Homer Spit.** Don't feel obligated to follow the crowds; this 5 mi. strip of land, composed entirely of gravel, RVs, and the smoldering remains of Icicle Seafoods, is one of the most heinous tourist traps in the state. While there is no denying that the Spit offers some great views, the utter lack of greenery and the sheer concentration of vehicles makes it a virtual parking lot. To actually get your own patch of sand, head to **Bishop's Beach;** take Main St. toward the water, and follow the signs to the left on Bunnell Ave.

About the only good justification for visiting the Spit, beyond the food, is to leave it again via boat, the vast majority of which are halibut charters. On a good day, as many as 90 cast off in search of the big fish. Choosing a charter, like fishing itself, can be a crap shoot. Although most charter companies are reputable businesses, there are a few that strip their customers more cleanly than a halibut fillet. Many of the boats are booked through **Central Charters** (235-7847; email central@ptialaska.net; http://www.ptialaska.net/~central), near the middle of the Spit. Full-day trips start at $150, with all tackle and bait included, and a refund policy for foul weather. **Fishing licenses** (3 days $15) allow a daily one-fish limit (see **Practical Information,** above). Check with the tourist office for a list of companies; not every reliable business will necessarily be a member, but those that are should be reputable.

For those without enough cash to chase after the big sea monsters, there's always the **fishing hole** near the start of the Spit, where anyone who can hold a rod can probably catch a salmon. A stocking program plants fry in this tidal lagoon. They return years later to spawn, but the lagoon is unsuitable for spawning, and pitiless anglers manage to hook or snag most of the hapless fish that return. **Sportsman's Supplies,** the white building near the fishing hole, rents poles and tackle for $10 per day.

The killer **East Hill Rd.,** to the east of town off East End Rd., snags a panorama of the Kenai Mountains. The road levels out to quiet, flat gravel and is flanked by fields of fireweed and other wildflowers. By foot, take to the beach or the 6 mi. **Homestead Trail,** west of town. The trail has three different access points; check the *Homer Tourist Guide* for details and info on how to identify the arctic star flowers, marsh violets, green rein orchids, and other wildflowers that bloom along the way. Mark, at **Trail's End Horse Adventures** (235-6393), leads horseback forays. *($20 per hr., each additional hr. $15, $65 for 4hr., $110 per day.)*

ENTERTAINMENT AND NIGHTLIFE

The town's hyperactive drama group performs at **Pier One Theater,** P.O. Box 894 (235-7333; www.alaska.net/~wmbell), one of the first structures built on the Spit. Catch plays on the mainstage throughout the summer. *(Shows Th and Su at 7:30pm, F-Sa at 8:15pm. $11, seniors $10, children $7. Th all seats $8.)* A series of other performances take place Sunday through Thursday, many featuring Homer's most famous son (only outdone by its still-more-famous daughter): Tom Bodett, of National Public Radio and Motel 6 ("We'll leave the light on for ya") fame. Check the *Homer News* for schedules. The **Homer Family Theater** (235-6728), at Main St. and Pioneer Ave., features current blockbusters and feel-good flicks for $6.

The sun never sets on Homer summers, figuratively and almost literally. Nightlife ranges from beachcombing in the midnight sun to hanging at the combination tourist trap and local joint, the **Salty Dawg Saloon** (235-9990), under the log lighthouse near the end of the Spit. *(Open 11am-whenever.)* Generations of business cards are tacked to the wall behind the right end of the bar, amid other cards, napkins, and bills, giving the Dawg the feel of a 3D, semi-historical message board (or the *Sgt. Pepper* album cover). **Alice's Champagne Palace,** 196 Pioneer Ave. (235-7650), is a wooden barn with diverse live music and lots of young locals. *(Open Tu-Sa 2pm-morning.*

■ Near Homer: Kachemak Bay State Park

Locals are vocal in their praise of **Kachemak Bay State Park**—most maintain that a visit to Homer is not complete without a trip across the bay. One of the largest coastal parks in the country, the area contains about 375,000 acres of beaches, tide pools, mountains, and glaciers, and includes one of the northernmost temperate rainforests in the world. Stop by the **Southern District Ranger Station** (see **Practical Information,** above) for info on the park's myriad hiking and camping opportunities. **Saint Augustine's Charters** (235-6126) offers regularly scheduled water taxi service to the park (daily 9am and 4pm; round-trip $45). Personalized service is also available; call **Inlet Charters** (235-6126 or 800-770-6126) for reservations. **Mako's Water Taxi** (399-4133; http://akms.com/makotaxi) and **Rainbow Tours** (235-7272) offer similar services for about the same cost, but price varies depending on the number of passengers and the specific destination. Rainbow offers a 1½-hour cruise from the Spit to **Gull Island,** home to murres, cormorants, guillemots, other birds with strange names, a few puffins, and about sixteen bijillion gulls (9am and 4:30pm; $15, seniors $12.50, under 12 $10). The 30s-era **St. Augustine's Fire,** a gorgeous wooden sailing yacht, ferries passengers in the lap of nautical luxury (2hr.; $35). Call **Inlet Charters** (see above) to book. For a self-powered water adventure, consider a full-day kayak trip with **True North Kayak Adventures,** P.O. 2319 (book through **Trips,** 235-0708). The tour, although expensive, comes with a great lunch and a host of sea otters ($125, including round-trip water taxi).

■ Near Homer: Halibut Cove

Yet another great way to spend an expensive afternoon in the Homer area is with **Danny J. Tours** (235-7847), visiting the colorful artist/fishing colony of Halibut Cove and its few dozen residents. Early trips leave the Spit daily at noon, and make a short visit to Gull Island (see above) before dropping passengers off at the village for 2½ hours (round-trip $42, seniors $34, children $21). The evening run (departure 5pm, return 10pm; $21) requires a reservation. Visit **Saltry** (296-2223), the cove's only restaurant, to eat fish, both cooked and raw; halibut salad is $8 and *nori maki* costs $10 (open 1-5pm and 6-9pm). A raised boardwalk leads to the **Halibut Cove Art Gallery's** collection of works by residents. At **Diana Tillion's Cove Gallery,** Diana extracts ink with a hypodermic needle from stranded octopi, eats the octopi, and paints with their body fluids. Farther down the path, past the resident dock, the **six-foot-tall portrait of Alex Duff Combs' head** welcomes visitors to his gallery. World-traveled and universally acclaimed, Combs' pottery and painting now rest in a house filled with faded buoys and peacock feathers. Several hiking trails surround the town, winding away from art toward animalia. The most convenient is the 1 mi. **Saddle Trail,** which departs from behind the Saltry, rambles along a ridge past intriguing rock formations, and reaches an overlook of the cove.

■ Seldovia

Virtually untouched by the tourist mania rampant on the rest of the Kenai peninsula, this isolated hamlet combines marine charm, slow-paced life, and funky ambience à la Homer. The Russians named Seldovia for its herring, and the fish have lived up to their reputation for centuries, buoying the town's economy. Unique geological features surround the town and broaden the horizons of Seldovia's fishophilic visitors. Seldovia overlooks four active volcanoes: Augustine, Iliamna, Redoubt, and Spur.

PRACTICAL INFORMATION Bring money to Seldovia; there are **no banks,** and few stores accept credit cards.

> **Airplanes:** The **airport** is less than 1 mi. out of town on Airport Ave. **Homer Air** (235-8591) flies to Homer ($29, round-trip $55). **Southcentral** (800-478-2550) also flies to Homer ($28, round-trip $51). **Great Northern Airlines** (800-243-1968) flies daily to Anchorage (one-way $33).
>
> **Ferries: Alaska Marine Highway** (235-8449 or 800-382-9229) chugs from Homer to Seldovia twice per week (Tu 12:30pm and Su 3am; one-way $18), and lingers for 4hr. before heading back.
>
> **Harbormaster:** 234-7886; VHF 16, CB 3.
>
> **Visitor Information:** The **Chamber of Commerce** (234-7612) is stacked to the rafters with info, including a free and detailed map. Open daily Memorial Day to Labor Day 11am-5pm; in winter M-F 11am-5pm, Sa-Su 11am-4pm.
>
> **Tours:** Three tour boats cruise daily to Homer. None of the tour commentary is worth paying for, but this might be the only way out. **Rainbow Tours** (235-7272) offers the least expensive service (one-way $25, round-trip $40; seniors $36; youth $25). **Jakolof Bay Express** (234-7660) provides eco-friendly and just plain friendly ferry/bus service ($45). Call **Trips** (235-0708) for reservations.
>
> **Taxis: Southshore Cab,** 234-8000. $6 from town to the outer beach campground. Open daily 8am-2am.
>
> **Equipment Rental: Rocky Raven's** (234-7810). Bikes $4 per hr., $15 per day. Open daily 10am-6pm. **The Buzz** (234-7479), on the harbor side of Stamper's Market on Main St., rents more expensive bikes ($20 per day, $25 per 24hr.) and fishing tackle ($15 per day; $25 deposit). Open daily 6am-6pm. **Kayak'atak** (234-7425; http://www.alaska.net/~kayaks) rents kayaks. Singles $45 per day; doubles $70 per day. Call any time.
>
> **Bookstore: Lost Horizons Books,** 235 Main St. (234-7839; email lsthoriz@alaska.net). Open Memorial Day to Labor Day M-Sa 10am-5pm, Su 11am-5pm.

Library: On Seldovia St. near Main St. Open Tu 2-4:30pm and 7:30-9:30pm, Th 3:30-6pm and 7:30-9:30pm, Sa 11:30am-4:30pm.
Laundromat and Public Showers: Harbor Laundromat (see **Food,** below).
Emergency: 911. **Police:** 234-7640. **Fire:** 234-7812.
Medical Services: Seldovia Medical Clinic (234-7825). Open M, W, F 9am-4pm.
Post Office: (234-7831), at Main and Seldovia St. Open M-F 9am-5pm. **ZIP Code:** 99663.
Area Code: 907.

ACCOMMODATIONS, CAMPGROUNDS, AND FOOD Dancing Eagles Lodge

(234-7627), at the end of Main St. by the boardwalk, offers rustic cabins, a private extension of the town boardwalk, a hot tub, and a terrific view of the bay (from $45). Less attractively situated cabins overlook the airport at **Seldovia Seaport Cottages,** 313 Shoreline Dr., Box 118 (234-7483; wheelchair accessible). Pleasant interiors frame kitchenettes and double or twin beds (singles or doubles $60, each additional person $10). The chamber of commerce (234-7612) keeps a list of Seldovia's **B&Bs,** most of which cost $60-85. **Outside Beach,** 1mile from town, has free tent sites, pit toilets, and close encounters with sea otters; turn left off of Jakolof Bay Rd. at the "Narrow Road" sign. Stay on Jakolof road for another ½ mile for access to **Wilderness Park** (RV sites $8); permits are available at the city office (234-7643).

Seldovia Market (234-7633), on Main St., stocks a modest supply of groceries, hardware, tackle, liquor, and pharmaceuticals (open M-Sa 9am-8pm, Su noon-5pm). Frozen dairy treats, comforting hot showers, and laundry services mingle in bizarre but happy matrimony at the sparkling **Harbor Laundromat** (234-7420), also on Main St. (showers $4 per 10min., towel and soap included; wash $2-4, dry 25¢ per 5min.). Enjoy a delicious cone ($1.75) or a smacktastic milkshake ($3.50) while toweling off or folding clothes (open M-Sa 10am-9pm, Su 11am-7pm; call for winter hours; last shower 8:30pm). **The Buzz** (234-7479) serves coffee, espresso, and great food in a nice rainy-afternoon loitering space. Calzones ($6.25), quiche slices ($4.75), local art, and aromatherapy oils abound (open daily 6am-6pm; in winter 8am-4pm; credit cards accepted). The new **Crab Pot Cafe** (234-7440), on Main St. next to the post office, serves deli sandwiches on freshly baked bread (from $4) and a handy breakfast of biscuits and gravy ($5; open daily 7am-8pm). **Pumi's Oriental Barbecue** (234-7558), next to the harbormaster's office, cooks up verdant green broccoli and garlic sauce ($6), including egg roll and rice (open M-Sa 10am-9pm; wheelchair accessible).

SIGHTS, OUTDOORS, NIGHTLIFE, AND ENTERTAINMENT Seldovia's quiet, col-

orful homes, well-manicured streets, and beautiful harbor make for a peaceful evening stroll. Stop by the small **museum,** 328 Main St. (234-7898), sponsored by the Seldovia Native Association. *(Open M-F 8am-5pm.)* The adjacent **Berry Kitchen/Museum Gift Shop,** 328 Main St. (234-7898), in the Seldovia Native Association Building, whips up a mean blueberry jam. *(Open daily 10am-2pm.)* The native houseboat grounded at Anderson Way also houses a small **museum,** with a collection that includes an antique broad axe and a meteorite; call 234-7496 for tours. *(Open Tu-Su noon-4:30pm. Free.)* **St. Nicholas Orthodox Church,** built in 1891, peers out over the town from a hilltop. Tours are given by Fred and Tinette Paulson (234-8000), who provide commentary at any time (donation requested).

The **Otterbahn Hiking Trail,** starting at the Susan B. English School near Winifred Ave., winds 1 mi. to Outside Beach, leading to a small lighthouse perched above cliffs that plunge into the bay. Clear days grant a magnificent view of the volcanoes. There is also a 6 mi. hike up the bay on the dirt extension of **Rocky St.;** consult the map of Seldovia at the visitor center for a detailed orientation. For indoor kicks, head to the **Linwood Bar** (234-9906; open 10am-2am) or the brews and country music at the **Seldovia Lodge** (234-7673; open 4pm-2am; wheelchair accessible).

Seldovia triples in size on **Independence Day** (July 4). An old-fashioned celebration draws hundreds of visitors (a mob, in Seldovian terms) from all over the peninsula, and includes parades, the 5K Salmon Shuffle, a horseshoe tournament, and a pancake feed at the fire hall. The entire town sits on the breakwater to observe and cheer the canoe-jousters and log-rollers. (*Let's Go* whole-heartedly recommends rolling off a log into 40°F water in order to become something of a local hero.)

KODIAK ISLAND

In this century, Kodiak Island has been rocked by earthquakes, engulfed by tsunamis, doused in the oil of the Exxon *Valdez*, and blanketed in nearly two feet of volcanic ash. The island receives about 180 days of rain each year, and its rolling green hills earn it the name "Emerald Isle of Alaska." Kodiak shelters the Kodiak National Wildlife Refuge, home to about 3000 Kodiak brown bears, the world's largest carnivorous land mammals. The refuge's 800 mi. of coastline encircle the island's sharp inland peaks, pushing Kodiak's human population onto the eastern shore. Rich surrounding waters have made the island's fishing fleet the most productive in the state, drawing tidal waves of young people each summer to work its canneries. Islanders take their seafood seriously, and until recently, tourism has been only an afterthought.

■ Kodiak

Kodiak was the first capital of Russian Alaska before Alexander Baranof moved the Russian-American Company to Sitka. The glittering ladies of St. Petersburg dressed to the hilt back in the colonial day, thanks to Russian enslavement of the native Alutiiq people, who were forced to hunt local otters to near extinction.

Nearby Novarupta Volcano is anything but extinct. It erupted in 1912 with a force 10 times greater than the 1980 eruption of Mount St. Helens, spewing so much ash that, for two days, residents could not see a lantern held at arm's length. In 1964, the Good Friday earthquake shook the area, causing $24 million in damage and creating a tsunami that destroyed much of downtown Kodiak. When the swamped fishing port was rehabilitated by the Army Corps of Engineers, one 200 ft. vessel, *The Star of Kodiak*, was cemented into the ferry dock and converted into a cannery.

Local color is hard to find here, since so many of Kodiak's inhabitants are seasonal. Until the next natural disaster livens things up, Kodiak's prime excitement lies in its outdoor opportunities. The gorgeous northern shorelines are virtually inaccessible without a car, though, and nobody on the island rents to travelers under 25.

ORIENTATION AND PRACTICAL INFORMATION

The city of Kodiak is on the eastern tip of Kodiak Island, roughly 250 mi. south of Anchorage. Paved and rutted gravel roads run 100 mi. along the scenic coastlines north and south of the city. **Chiniak Rd.,** which heads south for 42 mi., makes an especially impressive trip. In town, the main drag is **Center St.,** which starts at the ferry terminal and heads inland, ending at the intersection with **Rezanof Dr.** to the left and **Lower Mill Bay Rd.** to the right.

Airplanes: The **airport** is 5 mi. southwest of town on Rezanof Dr. **Era Aviation** (800-866-8394) flies to Anchorage (1hr., 5-7 per day, round-trip $240). **Pen Air** (487-4014) flies to Karluk (round-trip $150); Port Lions (round-trip $60); Larsen Bay (round-trip $120). Office open daily 5am-10pm.

Ferries: Alaska Marine Highway (800-562-6731; fax 486-6166). Ferries depart Kodiak May-Sept. 1-3 times per week, and less frequently in winter. To: Homer ($48); Seward ($54); Valdez ($98); Cordova ($98). 5-day round-trip to Dutch Harbor, Aleutian Islands (1 per month, $202). The terminal is next to the visitors bureau. Open M-F 8am-5pm, Sa 8am-4pm, and when ferries are in.

Harbormaster: 403 Marine Way (486-8080). VHF 12.

Taxis: A&B Taxi (486-4343) and **AAA Ace Mecca Taxi** (486-3211). $3 fare plus $2 per mi. $13 to the airport. Runs 24hr. **Airporter** (486-7583) offers a $5 shuttle to the airport from downtown. Call ahead.

Car Rental: Budget, 516 Marine Way (486-8500), or at the airport (487-2220). From $51 per day; unlimited mileage. **Rent-a-Heap** (486-8550). $29 per day, 29¢ per mi. Must be 25 with credit card. Downtown office open M-Su 9am-7pm. Airport office open daily 6:30am-10pm.

Car Repair: R.C. Enterprises, 2017 Mill Bay Rd. (486-8476). Open M-F 9am-6pm, Sa 10am-2pm.

Visitor and Financial Information

Visitor Information: Kodiak Island Convention and Visitors Bureau, 100 Marine Way (486-4782; fax 486-6545; http://www.kodiak.org), in front of the ferry dock. Hunting and fishing info, charter and accommodations arrangements, and an inconveniently enormous map. Open daily 8am-5pm, and for most ferry arrivals; in winter M-F 8am-noon and 1-5pm.

Outdoor Information: Fish and Wildlife Service and Wildlife Refuge Visitor Center, 1390 Buskin River Rd. (487-2600), just outside Buskin State Recreation Site, 4 mi. southwest of town on Rezanof Rd. Offers wildlife displays, stuffed brown bears, nature films, and info on Kodiak National Wildlife Refuge and its cabins. Open M-F 8:30am-4:30pm. **State Department of Parks,** 1200 Abercrombie Dr., S.R. Box 3800 (486-6339), at Fort Abercrombie, has info on local state parks and campgrounds. Open M-F 8am-5pm, Sa noon-5pm.

Fishing Information: Alaska Department of Fish and Game, 211 Mission Rd., Box 686 (486-1880, recording 486-4559), has info on regulations and seasons. Open M-F 8am-4:30pm. **Licenses** are available at all local sporting goods stores (1 day $10, 3 days $20, 7 days $30, 14 days $50).

Employment: Alaska State Employment Service, 305 Center St. (486-3105), in Kodiak Plaza. First stop for fish-canners. Open M-F 8am-5pm.

Banks: National Bank of Alaska, 202 Marine Way (486-3126). Open M-Th 10am-5pm, F 10am-6pm, Sa 10am-2pm. **First National Bank,** 202 Marine Way (486-3251). Open M-F 10am-5pm, Sa noon-4pm. Both have 24hr. ATMs.

Local Services

Equipment Rental: Mack's Sports Shop, 117 Lower Mill Bay (486-4276), at end of Center Ave. Open M-Sa 7am-7pm, Su 8am-6pm. **Cy's Sporting Goods,** 202 Shelikof St. (486-3900), near the harbor. Open M-F 8am-7pm, Sa 8am-7pm, Su 9am-6pm.

Bookstore: Shire Bookstore, 104 Center Ave. (486-5001). Mystery and romance sections, plus a coffee bar. Open M-Sa 9am-6pm, F 9:30am-9pm. Su noon-5pm.

Library: 319 Lower Mill Bay Rd. (486-8686). Open M-F 10am-9pm, Sa 10am-5pm, Su 1-5pm. Internet access available.

Public Radio: KMXT 100.1 FM.

Laundromat and Public Showers: Ernie's, 218 Shelikof (486-4119), across from the harbor. Wash $3, dry 25¢ per 4min. Showers $4 per 20min., towel $1. Open daily 8am-8pm; last wash 6:30pm; last shower 7:30pm.

Emergency and Communications

Emergency: 911. **Police:** 217 Lower Mill Bay Rd. (486-8000). **Fire:** 219 Lower Mill Bay Rd. (486-8040).

Crisis Line: 486-3625. **Women's Crisis Line:** 422 Hillside Dr. (486-6171). **AIDS Helpline:** 800-478-2437.

Pharmacy: Wodlinger Drug and Photo, 312 Marine Way (486-4035), across from the harbormaster. Pharmacy open M-F 10am-6pm. Store open M-Sa 9:30am-6:30pm, Su noon-4pm.

Hospital: Kodiak Island Hospital, 1915 E. Rezanof Dr. (486-3281).

Post Office: 419 Lower Mill Bay Rd. (486-4721). Open M-F 9am-5:30pm. **Downtown Contract Station,** in the AC Grocery. Open M-Sa 10am-6pm. **ZIP Code:** 99615.

Internet Access: See **Library,** above.

Area Code: 907.

ACCOMMODATIONS AND CAMPGROUNDS

Kodiak has no hostel and no true budget accommodations. Cheap motels can be convenient, and many B&Bs are far away from the ferry and airport. Finding a room becomes almost impossible when the airport shuts down due to bad weather, and this happens often. Kodiak has a brutal 11% hotel tax. Campers can head for **Gibson Cove,** 2 mi. west of Kodiak on Rezanof Dr. Built by the city for transient cannery workers, Gibson Cove looks, feels, and smells like a gravel parking lot soaked in fish innards. In fact, it *is* a gravel parking lot soaked in fish innards, but at $2 per night with free hot showers, nobody quibbles. Better scenery and more breathable air can be found slightly farther away at two pleasant state-run facilities.

⊛Lakeview Terrace B&B, 2426 Spruce Cape Rd., P.O. Box 3107 (486-5135); take Mission St. 2½ mi. northeast of town until it becomes Spruce Cape Rd. Large, spotless rooms contain comfortable queen beds, cable, private sinks, semi-private bath, breakfast, and friendly felines. Singles $45; doubles $55; tax included.

Shelikof Lodge, 211 Thorsheim Ave. (486-4141; fax 486-4116), on a small street to the right of McDonald's. A remodeling job has perked up this otherwise generic motel, whose comfortable green rooms have cable. Singles $60; doubles $65. Courtesy van to the airport M-F 8:30am-4:30pm. Open only in summer.

Russian Heritage Inn, 119 Yukon (486-5657; fax 486-4634), off Lower Mill Bay Rd. near Mark's Sports Shop. Nothing Russian besides the little blue domes on the doors. Congenial owner offers recently remodeled rooms with big cable TVs; about half have fridges. Tiny room $60 plus tax; larger rooms $75-85 plus tax, regardless of number of occupants. Laundry service (wash or dry $1.50).

Fort Abercrombie State Park (486-6339), 4 mi. northeast of town on Rezanof-Monashka Rd. Water, shelters, and toilets. No RV hookups; designed for backpackers. WWII ruins, trails, a trout-fishing lake, and spectacular sunsets. 13 sites: $10. 7-night max. stay. Open to motor traffic in summer only; walk-ins year round.

Buskin River State Recreation Site (486-6339), 4½ mi. southwest of town, off Rezanof Dr. Water and pit toilets, RV dump station. Over 50% of Kodiak's sport fish are caught on the nearby Buskin River. 15 sites: $10. 14-night max. stay.

FOOD

AC Grocery, 111 Rezanof Dr. (486-5761), is a convenient supplier (open M-Sa 7am-10pm, Su 7am-9pm). The Chinese deli at **Safeway,** 2685 Mill Bay Rd. (486-6811), 2 mi. from town, has accrued great raves (open daily 6am-midnight). **Cactus Flats Natural Foods,** 338 Mission St. (486-4677), sells vitamins, too (open M-Sa 10am-6pm).

Harborside Coffee and Goods, 216 Shelikof (486-5862), packs the most flavor in Kodiak. Proximity to the harbor makes it a popular destination for the summer fishing crowd. Ham and cheese croissant sandwich $3.25; soup and bread $4. Tea comes in a big, beautiful earthenware mug ($1.25). Open M-Th 6:30am-9pm, F and Sa 6:30am-10pm, Su 7am-8pm.

El Chicano, 103 Center Ave. (486-6116). Pinkish stucco, ultra-padded booths, and guitar music back up acceptable Mexican offerings. Black bean soup with home-made Mexican bread $4.75; enormous burrito $8.75. Open Su-Th 7am-9:30pm, F-Sa 7am-10pm, Su 4-9pm.

Henry's All-Alaskan Sports Cafe (486-8844), in the mall on Marine Way. Pasta entrees from $10; burgers and other excellent sandwiches $6-9; breakfast steak-n-eggs $10. Drink slowly, since Alaskan Amber costs $4.50 per pint. Open M-Th 7am-10:30pm, F-Sa 7am-11:30pm, Su 8am-9:30pm.

Beryl's, 202 Center Ave. (486-3323), to the right of the First National Bank. Attractive wooden furniture and an array of crafts provide whatever earthiness there is in Kodiak. Fine sandwiches ($6), pineapple milkshakes ($2.75), plus a variety of ice cream and sweets. Open M-F 7:30am-6pm, Sa 10am-6pm.

SIGHTS, ENTERTAINMENT, AND EVENTS

Built in 1808 as a storehouse for sea otter pelts, the **Baranov Museum,** 101 Marine Way (486-5920), is housed in the oldest Russian structure standing in Alaska and the oldest wooden structure on the U.S. West Coast. *(Open Memorial Day to Labor Day M-Sa 10am-4pm, Su noon-4pm; Labor Day to Jan. and March to Memorial Day M-W and F 10am-*

3pm, Sa noon-3pm. $2, under 12 free.) The museum displays a collection of Russian and Native Alaskan artifacts; the library has photos and literature ranging from the Russian period to the present. The **Holy Resurrection Russian Orthodox Church** (486-3854), just in front of the museum, oversees the oldest parish in Alaska. Built in 1794 and rebuilt after a fire shortly before WWII, its elaborate icons date back to the early 1800s. Although it's no longer open to the public, try stopping by 15 minutes before vespers (Sa and Th at 6:30pm) to chat with the priest and take in the interior.

The **Alutiiq Museum and Archaeological Repository,** 215 Mission Rd. (486-7004), built with payback funds from the Exxon *Valdez* oil spill, houses displays and artifacts documenting the 7000-year-old culture of the Alutiiq. *(Open M-F 10am-6pm, Sa 10am-4pm, Su 11am-4pm. $2.)* The **Kodiak Alutiiq Dancers,** 713 E. Rezanof Dr. (486-4449), at the Tribal Council, provide a more animated glimpse of native culture. *(Shows June 1 to Sept. 1 daily at 3:30pm. $15.)* Modern animation and other films appear at the **Orpheum Theatre,** 102 Center Ave. (486-5449). *(2 shows per night. $5.50.)*

The five-day **Kodiak Crab Festival** (486-5557), held just before Memorial Day, celebrates a bygone industry with parades, fishing derbies, and kayak, bike, foot, crab, and "survival suit" races. The festivities culminate with the **Chad Ogden Ultramarathon,** a superhuman race along 43 mi. of hilly roads from Chiniak to Kodiak. **St. Herman's Days** (486-3854), held on the weekend closest to August 9, honors the first saint of the Russian Orthodox Church in North America, canonized in 1970. On one of these days, depending on the weather, visitors are welcome to join the annual pilgrimage to St. Herman's former home on Spruce Island.

OUTDOORS

Beautiful **Fort Abercrombie State Park** (486-6339), 3½ mi. north of town, was the site of the first secret radar installation in Alaska, plus a WWII defense installation. After Attu and Kiska in the Aleutian Islands were attacked and occupied by the Japanese in 1942, Kodiak became a major staging area for the lesser-known North Pacific Campaign. Both installments are in severe disrepair; check them out along one of the park's beautiful **hiking trails.** Bunkers and other reminders of the Alaskan campaign remain elsewhere as well, including an old naval station 6½ mi. southwest of Kodiak.

On the rare clear day, hikers can take in a view stretching from the Kenai Peninsula to the Alaska Peninsula atop **Barometer Mountain.** To reach the trailhead, head west out of town on Rezanof Dr., then take the first right past the end of the airport runway, and go about 5 mi. from town; look for the trailhead on the left. After passing a stand of thick alders, the trail climbs steadily and steeply along a grassy ridge before arriving at the summit. Most hikers take about two hours to make the 5 mi. climb to the top, and descend in half that time. The trail up **Pyramid Mountain,** beginning from the parking lot at the pass on Anton Larsen Bay Rd., is about 11 mi. from town. At the top shoulder of alpine tundra, a nice view precedes the rugged final ascent. The hike covers 4 mi., and takes two to four hours. **Termination Point** pokes out into the ocean at the end of Monashka Bay Rd. Cross the creek and head to the beach, where hikers can either stroll in the sand or choose one of several paths that parallel the water for 3 mi. past a Russian Orthodox monastery. A return path detours to an old cabin at the edge of the forest, and then past several moss-coated beaver ponds before arriving back at the parking lot. Ask at the visitor center (see **Practical Information,** above) about the *Trail Guide* ($5) prepared by local outdoor wanderers.

The island's 100 mi. road system gives access to several good **salmon streams.** In Kodiak, surfcasting into Mill Bay at high tide often yields a pink or silver. Red salmon, running from early June to early August, appear in the Buskin and Pasagshak Rivers. Pinks run up the Buskin, Russian, American, and Olds Rivers in astounding numbers from mid-July to mid-September. Better-tasting but scarcer silver salmon run up the same rivers from late August to early October. Dolly varden, the most frequently caught fish on Kodiak, can be hooked year-round from Pasagshak and Buskin Rivers.

Guided **sea kayaking** trips come eye-to-eye with sea otters, puffins, bald eagles, and, on lucky days, encounter giant Kodiak bears from a comfortable distance. **Wavetamer,** P.O. Box 228 (486-2604), leads two-hour tours of Near Island and Mill

ALASKA

Bay ($40), and five-hour coastal treks ($85). Gear is provided, and there is a two-person minimum. **Kodiak Kayak Tours** (486-2722) offers two daily trips, which explore much of the same territory for about three hours ($45). Trips typically start at 9am and 2pm, but they're flexible. Experience is not necessary. Call at least a day ahead.

If you have a vehicle, the 42 mi. coastal drive to **Chiniak** offers a chance to see beautiful seascapes of small offshore islets bathed in fog, and dozens of mufflers lying along the jarringly rough road. If the potholes haven't rearranged your dental work, stop in for a deluxe high-rise hamburger with fries ($5) at the **Road's End Restaurant and Bar,** 42 Road's End (486-2885), in Chiniak. They also serve a generous grilled-cheese sandwich with fries ($3.50) and premier pies ($3.50 per slice) of many varieties (open Tu-W 2-10pm, Th-Su noon-10pm).

■ Kodiak National Wildlife Refuge

Kodiak National Wildlife Refuge encompasses the western two-thirds of Kodiak Island. Since this is a refuge rather than a park, human recreational use is of secondary concern; no trails or roads lead into the region, and there are no official campgrounds. While the refuge contains seven public use cabins, only three can be reached by boat; the others require an expensive float plane ride (around $450).

Most visitors come to Kodiak to see the enormous bears. The numerous "guaranteed" brown-bear-viewing packages run $350-400 for a three- to four-hour float plane tour. Some of the prime viewing areas have visitor quotas, and reservations are made months ahead of time. Call the refuge visitor center (487-2600) for permits and suggestions on how to get to the bears for the least amount of money.

Ultimately, the closest most people get to the refuge is the **visitor center,** 4 mi. southwest of Kodiak (see **Kodiak: Practical Information,** above), which interprets this remarkable area through an array of videos and stuffed bears. This refuge is a beautiful place, but other beautiful places (such as Denali or Wrangell-St. Elias) host the same sort of sightseeing tours for less money.

PRINCE WILLIAM SOUND

▓ Valdez

Upon approaching Valdez from the icy waters of Prince William Sound, the city looks like a subarctic Garden of Eden—lush vegetation laces deep blue mountains, interrupted only by rushing waterfalls and cloud-covered peaks. Once in town, this land of milk and honey takes on a different hue: black. As the northernmost ice-free port in Alaska, Valdez is the terminus of the Alaska pipeline, and oil runs the show.

Historically, Good Friday has been anything but good to Valdez. The 1964 Good Friday earthquake leveled the entire town; it has since been moved and rebuilt in a more seismically friendly area. On the Good Friday of 1989, 25 years later, the infamous Exxon *Valdez* rammed into nearby Bligh Reef and spilled 11 million gallons of oil over 1640 sq. mi. of Prince William Sound. Oil washed up on over 1500 mi. of shoreline, and it is estimated that the casualties included 2000 sea otters, 300 seals, 250 bald eagles, and 250,000 sea birds. Locals say little about the environmental damage, but are sure to mention that the $2 billion dollar clean-up, which lasted over three years, brought thousands to the town and tripled its population.

In summer, Valdez's bountiful waters and natural setting attract a peculiar mix of visitors. College-aged adventurers seek very small fortunes in canneries, or "slime-houses," while living in a crowded tent city. Below, fleets of RVs teem in downtown parks, as their owners explore tax-free shopping in town. A handful of backpackers pass through, camping in the hills outside the city and exploring its lush surroundings. Each winter, Valdez receives an absurd amount of snow—330 in. on average—earning it the title "The Snow Capital of Alaska." Winter income for locals is scarce, but the frozen deluge brings a whole new set of outdoor sports and events.

ORIENTATION AND PRACTICAL INFORMATION

Valdez lies 304 mi. east of Anchorage, in the northeast corner of Prince William Sound. From Valdez, the spectacular Richardson Hwy. (Rte. 4) runs 119 mi. north to Glennallen, where it intersects with the Glenn Hwy. (Rte. 1), which heads southeast to Anchorage and northeast to Tok. Most of downtown Valdez lies on **Egan** (the main street), **Fairbanks,** and **Pioneer Dr.,** all of which run east-west between the north-south **Hazelet** and **Meals Ave.** The Richardson Hwy. enters into the east side of town, and turns into Egan Dr.

Airplanes: Valdez Airport, 4 mi. out of town on Airport Rd., off Richardson Hwy. **ERA Aviation** (835-2636) flies 3 times daily to Anchorage ($86 in advance).

Buses: Gray Line (800-544-2206) departs daily from the Westmark Hotel in Valdez at 8am, and arrives in Anchorage at 6pm ($66).

Ferries: Alaska Marine Highway, P.O. Box 647 (800-642-0066; http://www.dot.state.ak.us/external/amhs/home.html), at the city dock at the end of Hazelet Ave. To: Whittier ($58, ages 2-11 $30); Cordova ($30, ages 2-11 $16); Seward ($58, ages 2-11 $30); Bellingham, WA ($328, ages 2-11 $164).

Harbormaster: 300 N. Harbor Dr. (835-4981; VHF 16).

Taxis: Valdez Yellow Cab (835-2500). Between town and the airport $8, each additional person $1. Runs 24hr.

Car Rental: Valdez-U-Drive, P.O. Box 1396 (835-4402), at the airport. Local driving $40 per day, out of town $49; rates fluctuate. Must be 25 with major credit card, or 21 with proof of rental car insurance, a good driving record, and major credit card.

Car Repair: Tesoro (835-5300). Open M-Sa 6:30am-midnight, Su 6:30am-10pm.

Visitor Information: Valdez Convention and Visitors Bureau, P.O. Box 1603 (835-2984, 835-4636, or 800-770-5954), at Fairbanks St. and Chenega. Info on sights, accommodations, hiking, and camping. Open daily 8am-8pm; in winter M-F 9am-5pm. Free local phone.

Outdoor Information: Parks and Recreation Hotline, 835-3200. The free pamphlet *Valdez Fishing Facts and Hints* is available from the visitor center and at the many sporting goods stores in town. Most fishing stores sell **fishing licenses.**

Employment: Alaska Employment Service, P.O. Box 590 (835-4910; email aesv-ldz@alaska.net), on Meals Ave. in the State Office Bldg. Info on canneries and fish processors. Open M-F 8am-noon and 1-4:30pm.

Equipment Rental: The Prospector (835-3858), beside the post office on Galena Dr., has an immense supply of clothing, shoes, tarps, freeze-dried food, hunting gear, and fishing tackle. Open M-Sa 9am-9pm, Su 10am-6pm. **Beaver Sports** (835-4727), across from the post office on Galena, caters to eco-friendly hikers with high-quality backpacking gear. Bikes $5 per hr., $20 per 24hr. Open M-F 10am-7pm, Sa 10am-6pm. **Anadyr Adventures,** 217 N. Harbor Dr. (835-2814; email anadyr@alaska.net). Single kayaks $45 per day for first 2 days, $40 per each additional day; doubles $65 for first 2 days, $60 per each additional day. Rents to experienced kayakers only. Damage deposit ($200-300) or credit card required. 2hr. orientation class $55. 3hr. tours $55.

Bookstore: Chinook Books and Coffee (see **Food,** below).

Library: (835-4632), 200 Fairbanks Dr., beside the museum. Outstanding 3-floor library, with well-stocked Alaska Room and a selection of free books. Library offers free Internet access with 1hr. time limit. Call ahead; computers are limited. Open M and F 10am-6pm, Tu-Th 10am-8pm, Sa noon-5pm.

Laundromat: Like Home Laundromat, 121 Egan (835-2913). Wash $1.50, dry 25¢ per 7min. Open daily 8am-10pm.

Public Showers: Harbormaster (see above). $4 per 10min. **Bear Paw RV Park** (see below). $4 for spotless private bathrooms, sinks, and unlimited time.

Weather: 835-4505. **Time and Temperature:** 835-8463.

Emergency: 911. **Police:** 835-4560. **State Troopers:** 835-4307.

Crisis Line: 835-2999. 24hr.

Pharmacy: Village Pharmacy (835-3737), in the same building as Eagle Quality Center, at Pioneer and Meals. Open M-Th 9am-6pm, F 9am-7pm, Sa 11am-2pm.

Hospital: Valdez Community Hospital, 911 Meals Ave. (835-2249).

ALASKA

Post Office: 835-4449, at Galena and Tatitlek St. Open M-F 9am-5pm, Sa 10am-noon.
ZIP Code: 99686.
Internet Access: See **Library,** above.
Area Code: 907.

ACCOMMODATIONS AND CAMPGROUNDS

Finding a roof in Valdez is expensive and time-consuming. There are no hostels, and the cheapest indoor options are B&Bs (from $55). The free **reservation center** (835-4988) arranges B&Bs (and glacier tours, rafting trips, and helicopter rides). Although Valdez forbids camping in non-designated areas, insolvent sojourners sometimes camp illegally along **Mineral Creek,** a 15-minute walk from downtown; take Mineral Creek Dr. from Hanagita St.

Anna's B&B, 1119 Ptarmigan (835-2202), has brightly colored rooms with shared bath, and is rumored to serve the best breakfast in town. Singles $55; doubles $65.

L&L's B&B, 533 W. Hanagita St. (835-4447; http://www.alaskagold.com/landl/landl.html), provides clean, pretty rooms with a shared bath (from $60). L and L serve a help-yourself continental breakfast, offer free pick-up from ferries, tour boats, and buses, and their garage for hanging out soaked gear to dry.

Alaskan Artistry B&B, 732 Copper Dr. (835-2542). A lovely place to stay, though pricey. Rooms are large and well-decorated, each with TV and VCR. The lounge area is spacious and cozy, with big-screen TV and a good selection of videos and books. Mini-kitchen, toy room, and swing set. Singles from $65; doubles from $70.

Blueberry Lake State Recreation Site, 24 mi. up the Richardson Hwy. from town, perches near the top of Thompson Pass and looks over surrounding peaks and lakes. Sites $10. Pit toilets and water.

Valdez Glacier Campground (832-2282), 5½ mi. from town and 1½ mi. past the airport; look for a small sign on the left. Slightly inconvenient, but the sites are big, chock-full o' trees, and quieter than those in town. Bears aplenty—keep a clean camp. 101 sites: $10. Water and pit toilets. 15-night max. stay. No reservations.

Sea Otter RV Park (835-2787 or 800-831-2787), at the end of S. Harbor Dr. Pretty RV sites along the water, with a few grassy tent sites inside the RV-formed windblock. Very friendly management and pet rabbits. Tent sites $16-20; hookups $18-20. The RV Park offers by far the lowest gas prices in town, and has its own laundromat (see **Practical Information,** above).

FOOD AND NIGHTLIFE

Budget travelers can head to the **Eagle Quality Center** (835-2100), at Meals Ave. and Pioneer Dr. (open 24hr.). The **Sugar Loaf Saloon** (835-4600), on the corner of Meals and Egan St., is a good place to relax after a day on the road. Though not particularly original or Alaskan, it has an open atmosphere, a huge sports screen, and the largest selection of Alaskan microbrews in town (drafts from $3; open daily 11am-4:30am).

✺**Mike's Palace** (a.k.a. **Pizza Palace**), 201 N. Harbor Dr. (835-2365). The savory minestrone soup ($3) and varied Italian, Greek, and American chow (including good seafood) keep locals happy in this harborside restaurant. Lunch gyros $7; halibut olympia $14; baklava $3.25. Open daily 11am-11pm.

✺**Chinook Books and Coffee,** 126 Pioneer Dr. (835-4222). The friendly and energetic new owners of this shop present a fun, healthy menu, the largest book selection in Valdez, and plenty of advice on what to do while in town. Smoked salmon and cream cheese bagel $6.25; soup-in-a-bread-bowl $5.75; turkey sandwich $5; Very Manly Quiche of the Day $9. Open M-Sa 8am-5pm.

Fu Kung, 207 Kobuk St. (835-5255). Like the mirror room in Bruce Lee's *Enter the Dragon,* Fu Kung's quonset hut exterior is deceiving. Inside, this well-decorated Chinese restaurant serves lunch specials ($7) and savory almond chicken ($11), plus a wide range of vegetarian options. Open daily 11am-11pm.

Lisa's Kitchen (835-5633), wedged into a small trailer at the corner of Pioneer Dr. and Hazelet St., and soon moving to Fairbanks and Tatitlek. Miraculous, tangy Mexican grub for such a far northern seaport. Tamales $2.75; burritos $5.50. A polite *por favor* and *gracías* gains Lisa's good graces, and may put more salsa on your portion. Open May-Aug. M-Sa 11:30am-8pm.

Totem Inn Restaurant, 100 Totem Dr. (835-4443). For a quick and hearty hot breakfast, sit among locals and stuffed wildlife in a lodge-style atmosphere. Large menu includes light options and a salad bar ($5.75). Breakfast $5-9; dinner from $12. Breakfast served until 2pm. Open daily 5am-11pm.

SIGHTS, ENTERTAINMENT, AND EVENTS

The **Valdez Museum,** 217 Egan Dr. (835-2764), packs an impressive informational punch for its size; exhibits on both Good Friday debacles await. *(Open M-F 9am-6pm, Sa 8am-5pm. $3, seniors $2.50, ages 14-18 $2, under 14 free.)* On midsummer weekends, yuk-hunting travelers hit **The Acres** (info 835-3505, tickets 835-4988), at the intersection of the Richardson Hwy. and Airport Rd., for *Boom Town,* an all-singin', all-dancin' history of Valdez. The performance is predictably hokey and surprisingly informative. *(Tu-Sa at 8pm. $15, ages 6-12 $10, under 5 free.)* A 1964 **earthquake video** is shown daily at 4pm in the Totem Inn for free. The **Teen Center** (835-4526), on Hanagita and Hazelet, provides arcade-style fun with pool tables and video games. *(Open Tu-W 3:30-10:30pm, Th noon-6pm, F 3:30-11:30pm, Sa 5-11:30pm.)*

After an 800 mi. journey from the fields of Prudhoe Bay, the Alaska Pipeline (see p. 438) deposits a fifth of America's domestic oil into tankers waiting in Valdez. Unfortunately for penny-pinchers, **Valdez Marine Terminal** strikes a gusher in visitors' wallets with a two-hour, somewhat dry tour. *(4 tours daily depart from the airport. $15, ages 6-12 $7.50, under 6 free.)* A visit to the **pipeline visitor center** (835-2686) at the airport yields plenty of free pipelinalia, including construction-related films.

Gold Rush Days (on the first W-Su in Aug.) are a feast for budget travelers. The visitor center hosts a free salmon and halibut fry, along with a fashion show, dance, traveling jail bus, and **ugly vehicle contest.** Valdez makes the most of its massive snowfall and alpine setting with the annual **Snowman Festival,** held on the first weekend in March. A drive-in movie is projected onto a giant snowbank, where locals drive up and tune into the soundtrack on the local radio station. In the early 90s, Valdez built the largest snowman ever (although the record has since been broken in Japan), and the movie was projected on its ample belly while kids skied through the screen. In late March, Valdez holds the **World Extreme Skiing Championship** and the **King of the Hill Snowboard Competition,** rendering uncool people everywhere uneasy.

OUTDOORS

The **Solomon Gulch Trail** starts 150 yards northeast of the hatchery on Dayville Rd., near Valdez's hydroelectric plant. A mere 1.3 mi., this 2½-hour hike covers two steep inclines, ending at **Solomon Lake** with excellent views of Valdez Bay and the pipeline. The **Goat Trail** is more rigorous and farther from the city, though not exactly off the beaten path; the trail follows a Native Alaskan footpath that was once the only route from Valdez to the Interior. As it weaves through Keystone Canyon, the trail follows the **Lowe River** past glimpses of waterfalls. Look for the sign just past **Horsetail Falls** (Mile 13.5), and follow a dirt trail about ¼ mi. from the **Bridal Veil Falls** at Mile 18.2. Just north of downtown, the 5½ mi. **Mineral Creek Trail** leads through the mountains, with waterfalls and wildlife along the way. The first few miles are accessible by car, but the last part of the trail can only be walked, and leads to the **Old Gold Mine.** The **Shoup Bay Trail** is a new, approximately 6 mi. trail along the mountainside, waiting to be explored. Inquire at the visitor center or Beaver Sports (see **Practical Information,** above) for good info on other hikes.

Fishing is the big draw for many of Valdez's summer visitors. Fishing charter services outnumber RV parks and gift shops (compare prices at the visitor center), but some fish, especially pink salmon, bite as close as the town docks. To commune with fish instead of killing them, try **Anadyr Adventures** (see p. 435), which offers three-hour **kayaking** nature tours twice daily. *($55 per person, children and seniors $49.50.)* Beyond guided hiking, kayaking, and fishing trips, **Keystone Adventures** (835-2606

ALASKA

or 800-328-8460; email keystone@alaska.net; http://www.alaskawhitewater.com)
will lead **rafting** trips on any river in Alaska. Their 4½ mi. route through the Keystone
Canyon on the **Lowe River** runs through an exciting stretch of froth with breathtaking scenery, including a close look at the 900 ft. **Bridal Veil Falls.** They also provide a
full day of adventure on the whitewater of the **Tonsina River,** including a stop for
lunch. *(Lowe $35. Tonsina $85.)*

By boat, helicopter, or plane, and for a hefty price, visitors view the Prince William
Sound's most prized possessions: **Columbia** and **Shoup Glaciers.** The best budget
option is the **Alaska Marine Highway** ferry (see **Practical Information,** above),
which pauses in front of the face of the 3 mi. wide **Columbia Glacier** for 10 minutes
on its way to and from Whittier ($58). **Stan Stephens Charters** (835-4731 or 800-
992-1297; email ssc@alaska.net) offers an economy cruise to Columbia daily at
12:30pm. *(6½hr.; $65; ages 4-12 $45, under 3.)* **Captain Jim's Charter Company** (835-
2282) also offers a five-hour Columbia Glacier trip, a nine-hour **Meares Glacier** trip,
and wildlife cruises at similar prices. **The Chapel of the Sea** (800-411-0090) allows
the pious and penniless to board the *Lu-Lu Belle* cruise boat for a one-hour, non-
denominational church service in the sound. Show up Sunday by 7:30am at the dock
adjacent to the Westmark Hotel for an 8am departure; seats are limited, and the lu-lu-
of-a-cruise's sublime scenery could easily inspire a religious awakening. *(Free, though
offering collected.)*

Valdez's plentiful snowfall and prime coastal location, warming up to a balmy 25°F
in January, make the town a **skier's paradise.** There are no chairlifts in Valdez. Experienced skiers can charter helicopters to drop them for an extreme (-ly scary) adventure. Downhill skiers and snowboarders often drive, hitchhike, or "snowmachine"
(Alaskan for "snowmobile") up to **Thompson Pass,** and ski down to the town. *(Let's
Go does not recommend hitchhiking or plummeting down ridiculously steep mountains on skinny boards with wax on them.)* **Mt. Odyssey** also provides skiers with
gonzo terrain. There are also numerous **cross-country ski trails,** many of which start
at the Coast Guard Housing, on Anchor Crest at the western end of town. For more
details, pick up the free guide *Snowcountry* from the visitor center.

Take That, Freud

Everything is big in Alaska—even the mosquitoes are the size of small predatory
birds—and the 1968 discovery of oil in Prudhoe Bay was no exception, launching
a massive technological effort to build the most specialized pipeline in the world.
The oil may be crude, but the pipeline is not. The construction of the Trans-Alas-
kan Pipeline involved over 70,000 workers, $8 billion, the development of
advanced insulation technologies, and new roads, including the huge Dalton
Highway. Unique supports suspend half the pipeline above ground, a feature necessary since the oil's temperature could thaw permafrost, creating unstable
ground. In some places, the pipeline stands as high as 10 ft. to allow wildlife to
pass underneath. Even the zig-zag construction (not the brainchild of an inebriated engineer) was specially designed to enable the pipeline to withstand an
earthquake of up to 8.5 on the Richter scale. (Keep your fingers crossed on Good
Fridays.) Oil first flowed through the pipe in 1977, making the 6mph, five-day
ooze from Prudhoe Bay. After traversing 800 mi., three mountain ranges, and over
800 rivers, the pipeline spills its precious fluid in Valdez at a rate of up to 75,000
barrels per hour (over 60 million gallons per day).

■ Richardson Hwy. (Rte. 4) and Glenn Hwy. (Rte. 1): Valdez to Anchorage

The Richardson and Glenn Highways provide a paved, two-lane route through the
scenic 304 mi. between Valdez and Anchorage. The mile markers for the Richardson
Hwy. start 4 mi. from the current site of Valdez, since they begin counting at the original townsite, where everything was flattened by the 1964 earthquake. The highway

winds through the **Keystone Canyon,** surrounded by overwhelmingly green vegetation atop towering mountains, and passing untold waterfalls that cascade down the rocks from hundreds of feet above. **Thompson Pass,** at Mile 26, affords a stunning above-treeline view of the mountains, the canyon below, and wildflowers everywhere. Many say that this drive is the most scenic in the entire scenery-stuffed state.

Along both highways on this stretch, there are too many **state campgrounds** and **rest areas** to name. At Mile 115, the Richardson Hwy. junctions with the Glenn Hwy. in **Glennallen** (see below). Turn west onto the Glenn to continue the 189 mi. to Anchorage; mileposts measure distance from Anchorage. At Mile 160 is the turn-off for **Lake Louise Recreation Area,** 19 mi. off the highway. This area is known for its lake trout, its cross-country skiing, and its plump berries of late summer and early fall. The highway climbs to its highest elevation at Mile 129, the **Eureka Summit** (3322 ft.), from whence unfold the river valleys below, the **Chugach Mountains** to the south, and the **Talkeetnas** to the northwest. The agricultural town of **Palmer** lies at Mile 42 (see p. 409), and the scenic, lengthy drive from Valdez ends as the highway turns into 5th Ave. in downtown Anchorage.

■ Cordova

Fortified by rugged mountains of volcanic rock and waters teeming with salmon, Cordova lures nature lovers and anglers. Accessible only by sea or air, the town has preserved its natural beauty in a relatively tourist-free setting, and its rich hiking, biking, skiing, bird-watching, and fishing resources are blissfully uncrowded. Proposals to connect Cordova with the Interior's road network have met with strong opposition from the community—Cordovans would rather admit visitors in a manner compatible with their independent and low-key style. Residents have recently begun a four-year program that will focus on low-impact ecotourism rather than cruise ships and t-shirt kiosks. The movement was spearheaded by a former mayor who, until 1994 was the nation's highest elected Green Party official, and now owns the Orca Book Store. Cordova's only drawback is its weather. Many cloudy days and 150 in. of annual precipitation make this a damp paradise; June is the best month for staying dry.

ORIENTATION AND PRACTICAL INFORMATION

Cordova, on the east side of Prince William Sound at **Orca Inlet,** starts at the shore and ascends rapidly. Streets parallel the ocean, with **Railroad Ave.** at water level and numbered streets increasing up the hillside. **First St.** is the downtown shopping district and leads out of town to the ferry terminal. Railroad Ave. becomes **Copper Bay Hwy.** out of town toward the airport and Childs Glacier.

Airplanes: The **airport** is 13 mi. east of town on the Copper River Hwy. **Alaska Airlines** (424-3278 or 800-426-0333). To: Juneau ($187); Anchorage ($50-112). The **Airport Shuttle** (424-5356) meets all flights and runs to town for $9. Call ahead.

Ferries: Alaska Marine Highway, P.O. Box 1689 (424-7333 or 800-642-0066), 1 mi. north of town on Ocean Dock Rd. off 1st Ave. One-way to: Valdez ($30); Whittier ($58); Seward ($58); Kodiak ($98); Homer ($138).

Harbormaster: 424-6400; VHF ch. 16.

Taxis: Wild Hare Taxi Service, 424-3939. **Bow 'n' Arrow Taxi,** 424-5766. Both run 24hr.

Car Rental: Cordova Auto Rentals (424-5982, Su and after hours 424-7440), at the airport. $69 per day; unlimited free mileage. Must be 25 with major credit card.

Car Repair: Sharp Auto Clinic, 424-3330.

Visitor Information: Cordova Historical Museum, 622 1st St., P.O. Box 391 (424-6665; fax 424-6666; email cdvmsm@ptialaska.net). A handy map and friendly staff. Open M-Sa 10am-6pm, Su 2-4pm. **Cordova Chamber of Commerce,** P.O. Box 99 (424-7260), on 1st Ave. by the bank. Ample pamphlets. Open M-F 8am-4pm.

Outdoor Information: Chugach National Forest, Cordova Ranger District, Box 280 (424-7661), on 2nd St., between Browning and Adams, on the 2nd floor. Excellent info on hiking and fishing. Reserve any of 17 Forest Service **cabins** (no water) here.

Open M-F 8am-5pm. **Alaska Dept. of Fish and Game,** P.O. Box 669 (424-3215; recording 424-7535). **Fishing licenses** available at: **Davis' Super Foods** on 1st St. Open M-Sa 7:30am-9pm, Su 9am-8pm. **A.C. Company** (424-7141), in the small boat harbor. Open M-Sa 7am-10pm, Su 8am-9pm.

Banks: First National Bank of Anchorage (424-7521) and **National Bank of Alaska** (424-3258). Both on 1st St., with 24hr. **ATMs.** Banks open M-F 9am-5pm.

Equipment Rental: Cordova Coastal Outfitters (424-7424), in a yellow shack on the dock in the small boat harbor, across the street and down the ramp from A.C. Company. Mountain bikes $15 per day. Single kayaks $30 per day; doubles $45. Canoes $30 per day. Boats $85 per day. Inflatable Zodiacs $55 per day, with motor $85. Rents camping equipment, too.

Bookstore: Orca Book Store (424-5305), on 1st St. Small, quality selection, with ample balcony reading room. Ask the owner, Kelley Weaverling, about local wildlife and politics. Open M-Sa 8am-5pm.

Library: (424-6667), on 1st St. next to the museum. Open Tu-Sa 1-8pm.

Laundromat: Whirlwind Laundromat, 100 Adams St. (424-5110), at 1st St. Wash $3.25, dry 25¢ per 5min. Open M-Sa 8am-8pm, Su 9am-5pm; in winter daily 10am-6pm. **Club Speedwash,** behind the Club Bar on 1st St. Wash $2, dry 25¢ per 15min. Open daily 8am-8pm.

Showers: Club Speedwash (see above), has showers for $2.50 plus 25¢ per min. **Harbormaster's,** 602 Nicholoff Way (424-6400). $3 per 5min. Tokens available M-F 8am-5pm. Showers open 24hr.

Public Radio: KCHU 88.1 FM.

Emergency: 911. **Police:** (424-6100), next to the post office on Railroad Ave. **Fire:** 424-6117.

Crisis Line: 424-HELP/4357.

Pharmacy: Cordova Drug Co., P.O. Box 220 (424-3246), on 1st St. Open M-Sa 9:30am-6pm, Su 10am-1pm.

Hospital: Cordova Community, 602 Chase Ave. (424-8000), off Copper River Hwy.

Post Office: (424-3564), at Council St. and Railroad Ave. Open M-F 10am-5:30pm, Sa 10am-1pm. **ZIP Code:** 99574.

Area Code: 907.

ACCOMMODATIONS AND CAMPGROUNDS

Cordova has a few beautiful B&Bs. Camping near town is less idyllic; the municipal campground is a gravel parking lot. The residents of **Hippie Cove,** about 1½ mi out of town past the ferry terminal, may help friendly backpackers find a place to tent down in the peaceful bay, but camping there is officially illegal. None of Cordova's accommodations are wheelchair accessible.

Cannery Row Bed and Breakfast, 1 Cannery Row, P.O. Box 120 (424-5920; fax 424-5923), ¼ mi. out of town before the ferry dock. Travelers can experience Cordova's fishing history firsthand by staying in an immaculate refurbished cannery bunk house. The best indoor value in town, with fresh blue and white paint, fluffy quilts, and a continental breakfast. Shared baths; laundromat right next door. Singles $42; doubles $47. Credit cards accepted.

Northern Nights Inn (424-5356), at 3rd St. and Council Ave. Run by an enthusiastic and generous hostess, this meticulously restored home of a copper-era millionaire is now adorned with period antiques. Private baths, cable, VCRs, microwaves, and fridges. Singles $55; doubles $75. Provides referrals to Cordova's other B&Bs.

Alaskan Hotel and Bar, P.O. Box 484 (424-3299; fax 424-5276; email hotelak@ptialaska.net), on 1st St. Overall air of long-decayed elegance. Simple rooms line the upper floors; those above the bar get noisy at night. Singles and doubles $35, with private bath $55. Add $10 for 3 or more people.

City RV Park (424-6200), on Whitshed Rd. 1 mi. from downtown. 4 RV sites and a few tent spots in this city-sanctioned campground overlooking Orca Inlet. All gravel; bring tie-downs for tents. Toilets, showers, and water. Tent sites $3; RV hookups $12. 14-night max. stay.

FOOD

By small-town Alaska standards, Cordova has a terrific variety of affordable lunch options. The dinner scene is not as easy, since many restaurants close by mid-afternoon. The best selection of groceries is in the colossal **A.C. Company** (424-7141), on Nicholoff St., in the small boat harbor (open M-Sa 7am-10pm, Su 7am-9pm).

✪**Killer Whale Cafe** (424-7733), on 1st St. in the back of the groovy Orca Bookstore. It seems that every tiny Alaskan town has an earthy espresso-steeped cafe. This is one of the better ones. Eat in light-washed, wood-lined splendor on one of two inside decks overlooking the books. A hangout for the hip of all ages and origins. Homemade soup and croissant $3; killer sandwiches $5.50-8; cappuccino $2. Open M-F 7am-4pm, Sa 8am-3pm.

The Cookhouse Cafe, 1 Cannery Row (424-5926), ¼ mi. south of the ferry terminal. Good eats and bright decor make this a top spot. Come early to meet local fishermen, or come later and meet the cannery workers. Splendid breakfast, served all day Saturday. 3 hotcakes $4.50; *rigatoni al forno* $7. Open M-Sa 6am-3pm, Su 7am-2pm, plus some Sa nights for dinner; call or check local message boards for hours.

Baja Taco (424-5599), in a red bus by the small boat harbor. A rolling taco stand with a permanent al fresco dining stage. Heads south of the border in winter for research and development. Chicken burrito $6.50; breakfast burrito $6.50; espresso 50¢. Open M-Th 8am-4pm, F-Sa 8am-8pm, Su 10am-8pm.

SIGHTS, EVENTS, AND NIGHTLIFE

If it's raining (and it probably is), dry off in the **Cordova Historical Museum,** 622 1st St. (424-6665), in the same building as the library on 1st St. *(Open M-Sa 10am-6pm, Su 2-4pm. $1 donation suggested.)* The museum has living iceworms *(Mesenchytraeus solifugus)* that dwell inside the glaciers, plus Prince Willie, an erratic leatherback turtle who strayed several thousand miles and wound up in a local fisherman's net. Check out the hilariously dramatic "Story of Cordova," shown daily at 3pm. The museum also boasts an old printing press, the reconstructed business end of a lighthouse, and an Inuit kayak. **B Street Artworks** (424-5331), on Browning St., features local painting, pottery, sculpture, and design. *(Open W, F-Sa 1-5pm.)*

For 32 years, Cordova residents have held an **Iceworm Festival** in winter to relieve cabin fever and honor the semi-legendary squirmer. The celebration breaks loose the first weekend in February and includes a parading 100 ft. iceworm propelled by Cordova's children and the crowning of Miss Iceworm Queen. For the rest of the year, locals flee rainy nights at the original 1906 oak bar of the **Alaskan Hotel and Bar** (424-3288). Live blues and rock play from 10pm until closing four nights per week, including Friday and Saturday. *(Open M-Th 8am-2am, F-Sa 8am-4am, Su 10am-2am.)*

OUTDOORS

Near Cordova

The vast **Copper River Delta,** a preserve covering over 1100 sq. mi., parallels the Copper River Hwy. A simple drive or pedal along the highway reveals stunning vistas of mountains, wetlands, and glacial deltas. Any vantage point in this diverse land reveals granite peaks, sodden muskeg, and 50 ft. sand dunes. The delta swarms with bear, moose, wolves, coyotes, eagles, swans, sea otters, and millions of shorebirds.

The **Copper River Delta** is the largest contiguous wetland area on the entire Pacific Coast of North America, and supports the largest accumulation of shore birds in the world during the first two weeks of May. Birdwatchers flock to the annual **Shorebird Festival** in the first week of May. Call the visitor center (424-6665) or Kelley Weaverling at Orca Bookstore (424-5305) for more info.

Hiking in the delta is often wet and tough, but the neighboring **Chugach Mountains** provide dry trails and excellent climbing opportunities. Forest Service volunteers keep the trails very well-maintained. The popular and rewarding **Crater Lake Trail** takes around two hours one way. The trailhead is about 1½ mi. down Lake Ave., past the city airstrip, on the shore of **Lake Eyak.** Half-way up is a 1 mi. connecting trail to the front side of **Mt. Eyak,** with access to the peak for aggressive hikers. For a strenuous hike, continue on from Crater Lake among mountain goats along a 5½ mi. ridge to connect with the **Power Creek Trail.** This ridge route meets the trail midway on its 4 mi. ascent to one of the most spectacular Forest Service **cabins** in the state (one of three in the area accessible by foot). The Power Creek Trail begins at the end of Power Creek Rd., 7 mi. from town. The loop combining the Crater Lake and Power Creek trails is a 12 mi. hike. Other, shorter trails branch off the Copper River Hwy.; check with the Forest Service (see **Practical Information,** above) for an excellent free pamphlet on hiking around Cordova.

The Copper River Hwy. provides access to campgrounds, hiking trails, Childs Glacier, and a good biking trail to **McKinley Lake.** The trailhead is at Mile 21.6; the highway turns to gravel after Mile 12. About 15 mi. from town, the **Sheridan Glacier** lets hikers get up close and personal with an icy monolith. Left off the Copper River Hwy., just past the airport, follow Sheridan Glacier Rd. to its end, and pick up a marked trail. Walking out onto the glacier is dangerous, with snow-covered crevasses that can swallow hikers without a trace. Nevertheless, scores of locals and tourists venture onto Sheridan's broad back every summer, and many even return.

Kayaking in Prince William Sound and Orca Inlet is spectacular, and **Cordova Coastal Outfitters** (800-357-5145; email coastal@eagle.ptialaska.net) offers expertly guided tours. *(4hr. wildlife trip $60; 8hr. trip $95. All gear included.)* Drop-offs, gear rental, and trip-planning are also available. **Fishing** in Cordova is superb, as all five species of Pacific salmon spawn seasonally in the Copper River. Salmon and halibut have been caught right off the city dock, but fishing is usually better along Orca Inlet Rd., on the Eyak River, or at **Hartney Bay.** King salmon run in the winter, sockeye and dolly varden in summer and early fall, and coho salmon in late summer and fall.

In winter, the oldest chairlift in Alaska swings into action, shuttling telemark skiers up **Mt. Tripod.** *($15 per day.)* **Cross-country skiing** is free and excellent along the **Mt. Tripod Trail.** Highlights of the darker months include ice skating on Lake Eyak, and on Sheridan Glacier for the more adventurous/foolhardy.

Childs Glacier

Childs Glacier, at the end of the 50 mi. highway, is one of the most stupendous road-accessible sights in Alaska, and far more impressive than its famous cousin in Juneau, the Mendenhall. Under the heat of the summer sun, the glacier cleaves off 20-story chunks of ice that fall hundreds of feet before crashing into the Copper River's silty waters. The largest calvings send 20 ft. waves over the observation area on the opposite bank of the river, ¼ mi. from the glacier. Splintered trees and boulders strewn throughout the woods reveal the awesome power of these inland tsunamis. Although falls of this size are uncommon (maybe once a season), they are unpredictable and, as several alarming signs suggest, viewers should be prepared to run. Another set of signs prohibits harvesting the salmon flung into the woods by the waves and left high and dry. In lieu of a movie theatre, a popular local pasttime is to sit out at the glacier on a nice day, drink a few brews, and wait for the glaciers to calve.

The **Million Dollar Bridge,** only a few hundred yards from the viewing area, was considered an engineering marvel in 1910 because of its placement between two active glaciers. One has retreated, but Childs Glacier is now less than ½ mi. away. The bridge was heavily damaged in the 1964 quake, and a primitive patch job keeps it standing; many people drive safely across the span, but at their own risk. Legend has it that if you see an iceberg float under the bridge's upstream side, then dash across in time to drop a penny onto its icy back as it emerges, you'll be granted a wish.

The combined splendor of the delta and the glacier make the somewhat expensive trip worthwhile. If traveling with a group, rent a car (see **Practical Information,** above), pack a lunch (there's no food anywhere on the highway), and make a glorious day of it. Hitchhikers have been known to get stranded, since Childs is not a major tourist attraction. (Although *Let's Go* does not recommend hitchhiking, it still seeks to empathize with the neglected.) **Copper River and North West Tours** (424-5356) meets ferries with the offer of a narrative and a comfy round-trip bus ride. The Million Dollar tour lasts five to six hours and includes a delicious lunch during the three-hour stop at Childs ($40).

COPPER RIVER BASIN

■ Glennallen

Glennallen is not a major destination in itself, but serves as a base for entering Wrangell-St. Elias National Park (see p. 443) and for fishing in nearby rivers. Glennallen stands at the junction of the Richardson and Glenn Hwy., 120 mi. north of Valdez and 189 mi. east of Anchorage, making it a stop for countless RVs. The **Nabesna Road** lies to the north (see p. 444), and the turn-off for **Edgerton Highway** (leading to the **McCarthy Road**; see p. 445) is south of Glennallen on the way to Valdez.

The town **visitor center** (822-5555), a log cabin with a sod roof, lies at the intersection of the Glenn and Richardson Hwy., about a mile away from most of the other businesses in Glennallen, which are located on the Glenn (open daily May 15-Sept. 15 8am-7pm). The center is a flowing font of info on sights and activities in and near Wrangell-St. Elias, and proffers pamphlets on hiking and fishing in the Copper River Valley. **National Bank of Alaska** has an **ATM** next to the post office, and at Hub Maxi Mart (both 24hr.). The **library** (822-5226) is 1½ mi. from town on the Glenn Hwy. (open Tu-Th 1-6pm, F 1-8pm, Sa 11am-6pm), while the **laundromat** is next to Park's Place (open daily 7am-11pm). **Road Conditions:** 834-1039. **State Troopers:** 822-3263. The **Crossroads Medical Clinic** (822-3203) is 1 mi. from town on the Glenn. The **post office** (822-3273) is 2 mi. from the visitor center (open M-F 8am-5pm, Sa 9am-noon). **ZIP Code:** 99588. **Area Code:** 907.

Dry Creek State Campground, 3 mi. north of the visitor center on the Richardson Hwy., is a popular place with water, pit toilets, and 60 RV, tent, and walk-in sites ($10). There is also camping on the banks of the **Gulkana River,** near the bridge at Mile 127 on the Richardson Hwy., 19 mi. north of the visitor center. If the salmon are running, this place is guaranteed to be packed with fishy-smelling people in waders. The **Caribou Hotel** (822-3302 or 800-478-3302; fax 822-3711), at Glenn Mile 187 tucked behind the Caribou Cafe, has reasonably priced annex rooms with shared bathrooms (singles $49; doubles $59). **Carol's B&B** (822-3594 or 822-3600; fax 822-3800) serves a true Alaskan breakfast, and is centrally located in downtown Glennallen (singles $60; doubles $70). From the visitor center, follow the Glenn Hwy. about 2 mi., turn right on Birch St. just past the bank, and look for the house on the right with the log fence. Also in the heart of town is **Maranatha B&B**, 127 Terrace Dr. (822-3643; fax 822-5098; email pmkildal@alaska.net), which also serves a continental breakfast (singles and doubles $65); turn right off the Glenn Hwy. onto Terrace Dr., about 1 mi. from the visitor center. Grab grub at **Park's Place Groceries** (822-3334), just west of town on the Glenn Hwy. (open M-Sa 24hr., Su 7am-11pm).

■ Wrangell-St. Elias National Park

From its lowland web of sapphire ponds, open meadows, and dense brush, to its jagged snow-drenched peaks, glittering slopes, and mountain glaciers, Wrangell-St. Elias National Park is diverse, vast, and wild. In a state where the enormous is commonplace, Wrangell remains unique: the largest national park in the U.S., it is so big that six Yellowstone National Parks could fit within its boundaries. Within its 13.2 million acres, the Wrangell, St. Elias, Chugach, and Alaska Ranges converge. Nine peaks tower over 14,000 ft., including Mt. St. Elias, the second-highest mountain in the U.S. (18,008 ft.), and Wrangell Mountain, a volcano that last erupted in 1900.

ALASKA

Beyond towering peaks and extensive glaciers, Wrangell teems with wildlife: bears, Dall sheep, caribou, moose, bison, sea lions, and a host of birds all make the park their home. With only two rough roads that penetrate its interior, and almost no established trails, Wrangell's difficulty of access keeps many tourists well away. Only a fraction of Denali's visitor load even makes it within park boundaries, much less into the mind-boggling backcountry.

ORIENTATION AND GETTING THERE

Wrangell-St. Elias is in the southeast corner of Alaska's mainland, bordered by the **Copper River** to the west and the Yukon's **Kluane National Park** to the east (see p. 383). Travelers should stop to get info at the perimeter, since no ranger stations or services exist in the heart of the park. The two access routes to the park's interior are the **Nabesna Road** (see below), extending a grueling 46 mi. from the Richardson Hwy. (Rte. 4) into the park's northern portion, and the **McCarthy Road** (see p. 445), which plunges 60 mi. into the park from Chitina (CHIT-nuh) to McCarthy (see p. 446). **Ranger stations** lurk outside the park boundaries in **Copper Center** (822-7261), south of Glennallen (open 8am-6pm); **Chitina** (823-2205; open daily 10am-6pm); and **Slana** (822-5238), on the park's northern boundary (see below). They have the lowdown on all the must-knows and go-sees of the park, and sell invaluable topographical maps (entire park $9; quadrants $4). The visitor center in **Glennallen** (see above) is also a helpful resource.

Much of the land along the McCarthy Road and some along the Nabesna Road is private property, so be sure to check with one of the ranger stations before parking on the curb and heading off into the dense brush of the backcountry. Travelers with a little more spending money can fly into the wilderness. **Charter flights** from McCarthy or Nabesna start at around $60 per person (1-way), and increase in price depending on the destination. For any overnight trip, the ranger stations request a **written itinerary;** though not required, it could never be a bad idea. The park has few established trails, so **backcountry** hikers must be seasoned backpackers with extensive experience in route-finding, stream-fording, glacier-crossing, and other survival skills. All hikers should be aware of Wrangell's large and active bear population (see p. 47).

■ Wrangell-St. Elias: The Nabesna Road

Underappreciated and underused, this second access into Wrangell-St. Elias National Park is shorter, more scenic, and slightly less bone-jarring than the **McCarthy Road** (see below), and offers access to nearly a dozen trails of many lengths and difficulties. The turnoff for the Nabesna Rd. is located at **Slana** (rhymes with "bandana"), 65 mi. southwest of Tok (see p. 472) on the Tok Cutoff. Slana is the place to prepare and make last-minute provisions for a journey into the park, since **Nabesna,** at the end of the 42 mi. road, is little more than a mining ghost town. It is currently populated by the **Ellis family,** and pretty much no one else. The **Slana Ranger Station** (822-5238), right off the highway, sells topographic maps ($4-9) and provides info on weather, road conditions, bear behavior, and everything else under the sun (open in summer daily 8am-5pm; in winter by appointment only). **Fishing permits** cost $10 for a day, $20 for three days, and $100 for the entire season. Slana has **no clinic;** call 911 for **emergencies,** or stop by the ranger station. Slana's **post office** is 1 mi. down the Nabesna Rd., with a pay phone outside (open M, W, F 10am-2pm). **ZIP Code:** 99586.

For groceries, laundry, a shower, or camping, head to **Midway Services,** about 1 mi. northeast of the Nabesna cutoff. For a meal, travel 2 mi. farther northeast on the highway to **Duffy's Road House.** When you're not sleeping for free in the mountains and need to snooze in Slana (not too difficult), **Doubletree RV Park** (822-3973), 1 mi. down the Nabesna Rd. next to the post office, has tent sites ($18), hookups ($20), and showers ($3; guests only). Nestled in the forest, the family-run **Huck Hobbit's Homestead Retreat and Campground** (822-3196) rents bunk beds ($15), tent sites ($2.50), and cozy two-person log cabins ($25). The secluded cabins and bunkhouse are heated with wood-burning stoves, sport trapping decor, and are filled with relics from the last federal homestead (in Slana in the mid-1980s). The homestead is strikingly quiet, and there's no need to bring any bottled water, thanks to a clear, fresh spring. Solar showers are free, and the welcoming, friendly owners serve home-cooked meals (breakfast $5; dinner $7). **Canoe rental** (with drop-off and pick-up) costs $35 per day. To find the hobbits, head south on the Nabesna Rd., turn left at Four Mile Rd., then take the first right; follow the signs, then walk ¾ mi. up the trail.

Before driving the Nabesna Road, ask at the ranger station about the water levels of the three or four streams that car must pass along the way. For any crossing, it's best not to slow down, but to charge through the stream to avoid getting mired in wet gravel; go at least 10mph, but probably not 30 or 40mph. The gravel road in its entirety takes about 1½ hours to drive. In infinitesimal Nabesna, the **End-of-the-Road Bed and Breakfast** (822-5312, last-ditch messages 822-3426) has bunks ($20), singles ($55), and doubles ($65). Showers are available for general use, but the price ($3, towels $2) is not included with bunk accommodations. The family that owns the B&B also runs **horseback riding, hunting trips,** and an **air taxi** service in Nabesna (flightseeing $150 per hr. for 2 seats, $235 per hr. for 3 seats; call for reservations).

The Slana Ranger Station has a full list of **hikes** beginning at Nabesna or along the road. The **Caribou Creek Trail,** at Mile 19.5, is an extremely mild 4 mi. walk (one-way) past three shallow stream crossings to a primitive mining cabin with first-come, first-served bunks. Be wary of bears in the brushy areas, and savor the rare opportunity to sing as loudly and as poorly as you want. Those comfortable with trackless ridge-walking can make a 16 mi. loop starting from the **Lost Creek Trail** at Mile 31.2, and return on the redundantly named **Trail Creek Trail** at Mile 29.4, or vice-versa. The two are not directly connected; secure a detailed map and a chat with the rangers before setting out. The **Skookum Creek Volcanic Trail,** at Mile 36.8, is brand-new (courtesy of the Sierra Club) and begging to be explored, especially by geology buffs. The trail is 2½ mi. (one-way), and rises about 3000 ft. in elevation, traveling up a forested alluvial fan, along a stream following rock cairns, and then through unmarked, unmaintained tundra; ask your friendly ranger for details.

■ Wrangell-St. Elias: The McCarthy Road

Once the largest town in Alaska and heralded as its future capital, **Chitina** (CHIT-nuh) bucked the yoke of greatness. When the copper mines dried up, the town virtually disappeared, too. What's left is a flower child community of about 45 winter residents, with a **ranger station** (see above), a tiny **general store** with fuel (823-2211; open Su-Th 8am-9pm, F-Sa 8am-10pm), and the **It'll Do Cafe** (823-2244), which will have to, since it's the only one in town (open daily 7am-8pm; closed in winter). Penniless campers will delight in the spacious, free **campground** across the **Copper River** (pit toilets, no water), but be warned: the winds in the canyon are intense and can blow poorly staked tents miles down the river.

Starting at Chitina, the McCarthy Road follows the old roadbed of the Copper River & Northwestern Railway for 58 mi. to the **Kennicott River.** Severe washboard, rocks, potholes, and even an occasional railroad spike make this grueling three-hour drive arguably the roughest state road in Alaska. With normal tires, any speed over 20mph dramatically increases the chance of a blow-out; carrying at least one spare tire is strongly recommended. Bold and unflappable drivers will be rewarded with amazing views of the Copper River Delta. At Mile 17, the 525 ft. **Kuskulana Bridge** passes 238 ft. above the raging **Kuskulana River.** Summer thrill-seekers can **bungee jump** from the bridge thanks to **Club Way North** (783-1335), P.O. Box 1003, Girdwood 99857 (one jump $50, 2 jumps $80, **free if you jump naked,** although they hate to see the resulting rope burn). After jolting and rattling for 41 more miles, the road terminates on the western edge of the Kennicott River, where travelers must cross a foot bridge and walk ½ mi. into the town of McCarthy. Free parking is available another ½ mi. back before the river; the lot at the river charges $5 for 24hr.

ALASKA

■ McCarthy and Kennicott

Deep in the heart of Wrangell-St. Elias National Park, McCarthy and its sister town Kennicott are quiet today, but abandoned log-hewn buildings and forgotten roads straying off to points unknown bear witness to a boom town past. In the early 1900s, thousands of miners swarmed to the site of the purest copper ore ever discovered, between the Kennicott Glacier and McCarthy Creek, and the mill town of Kennicott was erected. The Copper River and Northwest Railway (CR&NWR), though currently dubbed the "Can't Run and Never Will," did run from the Kennicott mill to the port at Cordova, until the mine closed in 1938, and the everyone rolled out as quickly as they came. McCarthy sprouted up in the boom days as a free-wheeling, sin-celebrating alternative to stick-in-the-mud Kennicott, a company town where strict rules of conduct were enforced. Today, the saloons and brothels are gone, but the towns remain as a base for adventurous backpackers and a place of quiet remoteness.

PRACTICAL INFORMATION AND SIGHTS **Backcountry Connection** (822-5292, in AK 800-478-5292) offers shuttle service to McCarthy from Glennallen and Chitina. *(Departs Glennallen M-Sa 7am, Chitina 8:30am. Returning van departs McCarthy at 4pm. One-way from Chitina $45, round-trip $75-85.)* **Wrangell Mountain Air** (554-4411 or 800-478-1160) flies to McCarthy twice daily from Chitina. *(9:05am and 2:45pm. $130 round-trip from Chitina; $120 from Glennallen.)* Relatively regular traffic makes hitchhiking one possibility, though getting stranded is another. (*Let's Go* recommends neither hitchhiking nor getting stranded.) If you're driving and you plan on staying across the river, it's a good idea leave heavy, bulky luggage in the car, and only bring into McCarthy or Kennicott what you really need.

The first building on the way up from the river houses the **McCarthy-Kennicott Historical Museum**, filled with pictures and artifacts from the mining days. *(Open in summer daily 10am-6pm. $1 donation.)* It's also a good place to get general info about the area and pick up a map for a walking tour of the two towns. Regular **shuttle buses** run the 5 mi. from McCarthy to Kennicott. The river's tram station carries schedules, and there are copies posted throughout both towns. *($8 round-trip.)* Another shuttle goes from the footbridge to Kennicott. *($10 round-trip.)* To hike to Kennicott, take the **Old Wagon Trail** instead of the dusty main road; look for the sign on the left shortly after turning toward Kennicott at the fork.

ACCOMMODATIONS, CAMPGROUNDS, AND FOOD The newly opened **Kennicott River Lodge and Hostel**, P.O. Box 83225, Fairbanks 99708 (554-4441, in winter 479-6822; http://www2.polarnet.com/~grosswlr), right before the footbridge at Mile 58.7 (look for sign), offers several pine-fresh cabins ($25) with comfortable beds (bring your own sleeping bag) and a striking view of Kennicott River and Glacier. The hostel has no showers, but a sauna and a hot tub are in the works. The only indoor alternative across the bridge is the **McCarthy Lodge** (554-4402; fax 554-4404; singles $95; doubles $110). Non-guests can shower ($5) at the lodge, or breakfast (7am-10am; $4-9) and sup ($15-23, served at 7pm) in a rustic dining room with antique-covered walls (open daily 7am-10pm; bar opens at 3:30pm). The **Copper Point Tram Station** (554-4401, open 7am-11pm) oversees camping in the parking lot just west of the river, before the bridge to McCarthy ($10). Camping is free at the lot ½ mi. farther back toward Chitina (pit toilets, no water). Since almost all the land around McCarthy and Kennicott is privately owned, and local drinking water comes from creeks, camping is prohibited in all areas east of the river except on land north of Kennicott.

McCarthy has no general store, though the **Nugget Gift Shop** (554-4412) sells some snacks and camping supplies (open daily 9am-8pm). Scrumptious and cheap feasts are served at **Roadside Potato Head,** in a colorfully decorated van next to the tram station. Enjoy hearty potatohead burritos ($6), burgers ($5), and fantastic coffee ($1), as the congenial staff gives advice on local activities (open daily 9am-9pm). **Tailor-Made Pizza,** in Kennicott, fashions great-fitting pizzas (small pepperoni $15), though you may wish the prices were off-the-rack (open daily 10am-10pm). The **McCarthy Ice House,** across from the lodge, serves both ice ($2.25) and fantastic ice cream in home-made waffle cones ($3); you choose the flavor and they blend the ingredients into the ice cream (open 8am-9pm).

ORGANIZED ADVENTURE If you go flightseeing anywhere in Alaska, do it here. Even a short flight to 16,390 ft. Mt. Blackburn and the surrounding glaciers offers soul-stunning views. **Wrangell Mountain Air** (554-4411, reservations 800-478-1160; http://www.alaskaone.com/wma), makes a 35-minute tour of the amazing icefalls of the **Kennicott** and **Root Glaciers** ($50). The best bargain, a 70-minute trip, goes up the narrow **Chitistone Canyon** to view the thundering **Chitistone Falls,** over 15 gla-ciers, and five mountain peaks ($95). There is a two-person minimum on all flights. **McCarthy Air** (554-4440) offers similar tours and rates; charter flights into the back-country can also be arranged. **Copper Oar** (800-523-4453; email howmoz@aol.com), at the end of the McCarthy Rd., runs a two-hour **whitewater rafting** trip down the Class III Kennicott River, providing all of the necessary rain gear ($45).

St. Elias Alpine Guides (in McCarthy 554-4445; in Anchorage 345-9048) leads a three-hour tour of the historic buildings of Kennicott, including the eerie, rotting, 14-story **mill** that was abandoned when workers fled to catch the last train out of town in 1938 ($25). Kennicott was purchased in the summer of 1998 by the Park Service, making tour availability and the fate of the mill as yet uncertain.

St. Elias Alpine Guides also lead a variety of guided hikes and explorations, includ-ing two-hour nature hikes to ice fields ($25), stunning half-day walks with crampons on the **Root Glacier** ($50), and a morning of exploring the ice caves and moraines of the **Kennicott Glacier** terminus ($35). They also offer a number of longer hikes and fly-in adventures. **Kennicott Wilderness Guides** (800-664-4537; fax 554-4444; email crkmwg@aol.com; http://www.alaskaone.com/k-mcguides), in Kennicott, provides a variety of similar options for similar rates, including an evening glacier tour ($50).

OUTDOORS Landlubbers will find **mountain biking** an excellent way to explore the area. The **Copper Point Tram Station** (554-4401), at the end of McCarthy Road, rents bikes. *($15 for 6hr., $25 per day.)* Leisurely bikers can take **Old Wagon Trail Road** between McCarthy and Kennicott, a mild 5 mi. climb to Kennicott with occasion views of the grit-encrusted glacier. A more strenuous 9 mi. ride runs along the wooded **Dan Creek Road** to **Nizina River,** where the broken **Old Nizina River Bridge** rests, a victim of glacial flooding.

Many hikers and backpackers use McCarthy and the McCarthy Road as a base. The park maintains **no trails** around McCarthy, but miners from decades past and millen-nia of game have established various routes and obscure roads; be sure to consult with a ranger station before setting out. The most common route is a 16 mi. hike past Kennicott to the **Root Glacier,** which follows road-bed and glacial moraine with three moderate stream crossings. It is possible, though a bit challenging, to mountain bike this route as well. A hike to **Dixie Pass** has the advantage of accessibility, starting from Mile 13 on the McCarthy Road; hikers should allow three to four days for the 24 mi. round-trip. The rough trail travels through lowlands covered with willows and higher elevations of arctic tundra. The **Goat Trail** demands a little more money and strong hiking expertise (fly-in required). The trail is a 25 mi. trek from **Lower Skolai Lake** to **Glacier Creek,** and traverses the ridge high above **Chitistone Canyon and Falls,** one of the park's most spectacular features.

ALASKA

Interior Alaska

Alaska's vast Interior sprawls between the Alaska Range to the south and the Brooks Range to the north, covering 166,000 sq. mi. of America's wildest and most stunning terrain. Most of the Interior alternates between flat forest and marshy, treeless tundra, punctuated by immense mountain ranges. Moose, grizzlies, wolves, caribou, Dall sheep, lynx, beavers, and hares roam the Interior's parks and wild country, while the Yukon River, the Tanana River, and hundreds of other waterways have created the sloughs, inlets, lakes, and bogs that sustain a huge waterfowl population. The unofficial state bird, the mosquito, vastly outnumbers all other animals in summer. Outside of Fairbanks, Alaska's second-largest city, the region is sparsely peopled.

🖐 HIGHLIGHTS OF INTERIOR ALASKA

- America's answer to an African game reserve, the vast and varied landscape of **Denali National Park** (see below) is the state's huge crown jewel.
- The search for character ends in ridiculously hospitable **Talkeetna** (see p. 456) or the remote outpost of **Eagle** (see p. 474).
- Beyond containing a couple hundred Northernmost Entities, **Fairbanks** (see p. 459) hosts the excellent **University of Alaska Museum** (see p. 465) and provides access to the far-off but fortifying **Circle Hot Springs** (see p. 470).

▇ Denali National Park and Preserve

Denali National Park's six million acres of tundra and taiga, spanning an area larger than Israel or the state of Massachusetts, make up an incredible expanse of unspoiled wilderness. Grizzly bears and golden eagles; Dall sheep and wolves; birds visiting each summer from as far away as Africa, Argentina, or Antarctica; and countless species of glorious wildflowers all motivated the park's establishment, and might even outshine its 20,320 ft. centerpiece, the largest mountain on earth.

Although the U.S. Geological Survey names the peak Mt. McKinley, most Alaskans either dub it Denali or simply call it "the Mountain." A more specific description is unnecessary—the pure-white upper reaches of the Mountain, visible from as far away as Anchorage, dominate the park's skyline like a second sun. The Mountain is so big that it manufactures its own weather: when moist air from the Pacific Ocean collides with the cold mountaintop, sudden storms encircle the summit. As a result, Denali's face is only visible about 30% of the time in summer, and many visitors to the park will never actually see the peak.

In summer, especially between mid-June and mid-August, crowds and lines at the entrance are unavoidable. Shuttle buses into the park only run from late May until mid-September, so the window of relatively crowd-free access is small. Mid- to late August is an excellent time to visit—fall colors peak, berries ripen, mosquito season has virtually ended, and September's snows have not yet arrived. Whenever you go, though, the keys to enjoying Denali are planning, patience, and a desire to explore. Rules and permit limits that can seem so frustrating upon arrival make it possible to escape into the untrammeled wilderness, leaving the swarms of humanity behind.

GETTING THERE

The park is easily reached by road or rail. The **George Parks Highway** (Rte. 3) makes for smooth and easy traveling to the park entrance north from Anchorage (240 mi. or about 4hr.) or south from Fairbanks (120 mi. or about 3hr.). Leading east away from the park, the **Denali Highway** (Rte. 8) starts 27 mi. south of the park entrance at Cantwell, and proceeds 136 mi. to Paxson (see p. 455). This gravel road takes far longer to traverse than one might expect, and it's closed in winter.

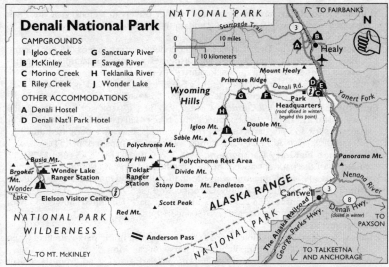

Denali National Park

CAMPGROUNDS
I Igloo Creek   G Sanctuary River
B McKinley   F Savage River
C Morino Creek   H Teklanika River
E Riley Creek   J Wonder Lake

OTHER ACCOMMODATIONS
A Denali Hostel
D Denali Nat'l Park Hotel

Several **shuttle bus** companies connect Denali with Anchorage and Fairbanks. **Parks Highway Express** (479-3065) runs to the park from Anchorage (4hr., $30) and from Fairbanks (3hr., $20); call for departure times. The **Alaska Backpacker Shuttle** (344-8775) runs between Anchorage and Denali ($40; bikes $5) and between Denali and Fairbanks ($20; bikes $5). **Fireweed Express** (458-8267) provides daily van service to Fairbanks ($25, round-trip $45, bikes $5). The **Alaska Railroad** (683-2233 or 800-544-0552) makes regular stops at Denali Station (open daily 10am-5pm), 1½ mi. from the park entrance, but is slower than shuttle services (see **Essentials: By Train,** p. 29). The railroad goes to: Fairbanks (1 per day, 3:45pm, $53) and Anchorage (1 per day; 12:30pm; $99, bikes $20). Reserve ahead, and check bags at least one hour before departure.

PRACTICAL INFORMATION

Buses: For **shuttle bus** info, see **Transportation within the Park,** below. The free **Riley Creek Loop Bus** runs between the visitor center, the Denali Park Hotel, the Alaska Railroad station, the Horseshoe Lake trailhead, and the Riley Creek campground (30min., 6am-9pm). Chalet-owned **courtesy buses** run from the Denali Park Hotel to the chalet near Lynx Creek Pizza, and to McKinley Village (6 mi. south of the park entrance) from 5am-midnight.

Taxis: Caribou Cab, 683-5000. **Denali Taxi Service,** 683-2504.

Summer Visitor Information: Denali Visitor Center (683-1266; http://www.nps.gov/dena), ½ mi. from the Parks Hwy. (Rte. 3). All travelers must stop here for orientation. The all-important **shuttle buses** are headquartered here. The park rangers provide ample maps and campsite info, interpretive walks, sled-dog demonstrations, and campfire talks. Their indispensable and free publication, the *Alpenglow,* includes event schedules and rates, as well as park history and biology. Most park privileges are distributed on a first-come, first-served basis; conduct all administrative business at the visitor center as early in the day as possible. An hourly 12min. **slide program** features the history of Denali and stunning pictures of the park. Theater open daily mid-Apr. to Sept. 7am-8pm. Lines for the shuttle often start forming by 6:30am, and shuttles depart as early as 5am in peak season. Lockers 50¢. **Eielson Visitor Center,** 66 mi. into the park, is accessible only by shuttle bus. Friendly rangers lead informative 45min. **tundra walks** daily at 1:30pm. No food is available here. None. Open daily in summer 9am-early evening. Write to **Denali National Park and Preserve,** P.O. Box 9, or the **Alaska Public Lands Information Center** (see p. 44).

ALASKA

Winter Visitor Information: Before any winter travels in Denali, visit the **Park Headquarters** (683-2294) at Mile 3.2 and on the left side of the park road. Open M-F 8am-4:30pm.

Fees and Permits: The Denali Visitor Center collects **entrance fees** ($5 per person, families $10; good for one week), and dispenses **permits** for camping in **campgrounds** (sites $6-12) or in the **backcountry** (free).

Bank: None in the park or vicinity. **Larry's Service Station,** 11 mi. north of the park entrance in Healy, has a temperamental **ATM**. Most park services take credit cards.

Equipment Rental: Denali Outdoor Center, P.O. Box 170 (683-1925), at Parks Mile 238.9, just north of the park entrance, rents bikes. Half-day $25; full day $40; 5 or more days for $35 per day. (Unlike private vehicles, bikes *are* permitted on all 89 miles of the park road.) Also leads rafting and kayaking trips (see p. 454).

Laundromat: McKinley Campground, P.O. Box 340, Healy 99743 (683-2379), 11 mi. north of the park entrance. The only public laundromat around. Wash $2; dry $1. Tokens sold daily June-Aug. 8am-10pm; in winter 8am-8pm. Machines 24hr.

Public Showers: At the **McKinley Campground** (see above). $2.50 per 7½min. **McKinley Mercantile** (683-2215), 1½ mi. into the park. Unlimited showers $3 with $5 key deposit. Showers open daily 7:30am-8:30pm.

Emergency: 911.

Medical Services: Healy Clinic (683-2211), 11 mi. north of the park entrance. Open only May-Sept. M-F 9am-5pm. Registered nurse on call 24hr.

Post Office: (683-2291), next to Denali National Park Hotel, 1 mi. from the visitor center. Open May-Sept. M-F 8:30am-5pm, Sa 10am-1pm; Oct.-Apr. M-Sa 10am-1pm. **ZIP Code:** 99755-9998.

Area Code: 907.

TRANSPORTATION WITHIN THE PARK

Denali National Park commands respect. Moving through it can be a complex, time-consuming, and confusing process. In order to protect the park's environment and to limit human impact on the land and wildlife, only the first 14 miles of the park are accessible by private vehicle; the remaining 75 miles of dirt road can be reached only by shuttle bus, camper bus, or bicycle (unless you're driving to the Teklanika campground, which requires a special permit). There is no required permit for driving or dayhiking in the first 14 mi., but you must pay a **$5 entrance fee** ($10 per family), good for one week. Because 98% of the park's landscape and wildlife lie beyond Mile 14 of the park road, a ride on the park shuttle is well worth abandoning the family camper or trusty 4x4.

There are two different services that plumb the park's interior, both in reconstituted schoolbuses. **Shuttle buses** leave from the visitor center (daily 5am-6pm), pause at the well-nigh inevitable sighting of any major mammal ("MOOOOOSE!"), and turn back at various points along the park road: **Toklat,** Mile 53 ($12.50); **Eielson,** Mile 66 ($21); **Wonder Lake,** Mile 85 ($27); and **Kantishna,** Mile 89 ($31). Ages 13-16 ride for half-price; ages 12 and under ride for free. Most buses are wheelchair accessible. The best views of Denali arise beyond Eielson, so if the sun and the wildlife are out, the 11-hour round-trip to Wonder Lake may be a good time investment. This long haul can be an utter washout, however, when Denali isn't visible—and that's true 70% of the time during the summer. In that case, you're probably better off getting off at Eielson and spending those saved three hours hiking instead.

Camper buses ($15.50) transport only those visitors with **campground permits** and **backcountry permits** (see **Practical Information,** above), and move faster than the shuttle buses. Both will stop to pick up dayhikers along the road on the way to the visitor center. Camper buses leave the center five times daily at 6:40, 10:40am, 2:40, 4:40, and 6:10pm. The final bus stays overnight at Wonder Lake and heads back at noon.

Tickets can be purchased by phone (272-7275 or 800-622-7275; fax 264-4684), or in person at the visitor center within two days of departure. Calling ahead is strongly recommended, since bus space fills up quickly. If you do wait until you reach the park to purchase tickets, arrive at the visitor center as close to opening (7am) as possible. Two highly valuable investments are the *Denali Road Guide* (available at the visitor center for $5) and **binoculars** (rented at the hotel gift shop for $6 per 24hr.).

ACCOMMODATIONS AND CAMPGROUNDS

With one exception, accommodations and campgrounds within the park are open in the summer only. Hotel rooms in or near the park are exorbitant. **Denali Park Resorts,** 241 W. Ship Creek Ave., Anchorage 99501 (800-279-2653), runs the park's tourist services, including the **Denali National Park Hotel** (683-9214), centrally located near the railroad station, airstrip, trails, park headquarters, and a grocery store. The hotel is not a budget option (singles $149; doubles $159). It's far cheaper to stay at the hostel or at one of the park's wonderful campgrounds, listed below.

Campers must obtain a **permit** from the visitor center, and may stay for up to 14 nights in park campgrounds. Forty percent of the sites at four of the seven campgrounds may be reserved by calling 800-622-7275 (272-7275 from Anchorage). If possible, make reservations in advance. First-come, first-served sites are distributed at the visitor center—get there up to a few days early for a better chance of grabbing a site.

Amenities are sparse in Denali. There are no hookups and only one dump station, at Riley Creek. RV drivers can pay $12 per night to park at **Riley Creek, Savage River,** and **Teklanika River,** or they can head to the numerous RV parks huddled near the park entrance. All campgrounds within the park are **wheelchair accessible,** except for Igloo Creek and Sanctuary River.

Denali Hostel, P.O. Box 801 (683-1295; fax 683-2106). Go 9.6 mi. north of the park entrance, turn left onto Otto Lake Rd., and drive 1.3 mi., continuing straight after the golf course (don't veer left); it's the 2nd house on the right, the log house with blue trim. Beautiful setting (oh, the sunsets!), international clientele, and helpful owners. Clean rooms, full kitchen, TV room, showers, and coin-operated laundry. Morning shuttles to the park, daily pick-ups from the visitor center at 5 and 9pm, and from the Alaska Railroad (Anchorage train only). Beds $24. Linen $3. Check-in 5:30-10pm. No curfew. No credit cards. Reservations wise. Open May-Sept.

Riley Creek, Mile 0.4 Denali Park Rd. The only year-round campground in Denali (no water in winter). All sites assigned at the visitor center. Close to the highway and the visitor center, Riley Creek is louder and more congested than the other campgrounds. Piped water, flush toilets, and sewage dump keep campers from getting riled up. 100 sites: $12.

Morino Creek, Mile 1.9 Denali Park Rd., next to the train tracks. 60 2-person sites for backpackers without vehicles. Water, chemical toilets. No open fires. Nearest showers at the Mercantile, ¼ mi. back up the road (see **Practical Information,** above). Backpackers who lack vehicles and are waiting for permits can set up camp here. Many travelers stay in Morino for the first day while they use the shuttle bus to preview potential campsites within the park. Self-registered sites $6.

Savage River, Mile 13 Denali Park Rd. High, dry country with easy access to popular Primrose Ridge. Complimentary shuttle to and from the visitor center. Flush toilets and water. Last area accessible by car without an access permit. 33 sites: $12.

Sanctuary River, Mile 23 Denali Park Rd. Quiet, wooded campsite with views of the river and neighboring mountains. Chemical toilets, but no water. No fires. Accessible only by bus. 7 tent sites: $6.

Teklanika River, Mile 29 Denali Park Rd. Popular with members of the Winnebago tribe. Piped water and flush toilets. Accessible by shuttle bus or by vehicle with permit. 53 tent and RV sites: $12. Minimum 3-night stay for vehicle campers.

Igloo Creek, Mile 34 Denali Park Rd. On lower ground, and therefore more likely to invite swarms of mosquitoes, and thus *less* likely to invite swarms of tourists; quiet and secluded. Pit toilets, no water. No fires. Accessible only by bus. 7 tent sites: $6.

Wonder Lake, Mile 85 Denali Park Rd. You are a happy camper indeed if you end up at Wonder Lake on a clear day. Spectacular, soul-searing views of the Mountain, a mere 27 mi. away. Piped water, flush toilets. No vehicles. About a kabillion mosquitoes, give or take a few zillion. 28 tent sites: $12. Wheelchair accessible.

ALASKA

FOOD

Food in Denali is expensive, making groceries a fruitfully frugal idea. Meager provisions are available from **McKinley Mercantile** (683-9246), at Mile 2 on Denali Park Rd. (open daily 7:30am-9:30pm). The **Lynx Creek Park-Mart** (683-2548; open June-Sept. daily 7am-11:30pm) and **Denali General Store** (683-2920; open May-Sept. daily 8am-9pm), 1 mi. north of the park entrance, stock similarly priced items. Once you board that park bus, there is no food available, anywhere.

Denali Smoke Shack (683-SMOK/7665), north of park entrance at Mile 238.5. Real Alaskan barbecue. The Smoke Shack's hip young waitstaff, friendly dog, decently priced food, and large vegetarian menu make it a local favorite. Cajun chicken sandwich $8; BBQ beef sandwich $9. Popular late-night scene with full bar and late hours. Open daily 5:30am-10:30am and noon-midnight. Bar open noon-2am.

Denali Crow's Nest & Overlook Bar and Grill (683-2723), 1 mi. north of park entrance, on the right. High on a hill, the Crow's Nest affords eagle-eye views of Mt. Healy. The fantastic burgers come with fries so greasy you may be able to see your reflection ($9). Draft beer from $3; the Frontier (an Alaskan specialty) $4.50. Grill open daily 11am-11pm; bar open until about 1am. Courtesy shuttle until 11pm.

McKinley/Denali Steak and Salmon Bake (683-2733), 1 mi. north of the park entrance, just after the Crow's Nest. A rustic lodge serving such hearty breakfasts as all-you-can-eat blueberry pancakes ($5), family-style. Call for free shuttle. Open daily 5am-10pm.

Lynx Creek Pizza (683-2547), 1 mi. north of the park entrance. Cheese-heavy pizza with a great crust (16 in. pie from $17.50), and imposing portions of Italian favorites ($7-8.50). More lodge decor! Daily lunch specials include a slice with Caesar Salad ($7). Open daily 11am-11pm. To get a beer with that, order to go and try the **Lynx Creek Pub** next door, open 4pm-midnight.

Denali Park Hotel (683-2215). The only sit-down dining option within the park. The **Dining Room** serves breakfast and lunch ($6-10) and dinner ($14-20). Open daily 7am-2:30pm and 5-10pm. The **Whistle Stop Snack Shop** vends pre-fab burgers ($6) and cold sandwiches ($5-7), but no fried green tomatoes. Open daily 5am-11pm. The **Espresso Station** sells muffins and cookies ($2) and espresso ($1.75).

DAYHIKING

The best way to experience Denali is to get off the bus and explore the land—feel the sun shining on your face, the wind whipping through your hair, the mosquitoes feasting on your blood.

Beyond Mile 14, the point which only shuttle and camper buses can cross, there are **no trails**. The park's backcountry philosophy rests on the idea that independent wandering creates more rewards and less impact than trail-bound hiking. In an effort to disperse hikers as widely as possible, rangers will not recommend specific routes, although they do suggest areas that meet hikers' desires and abilities. Only those who disembark from the bus can sit among wildflowers, meander across untouched tundra, feel the waters of a braided stream, or bask in the sun on a mountaintop.

You can begin dayhiking from anywhere along the park road by riding the shuttle bus to a suitable starting point and asking the driver to let you off. Don't feel obligated to get off at one of the designated rest stops (about every hour along the routes); drivers will be happy to drop you off anywhere that isn't restricted. Once you've wandered to your heart's content, head back to the road and flag down a shuttle bus heading in your direction. The first couple of buses that pass may be full, but it's rare to wait more than half an hour or so to find a ride. Many of the buses stop running fairly early, so be sure to check when the last buses will be passing your area.

One popular destination is **Primrose Ridge,** beginning at Mile 16 on the right side of the road. The area is bespangled with wildflowers and has spectacular views of the Alaska Range and the carpeted emerald valley below. A walk north from Mile 14

MCI Spoken Here

Worldwide Calling Made Simple

For more information or to apply for a Card call: **1-800-955-0925**

Outside the U.S., call MCI collect (reverse charge) at: **1-916-567-5151**

International Calling As Easy As Possible.

The MCI Card with WorldPhone Service is designed specifically to keep you in touch with the people that matter the most to you.

The MCI Card with WorldPhone Service....

- Provides access to the US and other countries worldwide.
- Gives you customer service 24 hours a day
- Connects you to operators who speak your language
- Provides you with MCI's low rates and no sign-up fees

For more information or to apply for a Card call:
1-800-955-0925

Outside the U.S., call MCI collect (reverse charge) at:
1-916-567-5151

Pick Up the Phone, Pick Up the Miles.

You earn frequent flyer miles when you travel internationally, why not when you call internationally? Callers can earn frequent flyer miles if they sign up with one of MCI's airline partners:

- American Airlines
- Continental Airlines
- Delta Airlines
- Hawaiian Airlines
- Midwest Express Airlines
- Northwest Airlines
- Southwest Airlines
- United Airlines
- USAirways

Your MCI Worldphone Access Numbers

COUNTRY	WORLDPHONE TOLL-FREE ACCESS #
#Singapore	8000-112-112
#Slovak Republic (CC)	00421-00112
#Slovenia	080-8808
#South Africa (CC)	0800-99-0011
#Spain (CC)	900-99-0014
#Sri Lanka	440100
(Outside of Colombo, dial 01 first)	
#St. Lucia ÷	1-800-888-8000
#St. Vincent	1-800-888-8000
#Sweden (CC) ♦	020-795-922
#Switzerland (CC) ♦	0800-89-0222
#Syria	0800
#Taiwan (CC) ♦	0080-13-4567
#Thailand ★	001-999-1-2001
#Trinidad & Tobago ÷	1-800-888-8000
#Turkey (CC) ♦	00-8001-1177
#Turks and Caicos ÷	1-800-888-8000
#Ukraine (CC) ÷	8♥10-013
#United Arab Emirates ♦	800-111
#United Kingdom (CC) To call using BT ■	0800-89-0222
To call using C&W ■	0500-89-0222
#United States (CC)	1-800-888-8000
#Uruguay	000-412
#U.S. Virgin Islands (CC)	1-800-888-8000
#Vatican City (CC)	172-1022
#Venezuela (CC) ÷ ♦	800-1114-0
Vietnam ●	1201-1022
Yemen	008-00-102

#	Automation available from most locations.
(CC)	Country-to-country calling available to/from most international locations.
✷	Limited availability.
▶	Wait for second dial tone.
◀	When calling from public phones, use phones marked LADATEL.
■	International communications carrier.
★ ♦	Not available from public pay phones.
	Public phones may require deposit of coin or phone card for dial tone.
● ▲ ÷	Local service fee in U.S. currency required to complete call. Regulation does not permit intra-Japan calls.
	Available from most major cities

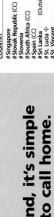

And, it's simple to call home.

1. Dial the WorldPhone toll-free access number of the country you're calling from (listed inside).

2. Follow the voice instructions in your language of choice or hold for a WorldPhone operator.
   - Enter or give the operator your MCI Card number or call collect.

3. Enter or give the WorldPhone operator your home number.

4. Share your adventures with your family!

MCI

The MCI Card with WorldPhone Service... The easy way to call when traveling worldwide.

MCI Calling Card
123 456 7890 1234
J.D. SMITH
WorldPhone

For more information or to apply for a Card call:
1-800-955-0925

Outside the U.S., call MCI collect (reverse charge) at:
1-916-567-5151

Please cut out and save this reference guide for convenient U.S. and worldwide calling with the MCI Card with WorldPhone Service.

COUNTRY	WORLDPHONE TOLL-FREE ACCESS #
American Samoa	633-2MCI (633-2624)
#Antigua	1-800-888-8000
(available from public card phones only)	#2
#Argentina (CC)	0800-5-1002
#Aruba ÷	800-888-8
#Australia (CC) ◆ To call using OPTUS ■	1-800-551-111
To call using TELSTRA ■	1-800-881-100
#Austria (CC) ◆	022-903-012
#Bahamas	1-800-888-8000
#Bahrain	1-800-888-8000
#Barbados	1-800-888-8000
#Belarus (CC) From Brest, Vitebsk, Grodno, Minsk	8-800-103
From Gomel and Mogilev	8-10-800-103
#Belgium (CC) ◆	0800-10012
#Belize From Hotels	815
From Payphones	557
#Bermuda ÷	1-800-888-8000
#Bolivia (CC) ◆	0-800-2222
#Brazil (CC)	000-8012
#British Virgin Islands ÷	1-800-888-8000
#Brunei	800-011
#Bulgaria	00800-0001
#Canada (CC)	1-800-888-8000
#Cayman Islands	1-800-888-8000
#Chile (CC) To call using CTC ■	800-207-300
To call using ENTEL ■	800-360-180
#China ✦ To call using a Mandarin-speaking Operator	108-12
	108-17
#Colombia (CC)	980-16-0001
Collect Access in Spanish	980-16-1000
#Costa Rica ◆	0800-012-2222
#Cote D'Ivoire	1001
#Croatia (CC) ★	0800-22-0112
#Cyprus ◆	080-90000
#Czech Republic (CC) ◆	00-42-000112
#Denmark (CC) ◆	8001-0022
#Dominica	1-800-888-8000
#Dominican Republic	1-800-888-8000
Collect Access	1121
#Ecuador (CC) ÷ Collect Access in Spanish	999-170
#Egypt (CC) ◆ (Outside of Cairo, dial 02 first)	355-5770
El Salvador	800-1767

— FOLD —

COUNTRY	WORLDPHONE TOLL-FREE ACCESS #
#Federated States of Micronesia	624
#Fiji	004-890-1002
#Finland (CC) ◆	08001-102-80
#France (CC) ◆	0800-99-0019
#French Antilles (CC) (includes Martinique, Guadeloupe)	0800-99-0019
#French Guiana (CC)	0-800-99-0011
#Gabon	00-005
#Gambia ◆	00-1-99
#Germany (CC)	0130-0012
#Greece (CC) ◆	00-800-1211
#Grenada ÷	1-800-888-8000
#Guam (CC)	1-800-888-8000
#Guatemala (CC)	99-99-189
Guyana	177
#Haiti ÷	193
Collect Access in French/Creole	190
Honduras ÷	8000-122
#Hong Kong (CC)	800-96-1121
#Hungary (CC) ◆	00▼800-01411
#Iceland (CC) ◆	800-9002
#India (CC) ◆	000-127
Collect Access	000-126
#Indonesia (CC) ◆	001-801-11
#Iran ÷	(SPECIAL PHONES ONLY)
#Ireland (CC)	1-800-55-1001
#Israel (CC)	1-800-940-2727
#Italy (CC) ◆	172-1022
#Jamaica ÷	1-800-888-8000
Collect Access (from public phones)	873
#Japan (CC) ◆ To call using KDD ■	00539-121▼
To call using IDC ■	0066-55-121
To call using ITJ ■	0044-11-121
#Jordan	18-800-001
#Kazakhstan (CC)	8-800-131-4321
#Kenya ◆ (Special Hotels only)	08001
#Korea ✦ To call using KT ■	009-14
To call using DACOM ■	0309-14
Phone Booths÷ Press red button, 03, then ★	
Military Bases	550-2255
#Kuwait	800-MCI (800-624)

— FOLD —

COUNTRY	WORLDPHONE TOLL-FREE ACCESS #
#Lebanon Collect Access	600-MCI (600-624)
#Liechtenstein (CC) ◆	0800-89-0222
#Luxembourg (CC)	0800-0112
#Macao	0800-131
#Macedonia (CC)	99800-4266
#Malaysia (CC) ◆	1-800-80-0012
#Malta	0800-89-0120
#Marshall Islands	1-800-888-8000
#Mexico ▲ Avantel	01-800-021-8000
Telmex ▲	001-800-674-7000
Collect Access in Spanish	01-800-021-1000
#Monaco (CC) ◆	800-90-019
#Montserrat	1-800-888-8000
#Morocco	00-211-0012
#Netherlands (CC) ◆	0800-022-9122
#Netherlands Antilles (CC) ÷	001-800-888-8000
#New Zealand (CC)	000-912
#Nicaragua (CC)	166
(Outside of Managua, dial 02 first)	
Collect Access in Spanish	
From any public payphone	*2
#Norway (CC) ◆	800-19912
#Pakistan	00-900-12-001
#Panama	108
Military Bases	2810-108
#Papua New Guinea (CC)	05-07-19140
#Paraguay ÷	05-812-800
#Peru	0-800-500-10
#Philippines (CC) ◆ To call using PLDT ■	105-14
To call using PHILCOM ■	1026-14
Collect Access via PLDT in Filipino	1237-77
Collect Access via ICC in Filipino	105-15
#Poland (CC) ÷	00-800-111-21-22
#Portugal (CC) ÷	05-017-1234
#Puerto Rico (CC)	1-800-888-8000
#Qatar ★	0800-012-77
#Romania (CC) ÷	01-800-1800
#Russia (CC) ÷ ◆ To call using ROSTELCOM ■	747-3322
(For Russian speaking operator)	747-3320
Collect Access via ROSTELCOM ■	747-3322
To call using SOVINTEL ■	960-2222
#Saipan (CC) ÷	950-1022
#San Marino (CC) ◆	172-1022
#Saudi Arabia (CC) ÷	1-800-11

If you're stuck for cash on your travels, don't panic. Millions of people trust Western Union to transfer money in minutes to 153 countries and over 45,000 locations worldwide. Our record of safety and reliability is second to none. So when you need money in a hurry, call Western Union.

WESTERN UNION | MONEY TRANSFER®

The fastest way to send money worldwide.®

along the **Savage River** provides a colorful, scenic stroll through this valley. A rigorous ascent up the tundra of **Dome Mountain,** at Mile 60, will reward hikers with close views of the Alaska Range, and on a clear day, Denali. The area surrounding **Wonder Lake** (Mile 85) is marshy and dense with willows but offers what may be the best view of the Mountain in the park. When trapped in visitor center limbo waiting for a hot date with the shuttle bus, don't despair. **Horseshoe Lake Trail** provides an easy-to-moderate 1½ mi. walk, with beautiful views of the mountains around a moose-attracting oxbow lake. The **Rock Creek Trail** runs 2.3 mi. from the hotel toward Park Headquarters, where the sled-dog demonstrations are held. Although conveniently located, its proximity to the road makes it noisy for a hike. The more challenging **Mt. Healy Overlook Trail** starts from the hotel parking lot and climbs steeply for 2½ mi. to an impressive view of the valley. The particularly ambitious can continue up the ridge to the 5700 ft. summit.

If you seek a more structured hiking experience, the park rangers will oblige. **Discovery hikes** ("disco hikes" to those in the know) are guided three- to five-hour hikes, departing on special buses from the visitor center. Topics vary; a ranger might lead you on a cross-country scramble or a moose trail excursion, providing a comprehensive introduction to local wildlife, flowers, and geological formations. The hikes are free but require reservations and a bus ticket fee. More sedate 45-minute **tundra walks** leave from Eielson Visitor Center daily at 1:30pm, and many other talks and naturalist programs are posted at the visitor center.

EXPLORING THE BACKCOUNTRY

Like boxing without gloves, like black coffee without a drop of sweetener, Denali's backcountry is the Real Thing. There are **no trails** in the backcountry. Intrepid outdoorspeople are free to explore this trackless wilderness on their own terms, with only grit, resilience, and ultra-high-tech Gore-Tex gear to aid them. While dayhiking is unlimited and requires no permit, only two to twelve backpackers can camp at one time in each of the park's 43 units. Overnight stays in the backcountry require a **free permit,** available no earlier or later than one day in advance at the **backcountry desk** in the visitor center. The **quota board** there reports which units are still available. Type-A hikers line up outside as early as 6:30am to grab permits for popular units. Talk to rangers and research your choices with the handy *Backcountry Description Guides* and *The Backcountry Companion*, available at the visitor center bookstore.

The park covers a variety of terrain, with varying implications for hiking. **River bars** are level and rocky, offering very good footing for hikers but potentially difficult stream crossings. **Low tundra,** in brushy, soggy areas above the treeline, is not easily navigable and makes for exasperating hiking under insect-infested conditions. **Alpine tundra,** or **dry tundra,** is higher and drier, meaning fewer mosquitoes. Generally, the southern reaches of the park contain dry tundra and river bars, opening wide vistas of the park. The northern reaches are brushier but include high points with incredible views of the Mountain. Some of the most enjoyable hiking and wildlife-viewing awaits in the middle of the park, near the **Toklat River** and **Polychrome Pass.**

The rangers will usually leave two or three zones open to unlimited backcountry camping, but these areas tend to be thick with mosquitoes and set back from the road behind other units. Some units are temporarily closed after a fresh wildlife kill or a bear encounter. **Sable Pass,** a veritable bear bastion, has been off-limits for years.

Backcountry campers must stay within the zone for which they registered, pitching tents at least ½ mi. from the road, and out of sight. The visitor center sells essential **topographic maps** ($4). Before campers head out, rangers provide a short introduction to bear management, and enforce some quality time with the center's interactive **backcountry simulator,** which allows virtual hikers to react to a melange of potentially dangerous wilderness situations. All but two zones require that food be carried in **bear resistant food containers (BRFC),** available for free at the backcountry desk. These are bulky things; be sure to leave space in your backpack (LSIYB).

McKinley or Not McKinley—That Is the Question

History has not been generous to William McKinley, the 25th president of the United States. Washington D.C. has no McKinley Memorial. Few have celebrated McKinley's birthday since he last marked the occasion himself in 1901. While Teddy Roosevelt, McKinley's Vice President and successor, is immortalized on South Dakota's Mt. Rushmore, McKinley doesn't even appear on a dime.

In Alaska, however, an attempt to memorialize McKinley was once made that would dwarf puny Mt. Rushmore. In 1896, a Princeton-educated prospector named the highest mountain in North America "Mt. McKinley," and with a little pressure on Congress, the name was made official. Of course, the mountain had a name long before any Ivy-league Republicans laid eyes on it. Athabascans, the native people of Alaska's Interior, called the 20,320 ft. giant Denali: "the Great One" or "the High One." Most Alaskans and many visitors use this name today.

The mountain certainly deserves its ancient title. At 18,000 ft. from base to summit, Denali has the greatest total altitude gain of any mountain in the world. Mt. Everest—originally Sagarmatha or Jomolungma—is higher, but rises only 11,000 ft. from its base on the Plateau of Tibet. In the same way that an adult is taller than the child who stands on a chair to get higher, Denali is the largest mountain on earth. In 1980, an official effort to rename the mountain Denali failed, but as a compromise the land on which it stands was designated Denali National Park. Today, almost everyone ignores the U.S. Geological Survey and uses the original Athabascan name. The upshot of all this is that you can comfortably call Denali— or Mt. McKinley—by many names. To avoid controversy altogether, call it simply "the Mountain," or just point. Everyone will know what you're talking about.

Denali's backcountry provides the ideal conditions for at least two major hazards: **hypothermia** and **mosquitoes.** With the park's cool, often drizzly weather and its abundant rivers and standing water, your feet *will* get wet, and hypothermia can set in quickly and quietly. It's a good idea to talk with the rangers about prevention and warning signs. The mosquito larvae thrive in the standing water and marshy ground, and grow to be nice and plump. They *will* find you, and when they do, impenetrable mosquito netting or clothes stinking of DEET can preserve your skin and sanity.

BIKES, RAFTS, KAYAKS, PLANES, AND DOG SLEDS

Unlike private vehicles, **bicycles** are permitted on the entire length of the park road, making them a perfect way to escape the shuttle-bus blues. Park at Savage River and ride into the heart of Denali. Most of the road is unpaved, so thick tires work well. Off-road biking is not permitted anywhere in the park. For bike rental info, see **Practical Information**, p. 450.

Several **rafting** companies run the rapids of Denali's Nenana River. The **Denali Outdoor Center** (see p. 450) boasts the most experienced guides on the river, and is the only source for drysuits—something you'll rapidly come to appreciate if you take a spill into the 36°F (2°C) water. A two-hour canyon run costs $45 per person in an oar boat, and $55 if you want to help paddle. The DOC also runs guided **kayak** tours for $75, with zero experience necessary. **McKinley Raft Tours** (683-2392) and **Denali Raft Adventures** (683-2234) offer rafting trips for $45, but with big, orange mustang suits or raingear instead of drysuits.

Flightseeing tours are a wonderful way to see the Mountain, especially on a clear day, but the park is ironically not the best place to do this. **Denali Air** (683-2261) will take you up for one hour ($160), but the town of Talkeetna, south of the park, has companies that offer more trips at lower rates (see p. 458).

Cross-country skiing and **dog sledding** allow visitors to see the park during the winter. Despite 20-hour nights and temperatures below -40°F, many people of perfect mental health consider winter the most beautiful time of year. If you plan to travel through Denali in the winter, you are *strongly encouraged* visit the visitor center and inform them of your route.

■ Denali Highway (Rte. 8)

The breathtaking Denali Highway runs west from **Paxson**, 80 mi. south of Delta Junction on the Richardson Hwy. (Rte. 4), to **Cantwell,** 27 mi. south of the Denali National Park entrance. Along the way, it skirts the foothills of the Alaska Range amid countless lakes and streams teeming with grayling, trout, and arctic char. Fortunately for solitary sorts, the highway's 115 mi. of gravel scare away most tour buses and RVs. This makes it a scenic road-less-traveled to Denali, while pristine free campgrounds and unique geological formations along the way make the road a destination in itself. Bullet-riddled road signs attest to the popularity of hunting in this area, but mountain bikers, hikers, fishermen, bird-watchers, and archeologists also frequent the region. Glaciers and permafrost have been up to geological mischief, creating bizarre mounds, ridges, and basins all along the highway. For explanations of these features and general highway info, pick up the Bureau of Land Management (BLM) guide *Denali Highway Points of Interest,* available at most local roadhouses, visitor centers, and pit stops. The Denali Highway is **closed** from October to mid-May. Except for the 21 mi. west of Paxson, it is entirely gravel. Rocks and potholes vigorously assert their presence along some stretches, wreaking havoc on windshields and suspension systems, but the road is well-maintained for the most part. **Mile markers,** where they exist, measure the distance from Paxson.

The **Tangle Lakes National Register District,** between Miles 17 and 37, serves as a base for mountain bikers, ATVers, and birders. Pick up the BLM's free *Trail Map and Guide to the Tangle Lakes National Register District* at the Tangle River Inn (see below) for trail details. The area is ecologically fragile and contains 400 archeological sites. For more info contact the **Bureau of Land Management (BLM)** at Box 147, Glennallen, AK 99588 (822-3217; http://www.glennallen.ak.blm.gov). At Mile 21 is the **Tangle Lakes Campground** (toilets, water pump), and ¼ mi. farther on is the **Tangle River Campground** (toilets, no water). Both are scenic and free, providing easy access to the 30 mi. **Delta River Canoe Route,** with one difficult stretch of Class III rapids, and the **Upper Tangle Lakes Canoe Route,** an easier paddle beginning at **Tangle River** and ending at **Dickey Lake,** 9 mi. to the south. Topographic maps are available from the BLM. For those who crave the great indoors, the **Tangle River Inn** (822-7304, 259-3970, in winter 895-4022), at Mile 20 across the highway from the boat launch, has private rooms ($45) and bunkhouse beds ($25) with shared baths and a common room with pool table, TV, and VCR; book ahead. The inn offers a cafe, a bar, gas, and canoe rental ($3 per hr., $24 per day). Birders, fishermen, and flora fans flock to the **Tangle River Lodge** (259-7302), at Mile 22, whose owners have the lowdown on the area's wildlife and canoe routes. The area hosts 140 different species of birds, including the arctic warbler and Smith's longspur (see http://www.alaskan.com/tanglelakes/cklist.htm for a **birding checklist**), and some of the best car-accessible arctic grayling fishing in the state.

Spectacular mountain scenery lines the rest of the highway, interrupted by an occasional roadhouse or cafe. The turn-off at Mile 35 leads to the **Maclaren Summit** (4086 ft.), from which the **Maclaren River** is visible flowing from the **Maclaren Glacier,** with the Alaska Range and wildflowers all around. At Mile 80, the highway crosses the beautiful **Susitna River.** At Mile 95, an unmarked turn-off and a gradual 600 yard ascent lead to a prime view of **Mt. Deborah** and the valley below. The turn-off at Mile 130, 5 mi. east of Cantwell, grants an excellent view of **Denali** on rare clear days.

▓ George Parks Highway (Rte. 3)

Joining the Glenn Highway (Rte. 1) 35 mi. from Anchorage, the George Parks Highway (Rte. 3) runs 323 mi. north to Fairbanks, linking Alaska's two largest cities. Called simply "The Parks" by locals, Rte. 3 passes through some of Alaska's finest, most mountainous country. Its two lanes are paved and in excellent condition, except for a few frostheaves. **Denali National Park** (see p. 448) and the spur road to **Talkeetna** (see below) are a few hours north of Anchorage on this route, so most tourists to

Alaska's Interior drive the Parks. With moose sightings, wolf crossings, and spectacular mountain views, the 113 mi. drive from Anchorage to Talkeetna is a visual feast.

At Mile 39.5, the Parks runs north past the town of **Wasilla,** offering the **last stop for a bank** until Fairbanks. A little farther on, the highway passes several scenic **state campgrounds** and **state recreation areas,** offering unlimited canoeing opportunities, although many of the lakes are also open to noisy jetskis and motorboats.

■ Talkeetna

Talkeetna (tah-KEET-nah) is a Tanaina word meaning "rivers of plenty" and an apt name for this eclectic settlement plunked at the confluence of the Talkeetna, Susitna, and Chulitna Rivers, with access to all five kinds of salmon. A cluster of narrow dirt roads lined with log cabins and clapboard stores, Talkeetna is home to an off-beat population. The wayward traveler may meet an amputee craftsman with a husky-pulled wheelchair, a woman who boasts of having skinned and cleaned 27 moose in a single winter, or a young man who scaled Denali at age 12. In 1923, President Warren G. Harding died after stopping in Talkeetna to hammer in the golden spike completing the railroad between Anchorage and Fairbanks. (The First Lady, on hearing of her husband's death, reportedly questioned, "How can they tell?") There was no evidence of foul play, but the rumor that President Harding was poisoned at the Fairview Inn has become a perverse point of local pride.

Because of its proximity to **Denali National Park,** only 60 mi. by air to the north, Talkeetna is a popular flight departure point for would-be climbers of the Mountain. Every year between April and July, over 1200 mountaineers from around the globe converge on Talkeetna with stories to tell, creating an unlikely international village. From the town, most climbers fly to a base camp on the Kahiltna Glacier at 7200 ft. After that, it's all uphill.

ORIENTATION AND PRACTICAL INFORMATION

Talkeetna lies at the end of the **Talkeetna Spur Rd.,** 14 mi. east off the Parks Hwy. from Mile 98.5. The town is 113 mi. north of Anchorage, 139 mi. south of the Denali National Park entrance, and 260 mi. south of Fairbanks.

Trains: The **Alaska Railroad** station (733-2268, 265-2615, or 800-544-0552; email reservations@akrr.com; http://www.akrr.com) is a platform ½ mi. south of town behind the Latitude 62° Motel. 1 train per day to: Denali ($60, off-season $53); Anchorage ($59, off-season $49); Fairbanks ($108, off-season $104).

Shuttle Buses: Parks Highway Express (479-3065). To: Anchorage ($25); Denali ($30); Fairbanks ($49). **Talkeetna Shuttle Service** (733-1725 or 888-288-6008; fax 733-2222; email tshuttle@alaska.net) runs daily service from Anchorage to Talkeetna ($40). **Alaska Backpacker Shuttle** (344-8775 or 800-266-8625; fax 522-7382; email abst@juno.com). To: Anchorage ($40); Denali ($20); Fairbanks ($45).

Visitor Information: Talkeetna Mountain Shop (733-1686), at Main St. and the Spur Rd., proffers pamphlets about local air charters and walking tours. Open daily May to mid-Sept. 10am-5:30pm. Next door, **Talkeetna Gifts and Collectibles** (733-2710) has most of the same information, plus a wide selection of knick-knacks made by local artisans. Open daily 9am-7pm; in winter 10am-5:15pm.

Outdoor Information: To reach the brand-spankin'-new **Talkeetna Ranger Station,** P.O. Box 588 (733-2231; fax 733-1465; email dena_talkeetna_office@nps.gov; http://www.nps.gov/dena), follow Main St. to its terminus and turn left; the station is on the left. Primarily used by climbers, it's also a tranquil place to plan a trip to Denali. Open daily mid-May to Aug. 8am-6pm; Sept. to mid-May M-F 8am-5pm.

Banks: There are **no banks** in town, but locals are in a joyful tizzy over the recent installation of an **ATM** ($2 surcharge) at the **Three Rivers Tesoro Gas Station** (733-2443), on Main St. Open daily 8am-9pm.

Equipment Rental: Talkeetna Outdoor Center (733-2230), on Main St. Mounds of mountaineering gear; limited camping supplies. Canoes $17 per 4hr., plus $1 per person per day. Open mid-Apr. to mid-Oct. daily 10am-6pm; off-season open on demand. **Crowley Guide Services** (733-1279; fax 733-1278; email c.g.s2@world-net.att.net), on Main St., rents mountain bikes (half-day $10, full day $15).

Library: (733-2359), 1 mi. from town on the Spur Rd. Open Tu noon-8pm, W-F 11am-6pm, Sa 10am-5pm.

Laundromat: At the gas station (see **Banks,** above). Wash $1.75, dry 25¢ per 6min.

Public Showers: At the gas station (see **Banks,** above). $2 per 8min.

Emergency: 911. **State Troopers:** Parks Mile 97.8 (733-2256).

Crisis Line: 733-1010.

Medical Services: Sunshine Community Health Clinic (733-2273), 9 mi. from town on the Spur Rd.

Post Office: (733-2275), in town on the Spur Rd. Open M-F 9am-5pm, Sa 10am-2pm. **ZIP Code:** 99676.

Area Code: 907.

ACCOMMODATIONS AND CAMPGROUNDS

Talkeetna Roadhouse (733-1351; fax 733-1353; email rdhouse@alaska.net), centrally located at Main and C St. A comfortable, homey establishment with shared bathrooms. Bunks $21; singles $47.25; doubles $63. During the climbing season, reservations should be made well in advance.

Swiss Alaska Inn, just beyond Main St. Take a right after the McKinley Deli (see **Food,** below), then an immediate left down the dirt trail; the inn is on the right. Geared toward climbers, with 20 beds ($20) split among 4 rooms, each with bathroom and shower. Towels are provided, but linens are not. Open Apr.-June 22. Reservations are essential; contact **K2 Aviation,** Box 545-B (733-2291 or 800-764-2291; fax 733-1221; email flyk2@alaska.net; http://www.alaska.net/~flyk2), ½ mi. south of town on the Spur Rd.

Fairview Inn, P.O. Box 645 (733-2423), at the beginning of Main St. The alleged site of Harding's undoing, with decent prices. Singles $42; doubles $52.50.

Talkeetna River Adventures (733-2604). Turn right off of the Spur Rd. at the airport, then turn left and follow the signs. Clean, quiet, and wooded area with water, outhouses, and easy river access. Restrooms, a pay phone, and groceries available in the Adventures office. Beginning at the railroad tracks across from the waiting booth, several paths make a convenient shortcut to town. 40 sites: $12; parking $6; showers $3. Registration required at the office.

River Park Campground, at the end of Main St. The town recently acquired this site and hopes to improve it. While beautiful, the area is a popular late-night hangout for local teens and may not be particularly serene. Sites $8. Call the **Chamber of Commerce** (733-1505) for reservations. Rumor has it that camping space can also be found along the river.

FOOD

A sparse selection of groceries inhabits the shelves at **Nagley's Store** (733-FOOD/3663), on Main St., where a latte or hot dog costs only $1 (open Su-Th 8am-10pm, F-Sa 8am-11pm; in winter Su-Th 8am-9pm, F-Sa 8am-10pm).

⊛Talkeetna Roadhouse Cafe (see **Accommodations,** above) offers family-style dining, with hot and hearty breakfast and soup ($6). The cafe bakes bread, cookies, cinnamon rolls, and a blueberry muffin with a history, made from geriatric sourdough starter dating back to 1902. Open Su-W 6am-4pm, Th-Sa 6am-10pm.

⊛McKinley Grille (355-8377), outside the deli (see above). Everyone in town raves about the fresh halibut and salmon grilled in summer. Open Tu-Su 11am-9pm).

McKinley Deli (733-1234), at Main and C St. Talkeetna's spot for pizza, sandwiches, and espresso. The spaghetti dinner with bread and salad makes a tasty deal ($7.50). Open Su-Th 11:30am-9pm, F-Sa 11:30am-10pm.

Sparkey's (733-1414), across from the Mountain Shop (see **Practical Information,** above). Speedy cheeseburgers $3.50; giant ice cream cones $1. Open daily May-Sept. 11am-11pm; closes earlier during the off-season.

SIGHTS AND EVENTS

The **Talkeetna Historical Society Museum** (733-2487), off Main St. between C and D St., houses modest displays of Alaskana, the town's oldest cabin, and a dramatic scaled-down model of the Mountain. *(Open May-Aug. daily 10:30am-5:30pm; Apr. and Sept. F-Su 11am-5pm; Feb.-Mar. and Oct.-Nov. Sa-Su 11am-5pm; Dec.-Jan. Sa 11am-5pm. $1.)* For life-size dioramas, authentic Alaskan noises, and updates on the most recent Bigfoot sightings, follow the moose tracks through the light-hearted **Museum of Northern Adventure** (733-3999), on the Spur Rd. next to Talkeetna Gifts and Collectibles. *(Open daily in summer 11am-7pm, but somewhat flexibly. $2.50, seniors $2, under 12 $1.50.)*

The second weekend in July brings Talkeetna's increasingly famous **Moose Dropping Festival.** Animal rights advocates need not fret: "moose dropping" in this context is a noun, not an activity. Thousands flock for the opportunity to enjoy live bagpipes, purchase various moose-nugget novelties, and compete in the moose dropping toss, certain to be an experimental sport in the 2000 Sydney Olympic Games. Early December brings the **Wilderness Women Contest,** with such events as wood-chopping, salmon-snagging, target-shooting, and sandwich preparation, plus the associated **Bachelor's Ball. Miner's Day,** every third weekend of May, promises tons of ore-related family fun. Bands from all over the state gather for the **Bluegrass Festival,** held on the first weekend in August by Hell's Angel Dirty Ernie.

FLIGHTSEEING AND OUTDOORS

Even if you can't climb Denali, you can look at it. Talkeetna's **Denali overlook,** 1 mi. down the Spur Rd., boasts one of Alaska's best car-accessible views of the Mountain; if the clouds cooperate, they'll unveil nearly 4 mi. of rock and ice climbing straight to the sky. This perspective pales in comparison, however, to the vistas seen by plane. **Flightseeing** sometimes costs less than a fortune, and to see the Mountain amid other sheer peaks and glaciers is an incomparable experience. Talkeetna's air services are actually closer to Denali than those at the park entrance, making flights cheaper. **Doug Geeting Aviation,** P.O. Box 42 (733-2366 or 800-770-2366; fax 733-1000; email airtours@alaska.net; http://www.alaska.net/~airtours) and **Hudson Air Service,** P.O. Box 648 (733-2321 or 800-478-2321; fax 733-2333; email hasi@customcpu.com; http://www.alaskan.com/hudsonair) offer one-hour tours starting at $65 and $75, respectively. **K2 Aviation** (see **Accommodations,** above), **McKinley Air Service** (733-1765 or 800-564-1765; fax 733-1765; email mckair@alaska.net; http://www.alaska.net/~mckair), and **Talkeetna Air Taxi** (733-2218 or 800-533-2219; fax 733-1434; email flytat@alaska.net; http://www.alaska.net/~flytat) offer similar services for comparable prices. While an hour is plenty of time to be overwhelmed by the view, another $30-45 extends the trip by half an hour to fly all the way around the summit, taking in all 14,000 feet of **Wickersham Wall,** the longest uninterrupted slope in the world. Most outfits also offer **glacier landings** near the base of the peak for anywhere from $15-45 extra. For quite a bit more money, they'll take you and a guide up for some summer **skiing** on the glaciers. Be wary of companies offering landings far into July, when snow conditions can become unsafe. If you come to Talkeetna hell-bent on flightseeing, plan on waiting a couple of days for the clouds to break. Call the flight outfits despite any foul weather in town; the mountains can bask in sunshine while clouds smother Talkeetna.

Fishing and **river tours** abound in the waterways around town. **Talkeetna River Guides,** P.O. Box 563 (733-2677 or 800-353-2677; email trg@alaska.net; http://www.alaska.net/~trg/trg_dir), on Main St., offers fishing tours and two-hour float trips with views of Denali and frequent wildlife sightings. *(Fishing ½-day $129, full-day $175. Float trip $39, under 15 $15.)* **Mahay's Riverboat Service,** P.O. Box 705 (733-2223; email uptz57a@prodigy.com), on Main St. just before downtown, leads tours geared more towards education, with a somewhat noisy 30-minute jet boat ride followed by a one-hour hike through the woods with a naturalist. *($45, ages 2-12 $22.50.)* To head out solo, rent a canoe from **Alaska Camp and Canoe** (733-CAMP/733-2267), on Railroad Ave., or the **Talkeetna Outdoor Center** (see **Practical Information,** above). There isn't much **hiking** or **cross-country skiing** right out of Talkeetna, save a 2.3km loop starting at the scenic overlook 1 mi. up the Spur Rd.

■ George Parks Highway (Rte. 3) and Nenana

From Talkeetna, the Parks Hwy. begins a gradual ascent into the Alaska Range, and offers some of the finest views of Mt. McKinley available from the ground. The **South Denali Viewpoint,** near the entrance to Denali National Park, offers a particularly spectacular profile of the 20,320 ft. peak, and keeps rubberneckers from running off the road. The turn-off to the viewpoint is just a few miles from the **Ruth Glacier,** but it may not be worth taking unless the frequent clouds have dissipated, usually between 10pm and 4am. **Denali State Park** (907-745-3975), at Miles 132-168, offers plenty of hiking trails and more solitude than the famous national park. Two pleasant **campgrounds** are accessible from the highway: **Troublesome Creek** (Mile 137.2; 10 sites; $6 per vehicle) and **Byers Lake** (Mile 147; $12). Both campgrounds have toilets and drinking water. The **Denali Viewpoint** is yet another pretty place to take a picture of the peak, and is only a 10-minute drive north of the state park.

From here, the road winds northward across the Alaska Range, passing over a few surprisingly steep creek canyons and through **Broad Pass,** the scenic high point of the road (Mile 201). The Parks Hwy. soon passes the turn-off for the **Denali Highway** (Rte. 8) a rocky road through the basins that drain the Alaska Range (see p. 455). It is about a 20-minute drive from this turn-off to Denali National Park (see p. 448). Leaving Denali, the highway winds north along the **Nenana River** for about 70 mi. to the town of the same name.

Nenana (ne-NAH-na), 53 mi. south of Fairbanks, plays host to the **Nenana Ice Pool.** Bored out of their skulls during the long winter, residents of Alaska and the Yukon bet on the precise minute when the Nenana River will thaw in the spring. The pot has amassed $300,000. Call 832-5446, email tripod@ptialaska.net, or write P.O. Box 272, Nenana 99760, to place a $2 bet. If waiting for the ice to break doesn't hold your interest, check out the free **Alaska State Railroad Museum** (832-5580), in the train depot at the end of A St., for exhibits on the construction of the Alaska Railroad.

Nenana, meaning "place to camp between two rivers," is just that. **Nenana Valley RV Park** (832-5230) has large grassy sites, laundry services (wash $2, dry $1), nice bathrooms, bicycle rentals ($1 per hr.) and free showers (tents $10; RVs $14; hookups $17). At Mile 302, the **Finnish Alaskan Bed and Breakfast** (832-5628) costs a pretty penny, but offers pretty rooms to match (singles or doubles with shared bath $50). The **Two Choice Cafe** (832-1010), located on A St., offers burgers ($5.50) and ice cream cones ($1.50; open daily 7:30am-2:30pm).

▒ Fairbanks

Had E.T. Barnette not run aground with his load of goods near the junction of the Tanana and Chena Rivers, and decided on the spur of the moment to set up a trading post, and had Felix Pedro, an Italian immigrant-turned-prospector, not unearthed a golden fortune nearby, Fairbanks might never have been born. But they did, it was, and today, Fairbanks stands unchallenged as North American civilization's northernmost hub—witness such landmarks as the "World's Northernmost Woolworth's," "World's Northernmost Denny's," and "World's Northernmost Southern Barbecue." From here, adventuresome travelers can drive, fly, or float to the Arctic Circle and into the tundra. Most do not make the long and arduous trip to Fairbanks merely to stay put; Fairbanks is a means, not an end. That said, the endless strip malls have a few original log cabins crammed between them, and even the omnipresent tourism industry can't hide the rough-and-ready flavor of this frontier town. Men noticeably outnumber women, the streets are filled with 4WD steeds, and any road leads out of town into utter wilderness in minutes. Through frigid winters and summer swarms of merciless mosquitoes, Fairbanks residents persevere and enjoy everything from moose hunting to Shakespeare in the Park.

TO CHENA HOT SPRINGS RD.

Old Steese Hwy.

Steese Expwy

Gaffney Rd.

Richardson Hwy.

TO NORTH POLE, DELTA JUNCTION

Slater Dr. W.

Clay St.

Noble St.

Steese Expwy

10th Ave.

12th Ave.

Cushman St.

Rent-a-Wreck

23rd Ave.

Illinois St.

Alaska Railroad Station

Alaska Public Lands Information Center

16th Ave.

19th Ave.

Gillam Ave.

Eastland St.

1st Ave.

2nd Ave.

Cowles St.

E Cowles St.

Gillam Way

17th Ave.

22nd Ave.

S. Lathrop St.

Chena River

Lathrop St.

Noel Wien Library

19th Ave.

Cowles St.

Johansen Expwy

College Rd.

Danby St.

Aurora Dr.

Esquire Ave.

Aspen St.

Hanson Rd.

Phillips Field Rd.

2nd Ave.

Alaskaland

Wilbur St.

23rd Ave.

Peger Rd.

Davis Rd.

Noyes Slough

College Rd.

Phillips Field Rd.

Airport Way

University Ave.

Farmer's Loop Rd.

Geist Rd.

Chena River

Airport Way

Fairbanks International Airport

TO LARGE ANIMAL RESEARCH STATION AND STEESE HWY.

University of Alaska Museum

Agriculture Experimental Station

University of Alaska Fairbanks

Yukon Dr.

Tanana Dr.

Geist Rd.

Chena Ridge Rd.

George Parks Hwy.

TO NENANA, ANCHORAGE

ALASKA

Fairbanks
Overview

ACCOMMODATIONS

F Alaska Heritage Inn Youth Hostel
D Aurora Motel and Cabins
C Billie's Backpackers Hostel
G Boyle's Hostel
A Chena River State Campground
H Grandma Shirley's Hostel
E Tanana Valley Campground
B Your Hostel in Fairbanks

1 mile

1 kilometer

ORIENTATION AND PRACTICAL INFORMATION

Fairbanks lies 358 mi. north of Anchorage via the George Parks Hwy. (Rte. 3), and 500 mi. south of Prudhoe Bay along the gravelly Dalton Hwy. (Rte. 11). Delta Junction is 98 mi. southeast of Fairbanks on the Richardson (Alaska) Hwy. Fairbanks itself can at first be a confusing city to navigate as it is difficult to identify "downtown" in its maze of urban sprawl. Most every tourist destination lies on one of four thoroughfares: **Airport Way, College Road, Cushman Boulevard,** and **University Way.** The city center lies in the vicinity of South Cushman, north of Airport Way. Fairbanks is a **bicycle-friendly** city, providing wide shoulders, multi-use paths, and sidewalks for its two-wheeled travelers. The urban routes aren't particularly scenic, but they're a lot quicker than walking. The visitor center has a guide to biking through Fairbanks, plus pamphlets mapping out self-guided walking and driving tours.

Transportation
Airplanes: Located 5mi. from downtown on Airport Way. Served by: **Delta** (800-221-1212) to the lower 48; **Alaska Air** (452-1661) to Anchorage ($91, round-trip $128) and Juneau ($185, round-trip $370); **Frontier Flyer Services** (474-0014) to smaller Bush towns such as Bettles ($248). Fares change at the drop of a hat, and cheaper fares are often possible with advance purchase. A number of other carriers also serve Fairbanks including **Northwest, United,** and **Reno Air** (see p. 26).

Trains: Alaska Railroad, 280 N. Cushman St. (456-4155; fax 265-2323; email reservations@akrr.com; http://www.alaska.net/~akrr), behind the Daily News-Miner building. An excellent way to see the wilderness. From mid-May to mid-Sept., 1 train daily to Anchorage ($112) and Denali National Park ($53). From mid-Sept. to mid-Oct. and from early Feb. to mid-May, a train leaves for Anchorage once per week ($105). No trains run to Anchorage in the winter. Ages 2-11 half-price. Depot open M-F 7am-3pm, Sa-Su 7am-11am.

Buses: Parks Highway Express (479-3065 or 888-600-6001; email parkshwy@aol.com) runs daily to Denali ($20, round-trip $35) and Anchorage (about 9hr., $49, round-trip $95) and 3 times per week to Glenallen ($55, round-trip $105) and Valdez (9hr., $75, round-trip $145). Pick-up at the Convention and Visitors Bureau (see below), and Billie's Backpackers Hostel (see **Accommodations,** below), and most other places requested along the way. **Alaskon Express** (451-6835 or 800-544-2206) runs to Haines (18hr., 3 per week, $180). **Alaska Direct** (800-770-6652) runs 3 buses per week to Tok (4hr., $40) and Anchorage (11½hr., $65). **Fireweed Express** (458-8267) runs daily van service to Denali ($25, round-trip $45), with pick up at Billie's Backpackers Hostel; call for times and reservations.

Public Transportation: Municipal Commuter Area Service (MACS) (459-1011), at 5th and Cushman St. runs 2 routes (red and blue) through downtown Fairbanks and the surrounding area. Fare $1.50; students, seniors, and disabled 75¢; under 5 free. Day pass $3. Transfers valid for another bus. Pick up a schedule at the Convention and Visitors Bureau (see below), the post office (see below), from any driver, in shopping malls, or at the transit park. Buses tend to run a little late and they don't run all that often, depending on the route.

Taxis: Diamond Taxi (455-7777), $1 base, $1.50 per mi. **King Cab** (452-5464). $1 base, $1.80 per mi. **Fairbanks Taxi** (452-3535). $2 base, $1.80 per mi. **Yellow Cab** (452-2121). 25¢ base, $2 per mi. All 24hr.

Car Rental: Nearly all national companies offer packages with free mileage, but they won't allow driving on dirt roads. Many smaller companies, on the other hand, charge hefty fees for extra mileage. **Rent-a-Wreck,** 21055 Cushman St. (452-1606). $39 per day, 30¢ per mi. after 100mi.; must be 21 with credit card. Local use only (as far as Denali), and no gravel highways. **U-Save Auto Rental,** 3245 College Rd. (479-7060). $35 per day, 26¢ per mi. after 100mi. Must be 21 and credit card "preferred"; can use cash if over 25. $250 deposit; under 25 $500 deposit.

Road Conditions: 800-478-7675; http://www.dot.state.ak.us.

Visitor and Financial Services

Visitor Information: Convention and Visitors Bureau Log Cabin, 550 1st Ave. (456-5774 or 800-327-5774), at Cushman. Distributes a free **Visitor's Guide** listing tourist offices, services, events, activities, and shops. Free local calls. Open daily 8am-8pm; Labor Day-Memorial Day M-F 8am-5pm. **Fairbanks Information Hotline** (456-INFO/4636) has a 24hr. recording for upcoming events.

Outdoor Information: Alaska Public Lands Information Center (APLIC), 250 Cushman St. #1A, Fairbanks 99707 (456-0527), in the basement of the Federal building at Cushman and 3rd, has info and maps on Alaskan parks, roads, and public lands, and happily bestows advice on hiking. Visit if you are considering a trip to either Gates of the Arctic National Park or the Arctic National Wildlife Refuge (see p. 169); the staff gives thorough, indispensable tips on how to navigate these immense expanses of wilderness. Open daily 9am-6pm; in winter Tu-Sa 10am-6pm.

Banks: First National Bank (452-1871), at 8th Ave. and Noble. Open M-F 10am-6pm. **National Bank of Alaska,** 34 College Rd. (459-4360). Open M-Th 10am-5pm, F 10am-6pm, Sa 10am-4pm. 2nd location at 794 University Ave. Open M-Th 10am-5pm, F 10am-6pm, Sa 10am-2pm. Both have 24hr. **ATMs.**

ATM Locations: 7-11 locations at 3569 Airport Way, 3679 College Rd., 2301 Cushman St., and 2110 Peger Rd. **AlaskaUSA FCU** locations at 1261 Airport Way and 407 Old Steese Hwy. **Carrs Foodland,** at the intersection of Gaffney and Lacey. **Mapco Express** gas stations: 1773 College Rd., 2300 Cushman St., 205 E. 3rd St., and 4105 Geist Rd. **Safeway** locations at 3627 Airport Way and 30 College Rd. See **Banks,** above. All open 24hr.

Local Services

Outdoor Equipment: Beaver Sports, 3480 College Rd. (479-2494), across from College Corner Mall. Mountain bikes $16 per 6hr., $20 overnight, $94 weekly; $250 deposit required (cash or credit). Canoes $24 per day, $17 per day for 3-6 days, $12 per day for 7-10 days; paddles and life jackets included; $500 deposit required per boat. Skates $13 per day; $125 deposit required. Open M-F 10am-8pm, Sa 9am-7pm, Su 1-5pm. **Rocket Surplus,** 1401 Cushman St. (456-7078), vends camping supplies. Open M-Sa 9am-6pm. **Apocalypse Design, Inc.,** 101 College Rd. (451-7555), at Illinois. Speedy repairs on zippers and straps. Open M-F 9am-6pm, Sa 10am-4pm.

Bookstore: Gulliver's New and Used Books, 3525 College Rd. (474-9574). A decent selection of new books, a large variety of used books, and free Internet access in the Second Story Cafe upstairs (see below). Open M-F 9am-10pm, Sa 9am-

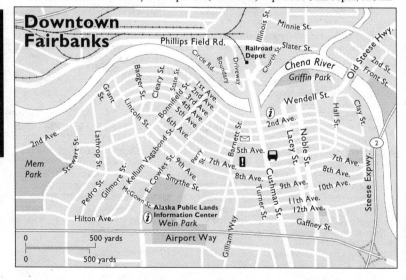

Downtown Fairbanks

8pm, Su 9am-6pm. Also in the **Shopper's Forum,** 1255 Airport Way (456-3657). Open M-F 10am-8pm, Sa 10am-6pm, Su noon-6pm.

Library: Noel Wien Library, 1215 Cowles St. (459-1020), at Airport Way. Open M-W 10am-9pm, Th-F 10am-6pm, Sa 10am-5pm. **University of Alaska at Fairbanks Rasmuson Library** (474-7481) is near the fountain on the eastern part of campus. Open M-Th 7:30am-8pm, F 7:30am-6pm, Sa-Su noon-5pm.

Laundromat and Showers: B&C (479-2696), at University and College, in Campus Mall. Wash $2, dry 25¢ per 8min. Showers $2.50, towels 50¢. Open M-Sa 8am-10:30pm, Su 9am-10:30pm. **B&L** (452-1355), at 3rd and Steese. Wash and dry each $1.50. Showers $3 per 20min. Open daily 8am-11pm.

Weather: 452-3553.

Emergency and Communications

Emergency: 911. **Alaska State Troopers:** 451-5333.

Crisis Line: 452-HELP/4357; also provides contact with **gay and lesbian groups. Rape Crisis:** 452-7273 or 800-478-7273. **Poison Control Center:** 456-7182.

Pharmacy: Payless Drugstore, 19 College Rd. (456-2151), at Steese and College, across from the Bentley Mall. Open M-F 9am-9pm, Sa 10am-7pm, Su 10am-6pm.

Hospital: Fairbanks Memorial, 1650 Cowles St. (452-8181), off Airport Hwy.

Post Office: 311 Barnette St. (452-3203). Entrance is in the back of the brown building at the corner of Barnette and 3rd, marked 315 Barnette. Open M-F 9am-6pm, Sa 10am-2pm. **ZIP Code:** 99707.

Internet Access: Noel Wien Library (see above). **Rasmuson Library** (see above). **Cafe Latte,** 519 6th Ave. (455-4898). $4 per hr.; 30min. free with coffee or food. **Second Story Cafe,** above Gulliver's Books on College Rd. (see above). One computer with free access.

Area Code: 907.

ACCOMMODATIONS AND CAMPGROUNDS

⊛**Grandma Shirley's Hostel,** 510 Dunbar St. (451-9816). From the Steese Expressway, turn right onto the Trainor Gate Rd., then left at E. St., and finally right on Dunbar St. Grandma beats out all other contenders to earn the title of Fairbanks Überhostel. (The painted bear on the bathroom door put her over the top.) Bedding, a spectacular kitchen, showers, a TV room, a big backyard, and free use of three old but road-worthy bikes. Men and women share a room with 9 beds. $15.

Billie's Backpackers Hostel, 2895 Mack Blvd. (479-2034; fax 457-2034; email akbillie@aol.com). Take Westwood Way 1 block off College to Mack Rd. Look for the house on the corner with the flags and the sign. Conveniently located near College Rd., Billie's maintains 3 rooms with 4 beds each, with hot shower and kitchen for each room. Somewhat cluttered, but a welcoming, cozy place to meet many international travelers. $18. $7 for a full breakfast and (occasionally) $10 for an all-you-can-eat, home-cooked dinner. Some tent spaces available.

Alaska Heritage Inn Youth Hostel (AAIH), 1018 22nd Ave. (451-6587). Take Cushman to 22nd Ave., then go west; the hostel is a large gray building on the right. The men's bunk room and facilities are a bit dim and cold while the women's room and facilities are brighter and cozier, in their own building to the side of the house. Space is somewhat limited in both bunk rooms. Common room with TV, picnic area, and 15 beds. $14, nonmembers $15 plus 8% bed tax; tent space $10.

North Woods Lodge, P.O. Box 83615 (479-5300 or 800-478-5305; fax 479-6888) on E. Chena Hill Dr. Take Roland Rd. west off Chena Pump Rd., then turn right on Chena Hills Rd. The lodge is ¼ mi. up the road on the right. A fair distance from the heart of Fairbanks; travelers will appreciate the quiet of North Woods. The wooden cabins are charming, clean, and have electricity but no running water. Small kitchen facilities; shared showers. The loft demands a sleeping bag. Free transportation between the lodge and the airport, bus, and train station. Nearby hiking trails; snowmobile rides in the winter. Cabins $40; double cabins $45; hostel dorms $15. Tent sites $12; 2 or more people $15.

Your Hostel in Fairbanks, 3412 College Rd. (479-0099), above The Marlin (see **Nightlife,** below). Located near the university and the many shops along College

Rd., easily accessible by bus. Showers, kitchen, and comfortable lounge area. Light sleepers may not enjoy the location (above a bar, on busy College Rd.). Dorms $15.

Chena River State Campground, off Airport Way on University Ave. With 2 or more people, this place is worth the $15 per night fee (walk-ins $10). Landscaped, clean, and situated on a particularly quiet stretch of the Chena River. 56 sites. In summer, 5-night max. per vehicle. $5 to use the dump station. Self-register.

Tanana Valley Campground, 1800 College Rd. (456-7956), by the fairgrounds on College Rd. near Aurora Ave. Somewhat noisy, but surprisingly grassy and secluded given its in-town location. Clean, spacious bathrooms. Managers hold an occasional barbecue for the campers and sell some staples. 33 sites: $12; hookups $15; walk-ins $6. Showers ($3 for non-campers). Laundromat (wash $2, dry $2).

FOOD

For an artery-blocking good time, look no farther than Airport Way or College Rd., where the Northernmost Franchises of almost every fast-food chain in existence lure burger lovers to their doom. Groceries are available 24hr. at **Carr's,** 526 Gaffney (452-1121); at **Safeway,** at University Ave. and Airport Way (479-4231); and in the **Bentley Mall,** at 30 College Rd. (451-6870). If you're really stocking up, **Sam's Club,** 48 College Rd. (451-4800), lets nonmembers buy in bulk for an additional 5% of the low, low total price (open M-Sa 9am-8pm, Su 10am-7pm). The **Farmers Market,** at the fairgrounds at Aurora and College (456-FARM/3276), is the place for fresh produce (open W 11am-6pm, Sa 9am-4pm).

Thai House, 528 5th Ave. (452-6123). The northernmost Thai restaurant never advertises, but it's jam-packed. Lunch $6-8, dinner starts at $8. Try the *param gai* (chicken with spinach and peanut sauce, $9) or the *pad thai* noodles ($7), but don't say spicy (*phet*) unless you mean it. Open M-Sa 11am-4pm and 5-10pm.

Gambardella Pasta Bella, 706 2nd Ave. (456-3417), at Barnette. Fresh flowers, an airy air, and excellent food make this classy family-run restaurant worth its heftier prices. The lunch menu offers subs for $4-7 and small pizzas for $6-8; a *bellisima* pasta dinner starts at $10. Stare down the "Mother of all Lasagnas" for $15 and enjoy the homemade bread. Open daily M-Sa 11am-10pm. Reservations recommended in summer.

The Pumphouse Restaurant and Saloon, Mile 1.3 Chena Pump Rd. (479-8452). The place is so popular that 1 of the city's bus lines goes out of its way to drop passengers here. Greeted by a 9ft. 3in. Kodiak brown bear when entering, you are quickly taken back to the gold rush days of Fairbanks, when fine restaurants were decorated with mining equipment. Lunch buffet $10. Dinner entrees average $18; the caribou stew is a hearty meal for $15. The deck and bar have a more limited but cheaper menu, including an Alaskan burger with fries ($7). Open daily 11:30am-11pm. Senator's Saloon inside (see **Nightlife,** below).

Pikes Landing, 4438 Airport Way (479-6500). Although fine (more expensive) dining is available inside, the deck or the screened-in patio are better places to eat and soak up some midnight sun. Dinner starts from $7; halibut fish-and-chips is a local favorite ($9.75), and the light fiesta chicken salad ($7.50) will light up your night. In June and July, diners can strut their golf skill, attempting to hole-out a 116-yd. shot over the river ($1 per ball, goes to charity). Deck open daily 2:30-11pm.

The Whole Earth, 1157 Deborah St. (479-2052), behind College Corner Mall. This health food store and deli could well have been a joint venture by Rachel Carson and Jane Fonda. Southwestern art and perhaps the only cacti in Alaska accompany organic coffee and a variety of good-for-you foods like the giant No Bull Burger ($4.75) and Anna's Hummus Sandwich ($3.75). Open M-Sa 9am-8pm, Su 11am-6pm. Hot food served 11am-7pm.

Alaska Espresso and Chowder House, 3226 Airport Way (474-0409), across from Sears. Sampling the tasty clam chowder (cup $2.50, bowl $4.50), it's difficult to believe that New England is 4000 mi. away. The House also offers deli sandwiches ($3.50 half, $5.50 whole), quiches ($3.95), and an impressive assortment of ice cream ($1.50). Open M-F 7am-9pm, Sa 9am-9pm, Su 10am-5pm.

Souvlaki, 310 1st Ave. (452-5393), a few blocks down the street from the visitor center. You can almost get your fill on the heavenly aroma alone. Succulent stuffed grape leaves (3 for $1.25), fresh falafel ($4.75), and homemade sourdough cinnamon rolls the size of Alaska itself ($1.75). Take-out available. Open M-F 10am-9pm, Sa 10am-6pm; in winter M-Sa 10am-6pm.

Little Saigon, 1753 College Rd. (452-4399), just east of Aurora Dr. The few locals who have discovered this small Vietnamese restaurant can't stop raving about it. Service is a bit slow, but the owner makes everything fresh and beautiful herself, and you'll be glad you waited to taste the *goi chon* spring rolls ($3 for 3 big rolls) or the *bún ga nuong,* a hearty serving of charcoal-broiled chicken with vermicelli ($4.95). Open daily noon-10pm.

BAKERIES AND COFFEEHOUSES

Wolf Run Dessert & Coffee House, 3360 Wolf Run (458-0636), just off University Way near Geist. Sweet tooths will love this rustic coffeehouse with its homemade, scrumptious desserts, plush chairs, and stone hearth fireplace with rocking chair. Sit at the outdoor patio seating overlooking a garden, while sampling some blueberry or peanut butter pie ($4.25) or 1 of the daily new cheesecake creations, tarts, and tortes. Espresso $1; latte $2.50. Open Tu-Th 11am-10pm, F-Sa 11am-midnight, Su noon-8pm.

Into the Woods, 3560 College Rd. (479-7701; email woods@polarnet.com). Greenwich Village meets the Klondike in this rustic log cabin coffeehouse. Relax in a large wicker chair, listen to a live guitarist, flip through a book from the bookstore or lending library, imbibe local art, go outside to the willow dome and catch a poetry reading, or sip a tall latte ($2) while perusing *Outhouses of Alaska.* Open in summer Su-Th 9am-midnight, F-Sa 9am-3am.

Bab's Bakery, 402 5th Ave. (457-1213), in the heart of downtown. Bab's Bakery bestows bunches of bagels (70¢ each) on blissfully breakfasting backpackers. Relaxed atmosphere and fresh baked goods make it an ideal breakfast stop. Grab Bab's bagel sandwich ($4), a latte ($2.25), or a dog treat (25¢). Open Tu-F 6:30am-6pm, Sa 8am-6pm; in winter Tu-F 6:30am-3pm, Sa 8am-3pm.

SIGHTS

One of Fairbanks's proudest institutions and main attractions is the **University of Alaska-Fairbanks (UAF),** at the top of a hill overlooking the flat cityscape. Both bus routes stop at the **Wood Campus Center** (474-7034), located on Yukon Dr. across from the fire station, which has pool tables, flyers advertising campus goings-on, and enough video games to entertain all the little brothers of the world. *(Open M-F 7am-7pm, Sa-Su 10:30am-6:30pm.)* The **Student Activities Office** (474-6027), located in the Wood Center, has the skinny on movies, music, and campus activities during the school year. *(Open M-F 8am-5pm.)* The **University of Alaska Museum** (474-7505; email fyuamvs@aurora.alaska.edu; http://www.uaf.alaska.edu/museum), a 10-minute walk up Yukon Dr. from the Wood Center, features exhibits including displays on the aurora borealis, gold collections, a thorough look at the Aleut/Japanese evacuation during WWII, and indigenous crafts. *(Open June-Aug. daily 9am-7pm; May and Sept. daily 9am-5pm; Oct.-Apr. M-F 9am-5pm, Sa-Su noon-5pm. $5, seniors $4.50, ages 13-18 $3, under 6 free.)* Blue Babe, an extremely rare 36,000-year-old steppe bison recovered from the permafrost, would be truly foolish to miss. The university offers free **tours** of the campus, beginning in front of the museum. *(2hr. M-F at 10am, weather permitting.)*

The search for a good picnic spot ends at the **Georgeson Botanical Gardens** (474-1944), on Tanana Dr. west of the museum. Tiptoe through the tulips (the best viewing time is late June through July) and enjoy the view of Fairbanks and the Alaska Range. Be sure to sit upwind of the bovine and porcine populations housed by the university's Agriculture Experimental Station. The **Large Animal Research Station** (474-7207) offers a rare chance to see baby musk oxen and other arctic animals up close. *(Tours June-Aug. Tu and Sa at 11am and 1:30pm, Th at 1:30pm; Sept. Sa 1:30pm. $5, students $2, seniors $4.)* Take Farmer's Loop to Ballaine Rd. and turn left on Van Kovich;

the farm is 1 mi. up on the right. If you miss the tour, grab some binoculars and ogle the musk ox, reindeer, and caribou from the viewing stand on Yankovitch Rd.

Alaskaland, P.O. Box 71267 (459-1095), on Airport Way, is a small-scale, would-be Arctic Disneyland, but it has just a train, a merry-go-round, and no pixie-dust. Overrun by kids, Alaskaland is a tourist trap of woolly mammoth proportions. There's no general admission charge, though, and the gates are open from 11am to 9pm, making for great night picnics. *(Rides and museums charge nominal fees.)* Featuring winners from the **International Ice Sculpting Competition,** the **Fairbanks Ice Museum** (451-8222), near the visitor center on 2nd Ave., demonstrates what a Fairbanks winter can do to the average under-stimulated sculptor. *(Open daily 10am-6pm. $6, seniors $5, ages 6-12 $4, under 6 free.)*

Well worth the 11 mi. trip north along the Steese Hwy. (Rte. 6) to **Fox, Gold Dredge #8** (457-6058) provides a day of panning and a guided tour. *(Open daily mid-May to mid-Sept. 9am-6pm. 4 tours daily. $19.50, ages 4-12 $12.50.)* Not only is it possible to earn the cost of admission back in gold, but fossilized fragments of mammoths, mastodons, and Keith Richards abound. An extra $8 ($6 for the kids) buys the "Miner's Lunch," served family-style.

OUTDOORS

In the winter, there are two mountains within a half-hour of Fairbanks open for **downhill skiing.** Twenty minutes northeast of Fairbanks, **Moose Mountain** (479-4732) offers over 20 trails. *(Lift tickets $25; college students, seniors, military, and ages 13-17 $20; ages 7-12 $15; under 6 or over 70 free. $5 off after 1pm or if the temperature is below 0°F.)* **Mt. Aurora Ski Land,** 2315 Skiland Rd. (389-3624), a half-hour north of Fairbanks, has trails for skiers of all levels. *(Adults $24, college students and military $20, students 13-17 and seniors $17, ages 7-12 $10, under 6 or over 70 $5.)* Take a right onto Fairbanks Creek Rd. off the Steese Hwy. (Rte. 6) at Mile 20½., make a left turn, and go up the hill about a mile.

Many **trails** stretch throughout Fairbanks for hikers, bikers, or cross-country skiers. Ideal for a leisurely stroll, **Creamer's Nature Path** starts at 1300 College Rd., and offers 2 mi. of trail through open pastures, home to various migratory birds and encircled by birch and spruce groves. The 3-12 mi. **Skailand Trails,** weaving through the hilly woods behind the university campus, visit several ponds and offer glimpses of the Alaska Range. Maps are available at the Wood Center in the Student Activities Office (see above). Multiple trails for **cross-country skiing** are on or near the UAF campus. A number of trails, ranging from 2-12 mi., begin and end at the University museum. Maps are available at the information desk in the Wood Center (see above). Many people who seek skiing near Fairbanks look to the **White Mountains National Recreation Area,** which has trails and cabins accessible from the Steese and Eliot Hwys. north of Fox. Others, looking for hiking or skiing trails, often travel to the **Chena River State Recreation Area** (see **Near Fairbanks,** p. 468). Maps for both areas are available at the Alaska Public Lands Information Center (see **Practical Information,** p. 462).

You can play a midnight round at the **Northstar Golf Club** (457-GOLF/4653), the northernmost golf course in the United States. *(Green fee for 9 holes $14; scorecards include a wildlife checklist with warnings about animals which will steal your ball if you hit it too far.)* Go north from Fairbanks on the Steese Hwy. (Rte. 6), get off at the Chena Hot Springs Rd. Exit and take a left. Make a right onto Old Steese Hwy., go about ¾ mi. and then turn left on Golf Club Dr.

NIGHTLIFE

⊛**Howling Dog Saloon** (457-8780), 11½ mi. north on the Steese Hwy. (Rte. 6) toward Fox, at the intersection of the Old and New Steese Hwys. Look for a colorful wooden structure in the middle of nowhere, circled by pick-up trucks. UAF students, military personnel, and just about everyone else carouse at the legendary Howling Dog. The summer crowd is especially diverse, described by management as "rough, tough, and good-lookin'." Rough and tough volleyball, pool, and horseshoe games go on until 4am or so. Live music W-Sa. Open May-Oct. Su-Th 4pm-around 2am, F-Sa 4pm-around 4am.

⊚**Blue Loon Saloon,** 2999 Parks Hwy. (Rte. 3) (457-5666), 5 mi. south of town on the Parks, near **Ester.** A free shuttle runs F-Sa after 9pm between the Marlin (under the same management), the Blue Loon, and the UAF Wood Center. There's always something (usually cool) happening at the Blue Loon. Live bands play 4 nights a week, drawing a mixed crowd of hippies, college students, and military types. Movies are shown 3 times a week, and the saloon holds multiple music festivals during the summer in its outdoor amphitheater. The building, huge even by bloated Fairbanks standards, houses a gigantic dance floor. Cover $3. Open M-F 5pm-1:30am, Sa-Su 5pm-3am.

Senator's Saloon, Mile 1.3 Chena Pump Rd. (479-8452), in the Pumphouse Restaurant. Where yuppies and oysters meet. If the portrait of Ronald Reagan affects your appetite, take drinks out to the deck and watch riverboats whiz by. Those with stronger stomachs should slurp the "oyster shooter," a live oyster in a shot glass, topped with cocktail sauce and lemon. Karaoke night (W at 8pm) draws a crowd, and in summer folks often stumble in from the Bar Boat which voyages from bar to bar along the river. Always humidfying its customers with a fine selection of cigars, the saloon's cigar-tasting night in January is a stogie smoker's dream. Happy hour daily 4-6pm and 10-11pm. Open Su-Th 11am-12:30am, F-Sa 11:30am-2am.

The Marlin, 3412 College Rd. (479-4646). Fairbanks's only jazz bar. Live music (Tu-Sa); open mike (Tu); blues (W); jazz (Th). Sit under the portrait of a favorite musician and enjoy the vibes. Open Su-Th 4pm-2am, F-Sa 4pm-3:30am.

Malemute Saloon (479-2500 or 800-676-6925), 7 mi. south of Fairbanks on the Parks Hwy. (Rte. 3). Follow signs to the one-time gold camp of Ester. This gold rush throwback with sawdust floors and swinging doors still draws as big a crowd as in the olden golden days, but today rowdy tourists have replaced burly miners. Every evening at 9pm (also 7pm in July), the saloon yucks up a vaudeville show with songs, dance numbers, and Robert Service. Tickets $12, children $6; dinner buffet (5-9pm) $15. Reservations required; complimentary bus service.

EVENTS

In mid-July Fairbanks citizens don old-time duds and whoop it up for **Golden Days,** a celebration of Felix Pedro's 1902 discovery that sparked the Fairbanks gold rush. Watch out for the traveling jail; without a silly-looking pin commemorating the event (sold at most businesses), an unknowing tourist may be taken prisoner and forced to pay a steep price to spring free. (The budget traveler might want to stay on board the paddywagon; it's a free ride and goes all over town.) Although its relation to the actual gold rush days is questionable, the **rubber duckie race** is one of the biggest events. For details, contact the visitors bureau (see **Practical Information,** p. 462) or call 452-1105. Be warned that Fairbanks teems with tourists during Golden Days; make hotel reservations several months in advance.

The summer solstice inspires some wild activity in Fairbanks. The **Yukon 800 Marathon Riverboat Race** sends high-horsepower competitors in low-slung powerboats on an 800 mi. quest up the Tanana and Yukon Rivers to the town of Galena and back. On June 20th, thousands of people will join in the **10km Midnight Sun Run** (452-8351), to run, walk, or compete in the costume division. The Fairbanks Goldpanners play their annual **Midnight Sun Baseball Game** on the solstice itself (June 19,1999). The game begins as the sun dips at 10:30pm, features a short pause near midnight for the celebration of the midnight sun, and ends at about 2am, in full daylight. The Goldpanners play more than 30 home games throughout the summer and have won five minor league national championships since 1970. Barry Bonds played here (perhaps the source for his massive taste for gold jewelry). Games are played at **Growden Memorial Park** (451-0095), near Alaskaland. *(Tickets $5.)*

For a true sports spectacular, see the **World Eskimo-Indian Olympics,** P.O. Box 2433 (452-6646), on July 15-18. *(Nightly pass $10, seniors and children $8. Season passes $20, seniors and children $15.)* Native Alaskans from all over the state compete for three days in traditional tests of strength and survival. Witness the **ear pull,** for which sinew is wrapped around the ears of contestants, who then tug to see who can endure the most pain. *Ears have been pulled off in this event.* Eat your heart out, Mike Tyson.

The **Tanana Valley Fair** (452-3750), August 6-14, is a traditional country fair with rides, lots of food, and competitions for "biggest cabbage" and "cutest baby." *(Tickets $7, seniors and ages 6-17 $3.)* Suggestions for replacing them with "biggest baby" and "cutest cabbage" have so far been ignored. If you're lucky, you'll be chosen as a contestant in the **kiss the cow contest,** although the cow herself is unfairly prohibited from being the judge. The fairground is at the intersection of College Rd. and Aurora.

On September 18, Fairbanks hosts the annual **Equinox Marathon** (452-8531), one of the top five most rigorous in the nation. About 300 hearty competitors run 26.2 mi. up Ester Dome, sometimes in blizzard conditions, gaining 3500 ft. in elevation. They usually return so delirious that they blabber about impending Persians, then shout "Nike!" and die.

In winter, February's **Yukon Quest Dog Sled Race** runs between Fairbanks and Whitehorse, starting in Fairbanks on even years. The Quest is considered more extreme, colder, and damnit, more *Alaskan* than the famous Iditarod. There are fewer dogs, fewer stops, and less concern for human welfare. For information, contact the Yukon Quest Business Office, 558 2nd Ave. (452-7954).

■ Near Fairbanks: Chena River and Environs

A short drive in any direction plunges travelers into genuine Alaskan wilderness. Within the vicinity of Fairbanks, you can soak your feet in hot spring-fed lakes, look for wildlife in a river basin, or hike up a ridge to view the Brooks or Alaska Ranges, both over 200 mi. away. Maps and detailed info on hikes are available at the Alaska Public Lands Information Center in Fairbanks (see **Practical Information,** p. 462). **Fishing** enthusiasts can find numerous places in and around Fairbanks to reel in a keeper. Along the **Chena River,** graylings are common, as are king salmon in early July. The **Chatanika River,** which runs along the Steese Hwy. (Rte. 6) between Miles 29 and 39, teems with shellfish and northern pike. Would-be Bob Izumis (you know, the fishing show guy) should stop by the visitor center (see **Practical Information,** p. 462) for licenses and information.

Chena Hot Springs Road branches off the Steese Hwy. (Rte. 3) at Mile 5; the **Chena River State Recreation Area** (451-2695) spills across the road between Miles 26 and

---

On the 157th Day of Christmas, My True Love Gave to Me...

The town of North Pole, AK celebrates Christmas 365 days a year. Santa officially came to town in 1953, when the sleepy little village of Moose Crossing changed its name as a gimmick to woo toy manufacturers. Town planners hoped that corporations would rush to display "made in the North Pole" on their products, but they somehow resisted this seduction. This hasn't stopped the North Pole's 1700 residents, most of them military personnel stationed at nearby Fort Wainwright, from transforming their town into a shrine to the jolly fat man. St. Nicholas Drive runs into Santa Claus Lane. Bus stops, lampposts, and shopping malls all reflect the Christmas theme. Holiday cheer is mandatory. The U.S. Postal Service redirected Santa's mail to the newly christened North Pole, and now Santa receives 20,000 letters each year—so many letters, in fact, that the merry old elf has recruited North Pole schoolchildren to help answer his mail.

When he's not finding out who's been naughty or nice, Santa moonlights as a North Pole entrepreneur. Eat Mexican at Santa's Tortilla Factory, do your duds at Santa's Suds, or go on a ride at Santaland Caravan Park. Best of all, anyone can get a personalized letter from Kris Kringle himself. Just send the recipient's name, age, sex, full mailing address, brothers' and sisters' names, favorite hobby, and anything special you would like Santa to write. The ruddy-cheeked elf demands $5 in return. His official address is 325 S. Santa Claus Lane, North Pole, AK 99705.

51. Encompassing almost 400 sq. mi. of wilderness, the area offers outstanding fishing, hiking, canoeing, and camping. Tent sites convenient to Chena Hot Springs Rd. are available at the quiet, secluded **Rosehip Campground** (Mile 27) and **Tors Trail Campground** (Mile 39). Both cost $8, including pit toilets and water.

The **Granite Tors Trail**, across the road from Tors Trail Campground, begins in boreal forest at river level and climbs past the treeline to a peak topped by giant granite pillars ("Tors") and blessed with fantastic views of Chena Dome to the north and Flat Top Mountain to the west. There are also excellent views of the Alaska Range between Miles 7 and 9 of the trail. In July and August, blueberries abound along the trail's first stretch. Rangers recommend taking the east trail (left) to do the 15 mi. loop clockwise. The **Angel Rocks Trail** (look for signs near Mile 49) follows the Chena River before turning up to the top of Angel Rocks, prominent granite slabs that offer views of the river valley and the Alaska Range. This 3½ mi. loop through exquisite wilderness and wildflowers makes a wonderful hike, but be sure to bring bug juice—it's mosquito country. The **Chena Dome Trail,** open to mountain bikers and horse riders, is the most spectacular trail in the park, a 29 mi. adventure that follows the high, rocky rim of the Angel Creek Valley. The trailheads are at Mile 50.5 and 49.1 on the Chena Hot Springs Rd. The climb from either trailhead is a steep one, and park rangers recommend starting from the northern trailhead for backpackers planning on covering the entire loop (about a 3-day trip). **Maps** and info on all these trails are available from **Tacks' General Store** at Mile 23, and at the Chena Hot Springs Resort.

Fifty-seven miles northeast of Fairbanks stands **Chena Hot Springs Resort** (369-4111, Fairbanks office 452-7867; http://www.chenahotsprings.com), luring travelers and Fairbanks residents to its steaming waters. In winter, scores of people shiver their way to the resort for its prime Northern Lights viewing. In summer, Lower 48ers and Europeans (outer 39ers) are more frequent guests. **Rooms** are dear (in summer: singles $85; doubles $95), but tent and RV **campsites** are available by the river (tentsites $15; RV sites $20; showers $3; water and dump station free); non-guests may use the indoor hot pool, too. (Pool open daily 9am-midnight; $8, seniors and ages 6-12 $6). The resort's **restaurant** serves excellent but pricey food, including quesadillas, exotic salads, and espresso. Lunch starts around $8, dinner entrees are $15-21, and the bar menu offers a burger and fries for $6.75 (open daily 7am-10pm). Nearby are hiking/biking trails, over 30 mi. of cross-country skiing trails, and fine fishing (once the water level has dropped from the spring snow melt). The resort rents bikes ($7.50 per hr., $25 per day); wheels are free for hotel guests.

The resort is a good place to plan and amass info on a number of gerunds (snowmobiling, dog sledding, rafting, fishing, horseback riding, ice skating, etc.), but it's not the only option for spending the night in the park. The **Angel Creek Lodge** (369-4128), at Mile 50 on the Chena Hot Springs Rd., provides more affordable accommodations. Its rustic cabins sleep three to five people, have electricity and access to free showers and a sauna, and range in price from $45 to $100 a night. The place really bustles in February as a checkpoint on the Yukon Quest Sled Dog Race (see p. 468).

■ Steese Highway (Rte. 6)

The Steese Hwy. heads northeast out of Fairbanks, 162 mi. to the town of Circle on the **Yukon River.** Just 5 mi. outside Fairbanks, the Steese meets **Chena Hot Springs Road,** where a right turn brings you toward Chena River Recreation Area and the Chena Hot Springs. The **Elliot Highway (Rte. 2)** comes hard on the heels of the Chena Rd. at Mile 11 in **Fox;** make a right turn at the intersection to stay on the Steese. Fox is the last place to fuel up for the next 117 mi. on the Steese until the town of **Central** (and gas is far from cheap in Central). For the next 20 mi., the highway winds through boreal forest, past two ski resorts, and into a region of stunted spruce and fir trees known as taiga. At Mile 16.5 is the **Felix Pedro Monument,** a plaque honoring Pedro's 1902 discovery of gold in the creek across the highway.

■ Steese Highway: Campgrounds and Outdoors

The **Upper Chatanika River Campground,** at Mile 39, provides secluded, woodsy campsites ($8). **Cripple Creek Campground,** at Mile 60, offers good fishing and recreational goldpanning (sites $6; walk-ins $3). Both campgrounds have access to the **Chatanika River Canoe Trail,** which parallels the Steese for nearly 30 mi. The easygoing stream is clear and Class II; its only treacherous obstacles are low water and overhanging trees. At Mile 45.4, just after the road goes from paved to unpaved, the **Long Creek Trading Post** (389-5287) stands on the left side of the highway (open 8am-noon daily). Here, you can rent a canoe for $30 per day, and a shuttle service will take you and your canoe wherever you want to go (first 15 mi., $1.50 per mi.; over 15 mi., $1 per mi.; $10 minimum). The trading post has a small general store, and is currently building both a bathhouse with laundry and an RV park with a dump station. The road begins to climb consistently at about Mile 70, and heads towards the highway's nicest scenery. The **White Mountain National Recreation Area** and the **Steese National Conservation Area** lie side-by-side to the north. (Warning: At this point in the drive, you may begin to feel that your vision has suddenly started to deteriorate. Don't worry. It hasn't. The street signs are simply filled with bullet holes.)

At Mile 86 is the trailhead for the **Pinnell Mountain Trail,** the most spectacular and popular hike in the vicinity of Fairbanks. The 27 mi. trail is a rugged walk entirely above treeline, passing among alpine tundra flora. With proper timing, you can bask in the midnight sun (June 18-24), witness an explosion of wildflowers (late June), or watch caribou migration in the valleys below (Aug.-Sept.). Allow three days for the entire trip. Two cabins are well spaced along the trail for both nights, but as the trail has no water, it's important to bring three to four days' worth per person. A stove and plenty of bug repellent are also strongly recommended. The trail ends up on the highway at Mile 107; most hikers hitch back to their cars. (*Let's Go* does not, of course, recommend hitchhiking.) Even if you don't have time to schlep 27 mi., a scramble up either end of the trailhead is worthwhile. For more info on the trail, call the Bureau of Land Management at 474-2200.

Several entry points between Mile 94.5 and 147 lead to **Birch Creek,** which offers whitewater enthusiasts a 127 mi. course including several Class III rapids. At Mile 108, the highway passes over **Eagle Summit** where the panoramic view of countless peaks and fragile tundra is well worth a stop.

■ Steese Highway: Central and Circle Hot Springs

Central (Mile 127), a small, pit-stop town of about 400 summer residents, is anything but central. The **Circle District Museum** displays beautiful native beadwork, a giant mammoth tusk and tooth, samples of local gold, and a playable pipe organ that was carried over the Chilkoot Trial and floated down the river to Circle. All of the displays are from the area, and most of the items were found in old cabins (open Memorial Day-Labor Day daily noon-5pm; $1, children 50¢). The **Central Motor Inn** (520-5228) serves nondescript meals (sandwiches $6, dinner from $8) and offers laundry and shower facilities (showers $3, wash and dry $2 each). **Gas** is available here and at **Crabb's Grocery,** just down the street.

From Central, the road gets considerably worse, winding its way down towards the **Yukon River Flats Basin.** Unless you are planning to float the mighty **Yukon River** or urinate into its great waters—an inexplicable activity favored by some tourists—there is little reason to drive the highway's final 34 mi. to **Circle.** Instead, follow the signs and veer right after downtown Central to the **Circle Hot Springs.** The springs are just 8 mi. from Central, and provide a pleasant reward for those who made the long drive down the mostly unpaved yet scenic Steese. The pool here is actually outdoors, and a day pass for non-guests at the **Arctic Circle Hot Springs Lodge** is $5 (open 8am-midnight). The lodge itself is charming, historic, boasts piping-hot spring-fed toilets, and is supposedly haunted by at least two ghosts. (One is "a real prankster."). The rooms are costly (singles $75; doubles $100), but the lodge has a hostel on the fourth floor, next to its library. The hostel rooms are small and carpeted, with low ceilings and no beds, but those who stay there get free usage of the pool (first person $20, each additional adult $15, under 9 $7.50; each room fits up to 4 people). The dining room (open 7am-9pm) offers a tasty lunch ($4-$7) or dinner ($10-$16), and **Cold Rush Ice Cream** offers an abundance of ice cream in a homemade waffle cone ($3.50).

■ Delta Junction

Aptly named the Crossroads of Alaska, Delta Junction's function is to serve the intersection of two major arteries. The **Alaska Hwy. (Rte. 2)** leads southeast 108 mi. to **Tok** (see below), while the **Richardson Hwy. (Rte. 4)** runs 100 mi. northwest to Fairbanks and 270 mi. south to Valdez. The huge post in front of the visitor center declares Delta Junction the terminus of the Alaska Hwy., though Fairbanks argues otherwise. For $1, you can buy a macho certificate of Alcan completion at Mile 1422. Towards Fairbanks, 8 mi. north of town, is **Big Delta Historic Park,** home of **Rika's Roadhouse** (895-4201), a restored homestead complete with barnyard and accompanying animals (free walking tour on request). Well-groomed lawns and a grand view of the river and pipeline make Rika's an ideal lunch spot (sandwiches $5; fresh muffins 75¢) or stretch break (open daily 9am-5pm). Free tours of the **Trans-Alaska Pipeline** are given several times per day (M-Sa); call the visitor center (see below) to make reservations. To catch a glimpse of the mighty bison, head to the **buffalo ranch,** 7 mi. toward Tok on the Alcan. Turn left on Clearwater Rd.; after 4 mi., turn left after the fire station and drive up to the fence to gaze upon the herd.

   Hendrick's Auto Parts and Garage (895-4221) is at Mile 269 on the Richardson Hwy. (open M-Sa 9am-6pm and Su 9am-5pm). The **visitor center** (895-5061 or 895-5063) stands at the intersection of the two highways (open daily mid-May to mid-Sept. 8am-8pm). A **health clinic** is reachable at 895-5100. The **post office** (895-4601) is just north on the east side of the highway (open M-F 9:30am-5pm, Sa 10:30am-noon). **ZIP Code:** 99737. **Area Code:** 907.

   Tenters can head to **Delta State Recreation Site,** ½ mi. north from the visitor center, for roomy, protected sites with drinking water and pit toilets ($8). No one has ever accused Delta Junction cuisine of being distinctive or unpredictable, but a few restaurants near the visitor center give a fair deal. At **Pizza Bella Restaurant** (895-4841 or 895-4524), across from the visitor center, hearty subs on homemade toasted rolls provide the highest nourishment-to-dollar ratio (half $5; whole $7). Locals favor the *bellissima* pizza (11 in. pies from $8; open Su-Th 11am-10pm, F-Sa 11am-11pm). Across from Pizza Bella, **Buffalo Center Drive-in** (895-4055) fills Delta Junction's meat quota, serving all manner of burgers (buffalo burgers $6; malts $2; open M-Sa 11am-10pm, Su noon-8pm). For the same kind of burgers and a sit-down meal, the **Buffalo Center Diner** (895-5089), two blocks up the Richardson Hwy. from the visitor center, also has steak, sandwiches, and local options (open daily 6am-10pm). Gung-ho grocery-grabbers should hit the **IGA Food Cache** (895-4653), just north toward Fairbanks (open M-Sa 7am-10pm, Su 8am-8pm).

A Case of the Runs

France hosts the Tour de France, Boston the Boston Marathon, and Delta Junction the Great Alaskan Outhouse Race. The most exciting event at the Deltana Fair, held in late July and early August since 1987, the race pits locals in a contest to see which team can most swiftly push or pull an occupied outhouse through a 1½ mi. course. The commodes are hand-crafted to achieve the speediest, lightest design possible. During the race, four competitors struggle with the ungainly box while one lucky teammate sits on the throne. Winners receive the exalted Golden Throne Award, a painted toilet with the team members' names engraved on the lid. The coveted Silver Plunger goes to the second place finishers, and the third place prize is the much-admired Copper Snake.

ALASKA

■ Tok

With the Alaska Highway (Rte. 2) running through the heart of town, Tok (TOKE), at Mile 1314, calls itself "Mainstreet Alaska." Like many small towns plunked along the highway, Tok is friendly, dull, and geared toward summer tourists. The town lies at the intersection of the Alcan and the **Tok Cutoff (Rte. 1),** which leads 64 mi. southwest to **Slana,** a gateway to Wrangell-St. Elias National Park (see p. 444), and continues 74 mi. farther to Glennallen (see p. 443). Tok is also conveniently situated 12 mi. from the Alcan's intersection with the **Taylor Highway (Rte. 5)** at **Tetlin Junction** (see p. 473). Those looking to kill some time in Tok can view yon Alaska Range, witness free **dog team demonstrations** at the **Burnt Paw Shop** (883-4121) in summer (M-Sa 7:30pm), and walk or bike along Tok's multi-use paved path, which runs for 13 mi. along the highway.

ORIENTATION AND PRACTICAL INFORMATION Fairbanks is 206 mi. northwest of Tok along the Alcan, and Whitehorse, YT is 387 mi. (619km) southeast. **40 Mile Air** (883-5191), at Alcan Mile 1313, flies to Fairbanks (1½hr., M-F, $130). It also serves smaller towns about two times per week, including Eagle ($150), Chicken ($45), Delta ($65), and Northway ($45). Call at least three days in advance for reservations. Hitchers struggle to catch a ride out of town. **Alaska Direct** (883-5059 or 800-770-6652) runs buses leaving from the front of **Northstar RV Park,** about ½ mi. south of the visitor center, at 2:30pm (W, F, and Su) to Fairbanks ($40), Anchorage ($65), and Whitehorse, YT ($80). **Alaskon Express** leaves three times per week from the Westmark Inn to Anchorage (9hr., $105), Fairbanks (5hr., $69), Valdez (7hr., $84), and Skagway (overnight in Beaver Creek, $162). A spacious new **visitor center** (883-5775; http://www.tokalaskainfo.com), near the west end of town, is the largest single-story log building in Alaska (open daily June-Labor Day 8am-8pm; in winter M-F 8am-4:30pm). With a **Public Lands Information Center** (883-5666 or 883-5667) in the same building, the complex offers a trip-planning room, free coffee, and free Alaska-promoting movies (7 per day). Across the highway is the **Tetlin National Wildlife Refuge Headquarters** (883-5312), which provides info on the waterfowl preserve (open M-F 8am-5pm). The Northstar RV Park (see above) houses a **laundromat** (wash $1.25, dry 25¢ per 8min.) and **showers** ($3.50). Call 800-472-0391 for a **weather report.** The **Public Health Clinic** (883-4101) is across from the visitor center (open M 8:30am-5pm, Tu-Th 7am-6pm, F 9am-5pm; hours may vary; call ahead). The **police** can be reached at 895-4344. The **post office** (883-5880) is near the intersection of the Tok Cutoff and the Alaska Hwy. (open M-F 8:30am-5pm, Sa 11am-3:30pm; no window services on Sa). **ZIP Code:** 99780. **Area Code:** 907.

ACCOMMODATIONS AND CAMPGROUNDS The **Tok Youth Hostel (HI-AYH)** (883-3745) is 8 mi. west of town in the woods. Going west, take Pringle Dr. on the left and follow it for ¾ mi. The hostel is an authentic medical tent from WWII, with limited conveniences (drinking water, no running water, solar showers, electric lights) but unlimited character ($10; open May-Sept.). In town, the **Golden Bear Motel & RV Park** (883-2561; fax 883-5950), ½ mi. south on the right side of the Tok Cutoff, has secluded tent sites ($15), including firewood, showers, laundry (wash $1.50, dry $1) and a lounge with VCR. A gas fill-up at **Saveway** (883-5389), next to the Golden Bear, earns free RV parking (no hookups) or a tent site with no facilities (except for the bathroom in this 24hr. store). Rooms are also available (singles $55; doubles $60; room without TV or phone $38). At **Gateway Salmon Bake** (883-5555), on the Alcan at the east end of town, an all-you-can-eat dinner (king salmon $16.50; chicken $11) gets patrons a free RV or tent site with flush toilets, hot water, showers, and no hookups (open May 15 to Sept. 15 M-Sa 11am-9pm, Su 4-9pm; without dinner, sites $10). The **Snowshoe Motel** (883-4511 or 800-478-4511; fax 883-4512), at Mile 1314 across from the visitor center, offers free continental breakfast and cable (singles $57; doubles $68). The **Tok River State Recreation Area Campground,** 4 mi. east of town, just across the Tok River on the north side of the highway, offers serene, woodsy riverside sites ($10).

Pannin' fer Goald I: Theory

Panning for gold is a bit like shampooing: lather, rinse, repeat. You'll need a 12- or 18-in. pan, easily found at local stores, and an unclaimed stretch of beach or river. Scoop up some likely-looking sand and gravel. Look for tree roots, turns in the river, and upstream ends of gravel bars, where heavy gold may settle. Swirl water, sand, and gravel in a tilted gold pan, slowly washing materials over the edge. Be patient, dreaming of how you'll spend your riches. Eventually you'll be down to black sand, and—hopefully—gold. Gold is shinier than brassy-looking pyrite (Fool's Gold), and it doesn't break down at the touch, like mica, another common glittery substance. Later, we'll practice this technique.

FOOD Tok serves up plenty of expensive, forgettable food. The atypical **Loose Moose Espresso Cafe** (883-JAVA/5282), ¼ mi. east and across the highway from the visitor center, is a refreshing alternative with a largely vegetarian repertoire, including quiche with salad ($4.75), a vast veggie sandwich ($5.50), and a sourdough waffle ($3.75; open May to mid-Sept. M-F 7am-7pm, Sa 7am-3pm). **Young's Cafe** (883-2233), across from the visitor center, serves large sourdough breakfasts all day long, sandwiches ($4-7), and sirloin steak ($12; open daily June to mid-Sept. 6am-9pm). At **Frontier Foods** (883-5195 or 883-5196), across from the visitor center, reasonably priced bulk items and fresh fruit abound (open daily 7am-11pm; in winter 8am-9pm).

■ Taylor Highway (Rte. 5): Tetlin Junction to Eagle

The Taylor proves that the term "highway" is used very loosely in the North. With dirt or gravel roadbeds and countless hairpin turns, the Taylor Highway is definitely not for the high-strung. Open only from April to October, the Taylor leads through some of the hairiest curves and carries some of the dustiest summertime RV caravans in the North. Beginning at **Tetlin Junction,** 12 mi. east of **Tok** (see p. 472), the highway is initially tolerable, with wide, smooth lanes. At Mile 96, the highway intersects with the **Top-of-the-World Highway (Hwy. 9)** (see p. 390), which careens 79 mi. east to Dawson City, YT (see p. 386). The Taylor continues north 64 mi. through worsening roads, until hitting the tiny town of **Eagle** (see below). If cutting off towards Dawson City, be prepared to cross the U.S./Canadian border, here open only from May through September (8am-8pm Alaska time). No scheduled buses serve the Taylor, although there is boat service between Eagle and Dawson City (see p. 387). Some car-less travelers hitchhike, but sparse RV traffic makes this difficult; most hitchers pack a good book and start early in the morning. (*Let's Go* does not recommend hitchhiking. It does recommend reading, which separates man from beast.) The border patrol can be hard on hitchhikers, and they take unfortunates to the station, on a high mountain pass in the middle of nowhere. Make sure to have proof of funds (see **Customs,** p. 7). Only the wooden and phoneless **Boundary Cafe,** a tad west of the border, will feed you or your car if you get stuck. **Chicken** (Mile 66; see below) has expensive **gas** and **auto repair** at and nowhere else; it's wise to start with a full tank.

From **Mile 0,** the Taylor Hwy. gradually climbs to over 3500 ft. as it rolls toward 5541 ft. Mt. Fairplay. These first 50 miles are the easiest to drive and the most scenic. A sign and rest stop just past the summit (Mile 35) explains the history of the highway (wheelchair accessible toilet available). At Mile 49, the Bureau of Land Management operates the **West Fork Campground,** with pit toilets, water, and private tree-filled sites, including 7 extra-long sites for pull-throughs (25 sites: $6, self registration).

The megalopolis of **Chicken,** rumored to have received the name after local miners couldn't spell their first choice, "Ptarmigan," lies at Mile 66. Each summer, Chicken's population explodes with an influx of gold miners from its usual 25 to upwards of 100. The **Chicken Creek Saloon** throws the wildest pre-solstice, solstice, and 4th of July parties in the region (open 8am-whenever). Pricey gas ($1.79 per gallon) and (hallelujah!) tire repair (about $17.50) can be found at the **Goldpanner,** on the Taylor south of the "downtown" turn-off (open May-Oct. daily 8am-8pm; Visa and Master-

ALASKA

Card accepted). Half-hour walking tours of old ghost-town Chicken leave daily at 2pm from in front of the store, and are the only way to see the original mining cabins (free, but donations encouraged). The Goldpanner also allows gold-panning at one well-panned stretch of water (free; pans loaned out from the store). Next to the Saloon, the pricey **Chicken Creek Cafe** serves up burgers and sandwiches from $7; two weighty flapjacks ($4.75) or a weiner with potato salad ($6) are more reasonable deals (daily 8am-6pm). If passing through in the evening, check out the nightly **Salmon Bake** (open in summer daily 4-8pm, $15). Tenters and RVs can set up on the lot next to the cafe for free, although the site is less than ideal. The **Chicken Mercantile Emporium** pushes plastic souvenirs aplenty and also sells gas for $1.70 per gallon (open summer daily 8am-8pm; Visa and MC accepted).

The **Jack Wade Dredge,** a huge machine used for placer mining, lies rusting away right next to the highway at Mile 86. The dredge has deteriorated considerably, and its safety is dubious, but that doesn't stop passersby from wandering around its eerie skeleton. From this point until Eagle, evidence of mining, both large and small-scale, abounds. At Jack Wade Junction the road forks north for Eagle and east for Dawson via the Top-of-the-World. For the last 64 mi. from the Eagle junction, the road tightropes and snakes along mountainsides and canyons of **Forty Mile River,** another popular, though difficult, spot for rafters (see **Eagle,** below, for canoe outfitters). This last portion of the highway can be an arduous, 2hr. test of drivers' grit, making them wonder if the tiny town at the end is really worth it. It is.

■ Eagle

Many of Eagle's 240 residents say there's no place they'd rather live than this unpretentious wilderness town. Connected to the outside world only by the Taylor Hwy. and only during the summer, Eagle is no tourist mecca, lacking both a town water and sewage system and a police department. Eagle's heyday was in 1899, when the Secretary of War established a military base here to keep the towns's booming gold rush population in check. In 1901, Eagle became the Interior's first incorporated city. The military went south after mining fizzled, but unlike other forts along the Yukon, several of Fort Egbert's buildings and paraphernalia remain untouched by marauding miners. Eager Eagle-ites have quick grins and plenty a tale about pioneer great-grandmothers to share with travelers passing through. They also have more enthusiasm for their town and way of life than perhaps any other northern community; during the long winters, when the only access is by plane, they proclaim: "We're not snowed in. You're snowed out!"

PRACTICAL INFORMATION Bo Fay, the proprietor of **Telegraph Hill Services** (947-2261), on the Taylor Hwy., is an unofficial visitor center. He knows and loves Eagle, and will readily provide coffee, conversation, gas, car repairs, and an indispensable map of the town (open daily 8am-6pm; in winter M-Sa 10am-5pm). The real **visitor center** (547-2233) is at the end of 1st St.; take a left toward the old grass airstrip (open summers daily 9am-5:30pm). The center works in conjunction with the **Yukon-Charley Rivers National Preserve Headquarters** (same phone) next door, which has the lowdown on canoe trips to Circle and beyond (see below). **Village Store and Hardware** (547-2270), on 1st St. towards the boat landing, is a good place to buy gas or other general supplies (open summer M-F 9am-8pm, Sa-Su 9am-6pm; in winter M-Sa 9am-6pm; credit cards accepted). In any **emergency,** call the **Village Protective Safety Officer** at 547-2285. The **post office** (547-2211) is on 2nd St. at Jefferson (open M-F 8:30am-4:30pm). **ZIP Code:** 99738. **Area Code:** 907.

The Taylor Hwy. closes from mid-October to mid-May, making Eagle only accessible by air or dog sled. **Tatonduk Air** (547-2285) flies twice daily to and from Fairbanks and Eagle ($77). Ask at the **Eagle Trading Co.** (see below) for details.

CAMPGROUNDS, ACCOMMODATIONS, AND FOOD Campers will rejoice upon finding the **Eagle BLM Campground,** a 1 mi. hike from town past Fort Egbert, or the first left after Telegraph Hill Services. Ask Bo—he knows (sites $6; no water; pit toilets). Several short hiking trails start here. The unremarkable-looking **Yukon Adventure Bed and Breakfast** (547-2221), sitting about ½ mi. east of town, sets a new standard for rural B&Bs. Facing away from the river, turn left on 1st Ave., and follow signs for the boat launch. Have a mental adventure on the sun deck, or watch a film from the wide selection of videos.There are only three rooms, so call in advance (singles $50; doubles $60). The **Eagle Trading Co.** (547-2220), on Front St., has it all: gas, groceries, high-pressure, hot showers ($4), laundromat (wash $4 per double load, dry 25¢ per 5min.), RV hookups ($15), and rooms for rent (singles $50; doubles $60; open in summer daily 8am-8pm; in winter 10am-6pm; no credit cards). The adjacent **Riverside Cafe** (547-2250) serves standard fare at reasonable prices (burgers with fries or salad $5, pancakes $3.50; cash only; open May-Oct. daily 7am-8pm).

SIGHTS No visit to Eagle is complete without the three-hour **walking tour** (547-2297 or 547-2325), offered daily in summer by the **Eagle Historical Society and Museums.** The tour leaves at 9am from the **Courthouse Museum** at 1st and Berry St., and includes the courthouse, customs house, and Fort Egbert, which can't be viewed otherwise. *($5, under 12 free; call to arrange a different time.)* Well-preserved relics of frontier life decorate the tour, from a birch bark canoe to experimental (failed) horse snowshoes. The guides harken to a time when permafrost ice cream was Eagle's dessert of choice, and king salmon were so plentiful that Eagle dogs ate it daily.

    Amundsen Park, on 1st St. at Amundsen, honors the Norwegian explorer of the same name who, in the winter of 1905, hiked several hundred miles across northern Canada into Eagle when his ship became locked in the ice floes of the Arctic Ocean. Amundsen used Eagle's new telegraph to cable his government for money, then mushed back to his ship and successfully completed the first northward journey from the Atlantic to the Pacific—the hitherto unthinkable Northwest Passage. The park commemorates his voyage with a glistening silver globe etched in relief.

FLOATING FROM EAGLE The Yukon River, 1,979 mi. long, is the fourth longest river in North America and has the fifth largest flow volume of any river on earth. No other American river is as undeveloped, and its entire length has become a cult experience. The trip takes about three to four months and ends 1200 mi. from Eagle near Nome at the Bering Sea. Don't despair if four months sounds daunting. The 154 mi. between Eagle and Circle (see p. 120) take only four to six days. The trip passes through the **Yukon-Charley Rivers National Preserve** and some of Alaska's wildest country, but remains relatively calm the whole way. Rumor has it that any decent boat or even Huck Finn-style raft could make the trip. Campers do their best to avoid bears and countless mosquitoes by pitching tents on the gravel bars along the river. For detailed info, visit the Eagle Visitor Center (see above) or write to the National Preserve at P.O. Box 167, Eagle, AK 99738. **Eagle Canoe Rentals** (547-2203) will set you afloat for the five-day trip to Circle. *($165; paddles, life jackets, and canoe return included.)* Getting back is up to you, but flights to Fairbanks are available from Eagle and Circle, as is the daily river trip from Eagle to Dawson City along the *M/V Yukon Queen. (5hr., 1 per day, US$82.)* **Eagle Commercial** (547-2355), next to Amundsen Park on First St., sells topographic maps of the river and region ($6.50-7.50) as well as maps for the Canadian portion ($9.50). *(Open June-Sept. daily 9am-7pm.).*

ALASKA

Pannin' fer Goald 11: Practice

Swish. Swish. Swish swish. Swish. "Nope." Swish swish swish. Swish. "Nope." Swish. Swish swish swish. Swish. Swish. "GO-ALD! It's goald, goald, I tells ya!"

Southeast Alaska

Southeast Alaska (a.k.a. "the Panhandle" or just "Southeast") spans a full 500 mi. from the basins of Misty Fiords National Monument, past the state capital at Juneau, to Skagway at the foot of the Chilkoot Trail. The waterways weaving through the Panhandle, collectively known as the Inside Passage, make up an enormous saltwater soup spiced with islands, inlets, fjords, and the ferries that flit among them. Hemmed in by glorious mountains, the Southeast is distinguished by a cold-temperate rainforest climate, over 60 major glaciers, and neverending stacks of sourdough pancakes. Some communities of Interior and Southcentral Alaska have experienced what Alaskans call urban sprawl, but Panhandle towns cling to narrow pockets of coast that provide little or no room for growth. The absence of roads in the steep coastal mountains has helped these towns maintain their small size and hospitable personalities.

🔊 HIGHLIGHTS OF SOUTHEAST ALASKA

- The hub town of **Ketchikan** (see below) leads to hiking in **Deer Mountain** (see p. 482) and kayaking through **Misty Fiords National Monument** (see p. 484).
- The **Mendenhall Glacier** in **Juneau** is Alaska's most famous; visitors can touch its face or hike alongside it on the **West Glacier Trail** (see p. 502).
- The **Sheldon-Jackson Museum** and **St. Michael's Cathedral** in **Sitka** (see p. 495) house some of the most striking artifacts in the state, both Russian and Tlingit.
- In **Haines,** the **Chilkat Dancers** (see p. 508) provide a fascinating evening's entertainment after a rigorous and incredible hike up **Mt. Ripinsky** (see p. 508).
- For those with the dollars and the desire, **Glacier Bay National Park** (see p. 503) stuns the senses in a symphony of sea and ice.
- **Skagway** (see p. 509) kicks off the hallowed **Chilkoot Trail** (see p. 513) with flavorful Gold Rush fanfare.
- **Whales, whales, and more whales.** The **ferries** from Juneau to Petersburg or Sitka ply waters filled with surface-slicing orcas and body-slamming humpbacks.

GETTING AROUND

The **Alaska Marine Highway** system (see p. 34) provides the cheapest, most exciting way to explore the Inside Passage. Nighttime ferry trips allow passengers to avoid pricey accommodations in towns without hostels by sleeping on deck, where only the swarms of bald eagles above outnumber the hordes of mummy-bagged travelers. The ample scenery and the whales are best viewed in sunlight, though.

■ Ketchikan

Ketchikan is the first stop in Alaska for most tourist-stuffed northbound cruise ships and ferries laden with would-be cannery workers. Despite crowds and notoriously bad weather—the town averages nearly 14 ft. of rainfall a year—Ketchikan remains a popular destination. Its location is the key: the city provides access to Prince of Wales Island, Metlakatla, and most notably, Misty Fiords National Monument. Ketchikan itself offers plenty of bike trails, campgrounds, and hiking trails in nearby Tongass National Forest, plus numerous native and historical attractions that get mobbed by thousands of tourists on summer days.

Over three miles long and several hundred yards wide, Ketchikan stretches along the coast in typical Panhandle fashion. The city is Alaska's fourth largest (pop. 15,000), split between a tourist-oriented historic district and long chains of unremarkable, weather-beaten stores and homes. Indigenous carvers and refugee artists from the Lower 48 make their livings within the confines of the historic district and nearby Saxman Village, while loggers and fisherfolk romp around the rest of the community.

Southeast Alaska

TO KLUANE
TO WHITEHORSE
YUKON TERRITORY Alaska Hwy.
CANADA
U.S.A.

Atlin

Haines Hwy.
Klondike Hwy.
Skagway
Haines
Lynn Canal

Atlin Prov. Park

Glacier Bay Nat'l Park & Preserve
Glacier Bay

Gustavus
Cross Sound
Pelican
Icy Strait
Hoonah
Chichagof Is.
Tenakee Springs
Chatham Strait

Juneau
Gastineau Channel
Douglas Is.

Dease Lake

Telegraph Creek

BRITISH COLUMBIA
ALASKA

Stikine River

Angoon
Admirality Is.
Stephens Passage

Mt. Edziza Prov. Park

Sitka
Baranof Is.

Kake

Cassiar Hwy.
37

Kuiu Is.
Kupreanof Is.
Petersburg
Mitkof Is.
Zarembo Is.
Wrangell
Wrangell Is.
Etolin Is.

ALEXANDER

Sumner Strait

Clarence Strait
Klawock
Thorne Bay
Craig
Hollis
Hydaburg

Hyder
37A
Stewart

Behm Canal
Revillagigedo Is.
Ketchikan
Misty Fiords Nat'l Monument

Gravina Is.
Annette Is.
Metlakatla

ARCHIPELAGO

Prince of Wales Island

Portland Inlet

Dundas Is.
Dixon Entrance

Yellowhead Hwy.

Chatham Sound
Prince Rupert
16

PACIFIC OCEAN

Graham Is.
Masset
Port Clements
16
Yellowhead Hwy.
Tlell
Queen Charlotte City
Skidegate
Sandspit

Porcher Is.
Grenville Channel
Banks Is.
Pitt Is.
TO BELLINGHAM

N

Queen Charlotte Islands

Moresby Is.

Hecate Strait

- - - - - Ferry Routes

0   50 miles
0   50 kilometers

Gwaii Hanas Nat'l Park Reserve

ALASKA

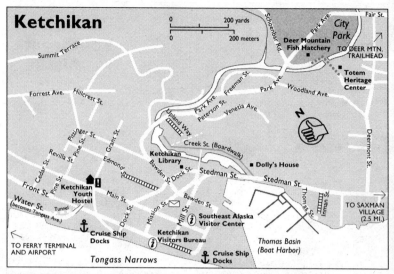

ORIENTATION AND PRACTICAL INFORMATION

Ketchikan rests on **Revillagigedo** (ruh-VIL-ya-GIG-a-doe) **Island,** 235 mi. southeast of Juneau, 90 mi. northwest of Prince Rupert, BC, and 600 mi. northwest of Seattle, WA. Upon reaching Ketchikan from Canada, **roll back your watch** by an hour to get in step with Alaska Time. Ketchikan caters to the travel elite, as revealed by the differing locations of the cruise ship docks (downtown) and the ferry docks (2 mi. north of town). The town is extremely spread out, making bike rental a wise option.

Transportation

Airplanes: A small ferry runs from the **airport,** across from Ketchikan on Gravina Island, to just north of the state ferry dock (every 15min.; in winter every 30min.; $2.50). **Ketchikan Airporter** (225-5429) carries people and bags between the airport and the ferries ($12.50). **Alaska Airlines** (225-2141 or 800-426-0333), in the mall on Tongass Ave. makes daily flights to Juneau ($80). Open M-F 9:30am-5pm. Air taxis and tours include **Taquan** (225-8800 or 247-6300; email taquan.ptialaska.net; http://www.alaskaone.com/taquanair), **Island Wings** (225-2444, 247-7432, or 888-854-2444), and **ProMech** (225-3845 or 800-860-3845).

Ferries: Alaska Marine Highway (225-6181; http://www.dot.state.ak.us/external/amhs/home.html), at the far end of town on N. Tongass Hwy. To: Wrangell ($24); Petersburg ($38); Sitka ($54); Juneau ($74); Haines ($88); Skagway ($92). Wheelchair accessible. Turn right from the terminal to reach the city center. Buses to town until 6:45pm. For more info, see **Essentials: By Ferry,** p. 34.

Harbormaster: 228-5632; VHF ch. 7. Electrical and water hookups $10.55.

Public Transportation: The main bus route runs a loop between the airport parking lot near the ferry terminal at one end, and Dock and Main St. downtown at the other. Stops about every 3 blocks. Fare $1, seniors and children 75¢. Every 30min. M-F 5:15am-9:45pm; 1 per hour Sa 6:45am-8:45pm, Su 8:45am-3:45pm.

Taxis: Sourdough Cab, 225-5544. **Alaska Cab,** 225-2133. **Yellow Taxi,** 225-5555. All run 24hr.; call ahead. A ride downtown from the ferry terminal costs $8.

Car Rental: Alaska Rent-A-Car, at the airport (225-2232), or at 2828 Tongass Ave. (225-5000 or 800-662-0007). Free local pick-up and delivery. $43 per day; unlimited mileage. Must be 21 or older. Open daily 6am-10:30pm.

Visitor and Financial Services

Visitor Information: Ketchikan Visitors Bureau, 131 Front St. (225-6166 or 800-770-3300), on the cruise ship docks downtown. Info, maps, and access to local charter and touring companies. Open daily May-Sept. 7am-5pm; limited winter hours. **Southeast Alaska Visitors Center (SEAVC)** (228-6220), on the waterfront next to the Federal Building, provides info on public lands around Ketchikan, including Tongass and Misty Fiords. The beautiful new ecology and native history exhibit is worth the $4 (free during off-season). SEAVC also provides an excellent trip-planning service, especially valuable for kayakers and fish fanciers heading out on their own, including maps, videos, and help from the knowledgeable staff. Open daily May-Sept. 8:30am-5pm; Oct.-Apr. Tu-Sa 8:30am-4:30pm.

Banks: National Bank of Alaska, 306 Olain St., at Dock St. 24hr. **ATM.** Bank open M-Th 9:30am-5pm, F 9:30am-6pm.

Local Services

Equipment Rental: Southeast Exposure, 507 Stedman St. (225-8829), across from the tunnel. Bikes $6 per hr., $22 per day. Kayak rentals require a 1½hr. orientation class ($30). Singles $35 per day, $30 per day for 6+ days; doubles $50 per day, $45 per day for 6+ days. $200 damage deposit. Open daily May-Sept. 7am-5pm. **The Pedalers** (225-0440), around the corner from the SEAVC, on the boardwalk. Bikes $6 per hr., $22 per day. Open daily 8am-5pm. **Southeast Sea Kayaks,** P.O. Box 7281 (225-1258 or 800-287-1607; email bbkayak@ktn.net; http://www.ktn.net/sea kayaks), in the visitors bureau. Singles $40 per day, $30 per day for 6+ days; doubles $50 per day, $40 per day for 6+ days. $200 damage deposit. Trip-planning service available. **Alaska Wilderness Outfitting,** 3857 Fairview (225-REEL/7335), rents camping kits including Coleman stove, lantern, mess kit, cooler, and assorted extras ($20 per day). Calls welcome daily 7am-10pm.

Bookstore: Parnassus, 5 Creek St. (225-7690). A special-subject book shop with an eclectic selection of used and new books. Talk to owner Lillian for the scoop on new publications, controversial politics, and local personalities. Open daily 8:30am-6pm; in winter closed M.

Library: Ketchikan Public Library, 629 Dock St. (225 3331), south of Creek St. and overlooking a waterfall. Free Internet access. Open M-W 10am-8pm, Th-Sa 10am-6pm, Su 1-5pm.

Laundromat: Highliner Laundromat, 2703 Tongass (225-5308). Wash $1.25, dry 25¢ per 7min. Showers $2 per 10min. Open 6am-10pm.

Public Showers: Seamen's Center (247-3680), on Mission St. next to St. John's. A warm, dry lounge for cleaning up and watching TV. Frequented by Ketchikan's down-and-out, but welcomes travelers. Showers $2.50, laundry 75¢. Volunteers help cook or clean for 2hr. any evening. Open daily June-Aug. 1-8pm; Sept.-May W and Sa-Su 4-7pm. **The Mat,** 989 Stedman (225-0628), ¾mi. from downtown, offers TV and a play area as well as showers ($2.50 per 15min.). Open daily 6am-11pm.

Public Pool: Kayhi Pool, 2160 4th Ave. (225-2010). **Valley Park Pool,** 410 Sihocubar Rd. (225-8755). Call for hours.

Public Radio: KRBD 105.9, 123 Stedman St. (225-9655; email rainbird@ktn.net).

Weather: 874-3232.

Emergency and Communications

Emergency: 911. **Fire:** 225-9616, on Main St. near Dock St. **Police:** 225-6631, at Main and Grant St., across from the hostel.

Senior Citizens' Helpline: 225-8080.

Pharmacy: Downtown Drugstore, 300 Front St. (225-3144). Open M-Sa 8am-6:30pm, Su 10am-6pm.

Hospital: Ketchikan General Hospital, 3100 Tongass Ave. (275-5171). **Clinic:** 3612 Tongass Ave. (225-5144). Open M-F 7:30am-6pm.

Post Office: (225-9601), next to the ferry terminal. Open M-F 8:30am-5pm. **Substation** at corner of Race and Tongass Ave. (225-4153). Open M-F 9am-6pm, Sa 9am-5pm. Another substation (225-2349) is in the Trading Post, at Main and Mission St. Open M-Sa 9am-5:30pm. **ZIP Code:** 99901.

Internet Access: See **Library,** above.

Area Code: 907.

ALASKA

ACCOMMODATIONS

The **Ketchikan Reservation Service** (800-987-5337; fax 247-5337) provides info on B&Bs (singles starting at $60). Because of boardwalk stairs, none of these accommodations are wheelchair accessible.

◉**Millar Street House,** P.O. Box 7281, 1430 Millar St. (225-1258 or 800-287-1607; email bbkayak@ktn.net). Call for directions. Excellent owners Kim and Greg fill 2 spacious rooms with cheer and the comforting smell from their extra-large bread machine. Just out of downtown, in a historic house overlooking the ocean. An essential stop for transplanted Aussies, or anyone else looking for a good time and a nice cup of tea. Singles $70; doubles $80.

Ketchikan Youth Hostel (HI-AYH), P.O. Box 8515 (225-3319), at Main and Grant St. in the First Methodist Church. Busy with hostelers of all ages, though the social scene is skimpy. The foam mats on the floor pass muster if you have a sleeping bag. Clean kitchen, common area, 2 showers, tea and coffee. Overflow sleeps in the church sanctuary. $8, nonmembers $11. 4-night max. stay, subject to availability. Strict lockout 9am-6pm. Lights out at 11pm-7am. Curfew 10:30pm. Baggage storage during lockout. Call ahead if you plan to arrive on a late ferry—the managers are extremely accommodating. Reservations advisable. Open June-Aug.

Innside Passage B&B, 114 Elliot St. (247-3700), on the stairway just above Tongass Ave., about ½ mi. from downtown, next to Panhandle Rigging Loft. Dark wood jacuzzi (with complimentary bubble bath) adds an exotic flourish to this simple, clean accommodation. Rooms overlooking the water make excellent eagle-watching perches. Singles $60; doubles $75. Reservations strongly recommended; mail a check in advance (no credit cards).

CAMPGROUNDS

Travelers who plan ahead can escape the lofty price for lodgings in Ketchikan by camping, although the city's infamous rain can make this a soggy, drippy chore. For supplies, check out **The Outfitter,** 3232 Tongass (225-6888; open M-F 8am-7pm, Sa 8am-6pm, Su 8am-4pm), or **Plaza Sports,** in the Plaza Mall (225-1587; open M-Sa 8am-8pm, Su 8am-5pm). Campgrounds usually have stay limits of a week or two, but cannery workers tent up in the public forests for up to a month. There is no public transportation from the town to the campgrounds, so plan on hiking, biking, or paying an exorbitant cab fare. The SEAVC (see **Visitor Information,** p. 478) provides information on all the campgrounds listed below, and on cabins with stoves ($25) in remote locations of the Tongass National Forest. Contact the SEAVC to get the late-breaking reservation phone number. Spaces fill rapidly in the summer.

A number of leafy, well-maintained campgrounds serve as a haven for counter-culture visitors to K-town. **Signal Creek** and **Three C's Campgrounds** sit across the street from each other on Ward Lake Rd. Drive north on Tongass Ave. and turn right at the sign for Ward Lake, approximately 5 mi. from the ferry terminal. The campgrounds share 28 spaces, water, and pit toilets (1-week max. stay; $8 fee May-Sept.). RVs should head one mile farther on Ward Lake Rd. to **Last Chance Campground,** where larger and recently landscaped sites cost $10 and are fully wheelchair accessible. Anyone can camp for up to 30 days in **Tongass National Forest,** but afterwards may not return for six months. Sites are not maintained, but any clearing is free.

FOOD

If there were a cure for the dread Northwest Thousand Island Disease, an affliction that leaves neither frankfurter nor falafel without a heart-stopping gob of mayo, Ketchikan would be first on the list for treatment. The restaurant scene follows a typical Panhandle pattern: one or two worthwhile establishments mingled with a heap of mediocre standard fare joints aimed at travelers just stepping off cruise ships. Stock up on groceries at **Ketchikan Market,** 3816 Tongass Ave. (225-1279; open daily 24hr.), or closer to downtown at **Tatsuda's,** 633 Stedman, at Deermount St. (225-4125; open daily 7am-11pm). The freshest seafood swims in **Ketchikan Creek;** in summer, anglers frequently hook king salmon from the docks by Stedman St. If you get lucky, **Silver Lining Seafoods,** 1705 Tongass Ave. (225-9865), will custom smoke your catch for $2.75 per lb. (open M-F 10am-6pm, Sa 10am-5pm, Su 11am-4pm).

5 Star Cafe, 5 Creek St. (247-7827). Not a dollop of killer mayo can be found in this oasis of health. The communal silverware drawer compliments the homey style of the black bean burrito with basmati rice ($6.75), soup of the day ($3), or banana *streusel* muffin ($1). Stenciled salmon swim up the wall, pointing the way to the upstairs Soho Coho, a local gallery. Open M-F 7:30am-5:30pm, Sa-Su 9am-5pm.

The Pizza Mill, 808 Water St. (225-6646), through the tunnel, 2 blocks north of downtown. Serves personal pan pizza with 2 toppings ($5.50). Jaded youths can split a trendy, 12 in., veggie-loaded "Generation X" with a disaffectedly hungry friend ($16). Open M-W 11am-11pm, Th-Sa 11am-3am, Su 11am-11pm.

Burger Queen, 522 Water St. (225-6060), 1 block past the tunnel. The regal veggie burgers, chicken troika sandwiches, and guacamole cheddar burgers can please even the pickiest palate. Everything in 3 sizes ($2-$8). Open in summer M-Sa 11am-8pm; off-season, closes at 4pm.

Jimbo's Cafe, 307 Mill St. (225-8499), across from the cruise ship docks. Where the inebriated stagger after the bars have closed. During more sober hours, tourists step up to the lunch counter. Try a 1 lb. Alaskan burger ($9), or a stack of 3 pancakes ($3.75). Free local calls. Open daily 6am until "very, very late."

SIGHTS

Every summer day, up to 6000 travelers tumble down gangplanks into downtown Ketchikan. With little time to spend exploring, they are immediately sucked into a vortex of horse-drawn carriages and chartered fishing boats, leaving more of Ketchikan for everyone else's romping pleasure. The official walking tour makes no distinction among good, bad, and ugly.

Ketchikan's primary cultural attraction is the **Saxman Native Village,** the largest totem park in Alaska, 2½ mi. southwest of town on Tongass Hwy. *($8 by cab, or a short ride on the highway bike path. Open M-F 9am-5pm, Sa-Su when a cruise ship is in.)* Founded at the turn of the century to preserve indigenous culture, the village has a traditional house, dancers, and an open studio where artisans create new totems. The poles on display represent both recent and historic carvings, some dating back150 years.

Know Your Totems

Totem poles are everywhere in this part of the world—lurking in primeval forests, planted in local cemeteries, decorating cheap motels, or poking out from tourist-happy McDonald's. Many indigenous peoples have long used these intricate sculptures both to honor each other and to transmit over a thousand years of history and culture; some mortuary poles even contain ancestors' ashes. Each of the figures vertically stacked on the totem has a specific significance, depending on the artist's tribe. The following symbols represent local Haida and Tlingit myths:

Raven: The creator of the tribes and a trouble-making trickster, identifiable by his long, straight beak. When the world was dark, Raven stole the sun from an old chief, and is often depicted with an orb in his beak.

Eagle: The second most important mythological figure, signifying peace and friendship. His hooked beak distinguishes him from Raven.

Bear-Mother: With one cub between her ears and another between her legs, she links the tribes of Eagle and Raven.

Beaver: His flat tail and two front chompers make him stand out from the rest. Beaver is often associated with Eagle.

Bear and Wolf: Remarkably similar, with sharp teeth and a high forehead. Both caused a lot of trouble (and still do) in their relationships with humans.

Killer Whale: Often shown with a seal in its mouth, the large-finned and razor-toothed orca stands for strength.

The **Totem Heritage Center,** 601 Deermount St. (225-5900), on the hill above downtown, houses 33 well-preserved totem poles from Tlingit, Haida, and Tsimshian villages. *(Open daily May-Sept. 8:30am-4:30pm. $4, under 13 free.)* It is the largest collection of authentic, pre-commercial totem poles in the U.S., but only a few are on display. An $8 combination ticket also provides admission to the **Deer Mountain Fish Hatchery and Raptor Center** (225-9533), across the creek. A self-guided tour explains artificial sex, salmon style. *(Open daily May-Sept. 8am-4:30pm.)* Unfortunately, visitors can only peer at the frothy action from a small central deck, though hungry eagles can be freely seen swooping down for fish entrails by the boats.

The colorful stretch of houses perched on stilts along **Creek Street** combats the otherwise unremarkably "historic" Ketchikan downtown. This festive area was once a thriving red-light district where, as tour guides quip, both sailors and salmon went upstream to spawn. Actresses in black fishnets and red-tasseled silk still celebrate this proud heritage of wenching, beckoning passers-by into **Dolly's House,** 24 Creek St. (225-6329), a brothel-turned-museum. *(Hours vary with cruise ship arrivals; typically open until 2:30 or 4:30pm. $4.)* Antiques nestle in secret hideaways where Dolly stashed money, bootleg liquor, and customers during police raids.

OUTDOORS (OR THE NEAREST APPROXIMATION)

Although Ketchikan offers boundless hiking and kayaking opportunities within the nearby Misty Fiords National Monument (see p. 484), hikers need only flirt with the city limits to find a trailhead. From Ketchikan, the 3001 ft. **Deer Mountain** makes a good dayhike. Walk up the hill past the city park on Fair St.; the marked trailhead branches off to the left just behind the dump. The ascent is steep but manageable, and on the rare clear day, the walk yields sparkling views of the town and the sea beyond. While most hikers stop at the 2½ mi. point, a longer route leads over the summit and past an A-frame overnight shelter that can be reserved at the SEAVC (see p. 478). The trail runs above treeline along a steep ridge, where snow and ice sometimes linger into the summer. At the peak, clear skies open upon a vista of mountains and lakes extending as far as Misty Fiords. **Blue Lake,** an alpine pond stocked with trout, shimmers in the middle of the ridge walk. Although there are no ski hills near Ketchikan, Deer Mountain has choice spots for **snowboarding** in winter. From the summit of the 3237 ft. **John Mountain,** the **John Mountain Trail** descends along the ridge, passing the **Stivis Lakes** on its way down to the **Beaver Falls Fish Hatchery** and the South Tongass Highway, 13 mi. from Ketchikan. This section of the hike is poorly marked and may test hikers' ability to read topographic maps. The entire hike, manageable in a tough full day, is 10 mi. long and requires a pick-up at the end.

A less strenuous and equally accessible outing is the trek along a boardwalk built over muskeg up to **Perseverance Lake.** The **Perseverance Trail,** beginning 10 mi. north of the city just before the Three C's Campground (see p. 480), climbs 600 ft. over 2.3 mi. to an excellent lake for **trout fishing.** Licenses can be purchased at the Outfitter or Plaza Sports (see **Campgrounds,** p. 480). *($10 per day, $15 for 3 days, $30 for 2 weeks, $50 for the season.)* By renting a boat and equipment from **Deer Mtn. Charters,** 939 Park Ave. (225-9800, 247-9800, or 800-380-3280; fax 225-8793; email deermtn@ktn.net), anglers can fish beyond the docks without forking over higher charter prices. *(Boats from $60 per day, rods from $5 per day.)*

For cold swimming, a sandy beach, and sheltered picnic tables, head to **Ward Lake,** at the Signal Creek Campground on Ward Lake Rd. (see p. 480). A 1.3 mi. trail around the grassy pond is perfect for first-time mountain bikers, while those with more experience can explore the surrounding logging roads. Defy the laws of rainy weather and gravity at **Kave Sport's indoor climbing gym,** 615 Stedman Ave. (225-KAVE/5283; email kavesp@hotmail.com). Over 2300 sq. ft. of climbing walls challenge beginners and expert climbers alike. *(Open M-Th 10am-10pm, F 10am-midnight, Sa 10am-10pm, Su noon-6pm. $6 per hr., $12 per day; equipment rentals $9.)*

NIGHTLIFE, ENTERTAINMENT, AND EVENTS

Scads of establishments allow Ketchikanians to drink like fish. Downtown is lined with tourist-oriented pubs, while every third building on Water St. houses a bar. Fisher-types crowd into **The Potlatch** (225-4855), on Thomas St., at the docks off Stedman St., just south of downtown. Uprooted railroad car seats grant a place to sip a beer and gander at the blackboard messages from one boat crew to another (open daily 11am-midnight or 2am, depending on the crowd). Younger, more diverse imbibers gather at the **First City Saloon** (225-1494), on Water St. toward the ferry terminal. First City serves Guinness, St. Pauli Girl, and a variety of microbrews (domestics $2-3). Local bands play here (Th-Su)—drink first (open daily 9am-2am). The hard-to-find **Hole in the Wall Marina,** 7500 S. Tongass (247-2296), is rich in local flavor. More varieties of beer (18) than chairs (4). Fish off the dock, then drink a pint or two while your catch cooks (open when you get there).

But, like Mom always said, you don't have to drink to have a good time. Ketchikan's **First City Players** present a variety of plays to sell-out crowds. On Fridays in July and August, check out the bawdy *Fish Pirate's Daughter,* a super-melodrama about Prohibition-era Ketchikan (Th-Sa at 8pm; $15, students $12). Shows go up at the **Main Street Theatre,** 338 Main St. (225-4792). The annual **Timber Carnival,** a spirited display of speed-chopping, axe-throwing virtuosity, coincides with Ketchikan's boisterous 4th of July celebration. On the second Saturday in August, the **Blueberry Festival** stuffs the streets with crafts, food, and live music, as well as a fierce **slug race.**

■ Near Ketchikan: Metlakatla

Metlakatla, where even the local dogs are too relaxed to open their eyes for passersby, offers a refreshing alternative to hyper-hyped Ketchikan. A few hours after you step off the floatplane or ferry, the whole town will know of your arrival. This is a good thing—smiling locals in the tiny town of "Met" often offer helpful tidbits of information or rides to good trailheads and campgrounds. Perched only 15 mi. southwest of Ketchikan on Annette Island, the town, whose name means "salt water channel passage" in Tsimshian (SIM-see-an), lies entirely within the **Tsimshian Reserve.** The community was founded in 1887, when Anglican lay-minister William Duncan led 800 Tsimshian to the island from British Columbia to escape religious persecution. During WWII, the village population swelled to 20,000 with military troops, but now has returned to its slow-paced origins, and is virtually untouched by tourism.

Staying for more than a day requires a permit, available at the **Municipal Office Building** (886-4441) on Upper Multon St. (open M-F 8am-4:30pm). Little else on the island takes much effort; Metlakatla is an easy, happy place to escape the Ketchikan

Come Closer, and Listen Well...

Those who brave the Alaskan outdoors usually fear only two animals—massive brown bears and vampire mosquitoes. Yet if you pay heed to the Tlingit stories told in hushed whispers around late-night fires, you will surely fear another. Some say the creatures are mere myths to scare the children, but anyone who's lived in the Southeast long enough, whether Tlingit, logger, or fisherman, isn't so quick to dismiss their existence—or their danger. According to Tlingit tales, if you wander too close to the water or too far into the woods, the Kushtakas (KOOSH-ta-kuz)—land otters by day, humans by night—will snatch you and turn you into one of their own. Paddling in skate-skin canoes under cover of night, the Kushtakas rescue fishermen lost at sea, only to take them to the eerie land of the otter people, never to be seen again. Then, disguised as these lost men, the otter people come ashore to ensnare the fishermen's loved ones. Recognize a Kushtaka in otter form by its faint two-toned whistle, or in human guise by the fur between its fingers. Just don't stare too long, or you'll be overwhelmed by its numbing power...

crowds. It's almost worth the trip solely for the bird's-eye view of incredible scenery on the float plane trip over. Travelers can stay in town to get in on the community's rich culture, or head to the hills for wilderness adventure (which may be tamer than usual, since Annette Island is bereft of bears).

PRACTICAL INFORMATION, CAMPGROUNDS, AND FOOD Pro-Mech Air (in Ketchikan 225-3845; in Metlakatla 886-3845; 800-860-3845) offers safety-conscious float plane flights (15min.; 4 per day; $19, $30 round-trip; no credit cards). **Taquan Air** (886-6868) offers comparable service for a slightly higher price. The **Alaska Marine Highway** (800-624-0066) makes six trips a week to the island, including two on Saturdays (75min.; $14). From the ferry terminal, it's a short walk to town; turn right upon arrival and follow the signs.

If you've got the money, you can buy a roof over your head, and if you've got the time, you might find a decent place to pitch a tent. **Camping** is free beyond the cemetery, heading out of town on Western Ave., though the underbrush is thick and the ground wet. A better bet may be to ride out toward the old military airport and **Point Davis,** where camping is acceptable out of sight of the road. Hitching is easiest on the weekends, when locals go out on picnics (although even then, *Let's Go* does not recommend it). **Ethel's B&B,** P.O. Box 526 (886-5275), on Western Ave. past the longhouse, serves a hot breakfast and dinner, as well as a bag lunch ($85; in winter $75).

Food options are predictably limited. **Leask's Mini Mart** (886-3000), at the south end of Upper Milton St., sells rolls of the egg ($2.25) or cinnamon ($1.75) variety, with an extensive fried-foods deli (open M-Sa 7:30am-10pm). To support the island grocery monopoly, a larger (but sadly roll-less) **Leask's Market** sits at the other side of town on Western Ave. (open M-F 10am-6pm, Sa 10am-5:30pm, Su noon-5pm).

OUTDOORS AND SIGHTS Perhaps the most enjoyable way to spend a languorous Metlakatla afternoon is to walk down the rocky beach that parallels Western Ave., past the cemetery to the newly-remodeled boardwalk, picnic tables, and ropeswing of **Pioneer Park.** For some upward mobility, a 30-minute trail up **Yellow Hill** offers splendid views of the island's west side. The trail starts about 1½ mi. south of town on Airport Rd.; look for the boardwalk on the right. A longer route leading to **Purple Lake,** where many a tasty trout has met its end, yields even more precious views per mile. The steep 3 mi. trail leads up a rocky mountainside that gushes waterfalls. Take Airport Rd. south for 2.7 mi., then continue another 1.8 mi. on Purple Mountain Rd. to the trailhead. A more convenient way up Purple Mountain begins by following the trail next to the water pipeline, which starts right next to the ferry dock. Once reaching the dam at the top, hikers can make the rest of the way on various unmarked trails. Bushwhacking through the oldgrowth is said to be quite painless, and the view from the top is ample reward for this all-day excursion.

A visit to Metlakatla would not be complete without seeing the art-filled **longhouse** on Western Ave. *(Open M-F 1-4:30pm.)* Locals have begun to bring in cruise ship tourists from Ketchikan in the summer to watch a **tribal dance performance;** stop by the longhouse in the late morning or call 247-8737 to spectate. The free **Duncan Museum** (886-7363), once the home of founding father William Duncan, features a collection of his personal effects and old photographs of the village. Look for the bright yellow cottage at the south end of town (open M-F 1-4pm) or peek at the exhibit in the front room of the longhouse.

■ Near Ketchikan: Misty Fiords National Monument

The jagged peaks, plunging valleys, and dripping vegetation of **Misty Fiords National Monument,** 20 mi. east of Ketchikan, make biologists dream and outdoors enthusiasts drool. Only accessible by kayak, power boat, or float plane, the 2.3-million-acre park offers superlative camping, kayaking, hiking, and wildlife viewing. Walls of sheer granite, scoured and scraped by retreating glaciers, rise up to 3000 ft., and encase saltwater bays. More than 12 ft. of annual rainfall and a flood of runoff from large icefields near the Canadian border feed the streams and waterfalls that empty into two long fjords, **Behm Canal** (117 mi. long) and **Portland Canal** (72 mi. long), on either side of the monument. **Camping** is permitted throughout the park, and the Forest Service maintains four first-come, first-served shelters (free) and 14 cabins ($25). Write directly to the **Misty Fiords Ranger Station** (225-2148) at 3031 Tongass Ave., Ketchikan, and ask ahead at the SEAVC (see p. 478).

Seasoned **kayakers** often paddle straight into the park, nimbly navigating the harsh currents between Ketchikan and Behm Canal. Kayaking neophytes might contact **Alaska Cruises**, 220 Front St., Box 7814 (225-6044), who will drop off both kayaker and kayak at the head of Rudyard Bay during one of their four weekly sightseeing tours ($175 per person). **Southeast Sea Kayaks** (225-1258 or 800-287-1607; email bbkayak@ktn.net; http://www.ktn.net/seakayaks), at the visitors bureau (see p. 478), will arrange similar transportation ($175-$200 per person), book forest service cabins, and sell a trip-planning package with topographical maps for kayaking, fishing, and other activities in the monument ($14). The trip-planning center at the SEAVC is also a comprehensive resource. **Walker Cove, Punchbowl Cove,** and **Rudyard Bay,** off Behm Canal, are choice destinations for paddlers, though the waters are frigid and wide stretches of coast lack good shelter or dry firewood.

A slew of expensive charter operations visit the monument, starting from at least $125. Alaska Cruises offers an 11-hour **boat tour** with three meals ($155). **Combination boat/flight tours** last six hours ($195). **Island Wings** (225-2444 or 247-7432) has the cheapest flightseeing trips ($125), but these airy jaunts still cost more than $1 per minute. Call the Ketchikan Visitors Bureau for more information.

■ Prince of Wales Island

Prince of Wales Island sits less than 30 mi. west of Ketchikan, beneath a thick rainforest canopy broken only by mountain peaks, patches of muskeg, and swaths of clearcutting. Tongass National Forest and Native American tribal groups manage most of the island, which is criss-crossed with roads built to facilitate logging. The industry has left some scars, but even so, a great deal of Prince of Wales Island remains swaddled in virgin forest.

On an island this large, smaller only than Hawaii and Kodiak in the U.S., exploration requires a good set of wheels. The 1800 miles of logging roads are perfect for mountain biking or tooling around in a 4x4 or all-terrain vehicle. Car rentals on the island are expensive, so it's less taxing to bring a bike or truck over on the ferry. Pricey charter companies reel in fishermen, hunters, kayakers, and scuba divers, though independent travelers can set off on their own with a few maps and some help from the Forest Service (see below). Be sure to get permits for fishing and hunting, and to know where tribal lands end and National Forest begins.

There are three main towns on Prince of Wales: Craig, Klawock, and Thorne Bay. Craig is on the west side of the island and sports most of the tourist resources. Underinspiring Klawock lies seven miles east, while less-than-lovely Thorne Bay is 43 miles farther east on the other side of the island. Hollis, where the ferry docks, is 31 miles southeast of Craig. There is only one main paved road connecting these towns—stick to it and you can't get lost.

■ Prince of Wales Island: Craig

Craig, on the west coast of the Island, is home to most charter services, the district ranger station, a number of very nice and pricey hotels, and one commendable restaurant. Outside of these niceties, there's little reason to linger. The surrounding area is heavily clearcut and there are no convenient hiking trails.

PRACTICAL INFORMATION
Airplanes: Float planes fly directly into Craig from Ketchikan. **Promech** (826-3845 or 800-860-3845). 2 per day, $69. **Taquan Air** (826-8800): 4 per day, $81.

Ferries: The **Alaska Marine Highway** (see Ketchikan listing, p. 478) runs from Ketchikan to Hollis (2¾hr.; 1 per day in summer; $20, ages 2-11 $12, car $41).

ALASKA

Taxis: Jackson Cab (755-2557) runs between Hollis and Craig for about $25.

Car Rental: Practical Rent-a-Car (826-3468) Small selection of much-needed cars and 4x4s. $40 per day, 40¢ per mi. 18-year-olds welcome. Open M-Sa 8am-5pm.

Harbormaster: 826-3404, at VHF ch. 16.

Visitor Information: Craig Chamber of Commerce (826-3870), on Easy St., cheerfully obliges requests for info. Open M-F 9:30am-4pm. Wheelchair accessible.

Outdoor Information: Forest Service Office (826-3271), at 9th Ave. and Main St., gives the skinny on caves, camping, and the 19 wilderness cabins on Prince of Wales Island. Open M-F 7am-5pm. The **Log Cabin** (826-2205) sells **fishing and hunting licenses.** Open M-Th and Sa 8am-6pm, F 8am-7pm, Su 10am-3pm.

Bank: National Bank of Alaska (826-3040), on Craig-Klawock St., by the post office. Open M-Th 10am-5pm, F 10am-6pm.

Bookstore: The Voyager, on Cold Storage Rd. in the Southwind Plaza. Sells cappuccino. Open M-Sa 7am-7pm, Su noon-5pm.

Library: (826-3281), on 3rd St.

Medical Services: Seaview Medical Center (826-3257), on 3rd St. Open M-F 9am-5pm, Sa 9am-2pm.

Emergency: 911. **Police:** (826-3330), across from the library on 3rd. St.

Post Office: (826-3298), on Craig-Klawock St. next to Thompson Supermarket. Open M-F 8am-5pm, Sa noon-2pm. **ZIP Code:** 99921.

Area Code: 907.

ACCOMMODATIONS, CAMPGROUNDS, AND FOOD Although most of the island falls within the free camping zone of Tongass National Forest, Craig is surrounded by private tribal lands where camping is prohibited. The **TLC Laundromat and Rooms** (826-2966), on Cold Storage Rd. behind the supermarket, offers affordable and legal slumber space (singles $40; doubles $50). The **laundromat** (wash $2, dry 25¢) also has **showers** ($2.50 per 5min.; open M-Sa 8am-8pm).

Once loaded up with supplies and food from Craig, campers should head north to **Tongass National Forest.** Visits may last up to one month, as long as campers spend no longer than two weeks at any site. Call or stop by the **Forest Service Station** (828-3304) for more information on the 12 **cabins** on Prince of Wales (open M-F 8am-5pm). **Eagles Nest Campground,** 12 mi. north of Thorne Bay, offers access to a bathroom, water, cooking grates, a canoe launch, picnic tables, and RV parking.

The only place in town to sit down for a tasty (if greasy) meal is **Ruth Ann's** (826-3376), on Front St., which offers affordable breakfast and lunch options ($6-8). Ruth Ann must make a bundle during dinner, though, when prices skyrocket to $18 and higher (open daily 6am-10pm). The best bet for supping is **Thompson Supermarket** (826-3394) on Craig-Klawock St., where a salad bar and a deli complement a good selection of groceries (open M-Sa 7:30am-8pm, Su 9am-7pm). Move them ever-lovin' feet to Easy St., where **TK Sub Marina** (826-3354) offers low-fat salads ($4) or full foot-long subs ($13).

OUTDOORS AND UNDERGROUND The **Craig Dive Center** (826-3481 or 800-380-DIVE/3483), at 1st and Main St. in Craig, offers a two-tank boat dive for groups of four ($125 per person). Owner Craig lives in Craig—coincidence or destiny? **Island Adventures** (826-2710) rents kayaks for $20 per day. **Log Cabin** (755-2205 or 800-544-2205), in Klawock, rents canoes for $20 per day. The Forest Service (see above) provides info about the island's nine **hiking trails,** plus tips on hiking and **biking** local logging roads without mishap. The cuddly rangers can also furnish maps for a number of established **canoe trails,** and reserve one of the **wilderness cabins** that line these watery routes ($25 per night).

The most distinctive of the island's attractions is **El Capitan Cave,** North America's deepest cavern. The cave bores into the limestone bedrock of Prince of Wales, and is adorned with striking marble outcroppings. Deep within the cave, speleologists (not to be confused with amateur spelunkers) have recently uncovered the remains of a 12,000-year-old grizzly bear. Free two-hour tours start behind the gate 150 feet inside the cave, and require a hard-hat and flashlight. *(Tours May-Sept., W-Su at noon, 1pm, and 3pm. Off-season tours available with 14-day advance notice.)* Make reservations with the **Thorne Bay Ranger District** (828-3304). The cave is about a three-hour drive from either Craig or Thorne Bay.

▨ Wrangell

Wrangell is the only spot in Alaska to have been ruled by four different nations. In 1834, the Russian-American Company ousted a Tlingit village on an island near the mouth of the Stikine River to build a fort. Six years later, the British-owned Hudson Bay Company took out a lease on the Russian garrison. When the United States purchased Alaska from Russia in 1867, Britain forked over control of the fort to the Americans. As the only entry between Prince Rupert and Skagway to Canada's interior, the Stikine River became a crucial transportation corridor during the three gold rushes of the next forty years. As miners traveled to and from the goldfields, they tramped through the little town that became Wrangell. Proto-ecologist John Muir was duly unimpressed with the result: "It was a lawless draggle of wooden huts and houses, built in crooked lines, wrangling around the boggy shores of the island." Now an orderly, prosperous lumber and fishing town with a picturesque harbor, Wrangell's attractions are convenient enough to allow a brief visit during a ferry layover, but plentiful enough to merit a night's stay. Note that locals take their day of rest very seriously: grocery stores, the museum, and the tourist office are all closed on Sundays.

PRACTICAL INFORMATION

Airplanes: Alaska Air (874-3309, recording 874-3308). 1 flight daily to: Petersburg ($72); Juneau ($125); Ketchikan ($109); Seattle, WA ($366). **Taquan Air** (874-8800) flies to: Ketchikan ($72); Juneau ($125). **Sunrise Aviation,** P.O. Box 432 (874-2319) offers flightseeing over the Stikine River ($285).

Ferries: Alaska Marine Highway (874-2021, recording 874-3711), at Stikine Ave. and McCormack St. Frequent service to: Sitka ($38); Juneau ($56); Ketchikan ($24). Open 1½hr. before arrivals. Lockers 25¢.

Taxis: Porky's Cab Co., 874-3603. **Star Cab,** 874-3622. Both 24hr.

Car Rental: Practical Rent-A-Car (874-3975; fax 874-3911), on Airport Rd. near the airport. Compact car $43 per day; van $46 per day; unlimited mileage. Must be 21.

Auto Repair: Wrangell Auto Body (874-3857), at Mile 2¼ of Zimovia Hwy.

Visitor Information: Chamber of Commerce (874-3901; email wrangell@wrangell.org; http://www.wrangell.org), on Front St. at the side of the Stikine Inn. Pick up *The Wrangell Guide* and its free map. Open Tu-F 9am-4pm.

Outdoor Information: Forest Service, 525 Bennett St., ¾mi. east of town (874-2323). Reserve cabins here. Open M-F 8am-5pm. **Alaska Department of Fish and Game** (874-3822), in the green Kadin Building on Front St. Fishing and hunting info. **Ottesen's True Value,** P.O. Box 81 (874-3377), on Front St., sells licenses.

Banks: National Bank of Alaska (874-3341), on Front St. Home of Wrangell's sole **ATM.** Bank open M-F 9am-5pm.

Library: (874-3535), on 2nd St. Free Internet access. Open M and F 10am-noon and 1-5pm, Tu-Th 1-5pm and 7-9pm, Sa 9am-5pm.

Public Radio: KSTK 101.7 FM

Laundromat: Thunderbird Laundromat, 233 Front St. (874-3322). Wash $2, dry 25¢. Open daily 6am-7pm.

Public Pool: (874-2444), indoors at Wrangell High School on Church St. Hours vary; closed Su. Pool, weight room, gym $2, under 18 $1.25; racquetball $6 per pair.

Public Showers: Hungry Beaver Pizza (see **Food,** below), on Shakes St. $3.

Emergency: 911. **Police:** 874-3304. **Fire:** 874-3223. Both the police and fire department are in the **Public Safety Building** on Zimovia Hwy.

Pharmacy: Stikine Drug, 202 Front St. (874-3422). Open M-F 10am-5:30pm, Sa 10am-2pm, Su 11am-6pm.

Hospital: (874-3356), at Bennett St. and 2nd Ave.

Post Office: (874-3714), at the north end of Front St. Open M-F 8:30am-5pm, Sa 11am-1pm. **ZIP Code:** 99929.
Internet Access: See **Library,** above.
Area Code: 907.

ACCOMMODATIONS AND CAMPGROUNDS

Wrangell Hostel, 220 Church St. (874-3534), 5 blocks from the ferry terminal; just look for the groovy neon cross. A surprisingly under-utilized resource—you may end up having the entire place to yourself. Showers, kitchen, and spacious common room with piano. 20 foam mats on the floor for $10 each; blanket and pillows $1. Daytime luggage storage. Reception open daily in summer 5pm-9am. 10pm curfew unless you're on a late ferry; call ahead. Closed in winter.

Harbor House B&B, 645 Shakes Ave. (874-3084 or 800-488-5107), across from the Hungry Beaver. Ahoy! Three rooms decked out with nautical antiques and a prime harborside location. Shared bath and small kitchen. Ride around town on complimentary "vintage" bikes. Continental breakfast included. Singles $55; doubles $70.

Rooney's Roost B&B, 206 McKinnon St. (874-2026 or 874-3622), at 2nd St. A step down in appearance and convenience; nevertheless, Rooney's is clean, with big breakfasts and comfortable beds. Singles $55; doubles $60. In July and Aug., reserve several weeks in advance.

City Park, 1½ mi. south of town on Zimovia Hwy., immediately beyond the cemetery and baseball field. (2nd St. changes names several times before becoming Zimovia Hwy. south of town—trust us.) Picnic tables, shelters, drinking water, and toilets of dubious comfort, but a beautiful view of the water. The price is right, too: free. 24hr. max. stay. Open Memorial Day-Labor Day.

Alaskan Water RV Park, 241 Berger St. (874-2378 or 800-FISH-INC/347-4462; fax 874-3133), off Zimovia Hwy., ½ mi. from town. Clean and convenient, but gravelly with scant privacy. 6 RV hookups: $12. Showers $2.50. Open mid-Mar. to mid-Oct.

FOOD

If you're not in the mood for pizzas or burgers, pick up some tasty deli sandwiches at **Benjamin's Groceries** (874-2341), on Outer Dr. (open M-Sa 8am-8pm) and picnic at **Kik Setti Totem Park,** around the corner at Front St. and Episcopal. For bulk organic grains, dried fruit and nuts, and healthy fruit juices, head to **Homestead Natural Foods** (874-3462), ½ mile north of town on Evergreen Ave., on the way to the petroglyphs. Call first on nice days, in case Rosemary decides to close up and go kayaking.

J&W's, 120 Front St. (874-2120). Good, messy burgers ($3.60) and fried mini-burritos ($1.65) are sold at the window. Local teeny-boppers congregate outside around the picnic tables. More creative alternatives include salmon or shrimp burgers ($5) and 13 flavors of shakes ($2.65). Open M-Sa 11am-7pm, Su noon-7pm.

Hungry Beaver Pizza/Marine Bar (874-3005), on Shakes St. near the island. Where guzzlers and high school grease-eaters mix. One-person pizzas from $5.50. Low-key waterfront bar is a last refuge for late-night diners. Kitchen open daily 4-10pm. Bar open daily 10am-2:30am. Showers $3. Pizza-eating can get messy, it seems.

SIGHTS

If the ferry schedule only gives you 45 minutes in Wrangell, a walk out to **Shakes Island** might be a good reason to rush. Follow Front St. to Shakes St., where a short bridge leads to the middle of Wrangell's snug harbor. Outdoor totems guard the **Shakes Tribal House** (874-2023), a meticulous replica of the communal home of high-caste Tlingits. *(Open in summer whenever a cruise ship docks for more than 1hr., or by appointment for a donation of $20 or more. Regular donation $2.)* A Civilian Conservation Corps work team built the house during the Great Depression without the aid of a sawmill or a single nail. Inside, finely carved totems stand below large timbers scarred by the original adze marks.

Stone carvings by the region's first inhabitants adorn **Petroglyph Beach,** ¾ mile north of the ferry terminal on Evergreen Ave. Some are simple circles and spirals, while others illustrate complex facial patterns, thought to represent spirits or totem animals. Archaeologists are uncertain about the age of these petroglyphs, but local tradition maintains that they were in place before the Tlingit reached the harbor. The **Wrangell Museum** (874-3770), temporarily dwelling in the basement of the community center on Church St., houses collections of Native American artifacts, a communications and aviation room, and an exhibit on the region's natural history. *(Open year-round Tu-F 10am-4pm, Sa 1-5pm. $2, under 16 free.)*

OUTDOORS

Hikers can follow in John Muir's footsteps, scrambling up nearby **Mt. Dewey** to an observation point with a commanding view of town and the Stikine River flats. Walking down 2nd St. toward the center of town, McKinnon St. is on the left. Follow McKinnon St. to a left on 3rd St., and look for a white sign marking the trailhead. The trail is primitive and not regularly maintained. Three miles beyond City Park on Zimovia Hwy., the **Rainbow Falls Trail** runs 0.7 mi to the top of a 40 ft. waterfall. The **Institute Creek Trail,** which breaks off from the Rainbow Fall Trail just before the top of the falls, is much more rewarding. The result of a Herculean trail-building effort, the route follows a boardwalk for 2.7 mi., paralleling a series of impressive waterfalls (50min. from trailhead) before breaking into several muskeg openings on a ridgetop. A three-sided Forest Service shelter, available for overnight stays on a first-come first-served basis, sits on the ridge at the end of the trail. Both taxi services go to the trailhead for $7-8. The **Wrangell Ranger District,** Box 51 (874-2323), has more info on trails, campsites, and cabins in the Wrangell area. *(Open M-F 8am-4:30pm.)*

The **Stikine River** is one of the fastest navigable rivers mentioned in this book. **Alaska Vistas** (874-2429 or 874-3006; email info@alakavistas.com; http://www.alaskavistas.com) rents kayaks (singles $40; doubles $50), and runs boat tours up the Stikine and over to **Garnet Ledge.** There are six Forest Service cabins throughout the Stikine Delta and two bathing huts at **Chief Shakes Hot Springs,** a few miles upriver. The **Anan Bear Observatory** is also accessible by boat—watch voracious bears feast on the pink salmon that climb the falls to spawn. Contact **Stickeen** [sic] **Wilderness Adventures,** Box 934, 107 Front St. (874-2085 or 800-874-2085; fax 874-2285), for info; they schedule departures around ferry schedules. *(Open M-F 9am-5pm. Daytrips $145 per person.)* For a full listing of charter boat services (Wrangell has over 24), contact the Chamber of Commerce (see **Practical Information,** above), which also provides info on **scuba-diving, whale-watching,** and **fishing and hunting** trips.

■ Petersburg

Drawing visitors and locals alike, the harbors of Petersburg teem with fresh salmon and generations of Norsk fisherfolk. In 1897, Norwegian immigrant Peter Buschmann noticed the natural harbor, abundant fish, and convenient glacier ice around Petersburg, saw an opportunity, and built a cannery. Now P-Burg claims one of the world's largest halibut fleets and a strong Scandinavian legacy, plus direct access to the humpback-filled Frederick Sound. The tiny Wrangell Narrows that lead to Petersburg are too small for the large cruise ships, sparing the fishing town from tourist trappings, but also inspiring little reason to accommodate budget travelers. There are no hostels or storage facilities for packs, but it's worth the effort to plant stakes in P-burg, where the houses are well groomed, the streets are clean, the scenery is pretty, the fish are fresh, the men are good-looking, and all the children are above average.

PRACTICAL INFORMATION AND ORIENTATION

Petersburg is located on **Mitkof Island.** If you're looking for **Nordic Drive, Main Street,** or **Mitkof Highway,** you're probably on it—the main drag goes by all three aliases. The ferry drops off 1 mi. south of downtown, but it's a painless walk. Cabs to the center run about $4, or $6 out to Tent City.

ALASKA

Airplanes: Alaska Airlines, 1506 Haugen Dr. (772-4255), 1 mi. from the Federal Bldg. To: Juneau ($114); Seattle, WA ($346; $181 with 2 wk. advance purchase). Next door, **Haines Air** (772-4200) often beats these prices with 3 daily flights to Juneau. For **flightseeing,** call **Temsco Air** (772-4780) or **Pacific Wing** (772-4258).

Ferries: Alaska Marine Highway, Mile 0.9 Mitkof Hwy. (772-3855), 1 mi. from the town center. To: Ketchikan ($38); Sitka ($26); Wrangell ($18); Juneau ($44). Open 1½hr. before ferry arrivals.

Harbormaster: 772-4688. Provides maps and brochures. Showers $1.

Taxis: City Cab, 772-3003. Rates start at $4. Runs 24hr. $6 from ferry to Tent City.

Car Rental: Allstar (772-4281 or 800-722-5006), at the Scandia House Hotel. $45 per day; unlimited mileage. Must be 21 with a credit card. Also rents 18 ft. **boats** ($150 per day, $125 for hotel guests).

Auto Repair: Mike's Autobody (772-3052), next to the post office (see below).

Visitor Information: P.O. Box 649 (772-4636; http://www.petersburg.org), at 1st and Fram St. Houses a replica of the world-record king salmon: 126½ lb. of fish. Reserve Forest Service cabins here, or pick up the free *Viking Visitors Guide,* featuring Sven the Friendly Viking. Open M-Sa 9am-5pm; in winter M-F 10am-2pm.

Outdoor Information: Forest Service, P.O. Box 1328 (772-3871), above the post office. Info on hiking and fishing, plus cabin reservations. Open M-F 8am-5pm.

Bank: National Bank of Alaska, 201 Nordic Drive. 24hr. **ATM.** Open M-Th 9am-5pm, F 9am-5:30pm.

Equipment Rental: Northern Bikes (772-3978), next to the Scandia House. $3 per hr., $20 per day. Open M-F 10am-5pm, Sa 10:30am-5pm. Flexible on returns.

Public Showers: The harbormaster office at North Harbor (see above) has what are rumored to be the longest, hottest showers in all of Southeast AK ($1). Also at **Glacier Laundry** ($2; towels $1), **Tent City,** and **Twin Creek RV Park** (see below).

Petersburg

N

Frederick Sound

TO SANDY BEACH

Eagle's Roost Park

Nordic Drive

Wrangell Ave.

Valkyrie St.

Lake St.

Balder St.

Charles W.

Dolphin St.

Nordic Drive

North Harbor

1st St.

Aaslaug St.

Clausen Memorial Museum

4th St.

Excel St.

Harbor Way

Fram St.

Gjoa St.

5th St.

6th St.

7th St.

8th St.

Haugen Dr.

TO AIRPORT AND TENT CITY

Ira St.

Sing Lee Alley

Hammer Slough

2nd St.

3rd St.

TO FERRY TERMINAL

Bookstore: Sing Lee Alley Books, 11 Sing Lee Alley (772-4440). Alaskana, children's books, classics, and pop/mid-brow contemporary. Open M-Sa 10am-5pm.

Library: (772-3265), at Haugen and Nordic Dr. above the Fire Hall. Free Internet access. Open M-Th noon-9pm, F-Sa 1-5pm.

Laundromat: Glacier Laundry (772-4400), at Nordic and Dolphin. Wash $2, dry 25¢ per 5min. Open daily 6am-10pm. Also at **Twin Creek RV Park** (see below).

Public Radio: KFSK 100.9 FM.

Employment: Petersburg Employment Service (772-3791), at Haugen Dr. and 1st St. Fish-steeped staff provide info on all three canneries. Call to request the lyrically succinct pamphlet *Alaska Job Facts and Seafood Processing Jobs in Alaska.* Open M-F 9-11am and noon-8pm, Sa 9-11am and noon-3pm.

Emergency: 911. **Police:** 16 S. Nordic Dr. (772-3838). **State Troopers:** 772-3100.

Alcohol and Drug Helpline: Changing Tides, 772-3552.

ALASKA

Pharmacy: Rexall Drug, 215 Nordic Dr., downtown. Open M-F 9am-6pm; Sa-Su noon-6pm.

Hospital: Petersburg Medical Center (772-4291), at Fram and N. 1st St.

Post Office: (772-3121), at Haugen and Nordic Dr. Open M-F 9am-5:30pm, Sa 11am-2pm. Lobby with stamps open M-F 7am-8pm, Sa 8am-6pm. **ZIP Code:** 99833.

Internet Access: See **Library,** above.

Area Code: 907.

ACCOMMODATIONS AND CAMPGROUNDS

Tent City, the only place near town for backpackers, is often crammed with summer cannery workers. Camping solo is impossible, since wet and untentable muskeg covers the entire area. The next nearest campground to Petersburg is 22 mi. away, but a short 8 mi. journey leads to the Tongass National Forest, Ohmer Creek, and its free, month-long camping. Contact the visitor center (see above) for comprehensive B&B listings, though prices can be appalling compared to nearby Sitka, thanks especially to Petersburg's 10% accommodations tax.

Nordic House B&B, 806 Nordic Dr., Box 573 (772-3620; fax 772-3673; email nordicbb@alaska.net), ¼ mi. north of the ferry terminal. Three lovely rooms, a large common kitchen and sparkling bath, and a sitting space with a fine view cheer Norwegians pining for the fjords. Continental breakfast, best eaten on the deck overlooking the fishing docks. Singles from $65; doubles from $75. Make reservations for July and Aug.

Harbor Day B&B, 404 Noseeum St., Box 1255 (772-3971). From ferry terminal, take a right onto Marian St. and keep your eyes peeled ½ mi. out of town for Noseeum. Noseeum? Keep looking. Fine Scandinavian-style rooms with a health-conscious breakfast, though without a sea-and-mountain view. Singles $55; doubles $70.

Water's Edge B&B, P.O. Box 1201 (772-3736 or 800-TO-THE-SEA/868-4373; email bbsea@alaska.net), 1½mi. north of town on Nordic Dr. A gorgeous setting, with huge bay windows overlooking Frederick Sound. Very clean and bright, and a continental breakfast, to boot. Singles $80; doubles $90. Reserve early.

Tent City (772-9864), on Haugen Dr. past the airport, 2 mi. from the ferry. Established by the city and administered by Parks and Recreation as a cannery workers' homestead, this ramshackle collection of tarps and wooden platforms rests atop a muskeg swamp. Recently added amenities (pay phone, griddle, hotplate, refrigerator, and a shelter) help establish order in a place that used to be largely self-governed. A new no-alcohol policy has mellowed things a bit, but Tent City is still not the friendliest or safest place in the world. Several sites are set aside for tourists and short-term visitors. Water, toilet, 4 showers (50¢), pit fires with wood. $5, $30 per week, $125 per month. Quiet hours 10pm-noon. Open May-Sept. Tents only.

Twin Creek RV Park, Box 90B (772-3244), at Mile 7 of Mitkof Hwy. The only home for a large RV in Petersburg. Steps away from foliage, fishing, and hiking. Showers, laundry, fishing tackle. Hookups $18.75.

Ohmer Creek Campground, at Mile 22 of Mitkof Hwy. Maintained by the Forest Service (772-3871). A long haul from town is rewarded by 10 free sites for tents or small RVs amid the lupine, columbine and wild iris of the woods. A gravel trail leads to choice fish-watching venues. Water, pit toilets. 14-day max. stay.

FOOD

Although swimming in fish, Petersburg still charges a bundle for seafood. **The Trading Union** (772-3881), on Nordic Dr. downtown, offers a selection of both marine and terrestrial groceries (open M-F 8am-7pm, Sa 8am-5:30pm, Su 9am-5pm).

⊛**Homestead Cafe** (772-3900), on Nordic Dr. at Excel St., across from the general store. Steeped in local flavor, run by fishermen's wives who understand large appetites, and frequented by fishermen who know how to eat. The good ol' boys of Petersburg play dice on the tables and chat at the counter. Just you try to finish their stack of pancakes ($3.50), or the prodigious plate of biscuits and gravy ($5.50). Open M-Sa 24hr.! Lunch begins at 11am.

ALASKA

Helse-Health Foods and Deli (772-3444), on Sing Lee Alley off Nordic Dr. With flowers, little wooden stools, and plenty of jazz, this place offers refuge from typical Alaskan *cuisine bourgeoise*. Soup and bread $5, "Cheese Breeze" (avocado, shrimp, mushrooms, and havarti) $6.75. Lots of juices. Open M-F 7:30am-5pm, Sa 10am-4pm; in winter M-F 7:30am-3pm, Sa 10am-3pm.

Alaskafé (772-JAVA/5282), on Excel St. above Costal Cold Storage. Globetrotting gourmets import panini to Petersburg. Overdosing on Norse culture? The Fellini—mozzarella and gorgonzola cheeses, artichoke hearts, and sun-dried tomatoes—should fix you right up (half $5.45, whole $7.75). Live band and jam session Sa nights. Open M-Th 7:30am-5pm, F-Sa 7:30am-6pm and Sa 8pm-midnight.

Java Fish, a green trailer on the corner of Excel St. and Harbor Way, across from the harbormaster. Unique, tasty take-out to fill the hungriest of fisherfolk and cannery workers. Cappuccino ($1.50), shrimp quesadilla ($6.50), halibut gyro ($6.50), and breakfast sandwiches (from $3). Open M-Th 7am-5pm, F-Sa 7am-8pm, Su 9am-3pm.

El Rincon (772-2255) sets up camp each summer inside Kito's Kave on Sing Lee Alley. Authentic, dirt-cheap tacos ($1.25) and burritos ($2.50). Open in summer M-Th 11am-10pm, F-Sa 11am-midnight, Su noon-midnight; migrates south with cannery workers in winter.

SIGHTS AND EVENTS

This is one of the best places on the Panhandle to see a fishing town at work, and there's always something biting. The epicenter of the year-round action is down at **North Harbor,** near the middle of town on Excel Ave. Wander the docks, talk to local fishermen, read the bulletin boards, and savor the aromatic catch. The **Clausen Memorial Museum,** 203 Fram St. (772-3598), at 2nd Ave., displays native artifacts and an inspiring history of fishing techniques. *(Open M-Sa 9:30am-4:30pm, Su 12:30-4:30pm; in winter W 9:30am-4:30pm, Su 12:30-4:30pm. $2, under 12 free.)* Outside the museum is the bizarre **Fisk Fountain,** a hulking metal monolith with an abstract array of fishies.

On the third full weekend in May, Petersburg joins its international brethren in joyous celebration of Norway's 1905 independence from Sweden. During this **Little Norway Festival,** mock Vikings dance, sing, parade, hunt their own furs, wear horns, sail in long boats, and violently board an airplane in traditional Viking style. Memorial Day weekend brings the hallowed **Salmon Derby.** This search for the specially tagged fish—and its accompanying $10,000 prize—has been sadly unsuccessful in recent years. Hold your nose and stay away from open spaces on the **4th of July** in Petersburg: celebrations feature a **competitive herring toss.**

OUTDOORS

The harbor island's fishing sites yield salmon, halibut, crab, shrimp, dolly varden, and cutthroat trout, while the land teems with black bears, deer, moose, and waterfowl. Wanna kill 'em? For more info, and to obtain Alaska state sportfishing and hunting licenses, contact the **Alaska Department of Fish and Game** (see p. 48). In the meantime, amateurs will discover that **jigging** for herring from the docks is alarmingly fun.

While the Petersburg area offers a multitude of hiking opportunities, only a handful of trails are readily accessible by foot. The 4 mi. **Raven's Roost Trail** leads to a Forest Service cabin by the same name. *($25 per night. Call 772-3871 well in advance for reservations.)* Another popular walk follows what locals call the **Loop.** From Nordic Dr., walk past the Eagle's Roost Picnic Area and Sandy Beach Park (where indigenous **petroglyphs** are visible on the beach at low tide), onto the Frederick Pt. Boardwalk, and back on Haugen Dr.; this all takes about 1½ hours. Pick up the *Petersburg Map* at the ferry terminal or visitor center (see **Practical Information,** above) for a complete illustration of the trails and logging roads on Mitkof Island.

The planked **Petersburg Creek Trail,** ½ mi. across the Wrangell Narrows on neighboring Kupreanof Island, runs 11½ mi. up to **Petersburg Lake,** through a wilderness area to another Forest Service cabin. If the tide is high enough, you can go up the creek a few miles by boat to make a mere 6½ mi. hike to the lake. Many charter operators in town ferry folks across the narrows and rent skiffs, but this can cost more than $100. Ask at the harbormaster's office about boats making the crossing with space for an extra passenger. A small number of people also live across the narrows and make the afternoon commute home.

Several area outfitters offer reasonably priced outdoor adventures. **Tongass Kayak Adventures,** 106 N. Nordic Dr., P.O. Box 707 (772-4600), offers guided sea kayak tours up Petersburg Creek. *(5hr. tours daily June-Aug. $55 per person, under 12 $30. Includes gear.)* Or do it yourself: kayak rentals cost $40 per day for a single or $50 for a double, with a three-day minimum.

■ Sitka

The turquoise water of the Pacific washes up college students, leather-faced fishermen, artists, and cruise-ship tourists onto the shores of a community that has regained its native name and long since strayed from its Russian roots. In 1802, the native Tlingit, resentful of a three-year Russian occupation, razed the settlement and massacred nearly every inhabitant. Two years later, the Russians returned and bombarded the Tlingit fort. After a bloody 10-day battle, the Tlingit ran out of ammunition and withdrew under cover of darkness. "New Archangel" quickly became a cultural and economic center, the capital of Russian America. Today, an influx of urbane ex-urbanites adds fresh flavor to a the ethnic and cultural mix.

PRACTICAL INFORMATION

Airplanes: Alaska Airlines (966-2266 or 800-426-0333; http://www.alaskaair.com). To: Juneau ($96); Ketchikan ($124). Also flies to Seattle, Anchorage, Wrangell, and Petersburg.

Ferries: Alaska Marine Highway, 7 Halibut Rd. (747-8737 or 800-642-0066), 7 mi. from town. To: Ketchikan ($54); Petersburg ($26); Juneau ($26). Open 2hr. before arrival until departure.

Harbormaster: 747-3439.

Local Transportation: Sitka Tours (747-8443) offers rides to the ferry terminal and the airport ($3). Open daily 7am-5pm, but hours vary. **Tribal Tours** maintains a **Visitor Transit System** (747-7290) which drives to and from all the major attractions, though most sights are within walking distance of each other. $5 per day.

Taxis: Sitka Taxi, 747-5001. $12.50 from Sitka to the ferry; $6 to the airport; 50¢ per additional person. Runs 24hr.

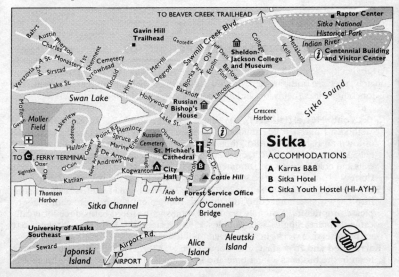

Car Rental: Advantage Car Rental (747-7557), at the airport. From $31 per day; unlimited mileage. Must be 21 with credit card.

Visitor Information: Sitka Convention and Visitors Bureau, P.O. Box 1226 (747-5940; email scub@ptialaska.net; http://www.ptialaska.net/~scub). The bureau's most convenient booth is in the **Centennial Building,** 330 Harbor Dr. Few brochures, but the volunteer staff is helpful. Open when cruise ships are in and when the Centennial Bldg. hosts events.

Outdoor Information: Sitka Ranger District, 201 Katlian, #109 (747-6671). Pick up *Sitka Trails* ($4) and pamphlets about cabins ($25 per night) in Tongass National Forest. Open M-F 8am-5pm.

Banks: On Lincoln St. behind the church: **Nations Bank of Alaska** (747-3226). Open M-Th 9:30am-5:30pm, F 9:30am-6pm. 24hr. **ATM.**

Equipment Rental: Southeast Diving and Sports, 329 Harbor Dr. (747-8279). Clunky old 5-speeds $5 per hr., $20 per day, $25 overnight. Open M-Sa 10am-5pm, Su 11am-5pm. **Baidarka Boats** (747-8996; email 72037.3607@compuserve.com; http://execpc.com/~bboats), on Lincoln St. above Old Harbor Books. Single kayaks $25 per half-day, $35 per day; doubles $30 per half-day, $45 per day; rates less with longer rentals. Required 1hr. instructional class for novices ($25). Guided half-day ($50-100) and full-day ($70-150) tours. Open daily 8am-6:30pm; in winter fewer hours and closed Su. **Mac's,** 213 Harbor Dr. (747-6970). Well stocked with gear for fish and humans. Open M-Sa 8am-6pm, Su 9am-5pm.

Luggage Storage: The **fire station,** on Halibut Point Rd. near downtown, stores backpacks for free, as does the **Centennial Building,** 330 Harbor Dr. The **ferry terminal** has 25¢ lockers. 24hr. max.

Bookstore: Old Harbor Books, 201 Lincoln (747-8808). Info on local arts events, marine charts, and **topographic maps.** Free copies of the *New York Review of Books,* the *New York Times Book Review,* and the *Bloomsbury Review.* Ecopolitical diatribes available on request. Open M-F 9am-6pm, Sa-Su 9am-5pm.

Library: Kettleson Memorial Library, 320 Harbor Dr. (747-8708). Open M-Th 10am-9pm, F 1-6pm, Sa-Su 1-5pm. Wheelchair accessible. Free Internet access.

Laundromats and Public Showers: Duds 'n' Suds Laundromat, 906 Halibut Point Rd. (747-5050), convenient to the hostel. Wash $1.75, dry 50¢ per 10min. Shower $2 per 10 min. Open M-F 7am-8pm, Sa-Su 8am-8pm.

Pharmacy: Harry Race Pharmacy, 106 Lincoln St. (747-8666), near Castle Hill. Also has 1hr. photo. Open M-Sa 9am-6pm, Su 9am-1pm.

Hospital: Sitka Community Hospital, 222 Tongass Dr. (747-3241).

Post Office: 338 Lincoln St. (747-5525). Open M-Sa 8:30am-5:30pm. **ZIP Code:** 99835.

Internet Access: See **Library,** above.

Area Code: 907.

ACCOMMODATIONS AND CAMPGROUNDS

To lure backpackers, the park service has renovated Sitka's two campgrounds. Unfortunately, they are both far, far away. Sitka also has 20 **B&Bs,** from $50 per night. The visitors bureau lists their rates and numbers (see **Practical Information,** above.)

Sitka Youth Hostel (HI-AYH), 303 Kimshan St., Box 2645 (747-8356), in the United Methodist Church at Edgecumbe St. and Kimshan. Find the McDonald's 1 mi. out of town on Halibut Point Rd., then walk 25 yards up Peterson St. to Kimsham. 20 cots, kitchen facilities, VCR, and several videos. Sleeping bags required. Free local calls and cold showers. $7, nonmembers $10. Lockout 8am-6pm, strictly enforced. Curfew 11pm. 3-night max. stay. Will store packs during the day. Open June-Aug.

Sitka Hotel, 118 Lincoln St. (747-3288; fax 747-8499; email mail@sitkahotel.com; http://www.sitkahotel.com), downtown. Convenient and homey, with eager-to-please proprietors. Tastefully decorated rooms with shared baths. Free local calls, cable, laundry. Singles $50; doubles $55. Private baths $10 extra; kitchens $10 extra. Reserve 2 weeks in advance and request a view.

Karras Bed and Breakfast, 230 Kogwanton St. (747-3978). Bertha and Pete have been in the business a long time and know how to please, with huge breakfasts, laundry, private entrances, and spacious living rooms with views of the harbor. Good for large groups. Singles from $55; doubles from $70 (includes tax).

Starrigavan Creek Campground, at the end of Halibut Point Rd., 1 mi. from the ferry, 8 mi. from town. Secluded sites for tents and RVs, under a canopy of trees. Water, pit toilets, picnic shelter, proximity to a scenic estuary trail. 30 sites: $8. 14-night max. stay. No vehicle access 10pm-7am. Wheelchair accessible.

Sawmill Creek Campground, 8½ mi. south of town. Take Halibut Point Rd. to Sawmill Creek Rd. junction in Sitka. Follow Sawmill Creek Rd. to the pulp mill, then take the left spur for 1.4 mi. Recently renovated 11-unit campground. Trees, stream, solitude, picnic tables, fireplaces, pit toilets, and decent fishing in nearby Blue Lake. Free. Quiet hours 10pm-6am. 14-night max. stay.

FOOD

Function clearly outweighs the aesthetic in Sitka's cuisine scene. Even posh restaurants rely solely on the waterfront to spice up their culinary creations. Find standard fare at **Lakeside Grocery,** 705 Halibut Point Rd. (747-3317; open daily 6am-midnight). Pick up fresh seafood along the docks or at **Seafood Producers Coop,** 507 Katlian Ave. (747-5811), where halibut and salmon run $2-3 per lb. (open daily 9am-5pm). **Evergreen Natural Foods,** 101 American Way (747-6944; open M-Sa 10am-6pm), vends granola ($2.50 per lb.).

The Backdoor, 104 Barracks St. (747-8856), behind Old Harbor Books. An amiable coffee shop and popular hostelers' hangout with attractive local art, unpredictable poetry readings, and occasional live accordion music. 12oz. Buzzsaw (coffee with espresso) $2.25; homemade soup with bread $4; scones $1. Open M-Sa 7am-5pm and frequently after-hours.

The Bayview Restaurant, 407 Lincoln St. (747-5440), upstairs in the Bayview Trading Company. Yet another great view. Food is well-prepared, but the portions are more modest than the prices. *Pirogies* (Russian dumplings) with salad and borscht $8. More than 25 variations on the hamburger trope. Open M-Sa 7am-8pm, Su 8am-3pm; in winter M-Sa 7am-7:30pm, Su 7am-3pm.

Van Winkle and Daigler, 228 Harbor Dr. (747-3396). A good place to splurge. Lunch specials from $9; dinner entrees from $13. Try the smoked salmon chowder ($3.95). Live music Sa night.

Lane 7 Snack Bar, 331 Lincoln St. (747-6310), near the bowling alley. The cheapest joint in town. Revel in the budget glory of $4 burgers and $2 curly fries, plus the best milkshakes around ($3). Lots of formica. Open daily 7am-11pm; in winter M-Sa 10:30am-11pm, Su 10:30am-10pm.

SIGHTS, EVENTS, AND ENTERTAINMENT

Sitka is one of the few cities in Southeast Alaska with indoor attractions that serve as more than just an excuse to get out of the rain. The onion-domed **St. Michael's Cathedral,** built in 1848 by Bishop Innocent, hearkens back to Sitka's Slavic era. *(Hours vary with cruise ship schedules; generally open M-Sa 11am-3pm, Su noon-3pm. $1 donation.)* Services are open to the public and conducted in English, Tlingit, and Old Slavonic amid haunting icons and neo-Baroque paintings. Two blocks down Lincoln St., the meticulously refurbished **Russian Bishop's House** (747-6281) is one of four remaining Russian colonial buildings in America. *(Open daily mid-May to Oct. 1 9am-1pm and 2-5pm; call for access off-season. Tours every 30min. Downstairs free. Chapel $3.)* The magnificent chapel upstairs, dedicated to the Annunciation of the Virgin Mary, is adorned with gold and silver icons. At the east end of Lincoln St., formerly the site of Baranov's Castle, the seat of Russian administration in Alaska, **Castle Hill** provides an easily accessible view of the cathedral and the Sound. *(Open daily 6am-10pm.)*

The **Sheldon-Jackson Museum** (747-8981), on the tidy Sheldon-Jackson College campus at the east end of Lincoln St., is one of Alaska's best museums for native artifacts and history. *(Open daily 8am-5pm; in winter Th-Sa 10am-4pm. $3, free with student ID.)* The collections date back to the 1880s and represent Athabascan, Aleutian, Inuit, and Northwest Coast artistic styles. Pull-out drawers hold Inuit children's toys and the raven helmet worn by Chief Katlean, the Tlingit hero of the 1804 battle against the Russians.

The manicured trails of the **Sitka National Historic Park** (747-6281), a.k.a. "Totem Park," lie a few minutes' walk down Lincoln St., ½ mi. east of St. Michael's. The trails pass 15 masterfully replicated totems, placed along the shoreline among old growth forest. At one end of the 1 mi. loop stands the site of the **Tlingit Fort** where the hammer-wielding Chief Katlean and his men almost held off the Russians in the battle for Sitka. The park **visitor center** shows a film about the fight, and houses the **Southeast Alaskan Native American Cultural Center** (747-8061), where woodcarvers, silversmiths, costume-makers, and weavers demonstrate their crafts. *(Open daily 8am-5pm.)*

Recovering bald eagles and owls perch dutifully for snapshots at the **Alaska Raptor Rehabilitation Center** (747-8662), on Sawmill Creek Rd. There are guided tours for $10, but visitors can get in for free with a donation of frozen mice or other appropriate raptor chow. *(Open daily 8am-5pm, and with cruise ships.)*

In June, the **Sitka Summer Music Festival**, P.O. Box 3333 (277-4852 or 747-6774), draws world-renowned chamber musicians to play at one of Alaska's most popular musical events. *(All shows $14, under 18 $7.)* The concerts, held in the Centennial Building on Tuesday, Friday, and some Saturday evenings, are often crowded; reservations are a good idea. Rehearsals, however, are free and rarely crowded.

OUTDOORS

The Sitka area offers excellent **hiking** opportunities. Rain gear and a copy of *Sitka Trails*, $4 at the Forest Service office or Old Harbor Books, prove invaluable on almost any hike. The boardwalked **Beaver Lake Trail**, a 2 mi. hike that rises only 200 ft. in elevation, is the easiest of the popular trails. Platforms overlooking serene **Beaver Lake** offer great fishing for grayling. The trailhead begins at the Sawmill Creek Campground (see **Campgrounds,** above), across the bridge over Sawmill Creek. A longer hike is the gentle and intimate **Indian River Trail,** a 5½ mi. riverside walk to the base of **Indian River Falls.** Take Sawmill Creek Rd. out of town and turn on Indian River Rd. before the bridge. The rocky **Three Sisters Mountains** occasionally come into view along the trail, as do spawning salmon in early fall.

Gavan Hill Trail is a more strenuous hike with easier access; the trailhead is near downtown, at the end of Baranof St. The majority of the 2500 ft. ascent is a boardwalk trail, making the three- to four-hour hike reminiscent of a stairmaster workout, and the perseverant are rewarded by a sensational view of the sound. The newly redone **Mount Verstovia Trail** provides an enjoyable hike with incredible panoramas. The trailhead is about 2 mi. east of town, right next to Rookie's Sports Bar and Grill on Sawmill Creek Hwy.; watch for the sign.

The Forest Service also maintains a number of **remote trails** in the Sitka region, most accessible only by boat or floatplane, and many leading to **wilderness cabins** ($25 per night). The most striking is the **Mt. Edgecumbe Trail,** a full-day, 7 mi. one-way clamber to the crater of Sitka's very own dormant volcano, whose broken cone dominates the view across the sound from Sitka. The trailhead lies behind Fred's Creek Cabin, a half-hour skiff journey from Sitka; a shelter for exhausted hikers sits another 3 mi. up the trail. The end of the hike offers stunning views of the Sitka region and a close look at the red volcanic ash spewed eons ago by Mt. Edgecumbe.

In addition to kayak and bicycle rental services, over 30 **charter operators** vie to separate you from Sitka and your money. The visitor center (see **Practical Information,** above) lists names, numbers, and prices. Options include deep-sea fishing, kayaking, whale-watching, flightseeing, and wilderness drop-offs.

■ Tenakee Springs

The largest town on the largely uninhabited Chichagof Island, Tenakee Springs has one street: a dirt path, populated by children pushing grocery-laden wheelbarrows, fisherman lolling outside the mercantile, and vehicles traveling under 10 mi. per hour. Residents thrive on the slow pace, cultivating gardens and friendships in this close-knit community of 100. Locals are quick to welcome visitors, even those heavy of pack and light of wallet. The few things to do here include sitting in the hot spring, talking to the locals, walking to Indian River, and sitting in the hot spring some more. The town and bath effectively slow down the pace, blissfully numb the mind, and soak away travel weariness.

PRACTICAL INFORMATION Both **Loken Aviation** (736-2306 or 800-478-3360) and **Wings of Alaska** (736-2247) fly from Juneau six or seven days per week ($60-65). The state ferry *LeConte* makes a short stopover in Tenakee on its route between Juneau and Sitka ($22 either way). Residents value their isolation and adamantly oppose Forest Service proposals to construct a road link with neighboring **Hoonah.** There are **no banks** in Tenakee and no one accepts credit cards.

There is very little plumbing in Tenakee. Everyone bathes in the hot spring, and a real toilet is available at the town **bakery**, provided it's open. Otherwise, use the dirty public outhouse, which sits behind the bakery and over the beach. To get to the **library** (736-2248), which is located in the same building as the **city office** (736-2207), take a left from the ferry, continue about ¼ mi., and enter the big wooden building on your right (open Tu and Th 11am-3pm, Sa noon-3pm). The weather forecast can be had at 800-472-0391. The **post office** (736-2236) is right off the dock (open M-F 7:30am-noon and 12:30-4:30pm, Sa 7:30-11:30am). **ZIP Code:** 99841. **Area Code:** 907.

ACCOMMODATIONS, CAMPGROUNDS, AND FOOD There are two places to stay in town, and one of them has a price tag in the thousands. The affordable option is to rent one of six available cabins from **Snyder Mercantile** (736-2205). The smaller, more basic cabins sleep one to two people comfortably (from $40). A larger cabin sleeps four to five (from $45). Both cabin-types have outhouses and cooking facilities, but no towels or bedding. A $65 cabin sleeps seven, with carpeting, fireplaces, and a flush toilet—a rare find in Tenakee. Reservations are essential in summer. **Camping** around Tenakee is bear intensive; Chichagof Island has about one bear per sq. mi.; only Admiralty Island has a denser population. Walking from the ferry dock to town, make a right turn on the dirt street. After about ¾ mi., a path to the left with boardwalks leads to Indian River. Camping is technically not permitted along this trail, although, ironically, there are tent sites, a shelter, and a picnic table on the trail near the river. If there have been bear sightings, though, it isn't wise to camp near the river. In that event, locals generally don't mind if campers tent in the cleared-out woods or on the beach near the boat harbor at the far east end of the street.

Other than the salmonberries along the main path, food in Tenakee can be difficult to find. **Snyder Mercantile,** next to the ferry dock, stocks a limited supply of groceries, including vegetables and fruit flown in weekly (open M-Sa 9am-noon and 1-5pm, Su 9am-2pm). **Partytime Bakery** (736-2305) cooks up fresh bread ($3.50) and sinful cinnamon rolls ($2.50), as well as a diverse lunch menu, including spinach calzones ($2.50) and a huge plate of biscuits and gravy ($5.25; open M and W-Su 8am-2pm). Next to the bathhouse is the **Blue Moon Cafe,** an unassuming Tenakee institution. If Rosie is there, and if she feels like cooking, try the french fries ($3.75), ham and eggs ($7.50), or chicken dinner ($9). Arrange in advance for anything other than a cheeseburger or cans of Rainier Beer ($1.50); Rosie needs time to thaw her ingredients.

THE HOT SPRING Tenakee's namesake is the town's epicenter, a natural sulfuric hot spring that feeds the public bath house at the end of the ferry dock, is the town's epicenter. You won't find this small, unglamorous blue bathhouse on any postcards, but miners and fishers have been soaking out aches and worries in these therapeutic 106°F (41°C) waters for more than a century, and the Tlingit maintained a winter settlement at the spring long before Europeans arrived. Since few homes have showers, this is where most of modern Tenakee's citizens take daily baths.

Men and women have separate bathing hours, largely because bathers are required to be nude (men 2-6pm and 10pm-9am; women 9am-2pm and 6-10pm). They are also required to be reasonably clean before entering; bring your soap. To get in on the town gossip, bathe when the spring is busiest at the start of each new gender shift. The bath is free, but donations are welcome at Snyder Mercantile across the street.

SIGHTS AND OUTDOORS Tenakee's only street extends several miles in either direction, and is closed off to motor vehicles after a short distance. To the west, the road leads along the water past a communal saw mill and small homesteads. Tread carefully around private land here; not everyone loves wanderers. Several miles from town, the path turns onto the shore of the inlet, where smooth rocks make good footing for an extended **beach walk.** In midsummer, silver salmon leap from the water. In town, outhouses and garbage detract from the beach's appeal. To the east, the wide beach makes for better walking than the faint path that parallels the shore through the woods. Bears have realized this too—use caution, and bring a camera.

A 15-minute **kayak** paddle from shore, a small reef gives a home to dozens of sea otters who will scrutinize paddlers from land before performing their water show. An excellent adventure begins in Hoonah and follows the long inlet of **Port Frederick** back to its end. From there, a 100-yard portage leads to the upper region of **Tenakee Inlet.** Paddlers can explore the unbroken shores and hidden coves of the inlet on their way out to Tenakee Springs. The 40 mi. trip could also be made in the reverse direction, but the hot springs are probably best savored at the end. **Mother Truckers** (736-2323) rents bicycles and kayaks. *(Bicycles $20 per day. Kayaks $50 per half-day, $75 per full day.)* Ferries from Juneau will take kayaks to Tenakee for $9.

For **chartered expeditions** to fish, view wildlife, and learn about the intricacies of the inlet from someone who has been on the water around Tenakee all his life, contact **Jason Carter** (736-2311). Jason runs half-day and full-day trips, and also transports kayaks. Fishing and hunting licenses are available at **Snyder Mercantile.**

■ Juneau

Alaska's state capital has an air of modernity and progressiveness usually not found in the rural fishing villages of Southeast Alaska. It has always been on the cutting edge, starting out as one of the first major Alaskan gold mining centers. Accessible only by water and air, Juneau has happily avoided the urban sprawl that plagues Anchorage. The tourist industry, however, has had no problem establishing its presence: Juneau is the second busiest cruise ship port in the U.S., after Miami. Hordes of travelers come to Juneau for the readily accessible Mendenhall Glacier, numerous hiking trails, and close access to Glacier Bay. Be prepared to share the beauty.

ORIENTATION AND PRACTICAL INFORMATION

Juneau sits on the Gastineau Channel opposite Douglas Island, 650 mi. southeast of Anchorage and 900 mi. northwest of Seattle. **Franklin St.** is the main street downtown. **Glacier Highway** connects downtown, the airport, the residential area of the Mendenhall Valley, and the ferry terminal. The ferry and airport are both annoyingly far from the glacier and downtown. Expect to wait a long time for the bus or pay through the nose for a taxi.

Transportation
Airplanes: Juneau International Airport, 9 mi. north of Juneau on Glacier Hwy. Served by Alaska Airlines, Delta Airlines, and local charters. **Alaska Airlines** (789-0600 or 800-426-0333), on S. Franklin St. at 2nd St., in the Baranov Hotel. To: Anchorage ($99-222); Sitka ($96); Ketchikan ($124); Gustavus ($65). Open M-F 8:30am-5pm. Check at the visitor center for schedules and routes for all airlines. **Island Waterways** provides transportation from the airport to downtown, though the bus is cheaper ($7, round-trip $12).
Buses: Capital Transit (789-6901). From downtown to Douglas, the airport, and Mendenhall Glacier. Hourly express service downtown (M-F 8:30am-5pm). The closest stop to the ferry is at Auke Bay, 2 mi. from the terminal.Runs M-Sa 7am-10:30pm, Su 9am-5:30pm. Fare $1.25; exact change required. **Schedules** available at municipal building, library, Davis Log Cabin, and on buses. **MGT Ferry Express**

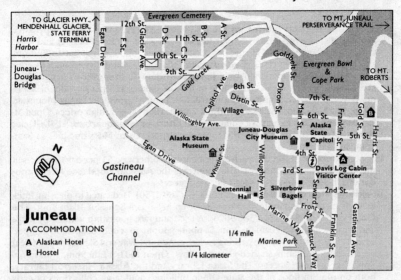

Juneau

ACCOMMODATIONS

A Alaskan Hotel
B Hostel

(789-5460). Meets all ferries and runs to downtown hotels or the airport ($5). Call 6-8pm a day in advance to reserve a ride from any major hotel to the airport or ferry (whether you're staying at a hotel or not). From the hostel, the Baranov is the closest hotel. Also offers a 2½hr. guided tour of Mendenhall Glacier ($12.50). Tour times vary; call ahead.

Ferries: Alaska Marine Highway, 1591 Glacier Ave., P.O. Box 25535, Juneau 99802-5535 (465-3941 or 800-642-0066; fax 277-4829). Ferries dock at the Auke Bay terminal, 14 mi. from the city on the Glacier Hwy. To: Ketchikan ($74); Sitka ($26); Haines ($20); Bellingham, WA ($226). Lockers are limited (25¢ per 48hr.).

Harbormaster: 586-5255, Auke Bay 789-0819.

Taxis: Capital Cab (586-2772) and **Taku Taxi** (586-2121). Both run a 1hr. charter from downtown to: Mendenhall Glacier (about $45); the ferry (about $25); the airport ($12). Exact services differ slightly; both let you split charter cost.

Car Rental: Rent-A-Wreck, 9099 Glacier Hwy. (789-4111), next to the airport. $35 per day plus 15¢ per mi. after 100 mi. Must be 21 with credit card or piles of cash. Open M-F 8am-6pm, Sa-Su 9am-5pm.

Car Repair: Sam's Auto Body, 8575 Airport Rd. (789-4114).

Visitor and Financial Services

Visitor Information: Davis Log Cabin Visitor Center, 134 3rd St., (888-581-2201 or 586-2201; fax 586-6304; email jcvb@ptialaska.net), at Seward St. Excellent source of pamphlets and maps on walking tours, sights, and natural wonders. Open June-Sept. M-F 8:30am-5pm, Sa-Su 9am-5pm; Oct.-May M-F 8:30am-5pm.

Outdoor Information: National Forest and National Park Services, 101 Egan Dr. (586-8751; fax 586-7928), at Willoughby in Centennial Hall. Staff provides info on hiking and fishing in the area, and reservations for Forest Service cabins in Tongass National Forest. Pick up a copy of the valuable *Juneau Trails* booklet ($4) listing many 5-12 mi. hikes. Open daily in summer 8am-5pm; in winter M-F 8am-5pm.

Alaska Dept. of Fish and Game, 1255 W. 8th St. (465-4112; licensing 465-2376), close to the bridge. Sells fishing licenses. Open 8am-5pm. **Fishing Information Hotline** (465-4116). Weather, licenses, and fish locations.

Bank: National Bank of Alaska, 123 Seward St. Open M-Th 9:30am-5pm, F 9:30am-6pm. Accepts most **ATM** cards.

Currency Exchange: Thomas Cook, 311 Franklin St. (586-5688). Sells MasterCard travelers checks. Open M-F 9am-5pm, Sa 10am-2pm.

American Express: 800-770-2750. Open M-F 10am-7pm, Sa 10am-6pm.

Local Services

Equipment Rental: Mountain Gears, 126 Front St. (586-2575), opposite McDonald's. Mountain bikes $6 per hr., $25 per 24hr. Includes helmet and lock. Open M-F 10am-6pm, Sa 10am-5pm. Call for advice on area trails or to find out about informal group rides. **Cycle Alaska** (364-3377) will deliver a bike to your door. $30 per 8hr. Open 9am-4pm. **Juneau Outdoor Center** (586-8220), on Douglas Island, delivers kayaks anywhere in Juneau. Singles $35 per day; doubles $45 per day. Experience required, but instruction happily provided. **Foggy Mountain Shop,** 134 N. Franklin St. (586-6780), at 2nd St. High quality, high prices. Open M-Sa 10am-6pm. Less expensive equipment at **Outdoor Headquarters,** 9131 Glacier Hwy. (800-478-0770 or 789-9785), near the airport. Open M-F 9am-8pm, Sa 8am-6pm, Su 11am-5pm.

Luggage Storage: At the hostel (free for boarders; otherwise $1 per bag). Lockers at the ferry terminal (see above). The counter at the **Alaskan Hotel** (see **Accommodations,** below) often stores for free. 24hr. access.

Bookstore: Hearthside Books, 254 Front St. (789-2750). Dedicated to pleasing intellectuals of the Panhandle year-round. Open M-Sa 9am-8pm, Su 10am-8pm. **The Observatory,** 235 2nd St. (586-9676). A used and rare bookstore with many maps and prints. Open M-F 10am-5:30pm, Sa noon-5:30pm; in winter M-Sa noon-5:30pm.

Library: (586-5249), over the parking garage at Admiral Way and S. Franklin St. Great views and a gorgeous stained-glass window. Open M-Th 11am-9pm, F-Su noon-5pm. Free Internet access. The **State Library** and the **Alaska Historical Library,** both on the 8th floor of the State Office Building, hold large collections of early Alaskan photographs. Both open M-F 9am-5pm.

HIV/AIDS Information and Counseling: Shanti's, 800-411-1331. 24hr.

Gay/Lesbian Information: Southeast Alaska Gay and Lesbian Alliance, 586-4297.

Laundromat and Public Showers: Dungeon Laundrette (586-2805), at 4th and Franklin St. Wash $1.50, dry $1.50. Open daily 8am-8pm. **Alaskan Hotel** (see **Accommodations,** below). Showers $3.12.

Events Hotline: 586-5866. **Weather:** 586-3997.

Emergency and Communications

Emergency: 911. **Police:** 210 Admiral Way (586-2780), near Marine Park. Permit available for 48hr. **parking** in a 1hr. zone. Open for permits M-F 8am-4:30pm.

Crisis Lines: Crisis and Suicide Prevention Hotline, 586-4357. Open M-F 9am-5pm. **Rape and Abuse Crisis Line (AWARE),** 800-478-1090. 24hr.

Pharmacy: Juneau Drug Co., 202 Front St. (586-1233). Open M-F 9am-9pm, Sa-Su 9am-6pm.

Hospital: Bartlett Memorial (586-2611), 3½ mi. north off Glacier Hwy.

Post Office: Main Office, 709 W. 9th St. (586-7987). Open M-F 9am-5pm, Sa 9am-1pm for parcel pick-up only. **Substation** (586-2214) for outgoing mail is at Heritage Coffee on S. Franklin. Open M-F 9:30am-5pm, Sa 9:30am-2pm. **ZIP Code:** 99801.

Internet Access: See **Library,** above.

Area Code: 907.

ACCOMMODATIONS AND CAMPGROUNDS

The few establishments that offer affordable options have them in limited quantities, so phone ahead. One of the best sources for rooming advice is the **Alaska Bed and Breakfast Association,** P.O. Box 2800 (586-2959; http://www.wetpage.com/bbaaip), which can help find a room downtown (from $65). While the Forest Service offers two beautiful campgrounds, neither is easily accessible without a car.

Juneau International Hostel (HI-AYH), 614 Harris St. (586-9559), at 6th St. atop a steep hill. A beautiful facility in a prime location with rigid management. Sweep the floor or be swept out the door. Common area with comfy couches. 48 beds: $7, nonmembers $10. Kitchen available 7-8:30am and 5-10:30pm. Coin-op laundry (wash $1.25, dry 75¢); small charges for sheets, towels, soap, and detergent. Strict lockout 9am-5pm and non-negotiable 11pm curfew. 3-night max. stay if they're full. Fills fast, but a $10 deposit mailed in advance serves as a reservation. No phone reservations. No wheelchair access.

Alaskan Hotel, 167 Franklin St. (586-1000, in the Lower 48 800-327-9347), right downtown. A handsome hotel built of dark wood, meticulously restored to original 1913 decor. Kitchenettes and TVs. Bar features live tunes and dancing. Hot tub with radio (noon-4pm $13 per hr., 4pm-2am $26.25 per hr.) Rooms $67-84; rates lower in winter. Free luggage storage for guests. Laundry (wash or dry $1).

Inn at the Waterfront, 455 S. Franklin (586-2050; fax 586-2999), over the Summit Restaurant. The classy-looking restaurant downstairs belies the inn's origins as a gold rush brothel. 14 clean, comfortable rooms; a few have shared baths. Singles $77; doubles $84. Ask for cheaper rooms specifically, or you might get one with several more stars and zeros attached. Continental breakfast included.

Mendenhall Lake Campground, on Montana Creek Rd. Take Glacier Hwy. north 9 mi. to Mendenhall Loop Rd.; continue 3½ mi. and take the right fork. If asked, bus drivers will stop within 2 mi. of camp (7am-10:30pm only). About 6 mi. from the ferry terminal. 60 newly renovated sites have stunning views of the glacier and convenient trails to go even closer. Fireplaces, water, flush toilets, showers, picnic tables, free firewood. Sites $8, seniors $4. 14-night max. stay. Reserve for an extra $7.50 by calling 800-280-2267.

Auke Village Campground (586-8800), on Glacier Hwy., 15 mi. from town and 1½ mi. west of the ferry terminal near a scenic beach. 12 sites to enclose a tent or RV in verdant seclusion. Fireplaces, water, flush toilets, picnic tables. Sites $8, seniors $4. No reservations. 14-night max. stay.

FOOD

Juneau accommodates seekers of anything from fresh salmon to filet-o'-fish sandwiches. **Juneau A&P Market,** 631 Willoughby Ave. (586-3101; fax 586-6775), near the Federal Building, is one of the best grocery stores in the region, with an extensive salad bar ($3.30 per lb.), and jumbo deli sandwiches ($4.50; open daily 24hr.). Costlier health food resides in **Rainbow Foods** (586-6476), at 2nd and Seward St. (open M-F 10am-7pm, Sa 10am-6pm, Su noon-6pm). The corner of Front and Seward St. is home to Juneau's fast food syndicate.

🍴**Armadillo Tex-Mex Cafe,** 431 S. Franklin St. (586-1880). A place for locals, even in the heart of the cruise ship souvenir-shopping district. Authentic Southwest paintings and a few kitschy plastic armadillos decorate this always packed cafe. Fast, saucy service and hot, spicy food. Heaping plateful of T. Terry's nachos $8; *chalupa* (corn tostada heaped with chicken, beans, guacamole, and cheese) $8; two enchiladas $6. Excellent free chips and salsa. Open M-Sa 11am-10pm, Su 4-10pm.

Fiddlehead Restaurant and Bakery, 429 W. Willoughby Ave. (586-3150), ½ block from the State Museum. Fern-ishings for affluent sprout-lovers, serving seafood, exquisite desserts, and fresh Alaskan sourdough. Wholesome sandwiches with soup or salad $7-10. Open daily 6:30am-10pm; in winter 6:30am-9pm. The **Fireweed Room** upstairs serves more expensive fare with smoke-free evening jazz in summer ($5 cover). Open M-F 11:30am-1pm and 5:30-9pm, Sa-Su 5:30-9pm.

Thane Ore House Salmon Bake, 4400 Thane Rd. (586-3442). One of many cruiseship oriented salmon bakes a few miles out of town, but Mr. Ore will pick you up at your hotel. All-you-can-eat salmon, halibut, ribs, and fixings ($18.50). Open May-Sept. daily 11:30am-9pm.

Cafes and Coffeehouses

🍴**Valentine's Coffee House and Bakery,** 111 Seward St. (463-5144). Mom's kitchen with a trendy feel and calico tablecloths. Fresh baked calzones $6; burritos $6.25; salads $5; all sorts of breads. Open M-F 7am-6pm, Sa 8am-6pm, Su 9am-3pm.

Silverbow Bagels, 120 2nd St. (586-YUMM/9866). In 1997, Jill and Ken serendipitously discovered a mythic silver bagel atop the Perseverance Trail, and were inspired to meet the needs of expatriate bagel connoisseurs. Scarf 75¢ bagels at 6am or quaff $1 Blue Willow tea at 5pm. Sandwiches $1-7. Open M-F 6:30-5pm, Sa-Su 7:30am-3:30pm.

Heritage Coffee Co., 174 S. Franklin St. (586-1087). A popular place to escape for an hour or two from Juneau's often wet and tourist-ridden streets. Easygoing staff assembles large sandwiches ($6.25) and pours fine coffee (espresso $1; cappuccino $1.75). Open M-F 6:30am-6:30pm, Sa-Su 7am-5pm.

SIGHTS

The excellent **Alaska State Museum,** 395 Whittier St. (465-2901), leads through the history and culture of Alaska's four major native groups: Tlingit, Athabascan, Aleut, and Inuit. *($3, seniors and children free. Open May 18 to Sept. 17 M-F 9am-6pm, Sa-Su 10am-6pm; Sept. 18 to May 17 Tu-Sa 10am-4pm.)* The museum houses the First White Man totem pole, a carved likeness of Abraham Lincoln, and traveling displays of photography and painting.

The hexagonal and onion-domed 1894 **St. Nicholas Russian Orthodox Church,** on 5th St. between N. Franklin and Gold St., holds rows of icons and a glorious altar. Services, held Saturday at 6pm and Sunday at 10am, are conducted in English, Old Slavonic, and Tlingit. Tours are open to the public. *($1 donation requested. Open daily in summer 9am-5pm.)* The **State Office Building** (the S.O.B.), on Willoughby St., has an 8th-floor **observation platform** overlooking Douglas Island and the channel. A large atrium on the same floor contains a totem pole and a pipe organ fired up for a **free concert** every Friday afternoon.

Between mid-July and September, **Gastineau Salmon Hatchery,** 2697 Channel Dr. (463-5113 or 463-4810), is the place to be. When the salmon are running, thousands pack into the parking lot; the salmon crammed into the spawning ladder are pretty impressive, too. The spectacle is free, but admission to the small aquarium inside is not. *(Open M-F 10am-6pm, Sa-Su noon-5pm. $2.75, children $1.)* The **Alaska Brewing Co.,** 5429 Shaune Dr. (780-5866), gives free tours (must be 21 or accompanied by a parent or guardian). *(Tours every 30min. May-Sept. M-Sa 11am-4:30pm; Oct.-Apr. Th-Sa 11am-4:30pm.)* Given the price of beer in Alaska, it's hard to turn down the free samples of its award-winning brews. To get there, take the hourly city bus to Lemon Creek, turn onto Anka Rd. from the Glacier Hwy., and right on Shaune Dr.

OUTDOORS

Juneau's trail system is extensive, well-documented, and crowded. To get the best view of the city, go to the end of 6th St. and head up the trail to the summit of **Mt. Roberts** (3576 ft.). It's a steep, 4 mi. climb, and higher elevations reveal panoramic views up the Gastineau Channel and west toward the Pacific, including nearby Mt. Juneau. A **tramway** also offers access to the vista. *(Trams run every half-hr. $1.50.)* The **West Glacier Trail** begins off Montana Creek Rd., by the Mendenhall Lake Campground. The five- to six-hour walk yields stunning views of **Mendenhall Glacier** from the first step to the final outlook. The 3½ mi., one-way trail parallels the glacier through western hemlock forest and up a rocky cairn-marked scramble to the summit of 4226 ft. **Mt. McGinnis.**

A number of excellent trails start at the end of Basin Rd. The **Perseverance Trail** leads to the ruins of the Silverbowl Basin Mine and booming waterfalls. The **Granite Creek Trail** branches off the Perseverance Trail and follows its namesake to a beautiful basin, 3.3 mi. from the trailhead. The summit of Mt. Juneau lies 3 mi. farther along the ridge and, again, offers terrific views. The shorter, steeper **Mt. Juneau Trail,** which departs from Perseverance Trail about 1 mi. from the trailhead, offers similar panoramas. For more details on area hikes, drop by the visitor center or any local bookstore to pick up *Juneau Trails,* published by the Alaska Natural History Association ($4). Rangers provide free copies of maps from this book at the Centennial Building (see **Practical Information,** above). All trails are well-maintained and excellent for **mountain biking.** Check with **Mountain Gears** (see **Practical Information,** above) for their difficulty rankings and suggestions. Biking off-road is sometimes prohibited. Whatever your mode of transport, be sure to keep the bears in mind.

The best excuse to spend money in town is on an incredible boat tour of **Tracy Arm,** a mini-fjord near Juneau. Known as "the poor man's Glacier Bay," Tracy Arm offers much of the same spectacular beauty and wildlife at well under half the cost. A typical tour includes sightings of humpback and killer whales, hundreds of seals, and bald eagles. The trip also passes by the **Sawyer Glaciers,** which frequently calve large chunks of ice into the sea, and leave massive icebergs glowing blue in the water. **Auk Nu Tours,** 76 Egan Dr. (800-820-2628), is the biggest tour company ($100). The huge boats and resulting impersonality might detract from the joy of the free lunch. **Bird's Eye Charters** (790-2510), whose small boats take only 16 passengers, is on the opposite end of the spectrum ($140), offering breakfast, lunch, snacks, and all the personal attention money can buy. A happy medium lies in **Adventure Bound,** 245 Marine Way. (463-2509 or 800-228-3875). Friendly owner Steve personally pilots a mid-sized boat with a maximum of 28 passengers. There's no free food, but snacks and simple sandwiches are available. *($100, under 18 $50. $20-off coupon in the Juneau visitor guide.)*

Kayak Express, 4107 Blackberry St. (780-4591; http://www.adventuresports.com/asap/kayak/express), allows kayakers and their craft to get beyond **Gastineau Channel,** running drop-offs and pick-ups at Gustavus, Hoonah, or Port Adolphus for $110 (round-trip $220), or at Oliver's Inlet, Port Couverden, St. James Bay, or Funter Bay for $75 (round-trip $150). **Alaska Discovery,** 5449 Shuane Dr. (780-6226 or 800-586-1911), provides both equipment and guides for its daily kayak trips through the inside passage north of Juneau. *($125 per person; transport from downtown $18.)* **Temsco Helicopters** (789-9501; fax 789-7989), at the airport, offers a one-hour flightseeing tour to the Mendenhall Glacier, or a 1½-hour glacier landing ($142).

In winter, the **Eaglecrest Ski Area,** 155 S. Seward St. (586-5284 or 586-5330), on Douglas Island, offers decent alpine skiing. *($24 per day, ages 12-17 $17, under 12 $12. Ski rental $20, children $14.)* The Eaglecrest ski bus departs from the Baranov Hotel at 8:30am and returns from the slopes at 5pm on winter weekends and holidays. *(Round-trip $6.)* In summer, the Eaglecrest **Alpine Summer Trail** is a good way to soak in the mountain scenery of virtually untouched Douglas Island.

NIGHTLIFE

The best bar in town is in the **Alaskan Hotel,** 167 Franklin St. It hosts frequent live Cajun and blues amid a lush gold rush decor, and manages to retain its local crowd year-round despite the shocking cost of beer. *(Bar open daily noon-midnight.)* Mosey on down to the **Red Dog Saloon,** 278 S. Franklin (463-9954), Juneau's most popular tourist trap, for live music on weekends. In the winter, locals return to their customary stools between walls lined with bear pelts and tourist pelts (a.k.a. money). Beer costs $3.50-4.50. *(Open Su-Th 10am-midnight, F-Sa 10am-1am; off-season Su-Th noon-midnight, F-Sa noon-1am.)* Inebriated and frenzied flocks of hard-partying youngsters congregate at the city's only club, **Penthouse** (463-4141), on the 4th floor of the Senate Building. *(Must be 21. $2 cover on weekends. Open Su-Th 9pm-1am, F-Sa 9pm-3am.)* **The Hanger on the Wharf,** on Marine Way, is another youth-magnet, with a huge selection of micro-brews and views of the Channel. *(Open M 4-11pm, Tu-W 11:30am-11pm, Th-Su 11:30am-1am.)*

■ Glacier Bay National Park

Glacier Bay was once referred to by explorer Jean François de Galaup de la Perouse as "perhaps the most extraordinary place in the world." The little-known Frenchman was right. Crystal monoliths, broken off from glaciers, float peacefully in fjords, while humpback whales maneuver the maze of the icy blue depths. Glacier Bay National Park encloses nine tidewater glaciers, as well as the **Fairweather Mountains,** the highest coastal range in the world. (Eat your heart out, Norway.) Charter flights, tours, and cruise ships all probe Glacier Bay, providing close encounters with glaciers, rookeries, whales, and seals. The bay itself is divided into two inlets: the west-

ALASKA

ward **Tarr Inlet** advances as far as the **Grand Pacific** and **Margerie Glaciers**, while the eastward **Muir Inlet** ends at the **Muir** and **Riggs Glaciers**.

Glacier Bay provides a rare opportunity to see geological and ecological processes radically compressed. A mere two centuries ago, the **Grand Pacific Glacier** covered the entire region under a sheet of ancient ice. Severe earthquakes separated the glacier from its terminal moraine (the silt and debris that insulates advancing ice from the relatively warm surrounding seawater), and the glacier retreated 45 mi. in 150 years—light speed in glacial time. As a result, the uncovered ground is virgin territory, colonized by pioneering vegetation.

Getting to **Bartlett Cove** is relatively easy: a plane or ferry takes visitors to **Gustavus,** and from there a taxi or shuttle (about $12) goes on to the **Glacier Bay Lodge** (800-622-2042), next to the cove. Once in the park, however, there are only a few ways to see the glaciers, and they're expensive. The simplest is by boat tour. The *Spirit of Adventure* is owned by the lodge, and offers six **sightseeing packages** to the glaciers, ranging in price and niceties from a half-day whale-watching trip ($78) to a package with flights to and from Juneau, a night at the B&B, and an eight-hour glacier tour ($379). The basic "see the glaciers" daytrip runs from the lodge ($80). The park offers great opportunities for independent explorers. Because there are boat quotas in the summer, people with their own boats must call ahead to the **Information Station** (697-2627) to book a visit.

Any visit to the park begins at the **Visitor Information Station** (697-2627), at the tour boat dock in **Bartlett Cove,** 10 mi. north of the town of Gustavus (see below), where rangers give a mandatory backcountry orientation and distribute permits (open daily 7am-9pm). Additional maps and wildlife info are available at the information center on the second floor of the **Glacier Bay Lodge** (697-2230 or 800-451-5952; open M-F 11:30am-2pm and 4-9pm).

In Bartlett Cove near the lodge, backpackers can stay in the free **campground,** which has 25 sites and is rarely full. Glimpses of orcas and humpback whales are common from the beachfront sites; whales sing the campers to sleep. Those without a tent can collapse in comfortable dorm beds at the **Glacier Bay Lodge** ($28). **Showers** ($1 per 5min.) and **laundry** ($2 wash, $1.25 dry) are available to all. Some visitors opt to stay in nearby **Gustavus,** and use it as their jumping-off point to the park.

Wilderness camping and **hiking** are permitted throughout the park, though there are no trails except the two near the lodge, and hiking is very difficult in most of the park because of thick alder brush. Tour-boat skippers drop passengers off at one of four points designated by the Park Service; arrange beforehand for pick-up. Drop-off, pick-up, and an unavoidable but spectacular tour cost $178 on the *Spirit of Adventure* (see above). Visitors should contact **Glacier Bay National Park,** P.O. Box 140, Gustavus 99826 (697-2230), for assistance with planning a backcountry trip. Glacier Bay is rapidly becoming *the* destination for extended kayak trips in the region.

Kayak rental is available at **Glacier Bay Sea Kayaks,** P.O. Box 26, Gustavus 99826 (697-2257; kayaks $35 per day for 1-2 days, $25 per day for over 3 days; double kayaks $50 per day for 1-3 days, $40 per day for 5-9 days, $35 per day for 10 days or more). **Sea Otter Kayaks** (967-3007; email seaotter@he.net; http://www.he.net/ ~seaotter) rents at the same rates, and also provides rain gear, drybags, and charts. Kayakers can start out directly from Bartlett Cove, but usually won't be able to paddle all the way up to the glaciers in a reasonable amount of time.

■ Gustavus

The gateway to Glacier Bay National Park, Gustavus is rarely noticed by glacier–greedy backpackers and ecotourists. Friendly locals are quick to share experiences and reveal secrets of the surrounding land, however, and their enthusiasm for the outdoors is infectious. The second graders of Gustavus Elementary School (and authors of the aptly titled pamphlet *Gustavus, the Way to Glacier Bay*) advise this: "In Gustavus there is no bank, no hospital, no toystore, no McDonalds, no other fast food places, and no zoo." Be prepared. The **Fireweed Gallery** (697-2325) displays local painting, sculpture, and handicrafts in an earthy setting (open M-F 1-5pm and by appointment). Besides the Fireweed, everything to see and do in Gustavus is outside. The boat dock offers astonishing purple-gold sunsets and 360° of mountain views. Logging roads that criss-cross the land beg for bike exploration.

Gustavus is situated on a crossroads called four corners. **Glacier Bay Lodge** and **Bartlett Cove,** the entrance to the park, lie 10mi. west of four corners, the **airport** 2mi. east, and the ferry 1½ mi. south. Gustavus is accessible only by boat or plane. The cheapest way to get there is via **Alaska Airlines** (800-426-0333; $39 from Juneau). Smaller, more expensive local airlines include **Air Excursions** (697-2375; $55 from Juneau), **Haines Air** (766-2646; $55 from Juneau), and **Wings of Alaska** (766-2030). They depart frequently from Juneau and Haines. Another option is the two-hour ferry ride from Auke Bay on **Auk Nu Tours** (800-820-2628; $45, round-trip $85). A **bus** from the Glacier Bay Lodge (see p. 504) meets every Haines Airways and Alaskan Airlines flight, and rolls on to Bartlett Cove ($12). If you've brought a bike, kayak, or more than two people, the cheaper option is **TLC Taxi** (697-2239), which charges $15 plus $7 per additional person, $5 per bike, and $10 per kayak. **Bud** (697-2403) rents midsize cars for $60 a day. Should a metaphorical elephant land on your toe, or other injury arise, visit the **Gustavus Clinic** (697-3008). The **post office** sits on the main road near the airport. **ZIP Code:** 99826. **Area Code:** 907.

Gustavus's second graders might have added that their town offers little in the way of budget accommodations. The cheapest quality B&B is **Good River Bed and Breakfast,** P.O. Box 37 (697-2241; http://www.goodriver.com), which offers free use of bikes, fishing gear, and raingear; call for directions. A beautifully kept lawn and garden complement cozy bedrooms and handmade quilts (singles $70; doubles $80). The **Bear's Nest** (697-2440) maintains two cabins, as does **A Puffin's B&B** (697-2260). Both offer complimentary breakfasts, bikes, and shuttle service. Some locals rent out cabins, which sleep two to four ($85 per night). There are **no campgrounds** in Gustavus, though tenters sometimes crash on the beach near the ferry dock.

The most affordable food in Gustavus comes from **Bear Track Mercantile,** ¼ mi. south of four corners (697-2358; open daily 9am-7pm). If peanut butter filled days don't cut it, the **Bear's Nest Cafe** (697-2440), 0.3 mi. north of four corners, serves lasagna ($8), enchiladas ($9), and espresso ($1.50; open 8am-8pm).

▓ Haines

The setting is superb: snowcapped mountains and crystal blue water surround Haines with breathtaking beauty. The weather is amazing: called "the sunny spot of Southeast," Haines gets less than half the rain of nearby Juneau. The locals are young and friendly: they're quick to share stories and trail advice. All of this and oodles of outdoor activities make Haines one of the most sublime stops in Southeast Alaska.

ORIENTATION AND PRACTICAL INFORMATION

Haines lies on a thin peninsula between the **Chilkat** and **Chilkoot Inlets,** just southwest of Skagway on the Chilkoot Inlet. Most of the Haines business district sits in a rectangle outlined by Main St. and the **Haines Highway** and their perpendiculars, **2nd** and **3rd Avenues.** Below this peninsula, the two inlets merge into **Lynn Canal.** There are U.S. (767-5511) and Canadian (767-5540) **customs offices** at Mile 42 of the Haines Hwy. (open daily 7am-11pm). Travelers must have at least $200 cash (though the requirement varies by destination), a credit card, and valid proof of citizenship to enter Canada, and rental cars are not always allowed across (see **Customs,** p. 7).

Airplanes: Haines Air (766-2646) and **LAB Flying Service** (766-2222 or 800-426-0543), both on Main St., offer comparable rates to: Juneau ($60-65); Skagway ($85-110); Glacier Bay ($85-110).

Buses: Alaska Direct (800-770-6652). Provides non-stop service to Anchorage ($150) and Fairbanks ($125), departing Haines Su, W, and F at 6am. Make reservations for **Alaskon Express** through **Ft. Seward Tours** (766-2000), in the lobby of the Hotel Hälsingland. Buses travel north Tu, Th, and Su, with an overnight stop in Beaver Creek, YT, near the Alaskan border. To: Anchorage ($189); Fairbanks ($180); Whitehorse, YT ($86). Open daily 9am-8pm.

Ferries: Alaska Marine Highway (766-2111). Terminal on Lutak Rd., 4 mi. from downtown. Daily to: Juneau ($20); Skagway ($14).

Harbormaster: 766-2046. Monitor VHF 16, working channel VHF 12.

Taxis: The New Other Guy's Taxi (766-3257). $6 from ferry to downtown. Long-term parking for ferry passengers $5 per day, $25 per week. Runs 24hr.

Car Rental: Eagle's Nest Car Rental (766-2891 or 800-354-6009), at Eagle's Nest Motel, west of town on the Haines Highway. Must be 21 with a major credit card. $45 per day, plus 35¢ per mi. over 100 mi. **Avis** (766-2733), at Hotel Hälsingland, grudgingly offers an 8hr. deal with unlimited mileage for $40. Must be 25 with a credit card. $65 per day late fee. Call ahead to reserve.

Car Repair: Charlie's Repair, 225 2nd Ave. (766-2494). Open M-F 8am-5pm.

Visitor Information: Haines Convention and Visitors Bureau (766-2234 or 800-458-3579; fax 766-3155; email hainesak@wwa.com; http://www.haines.ak.us), on 2nd Ave. near Willard St. Comprehensive info on accommodations, nearby hikes, and surrounding parks, including the free pamphlet *Haines is for Hikers.* Free tea and coffee. Open M-Th 8am-10pm, F 8am-8pm, Sa-Su 10am-6pm; in winter M-F 8am-5pm. Mobbed M-Th 7-10pm, when the cruise ship is docked.

Outdoor Information: State Park Information Office, 259 Main St., P.O. Box 430 (766-2292), above Helen's Shop between 2nd and 3rd Ave. Rangers tell all about area hiking, bears dangers, and the Chilkat Bald Eagle Preserve. Open Tu-Sa 8am-4:30pm, but call ahead; rangers are often out on patrol.

Bank: First National Bank of Anchorage, on Main St., is the only bank in town. ATMs 24hr. Open M-Th 10am-4pm, F 10am-5pm.

Equipment Rental: Sockeye Cycle (766-2869), on Portage St. in Ft. Seward. Bikes $6 per hr., $20 per 4hr., $30 per 8hr. Helmets and locks included. Also offers guided daytrips on and off road, led by the man who began the Kluane-Chilkat Bike Relay (see **Events,** p. 508). Open M-Sa 9am-6pm, Su 1-5pm. **Deishu Expeditions** (766-2427 or 800-552-9257; email paddle@seakayaks.com; http://www.seakayaks.com), on Portage St. near the cruise ship dock. Single kayaks $20 per day; doubles $40 per day. Open daily 9am-6pm; call to arrange pick-up or drop-off at other times. **Alaska Sport Shop** (766-2441), rents camping equipment and sells fishing licenses. Open M-Sa 8:30am-6pm, Su 10am-4pm; in winter M-Sa 10am-6pm.

Bookstore: The Babbling Book (766-3356), on Main St. near Howser's Supermarket. Good collection of Alaskana, current and non-fiction. Open M-Th 10am-9pm, F-Sa 10am-6pm, Su 11am-5pm.

Library: (766-2545), on 3rd Ave. Open M and W-Su 10am-9pm, Tu and Th 10am-4:30pm and 7-9pm, F 10am-4:30pm, Sa 1-4pm, Su 2-4pm.

Laundromat and Public Showers: Port Chilkoot Camper Park (766-2000), across from the Hälsingland Hotel. Wash $2, dry 25¢ per 7min. Showers $1.50. Open daily 7am-9pm. **Susie Q's** (766-2953), on Main St. near Front St. Wash $2, dry 50¢. Showers $2. Open daily 8am-8pm; in winter 8am-6pm.

Emergency: 911. **Police:** 766-2121. **Fire:** 766-2115.

Rape and Abuse Crisis Line: AWARE (800 478-1090).

Medical Services: Health Clinic (766-2521), on 1st Ave. next to the visitors bureau.

Post Office: On Haines Hwy., between 2nd Ave. and Front St. Open M-F 9am-5:30pm, Sa 1-3pm. **ZIP Code:** 99827.

Area Code: 907.

ACCOMMODATIONS AND CAMPGROUNDS

The weather is better in Haines than almost anywhere else in Southeast Alaska, and camping is usually a true pleasure. In addition to the private campgrounds listed below, there are several state campgrounds (with water and toilets) around Haines. **Chilkat State Park,** 7 mi. south on Mud Bay Rd., has guided nature walks and good king salmon and halibut fishing (32 sites: $6). **Chilkoot Lake,** 10 mi. north of town on Lutak Rd., provides views and sockeye salmon (32 sites: $10). **Mosquito Lake,** 27 mi. north on Haines Hwy., earns its name in late summer (13 sites: $6). Call the State Park Information Office (766-2292) (see **Practical Information,** above) for more info.

Bear Creek Camp and International Hostel, Box 1158 (766-2259), on Small Tracts Rd., 2 mi. out of town. From downtown, follow 3rd Ave. out Mud Bay Rd. to Small Tracts. Location is convenient to nothing; call ahead for ferry terminal pickup. A ring of basic cabins, each with its own unique odor. Spartan furnishings—a roof and a foam pads on bunks. Beds $14; family cabins $38; tent sites $8. No curfew.

Hotel Hälsingland, Box 1589 MD (766-2000; 800-542-6363, or 800-478-2525 in YT and BC; fax 907-766-2006). Old Ft. Seward officers' quarters, with original 30s decor that shows its age. Several small economy rooms with sinks and a shared bath. Singles $49; doubles $59. Call ahead for cheaper rooms; a bath doubles the price.

Fort Seward Lodge, P.O. Box 307 (766-2009 or 800-478-7772). A historic Fort Seward building, just beyond the post office above Haines. A bit dark, but clean and attractive with hand-finished furniture. Singles $45, with bath $60; doubles from $55, with bath from $75. $10 less Oct.-Apr. Not wheelchair accessible. .

Portage Cove, ¾ mi. from town on Beach Rd. Accepts only backpackers and cyclists. 9 grassy sites overlook the water ($6). Scant privacy, but other campers tend to be congenial. Pit toilets and a food-hanging site. 7-night max stay.

Port Chilkoot Camper Park, P.O. Box 41589 (766-2000 or 800-542-6363), across from Hotel Hälsingland. Tall pines evoke a shady forest right in town; pitch a tent at the far corner from the road for the most effect. Gravelly but well maintained and convenient to downtown. Laundromat and showers ($2). 60 sites: $8; full hookups $19. Open Apr.-Sept.

Salmon Run RV Campground (766-3240), at Lutak Inlet, 1.8 mi. past the ferry terminal, away from town. Wooded, with streams on grounds. Half of the sites overlook the beach. Restrooms. Sites $10. Open year-round.

FOOD

As new establishments strive to please outsiders' delicate palates, creative sandwiches and overstuffed burritos are beginning to replace steak and potatoes on Haines menus. Groceries are expensive; better to stock up in Juneau. Of the two markets in town, most locals prefer **Howser's Supermarket** (766-2040), on Main St. (open daily 8am-9pm). For fresh seafood, including salmon ($7 per lb.) and prawns ($13 per lb.), head to **Bell's Seafood** (766-2950), on 2nd Ave., under the Old City Jail and Firehouse sign (open Su-Tu and Th-Sa 9am-6pm, W 9am-10pm).

◉**Wild Strawberry,** 138 2nd Ave. (766-3608), off Haines Hwy. Sit out on the deck on a sunny Haines afternoon enjoying a loaded bagel sandwich ($6) or grilled seafood specials ($8), made with halibut and salmon fresh from Jim's boat. Espresso, candy, and ice cream ($2). Tastes and feels like Mom's kitchen, if your momma was a gourmand. Open M-F 7am-9pm, Sa 9am-9pm, Su noon-9pm.

Mountain Market (766-3340), on Haines Hwy. at 3rd Ave. Haines' health food grocery store and cafe serves sandwiches overflowing with sprouts and avocado from $5.50, with daily soup add 75¢. Standard espresso schtick. Open daily 6am-6pm.

Grizzly Greg's (766-3622), on the corner of 2nd Ave. and Main St. Classic pizzeria, complete with red-and-white-checked decor. Pizza by the slice ($2.50) and enormous calzones ($7). Ice cream, foosball, and oldies on the radio.

Chilkat Restaurant and Bakery (766-2920), on 5th Ave., near Main. Family-style, with healthy portions. Sugary baked goods available for takeout. All-you-can-eat soup-and-salad bar $9; basic sandwiches $5; creative sandwiches $8. Popular Mexican night on Friday. Open M-Sa 7am-8:30pm.

Bamboo Room (776-2800), on 2nd Ave. near Main St. This unpretentious diner is a favorite breakfast spot, crowded until 3pm with fisherfolk downing buckwheat hotcakes and coffee ($4.25). Lunch specials $6; dinner specials $9-10. No bamboo in sight. Open daily 6am-10pm.

SIGHTS, NIGHTLIFE, AND EVENTS

Fort William Seward, on the west side of town, was established in 1901 to assert American presence during a border dispute with Canada. With few duties other than shoveling snow and watching for fires, the colonial-style post quickly became known as a gentle assignment. Boredom was the soldiers' only enemy: "Even among men with the most modern arms, time is the hardest thing to kill," lamented one observer in a 1907 newspaper. After WWII, the fort shut down and five veterans bought the entire 400-acre compound, intending to form a commune. Their utopian venture never succeeded, but most of these settlers became enterprising members of the community. Today, Ft. Seward lies at the center of Haines' tourist activity, showing off a replicated **Totem Village** (766-2160), complete with a replicated tribal house.

The **Chilkat Dancers** perform traditional Tlingit dances with interpretive narration at the **Chilkat Center for the Arts.** *(Performances usually at 8pm, but revolve around cruise ship and ferry schedules. Call Hotel Hälsingland at 766-2000 for tickets. $10, ages 5-18 $5, under 5 free.)* The village is also home to **Sea Wolf Studio-Gallery** (766-2540), where artist Tresham Gregg carves Tlingit masks. *(Open M-F 9am until the last ship leaves.)* The **Alaska Indian Arts Center** (766-2160), at the far side of the fairgrounds, allows visitors to watch artisans in their workshops and marvel at the craft of totem pole carving. *(Open M-F 9am-noon and 1-5pm.)* The **American Bald Eagle Foundation Center,** P.O. Box 49 (766-3094), at the intersection of Haines Hwy. and 2nd Ave., offers an indoor look at Haines' wildlife and screens a film of the November bald eagle occupation. *(Open M-Sa 9am-6pm, Su 1-6pm, and to accommodate cruise ships. Free.)*

The three main watering holes in Haines are **The Fogcutter** on Main St., across from the bank, **Harbor Bar,** next to the small boat harbor, and the bar in the **Hälsingland Hotel.** Bars here have a unique system: while all open at around 11am, their closing times depend on where the crowd is, and the crowd follows the drink specials and live music. After midnight, once the party-spot has established itself, the barkeep calls the other two bars and they close up early. The fun roams around, but a good bet is to start out at the Fogcutter for a wide selection on tap and 50¢ pool.

Haines becomes party central in early summer with a **Craft Beer and Home-Brew Festival** (May 21-22 in 1999), a **Bald Eagle Run** and **Harley Davidson Rodeo** (May 21-23), and an Alaskan version of **Mardi Gras** (June 5). If wheels are your thing, but Hogs aren't, team up for the **International Kluane to Chilkoot Bike Relay** (June 19). The 153 mi. course covers the Haines Hwy. from Haines Junction, YT to Haines, AK, with checkpoints every 20 mi. to relieve saddle soreness. Call **Sockeye Cycle** (see **Practical Information,** above) for more info.

OUTDOORS

The **Haines Highway** winds 40 mi. from Haines into the **Chilkat Range** north through the Yukon, with views guaranteed to blow you through the back of your Winnebago, were you to drive such a vehicle. **Chilkat Bald Eagle Preserve,** 19 mi. drive or bike up the highway, protects the feeding grounds where thousands of eagles gather in November—the world's largest annual concentration. A handful of eagles make the preserve their year-round home. Call the **American Bald Eagle Foundation Center** (766-3094) for more information.

Three main trails head into the wilderness around Haines. The **Mt. Riley Trail** starts in several places and ends on a 1760 ft. summit with a panoramic view of the Lynn Canal, the Chilkoot and Chilkat Inlets, and everything else within 30 mi. The primary trailhead is marked by a large sign 3½ mi. from town, 1½ mi. down Mud Bay Rd. past the hostel. This route is steep for most of its 2 mi. and takes the average hiker about two hours. **Mount Ripinsky,** the 3920 ft. mountain looming over the north end of town, provides a challenging hike over two summits connected by an alpine ridge. On a clear day, the view from the ridge extends all the way to Juneau; on partly cloudy days, the summit is often shrouded, but the shorter Mt. Riley continues to provide excellent views. To reach Mt. Ripinsky's trailhead, follow 2nd Ave. north to Lutak Rd., branch off Lutak onto Young St. at the hill, then turn right along a pipeline for 1 mi. After cresting the 3610 ft. **North Summit,** the trail dips down along the ridge and may be difficult to follow in poor weather. At the end of the ridge, it climbs again to the 3920 ft. peak, and descends steeply to its end at Mile 7 of the Haines Hwy. This strenuous 10 mi. hike makes for a long day of walking or a relaxed overnight trip. Hey there, big fella, **Seduction Point Trail** offers 6¾ mi. of birds, beaches, ocean bluffs, berry picking, wildflowers, and alluring views of the **Davidson Glacier.** Take Mud Bay Rd. out of Haines 7 mi. to Chilkat State Park, and try to time the last part of the hike along **David's Cove** to coincide with low tide.

A local favorite swimming hole is **Chilkoot Lake,** 10mi north on Lutak Rd. Chilkat River hosts good kayaking and canoeing. Call **Deishu Expeditions** (see **Practical Information,** above) for rentals and trip recommendations.

■ Skagway

In August 1896, 500 mi. from Skagway, a Tlingit man named Skookum Jim was washing a pan in a tributary of the Klondike River when he discovered strips of gold so thick they looked "like cheese in a sandwich." By October, Skagway had swollen to a town of 20,000, as stampeders piled off boats and made provisions for the trek to Dawson City, YT. When the Nome gold rush began in 1900, Skagway lost its hub status and much of its population, surviving only as a port and the terminus of a railway over White Pass.

The railroad still runs today, but carries tourists rather than miners and supplies. Although Skagway's population is only 700, gargantuan Inside Passage cruise ships and ferries disgorge as many as 7000 passengers per day. Most tourists stay on Broadway Street, the town's renovated historic district, leaving the surrounding streets and trails (except the Chilkoot), relatively uncrowded. While July and August may not be the best time for serenity, Skagway's sky-meets-sea location and open-hearted hostel make any visit worthwhile.

ORIENTATION AND PRACTICAL INFORMATION

At the northernmost tip of the Inside Passage, Skagway is a terminus of the **Alaska Marine Hwy.** Drivers connect to the interior **Alaska Hwy.** (Hwy. 1) by taking the **Klondike Hwy.** (Rte. 98 in AK; Hwy. 2 in YT) 113 mi. to Whitehorse, YT. The first 66 mi. to **Carcross** snake gently alongside lichen-covered crags interspersed with waterfalls. Both Canadian and U.S. **customs** are passable 24 hours a day, although the U.S. office is not staffed between midnight and 6am (see **Customs,** p. 7). There are no services on the 66 mi. between Skagway and Carcross. **Haines** is 15 mi. away by water, 360 mi. by land. Hitchers say they do better spending $14 on the ferry to Haines, than thumbing the more heavily traveled **Haines Hwy.** to Kluane and Interior Alaska.

The **ferry** drops passengers off at the southern end of **downtown.** Skagway's main drag, **Broadway,** runs inland from the docks, is paralleled by **Spring St.** to the right, and **State** and **Main St.** to the left. Numbered **avenues** intersect these streets, with the numbers ascending as they move away from the water.

Skagway has a significant **city tax:** 4% on all merchandise, food, and services, and 8% on accommodations.

Transportation

Airplanes: Skagway Air Service (983-2218), on Broadway between 4th and 5th Ave. 8 per day to: Haines (8min., $35); Juneau (45 min., $75). Also several flights to Gustavus ($85) and tours of Glacier Bay ($120). Open daily 7am-9pm.

Trains: White Pass and Yukon Route, P.O. Box 435 (983-2217 or 800-343-7373), 1 block off Broadway, on 2nd Ave. toward the tracks. 3hr. round-trip excursion to White Pass Summit on one of the most scenic and steepest railroads in North America. Trains run May 12 to Sept. 24, leaving daily at 8:30am and 1pm, plus Tu-W at 4:30pm ($78, ages 3-12 $39). Accesses remote hiking trails along the route (see **Outdoors,** below). Combined train and bus service to Whitehorse, YT (5hr., daily at 12:40pm, $95, ages 3-12 $48). All trains wheelchair accessible, but bus service may not be.

Buses: Alaska Direct (983-2311 or 800-770-6652) runs vans daily by appointment from the ferry terminal, visitor center, and hostel to Whitehorse (4hr., $35, round-trip $50). Connections on W, F, and Su to Fairbanks ($120) and Anchorage ($145), require an overnight stay in Whitehorse. **Alaskon Express** (983-2241 or 800-544-2206), in the Westmark Inn, on 3rd Ave. between Broadway and Spring. Buses mid-May to mid-Sept. Su, Tu, and Th to: Anchorage ($209); Fairbanks ($205). Both trips require an overnight stop ($42.50) in Beaver Creek, YT. Also runs 1 per day in summer to Whitehorse, YT (3hr., 7:30am, $56).

Ferries: Alaska Marine Highway (983-2941 or 800-642-0066). 6 per week to: Haines ($14); Juneau ($26). Beware dockside ticket office's erratic hours. **Water Taxi** (983-2083, in AK or Canada 888-766-3395). 2 per day to Haines (1hr., $20, round-trip with 4hr. in Haines $32; under 12 half price). Open May-Sept. daily 9am-5pm.

Taxis: Frontier Excursions (983-2512), at 7th Ave. and Broadway. To the Chilkoot trailhead in Dyea ($10); pick-up at log cabin near trail's terminus ($20).

Car Rental: Sourdough Van & Car Rentals (983-2523, in AK 800-478-2529; email rental@ptialaska.net), at 6th Ave. and Broadway. From $30 per day, plus 30¢ per mi. over 100 mi. Drop-offs at Haines ($40) and Whitehorse ($100) by arrangement.

Auto Repair: Hoover's (983-2454), at 4th and Main St. Open M-Sa 7am-7pm, Su 8am-6pm.

Visitor and Financial Services

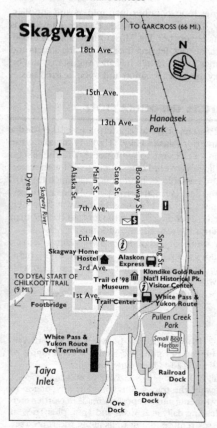

Visitor Information: Klondike Gold Rush National Historical Park Visitor Center (983-2921), at 2nd and Broadway. Free 45min. walking tours 4 times daily; self-guided tour brochures available. Open daily June-Aug. 8am-8pm; May and Sept. 8am-6pm. **Skagway Convention and Visitors Bureau** (983-2854; http://www.skagway.org), on 5th Ave. off Broadway. A ton of brochures and accommodations info. Open May-Sept. M-F 8am-6pm, Sa-Su 9am-6pm; Oct.-Apr. M-F 8am-noon and 1-5pm.

Outdoor Information: Trail Center (983-3655), across the street on Broadway, is a joint-run U.S./Canada Parks headquarters with info and maps on local hikes and the Chilkoot Trail. Sells **overnight permits** for the Canada side of the trail (CDN$35, under 16 CDN$17.50), keeps itinerary records, and sells a few trail guides. Open late May to mid-Sept. daily 8am-5pm.

Bank: National Bank of Alaska (983-2265), at Broadway and 6th Ave. Open M-F 9:30am-5pm. 24hr. **ATM.**

Local Services

Equipment Rental: Sockeye Cycle (983-2851; http://www.haines.ak.us/sockeye), on 5th Ave. off Broadway St. From $6 per hr., $30 per day, including helmet and lock. Guided tours available. Open May-Sept. daily 9am-6pm. **Skagway Hardware** (983-2233), on Broadway St. at 4th Ave., sells fishing permits ($10 per day, $100 per season; king salmon tag $100 extra), limited outdoor gear, and fix-its. Open mid-Apr. to Sept. M-Sa 8am-6pm, Su 10am-4pm; in winter M-Sa 8am-5pm. **The Sports Emporium** (983-2480), on 4th Ave. between Broadway and State, sells more high-tech gear. Open May to late Sept. daily 9am-6pm; in winter M-F noon-5pm.

Library: (983-2665), at 8th Ave. and State St. Internet access available. Open M-F 1-9pm, Sa 1-6pm.

Laundromat: Services Unlimited Laundromat (983-2595), at 2nd Ave. and State St. Wash $2, dry 25¢ per 5min. Open daily in summer 8am-8pm, last load 6:30pm; in winter F-Tu 9am-6pm. **Garden City RV Park** (983-2378), at State St. and 15th Ave. Wash $1.50, dry 25¢ per 5min. Open May-Sept. 7am-10pm.

Public Showers: Garden City RV Park (see **Laundromat,** above), 75¢ per 5min.

Emergency and Communications

Emergency: 911. **Police:** (983-2232), on 7th Ave. in City Hall.

Hospital: Skagway Medical Service (983-2255), on 11th Ave. between State and Broadway.

Internet Access: See **Library,** above.

Post Office: (983-2320), at Broadway and 6th, next to the bank. Open M-F 8:30am-5pm. Lobby open 24hr. **ZIP Code:** 99840.

Area Code: 907.

ACCOMMODATIONS AND CAMPGROUNDS

The Skagway Home Hostel is reason enough to visit the town, and if it weren't, the Golden North Hotel and Skagway Inn B&B would take up the slack. Unless you're camping, it's wise to make reservations at least one month in advance. Dyea, 9 mi. away, has the only available free tenting.

⊛**Skagway Home Hostel,** P.O. Box 231 (983-2131), on 3rd Ave. near Main St. This definition of Home Sweet Home invites travelers into a generous, idiosyncratic family. Kitchen and facilities shared by owners and guests alike. 21 beds ($15) and 1 private double ($40). Up to 10 may sign up for dinner before 4:30pm ($5; free if you cook). Showers, kitchen, bike use and plenty of Chilkoot Trail advice. Cash or travelers checks only. Chore required. Stores packs. Sheets and towels $1. Laundry $3 (wash, dry, and detergent.) Check-in 5:30-9pm. No lockout. Curfew 11pm (late ferries accommodated). Reservations advised (by mail only).

⊛**Skagway Inn Bed and Breakfast** (983-2289 or 800-478-2290), on Broadway at 7th Ave. Built as a brothel in 1897 and now respectably refurbished, each room retains the name of one of the brothel's illustrious women. Divine full breakfast served in an elegant dining room. Pick-up and delivery to ferry and airport. Shared baths. Singles $65; doubles $85; winter rates $10 less.

Golden North Hotel, P.O. Box 431 (983-2295), at 3rd Ave. and Broadway St. The classiest affordable hotel in Southeast Alaska and the oldest hotel in the state (since 1898). Each room in a period style, with canopy beds and antique furniture. Singles $55, with bath $75; doubles $65, with bath $85.

Dyea Camping Area, 9 mi. northwest of Skagway on Dyea Rd., near the start of the Chilkoot Trail. 22 spacious, woodsy sites. Pit toilets, fire rings, no drinking water or showers. 14-night max. stay. Not recommended for RVs. Free.

Pullen Creek RV Park (983-2768), on 2nd Ave. by the harbor. Small and noisy, but convenient, with an unobstructed view of the mountains. Bathrooms, coin shower. Sites $10 ($5 extra for vehicle); hookups $20. No open fires.

FOOD

With Skagway's status as a cruise ship magnet, eating and shopping can be expensive. The **Fairway Supermarket** (983-2220), at 4th Ave. and State St. sells groceries (open M-Sa 8am-9pm, Su 9am-6pm; in winter M-Sa 9am-6pm, Su 10am-4pm). **You Say**

ALASKA

Tomato (983-2784), on State St. at 9th Ave., sells dry, natural meals by the pound for backpackers. Bulk supplies can be special ordered at a 15% discount (open Apr.-Oct. daily 11am-7pm; call for winter hours).

Stowaway Cafe (983-3463), on 2nd Ave. by the small boat harbor. Though pricey, the Stowaway is ten steps above the Broadway mayhem. Fresh seafood gumbo $16; lunch veggie curry $7.50; unlimited bread made in heaven. Open May-Sept. daily 11am-10pm. Reservations suggested.

Klondike Kate's, on Broadway at 1st Ave. The cheapest fresh seafood deals in town, with outdoor seating and a great view of the mountains and harbor. Deep-fried halibut, tempura shrimp, or broiled Alaskan salmon each come with coleslaw for a measly $5. Open July-Aug. 11am-8pm.

Bonanza Bar and Grill (983-6214), on Broadway between 3rd and 4th Ave. As American as they come, with basic sports grill fare and a game on the big-screen TV. Nachos grande, pizza, or sandwiches from $7. Pitchers from $10. Open May-Sept. daily 10am-midnight.

Corner Cafe (983-2155), at 4th Ave. and State St. Where the locals head for basic grub. Open-air seating helps dissipate avoid the smoke. Listen to that fryer sizzle! Stack of sourdough pancakes $4, burgers $4.75-7. Open daily 6am-8pm.

Mabel G. Smith's, 342 5th Ave. (983-2609). Those avoiding Starbucks or the Love Boat stampede on Broadway get their caffeine here. Muffins and cookies ($1.30). Open May-Sept. M-F 6am-6pm, Sa 6am-4pm, Su 7am-4pm; call for winter hours.

SIGHTS AND ENTERTAINMENT

Most of Broadway St. is preserved in pristine 1898 form as the **Klondike Gold Rush National Historical Park.** The Park Service leases a restored vintage saloon and many other period buildings to local businesses. Polish up on gold rush trivia at the **Trail of '98 Museum** (983-2420), housed in the 1899 Arctic Brotherhood Hall, on Broadway between 2nd and 3rd. *(Open in summer daily 9am-noon and 1-5pm. $2, students $1.)* The hall's driftwood-coated facade is the state's most photographed building, a testament to Alaska's dearth of interesting architecture. Among the museum's offerings are the usual litany of native artifacts and one unique monstrosity, the world's only duck-neck robe. For more ribald history, head next door to the **Red Onion Saloon** (983-2222), Skagway's first bordello. *(Open May-Sept. daily 10am-late. Free.)* A century ago, the bartender marked each lady's availability by placing dolls on a rack downstairs in either an upright or prostrate position. Now the Red Onion is a popular bar with an enviable collection of bed pans adorning one wall. Come for live afternoon jazz (courtesy of cruise ship musicians) or for the open jam on Thursday nights, when the locals come out to play. For a little less ambience but a ton of taste, the **Skagway Brewing Company,** in the Golden North Hotel (see **Accommodations,** above) serves up seven drafts straight from its own in-house microbrewery. *(Open May-Sept. 11am-midnight.)* The Oosic Stout is named for the bone of a male walrus' nether regions.

Skagway's history is almost overshadowed by its shiny, packaged souvenir and jewelry shops. **Inside Passage Arts** (983-2585), at Broadway between 4th and 5th, is an artist-run gallery which sells work by local indigenous craftspeople. *(Open May-Sept. daily 9am-5pm.)* **Corrington Alaskan Ivory** (983-2580), at 5th Ave. and Broadway St., contains a copious display of expensive carved bone and fossilized ivory in their showroom and free museum. *(Open daily 9am-6pm.)*

The **Gold Rush Cemetery** on the inland edge of town retains an eerie serenity rare in other gold rush monuments. Take Main St. and head for the parking lot before the bridge and the sign indicating a dirt road; the cemetery is about 1½ mi. from down-

The Cleanest Con Man in the North

Skagway's most notorious ne'er-do-well, Jefferson Randolph "Soapy" Smith, got his name from his favorite scam, the "soap game." He would sit on a street corner selling a chance to pick a bar of soap from his collection for an outrageous $5. Each bar had some bill wrapped around it, with the bar and bill wrapped in cloth to obscure the denomination. With thousands of prospectors roaming the streets of Skagway any given day, it never took long before a crowd gathered, and some impetuous spenders would step forward to buy bars. As luck would have it, those first two or three invariably held very large bills and triggered a buying frenzy. Most purchasers ended up with only a bar of soap and a single greenback. The two or three lucky fellows (a.k.a. accomplices) would meet up with Soapy later and return the planted bills for a handsome payoff. Ultimately, Soapy Smith wasn't such a bad sort: he donated money to the community for a new church, started an adopt-a-dog program, and rarely robbed locals. In appreciation of his peculiar brand of philanthropy, the town named him a Marshal of the 4th of July parade in 1898. A few days later, Soapy died in a shootout, taking his adversary down with him. While Soapy was buried outside the limits of the town cemetery, the fickle public gave his killer a choice plot and a tombstone inscribed, "He gave his life for the honor of Skagway." Today, Soapy's spirit is celebrated each July at a debaucherous evening gathering called Soapy's Wake.

town. Soapy fans will have to pay their respects slightly beyond the cemetery boundaries. A short trail from the cemetery leads to **Lower Reid Falls,** which cascades 300 ft. down the mountainside.

Those wanting to enjoy Soapy's exploits without reading another pamphlet can head to the **Skagway Days of '98** show in the Eagles Hall (983-2545), at 6th and Broadway. *(Daily in summer; gambling 7:30pm, show 8:30pm. $14, children $7. Matinees $12, children $6.)* For over seven decades, the vaudeville show has featured song and dance, play-money gambling, and audience-actor interaction.

OUTDOORS

Backpacking buffs in Skagway won't pass up the **Chilkoot Trail** (see p. 383). Before going, pick up the Alaska National History Association's complete *Hiker's Guide to the Chilkoot Trail* ($2), available at the Trail Center (see **Practical Information,** above). Even if not camping out in Canada (permit CDN$35), hikers still need to register (CDN$10) at the Trail Center. Call 800-661-4086 or 867-667-3910 between 8am and 4:30pm. Only 50 people per day are allowed on the trail in summer—42 reserved and 8 walk-ons. Park officials patrol the trail, and rangers are also usually at the trailhead in Dyea. If you're planning to continue into British Columbia, give your name at the trail center before hiking, and then check in with customs in Fraser, BC (along the Klondike Highway) or Whitehorse, YT (867-667-3493; 8:30am-4:30pm PST) upon completion. Have a credit card, valid photo ID, and birth certificate or passport with you to cross the border. According to rangers, these requirements are enforced only on a whim, and are most likely to trip up the scruffy and potentially indigent.

Although the Chilkoot Trail is the marquee name in Skagway hiking, shorter local trails have inspiring views and fewer people around to block them. The **Dewey Lake Trail System** provides some of the best and closest hiking, ranging from a 20-minute stroll to a strenuous climb up to two alpine lakes at 3700 ft. To reach the trail system, walk east toward the mountains along 2nd. Ave.; follow the dirt path just before the railroad tracks to the left, and look for signs pointing out the trail on the right. **Lower Dewey Lake,** a long, narrow pond surrounded by woods, lies less than a mile up the trail. Here one trail branches to the lake (about 2 mi.), and another branches left toward **Icy Lake** and **Upper Reid Falls** (about 1½ mi.). Both of these walks are gentle, with little change in elevation. A third trail to **Upper Dewey Lake** branches off the Icy Lake trail near the northern end of Lower Dewey Lake. The first section of the 2¼ mi. trail is brutal, but the climb mellows out somewhat and switchbacks its way to the lake. Upper Dewey rests in a stunning amphitheater of serrated peaks. The total ascent from town takes about three hours. A small cabin, newly renovated with bunks and cooking utensils, has cramped space for four and is available on a first-come, first-served basis. The best tenting sites are along the opposite shore. A permit is necessary for overnight camping anywhere in the forests surrounding Skagway; get one free at the police station (see **Practical Information,** above). **Fishing** is available at both of the Dewey Lakes. The **Skyline Trail** leads up **AB Mountain,** named for the pattern created by melting snow on its side each spring. Both the directions to the trailhead and the challenging trail itself are confusing; pick up a **Skagway Trail Map** at the Trail Center. From town, it's about 5 mi. to the panoramic 3500 ft. summit; allow three to four hours for the steep ascent. Many other hikes start from trailheads in or near Skagway, some involving train pick-ups and drop-offs.

The Bush

Known as the Country or the Bush, this vast land of tundra and jagged coastline over-whelms the tiny settlements and narrow landing strips that hint at human presence. Polar bears ride ice floes and hundreds of thousands of caribou roam freely. Native Alaskan settlements are few and far between, accessible only by plane, boat, or snow-machine. Cannery workers and oil drillers swarm to remote settlements for big money, knowing it's theirs to save because there's nowhere to spend it. In Arctic Alaska, the crowning Brooks Range stretches from the far northwest to the Canadian border, while the North Slope's flat expanses spread northward from the Brooks to the Arctic Ocean and Barrow. Northwest Alaska includes the Seward Peninsula, a treeless, hilly projection of tundra, where Nome and Kotzebue lie on the storm-lashed Bering Sea. The Southwest includes the flat, soggy terrain of the Yukon-Kush-kowin delta, the mountainous Alaska Peninsula, and the Aleutian Islands, a volcanic archipelago with some of the worst weather on earth. Anyone who hopes to travel in the Bush must have a strong sense of adventure and self-reliance, or tons of money and trust in tour guides. Because all supplies, even gas, must be flown in from Fair-banks, transportation in the Bush is expensive. Once in the Bush, tour outfitters abound, ready and willing to take visitors into the wilds to fish, hunt, hike, kayak, or canoe in some of the most remote real estate on earth.

ARCTIC ALASKA

■ Dalton Highway (Rte. 11)

The Dalton Hwy. parallels the Alaska pipeline from Fairbanks to the Arctic Circle, then reaches all the way to Deadhorse and the gates of Prudhoe Bay, an oil field on the Arctic Ocean. Before considering the drive, check your wallet to see if a tour is possible. The **Northern Alaska Tour Company** (474-8600) offers a daytrip to the Arctic Circle boundary (departs 7am, returns 11pm; $99), and a three-day trip to Prudhoe Bay including everything but meals ($589). These tours, though pricey, are the best way to view the area while preserving both car and sanity; a flat tire halfway up the Dalton would be a far worse financial drain.

The entire Dalton Hwy. was opened to the public on January 1, 1995. Truckers predominate, spitting rocks and dust from their 36-wheel rigs; a tiny number of RVs, a handful of 4WD vehicles, and an occasional crazy motorcyclist constitute the tourist traffic. Some hitchers proceed on the logic that nobody would leave a person stranded in the middle of nowhere, yet truckers almost always do. The road is pass-able in a standard passenger car, but it's unwise to try it, and the visitor center in Fair-banks discourages ignorant hotheads from making the attempt. The sharp gravel road is interrupted by rocks, boulders, ditches, and mud deep enough to absorb a car. The Dalton can wreck a suspension and mercilessly puncture tires, especially at speeds over 50mph. The drive *is* breathtaking, though almost entirely without services. Bring two spare tires, a rabbit's foot or other superstitious talisman, and extra gas, tools, clothing, food supplies, and drinking water. Being towed back to Fairbanks costs around $7 *per mile*. The 498 mi. journey takes about four days round-trip.

■ Fairbanks to the Arctic Circle

A drive up the Dalton Hwy. begins with an 84 mi. jaunt from Fairbanks along the **Elliot Hwy.** to Mile 0 of the Dalton. Savor the pavement as you head out of Fairbanks; it's the last you'll see for almost 900 mi. The Dalton crosses the **Yukon River** at Mile 56, 140 mi. from Fairbanks. On the north side of the river is **Yukon Ventures** (655-9001), one of the highway's two (count 'em, two) service stations, which sells unleaded gas, rents rooms ($50), and has a small cafe (open daily in summer 7am-11pm; in winter 7am-9pm).

As it gains elevation, the road winds through its first alpine region; at Mile 97.5, it passes **Finger Rock** to the east and **Caribou Mountain** to the west. The **rest area** just past Finger Rock is an ideal place to calm pothole-jarred nerves and enjoy the view of the Brooks Range. Next comes the **Arctic Circle** (Mile 115), the southernmost point at which the sun does not set on the longest day of the year. A recently constructed pull-off has several picnic tables, and presents four displays on the Arctic seasons (summer, winter, winter, and winter). Thousands hunger for the enormous Arctic Circle sign photo op, and the spot offers good, free camping. Most folks are satisfied with merely reaching the Arctic Circle, and quickly retreat to Fairbanks; from here, the road only gets worse.

■ Arctic Circle to Deadhorse

Continuing north over **Gobblers Knob** (1500 ft.), the Dalton rattles past **Prospect Camp** and **Pump Station No. 5,** over the **Jim River** and the South Fork of the **Koyukuk River** to the town of **Coldfoot,** which has the last services available before Prudhoe Bay, 240 mi. away. Coldfoot, "the northernmost truck stop in North America," was originally a mining town that, at its peak, boasted one gambling hall, two road houses, seven saloons, and ten prostitutes. Its name originated in 1898, when a group of timid prospectors got cold feet about wintering above the Arctic Circle and headed south again. Just north of town is the **Coldfoot Visitor Center** (678-5209), an excellent source of info for travelers planning on intense hiking or paddling in the Brooks Range (open daily 10am-10pm; daily slide presentations 8:30pm). The **post office** (678-5204) is next to the general store (open M, W, and F 1:30-6pm). **ZIP Code:** 99701. Downtown is a huge, muddy parking lot. On its perimeter, the **Coldfoot Cafe** (678-5201) serves good, hot, and—surprise!—expensive food (open 24hr.). The **Slate Creek Inn** (678-5224) maintains several RV sites (electrical hookups $25) and **showers** ($5). There is **free camping** out of town; ask at a visitor center about nearby public land. Eight miles north of Coldfoot, the Bureau of Land Management (BLM) **Marion Creek Campground** has sites in muskeg forest with water and pit toilets ($6).

Twelve miles north of Coldfoot, at Mile 188.6, is the junction for the frontier village of **Wiseman.** Three miles off the beaten path, this town was seared into the American collective consciousness by Robert Marshall's 1933 work, *Arctic Village.* Perhaps the wildest road-accessible frontier town in Alaska, Wiseman is home to many of the canine stars in the movie version of *White Fang*—including W.F. himself. From Wiseman, the highway continues into the heart of the **Brooks Range,** a region frequented by moose, Dall sheep, bear, caribou, and hawks. At Mile 235, the last tree along the highway—a surprisingly tall and majestic spruce—marks the beginning of the steep and awe-inspiring ascent toward **Atigun Pass** (4752 ft.). The highway cuts steeply into the mountainside as it approaches the perennially snow-covered pass, granting spectacular views of the **Dietrich River Valley.** Once the mountains are breached, the long descent toward the Arctic Ocean begins.

In the highway's final stretch, the mountains gradually flatten into a broad expanse of monotonous tundra, perpetually brown except during a brief flourishing in July and August. The tundra is filled with bumps and lumps of moss called tussocks, and is underlaid by tremendous amounts of water unable to escape through the frozen ground. This guarantees wet, soggy, difficult walking, though hikers may be rewarded by seeing wildlife not found below the Brooks Range, such as musk oxen, arctic fox, snow owls, and tundra swans. Even under constant sunlight, the temperature is typically about 43°F (5°C) in summer.

Approximately 10 mi. from the highway's end, a layer of coastal fog enshrouds the land, blocking the sun and forcing the temperature to plummet. **Deadhorse** suddenly appears on the horizon, and 3 mi. beyond is **Prudhoe Bay.** And then you're there. At the Arctic Ocean. The northernmost point accessible by road in North America. Fun, wasn't it? Now you just have to get back.

■ Deadhorse and Prudhoe Bay

The camp of **Deadhorse,** on the southern perimeter of **Lake Colleen,** owes its name to the gravel company that brought the first road-building materials north, and whose motto was: "We'll haul anything, even a dead horse." The airport is served by **Alaska Airlines** (800-225-2752); a one-way flight from Fairbanks costs $284. In an **emergency,** call the ARCO operator at 659-5300; there are no public emergency services.

Prudhoe Bay, owned by oil companies and accessible only by guided tour, has no permanent residents. Every building, structure, and person contributes in some way to oil production. The Atlantic Richfield Co. (ARCO) runs a **visitor center** (659-5748). The **Arctic Caribou Inn** (659-2368) offers excellent three-hour tours twice daily ($60), allowing visitors to stand next to Mile 0 of the pipeline, check out the interior of the workers' surprisingly nice bunkhouses, get an in-depth tour of the oil fields, and dip their fingers into the icy waters of the Arctic Ocean. The inn also runs a shuttle to the ocean (80min.; 11am, 4pm, and 6pm; $25); this abbreviated version is mostly a driving tour of the oil fields, but still affords the chance to leap into the Arctic Ocean. Keep in mind that Prudhoe Bay is a "dry" "community." No alcohol or firearms are allowed. The **post office** (659-2669) is next to the Arctic Caribou Inn (open daily 1-3:30pm and 6:30-9pm). **ZIP Code:** 99734. **Area Code:** 907.

Old Pilots and Bold Pilots, But No Old Bold Pilots

Alaska has the highest per capita ownership of small planes, the greatest number of pilots, the highest number of float planes, and one of the nation's busiest airports (in Anchorage). Throughout much of the Interior, small planes aren't simply the best way to get there; they're the only way. Some of the state's most colorful lore is steeped in aviation—like the story of Alaska's third governor, who broke both ankles crash-landing his small plane to avoid endangering the children playing on the airstrip. Tales of unusual landings are as common as tales of unusual cargo: Bush pilots have been known to transport canoes, beer, furniture, and even moose to the farthest reaches of the state.

■ Brooks Range

Defining Alaska's North Slope, the magnificent Brooks Range makes a great semicircle from the Bering Strait in the west, through the **Noatak National Preserve** and **Gates of the Arctic National Park,** to the **Arctic National Wildlife Refuge (ANWR)** and the Canadian border in the east. This northern terminus of the Rocky Mountains covers gargantuan expanses of remote territory, and remains the last stretch of truly untouched wilderness in the U.S. Accessing the Brooks Range and the parks that protect it is both difficult and expensive. It's possible to hike into the mountains from the Dalton Hwy. near Wiseman (see p. 516), but to reach the best parts of the range, or even to get more than 10 mi. from the highway, most people fly in. Talk to park officials before planning a trip into the Brooks: the headquarters for both ANWR and the Gates are in Fairbanks (see p. 462), and the **Coldfoot Visitor Center** (see p. 516) can give specific info on where to hike into the range from the Dalton Hwy.

■ Anaktuvuk Pass

Many travelers heading into Gates of the Arctic National Park and Preserve fly to Anaktuvuk Pass, the only break in the 1000 mi. Brooks Range. Literally and politely translated, "Anaktuvuk" means "caribou crap," an appropriate name given the swarms of caribou that migrate through the pass every year. Though Anaktuvuk is within the park and protected by U.S. law, it is private land owned by the Nunamiut (NOON-ah-myoot). These inland Inuit people only began to make permanent settlements in the last 50 years. Surrounded by park lands and nestled in a mirage-like mountain pass in the tundra of the Arctic Divide, the Nunamiut struggle to maintain their lifestyle amid modern pressures and developments.

ALASKA

Until recently, the Nunamiut have been wary of opening up their land to tourist use. They manage the land, hunting and trapping aboard motorcycles and ATVs, and are careful not to overrun it, though the trail of ATV tracks around town can be initially startling. Travelers are welcome, but residents politely and steadfastly request that they use low impact camping techniques, do not litter, do not interrupt the activities of the Nunamiut, and absolutely never take pictures of local people without permission. The **Simon Paneak Memorial Museum** (661-3413) has extensive displays on traditional Nunamiut culture, and houses the **Hans van der Laan Brooks Range Library,** an interesting collection of material on the people and land of Alaska's far north (both open daily June-Aug. 8:30am-5pm; Sept.-May M-F; free, but $5 soon).

Larry's Flying Service (474-9169), one of the most well-respected Bush airlines, flies to Anaktuvuk Pass from Fairbanks (Tu and F, $198 round-trip), as do several others. The flight over the awe–inspiring Brooks Range is probably worth the money— wilderness this pristine and beautiful exists few places on earth. The **Washeteria** (661-9713), next to the enormous blue-roofed school, has free **showers** and **laundry** facilities (wash $1, dry 50¢ per 10min.; open M-Tu 8:30am-5pm, W-F 8:30am-9:30pm, Sa 1-9:30pm, Su 10am-6pm). **Police:** 911. **Medical/Fire:** 611. **Public Safety:** 661-3911. **Health Clinic:** 661-3914. The **post office** (661-3615) is next to the airstrip (open M-F 8:30-11:30am and 12:30-5:30pm). **ZIP Code:** 99721. **Area Code:** 907.

Anaktuvuk has no rooms for rent, but visitors can **camp** anywhere just outside of town. The hills on the other side of the **John River** have desirable sites. The **Nunamiut Corporation Store** (661-3327) sells groceries at prices as steep as the mountains (open M-F 10am-7pm, Sa noon-7pm). The **Nunamiut Corporation Camp Kitchen** (661-3123), a hole-in-the-wall restaurant on the south end of town, serves breakfast ($7) and burgers ($7.50; open daily 6:30-10am, 11am-1:30pm, and 3-7pm).

■ Gates of the Arctic National Park and Preserve and the Arctic National Wildlife Refuge

Established in 1980, **Gates of the Arctic National Park and Preserve** contains over 8.4 million acres of wilderness in the central Brooks Range. The park exists to protect the environment, not to maximize human pleasure—there are no trails or facilities in the park, and access is difficult and expensive. Nevertheless, the park's remote setting and untouched interior make it attractive to the most hard-core explorers of the outdoors. Six national wild and scenic rivers run through the park, providing excellent floating opportunities. Heavy glaciation has carved huge U-shaped valleys throughout the park that aid hiking and route-finding.

Covering a huge swath of northeast Alaska, the isolated **Arctic National Wildlife Refuge (ANWR)** encompasses more than 31,100 sq. mi., an area larger than Ireland, with the calving grounds of the teeming Porcupine caribou herd and the Brooks Range's highest mountains within its borders. Oil companies are close to winning their battle to move in for exploration, though, and this may alter the area forever. The park and refuge are most accessible to the powerfully determined and the decidedly wealthy. In a long and uncertain journey, budget backpackers sometimes hitch up the Dalton Hwy. and hike in from several access points along the road. (*Let's Go* recommends uncertainty, but not hitchhiking.) Those with a bit more money fly commercially into **Anaktuvuk Pass** (see above) and head out from there. Those with still more cash to burn can charter a plane and truly isolate themselves. The town of **Bettles** lies south of the mountains on the Middle Fork of the **Koyukuk River,** and is the jumping-off point for plane charters. Several companies offer charter service; ask around for the best deal, and expect to pay several hundred dollars per hour.

The Alaska Public Lands office suggests that only travelers with extensive backpacking background, wilderness survival skills, and experience in Alaska parks should enter Gates. For more info, contact **Park Headquarters,** 201 1st Ave. (456-0281), in Fairbanks. The Park Service also operates an info-bestowing **Gates of the Arctic Field Station** (692-5494) in Bettles (open daily 8am-5pm). In Bettles, **Sourdough Outfitters** (692-5252) rents canoes and other equipment, and its guides are extremely knowledgeable about the park (open M-F 9am-6pm, Sa 10am-6pm). The **post office** (692-5236) is at the northern end of town (open M 8am-noon and 1pm-5pm, Tu, Th, and F 8am-noon and 1pm-3pm, W 8am-noon and 1pm-4pm, Sa 1-4pm). **ZIP Code:** 99726. **Area Code:** 907.

Ask around for good places to pitch a tent. The **Bettles Lodge** (692-5111 or 800-770-5111) has a bunkhouse ($15, sleeping bag required), private rooms (singles $95; doubles $115), showers ($3.50; towel $1), laundry ($7.50 per load), and a restaurant with good cheeseburgers ($6.25; open daily 8-10pm). At the lodge, the **Bettles Trading Post/Sourdough Outfitters** (see above) sells expensive groceries.

■ Barrow

Huddled on flat brown tundra next to the icy waters of the Chukchi Sea, Barrow endures some of the harshest conditions in the world: temperatures below -60°F (-51°C) and months of unending twilight. Barrow is the northernmost point on the North American mainland, almost 330 mi. north of the Arctic Circle. Even more remarkable than the pluck it takes for locals to withstand nature's aggressions is how long Barrow natives have been doing so. As early as 2000 BC, the native Iñupiat roamed the area; by 1200 AD, Barrow had become their permanent home. Today, 60% of the 4000-person population is Iñupiat. As in ancient times, bowhead whaling remains an economic mainstay, with extensive hunts in the fall and spring. The native Iñupiat language is spoken as much as English, and ancient and modern customs co-exist. Fresh seal meat and bear hides hang out to dry beside $30,000 cars, all across the street from the local espresso shop. This blend gives Barrow a distinct flavor and smell, attracting the smattering of tourists who visit each year. After dipping their toes in the chilly arctic water and taking several pictures of Iñupiat dancing, however, most travelers content themselves with the fact that they've been to the "top of the world," and then head back south, leaving the persistent town to face a winter world of permafrost and pervasive gray.

ORIENTATION AND PRACTICAL INFORMATION

As with all true Bush communities, Barrow is only accessible by plane, and at quite a price. Buy a ticket far in advance; the earlier the reservation, the cheaper. Barrow itself is infinitely walkable.

Airplanes: The **airport** is downtown, a few blocks from the water on Ogrook St. **Alaska Airlines** (800-426-0333) flies several times daily from Anchorage ($378 round-trip).

Public Transportation: Buses depart across from the airport, and swing around town every 20min. Flag one down anywhere along the route. 50¢, seniors free.

Taxis: City Cab, 852-5050. **Arctic Cab,** 852-2227. Rides around Barrow $5-6, each additional person $1. Both run 24hr.

Car Rental: UIC Car Rental (852-2700). $75 per day, $20 extra if uninsured. Must be 25. Credit cards accepted.

Visitor Information: Top-of-the-World Hotel, at the corner of Stevenson and Agvik St. (see **Accommodations,** below), is the best source of local info, with walking maps of town. Lobby open 24hr. For employment and general info, contact the **North Slope Borough Public Information Office,** P.O. Box 69 (852-0215).

Tours: A package tour can actually be the cheapest way to see Barrow. Several companies offer 1-day and overnight packages that include guided tours and cost less than an independent ticket and hotel accommodation. **Alaska Airlines Vacations** (800-468-2248) offers 2 tours in conjunction with **Top-of-the-World Hotel** and **Tundra Tours.** Trips run mid-May through mid-Sept. Daytrip from Fairbanks $395. Overnight package includes accommodations at the Top-of-the-World Hotel ($438). To or from Anchorage, add $85. **Gray Line** (277-5581) offers similar services. 1-day package with 4hr. flightseeing tour from Anchorage $593. Overnight package $702 for one person, $636 per person for two people.

ALASKA

Library: Tuzzy Library (852-4042), on Stevenson St., three doors down from Polar Coffee Shop. Open M-Th noon-9pm, F-Sa noon-5pm.
Emergency: 911. **Police:** (852-0311), near the Top-of-the-World Hotel.
Crisis Line: 852-0267. 24hr.
Hospital: (852-4611), at the end of Agvik St., by the Middle Lagoon.
Post Office: 601 Cunningham St. (852-6800). Open M-F 10am-5:30pm, Sa 9am-1pm.
   ZIP Code: 99723.
Area Code: 907.

ACCOMMODATIONS AND CAMPGROUNDS

Accommodations in Barrow are outrageously expensive; if you're planning to stay the night, be prepared to pay an arm and a leg. Harsh weather makes camping a purgatory, but die-hard tenters can ask permission to camp on the beach outside the Top-of-the-World Hotel.

Top-of-the-World Hotel, P.O. Box 189 (800-882-8478, in AK 800-478-8520). The most prominent hotel in town, with full-service accommodations. Clean and bright rooms, with cable and refrigerators, brighten up the tundra-intensive view just outside the window. Many rooms overlook the icy waters of the Arctic Ocean. Singles $159; doubles $179.
Airport Inn, P.O. Box 933 (852-2525). Friendly and informative staff. Cheerful but plain 70s decor suggests a Motel 6 a loooong way from the Interstate. The prices do not. Singles $115; doubles $125. Kitchenettes available for no extra charge.

FOOD

Although costly, Barrow's food options are surprisingly good. Economy-minded travelers hunting groceries can mush to **Alaska Commercial** (852-6711), one block from Top-of-the-World Hotel on Agvik St. (open M-F 7am-11pm, Sa-Su 7am-10pm).

Arctic Pizza (852-4222 or 852-4223), at Ogrook and Apayauk St. A local favorite, this spacious oceanside restaurant serves a variety of seafood, Italian, and Mexican chow. Ignore the name and order Shrimp à la Arctic, Halibut à la Arctic, or Scallops à la Arctic (around $16). Hamburgers $6.50. Open M-Th 11:30am-10:45pm, F-Sa 11:30am-11:45pm, Su 4-10:45pm.
Polar Haven Coffee Company (852-BEAN/2326), across from the Top-of-the-World Hotel. A town with 85 straight days of darkness had better have some damn good coffee. Thanks to Polar Haven, Barrow does. Steaming hot lattes (tall $3.25) and cocoa ($1.75) in a country-style cafe, with bright decor and art books. Bagels with salmon $4.25; coffee shakes from $4. Open M-F 7am-6pm, Sa 8am-6pm.
Pepe's North of the Border Restaurant (852-8200). Prices are high at the world's northernmost Mexican restaurant. A la carte burritos $4.25; entrees around $15. The food is decent, but the ambience is far (4000 mi.) from authentic. Open M-Sa 6am-10pm, Su 8am-10pm.
Teriyaki House (852-2276), around the corner from the airport. The Bering Land Bridge is gone, but the Asian influence holds on in this modest downtown restaurant, which serves a host of Chinese and Japanese options (sushi from $6). Lunch specials like Kung Pao chicken with fried rice, egg roll, and soup ($8.50) offered M-F 11:30am-2pm. Open daily 11:30am-11:30pm.

SIGHTS AND EVENTS

The most obvious sight in Barrow is **Point Barrow,** the northernmost tip of the North American continent. The point is not accessible by car, so purists must walk the 2 mi. stretch or rent a Hummer to access the lonely land's end; follow Stevenson St. north. Those nostalgic for the days of Mutual Assured Destruction (or *Dr. Strangelove* fans) might appreciate a trip across town to the **DEW Line,** the Distant Early Warning system designed to detect Soviet missiles flying over the north pole.
   Across the street from Arctic Pizza at Apayauk and Ogrook St. are the **Mounds,** the site of Barrow's original Iñupiat settlement. Today, the ancient sod buildings lie

below a grassy knoll and offer little to see, but in 1982, five 650-year-old bodies were discovered here. The two women and three children, well preserved by permafrost, were dubbed the **Frozen Family.** In 1994, an even older body was discovered—a girl, still dressed in a hooded parka, from around 1200 AD.

The **jaws of a giant bowhead whale** sprout up from the ground on Eben Hopson St. Next to the whale-bone arch is **Brower's Store,** Barrow's original whaling station and the oldest wooden structure in the Arctic. The **Iñupiat Heritage Center,** across from the Alaska Commercial Company Store about 1 mi. from town, opened in the fall of 1998. The center includes historical displays, traditional arts, and a library. For more info, call the **Commission on Iñupiat History, Language, and Culture** (852-2611).

The **Nalukatag,** or "blanket toss festival," celebrates the end of a successful whaling season every June. In this important Iñupiat ritual, children are thrown high into the frigid air from hide blankets. In early August, on the first day that the sun sets, self-punishing travelers can take a short and ceremonial plunge into the icy arctic water.

NORTHWEST ALASKA

■ Nome

Nome owes its existence to the "three lucky Swedes" who discovered gold on nearby Anvil Creek in 1898, and its name to the poor penmanship of a British sailor. Baffled as to what to call this barren, weather-beaten camp at the edge of the sea, he scribbled "Name?" on his map. Cartographers back in England got his vowels confused, and Nome's name was born. Nome is home to a population of 4000, half of which is Native Alaskan. Buildings are elevated on pilings to prevent the permafrosted ground from thawing beneath them, and most have extremely ramshackle exteriors. Those who can afford to get here will find untamed wilderness surprisingly accessible by road, refreshingly non-commercialized relics of mining history, and a culture centered around the Iditarod dog sled race and the Midnight Sun Festival.

PRACTICAL INFORMATION

Airplanes: The **airport** is about 2 mi. west of town. **Alaska Airlines** (800-426-0333) flies from Fairbanks (round-trip $460); Anchorage (round-trip $360). **Alaska Airlines Vacations** (800-468-2248) offers circuit tours from Anchorage to Nome to Kotzebue. **Frontier Flying Services** (in Fairbanks 474-0014) flies from Fairbanks (round-trip $506, seniors and children $436), as does **Yute Air** (888-359-9883).

Taxis: Checker Cab, 443-5211. **Nome Cab,** 443-3030. $3 in town, $5 to the airport. Both run 24hr.

Car Rental: Stampede (443-3838), on Seppala Dr. 2WD pickup $65 per day; 4WD pickup, Bronco, or van $75 per day; unlimited mileage. Must be 25 with credit card or $100 cash deposit. **Alaska** (443-2939), corner of 4th and Steadman. 2WD pickup $75 per day; 4WD $85 per day. Also provides auto repair services. Open M-F 7am-9pm, Sa 7am-6pm. Must be 21. **Gas** sells for an alarming $2.14 per gallon.

Visitor Information: Nome Convention and Visitors Bureau, P.O. Box 240 (443-5535; http://www.alaska.net/~nome), on Front St. A wealth of info. Open in summer daily 9am-7:30pm; off-season 9am-6:30pm.

Outdoor Information: National Park Service (443-2522), on Front St. in the Sitnasuak Native Corp. Building. Info on Bering Land Bridge National Park and Preserve, plus local hiking and driving tips. Open M-F 8am-noon and 1-5pm, Sa 10am-noon and 1-6pm.

Bank: National Bank of Alaska, 250 Front St. (443-2223). Open M-Th 10am-5pm, F 10am-6pm.

Library: Kegoayah Kozga Library (443-5133), above the museum on Front St. Open in summer M-Th noon-8pm, F-Sa noon-6pm. Free Internet access.

Laundromat: Nome Washeteria (443-5335), at Seppala and C St. The only laundromat in town. Wash or dry $4. Open M-Sa 11am-8pm.

Public Showers: Rec Center (443-5431), at the northern edge of town on 6th Ave. Free with $4 admission. Rents cross-country skis and ice skates in winter.
Radio: KICY 100.3 FM, 850 AM. **KNOM** 780 AM.
Weather: 443-2321. Otherwise, check the box outside the visitors bureau.
Emergency: 911. **Police:** 443-5262.
Hospital: Norton Sound Hospital (443-3311), at the end of Bering St.
Post Office: 240 E. Front St. (443-2401). Open M-F 9am-5pm. **ZIP Code:** 99762.
Internet Access: See **Library,** above.
Area Code: 907.

ACCOMMODATIONS AND CAMPGROUNDS

Beds in Nome are costly, but **free camping** is permitted on the flat, sandy beaches, about 1 mi. east of town on Front St., past the sea wall. Gold miners dot the beaches; enjoy the company and hope to fall asleep despite the constant drone of their sluices. If you have a car, try **Salmon Lake,** at Mile 38 of the Taylor Hwy. (see **Outdoors,** below).

Betty's Igloo, P.O. Box 1784 (443-2419), at the eastern edge of town on 1st Ave. and K St. Clean and comfortable, with kitchen facilities, a spacious common room, and friendly hosts. Shared bath. Children not allowed. Singles $55; doubles $70; includes tax. Breakfast included. Reservations strongly recommended.

Weeks Apartments, 697 3rd. Ave. (443-3194), at G St. Dilapidated exterior, but clean inside. A mother lode of amenities: TV, maid service, kitchen, private bath, private washer and dryer. Singles $60; doubles $60-80. Call ahead.

FOOD

Stock up on groceries and supplies at **Eagle Quality Center** (443-5454), on Bering St. (open M-Sa 7:30am-9pm, Su 10am-7pm). The rowdy **bars** in town, grouped together on Front St., are always packed with locals.

⊛Java Hut (443-3990), on Bering St. across from the Eagle Quality Center. Nome's only flavorful food, with a young clientele and fresh atmosphere. Seawall Salmon Salad on a croissant $7.75; turtle cheesecake $2.50. Also serves cappuccino and espresso. Open M-Sa 7:30am-11pm.

Fat Freddie's (443-5899), next to the visitors bureau. A popular tour destination since it's clean, well-lit, and overlooks the ocean. Admire the blue expanses of the Bering Sea while chowing down on the soup and all-you-can-eat salad bar ($8). Breakfast omelettes $7. Open daily 6am-10pm.

Twin Dragon (443-5552), at the corner of Front St. and Steadman, has a bright, well-decorated interior. Extremely fresh vegetables—how'd they do that? Almond chicken or sweet and sour pork $12. Look for lunch specials. Open M-F 11am-11pm, Sa noon-11pm, Su 3-11pm.

Milano's (443-2924), on the corner of Front St. and Federal. Expensive pizza (medium $14) and Japanese fare (sushi dinner $15), with good service and a hint of dark ambience. Open M-Sa 11am-11pm, Su 3-11pm.

EVENTS

Isolation from the rest of the world makes people do strange things. The **Bering Sea Ice Golf Classic** is held in March on the frozen ocean. Contestants use bright orange balls and face a number of unique hazards: ice crevasses, bottomless snow holes, and frosted greens. Course rules dictate: "If you hit a polar bear (Endangered Species List) with your golf ball, you will have three strokes added to your score. If you recover said ball, we will subtract five strokes." The **Midnight Sun Festival** marks the summer solstice (June 19) with a parade, a barbecue, a simulated bank robbery, and a street dance, among other silliness. On Labor Day, the **Great Bathtub Race** sends wheeled bathtubs, filled with water, soap, and bather, hurtling down Front St. The biggest event of the year, however, is the **Iditarod** (800-545-MUSH/6874; http://www.iditarod.com). The world's foremost dog sled race begins in Anchorage and finishes here in mid-March, beneath the log arch visible year-round by City Hall. Thousands of out-of-town spectators journey in for the finish, and local accommodations can be booked nearly a year in advance.

OUTDOORS

Branching out into the surrounding wilderness, Nome's three highways are a godsend for the adventurous traveler. Though entirely gravel, all are generally well-maintained and navigable in a rental car. According to the visitors bureau, hitchers can usually find rides fairly easily up the Taylor or Council Highway on weekends, when many Nome residents head in that direction. There are excellent **fishing** rivers along the highways, including the **Nome** and **Pilgrim Rivers,** both accessible via the Taylor Hwy. Bring mosquito repellent or you will curse the day you ever heard of Nome.

Nome's outskirts are home to the remnants of over 40 abandoned **gold dredges.** The closest, **Swanberg's Dredge,** is about 1½ mi. from downtown on Front St., on the way to the Taylor Hwy. The **Taylor Highway** (also known as the Kougarok Rd.) heads north from Nome for 85 mi., then peters out without reaching any particular destination. Along the way is **Salmon Lake,** near Mile 38. Popular with locals, the lake offers fantastic fishing and primitive campsites. At Mile 53.6, an unmarked 7 mi. road leads to the **Pilgrim Hot Springs** area. The Catholic Church ran an orphanage here from 1917 to 1941, and many of the buildings are intact and undisturbed. This is private land, but the visitors bureau can provide the name and number of the caretaker for permission to soak in the hot springs. (Make sure to check first before driving out, or you may find the tubs drained for maintenance.) The **Kigluaik Mountains** are accessible via this highway, and offer some good hiking and wildflowers.

The **Council Highway** runs 73 mi. from Nome to **Council,** a ghost town and summer home for Nome residents, appealingly below the treeline. En route, the highway goes around **Cape Nome,** passing beaches, fishing camps, and the fascinating **Last Train to Nowhere** at Mile 33, a failed railroad lingering with an engine and cars that sit slowly rusting on the tundra. The **Nome-Teller Highway** winds west from Nome for 72 mi. to the tiny Alaska Native village of **Teller,** home to the friendly Joe Garnie of Iditarod fame.

Nome is also one of two departure points to the **Bering Land Bridge National Park and Preserve.** Allegedly the least visited park in the United States, the park encompasses the northern third of the Seward Peninsula, and contains lakes, lava fields, and ancient indigenous ruins. Stone tools, thousands of years old, rest untouched in a valley surrounded by granite spires. The most popular destination (relatively speaking) is the **Serpentine Hot Springs,** just inside the southern border of the park and about 30 mi. from the end of the Taylor Hwy. A primitive bathhouse contains the 140-170°F water and is open year-round. The park maintains a rustic sleeping cabin that sleeps 20 and cannot be reserved. The most common way to get there is by snowmobile in the winter. In summer, a charter flight can be taken to **Taylor;** from there, Serpentine lies 8 mi. over the tundra. Contact the Park Service office (443-2522) for topographic maps and more info.

■ Kotzebue

On the tip of the **Baldwin Peninsula,** 160 mi. northeast of Nome and 25 mi. north of the Arctic Circle, Kotzebue (KOTZ-ih-boo) is principally a transportation and commercial hub for native settlements and other small communities in Alaska's Arctic Northwest. The wind-buffeted village has little to offer independent travelers except access to three remote and wild national parklands, all above the Arctic Circle (see **Northwest Alaska Areas,** below). The **Northwest Alaska Native Corporation (NANA)** has its headquarters here. It takes a ton of money to reach Kotzebue, and

ALASKA

$20 more earns admission to the **NANA Museum's Iñupiaq Program** (info and reservations 442-3301), which teaches native dance and the ceremonial blanket toss.

The **airport** is on the west end of town, a 10-minute walk from Kotzebue's modest downtown. **Alaska Airlines** (442-3474 or 800-426-0333) flies four times per day to Anchorage (round-trip $386) and Nome (round-trip $320). **Polar Cab** runs lucratively around town (442-2233). The **Visitor Center and National Park Service** (442-3760) is two blocks from the Airport on 2nd Ave. (open daily 8am-7pm). The center is a stop-off for the bus loads of tourists staying at the local expensive hotel, but also has maps and info about charter planes that fly into the three parks of the Noatak River region. There is no place to do laundry; do not besmirch yourself.

Camping is difficult in Kotzebue. Some visitors befriend locals and pitch tents in their backyards. Others make their way to the fish camps 1 mi. either way on the beach. **Ofreida's B&B,** 667 Caribou Dr. (442-3366), is a relatively reasonable indoor option. Ofreida rents two rooms with shared bath, homey decor, and a big breakfast (singles $65; doubles $75). She also lets folks pitch a tent in her backyard; call ahead. **Hanson's,** on Shore Ave., stocks the usual groceries, but be warned: a gallon of milk costs $5.50. **Bayside Restaurant,** on Shore Ave. (442-3600), is a decent place to eat, with windows overlooking the whitecaps.

■ Northwest Alaska Areas

There are more than 14,000 sq. mi. of protected wilderness in Northwest Alaska; **Cape Krusenstern National Monument, Kobuk Valley National Park,** and **Noatak National Preserve** comprise 11% of all the land administered by the National Park Service. Local native people legally use the parks for subsistence hunting. This is wilderness at its wildest, and its remoteness all but guarantees that it will remain that way, accessible to only the most dedicated (and propertied) of outdoorspeople.

Cape Krusenstern National Monument was established primarily for archaeological reasons. Within its gravel, in chronological layers, lie artifacts from every known Inuit occupation of North America. The monument's marshy tundra borders the coastlines of the **Chukchi Sea** on the west and **Kotzebue Sound** to the south. Some hiking is possible in the rolling **Igichuk** and **Mulgrave Hills,** as is kayaking along the coast and in the numerous lagoons. The only way in is by charter plane from Kotzebue (about $250 per hr.).

The 2650 sq. mi. **Kobuk Valley National Park** occupies a broad valley along the central **Kobuk River,** 25 mi. north of the Arctic Circle. One of the park's more surprising features is the 25 sq. mi. **Great Kobuk Sand Dunes,** a small piece of the Sahara in Alaska's Arctic. The most popular park activity is floating the Kobuk. Popular put-in spots include the village of **Ambler** on the park's east edge, or at the river's headwaters in **Walker Lake,** deep in the Brooks Range. The sand dunes are accessible via a short overland hike from the Kobuk River, after floating within hiking range. The region is accessible via regularly scheduled flights from Kotzebue. **Yute Air** (442-3330) flies to Ambler from Kotzebue ($190).

The 10,200 sq. mi. **Noatak National Preserve** contains the broad, gently sloping **Noatak River Valley.** This westward-flowing river drains the largest undisturbed watershed in North America. Most visitors see the area from the water, floating along the Noatak from the arboreal forest's northern edge into a treeless expanse of tundra. Wildlife abounds, especially members of the region's 400,000-strong caribou herd. Fewer than 100 visitors float the Noatak each season. The only way in is by (you guessed it) airplane; there are some scheduled flights between **Noatak,** an outlying town on the preserve's western boundary, and Kotzebue (around $80).

ALEUTIAN ISLANDS

This is no place to go on a budget. At the fiery boundary between two tectonic plates, the string of snow-capped volcanoes that make up the Alaska Peninsula and the Aleutian Islands stretches more than 1000 mi. into the stormy North Pacific; the westernmost islands are within a few hundred miles of Kamchatka, Russia. The Aleutians are one of the most remote locations on earth, and the lava-scarred cones on these green but treeless isles are abused by some of the world's worst weather. Vicious storms packing winds well over 100mph can blow in at any time.

Recent archaeological findings suggests that the ancestors of today's Aleuts migrated between today's Russia and Alaska even earlier than 6000 B.C., by moving up through the islands, rather than across the Bering Land Bridge (see p. 527). In the 19th century, Russia used the Aleutians as stepping stones into Alaska, using native people for their otter and seal hunting abilities and attempting to spread the teachings of the Russian Orthodox Church. The next great invasion came in 1942, when the Japanese tried to divert American forces from the southern Pacific by bombing the island of Unalaska and occupying the outer islands of Attu and Kiska. As a so-called safety precaution, the U.S. Army evacuated Aleut residents from many of the islands and held them in relocation camps for three years. Only a portion of the Aleuts survived the internment and were able to return, only to find their property destroyed by the intruders. In 1943, U.S. forces stormed Attu and touched off a bloody if obscure battle, the only one fought in North America during WWII, leaving thousands of American and Japanese soldiers dead on the wind-swept tundra.

The Alaska Peninsula and the islands are home to Aleut villages, small military installations, and larger towns dedicated to serious deep-sea fishing. A few hundred tourists come each summer, despite the cost and time involved, to explore the natural beauty of this volcanic wilderness and to see millions of migratory seabirds. Several species of birds found here nest nowhere else.

GETTING THERE

The only two ways of reaching the Aleutian Islands are both alarmingly expensive. A one-way **flight** from Anchorage to Dutch Harbor, the largest town on the Aleutians, costs about $450 and lasts two to three hours. A round-trip ferry on the **Alaska Marine Highway** from Kodiak costs $404, and takes five to six days. The ferry is a more sensible choice, since the whole point of traveling to the peninsula and the Aleutians is not merely to reach the destination—there's really not much there—but to enjoy the unique panoramas and wildlife along the way. An **AlaskaPass** might make the ferry trip more affordable (see **Essentials,** p. 34). The Alaska Marine Highway makes this trip only seven times per year between April and September, and the weather is mildest in July. The boats fill quickly in summer; make reservations at least two weeks in advance. The *M/V Tustamena* serves the Aleutian chain from Kodiak. The ship is hardly a cruiseliner, and it's probably a good idea to try it out on a daytrip before committing for five days. It features showers, a dining room with limited hours and decent food (bringing groceries from Kodiak is a very good idea), and a lounge where an on-board naturalist regularly gives slide shows on the plants and wildlife visible from the ship. Passengers can sleep above deck, but the solarium is (cough) right next to the (ack) exhaust tower. An extra $564 buys a furnished four-person cabin (about $25 per person per night); call well in advance for reservations. Stock up on Dramamine or another seasickness remedy before leaving. The *Tustumena* weathers 5-15 ft. seas—they don't call it the "Vomit Comet" for nothing.

The trip is popular with senior citizens, who can take advantage of a 50% ferry discount, although this requires either a flight back to the mainland or a month-long wait for the next ferry. The cruises also host a handful of families, students, anglers, and maniacal birdwatcher types who run around with binoculars the size of small children screaming, "It's a whiskered auklet!" The ferry stops briefly at small towns ranging from fishing villages to prefabricated cannery quarters before reaching Dutch Harbor, the most interesting town in the Aleutians. Unfortunately, it only stops here for about five hours before turning around and heading back, which doesn't leave much time for exploration.

ALASKA

■ Unalaska and Dutch Harbor

Isolated in the Pacific Ocean, at the western limit of the Alaska Marine Highway's ferry service, Dutch Harbor and Unalaska (un-uh-LAS-ka) are about as remote a community of 4100 as you'll find in North America. The name Unalaska comes from the original Aleut name for the area, "Agunalaksh." When the Russians came to the island, this evolved into "Ounalashka" and by 1890, the current name presided. Even the locals are somewhat confused about where Dutch Harbor ends and Unalaska begins. Technically, Dutch Harbor is only a port, yet it has its own post office and ZIP code. A sort of Unalaskan suburb has been built on Amaknak Island, about 2 mi. from downtown Unalaska, and this area is often called Dutch Harbor. The two islands are connected by the Bridge to the Other Side.

Unalaska has been the top port in the nation for both seafood volume and value since 1992, and 90% of the community depends on the fishing industry. The development of the pollock fishery in 1988-1992 brought particularly rapid growth to the islands. While commercial fishing runs the town, recreational fishing is understandably popular; in 1996, a Fairbanks resident caught a 459-pound halibut, setting a new world record. The islands have no large game, but they seem to host as many bald eagles as urban centers have pigeons. There are no trees on which the eagles can perch, so they alight on ship masts, rooftops, and the domes of the Russian Orthodox Church. The regal American symbols are known to fight over fish being reeled in, and occasionally attack humans.

Unalaska is hardly a haven for the budget traveler. Prices stay high due to remoteness and unusually high incomes—over $130 million in seafood passes through this port every year. But the view of treeless, snow-capped mountains soaring thousands of feet from Unalaska Bay's chilly blue waters is always free.

ORIENTATION AND PRACTICAL INFORMATION
Unalaska lies about 300 mi. from the tip of the Alaska Peninsula. It is in the same time zone as the rest of the state.

Airplanes: The **airport,** about ¼ mi. from City Dock on the main road into town, is served by **Pen Air** (581-1383 or 800-448-4226), **Alaska Airlines** (266-7700 or 800-426-0333), and **Reeves** (581-3380). All offer flights to Anchorage at similar rates (about $425). The airport is often shut down by fog, and planes sometimes don't fly in or out for a week at a time. Pen Air flies smaller planes, and is the most likely of any of the airlines to get into or out of town.

Ferries: Alaska Marine Highway (800-642-0066) ferries stop at City Dock, 1½ mi. from Dutch Harbor and 2½ mi. from Unalaska. The *M/V Tustamena* arrives about once a month in the summer, departing one-way to Kodiak (2½-3 days, $202).

Taxis: Taxi service is available from five companies; locals are as baffled by that number as you are. **Harbor Express,** 581-1381. Ferry to town $5-10. Runs 24hr.

Visitor Information: Unalaska Convention and Visitors Bureau, P.O. Box 545 (581-2612; http://www.arctic.net/~updhcvb), in the Grand Aleutian Hotel, has general info. Open M-F 9am-5pm. The **Ounalashka Corporation** (581-1276), in a low, orange-roofed building near the Grand Aleutian, is also helpful. Open M-F 8am-noon and 1-5pm.

Equipment Rental: Aleutian Adventure Sports (581-4489), downtown at 4th and Broadway, rents mountain bikes ($30 per day), kayaks ($45 per half-day, $65 per day), and other outdoor equipment. They also lead a variety of guided trips.

Senior Center: Father Ishmail Gromoff Senior Center (581-5044), on the Unalaska side, by the lake. The Qawalangin Tribal Council sponsors a weekly Culture Night, with free classes on Aleut doll-making and other crafts (Sept.-May M 7-9pm). Open daily 8am-8pm.

Medical Services: Iliuliuk Family and Health Services (581-1202; after-hours 581-1233), in a big gray building around the corner from the police station. Open M-F 8:30am-6pm, Sa 1pm-5pm.

Emergency: 911. **Police:** (581-1233), 29 Safety Way, on the Unalaska side.

Post Office: Unalaska (581-1232). Dutch Harbor (581-1657). Both open M-F 9am-5pm and Sa 1-5pm. **ZIP Code:** Unalaska 99685. Dutch Harbor 99692.

Area Code: 907.

ACCOMMODATIONS AND CAMPGROUNDS Once again: it ain't cheap. The visitors bureau (see **Practical Information,** above) keeps a list of accommodations, including several guest houses. Most land in the area is owned by native corporations, with the notable exception of Summer Bay, and a fee is required for access or camping (land-use $5 per day, with camping $10 per day). Contact the Ounalashka Corporation or the visitors bureau for details. Camping is blissfully free at **Summer Bay.** From City Dock or the airport, hike 3½ or 4 mi. respectively through both Dutch Harbor and Unalaska, and follow Summer Bay Rd. along the shore for another 3½ mi. to Summer Bay. A bridge, some sand dunes, and a few picnic tables and barbecues mark the spot; there are no other facilities. Pitch your tent in a sheltered location, or the vicious wind gusts will introduce your possessions to Iliuliuk Bay. **The Bunkhouse,** P.O. Box 920185, Dutch Harbor, 99692 (581-4357), offers clean rooms with shared baths, a lounge with TV, phone, fridge and microwave, and laundry facilities (singles $42, $206 per week; doubles $53, $310 per week; meals upon request). From the airport, follow the Airport Rd. past the Dutch Harbor post office and take the first left, about ½ mi. down the road, on Gilman. The Bunkhouse is the two-story cream building, on the right next to Peking restaurant.

SIGHTS AND OUTDOORS A land use pass is required for any and all venturing off of the main roads; purchase one at the visitors bureau or the Ounalashka Corporation ($5 per day). If you have the good fortune to have your ferry layover in Unalaska on a sunny day, make haste to hike to the top of **Mt. Ballyhoo,** just behind the airport. The summit affords one of the most mind-bogglingly beautiful, amazingly awe-inspiring sights in the entire universe. Superlative overkill is not possible here. Amazing gold, red, and black rock formations jut out of a sheer cliff that drops 1634 ft. to the translucent green water of the ocean below. While the winners of an annual race make it to the summit in 26 minutes, a slightly saner pace takes 45 minutes to an hour. Ferry passengers can walk along the ridge for another 20 to 30 minutes past the summit, and still easily return to catch the boat. On the back side of Ballyhoo, a WWII road leads to a bunker, built on a cliff, with another great view.

If the weather is lousy, or the thought of climbing 1600 ft. is unpleasant, then grab a cab or walk the 4 mi. from the City Dock to the **Unalaska Cemetery** and **Memorial Park,** on the eastern edge of Unalaska. These two sites present a description of the Japanese air attacks of June 1942, and a giant propeller from one of the sunken ships. A mile down Summer Bay Rd. from Memorial Park lies Unalaska's **landfill,** another popular tourist destination. Many, many, many **eagles** search for food here, since Unalaska's waste is so fish-intensive. Also off of Summer Bay Rd. is a small trail leading to the top of **New Hall.** The full hike takes about two hours, and the last stretch is mighty steep, but even climbing the first 30 or 45 minutes of the trail provides one of the best views of the Unalaska valley.

Back toward Unalaska on Beach Front Rd. sits the impressive **Holy Ascension Orthodox Church,** built in 1824-27 and expanded in 1894, the oldest standing Russian-built church in the U.S. This area was the thriving center of Orthodox missionary activity in Alaska, and the once dilapidated church has recently been restored to its former splendor. On the way back to the ferry, right after the Bridge to the Other Side, is **Bunker Hill,** which was heavily fortified during WWII. Following either the construction road clockwise or the beach counter-clockwise to reach the old trail, a quick 420 ft. climb leads to a large concrete bunker affording a great view of the surrounding bays and mountains, and surrounded by wildflowers in summer.

Those planning to stay longer than three or four hours can ask locals or the visitors bureau about the numerous trails and military artifacts strewn across the local countryside. Check with **Aleutian Adventure Sports** (see **Practical Information,** above) for info on kayaking and other outdoor activities, or contact the visitors bureau about the various fishing charters. To participate in or to learn more about the **Margaret Bay Archaeological Dig,** which is challenging the Beringia Land Bridge theory, call 581-5150 or the visitors bureau. Next to the Ounalashka Corporation building, the **Museum of the Aleutians,** opening in December of 1998, will house returned Aleut artifacts and the latest archeological findings. Call Rick Knecht (581-5150) for hours.

ALASKA

APPENDIX

■ Holidays (1999)

USA		CANADA	
Date	**Holiday**	**Date**	**Holiday**
January 1	New Year's Day	January 1	New Year's Day
January 18	Martin Luther King, Jr. Day	April 5	Easter Monday
February 15	Presidents' Day	May 24	Victoria Day
May 31	Memorial Day	July 1	Canada Day
July 4	Independence Day	September 6	Labour Day
September 6	Labor Day	October 11	Thanksgiving
October 11	Columbus Day	November 11	Remembrance Day
November 11	Veterans' Day	December 25	Christmas Day
November 25	Thanksgiving	December 26	Boxing Day
December 25	Christmas Day		

■ Festivals (1999)

Date	Name & Location	Description
Beginning March 6	**Iditarod** AK: Anchorage to Nome	The bravest of the brave hitch up a team of hardy huskies and mush over tundra and mountains across 1150 mi. of Alaska.
First 3 weeks in June	**Rose Festival** Portland, OR	Portland goes to town, partying for a whole month. Oregonians crown a festival queen, have a few parades, detonate some fireworks, and run milk carton races.
July 1	**Canada Day** Anywhere in Canada	Canada's typically quiet demeanor struggles with an irresistible urge to whoop it up for the anniversary of Confederation.
July 4	**Independence Day** Anywhere in the U.S.	A pale imitation of Canada Day, celebrated 3 days late. Fireworks, fireworks, fireworks, fireworks, fireworks, hot dogs and hamburgers on the grill, and some fireworks.
July 9-11	**Oregon Country Fair** Eugene, OR	Craft booth concessionaires and earnest crystal-worshippers converge on Eugene to eat, play, discuss sustainable energy, and hug.
July 9-18	**Stampede** Calgary, AB	One of the biggest rodeos in the world, with international contestants, hundreds of thousands of visitors, and many cows.
Mid-July	**Folk Music Festival** Vancouver, BC	A modern-day Woodstock of the West, Vancouver attracts folk musicians from around the world to don their Birkenstocks and jam.
Third weekend in July	**Rhythm & Blues Festival** Winthrop, WA	Just what its name says. Ample rhythm and plentiful blues invade a self-proclaimed wild Western town.

Late August	**Lentil Festival** Pullman, WA	A "Tase T. Lentil" 5km fun run, lentil pancake breakfast, lentil parade, lentil pizza, lentil ice-cream, and no cholesterol. "There's a lentil dish for everyone."
September 4-6	**Bumbershoot** Seattle, WA	Seattle's block party for the arts draws hundreds of thousands of groovsters to watch every sort of big-name act, from Sir Mix-A-Lot to the Indigo Girls to Sky Cries Mary.
September 15-18	**Round-Up** Pendleton, OR	A whole week of tribal dances, bucking broncos, and country line dancing. Yeee-haw!
Mid-February to October	**Shakespeare Festival** Ashland, OR	Dude, that's a lot of drama.

■ Phrasebook

CANADIAN	AMERICAN
chesterfield	sofa
washroom	bathroom
cutlery	silverware
serviette	napkin
appy	appetizer
queue	line
touque	wool hat
balaclava	wool hat covering whole face
university	college
college	community college
invigilator	proctor
shit disturber	rabble rouser
busker	street performer
nummer nummer	delicious
hoser	loser
return trip	round-trip
candy floss	cotton candy
two-four	24-pack
pissed	drunk
angry	pissed
no worries	no problem
for sure	okay
eh?	huh?
First Nation	Native American
Yankee	American
Canadian	Who?
As Canadian as possible, under the circumstances	As American as apple pie

Mileage (Distances)

	Anchorage	Boise	Calgary	Dawson City	Edmonton	Fairbanks	Portland	Prince George	Prince Rupert	Prudhoe Bay	Seattle	Spokane	Vancouver	Whitehorse	San Fran.
Anchorage		2934 mi.	2160 mi.	515 mi.	1975 mi.	358 mi.	2610 mi.	1678 mi.	1605 mi.	847 mi.	2435 mi.	2578 mi.	2145 mi.	724 mi.	3153 mi.
Boise	4725km		828 mi.	2537 mi.	1011 mi.	2930 mi.	439 mi.	1128 mi.	2079 mi.	3419 mi.	499 mi.	379 mi.	642 mi.	2210 mi.	649 mi.
Calgary	3478km	1333km		1747 mi.	184 mi.	2038 mi.	859 mi.	493 mi.	950 mi.	2527 mi.	738 mi.	443 mi.	609 mi.	1436 mi.	1514 mi.
Dawson City	829km	4085km	2812km		1562 mi.	393 mi.	2197 mi.	1390 mi.	1192 mi.	882 mi.	2022 mi.	2200 mi.	1764 mi.	327 mi.	2830 mi.
Edmonton	3180km	1627km	296km	2515km		1853 mi.	1043 mi.	461 mi.	906 mi.	2342 mi.	790 mi.	628 mi.	722 mi.	1251 mi.	1698 mi.
Fairbanks	576km	4717km	3281km	633km	2983km		2455 mi.	1668 mi.	1483 mi.	489 mi.	2313 mi.	2456 mi.	2137 mi.	602 mi.	3121 mi.
Portland	4202km	707km	1383km	3537km	1679km	3953km		733 mi.	1208 mi.	2977 mi.	175 mi.	400 mi.	318 mi.	1886 mi.	655 mi.
Prince George	2701km	1816km	794km	2238km	742km	2686km	1180km		434 mi.	2074 mi.	558 mi.	663 mi.	486 mi.	983 mi.	1437 mi.
Prince Rupert	2584km	3347km	1529km	1919km	1459km	2388km	1945km	699km		1972 mi.	1033 mi.	1230 mi.	901 mi.	881 mi.	1880 mi.
Prudhoe Bay	1363km	5504km	4068km	1420km	3771km	787km	4793km	3339km	3175km		2802 mi.	2975 mi.	2541 mi.	1091 mi.	3610 mi.
Seattle	3920km	803km	1188km	3255km	1271km	3724km	282km	898km	1663km	4511km		282 mi.	143 mi.	1711 mi.	808 mi.
Spokane	4151km	610km	713km	3542km	1011km	3954km	644km	1067km	1980km	4790km	454km		400 mi.	1987 mi.	1055 mi.
Vancouver	3453km	1034km	981km	2840km	1162km	3440km	512km	782km	1451km	4091km	230km	644km		1450 mi.	973 mi.
Whitehorse	1166km	3558km	2312km	527km	2014km	969km	3036km	1583km	1418km	1756km	2755km	3199km	2334km		2519 mi.
San Fran.	5076km	1044km	2438km	4556km	2734km	5025km	1055km	2314km	3027km	5812km	1301km	1699km	1567km	4056km	

Index

A

AAA 30
Aberdeen, WA 215
accommodations 37
Adams, Bryan 248
adventure tours 49
aggression, U.S./Canadian 508
AIDS 15
air travel
  charter flights 27
  cheapest fares 25
  couriers 28
  from Asia, Africa, and
    Australia 26
  from Europe 26
  standby 28
  ticket consolidators 27
  within North America 25
Alaska 393, 396
  Aleutian Islands 525
  Arctic Alaska 515
  Bush, the 515
  Copper River Basin 443
  fish and game licensing 48
  geography 393
  history 396
  Interior Alaska 448
  Kenai Peninsula 411
  Kodiak Island 430
  Northwest Alaska 521
  practical information 398
  Prince William Sound 434
  reading 398
  recent events 398
  romance 408
  Southcentral Alaska 399
  Southeast Alaska 476
  tourism division 2
alaska 396
Alaska approaches 333
Alaska Highway (Hwy. 1), YT
  BC/Yukon Border to
    Whitehorse 381
  Sheep Mountain to the
    Alaska border 385
Alaska Highway (Hwy. 97), BC
  Dawson Creek to Fort St.
    John 342
  Fort Nelson to the Yukon
    border 343
Alaska Hwy. (Hwy. 2), AK 397
Alaska Hwy. (Hwy. 97), BC
  342
Alaska Marine Highway 34
  blockade of 248
Alaska Native Claims and
  Settlement Act 397
Alaska Public Lands
  Information Center 44
  APLIC Fairbanks 462
Alaska Railroad 29

Alaska, Southeast 476
Alaska, Southeastern
  Wrangell 487
AlaskaPass 34
Albany, OR 124
Alberta 347
  natural resource service 49
  provincehood 248
  provincial parks 44
  Travel Alberta 2
Alberta Badlands, AB 373
Alert Bay, BC 285
Aleutian Islands, AK 525
  Dutch Harbor 526
  Unalaska 526
Aleuts 396
Alexie, Sherman 55
alternatives to tourism 16
altitude sickness 13
Ambler, AK 524
American Automobile
  Association (AAA) 30
American Express 10
American Motorcyclist
  Association (AMA) 33
Amtrak 28
Anaktuvuk Pass, AK 517
Anchorage, AK 400
  accommodations and
    campgrounds 403
  cafes and coffeehouses 405
  entertainment 407
  food 404
  nightlife 408
  orientation 400
  outdoors 406
  practical information 400
  shopping 407
  sights 405
animals, imaginary
  10-legged polar bear 405
  First Nations mermaid 355
  Jake, the petrified alligator-
    man 216
  kushtakas 483
  lightning fish 211
animals, interesting
  Banff Springs snail 354
  iceworms 411, 441
  razor clams 329
Appendix 528
Arctic Circle 1, 391, 516
Arctic National Wildlife
  Refuge, AK 518
art, edible 426
arts
  Pacific Northwest 55
  Western Canada 248
Ashford, WA 223
Ashland, OR 105
Astoria, OR 80

  near Astoria 82
Athabasca 396
Atlin, BC 344
ATM cards 11
auto clubs 30
auto transport companies 32
Avon Skin-So-Soft 14

B

B&Bs 39
Bach Festival, OR 122
backpacks 18, 46
Bainbridge Island, WA 187
Baker City, OR 142
Bamfield, BC 289
banana belts, Alaska 422
banana slugs 216
Bandon, OR 102
Banff National Park 347
Banff-Windermere Hwy.
  (Hwy. 93), BC 308
bank machines 11
Barkerville, BC 312
Barrow, AK 519
BC Ferries 34
beaches, nude
  Teddy Bear Cove, WA 191
  Wreck Beach, BC 261
Bear 16 354
Bear Cove, BC 286
Bear Lake, BC 316
bear safety (if you're being
  mauled, you're too close) 47
Beaver Creek, YT 386
beaver fever 14
bed and breakfasts 39
Bee Stings 13
Bella Coola, BC 312
Bellevue, WA 174
Bellingham, WA 187
Bend, OR 131
Bering Land Bridge National
  Park, AK 523
Bering, Vitus 396
Berton, Pierre 249
Bettles, AK 518
big cheese of cheese 89
biking 33
Bikini Kill 184
Bill, Lightnin' 235
Bingen, WA 76
Birch Bay, WA 192
bisexual, gay, and lesbian
  travelers 21
Black Ball Transport 34
black gold 397
Blaine, WA 192
Blairmore, AB 376
blisters 13
Blue Mountains, WA 245
Bodett, Tom 427

INDEX

About Let's Go

THIRTY-NINE YEARS OF WISDOM

Back in 1960, a few students at Harvard University banded together to produce a 20-page pamphlet offering a collection of tips on budget travel in Europe. This modest, mimeographed packet, offered as an extra to passengers on student charter flights to Europe, met with instant popularity. The following year, students traveling to Europe researched the first, full-fledged edition of *Let's Go: Europe*, a pocket-sized book featuring honest, irreverent writing and a decidedly youthful outlook on the world. Throughout the 60s, our guides reflected the times; the 1969 guide to America led off by inviting travelers to "dig the scene" at San Francisco's Haight-Ashbury. During the 70s and 80s, we gradually added regional guides and expanded coverage into the Middle East and Central America. With the addition of our in-depth city guides, handy map guides, and extensive coverage of Asia and Australia, the 90s are also proving to be a time of explosive growth for Let's Go, and there's certainly no end in sight. The maiden edition of *Let's Go: South Africa,* our pioneer guide to sub-Saharan Africa, hits the shelves this year, along with the first editions of *Let's Go: Greece* and *Let's Go: Turkey.*

We've seen a lot in 39 years. *Let's Go: Europe* is now the world's bestselling international guide, translated into seven languages. And our new guides bring Let's Go's total number of titles, with their spirit of adventure and their reputation for honesty, accuracy, and editorial integrity, to 44. But some things never change: our guides are still researched, written, and produced entirely by students who know first-hand how to see the world on the cheap.

HOW WE DO IT

Each guide is completely revised and thoroughly updated every year by a well-traveled set of over 200 students. Every winter, we recruit over 160 researchers and 70 editors to write the books anew. After several months of training, researcher-writers hit the road for seven weeks of exploration, from Anchorage to Adelaide, Estonia to El Salvador, Iceland to Indonesia. Hired for their rare combination of budget travel sense, writing ability, stamina, and courage, these adventurous travelers know that train strikes, stolen luggage, food poisoning, and marriage proposals are all part of a day's work. Back at our offices, editors work from spring to fall, massaging copy written on Himalayan bus rides into witty yet informative prose. A student staff of typesetters, cartographers, publicists, and managers keeps our lively team together. In September, the collected efforts of the summer are delivered to our printer, who turns them into books in record time, so that you have the most up-to-date information available for your vacation. Even as you read this, work on next year's editions is well underway.

WHY WE DO IT

We don't think of budget travel as the last recourse of the destitute; we believe that it's the only way to travel. Living cheaply and simply brings you closer to the people and places you've been saving up to visit. Our books will ease your anxieties and answer your questions about the basics—so you can get off the beaten track and explore. Once you learn the ropes, we encourage you to put *Let's Go* down now and then to strike out on your own. You know as well as we that the best discoveries are often those you make yourself. When you find something worth sharing, please drop us a line. We're Let's Go Publications, 67 Mount Auburn St., Cambridge, MA 02138, USA (email: feedback@letsgo.com). For more info, visit our website, http://www.letsgo.com.

HAPPY TRAVELS!

Researcher-Writers

The Creation of A&P

Kristy Garcia   *Washington, Eastern Oregon*
A pet Let's Go vet, nimble Kristy was set to completely engage her terrain.
She conquered Seattle, with deserts did battle, and left many microbrews slain.
In love with small towns and enamored of dams, Kristy had the off-track racket mastered.
Her copious comments our minds did enliven; her postcards our office walls plastered.
Pal of the Palouse, a slug *connaisseuse*, she weathered each possible clime.
Enthused and amused, she never refused to pass up any groovy good time.

Anne Johnson   *Northern BC, Southeast AK, Southcentral AK, Northwest AK*
A Midwestern daughter, no stranger to water, our Anne in the past had left home
To sail through the Southeast, up to Scagway at least, but she hadn't yet made it to Nome.
So Anne seized the day, blazed her way through AK, and logrolled a path to town pride.
When Homer exploded, she laughed and reported the story for this very guide.
Anne hitchhiked a lot (although *Let's Go* would not), and she never did want for new friends.
From random alums to more intimate chums, the list of fine folks scarcely ends.

Jennifer Laine   *Southcentral AK, Interior AK, Arctic AK, Aleutian Islands*
From Anch'rage to Fairbanks, then out to Dutch Harbor, Ms. Laine made a dizzying circuit.
She tripped across trails with a well-trammeled tread; as for nightlife—she knew how to work it.
For she so loved this land that she carefully scanned it for nuggets to bury in prose,
And with uncanny stealth, she sniffed out some fine health food with one ever-vigilant nose.
With tire-popping gusto, she plowed through the dust, going anywhere lonely roads led,
Yet she still found the time for a brisk morning climb up a mountain with her grateful ed.

Thomas Lue   *Oregon, Central Washington*
Ticket agents were smitten and freebies were written when young Thomas Lue hit the ground.
He wielded his press pass with rapier precision, and snagged every bargain around.
Thomas fared very well in his sleek white Tercel, in the course of this spirited rambling.
He waxed very tender 'mid natural splendor, and railed like a priest against gambling.
At turns way sarcastic, then enthusiastic, Tom exercised excellent leadership.
Emitting a laugh, he'd cleave wheat from its chaff, leaving nothing but pearls for you readership.

Rebecca Reider   *Southern British Columbia, Alberta*
Sampling bars on the Island and greens on the Beach, and imbibing wee drams in the Valley,
Rebecca quoth, "Gee! These here folks of BC are as mellow as any in Cali!"
With a penchant to scare any errant black bear, Rebska raced across roadways pell-mell.
From crazed hostel owners to raw, unclothed stoners, she's got a few stories to tell.
Though the coast was sublime, it was only in time that she reached the true acme of being—
Aloft on the Rockies, she fused her deep loves of geology, splendor, and skiing.

Paul Todgham   *British Columbia, the Yukon, Interior Alaska*
And that leaves us with Paul, who plumb gave us his all, caring naught about washouts and mire.
From whitewater rafting to fine sentence-crafting, he never, no, never did tire.
Paul partied in Chicken and went on a-tickin', late into the light of the night.
He lapped up the miles with wide-open smiles and all of his SUV's might.
Yet come close and listen…the queerest tale's this'n: A cocktail Paul giddily sips,
And he turns to a star in a brothel-turned-bar, as a foul pickled toe meets his lips.

Acknowledgments

My deepest professional gratitude goes to Ben F. for making this happen with dutiful skill and excellence; to Anna for seasoned wisdom and truly inspired leadership; to Anne and the whole receptionist brigade for smoothly-running gears; to Irene and TJ for extra proofing; to Dan, Maryanthe, and Heath for productive salvation; to Dan, Derek, and Matt in the incomparable Mapland; to every last ME for everything; to the whole Domestic Room (Middle East inclusive) for decorative heaven and a lifetime of banter; to Heather Holmes for the whale story; to Barb Maynes for the goat scoop; and to our fantastic battalion of researchers for doing our dirty work so deliciously.

More profound thanks to Ben L. and Nate for movies, food, and more; to my family for keeping me well-loved and taking me way up north; to Erin for similarly precious love and escape; and to Michael, Jonathan, Elizabeth, Adam, Scott, and all other neglected friends. I am now ready to rejoin you all. —*DBR*

Thanks, and then some more thanks, to Doug, who had a vision of turning this book upside-down, and pulled it off with panache and an organizational scheme to make strong men cry. Also special thanks to Anna, who kept everything sane, dealt with everything we threw at her, and caught every non-italicized period. As for the Domestics, you all made this job something better than just a job (even if you did kill Gertie). To our RWs, you built this book. Thank you. Farbs, as usual, for listening. To TJ and John, the answer men, and co-envisioners of *Thermopylae, a Beach Story.* Lara, Esti, Sharmila, Ben Leems, what can I say? You made everything good, even if it was bad. To Irene, thank you. (Bet you weren't expecting that, were you, my dear?) To Marshall, Drake, Rebecca, Becky, see you all in a few weeks. I can't wait. To Mom, Dad, and Rache, for being the family of families. And again to Mom for teaching me a thing or two about baseball. To Josh, Kirsch, Sara, Mitch, Sheeba, and everyone else who I know will always be there. And to Elise, for being exactly who you are, impossible to sum up. —*BDF*

Editor	Douglas Rand
Associate Editor	Ben Florman
Managing Editor	Anna C. Portnoy
Publishing Director	Caroline R. Sherman
Publishing Director	Anna C. Portnoy
Production Manager	Dan Visel
Associate Production Manager	Maryanthe Malliaris
Cartography Manager	Derek McKee
Design Manager	Bentsion Harder
Editorial Manager	M. Allison Arwady
Editorial Manager	Lisa M. Nosal
Financial Manager	Monica Eileen Eav
Personnel Manager	Nicolas R. Rapold
Publicity Manager	Alexander Z. Speier
New Media Manager	Måns O. Larsson
Map Editors	Matthew R. Daniels, Daniel J. Luskin
Production Associate	Heath Ritchie
Office Coordinators	Tom Moore, Eliza Harrington, Jodie Kirshner
Director of Advertising Sales	Gene Plotkin
Associate Sales Executives	Colleen Gaard, Mateo Jaramillo, Alexandra Price
President	Catherine J. Turco
General Manager	Richard Olken
Assistant General Manager	Anne E. Chisholm

Thanks to Our Readers...

Mano Aaron, CA; Jean-Marc Abela, CAN; George Adams, NH; Bob & Susan Adams, GA; Deborah Adeyanju, NY; Rita Alexander, MI; Shani Amory-Claxton, NY; Kate Anderson, AUS; Lindsey Anderson, ENG; Viki Anderson, NY; Ray Andrews, JPN; Robin J. Andrus, NJ; L. Asurmendi, CA; Anthony Atkinson, ENG; Deborah Bacek, GA; Jeffrey Bagdade, MI; Mark Baker, UK; Mary Baker, TN; Jeff Barkoff, PA; Regina Barsanti, NY; Ethan Beeler, MA; Damao Bell, CA; Rya Ben-Shir, IL; Susan Bennerstrom, WA; Marla Benton, CAN; Matthew Berenson, OR; Walter Bergstrom, OR; Caryl Bird, ENG; Charlotte Blanc, NY; Jeremy Boley, EL SAL; Oliver Bradley, GER; A.Braurstein, CO; Philip R. Brazil, WA; Henrik Brockdorff, DMK; Tony Bronco, NJ; Eileen Brouillard, SC; Mary Brown, ENG; Tom Brown, CA; Elizabeth Buckius, CO; Sue Buckley, UK; Christine Burer, SWITZ; Norman Butler, MO; Brett Carroll, WA; Susan Caswell, ISR; Carlos Cersosimo, ITA; Barbara Crary Chase, WA; Stella Cherry Carbost, SCOT; Oi Ling Cheung, HK; Simon Chinn, ENG; Charles Cho, AUS; Carolyn R. Christie, AUS; Emma Church, ENG; Kelley Coblentz, IN; Cathy Cohan, PA; Phyllis Cole, TX; Karina Collins, SWITZ; Michael Cox, CA; Mike Craig, MD; Rene Crusto, LA; Claudine D'Anjou, CAN; Lizz Daniels, CAN; Simon Davies, SCOT; Samantha Davis, AUS; Leah Davis, TX; Stephanie Dickman, MN; Philipp Dittrich,GER; Tim Donovan, NH; Reed Drew, OR; Wendy Duncan, SCOT; Melissa Dunlap, VA; P.A. Emery, UK; GCL Emery, SAF; Louise Evans, AUS; Christine Farr, AUS; David Fattel, NJ; Vivian Feen, MD; David Ferraro, SPN; Sue Ferrick, CO; Philip Fielden, UK; Nancy Fintel, FL; Jody Finver, FL; D. Ross Fisher, CAN; Abigail Flack, IL; Elizabeth Foster, NY; Bonnie Fritz, CAN; J. Fuson, OR; Michael K. Gasuad, NV; Raad German, TX; Mark Gilbert, NY; Betsy Gilliland, CA; Ana Goshko, NY; Patrick Goyenneche, CAN; David Greene, NY; Jennifer Griffin, ENG; Janet & Jeremy Griffith, ENG; Nanci Guartofierro, NY; Denise Guillemette, MA; Ilona Haayer, HON; Joseph Habboushe, PA; John Haddon, CA; Ladislav Hanka, MI; Michael Hanke, CA; Avital Harari, TX; Channing Hardy, KY; Patrick Harris, CA; Denise Hasher, PA; Jackie Hattori, UK; Guthrie Hebenstreit, ROM; Therase Hill, AUS; Denise Hines, NJ; Cheryl Horne, ENG; Julie Howell, IL; Naomi Hsu, NJ; Mark Hudgkinson, ENG; Brenda Humphrey, NC; Kelly Hunt, NY; Daman Irby, AUT; Bill Irwin, NY; Andrea B. Jackson, PA; John Jacobsen, FL; Pat Johanson, MD; Russell Jones, FL; J. Jones, AUS; Sharon Jones, MI; Craig Jones, CA; Wayne Jones, ENG; Jamie Kagan, NY; Mirko Kaiser, GER; Scott Kauffman, NY; John Keanie, NIRE; Barbara Keary, FL; Jamie Kehoe, AUS; Alistair Kernick, SAF; Daihi Kielle, SWITZ; John Knutsen, CA; Rebecca Koepke, NY; Jeannine Kolb, ME; Elze Kollen, NETH; Lorne Korman, CAN; Robin Kortright, CAN; Isel Krinsky, CAN; George Landers, ENG; Jodie Lanthois, AUS; Roger Latzgo, PA; A. Lavery, AZ; Joan Lea, ENG; Lorraine Lee, NY; Phoebe Leed, MA; Tammy Leeper, CA; Paul Lejeune, ENG; Yee-Leng Leong, CA; Sam Levene, CAN; Robin Levin, PA; Christianna Lewis, PA; Ernesto Licata, ITA; Wolfgang Lischtansky, AUT; Michelle Little, CAN; Dee Littrell, CA; Maria Lobosco, UK; Netii Ross, ITA; Didier Look, CAN; Alice Lorenzotti, MA; David Love, PA; Briege Mac Donagh, IRE; Brooke Madigan, NY; Helen Maltby, FL; Shyama Marchesi, ITA; Domenico Maria, ITA; Natasha Markovic, AUS; Edward Marshall, ECU; Rachel Marshall, TX; Kate Maynard, UK; Agnes McCann, IRE; Susan McGowan, NY; Brandi McGunigal, CAN; Neville McLean, NZ; Marty McLendon, MS; Matthew Melko, OH; Barry Mendelson, CA; Eric Middendorf, OH; Nancy Mike, AZ; Coren Milbury, NH; Margaret Mill, NY; David H. Miller, TX; Ralph Miller, NV; Susan Miller, CO; Larry Moeller, MI; Richard Moore, ENG; Anne & Andrea Mosher, MA; J. L. Mourne, TX; Athanassios Moustakas, GER; Laurel Naversen, CA; Suzanne Neil, IA; Deborah Nickles, PA; Pieter & Agnes Noels, BEL; Werner Norr, GER; Ruth J. Nye, ENG; Heidi O'Brien, WA; Sherry O'Cain, SC; Aibhan O'Connor, IRE; Kevin O'Connor, CA; Margaret O'Rielly, IRE; Daniel O'Rourke, CA; Krissy Oechslin, OH; Johan Oelofse, SAF; Quinn Okamoto, CA; Juan Ramon Olaizola, SPN; Laura Onorato, NM; Bill Orkin, IL; K. Owusu-Agyenang, UK; Anne Paananen, SWD; Jenine Padget, AUS; Frank Pado, TX; G. Pajkich, Washington, DC; J. Parker, CA; Marian Parnat, AUS; Sandra Swift Parrino, NY; Iris Patten, NY; M. Pavini, CT; David Pawielski, MN; Jenny Pawson, ENG; Colin Peak, AUS; Marius Penderis, ENG; Jo-an Peters, AZ; Barbara Phillips, NY; Romain Picard, Washington, DC; Pati Pike, ENG; Mark Pollock, SWITZ; Minnie Adele Potter, FL; Martin Potter, ENG; Claudia Praetel, ENG; Bill Press, Washington, DC; David Prince, NC; Andrea Pronko, OH; C. Robert Pryor, OH; Phu Quy, VTNM; Adrian Rainbow, ENG; John Raven, AUS; Lynn Reddringer, VA; John Rennie, NZ; Ruth B.Robinson, FL; John & Adelaida Romagnoli, CA; Eva Romano, FRA; Mark A. Roscoe, NETH; Yolanda & Jason Ross, CA; Sharee Rowe, ENG; W. Suzanne Rowell, NY; Vic Roych, AZ; John Russell, ENG; Jennifer Ruth, OK; William Sabino, NJ; Hideki Saito, JPN; Frank Schaer, HUN; Jeff Schultz, WI; Floretta Seeland-Connally, IL; Colette Shoulders, FRA; Shireen Sills, ITA; Virginia Simon, AUS; Beth Simon, NY; Gary Simpson, AUS; Barbara & Allen Sisarsky, GA; Alon Siton, ISR; Kathy Skeie, CA; Robyn Skillecorn, AUS; Erik & Kathy Skon, MN; Stine Skorpen, NOR; Philip Smart, CAN; Colin Smit, ENG; Kenneth Smith, DE; Caleb Smith, CA; Geoffrey Smith, TX; John Snyder, NC; Kathrin Speidel, GER; Lani Steele, PHIL; Julie Stelbracht, PA; Margaret Stires, TN; Donald Stumpf, NY; Samuel Suffern, NY; Michael Swerdlow, ENG; Brian Talley, TX; Serene-Marie Terrell, NY; B. Larry Thilson, CAN; J. Pelham Thomas, NC; Wright Thompson, ITA; Christine Timm, NY; Melinda Tong, HK; M. Tritica, AUS; Melanie Tritz, CAN; Mark Trop, FL; Chris Troxel, AZ; Rozana Tsiknaki, GRC; Lois Turner, NJ; Nicole Virgil, IL; Blondie Vucich, CO; Wendy Wan, SAF; Carrie & Simon Wedgwood, ENG; Frederick Weibgen, NJ; Richard Weil, MN; Alan Weissberg, OH; Ryan Wells, OH; Jill Wester, GER; Clinton White, AL; Gael White, CAN; Melanie Whitfield, SCOT; Bryn Williams, CAN; Amanda Williams, CAN; Wendy Willis, CAN; Sasha Wilson, NY; Kendra Wilson, CA; Olivia Wiseman, ENG; Gerry Wood, CAN; Kelly Wooten, ENG; Robert Worsley, ENG; C.A.Wright, ENG; Caroline Wright, ENG; Mary H. Yuhasz, CO; Margaret Zimmerman, WA.

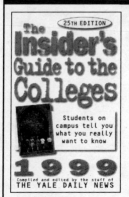

★Let's Go 1999 Reader Questionnaire★

Please fill this out and return it to **Let's Go, St. Martin's Press,** 175 Fifth Ave., New York, NY 10010-7848. All respondents will receive a free subscription to *The Yellowjacket*, the Let's Go Newsletter. You can find a more extensive version of this survey on the web at http://www.letsgo.com.

Name: _____

Address: _____

City: _____ **State:** _____ **Zip/Postal Code:** _____

Email: _____ **Which book(s) did you use?** _____

How old are you? under 19   19-24   25-34   35-44   45-54   55 or over

Are you (circle one)   in high school   in college   in graduate school
    employed   retired   between jobs

Have you used Let's Go before? yes no   **Would you use it again?** yes no

How did you first hear about Let's Go? friend   store clerk   television
    bookstore display   advertisement/promotion   review   other

Why did you choose Let's Go (circle up to two)? reputation budget focus
    price   writing style   annual updating   other: _____

Which other guides have you used, if any? Fodor's   Footprint Handbooks
    Frommer's $-a-day   Lonely Planet   Moon Guides   Rick Steve's
    Rough Guides   UpClose   other: _____

Which guide do you prefer? _____

Please rank each of the following parts of Let's Go 1 to 5 (1=needs improvement, 5=perfect). packaging/cover practical information
    accommodations   food   cultural introduction   sights
    practical introduction ("Essentials")   directions   entertainment
    gay/lesbian information   maps   other: _____

How would you like to see the books improved? (continue on separate page, if necessary) _____
_____

How long was your trip?   one week   two weeks   three weeks
    one month   two months or more

Which countries did you visit? _____

What was your average daily budget, not including flights? _____

Have you traveled extensively before? yes no

Do you buy a separate map when you visit a foreign city? yes no

Have you used a Let's Go Map Guide? yes no

If you have, would you recommend them to others? yes no

Have you visited Let's Go's website? yes no

What would you like to see included on Let's Go's website? _____
_____

What percentage of your trip planning did you do on the Web? _____

Would you use a Let's Go: recreational (e.g. skiing) guide gay/lesbian guide
    adventure/trekking guide   phrasebook   general travel information guide

Which of the following destinations do you hope to visit in the next three to five years (circle one)? Canada Argentina Perú Kenya Middle East
    Caribbean   Scandinavia   other: _____

Where did you buy your guidebook?   Internet   independent bookstore
    chain bookstore   college bookstore   travel store   other: _____

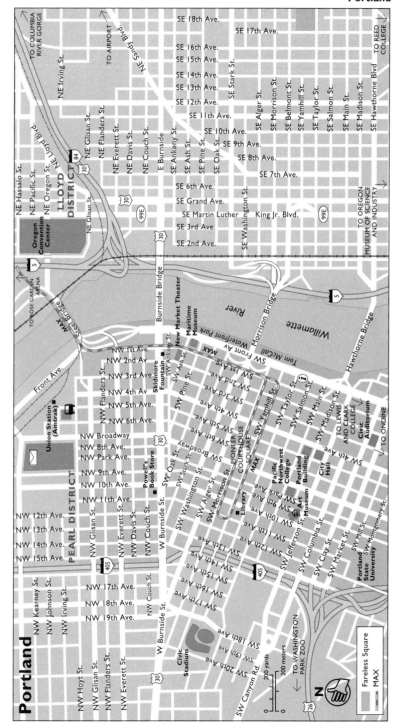

Seattle

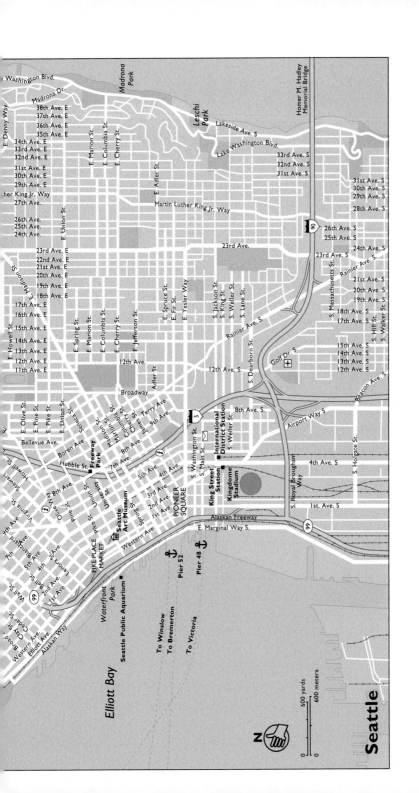

Seattle

Vancouver

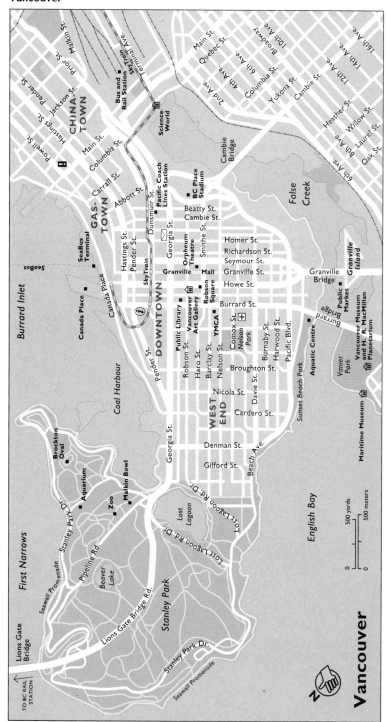